Religion in Early Stuart England
1603–1638

DOCUMENTS OF
ANGLOPHONE CHRISTIANITY

GENERAL EDITORS

Roger Lundin
Blanchard Professor of English
Wheaton College

Debora K. Shuger
Professor of English
University of California, Los Angeles

Religion in Early Stuart England
1603–1638

An Anthology of Primary Sources

Debora Shuger, editor

BAYLOR UNIVERSITY PRESS

Cover Design by Pam Poll

Library of Congress Cataloging-in-Publication Data

Religion in early Stuart England, 1603–1638 : an anthology of primary sources / [edited by] Debora Shuger.
     1021 pages cm
   ISBN 978-1-60258-298-9 (hardback)
1. England—Church history—17th century—Sources. I. Shuger, Debora K., 1953– editor of compilation.
  BR375.R45 2012
  274.206—dc23

                                        2012017928

TABLE OF CONTENTS

Introduction   xi
Abbreviations for Works Commonly Cited   xxi
Note on Nomenclature   xxiii

John Dod and Robert Cleaver   1
A plain and familiar exposition of the Ten Commandments
1604   3

Lancelot Andrewes   25
The copy of the sermon preached on Good Friday last before the King's Majesty
1604   29

William Bradshaw   42
*English puritanism: containing the main opinions of the rigidest sort of those
that are called Puritans in the realm of England*
1605 (rev. ed. 1641)   46

John Buckeridge   56
A sermon preached at Hampton Court before the King's Majesty
1606   59

Richard Field   68
Of the Church, five books
1606 (rev. ed. 1628)   71

Richard Corbett   100
"An elegy written upon the death of Dr. Ravis, Bishop of London"
ca. 1609   103

Lewis Bayly   105
The practice of piety directing a Christian how to walk that he may please God
1611–12 [first extant edition 1613]   108

Thomas Adams   141
The white devil, or the hypocrite uncased: in a sermon preached at Paul's Cross
1612, published 1613   144

Benjamin Carier   160
*A treatise written by M. Doctor Carier wherein he layeth down sundry learned
and pithy considerations by which he was moved to forsake the Protestant
congregation and to betake himself to the Catholic Apostolic Roman Church*
1614   163

John Howson   178
"Dr. Howson's answers to my Lord Grace of Canterbury{'s} accusations
before his Majesty at Greenwich"
June 10, 1615   182

Collegiate Suffrage   192
*The collegiate suffrage of the divines of Great Britain . . . delivered in the Synod
of Dort, March 6, anno 1619, being their vote or voice foregoing the joint and
public judgment of that Synod*   .
1619 (English trans. 1629)   197

Robert Sanderson   230
Sermon preached at a visitation at Boston
1619, published 1622   233

Richard Corbett   250
"The distracted puritan"
ca. 1620–21   250

John Cosin   253
*Sermon I: Preached at St. Edward's in Cambridge, January the 6th,
A.D. MDCXXI, and at Coton on the second Sunday after Epiphany*
1621   257

Appendix: Calvin's commentary on Isaiah 60:2-3   269

John Preston   270
Plenitudo fontis, or, Christ's fullness and man's emptiness
1621, published 1639 (rev. ed. 1644)   277

Humphrey Sydenham   287
*Jacob and Esau: election, reprobation, opened and discussed by way of sermon
at Paul's Cross, March 4, 1622*
published 1626   290

Michael Sparke   294
Crumbs of comfort, the valley of tears, and the hill of joy
1623   297

John Donne   301
Sermon preached at Whitehall, the first Friday in Lent
1623, published 1640   305

Lancelot Andrewes   320
A sermon preached before the King's Majesty at Whitehall, on the xiii of April,
A.D. MDCXXIII, being Easter Day
1623, published 1629   322

William Drummond of Hawthornden   335
A cypress grove
1623   338

George Wither   350
The hymns and songs of the Church
1623   354

William Laud   368
A relation of the conference between William Laud . . . and Mr. Fisher, the Jesuit
(Frequently referred to under the title *Conference with Fisher*)
1624 (rev. ed. 1639)   372

Richard Montagu   398
A gag for the new Gospel? No, A NEW GAG for an old goose
1624   402

Appello Caesarem: a just appeal from two unjust informers
1625   409

Appendix: William Barlow on falling from grace at the Hampton Court
Conference
1604   416

John Preston   418
Riches of mercy to men in misery; or, certain excellent treatises concerning
the dignity and duty of God's children
ca. 1625, published 1658   418

"The buckler of a believer"   418
"Self-seeking opposite to Christ's interest"   432
"Free grace magnified"   439

Phineas Fletcher   446
The locusts, or Apollyonists
1627   449

J. R.   486
The spy: discovering the danger of Arminian heresy and Spanish treachery
1628   489

John Earle   508
Microcosmography: or, a piece of the world discovered, in essays and characters
1628   513

William Prynne   519
God no impostor nor deluder
1629 (rev. ed. 1630)   521

Joseph Hall   530
*The estate of a Christian laid forth in a sermon preached at Gray's Inn
on Candlemas Day*
late 1620s   532

John Everard   537
The Gospel treasury opened
ca. 1625–36 (published in 1653)   543

"Of milk for babes; and of meat for strong men"   546
"All power given to Jesus Christ, in Heaven and Earth"   554

Richard Sibbes   568
The bruised reed and smoking flax
1630   570

The Little Gidding Story Books   590
*The story books of Little Gidding: being the religious dialogues recited
in the Great Room*
1631–32   596

Francis Quarles   617
Divine fancies: digested into epigrams, meditations, and observations
1632   620

John Cosin   629
Sermons preached at Brancepath
1632–33   631

Richard Corbett
"Upon Fairford windows"
ca. 1632–33   642

William Strode   644
"On Fairford windows"   647
"On the Bible"   649
"Justification"   650

"On the same M. M. P."
ca. 1625–45 650

Humphrey Sydenham 654
Jehovah-Jireh. God in his providence and omnipotence discovered: a sermon preached ad magistratum *at Chard in Somerset, 1633*
published 1637 654

Anthony Munday 664
The survey of London
1633 668

Samuel Hoard 726
God's love to mankind
1633 (1635?) 730

Thomas Laurence 763
The duty of the laity and privilege of the clergy
1634, published 1635 765

Francis Quarles 775
Emblems
1635 775

Robert Shelford 788
Five pious and learned discourses (with prefatory lyric by Crashaw)
1635 790

Robert Sanderson 803
A sovereign antidote against Sabbatarian errors
1636 804

Sidney Godolphin 807
"Lord, when the wise men"
ca. 1630–40 809

William Prynne 811
News from Ipswich
1636 816

John Hales 823
A tract concerning schism
ca. 1636, published 1642 828

"Letter to Archbishop Laud upon occasion of the Tract concerning schism"
ca. 1638, published 1716 834

Sermon on Luke 16:25 ("The danger of receiving our good things in this life")
ca. 1619–38, published 1660 838

Sermon on Galatians 6:7 ("Of inquiry and private judgment in religion")
ca. 1619–38, published 1660   843

Christopher Dow   851
Innovations unjustly charged upon the present Church and state
1637   854

William Chillingworth   891
The religion of Protestants a safe way to salvation
1637   897

Sir Kenelm Digby   933
A conference with a lady about choice of religion
1638   938

William Habington   952
Castara, 3rd ed.
1640   954

George Wither   957
Hallelujah: or Britain's second remembrancer
1641   957

Appendix I: List of Authors According to Birth Year   984
Appendix II: Topical Index   985

INTRODUCTION

The fifty-plus texts here folded into a single volume[1] provide an overview of the theological controversies and cultural forms of early Stuart Christianity—an overview of sufficient range and depth to serve as a source-book for scholars, but with sufficient annotation and standardizing of accidentals to be accessible to students and those not accustomed to the vagaries of early modern punctuation. Over half the books published in England during the period between James' 1603 accession to the English throne and the start of the Wars of the Three Kingdoms in 1639 (or approximately 30,000 titles) concern religion. The selections that follow are therefore necessarily selective. Omitted are all translations, all non-English-language texts (unless translated prior to 1638),[2] and material easily available in paperback editions (e.g., the poems of George Herbert). The works chosen, in turn, reflect three overlapping aims, the first being to elucidate the central theological creeds and controversies of the era; the second, to capture something of the variety of religious expression—the manual of private devotions, the Paul's Cross sermon, the doctrinal treatise, the conversion narrative, the popular poetry of the verse epitaph, and so on through a long list of possibilities; and, finally, to recover forgotten works of unusual beauty, intelligence, or simply interest.

---

[1] The phrasing alludes to T. S. Eliot's memorable lines, reflecting on the religious divisions that tore apart the early Stuart Church, from "Little Gidding," written in 1942—the final poem of his *Four Quartets*:

We cannot revive old factions
We cannot restore old policies
Or follow an antique drum.
These men, and those who opposed them
And those whom they opposed
Accept the constitution of silence
And are folded into a single party.
ll. 187–90

[2] The real loss here is Edward Herbert's *De veritate* (Paris 1624; London 1633), the only post-Christian (i.e., deist) treatise published in England during this period.

Numerous ways of organizing the volume's contents presented themselves: by genre, by theological position, by controversy handled, by venue or targeted audience. Since each of these required discarding half the selected texts for lack of a suitable niche, in the end chronology won out as the faute de mieux principle of order, although even this minimal structure proved not altogether straightforward: works written for print appear according to their initial date of publication; sermons, however, according to the date preached; manuscript poetry, which often circulated widely for years prior to print publication, according to the probable date of composition. The chronology thus, as a general rule, indicates the time (or time frame) of writing/speaking. In some cases this dating is perforce approximate, but only in one mere guesswork.[3]

Although chronology often yields meaningful order, it promises no more than one damn thing after another; hence, for the purposes of an introductory overview, it seems helpful to divide the anthologized texts into four loosely defined groups, beginning with works of theological definition and controversy, followed by pastoral and practical divinity, then sermons, and, finally, pieces written in literary genres or, which amounts to much the same thing, by laypersons.[4]

The earliest of the doctrinal/controversial writings, Bradshaw's 1605 *English puritanism*, turns out quite wonderfully also to be among the most radical: a salutary caution against any linear consensus-to-crisis historiographic model,[5] although the work was reprinted in the 1640s, with edits that mark the shift from the Reformation (and, indeed, medieval) contest between royal and ecclesiastical power to the Long Parliament's challenge to the intertwined powers of bishop and king. Like the Commons in the early 1640s, Bradshaw would dismantle episcopacy root and branch, but, unlike the radicals of four decades later, he has no qualms about transferring the Church's coercive powers to the Crown.

English puritanism is a protest against the emphases on the order, unity, and uniformity of an inclusive national Church that shaped ecclesiastical policy under Archbishops Whitgift and Bancroft: that is, from the mid-Elizabethan period to 1610. The other pre-1610 doctrinal text anthologized below, Richard Field's magisterial *Of the Church* (1606), stands at the opposite end of the ecclesio-political spectrum from Bradshaw's. Yet, in a different way, it too bears the impress of the Whitgift-Bancroft era, above all in its attempt to harmonize Reformed and patristic teaching. The work draws on the latter to defend the former against Roman Catholic charges of novelty and heresy, but the patristic material, whose un-Protestant contours Field's historicism exposes, strains against his Calvinist framework.

[3] See the introduction to John Hales <*infra*>.

[4] The notable exceptions, Donne and Herbert, are such as prove the rule, most of their sacred poetry having been written prior to ordination. The rule, however, does admit of true exceptions, as noted below.

[5] A principal reason for ending this volume in 1638 rather than a few years later was to escape the gravitational pull of this model; had it ended with the Civil War, the chronological sequence of readings would have *had* to explain why things fell apart; the endpoint, that is, would have made it hard not to select readings in order to show a rising trajectory of conflict and radicalization. (The other reason was to avoid overlap with the issues and controversies that will dominate the next volume.)

The next two texts in this category, Carier's 1614 apologia for his conversion to Rome and Howson's 1615 account of his "trial" for heresy and crypto-Catholic treason, both point to the role of George Abbot, Archbishop Bancroft's successor, in forcing a split between Reformed orthodoxy and a more patristic, sacramental, and traditionalist churchmanship. The 1619 canons drafted by the English delegation to the Synod of Dort (the *Collegiate suffrage*) and Montagu's 1624–25 assault on Calvinist pretensions to hegemony represent later stages in this conflict within the conformist mainstream over the theological identity of the English Church, although the fact that the English draft canons at points differ strikingly from those finally adopted by the Synod suggests that by the 1620s Reformed orthodoxy was itself more open-ended, tentative, and riven than either its adherents or enemies chose to note.

Montagu-style, patristic high-churchmanship became the main site of resistance to godly Calvinism, but Hoard's 1633 *God's love* and the sermons of Everard, which date from the same period, also mount significant, albeit wildly different, critiques. *God's love* is the earliest English-language defense of Arminianism, the liberal Protestant rationalism that condemned predestination and was, in turn, condemned by the Synod of Dort; Everard's sermons, among the earliest works of English antinomianism, the hyper-Protestant mysticism that proved mother-root to the radical religion of the Civil War sects, and whose focus on rapturous union with God—rather than on works of mercy or defeating the antichrist—bounds religion within the sphere of the purely private. Like Bradshaw's transfer of all coercive jurisdiction to the secular domain, only more so, Everard's gospel of the paradise within implies the retreat of the sacred from marketplace, forum, and polis. That both Bradshaw's congregationalism and Everard's antinomianism flourished during the Interregnum and, thereafter, in America makes perfect sense.

William Laud's actual conference with the Jesuit Fisher took place in 1622; his published account of their conference appeared in 1624, followed by a revised version in 1639, when Laud was archbishop of Canterbury, and had been for six years. To this second edition, written as the Caroline regime unraveled, Laud adds a preface explaining, and defending, his governance of the English Church. In both versions, however, the *Conference with Fisher* is, above all, an attempt to formulate an alternative to the promise of certainty offered, first, by the Roman Church's claim to infallibility, but also by Calvinist claims for the self-evident truth of Scripture (*Institutes* 1.7.2). Laud denies that any such self-evident, infallible foundation exists, but he also denies Fisher's corollary that, without this foundation, belief has nothing to rest on but private opinion. Instead he argues that, although we must perforce make do with intimations and probabilities—rational, cultural, experiential, supernatural, historical—these *taken together* constitute a sufficient basis for faith. This grounding of faith in multiple partial inducements and fallible authorities probably owes something to Richard Hooker's triad of reason, authority, and tradition, but it also bears the impress of the common-law principle that disparate circumstantial probabilities could, taken together, amount to full proof (whereas on the Continent, conviction required some piece of incontrovertible evidence).[6]

---

[6] The contrast here pertains only to the criminal law. See John Langbein, *Prosecuting crime in the Renaissance* (Harvard UP, 1974), 205.

The classic Laudian apologiae of the mid-30s—Shelford's *Five pious and learned discourses* and Dow's *Innovations*—likewise hinge on the conviction that faith has multiple bases: that Church, reason, indwelling Spirit, Scripture, conscience, nature, and a good deal else can become for us channels of grace and truth; and conversely that no one of these affords the only light in an otherwise naughty world. This sense of a world structured by multiple sacral loci is at the core of Laudianism's theological vision. Hence Shelford does not argue that sacraments are holier than sermons, but rather that sacraments and sermons, plus a dozen or so other things, are all, potentially, holy.[7] The epistemic and spiritual pluralism of the Laudian vision sets it against the sacred/profane binarism of the godly, but also apart from the rationalism of Great Tew, the Oxfordshire manor where, from 1633 to the Civil War, Lord Falkland hosted an informal collegium of statesmen, philosophers, priests, and poets (including, in this volume, Chillingworth, Earle, Hales, and Godolphin, but also Hobbes, Clarendon, and Jonson).

Chillingworth's *The religion of Protestants* (1637), the classic statement of Great Tew theology, opens with a defense of Laudian high-churchmanship and the beauty-of-holiness experiment. But, in contrast to Laud, Chillingworth insists on weighing religion in the scales of reason, and in the scales of reason alone. However Chillingworth's rationalism is softened by his conviction that "universal tradition" has real evidentiary weight—weighs enough in itself to tip the scales. The rationalism of John Hales, whose *Tract concerning schism* may have been written for Chillingworth, is harder, edgier: openly contemptuous of antiquity, orthodoxies, hierarchies. His insistence that all persons, including the young of both sexes, are to think for themselves, challenge their teachers, and take nothing on authority has obvious affinities with the radicalism of Milton's *Areopagitica*. Yet when sides had to be taken, Hales stood with the royalists.

Kenelm Digby's 1638 *Conference with a lady* provides a compact, lucid defense of the Roman Church's infallibility: the position with which both Laud and Chillingworth grapple. Digby's tract is of interest in part simply because it lays out the standard arguments of early seventeenth-century Catholic apologetics. Yet Digby is no stripping-of-the-altars nostalgic traditionalist, but, like Hales, an unconventional, at points heterodox, thinker of a distinctly modernist stripe with close personal and intellectual ties to both Hobbes and Descartes.

A second group of texts comprises the early Stuart best-sellers of Protestant spirituality and holy living: Dod and Cleaver's exposition of the *Ten Commandments*, Bishop Bayly's *Practice of piety*, Michael Sparke's *Crumbs of comfort*, and Richard Sibbes' *The bruised reed*. The first two, both classics of godly Calvinism from the early Jacobean period, turned out to be unexpectedly complex, both intellectually and genealogically, braiding together Sabbath-and-sermon zeal with magnificent word-paintings of the eternal and infernal kingdoms, swathes of medieval piety and scholastic ethics, plus a dozen or so further strands, ranging from humanist speculative chronology to orthodox Trinitarian dogmatics. One never knows what the next page will bring, and what one finds is more often Bonaventure than Beza. Sparke's much-reprinted 1623 anthology of private prayers, by

[7] See also the description of the proto-Laudian St. Giles-in-the-Fields in Munday's *Survey of London* <*infra*>.

contrast, is demotic Calvinist throughout, its devotions modeling for its target readership, but also for us, the popular voice of godly inwardness. Sibbes' 1630 *Bruised reed*, like Herbert's *Temple*, its lyrical soul mate, ranks among the masterpieces of Christian spirituality.[8] It is also, more specifically, a masterpiece of godly Calvinist spirituality, yet the work seems to wrestle with, and at points recoil from, the perfectionist evangel suffusing early Stuart Calvinism: the rigorism, both with respect to faith and conduct, conspicuous in the manuals of Dod, Cleaver, and Bayly.[9]

As frescos to early Renaissance churches, so sermons to early Stuart ones. Of those included in this volume, several have close ties to the doctrinal and practical writings just considered. (Indeed, the sermons of John Everard got transported into the doctrinal category as examples of pre–Civil War antinomianism.) John Cosin's 1632–33 Brancepath sermons address the Sabbatarian controversy, as do Dod's exposition of the *Ten Commandments*, Bayly's *Practice of piety*, and Robert Sanderson's 1636 tract, *A sovereign antidote*. Throughout the early Stuart period, but particularly after Charles reissued the Book of Sports in 1633, Sabbath observance became *the* wedge issue dividing the godly from the established Church. For the former, the Commandment to honor the Sabbath stood on a par with those against murder and adultery; one might accept, as most of the godly did, that adiaphora like vestments and polyphony, however distasteful, fell within the scope of human (i.e., ecclesiastical) law, but the Fourth Commandment was part of divine law, and non-negotiable. To an unexpected extent, Cosin, although a very high churchman, affirms the basic premise of the Sabbatarian position; and Sanderson, although a Calvinist, draws back in the name of universal catholic tradition. Sanderson's 1621 sermon on conformity pertains to Sabbatarianism, but, together with Buckeridge's 1606 Hampton Court sermon and, in part, the readings from Field, Laud, Laurence, Carier, and Dow, also engages the larger questions of authority, obedience, and the limits of each.

Most of the remaining sermons split apart into two distinct groups: on the one side, the Anglo-Catholic preaching of Andrewes, Laurence, and Cosin (the 1621 Epiphany sermon); on the other, the evangelical Calvinist sermons of Preston and Hall. The former seek to make us apprehend the divine order of things—the mysteries of salvation history, the numinous sanctity of the Church, the majestic splendor of the cosmos; the latter embody the Reformed understanding of the sermon as God's chosen means to work the salvation of his elect by breaking the hearts of sinners, healing the broken-hearted, denouncing wrath, urging repentance, promising eternal joy to all who find in themselves the triumphant assurance of saving faith and the new life of sanctifying grace.[10] The extraordinary diptych formed by Humphrey Sydenham's 1622 Calvinist sermon on divine power and his 1633 Laudian one on divine majesty exemplifies the contrast

---

[8] On the parallels between Sibbes and Herbert, see Richard Strier, *Love known: theology and experience in George Herbert's poetry* (Chicago UP, 1983).

[9] A similar rigorism surfaces in Calvinist preaching; it is a marked feature of the Calvinist sermons—those by John Preston and Joseph Hall <infra>.

[10] Preston's sermons had a major influence on the lawyer and controversialist William Prynne, visible in his 1629 *God no impostor* <infra>, which is not a sermon but a doctrinal tract, perhaps the period's only strictly doctrinal tract written by a layman.

between these two styles of preaching and their attendant theologies, yet the two sermons also betray an unmistakable kinship; they were, of course, written by the same person, but the continuities throw into sharper relief the sites of difference—most of which
seem to involve conceptualizations of power. Sanderson's lucid and tightly argued sermon
defending conformity, as noted above, does not fit this Laudian–Calvinist binarism, nor
does either Thomas Adams' rousing denunciation of the sins against social and economic
justice committed by godly, respectable Londoners, or Donne's moving sermon on Jesus
weeping before Lazarus' grave, whose grappling with the relation of the living to the dead
under the new Protestant dispensation gives the fullest expression to questions, fears, and
longings that echo throughout the volume's readings. Yet, although modern scholarship
does not know what to call them ("Anglican" having proven either meaningless or misleading),[11] these were eminent, influential, mainstream preachers, and that their churchmanship finds itself nameless and hence largely invisible suggests the extent to which the
historiography of belief still depends on the *arma virumque* model, in which the primary
task is to identify the two sides and then trace their conflict through its various stages.[12]

The last of this introduction's *pro tem* categories is the most diffuse and perhaps most
significant. The early Stuart period witnesses an extraordinary flowering of sacred literature, with an A-list that includes Herbert, Donne, Crashaw, Herrick, Browne, and the
young Milton. Of these six, four at some point took holy orders. Most of the era's sacred
literature, however, is lay-authored; indeed, this body of work constitutes the principal
surviving archive of lay piety,[13] one that preserves the elsewhere undocumented voices of
grocers, grandmothers, and young gentlewomen, intermingled with courtiers, Catholics,
libelers, lairds, lawyers, plus a sprinkling of clerics, playwrights, professional writers, and
even a lone bishop.

The bishop, Richard Corbett, contributes a couple of witty anti-puritan satires, but
also a moving elegy that ends with a remarkably early (1609) protest against the new
super-sized noble tombs dwarfing the altar—a practice later targeted by Laud. One of
Corbett's chaplains, William Strode, although now virtually unknown, was a far greater
poet, whose handful of exquisitely crafted sacred lyrics explore the entanglements of
art and faith. The austere and darkly powerful verse of the Catholic courtier, William
Habington, with its sense of the vastness of space-time and the nothingness of mortal
glory, provides an instructive contrast to that of Richard Crashaw, the period's one canonical Catholic poet, whose flamboyantly emotional style tends to be regarded as having
the same relation to his religion as smoke to fire. Habington, like Digby, complicates
the standard picture of early Stuart Catholicism. Strode and Habington wrote just a few
sacred poems; Sidney Godolphin only one, but a good one. Its insistence that the shepherds' adoration finds no less favor with God than the wise men's implicitly critiques the

[11] See the note on nomenclature following this introduction.

[12] The Latin, the first words of Vergil's *Aeneid*, means "arms and the man." Donne's sermons have obviously been of interest to literary scholars, although these have perhaps spent far too much mental energy
trying to assign them to one or another party. For Peter Lake's splendid essay on Sanderson, see the introduction prefacing the latter's 1619 sermon *<infra>*.

[13] This honor usually goes to the court records, yet these are by nature more attuned to the voices of
lay impiety.

sort of Protestant gnosticism exemplified by Bayly's *Practice of piety* with its sixty pages on the knowledge of the Trinity necessary for salvation, but the critique also speaks to the rationalism of Godolphin's own Great Tew circle—the rationalism of Hales' warning to the Eton schoolboys that God will not accept an unexamined faith.

With the exception of Habington's, these sacred lyrics were private poems, meant for manuscript circulation alone. George Wither and Francis Quarles, by contrast, wrote for the mass readership of print: the latter one of the most popular poets of the age; the former, among the most prolific. Although Quarles was a loyal Protestant in high regard among the godly, his poems seem, on the whole, neither theologically nor tonally Calvinist. One poem in his 1632 *Divine fancies* defends free will, and the verses on the infant Jesus achieve a level of sentimentality that Murillo would have found embarrassing. Both the visual design and spiritual psychodrama of Quarles' 1635 *Emblems* draw on Jesuit models, which, given the work's success, raises the possibility that seventeenth-century godly Protestants could both understand and speak the "soul's language" of Counter-Reformation Catholicism.[14] So too in Wither's 1623 *Hymns and songs*, continuity seems to predominate over rupture. The volume, which had King James' backing, was supposed to have become the first hymnal of the English Church; many of its hymns versify biblical texts, but there are also Christmas carols, Communion anthems, hymns for the great feasts of the liturgical year, for saints' days, for the Blessed Virgin. Over the following decades, Wither's stance, like Milton's, shifted increasingly toward the Protestant political left, the shift registered in his 1641 revised *Hymns and songs* (retitled *Hallelujah: Britain's second remembrancer*), dedicated to the Long Parliament. Yet the revisions take one by surprise, for Wither does not excise the hymns tied to the Prayer Book's distinctly un-Protestant liturgical calendar, but instead adds dozens upon dozens of new hymns intended not for public worship but for the sanctification of ordinary life: hymns dealing with everything from animal rights and companionate marriage to Englishness and Wednesday, although my favorite is the one thanking God for having been born male.

The unchurching of religion one detects in Wither may, in the end, have been among the more significant factors in the ensuing ecclesiastical meltdown, but it plays no role in the oppositional (and later, revolutionary) political imaginary of godly Calvinism, which, particularly after 1618, centers on international conspiracies of devils, Jesuits, Arminians, and, by 1636, Laudian bishops to destroy God's Church and persecute his saints. Given the incalculable (in both senses) impact of this apocalyptic reading of current history, the anthology includes three separate renderings. The earliest, Phineas Fletcher's *Locusts* (1627), a neo-Spenserian brief epic on the Gunpowder Plot, is a strange, powerful, haunting poem, ideologically riven by its incompatible commitments to the Jacobean peace and Protestant holy war. *The spy*, published abroad and anonymously the following year, describes (in reasonably competent neo-classical couplets) the massive popish plot against England or "Truth's Fortress," with particular emphasis on the treachery of crypto-Catholic bishops like Laud and Montagu. The poem is technically a seditious libel,

---

[14] This is a contested possibility, the alternative and widely-held view being that Protestantism involved "the creation of another religion . . . another personal relationship between man and God" (Paul Tillich, *A history of Christian thought*, ed. Carl Braaten [Simon & Schuster, 1967], 228). Note: the phrase in quotation marks above comes from Donne's "The ecstasy."

which is why it had to be printed overseas, but its allegations closely resemble those made by the Commons leadership during the Parliaments of 1628–29, until Charles shut them down for eleven years. One gust in the perfect storm that swept away the Caroline regime came with the third popish plot (in this case, popish–Laudian–bishop plot) text: Prynne's incendiary 1636 pamphlet, *News from Ipswich*, which precipitated the Star Chamber trial that made Prynne a puritan martyr but cost him his ears. It is a textbook example of the subversive underground literature of post–Reformation England.

The anthology's four other pieces of lay-authored sacred prose do not resemble Prynne, for which one may be grateful, but neither do they resemble one another—indeed, the final two are probably sui generis—and so we are dealing with a category suspiciously akin to the dogs of Borges' Chinese encyclopedia.[15] *Mea maxima culpa.* William Drummond's 1623 *A cypress grove*, a *contemptus mundi* dream vision (and model for Thomas Browne's *Urn-Burial*), weaves a dark and rich tapestry in which strands of Donne, *Hamlet*, and the new science thread through interlaced topoi of Renaissance Platonism and Spanish baroque spirituality; only the absence of specifically Roman Catholic motifs identifies the work as Protestant; like Quarles' *Emblems*, it points to the survival, at least among the laity, of a piety largely untouched by the Reformation. The religious portraits, both satiric and ideal, scattered among the Theophrastean characters of John Earle's *Microcosmography* (1628) evoke the Christian rationalism of the Great Tew circle in their muted and humane assessments of people who resemble neither saints nor demons—and who in this respect differ strikingly from the Calvinist portraiture of Joseph Hall's earlier adaptation of Theophrastus.[16] For Hall, as for the Catholic Digby, the transformative power of one's religion is the measure of its truth, and the more spectacular the transformation, the more evidently supernatural its source. These texts thus point to a relationship between conceptualizations of selfhood and confessional stance, but also to a second, more problematic, interplay between conceptualization of selfhood and confessional apologetics.

The final two texts have the grocers and gentlewomen. *The Little Gidding story books* record conversations that took place in late 1631 among a half dozen or so members of a semi-monastic community, most of them women; two of the women, together with their uncle Nicholas Ferrar, reworked the shorthand notes taken vive voce into manuscript volumes, volumes that have a good claim to be the single most important body of women's writing since Julian of Norwich's *Showings* over two hundred years before. The *Story books* bespeak the community's austere, ascetic piety and Anglo-Catholic traditionalism, yet the conversation has a free-form analytic intensity driven by an explicit commitment to questioning received ideas, values, and practices; indeed, in their defense of private inquiry and judgment in matters of religion, the Little Gidding women sound remarkably like John Hales. The voices preserved by the minor playwright Anthony Munday in his

---

[15] For Borges' dogs, see www.multicians.org/thvv/borges-animals.html (accessed December 10, 2010) or "John Wilkins' Analytical Language," in *Selected nonfictions: Jorge Luis Borges*, ed. Eliot Weinberger (Penguin, 1999), 231 (a translation of "El idioma analítico de John Wilkins," *La Nación*, February 8, 1942). My category becomes even less coherent if one adds the two prose works by laypersons mentioned earlier: Prynne's *God no imposter* and Digby's *Conference with a lady.*

[16] The introduction to the Earle selections <*infra*> reprints relevant passages from Hall and other early seventeenth-century character-writers.

1633 revision of Stow's *Survey of London* span the demographic gamut (minus kings and beggars); they speak from the tombs and memorials whose inscriptions, often in verse, Munday recorded in his comprehensive overview of the waves of restoring, enlarging, and adorning that from the mid-Jacobean period on worked a sea-change in the decaying fabric of London's churches. With a couple of exceptions, the changes display neither Laudian nor godly Calvinist markings, but instead seem to embody a mainstream Protestant churchmanship largely invisible in the historical scholarship, where narrative structure requires faction and friction. Moreover, this churchmanship seems to register specifically lay convictions and commitments. The ecclesiastical architecture and inscriptions Munday describes memorialize the churchwardens who oversaw the renovations; the collective generosity of the parish; the charitable gifts, large and small, of individual laypersons; and, on tombs, walls, and windows, the love binding the living and the dead: a wife's love for her two husbands, between whom she asks to be buried; a young man's love for the girl who in a few weeks would have been his bride; an old woman's love for her precious granddaughter. These churches presumably had ministers, but Munday rarely gives even their names.

The *Survey* here finds itself grouped with works of religious literature, but its inscriptions were contemporary with Dort, the Spanish Match, *The spy*, Laud's conference with Fisher, and Donne's sermon on the loves swallowed up in death. The selections are meant to be read against each other and parsed into myriad groupings, each, like a kaleidoscope's shifting configurations of many-splendored fragments, actualizing a different possible pattern. And they are meant to be read against the great canonical literary texts this anthology does not include.

The individual readings are each prefaced by an introduction and a bibliography of sources consulted. The texts that follow their respective introductions have been modernized throughout: the words are unchanged—those now unfamiliar have glosses—but spelling, punctuation, capitalization, and such-like accidentals have been modified in the interests of readability.[17] However, if a sermon's punctuation seemed to mark the rhythms of oral delivery (e.g., those by Andrewes and Preston), I kept most of the original pointing; similarly, where capital letters and boldface seemed signifiers rather than typographic convention (e.g., Prynne's *News from Ipswich*), a fair amount remains. Many of the theological tracts included extensive marginalia and footnotes, 90 percent of which lie on the cutting room floor, leaving only a representative remnant to suggest the range of authorities and sources cited.

The volume's own conventions are few and simple. *Everything* in braces is an editorial addition, whether in the text or in the notes. Square brackets sometimes indicate notes or emendations added by earlier editors; more often, they indicate that the bracketed material was originally a marginal annotation, although now placed within the text or below it. Omissions, as usual, are indicated by ellipses, supplemented by ‡ to signify

---

[17] Note: readability is not the same as correctness. In repunctuating, I have striven throughout for clarity, even if it meant adding non-regulation commas.

gaps of considerable length. I retained the early modern use of italics to indicate quotations or near-quotations and likewise followed early modern usage in not capitalizing pronouns referring to God. It seemed helpful, however, to use capitalization to distinguish the Fathers (patristic theologians), and the Father (God), from father (male parent); similarly "Church" refers to the mystical body of Christ or any of its visible branches, whereas a "church" is an ecclesiastical building. "Communion" is capitalized when signifying a Eucharistic celebration, otherwise not.[18]

All this should prove fairly self-evident. The one slightly puzzling convention arose from the need to clarify whether a note such as "see Prynne, *News*, 125" referred to the portion of Prynne's *News from Ipswich* reprinted in this volume or to the 1636 original. If the former, the citation will be followed by <*supra*> or <*infra*>, or the specific page numbers will themselves be given in angle brackets (e.g., Prynne, *News* <125>). If the citation does not use angle brackets, then it refers to the free-standing work: unless otherwise indicated, to the edition that the anthology uses as its base text; i.e., the edition specified at the conclusion of each of the readings. *Everything* in angle brackets, however, refers to this volume.

The early seventeenth-century English of the readings should not present much difficulty. The handful of unfamiliar words have been glossed, as likewise the occasional syntactic snarl. However, a few familiar-looking words have shifted meaning over time, and these have the potential to cause serious confusion. The reader should therefore keep in mind that in early modern English:

1. "want" means *lack*, not desire.
2. "pretend" can mean simply *claim* or *allege* (it can also, however, have the pejorative modern sense of *declare falsely, use as pretext, feign*).
3. "issue" and "event" often mean *outcome, result*.

A few other features of early modern English also deserve comment:

1. Sometimes nouns retain their Latin genders; in particular, the soul and the church, both of which are feminine in Latin, are often referred to as "she."
2. "Which" can be used as a personal pronoun; thus in the 1559 Book of Common Prayer, the Lord's Prayer begins "Our Father, which art in heaven."
3. Names of biblical books and saints often take an unfamiliar form: thus "Isaiah" is rendered "Esay"; Jerome becomes "Hierome"; Augustine appears as "Austin," etc.
4. The internal numbering of points within a text is often singularly unhelpful. Sometimes (e.g., Chillingworth's *The religion of Protestants*) the numbering is careful and systematic, but I have kept the original numbering throughout, even where it makes no apparent sense.

---

[18] So to (following early modern usage), "the Apostle" refers to St. Paul, "the Prophet" to Isaiah.

ABBREVIATIONS FOR WORKS
COMMONLY CITED

Collinson, *Religion of Protestants* Patrick Collinson, *The religion of Protestants: the Church in English society, 1559–1625* (Clarendon, 1982)

Como, *Blown by the Spirit* David Como, *Blown by the Spirit: Puritanism and the emergence of an antinomian underground in pre–Civil War England* (Stanford UP, 2004)

Donne, *Sermons* John Donne, *Sermons*, ed. George Potter and Evelyn Simpson, 10 vols. (U California P, 1953–62)

DNB *Dictionary of national biography*, ed. Leslie Stephen and Sidney Lee, 63 vols. (London: Smith, Elder, 1885–1900)

EEBO Early English books online (1998–)

Hooker, *Works* Richard Hooker, *The works of . . . Richard Hooker*, 3 vols., ed. John Keble, rev. R. W. Church & F. Paget, 7th ed. (Clarendon, 1888)

Kendall, *Calvin and English Calvinism* R. T. Kendall, *Calvin and English Calvinism to 1649* (Oxford UP, 1979)

Lake, *Moderate puritans* Peter Lake, *Moderate puritans and the Elizabethan Church* (Cambridge UP, 1982)

Lake, *Boxmaker's revenge* Peter Lake, *The boxmaker's revenge: "orthodoxy," "heterodoxy," and the politics of the parish in early Stuart London* (Manchester UP, 2001)

Laud, *Works* William Laud, *The works*, ed. William Scott and James Bliss, 7 vol. in 5 (Oxford: John Henry Parker, 1847–60)

McGee, *Godly man* J. Sears McGee, *The godly man in Stuart England: Anglicans, Puritans, and the two tables, 1620–1670* (Yale UP, 1976)

Milton, *Catholic and Reformed* — Anthony Milton, *Catholic and Reformed: The Roman and Protestant Churches in English Protestant thought, 1600–1640* (Cambridge UP, 1995)

Moore, *English hypothetical universalism* — Jonathan Moore, *English hypothetical universalism: John Preston and the softening of Reformed theology* (Eerdmans, 2007)

ODNB — *Oxford dictionary of national biography: online edition* (Oxford UP, 2004–)

OED — *Oxford English dictionary: online edition* (Oxford UP, 2000–)

Quantin, *Christian antiquity* — Jean-Louis Quantin, *The Church of England and Christian antiquity* (Oxford UP, 2009)

Shuger, "Faith and assurance" — Debora Shuger, "Faith and assurance," in *A companion to Richard Hooker*, ed. Torrance Kirby, 221–50 (Brill, 2008)

Shuger, *Censorship* — Debora Shuger, *Censorship and cultural sensibility: the regulation of language in early modern England* (U Pennsylvania P, 2006)

Shuger, "Protesting" — Debora Shuger, "A protesting catholic puritan in Elizabethan England," *Journal of British Studies* 48.3 (2009): 587–630

Shuger, "Reformation of penance" — Debora Shuger, "The reformation of penance," *Huntington Library Quarterly* 71.4 (2008): 557–72

Spinks, *Sacraments* — Bryan Spinks, *Sacraments, ceremonies and the Stuart divines: sacramental theology and liturgy in England and Scotland 1603–62* (Ashgate, 2002)

Tyacke, *Anti-Calvinists* — Nicholas Tyacke, *Anti-Calvinists: the rise of English Arminianism, c. 1590–1640* (Oxford UP, 1987)

NOTE ON NOMENCLATURE

In the 1980s, the familiar Anglican–Puritan dichotomy collapsed under the realization that a significant percentage of law-abiding mainstream Christians (i.e., Anglicans) in early Stuart England, parishioners and ministers alike, consisted of evangelical Calvinists (i.e., Puritans). The terminology remains in flux—and contentious, because naming implies narrative. So, for example, calling those whose churchmanship resembles Archbishop Laud's "Arminians" implies, among other things, that such churchmanship is a seventeenth-century development.[1] The use of "avant-garde" to designate the same churchmanship likewise, but more overtly, renders it *by definition* a new phenomenon, a break with the theological traditions of the Elizabethan Church and the English Reformation.[2] Naming implies narrative.

The names themselves, however, probably constrain narrative possibilities less than do their number. Most historical narratives use a two-term model: Anglicans/Puritans, Calvinist/anti-Calvinist, North/South, etc. As the examples suggest, two-term models have, it would seem invariably, an oppositional structure. Since conflict shapes much of human history, histories tend to foreground conflict, for which a two-term model generally proves satisfactory. That the Reformation triggered over a century of bitter and often bloody religious conflict will be denied by no one, and several of the readings in this volume (e.g., *The spy*) clearly construe their world in terms of a single overarching binary opposition. Yet many, and perhaps most, of the readings do not, even in their disagreements. The draft canons the English delegation submitted to the Synod of Dort (*The collegiate suffrage*) differ in crucial respects from those the Synod finally adopted, yet the draft canons of

---

[1] The controversy sparked by Jacob Arminius' (1560–1609) teaching on predestination postdates his 1603 appointment as divinity professor at Leiden.

[2] See Tyacke, *Anti-Calvinists*; Peter Lake, "Lancelot Andrewes, John Buckeridge, and avant-garde conformity at the court of James I," in *The mental world of the Jacobean court*, ed. Linda Levy Peck, 113–33 (Cambridge UP, 1991); and Lake, "Puritan identities," *Journal of Ecclesiastical History* 35.1 (1984): 112–13.

the other delegations also differed, and differed along different lines, and in the end all the delegations subscribed to the official canons.[3] There were divisions among them, but multiple, irregular, fairly narrow fissures, not one long weaponized trench bisecting the playing field. The Synod itself, of course, does belong to the annals of confessional warfare (it was called to defend Calvinist orthodoxy against Arminianism). Yet most varieties of religious experience lack battlefield analogues: Francis Quarles' popular-Protestant *Emblems* (1635) draws heavily on Counter-Reformation materials, and even *The collegiate suffrage* at one point invokes the Thomist evidence-adherence distinction central to the very different theologies of Richard Hooker and William Laud.[4] The domain of early Stuart religion reveals multiple fissures, but also an extensive commons, as well as a couple of deep channels across the length of a darkling plain.[5]

The way to escape the polarization built into a two-term model is, rather obviously, to use a richer, more descriptive terminology. The terminology need not be that of the period, given that most early Stuart religious labeling is hostile, polemical, and anything but descriptive. Instead, the anthology follows current scholarly usage, but inflected by two further considerations: that the terms used be consistent with the *self*-understanding of those to whom they refer (hence the avoidance of "Arminian" for those who would have disowned the kinship), and second, that their connotations be neutral (hence the preference for "Roman Catholic" over "Catholic" and "churchman" over "conformist").[6] However, since current scholarly usage is itself neither stable nor uniform, some definition of key terms seems in order.

Throughout the volume, "godly Calvinism" (or, less often, "evangelical Protestantism" and "experimental predestinarianism") designates the pietistic Calvinism centering on personal assurance, with an emphasis on sermons and Sabbath, that made up a broad current within the mainstream of the early Stuart Church. "Puritanism" (which between 1603 and 1638 seems more a tendency than a party and is therefore generally lower-cased) refers to "the sharp cutting edge" of this evangelical Protestantism, to an "oppositionist movement against the established Church," usually from within, although some puritans (Bradshaw, for example) were non-conformists.[7] Under Elizabeth, and again in the 1640s, this cutting edge struck at episcopacy, at the set liturgy of the Prayer Book, at the ecclesiastical courts. For much of the early Stuart period, however, frontal attacks on the established Church subside; instead, against the backdrop of the Palatinate crisis, the oppositionist energies within evangelical Protestantism fuse into an apocalyptic anti-Catholicism that saw Spain, the papacy, Arminians and, increasingly, Anglo-Catholic churchmen as allies in a dark conspiracy against God's people.

[3] For elaboration of this and the other specifics in this paragraph, see the introductions and notes to the individual selections.

[4] See the Anthony Milton "A qualified intolerance: the limits and ambiguities of early Stuart anti–Catholicism," in *Catholicism and anti-Catholicism in early modern English texts*, ed. A. F. Marotti, 85–115 (Macmillan, 1999).

[5] The allusion is to the final lines of Matthew Arnold's "Dover Beach."

[6] These are considerations not rules; it would be mere clumsy pedantry to use "experimental predestinarians" rather than "the godly" on a regular basis, as likewise to eschew "Catholic" where it is clearly shorthand for "Roman Catholic."

[7] Peter Lake, "Puritan identities," *Journal of Ecclesiastical History* 35.1 (1984): 113.

"Arminian" refers to those anti-Calvinists who affirmed the view of predestination held by the Dutch followers of Jacobus Arminius. John Playfere's invaluable survey of the various post-Reformation strands of predestinarian teaching identifies Arminianism with the position that God elected "those to life, whom he foreknew would believe and persevere under the means and aids of grace"—a position, Playfere notes, also held by humanist Lutherans like Melanchthon and Hemingsen, as well as by "many Papists"[8]—and John Milton. During the period covered by this volume, only Samuel Hoard's *God's love* is openly Arminian: before 1621, head-on challenges to fundamental Calvinist teaching would almost certainly have been blocked by the licensers;[9] after 1626, a royal proclamation forbade all public debate on predestination. Hence we do not really know whether there were more than a handful of English Arminians. Puritan controversialists, however, used "Arminian" as a catchall smear for high (or simply non-Calvinist) churchmen, because a 1618 Dutch cause célèbre linked Arminianism with treason and popery,[10] a usage recent scholarship has revived (albeit for different reasons). Yet Dutch Arminians do not seem to have been liturgically "high," and early Stuart high churchmen rarely treat predestination.

Having now brought up high churchmanship, some explanation should be attempted. "High church," "Anglo-Catholic," and "Laudian" designate overlapping categories and often function as near-synonyms; yet they do point to different aspects or phases of a current within the English Church going back to the Henrician Reformation. High churchmanship has to do with ritual, ceremony, and the sensuous enhancement of worship. It proved controversial because it involved reintroducing pre–Reformation ceremonies, ornaments, and practices (e.g., choral polyphony, altar candles, sacred images) and because it shifted the focus of worship from sermon to prayer and sacrament. Hence, high churchmanship generally presupposed the distinctive Anglo-Catholic vision of the post–Reformation English Church as continuous with the totality of the Christian past and heir to all that was good in medieval Christendom.[11] For most Calvinists, by contrast, and all puritans, the primary bonds of imagined community did not extend back through the centuries but stretched across the Channel to the Reformed Churches of the Continent. William Laud was both a high churchman and an Anglo-Catholic, but Laud remained a minor figure into the late 1620s, so that to use "Laudian" in Jacobean contexts seems misleading. The label does, of course, refer to those in basic agreement with Laud's policies during his years in power. Yet it can also refer to a distinctive theological outlook; the anthologized selections written by Laud's allies (and by Laud himself) share salient features: in particular, a stress on the mystery and beauty of holiness, but also the insistence noted in the introduction on the multiple strands of sacred truth, sacred authority, sacred

---

[8] John Playfere, *Appello Evangelium* (ca. 1625; 1st publ. London, 1652), 34–35; according to Playfere, Arminius' own position, although also hinging on divine foresight of faith, was more complicated (38–40).

[9] The licensers were chaplains to the archbishop of Canterbury and the bishop of London; from 1611 to 1633 the dogmatically Calvinist George Abbot was archbishop; from 1611 to 1621 the somewhat less dogmatic Calvinist, John King, was bishop of London.

[10] See the introductions to *The collegiate suffrage* <infra, n. 3> and *The spy* <infra>.

[11] Hence the high-church preference for English gothic over the new baroque styles of continental Catholicism (see Graham Parry, *The arts of the Anglican Counter–Reformation* [Boydell, 2006], 190–91).

presence—strands which singly have little force but woven together make whole cloth. This cluster of features, which is not typical of earlier high churchmen (e.g., Richard Montagu or Lancelot Andrewes), is also properly termed "Laudian."[12]

None of the authors anthologized here upholds reason against revelation; "rationalism" in early Stuart contexts means upholding the authority of individual reason against that of custom, tradition, councils, consensus, and every human ipse dixit. This is the rationalism of Milton's *Areopagitica*, but also of the Great Tew circle and, with qualifications, of Little Gidding.

"Roman Catholic" is, for the purposes of this volume, a straightforward category comprised of all those who considered themselves Roman Catholics.

The most problematic category is the last. Because the main "oppositionist movement" within the English Church from the Elizabethan Settlement to the Civil War was strongly Calvinist and fiercely hostile to whatever smacked of medieval Catholicism, predestination and "popishness" became the dual foci around which controversies revolved and parties crystallized. These parties have labels: the godly, Anglo-Catholic, etc. However, looking down the table of contents, one sees that perhaps a third of the names fit none of the labels adduced thus far, including big names like Sanderson and Donne. Early Stuart religion, like early Stuart politics, was not, on the whole, conceived in terms of parties (Democrat, Republican) or ideological groupings (blue-collar Democrat, free-market conservative). Parties do form around a few controverted issues, parties involving some number of persons with strong commitments to one or another position on these issues, but alongside this (to us) familiar way of structuring political and religious identity, one finds a quite different model, which seems to have been the normative one, since it goes unnoticed. This model assumes (in fact, requires) that everyone affirm a common core of beliefs or principles—thus from 1583 on, all clergy had to accept the royal supremacy, the Book of Common Prayer, and the Thirty-nine Articles—but this was, and was meant to be, a small core that left wide latitude for *individual* inflection and reflection. That is (an analogy may prove helpful here), instead of the species/breed model (dog/poodle) of modern party or denominational identity, what one finds is a species/individual structure (dog/short wire-haired dog, huge shaggy dog with one white paw, flop-eared brown dog). On the species/breed model, a thing's (or person's) identity is primarily a matter of the right-hand category: to the question "what is it," the answer is "a poodle," not "a dog." On the species/individual model, however, there is no right-hand category; "huge shaggy dog with one white paw" is not a category. Hence, identity has to ground itself in the common-denominator attributes of the left-hand side. What is it? It's a dog. Or, if one is speaking about early Stuart figures like Sanderson and Donne, the answer, it would seem, has to be that these are conformists or churchmen. It is the answer Francis Quarles' widow gave concerning her husband: "For his religion, he was a true son of the Church of England." Of the authors in this volume, besides those just mentioned, Field, Adams, Munday, and the early Wither fall within this category, as do a succession of Anglican worthies: John

[12] See Peter Lake, "The Laudian style," in *The early Stuart Church*, ed. K. Fincham, 51–70 (Stanford UP, 1993).

[13] Kenneth Fincham and Peter Lake, "The ecclesiastical policies of King James I," *JBS* 24 (1985): 169–207.

Jewel and John Whitgift, George Herbert and King James;[13] plus the thousands of ordinary parishioners whom Judith Maltby termed "Prayer Book Protestants." Setting aside the latter, about whom we know so little, it is clear that these do not constitute a party in the modern sense; their emphases are different, their voices distinctive, individual. What binds them together, as the foregoing implies, is a baseline commitment to an inclusive national Church at once Catholic and Reformed.[14]

---

[14] As a thought-experiment in political analogy, imagine that 40 percent of U.S. citizens identified themselves neither as Democrats or Republicans, liberals or conservatives; surveys showed that the actual views of these citizens differed quite widely, although they shared a basic commitment to democracy, to their country and its institutions, and to human rights; if asked, they generally called themselves "Americans." Such a cohort does not exist, of course, because in a two-party democracy *centered on the ballot box*, political participation virtually requires identifying with a side.

JOHN DOD*
(1550–1645)

The youngest of seventeen children, Dod's conversion took place during his years at Jesus College, Cambridge (BA 1576; MA 1579), where he formed lasting ties both to the nonconformist Thomas Cartwright and to leading moderate puritans like William Whitaker and Laurence Chaderton. Ordained in 1580, in 1585 he resigned the fellowship he had held since 1578 to take up a living in Hanwell, Oxfordshire, alongside Robert Cleaver (b. 1562) who served in the neighboring parish of Drayton. At Hanwell, Dod inaugurated a distinctive and demanding puritan ministry, including two Sunday sermons, a Wednesday lecture, seated communion around an ordinary table set up in the chancel, public fasts, and regular combination lectures with Cleaver and other ministers at Banbury.[1] It was also at Hanwell that Dod and Cleaver wrote *A plain and familiar exposition of the Ten Commandments*, first published in 1604 and running through nineteen editions over the next thirty years. Both men refused to subscribe to the three articles mandated by the 1604 Canons[2] and both were therefore suspended. After a three-year suspension, Dod was finally ejected in 1607, but soon thereafter found refuge with Sir Erasmus Dryden at his chapel of Canons Ashby in Northamptonshire, where he and Cleaver continued their collaboration, publishing an influential series of tracts and handbooks on godly living. At King James' insistence, however, in 1614 Bishop Dove forbade Dod's unlicensed preaching, at which point he seems to have gone to London and perhaps to have flirted with separatism (a path he ultimately chose not to follow). At James' death, Archbishop Abbot lifted Dod's suspension without requiring the old man to subscribe—a toleration that Laud too apparently extended, since his 1635 visitation notes Dod's decades of

---

* The very little that is known about Robert Cleaver, Dod's co-author, has been incorporated into the following sketch of the latter's career.

[1] On puritan fasts and lectures, see Patrick Collinson, *The Elizabethan puritan movement* (U California P, 1967).

[2] The canons of 1604 ratified Whitgift's 1583 rule that all candidates for holy orders affirm in writing 1. the royal supremacy over the English Church; 2. their commitment to the Prayer Book; 3. their belief that nothing in the Thirty-nine Articles conflicted with the Word of God.

nonconformity, and yet two years later Dod became the titular incumbent of Fawsley (where he had been serving as de facto vicar since 1625) without any known objection from his Archbishop, although Dod was a vocal opponent of Caroline policy. His eminence as a godly pastor can be gauged by the fact that the dying John Preston <infra> retired to Fawsley in 1628 to be under Dod's spiritual guidance. Dod remained in his parish throughout the Civil War, dying two months after the Battle of Naseby in his ninety-fifth year. It is not known when Cleaver died; his last publication, *A declaration of the Christian Sabbath*, came out in 1625.

In the selections from *A plain and familiar exposition* that follow, one can scarcely miss the distinctive creed and code of English puritanism: the extraordinary stress placed on Sabbath observance, the defense of personal assurance and final perseverance, the prohibition of religious images (including a moving and unexpected response to the question of where, except in the crucifix, we can *see* Christ in this world), and the sacramental, almost mystical, value attached to Bible-reading as both teaching God's will and transforming us into his likeness. One notes too the pervasive legalism—Scripture as rule-book; holiness as obedience—although balanced both by a Lutheran understanding of law as the mirror of our inescapable sinfulness, and also by a recognition of the painful imperfection of even God's best-beloved children. Its section on loss of faith and the terror of dereliction speaks in the same pastoral accents as Sibbes' *Bruised reed <infra>*.

Yet much of Dod and Cleaver's teaching is not distinctively puritan but, as the title states, "familiar"—familiar from scholastic ethics and numberless pre–Reformation sermons: the passages dealing with nasty gossip, with revenge, with filial and servile fear, with works of mercy, with economic justice, with fasting, prayer, and sacraments have very long pedigrees. The work makes hay of the old and oft–repeated charge that Protestant solifidianism dissolved the link between Christian holiness and social ethics.[3]

Part of the text's rhetorical power and historical interest, however, lies in its voicing of anticipated objections to its own teaching, objections that vividly register the attitudes and values informing the secular culture of the age—or at least what those attitudes and values were felt to be. The imagined objections identify the flashpoints (the most obvious being the legitimacy of pay-back for injuries and affronts) where that culture resisted the demands not just of puritanism, but of serious Christianity.[4]

SOURCES: *ODNB*; Jean Delumeau, *Catholicism between Luther and Voltaire* (London: Burns & Oates, 1977); William Haller, *The rise of puritanism* (Columbia UP, 1957); Shuger, "Reformation of penance"; John Spurr, *English puritanism, 1603–1689* (Macmillan, 1998); Hanwell Village Home: www.hanwellvillage .com/st_peters_church.html (accessed October 19, 2010).

---

[3] As, e.g., the charges made by Hoard <746–47, 758–60>, Dow <886>; also James Simpson, *The Oxford English literary history*, vol. 2: *1350–1547: reform and cultural revolution* (Oxford UP, 2004), 355–68. On the puritan-Protestant commitment to a conservative social ethics, see Collinson, *Religion of Protestants*, 150–82 *et passim*.

[4] See the *Little Gidding story books <infra>*.

JOHN DOD AND ROBERT CLEAVER

A plain and familiar exposition of the Ten Commandments
London, 1604

Exod. 20:1
God spake all these words and said, I am the Lord thy God, which brought thee out of the land of Egypt, out of the house of bondage.

These words contain a preparation to stir us up with all care and conscience to keep the law of God, which partly concerneth the observing of all the Commandments in general, and more especially the keeping of the first. That preparative which pertaineth to all is in these words (*God spake*): that is, that seeing they have God for their author and immediate teacher of them, even by his own voice, therefore we must settle ourselves to obey them without resistance or gainsaying. That which belongeth to the first is drawn, first, from the nature of God being Jehovah, which signifieth the essence and being incommunicable to any creature; and secondly, from his benefits: either general, in these words (*thy God*), that is, one that have bound myself in covenant with thee, to be thine, to deliver thee from all evils of soul and body, and to do thee all good for this life and that which is to come; or else special, in the last words (*which have brought thee out of the land of Egypt*), {which} signified that he had shewed and proved himself to be their God by drawing them out of that place which was wholly addicted to idolatry and superstition, and out of that condition and state which was full of misery and bondage. Since therefore this wonderful deliverance doth abundantly testify his love and goodness towards them, therefore they should wholly submit themselves unto him, & acknowledge him, and him only, to be their God.

God spake all these words.

In that he bringeth in the author of these words, saying *God spake* them, we are taught that God is after a peculiar manner the author of the Ten Commandments. As all Scripture is to be regarded as proceeding from God, so more nearly these ten words, because they be after a more special sort his words.

   . . .

3

. . . whereas the ceremonial and judicial laws were delivered by the ministry of angels, and the other Scriptures by the means of the men of God, the prophets, these words and these Commandments, God himself in his own person, full of majesty and terror, accompanied with his glorious angels, in a flame of fire, did pronounce so terribly in the hearing of them all, as that they trembled and came to Moses, requesting him that they might no more hear God speaking on this manner. . . .

. . .

And besides this testimony, divers reasons may be used to shew that these are God's own will and words after an extraordinary manner.

For the wonderful and perfect holiness that is contained in them sheweth who is the maker of them, because there is no good duty which God bound Adam to perform but is comprehended and commanded in one of these; and there is no sin that we are bound to abstain from and eschew which is not forbidden in some of these ten words. It was above the wit of men or angels to contain in so few words the whole perfection of our duty to God and man.

. . . this law is so absolute, and doth set out so full and complete a righteousness, that if one could fulfill them all, he should be fully acceptable unto God and needed not fly to Christ to be his redeemer. For indeed this meeteth with all sins, yea with the first and least motions; as Paul saith that he had not known that lust (meaning the motions of original concupiscence) had been sin but that the law saith *thou shalt not lust*. . . . so further this will prove them to be the words of God, because they be written and engraven in every man's conscience; so that, let wicked men strive and labor and do what they can to make themselves atheists, yet it will not be; they cannot blot out God's writing. These laws stick imprinted in their hearts and souls so firmly that they cannot be removed. For, as Paul saith, God hath not left himself without witness, but in every man's bosom and everyone's nature hath planted so much of his law as will serve to leave them without excuse, and to condemn them. . . .

. . .

Lastly, Christ himself came into the world to keep these laws. For they require a perfect and absolute obedience, as they are perfect; which, seeing no man could do, therefore Christ took our flesh upon him to fulfill them. . . . and he came not only to perform them himself fully, but also to make his saints able to obey them, though not in perfection and without any defect (for that only he himself can do), yet in truth and sincerity, for that he requireth of all his members.

Since therefore God hath such special regard in delivering these laws, we must hence learn with all reverence to hearken unto them, & willingly to bear the admonitions & rebukes that are contained in them, whosoever we be, and whatsoever he is that applieth them and speaketh them unto us. And in so doing we shall in truth shew ourselves to believe that God is the author of these words, if we can be content to endure that these precepts should be pressed and urged upon us, though by one that is our inferior, and baser in outward respects than ourselves. . . . And this affection was in Job, as he testifieth of himself in his 31 chapt., 33 verse: that though he was a man of much wealth and authority as that he could have made afraid a great multitude and could have crushed them by his power, yet the poorest and most contemptible might have dealt with him. . . . He would not chafe with those that brought God's rebukes unto him and say, "What have you to do to meddle with me? Who gave you authority to control your betters?" but controlling himself, kept within his own doors to humble his soul before God and to seek reconciliation with him.

. . .

Secondly, we may learn not to be afraid or ashamed to stand for them {the Commandments}, as also to practice them in our lives, though the atheists and profane sinners of the world mock and scoff at us never so much for the same. For what need we be ashamed to maintain those words which God himself was not ashamed in his own person to speak? . . .

This serveth therefore exceedingly to condemn their dastardliness that are afraid to keep the Sabbath or to do any such duty because they should be counted puritans. But is it not better that men should hate us without cause than that God should have a quarrel against us upon a just cause?

. . .

Thirdly, this serves to teach us to keep this law spiritually, because it is spiritual; for such as God is that made the law, such is the law which he made. It reacheth therefore to the inward parts of every man, and lieth close upon his conscience. And indeed in this it doth especially differ from the laws of men: for they do tie the hand and the tongue and the foot to the good abearing,[1] and take notice if any of these be faulty against them; but they meddle not with the heart and make no question of the inward motions of the soul, because man can bring in no proof of such a breach of the law, neither can he have any witness against the inward corruptions. But God searcheth the hearts and trieth the reins and entereth into the secrets of the soul.[2] . . . Now then our obedience shall be spiritual when it proceedeth from the soul and is done to a good end. But whatsoever is done for merit, as the Papists do, or for vainglory, as the Scribes and Pharisees did, this is not spiritual; this proceedeth not from the love of God but from self-love. This is a reflective kind of friendship that maketh us do something unto others that they may recompense us again with the like or a better reward. But then is our obedience true and upright when it cometh from a good heart, with desire and purpose to shew our obedience to God and our love to men.

. . .

. . . whosoever seemeth to keep all the other Commandments and yet will willingly maintain and bear with himself in the breach of one, he did never perform any true obedience unto any. Though one be no thief, yet if he be a Sabbath-breaker, he breaketh the whole law. For if one ask him, why do not you commit adultery? and he say, because God commandeth that I should not, then he would keep the Sabbath also; for they be both alike the Commandments of God. But if it be not because God commandeth, then he doth not obey the law but serve himself. . . .

The use of this is, first, to confute popish religion . . . because for the Second Commandment they do wholly allow themselves to break it. For the scope and sum of that Commandment is that we should serve God, not according to our own invention, but

---

[1] {to their good behavior}

[2] {On the medieval background to this, see Harold Berman, *Law and revolution: the formation of the western legal tradition* (Harvard UP, 1983), 187–88.}

according to his will. But their religion, what is it but a mere device of men's brains? . . . For where doth the word of God teach them to make images lay-men's books? . . . And most of them have no care of the Sabbath, but have more regard of their idol holy days, which the pope hath appointed, than of the Sabbath day, which God hath commanded. So for most carnal professors among us, who almost is there that regardeth the Sabbath and feareth to break it any further than the law of man will take hold of them? . . . But if they could keep themselves close from the magistrate & minister, would not most men willingly be following their business that day? This is to proclaim themselves hypocrites, & that they have no fear of God nor regard of him in their hearts. Oh but they hope they are good Christians and do keep the law of God, for they do not steal nor swear nor lie. But do they not know that God spake all these words, & therefore he hath no sound heart that addicteth not himself to keep them all?

This must teach us also that when we see that God doth not bless us according to his promises made to those that fear him, then we must examine ourselves diligently concerning our obedience to this his law, whether we live not in some sin, or whether some old sin lie not in us which hath never been repented of: for certainly God layeth no punishment upon us but only for contempt or neglect of his law. Wherefore, when he strikes us, we must begin to examine our obedience. . . .

. . .

. . . Then the question is, whether he be Jehovah or not, whether the same forever, without any change. If he be (as sure he is), then he must deliver us also when we call upon him. But are we sure to be delivered out of this trouble and to be set out of this debt or temptation if we call unto God? This we are sure of, that if we cry to God, he will deliver us from our sin, and from the punishment of it; or if the cross do hang still upon us, he will sweeten it with some spiritual comfort, and strengthen us that we shall be able to endure it, and so recompense it with heavenly grace that we shall gain more in the spirit than we lose in the flesh. But unless that we believe that God is Jehovah and immutable, all the histories of the Scripture are made unprofitable unto us; then we have no use nor comfort of those things which we hear and read: as how God blessed Abraham and delivered Jacob and did many wonderful things for his people in former times. But if we hold this firmly, that God is the same forever, this is sure: that whatsoever good thing he did for them, he will do the like for us, if we use the same means. So also if anyone hath found in himself, that at such a time I was in great troubles and terrors, and then I prayed unto God, and I know that he heard my prayer and helped me. Are you certain that God did hear you when you cried heretofore? Then you may be far more sure of this: that if you cry again, he will hear you again, else he should not be Jehovah. If he have been yours once, he is yours still, and will be yours forever.

This is also for the terror of the wicked. Is God Jehovah, constant and unchangeable in his judgments? Then look what plagues proud persons have had heretofore, the same shall they have now, so sure as God is true, unless they repent and get pardon in Christ. . . . Many that did steal before and were brought to shame and could scarce save their lives, yet when they are delivered will fall to it again, but yet far more closely (as they imagine) and with much greater skill in the trade; and then they think all shall be well. But who found them out before? Did not the righteous God, that will reward wicked men according to their wickedness? . . . Let not them look for better success in their latter sins than in the former, since God remaineth constant and is both able and ready to punish them.

Some have played the filthy persons, and God hath shewed it to men to their discredit. Will they then fall to it again and think they can hide it? No, they shall not, for God will reveal it. . . . As sure as he is Jehovah that brought them into the pikes[3] before; so sure, if they turn again to their filthy vomit, he will bring them to shame again: either in this life, to make them repent and judge themselves; or if not, then sure in the life to come, where the burden shall be much more heavy and intolerable upon their conscience, and shall press them down to hell. It is a wholesome medicine for such sinners to come to shame here, that, if it may be, they may be brought to repentance and amendment.

Thy God

The former argument of obedience was taken from God's nature, that he was eternal in justice to punish sinners, and in mercy to reward his children. Now this is from his goodness: *I am thy God.* Almighty indeed I am . . . yet so as that I abase myself to take care for thee, to have a loving heart toward thee, and to be thy father, and to make thee my child; to be thine husband also, and to make thee my spouse. . . .

The doctrine hence gathered is that if ever we will obey God in soundness, then we must know him to be our God, to have tender care of us, to love us, and that we shall speed best when we yield most obedience to him. . . .

Reason will shew this: for if we hear that God is infinite in power, and do not withal know that he is our God to use his power for our good, then it makes us fear . . . as nothing vexeth the thief more than to hear of a just judge, for then he hath no hope of escaping, unless he have a pardon and know that the judge comes to deliver him and to do him good. Also when we hear of God's patience and goodness and mercy, this will be but a vexation to us, unless we know that he is good and merciful to us. This addeth to the grief, to hear that God is good, if we must not feel it. For then the wicked heart objects thus: They preach much that God is merciful, gracious, &c. But what is this to me, that he is so to others? I am sure he is not so to me. I shall fare never the better for it. . . . As for a beggar that hath nothing, to hear tell of large possessions and great revenues that must be left to such and such a one; this is tedious unto him and makes his misery more bitter. And in this case, till men be persuaded that God is their God, they count it bootless to pray; and as for giving of thanks, they want matter and arguments. . . .

. . .

Secondly, God sheds his love abroad in the hearts of his children and makes them cry *Abba*, Father. This is not so in men. They, when they beget a son, cannot beget a childlike affection in him; but oft times the children are rebellious and stubborn. But if God beget a child to himself by the seed of his word, he makes him affected to him as to his father. If then we have this affection to God, that we love him as our father, certainly this is his work, and we are his children.

Also God the Son, Christ Jesus, where he comes, he kills sin; he abates our lust and worldliness, and works a fresh spring of grace and holiness. But if we feel no work of his death in us to mortify our sin, then how can we know that he died for us? . . . But if God's

---

[3] {into danger}

spirit reprove and check thee for thy sin and make thee fear, blessed art thou, for God is thy God.

Oh, but I am more troubled and terrified now than I was before. True. And it must be so. For God's spirit, where it takes place, must needs convince men of sin. For it is not (as many think) a matter of wit to stand in defense of sin and be able to speak for a bad thing, but it is a matter of lust; for where lust hath dominion, it whets the wit to speak for it, and the devil helps. But if God's spirit come once, it drives to a plain confession. . . . Then try thyself in these things, not to have beauty and strength . . . but to have patience and gentleness and a moderate spirit to adorn thy mind; these be sure signs of God's spirit. Also the Holy Ghost makes us able to cry *Abba*, Father. . . . If we have this spirit of prayer, then it is plain the Holy Ghost is ours. . . .

But men will say they have a faith and believe in God, which if they had, it would bring forth obedience and have works. For how can they choose but obey God, if they hold this sure, that God loveth and regardeth them, and will give them a reward for every good thing that they do? And this everyone must perform that will say, God is my God.

And here is to be removed the injurious dealing of the Papists, who, as themselves are justly debarred from the assurance of God's mercy because they rest on their own merits, so would they deprive all others of the comfort of perseverance, making this a certain point of their religion, that no man stands certain of salvation. And by this means they hinder men from cheerful obedience and cut off all sound thankfulness.

. . .

So that if Christ have washed us from our sin, the worst and sorest enemy (for all the world cannot wash away one sin), then never fear these less matters.

Oh, but this makes me doubt whether I am God's child or not, because I have such long and fiery troubles. If God loved me, would he afflict me thus? Then look to this people here. They were the best nation under the sun, and none so good as Israel, even then when they were thus pressed under Pharaoh's cruelty. All other people were but as thorns; they were the rose. Other were but harlots; they the Lord's spouse. Yet they were afflicted, and that indeed to keep them from ungodliness and worldly lusts, and consequently their own damnation. So that outward ease is no sure sign of God's favor, else none should have been so much in God's favor as the Sodomites, Canaanites, and such like, for they had all the ease, wealth, and outward prosperity of the world. And before the flood, Cain's children had all the glory of the world on their side. They found out music and keeping of cattle and other arts, and all must be beholding to them. But let us keep God's favor; let us fear him and pray unto him, and then our long and strong crosses shall bring long and strong comforts.

Secondly, let us learn hence to prepare for crosses, since God's children may be sore afflicted; else little do we know how they will sting us when they come. . . .

Prepare therefore for crosses, and we shall be able to bear them. But if we go on in a fool's paradise and think, indeed this world is a vale of tears to others, but to me it shall be a place of pleasure; they must have trouble, but I must have ease, then, when instead of joy we find grief that we looked not for, and we dreamed of credit but there comes nothing but contempt, we imagined that God should lift us up higher and higher, and he casts us down lower and lower, this casts us into such desperate passions that we are neither fit to serve God nor man.

All this would be helped, if we could think God's children have in all times suffered afflictions; it is the lot of the righteous, and I must look to taste of the same cup; and therefore labor beforehand to get patience and to trust God and to look for help at his hands. . . . .

The First Commandment

Now follow the Commandments, whereof the first is contained in these words:

Exod. 20:3: *Thou shalt have none other gods before my face*

. . .

First, of the negative part: to *have none other gods* is not to have anything whereon we set our delight or which we esteem more than God. The doctrine from hence is that we must suffer nothing to withdraw our soul, or anything in our body or soul, from God. For whatsoever withdraweth anything in us from God, that is a strange god unto us. That is every man's god, that every man's heart is most set upon. Whatsoever the mind of man is more carried after than the glory and service of God, that is another GOD unto him. As for matter of commodity, if a man set his hope and his trust and his heart upon his wealth, this is idolatry. As in Job 31:24: if *I made gold my hope*, &c. So the rich man in the Gospel made his wealth an idol, because he trusted in it and did worship to it; for here he speaks of the inward worship of GOD in the soul. If one then rely upon wealth and think himself safe when he hath it and undone if it be taken from him, this is to make goods his gods and gold his hope. . . . So covetousness is called idolatry, not that men bow down their bodies to it, but (which is worse) their souls and affections, their wit, memory, understanding, yea all their faculties stoop to that, which should only stoop to God. So that he that loves riches above measure and sets his heart upon earthly things is one of the worst sort of idolaters.

In like manner, pleasure, and what other thing so ever a man hunts after more than after God's glory, is another god unto him. As the Apostle speaks of some voluptuous persons, who would have thought it an injury if one had told them that they worshipped not God but their bellies; for they, no doubt, took themselves to be professors of religion and servants of God as well as the best; howbeit, the Apostle saith in plain words that they made their belly their god. For though they did not kneel down and hold up their hands to their belly, yet they set themselves more earnestly to feed themselves than to glorify God, and were more grieved if they were pinched in a matter of victuals and good cheer than to see the name of God dishonored and blasphemed or any sin committed. . . .

All these ungodly men then be worshippers of false gods and make those vain things idols to themselves. So even Eli was said to honor his sons more than God. Though he were a good and holy man, yet being too indulgent to his children, in that he contented himself only to have admonished them for their faults, and did not proceed to punish them when admonition would not prevail (as became him, being a magistrate), he honored his children more than God. . . .

The use of this is, first, to reprove all ignorant men and unregenerate persons. It is certain they have other gods. For every unregenerate man depends either upon himself or some other thing else, never upon God: as he saith of such, *they sacrifice unto their nets*

[Hab. 1:16]. . . . So that every carnal man sets up himself; he doth nothing but seek and serve himself, and therefore is his own idol, and another god unto himself.

This serves also to humble God's children daily with the consideration of it, for who lives so holily that doth not sometimes fear men more than God, and that doth not often depend too much upon outward means, and hath not too great a love of earthly things?

. . .

Before my face

Because this is the most spiritual commandment and doth most press upon the heart, and we are most ready in this matter to dissemble with men and deceive our own souls, therefore God doth more nearly urge it, and saith, *before me.*

Hence we learn that it is not enough so to behave ourselves as that no impiety break forth from us before men, but we must look to our hearts and see that no impiety come in God's sight. . . . For men first look to the outward behavior and hence descend to judge of the heart, but God first approves the heart and then the outward action. If we see good things outwardly, we are bound in conscience to think well of that man; but God will first see uprightness, and then he will account well of the practices that we do outwardly. . . .

. . .

Secondly, this teacheth us to carry ourselves warily, and to fear as well secret as open sins, because all secrets are open to God, and every hidden thing is manifest before his face. . . . But the want of this persuasion, that God looks always full upon us, is the cause why men have so many covetous, so many crafty and cruel thoughts, and such impure cogitations; yea, men are now come almost to this height of atheism thereby as to think and say that thought is free. But they shall find that though it be free from men, it is not free from God; and that they shall be liable to the sentence of everlasting death and condemnation before God's judgment seat, unless they be as careful to cherish holy thoughts within themselves, as honest actions; and as diligent in purifying their hearts in the sight of God, as in walking civilly in the sight of men.

. . .

. . . For why do men so willingly serve great personages and are ready to employ themselves in their business but because they think that hence they shall have honor and credit as a reward of their services. If then we did faithfully consider that God giveth such excellent wages as that no man can give the like (for what doth he not bestow on them that fear him? He gives his Son, he gives them his Spirit, and grace in their heart, he gives them the blessings of this life, and eternal in the world to come), we would surely serve him with a willing mind.

But on the contrary, the cause and fountain of all disobedience against God is because there is no right knowledge of God. As Hosea complains in his 4 chapter, verse 2, that *they lie, they steal, they commit adultery, and blood toucheth blood.* But what is the cause of this confusion? Because there was *no knowledge of God in the land*; and where men know not God, what can be looked for else but all impiety against God, all unrighteous dealing against men?

This plain reproves all ignorant persons that know not how many persons there be in the Trinity, or at least they cannot tell what any of them did for them. They are not acquainted with the properties of God, nor with his actions; they never thought on his name nor pondered on his truth, justice, power, mercy, and such like things. These may brag of love and faith and hope and confidence and patience, but they have none of them, for all good things flow from this, that we know God. . . . Therefore an ignorant heart is always a sinful heart, and a man without knowledge is a man without grace. . . .

And on the other side, this must stir us up to call for wisdom and to cry for understanding, to seek for it and to dig for it as for gold and precious stones. We must often read God's word, and confer and meditate upon it; which, if we do, it will give us understanding, and then we shall see God's properties, his goodness, his love, his ability and readiness to help us, and so we shall be effectually drawn to trust in him. And indeed this often meditating and thinking upon God's word is the next way to make us like God and to renew and repair the image of God in us. For by seeing Christ in the Gospel, we are changed from glory to glory; & the more we know him, the more we increase in being like to him. . . .

The next duty is love. That we must *love God with all our hearts and all our souls*. . . . And indeed this is the chief duty & the best fruit of knowledge; for this worketh all cheerfulness to obey, constancy to obedience, patience in our suffering, and procureth acceptation from God for all our service. But because it is so plain a duty as that no man will deny it, it is best for us to shew some marks whereby we may see in what measure we have attained to love God.

The first may be, how we delight to seek God in the means wherein he hath appointed to meet us. For in what measure we can offer ourselves to God in those things wherein he offereth himself to us, in that measure we love him. If we be willing to ask all good things and to seek comfort at his hands by prayer, and to lay open our wants to him and as it were to confer with God; if we be desirous to come to hear his word, wherein we may see his wisdom for our direction, his mercy for our comfort, his power for our defense and for the subduing of our sins, and his riches to make us rich and to supply all our wants, then we do indeed love God. . . . So for the word and sacraments, wherein Christ Jesus offereth himself unto us, to make us partakers of his body and blood. Would we then try how we love God? We may try it by examining what desire we have to these things. . . .

. . .

A third note whereby we may discern our love to God is the love we bear to his servants. 1 John 5:1: *He that loves him that begets, will love him that is begotten of him.* If then we find in our hearts a good affection to Christians, because they are Christians, without any respect what they have been or may be unto us; if we esteem of them because they bear a love to God's word and have the virtues of Christ shining forth in their lives—as love, patience, meekness, temperance, and such like—it is an undoubted testimony unto us of our true love to God.

A fourth mark is if we love his coming, if we can willingly desire the appearance of Christ to judge the quick and the dead. For whatsoever our heart is truly set upon, we cannot but be exceeding desirous to have it with us. Love is such a band as doth tie and draw the mind unto that which is loved. . . . And even in the natural marriage, in which the love is much more weak and slender, this is manifest, that if the wife love her husband, when he is gone far off, she will be very desirous of his return. If this be so in this marriage (where there be many infirmities and crosses), that they long and wish for the company of one another, how much more in the spiritual? where there is perfection already on the one party, as that he is full of love and mercy, and will likewise free the other party from all miseries, wants, & infirmities (when they shall be joined fully together), and fill them full of all virtues and graces. In this marriage, I say, how can one choose but long after this perfect and happy meeting? How can he that hath any love and assurance of these things stay himself? but he shall be ready to fly up into heaven, and the flame of his desire will burn above the clouds to wish that God would come and dwell with us. . . .

. . .

The next duty here commanded is the fear of GOD, which also proceeds from knowledge. For the sight of God's goodness and mercy and truth will inflame the heart with a love of him; so if one consider his greatness, power, and excellency above all his creatures, this will strike his heart with a wonderful reverence and a great fear of his majesty.

But for this fear, an objection must first be answered. For 1 John 4:18, he saith, *Perfect love casteth out fear*, and Luke 1:74, *We are delivered from all our enemies that we might serve him without fear.* To this we answer that perfect love casteth out a slavish fear indeed, and such as is in the devils, who tremble before God, but so as they run from him; such as is in wicked men when the threatenings of God arrest their evil consciences . . . and make them therefore not to love God's word and the ministry, but to hate it, & cast off all care of godliness & religion from them.

But it is true that whosoever loveth God cannot choose but in the same measure also {to} fear him. For the spirit of God that persuadeth them of his favor and worketh love will declare his power and greatness, which will work a fear and awe of him. It casteth out therefore the hellish fear that makes one flee from God, but it causeth that holy fear that makes one more careful to come unto him and to worship him. . . . This is commanded, Esay 8:13, *Sanctify the Lord in your hearts, and let him be your fear & your dread.* The occasion of this precept was this.

Before in the chapter he shews that there were stirs and rumors of wars in the land, whereupon the people and king and all did shake as leaves shaken with the wind by reason of the great fear which was in them. . . . But in the 12 verse, the Prophet saith, You that be God's children, do not you fear their fear. Fear not you the fears of wicked men, for they fear nothing but poverty and outward disgrace and a temporal death; these be base fears and not worthy that the hearts of the children of God should be taken up with them, being but trifles. . . . fear neither the fears that wicked men fear, nor yet them themselves. But now because the heart of man will fear something, and unless it be very well armed, it will fear man and the fears of man; therefore he sheweth a means how to keep us from all infection of such foolish terrors, and that is to sanctify God in our heart, and to let him be our dread: that is, to give him the praise of his power, mercy, and truth, and of all his attributes, and then he shall be our dread. . . .

. . .

Secondly, the fear of God, if it once thoroughly do possess the heart, will make one pliable and frameable to God's will, though it be never so contrary to his nature and former behavior. . . .

So Isaiah 6:5: God did send him about such a message as he knew would be full tedious unto him and go against his stomach: namely, that he must preach to harden the hearts of the people and be a minister of death to his hearers, which was as bitter as death to him, so as he could never have yielded to it. But now God comes not with the bare precept, for that would have done little good, the thing was so contrary to Isaiah. Therefore he shews himself to him in a vision and lets him see his majesty in such a fearful sort, as that he cries out, *What shall I do? I am a man of polluted lips and dwell among a people of polluted lips. I shall surely die, for I have seen the Lord.* When he was thus thoroughly terrified, and the pride of his flesh was beaten down with the apprehension of God's fearful majesty, then when God asks, *Who will go?* he is ready, and saith, *Lord, send me.* And so God sends him, and he goeth immediately, and willingly.

There is no disputing now, nor reasoning of the matter. For all the objections that men make (that they think that God's commandments be hard and grievous, and why should they deny themselves? Why should not they have their pleasure?) come hence: that they fear not God, nor think of his greatness. For if they could bring their hearts once to consider of his wonderful power, they would soon stoop; all arguments would fall to the ground, and all would be quiet and still. For this will tame the fierceness and boisterousness that is in men's hearts, and make them gentle and calm. As we see in Job, though he was a very good and patient man, yet when his flesh began a little to work and his heart was disquieted and vexed by the words of his friends, then he would needs be dealing with God; he thought he had reason to speak and imagined that he could say much for himself; he would have his mouth full of arguments and fain would have God to come to hear what he could speak in his own defense and to shew what wrong was done to him. But now when God comes and declares his workmanship in the snow and ice and some other of his creatures, as it were to let him see how childish he was in the smaller matters and ignorant of the creation and preservation of these least things, and therefore he was a most unmeet man to call God to account and that God must come to give his answer before him, that he should sit in the seat of judgment and on the bench, and GOD stand at the bar—he was like to dispute well with God his Creator that did not know the nature of the least of his creatures. When God had argued with him thus a while, and he saw how great God was and how excellent, Job had no more to say, but now indeed he confesseth that he had spoken foolishly, but he would do so no more; he would now be still and content to bear God's hand, let him do what he would; if he would kill him, he was content to die, but he would never dispute with God anymore. So we see how quiet Job was now, and what good and notable effects this fear of GOD will work in our hearts, if it once soundly and thoroughly possess them.

. . .

The way to attain to this is, first, to deny ourselves quite, to renounce utterly our carnal wisdom. . . . If one will debate the matter according to the fleshly wisdom of men, and say he hath reason to do that he doth, then surely he will never have reason to be religious and serve God, for that is against his reason. . . . for the wisdom of the flesh is enmity to God in all things. Yea, the carnal wisdom of a spiritual man is enmity to God and goodness, and so long as one follows it, he shall never fear God. As we may see in Eve, when she would go and consult with that carnal reason that the devil had put into her head, and began to think with herself, Surely this fruit hath a good color to the eye, and it is like it will prove pleasant to the taste, and I shall get much knowledge by it and be made like God, so that my state shall be much amended. . . .

. . .

The great fear of man's power ariseth from the forgetting of God's infinite power. When one is in such a terror of man that is but dust and cannot defend himself against worms but they shall creep in his bowels and eat up his heart, it comes from hence, that one doth quite forget that there is such a God as was able to make heaven and earth of nothing and that hath grievous judgments laid up for sinners. . . . Therefore in the Rev{elations}, when he reckoneth up a great rabble of reprobates & the whole host of damned sinners, he puts the *fearful* in the forefront & makes them the captains & ring-leaders of all the rest. . . . They be afraid to keep the Sabbath or go to hear sermons lest they should be counted too precise; they will not serve God lest their old acquaintance and friends should forsake them and their neighbors should jest and laugh at them. This dastardliness and coldness to do good, but courage and readiness to do evil, shews plainly that they be void of the true fear of God. . . .

Hence then the best man in this world may learn to confess his weakness and to acknowledge his wants and defects in this behalf: for that so much fear of death, poverty, disgrace, and of men shews a great want of the fear of God. This trembling at men's threat-enings so much and at God's threatenings so little, that is in all men by nature . . . testifi-eth to our faces and sheweth plainly that we have but a very little spark of the fear of God.

These wants we must see and confess, and run unto Jesus Christ, that made a perfect and absolute satisfaction that he might supply our imperfections; and then of his fullness we shall have enough to fulfill that wherein ourselves come short.

. . .

. . . Now some of the marks whereby we may know that we do indeed, and not in word only, trust and rely upon God alone are these:

The first is to use all good means faithfully to serve God's providence. No man is more diligent in putting all good means in practice than he that hath a most constant and firm faith in God, as we see that in Jacob. He had a promise that he should prevail with men sith he had prevailed with God. . . . When Jacob received this promise and did fully trust in God for his deliverance, yet he was not slack in using all means that might pacify Esau. Nay, who could have used more wise and good means than he did? but still honest means. For forthwith he sends him presents to assuage his wrath, and sends them not all together, but sets a distance betwixt one and other, that so this pause might make him to digest them the better, and his wrath might by little and little go out. . . . And then he bids them all to do obeisance and call him *my lord Esau*, in great wisdom and discretion; for, give a covetous man wealth enough, and an ambitious man honor enough, and you may lead them whither you will.

Likewise Paul, when God had promised to bestow upon him all that were in the ship, he would not neglect the means. For when the mariners would craftily have got-ten themselves away in the boat, he suffered it not, but tells them that if they went away, they should be all drowned, as they should indeed. For as God had appointed to save all, so he had appointed to save them all together, and by their staying together, one to help another. . . . So for the soul, if you say, I trust God will give me everlasting life, then you will pray, then you will hear the word, then you will meditate upon the word and receive the sacraments. . . .

A second note of this true confidence is not to be discouraged when we want the means. As when we have them we will not trust in them, so when we want them we will not be dismayed, if we put our confidence in God; for the heart is never dismayed till the hope be gone, and if God be our hope, then so long as he remains, our comfort remains. But this is the miserable corruption of our nature, that if all these outward things be gone, then we sit down discontented and discouraged and think that our case is desperate and we undone; but if riches and outward matters flow in, and we have the world at will, then as the rich man in the Gospel, we say . . . *soul, take thine ease; thou hast store laid up for many years. . . .*

Therefore Job proveth by this that he did trust in God, for he did not rejoice in his goods; he was not glad that he had much gold and many cattle and grounds, for he knew that God did not love him one jot the better for that, and all his wealth could not keep one cross from him or prolong his life one minute of an hour, and therefore he did not much rejoice to see these things come in by heaps; and so when all was gone, he had soon made his accounts, *God hath given, God hath taken, blessed be the name of the Lord. . . .* If God be our father and undertake to maintain us, why are we not content with his promises? What though he keeps things in his own hands? It is because we know not how to use them. But this is the matter: we would be our own gods (as it were) and live at our own finding. And in this case we be far more foolish than our children, for they do not trouble themselves to think, how shall I bring the year about? how shall I get provision for the next year? or, what if ill weather come? &c. But they are merry and fresh and think not upon these matters, but make account that their parents will see them provided for . . . and therefore when they need, they go to them with hope, and have success accordingly.

. . .

The Second Commandment

Exod. 30:4: *Thou shalt not make to thyself any graven image, nor the {likeness of any thing in heaven}, &c.*

In all which words is shewed by what means we must worship God: namely, not after the inventions of the flesh and blood, but according to the direction of his holy word. And here is set down a prohibition forbidding us to make any image to represent God or to help us in his worship, or to have any superstitious or will-worship thereby to please him the better. . . .

. . .

Therefore it is a most blasphemous debasing of his majesty to go about any such resemblance, and is so far from lifting up our hearts unto him that it draws our hearts down from him, making us conceive carnally of him as of those things which we see with our natural eyes. If we should see a man bow down to snakes and toads . . . in honor and reverence to his prince, because these did resemble him, were he not to be condemned of great abuse and dishonor to his prince? For these base and vile things are no way fit to put us in mind of our honorable sovereign. . . . Now there is a thousand times more agreement betwixt the mightiest man and a toad than betwixt God and an idol. For a toad is a creature of God, as well as the greatest potentate; but an idol is the work of man's fingers and an invention of the devil. . . . But here some object that indeed God the Father and the Holy Ghost be merely spirits and cannot be represented by any thing, but what say you of God the Son? He took upon him the nature of man. May not one make an image of him? But can we make an image of Christ unless we leave out the chief part of him, which is his divinity? . . . Therefore this is an absurd and wretched resemblance.[4] But if we would see an image of Christ, look upon poor Christians that walk up and down amongst us, for they be flesh of his flesh & bone of his bone, and in them is a lively resemblance of him, and they have a body and a reasonable soul, as he hath, and the graces of his spirit in them. . . . But would we see Christ crucified before our eyes, & withal be made partakers of the merit and efficacy of his death and passion? Look upon him in the ministry of the word and sacraments, and there we shall not only behold him, but also enjoy a blessed communion with him.

. . .

Visiting the sins of the fathers on the children

First it may be objected how God can in justice do this, and punish the children for the father's fault? But to that we may answer as God doth in Hos. 2:2, speaking to the Jews: he bids them plead with their mother, comparing himself to an husband; he shews that there is no fault in him, but all the blame lies on the adulterous mother. For as an husband may without any fault put away the wife that hath dealt treacherously, and her adulterous brood too, because they be none of his children, so God may justly plague and forsake both the parents and the wicked children of wicked parents.

. . .

So Cham's posterity, for many generations, bare the curse upon them for the impiety of their wicked father.

This serves to rebuke those parents that think and {*sic*} go about by oppression, by wrongful and injurious dealing, and such wicked courses to better the estate of their children, and hope by these means to make their seed great upon the earth after them. Nay, this is the way to bring the curse of God, and consequently destruction, upon their family. . . . As God's daily judgment upon enclosers[5] and oppressors in our days shews it, for when they begin to molest poor men, to unpeople towns, to seek how they may dwell alone in the land, this enclosing doth but exclude them and theirs, so that if men would but mark and observe it, they should see before their faces how God plagues their sins, both in themselves and their houses.

‡

The Sixth Commandment

Thou shalt not kill

This Commandment respects the person of our neighbor, requiring us to procure his welfare and safety both in soul and body, and to avoid all kind of cruelty and unmercifulness.

. . .

---

[4] {It is not clear how strictly this prohibition was understood; the frontispiece to this edition shows Christ the Good Shepherd bringing home the lost sheep on his shoulders. The principal objection was to religious images in churches.}

[5] {See the Wikipedia article on "enclosure": http://en.wikipedia.org/wiki/enclosure.}

What the things of omission be that are forbidden concerning the body, it may appear in Matt. 25, where Christ condemns some as goats, limbs of the devil, and fire-brands of hell, because they gave not meat to the hungry and drink to the thirsty and clothed not the naked and visited not the sick and imprisoned, and such like. So that the neglecting of these duties of mercy is sufficient to condemn them as guilty and worthy of eternal death and hell-fire. . . . Another thing of omission is when one neglects to pay the due wages and recompense for the work of any poor man. For if it be a miserable sin not to do good freely where need requireth, it is much more abominable and damnable not to give a due debt and reward of the work when it is deserved. . . . For two special sins there be in the second table that make the land cry to God, that he can have (as it were) no rest until he take vengeance: the one, sodomy; and the other, oppression and cruelty against this Commandment. As afore in Deut{eronomy}, so in James, he saith, *Howl ye rich men.* And why? What misery is near? The cry of the poor, oppressed by you, is come up into the ears of the Lord of hosts. When one gets his goods so ill and enricheth himself by withholding other men's dues, though the men should be silent and say nothing, yet his necessity, his belly and his back, would make an hideous outcry before God till he had executed his vengeance. . . .

. . .

The first thing of practice that is here forbidden is inward, and that is hasty and unadvised anger, rash and unjust wrath. . . . That which was (for the sudden and present passion) natural, if it lie soaking and lingering, and sink deep into the heart, it grows then to be devilish. And so if one's anger be above that that the quality of the fault requires, this is rash, and comes not through the folly of the party with whom he is angry, but through his folly that is angry. Therefore we must look that we be never moved without a just cause. And then that we proportion our anger to the sin committed against God, and not to the injury done to us, for that proceeds from pride and is no better than revenge; and therefore we must more be grieved at those things that break the first than at those that break the second table; and always that that doth most displease God and is most odious to him must be most grievous to us. And yet let not the sun go down upon it, but let it quicken us to prayer for the person, and that with a zeal of God's glory.

Now the means to keep us from this foolish passion of rash anger are these: first, often to meditate upon our own sin and vileness. . . . So that could we consider our own offences, how rebellious we have been against God and how often injurious to men, this would make us more quiet & to take more deliberation before we were offended so much with our neighbor. It will assuage, delay, and take away the edge of our rash anger against the weaknesses of others.

Second, labor to get wisdom always, and in everything to behold God's providence, to see his hand ruling everything, and to persuade ourselves that all things come to pass according to his purpose and direction; and then we shall not so soon fret against men. . . .

. . .

Now it followeth how it {the Sixth Commandment} is broken in deed: and that is when one strikes to hurt, without death. This hurting our neighbor in revenge, God hath appointed to be punished by the magistrate, by inflicting the same hurt upon him that he in his heat of revenge hath done to another: *an eye for an eye, hand for hand, foot for foot, &c.* And this is most just that he should drink of his own cup. He makes it a light matter in his passion to strike out one's eye; therefore he shall feel himself how small a thing it is. He makes it a small thing to cut off a leg or an arm; well, if he like it so well, he shall make trial in himself how good it is. All which shews that God doth exceedingly hate this fierceness of men to run upon their brother in revenge.

And that we may the better see the unlawfulness of this sin of revenge, consider what wrong he doth to the party and unto God and to himself that would be revenged. First, concerning the person on whom he seeks revenge: he takes upon him to punish him without any calling or authority, and therefore is injurious. But, may I not do to him as he did to me? No. God gives no such allowance, but bids us do as we would be done unto. Therefore one goes beyond his commission, and for this cause doth injury. Then to himself he doth wrong that seeks revenge, for it embitters his enemy more and makes him more mad against him; and then he is not sure to speed better, but he may get more hurt to himself; and if he be too strong for the other, yet he hates him more and watches to do him mischief. And besides, he strips himself of God's protection. . . .

Lastly, he wrongs God most of all, for he takes his office out of his hand; for God hath said *vengeance is mine, and I will repay.* Who made you a magistrate to take God's room? What commission have you to lay hands upon his image? But if I suffer this, he would always be meddling and quarrelsome; I should not have any quiet by him. But God saith, *I will repay.* Think you God hath left governing the world? Or is he asleep, that he cannot see these troublesome persons? Or doth he want justice, or power, that he cannot or will not punish them sufficiently, but you must needs rush upon the bench, and be plaintiff, judge, and executioner yourself? Nay, you do great wrong. He hath said, I will do it; and will you presume to step before him and say, I will do it myself? But God is fittest to reward and revenge injuries, for he is not partial, and he tries the hearts and sees all circumstances why he hated you, how long, and with what mind he did thus and thus unto you; and he also can and will proportion the punishment to the fault; whereas (commonly) if men might carve to themselves here, they would cut a great deal too deep, or else be too sparing. But sith God can do it in best time, in best measure, and in best manner—and hath said he will do it—what should you do meddling with revenge, unless you will hurt yourself, wrong another, and shoulder God out of his place?

. . .

The thing commanded generally is to love the welfare and safety of our neighbor's soul and body as our own; and the particular duties that in it are given in charge are either inward or outward. The inward are two: meekness and compassion. Meekness is a mild, quiet, and loving disposition of the heart, and a kind and courteous affection to our neighbor. . . . This courtesy he opposeth to anger and bitterness, which he had named in the former verse as breaches of this Commandment. And there be reasons why men should carry tender and meek affections toward their neighbor. The first may be gathered out of Esay 58:7, *Hide not thyself from thine own flesh.* We have one God, one Father, and are (as it were) one body; and therefore must be like affected one to another as members of one body. . . .

Now the branches and parts of this meekness are, first, to forgive one another, as in the place of the Ephesians before: *Be ye courteous, forgiving one another, as God for Christ's sake forgave you.* Meeting with an objection that might be made: Why, I am as gentle, affable, and quiet as any man can be, so long as you do not wrong me nor disgrace me;

but indeed if you do me injury or cross me of my will, then (you must pardon me) I am something passionate; I cannot endure it. Can you not endure it? What can you endure then? Surely no more than a bear or a lion or a beast can. But a Christian meekness will forgive and forget injuries and wrongs. It will not only be kind to the kind, and shew courtesy for courtesy (for this the veriest reprobate and deepest dissembler in the world may do), but it will overcome evil with good; it will be kind to the unkind and put up wrongs and offenses. . . .

A second branch, and indeed an effect, of this kindness is to construe all things in the best part, to take things in the best sense and meaning we can, not to be suspicious and misdeeming.[6] For this ill construction and wrong interpretation of things, by haling and wresting them to the worst sense, is a means to fill our own hearts full of bitterness and make us ready upon every occasion to fall to brawling and contention with other men. When one shall have these doubts—perhaps he thinketh thus of me; it may be he had this meaning or did it to this ill intent—this will marvelously infect and leaven the heart with malice and hatred. . . .

But a courteous and a meek man will be sure, if a thing may be expounded one way better than another, to take it in the best sense, and make the best of it.

. . .

Now the outward duties follow, and they are three in number specially to be regarded. The first is an amiable and loving behavior of oneself towards others. For, as a sour look and an austere contemptuous gesture breaks this Commandment (because it alienates men's affections from us and is a preparative to hatred), so it is a fruit of love and a part of keeping this Commandment that one should, by all good and gentle carriage of himself, shew his readiness and willingness to do good, so near as he can, to all. And this is a thing noted in Abraham as a matter of commendation and a testimony of his humble and loving heart: that where he came, he was very courteous to all men, even to infidels and men of false religion, and did carry himself in all good sort unto them. As when he had to deal with the Hittites, first he boweth himself in all courteous manner, and then his words were gentle, and all his persuasions mild and kind. And when they willed him to bury his dead in any of their sepulchers, he gives them hearty thanks, and with the like courtesy and good speech as afore propounds his request. And this gentle dealing did so win the hearts of these heathen people, and made him so well esteemed and accounted of amongst them, as they say to him, thou art a prince of God amongst us, and would deny him nothing. . . .

. . .

The second outward duty is to defend the oppressed and succor those that suffer wrong: a thing much commended in Job, that he pulled prey out of the lion's mouth and sought out the cause of the poor; he was a father to the fatherless and husband to the widow. And this did comfort him in time of his trouble more than all the wealth in the world. . . . If we see those that be unrighteously drawn to death and oppressed, we must not stand by and say, Alas, who ever saw such a world as this is? who ever saw such dealing? but we must put to our helping hand and labor to our power and as far as we can

---

[6] {In both English and Continental law, this is known as the *mitior sensus* rule. See Shuger, *Censorship*, 129, 183–94, 202–8, 223–25.}

to rescue them and deliver them. . . . Know you not that God recompenseth men according to their works? that he causeth them to reap like for like? and may not you come to the like misery yourself? and then, because you had no heart nor will to help another, you shall see others sit as quietly by you and not venture to minister any succor unto you. . . . But most men bear this mind, that they could take more pains and be at more cost to pull one of their own beasts out of the ditch than to pull a poor wronged Christian out of the paws of the persecutor. But Jonathan was not of this mind; he ventured his own life to save David's, and delivered him out of the hand of Saul his father, though it seemed David only stood betwixt him and the crown. . . .

. . .

Now certain things must be avoided, where are occasions of the breach of it {the Sixth Commandment} and hinder the keeping of it. And the first of these is pride: for so much pride as there is in any, so much occasion there is of the beach of this Commandment. For so the Holy Ghost saith that only from pride, contention comes. He that is proud is always ready to stir up strife, for he will do wrong to any, but he will be admonished by none. Secondly, he so spends and ruinates his estate by serving his proud lust that he hath nothing to bestow in works of mercy; by setting himself so high, he brings his estate so low that he cannot afford to do any good; he is always in want and need, still shifting and cast behindhand because he is too lavish in spending upon needless things to serve himself. As the Sodomites, though they lived in the most rich and plentiful country under the sun, and that which was fruitful of all increase, yet they could shew no work of mercy, no good that they could do. Why? Because they were proud and thought all too little that came to themselves and for their own delights, and therefore could spare nothing to supply another's need. So it is seen that many poor men are able to do more good, have more to lay out upon mercy, than many that have rich revenues. And why? . . . Is it not therefore because they have fed the wasting humor of pride? And that eats up all which they should bestow on God's poor saints. . . .

‡

The Ninth Commandment

Thou shalt not bear false witness against thy neighbor

The former Commandment concerning our own and our neighbor's goods, this requireth that we hurt not our neighbor's nor our own good name, but (as occasion shall be given) maintain and increase it.

The inward breach of this Commandment consisteth in the ungrounded suspicion which groweth commonly by the unjust judging and condemning of our neighbors, contrary to the express commandment of our Savior, Matt. 7:1: *Judge not, and ye shall not be judged. For with what judgment ye judge, ye shall be judged; and with what measure ye mete, it shall be measured to you again.* As if he should have said: if you would have your own infirmities pitied and your words and deeds construed in the best sense, then shew the like kindness unto others. Take nothing in the worst part; let not the dislike of your neighbors arise from any want of true love in you, but only from evident tokens of wickedness in them. For this is most righteous and ordinarily comes to pass, that none are more hardly censured than they that are the bitterest and eagerest censurers. . . . How hateful and hurtful this inward suspicion and causeless misdeeming is may better appear by the causes from whence it springeth. The first is want of godly and Christian love. As 1 Cor. 13:7. For where we love, we hope well. As may be seen in the Pharisees quarrelling against and stumbling at every word and work of Christ. . . .

. . .

The next cause is want of wisdom and good discretion. As Acts 28:4: the rude barbarians seeing the viper to hang on Paul's hand judged him presently thereupon to be a murderer. . . . And Job's friends, beholding his extraordinary afflictions, conclude that he was an extraordinary sinner.

The third cause hereof is an ill conscience and guiltiness in the judgers themselves. As Saul was always suspicious of David as though he had sought his life, because he had deserved evil at his hands. And, having dealt cruelly and craftily with him, suspected the like measure from him.

. . .

The use of all this is that if we would not be found culpable of the breach of this Commandment nor transgressors against the name and fame of our brethren, then must we not give ourselves allowance to conceive an evil opinion of them without a sufficient warrant and due ground for the same. For, though the thing be so indeed, yet it is a sin in us so to conceive of it, unless there be sufficient evidence and reason to lead us thereunto. For what though it be so? yet in matters of our neighbor's credit we must not take such light conjectures as a sufficient cause to move a suspicion. We must do as we would be done by. And therefore, as we would not be condemned of others upon every shew of evil and slight occasion, so let every man look to himself that he build not an ill conceit against his neighbor upon a false foundation. Never think ill of any till he have deserved it and given sufficient cause thereof. But yet this must be known by the way: that though love will not allow suspicion, yet it doth not thrust out discretion. It judgeth not rashly, but it judgeth justly. It is not so sharp-sighted as to see a mote where none is, nor so purblind but it can discern a beam where it is. . . . Which must be observed against many men that by this doctrine (and indeed wresting it, as evil men do all Scripture) take occasion to thrust admonition out of the doors, and think all men should be blind because God will have all men be charitable. For so when they have broken forth openly into gross wickedness, and all their life sheweth them to be profane, ungodly, covetous, and deceitful, and without the fear of God; come now and charge them that certainly they be wicked persons and have no true faith nor repentance, presently you shall have this first defense: Oh, God knoweth mine heart; you must not judge, you must not search into a man's heart. But a Christian may judge wisely, though not rashly. He may judge by the fruit, though not by the sap. If one's wickedness be hidden, then God would not have men censure. But if it break forth, he would have men to take heed, and reprove also. . . .

So others boast that they have a good faith and a good hope; they hope to be saved as well as the best, if one will believe them; and if you will not credit them, they take it as a great injury done to them. But what reason can they give of their hope? What sound cause can they allege why they should be saved rather than Judas, and not go to hell as well as Cain? Surely, they can yield no reason of their faith; they be not learned, but (they say) they have a good heart and a good hope that God will save them. Nay, they neither have a good heart nor good hope. For a good hope is always upheld by good reasons; and a strong faith by strong grounds out of God's word. Else a man may talk of hope, of faith, and a good heart, and be yet far from all; unless he shew upon what ground he buildeth his hope, it is but presumption. When sin and death shall assault him, his strength and hope shall fail him and all comfort will forsake him. So for the sacrament. It is a common custom of men, a day or two before they come to the Communion, to wrap up many reckonings and foul matters among themselves and to rake up the coals of their malice under the ashes so closely as that one would hope there were no spark left to kindle contention again. But a day or two after, they be as full of craft, brawling, and deceitfulness as ever before.[7] Then one may boldly say, You have polluted the holy sacrament. . . .

. . . For one may be as grievous a transgressor of this Commandment in speaking nothing but the truth, in some cases, as if he had raised an unjust and false report against another.[8] And this kind of truth, if it be put in one end of the balance of God's judgment, will weigh as heavy as falsehood in the other. If one speak the truth without discretion, unseasonably, out of time and place; if his words be true but his end evil and wicked, he is as cruel and malicious an enemy to the name and credit of his neighbor, and as vile a slanderer in the sight of God, as if he spake that which was false. . . .

. . . So in these times, some men there be that if they know any private fault in any man, then without any regard of time and place, they proclaim their neighbor's infirmities to the wide world, and care not before what company, amongst what persons, they blaze out his weakness. . . .

They then are here to be reproved, that will not (as God commands them) tell their neighbor plainly of his fault and not hate him in their hearts. But if they know a fault by him, straight they set him on the stage, make him known to all men, never leave talking of it: which sheweth plainly that in truth they hate their neighbor. For if they would (as God bids) tell the party, this would heal the soul and cover his sin, and make him amend. . . .

. . .

Thirdly, a man lies against himself by accusing: as when men in a kind of proud humility will deny their gifts with an intent to get more credit. Alas! I have no gifts, no wit, no learning; a simple scholar, and weak memory; and such like, contrary to that one knows and thinks. Now this dispraising oneself falsely is not humility but iniquity. For one should make himself neither better nor worse than God hath made him. . . . But a man must neither wrong God nor himself in diminishing and concealing the things that God in goodness hath given him; he ought not to deny them but to use them to God's glory. And so, come to men for works of mercy, persuade them to do good and distribute, and presently they begin to complain how poor they be, what great charge they have, what losses they have sustained, and I know not what; whereas their own soul beareth them witness that they are wealthy and have much more than many men that do a great deal more good than themselves.

Therefore, though a man do not slander his neighbor, yet if he slander himself, he is to be reproved as a liar. Herein divers of God's children fail much in time of temptation.

---

[7] {The prefatory rubrics to the Communion service in the 1559 Book of Common Prayer required the minister not to permit those *"betwixt whome he perceyveth malice and hatred to raigne . . . to be partakers of the Lordes table untyll he know them to be reconciled."* See also John Bossy, *Peace in the post–Reformation* (Cambridge UP, 1998).}

[8] {See Shuger, *Censorship* 129, 154, 171–79.}

Those that have been and are sound and true-hearted Christians, if they have lost their feeling a while, and cannot find that rejoicing in God and comfort in good things that in former times they had, then comes the accuser of the brethren, Satan, that old and subtle serpent, and he strives to make them accuse themselves falsely. Oh, saith he, if you had been good indeed, & had borne a true heart to God, he would never have forsaken you thus and given you over to such a deadness; and then, through weakness, God's children are ready to join with the devil against themselves and to think, it is true; sure I was but an hypocrite and hollow-hearted; my former comforts were delusions and presumptions; if they had been true, I should not have lost them. But in so judging, you wrong yourself. You ought to remember that temptations be not truths but false accusations. And therefore, if Satan strive to accuse, do you strive to excuse. And if he would cast you down, by so much the more lift up yourself by reasons out of God's word and by former experience in yourself and other Christians. For that is no good reason: because you have no feeling, therefore you have no faith; and because you have lost the sense of your comfort, therefore it was not true comfort. This is no true conclusion. For one may lose his feeling and yet retain lively and effectual faith (Cant. 3:1 &c). And one may have the true Comforter in his soul, and yet for a time be without sense of comfort, as is to be seen in our Savior Christ (Luk. 22:44, Matt. 27:46).

Take heed, therefore, of making such conclusions. For a man may want the feeling of his faith, and cry and call again and again for it, and feel nothing all this while; and yet nevertheless have true and sound faith. For the feeling of and mourning for the want of faith, and the earnest and constant desire of it, is an infallible sign of faith. For this is a sure rule, that so long as one feels himself sick, he is not dead. And the high estimation of the fruits of faith, joined with a vehement desire thereof, is a singular evidence that there is a sound and lively root of faith in the heart. Do not therefore agree with the devil to persecute yourself. Fight against him, and take not his part against your own soul. You shall find he is strong enough alone; you had not need join with him, but rather to resist him. If one be once the child of God in truth, he is so forever. . . .

. . .

. . . And as the former persons were so easily seduced in matter of their commendation, because they seldom or never look over their sins, so these are quickly put in doubt of their uprightness, because they do not use to mark what good works they do and consider what graces God hath bestowed upon them. For if men would not be always looking and searching into their infirmities, but sometimes lift up their eyes to the mercies of God, to that strength which he hath given against sin, and power to do some good things, and take as diligent a survey of God's benefits as of their afflictions and miseries, they would not be so soon driven from their hope and put out of comfort.

‡

The Tenth Commandment

Thou shalt not covet thy neighbor's house, neither shalt thou covet thy neighbor's wife, nor his man-servant, nor his maid, nor his ox, nor his ass, nor anything that is thy neighbor's

This last Commandment forbids the least thoughts and motions of the heart against our neighbor, though there be neither consent nor yielding of the will. And this requires such a contentedness with our estate as that we never have the smallest motion tending to the hurt of our neighbor in any sort. Yea, that we have such a love of our neighbor as never to think of him, or anything belonging to him, but with desire of his good every way. To covet, in this place, signifies to have a motion of the heart, without any settled consent of will.

From this, then, that God here forbids coveting, we learn that the first motion and inclination of the heart to any sin, though a man never yield to it nor cast about how to bring it to pass, is a sin.[9] And the reasons are plain: first, because God hath forbidden it. As Paul saith, he had not known lust to be a sin but that the law saith *Thou shalt not lust*. He knew, and many heathen men that never heard of God's law did confess, that the inward thoughts joined with consent and full purpose to do them if occasion served were sins. But for those motions that did but (as it were) pass through the heart and stayed not there and had no place of abode yielded to them, but were shut out so soon as they entered in, he could never have been persuaded that these were faults and provoked God's wrath but that he knew and believed that the law of God condemned them. . . .

. . .

The use that we should make of this is our continual humiliation; for that our nature and the whole frame of our soul and body is such as no minute almost goes over our head but some evil & vain motion or other goes through our heart and springeth out of the sink and puddle of our flesh. Our nature is like a great firebrand, that if it be never so little stirred, sends forth many sparks on every side. Therefore we must learn in this regard to deny ourselves and humbly to fall down before GOD, beseeching him to heal our corrupt nature and to wash and cleanse it more and more by his Holy Spirit. Then we have made one good use of the Law, when we are so touched with the sight of our sins as that we go quite out of ourselves, then the Law hath so stopt our mouth as that we can allege nothing in ourselves wherefore we should not be damned, but rely and cast ourselves only on the mercies of God in the merit of Christ. Again, this teacheth to use all good means to keep our heart from these ill motions and hinder this firebrand from sparkling abroad. First, make a covenant with our eyes to look upon nothing, & our ears to hear nothing, and all our senses to admit nothing into the heart that may stir up and provoke the naughtiness of it. Secondly, take down the flesh often by fasting, prayer, and hearing, and such other spiritual exercises. For this is the cause why our corruption grows so strong, because we do not set ourselves to resist & fight against it. . . .

━━◦━━

Text: EEBO (STC [2nd ed.] / 6971.3)

John Dod and Robert Cleaver, *A plain and familiar exposition of the Ten Commandments, with a methodical short catechism, containing, briefly all the principal grounds of Christian religion. Newly corrected by the author* (London: Printed by Thomas Haveland, for Thomas Man, 1610), 1–9, 11–12, 15–39, 41–45, 49–57, 66–68, 79–81, 256–57, 259–60, 265–70, 274–77, 282–83, 331–40, 342–43, 358, 365–67.

[9] On this point, Dod, and mainline Protestantism in general, differs sharply from the dominant Catholic (and pre-Reformation) position, which makes the will's consent to evil part of the definition of sin.

LANCELOT ANDREWES
(1555–1626)

Born in 1555, the eldest child of a moderately prosperous London mariner, Andrewes entered Merchant Taylors' School around 1565, where, under its master, Richard Mulcaster, he studied Greek, Hebrew, oratorical declamation, and music theory, along with the more conventional Latin curriculum. A brilliant student, in 1571 he received one of the six newly endowed Greek scholarships at Pembroke; and so, together with his classmate Edmund Spenser, Andrewes found himself in Cambridge, where Whitgift was still Master of Trinity, on the eve of the Admonitions controversy.[1] During his years at Pembroke, Andrewes mastered foreign languages (fifteen according to Buckeridge). In 1575 he received his BA and a college fellowship; the MA came three years later, at which date he also became Pembroke's catechist, delivering a highly successful series of lectures, posthumously published as *The pattern of catechistical doctrine* (1630, 1641).[2] Having been ordained in 1580, he received his BD in 1585, writing a thesis against usury.His public career began shortly thereafter. In 1586 he was appointed chaplain to the Earl of Huntingdon, who brought him to northern England, where he preached to and conferred with Catholic recusants, apparently with some success. His principal patron during the late 1580s, however, was puritan-leaning Walsingham, who, despite their confessional differences, nominated Andrewes to the vicarage of St. Giles, Cripplegate, and to prebends at St. Paul's and Southwell Minster in 1589—the same year Andrewes also became Master of Pembroke.

Soon after Walsingham's death in 1590, Andrewes became chaplain to Archbishop Whitgift (in whose household he met Buckeridge and Neile) and to Queen Elizabeth, before whom he began his career as a court preacher in Lent of 1590. During the following

---

[1] M. M. Knappen, *Tudor Puritanism* (Chicago UP, 1939); Patrick Collinson, *The Elizabethan Puritan Movement* (U California P, 1967).

[2] A fuller version was published in 1642 as *The moral law expounded*, which shows that Andrewes took a strong Sabbatarian position (in the 1570s and 1580s, this was, however, not yet a puritan stance), but also that his views on liturgy, ceremony, and the sacraments had already assumed a high-church cast (see McCullough, *Lancelot Andrewes* xvi).

decade, Andrewes served in his London parishes, composing a manual of pastoral care for the sick and dying, instituting a monthly communion, hearing private confession, and restoring St. Giles' chancel and railing its altar.[3] His *Judgment of the Lambeth Articles*, written ca. 1595 but not published until the Restoration, takes issue with the central tenets of doctrinal Calvinism. In 1596 Elizabeth offered him the bishopric of Salisbury, in 1599 of Ely, both which Andrewes refused, because the offer was conditional, as most such offers under Elizabeth were, on his alienating their episcopal revenues, which Andrewes viewed as sacrilege. He did, however, accept honorary membership in Gray's Inn (1590) and a prebend at Westminster (1597).

In 1601 Andrewes sparked a minor uproar by preaching in defense of priestly absolution. The same year, Robert Cecil, on Fulke Greville's recommendation, nominated him for dean of Westminster. His students later gratefully described how Andrewes "never walked to Chiswick for his recreation without a brace of young fry" clustering around him for informal lessons, how he would teach Hebrew and Greek in the evenings to the older boys "without any compulsion of correction." Camden was headmaster at the time and Hakluyt became prebendary in 1602. Andrewes was drawn into their intellectual orbit, in 1604 becoming a member of the Society of Antiquaries (shortly thereafter dissolved by James). Their works were among the few secular texts in Andrewes' library at the time of his death.

Although Andrewes was forty-eight when Elizabeth died, one thinks of him as a Jacobean churchman. He quickly rose to national prominence under the new King. At the Hampton Court Conference in 1604 he defended the sign of the cross in baptism, and at the Conference's conclusion was appointed director of one of the committees entrusted with preparing a new translation of Holy Scripture. For most of James' reign, beginning with the 1604 Good Friday sermon reprinted below, Andrewes preached at court at Christmas, Easter, Pentecost, the anniversaries of the Gunpowder and Gowrie plots, and, less regularly, on Good Friday or during Lent—sermons that became "highlights of the court season, drawing large crowds . . . [and] royal accolades far greater than any known from James for other forms of literature" (*ODNB*).[4]

In 1605 he accepted the bishopric of Chichester; four years later, he received the far more valuable see of Ely. He paid a price for these promotions, although not the Elizabethan kind.[5] The Oath of Allegiance, imposed by James after the Gunpowder Plot and firmly opposed by the Papacy, provoked a pan-European controversy over the proper boundaries between civil and ecclesiastical power. The King himself wrote the first defense of the Oath in 1608, but then assigned Andrewes to respond to Bellarmine's answer—an honor Andrewes apparently would have gladly forgone, one of his friends noting that it was "contrary to his [Andrewes'] disposition and course to meddle with controversies" (Chamberlain 1:264). He did, however, produce two long Latin tracts on obedience to princes: *Tortura torti* (1609) and *Responsio ad apologiam Cardinalis Bellarmini* (1610). These, and Andrewes' other gifts, made him the favored candidate for archbishop of Canterbury in 1610. However, from his deathbed, the Earl of Dunbar ordered his

---

[3] Notes of the 1590s St. Giles sermons were printed in 1657 as *Apospasmatia sacra*.

[4] A principal duty of the Lord Almoner, a post Andrewes held from 1605 to 1619, was to preach at court on the major feasts of the Church year.

[5] Elizabeth regularly demanded candidates for the episcopate to agree to cede a valuable piece of church property to the Crown (or a favored courtier) as a condition of their elevation.

servants to remove his heart (after his death) and present it to James in a golden cup with the sole request that George Abbot, then bishop of London, be elevated to Canterbury.[6] So Andrewes remained at Ely, often in the company of the great Protestant philologist, Isaac Casaubon, who had emigrated to England in 1610 and quickly become Andrewes' intimate friend. Four years later, the dying Casaubon called for Andrewes to administer his final Communion.

In 1613 Andrewes was appointed to the commission looking into the Essex divorce, to which divorce, under considerable royal pressure, he acceded—a capitulation that the wisdom of hindsight has deplored. Three years later, James made him a member of the Privy Council and then, in 1619, bishop of Winchester and dean of the Chapels Royal. At the age of seventy Andrewes retired from public life, too ill even to attend James on his deathbed. He died on September 25, 1626, and was buried in the church of St. Saviour's, Southwark, Buckeridge preaching the funeral sermon.

The *ODNB* describes Andrewes as "a man of immense scholarship and spiritual devotion, whose character was marked by charity, moral rectitude, and selflessness." For his own generation, he exemplified the saintly scholar-bishop, still a potent cultural ideal in early Stuart England. Contemporary memorials eulogize him not as an influential court prelate but as a holy bishop, spending his mornings and evenings in study and prayer— this last occupation recorded in his *Preces privatae*, the austere and moving trilingual devotions composed for his own use. The early biographies likewise stress his generosity to poor parishioners and struggling scholars, much of it given anonymously, as well as his open-handed hospitality. Now primarily treated as the spiritual father of Laudianism, he was also one of the very few early modern Englishmen to achieve a European reputation for learning. Although primarily an orientalist and patristic scholar, his interests extended to scientific and historiographic fields. Bacon consulted Andrewes about the *Advancement of learning* and dedicated the *Advertisement touching an holy war* to him. Andrewes was apparently also the only clergyman to comment favorably on Selden's highly learned, controversial, and anti-clerical *History of tithes*. Andrewes' own *Two answers to Cardinal Perron* (ca. 1618; pub. 1629) is itself a good example of humanist-historicist scholarship.

Andrewes, together with Neile, Overall, Laud, and Cosin, was a principal architect of English high churchmanship, or whatever one wishes to call this more liturgical, patristic, sacramental, and traditionalist strain in the post–Reformation English Church. His private chapel at Ely Palace, where he reintroduced the more elaborate ceremonial and ornament of pre–Reformation worship, became a model for subsequent experiments in the beauty of holiness.

Andrewes' reputation, then and now, rests principally on the great festal sermons preached at court, the ninety-six sermons published by Laud and Buckeridge in 1629.[7] These recall the rich mysterious textures of ancient and medieval Christian preaching: the Latin Fathers' elaborate word-play, the antithetic rhetoric of Christian paradox, the haunting

---

[6] See the *ODNB* entry for George Abbot.

[7] For their influence on later preaching, particularly in the high church tradition (e.g., Cosin's Epiphany sermon *<infra>*), see Mitchell 133–69.

personifications of late-antique allegoresis. Of the two sermons included in this volume, the 1604 Good Friday homily is the first of Andrewes' Jacobean court sermons, the 1623 Easter one, among the last. Like most of Andrewes' festal preaching, both draw on patristic exegesis; both are typological, allegorical, and christological—indeed both begin with an hermeneutic prelude defending spiritual exegesis against literal–historical readings. Both are intensely visual: the Good Friday sermon insists that we mark, behold, regard the dying Christ it sets before us, fashioning a crucifix of words rather than wood; the Easter sermon renders salvation history through the scarlet of Christ's cloak, the purple of grapes, of the feet trampling the grapes, of the wine of the Eucharist, the red porridge for which Esau sold his birthright, shame's blush, the blood of Christ. In both sermons, time collapses: Jeremiah describes the Crucifixion, Isaiah encounters Christ returning from the harrowing of hell, and we hear them speaking. Sacred history occurs in an eternal present that is the temporal counterpart to sacred textuality—to Holy Scripture read as a single poem of infinite intricacy and depth. Andrewes' sermons, in turn, reproduce this vision of history as symbolic structure rather than causal sequence; Peter MacCullough likens them to Bach's canonic fugues (xxix).

Both sermons exemplify Andrewes' distinctive prose style, with its asyndetic staccato clauses fused into highly formalized verbal patterns that combine antithetic point, schematic parallelism, and multilingual wordplay—the leitmotifs "regard" and *"non sicut"* of the Good Friday sermon; its teasing out the christological symbolism lodged in the etymological core of the Hebrew. This use of verbal patterning to articulate the order of things, which characterizes the sermons, presupposes a pre-referential view of language, in which the thing is implicit in the name, in which words—their sounds, stems, etymologies—disclose the rhythms and relations structuring sacred history. As T. S. Eliot remarked, "Andrewes takes a word and derives the world from it" (305).

NOTE ON THE TEXT: manuscript evidence indicates that Andrewes prepared polished final drafts of his sermons, with careful attention to pointing and layout (MacCullough li). The Laud and Buckeridge edition, *XCVI sermons* (the text for the 1623 Easter sermon), follows the authorial manuscript, and the conventions of the 1604 sermon are sufficiently similar to assume that it too reproduces Andrewes' distinctive formatting. Early modern punctuation indicates breath-pauses; when authorial, it signals the intended rhythms of oral delivery. Therefore, although I have modernized the punctuation somewhat,[8] it remains largely Andrewes' own.

SOURCES: *ODNB*; John Chamberlain, *The letters*, 2 vols. ed. Norman MacClure (American Philosophical Society, 1939); T. S. Eliot, *Selected essays* (Harcourt, Brace, 1960); Nicholas Lossky, *Lancelot Andrewes, the preacher (1555–1626): the origins of mystical theology of the Church of England* (Clarendon, 1991); Peter Mac-Cullough, ed., *Lancelot Andrewes: selected sermons and lectures* (Oxford UP, 2005); Elizabeth McCutcheon, "Recent studies in Andrewes," *English Literary Renaissance* 11 (1991): 96–108; W. Fraser Mitchell, *English pulpit oratory from Andrewes to Tillotson: a study of its literary aspects* (SPCK, 1932); Debora Shuger, "Lancelot Andrewes," *Dictionary of literary biography: sixteenth-century non-dramatic writers*, ed. David Richardson (Detroit: Gale Research, 1996), and *Habits of thought in the English Renaissance* (U California P, 1990), chaps. 1–2.

[8] The early modern colon functioned more like a modern comma or semicolon—it indicates a breath-pause between clauses (*kola*)—and so has been replaced by one or another of these latter options.

LANCELOT ANDREWES

The copy of the sermon preached on Good Friday last before the King's Majesty
1604

Have ye no regard, ô all ye that pass by the way? Consider, and behold, If ever there were sorrow like my sorrow, which was done unto me, wherewith the Lord did afflict me in the day of the fierceness of his wrath.[1]

Lament. Jerem. 1:12

At the very reading or hearing of which verse, there is none but will presently conceive, it is the voice of a party in great extremity. In great extremity two ways. First, in such distress, as never was any, *If ever there were sorrow like my sorrow?* And then, in that distress having none to regard him: *Have ye no regard all ye?*

To be afflicted, and so afflicted, as none ever was, is very much. In that affliction to find none to respect him or care for him, what can be more? In all our sufferings it is a comfort to us that we have a *sicut*: that nothing hath befallen us, but such as others have felt the like [1 Cor. 10:13]. But here, *si fuerit sicut?* If ever the like were: that is, never the like was.

Again, in our greatest pains, it is a kind of ease, even to find some regard. Naturally we desire it, if we cannot be delivered, if we cannot be relieved, yet to be pitied. It sheweth there be yet some, that are touched with the sense of our misery, that wish us well, and would give us ease if they could. But this afflicted here, findeth not so much, neither the one nor the other, but is even as he were an outcast both of heaven and earth. Now verily a heavy case, and worthy to be put in this book of Lamentations.

---

[1] {This is the Geneva translation, which Andrewes used throughout his life in his preaching. The sermon also repeatedly echoes the Latin Vulgate of this passage, which reads: *O vos omnes, qui transitis per viam, attendite et videte si est dolor sicut dolor meus: quoniam vindemiavit me ut locutus est Dominus in die irae furoris sui.* Andrewes always read the pericope both in English and Latin at the beginning of each sermon (MacCullough xxxv).}

I demand then, of whom speaketh the Prophet this? Of himself, or of some other? This I find, there is not any of the ancient writers, but do apply, yea, in a manner appropriate this speech to our Savior Christ; and that, this very day, the day of his Passion (truly termed here *the day of God's wrath*). And wheresoever they treat of the Passion, ever this verse cometh in. And (to say the truth) to take the words strictly as they lie, they cannot agree, or be verified of any, but of him, & him only. For though some other, not unfitly, may be allowed to say the same words, it must be in a qualified sense; for, in full and perfect propriety of speech, he, and none but he; none can say (neither Jeremy nor any other) *Si fuerit dolor, sicut dolor meus*, as Christ can: no day of wrath, like to his day; no sorrow to be compared to his (all are short of it), nor his to any; it exceedeth them all.

And yet, according to the letter, it can not be denied but they be set down by Jeremy, in the person of his own people, being then come to great misery, and of the holy city, then laid waste and desolate by the Chaldees. What then? *Ex Aegypto vocaui Filium meum; out of Egypt have I called my Son*, was literally spoken of this people too; yet is by the Evangelist applied to our Savior Christ. *My God, my God, why hast thou forsaken me?* at the first uttered by David, yet the same words our Savior taketh to himself, and that more truly and properly, than ever David could; and of those of David's, and of these of Jeremy's, there is one and the same reason.

Of all which the ground is that correspondence which is between Christ and the patriarchs, prophets, and people before Christ, of whom the Apostle's rule is, *Omnia in figura contingebant illis*; that they were themselves types, and their sufferings, forerunning figures of the great suffering of the Son of God; which maketh Isaac's offering and Joseph's selling, and Israel's calling from Egypt, and that complaint of David's, and this of Jeremy's, appliable to him; that he may take them to himself, and the Church ascribe them to him, and that in more fitness of terms, and more fullness of truth, than they were at the first spoken by David, or Jeremy, or any of them all.

And this rule, and the steps of the Fathers proceeding by this rule, are to me a warrant, to expound and apply this verse (as they have done before) to the present occasion of this time, which requireth some such Scripture to be considered by us, as doth belong to his Passion, who this day poured out his most precious blood as the only sufficient price of the dear purchase of all our redemptions.

Be it then to us (as to them it was, and as most properly it is) the speech of the Son of God, as this day hanging on the Cross, to a sort of careless people that go up and down without any manner of regard of these his sorrows and sufferings, so worthy of all regard. *Have ye no regard? ô all ye that pass by the way, consider and behold, if ever there were sorrow, like to my sorrow, which was done unto me, wherewith the Lord afflicted me in the day of the fierceness of his wrath.* Here is a complaint, and here is a request. A complaint, that we have not; a request, that we would have the pains & passions of our Savior Christ in some regard. For first he complaineth (and not without cause) *Have ye no regard?* And then (as willing to forget their former neglect, so they will yet do it) he falleth to entreat, *ô consider and behold!*

And what is that we should consider? The sorrow which he suffereth; and in it, two things: the quality and the cause. 1. The quality, *si fuerit sicut*: if ever the like were; and that either in respect of *dolor*, or *dolor meus*; the sorrow suffered, or the person suffering. 2. The cause: that is God, that in his wrath, in his fierce wrath, doth all this to him, which cause will not leave us, till it have led us to another cause in ourselves, and to another yet in him. All which serve to ripen us to *regard*.

These two then specially we are moved to regard. *Regard* is the main point. But, because therefore we regard but faintly, because either we consider not, or not aright, we are called to consider seriously of them. As if he should say, *Regard you not?* If you did *consider*, you would; if you *considered* as you should, you would *regard* as you ought. Certainly the Passion, if it were thoroughly *considered*, would be duly *regarded. Consider* then.

So the points are two: the *quality* and the *cause* of his suffering; and the duties two: to *consider* and *regard*. So to *consider*, that we *regard* them, & him for them.

‡

Have ye no regard? &c.

To cease this complaint, and to grant this request, we are to regard; and that we may regard, we are to consider the pains of his Passion. Which, that we may reckon no easy common matter of light moment, to do, or not do, as we list, first, a general stay is made of all passengers, this day. For (as it were from his Cross) doth our Savior address this his speech to them that go to and fro, the day of his Passion, without so much as entertaining a thought, or vouchsafing a look that way: *O vos qui transitis!* ô you that pass by the way, stay and consider. To them frameth he this speech, that pass by; to them, and to them all. *O vos omnes, qui transitis*, ô all ye that pass by the way, stay and consider.

Which very stay of his, sheweth it to be some important matter, in that it is, of all. For, as for some to be stayed, and those the greater some, there may be reason; the most part of those that go thus to and fro may well intend[2] it; they have little else to do. But to except none, not some special persons, is hard. What know we their haste? Their occasions may be such, & so urgent, as they cannot stay. Well, what haste, what business soever, pass not by; stay though. As much to say, as, Be they never so great, your occasions, they are not, they cannot be so great as this. How urgent soever, this is more, and more to be intended. The regard of this is worthy the staying of a journey. It is worth the considering of those, that have never so great affairs in hand. So material is this sight in his accompt; which serveth to shew the exigence of this duty. But as for this point it needeth not to be stood upon to us here at this time; we are not going by, we need not to be stayed; we have stayed all other our affairs, to come hither, and here we are all present before God, to have it set before us, that we may consider it. Thither then let us come.

That which we are called to behold and consider, is his *sorrow*. And sorrow is a thing, which of itself nature inclineth us to behold, as being ourselves in the body which may be one day in the like sorrowful case [Hebr. 13:3]. Therefore will every good eye turn itself, and look upon them that lie in distress. Those two in the Gospel that passed by the wounded man, before they passed by him (though they helped him not as the Samaritan did), yet they looked upon him as he lay. But this party here lieth not; he is lift up, as the serpent in the wilderness, that unless we turn our eyes away purposely, we can neither will nor choose but behold him.

---

[2] {to direct the eyes or mind to something}

But because to *behold*, and not to *consider*, is but to gaze; and gazing the angel blameth in the apostles themselves, we must do both: both *behold*, and *consider*; look upon, with the eye of the body (that is, *behold*); and look into with the eye of the mind (that is, *consider*). So saith the Prophet here. And the very same doth the Apostle advise us to do: First, ἀφορᾶν, to look upon him (that is, to *behold*), and then ἀναλογίζεσθαι, to think upon him, that is, to *consider* his *sorrow*. Sorrow sure would be considered.

Now then, because as the quality of the sorrow is, accordingly it would be considered (for if it be but a common sorrow, the less will serve; but if it be some special, some very heavy case, the more would be allowed it: for proportionably with the suffering, the consideration is to arise), to raise our consideration to the full, and to elevate it to the highest point, there is upon this sorrow set a *si fuerit sicut*, a note of highest eminency: for *si fuerit sicut*, are words that have life in them, & are able to quicken our consideration, if it be not quite dead. For, by them we are provoked, as it were, to *consider*, and considering, to see whether ever any *sicut* may be found to set by it, whether ever any like it.

For if never any, our nature is, to regard things exceeding rare and strange; and such as the like whereof is not else to be seen. Upon this point then, there is a case made, as if he should say, If ever the like, *regard* not this; but if never any, be like yourselves in other things, and vouchsafe this (if not your chiefest) yet some *regard*.

To enter then this comparison, and to shew it for such—that, are we to do, three sundry ways: for three sundry ways, in three sundry words, are these sufferings of his here expressed; all three within the compass of the verse.

The first is מכאוב Mac-ob (which we read *sorrow*), taken from a wound or stripe, as all do agree.

The second is עולל Gholel, we read *done to me*, taken from a word that signifieth *melting* in a furnace; as S. Hierom noteth out of the Chaldee (who so translateth it).

The third is חוגה Hoga, where we read *afflicted*, from a word which importeth *renting off*, or *bereaving*. The old Latin turneth it, *Vindemiauit me*, as a vine whose fruit is all plucked off. The Greek with Theodoret, ἀπεφύλλισέ με, as a vine or tree whose leaves are all beaten off, and it left naked and bare.

In these three are comprised his sufferings: *wounded, melted, & bereft*, leaf and fruit—that is, all manner of comfort.

Of all that is penal, or can be suffered, the common division is, *sensus, & damni*, grief for that we feel, or, for that we forgo. For that we feel, in the two former: *wounded* in body, *melted* in soul. For that we forgo, in the last: *bereft all*, left neither fruit, nor so much as a leaf to hang on him.

According to these three, to consider his sufferings, & to begin first with the first. The pains of his body, his wounds and his stripes.

Our very eye will soon tell us, no place was left in his body, where he might be smitten & was not. His skin and flesh rent with the whips & scourges, his hands and feet wounded with the nails, his head with the thorns, his very heart with the spear point. All his senses, all his parts loden with whatsoever wit or malice could invent. His blessed body given as an anvil to be beaten upon, with the violent hands of those barbarous miscreants, till they brought him into this case, of *si fuerit sicut*. For, Pilate's *Ecce Homo!*, his shewing him with an *Ecce*, as if he should say, Behold, look if ever you saw the like rueful spectacle: this very shewing of his sheweth plainly, he was then come into a woeful plight—so woeful, as Pilate verily believed, his very sight so pitiful, as it would have moved the hardest heart of them all to have relented and said, *This is enough, we desire no more.* And this for the wounds of his body (for on this we stand not).

In this one, peradventure, some *sicut* may be found, in the pains of the body. But in the second, the sorrow of the soul, I am sure, none. And indeed, the pain of the body is but the body of pain; the very soul of sorrow and pain, is the soul's sorrow and pain. *Give me any grief, save the grief of the mind*, saith the wise man {Ecclesiasticus 25:13}. *For* (saith Solomon) *the spirit of a man will sustain all his other infirmities, but a wounded spirit, who can bear?* And of this, this of his soul, I dare make a case, *si fuerit sicut.*

He began to be troubled in soul, saith S. John; *To be in an agony*, saith S. Luke; *To be in anguish of mind and deep distress*, saith S. Mark. To have his soul round about on every side environed with sorrow, and that, sorrow to the death, Here is *trouble, anguish, agony, sorrow* and *deadly sorrow*; but it must be such, as never the like. So it was too.

The estimate whereof we may take from the second word, of *melting*, that is, from his sweat in the Garden; strange and the like whereof was never heard or seen.

No manner violence offered him in body; no man touching him, or being near him; in a cold night (for they were fain to have a fire within doors), lying abroad in the air, and upon the cold earth, to be all of a sweat, and that sweat to be blood; and not as they call it, *diaphoreticus*, a thin faint sweat; but *grumosus*, of great drops, and those so many, so plenteous, as they went through his apparel and all; and through all, streamed to the ground, & that in great abundance; read, inquire, and consider, *si fuerit sudor sicut sudor iste*; if ever there were sweat like this sweat of his? Never the like sweat certainly, and therefore never the like sorrow. Our translation is, *Done unto me*, but we said, the word properly signifieth (and so S. Hierome & the Chaldee Paraphrast read it) *melted me.* And truly it should seem by this fearful sweat of his, he was near some furnace, the feeling whereof was able to cast him into that sweat, and to turn his sweat into drops of blood. And sure it was so. For see, even in the very next words of all to this verse, he complaineth of it: *Ignem misit in ossibus meis*, that a fire was sent into his bones which melted him, and made that bloody sweat to distil from him. That hour, what his feelings were, it is dangerous to define; we know them not, we may be too bold to determine of them. To very good purpose it was, that the ancient Fathers of the Greek Church in their liturgy, after they have recounted all the particular pains as they are set down in his Passion, and by all, and by every one of them, called for mercy; do, after all, shut up all with this, Δὶ ἀγνώστων κόπων καὶ βασάνων ἐλέησον καὶ σῶσον ἡμας, *By thine unknown sorrows and sufferings felt by thee, but not distinctly known by us, have mercy upon us and save us.*

Now, though this suffice not, nothing near; yet let it suffice (the time being short) for his pains of body and soul. For those of the body, it may be some may have endured the like; but the sorrows of his soul are unknown sorrows, & for them, none ever have, ever have or ever shall, suffer the like; the like, or near the like in any degree.

And now to the third. It was said before, to be in distress, such distress as this was, & to find none to comfort, nay not so much as to regard him, is all that can be said to make his sorrow a *non sicut.* Comfort is it, by which in the midst of all our sorrows, we are *confortati*, that is, strengthened & made the better able to bear them all out. And who is there, even the poorest creature among us, but in some degree findeth some comfort, or some regard at somebody's hands? For if that be not left, the state of that party is here in the third word said to be like the tree whose leaves and whose fruit are all beaten off quite, and itself left bare and naked both of the one and of the other.

And such was our Savior's case in these his sorrows this day, and that so, as what is left the meanest of the sons of men, was not left him: *not a leaf.* Not a leaf! Leaves I may well call all human comforts and regards, whereof he was then left clean desolate. *His own,* they among whom he had gone about all his life long, healing them, teaching them, feeding them, doing them all the good he could, it is they that cry, *Not him, no, but Barabbas rather. Away with him, his blood be upon us and our children.* It is they that in the middest of his sorrows, shake their head at him and cry, *Ah thou wretch*; they that in his most disconsolate estate cry *Eli, Eli* in most barbarous manner; deride him and say, *stay, and you shall see Elias come presently and take him down.* And this was their regard.

But these were but withered leaves. They then that on earth were nearest him of all, the greenest leaves & likest to hang on, and to give him some shade: even of them, some bought and sold him, others denied & forswore him, but all fell away & forsook him. Ἀπεφύλλισέ με (saith Theodoret); not a leaf left.

But, leaves are but leaves, and so are all earthly stays. The fruit then, the true fruit of the vine indeed, the true comfort in all heaviness, is *desuper*, from above; is divine consolation. But *vindemiauit me* (saith the Latin text), even that was in this his sorrow, this day, bereft him too. And that was his most sorrowful complaint of all others: not that his friends upon earth, but that his Father from heaven had forsaken him; that neither heaven nor earth yielded him any regard; but that between the passioned powers of his soul, and whatsoever might any ways refresh him, there was a traverse[3] drawn, & he left in the estate of a weather-beaten tree, all desolate and forlorn. Evident, too evident, by that his most dreadful cry, which at once moved all the powers in heaven and earth, *My God, my God, why hast thou forsaken me?* Weigh well that cry, consider it well, and tell me, *si fuerit clamor sicut clamor iste*; if ever there were cry, like to that of his. Never the like cry, and therefore never the like sorrow.

It is strange, very strange, that of none of the martyrs the like can be read, who yet endured most exquisite pains in their martyrdoms; yet we see with what courage, with what cheerfulness, how even singing they are reported to have passed through their torments. Will ye know the reason? S Augustine setteth it down, *martyres non eripuit, sed nunquid deseruit?* He delivered not his martyrs, but did he forsake them? He delivered not their bodies, but he forsook not their souls, but distilled into them the dew of his heavenly comfort; an abundant supply for all they could endure. Not so here. *Vindemiauit me* (saith the Prophet); *dereliquisti me* (saith he himself). No comfort, no supply at all.

Leo it is that first said it (and all antiquity allow of it): *non soluit unionem, sed subtraxit visionem.* The union[4] was not dissolved; true, but the beams, the influence was restrained, and for any comfort from thence, his soul was, even as a scorched heath ground, without so much as any drop of dew of divine comfort; as a naked tree, no fruit to refresh him within, no leaf to give him shadow without; the power of darkness let loose to afflict him; the influence of comfort, restrained to relieve him. It is a *non sicut* this. It cannot be expressed as it should, and as other things may. In silence we may admire it, but all

---

[3] {curtain, screen, barrier}
[4] {the hypostatic union of the divine and human natures in the person of Christ}

our words will not reach it. And though to draw it so far as some do, is little better than blasphemy;[5] yet on the other side, to shrink it so short, as other some do, cannot be but with derogation to his love, who to kindle our love and loving regard, would come to a *non sicut* in his suffering. For, so it was, and so we must allow it to be. This in respect of his Passion. *Dolor.*

Now in respect of his person, *dolor meus.* Whereof, if it please you to take a view, even of the person thus wounded, thus afflicted and forsaken, you shall then have a perfect *non sicut.* And indeed, the person is here a weighty circumstance; it is thrice repeated, *Meus, Mihi, Me.* And we may not leave it out. For, as is the person, so is the passion; and any one, even the very least degree of wrong or disgrace, offered to a person of excellency, is more than a hundred times more, to one of mean condition, so weighty is the circumstance of the person.[6] Consider then, how great the person was. And I rest fully assured, here may we boldly challenge, and say, *si fuerit sicut.*

Ecce homo, saith Pilate first, a man he is, as we are; and were he but a man, nay, were he not a man, but some poor dumb creature, it were great ruth to see him so handled, as he was.

A man, saith Pilate, and *a just man*, saith Pilate's wife. *Have thou nothing to do with that just man.* And that is one degree further. For though we pity the punishment even of malefactors themselves, yet ever most compassion we have of them that suffer, and be innocent. And he was innocent. Pilate, and Herod, and the prince of this world, his very enemies, being his judges.

Now, among the innocent, the more noble the person, the more heavy the spectacle; and never do our bowels earn[7] so much, as over such. *Alas, alas for that noble prince*, saith this prophet [Jer. 22:18]: the style of mourning for the death of a great personage. And, he that suffereth here, is such, even a principal person among the sons of men, of the race royal, descended from kings; Pilate styled him so in his title, and he would not alter it.

Three degrees. But, yet we are not at our true *quantus.* For he is yet more: more than the highest of the sons of men, for he is THE SON OF THE MOST HIGH GOD. Pilate saw no further but *Ecce homo.* The centurion did: *Verè Filius Dei erat hic*; now truly this was the Son of God. And here, all words forsake us, and every tongue becometh speechless.

We have no way to express it but *à minore ad maius.* Thus, of this book, the book of Lamentations, one special occasion was the death of King Josias. But behold, a greater then Josias is here.

Of King Josias (as a special reason of mourning) the Prophet saith, *spiritus oris nostri, christus Domini*; the very breath of our nosethrils, the Lord's anointed (for so are all good kings in their subjects' accompts), he is gone. But behold, here is not *christus Domini*, but *Christus Dominus*; {not} the Lord's christ, but the Lord Christ himself. And that, not coming to an honorable death in battle, as Josias did; but, to a most vile reproachful death, the death of malefactors in the highest degree. And not slain outright, as Josias was; but

---

[5] {This would seem to refer to Calvin's claim that on the Cross, Christ suffered the agonies of the damned.}

[6] {A Roman law principle; see the discussion of *atrox iniuria* in Justinian's *Institutes* 4.4.}

[7] {to feel compassion and poignant sorrow}

mangled and massacred in most pitiful strange manner; wounded in body, wounded in spirit, left utterly desolate. O consider this well, and confess the case is truly put, *si fuerit dolor sicut dolor meus.* Never, never the like person. And if, as the person is, the passion be, never the like passion to his.

It is truly affirmed, that any one, even the least drop of blood, even the least pain, yea of the body only, of this so great a person; any *dolor* with this *meus*, had been enough to make a *non sicut* of it. That is enough, but that is not all: for add now the three other degrees. Add to this person, those wounds, that sweat, and that cry, and put all together: and, I make no manner question, the like was not, shall not, cannot ever be. It is far above all that ever were, or can be. *Abyssus est.* Men may drowsily hear it, and coldly affect it, but Principalities and Powers stand abashed at it. And for the quality, both of the passion & of the person, that never the like, thus much.

‡

Now to proceed to the cause, and to consider it: for without it, we shall have but half a *regard*, and scarce that. Indeed, set the cause aside, and the Passion (as rare as it is) is yet but a dull and heavy sight; we list not much look upon spectacles of that kind, though never so strange; they fill us full of pensive thoughts, and make us melancholic; and so doth this, till upon examination of the cause, we find it toucheth us near. And so near so many ways, as we cannot choose, but have some regard of it.

What was done to him we see. Let there now be a quest of inquiry, to find who was the doer of it. Who? Who but the power of darkness, wicked Pilate, bloody Caiaphas, the envious priests, the barbarous soldiers? None of these are returned[8] here. We are too low, by a great deal, if we think to find it among men. *Quae fecit mihi Deus.* It was God that did it. An hour of that day was the hour of the power of darkness; but the whole day itself, is said here plainly, was the day of the wrath of God. God was a doer in it: *Wherewith God hath afflicted me.*

God afflicteth some in mercy, and others in wrath. This was in his wrath. In his wrath God is not alike to all; some he afflicteth in his more gentle and mild, others in his fierce wrath. This was in the very fierceness of his wrath. His sufferings, his sweat, and cry, shew as much: they could not come but from a wrath *si fuerit sicut* (for we are not past *non sicut*; no, not here in this part; it followeth us still, and will not leave us in any point, not to the end).

The cause then in God, was wrath. What caused this wrath? God is not wroth, but with sin; nor grievously wroth, but with grievous sin. And in CHRIST there was no grievous sin. Nay, no sin at all. God did it (the text is plain). And in his fierce wrath he did it. For what cause? For, God forbid, God should do as did Annas the high priest, cause him to be smitten without cause. God forbid (saith Abraham) the judge of the world should do wrong to any. To any, but specially to his own Son: that his Son, of whom with thundering voice from heaven, he testifieth all his joy and delight were in him, in him only he was well pleased. And how then could his wrath wax hot, to do all this unto him? There is no way to preserve God's justice, and Christ's innocency both, but to say as the angel said of

---

[8] {Used in legal sense, linking up with "quest of inquiry," to mean "reported in answer to a writ or to some official demand for information."}

him to the prophet Daniel, *The Messias shall be slain,* ואין לו ve–en lo, *shall be slain, but not for himself.* Not for himself? For whom then? For some others. He took upon him the person of others; and so doing, justice may have her course and proceed.

Pity it is to see a man pay that he never took; but if he will become a surety, if he will take on him the person of the debtor, so he must.[9] Pity to see a silly poor lamb lie bleeding to death; but if it must be a sacrifice (such is the nature of a sacrifice), so it must. And so Christ, though without sin in himself, yet as a surety, as a sacrifice, may justly suffer for others, if he will take upon him their persons; and so, God may justly give way to his wrath against him.

And who be those others? The prophet Esay telleth us, and telleth it us seven times over for failing, He took upon him our infirmities and bare our maladies; he was wounded for our iniquities, and broken for our transgressions. The chastisement of our peace was upon him, and with his stripes were we healed. All we as sheep were gone astray, and turned every man to his own way; and the Lord hath laid upon him the iniquities of us all. All, all, even those that pass to and fro and, for all this, regard neither him nor his Passion.

The short is: It was we, that for our sins, our many, great, and grievous sins (*si fuerint sicut,* the like whereof never were), should have sweat this sweat, and have cried this cry; should have been smitten with these sorrows by the fierce wrath of God, had not he stepped between the blow and us, and latched it in his own body and soul, even the dint of the fierceness of the wrath of God. O the *non sicut* of our sins, that could not otherwise be answered!

To return then a true verdict. It is we (we wretched sinners that we are) that are to be found the principals in this act; and those on whom we seek to shift it, to derive it from ourselves, Pilate and Caiaphas and the rest, but instrumental causes only.[10] And it is not the executioner that killeth the man properly (that is, they); no, nor the judge (which is God in this case); only sin, *solum peccatum homicida est,* sin only is the murderer (to say the truth); and our sins the murderers of the Son of God; and the *non sicut* of them, the true cause of the *non sicut* both of God's wrath, and of his sorrowful sufferings.

Which bringeth home this our text to us, even into our own bosoms; and applieth it most effectually, to me that speak, and to you that hear, to every one of us; and that with the prophet Nathan's application: *Tu es homo;* thou art the man, even thou, for whom God in his fierce wrath thus afflicted him. Sin then was the cause on our part, why we, or some other for us.

But yet, what was the cause why he on his part? What was that that moved him thus to become our surety, and to take upon him our debt and danger? That moved him thus to lay down his soul, a sacrifice for our sin? Sure, *oblatus est quia voluit,* saith Esay again; offered he was for no other cause, but because he would. For unless he would, he needed not; needed not, for any necessity of justice, for no lamb was ever more innocent; nor for any necessity of constraint, for twelve legions of angels were ready at his command. But, because he would.

[9] {This was English law in Andrewes' day; see Craig Muldrew, *The culture of obligation* (Palgrave, 1998), 160.}

[10] {See the homily for Good Friday in the Elizabethan *Book of homilies*.}

And why would he? No reason can be given, but, because he regarded us (mark that reason). And what were we? Verily, utterly unworthy even his least regard; not worth the taking up, not worth the looking after: *Cum inimici essemus* (saith the Apostle); we were his enemies when he did it [Rom. 5:8]; without all desert before, and without all regard after he had done and suffered all this for us; and yet he would regard us, that so little regard him. For when he saw us (a sort of forlorn sinners) *non priùs natos, quàm damnatos*, damned as fast as born, as being by nature children of wrath, and yet still heaping up wrath against the day of wrath, by the errors of our life, till the time of our passing hence; and then the fierce wrath of God, ready to overwhelm us, and to make us endure the terror & torments of a never dying death (another *non sicut* yet): when (I say) he saw us in this case, he was moved with compassion over us, and undertook all this for us. Even then, in his love he regarded us, and so regarded us, that he regarded not himself, to regard us.

Bernard saith most truly, *dilexisti me, Domine, magis quam te, quando mori voluisti pro me*; in suffering all this for us, thou shewedst (Lord) that we were more dear to thee, that thou regardest us more than thine own self. And shall this regard find no regard at our hands?

It was sin then, and the heinousness of sin in us, that provoked wrath and the fierceness of his wrath in God. It was love, and the greatness of his love in Christ, that caused him to suffer these sorrows, and the grievousness of these sorrows, and all for our sakes.

And indeed, but only to testify the *non sicut* of this his love, all this needed not, that was done to him. One, any one, even the very least of all the pains he endured, had been enough; enough, in respect of the *meus*; enough, in respect of the *non sicut* of his person. For that which setteth the high price on this sacrifice, is this: that he which offereth it unto God, is God. But, if little had been suffered, little would the love have been thought, that suffered so little; and as little regard would have been had of it. To awake our regard then, or to leave us excuseless, if we continue regardless, all this he bare for us, that he might as truly make a case of *si fuerit amor, sicut amor meus*, as he did before, of *si fuerit dolor, sicut dolor meus*. We say we will regard love. If we will, here it is to regard.

So have we the causes all three: wrath in God, sin in ourselves, love in him.

Yet have we not all we should. For, what of all this? What good? *Cui bono?* That, that is it indeed that we will regard, if anything, as being matter of benefit—the only thing in a manner the world regardeth, which bringeth us about to the very first words again. For, the very first words which we read, *Have ye no regard?* are in the original, לוֹא אֲלֵיכֶם lo alechem, which the Seventy[11] turn (word for word) οὐ πρὸς ὑμας; and the Latin likewise, *nonne ad vos pertinet?* Pertains it not to you, that you regard it no better? For these two, pertaining and regarding, are folded one in another, and go together so commonly, as one is taken often for the other. Then to be sure to bring us to regard, he urgeth this, *pertains not all this to you?* Is it not for your good? Is not the benefit yours? Matters of benefit, they pertain to you, and without them, love, and all the rest, may pertain to whom they will.

Consider then, the inestimable benefit that groweth unto you, from this incomparable love. It is not impertinent this, even this: that to us hereby, all is turned about clean contrary; that by his stripes, we are healed; by his sweat, we refreshed; by his forsaking, we

[11] {The earliest translators of the Hebrew Scriptures into Greek (ca. 200 B.C.), the translation known as the Septuagint.}

received to grace. That this day, to him the day of the fierceness of God's wrath, is to us the day of the fullness of God's favor; as the Apostle calleth it, a day of salvation. In respect of that he suffered (I deny not), an evil day, a day of heaviness. But, in respect of that, which he, by it, hath obtained for us, it is (as we truly call it) a good day, a day of joy and jubilee. For it doth not only rid us of that wrath, which pertained to us for our sins; but, further, it maketh that pertain to us, whereto we had no manner of right at all.

For, not only by his death, as by the death of our sacrifice; by the blood of his Cross, as by the blood of the paschal lamb, the Destroyer passeth over us, and we shall not perish; but also by his death, as by the death of our high priest (for he is priest and sacrifice both), we are restored from our exile, even to our former forfeited estate in the land of promise. Or rather (as the Apostle saith) *non sicut delictum, sic donum*; not to the same estate, but to one nothing like it: that is, one far better than the estate our sins bereft us: for they deprived us of Paradise, a place on earth; but by the purchase of his blood, we are entitled to a far higher, even the kingdom of heaven; & his blood, not only the blood of remission to acquit us of our sins, but the blood of the Testament too, to bequeath us, and give us estate in, that heavenly inheritance.

Now whatsoever else, this (I am sure) is a *non sicut*: as that which the eye, by all it can see; the ear, by all it can hear; the heart, by all it can conceive, cannot pattern it, or set the like by it. Pertains not this unto us neither? Is not this worth the regard? Sure if anything be worthy the regard, this is most worthy of our very worthiest and best regard.

Thus have we considered and seen, not so much as in this sight we might or should, but as much as the time will give us leave. And now, lay all these before you (every one of them a *non sicut* of itself): the pains of his body, esteemed by Pilate's *Ecce*; the sorrows of his soul, by his sweat in the Garden; the comfortless estate of his sorrows, by his cry on the Cross. And with these, his person, as being the Son of the great and eternal God. Then join to these, the cause: in God, his fierce wrath; in us, our heinous sins deserving it; in him, his exceeding great love, both suffering that for us which we had deserved; and procuring for us, that we could never deserve; making that to appertain to himself, which of right pertained to us; and making that pertain to us, which pertained to him only, and not to us at all, but by his means alone. And after their view in several, lay them all together, so many *non sicuts* into one, and tell me, if his complaint be not just, and his request most reasonable.

Yes sure, his complaint is just, *Have ye no regard?* None? And yet never the like? None? And it pertains unto you? *No regard?* As if it were some common ordinary matter, and the like never was? *No regard?* As if it concern'd you not a whit, and it toucheth you so near? As if he should say: rare things you regard, yea though they no ways pertain to you; this is exceeding rare, and will you not regard it? Again, things that nearly touch you, you regard, though they be not rare at all; this toucheth you exceeding near, even as near as your soul toucheth you, and will you not yet regard it? Will neither of these by itself, move you? Will not both these together move you? What will move you? Will pity? Here is distress, never the like. Will duty? Here is a person, never the like. Will fear? Here is wrath, never the like. Will remorse? Here are sins, never the like. Will kindness? here is love, never the like. Will bounty? Here are benefits, never the like. Will all these? Here they be all, all above any *sicut*, all in the highest degree.

Truly the complaint is just, it may move us; it wanteth no reason, it may move; and it wanteth no affection in the delivery of it to us, on his part to move us. Sure it moved him exceeding much, for among all the deadly sorrows of his most bitter Passion, this, even this, seemeth to be his greatest of all, and that which did most affect him, even the grief of the slender reckoning most men have it in; as little respecting him, as if he had done, or suffered nothing at all for them. For lo, of all the sharp pains he endureth, he complaineth not; but of this he complaineth, of *no regard*. That, which grieveth him most, that, which most he moaneth, is this. It is strange, he should be in pains, such pains as never any was, and not complain himself of them, But, of want of regard only. Strange, he should not make request, ô deliver me, or relieve me; but only, *ô consider and regard me.* In effect, as if he said, none, no deliverance, no relief do I seek; regard I seek. And all that I suffer, I am content with it; I regard it not; I suffer most willingly, if this I may find at your hands, regard.

Truly, this so passionate a complaint may move us; it moved all but us. For most strange of all it is, that all the creatures in heaven and earth seemed to hear this his mournful complaint, & in their kind, to shew their regard of it: the sun in heaven shrinking in his light; the earth trembling under it; the very stones cleaving in sunder, as if they had sense and sympathy of it; and sinful men only, not moved with it. And yet it was not for the creatures, this was done to him; to them it pertaineth not. But for us it was, and to us it doth. And shall we not yet regard it? Shall the creature, and not we? Shall we not?

If we do not, it may pertain to us, but we pertain not to it. It pertains to all, but all pertain not to it. None pertain to it, but they that take benefit by it; and none take benefit by it, no more than by the brazen serpent, but they that fix their eye on it. Behold, consider, and regard it: the profit, the benefit is lost without regard.

If we do not, as this was a day of God's fierce wrath against him, only for regarding us; so there is another day coming, and it will quickly be here, a day of like fierce wrath against us, for not regarding him. And who regardeth the power of this wrath? He that doth, will surely regard this.

In that day, there is not the most careless of us all, but shall cry as they did in the Gospel, *Domine, non ad te pertinet, si perimus?* Pertains it not to thee, carest thou not that we perish? Then would we be glad to pertain to him, and his Passion. Pertains it to us then, and pertains it not now? Sure now it must, if then it shall.

Then, to give end to his complaint, let us grant him his request, and regard his Passion. Let the rareness of it, the nearness to us; let pity, or duty; fear, or remorse; love, or bounty. Any of them, or all of them. Let the justness of his complaint. Let his affectionate manner of complaining of this, and only this. Let the shame of the creatures' regard. Let our profit, or our peril. Let some thing prevail with us, to have it in some regard.

Some regard! Verily, as his sufferings, his love, our good by them are, so should our regard be, a *non sicut* too; that is, a regard of these, and of nothing in comparison of these. It should be so; for with the benefit, ever the regard should arise.

But God help us poor sinners, and be merciful unto us. Our regard is a *non sicut*, indeed; but it is backward, & in a contrary sense: that is, nowhere so shallow, so short, or so soon done. It should be otherwise, it should have our deepest consideration, this; and our highest regard.

But if that cannot be had (our nature is so heavy, and flesh and blood so dull of apprehension in spiritual things), yet at leastwise some regard. Some, I say: the more the better; but in any wise some. And not as here, no regard, none at all. Some ways to shew we make accompt of it: to withdraw ourselves, to void our minds of other matters, to set this before us, to think upon it, to thank him for it; to regard him, and stay and see, whether he will regard us, or no. Sure he will, and we shall feel our hearts pricked with sorrow, by consideration of the cause in us, our sin. And again, warm within us, by consideration of the cause in him, his love; till by some motion of grace he answer us, and shew, that our regard is accepted of him. And this, as at all other times (for no day is amiss, but at all times, some time to be taken for this duty), so specially on this day; this day which we hold holy to the memory of his Passion, this day to do it; to make this day, the day of God's wrath and Christ's suffering, a day to us of serious consideration and regard of them both.

It is kindly to consider *opus diei in die suo*, the work of the day, in the day it was wrought; and this day it was wrought. This day therefore, whatsoever our business be, to lay them aside a little; whatsoever our haste, yet to stay a little, and to spend a few thoughts in calling to mind and taking to regard, what this day the Son of God did and suffered for us: and all for this end, that what he was then, we might not be; and what he is now, we might be for ever.

Which, Almighty God grant we may all do, more or less, even every one of us, according to the several measures of his grace in us, &c.

✄∽⁓✄

Text: EEBO (STC [2nd ed.] / 597)

The copy of the sermon preached on Good Friday last before the King's Majesty, by D. Andrewes, Dean of Westminster, 6 April 1604 (London: Printed by R. Barker, Printer to the King's most excellent Majesty, 1604).

WILLIAM BRADSHAW
(ca. 1570–1618)

A poor man's son, Bradshaw completed grammar school thanks to the generosity of the puritan headmaster at Ashby-de-la-Zouch, where Joseph Hall was a fellow-student; the two entered Emmanuel in 1588. With the son of Marian exile and puritan leader, Anthony Gilby, for his tutor, Bradshaw soon found patrons and friends among the godly, including the puritan activists Sir Francis and Sir Edward Hastings, sons of the second Earl of Huntingdon; Arthur Hildersham, like Gilby, a prominent godly minister; Laurence Chaderton, the master of Emmanuel; and Thomas Cartwright, the presbyterian éminence grise. Bradshaw took his BA in 1593, his MA in 1596. In 1598 he took up a fellowship at the new college of Sidney Sussex, and within a year was publishing (anonymously) against subscription to Whitgift's three articles,[1] urging fellow-puritans to stand firm in their non-conformity on the grounds that the ceremonies mandated by the Book of Common Prayer were not indifferent (*adiaphora*) but popish superstitions odious to God. He soon found himself in trouble with the Cambridge authorities and in 1601 left the University for a lectureship in Chatham, Kent. However, since Bradshaw refused to subscribe, Whitgift disallowed the appointment, despite a letter from Sir Francis Hastings assuring the Archbishop that the young minister did not intend to disturb the peace of the Church. Shortly thereafter, through Hildersham's good offices, Bradshaw entered the household of Alexander Redrich, a puritan gentleman from Derbyshire, obtaining a preaching license from the lax, careerist bishop of Lichfield and Coventry, William Overton. Bradshaw's circle was actively involved in the petitioning campaign of 1603 urging the new King to remodel the English Church along puritan lines—the campaign that met a stinging defeat at Hampton Court the next year.[2]

English puritanism was Bradshaw's response to this debacle. In order to outflank the conformist charge that presbyterianism threatened monarchy (famously encapsulated in

---

[1] On these, see introduction to Dod and Cleaver's *A plain and familiar exposition*, n. 3 <*supra*>.
[2] For the fullest (and semi-official) account of the Hampton Court Conference, see Barlow.

James' "no bishop, no king"), Bradshaw dropped both the hierarchical synodal structure that English puritanism had inherited from Calvin and the entire system of ecclesiastical courts, leaving only individual parishes, each of which for him constituted an autonomous visible church—although such churches would share a common order of worship and the same three-fold ministry of pastor, doctor, and elder. All the institutional weight and coercive jurisdiction enjoyed by the bishops and sought by Elizabethan presbyterians for their synods would, on Bradshaw's plan, revert to the king. Although the work apparently failed to convince James that puritanism enhanced royal power, it did become one of the founding texts of congregationalism. A Latin translation appeared in 1610, and then, in the early 1640s as the English Church was being dismantled, two further editions of the 1605 text (with some interesting deletions) came out.

After 1605 Bradshaw turned his energies back to his pastoral ministry in Derbyshire, writing godly tracts on human mortality and holy matrimony. He was a respected figure in London's tight-knit, if fractious, godly community. Despite his radicalism and unbending non-conformity, he remained within the Church of England, carrying on his ministry largely unmolested, although Overton had been succeeded at Lichfield by the high-church bishops, Richard Neile and John Overall. Death overtook Bradshaw during a trip to London, whose godly community poured out to pay their solemn tribute at his funeral.

⚬⚬⚬

Much in *English puritanism* fulfills the claim of its title. The work strikes a long sequence of characteristic puritan notes: a deep and dire anti-Romanism that views the pope as antichrist, his followers as heretics; a hard-core biblicism that denounces all rites, all piety, all religion not mandated by Scripture as mere traditions of men, and, as such, odious in God's eyes; an indifference bordering on contempt for ecclesiastical tradition, including the patristic; the rejection of the whole notion of adiaphora, since with respect to the service of God there are no things indifferent—whatever Scripture does not authorize, it disallows. The theology, with its attendant hermeneutic, is thus voluntarist: God reveals his will in Scripture's commands and binding precedents; God's people are to hear and obey. Preaching, the explication and application of Scripture, is the principal office of the Church and its ministry.

Yet the centerpiece of Bradshaw's tract—his claim that each congregation constitutes an autonomous visible church, answerable only to God and the civil magistrate, who alone can impose coercive sanctions—is scarcely classic puritanism. It seems rather to jettison the core ideal of sixteenth-century puritanism: the Genevan discipline enforced through the Consistory, whereby the reformed Church might in turn reform and renew the social order (Collinson). By divesting churches of any coercive authority, Bradshaw's proposal goes a fair way down the long path separating Calvinist theocracy from modern voluntary religion.

One can also, of course, see his proposal as a sellout of the Church to secular power—the risks involved evident by 1641, which is presumably why the edition of that year deletes some of Bradshaw's most extreme concessions to the king (who, it is worth noting, Bradshaw sees not as godly prince or *caput ecclesiae*, but simply as civil magistrate); although, significantly, none of these changes even partially restores the Church's power over the laity: no pecuniary mulcts, no wearing the white sheet, no public penances, no corporeal punishments; if a sinner repents, nothing more will be required; if he does not, the congregation can expel him from their communion, but that is all. As Peter Lake comments, "Bradshaw was quite ready to claim that the puritan position was infinitely more compatible with the hierarchies of lay society than the present episcopal structure of the church" (271).

Bradshaw made these concessions, one presumes, in order to win the governing elite, James above all, to support what for Bradshaw mattered more than a million church courts: the restoration of pure worship, unpolluted by Romish superstitions. Indeed, its not clear that the concessions were ever seriously meant, given that Bradshaw makes no attempt to deal with such obvious issues as how to preserve uniformity of worship across the hundreds of English parishes or the nature of royal jurisdiction vis-à-vis the Church: will the king make ecclesiastical law, or merely enforce it? and if the latter, where do the laws he enforces come from? The holes in Bradshaw's platform raise the possibility that its function was primarily rhetorical: an attempt to seize the royalist high ground from the episcopal party along lines that anyone familiar with act I, scene i of *King Lear* will instantly recognize. It is also, of course, possible that the holes were not so visible in 1605 as they would be by 1641 and thereafter.

Chapter V of Bradshaw's tract, which concerns canonical procedure and the ex officio oath used in the church courts, requires a far fuller contextualization than can be provided here, but a few brief observations may prove helpful. The ex officio oath bound the accused to answer truthfully the questions put to him, including the self-incriminating ones. In common-law criminal trials, the accused was not under oath; hence, while he had no right to remain silent, lying was not technically perjury. However, for clergymen—as for all serious Christians—the distinction amounted to little, since perjury and falsehood are both sins. The Catholic recourse to equivocation was designed to avoid incriminating oneself and one's confederates in common-law trials; Protestant non-conformists, who generally found themselves in the church courts, sought to avoid self-incrimination by protesting that the oath violated the law of nature, rendering it ipso facto invalid. By far the best contemporary explanation of church court procedures is to be found in Richard Cosin's *Apologie of, and for, sundrie proceedings by jurisdiction ecclesiasticall* (1591, rev. ed. 1593). The ex officio oath also came up during the Hampton Court conference (Barlow, 92–93).[3] Also worth noting is the little-known *New art of lying* (1620) by the Jacobean conformist Henry Mason, a work which argues that it is morally permissible to *mislead* the courts in order to avoid self-incrimination, as long as such misdirection does not amount to outright falsehood.

Bradshaw's claim that Scripture has only a single literal sense, and that its meaning, like the meaning of every other text, is a matter of historico-grammatical analysis, should be set against Field's chapters in *Of the Church*—but also against Calvin's *Institutes* I.10 (on which, see also Muller).

---

[3] The best modern discussion is Helmholz's. On self-incrimination at common law, see the opening chapter of Langbein.

⟩⟨

Sources: William Barlow, *The sum and substance of the conference . . . at Hampton Court* (London, 1604); Patrick Collinson, *The Elizabethan puritan movement* (U California P, 1967); Richard Cosin, *Apologie* (London, 1591); Thomas Gataker, "The life and death of Master William Bradshaw," in *The lives of thirty-two English divines*, printed at the end of Samuel Clarke's *A general martyrology* (London, 1677), 25–60; Richard Helmholz, "The privilege and the *ius commune*: the Middle Ages to the seventeenth century," in *The privilege against self-incrimination: its origins and development*, ed. R. H. Helmholz et al. (Chicago UP, 1997), 17–46; Peter Lake, *Moderate puritans*; John Langbein, *The origins of the adversary criminal trial* (Oxford UP, 2003); Henry Mason, *The new art of lying* (London, 1620); Richard Muller, "Calvin's exegesis," in *The Bible in the sixteenth century*, ed. David Steinmetz (Duke UP, 1990), 68–82.

WILLIAM BRADSHAW

English puritanism: containing the main opinions of the rigidest sort of those that are called Puritans in the realm of England

1605 (rev. ed. 1641)

To the indifferent reader:

It cannot be unknown unto them that know anything that those Christians in this realm which are called by the odious and vile name of Puritans are accused by the prelates to the King's Majesty and the state to maintain many absurd, erroneous, schismatical, and heretical opinions concerning religion, church-government, and the civil magistracy: which hath moved me to collect (as near as I could) the chiefest of them, and to send them naked to the view of all men, that they may see what is the worst that the worst of them hold. It is not my part to prove and justify them. Those that accuse and condemn them must in all reason and equity prove their accusation, or else bear the name of unchristian slanderers. I am not ignorant that they lay other opinions (yea, some clean contradictory to these) to the charge of these men, the falsehood whereof we shall (it is to be doubted) have more and more occasion to detect. In the meantime, all enemies of divine truth shall find that to obscure the same with calumniation and untruths is but to hide a fire with dry straw or tow upon it. But thou mayest herein observe what a terrible popedom and primacy these rigid presbyterians desire, and with what painted bug-bears and scarecrows the prelates go about to fright the states of the kingdom withal, who will no doubt one day see how their wisdoms are abused.

Farewell.

CHAP. I

Concerning religion, or the worship of God in general

IMPRIMIS, they hold and maintain that the word of God contained in the writings of the prophets and apostles is of absolute perfection, given by CHRIST the head of the Church to be unto the same the sole canon and rule of all matters of religion and the worship and service of God whatsoever. And that whatsoever done in the same service and worship {that} cannot be justified by the said word is unlawful. And therefore that it is a sin to force any Christian to do any act of religion or divine service that cannot evidently be warranted by the same.

2. They hold that all ecclesiastical actions invented and devised by man are utterly to be excluded out of the exercises of religion: especially such actions as are famous and notorious mysteries of an idolatrous religion and in doing whereof the true religion is conformed (whether in whole or in part) to idolatry and superstition.

3. They hold that all outward means instituted and set apart to express and set forth the inward worship of God are parts of divine worship, and that not only all moral actions, but all typical rites and figures ordained to shadow forth in the solemn worship and service of God any spiritual or religious act or habit in the mind of man are special parts of the same, and therefore that every such act ought evidently to be prescribed by the word of God or else ought not to be done—it being a sin to perform any other worship to God, whether external or internal, moral or ceremonial, in whole or in part, than that which God himself requires in his word.

4. They hold it to be gross superstition for any mortal man to institute and ordain as parts of divine worship any mystical rite and ceremony of religion whatsoever, and to mingle the same with the divine rites and mysteries of God's ordinance. But they hold it to be high presumption to institute and bring into divine worship such rites and ceremonies of religion as are acknowledged to be no part of divine worship at all, but only of civil worship and honor: for they that shall require to have performed unto themselves a ceremonial obedience, service, and worship, consisting in rites of religion, to be done at that very instant that God is solemnly served and worshipped, and even in the same worship, make both themselves and God also an idol. . . .

5. They hold that every act or action appropriated and set apart to divine service and worship, whether moral or ceremonial, real or typical, ought to bring special honor unto God, and therefore that every such act ought to be apparently commanded in the word of God, either expressly or by necessary consequent. . . .

. . .

CHAP. II

Concerning the Church

1. They hold and maintain that every company, congregation, or assembly of true believers, joining together according to the order of the Gospel in the true worship of God, is a true visible Church of Christ; and that the same title is improperly attributed to any other congregations, synods, societies, combinations, or assemblies whatsoever.

2. They hold that all such churches[1] or congregations, communicating after that manner together in divine worship, are in all ecclesiastical matters equal and of the same power and authority; and that by the word and will of God, they ought to have the same spiritual privileges, prerogatives, officers, administrations, orders, and forms of divine worship.

3. They hold that Christ Jesus hath not subjected any church or congregation of his to any other superior ecclesiastical jurisdiction than unto that which is within itself. So

---

[1] {Since by "church," Bradshaw usually means a specific congregation rather than the mystical body of Christ or a denomination, I have generally left it lowercase.}

that if a whole church or congregation shall err in any matter of faith or religion, no other churches or spiritual church-officers have (by any warrant from the word of God) power to censure, punish, or control the same; but are only to counsel or advise the same, and so to leave their souls to the immediate judgment of Christ and their bodies to the sword and power of the civil magistrate, who alone upon earth hath power to punish a whole church or congregation.

. . .

5. They hold that every established Church ought (as a special prerogative wherewith she is endowed by Christ) to have power and liberty to elect and choose their own spiritual and ecclesiastical officers, and that {it} is a greater wrong to have any such forced upon them against their wills than if they should force upon men wives, or upon women husbands, against their will and liking.

6.[2] They hold that if in this choice any particular churches shall err, that none upon earth but the civil magistrate hath power to control or correct them for it. And that, though it be not lawful for him to take away this power from them, yet when they or any of them shall apparently abuse the same, he stands bound by the law of God and by virtue of his office (grounded upon the same) to punish them severely for it, & to force them under civil mulcts to make better choice.

6. They hold that the ecclesiastical officers and ministers of one church ought not to bear any ecclesiastical office in another; neither, as they are officers in one congregation, can they officially administer in another, but ought to be tied unto that congregation of which they are members and by which they are elected into office.

And they are not (without just cause, and such as may be approved by the congregation) to forsake their callings—wherein, if the congregation shall be perverse and will not hearken to reason, they are then to crave the assistance and help of the civil magistrate, who alone hath power and who ought, by his civil sword and authority, procure to all members of the church, whether governors or others, freedom from all manifest injuries and wrongs.

7. They hold that the congregation, having once made choice of their spiritual officers, unto whom they commit the regiment of their souls, they ought not (without just cause, and that which is apparently warrantable by the word of God) to discharge, deprive, or depose them; but ought to live in all canonical obedience and subjection unto them, agreeable to the word of God.

9. They hold that, though one church is not to differ from another in any spiritual, ecclesiastical, or religious matters whatsoever, but are to be equal and alike, yet that they may differ and one excel another in outward civil circumstances of place, time, person, &c. So that, although they hold that those congregations of which kings and nobles make themselves members ought to have the same ecclesiastical officers, ministry, worship, sacraments, ceremonies, and form of divine worship that the basest congregation in the country hath—and no other—yet they hold also that, as their persons in civil respects excel, so in the exercises of religion in civil matters they may excel other assemblies. Their chapels and seats may be gorgeously set forth with rich arras and tapestry. Their fonts may be of silver. Their communion tables of ivory &, if they will, covered with gold. The

---

[2] {The underlined passages appear in the original 1605 edition, but have been omitted from the 1641.}

cup out of which they drink the sacramental blood of Christ may be of beaten gold set about with diamonds. Their ministers may be clothed in silk & velvet: so themselves will maintain them in that manner. Otherwise, they think it absurd and against common reason that other base and inferior congregations must by ecclesiastical tithes and oblations maintain the silken and velvet suits & lordly retinue of ministers and ecclesiastical officers of princes and nobles.

8. They hold that the laws, orders, and ecclesiastical jurisdiction of the visible churches of Christ, if they be lawful and warrantable by the word of God, are no ways repugnant to any civil state whatsoever, whether monarchical, aristocratical, or democratical, but do tend to the further establishing and advancing of the right and prerogatives of all and every of them. And they renounce and abhor from their souls all such ecclesiastical jurisdiction or policy that is any way repugnant to any civil state whatsoever, whether monarchical, aristocratical, or democratical, but do tend to the further establishing and advancing of the right and prerogatives of all and every of them. And they renounce and abhor from their souls all such ecclesiastical jurisdiction and policy that is any way repugnant and derogatory to any of them, especially to the monarchical state, which they acknowledge to be the best kind of civil government for this kingdom.

9. They hold and believe that the equality in ecclesiastical jurisdiction and authority of churches and church-ministers is no more derogatory and repugnant to the state and glory of a monarch than the parity or equality of schoolmasters of several schools. . . . Yea, they hold the clean contrary: that inequality of churches and church-officers in ecclesiastical jurisdiction and authority was that principally that advanced Antichrist unto his throne and brought the kings and princes of the earth unto such vassalage under him; and that the civil authority and glory of secular princes and states hath ever decayed and withered, the more that the ecclesiastical officers of the Church have been advanced and lifted up in authority, beyond the limits and confines that Christ in his word hath prescribed unto them.

CHAP. III

Concerning the ministers of the Church

1. They hold that the pastors, teachers, and ruling Elders[3] of particular congregations are, or ought to be, the highest spiritual officers in the Church, over whom (by any divine ordinance) there is no superior pastor, but only Jesus Christ; and that they are led by the spirit of Antichrist that arrogate or take upon themselves to be pastors of pastors.

. . .

4. They hold that if there were a supreme national ecclesiastical minister or pastor that should be the prince of many thousand pastors, that then also Christ (as he did in the Jewish Church) would have appointed a solemn national or provincial liturgy or worship, unto which at some times of the year the whole body of the people should ascend—and that unto the metropolitan city, as unto a Jerusalem—and that he would (as he did in the Jewish Church) more precisely and particularly have set down the manner of solemnization thereof than of his parochial worship. Forasmuch therefore as they cannot read in

---

[3] {"teachers and ruling Elders"—not in 1605 ed.}

the New Testament of any higher or more solemn worship than of that which is to be performed in a particular congregation, they cannot be persuaded that God hath appointed any higher ministers of his service and worship under the New Testament than the elect ministers of particular congregations. . . .

5. They hold that no ecclesiastical minister {"pastor"—1605} ought to exercise or accept of any civil public jurisdiction and authority, but ought to be wholly employed in spiritual offices and duties to that congregation over which he is set. And that those civil magistrates weaken their own supremacy that shall suffer any ecclesiastical pastor to exercise any civil jurisdiction within their realms, dominions, or seignories.

6. They hold that the highest and supreme office and authority of the pastor is to preach the Gospel solemnly and publicly to the congregation, by interpreting the written word of God and applying the same by exhortation and reproof unto them. They hold that this was the greatest work that Christ and his apostles did, and that whosoever is thought worthy and fit to exercise this authority cannot be thought unfit and unworthy to exercise any other spiritual or ecclesiastical authority whatsoever.

7. They hold that the pastor or minister of the word is not to teach any doctrine unto the church grounded upon his own judgment or opinion or upon the judgment or opinion of any or all the men in the world, but only that truth that he is able to demonstrate and prove evidently and apparently by the word of God soundly interpreted; and that the people are not bound to believe any doctrine of religion or divinity whatsoever, upon any ground whatsoever, except it be apparently justified by the word or by necessary consequent deduced from the same.

8. They hold that in interpreting the Scriptures and opening the sense of them, he ought to follow those rules only that are followed in finding out the meaning of other writings: to wit, by weighing the propriety of the tongue wherein they are written, by weighing the circumstance of the place, by comparing one place with another, and by considering what is properly spoken, and what tropically or figuratively. And they hold it unlawful for the pastor to obtrude upon his people a sense of any part of the divine word for which he hath no other ground but the bare testimonies of men, and that it is better for the people to be content to be ignorant of the meaning of such difficult places than to hang their faith in any matter in this case upon the bare testimony of man.

9. They hold that the people of God ought not to acknowledge any such for their pastors as are not able by preaching to interpret and apply the word of God unto them in manner and form aforesaid. And therefore that no ignorant and sole reading priests[4] are to be reputed the ministers of Jesus Christ, who sendeth none into his ministry and service but such as he adorneth in some measure with spiritual gifts. . . .

10. They hold that in the assembly of the church, the pastor only is to be the mouth of the congregation to God in prayer, and that the people are only to testify their assent by the word Amen.[5] And that it is a Babylonian confusion for the pastor to say one piece

---

[4] {i.e., clergy who were not licensed to preach, but allowed only to read the Prayer Book liturgy and the sermons printed in the Book of Homilies}

[5] {See Ramie Targoff, *Common prayer: the language of public devotion in early modern England* (Chicago UP, 2001), 38–47.}

of a prayer and the people with mingled voices to say another, except in singing, which by the very ordinance and instinct of nature is more delightful and effectual the more voices there are joined and mingled together in harmony and consent.

. . .

12. They hold that it is as great an injury to force a congregation or church to maintain as their pastor, with tithes and such like donations, that person that either is not able to instruct them or that refuseth in his own person ordinarily to do it, as to force a man to maintain one for his wife that either is not a woman or that refuseth in her own person to do the duties of a wife unto him.

13. They hold that by God's ordinance there should be also in every church a doctor, whose special office should be to instruct by opening the sense of the Scripture[6] to the congregation (and that particularly) in the main grounds and principles of religion.

CHAP. IIII

Concerning the Elders

1. For as much as through the malice of Satan there are and will be in the best churches many disorders and scandals committed that redound to the reproach of the Gospel & are a stumbling block to many both without and within the Church, and sith they judge it repugnant to the word of God that any minister should be a sole ruler and, as it were, a pope so much as in one parish (much more that he should be one over a whole diocese, province, or nation), they hold that by God's ordinance the congregation should make choice of other officers as assistants unto the ministers in the spiritual regiment of the congregation, who are by office jointly with the ministers of the word to be as *monitors* and overseers of the manners and conversation of all the congregation, and one of another; that so every one may be more wary of their ways, and that the pastors and doctors may better attend to prayer and doctrine, and by their means may be made better acquainted with the estate of the people when others' eyes besides their own shall wake and watch over them.

2. They hold that such only are to be chosen to this office as are the gravest, honestest, discreetest, best-grounded in religion, and the ancientest professors thereof in the congregation, such as the whole congregation do approve of & respect for their wisdom, holiness, and honesty; and such also (if it be possible) as are of civil note and respect in the world, and able (without any burden to the church) to maintain themselves either by their lands or any other honest civil trade of life. Neither do they think it so much disgrace to the policy of the church that tradesmen and artificers (endowed with such qualities as are above specified) should be admitted to be overseers of the church as it is that persons both ignorant of religion and all good letters, and in all respects for person, quality, and state, as base and vile as the basest in the congregation, should be admitted to be pastors and teachers of a congregation. . . .

---

[6] {"to instruct by way of catechizing the ignorant of the congregation"—1605}

CHAP. V

Concerning the censures of the Church

1. They hold that the spiritual keys of the Church are by Christ committed to the aforesaid spiritual officers and governors, and unto none other. Which keys they hold that they are not to be put to this use: to lock up the crowns, swords, or scepters of princes and civil states; or the civil rights, prerogatives, and immunities of civil subjects in the things of this life; or to use them as picklocks to open withal men's treasuries & coffers; or as keys of prisons to shut up the bodies of men—for they think that such a power and authority ecclesiastical is fit only for the Antichrist of Rome and the consecrated governors of his synagogues, who, having no word of God, which is the sword of the Spirit, to defend his and their usurped jurisdiction over the Christian world, doth unlawfully usurp the lawful civil sword and power of the monarchs and princes of the earth, thereby forcing men to subject themselves to his spiritual vassalage and service, and abusing thereby the spiritual keys and jurisdiction of the Church.

2. They hold that by virtue of these keys they are not to make any curious inquisitions into the secret or hidden vices or crimes of men, extorting from them a confession of those faults that are concealed from themselves and others; or to proceed to molest any man upon secret suggestions, private suspicion, or uncertain fame, or for such crimes as are in question whether they be crimes or no. But they are to proceed only against evident and apparent crimes, such as are either granted to be such of all civil honest men or of all true Christians—or at least such as they are able by evidence of the word of God to convince to be sins to the conscience of the offender; as also such as have been either publicly committed or, having been committed in secret, are by some good means brought to light, & which, the delinquent denying, they are able by honest and sufficient testimony to prove against him.

3. They hold that when he that hath committed a scandalous crime cometh before them and is convinced {convicted} of the same, they ought not (after the manner of our ecclesiastical courts) scorn, deride, and taunt, and revile him with odious and contumelious speeches; eye him with big and stern looks; procure proctors to make personal invectives against him; make him dance attendance from court day to court day and from term to term, frowning at him in presence and laughing at him behind his back; but they are (though he be never so obstinate and perverse) to use him brotherly, not giving the least personal reproaches or threats; but, laying open unto him the nature of his sin by the light of God's word, are only by denouncing the judgments of God against him to terrify him, and so to move him to repentance.

4. They hold that if the party offending be their civil superior, that then they are to use, even throughout the whole carriage of their censure, all civil compliments, offices and reverence due unto him; that they are not to presume to convent {summon} him before them, but are themselves to go in all civil and humble manner unto him, to stand bare {hatless} before him, to bow unto him, to give him all civil titles belonging unto him. And if he be a king and supreme ruler, they are to kneel down before him and in the humblest manner to censure his faults; so that he may see apparently that they are not carried with the least spice of malice against his person, but only with zeal of the health and salvation of his soul.

5. They hold that the ecclesiastical officers laying to the charge of any man any error, heresy, or false opinion whatsoever do stand bound themselves, first, to prove that he holdeth such an error or heresy; and secondly, to prove directly unto him that it is an error by the word of God and that it deserveth such a censure, before they do proceed against him.

6. They hold that the governors of the Church ought with all patience and quietness hear what every offender can possibly say for himself, either for qualification, defense, apology, or justification of any supposed crime or error whatsoever; and they ought not to proceed to censure the grossest offence that is, until the offender have said as much for himself in his defense as he possibly is able. And they hold it an evident character of a corrupt ecclesiastical government, where the parties convented may not have full liberty to speak for themselves, considering that the more liberty is granted to speak in a bad cause (especially before those that are in authority and of judgment), the more the iniquity of it will appear, and the more the justice of their sentence will shine.

7. They hold that the oath ex officio, whereby popish and English ecclesiastical governors, either upon some secret informations or suggestions or private suspicions, go about to bind men's consciences to accuse themselves and their friends of such crimes or imputations as cannot by any direct course of law be proved against them, and whereby they are drawn to be instruments of many heavy crosses upon themselves and their friends—and that often for those actions that they are persuaded in their consciences are good and holy—I say, that they hold that such an oath (on the urger's part) is most damnable and tyrannous, against the very law of nature, devised by Antichrist through the inspiration of the devil, that by means thereof the professors and practicers of the true religion might either, in their weakness, by perjury damn their own souls, or be drawn to reveal to the enemies of Christianity those secret religious acts and deeds that, being (in the persuasion of their consciences) for the advancement of the Gospel, will be a means of heavy sentences of condemnation against themselves and their dearest friends.[7]

8. They hold that ecclesiastical officers have no power to proceed in censure against any crime of any person after that he shall freely acknowledge the same and profess his hearty penitency for it. And that they may not, for any crime whatsoever, lay any bodily or pecuniary mulct upon them or impose upon them any ceremonial mark or note of shame, such as is the white sheet, or any such like; or take fees for any cause whatsoever, but are to accept of, as a sufficient satisfaction, a private submission and acknowledgement, if the crime be private; and a public, if the crime be public and notorious.

9. They hold that if a member of the church be obstinate and shew no signs and tokens of repentance of that crime that they by evidence of Scripture have convinced to be a *crime*, that then by their ecclesiastical authority <u>they are to deny unto him the sacrament of the Supper. And if the suspension from it will not humble him, then (though not without humbling themselves in prayer, fasting, and great demonstration of sorrow for him)</u> they are to denounce him to be as yet no member of the kingdom of heaven nor of that congregation, and so are to leave him to God and the king. And this is all the ecclesiastical

---

[7] {I.e., if the accused answer the interrogatories, confessing to the illegal religious practices and revealing the names of the other participants, they will bring sharp penalties upon their own and their coreligionists' heads—their only offense being to have sought "the advancement of the Gospel."}

authority and jurisdiction that any spiritual officers of the church are to use against any man for greatest crime that can be committed.

10. They hold that the officers of the church are not to proceed unto excommunication[8] against any man without the <u>free</u> consent of the whole congregation itself, first called for in public assembly.[9]

11. They hold that the minister, or any other particular officer, offending, is as subject to these censures as any other of the congregation.

12. They hold that if any member of the congregation, having committed a scandalous sin, shall of himself forsake the worship of God and the spiritual communion with the church, that the church shall then send for the said person, and if he refuse to come, they shall (after much seeking and long patience) openly declare that he hath no part nor portion in the holy things of God among them;[10] that then the ecclesiastical officers have no authority or jurisdiction over him, but only the civil magistrate and those unto whom he oweth civil subjection, as parents, masters, landlords, &c.

CHAP. VI

Concerning the civil magistrate

1. They hold that the civil magistrate, as he is a civil magistrate, hath and ought to have supreme power over all the churches within his dominions in all causes whatsoever. And yet they hold that, as he is a Christian, he is a member of some one particular congregation and ought to be as subject to the spiritual regiment thereof prescribed by Christ in his word as the meanest subject in the kingdom; and they hold that this subjection is no more derogatory to his supremacy than the subjection of his body in sickness to physicians can be said to be said to be derogatory thereunto. . . .

4. <u>They hold that the civil magistrate is to punish with all severity the ecclesiastical officers of churches if they shall intrude upon the rights & prerogatives of the civil authority & magistracy and shall pass those bounds & limits that Christ hath prescribed unto them in his word.</u>

4. They hold that the pope is that Antichrist, and therefore that Antichrist, because, being but an ecclesiastical officer, he doth in the height of the pride of his heart make claim unto and usurp the supremacy of the kings and civil rulers of the earth. And they hold that all defenders of the popish faith, all endeavourers of reconcilement with that Church, all plotters for toleration of the popish religion, all countenancers and maintainers of seminary priests and professed Catholics, and all deniers that the pope is that Antichrist are secret enemies to the king's supremacy.

5. They hold that all archbishops, bishops, deans, officials, &c. have their offices and functions only by will and pleasure of the king and civil states of this realm; and they hold that whosoever holdeth that the king may not without sin remove these officers out of the Church and dispose of their temporalities and maintenance according to his own

---

[8] {"the extremest censure"—1605}

[9] {This final clause is not in the 1605 ed.}

[10] {From "that the church shall then send,"—not in the 1605 ed.}

pleasure, or that these offices are *jure divino* and not only or merely *jure humano*—that all such deny a principal part of the king's supremacy.

6. They hold that not one of these opinions can be proved to be contrary to the word of God; and that if they might have leave, that they are able to answer all that hath been written against any one of them.

FINIS.

TEXT: EEBO (Wing / B4158)

William Bradshaw, *English puritanism containing the main opinions of the rigidest sort of those that are called Puritans in the realm of England / written by William Ames* (London, 1641).

Checked against William Bradshaw, *English puritanism containing the main opinions of the rigidest sort of those that are called Puritans in the realm of England* (London, 1605) (STC [2nd ed.] / 3516).

JOHN BUCKERIDGE
(ca. 1562–1631)

Buckeridge took his BA from St. John's, Oxford, in 1582, his MA in 1586; three years later he was appointed tutor to William Laud, to whom he imparted a "reverence for patristic learning, liturgical ceremonialism, anti-Calvinist views on grace, and hatred of puritanism" (*ODNB*). The two remained close throughout their lives.

Having received his BD in 1592 and ordination shortly thereafter (his DD would come in 1599), Buckeridge left Oxford in 1595 to serve as chaplain to the Earl of Essex, and then in 1596 to Archbishop Whitgift, in whose household he encountered Lancelot Andrewes, another of the Archbishop's chaplains. Twenty years later, Buckeridge would preach at Andrewes' funeral and, together with Laud, publish his collected sermons. From 1597 to 1631 Buckeridge was, like Andrewes, a celebrated court preacher and, from 1606 to 1611, a college head. By 1610 he had become part of Bishop Neile's high-church community at Durham House, and upon Neile's translation to Coventry and Lichfield in 1611, Buckeridge succeeded to the see of Rochester. In 1614 he published a Latin tract against papal claims to temporal authority, *De potestate papae*; this, together with a 1618 treatise defending kneeling at Communion and the 1606 sermon reprinted below, make up the sum of his publications. Buckeridge supported Montagu during the bitter fracas sparked by the *New gagg* and *Appello Caesarem*. His last three years were spent as bishop of Ely.

<hr/>

One typically, and rightly, thinks of Buckeridge as a proto-Laudian, and there are moments in the 1606 Hampton Court sermon that bespeak a high-church stance. Yet in the main the work defends the classic Elizabethan understanding of the royal supremacy as set forth in the thirty-seventh of the Thirty-nine Articles. There is little in the sermon to which Caroline Parliamentary firebrand William Prynne could not have said *amen*. The beginning seems to take a much higher line, and one's initial impression is that Buckeridge regards all disobedience to superiors as rebellion against God. However, Buckeridge is preaching less than a year after the Gunpowder Plot, and the opening turns out to assert only the uncontroversial absolute prohibition of violent resistance—not the hyper-absolutist thesis that subjects are bound in conscience to obey whatever their princes command. Thus, after a very interesting bridge passage on private conscience, Buckeridge starts outlining the "rules or causes" a law must have *in order* to be morally binding. It cannot "cross the will of God" or violate natural law; moreover, for a law to bind in conscience, it must have "a due end: public good and not private . . . the increase of good religion and safety of the commonwealth." This (quite traditional) insistence that the legitimacy of a law depends as much on its end as on its source, although not necessarily anti-absolutist,[1] is markedly anti-authoritarian—and, potentially, a huge concession.[2] Buckeridge's observation that such binding laws may concern adiaphora (i.e., things indifferent in themselves)—and indeed that human laws *principally* concern adiaphora, since that which is intrinsically evil needs no statute to be forbidden—restates the standard centerpiece argument for conformity.

The second half of the sermon turns to the civil magistrate's role vis-à-vis ecclesiastical polity, defending the royal supremacy against the papal claims for the Church's autonomy from and superiority to the state. The swipe at presbyterians or puritans (the terms were near-synonyms at the time) as seeking a quasi-papal clerical autocracy[3] was scarcely original with Buckeridge: it was a staple of conformist polemic and, in addition, the stated opinion of the new King, who referred to Jesuits as "puritan-papists" and mocked the "preposterous humility" of puritans "crying, we are all but vile worms, and yet will judge and give law to their king, but will be judged nor controlled by none" (Sommerville 44).[4]

For Buckeridge, civil power differs from ecclesiastical in that the former alone may use force and impose taxes—*not* in that the former deals with temporal matters, the latter with spiritual. Rather, the sermon, like so much conformist political thought, proclaims the ideal *union* of secular and religious authority, an ideal embodied in the figure of the godly prince:

> In most political philosophy between Dante and Hegel, the primary drama of Christendom was the liberation of the prince . . . from the priest. . . . Godly people began to seek their fulfillment not in the church-state, but in the state-church. . . . The considerable stress in modern scholarship on the emergence of the rights of private religious experience and of toleration in the Reformed tradition obscures the degree to which Reformed thought remained Erastian, and continued to be a theory about the civil state's embodiment of "true religion." (Goldie 200–201)

Buckeridge, however, does not see royal supremacy as post-Reformation Erastianism but as the ancient and "natural" form of government: originally, all kings were also priests.[5]

---

[1] When Charles resorted to extra-Parliamentary taxation to meet the costs of national defense, he defended such expedients precisely on the grounds that the king had a duty to protect the "safety of the commonwealth," with or without Parliamentary support.

[2] Those who urged resistance to the Crown in 1641 and in 1776 justified rebellion on the grounds that the laws being enforced violated natural law, the public good, and (at least in 1641) true religion.

[3] Later, opponents of Laudianism and divine right episcopacy turned the charge back on the bishops, charging that it was they who posed the real threat to royal sovereignty (see Prynne, *News* <infra>).

[4] Bradshaw's *English puritanism* <supra> is largely an attempt to meet this charge.

[5] His invocation of Aristotle in support of this view is a bit disingenuous, given that Aristotle describes

He does not, of course, hold that English monarchs may exercise sacerdotal functions, but follows Tudor-Stuart orthodoxy in confining the prince's authority to matters of discipline and external government.

A Calvinist conformist might have eschewed Buckeridge's appeals to the laws of reason and nature, but the only point at which the sermon takes on an unmistakeably high-church cast is the concluding declaration that "we should conform ourselves *ad regulam antiquorum*," to the teaching of the Greek and Latin Fathers, and not modern Protestant divines. Although Stuart Calvinists do cite the Fathers (and Laudians cite Calvin), a commitment to patristic authority—and, more generally, to continuity with the pre-Reformation Church—is as much a hallmark of one strand of early Stuart Protestantism as solidarity with the Reformed Churches across the Channel is of the other.[6] (There are various reasons for this, the most obvious being that the core tenets of the Reformed platform have very little patristic basis other than two late tracts by Augustine.)

SOURCES: Collinson, *Religion of Protestants*; Mark Goldie, "The civil religion of James Harrington," in *Languages of political theory in early modern Europe*, ed. Anthony Pagden (Cambridge UP, 1990), 197–222; Peter Lake, "Lancelot Andrewes, John Buckeridge, and avant-garde conformity at the court of James I," in *The mental world of the Jacobean court*, ed. Linda Levy Peck (Cambridge UP, 1991), 113–33; William Lamont, *Godly rule: politics and religion 1603–1660* (Macmillan, 1969); C. H. McIlwain, *The political works of James I* (Harvard UP, 1918); Johann Sommerville, ed., *King James VI and I: political writings* (Cambridge UP, 1994).

---

these priest-kings as characteristic of primitive societies and distinctly unsuited for more advanced cultures (*Politics* 3.14–15).

 [6] Richard Field *<infra>* would seem to be a rule-proving exception, since the revisions to *Of the Church* suggest that his patristic scholarship finally got the better of his Calvinist orthodoxy; the tension between them is evident in the selections concerning prayers for the dead.

JOHN BUCKERIDGE

A sermon preached at Hampton Court before the King's Majesty
1606

Quapropter necesse est subijci, non solùm propter iram, sed etiam propter conscientiam.
Wherefore you must needs be subject, not only for wrath, but also for conscience.

Rom. 13:5

These words are a conclusion of this discourse of the Apostle concerning the obedience of Christians towards their superiors, the process {argument} of which Scripture is grounded upon many reasons: 1. *ab authore*, from the first founder and author of all power. *Omnis potestas est à Deo*; all power is of God, to whom, in himself and in his ordinance, all creatures must be subject, wherein—although it sometime happen that *Potens*, the ruler, is not of God (as the Prophet saith, They have reigned and not by me [Hosea 8:4]); and likewise *modus assumendi*, the manner of getting kingdoms, is not of God always, because it is sometimes by sinful means—yet *potestas*, the power itself, is ever from God. The 2. *à bono ordinis*, from the good of order; and the Lord calls himself the God of order, not of confusion. And *ordo est uniuscuiusque bonum*, order is the good of every creature, with whom it is better not to be than to be out of order. And *potestates quae sunt à Deo, ordinatae sunt*, the powers that are of God, are ordained or ordered. The 3. is *à malo culpae*, to disobey God in his ordinance is a sin; he that resisteth, resisteth the ordinance of God. The 4. is *à malo poenae*, they that disobey . . . willingly pull upon themselves damnation {condemnation}: temporal, in which God is more quick to revenge the wrong and treasons committed against his lieutenants and viceroys than the greatest sins against himself; and also eternal, as is manifest in Korah, Dathan, and the rest, that went down quick {alive} to hell; and, *non est damnatio sine peccato*, there's no damnation but for sin. The 5. is *à bono societatis*, from the good of peace, protection, justice, religion and the like, which man receives by government. He is God's minister for their good. If he be a good prince, *causa est*, he is the cause of thy good, temporal and eternal; if an evil prince, *occasio est*, he is an occasion of thy eternal good, by thy temporal evil. . . . If he be a good king, he is thy nurse; receive thy nourishment with obedience. If he be an evil prince, he is thy tempter;

receive thy trial with patience. So there's no resistance: either thou must obey good princes willingly or endure evil tyrants patiently. The 6. is *à signo*, from a sign . . . you pay tribute & custom and subsidies of duty and justice; you give them not of courtesy; and they are . . . the king's stipend or pay, not his reward. . . . They are God's ministers, serving for that purpose: not to take their own ease and pleasure, but to govern others, waking when others sleep, and taking care that all men else may live without care.

All these arguments the Apostle, in the words of this text, concludes with an *ideo*, wherefore: Because all powers are of God, because all powers bring with them the good of order, because it is a sin to disobey, because judgment and damnation temporal and eternal is the punishment of this sin, because government is the means to enjoy all the benefits of life, because kings are hired by tribute and custom by governing to serve their servants and subjects: *ideo necessitate subditi estote*, therefore you must be obedient of necessity, not only for wrath but also for conscience sake. Wrath is *forum externum*, that external court that contains all outward arguments *à praemio & poena*, from reward and punishment of God and man. *Non sine causa gladium portat*, he carries not the sword in vain; he is to reward or punish. And this is the servants' and hirelings' argument, which keeps base affections within compass and prepares the way to charity itself, *ut seta filum introducit*, as the needle or bristle brings in the thread;[1] wherein although he that obeys for wrath hath not the virtue of obedience, and so *bene non agit, quia ex voluntate non agit*, he doeth not well because he doeth not with his will or from the heart; yet *quia bonum agit, timor servilis bonus est*, because the act of obedience is good and a political virtue, this servile fear for wrath is good, proceeding sometimes from the Holy Ghost, and of great consequence in Church and commonwealth.

Conscience is that *forum internum*, that inward court wherein God sits and either by the principles of reason or by the laws of the Holy Ghost governs and judges all our actions done or to be done, and either accuseth or excuseth. It is *iudicatorium rationale*, not an affectionate or willful, but a reasonable judge [Bern. *De domo interiori*, cap. 28]. . . . It is the book of the soul—for the examining and amending whereof all books were written—in which are registered all our thoughts, words, and deeds: what we have done, what we must receive, and whither we must go, to heaven or hell; and when we must leave all other books, this book will not leave us, but bring us to God's tribunal, where it shall be laid open and judge us. *Haec est privata lex hominis*, this is every man's private law, against which whosoever doeth anything, sins; and therefore in some cases *conscientia etiam erronea ligat*, an erroneous conscience doth bind.

The process of this conscience is by way of syllogism. The proposition is framed by the *synderesis*[2] of the soul, which cannot be deceived: "all good is to be done, all evil is to be avoided." The assumption[3] is the discourse of reason, and therefore many times is

---

[1] {On a coerced obedience modulating into charity, see Augustine, *Ep.* 173.10, "the sheep which is compelled is driven whither it would not wish to go, but after it has entered, it feeds of its own accord in the pastures to which it was brought" (http://www.newadvent.org/fathers/1102173.htm). *Pace* Foucault, the reconfiguration of punishment as discipline was not an eighteenth-century development.}

[2] {A medieval scholastic term denoting the principles of right and wrong innate in the moral consciousness of every person.}

[3] {the minor premise of a syllogism}

erroneous: "this is good, or this is evil." The conclusion is the collection of conscience: "therefore this is to be done, or that is to be avoided." Wherein because the discourse of reason being erroneous makes an erroneous conscience, therefore, that the laws of men be not exorbitant, it shall be needful to prescribe certain rules or causes that must concur in all laws, civil and ecclesiastical, that they may bind the conscience.[4]

First there must be *materia debita*, a due matter, that is just and lawful or else indifferent in itself: for in things simply good or evil, which are commanded or forbidden by God and nature, no man hath power to cross the will of God. And in these things, man's power is declaratory and executory, not sovereign of itself. In things indifferent there is a power to command for circumstances of time, place, order, and the like; and there is a necessity of obedience, and that for conscience sake, else man hath no power to command anything of himself; and yet it is the sin of disobedience *non solùm malum, sed & vetitum facere*, not only to do that which is evil, but that also which is forbidden.

The 2. is *forma debita*, a due form, an equal proportion of honors & burdens, according to the difference & degrees of several estates, conditions, and qualities; as also a due order of proceeding in law-making, without tumult or confusion, without malice, spleen, or revenge. The 3rd is *efficiens debitum*, a due efficient, or a sufficient, power to whom the care of law-making is delegated. For as the sentence of him that is no judge is no sentence, so the law of him that is not authorized to decree laws is no law. The 4th is *finis debitus*, a due end: public good and not private. For as a tyrant herein differeth from a king, that the tyrant intendeth his private good & the king proposeth the public; so evil laws aim at private and bad ends, and good laws propose the most public and best ends: the increase of good religion and safety of the commonwealth. And these causes concurring . . . the laws of man must be obeyed not only for wrath but for conscience, which is the greatest obligation on earth; for . . . no man contemns the power of man, unless he first have contemned the power of God.

. . . Let us consider two points: the persons, and the necessity of obedience. The persons are two: subjects that must obey and higher powers that must govern and command. The necessity will bring us to the circuit and causes in which we must obey.

The subjects are set down in the first verse with a note of universality: *omnis anima*, let every soul be subject, not only heathen but Christians and clerks also; they have no exemption. . . . The soul of the priest and ecclesiastical person, as well as the soul of the layman, must be subject to the higher powers. For why? S. Paul in this epistle wrote as well to the clerks & priests or bishops of Rome (if there were any then resident at Rome) as to the people. . . . Chrysostom saith upon this place . . . Be thou an apostle, an evangelist, a prophet, or whosoever thou art, thou owest this subjection; his reason is, *neque enim pietatem subvertit ista subjectio*, for this subjection doth not overthrow true godliness. . . . The Apostle S. Paul appealed to Caesar, to his lawful superior. The martyrs and confessors and godly bishops never pleaded this exemption against their persecutors, until the bishop of Rome, like the ivy that growing by the wall eateth out the wall, so he growing by the Roman Empire had eaten out the Empire, and then he did exempt himself and his clergy from the higher powers ordained of God.

---

[4] {For these rules, see Aquinas, *Summa theologiae* 1.2.96.4.}

For so they are higher, and indeed highest powers next under God: that is the next thing to be considered in the persons. Powers they are, and therefore governors, for . . . the power is the power of governing. And civil powers they are . . . and that appeareth by two circumstances: they bear the sword and they receive tribute, neither of which belongs to the priest's office. And they be higher powers . . . inferior peradventure to some in graces and virtues, but in dignity and authority superior to all . . . carrying that sword, *quo omnes corrigendi*, with which all men are to be corrected. . . . And kings and emperors, as they have their calling immediate from God, so they admit no superior on earth but God, to whom only they must make their accompt.[5] And so much Tertullian acknowledged: *colimus imperatorem vt hominem à Deo secundum, & solo Deo minorem*, we Christians honor our emperor as the second man after God, and minor to none but to God. *Super imperatorem non est nisi solus Deus qui fecit imperatorem*, saith Optatus; the emperor admits no superior but that God that made the emperor. And in that place he accuseth Donatus that he esteemed himself as God and not a man: *dum se Donatus super imperatorem extollit. Dum se episcopus Romanus*, or *dum presbyterium*, he might have said; either while Donatus, the bishop of Rome, or the presbytery—one pope or many popes—doth extol himself above the emperor. . . . Wherein let no man mistake: when we call emperors and kings supreme governors, we do not extol them above God, or his law or word . . . And if they command anything against God, their authority comes too short; in such things it is better to obey God than man. And yet in these things, though we may not obey, yet we may not resist but suffer; as Julian's soldiers would not sacrifice at his command, yet when he led them against an enemy, they obeyed most readily. . . . They made a difference between their temporal lord and their eternal Lord, and yet for their eternal Lord's sake, they were subject to their temporal lord . . . . So in causes ecclesiastical they are likewise supreme on earth, yet not above God nor Christ; they are *ministri Dei, non papae, non presbyterij*; they are God's immediate ministers of whom they hold in *capite*,[6] not man's, not the pope's, not the presbytery's, to draw their swords at their command. . . . According to the School[7] there is *duplex necessitas*, a double necessity. There is *necessitas naturae*, the necessity of nature: as the fire is necessarily hot by nature, and if it cease to be hot, it ceaseth to be fire. And there is *necessitas praecepti & finis*, the necessity of the precept and the end, for all precepts are necessarily to be kept in respect of the end. . . . So subjection to higher powers is necessary in Christians . . . by the necessity of the end: peace and tranquility and religion in this life, and life everlasting after death. . . . Now because government and obedience are relatives of equal extent, so far must we obey as[8] their commission is to govern. And the precept of their authority extends not only to civil causes in the second table, but also to religion in the first. And this precept, according to the difference of times, is threefold: natural, legal, and evangelical. In the law of nature it can be no question but causes civil and ecclesiastical belonged both to one man, since the

---

[5] {The principal target is the papal claim to jurisdiction over temporal rulers, including the authority to depose them, but see also Bradshaw <5.4> regarding the presbyterian/puritan tenet that made princes subject to ecclesiastical discipline.}

[6] {Law: land held *in capite* is held directly of the king—or in this case, the King of kings.}

[7] {i.e., scholastic philosophy}

[8] {i.e., we must obey only to the extent that . . .}

calling of king and priest was united in one man: the prince of the family was both chief magistrate and priest, & had the supremacy in both, which Aristotle well observed when he said . . . things pertaining to God's worship are committed to kings as a part of their charge. . . . And this was practiced by all nations: Assyrians, Medes, Persians, Grecians, Romans, Jews and gentiles, pagans and Christians, all which did establish religion by their public laws and maintained it by the magistrate's sword. Justinian said, *Nos maxima sollicitudine*, the true religion of God and the honest conversation of priests is our greatest care. *Rex servit Deo, aliter quâ homo aliter quâ rex* (saith S. Augustine), the king doth serve God as a man and as a king [August Epist. 50]: as a man he serveth God by living holily; as a king he serveth God by making (ecclesiastical) laws with convenient rigor and severity, that shall command that which is just and forbid that which is contrary. His examples are Ezekias and Josiah that destroyed idols and reformed the worship of God. And also among the heathen, first Nabuchodonosor, who, being instructed by the miracle of the fiery furnace, made a law for the worshipping of Daniel's God; next Darius, who, by occasion of a like miracle, made a decree that all men should fear and tremble before the God of Daniel; and last of the King of Nineveh, who at Jonah's preaching proclaimed a fast and commanded all the city, man and beast, to fast and to *cry mightily to God, and to turn from their wicked ways*. And these three did this not out of a prophetical spirit, as some pretend that David and Salomon and Josiah did, but as belonging to their function royal by the light of nature. Wherein if any shall say that servitude is the punishment of sin, and so this proceedeth out of nature corrupted, not pure, I answer . . . sin brought in tyranny and slavery . . . but order of superiority and subjection is the instinct of purest nature. For in heaven there is order among blessed angels, and some are higher and some lower, and they obey one another, if not *ex praecepto* yet *ex consilio*; if not by precept and command, yet by counsel and direction. And in the state of innocence there was superiority and subjection not only between man and all other creatures, but between man and woman; and had they lived in Paradise till they had been father and son, there should have been *patria potestas*; and being many families, there must necessarily have been *regia potestas*, else the best and most happy life must have been without the greatest happiness of life, and that is order.[9] And this superiority and subjection remained not only in the profane and wicked, but also in the line of the godly and the Church, until the law of nature, which was daily adulterated and corrupted by the affections and traditions of men, was written by Moses in tables of stone: which is the second precept of this subjection.

And this Law of Moses did renew the law of the kingdom, and ordained that the king should have a book of the Law written by the priests and delivered him at his coronation, in which he is commanded to read all the days of his life that he may learn to fear the Lord his God and to keep all the words of this Law. . . . And in this ordinance the king is made *custos legis divinae*, the guardian of God's Law, and the whole Law is committed to his charge: the first table that concerns God's worship and causes ecclesiastical, as well as the second table that concerns civil conversation and causes secular. By virtue of which commission, when the kingdom & priesthood were divided in Moses and Aaron, Moses the civil magistrate exercised a supremacy over Aaron the high priest in causes ecclesiastical,

---

[9] {This is Aquinas' position; see *Summa theologicae* 1.96.3-4.}

whom he reproved for making the golden calf; and in his time, the breach of the Sabbath by gathering of sticks was punished by the civil sword.

Joshua, a prince and no priest . . . succeeded Moses in this charge, and by this commission he circumcised the sons of Israel, erected an altar of stone, read the Law, did execution on him that concealed the things dedicated to idols, caused the people to put away strange gods, and renewed the covenant between God and the people. And these are causes ecclesiastical.

. . .

Salomon by this commission built the Temple and dedicated it; he deposed Abiathar the high priest, and placed Zadok in his room. I hope this is a matter and argument of great supremacy.

. . .

The last example I will trouble you with is Josiah. He purged Judah and Jerusalem from high places, groves, and images; he gathered all Israel, read the Law, renewed the covenant, and caused all Israel to stand to the covenant, and he compelled them to serve the Lord. He kept the famous Passover, and reduced the priests and Levites to their courses set by David and Salomon. These and many more are the acts of famous kings in the time of the Law, done by their royal authority, not at the appointment and command of the priests. . . . Yea, Solomon did depose Abiathar the High Priest; and they {kings} forced and compelled both priest and people to serve the Lord and to abolish idolatry and superstition: and therefore this is a power of jurisdiction over persons ecclesiastical in causes of religion.

. . .

When the Donatists pleaded that kings were to meddle with civil causes of the second table, and not with ecclesiastical causes of the first, Optatus held it to be a madness in Donatus. . . . Donatus, inflamed with his accustomed fury, brake forth into these words, *What hath the emperor to do with the Church?* But, saith Optatus . . . the commonwealth is not in the Church, but the Church is in the commonwealth, that is, in the Roman emperor. . . .

But it will be said, indeed the kingdom was above the priesthood in the Law, but in the Gospel the priesthood is above the kingdom; and therefore though kings in the Law meddled with ecclesiastical persons and causes *necessitate praecepti*, yet in the Gospel their authority is confined only to causes civil. The Church that was governed 300 years before any king was Christian hath no need of their supremacy; there is no precept of obedience in the Gospel which imposeth this necessity. Indeed if the Gospel were either a revocation or limitation of their commission granted in the Law, it were somewhat.

But when the rule holds . . . the Gospel doth not take away the precepts of nature and the moral law, but perfect them, the commission of kings granted in the Law standeth good to the world's end. And Christ came *ut tolleret peccata non iura mundi*, not to take away the laws and societies, but the sins of the world. And he renewed the precept . . . *Give to Caesar the things which are Caesar's* by the law of nature and Moses. And the apostles do often and almost every one of them in their writings double the precept. . . . One place shall serve for all: 1 Tim. 2, he ordaineth that Christians shall *pray for kings and men in authority.* The reason is, *that we may live a quiet and peaceable life under them;* and the compass is, *in all godliness and honesty.* Therefore godliness and honesty belongeth to the king's charge. . . . And Esay prophesied that in the Gospel *kings should be nursing fathers and queens should be nursing mothers* of the Church, and they must nourish by their milk. And internal milk of the word and sacraments they cannot give. . . . Neither can they give commission or power to any man to preach or minister the sacraments, which is an authority derived from God by imposition of hands. . . . Their authority is a permission or license to preach in their dominions, not a power of mission or ordination. And therefore, since they cannot give the internal milk of the word and sacraments, they must give the external milk of discipline and government. . . . And therefore as soon as Constantine became a Christian, he assumed this supremacy: he put down idolatry, he established Christian religion, composed differences of bishops, suppressed heresy and schisms, called councils and gave his suffrage in them; he heard causes of religion & judged them in his own person; he made laws, decrees, edicts, and orders for religion. . . .

To reduce these things to certain heads: the first work of this supremacy is *reformatio Ecclesiae*, the reformation of the Church by abolishing idolatry, superstition, and heresy; and placing of true religion; practiced by Constantine and all the godly emperors his successors: a matter so evident both in the Law & the Gospel that it needeth no proof. . . .

The second work of this supremacy is *convocatio synodorum*, the calling of councils and synods: as the four first general councils were called by four emperors. . . . But I note rather the weak allegation of Cardinal Bellarmine, that all these councils and many more were called by emperors, but *authoritate papae*, by the authority of the bishop of Rome (or the presbytery, if there were any such thing then in being), as if in those times emperors had been vassals to the bishops of Rome. Whereas Leo Magnus[10] made supplication to Theodosius . . . that the Emperor would call a council in Italy; but the Emperor called it at Ephesus, and the bishops of Italy could not come in time, and Eutyches' heresy was there countenanced. . . . Then Leo made a second supplication, and alleged the sighs and tears of all the clergy, for to obtain a council in Italy. He solicited the Princess Pulcheria to further his supplication to the Emperor; he wrote to the nobles, clergy, and people of Constantinople to make like supplication to the Emperor; yet he could not obtain it in the time of Theodosius. When Martian succeeded (by the favor of Pulcheria), a council was granted, not in Italy but at Chalcedon. Then Leo made a fresh suit, that the Emperor would command the bishops of the Council that the faith of the Nicene Council might stand in full force unaltered, which the Emperor did at his request. And the Emperor's oration to that purpose is extant. Now, if supplication, intercession of friends, sighs and tears of priests be the authority of the pope, then the pope used his authority and commanded the emperor to call councils. . . .

The third work is *promulgatio legum*, the promulgation of church laws and edicts, commanding or forbidding things expedient or hurtful for the Church's government, whereof the church stories are full. . . . Eusebius mentioneth two laws: one that abolished idolatry, images, sacrifices, and divinations; another concerning building & enlarging of churches at the emperor's charge. Theodosius made a law against the Arians; the manner of it is worth the repeating. Amphilochus Bishop of Iconium had been a long suitor in vain; at last he used this stratagem: he came into the Court and saluted the Emperor, but would not salute the Emperor's son Arcadius, newly created Caesar. Theodosius, thinking

[10] {Pope Leo the Great (d. 461)}

he had not seen his son, shewed him his son and bid him salute and kiss him. Amphilochus answered, it is enough to honor the father. Theodosius, interpreting it as a contempt of his son, grew very angry, whereupon Amphilochus discovering himself said, *Art thou offended, O Emperor, that I reverence not thy son, and thinkest thou that God is not offended with the Arians, the blasphemers of his Son?* The Emperor, overcome with these words, *legem scribit*, made a law presently forbidding the assemblies of the Arians. I should tire myself and your patience if I should enter particulars, only I must refer you to the titles of the Civil Law, *De summa Trinitate & fide Catholicâ, de sacrosanctis ecclesijs, de episcopis & clericis, de haereticis,*[11] *&c.* . . . . There is a collection of ecclesiastical laws made by Charles the Emperor {Charlemagne}. . . . In the preface, the Emperor Charles professeth . . . *Therefore we have directed our commissioners unto you* (here you see king's high commissioners and visitors are ancient)[12] *that shall join with you to redress those things which need reformation, according to our canonical constitutions, in our name and by virtue of our authority.*

And these laws were of that force in those days, that when Mauritius the Emperor that made a law that . . . no man entangled with public charge should be advanced to an ecclesiastical office, S. Gregory approved this part of the law, because many under this color did *mutare seculum,* not *relinquere.*[13] And further, the law forbade any soldier to enter a monastery till his warfare was expired. S. Gregory, though he wished not any to fly the wars or not pay their debts under the name of a cloister, yet because he saw it hindered many from the warfare and service of God, wrote an humble letter to Mauritius and another to Theodorus, the Emperor's physician, to entreat the revocation of this law invented by Julian, in a very submiss style: *Ego quidem iussioni vestrae subjectus,* I your servant and subject to your command, have sent this law to many parts of the world, and now I write my opinion to your Majesty. . . . In both I have done my duty; I have performed my obedience to the emperor, and I have not concealed what I thought fit for God's cause. . . .

The fourth work of this supremacy is receiving of appeals and giving decisions, restitutions, and deprivations, and other punishments of bishops for causes ecclesiastical. Wherein, although Constantine at the first, in modesty and a desire to suppress the calumniations of bishops and being not yet so fully instructed in Christian faith, took the papers and articles of the bishops and burnt them in the Nicene Council;[14] yet being better instructed, and seeing the necessity of his authority in these causes, he judged Cecilianus' cause himself. Donatus procured Cecilianus to be condemned by 70 African bishops for certain crimes objected against him. . . . And in a tumult they {Donatus' party} set up another bishop of Carthage against him. Then they appealed to Constantine and desired him to assign them judges . . . who gave sentence for Cecilianus. Upon a second appeal, Constantine made a second delegacy to Chrestus Bishop of Syracuse . . . who likewise gave sentence with Cecilianus. Upon the third appeal . . . the Emperor called

---

[11] {These are all titles from the *Codex,* the third book of the *Corpus iuris civilis.*}

[12] {High Commission, whose authority derived from the monarch in his/her role of supreme governor of the English Church, was the only ecclesiastical court that had coercive powers, and was therefore much disliked by religious dissidents.}

[13] {change with the times, not renounce the world}

[14] {i.e., Constantine refused to sit in judgment on the bishops but had the accusations against them destroyed; see Shuger, *Censorship,* 153–56.}

both parts before him and gave final sentence for Cecilianus, and made a severe law against the Donatists; by which law many Donatists were brought home to the Catholic Church. . . . I must here omit infinite other matters of facts and punishments, and many objections, and conclude with a question that Theodosius proposed. . . . What accompt (saith Theodosius) make you of the doctors and histories of the Church that are unpartial and lived before these questions were moved? If it be answered, as then it was, *Habemus tanquam magistros*, we esteem them as our fathers and masters, the cause is clear: they give witness on our side. If they reject them, it is a matter of great deliberation whether a man would be of such a Church whereof never any man was before themselves. In which case it seemeth more than reasonable that, in a reformation, we should conform ourselves *ad regulam antiquorum*, to the rule of the ancient Scriptures, Apostles, and Fathers— Chrysostom, Nazianzen, Basil, Ambrose, Hierome, Augustine, Gregory & the like— rather than after the new cut of those who have not above the life of a man on their backs, sixty or seventy years. And surely the rule of charity is, that since all the question is of the Church's regiment—not so much who should feed and rule the Church, for so must both prince and priest, but who should rule & govern most—we should every one lay down all contentious humors and join hand and heart to feed and govern God's inheritance, and strive rather in deeds than words who shall most carefully do that duty which God hath laid upon him[15] *necessitate praecepti*, by this triple necessity of his precept, that so we may be all partakers of the end: peace and tranquility and religion in this life, and life everlasting in the kingdom of heaven, which God grant, Amen.

Text: EEBO (STC [2nd ed.] / 4002.5)
A sermon preached at Hampton Court before the King's Majesty, on Tuesday the 23 of September, anno 1606. By John Buckeridge, D. of Divinity (London: Robert Barker, Printer to the Kings most Excellent Majesty, 1606).

---

[15] {i.e., on each of us}

RICHARD FIELD
(1561–1616)

Field matriculated at Magdalen Hall, Oxford, in 1577, receiving his BA in 1581, his MA in 1584, and his BD in 1592—and attaining, in the process, considerable renown for his prowess in disputation and school divinity. In 1594 he was made divinity lecturer at Lincoln's Inn (a post that Donne would hold from 1616 to 1622).[1] In 1595 he was presented to a rural Hampshire living, where he was resident at least part-time until his death. However, in 1598 Elizabeth made him one of her chaplains-in-ordinary, and in 1604 he became a prebendary at Windsor, in 1609 dean of Gloucester; it was during these years that he wrote his monumental *Of the Church*. He preached regularly at court under James, who both enjoyed his company and admired his intellect—as did Richard Hooker. At his death in 1616 he had largely completed a massive study of the religious controversies roiling his era, of which only a noble and intelligent preface survives as part of Nathaniel Field's *Some short memorials concerning the life of that reverend divine, Doctor Richard Field*, first published in 1716.[2]

The first four books of Field's *Of the Church* came out in 1606 (with a corrected edition of 1614, bearing the 1606 title page), the final book in 1610. Richard's son Nathaniel brought out a revised edition in 1628, in which two chapters from book 3 had been substantially expanded: 3.1 dealing with the theologies and practices of the Eastern and African churches, and upholding their claims (contra Roman exclusivity) to be part of the true visible Church; and 3.23 grappling with the charge that Protestantism makes God the author of sin. In 1641 Robert Baillie accused Laud of smuggling his own views into Field's text, but the allegation seems baseless: the additions to 3.1 do not change the thesis of the 1606 version, and the highly technical discussion of divine causality in 3.23 bears no resemblance to anything Laud wrote.

---

[1] Donne was at Lincoln's Inn from 1592 to 1594, but there's no evidence that he and Field crossed paths.
[2] This is our source for the friendship between Hooker and Field.

Field's treatise offers a magisterial defense of the English Church as a true Catholic Church, heir to the faith of patristic and medieval Christendom.[3] As the selections below make clear, *Of the Church* defends Calvin and English Calvinist theology against the attacks of Rome. It upholds the Reformed position on predestination, perseverance, the invocation of saints, prayers for the dead, justification by faith, and virtually every other controverted topic that it treats. Yet, from the neo-platonism of its opening chapter through the recuperation of medieval four-fold exegesis in book 4, Field's commitment to the historical continuity of the visible Church complicates the austere architectonics of Reformed theology and resists its whitewashing of the past. (See, for example, his medieval/Augustinian understanding of works not as evidence of election, but as the basis of reward.) Field is not, or is not simply, a traditionalist; his historical awareness is too strong. The chapter on prayers for the dead thus shows not only that the Roman Church's position departs from patristic soteriology, but that Reformed orthodoxy does so as well: if the Fathers did not believe in purgatory, neither did they limit themselves to heaven and hell, but placed the souls of the faithful in some indeterminate middle place until the final Judgment.[4] Field's historicism—his recognition of and allowance for historical difference—resembles Hooker's, as does his insistence on the bounded but real rights of individuals to interpret Scripture and to disregard bad laws. His chapters on the Church's power to ordain forms of worship, which condemn only those forms that pretend to quasi-sacramental efficacy, allow, at least in principle, for organs, chanting, incense, candles, and whatever serves to instill reverence and inspire devotion—scarcely the standard Reformed position. Field's striking argument for the existence, and co-existence, of different bases of interpretive authority—ranging from private judgment to ecclesiastical pronouncement to the clear and distinct *sensus litteralis* of Scripture—parallels Laud's equally impressive defense of the multiple bases of faith <infra>: both upholding, as it were, a checks-and-balances constitutionalist epistemology[5] against the Jesuit claim that sovereignty is by nature indivisible so that the Church's teaching authority must either be infallible or cease to exist,[6] but also, implicitly, against a Scripture-only fundamentalism.[7]

One could, I suppose, call Field's position "Calvinist highchurchmanship"; it was probably a far more important strand in Jacobean Christianity than modern scholarship (with the signal exception of Collinson's *Religion of Protestants*) would lead one to suspect.

[3] Its argument is thus a vastly expanded version of Jewel's thesis in his seminal 1563 *Apology of the Church of England* that the English Church, not the papal one, stood in the line of continuity from the New Testament through the Fathers of the first six centuries.

[4] When John Overall tried to defend this view in the Divinity Act at Cambridge in 1600, the Calvinist heads sought to have him expelled (see his *Praelectiones*).

[5] Re the constitutionalism of the Caroline divines, one might note Laud's pervasive debt to Gerson, Ockham, and conciliarist republicanism (see the notes to his *Conference with Fisher*, 1639 <infra>). The concept of checks and balances comes from Polybius, whom King James greatly admired. The "absolutist" position that sovereignty must by definition be undivided (*somebody* [or *some body*] has to decide the exception) comes from Bodin's 1576 *Les six livres de la République*. (Whatever Laud's secular politics, his ecclesiology explicitly upholds a conciliarist, republican position against the claims of papal monarchy.)

[6] See selections from Carier and Digby <infra>.

[7] E.g., Bradshaw <supra>.

Sources: *ODNB*; Paul Avis, *Anglicanism and the Christian Church*, 2nd ed. (Continuum, 2002); Robert Baillie, Ladensium autokatakrisis, *the Canterburians self-conviction* (London, 1641), 103; W. Speed Hill, ed. *Studies in Richard Hooker: essays preliminary to an edition of his works* (UP of Case Western Reserve, 1972); Anthony Milton, *Catholic and Reformed*; John Overall, "*Praelectiones seu disputations academicae . . . de Patrum & Christi anima . . . in Cantabrigiensis Academiae comitiis aliquando ab ipso habitae*," appendix to Archibald Campbell, Bp. of Aberdeen, *The doctrines of a middle state between death and the resurrection* (London, 1731), 203–26.

RICHARD FIELD

Of the Church, five books
1606 (rev. ed. 1628)

TO THE
MOST REVEREND FATHER IN GOD,
MY VERY GOOD LORD, THE
LORD ARCHBISHOP OF CANTERBURY
HIS GRACE,
PRIMATE AND METROPOLITAN OF ALL ENGLAND[1]

Most Reverend In Christ, the consideration of the unhappy divisions of the Christian world, and the infinite distractions of men's minds, not knowing, in so great variety of opinions, what to think or to whom to join themselves (every faction boasting of the pure and sincere profession of heavenly truth, challenging to itself alone the name of the Church, and fastening upon all that dissent or are otherwise minded the hateful note of schism and heresy), hath made me ever think that there is no part of heavenly knowledge more necessary than that which concerneth the Church. For, seeing the controversies of religion in our time are grown in number so many, and in nature so intricate, that few have time and leisure, fewer strength of understanding, to examine them, what remaineth for men desirous of satisfaction in things of such consequence but diligently to search out which, amongst all the societies of men in the world, is that *blessed company of holy ones*, that *household of faith*, that *spouse of Christ*, and *Church of the living God*, which is *the pillar and ground of truth*; that so they may embrace her communion, follow her directions, and rest in her judgment. Hence it cometh, that all wise and judicious men do more esteem books of doctrinal principles than those that are written of any other argument, and that there was never any treasure holden more rich and precious, by all them that know how to prize and value things aright, than books of prescription against the profane novelties of heretics: for that thereby men that are not willing or not able to examine the infinite differences that arise amongst men concerning the faith have general directions what to follow and what to avoid. We admit no man, saith Tertullian in his *Book of prescriptions*,

---

[1] {This dedication was part of the 1606 edition, so the archbishop addressed is Bancroft.}

to any disputation concerning sacred and divine things, or to the scanning and examining of particular questions of religion, unless he first shew us of whom he received the faith, by whose means he became a Christian, and whether he admit and hold the general principles wherein all Christians do and ever did agree. . . . But as in the days of the Fathers, the Donatists and other heretics . . . rejected all other from the unity of the Church, excluded them from hope of salvation, and appropriated all the glorious things that are spoken of it to themselves alone; so in our time, there are some found so much in love with the pomp and glory of the Church of Rome that they fear not to condemn all the inhabitants of the world and to pronounce them to be anathema from the Lord Jesus, if they dissent from that Church and the doctrine, profession, and observations of it; so casting into hell all the Christians of Grecia, Russia, Armenia, Syria, and Ethiopia, because they refuse to be subject to the tyranny of the pope and the court of Rome, besides the heavy sentence which they have passed against all the famous states and kingdoms of Europe which have freed themselves from the Egyptiacal bondage they were formerly holden in. These men abuse many with the glorious pretences of antiquity, unity, universality, succession, and the like; making the simple believe that all is ancient which they profess, that the consent of all ages is for them, and that the bishops succeeding one another in all the famous Churches of the world never taught nor believed any other thing than they now do; whereas it is easy to prove that all the things wherein they dissent from us are nothing else but novelties and uncertainties; that the greatest part of the Christian world hath been divided from them for certain hundreds of years; that none of the most famous and greatest Churches ever knew or admitted any of their heresies; and that the things they now publish as articles of faith to be believed by all that will be saved are so far from being catholic that they were not the doctrines of that Church wherein they and we sometime lived together in one communion, but the opinions only of some men in that Church, adulterating the doctrine of heavenly truth, bringing in and defending superstitious abuses disliked by others, and serving as vile instruments to advance the tyranny of the bishop of Rome. Wherefore, for the discovery of the vanity of their insolent boastings, for the confirming of the weak, the satisfying of them that are doubtful, and that all men may know that we have not departed from the ancient faith or forsaken the fellowship of the catholic Church, but that we have forsaken a part to hold communion with the whole (led so to do by the most prevailing reasons that ever persuaded men, and the greatest authority on earth), I resolved to communicate to others what I had long since in private for mine own satisfaction observed touching the nature of the Church, the notes[2] whereby it may be known, and the privileges that pertain to it. . . . Thus craving pardon for this my boldness, and humbly beseeching Almighty God long to continue your Grace's happy and prosperous estate, and to make you a glorious instrument of much good to his Church, I rest,

Your Grace's in all duty,

RICHARD FIELD.

---

[2] {A "note" in this sense is any of certain characteristics, as unity, sanctity, catholicity, and apostolicity, by which the true Church may be known (*OED*).}

BOOK I

Chapter 1

Of the Church consisting of men and angels in the day of their creation

. . .

The most perfect and excellent creatures in the world below the condition of man have not a general apprehension of all things, but only of some outward sensible things, in the getting or declining whereof their good doth stand and consist;[3] and, therefore, have their desires likewise contained within the same straits, and are like prisoners, subject to the will of him that restraineth them, which cannot go at large whither they will. But man is by condition of his creation free, having no bounds of any one kind of good things within the compass whereof he is enclosed; but as his understanding is so large that it reacheth to all things that are, though in kind never so different and number never so numberless, so his desires have no limitation to things of any one kind alone, but are freely carried to the desiring of whatsoever in any kind or degree of goodness appears to be good. And because in this multiplicity of good things, nothing is good but as partaking of the chief good; nothing better than other but as coming nearer unto it; therefore, for the direction of all his desires, that he may rightly value and prize each thing, either preferring or less esteeming it according to the worth thereof, it is necessary that he know and desire as the chief good that which indeed is the chief and principal good, the measure of all the rest, before he can rightly discern the different degrees of goodness found in things, and so rightly prefer one before another.

And this, doubtless, is the reason why no other creatures but only men and angels are capable of felicity and bliss: because the greatest good they know or desire is but some particular thing, and that no better than themselves; but men and angels, in whom so great perfection of knowledge is found that they apprehend the whole variety and multiplicity of things and all the different degrees of goodness in them, never have their desires satisfied till they possess and enjoy that sovereign, infinite, and everlasting good, by participation whereof all things else in their several kinds and degrees are judged good. This glorious society of men and angels, whom the Most High God, passing by all his other creatures, made capable of felicity and bliss, calling them to the view, sight, and enjoying of himself, is rightly named *Ecclesia, coetus evocatus*, the Church of the living God, the joyful company of them among whom his greatness is known and his name called upon, the multitude which by the sweet motions of his divine grace he hath called out to the participation of eternal happiness.

Chapter 2

Of the calling of grace, whereby God called out both men and angels from the rest of his creatures to be unto him a holy Church; and of their apostasy

All other things seek no higher perfection nor greater good than is found within the compass of their own nature, by nature's guiding, without the help of any other thing, attaining thereunto; but men and angels, which seek an infinite and divine good, even

---

[3] Contarini, *De libero arbitrio* 599.

the everlasting and endless happiness which consisteth in the vision of God, *at whose right hand are pleasures for evermore*, cannot attain their wished good, which is so high and excellent and far removed from them, unless, by supernatural force, which we call *grace*, they be lifted unto it.[4] For though, by nature, they know God so far forth as by his effects and glorious works he may be known; yet, as he is in himself, they know him not further than in the light of grace and glory he is pleased to manifest himself unto them, thereby admitting them to the joyful sight and blessed view of his glorious majesty, *which dwelleth in light that no creature*, by itself, *can approach unto*. This is true and perfect happiness, to see the face of God, which to behold is the height of all that good which any creature can desire. To this the angels may be lifted up; to this they cannot ascend by themselves. To this man cannot go; to this he may be drawn, according to that our Savior delivereth of himself, *No man cometh unto me, unless my Father draw him.* Those things which are inferior unto man can neither attain by themselves, nor be drawn nor lifted up to the partaking of this so happy and joyful an estate. The vapor of water goeth up on high, but not unless it be drawn with the beams and sweet influence of the sun; but more gross and earthly things can neither ascend of themselves nor admit into them these heavenly beams to raise and draw them up. Among bodily substances, some are carried only with a straight and direct motion, either to the highest or lowest places of the world, which motion expresseth the condition of those things to the which God hath denied the knowledge and immediate enjoying of himself, which are established in the perfection of their own nature and therein rest without seeking any further thing; some with circular motion, by which they return to the same point whence they began to move. The motion of these expresseth the nature and condition of men and angels, who only are capable of true happiness, whose desires are never satisfied till they come back again to the same beginning whence they came forth, till they come to see God, face to face, and to dwell in his presence. None but immortal and incorruptible bodies are rolled with circular motions; none but angels that are heavenly spirits, and men whose souls are immortal, return back to the sight, presence, and happy enjoying of God their Creator. Each thing is carried in direct motion by nature's force; in circular, by heavenly movers. Every thing attaineth nature's perfection by nature's force and guidance; but that other, which is divine and supernatural, consisting in the vision and fruition of God, they that attain unto it must impute it to the sweet motions and happy directions of divine grace.[5]

This grace God vouchsafed both men and angels in the day of their creation, thereby calling them to the participation of eternal happiness, and giving them power that they might attain to the perfection of all happy and desired good if they would, and everlastingly continue in the joyful possession of the same. But such was the infelicity of these most excellent creatures, that, knowing all the different degrees of goodness found in things and having power to make choice of what they would, joined with that mutability of nature which they were subject unto in that they were made of nothing, they fell from the love of that which is the chief and greatest good to those of meaner quality, and thereby deprived themselves of that sweet and happy contentment they should have found in God.[6] And denying to be subject to their great sovereign and to perform that duty they

[4] Alex. de Hales, pars iii.
[5] Joan. Picus Mirandula, *Heptaplus* 1. vii.

owed unto him, were justly dispossessed of all that good which from him they received and under him should have enjoyed; yea, all other things which were made to do them service lost their native beauty and original perfection and became feeble, weak, unpleasant, and intractable, that in them they might find as little contentment as in themselves. For seeing nothing can prevail or resist against the laws of the omnipotent Creator, no creature is suffered to deny the yielding of that which from it is due to God. For either it shall be forced to yield it by right using of that which from him it received or by losing that which it would not use well; and so, consequently, if it yield not that by duty it should, by doing and working righteousness, it shall by feeling smart and misery. This then was the fall of men and angels from their first estate, in that by turning from the greater to the lesser good, they deprived themselves of that blessedness, which, though they had not of themselves, yet they were capable of, and might have attained unto by adhering to the chief and immutable good; and so by their fault fell into those grievous evils they are now subject unto, yet in very different sort and manner.

Chapter 3

Of the Church, consisting of those angels that continued in their first estate by force of grace upholding them, and men redeemed

. . .

So that as God in the day of the creation called forth all, both men and angels, from among the rest of his creatures to whom he denied the knowledge and enjoying of himself, that these only might know, fear, and worship him in his glorious temple of the world, and be unto him a selected multitude and holy Church; so when there was found amongst these a dangerous apostasy and departure from him, he held of the angels so many as he was pleased, and suffered them not to decline or go aside with the rest; and raised up and severed out of the mass of perdition whom he would among the sons of men. The angels now confirmed in grace and those men whom in the multitude of his mercies he delivereth out of the state of condemnation and reconcileth to himself do make that happy society of blessed ones, whom God hath loved with an everlasting love. This society is more properly named the Church of God than the former (consisting of men and angels in the state of that integrity wherein they were created), in that they which pertain to this happy company are called to the participation of eternal happiness with the calling of a more mighty, potent, and prevailing grace than the other. For whereas they were partakers only of that grace which gave them power to attain unto and continue in the perfection of all happy good if they would, and then *in tanta felicitate et non peccandi facilitate*, in so great felicity and facility of not offending, left to themselves to do what they would and to make their choice at their own peril; these are partakers of that grace which winneth infallibly, holdeth inseparably, and leadeth indeclinably in the ways of eternal blessedness.

---

[6] August. *De civitate Dei* lib. xii.

Chapter 4

Of the Church of the redeemed

All these, as well angels that stood by force of grace upholding them as men restored by renewing mercy, have a most happy fellowship amongst themselves and therefore make one Church of God. Yet, for that the sons of men have a more full communion and perfect fellowship, being all delivered out of the same miseries by the same benefit of gracious mercy; therefore, they make that more special society, which may rightly be named the Church of the redeemed of God. This Church began in him in whom sin began, even in Adam, the father of all the living, repenting after his fall and returning to God. For we must not think that God was without a Church among men at any time; but so soon as Adam had offended and was called to give an account of that he had done (hearing that voice of his displeased Lord and Creator, *Adam, where art thou?* that so he might know in what estate he was by reason of his offence), the promise was made unto him *that the seed of the woman should break the serpent's head.* Yet for that Abel was the first that the Scripture reporteth to have worshipped God with sacrifice and to have been divided from the wicked in whom God had no pleasure, even *cursed Cain* that afterwards shed his innocent blood, therefore we usually say the Church or chosen company of the redeemed of the Lord began in Abel. . . .

. . .

Chapter 5

Of the Christian Church

The society of this new and blessed people began in the apostles, whom Christ the anointed Savior of the world did choose to be his followers, and to be witnesses of all the things he did and suffered among sinful men. . . .

And though the Church of the Old and New Testament be in essence the same, yet for that the state of the Church of the New Testament is in many respects far more glorious and excellent, the Fathers and ecclesiastical writers for the most part appropriate the name of the Church to the multitude of believers since the coming of Christ, and call the faithful people that were before by the name of the Synagogue. If this difference of names be retained only for distinction sake (that men may know when we speak of that moiety of the people of God that was before, and when of that other that is and hath been since the coming of Christ), we dislike it not.

The Greek words which we turn *Church* and *Synagogue*, the one originally and properly signifieth a multitude called out or called together, which is proper to men; the other a multitude congregated and gathered together, which is common to men with brute beasts. If any man, having an eye to the different original significations of these words, do thereupon infer that the people of God before the coming of Christ did seek nothing but earthly, outward, and transitory things, and so were gathered together like brute beasts and like oxen fatted to the day of slaughter, we detest and accurse so wicked and damnable a construction. And herein surely the Catechism of Trent cannot well be excused, which, abusing the authority of St Augustine upon the Psalm lxxvii and lxxxi, affirmeth that *the name of Synagogue is therefore applied to the people that were under the Law, because, like brute beasts, which most properly are said to be congregated or gathered together, they respected, intended, and sought nothing but only outward, sensible, earthly, and transitory things.* Which unadvised speech, how much it advantageth the anabaptists, who think the faithful people before Christ did only taste of the sweetness of God's temporal blessings without any hope of eternal happiness, any man of mean understanding may easily discern.[7] It is, therefore, not to be doubted but that the faithful, before the manifestation of Christ in the flesh, were so instructed of the Lord that they assured themselves there was a better life for them elsewhere; and that, neglecting this earthly, momentary, and wretched life, they principally sought the other, which is divine and heavenly. . . .

. . .

Chapter 6

Of the definition of the Church

Concerning the Church, five things are to be observed. First, what is the definition of it, and who pertain unto it. Secondly, the notes whereby it may be known. Thirdly, which is the true Church demonstrated by these notes. Fourthly, the privileges that do pertain unto it. Fifthly, the divers degrees, orders, and callings of those men to whom the government of this Church is committed.

Touching the first, the Church is the multitude and number of those whom Almighty God severeth from the rest of the world by the work of his grace and calleth to the participation of eternal happiness by the knowledge of such supernatural verities as concerning their everlasting good he hath revealed in Christ his Son and such other precious and happy means as he hath appointed to further and set forward the work of their salvation. So that it is the work of grace and the heavenly call that give being to the Church, and make it a different society from all other companies of men in the world that have no other light of knowledge nor motion of desire but that which is natural; whence, for distinction from them, it is named *ecclesia*, a multitude called out.

Chapter 7

Of the divers sorts of them that pertain to the Church

They that are partakers of the heavenly calling and sanctified by the profession of divine truth and the use of the means of salvation are of very divers sorts. For there are some that profess the truth delivered by Christ the Son of God, but not *wholly* and *entirely*, as heretics; some that profess the whole saving truth, but not in *unity*, as schismatics; some that profess the whole saving truth in unity, but not in *sincerity* and singleness of a good and sanctified mind, as hypocrites and wicked men not outwardly divided from the people of God; and some that profess the whole saving truth in unity, and sincerity of a good and sanctified heart.

All these are partakers of the heavenly calling and sanctified by the profession of the truth, and consequently are all in some degree and sort of that society of men whom God

---

[7] Calvin. *Institut.* lib. ii. cap. 10.1.

calleth out unto himself and separateth from infidels, which is rightly named the Church. These being the different ranks of men made partakers of the heavenly calling and sanctified by the profession of saving truth, there are divers names by which they are expressed and distinguished one from another.

For as the name of the Church doth distinguish men that have received the revelation of supernatural truth from infidels; and the name of the Christian Church, Christians from Jews; so the name of the orthodox Church is applied to distinguish right believing Christians from heretics; the name of the catholic Church, men holding the faith in unity, from schismatics; the name of the invisible Church, *the Church of the first-born whose names are written in heaven*, the mystical body of Christ, and the like, to distinguish the elect from all the rest. So that many were of the Church which were not of the Christian Church, as the Jews before the coming of Christ; many of the Christian Church that are not of the orthodox; many of the orthodox that are not of the catholic; and many of the catholic that are not of the invisible and Church of the first-born whose names are written in heaven.

Thus then, the Church having her being and name from the calling of grace, all they must needs be of the Church whom the grace of God in any sort calleth out from the profane and wicked of the world to the participation of eternal happiness by the excellent knowledge of divine, supernatural, and revealed verity, and use of the good, happy, and precious means of salvation: but they only perfectly and fully in respect of outward being, which profess the whole truth in unity; and they only principally, fully, and absolutely are of the Church, whom divine grace leadeth infallibly and indeclinably by these means to the certain and undoubted possession of wished blessedness; because in them only grace manifesteth her greatest and most prevailing force, without which efficacy of grace, winning infallibly, holding inseparably, and leading indeclinably, no man ever attained to salvation; and of which whoso is partaker shall undoubtedly be saved.

In the benefits of this grace none but the elect and chosen of God, whom he hath loved with an everlasting love, have any part or fellowship, though others concur with them in the use of the same means of salvation and be partakers with them of sundry inward motions inclining them to good. When we say, therefore, none but the elect of God are of the Church, we mean not that others are not at all nor in any sort of the Church, but that they are not *principally, fully, and absolutely*; and that they are not of that especial number of them who partake and communicate in the most perfect work, force, and effect of saving grace.

. . .

Chapter 10

Of the visible and invisible Church

Hence it cometh that we say there is a visible and invisible Church, not meaning to make two distinct Churches, as our adversaries falsely and maliciously charge us, though the form of words may serve to insinuate some such thing, but to distinguish the divers considerations of the same Church; which though it be visible in respect of the profession of supernatural verities revealed in Christ, use of holy sacraments, order of ministry, and due obedience yielded thereunto, and they discernible that do communicate therein; yet in respect of those most precious effects and happy benefits of saving grace, wherein only the elect do communicate, it is invisible; and they that in so happy, gracious, and desirable things have communion among themselves are not discernible from others to whom this fellowship is denied, but are known only unto God. That Nathaniel was an Israelite all men knew; that he was *a true Israelite, in whom was no guile*, Christ only knew.

The persons, then, of them of whom the Church consisteth are visible; their profession known even to the profane and wicked of the world, and in this sort the Church cannot be invisible, neither did any of our men teach that it is or may be. For seeing the Church is the multitude of them that shall be saved, and no man can be saved unless he make confession unto salvation (for faith hid in the heart and concealed doth not suffice), it cannot be but they that are of the true Church must by the profession of the truth make themselves known in such sort that by their profession and practice they may be discerned from other men.

Notwithstanding, because the truth and excellence of the faith and profession of Christians is not discerned by the light of nature, but by faith alone; the excellency of this society of Christians above other profane companies in the world, and their happiness that are of it, is invisible, hidden, and unknown to natural men, and is known only to them that are spiritual. And who they are that have fellowship among themselves, not only in the profession of heavenly verities and outward means of salvation, but also in the benefits of effectual and saving grace, is known neither to the natural nor spiritual man, but to God alone.

‡

BOOK III

Chapter 1

*Of the division of the Christian world into the Western or Latin Church
and the Oriental or East Church*

. . .

Out of all that which hath been said, two things are observable.[8] First, that by the merciful goodness of God, all these different sorts of Christians—though distracted and dissevered by reason of diversity of ceremonies and outward observations, different manner of delivering certain points of faith, mistaking one another, or variety in opinion touching things not fundamental—do yet agree in one substance of faith and are so far forth orthodox that they retain a saving profession of all divine verities absolutely necessary to salvation and are all members of the true catholic Church of Christ. The second, that in all the principal controversies touching matters of religion between the Papists and those of the Reformed Churches, they give testimony of the truth of that we profess. For, first, they all deny and impugn that supreme universality of ecclesiastical jurisdiction which the bishop of Rome claimeth. Secondly, they think him subject to error as all other bishops are. Thirdly, they deny that he hath any power to dispose the principalities and

---

[8] {This concluding paragraph, and most of chapter's long discussion of the theologies and practices of the Orthodox, Ethiopian, Assyrian, Coptic, and Armenian Churches, first appears in the 1628 edition.}

kingdoms of the world or depose kings. Fourthly, they acknowledge all our righteousness to be imperfect, and that it is not safe to trust thereunto, but to the mere mercy and goodness of God. Fifthly, they admit not the merit of congruence, condignity, nor works of supererogation. Sixthly, they teach not the doctrine of satisfactions,[9] as the Romanists do. 7. They believe not purgatory, neither pray to deliver men out of temporal punishments after this life. 8. They reject the doctrine of the Romanists touching indulgences and pardons. 9. They believe not there are seven sacraments. 10. They omit many ceremonies in baptism which the Roman Church useth, as spittle, &c. 11. They have no private masses. 12. They minister the Communion in both kinds to all communicants. 13. They believe not transubstantiation, nor the new real sacrificing of Christ. 14. They have the divine service in the vulgar tongue. 15. Their priests are married, and though they permit them not to marry a second wife without special dispensation, yet if any do, they do not void nor dissolve the marriage. 16. They make no image of God. 17. They have no massy {sculpted} images but pictures only. 18. They think that properly God only is to be invocated, and howsoever they have a kind of invocation of saints, yet they think that God only heareth them and not the saints.

‡

Chapter 17

Of prayer for the dead, and merit

The next calumniation[10] is concerning prayer for the dead. Let the reader observe what it is that Bellarmine is to prove, and he shall find that he doth nothing but trifle. For he is to prove that Calvin confesseth that more than a thousand and three hundred years since, the popish doctrine and custom of prayer for the dead did prevail and was generally received in the whole Church of God throughout the world. This if he will prove, he must reason thus: the custom of praying to deliver the souls of men out of the pains of purgatory is the custom and practice which the Roman Church defendeth and Calvin impugned; but this custom Calvin confesseth to have been in use more than a thousand and three hundred years since; therefore he acknowledgeth the doctrine and practice of the Roman Church to be most ancient and to have been received a thousand and three hundred years ago. The minor proposition of this reason is false, and Calvin, in the place cited by Bellarmine, protesteth against it, most constantly affirming that the Fathers knew nothing of purgatory, and therefore much less of prayer to deliver men from thence. But Bellarmine will reply that the custom of praying for the dead was most ancient. We answer, the custom of remembering the departed, naming their names at the holy table in the time of the holy mysteries, and offering the Eucharist (that is, the sacrifice of praise) for them was a most ancient and godly custom, neither is it any way disliked by us. And surely it appears this was the cause that Aerius was condemned of heretical rashness, in that he durst condemn this laudable and

---

[9] {I.e., the doctrine that a sin, even after repentance and (where appropriate) restitution, leaves one indebted to divine justice, which must be satisfied (normally by performing the penance imposed in confession).}

[10] {In these chapters, Field is attempting to refute Bellarmine's allegations (calumniations) that Protestants have abandoned the faith and worship of Christian antiquity—the ancient faith and worship of the Church being preserved, according to Bellarmine, only in the Roman communion.}

ancient custom of the commemoration for the dead. In this sort they did most religiously observe and keep, at the Lord's table, the commemoration of all patriarchs, prophets, apostles, evangelists, martyrs, and confessors;[11] yea, of Mary the mother of our Lord: to whom it cannot be conceived that by prayer they did wish deliverance out of purgatory, since no man ever thought them to be there; but if they wished anything, it was the deliverance from the power of death which as yet tyrannizeth over one part of them; the speedy destroying of the last enemy, which is death; the hastening of their resurrection and joyful public acquittal of them in that great day wherein they shall stand to be judged before the Judge of the quick and dead. This was the practice of the whole Church and this the meaning of their commemorations and prayers, which was good and no way to be disliked.

Notwithstanding, it is most certain that many particular men extended the meaning of these prayers further, and, out of their own private errors and fancies, used such prayers for the dead as the Romanists themselves, I think, dare not justify. And so it is true that Calvin saith that *many* of the Fathers were led into error in this matter of prayer for the dead, and not that *all*—as if the whole Church had fallen from the truth, as Bellarmine falsely imputeth unto Calvin, who saith no such thing.

First, therefore, it was an opinion of many of the Fathers that there is no judgment to pass upon men till the last day; that all men are holden either in some place under the earth or else in some other place appointed for that purpose, so that they come not into heaven nor receive the reward of their labors till the general judgment. Out of this conceit grew that prayer in James' liturgy, that God would remember all the faithful that are fallen asleep in the sleep of death since Abel the just till this present day; that he would place them in the land of the living, &c. And the like are found in the mass-book. Of this opinion was Justin Martyr, Tertullian, Clemens Romanus, Lactantius, Victorinus Martyr, Ambrose, Johannes Romanus Pontifex, and sundry others.[12]

The second opinion was that men may be delivered from the punishments of sin after this life, if they die in the profession of the true faith, how wickedly so ever they lived; or at least, if the punishment of such be eternal and cannot be ended, yet it may be deferred or mitigated. How many of the Fathers were in this error and made prayers for the dead upon this false persuasion that all Christians, how wickedly so ever they lived, may find mercy at God's hands in the world to come at the entreaty of the living, they that have read anything can soon report.

Thirdly, whereas there are three estates of the souls of men: the first, in the body; the second, when they are severed from the body and stand before God immediately and instantly upon the dissolution; and the third, after they have received their particular judgment; the godly do not only recommend them unto God while they are yet in their bodies; but when, departing thence, they go to stand before the judgment-seat of God, they accompany them with their prayers and best good wishes, even to the presence of the Lord. Hence were all those prayers that were used on the days of the obits[13] of the

---

[11] Liturgia Chrysostomi.

[12] Sixtus Senensis {Sixtus of Siena (1520–69), Dominican theologian}, *Bibliothec. Sanct.*, lib. vi. annot. 345; {Jean} Gers{on}, *Serm. in Festo Paschae*.

[13] {Either a ceremony or office performed at the burial of a deceased person, or a service, usually a Mass, held to pray for the soul of, or otherwise commemorate, a deceased person on the anniversary of his or her death or at some other appointed time (*OED*).}

saints conceived respectively to[14] their passage out of this world and the dangers they do, by the goodness of God, escape in that fearful hour of their dissolution—which prayers were again repeated in the anniversary remembrances of their obits. Of this sort was that prayer in the mass-book. *Libera, Domine, animas omnium fidelium defunctorum de poenas inferni, et de profundo lacu: libera eas de ore leonis, ne absorbeat eas Tartarus, ne cadant in obscurum,* etc. *Deliver, O Lord, the souls of all faithful ones departed, from the pains of hell and the deep lake; deliver them from the mouth of the lion, that hell swallow them not up, and that they fall not into the dungeon of utter darkness.* How hard this was to use these prayers in a set course . . . and so to pray for them long after their death as if they were but even then in the passage and so in danger of falling into the hands of their ghostly enemies and not yet secure and assured of their eternal future state (which, yet, Bellarmine confesseth, is the best construction that can be made of them), I leave to the consideration of the wise. These are the several kinds of praying for the dead; all which, I hope, Bellarmine dareth not justify. But for the Romish manner of praying for the dead, it hath no certain testimony of antiquity—no man ever thinking of purgatory till Augustine, to avoid a worse error, did doubtingly run into it,[15] after whom many in the Latin Church embraced the same opinion; but the Greek Church never received it to this day. Thus, then, we see how unjustly Calvin is traduced by Bellarmine in this matter of prayer for the dead; and how weakly he proves that it is confessed that their opinion and the doctrine of antiquity is the same. . . .

‡

Chapter 20

Of the invocation and adoration of saints, touching which the Century *writers[16] are wrongfully charged to dissent from the Fathers*

Thus, then, I hope it appeareth that Calvin doth not confess that the doctrine of the Romanists hath any testimony or approbation of antiquity. Bellarmine, therefore, passeth from him to the writers of the *Centuries,* in whom he hopeth to find something for his purpose, but they stead him as little as Calvin did. Let us therefore take a view of that he saith. Touching free-will, justification, merits, and the like, there is nothing in them but that which hath been sufficiently, I hope, cleared in Calvin; the things they say being the same. Only two things I find imputed to them by Bellarmine, and not to Calvin. For first they are supposed to acknowledge the popish invocation of saints to have been in the time of the Fathers, and allowed by them. Secondly, they are charged to blame the Fathers for magnifying too much the excellency of martyrdom, the praises whereof, Bellarmine saith, they dislike because they will not admit that martyrdom is a kind of baptism serving for the expiation and washing away of sin.

---

[14] {with respect to}

[15] [in Ps. xxxvi. §3 {The bracketed notes are those added in the 1847 ed.}]

[16] {The 16th-century Lutheran authors of the *Magedeburg Centuries* (pub. 1559–74), the first Protestant universal history, whose disparagement of patristic authority proved very awkward for subsequent Protestant apologists.}

Touching the invocation of saints, it is evident it was not known in the first ages of the Church nor approved by the primitive Fathers. But because it hath mightily prevailed in these latter times, and the superstition and idolatry therein committed hath been such as cannot be excused, therefore, for the better answering of Bellarmine's cavils and the satisfying of ourselves and others, let us consider from what grounds and by what degrees it entered into the Church.

First, there was in the Church from the beginning a true and certain resolution that the saints departed do, in general, tender, respect, and wish well unto their brethren and fellow-servants whom they have left behind them in the warfare of Christ in this world. Secondly, men grew afterwards to think that men departing out of this world carry with them the remembrance of the state of things wherein, departing hence, they leave them; and that out of their love, which never falleth away, they do most carefully recommend unto God the particular necessity of their brethren made known unto them while they lived there. Thirdly, from hence it came that men entreated their friends yet living that if they prevented them and came before them into Christ their master's joyful and happy presence, being freed from the dangers, miseries, and evils of this present life, they would not forget to recommend them unto God that are in them still. Fourthly, whereas by an ancient custom they did remember the names of the departed at the Lord's table, giving thanks unto God that had made them so glorious in their life and death through his goodness, and praying him by their examples to frame them to the like; and, besides, kept the anniversary remembrances of the days of their death, as if they had been their birth-days, with all tokens of joy;[17] in the orations they made to set forth the goodness of God towards them and to propose their example for imitation, they did sometimes, by way of apostrophe, speak unto them as if they had been present and had sense and apprehension of that they spake (whereof they were yet doubtful, as appeareth by Gregory Nazianzen, Jerome, and others); and, not contented thus to commune with them, they entreated them, if they had any sense or knowledge of things in this world, to be remembrancers for them and the Church here below. This was a kind of doubtful compellation[18] and solic-iting of them, if their state were such as that they could take notice of these things, that they would not forget to procure the good of their brethren; but was no invocation, which is a retiring[19] of ourselves in all our needs, necessities, and distresses, with assured hope of help, to him that we hope can stead us in what distress so ever we be.

This, then, though the Fathers did sometimes—when they had particular occasion to remember the saints and to speak of them, by way of apostrophe turn themselves unto them and use words of doubtful compellation, praying them, if they have any sense of these inferior things, to be remembrancers to God for them—yet shall our adversaries never prove that they did prostrate their bodies, bow their knees, or make prayers to them in a set course of devotion; but this both adoration and invocation of saints and angels was directly condemned by them. We honor the saints, saith Jerome, but do not worship or adore any creature, neither angels, archangels, nor any name that is named in this

---

[17] Cypr. *Epist.* lvii and xxxiv.

[18] {direct address to another person or persons}

[19] {retreating to a place for seclusion, security, or privacy (*OED*)}

world or that which is to come. The Council of Laodicea, reported by Theodoret, directly condemneth this kind of adoration and invocation, not of saints only, but of angels also.

. . .

Wherefore, to conclude this matter concerning the invocation and adoration of saints and angels, seeing the Fathers did not in their set courses of devotion make prayers to the saints . . . seeing, for aught we know, the saints are not particularly acquainted with the state of things here below; seeing no degree of spiritual worship is to be given to any creature; we invocate them not, but pray unto God only, assuring ourselves that, if they can hear us or any way further our suits, they will do it when we pray unto God, as Augustine rightly observeth.

We adore them not, but rest in the judgment of the same Augustine, that the saints are to be honored for imitation, but not to be adored for religion; that they do not seek, desire, or accept any such honor, but will have us to worship God only, being glad that we are their fellow-servants in well-doing. The Romanist evasion, that God is only to be adored with that highest kind of religious worship which is named *latria*, which yieldeth to him that is worshipped infinite greatness; but the saints may be adored with an inferior kind of religious worship, named *doulia*, is directly contrary to Augustine, who, speaking of saints and angels, saith: *Honoramus eos charitate, non servitute; We honor them with the honor of love, but not of doulia or service.* If they say they have this distinction from Austin, it is true: but he doth not use it to this purpose, to make difference of two sorts of religious or spiritual worship, the highest degree whereof should be *latria*, the lowest *doulia*; neither doth he anywhere call the honor given to saints *doulia*, but nameth it the honor of love and fellowship. But he useth to distinguish religious worship (every degree whereof he calleth *latria*) from the external and civil worship, duty, and service that men yield to their princes, masters, and rulers, which is fitly named *doulia*, a service; but it is *servitus corporis, non animae*, a service of the body, and not of the mind. For men, notwithstanding this servitude, have their minds and their thoughts free, as being known to none nor overruled by none but God only. But the service of the spirit and mind, in the lowest degree that can be imagined, is due unto God only, and not to be given to any creature: for no creature knoweth the secrets of our hearts; no creature can prescribe laws touching the inward actions and thoughts of the mind, not having knowledge of them nor power to punish them that should offend.

It is therefore an impious conceit of the papists that the saints both can and do know all our inward actions and secret thoughts . . . and that, therefore, they are to be honored and worshipped with spiritual service, or service of the spirit and mind. Thus then it is true the *Century*-writers report, that in the third and fourth age after Christ there were some beginnings of that superstition which afterwards grew to be intolerable in the adoration and invocation of saints and angels; but neither they nor we are so ignorant as to think that the invocation of saints or the adoration of them prevailed in the Church within the compass of the first six hundred years; neither do they, as Bellarmine is pleased to slander them, tax that as idolatry in the Roman Church, which they find to have been the practice of all the Fathers; for they find nothing of the Romish idolatry in these glorious lights of the Christian world.

. . .

Chapter 22

Wherein is examined their proof of the antiquity of their doctrine, taken from a false supposal that our doctrine is nothing else but heresy long since condemned

. . .

Luther, saith he {Bellarmine}, pronounceth that there is no way to have access unto God, to treat with him touching reconciliation and acceptation into his favor, but by faith; that God regardeth not works; that a true Christian is so rich in faith that he cannot perish though he would nor how wickedly so ever he live, unless he refuse and cease to believe.

For the clearing of these places of Luther, we must remember that which Illyricus hath fitly noted to this purpose: that there are two courts of God's judgments and most righteous proceeding towards the sons of men: the one, he calleth *forum justificationis*; the other, *novae obedientiae*. In the first, he saith, God requireth perfect righteousness, fully answering that his law prescribeth; which being nowhere to be found but in Christ, is no way apprehended but by faith. In this respect, and sitting in this court of exact trial, he regardeth no works, virtues, or qualities—finding nothing of worth or worthy to be respected—but looking to our faith only; and for Christ's sake only, at the sole and only suit of faith, forgiving sin and imputing righteousness. Notwithstanding, because he never saith to any sinner, *Thy sins are remitted*, but that he addeth, *Go, and sin no more*, and that upon peril of forfeiting the benefit received and that some worse thing should betide unto him, therefore there is another court wherein he sitteth and giveth commandment for new obedience and works of righteousness, though not requiring so strictly that perfection which formerly he did, but accepting our weak endeavors and study of well doing; and in this sort it is that he will judge us in the last day according to our works.

Thus then we see how that, though faith be never alone, yet in procuring us acceptation with God, it is alone; and that, though God regard none of our virtues, actions, and qualities as being of any worth in the strictness of his judgment, but reject them as unpure and unclean, and respect nothing but the humble suit and petition of faith for the purpose of justification; yet, when we are justified, he requireth of us a new obedience, judgeth us according to it, and crowneth us for it. That which Luther addeth, that a man cannot perish though he would and how wickedly so ever he live, unless he cease to believe, may seem hard at the first sight, but not to them that do know that Luther is far from thinking that men may be saved how wickedly so ever they live, for he constantly teacheth that justifying faith cannot remain in that man that sinneth with full consent, nor be found in that soul wherein are *peccata vastantia conscientiam* (as Melanchthon speaketh, following Augustine), that is, {sins} raging, ruling, prevailing, laying waste and destroying the integrity of the conscience, which should resist against evil and condemn it.

This is all, then, that Luther saith: that no wickedness with which faith may stand can hurt us, so long as faith continueth; but if sin once become regnant, and so exclude faith, we are in the state of damnation. Against this doctrine of Luther, or any part thereof, neither Bellarmine nor the gates of hell shall ever be able to prevail. . . .

‡

BOOK IV

Chapter 16

Of the interpretation of Scripture, and to whom it pertaineth

Touching this point, there are two questions usually proposed: the one, to whom the interpretation of the Scripture pertaineth; the other, by what rules and means men may find out the true meaning of it. Touching the first, our adversaries jangle much with many declamations against private interpretations and interpretations of private spirits, and make the world believe that we follow no other rule of interpretation but each man's private fancy.

For answer hereunto, we say with Stapleton[20] that interpretations of Scripture may be said to be private, and the spirits whence they proceed named private, either . . . in respect of the person who interpreteth, the manner of his proceeding in interpreting, or the end of his interpretation. A private interpretation, proceeding from a private spirit in the first sense, is every interpretation delivered by men of private condition. In the second sense, is that which men of what condition so ever deliver, contemning and neglecting those public means which are known to all and are to be used by all that desire to find the truth. In the third sense, that which, proceeding from men of private condition, is not so proposed and urged by them as if they would bind all other to receive and embrace it, but is intended only to their own satisfaction.

The first kind of interpretation (proceeding from a private spirit) is not to be disliked, if the parties so interpreting neither neglect the common rules & means of attaining the right sense of that they interpret, contemn the judgment of other men, nor presumptuously take upon them to teach others and enforce them to believe that which they apprehend for truth, without any authority so to do. But private spirits in the second sense, that is men of such dispositions as will follow their own fancies and neglect the common rules of direction, as enthusiasts, and trust to their own sense without conference and due respect to other men's judgments, we accurse. This is all we say touching this matter—wherein I would fain know what our adversaries dislike. Surely nothing at all, as it will appear to every one that shall but look into the place above alleged out of Stapleton.

But, say they, there must be some authentical interpretation of Scripture, which every one must be bound to stand unto, or else there will be no end of quarrels and contentions.

The interpretation of Scripture is nothing else but the explication and clearing of the meaning of it. This is either true or false. The true interpretation of the Scripture is of two sorts. For there is an interpretation which delivereth that which is true and contained in the Scripture (or from thence to be concluded), though not meant in that place which is expounded.[21] This is not absolutely and perfectly a true interpretation, because, though it truly delivereth such doctrine as is contained in the Scripture and nothing contrary to the place interpreted, yet it doth not express that that is particularly meant in the place expounded. There is therefore another kind of true interpretations, when not only that is delivered which is contained in the Scripture, but that which is meant in the particular places expounded.

---

[20] {Thomas Stapleton (d. 1598), English Catholic controversialist and professor at Louvain.}

[21] {On these two sorts of true interpretation, see Augustine, *De utilitate credendi*.}

Likewise false interpretations are of two sorts: some delivering that which is utterly false and contrary to the Scripture; some others only failing in this, that they attain not the true sense of the particular places expounded. An example of the former is that interpretation of that place of Genesis, *The sons of God saw the daughters of men, &c.* which some of the Fathers have delivered, understanding by *the sons of God*, the angels of heaven, whose fall, they suppose, proceeded from the love of women. Which error they confirm by that of the Apostle, that women must come veiled into the Church for the angels: that is, as they interpret, lest the angels should fall in love with them. A false interpretation of the later kind . . . some think that exposition of the words of the Prophet Esay . . . *Who shall declare his generation*, delivered by many of the Fathers, understanding thereby the eternal generation of the Son of God which no man shall declare; whereas, by the name of *generation*, the Prophet meaneth that multitude that shall believe in Christ, which shall be so great as cannot be expressed.

An authentical interpretation is that which is not only true, but so clearly and in such sort, that every one is bound to embrace and to receive it. As before we made 3 kinds of judgment, the one of discretion common to all, the other of direction common to the pastors of the Church, and a third of jurisdiction proper to them that have supreme power in the Church; so likewise we make three kinds of interpretation: the first private, and so every one may interpret the Scripture—that is, privately with himself conceive, or deliver to other, what he thinketh the meaning of it to be; the second of public direction, and so the pastors of the Church may publicly propose what they conceive of it; and the third of jurisdiction, and so they that have supreme power, that is the bishops assembled in a general council, may interpret the Scripture, and by their authority suppress all them that shall gainsay such interpretations and subject every man that shall disobey such determinations as they consent upon to excommunication and censures of like nature.

But for authentical interpretation of Scriptures, which every man's conscience is bound to yield unto, it is of an higher nature; neither do we think any of these to be such as[22] proceeding from any of those before named & specified, to whom we grant a power of interpretation. Touching the interpretations which the Fathers have delivered, we receive them as undoubtedly true in the general doctrine they consent in, and so far forth esteem them as authentical; yet do we think that, holding the faith of the Fathers, it is lawful to dissent from that interpretation of some particular places which the greater part of them have delivered, or perhaps all that have written of them, and to find out some other not mentioned by any of the ancient.

Chapter 17

Of the interpretation of the Fathers, and how far we are bound to admit it.

The Fathers (saith Andradius),[23] especially they of the Greek Church, being ignorant of the Hebrew tongue, following Origen did rather strive with all their wit and learning to devise allegories and to frame the manners of men than to clear the hard places of the Law and the Prophets. Nay, even Hierome himself, who more diligently than any of the rest sought out the meaning and sense of the prophetical and divine oracles, yet often to avoid

[22] {by virtue of}
[23] {Diego Payva d'Andrada (b. 1528), Portuguese Tridentine theologian and Jesuit scholar}

the obscurities of their words, betaketh himself to allegories. In this sense it is that Cardinal Cajetan saith he will not fear to go against the torrent of all the Doctors; for which saying Andradius sheweth that Canus[24] and others do unjustly blame him. For though we may not go from the faith of the Fathers nor from the main truth of doctrine which they deliver in different interpretations, yet may we interpret some parts of the Scripture otherwise than any of the ancient ever did, weighing the circumstances of places, the nature and force of words in the original, and having other helps necessary.

Neither is this to contemn the uniform and main consent of the Fathers, but rather more exactly to illustrate and explain those things which they did allegorically understand or not so diligently travail in as is fit for them that come after to do. It is not then so strange a thing to say that there are many places of Scripture, the true, literal, and natural sense whereof we cannot find in any of the ancient. Neither is this to charge them with error in faith, seeing the sense they give tendeth to the furtherance of the true faith and the better forming of men's manners to godliness. Wherefore we fear not to pronounce with Andradius that whosoever denieth that the true and literal sense of sundry texts of Scripture hath been found out in this last age (wherein as Guido Fabritius[25] rightly noteth, all things seem to be renewed, and all learning to be newly born into the world, that so Christ might be newly fashioned in us and we new born in him) is most unthankful unto God, that hath so richly shed out his benefits upon the children of this generation, & ungrateful towards those men who with so great pains, so happy success, and so much benefit to God's Church have travailed therein.

Neither is Andradius only of this opinion, but Jansenius & Maldonatus[26] also, who both of them do in sundry places profess they rest not satisfied in any interpretation given by the Fathers, but prefer other found out in this age. For example, in the explication of that place of John, *Of his fullness, we have all received, grace for grace*, Maldonatus refuseth all the interpretations of the Fathers and giveth this of his own: we have received of Christ's fullness most excellent gifts of grace, yet no man hath received all, but every one is defective; yea, everyone lacketh something that another hath; but he may acknowledge the goodness of God towards him, in that he hath some other in stead of it, which the other hath not, and so may rightly be said to have received grace for grace, because in stead of that grace he wanteth and another hath, he hath received some other which the other wanteth. Many other instances might be given out of Cajetan . . . and other worthy divines of the Church of Rome, but this may suffice.

Chapter 18

Of the divers senses of Scripture

Thus having set down to whom the interpretation of the Scripture pertaineth, it remaineth that we speak of the rules, directions, and helps that men have to lead them to the finding out of the right meaning of it. But, because some suppose the Scripture hath many & uncertain senses, before we enter into the discourse of the rules which must direct us in

---

[24] {Melchior Cano (1509–60), Dominican theologian and bishop}

[25] {Guy Le Fèvre de la Boderie (1541–98), French Catholic scholar and Orientalist}

[26] {Cornelius Jansen, Bishop of Gent (1510–76) and Juan Maldonato (1533–83): both eminent Roman Catholic biblical scholars}

interpreting, we must speak something of the multiplicity of senses supposed to be in the words of Scripture, which may seem to contrary all certainty of interpretation. There is therefore a double sense of the sacred words and sentences of Scripture, for there is a literal sense and a spiritual or mystical sense. The literal sense is either proper (or native) when the words are to be taken as originally in their proper signification they import, or figurative when the words are translated from their natural and proper signification to signify something resembled by those things they do primarily import, as when Christ saith, *he hath other sheep, which are not of this fold.*

The spiritual or mystical sense of the Scripture is when the words either properly or figuratively signify some things which are figures and significations of other things. This is threefold: allegorical, tropological, anagogical. The first is when things spoken of in the Old Testament are figures of some things in the New. So it was literally true that Abraham had two sons, the one by a bond-woman, the other by a free, but these two sons of Abraham imported some other thing in the state of the New Testament: to wit, two different sorts of men.[27] And here we may observe the difference between an allegory and a type. A type is when some particular person or fact in the Old Testament demonstrateth and shadoweth out unto us some particular person or fact in the New. An allegory, when something in the Old Testament in a spiritual and mystical sort shadoweth out unto us in a generality things in some proportion answering in the New. So David overcoming Goliath was a type of Christ, and allegorically did shadow out that victory which we obtain in the state of the New Testament over those ghostly enemies that rise up against us.

The tropological sense of Scripture is when one thing delivered and reported in the Scripture signifieth some other thing pertaining to the behavior and conversation of men: as when God forbad to *muzzle the mouth of the ox that treadeth out the corn.* This prohibition did literally signify that God would not have laboring oxen restrained from feeding while they were treading out the corn. But this respect which God had unto these his creatures of inferior condition did signify that much less they which labor for our souls' good are to be denied the things of this life.

Anagogical, when the things literally expressed unto us do signify something in the state of heaven{ly} happiness. *God sware in his wrath,* to the Israelites, *that they should not enter into his rest,* meaning the land of Canaan, but the Apostle from thence concludeth that unbelievers shall not enter into that eternal rest of the saints in heaven; because the rest of the Israelites in the land of Canaan after their manifold dangers, vexations, and travails was a figure of the eternal rest in heaven. This division of the manifold senses of Scripture is taken out of Eucherius.[28]

Hierome maketh three kinds of exposition of Scripture: historical, tropological, and spiritual; that which he nameth spiritual comprehendeth both those before expressed by Eucherius, to wit, allegorical & anagogical. Augustine maketh the exposition of the Scripture to be twofold, historical & allegorical. The former he maketh to be twofold: to

---

[27] [{Flacius} Illyrycus *in Clave Scripturae, de multiplici sacrarum literarum sensu, haec doctissimè tradit collecta ex varijs authoribus.*]

[28] {Saint Eucherius (ca. 380–ca. 449), Bishop of Lyon and author of *Liber formularum spiritalis intelligentiae,* a defense of allegorical exegesis}

wit, analogical & etiological; and the later he maketh to comprehend that which properly is called allegorical and the other two, to wit, tropological and anagogical.

The reason of this diversity of mystical senses is because the Old Testament was a figure of the New; and the New, of future glory. This multiplicity of senses breedeth no uncertainty in the Scripture, nor equivocation, because the words of the Scripture do not doubtfully signify so divers and different things; but the things certainly signified by the words are signs & significations of divers things. All these are founded upon one literal & certain sense, from which only, in matter of question and doubt, an argument may be drawn. The thing wherein Origen offended was not that he found out spiritual and mystical senses of the divine Scripture, but because he thought there is no literal true sense of them but mystical only, so overthrowing the truth of the sacred history of the book of God. And the fault of many others in former times was, that following him too much, they neglected the literal sense and over-curiously sought out allegories and mystical senses; whereas yet the literal sense alone hath force and power to establish truth and improve {refute} error.[29] And this doubtless is the first and chiefest use and necessity of following the literal sense. Another is for that, being the foundation of the mystical, if we find it not out, we may run into many errors. The Manichees out of those words of the Psalmist, where he saith that *God hath made a tabernacle for the sun in heaven, out of which, it cometh in the morning, as a bridegroom out of his chamber, to shew the brightness of his countenance to the sons of men*—reading *posuit tabernaculum suum in sole; God placed his tabernacle, or appointed and made himself a tabernacle, in the sun*—inferred that Christ ascended into the highest heavens without our flesh, leaving his body behind him within the compass of the globe of the sun, so that his flesh is to be adored in the sun as in a tabernacle wherein it resteth and remaineth.[30] Now as their course is not to be excused which follow the mystical sense only & neglect the literal; so they are no less faulty that follow the literal sense only and do not at all consider the mysteries of spiritual understanding and information {forming} of Christian and godly conversation {conduct} which in the word of God do offer themselves unto them. For they make the Scriptures, especially of the Old Testament—where so many things of outward observation, ceremony, and purification were prescribed—unsavory, and to seem less divine than the laws and prescriptions of the gentiles (as the Athenians, Lacedaemonians, and other), and the manifold histories of former times to serve little to edification.

Between both these extremes, a mean is to be kept, that neither the one nor the other be neglected: so that we must neither be like them that, rejecting the literal exposition, seek out fond and childish allegories and so overthrow the truth of the divine history, as Origen did; or neglect the knowledge of it, publishing their own idle and ridiculous conceits as if they were the great & hidden mysteries of the Christian faith and religion; nor like those which rest in the bare and naked words and syllables, without collecting from thence such instructions as are fit. The former (saith Sixtus Senensis) are to know that howsoever they imagine the literal exposition of the Scripture to be easy, obvious, and trivial, yet it is indeed the hardest of all other. Whereupon, both Hierome and Augustine

---

[29] [Sixtus Sennens {i.e., of Siena}, *Bibliothecae* l.3. de vsu & vtilitate historicae & mysticae expopositionis] {This is also Aquinas' position; see his *Summa theologicae* 1.1.10.}

[30] [Greg. moral. l 21. in cap. 31. cap. 1]

confess that at first, to decline the obscurities and difficulties of the text of Scripture, they followed mystical senses as being more easy; but afterward when they grew in age & so in ripeness of judgment, they sought out the other, which is literal.

Thus we see the difference between the literal and mystical sense of Scripture, and how and in what sort the one is the ground of the other. Which that we misconceive not, nor take one for another, we must remember that by the literal sense of Scripture, we understand not that only which the words do properly afford, but which they primarily afford according to the intention of him that useth them and the construction of them that hear them. The mystical sense opposite hereunto is that which is not primarily intended by him that speaketh words having such mystical sense. All the allegories, therefore, parables, and enigmatical speeches which are used in Scripture, not being verified either in the intention of the speaker or construction of the hearer in sort as the words properly import but as signifying things resembled by the things they properly import, do literally signify that which by comparison of such things they make us understand.[31]

Here it is not out of place to observe the difference between a proverb, parable, allegory, and enigmatical speech or riddle. A proverb is a sententious saying, much in use and famous, for the most part somewhat obscure, by metaphorical words expressing something to us and alluding to something not distinctly expressed—though sometimes any famous and common saying be named a proverb. A parable is when one thing is compared and resembled to another; so Christ compared the kingdom of heaven to leaven, to a grain of mustard seed, to ten virgins, to a net cast into the sea. Though sometimes the similitude of a thing, and not any such speech wherein comparison is made between one thing and another, is named a parable: *Abraham recepit filium suum in parabola*, that is, *Abraham received his son from such an estate as was most like to the state of the dead.*

An allegory is when he that speaketh intendeth to signify and insinuate some other thing than his words in their primary use and signification do import. *Behold*, saith Christ, *the sower went out to sow, &c.* A riddle, or enigmatical speech, is an obscure allegory: *The trees went forth to anoint them a king*; and again, *Out of the eater came meat, & out of the strong came sweetness.* The Scripture is full of these allegories, parables, proverbial and enigmatical speeches: GOD, in teaching us, taking that course he knoweth fittest for us, and making us understand things heavenly and invisible by those that are earthly and visible.

And as God doth thus speak unto us in parables, allegories, and riddles, so did he shew the prophets of old in dreams and visions the things that are heavenly by those that are earthly, and the things that are invisible by those that are visible: as in the Revelation, Saint John *saw seven golden candlesticks, and one like the Son of man walking in the midst of them.*[32] There is none of these enigmatical, allegorical, or parabolical speeches, nor none of these visions, but either by some things known to them to whom they were proposed, or by special explication added to them, or *per novi facti exhibitionem*, by seeing the thing performed that was so obscurely shadowed only, may be understood. From these, without these helps of understanding, we can conclude nothing that is {not} doubtful. An example of understanding enigmatical and hard speeches by force of some things known unto us,

---

[31] {I.e., when a speech is intended figuratively (e.g., "I am the true vine"), its literal sense is figurative.}
[32] [Occam l. 3. tract. part. 3. c. 19]

giving light unto them, is the riddle of Samson, *Out of the eater came meat*, &c., which anyone knowing that out of a lion he had taken honey would understand, but another could not. By explication added, as the mystery of the seven stars and seven golden candlesticks is expounded to John that saw the vision of them. By evidence of the thing exhibited and performed, *Destroy this temple* (saith Christ), *and in three days I will build it and raise it up again. The disciples after they saw him risen from the dead, remembered these words & understood that they were spoken of our Savior of the temple of his body* and the resurrection of it. So likewise, when they saw the miserable and abominable overthrow of Jerusalem and the Temple, they could not but understand what was meant by the prophecy of Daniel touching the abomination of desolation standing in the holy place.

Thus having cleared that doubt which some make touching the multiplicity of senses of the words of Scripture, as if there were no certain meaning of them, and having shewed which is that sense we must principally seek after, as being the foundation of the rest, it remaineth that we come to speak of the rules of direction & the helps we have to attain to the understanding of the true meaning of the Scripture. For as Hierome fitly noteth . . . *We must not think that the Gospel consisteth in the words of Scripture, but in the sense and meaning; not in the outward rind and skin, but in the inward pith and marrow; not in the leaves of the words, but in the root and ground of reason.*

‡

Chapter 31

Of the bounds within which the power of the Church in making laws is contained, and whether she may make laws concerning the worship of God

Touching the first, the question is usually proposed whether the rulers of God's Church and people may make laws concerning God's worship and service. For the clearing whereof, Stapleton distinguisheth the things pertaining to the worship and service of God into three sorts. The first, such as are seals, assurances, and, in their sort and kind, causes of grace: as the sacrifices in old time and the sacraments now. The second, such as remove the impediments of grace, dispose to the receipt of it, and work other spiritual and supernatural effects, though they give not grace in so high degree as the first: as the signing with the sign of the cross, sprinkling with holy water, and the like. The third, such as are used only for order and comeliness in the performance of the principal and essential duties of God's worship and service. These being the diverse sorts of things pertaining to the worship and service of God, the question and controversy between us and our adversaries is only touching things of the second rank.[33] For they confess the Church hath no power to institute things of the first sort, and we willingly grant unto it a most ample power in things of the third sort. Let us first therefore lay down their opinion, and then examine the truth or falsehood of it.

Their opinion is that the Church hath power to institute ceremonies and observations, though not to justify and give grace, as do the sacraments, yet to cure diseases, drive away devils, purge out venial sins, and to work other the like spiritual and supernatural

[33] {See Keith Thomas, *Religion and the decline of magic* (Oxford UP, 1971), 3–50; Eamon Duffy, *Stripping of the altars* (Yale UP, 1992), 155–298.}

effects; and that not only by way of impetration and by force of the prayers of the Church which hath prayed that they that use such things may enjoy such happy benefits, but *ex opere operato*, by the very work wrought: the use of these things applying the merits of Christ to the effecting of these inferior effects, as the sacraments do to the effects of justification and remission of sins.

The sign of the cross, saith Bellarmine, driveth away devils three ways: first, by the devotion of them that use it, it being a kind of invocation of his name that was crucified for the redemption of the world, expressed not by words but by this sign; secondly, by the impression of fear, which the very sight and apprehension of it worketh in the devil, as being the thing whereby Christ wrought his overthrow; thirdly, *ex opere operato*, in which sort infidels using this sign have wrought these effects.

The Rhemists[34] upon 1 Tim. 4:5, *Every creature is good, &c.* have these observations: first, that every creature is by nature and condition of creation good. Secondly, that Satan unjustly usurpeth upon these creatures, in & by them seeking to hurt the bodies and souls of men. Thirdly, that by prayer and invocation of God's name, notwithstanding the curse upon all creatures & Satan's readiness to do us harm, they are good and comfortable to us, so that in them we taste the sweetness of divine goodness. Fourthly, that the blessings of God's Church and her ministers do not only stay and hinder Satan's working, remove the curse, and make the creatures serve for our good accordingly as at the first they were appointed, but apply them also to so sacred uses, as to be instruments of remission of sins, justification, and infusion of grace—as appeareth in the sacraments instituted by Christ. Fifthly, that besides and out of the use of sacraments, the prayers and blessings of the Church do sanctify divers creatures to the working of spiritual and supernatural effects, as to expel devils, cure diseases, and remit venial sins: and that not only as sanctified things are wont to do in that they stir up and increase devotion and the fervor of piety, but in that the ministers of the Church, by their sovereign authority, have annexed to the use of them power to work such effects. This last proposition containeth the whole matter of difference between them and us; for touching all the former, we consent and agree with them.

For clearing of this point, we lay down these propositions: first, that by ordinary prayers the creatures of God are sanctified to ordinary uses. Secondly, that the presenting them, or some part of them, in holy places and to holy persons to be blessed of them maketh the use of them more comfortable than the former blessing, but addeth no supernatural force, efficacy, or grace unto them. Thirdly, that Christ appointed, and the Church daily sanctifieth, the creatures of God and elements of this world to be the matter of his sacraments. Fourthly, that bread being appointed to be the matter of the sacrament of the body of Christ, and water of baptism, the Christians in ancient time held that bread which had been offered and presented at the Lord's table (out of which a part was consecrated for the use of the sacrament) more holy than other bread. And this is that bread, Augustine saith, was given to the catechumens; as also they religiously kept of that water which had been hallowed for the use of baptism, and by the use of it strengthened their assurance of enjoying the benefits which are bestowed on men in baptism. Neither can our adversaries clearly prove any separate sanctifying of water to have been used in the primitive Church.

---

[34] {Members of the English Catholic seminary at Douai, Rheims, whose heavily annotated English translation of the Old Testament came out in 1610.}

If they could, it were nothing else but the bringing of some part of this element into holy places, with humble desire that they which in memory of baptism should use it, and so have their faith strengthened, might more and more receive the effects of saving grace, as the Christians of Russia and Ethiopia unto this day on the Epiphany, on which day they remember the baptism of Christ, go into the water, praying unto God that the effects of the sacrament of baptism may more & more be seen and appear in them. Fifthly, that the Church consecrateth sundry outward things to the use of God's service, not giving them any new quality, force, or efficacy, but only praying that God will be pleased to accept that which is done in or with them, and to work in us that the use of them importeth. Sixthly, holy men having the gift of miracles did use sometimes water, sometimes oil, sometimes other things, and gave them to be used by other, for the working of miraculous effects, after the example of Elizeus and Christ himself: of which sort is that of Joseph mentioned by Epiphanius, who filling a vessel with water, signing it with the sign of the cross, and casting it into a certain fire, caused it to burn, though Satan hindered it before that it could not burn; as likewise that of Hilarion, who gave a kind of hallowed oil to certain, who, by using it, were cured of their diseases. But the consecrating of oil, salt, water, and the like things by men not having the gift of miracles, to drive away devils, cure diseases, remit venial sins, and work other spiritual and supernatural effects *ex opere operato*, by application of the merits of Christ, was never known in the primitive Church, nor any such form of exorcising or blessing as they now use.

That which the Rhemists allege touching the liver of a fish used by Tobie, the piece of the holy earth where Christ was buried preserving a man's chamber from the infestation of devils, and the force of holy relics tormenting them, maketh nothing to this purpose, all these examples being miraculous. Touching the harp of David quieting Saul, there is a reason for it in nature, though the repressing of Satan's rage were miraculous. That infidels have sometimes driven away devils by the sign of the cross, it was by the special dispensation of Almighty God, who would thereby glorify his Son, whose cross the world despised; and not as if this ceremony had force *ex opere operato* to work such effects. That the name of Jesus did miraculously cast out devils in the primitive Church (which is the next allegation) who ever made doubt? but what maketh this to the purpose? That which they allege, that Saint Gregory did usually send his benediction and remission of sins in and with such tokens as were sanctified by his blessing and touch of the martyrs' relics, as now his successors do the like hallowed remembrances of religion, is very vain. For Gregory did not send any such blessing of his own or remission of sins by force of it, as now his successors do, but only certain things that had pertained to Christ or his apostles, as part of the wood of the cross of Christ or of the chains wherewith the apostles were bound[35]—and, with them, the blessing of Christ and those apostles to such as should conform themselves to his sufferings or their faith. . . .

Thus we see, our adversaries cannot prove that the Church hath power to annex unto such ceremonies and observations as she deviseth the remission of sins and the working of other spiritual and supernatural effects, which is the only thing questioned between

[35] [These were often accompanieed with miraculous effects in those times, as appeareth by Gregory in the places cited.]

them and us touching the power of the Church. So that all the power the Church hath, more than by her authority to publish the commandments of Christ the Son of God and by her censures to punish the offenders against the same, is only in prescribing things that pertain to comeliness and order.

Comeliness requireth that not only that {*sic*} gravity and modesty do appear in the performance of the works of God's service that beseemeth actions of that nature, but also that such rites and ceremonies be used as may cause a due respect unto and regard of the things performed, and thereby stir men up to greater fervor and devotion. *Caeremoniae*, ceremonies, are so named, as Livy thinketh, from a town called Caere, in the which the Romans did hide their sacred things when the Gauls invaded Rome. Other think ceremonies are so named a *carendo*, of abstaining from certain things, as the Jews abstained from swine's flesh and sundry other things forbidden by God as unclean.

Ceremonies are outward acts of religion, having institution either from the instinct of nature, as the lifting up of the hands and eyes to heaven, the bowing of the knee, the striking of the breast, and such like; or immediately from God, as the sacraments; or from the Church's prescription—and either only serve to express such spiritual and heavenly affections, dispositions, motions, and desires as are or should be in men; or else to signify, assure, and convey unto them such benefits of saving grace as God in Christ is pleased to bestow on them. To the former purpose and end, the Church hath power to ordain ceremonies; to the latter, God only.

Order requireth that there be set hours for prayer, preaching and ministering the sacraments, that there be silence and attention when the things are performed, that women be silent in the Church, that all things be administered according to the rules of discipline. Thus we see within what bounds the power of the Church is contained, and how far it hath authority to command and prescribe in things pertaining to the worship and service of God.

Chapter 32

Of the nature of laws, and how they bind

Now it remaineth that we examine how far the band of such laws extendeth as the Church maketh, and whether they bind the conscience or only the outward man. For the clearing whereof, first we must observe in what sense it is that laws are said to bind; and secondly, what it is to bind the conscience. Lawgivers are said to bind them to whom they give laws when they determine and set down what is fit to be done, what things they are the doing whereof they approve and the omission whereof they dislike, and then signify to them whom they command, that though they have power and liberty of choice to do or omit the things prescribed, yet that they will so and in such sort limit them in the use of their liberty as that either they shall do that they are commanded or be deprived of the good they desire and incur the evils they would avoid. None can thus tie and limit men but they that have power to deprive them of the good they desire and bring upon them the contrary evils. So that no man, knowing what he doth, prescribeth or commandeth anything under greater penalties than he hath power to inflict, nor anything but that whereof he can take notice whether it be done or not, that so he may accordingly reward or punish the doing or omission of it.

Hence it followeth that mortal men forget themselves and keep not within their own bounds when either they command under pain of eternal damnation, which none but God can inflict . . . or take upon them to prescribe inward actions of the soul or spirit, or the performance of outward actions with inward affections; whereas none but God that searcheth the heart can either take knowledge of things of this kind or convent {summon} the offenders, and judge and try them. Thus then we see what it is to bind, and that none can bind men to the performance of anything but by the fear of such punishments as they have power to inflict.

Chapter 33

Of the nature of conscience, and how the conscience is bound

In the next place we are to see what the nature of conscience is and how the conscience is bound. Conscience is the privity the soul hath to things known to none but to God & herself. Hence it is that conscience hath a fearful apprehension of punishments for evils done, though neither known nor possible to be known to any but God and the offender alone. The punishments that men can inflict we never fear unless our evil doings be known to them. For, though we have conscience of them & be privy to them, yet if they be hidden from them, we know they neither will nor can punish us. To bind the conscience then, is to bind the soul and spirit of man with the fear of such punishments (to be inflicted by him that so bindeth) as the conscience feareth—that is, as men fear though none but God & themselves be privy to their doings. Now these are only such as God alone inflicteth; & therefore, seeing none have power to bind but by fear of such punishments as they have power to inflict, none can bind the conscience but God alone.[36] Neither should the question be proposed whether human laws bind the conscience, but whether binding the outward man to the performance of outward things by force & fear of outward punishments to be inflicted by men, the not-performance of such things (or the not-performance of them with such affections as were fit) be not a sin against God of which the conscience will accuse us, he having commanded us to obey the magistrates and rulers he hath set over us. For answer whereunto, we say there are three sorts of things commanded by magistrates.[37] First, evil and against God. Secondly, injurious in respect of them to whom they are prescribed, or at least unprofitable to the common-wealth in which they are prescribed. Thirdly, such as are profitable and beneficial to the society of men to whom they are prescribed. Touching the first sort of things, God hath not commanded us to obey, neither must we obey, but rather say to them that command us such things (with the apostles), whether it be fit to obey God or men, judge you. Yet we must so refuse to obey that we shew no contempt of their office and authority, which is of God, though they abuse it. Touching the second sort of things, all that God requireth of us is that we shew no contempt of sacred authority, though not rightly used, that we scandalize not others, and that we be subject to such penalties and punishments as they that command

---

[36] [Gers. *de vita spirituali anim.* lect. 4. corol. 5. *ubi reprehendit eos qui fulminant et tot condunt leges, quot nunquam legere possumus.*]

[37] {Regarding whether human laws bind in conscience, see also Buckeridge <supra> and Dow <infra>.}

such things do lay upon us. So that God requireth our willing and ready obedience only in things of the third sort. The breach & violation of this kind of laws is sin, not for that human laws have power to bind the conscience, or that it is simply and absolutely sinful to break them, but because the things they command are of that nature that not to perform them is contrary to justice, charity, and the desire we should have to procure the common good of them with whom we live. We are bound then sometimes to the performance of things prescribed by human laws in such sort that the not-performance of them is sin; not *ex sola legislatoris voluntate, sed ex ipsa legum vtilitate*, as Stapleton rightly observed.[38] But some man will say, What do the laws then effect? seeing it is the law of justice and charity that doth bind us, and not the particularity of laws newly made. To this we answer that many things are good and profitable if they be generally observed, which without such general observation will do no good: as for one man to pay tribute . . . is no way beneficial to the common-wealth; which would be very profitable, if all did so. Now the law procureth a general observation; whence it cometh that a man is bound by the law of charity and justice to that, after the making of a law, which before he was not bound unto.

And this is it that Stapleton meaneth, when he saith that human laws do bind the conscience not *ex voluntate legislatoris, sed ex ipsa legum vtilitate & ratione*. Not because they prescribe such things, but because the things so prescribed, if they be generally observed, are profitable to the commonwealth.

By this which hath been said, it appeareth that they do impiously usurp and assume to themselves that which is proper to God, who will have all their laws taken for divine laws and such as bind the conscience no less then the laws of God; who publish all their canons and constitutions in such sort that they threaten damnation to all offenders.[39] Whereas no creature hath power to prescribe, command, or prohibit anything under pain of sin and eternal punishment, unless the party so commanded were formerly—either expressly or by implication, either formally or by force and virtue of some general duty— bound unto it by God's law before; because God only hath power of eternal life or death.

The soul of man, as it receiveth from God only the life of grace, so it loseth the same when he, for the transgression of his laws and precepts, forsaketh it. For as none but he can give this life, so none but he can take it away. . . . Hence it followeth that no lawgiver may command anything under pain of eternal punishment but God only, because he only hath power to inflict this kind of punishment. And that no man incurreth the guilt of eternal condemnation but by violating the laws of God. Whereupon Augustine defineth sins to be thoughts, words, and deeds against the law of God.

That men do sin in not keeping and observing the laws of men, it is because, being generally bound by God's law to do those things which set forward the common good, many things, being commanded and so generally observed, grow to be beneficial, which without such general observation flowing from the prescript of law were not so; and so, though not formally, yet by virtue of general duty, men are tied to the doing of them under pain of sin and the punishments that deservedly follow it.

---

[38] {translated in the following paragraph}
[39] [Gers. *de auferribilitate Papae considerat.* 8]

Chapter 34

Of their reasons, who think that human laws do bind the conscience

The reasons which Bellarmine and other of that faction bring to prove that human laws do bind the conscience are so vain and frivolous that they deserve no answer; yet lest our adversaries should think we therefore pass them over without examination because we fear the force and weight of them, I will briefly take a view of them and let the reader see their weakness. To bind, saith Bellarmine, is either the essence or essential property of a law; therefore all laws, whether they be of God or of men, do bind in the same sort. He should have said, therefore all laws do bind, whether they be of God or of men. . . . His next reason is more childish than this: for he reasoneth thus, If laws do bind only in that they are divine, then all divine laws should equally bind. This reason concludeth nothing against us. For first, no man saith that laws bind only because divine (for it is essential to every law to bind), but that they bind the conscience because they are divine. . . .

. . .

. . . His last reason is taken from that place of the Apostle where he requireth us to be subject to power and authority for conscience sake. To this we answer, first, that it is a matter of conscience to be subject in all things, for subjection is required generally and absolutely, where obedience is not. Secondly, we say that it is a matter of conscience to seek and procure the good of the commonwealth; and that therefore it is a matter of conscience to obey good and profitable laws so far as we are persuaded our obedience is profitable. Thus have we briefly examined their reasons, who think that human laws bind the conscience, the weakness whereof, I hope all men of any judgment will easily discern.

Wherefore, to conclude this matter touching the Church's power in making laws, there are three things which we dislike in the doctrine & practice of the Roman Church. First, that they take upon them to prescribe ceremonies and observations having power to confer grace for the remission of venial sins and the working of other spiritual & supernatural effects. Secondly, that they assume unto themselves that which is proper unto God & seek to rule in the conscience. Thirdly, that by the multiplicity of laws, they dangerously ensnare the consciences of men and oppress them with heavy burdens. To this purpose is the complaint that Gerson long since made, that the laws of the Church were too many, and in a great part childish and unprofitable, bringing us into a worse estate than that of the Jews. . . . Neither, saith Gerson, are they content to burden us with the multiplicity of their laws, but, as if they preferred their own inventions before the laws of God, they most rigorously exact the performance of the things their own laws prescribe, & neglect the laws of God—as Christ told the Pharisees and hypocrites of his time, pronouncing against them that by their vain traditions they made the laws of God of none effect. To shew how unjust and unreasonable the Roman lawgivers are in burdening men with so many traditions, the same Gerson fitly observeth that Adam in the time of his innocency had but one commandment, which yet unhappily he brake; and that therefore, they seem to have no sense of man's miserable & wretched condition, nor any way to compassionate his infirmity, that charge him with so many precepts besides those of God and nature. Whereupon he gravely and wisely concludeth that he supposeth that the wisest and best amongst the guides of God's Church had not so ill a meaning as to have all their constitutions & ordinances taken for laws properly so named, much less strictly binding the conscience, but for threatenings, admonitions, counsels, and directions only. And that, when there groweth a general neglect, they seem to consent to the abolishing of them again. For seeing . . . laws are made when they are published by such as have authority, but have life, force, and vigor when the manners of men, receiving and obeying them, give them allowance; general & long continued disuse is, and justly may be thought, an abolishing and abrogating of human laws. Whereas, contrariwise, against the laws of God and nature, no prescription[40] or contrary use doth ever prevail, but every such contrary custom or practice is rightly judged a corruption and fault.

TEXT: *Of the Church, five books. By Richard Field, D.D., Dean of Gloucester* (Cambridge: Printed at the University Press for the Ecclesiastical History Society, 1847) [for Books I–III].

    Supplemented by *Of the Church, five books. By Richard Field, Doctor of Divinity and sometimes Dean of Gloucester* (Oxford: Imprinted by William Turner, printer to the famous University, 1628) STC (2nd ed.) / 10858 [for Books III.1 and IV].

[40] {Limitation or restriction of the time within which an action or claim can be raised; the extinction of a title or right by failure to claim it or exercise it over a long period; a restriction of this nature (*OED*).}

RICHARD CORBETT
(1582–1635)

Corbett's father, often described as a "gardener," was a property-owning gentleman, albeit on a modest scale, with a life-long interest in horticulture. Educated first at Westminster School, in 1598 Corbett entered Broadgates Hall, Oxford, and then in the same year transferred to Christ Church, graduating BA in 1602 and MA in 1605. At Oxford, Corbett was "esteemed one of the most celebrated wits in the university, as his poems, jests, romantic fancies, and exploits, which he made and perform'd extempore, shew'd" (*ODNB*); he was also renowned as an amateur ballad singer. In 1613 he took holy orders, becoming the least stuffy English cleric at least since the Reformation. His Passion sermon for that year defended (against Calvin) Christ's descent into hell—the position taken by most high-church divines. It is, however, unlikely that he was a protégé of Laud, who would probably not have "found much to commend in a young clergyman whose chief reputation was for light verse, practical jokes, and tavern escapades" (Bennett and Trevor-Roper xvii). Corbett's May 1617 BD thesis upheld the standard Protestant view that the sacraments do not confer grace *ex opere operato*. He simultaneously proceeded to a DD, "and one day (we are told), when already Doctor of Divinity, he distinguished himself by putting on the leather jacket of a professional balladist who had excited scant attention and drawing crowds to hear him singing ballads outside a tavern in Abingdon" (Bennett and Trevor-Roper xiv).

In 1620 his long-standing friendship with Sir Thomas Aylesbury drew Corbett within the orbit of Buckingham's patronage. On June 24, he became dean of Christ Church, having already received a canonry at Salisbury and a Berkshire vicarage. Around the same time, King James, who admired his "fine fancy and preaching," made him a royal chaplain. He was, however, less famous as a preacher than as a poet, specializing in "a rollicking satiric vein" (*DNB*), so that when he and Donne became deans in quick succession, Chamberlain observed that "if Ben Jonson might be made dean of Westminster, that place, Paul's, and Christ Church should be furnished with three very pleasant poetical deans" (Bennett and Trevor-Roper xx). Jonson was in fact Corbett's friend and a regular guest at the Christ Church deanery.

Together with Laud and several other divines, Corbett played a role in dissuading Buckingham from Catholicism in 1622–23. His next promotion, however, came only in 1628, when he was nominated bishop of Oxford, the "newest, smallest, and poorest of English dioceses," lacking even a single episcopal residence (Bennett and Trevor-Roper xxix). As bishop, he proved a committed Laudian, despite a certain tolerant laxity in matters of discipline and a liking for "jollity, fatness, and hospitality" (Bennett and Trevor-Roper xxxiv). His chaplains, who seem to have been kindred spirits, included William Strode <*vide infra*> and Thomas Lushington (whose pupil, Sir Thomas Browne, followed his tutor to Norwich after Corbett was translated there in 1632). Lushington and Corbett were "great bowlers together and, in a tight spot, used to calling for the resin for their hands. During a confirmation service, Bishop Corbett came to a candidate's head at the altar rail glistening in its baldness. Laying both hands upon it, the Bishop was heard to whisper to his clerical assistant. 'Some dust, Lushington!'" The most recent version of this story ends with the teller's pious hope that "the new communicant received a bias toward heaven" (Huntley 18).

The record of his brief episcopate at Norwich does not suggest any great administrative talents, especially regarding diocesan finance, although he did zealously seek contributions for the rebuilding of St. Paul's, contributing £400 himself, as well as reportedly giving money to poor ministers for them to contribute in their own names in the hope that their generosity might loosen the purse strings of richer parishioners (Bennett and Trevor-Roper xxxix). Given the anti-puritanism of Corbett's verse, his dealings with Norwich's non-conforming ministers seem unexpectedly pastoral. Only two ministers were suspended, both temporarily; upon hearing that one had agreed to conform, Corbett wrote:

> My worthy friend:
>
> I thank God for your conformity, and you for your acknowledgment. Stand upright to the Church wherein you live; be true of heart to her governors; think well of her significant ceremonies; and be you most assured I shall never displace you of that room which I have given you in my affection. Prove you a good tenant in my heart, and no minister in my diocese hath a better landlord. Farewell. God Almighty bless you with your whole congregation.
>
> From your faithful friend to serve you in Christ Jesus,
>
> Rich. Norwich[1]

He died after only four years at Norwich. One late seventeenth-century account records that his last words were "Good night, Lushington" (Bennett and Trevor-Roper xli).

Corbett, whom a contemporary named "the best poet of all the bishops of England" (Bennett and Trevor-Roper xl), wrote strictly for manuscript publication. The first printed edition, brought out by John Donne the younger, dates from 1647. The early editions make no attempt to order the poems, but in 1955 J. A. W. Bennett and Hugh Trevor-Roper

---

[1] Bennett and Trevor-Roper, xxxvi (modernized). The minister was Samuel Ward, whose encounter with Corbett's successor, Matthew Wren, ended less happily (see Collinson, *Religion of Protestants*, 153–54, 175–78).

produced a scholarly edition, with the poems arranged, as far as could be determined, chronologically. The three included in this volume appear under their approximate dates, spanning two decades (1609, ca. 1620, and ca. 1630).[2]

The elegy on Dr. Ravis, Bishop of London—and Dean of Christ Church during Corbett's undergraduate days—was written shortly after Ravis' death in 1609 (see the notes to the text below). Ravis was an uncompromising conformist, but also, in the words of the *ODNB*, "an unreconstructed Calvinist," giving a further unexpected twist to the surprisingly early high-church language of "host" (from *hostium*, sacrificial victim) and "altar" with which the poem concludes. The controversies over predestination that roiled late Elizabethan Cambridge had no Oxford counterpart, and seem never to have been central to Corbett's brand of high churchmanship.

Sources: *DNB*; *ODNB*; J. A. W. Bennett and Hugh Trevor-Roper, *The poems of Richard Corbett* (Clarendon, 1955): Frank Huntley, "Dr. Thomas Lushington (1590–1661): Sir Thomas Browne's Oxford tutor," *MP* 81.1 (1983): 14–23; Quantin, *Christian antiquity.*

---

[2] I did not include Corbett's wonderful ballad of Catholic nostalgic, "The Fairies Farewell," simply because it is so well known and often reprinted.

RICHARD CORBETT

An elegy written upon the death of Dr. Ravis, Bishop of London[1]
ca. 1609

When I past Paul's, and travel'd in that walk
Where all our Britain-sinners swear and talk[2]—
Old Harry-ruffians, bankrupts, soothsayers,
And youth, whose cozenage is as old as theirs—
And then beheld the body of my lord
Trod under foot by vice that he abhorr'd,
It wounded me the Landlord of all times
Should let long lives[3] and leases to their crimes,
And to his springing honor did afford
Scarce so much time as to the prophet's gourd.[4]
Yet since swift flights of virtue have apt ends
(Like breath of angels, which a blessing sends
And vanisheth withal), whilst fouler deeds
Expect a tedious harvest for bad seeds,[5]
I blame not Fame and Nature if they gave,
Where they could give no more, their last, a grave.
And wisely do thy grievèd friends forbear
Bubbles and alabaster boys[6] to rear

---

[1] {Ravis, whom Corbett had known at Oxford, died in 1609. Gilchrist notes that the poem must have been written shortly thereafter, since "towards its conclusion he complains that no tomb was raised over his remains; a complaint which was soon after obviated, when a fair monument was erected."}

[2] {Saint Paul's cathedral was in Corbett's time the resort of the idle and profligate of all classes [Gilchrist note].}

[3] {Leases and grants were made for periods of time specified in terms of some number of lives.}

[4] {Jonah 4:6-7; the gourd lasted a single night}

[5] {"expect" has the sense of "await"; "tedious" means both "disagreeable" and "slow" or "late"; "for" might conceivably be a misprint for "from."}

6 {i.e., carved marble *putti*}

On thy religious dust; for men did know
Thy life, which such illusions cannot show.
For thou hast trod among those happy ones
Who trust not in their superscriptions,
Their hired epitaphs, and perjured stone,
Which oft belies the soul when she is gone;
And durst commit thy body, as it lies,
To tongues of living men, nay unborn eyes.
What profits thee a sheet of lead? What good
If on thy corpse a marble quarry stood?
Let those that fear their rising, purchase vaults,
And rear them statues to excuse their faults;
As if, like birds that peck at painted grapes,
Their Judge knew not their persons from their shapes.
Whilst thou assured,[7] through thy easier dust
Shall rise at first;[8] they would not, though they must.
Nor needs the Chancellor boast, whose pyramis
Above the host and altar rearèd is;[9]
For though thy body fill a viler room,
Thou shalt not change deeds with him for his tomb.

TEXT: *The poems of Richard Corbet, late Bishop of Oxford and of Norwich*, 4th ed. Octavius Gilchrist (London, 1807).

Checked against J. A. W. Bennett & Hugh Trevor-Roper, eds., *The poems of Richard Corbett* (Clarendon, 1955).

---

[7] {safe, secure}

[8] {Because Ravis' dust is not weighted down by lead or marble, it will have less difficulty rising.}

[9] {Gilcrest notes that the reference is to Sir Christopher Hatton's extravagant monument. The use of "host" and "altar," together with the censure of the post-Reformation encroachment of aristocratic memorials on the spaces of sacramental presence—all hallmarks of Laudian churchmanship—make a remarkably early showing in this poem.}

LEWIS BAYLY
(ca. 1575–1631)

He was born in Carmarthen, Wales—probably the son of the parish curate. No record of his earlier education survives, but in 1611 he received his BD from Oxford, followed by his DD in 1613. He had been a parish priest from the mid-1590s (the sermons he preached while in Evesham, Worcestershire, form the core of *The practice of piety*) until shortly after James' accession, when he was appointed chaplain to Prince Henry, with a further appointment as treasurer of St. Paul's coming in 1611. Two weeks after the Prince's death on November 6, 1612, Chamberlain wrote to Carleton that Bayly had been called before the Archbishop and Privy Council for having declared in the pulpit that "divers councilors hear Mass in the morning . . . and then tell their wives what passes {in Privy Council}, and they carry it to their Jesuits and confessors." A follow-up letter reported that Bayly was ordered to preach another sermon explaining himself, whereupon, instead of backpedaling, Bayly apparently "made the matter much more than plain, relating the whole matter as it passed at the council-table, with justifying, offering to make proof, or bring his authors for what he said" (Birch, *James*, 1:208–13). This display of parrhesia apparently brought no reprisals. Instead, within a year Bayly found himself rector of a London parish (St. Matthew's Friday Street). In 1616 James made him a royal chaplain; soon thereafter, he was created bishop of Bangor, at which post he remained until his death a quarter-century later. He had a difficult time in Bangor, where he got caught up in longstanding personal and political quarrels—quarrels that would seem to lie behind the several accusations of grave misconduct made against him. In the 1626 Parliament, a Welsh MP charged him with simony, incontinency, licensing incestuous marriages, bribery, and extortion (Birch, *Charles*, 1:96); since the matter was allowed to drop, it is impossible to know to what extent the allegations were malicious. In 1621 Bayly did end up in Fleet prison, but this was for opposing the Book of Sports.

~~~

Bayly's title to the House of Fame rests solely on *The practice of piety*, which probably dates from 1611 to 1612 and by 1821 had come out in at least seventy-four editions and been translated into a half-dozen languages, including, in 1665, Algonquin. Bayly dedicated the volume to Prince Charles;[1] a copy of one of its morning prayers in the royal hand survives among the state papers—and at the close of *Eikon Basilike*, in the section entitled "Prayers used by his Majesty in the time of his suffering," where it follows the prayer from Sidney's *Arcadia* that so offended Milton (Smart).

The work is generally considered a classic of puritan spirituality. Bayly is an unbending Sabbatarian and enemy of profane amusements like play-going, dancing, bear-baiting, and maypoles; he extols preaching, depicts good works as signs of election, treats faith as assurance of one's own election, regards the elect as a tiny minority even among professed Christians, and requires for salvation a quite extraordinary theological competence (see the eighty pages of Trinitarian speculation with which *The practice of piety* begins). At moments, puritanism's subversive edge makes itself felt—as, for example, in Bayly's claim that the religion of England's governing elite carries "the multitude down right to hell" <130>. It was precisely Prynne's analogous insinuations in *Histriomastix* that cost him his ears in 1632.

Yet these puritan threads are woven into a more complex and multi-stranded fabric. Long stretches of *The practice of piety* lack distinctive godly coloration. Much of the work could have been written (and, indeed, often was written) centuries earlier: Bayly's flat-earth arguments for the Last Judgment's occurring near Jerusalem sound more Carolingian than Calvinist <121>. Indeed, Bayly himself takes pains to insist that the work was not a *parti-pris* contribution to post-Reformation apologetics but rather an attempt to recover "the *old Practice of true PIETY*, which flourished before these controversies were hatched" <Ep. ded.>. His picture of the wretchedness of fallen existence, graphic depictions of heaven and hell, and ascetic ideal of holiness all have roots extending deep into the Middle Ages. Elsewhere Calvinist and pre-Reformation formulations sit side by side without noticeable tension: the same chapter that treats works as signs of election also speaks of them *Everyman*-style as accompanying souls to heaven to "receive their reward" <118>. Moreover, although Bayly argues passionately for strict Sabbath observance, he betrays a striking ambivalence about core Reformation doctrines; he says almost nothing about free grace or justification by faith alone, but instead devotes one chapter after another to sanctification, the necessity of works for salvation,[2] and *fides caritate formata*, as well as strongly implying that grace is not irresistible: that those damned for their sins could have done otherwise, that they had grace sufficient to have done otherwise <127–28>.[3] Bayly often seems to share Christopher Dow's concern that solifidianism encouraged moral laxity and presumptuous security. *The practice of piety* urges legalism and anxiety.

The work feels, as it were, puritanical, but not exactly Protestant. Yet I do not at all mean to imply that Bayly was, without knowing it, of the Arminian party. *The practice* is not arguing against theological error but against secularism: the love of this world and its pleasures. The historiographic focus on doctrinal controversy and denominational

---

[1] Since Bayly served as chaplain to Prince Henry, the dedication to Charles suggests that the first edition came out after the former's death in late 1612.

[2] On antinomianism as a reaction against precisely this sort of godly piety, see the works by Como and Bozeman listed under Sources for the John Everard readings.

[3] Peter Lake notes a similar phenomenon in Elizabethan Calvinist preaching (*Moderate puritans* 151–53); see also Preston's *Plenitudo fontis* <infra>.

identities has left worldliness a non-issue, yet Bayly was scarcely the only early Stuart writer to identify this as the great spiritual danger of the age.[4] This targeting of worldliness—of carnal security, religious indifference, and absorption in the things of this life—explains the terror tactics of Bayly's rhetoric, which uses the full acoustic and dramatic resources of the grand style to shake the soul with violence sufficient to make it take heed.

Two further aspects of Bayly's manual deserve brief comment. First, its brief discussion of how to read Holy Scripture has nothing in common with the literal-historical hermeneutic often associated with Protestantism; it does, however, closely resemble the intensely personalized textual engagements of George Herbert's "The Holy Scriptures":

> for in ev'ry thing
> Thy words do find me out, and parallels bring,
> And in another make me understood.

Second, Bayly's chapters defending Sabbatarianism mix the expected biblical proof-texting and theater-of-God's-judgments providentialism with appeals to both ecclesiastical tradition and the cutting-edge chronological scholarship of the *res publica litterarum*.

Sources: *ODNB*; Thomas Birch, *The court and times of James the First*, 2 vols. (London, 1848) and *The court and times of Charles the First*, 2 vols. (London, 1848); Andrew Clark, ed., *Register of the University of Oxford*, vol. 2, pt. 1 (Oxford UP, 1887); Anthony Grafton, *Joseph Scaliger: a study in the history of classical scholarship*, 2 vols. (Oxford UP, 1983–93); Shuger, *Censorship*; James Simpson, *Burning to read: English fundamentalism and its Reformation opponents* (Harvard UP, 2007); John S. Smart, "Milton and the King's prayer," *RES* 1.4 (1925): 385–91.

---

[4] It is perhaps above all in lay-authored texts that worldliness presents itself as the main threat to Christianity (see, e.g., such early Stuart plays as Philip Massinger's *Renegado* and Thomas Dekker's *The virgin martyr*).

LEWIS BAYLY

The practice of piety directing a Christian how to walk that he may please God
1611–12 [first extant edition, 1613]

To the high and mighty Prince CHARLES, Prince of WALES:

CHRIST JESUS, the Prince of princes, bless your Highness with length of days and an increase of all graces, which may make you truly prosperous in this life and eternally happy in that which is to come.

Jonathan shot three arrows to drive David further off from Saul's fury, and this is the third epistle which I have written to draw your Highness nearer to God's favor, by directing your heart to *begin* (like Josiah) *in your youth to seek after the God of David* (and of Jacob) *your father.* Not but that I know that your Highness doth this without mine admonition, but because I would with the Apostle have you *to abound in every grace, in faith and knowledge, and in all diligence, and in your love to God's service and true religion.* Never was there more need of plain and unfeigned admonitions, for the Comic in that saying seems but to have prophesied of our times: *Obsequium amicos, veritas odium parit.*[1] And no marvel, seeing that we are fallen into the dregs of time, which being the last, must needs be the worst days. And how can there be worse, seeing vanity knows not how to be vainer, nor wickedness how to be more wicked? And whereas heretofore those have been counted most holy who have shewed themselves most zealous in their religion; they are now reputed most discreet who can make the least profession of their faith. And that these are the last days appears evidently, because that security of men's eternal state hath so overwhelmed (as CHRIST foretold it should) all sorts, that most who now live are become *lovers of pleasures more than lovers of God.* And of those who pretend to love GOD, O God, what sanctified heart can but bleed to behold how seldom they come to prayers? how irreverently they hear God's word? what strangers they are at the Lord's table? what assiduous spectators they are at stage-plays? where, being Christians, they can sport themselves to hear the vassals of the devil scoffing religion and blasphemously abusing phrases

---

[1] {Flattery finds one friends; truth, hatred (Terence, *Andria*)}

108

of holy Scripture on their stages as familiarly as they use their tobacco-pipes in their bibbing-houses.[2] So that he who would nowadays seek in most Christians for the power, shall scarce almost find the very shew of godliness. . . . And if the Bridegroom should now come, how many (who think themselves wise enough, and full of all knowledge) would be found foolish virgins, without one drop of the oil of saving faith in their lamps? For the greatest wisdom of most men in this age consists in being wise, first, to deceive others, and, in the end, to deceive themselves.

And if sometimes some good book haps into their hands or some good motion comes into their heads, whereby they are put in mind to consider the uncertainty of this life present or how weak assurance they have of eternal life if this were ended, and how they have some secret sins for which they must needs repent here or be punished for them in hell hereafter, Security then forthwith whispers the hypocrite in the ear that, though it be fit to think of these things, yet *it is not yet time*, and that he is yet *young enough* (though he cannot but know that many millions as young as himself are already in hell for want of timely repentance). Presumption warrants him in the other ear that *he may have time here-after at his leisure to repent*, and that howsoever others die, yet he is *far enough* from *death* and therefore may *boldly* take yet a *longer time to enjoy his sweet pleasures and to increase his wealth and greatness.* And hereupon, like Solomon's sluggard, he yields himself to *a little more sleep, a little more slumber, a little more folding of the hands to sleep* in his former sins; till at last Despair (Security's ugly handmaid) comes in unlooked-for & shews him his hour-glass, dolefully telling him that *his time is past* and that nothing now remains but to die and be damned. Let not this seem strange to any, for too many have found it too true; & more, without more grace, are like to be thus soothed to their end; and in the end, snared to their endless perdition.

In my desire therefore of the common salvation, but especially of your Highness' ever-lasting welfare, I have endeavored to extract out of the chaos of endless controversies, the *old Practice of true PIETY*, which flourished before these controversies were hatched. . . . If to be pious hath in all ages been held true honor, how much more honorable is it, in so impious an age, to be the true patron and pattern of piety? Piety made David, Solomon, Jehoshaphat, Ezekias, Josiah, Zerubbabel, Constantine, Theodosius, Edward VI, Queen Elizabeth, Prince Henry, and other religious princes to be so honored that their *names* (since their deaths) *smells* in the Church of God like a *precious ointment*, and *their remembrance is sweet as honey in all mouths, and as music at a banquet of wine*; when as the lives of others who have been godless and irreligious princes do rot and stink in the memory of God's people. And what honor is it for great men to have great titles on earth, when God counts their names unworthy to be written in his *book of life* in heaven?

It is piety that embalms a prince his good name and makes his face to shine before men and glorifieth his soul among angels. For as Moses' face by *often talking* with God shined in the eyes of the people, so by *frequent praying* (which is our talking with God) and *hearing the word* (which is God's speaking unto us), *we shall be changed from glory to glory by the Spirit of the Lord, to the image of the Lord.* And seeing this life is uncertain to all (especially to princes), what argument is more fit both for princes and people to study

---

[2] [Therefore Tertullian in cap. 26 calls the stage *diaboli ecclesiam* and *cathedram pestilentiarum* {the church of the devil and seat of plagues}.]

than that which teacheth sinful man to deny himself by mortifying his corruption, that he may enjoy Christ, the author of his salvation? To renounce these false and momentary pleasures of the world, that he may attain to the true and eternal joys of heaven? . . . How can piety but promise to herself a zealous patron of your Highness, being the sole son and heir of so gracious and great a monarch, who is not only the defender of the faith by title, but also a defender of the faith in *truth*, as the Christian world hath taken notice by his learned confuting of Bellarmine's overspreading heresies and his suppressing in the blade of Vorstius' athean[3] blasphemies?[4] . . . And let that exhortation of David to his son Solomon be ever in your princely mind: *And thou Solomon my son, know thou the God of thy Father, and serve him with a perfect heart, and with a willing mind: for the LORD searcheth all hearts and understandeth all the imaginations of the thoughts; if thou seek him, he will be found of thee, but if thou forsake him, he will cast thee off forever.*

To help you the better to seek and to serve this GOD Almighty, who must be your chief protector in life and only comfort in death, I here once again, on my bended knees, offer my old mite new stampt into your Highness' hands: daily for your Highness offering up unto the most HIGH, my humblest prayers that as you *grow in age and stature*, so you may (like your Master) *increase in wisdom and favor with God and all good men.* This suit will I never cease. In all other matters I will ever rest,

Your Highness' humble servant, during life, to be commanded. Lewis Bayly.

><><

Ad CAROLVM Principem.

Tolle malos, extolle pios, cognosce teipsum.
Sacra tene, paci consule, disce pati.[5]

THE PRACTICE OF PIETY
Directing a CHRISTIAN how to walk, that he may please GOD

Whoever thou art that lookest into this book, never undertake to read it unless thou first resolvest to become from thy heart an unfeigned practitioner of piety. Yet read it, and that speedily, least before thou hast read it over, God (by some unexpected death) cut thee off for thine inveterate impiety.

Unless that a man doth truly know God, he neither can nor will worship him aright: for how can a man love him whom he knoweth not [Bucer in Ps. 115]? and who will worship him, whose help a man thinks he needeth not? and how shall a man seek remedy by

---

[3] {atheistic}

[4] {Conrad Vorstius (1569–1622) was a Dutch Arminian theologian whose books King James had had publicly burned in 1612, apparently because some of his views seemed to nibble away at the divinity of Christ.}

[5] {To Prince Charles. Banish the wicked, embrace the good, know yourself. Hold fast to that which is holy, seek peace, learn to suffer.}

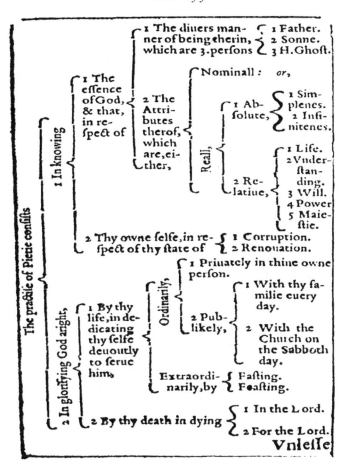

grace, who never understood his misery by nature? Therefore (saith the Apostle) *he that cometh to God must believe that God is and that he is a rewarder of them that seek him.*

And for as much as there can be no true piety without the knowledge of GOD, nor any good practice without the knowledge of a man's own self, we will therefore lay down the knowledge of God's majesty and man's misery as the first and chiefest grounds of the *practice of piety.*

A plain description of the essence and attributes of GOD out of the holy Scriptures, so far forth as every Christian must competently know and necessarily believe that will be saved

Although no creature can define what God is because he is incomprehensible and dwelling in inaccessible light, yet it hath pleased his Majesty to reveal himself in his word unto us so far as our weak capacity can best conceive him. Thus:

God is that one spiritual and infinitely perfect essence, whose being is of himself eternally.

In the divine essence we are to consider two things: first, the divers manner of being therein; secondly, the attributes thereof.

The divers manner of being therein are called Persons.

A Person is a distinct subsistence of the whole Godhead.

111

There are three divine Persons: the Father, the Son, and the Holy Ghost. These three Persons are not three several substances, but three distinct subsistences or three divers manner of beings of one and the same substance and divine essence. So that a Person in the Godhead is an individual understanding and incommunicable subsistence, living of itself, and not sustained by another.[6]

‡

Meditations of the misery of a man not reconciled to God in Christ

O wretched man, where shall I begin to describe thine endless misery! Who art condemned as soon as conceived, and adjudged to eternal death before thou wast born to a temporal life [*damnatus antequam natus.* Aug.]. A beginning indeed I find but no end of thy miseries. For when Adam and Eve being created after God's own image and placed in Paradise that they and their posterity might live in a blessed state of life immortal, having dominion of all earthly creatures and only restrained from the fruit of one tree as a sign of their subjection to their Almighty Creator, though God forbad them this one small thing under the penalty of eternal death, yet they believed the devil's word before the word of God, making God (as much as in them lay) a liar. And so being unthankful for all the benefits which God bestowed on them, they became malcontented with their present state, as if God had dealt enviously or niggardly with them; and believed that the devil would make them partakers of far more glorious things than ever God had bestowed upon them; and in their pride they fell into high treason against the most high, and disdaining to be God's subjects, they affected blasphemously to be gods themselves, equals unto God. Hence, till they repented (losing God's image), they became like unto the devil: and so all their posterity, as a traitorous brood (whilest they remain impenitent, like thee), are subject in this life to all cursed miseries, and in the life to come to the everlasting fire prepared for the devil and his angels.

Lay then aside for a while thy doting vanities, and take a view with me of thy doleful miseries; which daily surveyed, I doubt not but that thou wilt conclude that it is far better never to have nature's being than not to be by grace a practitioner of religious piety.

. . .

Meditations of the misery of infancy

What wast thou being an infant but a brute having the shape of a man? Was not thy body conceived in the heat of lust, the secret of shame, and stain of original sin? And thus wast thou cast naked upon the earth, all imbrued in the blood of filthiness (filthy indeed, when the Son of God, who disdained not to take on him man's nature and the infirmities thereof, yet thought it unbeseeming his holiness to be conceived after the sinful manner of man's conception), so that thy mother was ashamed to let thee know the manner thereof. What cause then hast thou to boast of thy birth, which was a cursed pain to thy

---

[6] {This summary of the knowledge that all adult Christians must have as a prerequisite for salvation continues for another 68 pages (see Dod <11>). Bayly's sources, given in the margins, include Augustine, Gabriel Biel, Hermes Trismegistus, Zanchius, Scaliger, Aquinas, Anselm, Bartholomew Keckerman, pseudo-Aristotle, St. Bernard, Johan Heinrich Alsted, Justin Martyr, Dionysius the Areopagite, Thomas à Kempis, and Boethius.}

mother and to thyself the entrance into a troublesome life? the greatness of which miseries, because thou couldst not utter in words, thou didst express (as well as thou couldest) in weeping tears.

Meditations of the miseries of youth

What is youth but an untamed beast, all whose actions are rash and rude, not capable of good counsel when it is given, and ape-like delighting in nothing but in toys and baubles? Therefore thou no sooner beganst to have a little strength and discretion, but forthwith thou wast kept under the rod and fear of parents and masters, as if thou hadst been born to live under the discipline of others rather than at the disposition of thine own will. No tired horse was ever more willing to be rid of his burthen than thou wast to get out of the servile state of this bondage. A state not worth the description.

Meditations of the miseries of manhood

What is man's state but a sea wherein (as waves) one trouble ariseth in the neck of another, the latter worse then the former? No sooner didst thou enter into the affairs of this world, but thou wast enwrapped about with a cloud of miseries. Thy *flesh* provokes thee to lust, the *world* allures thee to pleasures, and the *devil* tempts thee to all kind of sins; fears of enemies affright thee, suits in law do vex thee, wrongs of ill neighbors do oppress thee, cares for wife and children do consume thee, and disquietness twixt open foes and false friends do in a manner confound thee. Sin stings thee within, Satan lays snares before thee, conscience of sins past dogs behind thee. Now adversity on thy left hand frets thee; anon prosperity on thy right hand flatters thee. Over thy head God's vengeance due to thy sins is ready to fall upon thee; and under thy feet hell-mouth is ready to swallow thee up. And in this miserable estate, whither wilt thou go for rest and comfort? The house is full of cares, the field full of toil, the country of rudeness, the city of factions, the Court of envy, the Church of sects, the sea of pirates, the land of robbers. Or in what state wilt thou live, seeing wealth is envied and poverty is contemned; wit is distrusted and simplicity is derided; superstition is mocked and religion is suspected; vice is advanced and virtue is disgraced? Oh with what a body of sin art thou compassed about in a world of wickedness? What are thine eyes but windows to behold vanities? What are thine ears but flood-gates to let in the stream of iniquity? What are thy senses but matches to give fire to thy lusts? What is thine heart but the anvil whereon Satan hath forged the ugly shape of all lewd affections? Art thou nobly descended? Thou must put thyself in peril of foreign wars to get the reputation of earthly honor, oft times hazard thy life in a desperate combat to avoid the aspersion of a coward. Art thou born in mean estate? Lord! what pains and drudgery must thou endure at home and abroad to get maintenance, and all perhaps scarce sufficient to serve thy necessity? And when after much service and labor a man hath got something, how little certainty is there in that which is gotten—seeing thou seest by daily experience that he who was rich yesterday is today a beggar; he that yesterday was in health, today is sick. . . . and thou knowest not how soon nor in what manner thou shalt die thyself. And who can enumerate the losses, crosses, griefs, disgraces, sickness, and calamities which are incident to sinful man? To speak nothing of the death of friends and children, which oft times seems to be unto us far more bitter than present death itself. . . .

‡

Meditations of the misery of a man after death, which is the fullness of cursedness

. . .

[The damned soul's apostrophe to her body at their second meeting]: O sink of sin, O lump of filthiness (will the soul say unto her body), how am I compelled to re-enter unto thee, not as an habitation to rest but as a prison to be tormented together? How dost thou appear in my sight like Jephthah's daughter, to my greater torment {Judges 11:35}? Would God thou hadst perpetually rotted in thy grave, that I might never have seen thee again! How shall we be confounded together to hear, before God, angels, and men laid open, all those secret sins which we committed together! Have I lost heaven for the love of such a stinking carrion? Art thou the flesh for whose pleasures I have yielded to commit so many fornications? O filthy belly! how became I such a fool as to make thee my God? How mad was I for momentary joys to incur these torments of eternal pains? *Ye rocks and mountains, why skip ye so like rams* (Psal. 114:4) and will not fall upon me to hide me from the face of him that comes to sit on yonder throne; for the great day of his wrath is come, and who shall be able to stand (Apoc. 6:16-17)? *Why tremblest thou thus, O Earth, at the presence of the Lord*, and wilt not open thy mouth and swallow me up as thou didst Korah, that I be seen no more?

O damned Furies! I would ye might without delay tear me in pieces, on condition that you would tear me unto nothing! But whilest thou art thus in vain bewailing thy misery, the angels hale thee violently away from the brink of thy grave to some place near the tribunal seat of Christ, where . . . Christ shall rip up[7] all the benefits he bestowed on thee and the torments he suffered for thee and all the good deeds which thou omitted and all the ungrateful villainies which thou didst commit against him and his holy laws.

Within thee thine own conscience (more then a thousand witness) shall accuse thee. The devils who tempted thee to all thy lewdness shall on the one side testify with thy conscience against thee; and on the other side shall stand the holy saints and angels approving Christ's justice and detesting so filthy a creature. Behind thee an hideous noise of innumerable fellow-damned reprobates tarrying for thy company. Before thee all the world burning in flaming fire. Above thee, an ireful Judge of deserved vengeance ready to pronounce his sentence upon thee. Beneath thee, the fiery & sulphurous mouth of the bottomless pit gaping to receive thee. In this woeful estate, to hide thyself will be impossible (for on that condition thou wouldest wish that the greatest rock might fall upon thee); to appear will be intolerable, and yet thou must stand forth to receive with other reprobates this thy sentence: *Depart from me ye cursed, into everlasting fire, prepared for the devil and his angels* [Bonavent. *postill. Dom. 3. post Pent. Serm. 2*].

. . .

O terrible sentence! from which the condemned cannot escape; which being pronounced cannot possibly be withstood; against which a man cannot except, and from which a man can nowhere appeal. So that to the damned nothing remains but hellish torments, which knows neither ease of pain nor end of time. From this judgment-seat thou must be thrust by angels (together with all the damned devils and reprobates) into the bottomless lake of utter darkness that perpetually burns with fire and brimstone. Whereunto as they shall be thrust, there shall be such weeping, woes, and wailing, that

---

[7] {disclose, lay bare}

the cry of the company of Korah, Dathan, & Abiram when the earth swallowed them up was nothing comparable to this howling. Nay, it will seem unto thee a hell, before thou goest into hell, but to hear it.

Into which bottomless lake after that thou art once plunged, thou shalt ever be falling down and never meet a bottom; and in it, thou shalt ever lament, and none shall pity thee; thou shalt always *weep* for the pain of fire and yet gnash thy teeth for the extremity of cold. Thou shalt *weep* to think that thy miseries are past remedy; thou shalt *weep* to think that to repent is to no purpose; thou shalt *weep* to think how for the shadows of short pleasures, thou hast incurred these sorrows of eternal pains; thou shalt *weep* to see how that *weeping* itself can nothing prevail. Yea, in *weeping* thou shalt *weep* more tears than there is water in the sea; for the water of the sea is finite, but the *weeping* of a reprobate shall be *infinite*.

There thy lascivious eyes shall be afflicted with sights of ghastly spirits, thy curious ears shall be affrighted with hideous noise of howling devils and the gnashing teeth of damned reprobates; thy dainty nose shall be cloyed with noisome stench of sulphur; thy delicate taste shall be pained with intolerable hunger; thy drunken throat shall be parched with unquenchable thirst. Thy mind shall be tormented to think how for the love of abortive pleasures, which perished ere they budded, thou so foolishly lost heaven's joys and incurred hellish pains which last beyond eternity. Thy conscience shall ever sting thee like an adder when thou thinkest how often Christ by his preachers offered the remission of sins and the kingdom of heaven freely unto thee, if thou wouldest but believe and repent, and how easily thou mightest have obtained mercy in those days, how near thou wast many times to have repented, and yet didst suffer the devil and the world to keep thee still in impenitency; and how the day of mercy is now past and will never dawn again.

How shall thy understanding be racked to consider how for momentary riches thou hast lost the eternal treasure and changed heaven's felicity for hell's misery, where every part of thy body without intermission of pain shall be continually tormented alike.

In these hellish torments thou shalt be forever deprived of the beatifical sight of God, wherein consists the sovereign good and life of the soul. Thou shalt never see light, nor the least sight of joy, but lie in a perpetual prison of utter darkness, where shall be no order but horror, no voice but of blasphemers & howlers, no noise but of torturers and tortured—no society but of the devil and his angels, who being tormented themselves, shall have no other ease but to wreak their fury in tormenting thee. Where shall be *punishment* without *pity*, *misery* without *mercy*, *sorrow* without *succor*, *crying* without *comfort*, *mischief* without *measure*, *torment* without *ease*: where the *worm dieth not, and the fire is never quenched*; where the wrath of God shall seize upon thy soul and body as the flame of fire doth on the lump of pitch or brimstone, in which flame thou shalt ever be burning and never consumed, ever dying and never dead . . . nor knowing end of thy pains: so that after thou hast endured them so many thousand years as there are grass on the earth or sands on the sea-shore, thou art no nearer to have an end of thy torments than thou wast the first day that thou wast cast into them. Yea, so far are they from ending, that they are ever but beginning. But if after a thousand times so many thousand years, thy damned soul could but conceive a hope that those her torments should have an end, this would be some comfort, to think that at length an end will come. But as oft as the mind thinketh of this word *Never*, it is as another hell in the midst of hell.

This thought shall force the damned to cry όιαì, όιαì,[8] as much as if they should say, όυν άεì όυν άεì, O Lord, *not ever, not ever* torment us thus; but their *conscience* shall answer them as an echo άεì άεì, *ever, ever*. Hence shall arise their doleful όυαì, *woe* and *alas* for evermore!

This is that second death, the general perfect fullness of all cursedness and misery, which every damned reprobate must suffer so long as God and his saints shall enjoy bliss and felicity in heaven for evermore.

Thus far of the misery of man in his state of corruption, unless that he be renewed by grace in Christ.

Now follows the knowledge of man's self in respect of his state of regeneration by Christ.

Meditations of the state of a Christian reconciled to God in Christ

Now let us see how happy a godly man is in his state of renovation, being reconciled to God in Christ.

The godly man whose corrupt nature is renewed by grace in Christ and become a new creature is blessed in a three-fold respect. First, in his life. Secondly, in his death. Thirdly, after death.

His blessedness during this life is but in part, and that consists in seven things:

1. Because he is conceived of the Spirit in the womb of his mother, the Church, and is born not of *blood nor of the will of the flesh nor of the will of man but of* GOD, who in Christ is his father. So that the image of God his Father is renewed in him every day more and more.

2. He hath, for the merits of Christ's sufferings, all his sins, original and actual, with the guilt and punishment belonging to them, freely and fully forgiven unto him. And all the righteousness of Christ as freely and fully imputed unto him; and so God is reconciled unto him and approveth him as righteous in his sight and account.

3. He is freed from Satan's bondage and is made a brother of Christ, a *fellow heir* of his heavenly kingdom, and a *spiritual king* and *priest* to offer up *spiritual sacrifices* to God by Jesus Christ.

4. God spareth him as a man spareth his own son that serveth him. And this sparing consists in:

    1. not taking notice of every fault, but bearing with his infirmities (Exod. 34:6-7). A loving father will not cast his child out of doors in his sickness.

    2. not making his punishment when he is chastened as great as his deserts (Psalm 103:10).

    3. chastening him moderately when he seeth that he will not by any other means be reclaimed (2 Sam. 7:14, 15; 1 Cor. 11:32).

    4. graciously accepting his endeavors, notwithstanding the imperfection of his obedience; and so preferring the willingness of the mind more than the worthiness of the work (2 Cor. 8:12).

---

[8] {Alas, woe is me (Rev. 8:13).}

5. turning the curses which he deserved to crosses and to fatherly corrections: yea, all things, all calamities of this life, death itself; yea, his very sins unto his good.

5. God gives him his Holy Spirit, which

   1. sanctifieth him by degrees throughout, so that he doth more and more die to sin and live to righteousness.

   2. assures him of his adoption and that he is by grace the child of God.

   3. encourageth him to come with boldness and confidence into the presence of GOD.

   4. moveth him without fear to say unto him *Abba, Father.*

   5. poureth into his heart the gift of sanctified prayer.

   6. persuadeth him that both he and his prayers are accepted and heard of God, for Christ his Mediator's sake.

   7. fills him with

      1. peace of conscience.

      2. joy in the Holy Ghost, in comparison whereof all earthly joys seem vile & vain unto him.

6. He hath a recovery of his sovereignty over the creatures, which he lost by Adam's fall; & from thence, free liberty of using all things which God hath not restrained, so that he may use them with a good conscience. For to all things in heaven and earth he hath a sure title in this life, and he shall have the plenary and peaceable possession of them in the life to come. Hence it is that all reprobates are but usurpers of all that they possess and have no place of their own but hell.

7. He hath the assurance of God's fatherly care and protection day and night over him; which care consisteth in three things.

   1. in providing all things necessary for his soul and body concerning this life and that which is to come, so that he shall be sure, ever, either to have enough or patience to be content with that he hath.

   2. in that God gives his holy angels, as his ministers, a charge to attend upon him always for his good: yea, in danger, to *pitch their tents about him for his safety* wherever he be. Yea, God's protection shall defend him as a *cloud by day and as a pillar of fire by night*, and his providence *shall hedge him from the power of the devil.*

   3. in that the *eyes of the Lord are upon him and his ears continually open to see his state* and to hear his complaint, and in his good time to deliver him out of all his troubles.

Thus far of the blessed estate of the godly and regenerated man in this life. Now of his blessed estate in death.

Meditations of the blessed estate of a regenerate man in his death

When GOD sends death as his messenger for the regenerated man, he meets him half the way to heaven, for his conversation {conduct} and affection is there before him. . . . To die, unto him, therefore, is nothing else in effect but to rest from his labor in this world, to go home to his *father's house*, unto the *city of the living God, the heavenly Jerusalem, to an innumerable company of angels, to the general assembly and Church of the first born, to God the judge of all, and to the spirits of just men made perfect, and to Jesus the Mediator of the New Testament.* Whilest his body is sick, his mind is sound, for God maketh all his bed in his sickness and strengtheneth him with faith and patience upon his bed of sorrow; and when he begins to enter into the *way of all the world*, he giveth (like Jacob, Moses, and Joshua) to his children and friends, godly exhortations and counsels to serve the true God, to worship him truly all the days of their life. His blessed soul breatheth nothing but blessings and such speeches as savors a sanctified spirit. As his outward man decayeth, so his inward man increaseth and waxeth stronger. When the speech of his tongue faltereth, the sighs of his heart speaketh louder unto God; when the sight of the eyes faileth, the Holy Ghost illuminates him inwardly with abundance of spiritual light. . . . And when the appointed time of his dissolution is come, knowing that he goeth to his Father and Redeemer in the peace of a good conscience and the assured persuasion of the forgiveness of all his sins in the *blood of the Lamb*, he sings with blessed old Simeon his *Nunc dimittis: Lord, now lettest thou thy servant depart in peace, &c.* And surrenders up his soul, as it were with his own hands, into the hands of his heavenly Father. . . . He no sooner yields up his sacred ghost but immediately the holy angels, who attended upon him from his birth unto his death, carry and accompany his soul into heaven, as they did the soul of Lazarus into Abraham's bosom, which is the kingdom of heaven, whither only good angels and good works do accompany the soul: the one to deliver their charge, the other to receive their reward.

. . .

Meditations of the blessed estate of the regenerated man after death

This state hath three degrees:

1. from the day of death to the resurrection.
2. from the resurrection to the pronouncing of the sentence.
3. after the sentence, which lasts eternally.

As soon as ever the regenerated man hath yielded up his soul unto Christ, the holy angels take her[9] into their custody and immediately carry her into heaven, and there present her before Christ, where she is crowned with a crown of righteousness and glory—not which she hath deserved by her good works, but which God hath promised of his free goodness to all those who, of love, have in this life unfainedly served him and sought his glory.

Oh, what joy will it be to thy soul, which was wont to see but misery, and sinners, now to behold the face of the God of glory! Yea, to see Christ welcoming thee as soon as thou art presented before him by the holy angels, with an *Euge bone serve! Well done and well-come, good and faithful servant, &c. Enter into thy master's joy!* And what joy will this be, to behold *thousand thousands* of *Cherubims, Seraphims, Angels, Thrones, Dominions, Principalities, Powers*; all the *holy patriarchs, priests, prophets, apostles, martyrs, professors*, and all the *souls* of thy *friends, parents, husbands, wives, children*, and the rest of God's *saints* who departed before thee in the true faith of Christ, standing before God's throne in bliss and glory? If the Queen of Sheba, beholding the glory and attendance given to Solomon, as it were ravished therewith, brake out and said, *Happy are thy men, happy are these thy servants, which stand ever before thee and hear thy wisdom!* how shall thy soul be ravished

[9] {i.e., the soul}

to see herself by *grace* admitted to stand with this glorious company! to behold the blessed face of Christ, and to hear all the treasures of his divine wisdom! How shalt thou rejoice to see so many thousand thousands welcoming thee into their heavenly society! for as they all rejoiced at thy conversion, so will they now be much more joyful to behold thy coronation and to see thee receive thy crown which was laid up for thee against thy coming. For there the crown of martyrdom shall be put on the head of a martyr who for Christ's Gospel's sake endured torments; the crown of virginity on the head of a virgin, which subdued concupiscence; the crown of piety and chastity on the head of them who sincerely professed Christ and kept their wedlock-bed undefiled; the crown of good-works on the good alms-giver's head who liberally relieved the poor; the crown of incorruptible glory on the head of those pastors, who by their preaching and good example, have converted souls from the corruption of sin to glorify God in holiness of life. Who can sufficiently express the rejoicing of this heavenly company to see thee thus crowned with glory, arrayed with the shining robe of righteousness, and to behold the palm of victory put into thy hand? Oh what gratulation will there be that thou hast escaped all the miseries of the world, the snares of the devil, the pains of hell, and obtained with them thy eternal rest and happiness! For there everyone joyeth as much in another's happiness as in his own, because he shall see him as much loved of God as himself. Yea, they have as many distinct joys as they have copartners of their joy. And in this joyful and blessed state, the soul resteth with Christ in heaven till the resurrection when as the number of her fellow-servants and brethren be fulfilled, which the Lord termeth but a *little season*.

The second degree of man's blessedness after death is from the resurrection to the pronouncing of the final sentence. For at the last day:

1. The elementary {material} heavens, earth, and all things therein shall be *dissolved*, and *purified with fire*.
2. At the sound of the *last trumpet* or voice of Christ the Archangel, the very same bodies which the elect had before (though turned to dust and earth) shall arise again; and in the same instant every man's soul shall re-enter into his own body, by virtue of the resurrection of Christ their head, and be made alive and rise out of their graves as if they did but awake out of their beds. And howsoever tyrants bemangled their bodies in pieces or consumed them to ashes, yet shall the elect find it true at that day, that *not a hair of their head is perished*.
3. They shall come forth out of their graves like so many Josephs out of prison or Daniels out of the lion's dens or Jonahs out of whales' bellies.

   . . .

5. The bodies of the elect being thus raised shall have four most excellent and supernatural qualities. For

   1. they shall be raised in power, whereby they shall forever be freed from all wants and weakness, and enabled to continue without the use of meat, drink, sleep, and other former helps.
   2. in incorruption, whereby they shall never be subject to any manner of imperfections, blemish, sickness, or death.
   3. in glory, whereby their bodies shall shine as bright as the *sun in the firmament*; and which being made transparent, their souls shall shine through far more

glorious than their bodies. Three glimpses of which glory was seen: first, in Moses' face; secondly, in the Transfiguration; thirdly, in Stephen's countenance. Three instances and assurances of the glorification of our bodies at that glorious day. Then shall David lay aside his shepherd's weed and put on the robe of the king's son, Jesus, not Jonathan. Then every true Mordecai, who mourned under the sackcloth of this corrupt flesh, shall be arrayed with the king's royal apparel and have the crown royal set upon his head, that all the world may see *how it shall be done to him whom the King of kings delighteth to honor.* If now the rising of *one sun* makes the morning so glorious, how glorious shall that day be when innumerable *million* of *millions* of bodies of *saints* and *angels* shall appear more glorious than the *brightness* of the *sun,* the *body* of *Christ* in glory surpassing all.

4. in agility, whereby our bodies shall be able to ascend and to *meet the Lord at his glorious coming in the air. . . .* To this agility of the saints' glorious bodies the Prophet alludes, saying: *They shall renew their strength; they shall mount up with wings as eagles; they shall run and not be weary; they shall walk, and not faint.* And to this state may that saying of Wisdom be referred: *In the time of their vision they shall shine and run too and fro, as sparks among the stubble.*

And in respect of these four qualities, Paul calleth the raised bodies of the elect "spiritual": for they shall be spiritual in qualities, but the same still in substance.

And howsoever sin and corruption makes a man in this state of mortality *lower than angels,* yet surely when God shall thus *crown him with glory and honor,* I cannot see how man shall be any thing inferior to angels. For are they spirits? So is man also in respect of his soul. Yea more then this, they shall have also a spiritual body *fashioned like unto the glorious body* of the Lord Jesus Christ, in whom man's nature is exalted by a personal union into the glory of the Godhead and individual {indivisible} society of the blessed Trinity. An honor which he never vouchsafed angels. And in this respect man hath a prerogative above them. Nay, they are but spirits appointed to be ministers unto the elect, and as many of them who at the first disdained this office and would not keep their first standing were, for their pride, hurled into hell. This lesseneth not the dignity of angels, but extols the greatness of God's love to mankind.

. . .

Then shall the soul with joyfulness greet her body, saying: Oh well met again, my dear sister, how sweet is thy voice! how comely is thy countenance, having lain hid so long in the clefts of the rocks and in the secret places of the grave! Thou art indeed an habitation fit, not only for me to dwell in, but such as the Holy Ghost thinks meet to reside in as his temple forever. The winter of our affliction is now past; the storm of our misery is blown over and gone. The bodies of our elect brethren appear more glorious than the lily flowers on the earth; the time of singing *Hallelujah* is come; and the voice of the trumpet is heard in the land.[10] Thou hast been my yoke-fellow in the Lord's labors and companion in persecutions and wrongs for Christ and his Gospel's sake; now shall we enter together into our *Master's joy.* As thou hast borne with me the *cross,* so shalt thou now wear with

---

[10] {The paragraph up to this point is a pastiche of quotations and half-quotations from Canticles.}

me the *crown*; as thou hast with me sowed plenteously in *tears*, so shalt thou *reap* with me abundantly in *joy*. O blessed, aye blessed be that God, who (when yonder reprobates spent their whole time in pride, fleshly lusts, eating, drinking and profane vanities) gave us grace to join together in watching, fasting, praying, reading the Scriptures, keeping his Sabbaths, hearing sermons, receiving the holy Communion, relieving the poor, exercising in all humility the works of piety to God, and walking conscionably in the duties of our calling towards men. Thou shalt, anon, hear no mention of thy sins, for they are remitted and covered; but every good work which thou hast done for the Lord's sake shall be rehearsed and rewarded.

Cheer up thy heart, for thy judge is *flesh* of thy *flesh*, and *bone* of thy *bone*. Lift up thy head: behold these glorious angels, like so many Gabriels, flying towards us to tell us that the day of our redemption is come, and to convey us in the clouds, to meet our Redeemer in the air. Lo, they are at hand. *Arise therefore my dove, my love, my fair one, and come away*; and so like *roes* or young *harts*, they run with *angels* towards *Christ* over the trembling mountains of Bether [Cant. 2:17].

. . .

The place whither they shall be gathered unto Christ, and where Christ shall sit in judgment shall be in the air over the valley of Jehoshaphat, by Mount Olivet near unto Jerusalem, eastward from the Temple, as it is probable for four reasons:

1. Because the holy Scripture seems to intimate so much in plain words: *I will gather all nations into the valley of Jehoshaphat.* . . .

2. Because that, as Christ was there-abouts crucified and put to open shame, so over that place his glorious throne should be erected in the air when he shall appear in judgment to manifest his majesty and glory; for it is meet that Christ should in that place judge the world with righteous judgment, where he himself was unjustly judged and condemned.

3. Because, that seeing the angels shall be sent to *gather together the elect from the four winds* . . . it is most probable that the place whither they shall be gathered to shall be near Jerusalem and the valley of Jehoshaphat, which cosmographers describe to be in the midst of the superficies of the earth [the sea beyond Jordan towards Tyre cutteth the midst of the world; and Ezekiel saith of Jerusalem, *In medio gentium posui eam*:[11] that from Zion, as from a center, the Law should be published to all nations, and there all nations shall be judged according to the Law (Rom. 2:12)]. . . .

4. Because the angels told the disciples that, as they saw Christ ascend from Mount Olivet, which is over the valley of Jehoshaphat, so he shall in like manner come down from heaven. This is the opinion of Aquinas and all the Schoolmen, except Lombard and Alexander Hales.

5. Lastly, when Christ is set in his glorious throne and all the many thousands of his saints and angels, shining more bright than so many suns, in glory sitting about him, and the body of Christ in glory and brightness surpassing them all . . . Christ will first pronounce the sentence of absolution and bliss upon the elect.

---

[11] {I have placed her in the midst of the gentiles.}

First, because he will thereby increase the grief of the reprobate that shall hear it; secondly, to shew himself more prone to mercy than to judgment. And thus from his throne of majesty in the air, he shall in the sight and hearing of all the world pronounce unto his elect: *Come ye blessed of my Father, inherit the kingdom prepared for you from the beginning of the world, for, &c.*

   . . .

From this tribunal seat, Christ shall arise and with all his glorious company of elect angels and saints, he shall go up triumphantly in order and array unto the heaven of heavens, with such a heavenly noise and music that now may that song of David be truly verified: *God is gone up with a triumph, the Lord with the sound of the trumpets. Sing praises to God, sing praises; sing praises unto our King, sing praises; for God is the King of all the earth; he is greatly to be exalted.* And that marriage song of John: *Let us be glad and rejoice, and give honor to him, for the marriage of the Lamb is come, and his wife hath made herself ready, Alleluia; for the Lord God omnipotent reigneth.*

The third and last degree of the blessed state of a regenerated man after death begins after the pronouncing of the sentence, and lasteth eternally without all end.

Meditations of the blessed estate of a regenerated man in heaven after he hath received his sentence of absolution before the tribunal seat of Christ at the Last Day of Judgment

Here my meditation dazzleth, and my pen falleth out of my hand: the one being not able to conceive, nor the other to describe that most excellent bliss and *eternal weight of glory* (whereof *all the afflictions of this present life are not worthy*), which all the elect shall with the blessed Trinity enjoy from that time that they shall be received with Christ as joint heirs into that everlasting kingdom of joy.

   Notwithstanding, we may take a scantling thereof, thus.

   . . .

1. Of the Place

The place is the *heaven of heavens*, or the third heaven, called Paradise, whither Christ (in his human nature) ascended far above all visible heavens; *the bridegroom's chamber*, which by the firmament, as by an azured curtain spangled with glittering *stars* and glorious *planets*, is hid that we cannot behold it with these corruptible eyes of flesh. The Holy Ghost (framing himself to our weakness) describes the glory of that place which no man can estimate by such things as are most precious in the estimation of man, and therefore likeneth it to a great and a holy city, named the *heavenly Jerusalem*; where only God and his people who are saved and written in the Lamb's book do inhabit: *all built of pure gold, like unto clear glass or crystal; the walls of jasper stone; the foundations of the walls, with twelve manner of precious stones; having twelve gates, each built of one pearl: three gates towards each of the four corners of the world, and at each gate an angel* (as so many porters), *that no unclean thing should enter into it. It is four square, therefore perfect, the length, the breadth, and height of it are equal, 12000 furlongs every way; therefore glorious and spacious. Through the midst of her streets ever runneth a pure river of the water of life, as clear as crystal; therefore wholesome. And of either side of the river is the tree of life, ever growing, which bears twelve manner of fruits, and gives fruit every month; therefore fruitful. And the leaves of the tree is health to the nations; therefore healthy.* There is therefore no place so glorious by creation, so beautiful with delectation, so rich in possession, so comfortable for habitation. For there the king is Christ; the law is love; the honor, verity; the peace, felicity; the life, eternity. There is light without darkness, mirth without sadness, health without sickness, wealth without want, credit without disgrace, beauty without blemish, ease without labor, riches without rust, blessedness without misery, and consolation that never knoweth end. How truly may we cry out (with David) of this city: *glorious things are spoken of thee, O thou City of God!*...

2. Of the Object

The blissful and glorious object of all intellectual and reasonable creatures in heaven is the Godhead, in Trinity of Persons, without which there is neither joy nor felicity: but the very fullness of joy consisteth in enjoying the same.

This object we shall enjoy two ways:

1. by a beatifical vision of God.
2. by possessing an immediate communion with his divine nature.

The beatifical vision of GOD is that only that can content the infinite mind of man.[12] For everything tendeth to his center. GOD is the center of the soul; therefore (like Noah's dove) she cannot rest nor joy till she return and enjoy him. All that God bestowed upon Moses could not satisfy his mind, unless he might see the face of God. Therefore the whole Church prayeth so earnestly: *God be merciful unto us and bless us & cause his face to shine upon us*. . . . And Christ prayed for all his elect in his last prayer that they might obtain this blessed vision: *Father, I will that they which thou hast given me be* (where?) *even where I am.* (To what end?) *That they may behold that my glory, &c.* If Moses' face did so shine when he had been with God but forty days and seen but his *back parts*, how shall we shine when we shall see him *face to face* forever? and *know him as we are known, and as he is?* Then shall the *soul* no longer be termed *Marah*, bitterness, but *Naomi*, beautifulness: for the Lord shall turn her short bitterness to eternal beauty and blessedness (Ruth 1:20).

The second means to enjoy this object is by having an immediate and an eternal communion with GOD in heaven. . . . And Christ prayeth for his whole Church to obtain it. This communion Saint Paul expresseth in one word, saying *that God shall be all in all unto us*. Indeed, God is now all in all unto us—but by means and in a small measure. But in heaven, God himself immediately (in fullness of measure, without all means) will be unto us all the good things that our souls and bodies can wish or desire. . . . Yea all the strength, wit, pleasures, virtues, colors, beauties, harmony, & goodness that are in men, beasts, fishes, fowls, trees, herbs, and all creatures are nothing but sparkles of those things which are in infinite perfection in GOD.[13] And in him we shall enjoy them in a far more perfect and blessed manner. He himself will then supply their use. Nay, the best creatures (which serve us now) shall not have the honor to serve us then. There will be *no need of the*

---

[12] [*Fecisti nos domine ad te: inquietum igitur est cor nostrum donec requiescat in te* (Aug. *Conf.* lib. 1. cap. 1) {Lord, thou hast made us for thyself, and our hearts are restless until we find our rest in thee.}]

[13] [*Non potest summus rerum conditor in se non habere, quae rebus a se conditis dedit: quemadmodùm sol astris* (Hugo lib. 4 *de anima* cap. 15) {The great Creator of all things cannot lack in himself that which he bestows upon his creation, as the sun [has in itself the light that it bestows upon] the stars.}]

sun nor of the moon to shine in that city, for *the glory of God doth light it*. No more will there be any need or use of any creature when we shall enjoy the Creator himself.

When therefore we behold any thing that is excellent in any creatures, let us say to ourselves: how much more excellent is he who gave them this excellency! When we behold the wisdom of men who over-rule creatures stronger than themselves, out-run the sun and moon (in discourse prescribing many years before in what courses they shall be eclipsed), let us say to ourselves: how admirable is the wisdom of GOD, who made men so wise [Seneca *de beneficiis*, lib. 2. cap. 29]! When we consider the strength of whales and elephants, the tempests of winds & terror of thunder, let us say to ourselves: how strong, how mighty, how terrible is that God that makes these mighty & fearful creatures! When we taste things that are delicately sweet, let us say to ourselves: oh, how sweet is that God from whom all these creatures have received this sweetness! When we behold the admirable colors which are in flowers and birds, and the lovely beauty of women, let us say, how fair is that God that made these so fair!

And if our loving God hath thus provided us so many excellent delights for our passage through this Bochim or valley of tears, what are those pleasures which he hath prepared for us when we shall enter into the palace of our *Master's joy*! How shall our souls be there ravished with the love of so lovely a God! So glorious is the object of heavenly saints! So amiable is the sight of our gracious Savior!

Of the prerogatives which the Elect shall enjoy in heaven

By reason of this communion with God, the elect in heaven shall have four super-excellent prerogatives:

1. They shall have the kingdom of heaven for their inheritance, and they shall be free denizens of the heavenly Jerusalem. . . .
2. They shall be all kings and priests: spiritual kings, to reign with Christ and to triumph over Satan, the world, and reprobates; and spiritual priests, to offer unto God the spiritual sacrifice of praise and thanksgiving forevermore. And therefore they are said to wear both crowns and robes. Oh what a comfort is this to poor parents that have many children! If they breed them up in the fear of God to be true Christians, then are they parents to so many kings and priests.
3. Their bodies shall shine as the brightness of the sun in the firmament: like the glorious body of CHRIST, which shined brighter than the sun at noon when it appeared to Paul. A glimpse of which glorious brightness appeared in the bodies of Moses and Elias transfigured with our Lord in the holy Mount. Therefore (saith the Apostle) it shall rise a *glorious body*; yea, a *spiritual body*, not in substance but in quality, preserved by spiritual means and having (as an angel) agility to ascend or descend. . . .
4. Lastly, they (together with all the holy angels) there keep (without any labor to distract them) a *perpetual Sabbath* to the glory, honor, and praise of the aye blessed Trinity for the *creating, redeeming*, and *sanctifying* of the Church; and for his power, wisdom, justice, mercy, and goodness in the *government* of heaven and earth. When thou hearest a sweet consort of *music*, meditate how happy thou shalt be when (with the choir of heavenly *angels* and *saints*) thou shalt sing a part in that spiritual *Alleluia*, on that eternal blessed Sabbath where there shall be such

variety of pleasures and *satiety* of joys as never know *tediousness* in doing nor *end* in delighting.

Of the effects of those prerogatives

From these prerogatives there will arise to the elect in heaven five notable effects.

1. They shall know God with a perfect knowledge, so far as creatures can possibly comprehend the Creator. . . . And in him we shall know not only all our friends (who died in the faith of Christ) but also all the faithful that ever were or shall be. For

   1. Christ tells the Jews that they shall see Abraham, Isaac, and Jacob, and all the prophets, in the kingdom of God; therefore we shall know them.
   2. Adam in his innocency knew Eve to be *bone of his bone* and *flesh of his flesh* as soon as he awaked. Much more then shall we know our kindred when we shall awake perfected and glorified in the resurrection.
   3. The apostles knew Christ after his resurrection and the *saints which rose with him and appeared in the holy city.*

       . . .

   6. Christ saith that the twelve apostles shall sit upon twelve thrones to *judge* (at that day) *the 12 Tribes*: therefore they shall be known, and consequently the rest of the saints.
   7. Paul saith that at that day *we shall know as we are known of God*, and Augustine (out of this place) comforteth a widow, assuring her that, as in this life she saw her husband with external eyes, so in the life to come she should know *his heart and what were all his thoughts and imaginations.* Then husbands and wives, look to your actions and thoughts, *for all shall be made manifest one day.* See 1 Cor. 4:5.
   8. The faithful in the Old Testament are said to be gathered to their fathers; therefore the knowledge of our friends {kinfolk} remains.[14]
   9. *Love never falleth away*; therefore knowledge, the ground thereof, remains in another life.

. . . Though the respect of diversities of degrees and callings in magistracy, ministry, and oeconomy shall cease. Yea, Christ shall then cease to rule as he is Mediator, and rule all in all as he is God equal with the Father and the Holy Ghost.

   . . .

5. Lastly, they shall enjoy this blissful and glorious estate forevermore. Therefore it is termed *everlasting* life, and Christ saith *that our joy shall no man take from us.* All other joys (be they never so great) have an end. Ahasuerus' feast lasted an hundred and eighty days; but he, and it, and all his joys are gone. For mortal man to be assumed to heavenly glory, to be associated to angels, to be satiated with all delights and joys (but for a time) were much; but to enjoy them forever, without intermission of end, who can hear it and not admire it! who can muse of it and not be amazed at it! All the saints of Christ (as soon as they felt once but a true

---

[14] {On our relation to the dead and the survival of human ties into eternity, see, in this volume, the selections from Donne, Field, and *The survey of London.*}

taste of these eternal joys) counted all the riches and pleasures of this life to be but *loss* and *dung* in respect of that. And therefore (with incessant prayers, fasting, alms-deeds, tears, faith, and good life) they labored to ascertain themselves of this eternal life, and (for the love thereof) they willingly either sold or parted with all their earthly goods and possessions.

‡

Meditations on the hindrances which keep back a sinner from the practice of piety

Those hindrances are chiefly seven.

I. An ignorant mistaking of the true meaning of certain places of the Holy Scripture, and some other chief grounds of Christian religion.

The Scriptures mistaken are these.

1) Ezek. 33:14-16. *At what time soever a sinner repenteth him of his sin, I will blot out all, &c.* Hence the carnal Christian gathereth *that he may repent when he will.* It is true, whensoever a sinner doth repent, God will forgive, but the text saith not that a sinner *may* repent *whensoever* he will, but when God will give him grace. Many (saith the Scripture), when they would have repented, were rejected, and *could not repent though they sought it carefully with tears.* What comfort yields this text to thee, who hast not repented nor knowest whether thou shalt have grace to repent hereafter?

   . . .

4) 1 Tim. 1:15. *Christ Jesus came into the world to save sinners, &c.* True. But such sinners who like Paul are converted from their wicked life, not like thee who still continuest in thy lewdness. For that *grace of God which bringeth salvation unto all men teacheth us that, denying ungodliness and worldly lusts, we should live soberly, righteously, and godly in this present world.*

   . . .

6) Isai. 64:6. *All our righteousness are as filthy rags.* Hence the carnal Christian gathers that, seeing the best works of the best saints are no better, then his are good enough, and therefore he needs not much grieve that his devotions are so imperfect. But Isaiah means not in this place the righteous works of the regenerate—as fervent prayers in the name of God, charitable alms from the bowels of mercy, suffering in the Gospel's defense the spoil of goods and spilling of blood, and such works, which Paul calls the fruit of the Spirit. But the Prophet, making an humble confession in the name of the Jewish Church when she had fallen from God to idolatry, acknowledgeth that whilest they were by their filthy sins separated from God, as lepers are by their infected sores and polluted clothes from men, their chiefest righteousness could not be but abominable in his sight. And though our best works, compared with Christ's righteousness, are no better then *unclean rags*, yet in God's acceptation, for Christ's sake, they are called *white raiment*: yea, *pure fine linen and shining*, far unlike thy leopard's spots and filthy garments.

7) Jam. 3:2. *In many things we sin all.* True. But God's children sins not in all things as thou dost, without either bridling their lusts or mortifying their

corruptions. And though the relics of sin remain in the dearest children of God, that they had need daily to cry, *Our Father which art in heaven, forgive us our trespasses*, yet in the New Testament none are properly called sinners but the unregenerate. But the regenerate, in respect of their zealous endeavor to serve God in unfeigned holiness, are every where called *saints*. Insomuch that Saint John saith that *whosoever is born of God sinneth not.* That is, liveth not in willful filthiness, suffering sin to reign in him, as thou dost. Deceive not thyself with the name of a Christian. Whosoever liveth in any customary gross sin, he liveth not in the state of grace. . . .

. . .

The grounds of religion mistaken are:

I. From the doctrine of justification by faith only, a carnal Christian gathereth *that good works are not necessary.* He commends others that do good works, but he persuades himself that he shall be saved by his faith, without doing any such matters. But he should know that, though good works are not necessary to justification, yet they are necessary to *salvation.* For *we are God's workmanship, created in Christ Jesus unto good works, which God hath predestinated that we should walk in them.* Whosoever therefore in years of discretion bringeth not forth good works after he is called, he cannot be saved, neither was he ever predestinated to life eternal. Therefore the Scripture saith that *Christ will reward every man according to his works.* Christ respects in the angels of the 7 churches nothing but their works. And at the last day he will give the heavenly inheritance only to them who have done good works in feeding the hungry, clothing the naked, &c.[15] At that day, righteousness shall wear the crown. No righteousness, no crown. No good works (according to a man's talent), no reward from God—unless it be vengeance. To be rich in good works is the surest foundation of our assurance to obtain eternal life. For good works are the true fruits of a true faith which apprehendeth Christ and his obedience unto salvation. And no other faith availeth in Christ *but that which worketh by love.* . . . and that faith which doth not justify herself by good works before men is but a dead faith, which will never justify a man's soul before God. But a justifying faith *purifieth the heart* and sanctifieth the whole man throughout.

II. From the doctrine of God's eternal predestination and unchangeable decree, he gathereth that *if he be predestinated to be saved, he cannot but be saved; if to be damned, no means can do any good*; therefore all works of piety are but in vain. But he should learn that *God hath predestinated to the means as well as to the end.* . . . And *they* (saith Peter) *who are elect unto salvation are also elect unto the sanctification of the Spirit.* [*Noli te in Deo primum quaerere, sed in Christo, in quo si te per fidem inveneris, certus esto, te esse electum.*[16]] If, therefore, upon thy calling thou conformest thyself to the word and example of Christ thy master, & obeyest the good motions of the Holy Spirit in leaving sin and living a godly life, then assure thyself that thou art one of those who are infallibly predestinated to everlasting salvation. If otherwise, blame not God's predestination but thine own sin and rebellion. Do thou but return unto God, and God will graciously receive thee, as the

---

[15] {The evocation of the seven corporal works of mercy here has a parallel in Spenser's *Faerie Queene* bk. 1, canto 10, st. 34-43.}

[16] {Do not seek yourself first in God, but in Christ, in whom, if you find yourself by faith, assure yourself that you are chosen.}

father did the prodigal son, and by thy conversion it shall appear both to angels and men that thou didst belong to his election. If thou wilt not, why should God save thee?

III. When a carnal Christian hears *that man hath not free-will unto good*, he looseth the reins to his own corrupt will, as though it lay not in him to bridle or to subdue it, implicitly making God the author of sin in suffering man to run into this necessity. But he should know that GOD gave Adam free-will to stand in his integrity if he would; but man abusing his free-will lost both himself and it. Since the Fall, man in his state of corruption hath free-will to evil, but not to good; for in this state, *we are not* (saith the Apostle) *sufficient to think a good thought*. And God is not bound to restore us what we lost so wretchedly and make no more care to recover again. But, as soon as a man is regenerated, the *grace of God freeth his will unto good*, so that he doth all the good things he doth with a free-will. . . . And in this state, every true Christian hath free-will, and as he increaseth in grace, so doth his will in freedom. For *when the Son shall make us free, then shall we be free indeed*; and, *where the Spirit of the Lord is, there is liberty*, for the Holy Spirit draws their minds not by coaction but by the *cords of love* (Cant. 1:4), by illuminating their minds to know the truth, by changing their hearts to love the known truth, and by enabling every one of them, according to the measure of grace which he hath received, to do the good which he loveth. But thou wilt not use the freedom of thy will so far as God hath freed it, for thou doest many times willfully against God's law to the hazard of thy soul that, which if the king's law forbad under the penalty of death or loss of thy worldly state, thou wouldest not do. Make not therefore thy want of free-will unto good to be so much the cause of thy sin as thy want of a loving heart to serve thy heavenly Father.

IIII. When the natural man hears *that no man since the Fall is able to fulfill the Law of God and to keep all his commandments*, he boldly presumes to sin as others do. He contents himself with a few good thoughts, and if he be not altogether as bad as the worst, he concludes that he is as truly regenerate as the best. And every voluntary refusal of doing good or withstanding evil he counts the impossibility of the Law. But he should learn that though, since the Fall, no man but Christ, who was both God and man, did or can perfectly fulfill the whole Law, yet every true Christian, as soon as he is regenerated, begins to keep all God's commandments in truth, though he cannot in absolute perfection. . . . And then the spirit of grace which was promised to be more abundantly poured forth under the Gospel helpeth them in their good endeavors and assisteth them to do what he commands them to do. And in so doing, God accepteth their good will and endeavor instead of perfect fulfilling of the Law, supplying out of the merits of Christ, who fulfilled the Law for us, whatsoever wanteth in our obedience. . . .

. . .

V. When the unregenerated man hears that God *delighteth more in the inward mind than in the outward man*, then he feigneth with himself that all outward reverence and profession is but either superstitious or superfluous. Hence it is that he seldom kneeleth in the church, that he puts on his hat at singing of Psalms and the public prayers—which the profane varlet would not offer to do in the presence of a prince or a nobleman. And so that he keep his mind unto God, he thinks he may fashion himself in other things to the world. He divides his thoughts, and gives so much to God and so much to his own lusts; yea, he will divide with GOD the Sabbath and will give him almost the one half, and spend the other wholly in his own pleasures. But know, ô carnal man, that Almighty

GOD will not be served by halves, because he hath created and redeemed the whole man. And as God detests the service of the outward man without the inward heart as hypocrisy, so he counts the inward service without all external reverence to be mere profaneness. He requireth both in his worship. In prayer therefore bow thy knees in witness of thy humiliation; lift up thine eyes and thy hands in testimony of thy confidence; hang down thy head & smite thy breasts in token of thy contrition; but especially call upon God with a sincere heart: serve him holy, serve him wholly, serve him only; for God and the prince of this world are two contrary masters, and therefore no man can possibly serve both.

VI. The unregenerated Christian holds the *hearing of the Gospel preached to be but an indifferent matter*, which he may use or not use at his pleasure; but whosoever thou art that will be assured in thy heart that thou art one of Christ's elect sheep, thou must make a special care and conscience (if possibly thou canst) to hear God's word preached. For first, the preaching of the Gospel is the chief ordinary means which GOD hath appointed to convert the souls of all that he hath predestinated to be saved. . . . If the hearing of Christ's voice be the chief mark of Christ's *elect sheep* and of the *Bridegroom's friend*, then must it be a fearful mark of a reprobate goat either to neglect or contemn to hear the preaching of the Gospel. . . .

. . .

VII. The opinion that the sacraments are but *bare signs & seals of God's promise and grace unto us* doth not a little hinder piety. Whereas indeed they are seals as well of our service and obedience unto God—which service if we perform not unto him, the sacraments seal no grace unto us. But if we receive them upon the resolution to be his faithful and penitent servants, then the sacraments do not only signify and offer, but also seal and exhibit indeed the inward spiritual grace which they outwardly promise and represent. And to this end baptism is called the *washing of regeneration and renewing of the Holy Ghost*; and the Lord's Supper, *the communion of the body and blood of Christ*. Were this truth believed, the holy sacrament of the Lord's Supper would be oftener and with greater reverence received.[17]

VIII. The last and not the least block whereat piety stumbleth in the course of religion is by adorning vices with the names of virtues: as to call drunken carousing, drinking of health; spilling innocent blood, valor; gluttony, hospitality; covetousness, thriftiness; whoredom, loving a mistress; simony, gratuity; pride, gracefulness; dissembling, compliment. . . . So, on the other side, to call sobriety in words and actions, hypocrisy; alms-deeds, vain-glory; devotion, superstition; zeal in religion, puritanism; humility, crouching; scruple of conscience, preciseness, &c. and whilest thus we call evil, good, and good, evil, true piety is much hindered in her progress. And thus much of the first hindrance of piety, by mistaking the true sense of some special places of Scripture and grounds of Christian religion.

The second hindrance of piety

The evil example of great persons, the practice of whose profane lives they prefer for their imitation before the precepts of God's holy word. So that when they see the greatest men

---

[17] {On Protestant sacramental theologies, see Bryan Spinks. *Sacraments, ceremonies, and the Stuart divines: sacramental theology and liturgy in England and Scotland, 1603–1662* (Ashgate, 2002). "Exhibit" (*exhibere*), a term Calvin uses, means offer, not simply represent.}

in the state & many chief gentlemen in their country to make neither care nor conscience to hear sermons, to receive the Communion, nor to sanctify the Lord's Sabbaths, &c., but to be swearers, adulterers, carousers, oppressors, &c., then they think that the using of these holy ordinances are not matters of so great moment: for if they were, such great and wise men would not set so little by them. Hereupon they think that religion is not a matter of necessity. And therefore, where they should like Christians row against the stream of impiety towards heaven, they suffer themselves to be carried with the multitude down right to hell, thinking it impossible that God will suffer so many to be damned. Whereas if the God of this world had not blinded the eyes of their minds, the holy Scriptures would teach them that *not many wise men, after the flesh, not many mighty, not many noble are called, &c.*, but that for the most part the *poor receive the Gospel*, and that few rich men shall be saved. And *that howsoever many are called, yet the chosen are but few.* Neither did the multitude ever save any from damnation. As God hath advanced men in greatness above others, so doth God expect that they in religion and piety should go before others. . . . The multitude of sinners doth not extenuate but aggravate sin, as in Sodom. Better it is, therefore, with a few to be saved in the Ark than with the whole world to be drowned in the Flood. Walk with the few godly in the Scriptures' *narrow path* to heaven, but crowd not with the godless multitude in the *broad way* to hell. Let not the examples of irreligious great men hinder thy repentance, for their greatness cannot at that day exempt themselves from their own most grievous punishments.

The third hindrance of piety

The long escaping of deserved punishment in this life. *Because sentence* (saith Solomon) *is not speedily executed against an evil worker, therefore the hearts of the children of men are fully set in them to do evil, not knowing that the bountifulness of God leadeth them to repentance.* But when his patience is abused, and man's sins are ripened, his justice will at once both begin and make an end of the sinner; and he will recompense the slowness of his delay with the grievousness of his punishment. Though they were suffered to run on the score[18] all the days of their life, yet they shall be sure to pay the utmost farthing at the day of their death. And whilest they suppose themselves to be free from judgment, they are already smitten with the heaviest of God's judgments: a heart that cannot repent . . . .

. . .

The fourth hindrance of piety

The presumption of God's mercy. For when men are justly convinced of their sins, forthwith they betake themselves to this shield, *Christ is merciful*, so that every sinner makes Christ the patron of his sin, as though he had come into the world to bolster sin, and not to destroy the *works of the devil*. Hereupon the carnal Christian presumeth that, though he continueth a while longer in his sin, God will not shorten his days. But what is this but to be an implicit atheist: doubting that either GOD seeth not his sins, or, if he doth, that he is not just? For if he believeth that God is just, how can he think that God, who for sin so severely punisheth others, can love him who still loveth to continue in sin. True it is, Christ is merciful. But to whom? Only to them that repent *and turn from iniquity in Jacob.*

---

[18] {defer payment}

Despair is nothing so dangerous as presumption. For we read not in all the Scriptures of above three or four whom roaring despair overthrew. But secure presumption hath sent millions to perdition without any noise. As therefore the damsels of Israel sang in their dances, *Saul hath killed his thousands, and David his ten thousands,* so may I say that despair of God's mercy hath damned thousands, but the presumption of God's mercy hath damned ten thousands and sent them quick to hell, where now they remain in eternal torments without all help of ease or hope of redemption. God spared the thief, but not his fellow. God spared one, that no man might despair. God spared but one, that no man should presume. Joyful assurance to a sinner that repents; no comfort to him that remains impenitent. God is infinite in mercy, but to them only who turn from their sins to serve him in holiness, *without which no man shall see the Lord* (Heb. 12:14). To keep thee therefore from the hindrance of presumption, remember that as Christ is a Savior, so Moses is an accuser. Live therefore as though there were no Gospel. Die as though there were no Law. Pass thy life as though thou wert under the conduct of Moses. Depart this life as if thou knewest none but Christ, and him crucified. Presume not if thou wilt not perish. Repent if thou wilt be saved.

The fifth hindrance of piety

Evil company, commonly termed *good fellows,* but indeed the devil's chief instruments to hinder a wretched sinner from repentance and piety. The first sign of God's favor to a sinner is to give him grace to forsake evil companions, such who willfully continue in sin, contemn the means of their calling, gibing at the sincerity of profession in others and shaming Christian religion by their own profane lives. These sit in the seat of the scorners. For as soon as God admits a sinner to be one of his people, he bids him *Come out of Babylon.* Every lewd company is a Babylon. . . .

The sixth hindrance of piety

A conceited fear lest the practice of piety should make a man (especially a young man) to wax too sad and pensive; whereas indeed none can better joy nor have more cause to rejoice than the pious and religious Christian. For as soon as they are justified by faith, they have peace with God, than which there can be no greater joy. . . .

. . .

These are the seven chief hinderers of piety which must be cast out like Mary Magdalen's seven devils before ever thou canst become a true practicer of piety or have any sound hope to enjoy either favor from Christ by grace or fellowship with him in glory.

The Conclusion

TO conclude all: forasmuch as thou seest that without Christ thou art but a slave of sin, death's vassal, and worm's meat, whose thoughts are vain, whose deeds are vile, whose pleasures have scarce beginnings, whose miseries never know end: what wise man would incur these hellish torments, though he might by living in sin purchase to himself for a time the empire of Augustus? . . . For what should it avail a man (as our Savior saith) *to win the whole world for a time, and then to lose his soul in hell forever.*

. . .

Let then (ô sinner) *my counsel be acceptable unto thee: break off thy sins by righteousness, and thine iniquities by shewing mercy towards the poor. Oh let there at length be an healing of thine error.* Nathan used but one parable, and David was converted. . . . Christ looked but once on Peter, and *he went out and wept bitterly.* And now that thou art oft & so lovingly entreated, not by a prophet but by Christ, the Lord of prophets . . . leave thy wicked companions and weep bitterly for thine offences.

Content not thyself with that formal religion which unregenerated men have framed to themselves instead of sincere devotion, for in the multitude of opinions most men have almost lost the practice of true religion. Think not that thou art a Christian good enough, because thou doest as the most, and art not so bad as the worst. No man is so wicked that he is addicted to all kind of vices (for there is an antipathy twixt some vices). But remember that Christ saith, *except your righteousness shall exceed the righteousness of the Scribes and Pharisees, ye shall in no case enter into the kingdom of heaven.* Consider with thyself how far thou comest short of the Pharisees in fasting, praying, frequenting the church, and in giving of alms. Think with thyself how many pagans, who never knew baptism, yet in moral virtues and honesty of life do go far beyond thee. . . . A true Christian must have respect to walk, in the truth of his heart, in all the commandments of God alike; for, saith Saint James, *he that shall offend in one point of the Law* (willfully) *is guilty of all.* . . . The way to heaven is not easy or common, but *strait* and *narrow*; yea, so narrow that Christ protesteth that *a rich man shall hardly enter into the kingdom of heaven*, and that those who enter are but few; and that those few cannot get in but by striving; and that some of those who strive to enter in shall not be able. This all God's saints (whilest they here lived) knew well, when with so often fastings, so earnest prayers, so frequent hearing the word and receiving the sacraments, and with such abundance of tears they devoutly begged at the hands of God, for Christ's sake, to be received into his kingdom. . . .

How a private man must begin the morning with piety

As soon as ever thou awakest in the morning, keep the door of thy heart fast shut, that no earthly thought may enter before that God be come in first, and let him before all others have the first place therein. So all evil thoughts either will not dare to come in or shall the easier be kept out, and the heart will more savor of piety and godliness all the day after. But if thy heart be not at thy first waking filled with some meditations of God and his word, and dressed like the lamp in the tabernacle every morning and evening with the oil olive of God's word, and perfumed with the sweet incense of prayer, Satan will attempt to fill it with worldly cares or fleshly desires, so that it will grow unfit for the service of God all the day after, sending forth nothing but the stench of corrupt and lying words and of rash and blasphemous oaths.

Begin therefore every day's work with God's word and prayer. And offer up unto God upon the altar of a contrite heart the groans of thy spirit and the calves of thy lips as thy morning sacrifice and the first fruits of the day, and as soon as thou awakest say unto him thus:

A short soliloquy when one first wakes in the morning

My soul waiteth on thee, O Lord, more than the morning-watch watcheth for the morning. O God therefore be merciful unto me, and bless me, and cause thy face to shine upon me; fill me with thy mercy this morning, so shall I rejoice and be glad all my days.

Meditations for the morning. Then meditate.

1. How Almighty GOD can (in the resurrection) as easily raise up thy body out of the grave from the *sleep of death* as he hath this morning wakened thee in thy bed out of the sleep of nature. At the dawning of which resurrection day, *Christ shall come to be glorified in his saints*, and every one of the bodies of the thousands of his saints, being fashioned like unto his glorious body, shall shine as bright as the sun. All the angels shining likewise in their glory, the body of Christ surpassing them all in splendor and glory, and the God-head excelling it. If the rising of one sun make the morning sky so glorious, what a bright shining and glorious morning will that be when so many thousand thousands of bodies, far brighter then the sun, shall appear & accompany Christ as his glorious train, coming to keep his general session of righteousness, and to judge the wicked angels and all ungodly men? . . .

    . . .

4. Remember that Almighty God is about thy bed and seeth thy down lying and thy uprising, understandeth thy thoughts, and is acquainted with all thy ways. Remember likewise that his holy angels who guarded and watched over thee all night do also behold how thou wakest and risest. Do all things therefore as in the aweful presence of GOD and in the sight of his holy angels.

5. As thou art putting on thine apparel, remember that they were first given as coverings of shame, being the filthy effect of sin, and that they are made but of the offals and excrements of dead beasts. Therefore . . . thou hast great cause to be humbled at the sight and wearing of them, seeing the richest apparels are but fine covers of the foulest shame. Meditate rather that as thine apparel serves to cover thy shame and to fence thy body from cold, so thou shouldest be as careful to cover thy soul with that wedding garment which is the righteousness of Christ. . . .

    . . .

Brief directions how to read the holy Scriptures once every year over with ease, profit, and reverence

But forasmuch that as faith is the soul, so reading and meditating of the word of God are the parents of prayer, therefore before thou prayest in the morning, first read a chapter in the word of God; then meditate a while with thyself how many excellent things thou canst remember out of it:

As, first, what good counsels or exhortations to good works and to holy life.

Secondly, what threatnings of judgments against such and such a sin, and what fearful example of God's punishment or vengeance upon such and such sinners.

Thirdly, what blessings God promiseth to patience, chastity, mercy, alms-deeds, zeal in his service, charity, faith and trust in God, and such like Christian virtues.

hath wrought and what special blessings he
nd zealous servants.
art, and read not these chapters as matters
any letters or epistles sent down from God
en, *is written for our learning* (Rom. 15:4).

Sixthly, read them therefore with that reverence as if God himself stood by and spake these words unto thee . . . assuring thyself that if such sins (as thou readest there) be found in thee without repentance, the like plagues will fall upon thee, but if thou dost practice the like piety and virtuous deeds, the like blessings shall come unto thee and thine.

In a word, apply all that thou readest in the holy Scripture to one of these two heads chiefly: either to confirm thy faith or to increase thy repentance. For as *sustine & abstine, bear & forbear* [*Epicteti dict.*] was the epitome of a good philosopher's life, so *creda & resipice, believe and repent,* is the whole sum of a true Christian's profession. One chapter thus read with understanding and meditated with application will better feed and comfort thy soul than five read and run over without marking their scope or sense, or making any use thereof to thine own self. . . .

‡

Ten reasons demonstrating the Commandment of the Sabbath to be moral[19]

1. Because all the reasons of this Commandment are moral and perpetual, and God hath bound us to the obedience of this Commandment with more forcible reasons than to any of the rest. First, because he did foresee that irreligious men would either more carelessly neglect or more boldly break this Commandment than any other. Secondly, because that in the practice of this Commandment, the keeping of all the other consisteth; which makes God so often complain that all his worship is neglected or overthrown when the Sabbath is either neglected or transgressed. It would make a man amazed (saith Mr. Calvin) to consider how oft, and with what zeal & protestation, God requireth all that will be his people to sanctify the seventh day. Yea, how the God of mercy mercilessly punisheth the breach of this Commandment with cruel death, as though it were the sum of his whole honor and service.[20]

And it is certain that he who makes no conscience to break the Sabbath will not (to serve his turn) make any conscience to break any of the other Commandments, so he may do it without discredit of his reputation or danger of man's law. Therefore God placed this Commandment in the midst of the two Tables, because the keeping of it is the best help to the keeping of all the rest. The conscionable keeping of the Sabbath is the mother of all religion and good discipline in the Church. Take away the Sabbath and let every man serve God when he listeth, and what will shortly become of religion . . . ? The Sabbath day is God's market day for the week's provision, wherein he will have us to come unto him, and *buy of him, without silver or money,* the *bread of angels* and *water of life,* the wine of the sacraments and milk of the word, to feed our souls. . . . He is not far from true piety who makes conscience to keep the Sabbath day; but he who can dispense with his conscience to break the Sabbath for his own profit or pleasure, his heart never yet felt what either the fear of God or true religion meaneth. For of this Commandment may that speech of S. James be verified: *he that faileth in one is guilty of all.* Seeing therefore that GOD hath fenced this Commandment with so many moral reasons, it is evident that the Commandment itself is moral.

[19] {On English Sabbatarianism, see Collinson, *Religion of Protestants,* 146–47; Kenneth Parker, *The English Sabbath* (Cambridge UP, 1988).}

[20] [Bodin *de Repub.* lib. 4. cap. 2]

. . .

4. Because Christ professeth *that he came not to destroy the moral law*, and that the least of them should not be abrogated in his kingdom of the New Testament. Insomuch, that *whosoever breaketh one of the least of these Ten Commandments and teacheth men so, he should be called the least in the kingdom of heaven*: that is, he should have no place in his Church. Now the moral law commandeth one day of seven to be perpetually kept a holy Sabbath. And Christ himself expressly mentioneth the keeping of a Sabbath among his Christians at the destruction of Jerusalem, about 42 years after his Resurrection—by which time all the Mosaical ceremonies (except eating of blood and things strangled) were by a public decree of all the apostles quite abolished and abrogated in Christian Churches. And therefore Christ admonished his disciples *to pray that their flight be not in the winter nor on the Sabbath day*. Not in the winter, for that (by reason of the foulness of the ways and weather) their flight should be more painful and troublesome unto them; not upon the Sabbath, because it would be more grievous to their hearts to spend that day in toiling to save their lives which the Lord had commanded to be spent in holy exercises to comfort their souls. Now if the sanctifying of the Sabbath on this day had been but ceremonial, it had been no grief to have fled on this day no more than on any other day of the week.

. . . If then a Christian should not without grief of heart fly for the safety of his life on the Lord's Day, with what joy or comfort can a true Christian neglect the holy exercises of God's worship in the church, to spend the greatest part of the Lord's Day in profane and carnal sports or servile labor? And seeing the destruction of Jerusalem was both a type and an assurance of the destruction of the world, who seeth not but that the holy Sabbath must continue till the very end of the world?

5. Because that all the ceremonial law was enjoined to the Jews only and not to the gentiles, but this Commandment of the holy Sabbath (as matrimony) was instituted of God in the state of innocency when there was but one state of all men, and therefore enjoined to the gentiles as well as to the Jews. . . . All the ceremonies were a partition wall to separate Jews and gentiles. But seeing the gentiles are bound to keep this commandment as well as the Jews, it is evident that it is no Jewish ceremony. And seeing the same authority is for the Sabbath that is for marriage, a man may as well say that marriage is but a ceremonial law, as the Sabbath. . . .

The corruption of our nature found in the manifest opposition of wicked men and in the secret unwillingness of good men to sanctify sincerely the Sabbath [*Nitimur in vetitum*. Hor.[21]] sufficiently demonstrateth that the commandment of the Sabbath is spiritual and moral.[22]

7. Because that as God by a perpetual decree made the sun, the moon, and other lights in the firmament of heaven not only to divide the day from the night but also to be for signs [to distinguish twixt spring and harvest, summer and winter, and to foreshew judgments to come] . . . so he ordained in the Church on earth the holy Sabbath to be not only the appointed season for his solemn worship but also the perpetual rule and measure of time. So that as seven days make a week, four weeks a month, twelve months a year;

---

[21] {We seek that which is forbidden. . . . Bayly's memory has repressed the actual source, which is not Horace but Ovid, *Amores* 3.4.17.}

[22] {There is no §6 in the original text.}

so seven years make a Sabbath of years, seven Sabbaths of years a Jubilee. Or 80 Jubilees or 4000 years—or, after Ezekiel, 4000 cubits—the whole time of the Old Testament, till Christ by his baptism and preaching began the state of the New Testament. Neither can I here pass over without admiration how the sacrament of circumcision continued in the Church 39 Jubilees from Abraham, to whom it was first given, unto the baptism of Christ in Jordan, which was just so many Jubilees (after Bucholcerus' compt) as the world had continued before from Adam to the birth of Abraham[23]. . . . The most of all the great alterations and strange accidents which fell out in the Church came to pass either in a Sabbatical year or in a year of Jubilee. For example,

The 70 weeks of Daniel, beginning the first year of Cyrus and 3430 year of the world, contain so many years as the world did weeks of years unto that time, and so many weeks of years as the world had lasted Jubilees. . . . So that to comfort the Church for their 70 years' captivity which they had now, according to Jeremy's prophesy, endured in Babylon, Gabriel tells Daniel that at the end of 70 weeks or Sabbaths of years—that is, 70 times seven years, or 490 years—their eternal redemption from hell should be effected by the death of Christ. . . . From the death of Christ, or the last end of Daniel's weeks, to the 71 year of Christ, the world is measured by seven seals, or seven Sabbaths of years, making one complete Jubilee. From the end of those 7 seals, the world is measured to her end by 7 trumpets, each containing 245 years [Napier on the Apoc.][24]. . . .

And the year of our Savior Christ's birth, being the 3948 of the world, was at the end of a Sabbatical year and the 524 septenary of the world. Moses maketh the common age of all men to be ten times seven (Psal. 90), & every seventh year commonly produceth some notable change or accident in man's life.[25] And no wonder. For as Hippocrates affirmeth that a child in his mother's womb on the seventh day of his conception hath all his members finished, and from that day groweth to the perfection of birth. . . . At 7 years old the child casts his teeth and receives new. And every seventh year after there is some alteration or change in man's life, especially at nine times seven, the climacteric year, which by experience is found to have been fatal to many of those learned men who have been the chiefest lights of the world [Aristotle, Cicero, Bernard, Bocace, Erasmus, Luther, Melanchthon, Sturmius, &c]. . . . And indeed the whole life of a man is measured by the Sabbath: for how many years soever a man liveth here, yet his life is but a life of 7 days multiplied, so that in the number of 7 there is a mystical perfection, which our understanding cannot attain unto.

All which divine disposition of admirable things so oft by sevens call upon us to a continual meditation of the blessed seventh day Sabbath, in knowing and worshipping God in this life, that so from Sabbath to Sabbath we may be translated to the eternal glorious Sabbath of rest and bliss in the life to come.

By the consideration whereof, any man that looketh into the holy history may easily perceive that the whole course of the world is drawn and guided by a certain chain

[23] {Abraham Bucholcerus (1529–84), *Index chronologicus monstrans annorum seriem a mundo condito*. . . . The earliest edition I know of is from 1599.}

[24] {John Napier (1550–1617), *A plaine discovery of the whole Revelation of St. John* (1593). Napier was a Scottish mathematician and inventor of logarithms. On the early modern fascination with such mystical chronology, see the second volume of Anthony Grafton, *Joseph Scaliger*, 2 vols. (Clarendon, 1983–93).}

[25] [A. Gellius lib. 1.15. c. 7; Bodin *de Repub.* lib. 4. cap. 2]

of God's providence, disposing all things in *number, measure,* and *weight.* All times are therefore measured by the Sabbath, so that time and the Sabbath can never be separated. And the angel swears that *this measuring of time* shall continue till that time shall be no more. . . . As well therefore may they pull the sun, moon, and stars out of the heavens, as abolish the holy Sabbath (time's mete rod) out of the Church, seeing the Sabbath is ordained in the Church (as well as the sun and moon in the firmament) for the distinction of times.

8. Because that the whole Church, by an universal consent, ever since the apostles' time have still held the commandment of the Sabbath to be the moral and perpetual law of God, and the keeping of the Sabbath on the first day of the week to be the institution of Christ and his apostles.

The synod called Synodus Coloniensis saith that the Lord's Day hath been famous in the Church ever since the apostles' time. Ignatius, Bishop of Antioch, living in S. John's time, saith: *Let every one that loveth Christ keep holy the Lord's Day, renowned by his Resurrection, which is the queen of days, in which death is overcome and life is sprung up in Christ.* Justin Martyr, who lived not long after him, sheweth how the Christians kept their Sabbath on the Lord's Day as we do. . . .

As therefore David said of the City of God, so may I say of the Lord's Day: *Glorious things are spoken of the day of the Lord,* for it was the birth-day of the world, the first day wherein all creatures began to have being. In it light was drawn out of darkness. In it the Law was given on Mount Sinai. In it the Lord rose from death to life. In it the saints came out of their graves, assuring that on it Christians should rise to newness of life. In it the Holy Ghost descended upon the apostles. And it is very probable that on the seventh day when the 7 trumpets have blown, the cursed Jericho of this world shall fall, and our true Jesus shall give us the promised possession of the heavenly Canaan.

He that would see the uniform consent of Antiquity and practice of the primitive Church in this point, let him read Eusebius' *Ecclesiastical history* . . . Tertullian, *lib. de idololatria* . . . Chrysost. *Serm. 5, de resurrectione* . . . Cyril *in Johan.* . . . Of this judgment are all the sound new writers: see Foxe on the Apoc. 1:10, Bucer in Matt. 12:11 . . . Fulke on the Rhemish Test. . . . innumerable others. Learned Junius shall speak for all. . . . *Wherefore seeing the Lord's Day is both by the fact of Christ . . . by the example and institution of the apostles, and by the continual practice of the ancient Church, and by the testimony of the Scripture observed and substituted into the place of the Jewish Sabbath:* inepté faciunt, *they do foolishly who say that the observation of the Lord's Day is of tradition and not from the Scripture, that by this means they might establish the traditions of men.* . . .

9. . . . The Holy Ghost notes it as one of Jeroboam's greatest sins: that he ordained a feast from the *device of his own heart* (1 Kings 12:33). And God threateneth *to visit Israel for keeping the days of Baalim*—that is, of lords—as papists do of saints (Hos. 2:13), but saith that *such forget him.* And so indeed none are less careful in keeping the Lord's Sabbath than they who are most superstitious observers of men's holy days.[26] The Church of Rome therefore commits gross idolatry . . . in exacting on these days of men's invention, a greater measure of solemnity and sanctification than upon the Lord's Day, which is God's commandment: which in effect is to prefer Antichrist before Christ. Our Church hath

---

[26] {For the opposing view, see John Cosin's sermons on the Fourth Commandment *<infra>*.}

justly abolished all superstitious and idolatrous feasts, and only retains a few holy days to the honor of God alone, and easing of servants . . . though long custom forceth to use the old names for civil distinction, as Luke used the profane names of Castor and Pollux. . . .

10. Lastly, the examples of God's judgments on Sabbath-breakers may sufficiently seal unto them, whose hearts are not seared, how wrathfully Almighty God is displeased with them who are willful profaners of the Lord's Day.

The Lord (who is otherwise the God of mercy) commanded Moses to stone to death the man who of a presumptuous mind would openly go to gather sticks on the Sabbath day. The fact was small, true; but his sin was the greater, that (for so small an occasion) would presume to break so great a commandment.

Nichanor, offering to fight against the Jews on the Sabbath day, was slain himself, and 35,000 of his men.

A husbandman grinding corn upon the Lord's Day had his meal burned to ashes.

Another carrying corn on this day had his barn and all his corn therein burnt with fire from heaven the next night after.

Also a certain nobleman (profaning the Sabbath usually in hunting) had a child by his wife with a head like a dog, and with ears and chaps, crying like a hound.

. . .

On the 13 of January, anno Dom. 1582, being the Lord's Day, the scaffolds fell in Paris Garden under the people at a bear-baiting, so that 8 were suddenly slain, innumerable hurt & maimed: a warning to such who take more pleasure on the Lord's Day to be in a theater beholding carnal sports than to be in the church serving God with the spiritual works of piety.

Many fearful examples of God's judgments by fire have in our days been shewed upon divers towns where the profanation of the Lord's Day hath been openly countenanced.

Stratford upon Avon was twice on the same day twelve-month (being the Lord's Day) almost consumed with fire, chiefly for profaning the Lord's Sabbaths and for contemning his word in the mouth of his faithful ministers.

Teverton in Devonshire (whose remembrance makes my heart bleed) was often times admonished by her godly preacher that God would bring some heavy judgment on the town for their horrible profanation of the Lord's Day, occasioned chiefly by their market on the day following. Not long after his death . . . GOD, in less than half an hour, consumed with a sudden and fearful fire the whole town, except only the church, the courthouse, and the alms-houses, or a few poor people's dwellings; where a man might have seen 400 dwelling houses all at once on fire and above 50 persons consumed with the flame. And now again since the last edition of this book, on the fifth of August last, 1612, 14 years since the former fire, the whole town was again fired and consumed, except some 30 houses of poor people, with the schoolhouse and alms-houses. [Whilest the preachers cried in the church, *profaneness, profaneness, gain* would not suffer them to hear; therefore, when they cried *fire, fire* in the streets, God would not suffer any to help.] They are blind who see not in this the finger of GOD. God grant them grace, when it is next built, to change their market-day. . . .

Many other examples of God's judgments might be alleged, but if these are not sufficient to terrify thy heart from the willful profanation of the Lord's Day, proceed in thy profanation. It may be the Lord will make thee the next example to teach others to keep his Sabbath better.

. . .

The true manner of keeping holy the Lord's Day

Now the sanctifying of the Sabbath consists in two things: first, the resting from all servile and common business pertaining to our natural life. Secondly, in consecrating that rest wholly to the service of God, and the use of those holy means which belong to our spiritual life.

For the first.

1. *The servile and common works from which we are to cease are generally all civil works, from the least to the greatest.* More particularly,

First, from all the works of our calling, though it were reaping in the time of harvest.

Secondly, from carrying burthens as carriers do, or riding abroad for profit or for pleasure. God hath commanded that the beasts should rest on the Sabbath day, because all occasion of travailing or laboring with them should be cut off from man. God gives them that day a rest; and he that *without necessity* deprives them of their rest on the Lord's Day, the groans of the poor tired beasts shall in the day of the Lord rise up in judgment against him. Likewise such as spend the greatest part of this day in trimming, painting, and pampering of themselves, like Jezebels, doing the devil's work upon God's day.

Thirdly, from keeping of fairs or markets, which for the most part God punisheth with pestilence, fire, and strange floods.

Fourthly, from studying any books or science but the holy Scriptures & divinity. For our study must be *to be ravished in spirit upon the Lord's Day.* In a word, thou must on that day cease in thy calling to do thy work, that the Lord by his calling may do his work in thee. . . . And if Christ scourged them out as thieves who bought and sold in his Temple (which was but a ceremony shortly to be abrogated), is it to be thought that he will ever suffer those to escape unpunished who, contrary to his Commandment, buy and sell on the Sabbath day, which is his perpetual law? Christ calleth such, sacrilegious thieves; and as well may they steal the communion cup from the Lord's Table as steal from God the chiefest part of the Lord's Day to consume it in their own lusts. . . .

Fifthly, from all recreations and sports which at other times are lawful: for if lawful works be forbidden on this day, much more lawful sports, which do more steal away our affections from the contemplation of heavenly things than any bodily work or labor. Neither can there be unto a man that delighteth in the Lord any greater delight or recreation than the sanctifying of the Lord's Day. For can there be any greater joy for a person condemned than to come to his prince his house to have his pardon sealed? . . . If thou wilt allow thyself or thy servant recreation, allow it in the six days which are thine. . . . No bodily receation, therefore, is to be used on this day, but so far as it may help the soul to do more cheerfully the service of the Lord.

. . .

If then those recreations which are lawful at other times are on the Sabbath not allowed, much more those that are altogether at all times unlawful. Who without mourning can endure to see how in most places Christians keep the Lord's Day as if they celebrated a feast rather to Bacchus than to the honor of the Lord Jesus, the Savior and Redeemer of the world? For having served God but an hour in outward shew, they spend the rest of the Lord's Day in *sitting down to eat and drink, and rising up to play.* . . . Against which profanation, all holy divines, both old and new, have in their times most bitterly inveighed. Insomuch, that August. affirmeth that *it was better to plow than to dance upon the Sabbath day.*

Now, in the name of Almighty God (who rested, having created heaven and earth) . . . I require thee who readest these words, as thou wilt answer before the face of Christ and all his holy angels at that day, that thou better weigh and consider whether dancing, stage-playing, masking, carding, dicing, tabling, chess-playing, bowling, shooting, bear-baiting, carowsing, tippling, and such other fooleries of Robin-Hood, morris-dances, wakes, and May-games be exercises that God will bless and allow on the Sabbath day? . . . Hear this and tremble at this, O profane youth of a profane age!

O heart all frozen and void of the feeling of the grace of God! that having every day in six, every hour in every day, every minute in every hour, so tasted the sweet mercy of thy God in Christ, without which thou haddest perished every moment, yet canst not find in thy corrupt and irreligious heart to spend in thy Master's service that one day of the week which he hath reserved for his own praise and worship! Let men in defence of their profaneness object what they will . . . yet I would wish them to remember, that seeing it is an ancient tradition in the Church, that the Lord's Second Coming shall be upon the Lord's Day, how little joy they should have to be overtaken in those carnal sports to please themselves, when their Master should find them in spiritual exercises serving him? The profanest wretch would then wish rather to be taken kneeling at prayers in the church than skipping like a goat in a dance. If this cannot move, yet I would wish our impure gallants to remember that whilest they thus dance on the Lord's Day contrary to the Lord's Commandment, they do but dance about the pit's brink, and they know not which of them shall first fall therein. Whereinto being once fallen without repentance, no greatness can exempt them from the vengeance of that great GOD, whose Commandment (contrary to their knowledge and conscience) they do thus presumptuously transgress. If then God's Commandment cannot deter thee nor God's word advise thee, I say no more but what Saint John said before me, *he which is filthy, let him be filthy still.*

⟡⟡⟡

TEXT: EEBO (STC [2nd ed.] / 1602)

Lewis Bayly, *The practise of piety directing a Christian how to walk that he may please God,* 2nd ed. (London: printed for John Hodgets, 1613), 1, 3–6, 75–86, 114, 118–52, 155–64, 166–70, 178–203, 210–12, 222–29, 232–42, 246–60, 262–69, 290–91, 294–308, 310–14, 511–29, 532–54, 563–75. [NOTE, the pagination is not perfectly sequential.]

THOMAS ADAMS
(1583–1652)

Little more is known of Adams' early life than that he entered Trinity College, Cambridge, in 1598, received his BA in 1602, was ordained in 1604, and went on to take an MA from Clare Hall in 1606. From 1605 to 1611 he served as curate in a Bedfordshire parish until ousted by its new patron, his dismissal provoking a warmly supportive testimonial letter from his erstwhile parishioners. Within the year, however, he was preaching at Paul's Cross—the selection below is from a 1612 Paul's Cross sermon—and had come to the admiring attention of the Lord Chancellor, Baron Ellesmere, who soon after secured his appointment as vicar of two rural parishes. By 1619, however, he had come to London, where he served as vicar of St. Benet Paul's Wharf and St. Benet Sherehog, as well as lecturer at St. Gregory by Paul's, his stipend for all three parishes coming largely from the dean and chapter of St. Paul's Cathedral.[1] The 1633 revision of Stow's *Survey of London* describe all three parishes as having had "no repair or beauty bestowed" on them during Adams' tenure, but whether this neglect bespeaks under-funding or anti-Laudianism (or both) is hard to say.[2]

From 1612 through the early 1630s, Adams published sermons and sermon series on close to an annual basis, many going through multiple editions—"The White Devil" alone garnering five editions between 1613 and 1621. He was, as the following selection from that sermon makes evident, a superb stylist: according to one nineteenth-century critic, a puritan Shakespeare, although a low-church Andrewes seems closer to the mark. Adams' prose, like that of Andrewes, fuses the wit, brevity, and point of Renaissance Senecanism with the sound play and paradoxes of medieval *Kunstprosa* (see, e.g., his Epiphany sermon, "Christ's star," with its intercalated snatches of patristic Latin and Aquinas' Corpus Christi hymn [*Works* 2:4–7]), although Adams' sermons also flaunt their kinship

[1] Hence his dedication of a sermon to Donne and the prebends of the cathedral as his "very good patrons" ("The Barren Tree" [London, 1623]).

[2] John Stow, Anthony Munday, et al. *The survey of London* (London, 1633), 829, 836.

to the Theophrastean character and to classical verse satire. Plus, as Sears McGee notes, "Adams never met a pun he could resist."

Except for a slender volume that appeared shortly before his death in 1652, Adams abruptly stopped publishing in 1633. Since this silence coincides with Laud's elevation to Canterbury, a connection between these two events has long been suspected, especially given Adams' stated view that "the nearer to perfection, the fewer ceremonies" (*Happiness* 116). Laud, however, had been bishop of London since 1628, yet Adams published his massive collected sermons in 1630 and a biblical commentary in 1633 notwithstanding. We do not know why Adams withdrew from print thereafter. When the war came, he apparently sided with the King, since sometime around 1645 he was sequestered as "a loose-liver, a temporizing ceremony-monger, and malignant against the Parliament" (McGee 404). He died in poverty in November of 1652.

The nineteenth century saw Adams as a puritan. More recent scholarship notes that, despite his conspicuous lack of sympathy with the Laudian programme (except apropos the reendowment of the Church), Adams' name nowhere appears in the extensive archives of London's godly community. His scattered statements on predestination, ceremonies, episcopacy, and other such controverted topics place him in the mainstream of Jacobean churchmanship: a solid Protestant episcopalian, hewn from the same block as a long line of distinguished Calvinist bishops, from Toby Matthew and Edwin Sandys to Joseph Hall and John Davenant. Yet, in truth, Adams has little to say on these controverted topics—a principled silence, as he explains in 1633:

> But woe to them that break the peace of the Church, that blend religion with contention, put those asunder which God hath joined together—Truth and Peace! With what violent passions do men bandy controversies! How they do wrangle in print, and fight with their pens as soldiers with their pikes—all wounding the peace of the Church! With what bitterness of spirit do they defy one another! I would to God we had less of the polemical and more of the positive divinity. . . . Why should we answer every dog that barks with barking again? Why should we think the truth utterly lost unless we weary the press with indications of it? The tongue is afire, but the pen goes further; adds fuel to this fire, and shoots it abroad where the tongue cannot reach—of all which . . . if there were a good fire made, the Church might well endure to warm her hands at it; for it were certainly better for us to want some truth than to have no peace; and a man that never studied controversies may, without controversy, be saved.[3] (*An exposition*, 759)

In the words of one of Adams' early editors, he was "a man little addicted to parties" (Stowell lviii).

[3] The preceding paragraph, interestingly enough, derives from Donne's 1622 Paul's Cross sermon defending the Jacobean crack-down on militant Protestant preaching: compare Adams' "Be the garden never so fair, they would make the world believe that there is a snake under every leaf. Be the intention never so sincere, they will prognosticate and divine sinister and mischievous effects from it" (759) with the corresponding passage in Donne (*Sermons*, 4:197).

Adams' preaching, as the selections below illustrate, takes aim not against the errors of one or another faction of theologians but against the sins of the pious Protestant citizens composing his auditory at Paul's Cross and his several London parishes: the sharp practices of city merchants, shopkeepers, and tradesmen; the hypocrisy of godly gentlemen living high in London off the profits derived from enclosing, engrossing, and rack-renting on their country estates—the sins of *homo economicus*, especially *homo economicus* disguised in saint's clothing. This is Adams' "white devil." He attaches relatively little importance to the reformation of private manners; his white devils do not fornicate, dance, or drink; they grind the faces of the poor. The emphasis on charity—on charity understood as socio-economic practice, on charity as the equitable and compassionate ordering of manor and marketplace—is wholly traditional. It was also, however, polemical: directed against the pervasive post-Reformation tendency to elevate this or that controverted point—Sabbath observance, kneeling for Communion, papal infallibility—to the *unum necessarium*. Yet, as his publishing record attests, Adams was scarcely a voice crying in the wilderness, and his sermons may well be fairly typical of early Stuart parish preaching, so little of which—at least in comparison to court sermons and theological controversy—survives.

Sources: ODNB; Thomas Adams, *The happiness of the Church* (London, 1618); *An exposition upon the second epistle general of St. Peter*, ed. James Sherman (London, 1848); and *The works of Thomas Adams: being the sum of his sermons, meditations, and other divine and moral discourses*, 3 vols. (Edinburgh, 1861–62); Judith Maltby, *Prayer Book and people in Elizabethan and early Stuart England* (Cambridge UP, 1998); Sears McGee, "On misidentifying puritans: the case of Thomas Adams," *Albion* 30.3 (1998): 401–18; John Donne, *Sermons*, 10 vols., ed. George Potter and Evelyn Simpson (U California P, 1953–62); W. H. Stowell, intro. to Thomas Adams, *The three divine sisters* (London, 1847).

THOMAS ADAMS

The white devil, or the hypocrite uncased: in a sermon preached at Paul's Cross
1612, published 1613

To the Reader

Honest and understanding reader (if neither, hands off), I never saluted thy general name by a special epistle till now; and now, perhaps, soon enough. But if honesty be usher to thy understanding, and understanding tutor to thy honesty, as I cannot fear, so I need not doubt or treat with thee for truce. Truce, of what? Of suspense, not of suspension (it belongs to our betters).[1] *Suspend* thy censure; do not *suspend* me by thy censure. I do not call thee aside to ask with what applause this sermon passeth but . . . with what benefit. I had rather convert one soul than have an hundred praise me. Whereof, if I were (so besotted to be) ambitious, by this I could not hope it, for it pulls many tender and tendered sins out of their downy nests; and who strikes vice, and is not stricken with calumnies? I must rather think it hath passed from one press to another, to a worse, hazarding itself to be pressed to death with censures.[2] Which yet (though I lowly hope better) I cannot fear, since it speaks no more, nor other, than justifiable truth. What hath been objected already, I must briefly answer. It is excepted that I am too merry in describing some vices. Indeed, such is their ridiculous nature that their best conviction is derision, yet I abominate any pleasantness here but Christian; and would provoke no smile but of disdain, wherein the gravity of matter shall free my form of words from lightness. Others say I am other-where too satirically bitter. It is partly confessed: I am bitter enough to the sins, and therein (I think) better to the sinners, more charitable to the persons. Some wish I would have spared the Church-thieves because it is not yet generally granted that impropriations of tithes are appropriations of wrongs; but if there be a competent maintenance to the minister—and not to him neither, except of worthy gifts (provided that they judge of

---

[1] {There are multiple puns here; "suspense" can mean, among other things, expectation or uncertainty; "suspend" can refer to hanging, the usual form of capital punishment in Adams' day; "suspension" for a minister meant being debarred the exercise of his ministry.}

[2] {Here "pressing" refers both to the printing press and to a particularly grisly form of capital punishment; see http://en.wikipedia.org/wiki/Peine_forte_et_dure (accessed November 14, 2010).}

his gifts and competency)—it is enough. Well, if any such be grieved, let him allow his minister a sufficiency—under which he cannot live without want to his family or disgrace to his profession (at least, so taken)—and hereof certified, I will take counsel to draw the books and put his name out of the catalogue of thieves. But it would be strange if any of these Zibas should yield to Mephibosheth a division of his own lands or goods {2 Sam. 9:1–19:30}. When they do, I will say David is come again to his kingdom, or rather, the Son of David is come to Judgment. Others would have enclosers put out, because (commonly) great men, but therefore the greater their sins and deserving the greater taxation.[3] Nay, some would persuade usury to step in to traverse[4] his indictment and prove himself no thief by the verdict of the country, because *sub judice lis est*; it is not yet decided that usury is a sin.[5] It is *sub Judice* indeed, but the Judge hath already interposed his interlocutory[6] and will one day give his definitive sentence, that usury shall never dwell in his holy mountain. . . . Others affirm that I have made the gate of heaven too narrow, and they hope to find it wider; God and the Scriptures are more merciful. True it is, that heaven-gate is in itself wide enough, and the narrowness is in respect of the enterer; and though thy sins cannot make that too little to receive thee, yet they make thee too gross and unfit to get into that. Thus the straitness ariseth from the deficiency (not of their glory, but) of our grace. Lastly, some have the title sticking in their stomachs, as if Christ himself had not called Judas a *devil* and likened an hypocrite to a *whited sepulcher*; as if Luther did not give Judas this very attribute, and other Fathers of the Church, from whom Luther derives it. Good Christian reader, leave cavils against it and fall to caveats in it. Read it through. If there be nothing in it to better thee, either the fault is in my hand or in thy heart. Howsoever, give God the praise; let none of his glory cleave to us earthen instruments. If thou likest it, then . . . with the same affection thou readest it, remember it; and with the same thou remembrest, practice it. In hope of this and prayer for this, I commend this book to thy conscience, and thy conscience to God.

Willington, March. 27, 1613
Thine if thou be Christ's, T. A.

THE WHITE DEVIL OR THE HYPOCRITE UNCASED:
In a Sermon preached at PAUL'S CROSS,
March the seventh, 1612

This he said, not that he cared for the poor, but because he was a thief, and had the bag,
and bare what was put therein.
John 12:6

I am to speak of Judas, a devil by the testimony of our Savior—*have I not chosen you twelve, and one of you is a devil?* [John 6:70]—yet so transformed into a shew of sanctimony that he who was a devil in the knowledge of Christ seemed an angel in the deceived

---

[3] {censure}
[4] {contest}
[5] {literally, the controversy is "under" (i.e., being reviewed by) the judge}
[6] {provisional decree}

judgment of his fellow-apostles. A devil he was, black within and full of rancor, but white without and skinned over with hypocrisy; therefore, to use Luther's word, we will call him the *white devil*. Even here he discovers himself and makes good this title. Consider the occasion thus:

> Christ was now at supper among his friends, where everyone shewed him several kindness; among the rest Mary pours on him a box of ointment. Take a short view of her affection. 1. She gave a precious unction, spikenard . . . as if she could not be too prodigal in her love. 2. She gave him a whole pound . . . she did not cut him out devotion by piecemeal or remnant, nor serve God by the ounce, but she gave all; for quality, precious; for quantity, the whole pound. Oh that our service to God were answerable! We rather give one ounce to lust, a second to pride, a third to malice &c., so dividing the whole pound to the devil; she gave all to Christ. 3. To omit her anointing his feet and wiping them with the hairs of her head. . . . the beauty of her head to serve Christ's feet; *she brake the box tanquam ebria amore,*[7] and this of no worse than alabaster, that Christ might have the remaining drop; and *the whole house was filled with the odor.* At this repines Judas, pretending the poor, for he was white; intending his profit, for he was a *devil*.

. . .

1. Observe that Saint John lays this fault on Judas only, but Saint Matthew and Mark charge the disciples with it and find them guilty of this repining, and that . . . not without indignation [Matt. 26:8; Mark 14:4]. This knot is easily untied: Judas was the ring-leader, and his voice was the voice of Jacob, all charitable; but his hands were the hands of Esau, rough and injurious. Judas pleads for the poor; the whole synod likes the motion well; they second it with their verdicts. Their words agree, but their spirits differ; Judas hath a further reach: to distill this ointment thorough the limbic of hypocrisy into his own purse; the apostles mean plainly. Judas was malicious against his Master; they simply thought the poor had more need. So sensible and ample a difference do circumstances put into one and the same action: presumption or weakness, knowledge or ignorance, simplicity or craft do much aggravate or mitigate an offence. The apostles consent to the circumstance, not to the substance, setting (as it were) their hands to a blank paper. It was in them pity rather then piety; in Judas neither pity nor piety, but plain perfidy . . . It is a true rule even in good works: *finibus non officiis discernendae sunt virtutes a vitiis,* virtues are discerned from vices not by their offices, but by their ends or intents. Neither the outward form, no nor (often) the event, is a sure rule to measure the action by: the eleven Tribes went twice by God's special word and warrant against the Benjamites, yet in both assaults received the overthrow. . . .

I might here first lead you into the distinction of sins. . . .

But that which I fasten on is the power and force of example. Judas with a false weight sets all the wheels of their tongues a going. The steward hath begun a health to the poor, and they begin to pledge him round. Authority shews itself in this to beget a likeness of manners: *Tutum èst peccare autoribus illis;* it is safe sinning after such authors; if the steward say the word, the *fiat* of consent goes round. *Imperio maximus, exemplo maior;* he that

---

[7] {as though drunk with love}

is greatest in his government is yet greater in his precedent. A great man's livery is countenance enough to keep drunkenness from the stocks, whoredom from the post, murder
and stealth from the gallows. Such double sinners shall not escape with single judgments;
such leprous and contagious spirits shall answer to the justice of God, not only for their
own sins, but for all theirs whom the pattern of their precedency hath induced to the like.
. . . The imitation of our governors' manners, fashion, vices is styled obedience. If Augustus Caesar loves poetry, he is nobody that cannot versify. Now (saith Horace)

Scribimus indocti, doctique poemata passim.[8]

When Leo[9] lived, because he loved merry fellows and stood well affected to the
stage, all Rome swarmed with jugglers, singers, players. To this, I think, was the proverb
squared: *Confessor Papa, confessor populus*; if the pope be an honest man, so will the people
be. *In vulgus manant exempla regentum* [Cypr.]. The common people are like tempered
wax whereon the vicious seal of greatness makes easy impression. . . . Judas' train soon
took fire in the suspectless disciples; and Satan's infections shoot through some great star
the influence of damnation into the air of the communality. Let the experience hereof
make us fearful of examples.

Observe, that no society hath the privilege to be free from a Judas: no, not Christ college itself: *I have chosen you twelve, and behold one of you is a devil*, and this no worse man
than the steward, put in trust with the bread of the prophets. The synod of the Pharisees,
the convent of monks, the consistory of Jesuits, the councils of bishops, the holy Chair at
Rome, the sanctified parlor at Amsterdam is not free from a Judas. Some tares will shew
that *the envious man* is not asleep. . . . What, among saints? *Is Saul among the prophets*
[1 Sam. 10:12]? Among the Jews, a wicked publican, a dissolute soldier was not worth the
wondering at. . . . But amongst the sober, chaste, pure, precise Pharisees to find a man
of sin was held uncouth, monstrous. They run from their wits, then, that run from the
Church because there are Judases. Thus it will be till the great Judge *with his fan shall purge
his floor*; till the *angels shall carry the wheat into the barn of glory*. Until that day comes some
rubbish will be in the net, some goats among the sheep, some with the mark of the Beast
in the congregation of saints; one Ishmael in the family of Abraham, one without his wedding garment at the marriage feast; among the disciples, a Demas; among the apostles, a
Judas. Thus generally.

Observe: Judas is bold to reprove a lawful, laudable, allowable work. . . . Because his
mouth waters at the money, his teeth rankle the woman's credit; for so I find malignant
reprovers styled: *corrodunt, non corrigunt; correptores, immo corruptores*: they do not mend
but make worse; they bite, they gnaw. . . .

I could here find cause to praise reprehension, if it be reasonable, seasonable, well
grounded for the reprover, well conditioned for the reproved. I would have no profession more wisely bold than a minister's; for sin is bold, yea saucy and presumptuous: it is
miserable for both when a bold sinner and a cold priest shall meet, when he that should
lift up his voice like a trumpet doth but whisper through a trunk.[10] Many men are dull

---

[8] {Horace, *Epist.* 2.1.117: absolutely all of us, learned and unlearned, write poetry.}

[9] {Pope Leo X (d. 1521?)}

[10] {a pipe used as a speaking-tube or ear-trumpet (*OED*)}

beasts without a goad. . . . our connivance is sinful, our silence baneful, our allowance damnable. Of sin neither the fathers, factors, nor fautors[11] are excusable: nay, the last may be worst, whiles they may, and will not, help it [Rom. 1:32]. . . . there is little difference between permission and commission, between the toleration and perpetration of the sin. He is an abettor of the evil that may, and will not, better the evil. *Amici vitia, si feras, facis tua*; thy unchristian sufferance adopts thy brother's sins for thine own, children of thy fatherhood. Of so great a parentage is many a sin-favoring magistrate; he begets more bastards in an hour than Hercules did in a night; and except Christ be his friend, God's sessions[12] will charge him with the keeping of them all. No private man can plead exemption from this duty, for *amicus* is *animi custos*; he is thy friend that brings thee to a fair and free end. Doth human charity bind thee to reduce[13] thy neighbor's straying beast, and shall not Christianity double thy care to his erring soul? *Cadit asina, & est qui sublevet; perit anima, non est qui recogitet.* The fallen beast is lifted up; the burdened soul is let sink under her load.

. . .

Nay observe: he would hinder the works of piety thorough color of the works of charity, diverting Mary's bounty from Christ to the poor, as if respect to man should take the wall of God's service. Thus he strives to set the two tables of the Law at war, one against the other, both which look to God's obedience as the two cherubim to the mercy-seat; and the catholic Christian hath a catholic care. I prefer not the laws of God one to the other; *one star* here *differs not from another star in glory*. Yet I know the best distinguisher's caution to the lawyer: *this is the great commandment, and the other is* (but) *like unto it* [Matt. 22:38]. Indeed I would not have *Sacrifice* turn *Mercy* out of doors, as Sara did Hagar; nor the fire of zeal drink up the dew and moisture of charity, as the fire from heaven dried up the water at Elijah's sacrifice [1 Kings 18:31]; neither would I that the precise observation of the second table should gild over the monstrous breaches of the first. Yet I have heard divines (reasoning this point) attribute this privilege to the first table above the second: that God never did (I will not say, never could) dispense with these Commandments which have himself for their proper and immediate object. For then (say they) he should dispense against himself or make himself no God, or more; he never gave allowance to any to have 1. another God, 2. another form of worship, 3. *the honor of his name he will not give to another*, 4. nor suffer the profaner of his holy-day to escape unpunished. For the second table, you have read him commanding the brother *to raise up seed to his brother*, notwithstanding the law, *Thou shalt not commit adultery* [Deut. 25:5; Matt. 22:24]; commanding the Israelites to rob the Egyptians without infringing the law of stealth [Exod. 11:2]: all this without wrong, for *the earth is his and the fullness thereof*. . . .

Let not, then, oh Judas, charity shoulder out piety. . . . Faith and love are like a pair of compasses: whilst faith stands perfectly fixed in the center, which is God, love walks the round and puts a girdle of mercy about the loins. There may indeed be a shew of charity without faith, but there can be no shew of faith without charity. Man judgeth by the hand, God by the heart.

---

[11] {approvers, flatterers}

[12] {a sitting of a judge or judges to determine causes; a judicial trial or investigation (*OED*)}

[13] {bring back}

Hence our policies[14] in their positive laws lay severe punishments on the actual breaches of the second table, leaving most sins against the first to the hand of the Almighty Justice. Let man's name be slandered, *currat lex*, the law is open; be God's name dishonored, blasphemed, there is no punishment but from God's immediate hand. . . . The poor slave is convented to the spiritual court and meets with a shrewd penance for his incontinence; the rich noble man, knight, or gentleman (for Papists are no beggars) breaks the commissary's cords as easily as Sampson the Philistine's withes, and puts an excommunication in his pocket. All is answered, *who knows the spirit of man, but the spirit of man?* and *he stands or falls to his own master* [Rom. 14:4]. Yet, again, who knows whether bodily stripes may not procure spiritual health, and a seasonable blow to the estate may not *save the soul in the day of the Lord Jesus* [1 Cor. 5:5]. Often *detrimentum pecuniae & sanitatis propter bonum animae*, a loss to the purse or a cross to the corps {body} is for the good of the conscience [Th. Aquin.]. Let me then complain: 1. Are there no laws for atheists that would scrape out the deep-engraven characters of the soul's eternity out of their consciences and think their souls as vanishing as the spirits of dogs, not contenting themselves to lock up this damned persuasion in their own bowels, but belching out this unsavory breath to the contagion of others. . . . 2. Are there no laws for image-worshippers, secret friends to Baal, that eat with us, sit with us, play with us, not pray with us, nor for us, unless for our ruins. Yes, the sword of the law is shaken against them (alas that, but only shaken), but either their breasts are invulnerable or the sword is obtuse or the strikers troubled with the palsy & numbness in the arms. 3. Are there no laws for blasphemers, common swearers. . . . 4. Are there no laws to compel them on these days, *that God's house may be filled* [Luke 14:23]? No power to bring them from *the puddles to the springs* [Jer. 2:13]? From walking the streets, sporting in the fields, quaffing in taverns, slugging, wantonizing on couches, to watch with *Christ one hour in his house of prayer* [Matt. 26:40]? Why should not such blisters be lanced by the knife of authority which will else make the whole body of the commonwealth (though not incurable, yet) dangerously sick? I may not seem to prescribe; give me leave to exhort. *Non est meae humilitatis dictare vobis &c* [Bern.]; it suits not with my mean knowledge to direct you the means, but with my conscience to rub your memories. Oh let not the pretended equity to men countenance out our neglected piety to God![15]

Lastly observe his unkindness to Christ. What, Judas, grudge thy master a little unction? . . .

Nay, he terms it no better than a waste and a loss . . . *ad quid perditio haec? Why is this waste* [Matt. 26:8]? What, lost and given to Jesus? Can there be any waste in the creature's due service to the Creator? No, *pietas est, pro pietate sumptus facere*; this is godliness, to be at cost with God. Therefore our fathers left behind them *deposita pietatis*, pledges, evidences, sure testimonies of their religion, in honoring Christ with their riches. (I mean not those in the days of popery, but before ever the locusts of the papal See made our nation drunk with her enchanted cup.) They thought it no waste either . . . to build new monuments to Christ's honor. . . . In those days, charity to the Church was not counted waste.

[14] {polity, civil order; an organized and established system or form of government or administration, esp. in a state or city ("policy": *OED* 2b)}

[15] {The desire that the civil sword be employed to punish violations of the first table seems to have been peculiar to no party; see, in this volume, the selections from Bradshaw <2.6, 6.4> and Laud <373–75>.}

The people of England, devout like those of Israel, cried one to another, *"Afferte,"* Bring ye into God's house; till they were stayed with a statute of mortmain,[16] like Moses' prohibition, *the people bring too much* [Exod. 36:5-6]; but now they changed a letter, and cry, *"Auferte,"* take away as fast as ever they gave, and no inhibition of God or Moses, Gospel or statute, can restrain their violence till the alabaster box be as empty of oil as their own consciences are of grace. We need not stint your devotion, but your devoration; every contribution to God's service is held waste: *ad quid perditio haec? . . .* Gentlemen in these cold countries have very good stomachs; they can devour (and digest too) three or four plump parsonages . . . and they have fed so liberally that their poor servitors (ashamed I am to call them so), the vicars, have scarce enough left to keep life and soul together: not so much as *sitis & fames & frigora poscunt,*[17] the defense of hunger and thirst and cold requires . . . I will not censure you in this, ye Citizens; let it be your praise, that though you *dwell in ceiled houses* yourselves, *you let not God's house lie waste* [Hag. 1:4]. Yet sometimes it is found that some of you so careful in the City are as negligent in the country where your lands lie; and there the temples are often the ruins of your oppression; your poor, undone, blood-sucked tenants not being able to repair the windows or the leads to keep out rain or birds. If a levy or taxation would force your benevolence, it comes malevolently from you, with a Why is this waste? Raise a contribution to a lecture, a collection for a fire, an alms to a poor destitute soul, and lightly there is one Judas in the congregation to cry, *ad quid perditio haec? why is this waste?* Yet you will say, if Christ stood in need of an unction, though as costly as Mary's, you would not grudge it nor think it lost. Cozen not yourselves, ye hypocrites; if ye will not do it to his Church, to his poor ministers, to his poor members, neither would you to Christ; if you clothe not them, neither would you clothe Christ if he stood naked at your doors. Whiles you count that money lost which God's service receiveth of you, you cannot shake away Judas from your shoulder. . . . If God thought it no waste to give you plenty, even all you have, think it no waste to return him some of his own. Think not the oil waste which you pour into the Lamp of the Sanctuary. . . . Think nothing lost whereof you have feoffed God in trust. But let me teach you soberly to apply this, and tell you what indeed is waste.[18]

1. Our immoderate diet. . . .

2. Our unreasonable ebrieties {drinking}. . . . Temperance, the just steward, is put out of his office. What place is free from these ale-house recusants that think better of their drinking-room than Peter thought of Mount Tabor: *bonum est esse hîc, it is good being here* [Matt. 17:4], *vbi nec Deus nec daemon,* where both God and the devil are fast asleep? It is a question whether it be worse to turn the image of a beast to God, or the image of God to a beast. If the first be idolatry, the last is impiety. A voluptuous man is a murderer to himself; a covetous man, a thief; a malicious, a witch; a drunkard, a devil—thus to drink away the poor's relief, our own estate. *Ad quid perditio haec? why is this waste?*

3. Our monstrous pride that turns hospitality into a dumb shew. That which fed the belly of hunger now feeds the eye of lust. Acres of land are metamorphosed into

---

[16] {late 14th-century statute forbidding alienation of real property to the Church}

[17] {Juvenal, *Sat.* 14}

[18] {To "feoff in trust" is to transfer legal title to a trustee, who will administer the estate for the donor's benefit.}

trunks of apparel; and the soul of charity is transmigrated into the body of bravery. *This is waste. . . .* One man wears enough on his back at once to clothe two naked wretches all their lives. *Ad quid &c., Why is this waste?*

4. Our vainglorious building to emulate the skies, which the wise man calls *the lifting up of our gates too high* [Prov. 17:19]. Houses built like palaces. . . . Whole towns depopulate to rear up one man's walls; chimneys built in proportion, not one of them so happy as to smoke; brave gates, but never open; sumptuous parlors, for owls and bats to fly in. Pride begun them, riches finished them, beggary keeps them: for most of them molder away. . . . This is waste, and waste indeed, and these worse than the devil: the devil had once some charity in him, to turn stones into bread [Matt. 4:3], but these men turn bread into stones—a trick beyond the devil: *ad quid perditio haec? Why is this waste?*

5. Our ambitious seeking after great alliance: the *son of the Thistle must match with the Cedar's daughter* [2 Kgs 14:9]; the father tears dear years out of the earth's bowels and raiseth a bank of usury to set his son up on, and thus mounted, he must not enter save under the noble roof; no cost is spared to ambitious advancement: *ad quid &c. Why is this waste?*

Shall I say our upholding of theaters to the contempt of religion, our maintaining ordinaries[19] to play away our patrimonies, our four-wheeled porters, our antic the fashion, our smoky consumption,[20] our perfumed putrefaction: *ad quid perditio haec?* Why are these wastes? Experience will testify at last that these are wastes indeed, for they waste the body, the blood, the state, the freedom, the soul itself; and all is lost, thus laid out. But what is given (with Mary) to Christ is lost like sown grain, and shall be found again at the harvest of joy.

. . .

2. *Observe*: it is the nature of the wicked to have no care of the poor. *Sibi nati, sibi viuunt, sibi moriuntur, sibi damnantur*; they are all for themselves, they are born to themselves, live to themselves, (so let them) die for themselves, and go to hell for themselves. The fat bulls of Bashan, love *the lambs from the flock, and the calves from the stall &c.*, but *think not on the affliction of Joseph* [Amos 6:4]. Your gallant thinks not the distressed, the blind, the lame to be part of his care; it concerns him not. True, and therefore heaven concerns him not. It is infallible truth, if they have no feeling of others' miseries, they are no members of Christ. Go on now in thy scorn, thou proud roister, admire the fashion and stuff thou wearest, whiles the poor mourns for nakedness. Feast royally, Dives, whiles Lazarus can get no crumbs. Apply, Absalom, thy sound, healthful limbs to lust and lewdness, whiles the lame, blind, maimed cannot derive a penny from thy purse, though he move his suit in the name of Jesus; thou givest testimony to the world, to thy own conscience, that thou art but a Judas. Why, the poorest and the proudest have, though not *vestem communem*, yet *cutem communem*. There may be difference in the fleece, there is none in the flesh. Yea perhaps, as the gallant's perfumed body is often the sepulcher to a putrefied soul, so a white, pure, innocent spirit may be shadowed under the broken roof of a maimed corps. Nay, let me terrify them: not many rich, not many mighty, not many noble are called. . . .

[19] {inn, tavern}
[20] {tobacco}

Oh, how unfit is it among Christians, that some should surfeit, whiles others hunger? That one should have two coats, and another be naked, yet both one man's servants? Remember that God hath made many his stewards, none his treasurer; he did not mean thou shouldest hoard his blessings, but expend them to his glory. He that is infinitely rich, yet keeps nothing in his own hands but gives all to his creatures, at his own cost and charges he hath maintained the world almost 6000 years. He will most certainly admit no hoarder into his kingdom. Yet, if you will needs love laying up, God hath provided you a coffer: the poor man's hand is Christ's treasury. The besotted worldling hath a greedy mind to gather goods, and keep them; and lo, his keeping loseth them; for they must have either . . . thy end, or their end. Job tarried, and his goods went; but the rich man went, and his goods tarried [Luke 12]. *Si vestra sunt, tollite vobiscum*: if they be yours, why do you not take them with you? No, *hîc acquiruntur, hîc amittuntur*; here they are gotten, here lost. But God himself being witness (nay, he hath past his word), what we for his sake give away here, we shall find again hereafter; and the charitable man dead and buried is richer under the ground than he was above it. It is an usual song which the saints now sing in heaven:

That we gave;
That we have.

. . .

Judas cares not for the poor: Judas is dead, but this fault of his lives still. The poor had never more need to be cared for. But how? There are two sorts of poor, and our care must be proportionable to their conditions. There are 1. some poor of God's making; 2. some of their own making. Let me say, there are God's poor and the devil's poor; those the hand of God hath crossed; these have forced necessity on themselves by a dissolute life. The former must be cared for by the compassion of the heart and charity of the purse; God's poor must have good alms, a seasonable relief according to thy power, or else the Apostle fearfully and peremptorily concludes against thee: *the love of God is not in thee* [1 John 3:17]. . . .

For the other poor, who have pulled necessity on themselves with the cords of idleness, riot, or such disordered courses, there is another care to be taken: not to cherish the lazy blood in their veins by abusive mercy, but rather chafe their stonied sinews by correction—relieve them with punishment, and so recover them to the life of obedience. *The sluggard lusteth*, and hath an empty stomach; he loves sustenance well, but is loath to set his foot on the cold ground for it. The laws' sanction, the good man's function saith, *if he will not labor, let him not eat* [2 Thess 3:10]. . . . Sin's chief encouragement is the want of punishment: favor one, hearten many. It is fit, therefore, that *poena ad paucos, metus ad omnes perveniat*: penalty be inflicted on some to strike terror into the rest.

. . .

Of all bodily creatures, man (as he is God's image) is the best; but basely dejected, degenerated, debauched, the (simply) worst: of all earthly creatures, a wicked man is the worst; of all men, a wicked Christian; of all Christians, a wicked professor; of all professors, a wicked hypocrite; of all hypocrites, a wicked, warped, wretched Judas. Take the extraction or quintessence of all corrupted men, and you have a Judas. This then is Judas: a man degenerate, a Christian corrupted, a professor putrefied, a gilded hypocrite, a white-skinned devil. I confess I am sparingly affected to this point, and would fain shift my hands of this monster and not encounter him: for it is not to fight with the *unicorns of Assyria*, nor *the bulls of Samaria*, nor *the beasts of Ephesus*—neither absolute atheists, nor dissolute Christians, nor resolute ruffians, the horns of whose rapine and malice are no less manifest than malignant, but at once imminent in their threats and eminent in their appearance—but to set upon a beast that hath, with the heart of a leopard, the face of a man, of a good man, of the best man; a star placed high in the orb of the Church, though swooped down with the Dragon's tail because not fixed; a darling in the mother's lap, blessed with the Church's indulgence, yet a bastard; a brother of the fraternity, trusted sometimes with the Church's stock, yet no brother but a broker of treacheries, a broacher of falsehoods. I would willingly save this labor but that the necessity of my text overrules my disposition.

I know, these times are so shameless and impudent that many strip off the *white*, and keep the *devil*. Wicked they are and without shew of the contrary; men are so far from giving house-room to the substance of religion, that they admit not an out-room for the shew; so backward to put on Christ, that they will not accept of his livery. . . They salute not Christ at the Cross, nor bid him good morrow in the Temple,[20] but go blustering by, as if some serious business had put haste into their feet, and God was not worthy to be stayed & spoke withal. If this be a riddle, shew me the day shall not expound it by a demonstrative experience. For these I may say, I would to God they would seem holy and frequent the places where sanctimony is taught, but the devil is a nimble, running, cunning fencer, that strikes on both hands, *duplici ictu*, and would have men either . . . not holy or not a little holy in their own opinion and outward ostentation: either no fire of devotion on the hearth, or that that is, in the top of the chimney. That subtle *winnower* persuades men that they are all chaff and no wheat, or all wheat and no chaff; and would keep the soul either lank with ignorance or rank with insolence. Let me therefore woo you, win you, to reject both these extremes, between which your hearts lie as the grain betwixt both the millstones.

Shall I speak plainly? You are sick at London of one disease (I speak to you settled citizens, not extravagants[21]) and we in the country of another; a sermon against hypocrisy in most places of the country is like phlebotomy to a consumption (the spilling of innocent blood); our sicknesses are cold palsies and shaking agues. Yours in the city are hotter diseases: the burning fevers of fiery zeal, the inflammations and impostumes of hypocrisy. We have the frosts, and you have the lightnings; most of us profess too little, and some of you profess too much, unless your courses were more answerable. I would willingly be in none of your bosoms, only I must speak of Judas. . . .

. . .

. . . This is the hypocrite's misery: because he wears God's livery, the world will not be his mother; because his heart, habit, service is sin-wedded, God will not be his father. He hath lost earth for heaven's sake, and heaven for earth's sake; and may complain with *Rebecca's* fear of her two sons: *why should I be deprived of you both in one day?* [Gen 27:45].

---

[20] {"Cross" and "Temple" have their biblical meanings, but with a probable allusion to the Cheapside Cross (on which, see http://mapoflondon.uvic.ca/ELEA1.htm) and the Inn of Court called The Temple.}

[21] {wayfarers, visitors}

. . . Thus an open sinner is in better case than a dissembling saint. There are few that seem worse to others than they are in themselves; yet I have both read and heard of some that have with broken hearts and mourning bowels sorrowed for themselves as if they had been reprobates, and not spared so to proclaim themselves, when yet their estate was good to God-ward, though they knew it not. Perhaps their wickedness and ill life hath been grievous, but their repentance gracious. I may call these *black saints*. The hypocrite is neat and curious in his religious outside, but the linings of his conscience are *filthy and polluted rags* [Esay 64:6]. Then I say still, a *black saint* is better than a *white devil.*

. . .

I speak not to discourage your zeal, but to hearten it, but to better it. Your zeal goes through the world, ye worthy citizens. Who builds hospitals? The City. Who is liberal to the distressed Gospel? The City. Who is ever faithful to the Crown? The City. Beloved your works are good; oh, do not lose their reward through hypocrisy. I am not bitter, but charitable. I would fain put you into the chariot of grace with Elias, and only wish you to put off this mantle. Oh, that it lay in my power to prevail with your affections as well as your judgments: you lose all your goodness if your hearts be not right; the ostentation of man shall meet with the detestation of God. You lose your attention now, if your zeal be in your eye more than heart. You lose your prayers, if, when the ground hath your knee, the world hath your conscience, as if you had two gods: one for Sundays, another for work days; one for the Church, another for the Change.[22] You lose your charity whiles you give glozingly, illiberally, too late. Not a window you have erected, but must bear your names; but some of you rob Peter to pay Paul, take tenths[23] from the Church, and give not the poor the twentieths of them. It is not seasonable nor reasonable charity to undo whole towns by your usuries, enclosings, oppressions, impropriations; and for a kind of expiation, to give three or four the yearly pension of twenty marks. An almshouse is not so big as a village, nor thy superfluity, whereout thou givest, like their necessity, whereout thou extortest.[24] He is but poorly charitable, that having made a hundred beggars, relieves two. You lose all your pious observations whiles you lose your integrity; your solemn censuring, mourning for the time's evil, whiles yourselves are the evil cause thereof; your counterfeit sorrow for the sins of your youth, whiles the sins of your age are worse; your casting salt and brine of reproof at others' faults, whiles your own hearts are most unseasoned. All these artificial whitings are but thrifty leasings,[25] sick healths, bitter sweets, and more pleasing deaths. Cast then away this bane of religion, hypocrisy; this candle with a great wick and no tallow, that often goes out quickly, never without stench; this fair, flattering, *white devil*. How well have we bestowed this pains, I in speaking, you in hearing, if this devil be cast out of your consciences, out of your conversations. It will leave some prints behind it in the best, but bless not yourselves in it, and God shall bless you from it. *Amen.*

. . .

There are two sorts of thieves: public ones, that either with a violent hand take away the passengers' money or rob the house at midnight. . . . I will say little of these, as not

---

[22] {the Exchange—a place where merchants met to do business}

[23] {I.e., tithes: the reference is to the lay impropriation of parochial tithes.}

[24] {See Brian Tierney, *Medieval poor law* (U California P, 1959), 35–37, 117, 125.}

[25] {lies}

pertinent to my text, but leave them to the jury. And speak of thieves like Judas: secret robbers, that do more mischief with less present danger to themselves. . . .

To define this manner of thieves: a private thief is he that without danger of law robs his neighbor: that sets a good face on the matter, and hath some profession to countenance it. A justifiable cloak hides a damnable fraud: a trade, a profession, a mystery—like a Rome-hearted Protestant hides this devilish seminary under his roof without suspicion. To say truth, most of our professions (thanks to ill professors) are so confounded with sins as if there went but a pair of shears between them. Nay they can scarce be distinguished; you shall not easily discern between a hot, furious professor[26] and an hypocrite, between a covetous man and a thief, between a courtier and an aspirer, between a gallant and a swearer, between an officer and a bribe-taker, between a servitor and a parasite, between farmers[27] and poor-grinders, between gentlemen and pleasure-lovers, between great men and mad men, between a tradesman and a fraudsman, between a moneyed man and an usurer, between an usurer and the devil. In many arts, the more skilful, the more ill-full; for nowadays *armis pollentior astus*, fraud goes beyond force; this makes lawyers richer than soldiers, usurers than lawyers, the devil than all. . . . Grieved devotion had never more cause to sing, *Mundum dolens circuivi; fidem undique quaesivi*, &c.

> The world I compassed about,
> Faith and honesty to find out:
> But Country, City, Court, and all
> Thrust poor Devotion to the wall:
> The Lawyer, Courtier, Merchant, Clown
> Have beaten poor Devotion down,
> All wound her; till for lack of breath,
> Fainting Devotion bleeds to death.

But I am to deal with none but thieves, and those private ones; and because Judas is the precedent, I will begin with him that is most like him . . . Let me only change the names: *Either Judas played the pope, or the pope plays the Judas.* This is the most subtle thief of the world, and robs all Christendom under a good color . . .

. . . Judas pretended the poor and robbed them, and doth not the pope, think you? Are there no alms-boxes rifled and emptied into the pope's treasury? . . . Some by pardons he prevents from hell; some by indulgences he lifts up to heaven; and infinite by merits he ransoms from purgatory: not a jot without money: *cruces, altaria, Christum*; he sells Christ's cross, Christ's blood, Christ's self, all for money. Nay, he hath rent from the very stews {brothels}, a hell above ground, and swells his coffers by the sins of the people. . . .
. . .

I come to ourselves. There are many kinds of private thieves in both the houses of Israel and Aaron: *in foro & choro*, in Change and chancel, commonwealth and church. I can tax {censure} no man's person. If I could, I would abhor it, or were worthy to be abhorred. The sins of our times are the thieves I would arraign, testify against, condemn, have executed. The persons I would have saved *in the day of the Lord.*

---

[26] {Here "professor" refers to one who (noisily) professes piety, whereas above it meant something close to a professional.}

[27] {tax-collector}

1. If there be any magistrates (into whose mouths God hath put the determination of doubts, and the distribution of right into their hands) that suffer popularity, partiality, passion to rule, overrule their judgments, these are private thieves; they rob the poor man of his just cause and equity's relief, and no law can touch them for it. Thus may causes go, not according to right, but friendship. . . .

. . .

4. There is *thievery* too among tradesmen, and who would think it? . . . This web of theft is may ways woven in a shop or warehouse, but three especially:

    1. By a false weight and no true measure . . . or the cunning conveyances in weighing or meating,[28] such as cheat the buyer. Are not these pretty tricks to pick men's purses? The French word hath well exprest them: they are *Lieger dumaines*. Now had I not as good lose my purse on Salisbury Plain as in London Exchange? Is my loss the less because violence forbears and craft picks my purse? The highway thief is not greater abomination to God than the shop-thief; and for man, the last is more dangerous: the other we knowingly fly, but this laughs us in the face whiles he robs us.

    2. By insufficient wares. . . .

    3. By playing, or rather preying upon men's necessities. . . .

. . .

5. There are thieves crop into the Church too; or rather they encroach on the Church; for ministers cannot now play the thieves with their livings; they have nothing left to steal; but there are secret Judases can make shift to do it. . . . The Church was once rich, but it was *diebus illis*, in the golden time when honesty went in good clothes and ostentation durst not give religion the check-mate. Now they plead prescription, and prove them their own by long possession.[29] I do not tax all these for private thieves that hold in their hands lands and possessions that were once the Church's, but those that withhold such as are due to churchmen. . . . I complain not that . . . abbeys are turned into gentlemen's houses . . . but that men rob *aram dominicam*, God's house, to furnish *haram domesticam*, their own house: this is theft, and sacrilegious theft. . . .

. . .

6. There is more store of thieves yet: covetous landlords that stretch their rents on the tenterhooks of an evil conscience and swell their coffers by undoing their poor tenants; these sit close and stare the law in the face; yet, by their leave, they are thieves. I do not deny the improvement of old rents, so it be done with old minds: I mean, our forefathers' charity. But, with the devil, to set right upon the pinnacles[30] and pitch so high a price of our lands that it strains the tenants' heart-blood to reach it is theft, and killing theft. What all their immoderate toil, broken sleeps, sore labors can get, with a miserable diet to themselves, not being able to spare a morsel of bread to others, is a prey

---

[28] {measuring (from "mete")}

[29] {"Prescription," in English law is the uninterrupted use or possession from time immemorial or for a period fixed by law as giving a title or right (*OED*). I.e., the laymen who benefited from the despoliation of the Church at the Reformation argue that they have a *right* to the church lands their ancestors seized because they have occupied them for a sufficiently long time.}

[30] {See Luke 4:9.}

to the landlord's rapine: this is to rob their estates, grind their faces, suck their bloods. These are thieves.

7. Engrossers, that hoard up commodities and by stopping their propagation raise the price, these are thieves. Many block-houses in the city, monopolies in the court, garners in the country can testify there are now such thieves abroad. We complain of a dearth; sure the heavens are too merciful to us that are so unmerciful one to another. Scarcity comes without God's sending. Who brings it then? Even the devil and his brokers, engrossing misers. The commonwealth may often blow[31] her nails, unless she sit by an engrosser's fire; her limbs may be faint with hunger, unless she buy grain at an engrosser's price. I confess, this is a sin which the law takes notice of, but not in the full nature, as theft. The pick-purse (in my opinion) doth not so much hurt as this general robber, for they rob millions. These do not, with Joseph, buy up the superfluity of plenty to prevent a dearth, but hoard up the store of plenty to procure a dearth. Rebels to God, trespassers to nature, thieves to the commonwealth—if these were apprehended and punished, neither city nor country should complain as they do. Mean time, the people's curse is upon them, and I doubt not but God's plague will follow it, if repentance turn it not away: till when, they are private thieves.

8. Enclosers, that pretend a distinction of possessions, a preservation of woods—indeed to make better and broader their own territories, and to steal from the poor commons[32]—these are horrible thieves. The poor man's beast is his maintenance, his sustenance, his life; to take food from his beast is to take the beast's food from his belly. So he that encloseth commons is a monstrous thief, for he steals away the poor man's living and life. Hence many a cottager, nay perhaps farmer, is fain (as the Indians do to devils) to sacrifice to the lord of the soil a yearly bribe for a *ne noceat*. For though the law forbids such enclosures, yet *quod fieri non debet, factum valet*: when they are once ditcht in, say the law what it will, I see no throwing out; force bears out what fraud hath borne in. Let them never open their mouths to plead the commonwealth's benefit; they intend it as much as Judas did when he spake for the poor. No, they are thieves, the bane of the common good, the surfeit of the land, the scourge of the poor: good only to themselves, and that in opinion only, for they do it *to dwell alone* [Esai. 5:8], and they dwell alone indeed, for neither God nor good angel keeps them company—and for a good conscience, it cannot get through their quick-sets.[33] These are thieves, though they have enclosed their theft to keep the law out and their wickedness in. Yet the day shall come, their lands shall be thrown out, their lives thrown out, their souls thrown out: their lands out of their possessions, their lives out of their bodies, their souls out of heaven—except repentance and restitution[34] prevail with the great Judge for their pardon. Mean time, they are thieves.

. . .

The *bag* is most usually given to the worst men; of all the apostles, he that was to betray Christ is made his steward. Goods are in themselves good. . . . since wealth well

---

[31] {blow upon [to keep warm]}

[32] {The "commons" are the common people, but also the unenclosed land that the entire community used in common, often the land on which villagers grazed their cattle.}

[33] {the hedges with which fields were enclosed}

[34] {On restitution, see Shuger, "Reformation of penance."}

employed comforts ourselves, relieves others, and brings us (as it were) the speedier way to heaven—and perhaps, to a greater portion of glory. But for the most part, the rich are enemies to goodness, and the poor friends. . . .

. . .

Surely God is wise in all his ways; he knows what he does: Judas shall hence bag up for himself the greater damnation. It is then no argument of God's favor to be his purse-bearer—no more than it was a sign that Christ loved Judas above the other apostles because he made him his steward. He gave the rest grace; and him, the *bag*. Which sped best? These outward things are the scatterings of his mercies, like the gleaning after the vintage. The full crop goes to his children. . . .

I would have no man make his riches an argument of God's disfavor and his own der-eliction—no, but rather of comfort, if he can find his affections ready to part with them at Christ's calling. I never was in your bosoms. How many of you lay up this resolution in your closet[35] among your bags? How many (*resolve* said I), nay, perform this? You cannot want opportunity in these days. I would wish you to try your hearts that you may secure your consciences of freedom from this *Judasme*.[36] . . .

. . .

Thus he runs from sin to sin, and needs he must: for he that the devil drives feels no lead at his heels. Godliness creeps to heaven, but wickedness runs to hell. Many Parlia-ment Protestants go but a statute-pace yet look to come to heaven; but without more haste, it is like to be when the Pharisees come out of hell. But *facilis descensus Averni*[37]. . . . It is but slipping down a hill, and hell stands at the bottom. This is the cause that Judas runs so fast.

. . .

Thus because the ways to hell are full of green, smooth, soft, and tempting pleasures, infinite run apace with Judas till they come to *their own place*. But heaven's way is harsh and ascending, and the gate narrow. Indeed, the city of glory is capacious and roomy: *in my Father's house there are many mansions*, saith Christ. It is *domus speciosa & domus spa-tiosa*, not either scant of beauty or pent of room. But the gate hath two properties: it is 1. low; 2. strait—and requires of the enterers: 1. a stooping; 2. a stripping.

Low. Pride is so stiff that many a gallant cannot enter. You have few women with the top-gallant head-tires get in here; they cannot stoop low enough; few proud in and of their offices, that have eaten a stake, and cannot stoop . . . This low gate and an high state do not accord. Wretched fools, that rather refuse the glory within than stoop for entrance: as if a soldier should refuse the honor of knighthood because he must kneel to receive it.

Strait, or narrow. They must stoop that enter this low gate, so they must strip that enter this strait gate. No makebates[38] get in: they are too full of tales and lies. God by word of mouth excludes them. *Into it shall enter none unclean thing, or that worketh abomina-tion or lies* [Rev. 21:27]. Few litigious neighbors: they have so many suits, contentions,

---

[35] {private office or study. . . . Since there were no banks in this period, one's cash reserves would have been kept in bags or chests in the home.}

[36] {i.e., Judas-ism, but almost certainly a pun on Judaism}

[37] {The descent to hell is easy (Vergil, *Aen.* 6.126).}

[38] {fomenters of strife and discord}

nisi-priuses on their backs that they cannot get in. Some lawyers may enter, if they be not over-laden with fees. You have few courtiers taken into this Court, by reason there is no coach-way to it; the gate is too narrow. No officers that are big with bribes. Not an encloser; he hath too much of the poor's commons in his belly. The usurer hath no hope, for besides his bags, he hath too much wax and paper about him. The citizen hopes well, but a false measure sticks so cross in his mouth that he cannot thrust in his head. The gentleman makes no question, and there is great possibility—if two things do not cross him: a bundle of racked rents or a kennel of lusts and sports. The plain-man is likely, if his ignorance can but find the gate. Husbandmen were in great possibility but for the hoarding of corn and hoysing[39] of markets. Tradesmen, if they would not swear good credit into their bad wares, might be admitted. Ministers may enter without doubt or hindrance, if they be as poor in their spirits as they are in their purses. But impropriators have such huge barns-full of church-grains in their bellies that they are too great. Let all these take the physic of repentance to abate their swollen souls, or there will be no entrance.

You hear how difficult the way is to heaven, how easy to hell; how fast sin runs, how slowly godliness creeps: what should you then do but *strive to enter in at the narrow gate*— which you shall the better do, if you lighten yourselves of your bags. Oh, do not (Judas-like) for the bag sell your honesty, conscience, heaven. The bag is a continent {container} to money, and the world is a continent to the bag, and they shall all perish. *Meat for the belly, and the belly for meat*; gold for the purse, and the purse for gold; *and God shall destroy them both* [1 Cor. 6:13]. Trust not then a wealthy bag, nor a wealthy man, nor the wealthy world; all will fail. But trust in God, whose *mercy endureth for ever*. The time shall come, that

> *Deus erit pro numine,*
> *Cùm mundus sit pro nomine,*
> *Cùm homo pro nemine.*

God shall be God, when the world shall be no world, man no man—or at least no man, no world of our expectation, or of ability to help us. *To God,* then, our only help, *be all praise, power, and glory, now and for ever. Amen.*

FINIS

✎⌒✐

Text: EEBO (STC [2nd ed.] / 131)

The white devil, or The hypocrite uncased: in a sermon preached at Paul's Cross, March 7, 1612, by Thomas Adams, Minister of the Gospel at Willington, in Bedford-shire (London: Printed by Melchisedech Bradwood for Ralph Mab, 1613), 1–15, 17–26, 28, 31–32, 34–43, 45–57, 55–57, 59–61.

---

[39] {jacking up prices in}

BENJAMIN CARIER
(ca. 1565–1614)

The son of a Kentish clergyman (and exact contemporary of William Shakespeare [1564–1616]), Carier attended King's School, Canterbury, and thereafter—like his classmate Christopher Marlowe—Corpus Christi, Cambridge, where he enrolled as a student-servant. He took his BA in 1587 and was made a fellow in 1589, proceeding MA in 1590, BD in 1597, and DD in 1602. The following year he lost a hard-fought contest for mastership of Corpus, in which battle he had the strong support of two leading anti-Calvinist dons, John Overall and Richard Clayton. Beginning in 1598, however, he did receive a number of livings in Kent and Sussex, including two from Archbishop Whitgift, whose chaplain Carier became during this period. It was Carier, along with Barlow and Buckeridge, whom the prelate chose to minister to him in his final illness. Following Whitgift's death in 1603, Carier became chaplain successively to Prince Henry and King James, the latter supplementing his parochial livings with a prebend at Canterbury Cathedral. In 1610 he became one of the first fellows of Chelsea College, the think-tank for Protestant controversialists set up by Matthew Sutcliffe with the strong backing of the King—despite the fact that Carier's first publication, the 1606 *Sermon preached before the Prince at Richmond*, explicitly rejects the typical Protestant understanding of concupiscence as per se sinful in favor of the Roman Catholic position that, although concupiscence often foments sin, sin itself necessarily involves wrong choice (Ci^r; see Shuger, "Gums," 6–8).

Prior to 1613, Carier's curriculum vitae traces the gentle ascent of a more-than-moderately successful Jacobean cleric. In April of that year, however, Carier, now forty-eight and ill, departed for Spa. Four months later he proceeded to Cologne, where the rector of the Jesuit college received him into the Roman Church. In December he wrote the King an open letter explaining the motives for his conversion and urging James to restore his Church to the Catholic fold—a version of which letter was published in 1614 as *A treatise written by M Doctor Carier*. The publication may have been posthumous, for in 1614 Carier died in Paris, where he had been a guest of Cardinal du Perron.

His Protestant countrymen predictably attributed Carier's defection to ambition, which, given his age and ill-health, seems unlikely. Abundant evidence indicates that he had long been an Anglo-Catholic (the 1606 sermon, the autobiographical portions of *A treatise*, a manuscript from ca. 1605 to 1613 attacking Calvinist teaching on grace—as well as his connections to Buckeridge, Neile, Laud, Howson, and Overall), but that in itself does not explain his conversion nor its timing. Carier's own explanation was that a Calvinist take-over in the English Church had newly thrust his traditionalist and patristic viewpoint out the door (see the prefatory letter to James and 1.8-10),[1] a claim supported by Ian Atherton's observation that one of Abbot's principal aims upon becoming archbishop in 1611 "was to use his new position and power at court to undermine a circle of 'avant-garde conformists' . . . [whose] sacramentalist and anti-Calvinist brand of piety threatened his own" (1242).[2] This Genevan drift in the English Church's mainstream, rendered urgent by the memento mori of age and illness, left Carier's position in the Church of England no longer tenable, either spiritually or politically.

A treatise, whose reprintings in 1632, 1649, and 1687 coincide with Laud's elevation to Canterbury, the regicide, and James II's Declaration of Indulgence, is a tightly argued apologia, largely free of the vitriol and mendacity disfiguring so much confessional polemic. Although its version of Calvinism bears no resemblance to the theology of mainline Calvinist divines <*vide* the selections from Dod, Preston, and Sibbes>, Carier does not attribute it to them; he is describing a strain of popular religion, the religion of "country Calvinists . . . especially when they are met in the alehouse" <2.12>, and recent scholarship bears out Carier's view that Jacobean godly piety "opened up many possibilities for disorder and mischief," including "a latent tendency towards ideological disintegration" (Atherton 1225–26).

The work presents a Roman Catholic perspective on the English Reformation, and, more broadly, on the relation of temporal to spiritual power—on the role of religion as the sole basis, other than brute coercion, of civil order. Yet since Carier's conversion was no Pauline volte-face but the outcome of long-held convictions, *A treatise* also illuminates the early Jacobean delineation of a distinctive high-church theology—in which regard, it is worth remembering that only seven years separate Carier from Laud.[3] Like Montagu's in the 1620s, Carier's position up to the moment of his exile rested on the premise that the Church of England was not—according to its official formularies—aligned with the Reformed tradition but rather kept the faith that "ever had been held in the Catholic Church" <1.7–8>.[4] Moreover, his comments on the relation between religion and polity

---

[1] Since *A treatise* has numbered sections and subsections, I will use these rather than page number to refer to specific passages.

[2] John Howson's account of the charges brought against him by the Archbishop and his brother <*vide infra*> likewise strongly corroborates Carier's version of things.

[3] See Questier 52; Shuger, "Protesting." However, Carier's characteristically Tridentine ahistoricism <1.2–3, 1.14> differentiates his theological position in a fairly fundamental way from English high-churchmanship with its debt to the historicist ecclesiology of Richard Hooker's *Laws*.

[4] A premise George Hakewill denies in his 1616 semi-official *An answer to a treatise written by Dr. Carier* (see Milton, *Catholic and Reformed* 383).

articulate with unusual clarity assumptions fundamental to the Laudian program: above all, a sense that Protestantism erodes the bases not only of monarchy but of all civil order, since its contempt for all that is hallowed and venerable in the Church inevitably breeds contempt for the ancient forms, customs, and institutions of secular authority as well <2.8>; as its demand for liberty of conscience, which configures any prohibition as persecution, inevitably fosters an anarchic and seditious sectarianism (<2.13>; *vide* Atherton 1226, 1250).

For Carier, secular order must ground itself in the mysteries of religion—which is emphatically not, in his eyes, equivalent to making religion the mystification of secular order, which is how he views the English Reformation <1.16, 2.22–26>. He never explains the difference, but it is implicit in his description of penance as regulating both people and rulers according to absolute moral norms <2.42>. In the English Reformation, by contrast, theological principles were jury-rigged to sanction *ragioni di stato*.

Although at moments Carier seems to be asking merely that English Catholics be permitted to worship in peace (as opposed to seeking legal recognition of papal supremacy), he explicitly disallows anything resembling a pluralist secular state <2.14, 2.42>; and his own description of Protestants as heretics who would crucify Christ given the chance <1.12> and whose religion amounted to devil-worship <2.7-8> makes it clear why the authorities regarded Catholic toleration as unworkable.[5]

SOURCES: *ODNB*; Ian Atherton, "The burning of Edward Wrightman: puritanism, prelacy, and the politics of heresy in early modern England," *English Historical Review* 120 (2005): 1215–50; Benjamin Carier, *A sermon preached before the Prince at Richmond this present year, 1606* (London: Printed by I. R. for Edmund Matts); Elizabeth Gilliam and W. J. Tighe, "To 'run with the time': Archbishop Whitgift, the Lambeth Articles, and the politics of theological ambiguity in late Elizabethan England," *The Sixteenth Century Journal* 23.2 (1992): 325–40; Anthony Milton, *Catholic and Reformed*; Michael Questier, "Crypto-Catholicism, anti-Calvinism, and conversion at the Jacobean court: the enigma of Benjamin Carier," *Journal of Ecclesiastical History* 47.1 (1996): 45–64; Shuger, "Protesting"; and "'Gums of glutinous heat' and the stream of consciousness: the theology of Milton's *Maske*," *Representations* 60 (1997): 1–21.

---

[5] Chillingworth's *Religion of Protestants* is precisely an attempt to refute the position that erroneous belief about God necessarily involved willful and malicious rebellion against him *<infra>*.

BENJAMIN CARIER

A treatise written by M. Doctor Carier wherein he layeth down sundry learned and pithy considerations by which he was moved to forsake the Protestant congregation and to betake himself to the Catholic Apostolic Roman Church
1614

The Preface to the Reader

Having exactly perused (good reader) this treatise here presented to thy view, and finding it both in stuff and style to be learnedly and eloquently contrived, I took myself in some sort obliged in Christian duty to divulge it in print to the world: unwittingly, I confess, to the author; howbeit encroaching upon his charitable consent, who, I am well assured, is most forward to defray his talent in ought wherein the Catholic Roman religion may be advanced. Of this full and firm resolution he hath made effective proof, not only in words, but also in works.

   . . .

⤝⤜⤙

Most Excellent and Renowned Sovereign:

It is not unknown to all that know me in England that for these many years I had my health very ill. And therefore, having from time to time used all the means and medicines that England could afford, last of all, by the advice of my physicians, I made it my humble suit unto your Majesty that I might travel unto the Spa for the use of those waters, purposing with myself that if I could be well I would go from thence to Heidelberg and spend this winter there. But when I was gone from the Spa to Aquisgrane[1] and so to Cologne, I found myself rather worse than better than I was before. And therefore I resolved with myself that it was high time for me to settle my thoughts upon another world. And seeing I was out of hope to enjoy the health of my body, at the least to look to the health of my soul, from whence both art and experience teacheth me that all my bodily infirmities have their beginning; for if I could by any study have proved Catholic religion to be false or by any means have professed it to be true in England, I doubt not but the contentment of my soul would have much helped the health of my body. But the more I studied the

---

[1] {Aachen}

Scriptures and most ancient Fathers to confute it, the more I was compelled to see the truth thereof. And the more I labored to reconcile the religion of England thereunto, the more I was disliked, suspected, and condemned as a common enemy. And if I would have been either ignorant or silent, I might, perhaps, with the pleasures and commodities of my preferments have in time cast off the care of religion. But seeing my study forced me to know, and my place compelled me to preach, I had no way to avoid my grief, nor no means to endure it. I have therefore apprehended the opportunity of my license to travel, that I may withdraw myself for a while from the sight and offence of those in England which hate Catholic religion, and freely and fully enjoy the presence of our blessed Savior in the unity of his Catholic Church, wherein I will never forget at the daily oblation of his most blessed body and blood to lift up my heart unto him and to pray for the admission of your Majesty thereunto. And in the meantime I have thought it my duty to write this short treatise with mine own hand, wherein, before I publish myself unto the world, I desire to shew to your Majesty these two things:

1. The means of my conversion unto Catholic religion.
2. The hopes I have to do your Majesty no ill service therein.

I humbly crave your Majesty's pardon, and will rest ever

Your Majesty's faithful and truly devoted servant, B. CARIER.

Liege, Decemb. 12, 1613

CHAP. I

The means of my conversion to Catholic religion

{1.} I must confess to God's honor, and my own shame, that if it had been in my power to choose, I would never have been a Catholic. I was born and brought up in schism, and was taught to abhor a papist as much as any puritan in England doth. I had ever a great desire to justify the religion of the state, and had great hope to advance myself thereby. Neither was my hope ever so great as by your Majesty's favor it was at the very instant of my resolution for Catholic religion. . . . And that it may appear that I have not respected anything so much in this world as my duty to your Majesty and my love to my friends and country, I humbly beseech you give me leave as briefly as I can to recount unto you the whole course of my studies and endeavors in this kind, even from the beginning of my life until this present.

2. I was born in the year 1566, being the son of Anty. Carier, a learned and devout man, who, although he were a Protestant and a preacher, yet he did so season me with the principles of piety and devotion as I could not choose but ever since be very zealous in matters of religion. Of him I learned that all false religions in the world were but policies invented of men for the temporal service of princes and states, and therefore that they were divers and always changeable according to the divers reasons and occasions of state. But true Christian religion was a truth revealed of God for the eternal salvation of souls, and therefore was like to God, always one and the same, so that all the princes and states in the world never have been nor shall be able to overthrow that religion. This to me seemed an excellent ground for the finding out of that religion wherein a man might find rest unto his soul, which cannot be satisfied with anything but eternal truth.

3. My next care then was, after I came to years of discretion, by all the best means I could to inform myself whether the religion of England were indeed the very same which, being prefigured and prophesied in the Old Testament, was perfected by our blessed Savior and delivered to his apostles and disciples to continue by perpetual succession in his visible Church until his coming again; or whether it were a new one for private purposes of statesmen invented and by human laws established. Of this I could not choose but make some doubt, because I heard men talk much of those days of the change of religion which was then lately made in the beginning of Queen Elizabeth's reign.

4. I was sorry to hear of change and of a new religion, seeing, me thought in reason, if true religion were eternal, then new religion could not be true. But yet I hoped that the religion of England was not a change or new religion, but a restitution of the old, and that the change was in the Church of Rome, which in process of time might perhaps grow to be superstitious and idolatrous; and therefore that England had done well to leave the Church of Rome and to reform itself, and for this purpose I did at my leisure and best opportunity, as I came to more judgment, read over the chronicles of England and observed all the alterations of religion that I could find therein; but when I found there that the present religion of England was a plain change, and change upon change, and that there was no cause of the change at all of the first, but only that King Henry VIII was desirous to change his old bedfellow that he might leave some heirs male behind him (for belike he feared that females would not be able to withstand the title of Scotland), and that the change was continued and increased by the posterity of his latter wives, I could not choose but suspect something, but yet the love of the world and hope of preferment would not suffer me to believe but that all was well and as it ought to be.

5. Thus I satisfied myself at school, and studied the arts and philosophy and other human learning, until being Master of Arts and fellow of Corpus Christi College in Cambridge, I was at the last by the statutes of that house called to the study of divinity and bound to take upon me the order of priesthood. Then I thought it my duty, for the better satisfaction of mine own soul and the saving of other men's, to look as far into the matter as possibly I could that I might find out the truth. And having the opportunity of a very good library in that college, I resolved with myself to study hard and, setting aside all respect of men then alive or of writers that had moved or maintained controversies (further than to understand the question which was betwixt them), I fell to my prayers and betook myself wholly to the reading of the church history and of the ancient Fathers which had no interest in either side; and especially I made choice of Saint Augustine, because I hoped to find most comfort in him for the confirming of our religion and the confuting of the Church of Rome.

6. In this sort I spent my time continually for many years, and noted down whatsoever I could gather, or rather snatch, either from the Scriptures or the Fathers to serve my turn. But when after all my pains and desire to serve myself of antiquity, I found the doctrine of the Church of Rome to be every where confirmed. . . .

7. Being thus perplexed with myself what course I were best to take, I reflected back again upon the Church of England, and because the most of those preachers which drew the people after them in those days were puritans and had grounded their divinity upon Calvin's *Institutions*, I thought peradventure that they, having gotten the multitude on their side, might wrong the Church of England in her doctrine, as well as they desired

to do in her discipline—which indeed upon due search I found to be most true. For I found the Common Prayer book and the catechism therein contained to hold no point of doctrine expressly contrary to Antiquity, but only that it was very defective and contained not enough. And that for the doctrine of predestination, sacraments, grace, free-will, sin, &c., the new catechisms and sermons of those preachers did run wholly against the Common Prayer book and catechisms therein, and did make as little account of the doctrine established by law as they did of discipline:[2] but in the one they found opposition by those that had private interest; in the other they said what they list because no man thought himself hurt.

8. . . . Nevertheless, having gotten this ground to work upon, I began to comfort myself with hope to prove that the religion established by law in England was the same, at the least in part, which now was and ever had been held in the Catholic Church—the defects whereof might be supplied, whensoever it should please God to move your Majesty thereunto, without abrogating of that which was already by law established, which I still pray for and am not altogether out of hope to see. And therefore I thought it my duty as far as I durst rather by charitable constructions reconcile things that seemed different, that so our souls might forever be saved in unity, than by malicious calumniations to maintain quarrels, that so men's turns might for a time be served in dissention.

9. In this course, although I did never proceed any farther than law would give me leave, yet I ever found the puritans and Calvinists, and all the creatures of schism, to be my utter enemies, who were also like the sons of Zeruiah, too strong for David himself, but I well perceived that all temperate and understanding men, who had no interest in the schism, were glad to hear the truth honestly and plainly preached unto them. And my hope was by patience and continuance I should in the end unmask hypocrisy and gain credit unto the comfortable doctrine of Antiquity, even amongst those also who out of misinformation and prejudice did as yet most dislike it. . . .

10. But when after my long hope, I at the last did plainly perceive that God for our sins had suffered the devil, the author of dissention, so far to prevail, as partly by the furious practice of some desperate Catholics, and partly by the fiery suggestions of all violent puritans, he had quite diverted that peaceable and temperate course which was hoped for, and that I must now either alter my judgment, which was impossible, or preach against my conscience, which was intolerable, Lord, what anxiety and distraction of soul did I suffer day and night, what strife betwixt my judgment, which was wholly for the peace and unity of the Church, and my affection, which was wholly to enjoy the favor of your Majesty and the love of my friends and country. . . .

11. And yet because I had heard often that the practice of the Church of Rome was contrary to her doctrine, I thought good to make one trial more before I resolved; and therefore, having the advice of divers learned physicians to go to the Spa for the health of my body, I thought good to make a virtue of necessity and to get leave to go, the rather

---

[2] {That is, Carier holds that the *official* doctrine of the English Church is, like its discipline (i.e., ecclesiastical polity), consistent with the teaching and practice of Christian antiquity; and that the same doctrinaire puritans whose presbyterianism threatened English episcopacy were teaching a Calvinist theology at odds with "Anglican" orthodoxy. For a very different view of the matter, see Patrick Collinson, *The Elizabethan puritan movement* (U California P, 1967), and Tyacke, *Anti-Calvinists*.}

for the satisfaction of my soul, hoping to find some greater offence in the service of the Church of Rome than I had done in her books, that so I might return better contented to persecute and abhor the Catholics at home after I should find them so wicked and idolatrous abroad as they were in every pulpit in England affirmed to be. For this purpose, before I would frequent their churches, I talked with such learned men as I could meet withal, and did of purpose dispute against them, and with all the wit and learning I had, both justify the doctrine of England established by law and object the superstition and idolatry which I thought they might commit either with the images in the church or with the sacrament of the altar.

12. Their common answer was that which by experience I now find to be true, *viz.* that they do abhor all idolatry and superstition, and do diligently admonish the people to take heed thereof. And that they use images for no other purpose but only for a devout memory and representation of the Church Triumphant, which is most fit to be made in the time and place of prayer, where after a more special manner we should with all reverence have our conversation amongst the saints in heaven.

And for the b{lessed} sacrament, they do not worship the accidents which they see, but the substance which they believe. And surely, if Christ be there truly and really present (as your Majesty seemeth to grant he is), he is as much to be worshipped as if we saw him with our bodily eyes. Neither is there any more idolatry in the one than in the other. If our blessed Savior himself should visibly appear in person as he was upon the earth, Jews and infidels would hold it for idolatry to worship him and would crucify him again, and so would all heretics also who refuse to worship him in the sacrament where he is really present.

13. After divers other objections which I made, not so much because I was not, as because I desired not to be satisfied, I came to the pope's supposed pride and tyranny over kings and princes, and told them of the most horrible treason intended & practiced by Catholics against your Majesty, which hath not yet been judicially condemned by the Church of Rome. They all seemed to abhor the fact as much as the best subjects in the world, and much more to favor and defend the authority of their kings and princes than the heretics do. And they said that although your Majesty were out of the Church, yet they doubted not but if complaint were made in a judicial proceeding, that fact should be judicially condemned. In the meantime it was sufficient that all Catholic writers did condemn it, and that the pope by his *breve*[3] had condemned it, exhorting the Catholics of England to all Christian patience and obedience. As for any other authority or superiority of the pope than such as is spiritual and necessary for the unity of the Church, I have met with none that do stand upon it.

14. So that, whereas my hope was that by finding out the corruptions of the Church of Rome, I should grow further in love with the Church of England and joyfully return home, and by inveighing against the papists both enjoy my present preferments and obtain more and more, I saw the matter was like to fall out clean contrary. It is true indeed that there are many corruptions in all states. God hath no wheat field in this world wherein the devil hath no tares growing, and there are no tares more rank than those that grow among the wheat. For *optimi corruptio pessima*, and where grace aboundeth, if it be

---

[3] {A *breve* or brief is a letter issued by the Apostolic Secretariate to transmit papal commands.}

contemned, there sin aboundeth much more. But seeing both my reading & experience hath now taught me that the truth of Christian religion taught and practiced at this day in the Church of Rome and all the obedient members thereof is the very same in substance which was prefigured and prophesied from the beginning of the world, perfected by Christ himself, delivered to his apostles, and by them and their successors perpetually and universally in one uniformity practiced until this day without any substantial alteration; and that the new religion of England, wherein it doth differ, hath no ground but either the pleasure of the prince and Parliament or the common cry and voice of the people, nor no constancy or agreement with itself; what should I now do? It is not in my power not to know that which I do know. . . .

15. These were my thoughts at the Spa. . . . In the meantime I thought with myself, it may be God hath moved his Majesty's heart to think of peace and reconciliation. I know his disposition was so in the beginning, and I remember Master Causabon told me, when I brought him out of France, that his errand was nothing else but to mediate peace between the Church of Rome and the Church of England. Therefore I thought, before I would submit myself to the Church of Rome, I would write unto Master Causabon such a letter as he might shew unto your Majesty, containing such conditions as I thought might satisfy your Majesty, if they were performed by the Church of Rome. The copy of which letter is too long here to set down. But when Master Causabon answered me that he knew your Majesty was resolved to have no society with the Church of Rome upon any condition whatsoever, and that it would be my undoing if those my letters should come to your Majesty's hands or of those that bare the sway, I began to despair of my return into England. . . .

16. There is a statute in England made by King Henry VIII to make him supreme head of the Church in spiritual and ecclesiastical causes, which statute enjoins all the subjects of England on pain of death to believe and to swear they do believe that it is true. And yet all the world knows, if King Henry VIII could have gotten the pope to divorce Queen Katherine that he might marry Anne Boleyn, that statute had never been made by him; and if that title had not enabled the King to pull down abbeys and religious houses and give them to laymen, the Lords and Commons of that time would never have suffered such a statute to be made. This statute was continued by Queen Elizabeth to serve her own turn, and it is confirmed by your Majesty to satisfy other men. And yet your Majesty yieldeth the Church of Rome to be the mother Church, and the bishop of Rome to be the chief bishop or primate of all the western Churches, which I do also verily believe; and therefore I do verily think he hath or ought to have some spiritual jurisdiction in England. And although in my younger days, the fashion of the world made me swear as other men did (for which I pray God forgive me), yet I ever doubted, and am now resolved, that no Christian man can take that oath with a safe conscience, neither will I ever take it to gain the greatest preferment in the world.

17. There is another statute in England, made by Queen Elizabeth and confirmed by your Majesty, that it is death for any Englishman to be in England, being made a priest by authority derived or pretended to be derived from the bishop of Rome. I cannot believe that I am a priest at all, unless I be derived by authority from Gregory the Great, from whence all the bishops in England have their being, if they have any being at all.

18. There is another statute in like manner made and confirmed, that it is death to be reconciled by a Catholic priest to the Church of Rome. I am persuaded that the Church of Rome is our mother Church, and that no man in England can be saved that continues willfully out of the visible unity of that Church, and therefore I cannot choose but persuade the people to be reconciled thereunto, if possibly they can.

19. There is another statute in like manner made and confirmed, that it is death to exhort the people of England to Catholic Roman religion. I am persuaded that the religion prescribed and practiced by the Church of Rome is the true Catholic religion, which I will particularly justify and make plain from point to point, if God give time and opportunity, and therefore I cannot choose but persuade the people thereunto.

It may be these are not all several statutes; some of them may be members of the same (for I have not my books about me to search); but I am sure all of them do make such felonies and treasons as were the greatest virtues of the primitive Church, and such as I must needs confess myself I cannot choose, if I live in England, but endeavor to be guilty of; and then it were easy to find puritans enough to make a jury against me; and there would not want a Justice of Peace to give a sentence; and when they had done, that which is worse than the persecution itself, they would all swear solemnly that Doctor Carier was not put to death for Catholic religion, but for felony and treason. . . . And therefore whilst the case so stands, I dare not return home again. But I cannot be altogether out of hope of better news before I die, as long as I do believe that the saints in heaven do rejoice at the conversion of a sinner to Christ, and do know that your Majesty by your birth hath so great an interest in the saints of heaven as you shall never cease to have until you cease to be the son of such a mother as would rejoice more then all the rest for your conversion. And therefore I assure myself that she with all the rest do pray that your Majesty before you die may be militant in the communion of that Church wherein they are triumphant.

. . .

CHAP. II

The hopes I have to do your Majesty no ill service in being Catholic

. . .

2. And although it be sufficient for a man of my profession to respect only matters of heaven and of another world, yet because this world was made for that other, I have not regarded mine own estate that I might respect your Majesty's therein, and after long and serious meditation which religion might most honor your Majesty even in this world, I have conceived undoubted hope that there is no other religion that can procure true honor and security to your Majesty and your posterity in this world but the true Catholic Roman religion, which was the very same whereby all your glorious predecessors have been advanced and protected on earth and are everlastingly blessed in heaven.

3. The first reason of my hope is the promise of God himself to bless and honor those that bless his Church and honor him, and to curse and confound those that curse his Church and dishonor him, which he hath made good in all ages. . . .

. . .

5. As for the honor and greatness of the Turk and other infidels, as it reacheth no farther then this life, so it hath no beginning from above this world; and if we may believe Saint Ambrose . . . those honors are conferred rather by God's permission than by his donation, being indeed ordained and ordered by his providence, but for the sins of the people conferred by the prince that rules in the air. It is true that the Turkish empire hath now continued a long time, but they have other principles of state to stand upon: the continual guard of an hundred thousand soldiers, whereof most of them know no parents but the emperor; the tenure of all his subjects who hold all *in capite ad volunta-tem domini* by the service of the sword;[4] their enjoined silence and reverence in matters of religion; and their facility in admitting other religions as well as their own to the hope of salvation, and to tolerate them so that they be good subjects.

These and such like are principles of great importance to increase an empire and to maintain a temporal state. But there is no state in Christendom that may endure these principles, unless they mean to turn Turks also, which, although some be willing to do, yet they will neither hold *in capite* nor hold their peace in religion nor suffer their king to have such a guard about him nor admit of Catholic religion so much as the Turk doth.

6. It is most true, which I gladly write . . . that I think there was never any Catholic king in England that did in his time more embrace and favor the true body of the Church of England than your Majesty doth that shadow thereof which is yet left. And my firm hope is that this your desire to honor our blessed Savior in the shadow of the Church of England will move him to honor your Majesty so much as not to suffer you to die out of the body of his true Catholic Church; and in the meantime to let you understand that all honor that is intended to him by schism and heresy doth redound to his great dishonor both in respect of his real and of his mystical body.

7. For his real body, it is not as the Ubiquitaries[5] would have it, everywhere, as well without the Church as within; but only where himself would have it and hath ordained that it should be, and that is only amongst his apostles and disciples and their successors in the Catholic Church to whom he delivered his sacraments & promised to continue with them until the world's end: so that although Christ be present in that schism by the power of his deity (for so he is present in hell also) yet by the grace of his humanity, by participation of which grace only there is hope of salvation, he is not present there at all, except it be in corners and prisons and places of persecution. And therefore whatsoever honor is pretended to be done to Christ in schism and heresy is not done to him, but to his utter enemies.

8. And for his mystical body, which is his Church and kingdom, there can be no greater dishonor done to Christ than to maintain schism and dissention therein. What would your Majesty think of any subjects of yours that should go about to raise civil dissention or wars in your kingdom, and of those that should foster and adhere unto such men? It is the fashion of all rebels when they are in arms to pretend the safety of the king and the good of the country; but pretend what they will, you cannot account such men

---

[4] {I.e., his subjects hold their land by a grant from the sultan, who can revoke it at will, in return for military service.}

[5] {I.e., Lutherans, who upheld the real presence of Christ's body and blood in the Eucharist on the grounds of this ubiquity.}

any better than traitors. And shall we believe that our blessed Savior, the King of kings, doth sit in heaven and either not see the practices of those that, under color of serving him with reformation, do nothing else but serve their own turns and distract his Church that is his kingdom on earth with sedition? Or shall we think that he will not in time revenge this wrong? Verily he seeth it, and doth regard it, and will in time revenge it.

. . .

[10.[6]] The second reason of my hope that Catholic religion may be a great means of honor and security to your Majesty's posterity is taken from the consideration of your neighbors, the kings and princes of Christendom, among whom there is no state ancient and truly honorable but only those that are Catholic. . . . And as for those that have rejected and opposed the rules of Catholic religion, they have been driven in short time to degenerate, and become either tyrannical or popular. Your Majesty, I know, doth abhor tyranny, but if schism and heresy might have their full swing over the seas, the very shadow and relics of majesty in England should be utterly defaced and quickly turned into Helvetian or Belgian popularity, for they that make no conscience to profane the majesty of God & his saints in the Church will, after they feel their strength, make no bones to violate the majesty of the king and his children in the commonwealth.

. . .

12. The third reason of my hope that Catholic religion should be most available for the honor and security of your Majesty and your children is taken from the consideration of your subjects, which can be kept in obedience to God and to their king by no other religion, and least of all by the Calvinists; for if their principles be received once and well drunk in and digested by your subjects, they will openly maintain that God hath as well predestinated men to be traitors as to be kings, and he hath as well predestinated men to be thieves as to be judges,[7] and he hath as well predestinated that men should sin as that Christ should die for sin: which kind of disputations I know by my experience in the country that they are ordinary among your country Calvinists that take themselves to be learned in the Scriptures, especially when they are met in the ale-house and have found a weaker brother whom they think fit to be instructed in these profound mysteries. And howsoever they be not yet all so impudent as to hold all these conclusions in plain terms, yet it is certain they all hold these principles of doctrine from whence working heads of greater liberty do at their pleasures draw these consequences in their lives and practices. And is this a religion fit to keep subjects in obedience to their sovereigns?

13. Here, I know, the great masters of schism will never leave objecting the horrible treason of certain Catholics against your Majesty, which if the devil had not wrote to their hands they had had little to say against Catholic religion before this day. But I humbly entreat that the fact of some few men may not be forever objected against the truth of a general rule. . . . There is no principle of any religion, nor no article of any faith, which a Calvinist will not call in question, and either altogether deny or expound after his own fancy; and if he be restrained, he cries out by and by that he cannot have the liberty of his conscience. And what bond of obedience can there be in such religion?

---

[6] {The printer now and then forgets to number a paragraph.}

[7] {*Vide* Falstaff's justification of his criminal career on the ground that "'tis no sin for a man to labor in his vocation" (*1 Henry IV*, act I, scene ii, lines 210–11).}

14. It is commonly objected by statesmen that it is no matter what opinions men hold in matters of religion so that they be kept in awe by justice and by the sword. . . . But in a peaceable government, such as all Christian kingdoms do profess to be, if the reins of religion be let loose, the sword commonly is too weak and comes too late, and will be like enough to give the day to the rebel. And seeing the last and strongest bond of justice is an oath, which is a principal act of religion and were but a mockery if it were not for the punishment of hell and the reward of heaven, it is impossible to execute justice without the help of religion. And therefore the neglect and contempt of religion hath ever been and ever shall be the fore-runner of destruction in all settled states whatsoever.

. . .

17. . . . Let them say what they list of their own honesty and of their exhortations to obedience, as long as they do freely infect the people's souls with such false opinions in religion, they do certainly sow the seeds of disobedience and rebellion in men's understandings, which if they be not prevented by your Majesty's giving way to Catholic religion, will in all likelihood spring up in the next generation to the great prejudice and molestation of your Majesty and your posterity. . . .

. . .

20. . . . But if your Majesty shall ever be pleased . . . to admit a conference of learned and moderate men on either side . . . it will also appear that there is not indeed any such irreconcilable opposition betwixt the Church of England and the Church of Rome as they that live by the schism do make the world believe there is, neither in matter of doctrine nor matter of state.

21. For matter of doctrine, there is no reason that your Majesty or the kingdom should be molested or burdened for the maintenance of Calvinism, which is as much against the religion of England as it is against the religion of Rome. . . .

The doctrine of England is that which is contained in the Common Prayer book and Church catechism, confirmed by act of Parliament and by your Majesty's edict, wherein all Englishmen are baptized and ought to be confirmed, and therefore there is some reason that this should be stood upon.

But this doctrine in most of the main points thereof, as hath been touched before and requireth a just treatise to set down in particular, doth much differ from the current opinions and catechisms of Calvinism, or doth very near agree with, or at least not contradict, the Church of Rome, if we list with patience to hear one another. And those points of doctrine where we are made to be at wars with the Church of Rome, whether we will or not, do rather argue the corruptions of that state from whence they come than are argued by the grounds of that religion whereupon they stand; and the contradiction of doctrine hath followed the alteration of state, and not the alteration of state been grounded upon any truth of doctrine.

22. For when the breach was resolved upon for the personal and particular ease of King Henry VIII and the children of his latter wives, it was necessary to give every part of the commonwealth contentment, for which they might hold out in the heat of affection and study to maintain the breach. . . .

23. Therefore to the lords and favorites of the Court were given the lands and inheritance of the abbeys and religious houses, that having once, as it were, washed their hands in the bowels and blood of the Church, both they and their posterity might be at utter

defiance therewith. And so having overthrown and profaned the good works of the saints, it was necessary for them to get them chaplains that might both dispute, preach, and write against the merits of good works, the invocation of saints, the sacrifice of the altar, prayer for the dead, and all such points of Catholic doctrine as were the grounds of those churches and religious houses which they had overthrown and profaned. And it was not hard for those chaplains, by some shew of Scripture, to prove that which their lords and their followers were so willing to believe.

24. To the commons was given great hope of relief for their poverty, ease of subsidies and of the burden of so great a clergy, and many other goodly gay Nothings. And for the present, they should have liberty and the benefit of common law: that is, leave to live by such laws as themselves list to make and to contemn the authority of the Church, which, although it were for their benefit every way, yet because it crossed their affections, like wayward children they could never abide it. And was not this reason enough for them to hold out the breach and to study Scripture themselves: that they might be able to confute confession, satisfaction, penance, and to declaim against all that tyranny of the Church of Rome whereby themselves and their forefathers had been kept in awe and obedience unto God, and their kings?

25. To the clergymen that would turn with the times, besides the possibility of present preferment by the alteration, was given shortly after leave to marry and to purchase and to enjoy the profit and pleasure of the world as well as the laity. And what carnal-minded monk or priest would not with might and main keep open the breach after he was once plunged in it, rather than be in danger to forgo so pleasing a commodity. Hence did arise a necessity of speaking and writing against vows, virginity, poverty, fasting, praying, watching, obedience, and all that austerity of life which is by the laws of the Church required in a monastical and priestly conversation.

26. Upon these conditions, the lords, the commons, and the clergy were content to believe that the king was supreme head of the Church of England. . . .

   . . .

32. Queen Elizabeth, although she were the daughter of schism, yet at her first coming to the crown, she would have the Common Prayer book and catechism so set down that she might both by English service satisfy the commons, who were greedy of alteration, and by Catholic opinions gave hope to her neighbor princes that she would herself continue Catholic. And all her life long she carried herself so betwixt the Catholics and the Calvinists as she kept them both still in hope.

But yet being the daughter of the breach-maker, and having both her crown and her life from the schism, it was both dishonorable and dangerous for her to hearken to reconcilement. And therefore after she was provoked by the excommunication of Pius Quintus, she did suffer such laws to be made by her Parliaments as might cry quittance with the pope and the Church of Rome. And this course seemed in policy necessary for her, who was the daughter of King Henry VIII by Anne Boleyn, born with the contempt of Rome, the disgrace of Spain, & the prejudice of Scotland.

33. But now that your Majesty is by the consent of all sides come to the crown, and your undoubted title settled with long possession, the case is very much altered, for your Majesty hath no need of dispensations, nor no will to pull down churches, nor no dependence at all on Henry VIII. . . .

34. . . .

. . . You are our sovereign lord. All our bodies and our goods are at your command. But our souls, as they belong not to your charge but as by way of protection in Catholic religion, so they cannot increase your honor or authority but in a due subordination unto Christ, and to those that supply his place in *ijs quae sunt iuris diuini.*[8] It was essential to heathen emperors to be *pontifices* as well as *reges* because they were themselves authors of their own religion. But among Christians, where religion comes from Christ, who was no worldly emperor (though above them all), the spiritual and temporal authority have two beginnings, and therefore two Supremes, who, if they be subordinate, do uphold and increase one another.[9] But if the temporal authority do oppose the spiritual, it destroyeth itself and dishonoreth him from whom the spiritual authority is derived. Heresy doth naturally spread itself like a canker and needs little help to put it forward, so that it is an easy matter for a mean prince to be a great man amongst heretics, but it is an hard matter for a great king to govern them. . . .

. . .

41. For wealth—the puritan unthrift that looks for the overthrow of bishops and churches cathedral, hopes to have his share in them if they would fall once; and therefore he cannot choose but desire to increase the schism that he may gain by it. But the honest Protestant that can endure the state of the Church of England as it is could be content it were as it was, for he should receive more benefit by it every way.

The poor gentleman and yeoman that are burdened with many children may remember that, in Catholic times, the Church would have received and provided for many of their sons and daughters so as themselves might have lived and died in the service of God without posterity and have helped to maintain the rest of their families, which was so great a benefit to the commonwealth, both for the exoneration[10] and provision thereof, as no human policy can procure the like. The farmer and husband-man who laboreth hard to discharge his payments and hath little or nothing left at the year's end to lay up for his children that increase and grow upon him may remember that in Catholic times there were better pennyworths to be had when the clergy had a great part of the land in their hands, who had no need to raise their rents themselves and did what they might to make other lords let at a reasonable rate, which was also an inestimable benefit to the commons. So that whereas ignorant men carried with envy against the clergy are wont to object the multitude of them and the greatness of their provisions, they speak therein as much against themselves as is possible.

For the greater the number is of such men as are *mundo mortuus,*[11] the more is the exoneration of the commons; and the more the lands is of such as can have no propriety in them, the better is the provision of the commons. For themselves can have no more but their food and regular apparel; all the rest either remains in the hands of the tenants, or returns in hospitality and relief to their neighbors, or kept as in a living exchequer for the service of the prince and country in time of necessity. So that the commons doth gain no wealth at all, but rather do lose much by the schism.

[8] {in those things which pertain to divine law}
[9] {For the contrary argument, see Buckeridge <61–67>.}
[10] {unburdening, relief}
[11] {dead to the world}

42. And as for liberty, they are indeed freed from the possibility of going to shrift, that is, of confessing their sins to God in the care of a Catholic priest and receiving comfort and counsel against their sins from God by the mouth of the same priest, which duty is required of Catholic people but only once in the year, but performed by them with great comfort and edification very often, so that a man may see and wonder to see many hundred at one altar to communicate every Sunday with great devotion, and lightly no day pass but divers do confess, are absolved, and receive the blessed sacrament.

The poor commons of England are freed from this comfort; neither is it possible, unless their ministers had the seal of secrecy for them to use it.[12] And what is the liberty that they have in stead thereof? Surely the servants have great liberty against their masters by this means, and the children against their parents, and the people against their prelates, and the subjects against their king, and all against the Church of Christ: that is, against their own good and the common salvation; for without the use of this sacrament, neither can inferiors be kept in awe but by the gallows, which will not save them from hell, nor superiors be ever told of their errors but by rebellion, which will not bring them to heaven. These and such like be the liberties that both prince and people do enjoy by the want of confession and of Catholic religion.

43. As for the liberty of making laws in Church matters, the common lawyer may perhaps make an advantage of it and therefore greatly stand upon it, but to the common people it is no pleasure at all, but rather a great burthen. For the great multitude of statutes which have been made since the schism (which are more than five times so many that ever were made before since the name of Parliament was in England) hath caused also an infinite number of lawyers, all which must live by the commons and raise new families, which cannot be done without the decay of the old. And if the canons of the Church and the courts of confession were in request, the lawyers' market would soon be marred.

And therefore, most of your lawyers in this point are puritans and do still furnish the Parliament with grievances against the clergy. . . .

. . .

45. There never was, is, nor shall be any well-settled state in the world, either Christian or heathen, but the clergy and priesthood was, is, and must be a principal part of the government, depending upon none but him only whom they suppose to be their God. But where Calvinism prevaileth, three or four stipendiary ministers, that must preach as it shall please Master Mayor and his brethren, may serve for a whole city. And indeed, if their opinions be true, it is but a folly for any state to maintain any more. For if God hath predestinated a certain number to be saved without any condition at all of their being in the visible Church by faith or their persevering therein by good works; if God hath reprobated the greatest part of the world without any respect at all of their infidelity, heresy, or wicked life; if the faith of Christ be nothing else but the assured persuasion of a man's own predestination to glory by him; if the sacraments of the Church be nothing but signs and badges of that grace which a man hath before by the carnal covenant of his parents'

---

[12] {*Pace* Carier, the English canons of 1603/4 do uphold the secrecy of confession (i.e., the seal of the confessional), except for confessions of treasonable plots or deeds; see *The Anglican canons, 1529–1947*, ed. Gerald Bray, Church of England Record Society 6 (Woodbridge: Boydell, 1998), 412–13.}

faith;[13] if priesthood can do nothing but preach the word (as they call it), which laymen must judge of (and may preach too, if they will, where occasion serves); if the study and knowledge of antiquity, universality, and consent be not necessary, but every man may expound Scripture as his own spirit shall move him; if, I say, these and such like opinions be as true as they are among the Calvinists in the world common, and in England too much favored and maintained, there will certainly appear no reason at all unto your Parliament, whensoever your Majesty or your successor shall please to ask them, why they should be at so great a charge as they are to maintain so needless a party as these opinions do make the clergy to be. They can have a great many more sermons a great deal better cheap; and in the opinion of Calvinism, the clergy do no other service. They that do in England favor and maintain those opinions, and suppress and disgrace those that do confute them, they, although themselves can be content to be lords and to go in rochets, are indeed the greatest enemies of the clergy.[14] . . .

. . . As for other clergymen that are conformable to the religion established by law, as well for their doctrine as for their discipline, if they be good scholars and temperate men (as I know many of them are), they cannot but in their judgments approve the truth of Catholic religion, and if it were not for fear of loss, or disgrace to their wives and children, they would be as glad as myself that a more temperate course might be held and more liberty afforded unto Catholics and Catholic religion in England.

These clergymen, I am and ever shall be desirous to satisfy (not only in respect of themselves but also in respect of their wives and children), whom I am so far from condemning and misliking as that I do account myself one of them; and I desire nothing more in this world than in the toleration of Catholic religion to live and die among them. And therefore I have had so great care in this point as, before I did submit myself to the Catholic Church, I received assurance from some of the greatest that if your Majesty would admit the ancient subordination of the Church of Canterbury unto that mother Church (by whose authority all other churches in England at the first were and still are subordinate unto Canterbury) and {allow} the first free use of that sacrament for which especially all the Churches in Christendom were first founded, the pope for his part would confirm the interest of all these that have present possession in any ecclesiastical living in England, and would also permit the free use of the Common Prayer book in English for morning and evening prayer with very little or no alteration. . . .

. . .

48. I have more things to write, but the haste of answering your Majesty's commandment, signified to me by Sir Thomas Lake his letters, have made me commit many faults in writing this very suddenly, for which I crave pardon, and cut off the rest.

But for my returning into England, I can answer no otherwise but thus: I have sent you my SOUL in this treatise, and if it may find entertainment and passage, my BODY

---

[13] {On the Calvinist claim that election ran in families, a claim that the English delegates to the Synod of Dort explicitly rejected, see John Hales, *Letters from the Synod of Dort to Sir Dudley Carlton* (Glasgow, 1765), 30–43.}

[14] {He's referring to Calvinist, or "puritan," bishops like George Abbot, the then-Archbishop of Canterbury. See John Howson's "trial" <infra>; see also Nicholas Tyacke, *Aspects of English Protestantism*, 164, and Collinson, *Religion of Protestants*.}

shall most gladly follow after. And if not, I pray God I send my soul to heaven and my body to the grave as soon as may be. In the meantime, I will rejoice in nothing but only in the cross of Christ, which is the glory of your crown. And therefore I will triumph therein, not as being gone from you to your adversary, but as being gone before you to your Mother,[15] where I desire and hope forever to continue.

Your Majesty's true servant and beadsman, B. CARIER.

Liege, Decemb. 12, An. 1613.

TEXT: EEBO (STC [2nd ed.] / 4623.5)

A treatise, written by M. Doctor CARIER, wherein he layeth down sundry learned and pithy considerations, by which he was moved to forsake the Protestant Congregation, and to betake himselfe to the Catholic Apostolic Roman Church. Agreeing verbatim with the written Copy, addressed by the said Doctor to the King his most Excellent MAJESTY (n.p., 1614),[16] 1–22, 25–29, 32–34, 40–42, 44–46.

[15] {the Roman Church, but perhaps with an allusion to James' biological mother, Mary Stuart, a devout Catholic}

[16] The STC gives "England: English Secret Press."

JOHN HOWSON
(1556/7–1632)

John Howson's record of his hearing before King James on charges
brought by Archbishop Abbot

On June 10, 1615, John Howson, DD, a prebendary of Christ Church, Oxford, obeyed
a summons to appear before the King to answer charges of heterodoxy, barratry,[1] and
high treason brought by Robert Abbot, Master of Balliol and Oxford's regius professor of
divinity—his brother George, Archbishop of Canterbury since 1611, prosecuting the case
coram rege. The chance survival of a letter by Bishop Neile discloses that William Laud,
then Master of St. John's, Oxford, also appeared before the King that June to answer
similar charges brought by the same accusers.

Neile's letter reveals only the outcome of Laud's hearing, but Howson wrote a blow-
by-blow account of his "trial" almost immediately thereafter. The hastily-written manuscript was almost certainly for Howson's own use—for his own protection; as the account
makes clear, Howson had a habit of recording such confrontations immediately after the
fact lest his adversaries subsequently misreport his words, or their own.

Howson's account is presumably not impartial, yet sufficient corroborating evidence
exists to confirm its basic accuracy. If Howson depicts himself as victor, the aftermath
bears out this impression, since, when the Bishop of Oxford died only three years later,
the King nominated Howson his successor; equally telling, James named none of the
Abbots' Oxford allies to the British delegation attending the Synod of Dort. Howson's
manuscript, as suggested by its modern editors, Nicholas Cranfield and Kenneth Fincham provides an extraordinary behind-the-scenes view of what would appear to be the
moment when the winds at court shifted in favor of the anti-Calvinists (326–27). If so,
this would be an unexpectedly early tipping-point, before the Synod of Dort and before

---

[1] Usually refers to the misuse of the courts to harass enemies by vexatious litigation, but can also concern the buying and/or selling of offices, or, more loosely, quarrelsomeness.

the Palatinate crisis. Howson describes a theological landscape in which fissures present from the outset have suddenly begun to deepen, although the conclusion of his narrative suggests why the center might nonetheless have held for a quarter-century.

Because the manuscript only reports who said what during a single meeting, some background regarding both the participants and the issues is needed. In 1615 Howson was nearly sixty.[2] He had taken his BA at Christ Church, Oxford, in 1578, his MA four years later. In the 1590s, he served as one of Elizabeth's chaplains and preached twice at Paul's Cross, while apparently continuing at Oxford, where he took his BD and DD together in 1601. By the next July he had become the University's vice-chancellor. Preaching at the University church of St. Mary the Virgin that November, Howson set off a firestorm by urging the observance of the Prayer Book's liturgical calendar, with its saints' days and Marian feasts, and elevating worship and prayer to an equality with sermons. The puritan provost of Queen's, Henry Airay, who viewed the Prayer Book ceremonies as the worship of Baal rather than Christ and held that bishops were neither *iure divino* nor apostolic, denounced the Vice-Chancellor, who in turn suspended Airay from preaching. Airay and a couple of young masters openly defied Howson's orders, precipitating a crisis that ended up before the Privy Council, which decided in Howson's favor, although Airay managed to avoid having to make a formal apology. Indeed, in 1606 Airay himself became vice-chancellor, and proceeded to make trouble for Laud over a sermon.

Between 1610 and 1612 Robert Abbot became a powerful figure on the University stage, George Abbot on the national. The former received the mastership of Balliol in 1610, the regius divinity professorship in 1612, while the intervening year saw the latter elevated to Canterbury. Both were, unlike Airay, conformists of long-standing, but otherwise cut from much the same cloth: namely, Perkins-style old-school double predestinarians of an experimental stripe. From 1610 to 1615 both campaigned vigorously to suppress Oxford's anti-Calvinist faculty. In 1610–11 George Abbot sought to tar Laud as a papist to keep him from becoming head of St. John's. Once at Lambeth, Abbot "dedicated himself to defending a narrow interpretation of reformed teaching and practice," using "his archiepiscopal powers and influential connections to oppose those who challenged this theology," and in particular "anti-Calvinist divines such as Howson and Laud whose teaching, Abbot maintained, represented a fatal backslide into Roman error" (Cranfield and Fincham 324). As the manuscript makes clear, Howson, who had been thirty years at Oxford, saw the Calvinist consensus the Archbishop sought to enforce as something new: before 1611, he maintains, Oxford divines might disagree (and often did), but there was no black-balling of colleagues who did not toe the party line nor the intimidation that left Howson's friends afraid to be seen in his company.[3] Before 1611 the University had room for Howson—and, Howson adds, for Benjamin Carier, until Abbot more or less thrust him into the arms of Rome *<vide supra>*.

Howson found himself next in the line of fire. A sermon he preached in 1612 criticized some marginal glosses in the Geneva Bible. Airay, Robert Abbot, and William

---

[2] George and Robert Abbot were in their late fifties; the King, 49; Laud, the youngest at 45.

[3] See the portion of the manuscript dealing with charge 9; one glimpses what Howson saw as the pre-Abbot academic culture of tough-minded yet collegial critique in his account of the vetting of Bishop Morton's treatise (charge 14).

Goodwin, Dean of Christ Church, complained to the Vice-Chancellor, who suspended Howson for heterodox preaching. This incident lies behind the charges the Archbishop brings in 1615, but the particulars of Howson's alleged heterodoxy do not figure in the discussion, at least not in the manuscript record of it. Nor do we know what it was about Laud's 1615 Shrove-Tuesday sermon that brought its preacher a similar fate. However, on Easter Sunday(!) Robert Abbot preached a ferocious counter-sermon, which the distraught Laud summarized in a letter to Bishop Neile.[4] Abbot had apparently alleged that Laud and his ilk

> under pretence of truth and preaching against the Puritans, strike at the heart and root of faith and religion now established among us. That this preaching against the Puritans was but the practice of Parsons and Campion's counsel, when they came into England to seduce young students; and when many of them {the students} were afraid to lose their places if they should professedly be thus, the counsel they {the Jesuits} then gave them was that they should speak freely against the Puritans, and that should suffice. And they cannot intend that they are accounted Papists because they speak against the Puritans. But because they indeed are Papists, they speak nothing against them. If they do at any time speak against the Papists, they do beat a little upon the bush, and that softly too, for fear of troubling or disquieting the birds that are in it.

Laud goes on to describe how he was "fain to sit patiently and hear myself abused almost an hour together, being pointed at as I sat," adding that "the whole University apply it to me, and my own friends tell me I shall sink my credit, if I answer not Dr. Abbot in his own"; the letter concludes by asking Neile "some direction what to do."[5]

The accusation Robert Abbot brought against Laud was thus identical to that George Abbot makes to the King against Howson <see charge 2, *infra*>, and the two suspected papists were jointly summoned to Greenwich in June so that the Archbishop could present the charges against them to the King. The outcome in both cases was identical: the King had both defendants reinstated, and Robert Abbot was told to apologize.

Howson's manuscript recounts the exchanges between Howson and George Abbot, punctuated by royal interjections, that eventuated in this stunning rebuke to the Archbishop. These exchanges, moreover, provide important evidence regarding the theological rift in the English Church as it appeared ca. 1615. The sides are usually labeled Calvinist and anti-Calvinist, which seems accurate but in need of further specification, since the import of these terms shifts over time. In Howson's case, the disputed issues did not, apparently,

---

[4] Prynne gives a much-expanded version of this letter that purports to recount all sorts of objections that Abbot made to Laud's theology, but Prynne is extraordinarily unscrupulous, and the additional material may be of his own making (*Canterburies Doome* [1646], 155; Cranfield and Fincham 323).

[5] John Rushworth, "Historical collections: 1621," *Historical collections of private passages of state*, vol. 1: *1618–29* (1721), 62, www.british-history.ac.uk/report.aspx?compid=70138&strquery=Laud (accessed July 24, 2010). According to Heylyn, Abbot directly addressed Laud from the pulpit, demanding whether he were "Romish or English? Papist or Protestant? . . . a mungrel or compound of both . . ." (*ODNB*, q.v. Robert Abbot).

include predestination. No one mentions the topic, nor, consequently, Arminianism.[6] Modern scholars writing on the Howson case, and probably Howson as well, see the underlying division as one between sermon-centered evangelical piety and a more liturgical and sacramental "Prayer Book Anglicanism" (Dent 208, 220). However, Howson's manuscript and Laud's account of Robert Abbot's sermon make quite clear that this is *not* how the Archbishop's side perceived the stakes. The Abbots do not see Laud and Howson as Prayer Book Anglicans but as crypto-Catholics: that is, as papal agents acting under Jesuit instructions whose mission is to undermine the foundations of the English Church under the pretext of attacking puritans. (In subsequent controversies, however, this fifth-column often goes under the label "Arminianism."[7]) The charges against Howson presuppose this crypto-Catholic reading. The Archbishop accuses him not of over-valuing ceremonies but of defending papal supremacy <charge 4>. The questions concerning Howson's ties to Carier <charge 10> have the same subtext.

The King obviously disagreed with Abbot's version of things, as he had in the past: in 1610, for example, selecting both Robert Abbot and John Howson as founding faculty for his beloved Chelsea College. Indeed, on the scales of sanity, charity, and humanity, James comes off by far the best in this exchange: Abbot seems truly dangerous, but Howson also reveals an unattractively pugnacious streak. That the King had long refused to endorse Abbot's brand of Calvinist consensus helps explain the Archbishop's astonishing volte-face at the meeting's end, where, while still insisting that he could prove Howson guilty of, among other things, high treason, he suddenly offers to make everyone friends, have his brother apologize, and put a stop to the attack-sermons.[8] Presumably Abbot believed, or half-believed, the apocalyptic world-picture underlying his charges against Howson, yet he also could not but know that this view was one his royal master did not share; and he seems capable of recognizing that his suspicions might be misplaced, and that if Laud and Howson were not covert papists, it was time for the mending of fences.

Sources: *ODNB*; Nicholas Cranfield and Kenneth Fincham, "John Howson's answers to Archbishop Abbot's accusations at his 'trial' before James I at Greenwich, 10 June 1615," *Camden Miscellany* 29, Camden 4th series, vol. 34 (1987): 319–41; Christopher Dent, *Protestant reformers in Elizabethan Oxford* (Oxford UP, 1983); Nicholas Tyacke, "Religious controversy," in *Seventeenth-century Oxford: the history of the University of Oxford*, vol. 4, ed. Nicholas Tyacke (Clarendon, 1997), 569–620.

[6] Howson may have been a doctrinal Calvinist; in a 1602 sermon he describes the Atonement as "sufficient for the whole world, but efficient to all the elect of God" (Tyacke 571). One finds the same position in many Jacobean Calvinists; yet the position is also Thomist. See Emile Boutroux, *Pascal*, trans. Ellen Margaret Creak (Manchester: Sherratt and Hughes, 1902), 117; Joseph Pohle, "Controversies on grace," *The Catholic Encyclopedia* (New York: Robert Appleton, 1909), www.newadvent.org/cathen/06710a .htm (accessed March 25, 2009).

[7] See, in this volume, *The spy* and Fletcher's *Locusts*; also, Shuger, *Censorship*, 42–47.

[8] Abbot's proposal is both so specific and so unexpected that I suspect he is echoing the King's verdict in Laud's case. We have no independent evidence that Laud's hearing preceded Howson's, but I can think of no other way to explain why Abbot seems so prepared for and resigned to James' ruling.

JOHN HOWSON

*Dr. Howson's answers to my Lord Grace of Canterbury{'s} accusations
before his Majesty at Greenwich*
June 10, 1615

The King began his preface against the factious preaching and personal reproving one
another {that} should be[1] lately used in Oxon.

Upon which occasion my Lord Grace {Abbot} began to set upon me and to affirm
that I was the most factious preacher that ever lived there; and condemned his brother for
nothing more than that he would have any business with me, whom he esteemed ever as
pitch and to be avoided, etc.

I answered his Majesty that I was not guilty of any of the personal invectives which
[h]is Majesty spake of, but tolerated them patiently now for three years; wherein they
had been used by Dr. Goodwin, Dr. Abbot, and their followers at all solemnities, etc.
So that I durst affirm that never any pulpits were so wickedly abused in all Christianity,
nor ever any subject so notoriously wronged, against all Christian charity and the laws
of the land. And censured shamefully without any article exhibited against me, though
often entreated. That it was a conspiracy against me, that Dr. Goodwin should begin, Dr.
Abbot second him. That letters came before that sermon to Dr. Goodwin, etc., that of
whatsoever subject my next sermon should be, I should be questioned for it. That Mistress
[   ] reported that she had seen them. That I was admonished by a letter sent me, a
little before I went into the pulpit, by some friend without name, that I should look well
to myself, for some mischief was intended by my enemies: which letter I laid by till the
sermon was done. And so proceeded with the narration of my suspension, etc., which
article drawn, etc.

My Lord Grace said that I was not suspended for any doctrine there delivered, but
because I would not deliver up my copies nor appear to answer objections, being legally
cited.

I offered to produce the article and shew that I was censured for sermons *minus ortho-
doxos* {insufficiently orthodox}. That I delivered the copy of my sermon for which I was

---

[1] {"should be" here means simply "had been"}

convented, which no statute required. He answered that I refused to give up the rest. I replied that they demanded all the sermons I had preached that year, without any reason or statute for it: that finding no just cause of my reproof in that sermon, they sought out matter in the precedent or posterior to make some shew for their former wrong. Notwithstanding, to satisfy them, I sent them the copy of the first of the 4 and signified to them that the other two original copies were sent to his Majesty, and were, as I thought, in the custody of the then Lord Bishop of Coventry,[2] whence they might call for them.

To the other objection, I said that I was never legally called, but suspended *de facto*; the Vice-Chancellor understanding by my letters that, if I were cited, it was likely that I would appeal to his Majesty as the Visitor[3] of Christ-Church, and so hold his hands. For the vice-chancellor had not to censure any offence committed in that church, or any private college.

When his Grace replied that I was subject to the vice-chancellor for any commission in those sermons, I offered to produce a paper full of reasons to prove the contrary.

Hereupon he took me off, and said that this was not the business now in hand. He had other matters of higher nature to object against me, and withal made his motion that his Majesty would not give credit to my answers, for I would protest, swear, and forswear anything that made against me.

I demanded if I were ever convicted of any such crime; and I hoped that his Majesty would not be moved with this unjust crimination, which took away all means of yielding satisfaction unto him. I added that I had ever lived orderly, never put to any purgation before any magistrate[4] for my manners or my religion; and therefore my Lord Grace much wronged me with so foul an imputation.

2. Then he demanded of me if ever I had preached against the papists, and willed me to name in what points. His Majesty willed me to bethink myself well, and speak a truth that I might justify. I answered that I preached against the pope's supremacy both in temporals and spirituals. The Archbishop asked where and when; I answered, in my last sermon at Christ Church. He said that he knew not that. Then I said, against transubstantiation. He demanded where; I said at Christ Church, at a Communion. The Archbishop beginning to cavil, his Majesty said there was no fitter time or place than at a Communion. I added that I had preached solemnly against auricular confession, popish penances, also merit of works, in divers sermons—I thought I could produce the copies; against the wicked practices of Jesuits and that profane order; against the Powder Treason, solemnly. My Lord Grace said there was no man but would preach against that.

I added that I preached not so often as some others against the papists, because in my time there were never above 3 or 4 at once that were suspected of popery, and there were 300 preachers who opposed them by sermons and disputations; contrarywise there were

[2] [Richard Neile, Bishop of Coventry & Lichfield, 1610–14]

[3] {The visitor was an outside person appointed to oversee a church or college to prevent (or reform) abuses.}

[4] {That is, he had never been required to produce oath-helpers, who would swear that they believed he was telling the truth, to support his word; rather, as in this exchange (e.g., regarding the 10th charge), when Abbot demands that Howson formally swear to the truth of his words, Howson's oath is taken as sufficient proof.}

ever 300 supporters of puritanizing, and but 3 or 4 to oppose. With both these assertions my Lord Grace was highly offended, and denied them.

Then my Lord Grace objected that I had lived in opposition with all the deans that were in my time, namely with Dr. James, Dr. Ravis, Dr. King, and Dr. Goodwin. I answered that I was no prebendary in Dr. James his time; that I lived very kindly and lovingly with Dr. Ravis, and wrought him much good; that the two latter *oderunt me gratis*,[5] and requited much kindness and love with as much ill and unkindness, etc.

3. He said that I was ever in opposition to all prebendaries, namely Dr. Thornton, Dr. White, Dr. Hutton, Dr. Weston, etc. Only used Dr. Perkin to abuse the deans. I answered that Dr. Thornton was never resident since I was prebendary. Dr. White came seldom, but was my good friend. Dr. Hutton my most familiar, and Dr. Weston would ever embrace me; they desired my company more, and shewed extraordinary affection externally towards me.

4. He said they complained often to the Dean {Goodwin} that they were weary of the diet[6] or my company, I did so trouble them with papistical disputations, especially maintaining the pope's monarchy and power over kings.

I answered that by reason of somewhat that passed sometimes in sermons and disputations, we used some discourse, being all doctors and divines, and most of them my seniors and betters, and some moderators in divinity;[7] but if I had maintained any point of popery, they could have convinced me.[8] As for the monarchy of Rome, I ever abhorred that and disputed against it. And that being a matter of treason,[9] it is likely the Dean, being Vice-Chancellor and my great enemy, would not have omitted either just reproof or just punishment for it. But I never heard of it until this day.

5. That for the space of xx[ty] years, I never preached sermon that was not factious; and that he had noted it before unto me at Lambeth, where he spent a quarter of an hour upon me, persuading me to quietness, etc. I replied that he spent an whole hour. He denied. I affirmed. He said his men could witness that stood by. I said none were present. He asked the King if he did not think that I raved. I still denied it. Except perchance they {Abbot's men} stood behind the arras to be witnesses against me, if perchance I should be moved with his so bitter speeches. For as soon as he called for them, they were upon me in an instant, as if they stood in the door, which was hard by. Then he demanded in what room it was; I told him I knew not the name; he asked whether a little room or a big. I say, little or great in comparison. I said it was little in comparison of the others, but it might, in respect of some other, be great. Then he asked me what his discourse was. I answered that I could presently shew him, for I had it in writing. He would not believe me, but began to repeat some of his speeches to the King. I acknowledged that, and said that he repeated it, as I thought, *verbatim*. Why then, said his Majesty, ye agree on the point. I answered

---

[5] {They hated me without cause (Ps. 109:3, which Jesus applies to himself at John 15:25).}

[6] {"Diet" here probably means regular assembly or meeting (of the prebendaries), although it could also refer to (Howson's) way of thinking.}

[7] {Moderators or determiners of the divinity disputations, a role allotted the most senior theology faculty.}

[8] {"Convinced" could mean either refuted or publicly reprehended.}

[9] {The Act of Supremacy made affirming the pope's jurisdiction in England high treason on a third conviction.}

he spake all that, but that was not all that he spake, as should appear by my book. Then I drew out my writings, and among them a book of 6 or 7 sheets of paper in folios. My Lord Grace asked what it was. I said the manner of the proceeding against me, which I writ down that I might be able to justify what I said, if ever my cause should be heard. The King took the book and turned it, but found not the place; then I took it, and for haste, could not find it, but affirmed constantly that there it was. In the meantime, I said I would tell him what I could remember; and beginning with a reproof of his {Abbot's} for a sermon preached xx[ty] years before at an Act[10] in Oxon, wherein I taxed the Geneva note for calling archbishops, bishops, doctors, etc. the locust of the bottomless pit, etc.[11] He asked the King if he thought that I was mad. I answered, that I confessed indeed that I did lack sleep; for hearing of his violent threatening and strange accusation of so high a nature, and that unto his Majesty, upon whose favor or displeasure depended my very life or death, though I had searched my heart, and my conscience accused me not of any one word or action that might work me prejudice, yet considering the nature of my enemies, fearing lest peradventure *fortiter calumniando*, somewhat might *haerere*,[12] I never took sleep nor food that did me good; yet the nature of this business is such that it will waken any sleepy man and stir up his spirits, though spent {exhausted} before.

Then I rehearsed more of his speeches: among them this, that he used then the same accusation which he did lately, vizt. that the prebendaries loved me not, besides st[ill?] held me for a papist. He denied it. I answered that at my return to Oxon, I reported the accusation to my fellows at the table, who protested their love and that they never had used any such words of me. Then I told his Majesty that it was no unusual thing to find variance in a dean and chapter; for Ariosto said that when the Turks were too strong for the Christians, God sent St. Michael down into the world to find out discord and to put her into the Turk's army; who, searching the world over and not finding her, being ready to ascend and return that answer, hearing of a dean and chapter not far off, thought he would search that place also. And there he found her sitting among them as they were choosing their officers.[13] In this discourse my Lord Grace shew'd himself very forgetful and very impatient, saying that he doubted not but God's judgments would be seen on me ere I died. I wished they might fall upon the offender.

6. He demanded how many sermons I had preached against Dr Robinson.[14] I answered so many as he preached against me. When I signified that he said in the pulpit that I was a favorer of the papists because I read in my text *schisms* for σχίσματα with the Rhemists,[15] and not rather *dissensions* with the Genevists, etc. The King said, he was a bishop

---

[10] {university disputation}

[11] {The note to Rev. 9:3 in the 1576 Geneva Bible glosses the locusts as "false teachers, heretics, & worldly subtle prelates, with monks, friars, cardinals, patriarchs, archbishops, bishops, doctors, bachelors, and masters which forsake Christ to maintain false doctrine" (this from the first English edition; many later editions of the Geneva Bible printed in England omit the note).}

[12] {fearing lest perchance by boldly hurling such slanders against me they might be able to make something stick}

[13] [Ariosto, *Orlando Furioso in English Heroical Verse by John Harington* (1591), 108, stanza XV, lines 64–74.]

[14] [Henry Robinson was Provost of The Queen's College from 1581 to 1599, and Bishop of Carlisle from 1598 until his death in 1616.]

[15] {translators of the Roman Catholic Bible}

and now no puritan. I said that he owed his conversion to me, as I thought; and therefore meeting me in the Court after he was bishop, asked me if I had any friends in his country, that in them he might testify his love to me; adding also that if he had any friend to send to Oxford, he would commend him to me before any other. My Lord Grace wondered at this, and asked me if I would set it down under my hand; I answered, both under my hand and seal.

7. He asked me how many sermons I had preached against Dr. Rainolds.[16] I said, so many as he brought reasons that a man might not use a Latin, Greek, or Hebrew word in an English sermon. For I confuted every reason with a Sunday sermon. He denied that to be questioned, saying never any man was so absurd as to hold that. The King said he knew puritans hold it. I also added that this opinion prevailed so far in our University, that Dr Childerly about that time, preaching at Paul's Cross and having occasion to use those words *loquere puer ut te videam*,[17] added therewith, *I beseech you good brethren pardon the Latin*. And that divers bachelors of divinity, after the preaching of those sermons, resorted to my chamber and thanked me for delivering them from so gross a foolery.

8. He objected that at one assizes I preached against lawyers and the laws of the land; and added that I told a tale, that sometimes the Isle of Wight was noted to have neither fox nor coney nor beggar, but now it abounded with lawyers, etc.[18] The King answered, there were everywhere too many of them.

9. He said that at another assizes I preached against Judge Perian,[19] so that he swore he would ride that circuit no more; and that I maintained in that sermon that it was lawful to play at bowls in the time of divine service on the Sabbath day. The King said he could not be persuaded that any Christian man would use any such words, nor any magistrate would suffer them to pass unpunished. And asked who was Vice-Chancellor. He answered, Dr. Lille, a man as good as himself. I said that, understanding that the judge was judaically affected in the observations of the Sabbaths, and troubled the poor people wheresoever he went, {I} took occasion to speak of the Sabbaths, and told him that it was first ordained for the service of God, which being done, it was lawful for the people honestly to recreate themselves, for that was the day of rest, etc. The King allowed well of that. And said he knew Perian to be a sour puritan, with other words of dislike.

Upon these criminations, I said that I marveled he would object those things as faults, which in those times were accompted virtues and commendations, and was glad that *cum omnia caveram*, he would *pro ornamenta ferire*,[20] saying that I did little in those days but by the commandment of the magistrate, and was justified and commended for them and commanded to print them, though I was hardly drawn to that; that all the archbishops

---

[16] {John Rainolds, President of Corpus Christi from 1598 to 1607; eminent Hebrew scholar, and one of the puritan representatives at the Hampton Court Conference.}

[17] {"Speak boy, that I may see you." The passage does not occur in the Vulgate; Cranfield and Fincham take it as a free rendering of Gen. 27:1.}

[18] {Camden notes that this was a popular saying among the inhabitants of the Isle of Wight (see Cranfield & Fincham, n. 11). This charge, like charge 4, seeks to bring Howson under suspicion of sedition and treason.

[19] [Chief Baron of the Exchequer from 1592 until his death in 1604.]

[20] {The Latin here is garbled; the sense would seem to be that Howson is glad that he had watched his steps so carefully that Abbot has to berate him for things that actually deserve commendation.}

and bishops of London since I was first a preacher, all the chancellors of our universities, all the heads of our colleges especially favored me; and all went current until his Grace, who was ever my professed enemy, came to his dignity, since which time I had endured that which I think was never offered to any Christian in any religion: condemned without articles, so that neither I could know how to reform myself, or others by my example to avoid the errors, which are the chief ends why punishments are inflicted, etc.[21] To this little was answered but that the Lord Buckhurst our Chancellor {1591–1608}, presently after my vice-chancery, being informed by Bishop Ravis what kind of man I was, did ever after detest the memory of me.

To which I replied that if any man wronged me to him, it was his Grace. Which I suspected also was done at his Majesty's being at Oxford {in 1605}, when, I confessed, the Lord Buckhurst gave me no countenance; but I ascribed it to his Grace in respect of the English pastoral, which I, by the appointment of our Dean and Chapter, caused to be made and repeated in my lodging.[22] Which I knew was very offensive to his Grace, as then appeared evidently. Wherefore fearing that your Grace had then done me some ill office, I wrote letters to the Lord our Chancellor the Lord Buckhurst, signifying that I feared some had wronged me, because I observed his countenance was not upon me as on others; whose answer, I said, would shew that his Grace's information now was not right, but that he highly esteemed of me many years after my vice-chancellorship; and so drew out the Lord Buckhurst{'s} answer written with his own hand, which his Majesty took and read aloud, and then observed the date and said that was 3 years after my office, and a worthy testimony.

10. He charged that my conversation was ever with suspected papists, as namely with Browne, with whom I was inwardly acquainted.[23] The King answered, God forbid that a man should answer for the faults of his acquaintance, except he can be proved to partake of them. Then he objected Dr. Carier *<vide supra>*. I said I had very little acquaintance with him, and that I never to my knowledge came under any roof with him but either of some church or some of his Majesty's houses. He asked if I would stand to that. I affirmed. He required my hand upon it, and I gave it unto him. I added that I thought he would have been a Protestant yet, if he had not been ill used; and that either his Grace (Abbot) or my Lord of London (King) reported that, were it not for my charge of family, I had been gone beyond sea ere this; belike you thought my burden unsupportable, and yet you add more.

11. He asked me what company I had ever kept, and which of the heads of colleges ever favored me. I answered that many loved me that durst not shew it for fear of his Grace and my Lord of London, who used to take exceptions to men that kept me company; and

---

[21] {This is the standard Tudor-Stuart view on the matter; in contrast to current jurisprudence, punishment was never understood as retribution; that is, as harm inflicted on the doer proportionate to the wrongness of his deed. See Richard Cosin, *An Apologie for sundrie proceedings by jurisdiction ecclesiastical* (London, 1591), 2.2–4; William Lambarde, *Eirenarcha: or of the office of the justices of peace* (London, 1581), 67; William Blackstone, *Commentaries on the laws of England*, 2 vols., ed. William Carey Jones (San Francisco: Bancroft–Whitney, 1916), bk. 4, chap. 1, pp. 2164–69.}

[22] [The pastoral included "five or six men almost naked."]

[23] [Walter Browne, Arminian tutor at Corpus Christi College, died in 1613. He was labeled a papist during Laud's trial in 1644.]

that thereupon I did forbear to live in the University that I might not wrong my friends. But heretofore I had the familiarity, of Dr. Bond, Dr. Lilly, Dr. Holland, Dr. Ryves, etc. and so continued with them, and Dr. Williams, as long as they lived.[24] Yea, said my Lord Grace, Dr. Williams was popishly affected, as well as yourself, and defended that the pope was not anti-Christ. The King said that is no point of popery, etc. I added that Dr. Robinson, when he was a puritan, preached so much in Oxford, and alleged Zanchius[25] for his opinion.

12. He charged me to have denied the King to be the author of the books that went under his name: namely 1. the *Apology*; then, the Monitory preface.[26] I answered as in my petition, and withal that there was no credit to be given to my Lord of London's accusation, because our quarrel was Decemb. 1606 and the Monitory preface was printed 1609, almost 3 years after, all which time there passed no familiarity between us. This business was easily passed over. The King desired me, if I had doubted of any point in it, to acquaint him with it, and he should take it very kindly.

13. Then he added that I had excepted against other books that defended the religion; namely that I had read over my Lord of Ely's book[27] and answered half of it in the margin. I protested that I never had but one copy of his books, which were now in my study and might be called for to try the truth of that accusation. And that there was no subject in the land whose persons {*sic*} and writings I honored more; that I had read them diligently to my great contentment and profit, and never examined but one place of it, and that for my better understanding. That this his (Abbot) accusation proceeded not from any great love to him {Andrewes}, for his {Abbot's} nearest friends laid aspersions of popery upon him and others of his rank who were never puritans. And when he began to bluster at that, I said some had spoken plainly that the papists would have given ten thousand pounds to have had him archbishop. He said, if he knew the man, he would surely punish him. I replied, he would not. He asked if he were so great. I answered again, I am sure you would not. . . .

14. Then he objected certain notes I had taken against Dr. Morton's books. I acknowledged that, and said that I did it at his {Morton's} own request by letters received from him.[28] And opening by chance his last great book, I found a place of Bellarmine quoted in the margin very truly, but very ill translated in the discourse, and for his advantage; hereupon I began, for my better understanding, to turn over the leaf to the beginning of

---

[24] {These were all senior divines and college heads; Holland had been regius professor of divinity; Williams, Lady Margaret professor of divinity.}

[25] {Hieronymus Zanchius (1516–90), Heidelberg professor and strong proponent of double predestination.}

[26] [James I, *An apologie for the Oath of Allegiance; first set forth without a name, now acknowledged. Together with a Premonition* (1609).]

[27] [Lancelot Andrewes, *Responsio ad Apologiam Cardinalis Bellarmini* (1610).]

[28] {Thomas Morton (1564–1659), who was Bishop of Durham when he died in his 95th year, was a moderate Calvinist. According to the *ODNB* entry on Morton, "during 1608 and 1609 Bancroft had presided over the most substantial publication with which Morton was to be associated. *A Catholic Appeale to Protestants* (1609) was a cooperative effort by 'a certain number of Divines then at hand.'" The title page bears Morton's name, but John Overall, who was not a Calvinist, may have written substantial portions. Several divines were asked to read and comment, including John Donne and Howson, whose account of the vetting process is given in the text above.}

the chapter that I might see the coherence, all which I much misliked for many respects. Wherefore I thought fit for my further satisfaction to examine a chapter in the beginning of the book, which finding exceeding faulty, I gave it over, and acquainted my Lord of Lincoln, then Dr. Barlow, with this proceeding, and desired him that better order might be taken for his books. He told my Lord of Canterbury (Bancroft) of it, and some other bishops assembled, whereupon the Archbishop willed him to send for those exceptions. I came and delivered them. There were 17 of them, saith my Lord Grace. I said, aye, but I could have delivered 17 more. And then I added that my Lord Grace then (Bancroft) allowed of them, and sent me to Dr. Morton to make them good, which I did, and we parted very good friends. Whereupon my Lord's Grace then committed to my perusing some other books, and among them the book which was read in the Convocation.[29] You had it 4 years, said my Lord Grace, and did nothing to it. I replied that I had it but 4 months and had noted much upon it. And then told his Majesty that my Lord Grace (Abbot) was no sooner out of Lambeth House but I recovered my Lord's (Bancroft's) favor in the highest degree, so that he made me many large promises to my future preferment.

15. He said, my Lord Grace (Bancroft) long before he died held me for a papist. I denied it, but said that I thought his Grace (Abbot) had done his best to persuade him (Bancroft) so. But I affirmed that when Bishop Bancroft was bishop of London, he held his Grace (Abbot) for a puritan, and said in my hearing that if he were not a dean already, he should never have dignity in the Church of England, if he or his friends could possibly hinder him. Then he (Abbot) appealed to his Majesty, if he (James I) knew not his (Bancroft's) love to him (Abbot). Yea, said his Majesty, but {Howson} speaketh when he (Bancroft) was bishop of London. I added that it was by reason of a tract which his Grace wrote against the Cross in Cheap, and that Bishop Ravis brought him into favor again. He denied that ever he wrote such a tract.[30] I affirmed it, and said that not long after, he riding to preach in Abington where the Cross was newly painted and much cost bestowed on it, one of the townsmen asked him how he liked of that; he answered, very well; but, said the townsman, here are many that except against it; whereto you replied, none but fools. So, saith he {Abbot} to the King, he {Howson} speaks now for me. I replied, the townsman laugh'd in his sleeve and told me that at the last you were of another mind.

16. That my Lord of London {King} had reproved me publicly at Sir William Greene's table for maintaining popery there. I answered that my Lord of London never reproved any one proposition that ever I made concerning religion for the space of our 30 years' familiarity. And added that that house was not a place to defend or propose any popery in, for the gentleman was a very great entertainer of preachers and a good Protestant. His Grace said he held him so. And yet, said I, my Lord, when the Bishop of Oxon {Bridges} last year preached there, seeing Sir William Greene at church, congratulated him for it. Sir William wondering at him said, My Lord, I do usually go to church and ever did, and

---

[29] {Cranfield and Fincham provisionally identify this as William Crashaw's *Newes from Italy of a second Moses* (1608).}

[30] {Abbot may be equivocating on "tract"; he and Bancroft had a falling out over the proposed restoration of the Cheapside Cross in 1601, and Abbot apparently had written a letter giving his arguments against it, but these were only published as a "tract" in 1641, under the title *Cheapside Crosse censured and condemned by a letter sent from the Vice-Chauncellor*" (Tyacke 572).}

all my family. Then my Lord of Oxon replied that some had wrong'd him; for, said he, being in the Presence {Chamber} at the Court, a very great man in state, whom I will not name, wished me to look well to you, for you were one of the most dangerous papists that were in the diocese. Was it I that said so, said the Archbishop. I answered, no man was named; but he {Greene} suspected the author, and thought this wrong was done him for his love to me. He replied, the Bishop of Oxon was old and knew not what he said or did.

When I saw he had done his accusations, I demanded of him how old the youngest was, for the eldest was 25 years old at least. He answered, 4 or 5 years old. I said a man might be a papist then, and yet a good Protestant now, his Majesty and others having written so effectually since that time. The King said he would not think the worse of any man that since that was converted, whatsoever he were before. I said I knew many puritans which would seem to be converted within that time.

I forgot many pretty passages, which I cannot set in the right place: as that his Grace told me that I thrust a man beside the pulpit, who was appointed to preach, and violently took possession of the place. I denied that. He said, he could shew the hands of 6 heads of houses to prove it. I said it was not possible: and then repeating the order of it, as that it was my own proper course, nor any man that looked after it. I said, indeed, his brother had affirmed that in the pulpit; and in the pulpit afterwards acknowledged his error, and referred the truth to his relation.

In conclusion, my Lord's Grace said that though he could prove all those articles by hands and witnesses, if that his Majesty would have them produced in a court, yet if it pleased his Majesty, he would thus end the business: 1. He would make them all friends. 2. His brother should go down to Oxford and acknowledge his fault. 3. He would write letters to the University that their pulpit controversies might utterly cease, etc.

His Majesty concluded that those kind of sermons which had been used were very wicked and unchristian. That accusations conceived so many years {ago} were not matters for courts.

That I had not done wisely, considering how clamorous the puritans were and forward to accuse men of popery, in not preaching more often against the papists, and join them together.[31]

That I should do well hereafter to use that course. I said I did ever intend it, and hoped that his Majesty did not enjoin me any such thing as a punishment. He said no. Bid me use my discretion how, when, and where.

He wished me to be wary that I did not fall into any of these things objected, for then it would be suspected these are true.

He said he used not to condemn any man without evident proof, and he needed not, for if rottenness were at the heart, it would break out again.

He wished that all that were not sound would depart his country, and that he thought better of the soul of Baronius, etc., than of Browne or Carier or Langworth, etc. My Lord Archbishop concluded that in Mr. Browne's study was found a paper against his Majesty's title to the crown.

---

[31] {I.e., the King advised Howson to preach sermons censuring both Roman Catholics and puritans; Howson did as requested the next year. The sermons were printed by royal command in 1622 as *Certaine sermons made in Oxford, Anno. Dom. 1616. Wherein, is proved that Saint Peter had no monarchicall power over the rest of the Apostles.*}

So his Majesty graciously dismissed me.

My Lord Grace denied there was any competition between him and me for Balliol College.

His Majesty said to my Lord Grace that he had given me liberty of speech and free audience because I came upon the disadvantage. He had many years to premeditate his objections; my answer was sudden. He was used to his presence; I a stranger, and peradventure fearful. He was accustomed to speak to him. I never before.

TEXT: *John Howson's answers to Archbishop Abbot's accusations at his "trial" before James I at Greenwich, 10 June 1615*, ed. Nicholas Cranfield and Kenneth Fincham, *Camden Miscellany* 29, Camden 4th series, vol. 34 (1987): 320–41.

COLLEGIATE SUFFRAGE

The collegiate suffrage of the divines of Great Britain concerning the five articles controverted in the Low Countries. Which suffrage was by them delivered in the Synod of Dort, March 6, anno 1619, being their vote or voice foregoing the joint and public judgment of that Synod

London, 1629

The Synod of Dort (Dordrecht) was called to end a controversy in the Dutch Church dating back to the 1590s, when a young Amsterdam minister, Jacob Arminius, found he could no longer accept Theodore Beza's supralapsarian view of the divine decrees, the view widely espoused by both Dutch and English Calvinists at the time. In 1603 Arminius became professor of theology at Leyden, the flagship university of the Dutch Republic, at which point the dispute began in earnest. For Arminius' position was vigorously and publicly challenged by his colleague, Franciscus Gomarus, the disagreement between the two theologians dividing the University and then spilling over into the political sphere by raising fraught questions about the limits of ecclesiastical and civil power, Arminius' party defending the authority of the civil magistrate; Gomarus' followers, the autonomy of the Church in all matters concerning doctrine.[1]

The year after Arminius' death in 1609, a group of forty-four ministers codified his position in a five-point Remonstrance to the States of Holland, affirming conditional election (i.e., election conditional on foresight of faith), the universality of Christ's Atonement, the resistibility of grace, and the possibility of falling from grace.[2] The document, which gained Arminius' followers the name "Remonstrants," spurred the Gomarists to a Counter-Remonstrance in 1611. Shortly thereafter, King James intervened, initially urging the States General to adopt a polity of mutual toleration; however, as the political crisis worsened, James came to the conclusion that only a national synod, which it was clear from the outset would side with the Counter-Remonstrants, could prevent the Dutch Church, and the fledgling Dutch Republic, from collapse.

In 1617 Maurice of Nassau, the statholder of the United Provinces and captain-general of its army, declared his support for the Counter-Remonstrants. The Arminian

---

[1] The same dispute crops up in England in 1624–29 and again with the calling of the Long Parliament, but with the theological sides reversed: the Laudians (and conformist churchmen generally) defending the authority of Convocation; the Calvinist leadership in the Commons arguing for Parliamentary jurisdiction.

[2] The text is available at www.crivoice.org/creedremonstrants.html (accessed June 5, 2012).

Advocat of Holland, Johan van Oldenbarnevelt, responded by authorizing Holland's cities to hire mercenary troops subject to civic, rather than national, control. Maurice answered this challenge by moving against the offending cities, purging their councils of Remonstrants, and finally, in August 1618, arresting van Oldenbarnevelt, along with his brilliant young colleague, Hugo Grotius.[3] The Remonstrant cause was thus lost before the Synod of Dort began: its purpose was not to debate the contested issues but to seal the Counter-Remonstrant victory.

When the Synod met in November, the Bohemian revolt that would precipitate the Thirty Years' War was already in full swing, although the Elector Palatine would not be offered the crown for another year. The Synod comprised nineteen delegations (or colleges): eleven Dutch, eight representing other Reformed states, including England—or, more properly, Britain, since the delegation chosen by James included a lone Scotsman, Walter Balcanquahall, fellow of Pembroke Hall, Cambridge, along with Samuel Ward and John Davenant, both Cambridge heads; George Carleton, Bishop of Llandaff, the only bishop present; and (after illness had forced Joseph Hall to return to England), Thomas Goad, one of Archbishop Abbot's chaplains. All the English delegates were Calvinists, although Davenant and Ward strongly favored a hypothetical universalist model of predestination.[4]

The Synod was charged with responding to the five Remonstrant articles of 1610.[5] The Remonstrants, however, refused to cooperate in their own condemnation, and their obstructionist tactics led to their dismissal in January 1619. From late January through late February the individual delegations drafted suffrages—the British delegation experiencing some dissent among its members over the extent of Christ's Atonement (article 2). From late February into early March, the Synod considered the various suffrages produced by these delegations; and then in late March, a committee that included Bishop Carleton drew up a draft of the final canons, which was circulated among the other delegates for comment and critique. This committee presented its revised text to the Synod in early April, and the final version of the canons, which abjures supralapsarianism but otherwise upholds high Calvinist orthodoxy,[6] was read in a public ceremony on April 26th. All the delegations subscribed, but the British refused to allow the canons to be called "the doctrine of the Reformed churches" or to affirm more than that they were "not repugnant to the Articles of the Church of England" (Milton 1).

An English translation of the official Dort canons appeared shortly thereafter, under the title *The judgement of the Synode holden at Dort, concerning the five Articles* (1619).[7] The British delegation's collegiate suffrage, along with those of the other delegations, was

---

[3] Van Oldenbarnevelt was the target of a vicious propaganda campaign that painted him as a papal agent. See Wilhemina Frijlinck, ed., *The tragedy of Sir John van Olden Barnavelt* (Amsterdam: H. G. van Dorssen, 1922), cxxxi–cxxxii; John Motley, *The life and death of John of Barneveldt* (Harpers, 1900), 4–6. The picture of Arminians as crypto-Catholic traitors had a long and poisonous English afterlife, as can be seen in both *The spy* and Fletcher's *The locusts <infra>*.

[4] On hypothetical universalism, see the Preston introduction <*infra*>.

[5] In both the *Collegiate suffrage* and the Dort canons, articles 3 and 4 are treated together.

[6] High Calvinist orthodoxy being the doctrines comprised under the wonderfully Dutch acronym TULIP: Total depravity, Unconditional election, Limited atonement, Irresistibility of grace, Perseverance of the saints.

published at Leyden in the *Acta* of the Synod (1620), but after Richard Montagu's assault on Calvinist orthodoxy in the mid-1620s *<vide infra>*, the British delegates defended their position by overseeing three London reprintings of their suffrage in the original Latin version (1626, 1627, 1633). The sole English translation (reprinted here) came out in 1629.[8]

Current scholarship on these canons proposed by the British delegation typically describes them as offering a softer brand of Calvinism—in contrast to the more hard-line position that the Synod ultimately endorsed (Milton xxx–xxxi). While both adopt a sublapsarian position, the *Collegiate suffrage* (like the Thirty-nine Articles) drops double predestination: God decrees to save some persons out of the mass of fallen humanity; the rest are merely passed over, with no second decree consigning them to perdition. So too the *Collegiate suffrage* edges away from the orthodox Calvinist view that Christ died only for the elect towards a hypothetical universalism *<II.3>*,[9] and it does hold that (in some sense) grace is "genuinely offered to all" (Milton xxxii). Yet the net effect seems problematic. As Peter Lake notes, the *Collegiate suffrage* lacks "the logical coherence which had characterized the {orthodox} Calvinist case" (58–59); nor does it compensate for the muddled logic by any gain in moral intelligibility.

The theology set forth in the *Collegiate suffrage* differs significantly from the position upheld by the Synod of Dort's official canons, which, for all their negative publicity, do make formal and ethical sense. According to Dort, the Fall left man with nothing but "horrible darkness, vanity, and crookedness of judgment" in his intellect; "in his heart and will, malice, rebellion, and obduration; and in all his affections, impurity" (3&4.i); all persons are now "forward to evil, dead in sins, slaves of sin," unable, without grace, to "set straight their own crooked nature; no, not so much as dispose themselves to the amending of it" (3&4.iii). Fallen man is thus justly hated by God, who nonetheless, of his free mercy, chooses to pardon some: for these Christ dies, and to these alone is given grace and the regenerating Spirit that heals the corrupt will, "whereby it is enabled, like a good tree, to bring forth the fruits of good works" (3&4.xi). The elect and reprobate are thus quite radically different *sorts* of people, so that, most of the time, assurance of one's own election seems reasonably straightforward. Even if a person does not feel very assured, if that person has ever experienced grace, if he desires to turn to God, if he longs for faith, he should be of good cheer, for "our merciful God hath promised that he will not quench the smoking flax nor break the shaken reed." The cast-offs are those who, "forgetting God and our Savior Jesus Christ, have wholly enthralled themselves to the cares of the world and pleasures of the flesh" (1.xvi).

The *Collegiate suffrage*, by contrast, eschews the language of total depravity, although it continues to speak of the non-elect as vessels of wrath, hated by God *<Ib.1, 2>*. Moreover, unlike the Dort canons, which never speak of grace given the reprobate, the British divines hold that God bestows "many gifts of grace" on the non-elect, but these gifts

---

[7] This is the text referred to in the discussion of the canons that follows.

[8] This historical overview is based on Benedict 305–11; Milton, *passim*; Lake 54–56.

[9] The numbering of the Canons of Dort in the paragraphs that follow is that of the 1619 text. For the *Collegiate suffrage*, however, the numbering, although based on the 1629 edition, has been added by the current editor and corresponds to the text printed in this volume. The former are in parentheses; the latter, in angle brackets.

inevitably prove insufficient to keep such from falling away of their own accord and thus making "themselves liable to just damnation" <Ib.4>.[10] The *Collegiate suffrage* develops these themes in two long sections that have no counterpart in the official canons. The first, "Of those things that go before conversion" <III–IVb>, maintains that elect and non-elect may experience, "by the virtue of the word and the Spirit," the same initial "enlightening and exciting" graces, including "some knowledge of divine truth, some sorrow for sin, some desire and care of deliverance"; the non-elect, however, do not receive the "special grace" of perseverance, and so, sooner or later, "resist the Spirit of God and his grace" and are "justly forsaken by God" <III–IVb.5-7>. The second section addresses the question whether any of the non-elect are finally saved <Va>, and avers that the non-elect can and often do yield "unfeigned assent" to the Gospel, and that this faith, in turn, produces some holy desires and amendment of life <Vb.2>, yet "at length they shew that they are lovers of themselves and lovers of pleasures rather than lovers of God" <Vb.4>.

The *Collegiate suffrage* makes no attempt to explain why God would bestow these supernatural gifts and graces on vessels of wrath.[11] The point is clearly to make the non-elect responsible for their own damnation, God having given them sufficient grace <II.5>, yet since the text describes God as hating the non-elect, all of whom are destined to burn eternally in hell, it is hard not to view the gifting as a bait-and-switch ruse. *Timeo deum et dona ferens.* Moreover, since the elect and non-elect share the same initial graces, and since both sometimes do good and both sometimes fall into grievous sin, the two groups become exceedingly hard to distinguish. The British divines try to address the problem by claiming that some inner states, mostly penitential ones, are felt only by the elect <Va.4>; yet, having insisted that saving faith *implies* assurance of election <Vc.1>, they at once go on to suggest that self-deception can never be ruled out <Vc.3>. The text couples assurance to election and yet makes the experiences of elect and non-elect overlap to such an extent that assurance seems impossible.

It is not clear why the *Collegiate suffrage* sought these modifications of Calvinist orthodoxy. The disquieting net effect was not necessarily intended. It may be, as Anthony Milton (who clearly has some experience of committee reports) conjectures, that the "uncomfortable compromises evident" in the text reflect "an attempted synthesis of the different strands of English protestant thought" that just did not work (xxxii). But Peter Lake notes that the net effect closely resembles the similarly disquieting "temporary faith" of Perkins-style experimental predestinarianism (on which, see Kendall), and may have a similar aim: "to screw the godly professor up to a fever pitch of spiritual and practical exertion, in pursuit of that assurance which as a formal doctrine was clear enough, but which as an experience was a good deal more elusive" (Lake 58). However, Va.3—which states that all whose outward conduct and profession of Christianity shows that they have received at least preparatory grace should, "by a charitable construction," be considered

---

[10] This is Augustine's position in his late *De dono perseverantiae* (Quantin 171–76), but Augustine does not link election to assurance. The sudden disappearance of references to Augustine in the section of the *Collegiate suffrage* dealing with assurance ("Of the certainty of perseverance in respect of ourselves") is telling; 90 percent of the notes overall cite Augustine, but on assurance, they amazingly switch to Chrysostom, whose position is far closer to that of the Remonstrants. See Milton 280–86.

[11] For an attempted explanation, see Prynne's *God no impostor* <infra>.

"believers"—suggests that the delegation's position may also have been motivated by ecclesiological concerns specific to *English* Calvinism. The existence of initial graces shared by elect and non-elect alike seems designed to underwrite an inclusive national Church; God's lambs look too much like the rest of the flock for actual separation to be feasible. Yet the distinction between initial graces and special grace implies that only the godly minority in any parish will be saved. Such a distinction would make sense of the evident fact that the garden-variety conformists who made up 90 percent of the population exhibited some sort of Christian faith and often seemed reasonably good people, while at the same time reserving heaven for the godly.[12]

Yet, whatever the British delegation's aim, its draft canons still present one with a God who instills unfeigned faith, holy desire, and sorrow for sin in people marked out as vessels of wrath. The delegation certainly did not seek to widen the Calvinist gap between human notions of justice and the ways of God to men, but, as Hales wrote from Dort regarding Gomarus' attempt to make moral sense of predestination, they so "mended the question as tinkers mend kettles, and made it worse than it was before" (96). The *Collegiate suffrage* surely made things no better. (That they recognized the problem comes through in the final caution to their fellow ministers that predestination "be touched warily," and reprobation "only handled sparingly.") Its failure—the real possibility that it exacerbated the doubts it sought to address—makes both intelligible and credible Laud's position, one shared by most high churchmen, that "something about these controversies is unmasterable in this life."[13] Such reticence before the *arcana Dei* had much to recommend it, and therefore need not be read (as modern scholarship has tended to do) as coded Arminianism.[14]

SOURCES: Philip Benedict, *Christ's Churches purely reformed: a social history of Calvinism* (Yale UP, 2002); John Hales, *Letters from the Synod of Dort to Sir Dudley Carlton* (Glasgow, 1765); R. T. Kendall, *Calvin and English Calvinism to 1649* (Oxford UP, 1979); Peter Lake, "Calvinism and the English Church," *Past & Present* 114 (1987): 32–76; Anthony Milton, ed. *The British delegation and the Synod of Dort (1618–1619)*, Church of England Record Society 13 (Woodbridge, Suffolk: Boydell Press, 2005); Quantin, *Christian antiquity*.

[12] See Preston, *Riches* <425, 427, 439–45>.

[13] Laud, *Works* 6.1.292.

[14] A few English divines—e.g., Samuel Hoard <*infra*> and Thomas Jackson—were Arminians. John Overall seems to have been the only high churchman to formulate a distinctive theory of predestination; see Debora Shuger, "Milton über Alles," *Studies in Philology* 107.3 (2010): 401–15.

COLLEGIATE SUFFRAGE

The collegiate suffrage of the divines of Great Britain concerning the five articles controverted in the Low Countries. Which suffrage was by them delivered in the Synod of Dort, March 6, anno 1619, being their vote or voice foregoing the joint and public judgment of that Synod[1]

1619 (English trans. 1629)

The Five Articles Controverted in the Low-Countries and Discussed in the Synod of Dort.

1. Concerning God's predestination.
2. Of Christ's death, and man's redemption thereby.
3. Of free-will in the state of corruption.
4. Of conversion unto God, and the manner thereof.
5. Of the perseverance of the saints.

THE SUFFRAGE OF THE DIVINES OF GREAT BRITAIN CONCERNING THE FIRST ARTICLE

. . .

{Ia. Of Election}

{Ia.1} *The first orthodoxal position*

The decree of election, or predestination unto salvation, is the effectual will of God, by which, according to his good pleasure, for demonstration of his mercy, he purposed the salvation of man being fallen, and prepared for him such means by which he would effectually and unfallibly bring the elect to the self-same end.

The exposition and confirmation of the position

We call this decree of election an effectual will of God, because it respects not merely and only a way set down and leading to life, leaving man so ordained in the power of his own free-will (after such manner as Adam was ordained to happiness), but it doth respect and fore-appoint the very issue {outcome} of this ordinance. For this will is conjoined with the

---

[1] {The numbering of the Articles (I, II, III–IV, V) is in the original, and corresponds to the Canons of Dort; the numbering of the individual points and subheads has been added, as the braces indicate.}

power of God, Esa. 14:24, *The Lord of hosts hath sworn, saying, Surely as I have thought, so shall it come to pass, and as I have purposed, so shall it stand.* Psal. 113, *Whatsoever the Lord would, that did he in heaven and in earth* (upon which place see St. Austin, *Enchirid.* c. 75). Rom. 8:30, *Whom he hath predestinated, those he glorified.* . . .

We acknowledge no other moving cause of this will besides the mere good pleasure of God. Rom. 1:18, *He hath mercy on whom he will have mercy.* . . . But God doth deal with certain men after this especial manner for manifestation of his own mercy. Rom. 9:23, *That God might make known the riches of his glory toward the vessels of mercy.* Yea, and to them considered in the state of Adam's fall: namely, for the freeing them out of the mass of perdition. . . .

Finally, lest God's working in time should vary from his eternal purpose, he who did effectually destinate the elect unto salvation, doth also afford them means agreeable to this foresaid intention: that is to say, those means which God knew would without fail bring them to salvation. . . . Ephes. 1:4, *He hath chosen us, that we might be holy and without blame.* Mat. 13:11, *To you it is given to know the mysteries of the kingdom of heaven.*

Out of which testimonies of Scripture, it is evident that God by his foregoing decree of election hath sub-ordained all these things (to wit, the knowledge of the Gospel, vocation, faith, justification, sanctification, and perseverance) for the obtaining of the foredetermined salvation.

. . .

{Ia.2} *The second position*

Christ is the head and foundation of the elect, so that all saving graces prepared in the decree of election are bestowed upon the elect only for Christ, through Christ, and in Christ.

God, in the eternal election of particular men, by one and the self-same act both doth assign Christ their head and also doth appoint them, according to his good pleasure, the members of Christ—out of which purpose, even before their vocation (which is afterward performed in time), God doth behold them as given unto Christ and chosen in him and accepted of himself. . . .

. . .

{Ia.3} *The third position*

Faith, perseverance, and all gifts of grace leading home unto salvation are the fruits and effects of election.

We acknowledge in some men certain gifts of grace which are to be reduced {ascribed} to the common supernatural providence of God. But those gifts which have an infallible connection with glory and do work effectually for the obtaining thereof (as justifying faith and persevering) are the very effects of eternal election. Act. 13:48, *As many as were ordained to eternal life, believed.* . . .

. . .

{Ia.4} *The fourth position*

The decree of election is definite, not conditional; it is irrevocable and immutable, so that the number of the elect can neither be increased nor yet diminished.

In predestination, the means to salvation are no less absolutely decreed than salvation itself. For howsoever salvation, in the execution thereof, dependeth upon the conditional use of the means, yet the will of God electing unto salvation is not conditional, incomplete, or mutable, because he hath absolutely purposed to give unto the elect both power and will to perform those very conditions: namely, repentance, faith, obedience, and perseverance. For the decree of God predestinating cannot be conceived after this form, "I will choose Peter to eternal life, if it shall so happen that he doth believe, and persevere"; but rather after this manner: I do choose Peter unto eternal life, which that he may infallibly obtain, I will give unto him persevering faith." 2 Tim. 2:19, *The foundation of God standeth sure, God knows who are his.* . . .

. . .

Erroneous Opinions or Unsound Doctrines concerning Election, Which We Reject.

{Ia.error1} *The first*

That the decree by which God hath purposed in Christ and for Christ to save those which repent and believe unto the end is the whole and entire decree of predestination unto salvation.

. . .

{Ia.error2} *The second erroneous opinion*

That the peremptory election of particular persons is made upon the foresight and consideration of their faith in Christ, and of their perseverance in the same faith, as upon a condition fore-required in electing.

. . .

1. . . . Since therefore perseverance in faith is grounded upon the election of God, election cannot proceed from the fore-required condition of persevering faith.
2. Furthermore, the decree of giving glory and salvation unto steadfast believers in the end of this life as the reward of faith and obedience performed, is an act of justice, or at least of faithfulness and truth. But according to the Scriptures, election is a free act, not of debt but of grace, an act of love and special mercy founded upon the mere good will of God. Luke 12:32, *It is your Father's good pleasure to give you the kingdom.* . . .
3. By the like reason, faith foreseen is to be excluded from election, as foreseen works: that is to say, God may be said as well to have elected holy men for the condition of sanctification, as believers for the condition of faith. For who seeth not that this faith foreseen doth in truth pass into the nature of a work? which appears more evidently by the annexed condition of perseverance, by which is intended nothing else but the fruits of obedience and holiness and the whole harvest of all good works.
4. Lastly, by granting this election upon God's foresight, it follows that Christ was chosen by us before we were chosen by him; contrary to that John 15:16, *Ye have not chosen me, but I have chosen you.* Which divine oracle is often urged by St. Augustine to this purpose.

. . .

{Ia.error6} *The sixth erroneous opinion*

That in this life no man can receive any fruit or perceive any sense of his own election, otherwise than conditional.

Filial adoption is the proper, natural, and unseparable fruit of election, and is to be perceived by the elect in this life, the spirit of adoption revealing it to their hearts. Gal. 4:6, *Because ye are sons, God hath sent forth the spirit of his Son into your hearts, crying Abba, Father. If a son, then an heir of God.* . . . . Neither is there any falsehood in this solid peace of conscience, in the glorying of the godly, or in this infused hope, because these gifts are both sent by God to the elect, and to this end are they fastened in their minds, that they may be certain arguments of their unchangeable election.

We confess, our election is not to be perceived by us *à priori*, by the causes; but the proper effects of it may be known. And from the proper effect upward to the cause, the argument is good.

We likewise grant that the assurance of election in the children of God themselves is not always so constant and continual, but that oftentimes it is shaken with temptations, and for a time suppressed, so that not only the degree of assurance is lessened, but even election itself, in respect of the sense and apprehension of the elect, seems uncertain and ready to vanish.

Lastly, we confess that the elect justified, when they fall into grievous sins and cleave unto them, are not only deprived of the present taste of their election, but also conceive a great fear of the contrary, namely of God's wrath and revenging justice: and that deservedly, seeing the Holy Ghost vouchsafes not to communicate this heavenly and sweet *manna* of comfort to a defiled conscience yet wallowing in its own filthiness, but only to a clean heart and such an one as exerciseth itself in the practice of faith, repentance, and holiness. But we think that the minds of the faithful, being wakened and rising out of their pollutions, are renewed by God and comforted again with a sweet sense of eternal life prepared for them before the foundation of the world and in due time undoubtedly to be conferred upon them.

. . .

{Ib} II. Of Reprobation

{Ib.1} *The first orthodoxal position*

Reprobation properly called, or not-electing, is the eternal decree of God by which out of his most free-will he hath decreed not so far to take pity of some persons fallen in Adam as to rescue them effectually through Christ out of the state of misery and without fail to bring them to bliss.

The proper act of reprobation, as it is opposed to election, we think to be no other than the denying of the same glory and the same grace which are prepared for the sons of God by election. But glory and effectual grace are prepared for them in the decree of election, and with this very intent that it should be effectual; that is, that by such grace the sons of God might without fail come to the foresaid glory. Such grace and glory to be prepared for reprobates, we deny.

This non-election, we avow to be grounded upon the most free-will of God. Rom. 9:11, *That the purpose of God, according to election might stand, not of works, but of him that calleth. It was said, Jacob have I loved, but Esau have I hated.* That is, I have not so loved him, as that through grace I should certainly bring him to glory. And v. 18, *He hath mercy on whom he will have mercy, and whom he will he hardeneth*: Again (vers. 21), *Hath not the potter power over the clay, of the same lump to make one vessel unto honor and another unto dishonor.* And Joh. 10:26, *ye believe not, because ye are not of my sheep.*

Moreover, the glory of heaven is due to none, but is the *free gift of God*, Rom. 6:23. Therefore God, according to his most free-will, can choose whom he will to glory, and overpass whom he will, and that without any aspersion of injustice or hard dealing, since that in the bestowing of free gifts there is no place left for injustice. Neither is it any inclemency or cruelty to deny that to any man which is no way due unto him; especially when in the person presented unto there is found the highest demerit or desert of punishment, which is so far from expecting free gifts that it cannot choose but call for most just judgments: of which sort is the whole state of mankind represented to God when he was to choose or refuse whom he would among them. And what is here said of the bestowing of glory is likewise to be understood of the giving effectual grace.

. . .

{Ib.2} *The second position*

This not electing or over-passing doth not presuppose in the man overpassed any quality or other condition than that which is in the elect, and which is common to the whole corrupted heap.

God choosing out of his mercy doth find every elect person in the corrupted heap, overwhelmed in the same misery with the rest, and, by his present condition, subject to death. . . .

So equal objects and persons of the same condition being propounded, why God should free some and not all, why these rather than them, he {St. Paul} does not fetch the reason out of any disparity among them, but only out of God's free pleasure to show forth here his rich glory, there his just wrath, when he makes these (such as they were not) vessels of mercy, those (such as they very near were) vessels of wrath.

. . .

{Ib.3} *The third position*

When God affordeth his saving Gospel to save nations, he doth not this out of consideration of special worth in them; and when he denies this benefit to others, there is always a concomitant unworthiness in them to whom it is denied. But the mere will of God is the only cause why to these he will not show that mercy which, out of his good pleasure, he vouchsafed to others no less unworthy thereof.

. . .

{Ib.4} *The fourth position*

To some of those to whom the Gospel hath shined, although they be endued with many gifts of grace, yet of their own accord, and withal infallibly, they, by God's permission, fall into those sins, in which being forsaken and so remaining till death, they make themselves liable to just damnation.

We do not deny but these, though being not elected, yet receive many effects of grace, such as reckoned up Heb. 6:4: *illumination, taste of the heavenly gift of the good word, and of the powers of the world to come*. All which they turn to their own greater destruction, being left to their own wills and not being founded upon Christ, according to the decree of election, Rom. 11:7, *The election hath obtained it, and the rest were blinded*.

He that falls away from Christ, and ends his life being an alien from grace, shall be damned for his last sins. And because his apostasy could not be hidden from God's foreknowledge nor frustrate the same, without doubt God never chose such a man; he never predestinated him; yea, he never set apart from eternal death him who was to perish [Prosp. *ad cap. Gall.* resp. 2].

Some receive the grace of God but for a time; they persevere not; they forsake God and are forsaken of him: for they are left to their own free-will [Aug. *De correp. et grat.*, cap. 13].

{Ib.5} *The fifth position*

God damns none, or destinates to damnation, except in consideration of sin.

1. God dispenseth the gifts of grace {according} to his free-will. . . . Yet he never appoints the evil of punishment but upon the foreseen guilt of men. . . .

2. Moreover, damnation is an act of vindicative justice and therefore it must necessarily presuppose a precedent fault.

. . .

{Ib.error3} *The third {erroneous opinion concerning reprobation}*

That no man after Adam's fall was overpassed by the mere will of God, but all reprobation of particular persons was made upon consideration of their antecedent infidelity and final perseverance in the same.

Most certain it is, that God from all eternity did know that those whom he should pass by would die in their infidelity. But it is false that this foreseen infidelity should be the cause of his not-electing them.

1. For all men, and every man in particular, if not elected to persevering faith, are foreseen as persevering in infidelity; and no man is foreseen as without fail persevering in his infidelity but he whom God, in the disposing of effectual grace by his antecedent decree, hath passed by: John 20:26, *Ye believe not, because ye are not of my sheep*. 1 John 2:19, *If they had been of us, they had continued with us*. The Apostle fetcheth this preterition or non-election from the mere will of God. . . .

2. To conclude, if we shall set down for a ground that no man is reprobated but for his foreseen impenitence and final incredulity, there should be no mystery in the decree of reprobation, nothing unsearchable, nothing beyond our reach; quite contrary to that of the Apostle, Rom. 11:33, *Oh the depth, &c.* . . .

We know that grace is not given to all men, and that where it is bestowed, it is not given according to the merit of their works, neither yet according to the merit of their will, to whom it is given [Aug. *Epist.* 107].

Many are not saved, not because they would not be saved, but because God will not. That is, because God is not pleased to bestow special effectual grace upon them [Ibid].

. . .

THE SUFFRAGE CONCERNING THE SECOND ARTICLE
{Of Christ's death and man's redemption thereby}

{II.1} *The first position*

Out of an especial love and intention both of God the Father and of Christ himself, Christ died for the elect, that he might effectually obtain for them and infallibly bestow on them both remission of sins and salvation.

. . .

{II.2} *The second position*

Out of the self-same love, by and for the merit and intercession of Christ, faith and perseverance are given to the same elect, yea and all other things by which the condition of the covenant is fulfilled and the promised benefit—namely, eternal life—is obtained.

This position sheweth that out of the death and intercession of Christ, those gifts of grace do flow to the elect, by which they are effectually brought to life eternal. . . . Heb. 8:10, *I will give my laws into their minds, and in their hearts I will write them.* For that grace, which is given unto the elect for the death of Christ, is the grace of effectual redemption. Now we understand by the grace of redemption not such a grace by which men may be redeemed if they will, but by which they are in event mercifully redeemed because God so willeth.

{II.3} *The third position*

God, taking pity on mankind being fallen, sent his Son, who gave himself a ransom for the sins of the whole world.

In this oblation of Christ we consider two things: the *manner* of calling of men to the actual participation of this sacrifice and the *benefit* divers ways redounding unto men by the same sacrifice.

As for the manner, there is no mortal man who cannot truly and seriously be called by the ministers of the Gospel to the participation of remission of sins and eternal life by this death of Christ. . . . John 3:17, *He that believes not is condemned, because he hath not believed in the Son of God.* There is nothing false, nothing colorably feigned in the Gospel, but whatsoever is offered or promised in it by the ministers of the word is after the same manner offered & promised unto them by the Author of the Gospel.

Touching the benefit by the death of Christ in which is contained an infinite treasure of merits and spiritual blessings, the actual fruit doth redound to men after that manner and that measure and by the same means as seems good to God himself.

Now it pleaseth God, even after the acceptation of this sacrifice, no otherwise to bestow actually upon any man remission of sins and eternal life than by faith in the same Redeemer. And here that same eternal and secret decree of election shews itself, inasmuch as that price was paid for all, and will certainly promote all believers unto eternal life; yet is not beneficial unto all, because all have not the gift of fulfilling this condition of the gracious covenant. Christ therefore so died for all, that all and every one, by the means of faith, might obtain remission of sins and eternal life by virtue of that ransom paid once for all mankind. But Christ so died for the elect that, by the merit of his death in special manner destinated unto them according to the eternal good pleasure of God, they might infallibly obtain both faith and eternal life.

{II.4} *The fourth position*

Upon this merit of Christ is founded that general promise of the Gospel, according to which all that believe in Christ may really attain remission of sins and eternal life.

That this promise is universal, and founded only upon the death of Christ, it is evident out of . . . Acts 10:43, *To him give all the prophets witness that they shall receive remission of sins by his name, as many as believe in him, &c.* . . . Therefore, although this promise be not divulged unto all in every time and place, yet it is of that nature that it may be truly published to all and every one: for the nature of the promise extends itself perpetually to mankind, although the knowledge of the promise, according to the special providence of God, is published sometimes to these, sometimes to other nations. . . .

{II.5} *The fifth position*

In the Church, wherein, according to the promise of the Gospel, salvation is offered to all, there is such an administration of grace as is sufficient to convince {convict} all impenitents and unbelievers that by their own voluntary default, either through neglect or contempt of the Gospel, they perish and come short of the benefit offered unto them.

Christ by his death not only established the evangelical covenant, but moreover obtained of his Father that wheresoever this covenant should be published, there also, together with it, ordinarily such a measure of supernatural grace should be dispensed as may suffice to convince all impenitents and unbelievers of contempt, or at least of neglect, in that the condition was not fulfilled by them.

Here two things are briefly to be explained, whereof the first we put down for a supposition: that some measure of grace is ordinarily offered by the ministry of the Gospel.

The second for a position: that that grace is sufficient to convince all impenitents and incredulous persons either of contempt or at least of neglect.

The first is plain out of the Scriptures: Esay 59{:21} . . . *This is my covenant with them, saith the Lord: my Spirit that is upon thee, and my word, which I have put in thy mouth, shall not depart out of thy mouth from henceforth, and for ever.* Hence it is evident that the word and the Spirit are inseparably joined together by the promise of God in the ministry of the word.

. . .

The second is proved out of . . . John 15:22, *If I had not come and spoken unto them, they had not had sin, but now have they no cloak for their sin.* Out of this place it is certain that Christ, in propounding the Gospel, did withal dispense that internal grace which so far forth sufficed that, in that they accepted not or rejected the Gospel, they might be justly taxed of positive infidelity. John 3:19, *This is condemnation, that light is come into the world, and men loved darkness rather than light.* So are men justly damned, because they turn away from the light of the Gospel. Heb. 2:3, *How shall we escape if we neglect so great salvation?* For the neglect of salvation offered in the Gospel, we are subject to just punishment; therefore salvation is offered in the Gospel.

Heb. 4:12, *The word of God is quick and powerful, and sharper than any two edged sword, piercing even to dividing asunder of soul and spirit, and of the joints and marrow, and is a discerner of the thoughts and intents of the heart.* Hence it comes to be manifest that there is such power and efficacy of the word that it insinuates itself even into the secretest closets of the soul, and as it doth without fail quicken those which truly believe, so it doth truly inflict a deadly wound upon the stubborn.

. . .

{II.6} *The sixth position*

Notwithstanding this general covenant of saving those that believe, God is not tied by any covenant or promise to afford the Gospel, or saving grace, to all and every one. But the reason why he affords it to some and passeth by others is his own mercy and absolute freedom. . . .

God promiseth in the Old Testament that the preaching of the Gospel should be communicated to the gentiles. In the New Testament the partition wall is broken down . . . but God nowhere promised that universally in the world, at one and the same time, it should be preached.

. . .

2. Moreover, it is plainly evident (notwithstanding this universal covenant, which was of force even in the Old Testament) that God revealed not the knowledge hereof unto the gentiles. . . . Yea, and in our days scarce the sixth part of the habitable world have given their names to Christ. But if in fact and event God hath never vouchsafed the preaching of the Gospel to all and every one, certainly then he is not bound so to afford it. For he doth whatsoever he hath bound himself to do.

The same also is to be said of saving grace. We nowhere in the Scriptures meet with any mention of any promise by which God hath bound himself to impart this grace to all and every one. Nay rather the Scripture makes mention of God's liberty in commiserating, Rom. 9:18, *God hath mercy on whom he will have mercy,* notwithstanding this covenant grounded in the blood of Christ. And although God doth bless with many benefits all men—yea even the most ungrateful which live without the lists {confines} of the Church—and although all men (as being sinners) stand in need of saving graces, yet is he obliged to none either to bestow the one or the other.[2]

3. Lastly, it is concluded out of the Holy Scriptures that some are judged and condemned for sins committed only against the law of nature (Rom. 2:14-15). Whereby is implied that upon invincible ignorance they are excused for not fulfilling the law of faith. Which excuse can have no place where God proclaims his law and men are bound to obey.

Erroneous Opinions {concerning the Second Article} Rejected by Us

{II.error1} *The first*

That Christ's death being granted, God hath no other intention of saving any particular persons than conditional, and suspended upon the contingent act of man's faith.

---

[2] {i.e., neither benefits nor saving graces}

. . .

3. Moreover, the house of God being to be built *ex hominibus*, of men, hath not sufficient firmness and solidity if it be built *ab hominibus*, by men: this fabric must be reared by God's own hand. . . . Ephes. 2:20, *Being built upon the foundation of the prophets and apostles, Christ himself being the chief corner stone; in whom all the building fitly framed together groweth unto an holy temple, &c. In whom you also are builded together.* . . . Therefore God, building a Church for himself, doth with his own hand prepare the stones, polish them, and cement them; he doth not expect that they should by haphazard fit themselves, and join themselves to the foundation.

. . .

{II.error2} *The second erroneous opinion*

That it was the proper and entire end of Christ's death that he might purchase right and power unto God the Father to save men upon what conditions he would.

. . .

{II.error3} *The third erroneous opinion*

That Christ's death hath obtained for all men restitution into the state of grace and salvation.

1. Salvation is a thing promised by the new covenant; neither is it promised but upon the condition of faith: *Whosoever believeth shall be saved.* Since therefore all men have not faith in Christ, under which only condition salvation is promised, it is certain that the death of Christ did not obtain for all, but for the faithful alone, a restoring into the state of grace and salvation. . . .

. . .

3. If so be the death of Christ hath obtained restitution for all, then are they restored either then when Christ from all eternity was destinated to death, which is false; for so no man should be born a child of wrath, neither should original sin any whit damage mankind. . . . Or else they were restored in the person of our first parents, when the promise of the seed of the woman was proclaimed; which cannot be, for our first parents were not restored into the state of grace but by faith in Christ, and consequently their posterity in like manner. . . . Or lastly, when Christ himself suffered death upon the Cross; which cannot be, for so no man before that moment should have been restored, which will not be granted by any; neither are all restored from that time, because without doubt even at that moment and afterward, the anger of God waxed hot against some of his accusers, condemners, crucifiers, and mockers.

THEIR SUFFRAGE CONCERNING THE THIRD AND FOURTH ARTICLES

{III–IVa} First, of the Strength of Free-will in Man after the Fall

{III–IVa.1} *The first position*

The will of man being fallen is deprived of the supernatural and saving graces with which it was endowed in the state of innocency, and therefore to the performing of any spiritual actions it is able to do nothing without the assistance of grace.

That the will of man was endowed with excellent graces, it is hence manifest, because man was made after the image of God. But the image of God had the prime place in the chief faculty of the soul; and what these graces were with which the will of man was beautified in the Creation, it is evident out of those things which are restored for the making whole again of this image: Ephes. 4:24, *Put ye on that new man, which after God is created in righteousness and true holiness.* And that this righteousness, holiness, and uprightness of our will was lost by the Fall, it is clear by this second receiving the same, being recovered by the grace of God in Christ. For we are to put on anew that which we put off in Adam when he was stript and left naked.

And that such a will as this of ours avails nothing to the performance of supernatural actions, the Scripture clearly witnesseth, John 15:5, *Without me you can do nothing.* Rom. 5:6, *When as yet we were of no strength, &c.* 2 Cor. 3:5, *We are not sufficient of ourselves to think anything, as of ourselves.*

. . .

{III–IVa.2} *The second position*

There is in the will of a man being fallen, not only a possibility of sinning, but also an headlong inclination to sin.

. . .

Neither can the case stand otherwise in corrupt man not yet restored by the grace of God, since that such is the nature of the will that it cannot remain single or utterly unfurnished, but falling from one object, to which it did adhere, it pursues another eagerly to embrace it. And therefore being by a voluntary apostasy habitually turned from God the Creator, it runs to the creature with an unbridled appetite and in a lustful and base manner commits fornication with it, being always desirous to set her[3] heart and rest on those things which ought only to be used on the by, and to attempt and accomplish things forbidden. What marvel then if such a will be the bond-slave of the devil? . . .

The will without charity is nothing but a vicious desire [Aug. *Retract.* 1.5].

{III–IVb} Of Those Things That Go before Conversion

{III–IVb.1} *The first position*

There are certain external works ordinarily required of men before they be brought to the state of regeneration or conversion, which are wont sometimes to be performed freely by them and otherwhiles freely omitted, as to go to church, to hear the word preached, or the like.

That such things are required it is manifest, Rom. 10:4, *How shall they believe in him, of whom they have not heard.* And that they are in our power, both reason tells us, seeing it is in every man's power to rule his moving faculty, and experience proves it, because we see in outward things, men, as they will, themselves do this or that, or omit both. They can therefore sit at home when they should go to church. It is in their power to stop their ears when the preacher speaks. . . .

---

[3] {"Her" refers to the will (*voluntas*, a feminine noun in Latin).}

{III–IVb.2} *The second position*

There are certain inward effects going before conversion (or regeneration) which by the power of the word and Spirit are stirred up in the hearts of men not yet justified: as are a knowledge of God's will, a sense of sin, a fear of punishment, a bethinking of freedom, and some hope of pardon.

The grace of God is not wont to bring men to the state of justification (in which we have peace with God through our Lord Jesus Christ) by a sudden enthusiasm or rapture, but by divers degrees of foregoing actions, taming and preparing them through the ministry of the word. . . .

2. This the very nature of the thing requires; for, as in the natural generation of man there are many previous dispositions which go before the bringing in of the form, so also in the spiritual generation, by many actions of grace which must go before, do we come to the spiritual nativity.

3. To conclude, this appears by the instruments which God uses for the regenerating of men. For he employeth the ministry of men and the instrument of the word. . . . But if God would regenerate or justify a wicked man immediately, being prepared by no knowledge, no sorrow, no desire, no hope of pardon, there would be no need of the ministry of men nor of the preaching of the word for this purpose; neither would any care lie upon the ministers, dividing the word of God aright, fitly and wisely first to wound the consciences of their auditors with the terrors of the Law, then to raise them up with the promises of the Gospel, and to exhort them to beg faith and repentance at God's hand by prayers and tears.

{III–IVb.3} *The third position*

Whom God doth thus prepare by his Spirit through the means of the word, those doth he truly and seriously call and invite to faith and conversion.

By the nature of the benefit offered and by the evident word of God, we must judge of those helps of grace which are bestowed upon men, and not by the abuse or the event. Therefore when the Gospel of its own nature calls men to repentance and salvation, when the incitements of divine grace tend the same way, we must not suppose anything is done feignedly by God. This is proved by those earnest and pathetical entreaties, 2 Cor. 5:20, *We pray you in Christ's stead, be ye reconciled unto God.* Those exhortations, 2 Cor. 6:1, *We beseech you that you receive not the grace of God in vain.* . . . Those promises, Apoc. 3:20, *Behold, I stand at the door and knock; if any man hear my voice and open the door, I will come in to him.*

But if God should not seriously invite all whom he vouchsafes this gift of his word and Spirit to a serious conversion, surely both God should deceive many whom he calls in his Son's name, and the messengers of the evangelical promises might be accused of false witness; and those who, being called to conversion, do neglect to obey, might be more excusable. For that calling by the word and the Spirit cannot be thought to leave men unexcusable, which is only exhibited to this end: to make them unexcusable.

{III–IVb.4} *The fourth position*

Those whom God hath thus disposed, he doth not forsake nor cease to further them in the true way to conversion, before he be forsaken of them by a voluntary neglect or repulse of this initial or entering grace.

The talent of grace once given by God is taken from none but from him who first *buries it* by his own fault (Mat. 25:28). Hence is it that in the Scriptures everywhere we are admonished that we *resist not the Spirit*, that we *quench not the Spirit*, that we *receive not the grace of God in vain*, that we *depart not from God*. Yea, that is most evidently noted to be the reason of God's forsaking man: because God is first forsaken by man. . . . But never in the Scriptures is there the least mention that God is wont or is willing at any time, without some fault of man going before, to take away from any man the aid of his exciting grace or any help which he hath once conferred toward man's conversion.

Thus the orthodox Fathers who had to do with the Pelagians ever taught, *It is the will of God that we continue in a good will, who before he be forsaken forsakes no man, and oftentimes converts many that forsake him.*

{III–IVb.5} *The fifth position*

These foregoing effects wrought in the minds of men by the power of the word and the Spirit may be stifled and utterly extinguished by the fault of our rebellious will, and in many are; so that some, in whose hearts by the virtue of the word and the Spirit some knowledge of divine truth, some sorrow for sin, some desire and care of deliverance have been imprinted, are changed quite contrary, reject and hate the truth, deliver themselves up to their lusts, are hardened in their sins, and, without all desire or care of freedom from them, rot and putrefy in them.

. . .

Many do quickly entertain the light of the mind, but the understanding itself hath not the same force or power in all; and many when they seem enriched with faith and understanding, yet they want charity and cannot hold fast to those things which they see by faith and understanding, because there is no persevering in that which is not loved with the whole heart [Prosp. *De vocat.*, lib. 2. cap. 2].

{III–IVb.6} *The sixth position*

The very elect, in those acts going before regeneration, do not carry themselves so, but that for their negligence and resistance they may justly be relinquished and forsaken of God; but such is the special mercy of God toward them, that, though they do for a while repel and choke the grace of God exciting or enlightening them, yet God doth urge them again and again, nor doth he cease to stir them forward till he have thoroughly subdued them to his grace and set them in the state of regenerate sons.

. . .

But if God should not go on thus to follow even those that hold off and retire from him, no calling would be effectual, there would be no filial adoption, and even election itself, grounded upon the good pleasure of God, would be frustrated.

Since the fall of man, God would have it ascribed to his grace that a man doth come unto him; neither will he have it ascribed to any thing but his grace, that a man doth not go from him [Aug. *De persev.*].

{III–IVb.7} *The seventh position*

Those that are not elected, when they resist the Spirit of God and his grace in these acts foregoing regeneration, and extinguish the initial effects of the same in themselves, by the fault of their own free-will are justly forsaken by God whensoever it pleases him—whom, by their own fault so forsaken, we truly pronounce to remain by the same demerit hardened and unconverted.

We think it to be without all doubt that no mortal man doth so carry himself toward God but that either by omitting that which he should have done or committing that which he should not have done, he deserves to have the grace taken from him which he hath. Which ground being forelaid, it is clear that God, without all injustice and cruelty, may take from such men that grace which he hath extended to them and leave them to the hardness of their own hearts: Rom. 9:18, *He hath mercy on whom he will have mercy, and whom he will he hardeneth.* God oweth this to no man, that when he resists enlightening & exciting grace and serves his own lusts, he should then soften and mollify him by that special grace which no hard heart doth resist. . . .

{III–IVc} Of Conversion, as It Designs[4] the Immediate Work of God Regenerating Men.

{III–IVc.1} *The first position*

God doth regenerate by a certain inward and wonderful operation the souls of the elect, being stirred up and prepared by the aforesaid acts of his grace; and doth, as it were, create them anew by infusing his quickening Spirit and seasoning all the faculties of the soul with new qualities.

. . .

This spiritual birth presupposes a mind moved by the Spirit, using the instrument of God's word—whence also we are said to be *born again by the incorruptible seed of the word* (1 Pet. 1:23)—which must be observed, lest any one should idly and slothfully expect an enthusiastical regeneration: that is to say, wrought by a sudden rapture without any foregoing action either of God, the word, or himself.

Furthermore, we conclude that the Spirit regenerating us doth convey itself into the most inward closet of the heart, and frame the mind anew by curing the sinful inclinations thereof. . . .

From this work of God cometh our ability of performing spiritual actions leading to salvation. As the act of believing. . . . Of loving, 1 John 4:7, *Every one that loveth is born of God.* Lastly, all works of piety, John 15:5, *Without me ye can do nothing.*

Prosper saith that *Grace creates good in us* [*De lib arb.*].

---

[4] {signifies}

The Schoolmen do not deny so manifest a truth. Thomas Aquinas affirms that this grace of which we speak doth give a *certain spiritual being to the soul*; that it is a *certain supernatural partaking of the divine nature*; that it is, *in respect of the soul, as health is in respect of the body* [*Quaest. disp. de verit.*, art. 2].

{III–IVc.2} *The second position*

In this work of regeneration, man is merely passive; neither is it in the power of man's will to hinder God regenerating thus immediately.

. . .

What doth free-will? I answer briefly: It is saved. This work cannot be effected without two: one by whom it is done, the other in whom it is done. God is the author of salvation; free-will is only capable of it [Bern. *De grat & lib. ar.*]. . . .

When God determineth to save, no will of man resisteth. [Aug. *De cor. & gra.*]

{III–IVd} Of Conversion, as It Imports What Man Himself Doth in Turning to God by Faith and Saving Repentance.

{III–IVd.1} *The first position*

Upon the former conversion followeth this our actual conversion, wherein, out of our reformed will, God himself draweth forth the very act of our believing and converting; and this our will, being first moved by God, doth itself also work by turning unto God and believing; that is, by executing withal its own proper lively act.

1. In order of time, the work of God converting man and the act of man turning himself to God can hardly be distinguished, but in order of causality or efficiency, God's work must needs go before, and ours follow. An evil tree, naturally bringing forth evil fruit, must needs be changed into a good tree before it can bear any good fruit; but the will of an unregenerate man is not only as a bad, but as a dead tree. Therefore, if it bring forth good fruit, it doth it not that thereby it may be bettered or that by its own cooperation it may be quickened, but it doth it because it is already changed and quickened.

. . .

2. Secondly, we say that God doth not only work this habitual conversion whereby a man gets new spiritual ability to believe and convert, but also that God doth, by a certain wonderful efficacy of his secret operation, extract out of our regenerated will the very act of believing and converting. . . .

But if God by infusing some strength into us should only give us a possibility or power of believing, a possibility or power of converting, and so leave the act to the free-will of men, surely we should all do as our first father did: by our free-will we should fall from God, neither should we ever bring this possibility into act. This therefore is that excellent special grace granted to the elect in Christ, whereby they not only can believe if they will, but also will believe then when they can. Phil. 2:13, *God worketh in us the will and the deed.* This working grace the Fathers of the Catholic Church have maintained against the Pelagians. . . .

. . .

God effecteth our faith, working in our hearts after a wonderful manner to make us believe [Aug., *De praedest. sanct.*].

3. Lastly, this also we add, that this action of God in producing faith doth not hinder, but rather is the cause that the will doth work together with God and produce its own act. And therefore this act of believing, howsoever it is sent from God, yet, because it is performed by man, is attributed to man himself. . . .

. . .

{III–IVd.2} *The second position*

This action of God doth not hinder the freedom of the will but strengthen it; neither doth it root out the vicious power we have to resist, but it doth effectually and sweetly bestow on a man a resolute will to obey.

1. Here we deny two things: first, that by the divine operation there is any wrong offered to the will. For God doth so work in nature, even when he raiseth and advanceth it above its proper sphere, that he doth not destroy the particular nature and being of any thing, but leaves to every thing its own way and motion to perform the action. When therefore God worketh in the wills of men by his Spirit of grace, he makes them move in their natural course, that is, freely; and then do they work the more freely, by how much they are the more effectually stirred up by the Spirit. John 8:36, *If the Son shall make you free, you shall be free indeed.* . . .

He doth what he pleaseth with the wills of men, and when he pleaseth: having an all-sufficient power to incline men's hearts which way he listeth [Aug. *De cor.*, c. 14].

. . .

2. A second thing which we here disclaim is the whole extirpation of corruption. For although God in the very act of regeneration doth work so powerfully upon the will that actually the present power to resist is suspended for that time, yet doth he not pluck up by the roots, no not for that time, the remote {underlying} power of resisting. . . . For so long as that root of corrupt and corrupting concupiscence remains in the soul of man, certain it is that there must needs be there withal not only a possibility but also a proneness to resist the motions of the Holy Spirit: Gal. 5:7, *The flesh lusteth against the spirit.* . . .

This grace cannot be resisted, because first it worketh in us to will, that is, not to resist: for he can no further resist, from whom to will to resist is taken away; as excellently writeth our reverend late Bishop of Salisbury [Robertus {Abbot} Sarisbur., *De veritate grat.*, pag. 20].

{III–IVd.3} *The third position*

God doth not always so move a converted and faithful man to godly ensuing actions that he takes from him the very will of resisting, but sometimes he suffers him, through his own weakness, to stray from the direction of grace and in many particular actions to follow his own concupiscence.

. . .

Erroneous Opinions {Concerning the Third and Fourth Articles} Which We Reject

{III–IV.error1} *The first {erroneous opinion}*

That the will is not capable of spiritual gifts, and that therefore there never were any spiritual gifts in the will of man before his Fall; that these graces were never severed from the will of man upon his Fall; and that such graces are never infused in regeneration into the wills of men.

. . .

1. But if any man shall refer these graces to the affections, and place them without the will, he shall (which were a foul enormity) settle the chiefest gifts of divine grace in the unreasonable part of the soul. Moreover, the very habitual conversion of the will unto God the Creator, & the aversion or turning away thereof from the inordinate desire it had to commit fornication with the creature, without doubt is to be counted a chief and principal gift. And that the will was capable of this gift, it doth hence plainly appear, because it was created with such uprightness. . . .

. . .

{III–IV.error2} *The second erroneous opinion*

That that grace by which we are converted is only a gentle and moral suasion or inducement.

We deny not but in the work of conversion, whether in fitting us for that future grace or in confirming us therein, as already performed, God useth the persuasive force of his threats, promises, & exhortations, by which he allureth, stirreth, and ploweth up the fallows of men's hearts. But moreover, for adding without fail the last close to this operation, he works more powerfully and unconquerably, *according to the exceeding greatness of his power and the working of his might* (Ephes. 1:19). Neither is suasion sufficient, which no more than contingently affecteth and inviteth the will.

1. For moral suasion moveth only by way of object, and so far forth as the end propounded can allure. But the philosophers rightly determine that, as the inclination of anyone is, accordingly he apprehends the end. So long, therefore, as a man is carnal and unregenerate, his will cannot so be affected with supernatural benefits proposed unto it, that by the desire of them he should be thoroughly enflamed to believe and convert. But the will must be overcome and changed by a powerful operation exceeding all suasion, that so it may effectually embrace the good represented unto it.

2. If men should be converted unto God only by a moral suasion, then this question, "why, upon proffer of equal grace, one man believes, another doth not," might be answered out of the free-will's own power of willing or nilling; neither should we have herein any cause to admire the unsearchable wisdom and justice of our God. . . .

3. If men were converted only by moral suasion, he which receives this suasive grace might truly say, *I have separated myself.* . . . To what purpose then is that of Saint Paul, *Who hath separated thee? What hast thou, which thou hast not received?*

. . .

{III–IV.error3} *The third erroneous opinion*

That, presupposing all the operations of grace which God useth for the effecting of this conversion, yet the will of man is still left in an equal balance either to believe or not to believe, to convert or not to convert itself to God.

1. If after all the workings of grace the will of man be left in even point, it will necessarily follow that, not God by his grace, but man by his free-will is the chief cause and author of the very act of believing and converting. For he who by the utmost dint and strain of his grace prevailed no further than to raise up a man's will to an indifference

or estate of equal balance, doth not concur as a principal and predominant, or over-ruler, but only as an associate, and contingently; that is, upon this condition, if so be that the will, by its own natural power, first shall have removed itself from that equality. That, therefore, which is of less moment, the will receives from God: namely, that it should be placed in a certain middle estate, equally inclined to believe or not to believe; but that which is of greater moment, as specifying the very event—that is, actually to believe—this the will by its own power hath performed.

2. It would else follow that God affordeth no more grace to the elect than to those who are not elected, and that those owe no more thank to God than the other, inasmuch as the hand of God hath wrought in both nothing else but an even stand of the will, which equally consists in a point and is not capable of any latitude or degree.

3. The grace of conversion is given with that intention, that it shall become effectual, and shall not only set a man forward on his way, but also bring him to perform the very act of faith; whither, although such grace might perchance sometime reach by the sway of man's will equally poised to embrace and follow the motions of grace, yet no less often should such grace be frustrated by reason of the same free-will, likewise placed at even balance, and freely thence settling itself to refuse grace and to resist it. For in level counterpoise there is always presupposed an equal hazard of settling to either side.

This grace is refused by no hard heart: for it is therefore given, that the hardness of the heart be first taken away [Aug. *De praedest. sanct.* c. 8].

{III–IV.error4} *The fourth erroneous opinion*

That a man cannot do any more good than he doth, nor omit any more evil than he doth omit.[5]

This is most false and absurd, whether it be spoken of an unregenerate and natural man or of one that is regenerate and supported by sanctifying grace.

1. First concerning the state of a natural man: although he cannot put off his inbred corruption nor shake off the dominion of sin in general, yet can he repress many outward actions in which he lets loose the reins to his own concupiscences. Corrupt concupiscence inclines a wicked man to all kind of evil, yet it doth not determine or confine him unavoidably to commit this or that sin in particular, as to act this murder, that robbery, that adultery.

2. This is manifest also in that the very lewdest men attempt their wickedness not without some precedent deliberation and most free contriving of the means tending thereto; and being ready to commit the act, they have power to hold in and restrain themselves, being awed by the reverence of some other man or through some present fear of danger.

3. Lastly, punishments by the laws of men should be without cause menaced, if no man could omit those crimes which he doth commit.

But as for actions which are in themselves good, certain it is that unregenerate men do omit many outward moral acts which, for the substance of the work, they could perform;

---

[5] {A position held by some hard-core Calvinists (e.g., Piscator), which the final Canons—to the dismay of the British delegates—did not finally condemn.}

and for the voluntary neglect of such actions they are justly condemned. Matt. 25:42, *I was an hungry, and ye gave me no meat; I was athirst, and ye gave me no drink, &c.*

Likewise the same is to be avowed concerning those that are regenerated and truly sanctified: to wit, that although they are freed from the dominion of sin . . . they can notwithstanding, and that voluntarily, step out of the straight path of righteousness, even then also when they do not transgress. In like manner then, when they fell or slipped, they were able by the help and power of grace, through their free (that is, freed) will, to have resisted their own concupiscence and to have avoided those manifest works of the flesh recounted, Gal. 5:9, *fornication, uncleanness, debate, contentions, &c.* What man of sound judgment will say that David could not but commit adultery, and, that being committed, that he could not choose but by a lewd and deliberate plot take away the life of him to whom he had offered that extreme wrong? But (that we go not far for examples) we appeal unto the consciences of all godly men: who is he that daily praying unto God, *forgive us our trespasses*, doth not also acknowledge that through the grace of God it was in his power to perform divers good works, which yet he hath omitted, and likewise to overcome divers temptations, to which he notwithstanding hath yielded. . . .

THEIR SUFFRAGE CONCERNING THE FIFTH ARTICLE
Which Is of the Perseverance of the Saints

In this Article, when question is made concerning the perseverance of the saints, it is to be understood that we treat of those saints only which are come to the use of reason and are justified by the act of faith formed in them by the preaching of the Gospel, and who are supposed by the act of their own wills to persevere in the same faith or else to fail in their perseverance.

. . .

Because in this Article two things there are which are usually questioned—the one, whether they who are not elect may ever come to the state of sanctification and justification whereby they may be reckoned among the number of the saints; the other, whether the elect, who are justified and sanctified, do at any time wholly fall off from this estate—therefore in the first place we set down those positions by which we shew how far they who are not elect may go on in the way.

{Va} Touching Those Who Are Not Elect

{Va.1} *The first position*

There is a certain supernatural enlightening granted to some of them who are not elect, by the power whereof they understand those things to be true which are revealed in the word of God and yield an unfeigned assent unto them.

. . .

. . . Which illumination proceeding from the Holy Ghost did beget a true knowledge in the minds of these men, out of which knowledge they, as occasion required, brought forth actions suitable to the same. Yea, it may come to pass that an heathen philosopher may apprehend more accurately and distinctly the mysteries of Christ's Incarnation, and in his understanding more subtly discern the unity of the person and distinction of natures than an unlearned Christian.

Concerning the unfeigned assent which may be, and often is, yielded to the Gospel by some who are not elected, there is the like evidence. Luk. 8:13, The seed which fell upon the stony ground noteth to us such hearers as *for a while believe*; that is, those which give assent to things revealed from above. . . . And thereby it is plain that this their assent was no way feigned, because they received the word with joy (Acts 8:30). . . .

All backsliders of this kind are justly reproved and punished, not because they feigned that faith they never had, but because they forsook the faith they had; and they sin in a far greater measure which depart from the grace of faith conferred upon them than they who never tasted of the glad tidings of the Gospel, as our Savior teacheth us (John 15:22).

{Va.2} *The second position*

In these fore-mentioned there doth arise out of this knowledge and faith, a certain change of their affections and some kind of amendment of their manners.

. . .

In these, as the enlightening and assent yielded to the truth revealed from above was not feigned but true in its own kind and degree, so likewise was the change of their affections and manners: namely these beginnings or entrances were not feigned or colorable, but proceeded out of the power of those dispositions unto grace and from the inspiration of the Holy Ghost which they felt in themselves for a time, as is evident by their affections, their joy, sorrow, and zeal, which they do not so much feign and make a shew of as find to be truly in themselves.

. . .

{Va.3} *The third position*

Upon those good beginnings, testified by the external works of obedience, they are reputed (and by a charitable construction ought to be taken for) believers: justified and sanctified men.

They, who to these inward gifts of the Holy Ghost have added the outward profession of a Christian faith together with the amendment of their lives, ought of right to be reckoned by us (who cannot find out or search into the inward secrets of men's hearts) in the number of the faithful, of the justified. . . . Saint Augustine speaking of those who were not elect. . . . *There are some who are called of us the sons of God because of the grace received by them for a time, but yet they are not the sons of God.*

{Va.4} *The fourth position*

They who are not elect (although they thus far proceed) yet they never attain unto the state of adoption and justification; and therefore by the apostasy of these men, the apostasy of the saints is very erroneously concluded.

Although they who are not elect, being brought up & cherished in the Church's bosom, are in their minds, will, and affections disposed by the aforesaid preparatives tending in some sort to justification, yet are they not thereupon placed in the state of justification or adoption. For they still retain thoroughly settled in their hearts the strings and roots of their lewd desires, to which they give themselves over; still they remain wedded to the love of earthly things, and the hardness lurking in the secret corners of their hearts is not taken away; so that either persecution or temptation arising, they retire from grace, and being either entangled with the love of pleasures and enticements of the flesh, or carried away with some other vicious affections, at length they shew that they are lovers of themselves and lovers of pleasures rather than lovers of God, and that they enjoy nothing less than God, howsoever they may flatter themselves, but indeed that *they would make use of God, that they may enjoy the world*, as S. Augustine speaks. Whence it is manifest that they never really and truly attain that change and renovation of the mind and affections which accompanieth justification; nay, nor that which doth immediately prepare and dispose unto justification. For they never seriously repent; they are never affected with hearty sorrow for this cause, they have offended God by sinning; nor do they come to any humble contrition of heart, nor conceive a firm resolution not to offend any more; unto them is not given *repentance unto life*. . . . Add also that such do never feel in themselves an earnest desire of reconciliation: *They do not hunger and thirst after righteousness. For such shall be filled* (Matth. 5:6). . . . Also they do neither deny themselves nor seriously bid defiance to their own lusts, nor do they once feel in their hearts any such *accounting of all things but loss that they may win Christ*, as the Apostle did (Phil. 3:8). And to conclude, they never attain to that unfeigned lively faith which justifieth a sinner, *and worketh through love* (2 Tim. 1:5). For this faith is the peculiar *of the elect*. . . .

. . .

4. Those adopted sons *are also heirs, heirs of God and coheirs with Christ, and do receive the earnest of their inheritance.* But they who are not elect are never regenerated by this incorruptible seed, neither have they the seed of God remaining in them, neither are they assigned to be heirs with Christ. . . .

Gabriel Biel saith, *It is plain that those whom God foresaw are not his adopted sons because they are not preordained by the will of God unto everlasting inheritance.*

Apostasy is only of those who never reached home to true justification and to the state of adoption. But as for those who are the chosen sons of God and endued with true sanctity, their perseverance is certain and undoubted. . . .

{Vb} Of Perseverance, as It Concerns the Elect, and of the Certainty Thereof in Itself

{Vb.1} *The first position*

Besides that dogmatical faith and some kind of amendment in affections and manners, there is in due time given to the elect justifying faith, regenerating grace, and all other gifts by which they are translated from the state of wrath unto the state of adoption and salvation.

When God dealeth with his elect, he stayeth not in certain preparatives and initial operations, but always finisheth his work by enduing them with a lively faith, by justifying and adopting them, and by changing them from the state of death to the state of life. This the Apostle sheweth, Rom. 8:30, *Whom he hath predestinated, those he also called; and whom he called, he hath also justified, and whom he hath justified, he hath also glorified.* . . . Out of which places it is plain that God giveth to all the elect a certain continued connection of spiritual benefits, which never leaves them, but plyeth them onward even unto the state of glory.

{Vb.2} *The second position*

Although the elect, being set in this estate, omit something in every good work by reason of the remainder of concupiscence, and commit daily smaller sins of surreption,[6] negligence, and inconsiderateness, yet neither from thence is the state of justification shaken, nor the benefit of their claim to the inheritance of the kingdom of heaven thereby interrupted.

According to the rigor of the Law, every sin, yea the very least, is mortal and excludes the offender from the favor of God and kingdom of heaven. But God never deals in that strict manner with his sons adopted and justified in Christ. There are indeed some sins for which God denounceth his anger and indignation upon these his sons, yea and threateneth banishment from heaven, and also eternal death. . . . There are again some other sins, for which our merciful God is not wont, no not for a time, to deprive his children of the light of his countenance, or to terrify them with the fear of death or damnation: of which kind are the rebelling motions of our concupiscence whereof the Apostle complains (Rom. 7); also the defects and stains which do cleave to the best works of the regenerate; lastly, those daily trippings and scapes of human infirmity which are committed without any determinate purpose of committing them and which are forgiven by our daily craving of pardon: of these St. James, chap. 3. v. 2, *In many things we offend all*: and St. John 1:8, *If we say that we have no sin, we deceive ourselves.* Notwithstanding these sins, every faithful man may rightly say, *There is no condemnation to them that are in Christ Jesus*; yea even in the midst of these infirmities, God saith to every justified man, as he said to the Apostle, *My grace is sufficient for thee; for my strength is made perfect in weakness.* And sure they cannot be said to fall by their infirmities from the state of justification, through whose weakness the power of God is made perfect, and who all this while may boast that *the power of Christ dwelleth in them*, as it is in the same place.

{Vb.3} *The third position*

These very same, thus regenerated and justified, do sometimes through their own default fall into heinous sins and thereby they do incur the fatherly anger of God; they draw upon themselves a damnable guiltiness and lose their present fitness to the kingdom of heaven.

It is manifest by the examples of David and Peter that the regenerate can throw himself headlong into most grievous sins, God sometimes permitting it, that they may learn with all humility to acknowledge that, not by their own strength or deserts, but by God's mercy alone, they were freed from eternal death and had life eternal bestowed upon them.

Whilest they cleave to such sins and sleep securely therein, God's fatherly anger ariseth against them . . .

Besides, they draw upon themselves damnable guilt; so that as long as they continue without repentance in that state, they neither ought nor can persuade themselves otherwise than that they are subject to eternal death. . . . although they are not as yet given over to death, nor about to be given (if we consider the fatherly love of God), but are first to be taken out of this sin, that they may also be rescued from the guilt of death.

. . .

---

[6] {An unperceived creeping or stealing upon one or into one's mind (of evil thoughts or suggestions); hence, a sudden or surprise attack (of temptation, sin) (*OED*).}

{Vb.4} *The fourth position*

The unalterable ordinance of God doth require that the faithful, so straying out of the right way, must first return again into the way by a renewed performance of faith and repentance before he can be brought to the end of the way: that is, to the kingdom of heaven.

By the decree of election, the faithful are so predestinated to the end that they are (as along the king's high way) to be led to this appointed end through the means set down by God, otherways not to attain the same. Nor are God's decrees concerning the means, manner, and order of such events less fixed and sure than the decrees of the end and of the events themselves. If any man therefore walk in a way contrary to God's ordinance, namely, that broad way of uncleanness and impenitency (which leads directly down to hell), he can never come by this means to the kingdom of heaven. Yea, and if death shall overtake him wandering in this by-path, he cannot but fall into everlasting death. This is the constant and manifest voice of the holy Scripture, *Except ye repent, ye shall all likewise perish.* . . . They are deceived therefore that think the elect wallowing in such crimes, and so dying, must notwithstanding needs be saved through the force of election. For the salvation of the elect is sure indeed, God so decreeing; but withal (by the decree of the same our God) not otherwise sure than through the way of faith, repentance, and holiness. . . .

As therefore it was sure out of the decree and promise of God that all those who sailed in the ship with Saint Paul should escape alive out of shipwrack; and notwithstanding, Paul's saying was also as certain, *Unless these remain in the ship, ye cannot be saved* [Acts 27:31]; so also it was certain that the elect servants of God, David and Peter, should come to the kingdom of heaven; yet withal it was no less certain that if they had remained unrepentant, the one in his homicide and adultery, the other in his denying and forswearing Christ, neither of them both could have been saved.

. . . But God's providence and mercy doth easily loose this knot by taking care that none of the elect die in such estate by which, according to some ordinance of God's will, he must be excluded from eternal life.

{Vb.5} *The fifth position*

In the meantime, between the guilt of a grievous sin and the renewed act of faith and repentance, such an offender stands by his own desert to be condemned; by Christ's merit and God's decree to be acquitted; but actually absolved he is not until he hath obtained pardon by renewed faith & repentance.

There can be no question of the merit of damnation for such a sin. . . . Notwithstanding, in such a guilt the faithful are not in the like case with the wicked. To the faithful the blood of Christ is a prepared antidote at hand ready to be applied, which, as soon as their faith is awaked and rouzed up, they can use to the overcoming of this deadly poison.[7] But to the unfaithful, this inward active cause is wanting (to wit, faith), without which, the remedy, though sovereign in itself, is as if it were laid afar off, out of reach, neither can it be made their own or actually applied to them.

---

[7] {If this refers to the Eucharist, it is the text's sole mention of the sacraments.}

And moreover hereunto God's special love, which, though it doth not hinder but that his fatherly indignation ariseth against an undutiful son, yet it keeps off hostile hatred such as carrieth with it a purpose of condemning. . . .

. . .

{Vb.6} *The sixth position*

In the foresaid space {prior to repentance}, the right to the kingdom of God is not taken away {from the elect}, universal justification is not defeated, the state of adoption remaineth undissolved, and, by the custody of the Holy Spirit, the seed of regeneration, with all those fundamental graces without which the state of a regenerate man cannot stand, is preserved whole and sound.

Our right to the kingdom of heaven is not founded on our actions but on the free gift of adoption and on our union with Christ. . . . The faithful may wander out of the way which leadeth to the kingdom of heaven, but he cannot be said to lose his right of inheritance to that kingdom. For as he which fell into a leprosy was debarred from his own house until he was cleansed and yet in the mean space lost not his right to his own house, so the adopted son of God taken with the leprosy of adultery or murder or any other grievous sin, cannot indeed enter into the kingdom of heaven unless he first be purged from this contagion by renewed faith and repentance; yet all this while his hereditary right is not quite lost.

. . .

The same case holds in adoption. For God never adopted to himself a son in Christ whom afterwards he either must or would disinherit and cast out of his family. The children of God may indeed sin, and that very grievously; but the providence and mercy of God will not suffer them so far to sin as that they should thereby be bereft of their heavenly home and Father. *The servant abideth not in the house forever, but the son abideth forever.* . . .

To conclude, the seed of regeneration, with those fundamental gifts (without which the spiritual life cannot subsist), are preserved in safety. This is hence evident, because that the same Holy Spirit who doth infuse this seed into the hearts of the regenerate, doth imprint into the same seed a certain heavenly and incorruptible virtue, and doth perpetually cherish and keep the same. . . .

. . .

{Vb.7} *The seventh position*

That the regenerate do not altogether fall from faith, holiness, and adoption proceeds not from themselves nor from their own will, but from God's special love, divine operation, and from Christ's intercession and custody.

. . .

{Vb.8} *The eighth position*

The perseverance, therefore, of holy men is the free gift of God, and is derived unto us out of the decree of election.

. . .

{Vc} Of the Certainty of Perseverance in Respect of Ourselves

{Vc.1} *The first position*

Every faithful man may be certainly persuaded that through the mercy of God his Father he shall be kept and be brought unto eternal life.

We treated before of perseverance in respect of the certainty of the object or thing itself. Now are we to treat of it in respect of the certainty of the subject: to wit, inasmuch as that thing which is certain in itself, is also by us, in whom it is brought to pass, apprehended as certain and infallible.[8]

We, admitting every one of the faithful into the partnership of this benefit, do avow it to be, not a privilege afforded to a few of the faithful, but a gift bestowed on all the faithful as they are faithful, without distinction.

Moreover, we say rather that the faithful may or can have within themselves this persuasion than that they are always actually so persuaded, because this certain persuasion, although it proceeds from the very nature of faith, yet doth it not always, as it might and ought, put forth into action, but is sometimes suppressed, as we will hereafter declare.

Nevertheless here we affirm that every true faithful man hath in readiness at home within himself always and upon all occasions such a foundation sure enough, whereupon, if he rightly weigh his own condition and God's promise and custody, he may build up this actual confidence of his own preservation in faith unto eternal life.

. . .

2. To Christ our Savior it was not sufficient to pray that Peter's faith might not fail . . . unless Saint Peter also should know it and thereupon enjoy in himself the full persuasion thereof, Luke 22:32, *I have prayed for thee, Peter, that thy faith fail not.*

3. It is not enough for us for our comfort, that we, being wafted in the ship of the Church, go on toward the haven of salvation, except also we be fully persuaded that we cannot by any tempest be defeated of our wished harbor. It was not enough for Noah to be shut up safe in the ark, but he was by the promise of God secured against shipwreck for the confirmation of his confidence. . . .

4. This assurance of persuasion doth flow from the very nature of special faith, which not only is directly carried unto that which is promised, but also doth reflect upon itself and its own apprehension. Of the former act are meant those speeches in the Scripture: Rom. 5:1, *Being justified by faith we have peace with God.* . . . Of the latter, those: 1 John 2:3, *We do know that we know him.* 1 John 5:10, *He that believeth on the Son of God hath the witness in himself.* . . . Therefore every faithful man, through the inmost operation of his own faith, believes the preservation of the same faith in himself.

5. The same is confirmed out of the testimonies of this faith. Spiritual joy is a manifest evidence. 1 Pet. 1:8, *Believing, ye rejoice with joy unspeakable and full of glory.* . . .

6. Lastly, the certainty, not only of perseverance, but also of the perseverer, is warranted by the mutual pledges laid down between God and the faithful: on that side, our pledge kept in the hand of God; on this side, God's earnest penny laid up in our hearts:

---

[8] {Note that the usage here approaches the modern contrast of "subjective" and "objective," although the terms themselves, in this sense, do not enter English until the Restoration.}

a double pledge is given for the securing, not both parties, but one only: to wit, us. And this double pledge, although it be possessed on both sides, yet is surely kept by the fidelity of one part only: to wit, of God.

. . .

{Vc.2} *The second position*

This persuasion of faith cannot come into the act and vigor without the endeavor of holiness and use of the means.

The firm persuasion of God's bestowing the gift of perseverance and of our attaining of life everlasting we attribute to the mercy of God alone, and the intercession of Christ, as to the original cause; but so as we withal refer it to sanctification as an unseparable companion and a most sure sign. This is laid down as an evidence of a solid faith, 1 John 2:3, *Hereby we are sure that we know him, if we keep his commandments.* . . .

But we measure this holiness not by the degrees of it, but by the endeavor and settled purpose of him that hath it; and withal we profess that this holiness and persuasion of faith may and ought to be forwarded and confirmed by watching, fasting, prayer, and mortifying the flesh, and other means thereto appointed by God. . . .

Now it is certain that this firm persuasion of which we speak cannot put forth itself without these holy endeavors.

1. Because sanctification (the companion of justification) cannot consist without the intent of obedience, an habitual purpose whereof (although interrupted by many slips) is sufficient to the elect for the maintaining the state of justification entire in itself. But for the present comfort of this confidence is necessarily required an actual purpose of such obedience; neither can any man, out of the testimony of the Spirit speaking to his heart, say "I do now confidently believe that I shall remain in the state of grace to the end," unless he also add out of the sincere intent of his mind, "I do now most constantly purpose with myself to walk in the ways of God's holy commandments."

. . .

{Vc.3} *The third position*

This persuasion hath not that degree of certitude that can always shut out all fear of the contrary, but is sometimes lively, sometimes languishing, sometimes (as in great temptations) none at all.

In spiritual gifts with which we are furnished in this life, sincerity is required; perfection of degrees is not to be expected. Even that gift {i.e., faith} which is the hand by which we lay hold on all the rest hath its diseases and weaknesses; so that the persuasion of the faithful concerning their own salvation and perseverance cannot always enjoy the highest degree of certitude.

1. The first infirmity ariseth out of the ground itself whereupon this personal confidence is built, which seems to be of lower degree than the certitude of dogmatical faith. For the articles of the Catholic faith do work upon our assent as immediate and original principles, but the truth of this special faith is not enforced thence as a necessary consequent, but is added thereto by way of assumption.[9] Therefore there can be no greater

---

[9] {The assumption is the minor premise of a syllogism, the premise specifying the application of the general.}

certainty of that conclusion, which frameth this persuasion, than such as is in the weaker of the premises. But that assumption is grounded upon experimental arguments, weighed and applied by a man's private conscience; which arguments or marks, since they are sometimes questioned whether or no they be true and concluding evidences—nay often times are hid under the cloud of temptation, so that they the while cannot shine forth to our present comfort—what wonder if so be the faithful have not always at hand a lively and firm persuasion concerning their eternal salvation.

Nay, which is more, the very principles of the Catholic faith, howsoever they are, by the light of revelation, clear in themselves, yet forasmuch as they are known to us by the certainty not of *evidence* but only of *adhesion*, they do not procure in us an assent of such uniform stability as is yielded unto mathematical demonstrations and inbred notions admitted by all men.[10] But in our contemplating these revealed principles, out of the remainder of our carnal diffidence sometime there arise (as we may so say) certain vapors or mists, through which the light of divine truth (in itself immutable) to our weak eyes seemeth to tremble and suffer a kind of refraction. How much more frequent and more lasting is that mistake which may betide any of the faithful in the viewing his own personal confidence? Their eyes truly would always waver, except both this common revelation of the Catholic faith and also that personal application made by the conscience were confirmed and sealed unto our hearts by the Holy Ghost, *bearing witness to our spirit that we are the sons of God*. And this very testimony of the Spirit, although the seed thereof be never utterly extinguished, yet in regard of the fruit and sense thereof, sometimes it either withdraws itself so that our own infirmity may be evident to us, or else for a time it is, as it were, raked up under the ashes by our rebellion and ingratitude.

2. Therefore that other weakness doth arise from temptations by which this persuasion is assaulted. And those are partly afflictions, which seem to menace us with the evil of punishment; and partly our own perverse concupiscences, which do brand our souls with the evil of sin and guilt thereof; and partly the snares and assaults of the devil, by which he doth set upon us in both those kinds. But the main skirmish consists in the mutual wrastling and struggling of the flesh and spirit. Whilst this wrastling lasts, our faith is weak; but if so be the spirit overcomes the flesh, then our spirit cheers up and triumpheth in this manner: *Who shall separate us from the love of Christ?* But if (which often falls out) the spirit, thus wearied and weakened, receive the foil for a time, being either overborn with the load of afflictions or tainted with the spots of heinous sins, then there remains no such actual persuasion, a stop is made of all spiritual comfort, and the light of God's countenance is hidden from us. Hence those mournful complaints of holy men: Job 6:4, *The arrows of the Almighty are within me, the poison whereof drinks up my spirit, the terrors of God set themselves in array against me.* Lament. 3:42, *We have transgressed and rebelled. Thou hast not pardoned, thou hast covered thyself with a cloud that our prayers should not pass through.* But if the waves of temptation arise yet higher, and the fiery darts of the devil do wound the conscience already pressed down with its own burden, then not only this sweet

---

[10] {This Thomist distinction between the certainty of evidence and adherence is wholly unexpected here, although it is central to the anti-Calvinist argument: see Richard Hooker, *A learned and comfortable sermon of the certaintie and perpetuitie of faith in the elect* (1586) and, in this volume, Laud <388, 390–91>, Chillingworth <909–10>. Also, Shuger, "Faith and assurance."}

persuasion is banished, but also a persuasion utterly contrary cometh instead thereof, by force whereof holy men, thus affrighted, do apprehend God as an angry judge, and seem to themselves to be now falling headlong into the open gates of hell. This case is set down in those almost despairing speeches of Job, *Let the day perish wherein I was born*; and that of David, *I said in my haste, I am cut off from before thine eyes.*

{Vc.4} *The fourth position*

When a faithful man, after much struggling, hath got the upper hand of these temptations, that act by which he doth apprehend the fatherly mercy of God toward him and eternal life to be conferred without fail upon him is not an act of floating opinion or of conjectural hope, such as may be built on a false ground, but it is an act of a true and lively faith, stirred up and sealed in his heart by the spirit of adoption.

As it fares in nature, so in grace: after the cloud is removed, the day is the clearer; and certain diseases, after they are overcome, prove occasions of future health. A faithful man, escaping out of the waves of great temptations, doth not only receive the confidence which was almost extinguished, but gains a greater measure thereof. For he is made stronger by the conflict, and more cheerful by the conquest. Nay, if in this wrastling some of his bones be broken, after they be set again, they will knit the stronger. . . .

1. Because the life and state of a regenerate man is spiritual, he may be said, while he is transported by the force of sin or temptation, to be withheld from his natural place. The spirit therefore doth easily return back again to his own bent, and again acknowledgeth his former confidence in the fatherly mercy of God. This is manifest out of the examples of the saints who have expressed their own vehement conflicts, still ending in the lively voice of faith. . . .

2. Because the panting soul, thirsting for God's fatherly reconciliation, doth run more greedily to the fountain of living waters and relisheth more sweetly that whereof it perceived itself for a time debarred, namely the fruition of God appeased. Thence it acknowledgeth in itself the seed of faith, by the force whereof it ariseth again to repair the very breaches made upon faith, whose root indeed spreadeth the further by this loosening, and sends forth new tendrils, from which sprout out new shoots of greater certainty. . . .

We have in David an example of this renewed and confirmed confidence after that his spot of that great sin was washed away (Psal. 51). After that the assault of that dangerous temptation was abated (Psal. 73). In both these cases, there are to be seen clearly shining forth the spirit of prayer, spiritual joy, and the seal of adoption. . . .

Erroneous Opinions {Concerning the Fifth Article} Rejected by Us

{V.error1} *The first*

That the perseverance of those who are truly faithful is not an effect of election but a benefit offered equally to all, upon this condition: namely, if they shall not be wanting unto sufficient grace.

. . .

3. It is false that perseverance is a grace offered upon condition; for it is a gift promised absolutely by God without any respect at all of condition. The reason is this: some promises of God are touching the end, others touching the means which conduce to the

end. The promises concerning the end, that is to say, salvation, are conditional: *Believe and thou shalt be saved. Be faithful unto the death* (that is, persevere), *and I will give thee the crown of life.* But forasmuch as no man is able to perform the conditions, God also hath made most free and absolute promises to give the very conditions, which he works in us, that so by them, as by means, we may attain the end. . . . God promiseth life to those that constantly fear him: the promise of life is conditional, but of constant fear, it is absolute: *I will put my fear in their hearts, that they may not depart from me.*

. . .

{V.error4} *The fourth*

That no true believer or regenerate person can be assured in this life of his perseverance and salvation without special revelation.

Of the first part of this position, we handled before in this Article. But now, that a man may know that his perseverance for the future may be secured *without any special revelation*, we prove by this reason. Tis confessed that some saints (especially Saint Paul) did obtain this certainty: Rom. 8, *I am persuaded that neither life nor death, &c.* But Saint Paul did not fetch this persuasion from extraordinary revelation, but from those grounds which are common to him with other the faithful: vers. 32, *He that spared not his own Son, but delivered him up for us all, how shall he not with him also freely give us all things? Who shall lay any thing to the charge of God's elect? It is God that justifieth.* Vers. 33, *It is Christ that makes intercession for us.* What? was Christ only given for Paul, and not for other believers also? Was Paul alone the elect of God? Doth God justify Paul only? Or doth Christ make intercession for Paul alone? Since therefore out of these premises common to the whole Church of the elect, Saint Paul in that place infers that confident conclusion, *Who shall separate us?* and, *I am persuaded, &c.*, certain it is that other believers also, who have interest to the same means of salvation, may hence deduce and apply unto themselves this full persuasion of their salvation and perseverance.

The same conclusion every faithful soul is able to make out of other ordinary premises:

1. From the faithfulness of God: 1 Cor. 10:13, *God is faithful, who will not suffer, &c.*
2. From experience of his former good will: Phil. 1:6, *Being confident of this very thing, that he, which hath begun a good work in you, will also perfect it, &c.*
3. From the practice of good works performed in faith: 2 Pet. 1:10, *If ye do these things, ye shall never fall*; and what those things are, tis evident out of the 5 and 6 verses.
4. From the testimony of the conscience: 1 John 3:21, *If our hearts condemn us not, then have we confidence toward God.*
5. By the testimony of former led life: 2 Tim. 4:7, *I have fought a good fight; henceforth is there a crown laid up for me.*
6. Lastly the testimony of the Spirit doth seal all these things to us: Rom. 8:16, *The Spirit itself beareth witness with our spirit, &c.*

These and other evidences of the like kind are obvious to every faithful soul, and therefore likewise the conclusion.

. . .

{V.error5} *The fifth*

That as often as any grievous carnal sin is committed, so often is the state of justification and adoption lost.

Against this opinion, these arguments, besides others, are of force.

1. Man cannot by any sin make void any act of God's. But justification and adoption are God's acts, and those flowing from his own good pleasure: *Ergo.* When therefore it is questioned whether or no there may be an intercision {cessation} of justifying grace caused by the sins of the flesh, the question is not only whether a man can lose any quality by sin, but we must fetch this question much further, to wit, whether man's sin be of force to make void God's acts or to alter that doom of God, by which he in himself hath already pronounced us just and adopted us into the right and title of sons. . . .

2. So far it is that every grievous sin of the flesh should altogether divest a faithful soul of the state of justification and adoption that, on the contrary, it is held, especially by practical divines, that God doth permit those sins very often in justified and adopted persons, that both their justification and adoption might be afterward the more confirmed unto them: according to that of the Prophet, Psal. 119:71, *It is good for me that thou hast humbled me, that I might learn thy statutes.* . . . We conclude therefore, that neither justification is broken off nor yet adoption lost by the falls of the saints, but that hence it comes to pass that, rising again, they do so much the more warily *work out their own salvation with fear and trembling.*

{V.error6} *The sixth*

That the doctrine of the certainty of perseverance and salvation is of its own nature both hurtful unto true piety and pernicious every way to religion.

Both God's truth and man's experience easily wipe off this aspersion. For this Christian persuasion of perseverance and salvation, not only in respect of its own nature, but also according to the very event in the Church, doth, by God's blessing, produce a quite contrary effect.

1. First in respect of the thing itself, the certainty of the end doth not take away, but establish, the use of the means. And the same holy men who upon sure grounds promise unto themselves both constancy in the way of this pilgrimage and fruition of God in their everlasting home, know also that these are not obtained without performance of the duties of holiness and the avoidance of contrary vices; and therefore they turn not their backs from these means, but industriously embrace and prosecute them. . . . The Apostle doth altogether reject this consequence of carnal security imputed to this doctrine, and that with a kind of indignation: Rom. 6:1, *Shall we continue in sin, that grace may abound? God forbid. How shall we, which are dead to sin, live any longer therein?* As if Saint Paul would intimate unto us, not only the incongruity, but also impossibility of such a sequel.

2. As touching the event, true it is that any the most wholesome truth of God may be perverted by the abuse of men. But upon this doctrine we cannot acknowledge that there groweth any such inconvenience: no not *de facto*, that is, in the event itself. Let us take a view of the Reformed Churches in which this confidence of perseverance and inviolable adoption is believed and maintained. Do we find that thereupon the bridle is let loose

unto riot? That piety is trampled down? We give thanks unto God through our Lord Jesus Christ that among ours (who enjoy this full persuasion of spiritual comfort, and are confident that there is an inheritance which cannot be lost laid up for them in heaven) there is not found less care of godliness nor less endeavor (so far forth as man's infirmity will suffer) to live an unblameable life than is to be found among any sort of those who pin their perseverance on their own free-will, and will not grant it to flow from any foregoing election of God.

⋙⋘

Thus have we set down our joint suffrage concerning these five controverted Articles; which our judgment we believe to be agreeable to the word of God and suitable to the Confessions of so many Reformed Churches—from which, that this one of the Low Countries should be separated, it neither will seem safe nor pious unto those who have any grain of wisdom or spark of true piety.

And this our most gracious and mighty King of Great Britain . . . hath especially aimed at when he gave in charge to us, appointed to be sent hither, that we should, as much as in us lieth, by our moderate advices set forward the public peace of your Church; and that we should exhort our reverend brethren assembled in this celebrious Synod that they should not determine anything in their synodical suffrages which might thwart the received doctrine which hath been established in so many public Confessions of the Churches.

This received doctrine hath, not long since, seemed distasteful to the palate of some ill-affected to innovation, which doctrine, though they have by all means and helps endeavored to disgrace and suppress, yet nevertheless, like a kind of heavenly fire, it hath sent forth the clearer rays by the very motion and agitation. We truly wish from our hearts unto our brethren called Remonstrants that the eyes of their understanding may be enlightened and that their minds may not be estranged from the study of peace—as also unto the rest of our reverend brethren, such charitable affection toward them that they may not cease to wish well unto the persons of those men whose errors they oppugn.

And here we crave leave a little to turn our speech to the most illustrious and mighty States, and to their most judicious delegates, and finally to all the rest that sit at the stern of the commonweal in this country. It is your parts (most noble Lords) no less to take care lest the orthodox religion, than the commonweal committed to your trust, should receive any damage. *For magistrates serve God in this, when for his service they do those things which none can do but magistrates.* In this case therefore there needs not only your piety and good example, but also your power and commands. Let your power restrain that which here goeth by the name of *liberty of prophesying*. Upon presumption whereof some are wont, first lightly to nibble at, than openly to impugn, and at last to cry down the most established grounds of our faith. If it shall be lawful for everyone to impeach the orthodox doctrine approved by the common consent of all the Reformed Churches, it is to be feared that they who through the connivance of the magistrate have begun to innovate in the Church, will afterward, against his prohibition, as occasion may serve, attempt the like in the commonwealth.

   . . .

And now, beloved brethren and fellow ministers, we will also in a few words address ourselves to you, from whose wisdoms it cannot be hid that among these principal controversies so much discussed, there be sometime slight questions intermingled which neither have the same certainty of belief nor are of any great moment to true piety. But as for those which are of that nature, that, unless they be maintained, the free grace of God in the provision for man's salvation is infirmed and the free-will of man set up in God's throne, for those you ought constantly to stand as for the freehold of religion; neither by any means ought you to endure that the certainty of our salvation should be revoked from the stability of God's purpose to the inconstancy of man's free-will. But if among these any questions come in which, being not yet determined by the Reformed Churches, are probably disputed by godly and learned men either way without any damage to the rule of faith, it becomes not grave and moderate divines to thrust upon other men's consciences, as determinations of faith, their own private opinions herein. In such tenets there is no danger, so long as you take heed that diversity of opinion do not either among the ministers dissolve the bond of peace or among the people sow the seeds of faction.

Moreover (that we may give no further caution) among those things which are certain and soundly grounded upon the word of God, some there be which are not to be inculcated to every auditory without difference, but only to be touched warily in due time and place. Among these is that high mystery of predestination, a most sweet doctrine and full of comfort, but to those only who are rooted in faith and exercised in piety: to which kind of men, in great conflict of conscience, it may be in stead of a strong tower of defense. But when they who have not yet well learned the first foundations of religion and whose minds are wholly carried away by their carnal affections are, by the indiscretion of some preachers, called on to dive into this depth, this cometh of it: that while they brabble about the secret decree of predestination, they neglect the saving knowledge of the Gospel, and while they dream of nothing else but predestination unto life, they never care to set foot in that way in which they must walk who are predestinated unto life.

And concerning the mystery of reprobation, greater care is to be had that it be, not only handled sparingly and prudently, but also in the explication thereof, those fearful opinions and such as have no ground in the Scriptures be carefully avoided, which tend rather unto desperation than edification, and do bring upon some of the Reformed Churches a grievous scandal.

Lastly, we are so to determine of the precious merit of Christ's death that we neither slight the judgment of the primitive Church nor yet the Confessions of the Reformed Churches, nor (which is the most principal point of all the rest) weaken the promises of the Gospel, which are to be propounded universally in the Church.

These brief admonitions are here given by us rather that we might testify our love toward our venerable brethren than that we thought they needed this our advice.

There remains nothing now but that we humbly beseech Almighty God that the counsels of the States, the endeavors of the ministers, the assistance of foreign divines, and the endeavors of all may aim at this, and obtain this end: that the Church of the Low Countries, all errors being rooted out and dissensions composed, may enjoy the orthodox faith and a settled peace forever, through him who is the Advocate of our peace, our Lord and Savior JESUS CHRIST. *Amen.*

Subscribed by

> *George Carleton*, D. in Divinity, Bishop of Llandaff, afterward Bishop of Chichester.
>
> *John Davenant*, D. in Divinity, now Bishop of Salisbury.
>
> *Samuel Ward*, the Lady Margaret's Professor of Divinity in the University of Camb. and Master of Sidney College there.
>
> *Thomas Goad*, D. in Divinity.
>
> *Walter Balcanqual*, then Bachelor in Divinity, since D. in Divinity, now Dean of Rochester.

～～

TEXT: EEBO (STC [2nd ed.] / 7070)

The collegiate suffrage of the divines of Great Britain, concerning the five articles controverted in the Low Countries. Which Suffrage was by them delivered in the Synod of Dort, March 6, anno 1619. *Being their vote or voice foregoing the joint and public judgment of that Synod* (London: Printed for Robert Milbourne, 1629).

ROBERT SANDERSON
1587–1663

The son of a Sheffield clergyman, Sanderson matriculated at Lincoln College, Oxford, in 1603, receiving his BA in 1605, his MA in 1607, and his BD in 1617. From 1606 to 1619 he was a fellow of the college and for several years its reader in logic, his lectures forming the basis of his popular *Logicae artis compendium* (1615). From 1619 to 1660 he served as rector in the tiny Lincolnshire village of Boothby Pagnall. The 1619 sermon reprinted below thus dates from the very beginning of his pastoral ministry, Sanderson having been invited to preach the visitation sermon to the local clergy and episcopal visitors assembled at the much larger Boston church of St. Botolph's. In 1629 he received a prebend at Lincoln Cathedral, followed by several further such posts over the next decade, including, in 1642, Oxford's regius professorship in divinity. From 1622 on, volumes of his sermons appeared in print at regular intervals, many of them preached at Paul's Cross, at the Lincolnshire assize, and at court. Sanderson took his DD in 1636, the same year he published his tract on Sabbatarianism *<vide infra>*, whose reliance on distinction—between, in this case, two types of divine law—to mediate between seemingly contradictory positions reflects the intellectual habits of the University disputation. In 1643 the Lords named Sanderson to the committee seeking to avert total ecclesiastical meltdown. Although the attempt failed, Sanderson's moderation led to an offer to join the Westminster Assembly—an offer not taken up. Instead, having refused the Covenant, in 1644 Sanderson was sequestered from his livings and seized by Parliamentary soldiers—although soon after exchanged for a puritan minister held by the Royalists under an agreement whereby both men regained their livings. Having returned to Boothby Pagnall, Sanderson left for Oxford in 1646 to take up his professorship and, a year later, to help compose the University's official refusal of the Solemn League and Covenant. Subsequently ejected from Oxford, he joined the King on the Isle of Wight. Sanderson spent the Interregnum writing a series of highly regarded casuistical tracts on oaths, political allegiance, and the obligations of conscience. He took the Engagement in 1650 to avoid yet another deprivation, which would have left his family destitute and his parish at the mercy of "ravening wolves" (Lake 108). At the Restoration, Sanderson, now seventy-three, found himself bishop of Lincoln, in which capacity he vigorously enforced the Act of Uniformity—and contributed to the 1662 revised Book of Common Prayer.

꙳꙳꙳

When Sanderson preached the 1619 visitation sermon, he was, as his parenthetic condemnation of Arminianism <246> indicates, a Calvinist; all the evidence suggests that he remained a Calvinist into the late 1650s. In 1619 he was preaching in the church of another Calvinist, John Cotton. Little more than a decade later, however, Cotton would depart for New England, while Sanderson, with Laud's backing, became a royal chaplain. The divergent trajectories of these two Calvinists divines raise questions about the Calvinist-puritan consensus supposed to characterize the early Stuart Church until the Arminian insurgency of the late 1620s; instead, as Peter Lake notes, their divergence conforms point for point to the old Anglican-versus-Puritan historiographic model, according to which the lines of division that emerged in the 1570s continue down the same channels into the 1640s. For indeed, Sanderson's position in this sermon is identical to Whitgift's, but it is also identical to Laud's. Had it been preached forty years earlier or fifteen years later, its context would be obvious, but 1619 should have been the high-water mark of the Jacobean Calvinist-conformist mainstream; Sanderson, however, makes it clear that *someone* is denouncing bishops as "locusts of the bottomless pit" and the like.[1] The someone, as Lake points out, was almost certainly John Cotton, whose Calvinism was decidedly of the non-conformist, experimental-predestinarian, godly-puritan type and whose ministry at Boston had left both his congregation and the town council split into hostile camps. The auditors in 1619 would have included Cotton's congregation—the sermon was given from Cotton's pulpit. Sanderson was venturing into a minefield, not preaching to the choir.

Under such circumstances, one can scarcely speak of a Calvinist-*puritan* mainstream. Sanderson and Cotton, despite their shared Calvinism, end up on opposite sides of the fence. The former's sermon suggests that the division hinged, above all, on the authority of the visible, institutional Church—vis-à-vis that of Scripture, but also vis-à-vis the authority of private conscience. The central claim of Sanderson's powerfully argued sermon[2] is that liberty of conscience does not extend to outward forms imposed merely for order's sake; rather, the principal role of all human authority is precisely to ordain matters that divine and natural law leave indifferent (clerical garb, property taxes). Sanderson's arguments regarding the *authority* of the visible Church target non-conformity; however, a secondary line of argument concerns the *nature* of the visible Church, and here the intended target seems larger. His "Anglican"[3] description of the "weak in faith" as a "brother" and fellow-Christian, who having "embraced the Gospel," belongs "within the

---

[1] The identification of bishops with said locusts, very popular in puritan circles through the 1640s, goes back to the Geneva Bible (see Howson, n. 11 <*supra*>), receiving a new lease on life in Thomas Brightman's commentaries on Revelations, all published overseas, the first appearing in 1611. See William M. Lamont, *Richard Baxter and the Millennium* (London: Croom Helm, 1979) and the relevant entries in the *DNB* and *ODNB*.

[2] Note the limpid, neo-classical plain style—the *genus tenue* whose principal aim is *docere*, to teach—a sort of prose one rarely finds before the Restoration.

[3] See Peter Lake, "Calvinism and the English Church," *Past and Present* 114 (1987): 38–43; Debora

pale of the Church" no less than the strong, implicitly counters the ecclesiology informing wide swaths of English Calvinism, which saw the national Church as composed, not
of stronger and weaker Christians, but as a little flock of "godly professors" intermingled
with the "unsanctified and profane" herd of "formalists."[4]

Sources: *ODNB*; Peter Lake, "Serving God and the times: the Calvinist conformity of Robert Sanderson," *JBS* 27 (1988): 81–116; Anthony Milton, *Catholic and Reformed*; Izaak Walton, *The lives of Mr. Richard
Hooker, Mr. George Herbert and Dr. Robert Sanderson* (London, 1833), 174–248.

Shuger, "Literature and the Church," in *The Cambridge history of early modern English literature*, ed. David
Loewenstein and Janel Mueller (Cambridge UP, 2002), 533–40.

[4] The quotations are all from the following sermon. However, see also, in this volume, Dod and Cleaver
<5–6>, Bayly <129–30, 134> (and, with antinomian twist, Everarde <553–54>).

ROBERT SANDERSON

Sermon preached at a visitation at Boston
1619, published 1622[1]

Let us follow after the things which make for peace;
and things wherewith one may edify another.
Rom. 14:19

To the right reverend Father in God, George, Lord Bishop of London, my singular good
Lord.[2]

My good Lord:

I had ever thought the interest of but an ordinary friend might have drawn me to that
whereto the despite of a right bitter foe should not have driven me, till the fate of these sermons hath taught me myself better, and now given me at once a sight both of my error and
infirmity. The improbity {persistence} of some good friends I had out-stood, who with all
their vexation could never prevail upon me for the publishing of but the former of them;
when lo, at length the restless importunity of hard censures hath wrung both it and the
fellow of it out of my hands. So much have we a stronger sense of our own wrongs than
of our friends' requests; and so much are we forwarder to justify ourselves than to gratify
them. However, if (by God's good blessing upon them) these slender labors may lend any
help to advance the peace & quiet of the Church in settling the judgments of such as are
more either timorous than they need be or contentious than they should be, I shall have
much cause to bless his gracious providence in it, who, with as much ease as sometimes he
brought light out of darkness, can out of private wrongs work public good. In which hope,
I am the rather content to send them abroad, though having nothing to commend them
but truth and plainness. Yet such as they are, I humbly desire they may pass under your
Lordship's protection, whereunto I stand by so many dear names engaged. . . .

---

[1] {First published in *Two sermons preached at two several visitations in Boston in the diocese and county of
Lincoln* (London, 1622).}

[2] {George Montaigne, bishop of London 1621–27, generally considered a high churchman; the dedication appears in the 1622 version.}

Your Lordship's chaplain in all dutiful observance,

Robert Sanderson

. . .

THE FIRST SERMON
[At a Visitation at Boston, Linc{oln}. 17 April, 1619]

Let not him that eateth, despise him that eateth not;
and let not him that eateth not, judge him that eateth.
Rom. 14:3

It cannot be avoided so long as there is or weakness on earth or malice in hell but that scandals will arise and differences will grow in the Church of God. What through want of judgment in some, of ingenuity[3] in others, of charity in almost all, occasions (God knoweth) of offence are too soon both given and taken whilest men are apt to quarrel at trifles and to maintain differences even about indifferent things. The primitive Roman Church was not a little afflicted with this disease, for the remedying whereof, S. Paul spendeth this whole chapter. The occasion, this: in Rome there lived in the apostles' times many Jews, of whom, as well as of the gentiles, divers were converted to the Christian faith by the preaching of the Gospel. Now of these new converts, some, better instructed than others as touching the cessation of legal ceremonies, made no difference of meats or of days, but used their lawful Christian liberty in them both, as things in their own nature merely indifferent. Whereas others, not so thoroughly catechized as they, still made difference for conscience sake both of meats, accounting them clean or unclean; and of days, accounting them holy or servile according as they stood under the Levitical law. These latter, S. Paul calleth . . . *weak in the faith*; those former then must by the law of opposition, be *strong in the faith*.

It would have become both the one sort and the other (notwithstanding they differed in their private judgments, yet) to have preserved the common peace of the Church and labored the edification, not the ruin, one of another: the strong, by affording faithful instruction to the consciences of the weak; and the weak, by allowing favorable construction to the actions of the strong. But whilest either measured other by themselves, neither one nor other did . . . walk uprightly according to the truth of the Gospel [Gal. 2:14]. Faults and offences there were on all hands. The strong faulty in contemning the weak; the weak faulty in condemning the strong. The strong proudly scorned the weak as silly and superstitious for making scruple at some such things as themselves firmly believed were lawful. The weak rashly censured the strong as profane and irreligious for adventuring on some such things as themselves deeply suspected were unlawful. The blessed Apostle, desirous all things should be done in the Church in love and *unto edification . . .* taketh upon him to arbitrate and to mediate in the business; and like a just umpire layeth his hand upon both parties, unpartially sheweth them their several oversights, and beginneth to draw them to a fair and an honorable composition, as thus: the strong, he shall

---

[3] {"Ingenuity" and "ingenuous" occur several times in the sermon; the term has a range of meanings, including generosity, honorableness, honesty, candor, good sense, and intelligence.}

remit somewhat of his superciliousness in disesteeming and despising the weak; and the weak, he shall abate somewhat of his edge and acrimony in judging and condemning the strong. If the parties will stand to this order, it will prove a blessed agreement, for so shall brotherly love be maintained, scandals shall be removed, the Christian Church shall be edified, and God's name shall be glorified. This is the scope of my text and of the whole chapter.

In the three first verses whereof, there is . . . in the first verse, the proposal of a general doctrine as touching the usage of weak ones, with whom the Church is so to deal as that it neither give offence to, nor take offence at, the weakness of any: *him that is weak in the faith receive you, but not to doubtful disputations.* Next, there is . . . in the second verse, a declaration of the former general proposal, by instancing in a particular case touching the difference of meats. There is one man *strong in the faith*; he is infallibly resolved there is no meat *unclean of itself,* or (if received with thankfulness and sobriety) *unlawful*; and because he knoweth he standeth upon a sure ground . . . he is confident he may eat any thing, and he useth his liberty accordingly. . . . There is another man *weak in the faith*; he standeth yet unresolved and doubtful whether some kinds of meats (as namely, those forbidden in the Law) be clean, or he is rather carried with a strong suspicion that they are unclean. Out of which timorousness of judgment, he chooseth to forbear those meats and contenteth himself with the fruits of the earth: *Another who is weak eateth herbs.* This is *species facti*; this the case. Now the question is, in this case what is to be done for the avoidance of scandal and the maintenance of Christian charity? And this question my text resolveth in this third verse, wherein is contained . . . Saint Paul's judgment—or his counsel rather, and advice upon the case: *Let not him that eateth despise, &c.* . . .

I have made choice to entreat at this time of Saint Paul's advice as useful for this place and auditory, and the present assembly. Which advice, as the parties and the faults are, is also twofold. The parties two: he that eateth (that is, the strong) and he that eateth not (that is, the weak). The faults likewise two: the strong man's fault, that's . . . despising of his brother's infirmity; and the weak man's faults, that's . . . judging of his brother's liberty. Proportionably, the parts of the advice, accommodated to the parties and their faults, are two. The one, for the strong, that he despise not: *Let not him that eateth, despise him that eateth not.* The other, for the weak, that he judge not: *Let not him that eateth not, judge him that eateth.* Of which, when I shall have spoken somewhat in their general use, I shall by God's assistance proceed by way of application to enquire how far the differences in our Church for *conforming* and *not conforming* agree with the present case of *eating* and *not eating*; and consequently how far forth S. Paul's advice in this case of *eating* and *not eating* ought to rule us in the cases of *conforming* and *not conforming* in point of ceremony. And first of the former rule or branch of the advice: *Let not him that eateth, despise him that eateth not.*

The terms whereby the parties are charactered, *he that eateth* and *he that eateth not,* have in the opening of the case been already so far unfolded as that I shall not need any more to remember you that by him that eateth must be understood the *strong in faith,* and by him that eateth not, the *weak.* And so reducing the words *ab hypothesi ad thesin,*[4] this part of the advice, *Let not him that eateth, despise him that eateth not,* beareth sense

---

[4] {from the specific instance to the general principle}

as if the Apostle had said *Let not the strong in faith despise the weak.* Weak ones are easily despised; strong ones are prone to despise; and yet despising is both a grievous sin in the despiser and a dangerous scandal to the despised. In all which respects, it was but needful the Holy Ghost should lesson us not to despise one another's weakness: *Let not him that eateth despise him that eateth not.*

Weakness and smallness, be it in what kind soever, is the fittest object to provoke contempt. As we travel by the way, if a fierce mastiff set upon us, we think it time to look about and to bestir ourselves for defense, but we take no notice of the little curs that bark at us, but despise them. . . . And though *wisdom be better than strength*, yet Solomon tells us, *the poor man's wisdom is despised, and his words are not heard* [Eccl. 9]. *I am small, and of no reputation*, saith David [Ps. 119]. And our Savior's caveat in the Gospel is especially concerning little ones, as most open to contempt: *Take heed that ye despise not one of these little ones.* But of all other, that weakness is most contemptible which is seen in the faculties of the understanding soul: when men are indeed weak in apprehension, weak in judgment, weak in discretion, or at leastwise are thought so. Far from any real weakness this way, or any other, was our blessed Lord and Savior Jesus Christ, *in whom were hid all the treasures of wisdom and knowledge*; yet because upon conference with him, he seemed such unto Herod, not answering any of his questions nor that expectation which the fame of his miracles had raised of him in Herod, Herod took him for some silly simple fellow, and accordingly used him: for he *set him at nought, and mocked him*, and put him in *a white coat* as he had been some fool, *and sent him back* as he came [Luke 23].

And of this nature is the weakness my text hath to do withal: a weakness in judgment; or as it is vers. 1, a *weakness in faith*: where by *faith* we are not to understand that justifying faith whereby the heart of a true believer layeth fast hold on the gracious promises of God and the precious merits of Jesus Christ for the remission of sins; nor by weakness in faith . . . when the faith of a true believer is sore shaken with temptations of incredulity and distrust. But by *faith* we are to understand an historical faith only, which is nothing else but a firm and secure assent of the judgment unto doctrinal truths in matter of faith or life; and by weakness in such faith, a doubtfulness and irresolution of judgment concerning some divine truths appertaining to the doctrine of faith or life, and namely, concerning the just extent of Christian liberty, and the indifferent or not indifferent nature or use of some things. Which weakness of judgment in faith, bewraying itself outwardly in a nice and scrupulous and timorous forbearance of some things for fear they should be unlawful (which yet in truth are not so, but indifferent), doth thereby expose the person in whom such weakness is to the contempt and despisings of such as are of more confirmed and resolved judgments, and are stronger in the faith.

Weakness then is in itself contemptible, yet not more than strength is contemptuous. Passive contempt is the unhappiness of the weak; but active, the fault of the strong. They that find truly, or but overweeningly conceit in themselves, abilities either of a higher nature or in a greater measure than in other men, be it in any kind whatsoever, it is strange to see with what scornful state they can trample upon their weaker and inferior brethren, and look upon them (if yet they will at all vouchsafe a look) from aloft, as upon things below them, which is properly & literally to despise. . . . And they are ever the likeliest thus to despise others that conceit something in themselves more than others. Wealth, honor, strength, beauty, birth, friends, alliance, authority, power, wit, learning, eloquence, reputation—any trifle can leaven our thoughts . . . and swell us and heave us up above our brethren; and because we think we do over-top them, we think we may over-look them too, and despise them as vulgar and contemptible. . . . All strength and eminency then, we see, be it in any little sorry thing, is apt to breed in men a despising of their weaker and meaner brethren, but none more than this strength of knowledge and of faith wherewith we now deal. It should be quite otherwise. Our knowledge should *prae-ferre facem*, hold the light before us and help us for the better discovery of our ignorance; and so dispose us to humility, not pride. But pride and self-love is *congenitum malum*; it is a close and a pleasing and an inseparable corruption, which by sly and serpentine insinuations conveyeth itself, as into whatsoever else is good and eminent in us and poisoneth it, so especially into the endowments of the understanding part. Sharpness of wit, quickness of conceit, faithfulness of memory, facility of discourse, propriety of elocution, concinnity {gracefulness} of gesture, depth of judgment, variety of knowledge in arts and languages, and whatever else of like kind are but as wind to fill the sails of our pride and to make us swell above our brethren in whom the like gifts are not, or not in like eminency. . . . It was not then without good need that Saint Paul should become a remembrancer to the *strong in faith* not to despise the weak. And there is as good need the very strongest of us all should remember it, and take heed of despising even the very weakest. This despising being hurtful both to the strong and weak: to the strong, as a grievous sin; and to the weak, as a grievous scandal.

Despising, first, is a sin in the strong. Admit thy weak brother were of so shallow understanding and judgment that he might say in strictness of truth, what Agur saith but in modesty . . . *that he had not in him the understanding of a man* [Prov. 30:2]; yet the community of nature and the common condition of humanity should be sufficient to free him from thy contempt. His body was formed out of the same dust, his soul breathed into him by the same God as thine were, and he is thy neighbor. Let his weakness then be what it can be, even for that relation of neighborhood, as he is a man, it is sin in thee to despise him. . . . But that's not all. He is not only thy neighbor as a man, but he is thy brother too, as a Christian man. He hath embraced the Gospel, he believeth in the Son of God; he is within the pale of the Church as well as thou, though he be not so exquisitely seen in some higher mysteries nor so thoroughly satisfied in some other points as thou art. If it have pleased God to endow thee with a larger portion of knowledge, thou oughtest to consider, first, that thou art bound to be so much the more thankful to him that gave it; and then secondly, that it is expected thou shouldest do so much the more good with it; and thirdly again, that thou standest charged with so much the deeper account for it. If the same God have dealt these abilities with a more sparing hand to thy brother, in despising his weakness what other thing doest thou than even despise the good Spirit of God, *that bloweth where he listeth?* . . . For though there be *diversities of gifts* (both for substance and degree) *yet it is the same Spirit*. And the contempt that is cast upon the meanest Christian reboundeth upwards again, and in the last resolution reflecteth even upon GOD himself, and upon his Christ. *He that despiseth, despiseth not man but God, who hath given unto us his Holy Spirit* [1 Thess. 4:8]. . . .

Thus you see despising is hurtful to the despiser, as a sin; it is hurtful also as a scandal to the despised. And therefore our Savior in Matt. 18, discoursing of *not offending little ones*, anon varieth the word and speaketh of *not despising* them, as if despising were an especial and principal kind of offending or scandalizing.[5] And verily so it is, especially to the weak. Nothing is more grievous to nature, scarce death itself, than for a man to see himself despised: *Ego illam anum irridere me vt sinam? Satius est mihi quouis exitio interire*, could he say in the comedy.[6] It is a thing that pierceth far and sinketh deep and striketh cold & lieth heavy upon the heart; flesh & blood will digest anything with better patience. The great philosopher for this reason maketh contempt the ground of all discontent, and sufficiently proveth it in the second of his *Rhetoric*: there being never anything taken offensively but *sub ratione contemptus*; nothing provoking to anger but what is either truly a contempt, or at leastwise so apprehended. We all know how tenderly every one of us would take it but to be neglected by others. . . . And yet this is but the least degree of contempt, a privative contempt only. How tenderly then may we think a weak Christian would take it, when to this privative he should find added a positive contempt also? When he should see his person and his weakness not only not compassioned, but even taunted and flouted and derided and made a laughing stock and a jesting theme? when he should see them strive to speak and do such things in his sight and hearing as they know will be offensive unto him, of very purpose to vex and afflict and grieve his tender soul? Certainly for a weak Christian newly converted to the faith, to be thus despised, it were enough, without God's singular mercy and support, to make him repent his late conversion[7]. . . . And he that by such despising should thus offend, though but *one of the least* and weakest of those *that believe in Christ*, a thousand times better had it been for him that he had never been born. . . . Despising is a grievous sin in the despiser, in the strong; and despising is a grievous scandal to the despised, to the weak. Let not therefore the strong despise the weak: *Let not him that eateth, despise him that eateth not.* And thus much for the former branch of Saint Paul's advice. The other followeth: *Let not him that eateth not, judge him that eateth.*

Faults seldom go single, but by couples at the least. Sinful men do with sinful provocations as ball-players with the ball: when the ball is once up, they labor to keep it up. Right so when an offence or provocation is once given, it is tossed to and fro, the receiver ever returning it pat upon the giver, and that most times with advantage; and so betwixt them they make a shift to preserve a perpetuity of sinning & of scandalizing one another. It is hard to say who beginneth oftener, the strong or the weak, but whether ever beginneth, he may be sure the other will follow. If this judge, that will despise; if that despise, this will judge; either doth his endeavor to cry quittance with other and thinketh himself not to be at all in fault, because the other was first or more. This Apostle, willing to redress faults in both, beginneth first with the strong, & for very good reason. Not that his fault simply considered in itself is greater (for I take it a certain truth that to judge one that is in the right is a far greater fault, considered absolutely, without relation to the abilities of the persons, than to despise one that is in the wrong), but because the strong through the ability of his judgment ought to yield so much to the infirmity of his weak brother, who

---

[5] {"scandalize" in the theological sense of occasioning another's spiritual downfall; see Aquinas, *Summa theologiae* 2.2.43.}

[6] [Plaut., *in Cistel* 4.1] {Trans: And shall I allow an old woman to mock me? I'd rather die.}

[7] {The "weak" in this passage would seem to be recent "converts" from Roman Catholicism, to whom the violent anti-popery of godly preaching might feel deeply offensive.}

through the weakness of his judgment is not so well able to discern what is fit for him to do. What in most other contentions is expected, should be done in this: not he that is most in fault, but he that hath most wit should give over first. . . . But where both are faulty, as it is not good to stand debating who began first, so it is not safe to strain courtesy who shall end and mend first. In the case of my text, both were faulty, and therefore our Apostle would have both mend. He hath schooled the strong and taught him his lesson, not to despise another's infirmity: *Let not him that eateth, despise him that eateth not.* Now the weak must take out his lesson too, not to judge another's liberty: *Let not him that eateth not, judge him that eateth.*

. . . The fault of these weak ones in the case in hand was that, measuring other men's actions and consciences by the model of their own understandings, in their private censures they rashly passed their judgments upon, and pronounced peremptory sentence against, such as used their liberty in some things concerning the lawfulness whereof themselves were not satisfied, as if they were loose Christians, carnal professors . . . and such as made either none at all or else very little conscience of their actions. This practice my text disalloweth . . . *We must not judge others.* The Scriptures are express: *Judge not, that ye be not judged* [Matt. 7]. *Judge nothing before the time, &c.* [1 Cor. 4:5]. *Thou art inexcusable, O man, whosoever thou art that judgest* [Rom. 2]. . . .

Not that it is unlawful to exercise civil judgment or to pass condemning sentence upon persons orderly and legally convicted, for such as have calling & authority thereunto in Church or commonwealth. For this public politic judgment is commanded in the word of God, and reason sheweth it to be of absolute necessity for the preservation of states and commonwealths. Nor that it is unlawful, secondly, to pass even our private censures upon the outward actions of men when the law of God is directly transgressed and the transgression apparent from the evidence either of the fact itself or of some strong signs and presumptions of it. For it is stupidity, and not charity, to be credulous against sense. Charity is ingenuous and will believe anything, though more than reason; but charity must not be servile, to believe anything against reason: shall any charity bind me to think the crow is white or the black Moor beautiful? Nor yet, thirdly, that all sinister suspicions are utterly unlawful, even there where there wanteth evidence either of fact or of great signs, if our suspicions proceed not from any corrupt affections, but only from a charitable jealousy of those over whom we have especial charge or in whom we have special interest, in such sort as that it may concern us to admonish, reprove, or correct them when they do amiss [Aquin. 2.2.60.4.3]. . . . But the judgment here & elsewhere condemned is either, first, when, in our private thoughts or speeches, upon slender presumptions we rashly pronounce men as guilty of committing such or such sins, without sufficient evidence. . . . Or, secondly, when upon some actions undoubtedly sinful . . . we too severely censure the persons, either for the future as reprobates and castaways and such as shall be certainly damned, or at leastwise for the present as hypocrites and unsanctified and profane and such as are in the state of damnation—not considering into what fearful sins it may please God to suffer, not only his chosen ones before calling [as Paul, Mary Magdalene, &c.], but even his holy ones too after calling [as David, Peter, &c.] sometimes to fall, for ends most times unknown to us, but ever just and gracious in him. Or thirdly, when for want either of charity or knowledge (as in the present case of this chapter) we interpret things for the worst to our brethren, and condemn them of sin for such actions as are not directly and in themselves necessarily sinful, but may (with due circumstances) be performed with a good conscience and without sin. Now all judging and condemning of our brethren in any of these kinds is sinful and damnable, and that in very many respects. Especially these four, which may serve as so many weighty reasons why we ought not to judge one another: the usurpation, the rashness, the uncharitableness, and the scandal of it.

First, it is an usurpation. He that is of right to judge must have calling and commission for it. *Quis constituit te?* sharply replied upon Moses [Exod. 2:14]: *who made thee a judge?* and *Quis constituit me?* reasonably alleged by our Savior [Luke 12:14]: *who made me a judge?* Thou takest too much upon thee then, thou son of man, whosoever thou art that judgest, thus saucily to thrust thyself into God's seat and to invade his throne. Remember thyself well, and learn to know thine own rank. *Quis tu? Who art thou that judgest another* [Jam. 4]? . . . Thou art his fellow-servant, not his lord. He hath another Lord, that can and will judge him; who is thy Lord too, and can and will judge thee. . . . God hath reserved three prerogatives royal to himself: vengeance, glory, and judgment. As it is not safe for us then to encroach upon God's royalties in either of the other two, glory or vengeance, so neither in this of judgment. *Dominus iudicabit*: the Lord himself *will judge his people* [Heb. 10:30]. It is flat usurpation in us to judge, and therefore we must not judge.

Secondly, it is rashness in us. A judge must understand the truth, both for matter of fact and for point of law; and he must be sure he is in the right for both before he proceed to sentence, or else he will give rash judgment. How then dare any of us undertake to sit as judges upon other men's consciences, wherewith we are so little acquainted that we are indeed but too much unacquainted with our own? We are not able to search the depth of our own wicked and deceitful hearts and to ransack thoroughly the many secret windings and turnings therein; how much less then are we able to fathom the bottoms of other men's hearts with any certainty to pronounce of them either good or evil? We must then leave the judgment of other men's spirits and hearts and reins to him that is *the Father of spirits*, and alone *searcheth the hearts and reins.* . . .

Thirdly, this judging is uncharitable. Charity is not easily suspicious but upon just cause; much less, then, censorious and peremptory. Indeed when we are to judge of things, it is wisdom to judge of them secundum quod sunt: as near as we can to judge of them just as they are, without any sway or partial inclination either to the right hand or to the left. But when we are to judge of men and their actions, it is not altogether so; there the rule of charity must take place: *dubia in meliorem partem sunt interpretanda* [Aquinas 2.2.60.4 *ad* 3]. Unless we see manifest cause to the contrary, we ought ever to interpret what is done by others with as much favor as may be. To err thus is better than to hit right the other way, because this course is safe, and secureth us, as from injuring others, so from endangering ourselves; whereas in judging ill, though right, we are still unjust . . . True charity is ingenuous; it *thinketh no evil* [1 Cor. 13:5]. How far then are they from charity that are ever suspicious and think nothing well? For us, let it be our care to maintain charity and to avoid, as far as human frailty will give leave, even sinister suspicions of our brethren's actions. . . . Let us at leastwise suspend our definitive judgment and not determine too peremptorily against such as do not in every respect just as we do, or as we would have them do, or as we think they should do [*Gloss. ordin.* in 1 Cor. 4]. It is uncharitable for us to judge, and therefore we must not judge.

Lastly, there is scandal in judging. Possibly he that is judged may have that strength of faith and charity that, though rash uncharitable censures lie thick in his way, he can lightly skip over all those stumbling blocks and scape a fall. Saint Paul had such a measure of strength: *With me it is a very small thing*, saith he, *that I should be judged of you, or of human judgment* [1 Cor. 4:3]. If our judging light upon such an object, it is indeed no scandal to him, but that's no thanks to us. We are to esteem things by their natures, not events; and therefore we give a scandal if we judge, notwithstanding he that is judged take it not as a scandal. . . . And thus we see four main reasons against this judging of our brethren: 1. We have no right to judge, and so our judging is *usurpation*. 2. We may err in our judgments, and so our judging is *rashness*. 3. We take things the worst way when we judge, and so our judging is *uncharitable*. 4. We offer occasion of offence by our judging, and so our judging is *scandalous*. *Let not him therefore that eateth not, judge him that eateth.*[8]

And so I have done with my text in the general use of it, wherein we have seen the two faults of despising and of judging our brethren laid open and the ugliness of both discovered. I now descend to make such application . . . unto some differences and to some offences given and taken in our Church in point of ceremony. The case ruled in my text was of eating and not eating; the differences which some maintain in our Church are many in the particular . . . but all these . . . may be comprehended in gross under the terms of conforming and not-conforming. Let us first compare the cases, that having found wherein they agree or disagree, we may thereby judge how far Saint Paul's advice in my text ought to rule us for not despising, for not judging one another. There are four special things wherein, if we compare this our case with the Apostle's, in every of the four we shall find some agreement, and some disparity also: 1. the nature of the matter, 2. the abilities of the persons, 3. their several practice about the things, and 4. their mutual carriage one towards another. And first, let us consider how the two cases agree in each of these.

First, the matter whereabout the eater and the not-eater differed in the case of the Romans was in the nature of it indifferent; so it is between the conformer and not-conformer in our case. As there fish and flesh and herbs were merely indifferent, such as might be eaten or not eaten without sin, so here cap and surplice, cross and ring, and the rest, are things merely indifferent, such as (in regard of their own nature) may be used or not used without sin, as being neither expressly commanded nor expressly forbidden in the word of God.

Secondly, the persons agree. For as there, so here also, some are strong in faith, some weak. There are many whose judgments are, upon certain and infallible grounds, assured and resolved, and that *certitudine fidei* {by the certainty of faith}, that cap and surplice and cross and the rest are things lawful and such as may be used with a good conscience. There are some others again, who through ignorance or custom or prejudice, or otherwise

---

[8] {The principles to which Sanderson appeals in this first half of his sermon—the wrongfulness of contempt, usurpation of authority, rash judgment, malicious/scandalous interpretation—also underlie much Tudor-Stuart censorship (see Shuger, *Censorship*, passim). On Sanderson's "Anglican" focus on moral duties—in contrast to the typical "Puritan" stress on pure worship—see McGee, *Godly man*.}

weakened in their judgments, cannot (or will not) be persuaded that these things are altogether free from superstition and idolatry; nor, consequently, the use of them from sin.

Thirdly, the practice of the persons are much alike. As there the strong did use his liberty according to the assurance of his knowledge . . . and did eat freely without scruple, and the weak did forbear to eat because of his doubting and irresolution; so here, most of us, in assured confidence that we may wear and cross and kneel and use the other ceremonies and customs of our Church, do willingly and *ex animo* {sincerely} conform ourselves thereunto; yet some there are who, out of I know not what niceness and scrupulosity, make dainty of them, and either utterly refuse conformity or at leastwise desire respite till they can better inform themselves.

Lastly, there is some correspondence also in the faulty carriage of the parties one towards another. For as there the eater despised the not-eater, and the not-eater judged the eater, so here, it cannot be denied but that some conformers (although I hope far the lesser, I am sure far the worser sort) do despise and scandalize the non-conformers more than they have reason to do or any discreet honest man will allow. But is it not most certain also that the non-conformers (but too generally, yea, and the better sort of them too but too often and much) do pass their censures with marvelous great freedom, and spend their judgments liberally upon, and against, the conformers? Hitherto the cases seem to agree. One would think, *mutatis mutandis*, the Apostle's rule would as well fit our Church and case as the Roman, and should as well free the non-conformers from our contempt as us from their censures. *Let not him that conformeth, despise him that conformeth not; and let not him that conformeth not, judge him that conformeth.*

But if you will please to take a second survey of the four several particulars wherein the cases seemed to agree, you shall find very much disparity and disproportion betwixt the two cases in each of the four respects. In the case of my text, the matter of difference among them was not only indifferent in the nature of it but it was also left as indifferent for the use: the Church (perhaps) not having determined anything positively therein; at least no public authority having either enjoined or forbidden the use of such or such meats. But in the case of our Church it is far otherwise. Cap, surplice, cross, ring, and other ceremonies . . . though they be things indifferent for their nature and in themselves, yet are not so for their use and unto us. If the Church had been silent, if authority had prescribed nothing herein, these ceremonies had then remained for their use, as they are for their nature, indifferent: lawful, and such as might be used without sin; and yet arbitrary, and such as might be also forborne without sin. But men must grant . . . that every particular Church . . . hath power for decency and order's sake to ordain and constitute ceremonies: which, being once ordained and by public authority enjoined, cease to be indifferent for their use, though they remain still so for their nature; and of indifferent become so necessary that neither may a man without sin refuse them, where authority requireth; nor use them, where authority restraineth the use.

Neither is this accession of necessity any impeachment to Christian liberty or ensnaring of men's consciences, as some have objected. For then do we ensnare men's consciences by human constitutions when we thrust them upon men as if they were divine, and bind men's consciences to them immediately as if they were immediate parts of God's worship or of absolute necessity unto salvation. . . . For, first, the liberty of a Christian to all indifferent things is in the mind and conscience, and is then infringed when the conscience is bound and straitened by imposing upon it an opinion of doctrinal necessity. But it is no wrong to the liberty of a Christian man's conscience to bind him to outward observance for order's sake, and to impose upon him a necessity of obedience. Which one distinction of doctrinal and obediential necessity, well-weighed and rightly applied, is of itself sufficient to clear all doubts in this point. For, to make all restraint of the outward man in matters indifferent an impeachment of Christian liberty, what were it else but even to bring flat anabaptism and anarchy into the Church, and to overthrow all bond of subjection and obedience to lawful authority? I beseech you consider, wherein can the immediate power and authority of fathers, masters, and other rulers over their inferiors consist, or the due obedience of inferiors be shewn towards them, if not in these indifferent and arbitrary things [Bernard. *Epist.* 7]? For things absolutely necessary, as commanded by God, we are bound to do whether human authority require them or no; and things absolutely unlawful, as prohibited by God, we are bound not to do whether human authority forbid them or no. There are none other things left then wherein to express properly the obedience due to superior authority than these indifferent things. . . . And again, secondly, men must understand that it is an error to think ceremonies and constitutions to be things merely indifferent—I mean in the general. For howsoever every particular ceremony be indifferent, and every particular constitution arbitrary and alterable, yet that there should be some ceremonies, it is necessary, *necessitate absoluta*, inasmuch as no outward work can be performed without ceremonial circumstances, some or other; and that there should be some constitutions concerning them, it is also necessary, though not simply & absolutely as the former . . . [see Calvin, 4 *Instit.* 10.27]. Otherwise, since some ceremonies must needs be used, every parish, nay every man, would have his own fashion by himself as his humor led him. Whereof what other could be the issue but infinite distraction and unorderly confusion in the Church? And again, thirdly, to return their weapon upon themselves: if every restraint in indifferent things be injurious to Christian liberty, then themselves are injurious no less by their negative restraint from some ceremonies: wear not, cross not, kneel not, &c. . . . Let indifferent men judge, nay let themselves that are parties judge, whether is more injurious to Christian liberty: public authority by mature advice commanding what might be forborne, or private spirits through humorous dislikes forbidding what may be used; the whole Church imposing the use or a few brethren requiring the forbearance of such things as are otherwise and in themselves equally indifferent for use or for forbearance?

But they say our Church maketh greater matters of ceremonies than thus, and preferreth them even before the most necessary duties of preaching and administering the sacraments, inasmuch as they are imposed upon ministers under pain of suspension and deprivation from their ministerial functions and charges. First, for actual deprivation, I take it unconforming ministers have no great cause to complain. Our Church, it is well known, hath not always used that rigor she might have done. Where she hath been forced to proceed as far as deprivation, she hath ordinarily by her fair and slow and compassionate proceedings therein sufficiently manifested her unwillingness thereto, and declared herself a mother every way indulgent enough to such ill-nurtured children as will not be ruled by her. Secondly, those that are suspended or deprived suffer it but justly for their obstinacy and contempt. For howsoever they would bear the world in hand that they are the *only persecuted ones* and that they suffer for their consciences, yet in truth they do but abuse the credulity of the simple therein—and herein (as in many other things) jump with the Papists, whom they would seem above all others most abhorrent from. For as seminary priests and Jesuits give it out they are martyred for their religion, when the very truth is, they are justly executed for their prodigious treasons and felonious or treacherous practices against lawful princes and estates [see Donne's *Pseudo-Martyr* . . . esp. c. 5], so the Brethren pretend they are persecuted for their consciences, when they are indeed but justly censured for their obstinate and pertinacious contempt of lawful authority. For it is not the refusal of these ceremonies they are deprived for, otherwise than as the matter wherein they shew their contempt; it is the contempt itself which formally and properly subjecteth them to just ecclesiastical censure of suspension or deprivation. And contempt of authority, though in the smallest matter, deserveth no small punishment: all authority having been ever solicitous (as it hath good reason) above all things to vindicate and pre-serve itself from contempt by inflicting sharp punishments upon contemptuous persons in the smallest matters above all other sorts of offenders in any degree whatsoever. Thus have we shewed and cleared the first and main difference betwixt the case of my text and the case of our Church, in regard of the matter: the things whereabout they differed being every way indifferent; ours, not so.

And as in the matter, so there is, secondly, much odds in the condition of the persons. The refusers, in the case of my text, being truly *weak in the faith*, as being but lately con-verted to the Christian faith and not sufficiently instructed by the Church in the doctrine and use of Christian liberty in things indifferent; whereas with our refusers it is much oth-erwise. First, they are not new proselytes. . . . yea many, and the chiefest of them, such as have taken upon them the calling of the ministry and the charge of souls, and the office of teaching and instructing others. And such men should not be weaklings. Secondly, ours are such as take themselves to have far more knowledge and understanding and insight in the Scriptures and all divine learning than other men: such as between pity and scorn seem most to wonder at the ignorance and simplicity of the vulgar, and to lament (which is, God knoweth, lamentable enough, though not comparable to what it was within not many years since) the want of knowledge and the insufficiency of some of the clergy in the land. And with what reason should these men expect the privilege of weak ones? Thirdly, our Church hath sufficiently declared and published the innocency of her purpose and meaning in enjoining the ceremonies. Nor so only, but hath been content to hear and receive and admit the objections and reasons of the refusers; and hath taken pains to answer and satisfy to the full all that ever yet could be said in that behalf. And therefore it is vanity for these men (or their friends in their behalf) to allege weakness, where all good means have been plentifully used for full information in the points in doubt. Lastly, upon the premises {foregoing}, it doth appear that the weakness of our Brethren, pretended by those that are willing to speak favorably of them, proceedeth for the most part not so much out of simple ignorance . . . as out of an ignorance at the best in some degree of willfulness and affectation in not seeking or not admitting such ingenuous satisfaction as they might have by reason, if not out of the poison of corrupt and carnal affections . . . of pride, of singularity, of envy, of contention, of factious admiring some men's persons. By which, and other like partial affections, men's judgments become oftentimes so blinded that of unwilling at the first, they become at length unable to discern things with that freedom and ingenuity they should. And so the cases differ in regard of the persons.

They differ, thirdly, in the practice of the persons. There the strong did eat because he was well assured he might do it . . . and the weak did no more but forbear eating, as indeed he might do, no authority interposing to the contrary. But here we conform not only because we know we may lawfully do it, but for that we know we must of necessity do it, as bound thereunto in obedience to lawful authority. . . . And the refusers do not only *de facto* not conform to the contempt of authority and the scandal of others, but they stand in it too, and trouble the peace of the Church by their restless *petitions* and *supplications* and *admonitions* and other publications of the reasons and grounds of their such refusal. . . .

Lastly, there is difference in the faulty carriage of the persons, and that on both parts, especially on ours. For though our non-conforming brethren condemn us with much liberty of speech and spirit . . . yet we do not despise them (I mean with allowance from the Church; if particular men do more than they should, it is their private fault . . .) but use all good means we can to draw them to moderate courses and just obedience, although they better deserve to be despised than the weak Romans did: they being truly weak, ours obstinate; they timorous, ours also contemptuous.

Now these differences are opened betwixt the case in my text and the case of our Church, we may the better judge how far forth S. Paul's advice . . . ought to rule us in our case of conforming and not-conforming in point of ceremony. And first of not-despising, then of not judging. The ground of the Apostle's precept for not despising him that ate not was his weakness. So far then as this ground holdeth in our case, this precept is to be extended, and no further. And we are hereby bound not to despise our non-conforming brethren so far forth as it may probably appear to us they are weak and not willful. But so far forth, as by their courses and proceedings it may be reasonably thought their refusal proceedeth from corrupt or partial affections or is apparently maintained with obstinacy and contempt, I take it we may, notwithstanding the Apostle's admonition in my text, in some sort even despise them.

But because they think they are not so well and fairly dealt withal as they should be, let us consider their particular grievances wherein they take themselves despised and examine how just they are. They say, first, they are despised in being scoffed and flouted and derided by loose companions and by profane or popishly affected persons, in being styled *puritans* and *brethren* and *precisians*, and in having many jests and fooleries fastened upon them, whereof they are not guilty. They are, secondly, despised, they say, in that when they are convented before the bishops and others in authority, they cannot have the favor of an indifferent hearing, but are proceeded against as far as suspension, and sometimes deprivation, without taking their answers to what is objected or giving answers to what they object. Thirdly, in that many honest and religious men of excellent and useful gifts cannot be permitted the liberty of their consciences and the free exercise of their ministry, only for standing out in these things which ourselves cannot but confess to be indifferent.[9]

To their first grievance, we answer that we have nothing to do with those that are popishly affected. If they wrong them, as it is like enough they will . . . we are not to be charged with that: let them answer for themselves. But by the way, let our brethren

---

[9] {For all these grievances, see Bradshaw, chap. 5 <*supra*>.}

consider whether their stiff and unreasonable opposing against those lawful ceremonies we retain may not be one principal means to confirm but so much the more in their darkness and superstition those that are wavering and might possibly by more ingenuous and seasonable insinuations be won over to embrace the truth which we profess. And as for loose persons and profane ones that make it their sport upon their ale-benches to rail and scoff at puritans, as if it were warrant enough for them to drink drunk, talk bawdy, swear and stare, or do any thing without control, because forsooth they are no puritans: as we could wish our Brethren and their lay-followers, by their uncouth and sometimes ridiculous behavior, had not given profane persons too much advantage to play upon them and through their sides to wound even religion itself,[10] so we could wish also that some men by . . . scoffing at them had not given them advantage to triumph in their own innocency and persist in their affected obstinacy. It cannot but be some confirmation to men in error to see men of dissolute and loose behavior with much eagerness and petulancy and virulence to speak against them. . . . I see not but that otherwise the name of *puritan* and the rest are justly given them. For appropriating to themselves the names of *brethren, professors, good men*, and other like as differences betwixt them and those they call *formalists*, would they not have it thought that they have a brotherhood and profession of their own, freer and purer from superstition and idolatry than others have that are not of the same stamp? And doing so, why may they not be called *puritans*? The name, I know, is sometimes fastened upon those that deserve it not [of late our English Arminians have got the trick to fetch in within the compass of this title of *puritans*, all orthodox divines that oppose against their semi-pelagian subtleties, of purpose to make sound truth odious and their own corrupt novelties more passable and plausible];[11] rascal people will call any man that beareth but the face of honesty a *puritan*, but why should that hinder others from placing it where it is rightly due?

To their second grievance, I answer: public means by conferences, disputations, and otherwise have been often used, and private men not seldom afforded the favor of respite and liberty to bring in the allegations. And I think it can be hardly, or but rarely, instanced that ever deprivation hath been used but where fatherly admonitions have first been used and time given to the delinquents to consider of it and inform themselves better. . . .

And as to their third grievance. First, for my own part, I make no doubt, neither dare I be so uncharitable as not to think but that many of them have honest and upright and sincere hearts to God-ward and are unfainedly zealous of God's truth and for religion. They that are such no doubt feel the comfort of it in their own souls; and we see the fruits of it in their conversation, and rejoice at it. But yet I cannot be so ignorant on the other side as not to know that the most sanctified and zealous men are men, and subject to carnal and corrupt affections, and may be so far swayed by them in their judgments as

---

[10] {See the verdicts of Laud and Neile in the 1632 Star Chamber case of *Smith v. Martin*, which concerned precisely such profane scoffing at puritans (*Reports of cases in the courts of Star Chamber and High Commission*, ed. S. R. Gardiner [Camden Society, 1886], 149–53).}

[11] {This marginalium is in the 1622 version, so it cannot refer to Richard Montagu's *New gag* and *Appello Caesarem*, although Montagu is usually the one accused of broadening the scope of "puritan" to include all Calvinists, which is what Sanderson means by "orthodox." It should be noted that Bishop Montaigne, to whom Sanderson dedicates this sermon, is now frequently classed as an Arminian—although presumably not the sort of Arminian to which Sanderson is objecting.}

not to be able to discern without prejudice and partiality truth from error. Good men and God's dear children may continue in some error in judgment, & consequently in a sinful practice arising thence, and live and die in it (as some of these men have done in disobedience to lawful authority), and that unrepented of otherwise than as in the lump of their unknown sins.[12] It is not honesty or sincerity that can privilege men from either erring or sinning. Neither ought the unreproved conversation {conduct} of men countenance out their opinions or their practices against the light of divine Scripture and right reason. . . . Secondly, though comparisons be ever harsh and most times odious, yet since honesty and piety is alleged (without disparagement be it spoken to the best of them), there are as good and honest and religious and zealous men every way of them that willingly and cheerfully conform as of them that do not. In the times of popish persecution, how many godly bishops and conformable ministers laid down their lives for the testimony of God's truth and for the maintenance of his Gospel. And if it should please God in his just judgment . . . to put us once again to a fierce trial . . . I make no question but many thousands of conformers would (by the grace of God) resist unto blood, embrace the faggot, and burn at a stake in detestation of all popish antichristian idolatry as readily and cheerfully and constantly as the hottest and precisest and most scrupulous non-conformer. But thirdly, let men's honesty and piety and gifts be what they can: must not men of honesty and piety and gifts live under laws? And what reason these, or any other respects, should exempt any man from the just censure of the Church in case he will not obey her laws and conform to her ceremonies: especially since such men's immunity would but encourage others to presume upon the like favor; and experience teacheth us that no men's errors are so exemplary and pernicious as theirs who, for their eminency of gifts or sanctity of life, are most followed with popular applause and personal admiration?

We see their grievances against us: how unjust they are in the matter of despising. I would they did no more despise the Church's authority than we do their infirmities! But in the matter of judging, see if we have not a just grievance against them. . . .

First, they judge our Church as half popish and antichristian for retaining some ceremonies used in popery, though we have purged them from their superstitions and restored them to their primitive use. Their great admired opener of the Revelation [Brightman in Apoc. cap. 3] maketh our Church the linsey-woolsey Laodicean Church, neither hot nor cold. And some of them have slovenly compared our late gracious sovereign Queen Elizabeth of most blessed memory to a sluttish housewife that having swept the house yet left the dust and dirt behind the doors—meaning thereby the ceremonies. If our Church were but half so ill as these men would make it, I think every honest religious man should hold himself bound to separate from it. . . .

Secondly, they judge our bishops and other church-governors as limbs of Antichrist, locusts of the bottomless pit, domineering lords over God's heritage, usurpers of temporal jurisdiction, spiritual tyrants over men's consciences, &c., seeking by all means to make the name of lord bishop odious to the gentry and commons. Witness their Marprelate and other infamous and scandalous libels in that kind. Having power in their hands, if

---

[12] ["*Sancti stante charitate possunt errare etiam contra Catholicam veritatem*," Ockham, *Dial.* part 1, lib. 2, cap. 4. {See also "A learned discourse of justification" (Hooker, *Works* 3.18:26), and Chillingworth <1.13. *Ad* § 17>.}]

the bishops should use more rigorous courses towards them than they have done, could ye blame them?

Thirdly, they judge those that subscribe and conform Machiavellian time-servers, formal Gospellers, state-divines: men that know no conscience but law, nor religion but the king's, and such as would be as forward for the Mass as the Communion if the state should alter.

Fourthly, all such ministers as are not endowed with gifts for the pulpit they damn as hirelings and not shepherds: calling them idol-shepherds, betrayers of Christ's flock . . . and I know not how many names besides. Yea, although they be such as are diligent according to their measure of gifts to perform such duties as the Church requireth: to present the prayers of the people to God, to declare (by reading the holy Bible and good homilies for that purpose appointed) the will of God to the people, to instruct the younger sort in the points of catechism, to visit and comfort the sick and afflicted, and to administer reverently and orderly the holy sacraments of baptism and the Lord's Supper.

Fifthly, they judge all such as interpose for the Church's peace and oppose their novelties as enemies to all goodness, men of profane minds, haters of religion, despisers of the word, persecutors of the Brethren, imps of Satan, instruments of hell, and such as utterly abhor all godly and Christian courses.

Sixthly and lastly (for I irk to rake longer in this sink) they bewray themselves to be manifest judges of all that are not of their stamp, by singling out unto themselves and those that favor them certain proper appellations of *brethren* and *good men* and *professors*—as if none had brotherhood in Christ . . . but themselves. . . .

But they will say these peremptory censures are but the faults of some few; all are not so hot and fiery; there be others that are more temperate in their speeches and moderate in their courses, and desire only they may be spared for their own particular, but they preach not against any of these things nor intermeddle to make more stirs in the Church.

I answer, first, it were lamentable if this were not so. If all were of that hot temper, or distemper rather, that many are, they would quickly tire out themselves without spurring. Far be it from us to judge men's hearts or to condemn men for that we know not by them. Yet of some that carry themselves with tolerable moderation outwardly, we have some cause to suspect that they do inwardly and in their heart judge as deeply as the hottest-spirited railers. And we gather it from their forwardness at every turn and upon every slender occasion obliquely to gird and indirectly to glance at our Church and the discipline and the ceremonies thereof, as far as they well dare. And if such men meddle no further, we may reasonably think it is not for want of good will to do it, but because they dare not.

. . .

Lastly, it is to be considered whether it may be enough for a pastor not to meddle with these things, & whether he be not in conscience bound, especially in case he live among a people distracted in opinions, to declare himself expressly either for them or against them. If they be utterly unlawful, and he know it so, how is he not bound in conscience to reprove those that use them or require them? Otherwise he betrayeth the *truth of God* by his silence, and suffereth men to go on in their superstition without rebuke. But if he be sufficiently resolved of their lawfulness, how is he not bound in conscience to reprove those that refuse them or oppose them? Otherwise he betrayeth the *peace of the Church* by his silence, and suffereth men to go on in their disobedience without rebuke. Nay more, every minister that hath received pastoral charge hath twice or thrice (if not oftener) witnessed his allowance of all and singular the 39 Articles of the Church of England. . . . By which subscription and approbation he hath not only acknowledged *in the Church the power of ordaining rites and ceremonies* [Art. 20] but he hath after a sort also bound himself *openly to rebuke such as willingly and purposely break the traditions & ceremonies of the Church, as offenders against the common orders of the Church and wounders of the consciences of the weak brethren* [Art. 34]. He then that for any respect whatsoever is mealy-mouthed in these things wherein he is bound both in *conscience* & by virtue of his own *voluntary act* to speak freely, neither is constant to his own hand and tongue nor is *faithful in God's cause* . . .

Thus have I endeavored . . . to deliver my opinion freely, so far as my text gave occasion, concerning the ceremonial constitutions of our Church, and therein labored to free, not only the conformer from all unjust censures, but even the non-conformer also, so far as he hath reason to expect it, from all scandalous despisings. I beseech you pardon my length, if I have been troublesome. I had much to say, and the matter was weighty; and I desired to give some satisfaction in it to those that are contrary-minded; and I have no purpose (for any thing I know) at all to trouble this place anymore hereafter. Let us all now humbly beseech Almighty God to grant a blessing to what hath been presently taught and heard, that it may work in the hearts of us all charitable affections one towards another, due obedience to lawful authority, and a conscionable care to walk in our several callings faithfully, painfully {diligently}, and peaceably, to the comfort of our own souls, the edification of God's Church, and the glory of the ever-blessed Trinity, the Father, Son, and Holy Ghost, three Persons and one God: to whom be ascribed by us and the whole Church, as is most due, the Kingdom, the Power, and the Glory, for ever and ever. Amen.

Text: EEBO (STC [2nd ed.] / 21705)

Ten sermons preached I. Ad clerum. 3. II. Ad magistratum. 3. III. Ad populum. 4. By Robert Saunderson Bachelor in Divinity, sometimes fellow of Lincoln College in Oxford (London: Printed for R. Dawlman, 1627), 1–14, 16–49.

RICHARD CORBETT[1]

The Distracted Puritan
ca. 1620–21

The Distracted Puritan

Am I mad, O noble Festus,[2]
    When zeal and godly knowledge
        Have put me in hope
        To deal with the Pope,
    As well as the best in the College?
Boldly I preach, hate a cross, hate a surplice,
    Miters, copes, and rotchets:
Come hear me pray nine times a day,
    And fill your heads with crotchets.

In the house of pure Emmanuel[3]
    I had my education;
        Where my friends surmise
        I dazzled mine eyes
    With the light of Revelation.
Boldly I preach, &c.

They bound me like a bedlam,
They lash't my four poor quarters;

---

[1] {The biographical introduction to Corbett can be found on page <100>, prefacing his 1609 elegy on Dr. Ravis. The 1955 Oxford edition of Corbett's poems notes that a satire dating from the late summer of 1621 would appear to parody the opening line of "The distracted puritan," which suggests that the poem was *au courant* and thus a tentative date of 1620–21 (Bennett and Trevor-Roper, 133, 141). The Bohemian crisis unleashed a flood-tide of apocalyptic speculation in the years around 1620, bolstering the case for a 1620–21 date—although admittedly decoding Revelations had long been a puritan (or at least stage-puritan) hallmark.}

[2] {Echoing St. Paul's words to the Roman governor of Judea, Porcius Festus, see Acts 26:25.}

[3] {the conspicuously puritan Cambridge college}

      Whilst this I endure,
      Faith makes me sure
To be one of Foxe's martyrs.
Boldly I preach, &c.

     These injuries I suffer
     Through Anti-Christ's persuasions.
       Take off this chain,
       Neither Rome nor Spain
Can resist my strong invasions.[4]
Boldly I preach, &c.

     Of the Beast's ten horns (God bless us!)
     I have knock't off three already;
       If they let me alone,
       I'll leave him none;
But they say I am too heady.
Boldly I preach, &c.

     When I sack'd the seven-hill'd City
     I met the great red Dragon;
       I kept him aloof
       With the armor of proof,
Though here I have never a rag on.
Boldly I preach, &c.

     With a fiery sword and target
     There fought I with this monster:
       But the sons of pride
       My zeal deride,
And all my deeds misconster.
Boldly I preach, &c.

     I unhorsed the Whore of Babel
     With a lance of inspirations;
       I made her stink,
       And spill her drink
In the cup of abominations.
Boldly I preach, &c.

     I have seen two in a vision,
     With a flying book between them;
       I have been in despair
       Five times a year,

[4] {Some editions reverse "persuasions" and "invasions."}

And cur'd by reading Greenham.[5]
Boldly I preach, &c.

I observ'd in Perkins' Tables[6]
The black lines of damnation:
      Those crooked veins
      So stuck in my brains,
That I fear'd my reprobation.
Boldly I preach, &c.

In the holy tongue of Canaan
I plac'd my chiefest pleasure,
      Till I prickt my foot
      With an Hebrew root,[7]
That I bled beyond all measure.
Boldly I preach, &c.

I appear'd before the archbishop,
And all the High Commission;
      I gave him no grace,
      But told him to his face
That he favor'd superstition.
Boldly I preach, hate a cross, hate a surplice,
    Miters, copes, and rotchets:
Come hear me pray nine times a day,
    And fill your heads with crotchets.[8]

TEXT: *The poems of Richard Corbet, Late Bishop of Oxford and of Norwich*, ed. Octavius Gilchrist, 4th ed. (London, 1807).
    Checked against J. A. W. Bennett & Hugh Trevor-Roper, *The poems of Richard Corbett* (Clarendon, 1955).

[5] {Richard Greenham (d. 1592), famous puritan spiritual director}

[6] {William Perkins' (d. 1602), "A survey or table declaring the order of the causes of salvation and damnation according to God's word" included in his *Golden Chain* (1599); see www.scribd.com/doc/23473884/William-Perkins-Chart.}

[7] {All Hebrew words are built around a three-letter consonantal root; to "prick" a Hebrew text is to add the vowel points. There may be an allusion here to the controversy over the antiquity of Hebrew vowel-points: Buxdorf's *Tiberius*, arguing for their antiquity, came out in 1620; Cappel's *Arcanum punctuationis revelatum*, which dated them from the 5th century AD, in 1624. The question had been debated, however, since the middle of the 16th century.}

[8] {Note that if the poem dates from ca. 1621, the archbishop of this stanza is not Laud, but Abbot, who is not known to have favored superstition, crosses, miters, copes, or rochets (although he did require the surplice). Indeed, since Corbett died only two years after Laud's elevation to Canterbury, and had largely ceased to write poetry once bishop of Norwich (Bennett & Trevor-Roper, xl), the objections to dating the poem after 1633 seem insuperable.}

JOHN COSIN
(1595–1672)

The son of a prosperous Norwich clothier, Cosin matriculated at Gonville and Caius, Cambridge, in 1610, receiving his BA in 1614, followed by the MA in 1617 and BD in 1623.[1] In 1616 Cambridge's leading anti-Calvinists, Lancelot Andrewes and John Overall, both sought Cosin as their episcopal librarian. He accepted the latter's offer, from 1617 until Overall's death in 1619 serving as the Bishop's librarian and secretary, while Overall, in turn, became Cosin's theological model and mentor.[2] Soon after Overall died, Cosin entered Bishop Neile's circle at Durham House, becoming Neile's chaplain and, in 1624, receiving a prebendal stall in Durham Cathedral, followed two years later by the richly endowed living of Brancepeth, whose church he adorned with a splendid display of Gothic woodwork: the first of many such refurbishments, for "Cosin's idea of the right ambience for worship expressed itself in woodwork of the most flamboyant kind, and wherever his words of authority or influence fell, a forest of boldly carved oak arose" (Parry 40–41).

By 1621 Cosin had also formed a close friendship with Richard Montagu, whom he introduced to the Durham House circle, whose members included Laud and Buckeridge. In the years that followed, Cosin served as sounding board and editor for Montagu's *New gag* and *Appello Caesarem*,[3] in 1626 speaking on Montagu's behalf at the York House Conference, whose discussion he recorded (the account later published under the title *The sum and substance of the Conferences lately held at York House concerning Mr. Mountague's books*). Cosin's reputation as a liturgist led Charles to ask him to compose a devotional manual for the Protestant ladies at court; the result, the 1627 *A collection of private devotions*, bore enough resemblance to a book of hours—and could be read as allowing prayers for the dead—to provoke angry accusations of popery from Henry Burton and William

---

[1] On the inclusive Anglo-Catholicism of Gonville and Caius, see Alan Bray, *The friend* (Chicago UP, 2003), 87–93.

[2] See the fine discussion of Overall in Anthony Milton's "'Anglicanism' by stealth: the career and influence of John Overall," *Religious politics in post-Reformation England*, ed. Kenneth Fincham and Peter Lake (Woodbridge, 2006), 159–66. In 1669 Cosin erected a monument in Norwich Cathedral honoring Overall.

[3] See the raft of letters concerning these works in Cosin, *Correspondence*, vol. 1.

Prynne; it received a better reception from other quarters, going through three editions in 1627 alone, with five more in Cosin's lifetime.

Back in Durham, Cosin encountered further opposition. In a 1628 sermon, Peter Smart, one of Cosin's fellow-prebendaries, denounced the "strange Babylonish ornaments" and liturgical elaborations introduced by his colleague. Some of the practices condemned as innovations may have predated Cosin's tenure, but the replacement of congregational psalm-singing with choral polyphony sung by the choir was his doing, and triggered a dispute with the new Bishop of Durham, John Howson *<vide supra>*, that proved all the more bitter for being so unexpected, for Howson was a high churchman and one of Cosin's "familiars" at Durham House (Cosin, *Correspondence*, 1:208); yet on this occasion Howson defended Smart and reinstated the metrical Psalms.[4] Both men appealed to Laud, who sided with Cosin and the choir. In the meantime, however, Smart, whom the cathedral chapter had expelled from his stall, drew up a petition against Cosin, charging him with misdeeds ranging from using a cope bearing an image of Christ with a red beard and blue cap, to introducing a special consecrated knife for the communion bread, to denying the king was head of the English Church (Cosin, *Correspondence*, 1:xxiv–xxvii, 147–52). The surviving depositions do not support Smart's version of things, but the charges came to the attention of the 1628 Parliament, which accused Cosin of high treason, ordered his *Collection* burned and Cosin himself punished as an "author and abettor of Popish and Arminian innovations" (*ODNB*). Charles, however, dissolved Parliament in March of 1629, and the matter was dropped.

The 1630s were good years for Cosin, who became a royal chaplain-extraordinary in 1633 and chaplain-in-ordinary in 1636. Having received his DD in 1630, in 1636 he was appointed master of Peterhouse, additionally serving as vice-chancellor for 1639: in both capacities displaying his love of both strong administration and the beauty of holiness. In its first week, however, the Long Parliament reactivated the charges against Cosin, whose attempt to smuggle the Peterhouse plate to Charles did not help his case. By 1644 he was with the royal court in Paris, where he proved, in Thomas Fuller's words, "the Atlas of the Protestant religion, supporting the same with his piety and learning, confirming the wavering therein, yea daily adding proselytes (not of the meanest rank) thereto" (*ODNB*). During the next decade and a half Cosin wrote a series of tracts defending the Church of England (see especially his *Regni Angliae religio catholica*) and critiquing Roman Catholic doctrine. During the same years he also developed warm collegial relations with the Orthodox archbishop of Trebizond and with the ministers at Charenton—the huge barn-like Reformed church serving the capital's Protestant community—especially Jean Daillé and Moses Amyraut, whose humanist and heterodox Calvinism differed so strikingly from that of the Westminster Assembly.[5]

---

[4] In Howson's letters to Laud, Cosin comes across as a troublemaker (Cosin, *Correspondence*, 1:208–9), yet he got on famously with Howson's successor, the Calvinist Thomas Morton (q.v. Brian Quintrell's entry on Morton in the *ODNB*)—a salutary reminder that not all conflicts bespeak ideological difference and that ideological differences need not produce conflict.

[5] Cosin's later writings also show a deep sympathy with the views of the Lutheran syncretist Georg Calixtus (1586–1656), a follower of Cassander, above all in his conviction that the Apostles' Creed contained all necessary saving truths (Laud's view as well *<vide infra>*) and could therefore provide the doctrinal basis for the reunion of Christendom.

The Restoration saw Cosin elevated to the See of Durham—and a major presence in the revision of the Prayer Book. As bishop, Cosin fought hard to reclaim the vast revenues of his diocese, which he then spent on restoring vandalized churches, refounding almshouses and schools, endowing university scholarships, and building the public library on the Durham Palace green that still bears his name —these multifarious gifts and endowments carefully itemized in his will to "satisfy the world" that no monies had gone to enrich himself or his family (Cosin, *Correspondence*, 2:296).

Twenty-three of Cosin's sermons, bound together in a small manuscript volume, survive. These, like much of Cosin's work, were first printed in the nineteenth-century Library of Anglo-Catholic Theology. The 1621 Epiphany sermon below is Cosin's earliest known piece. The manner is that of Andrewes' festal preaching: a blend of staccato parataxis, figural density, sound play, and interwoven poetic and colloquial registers that owes something to seventeenth-century Senecanism and more to medieval *Kunstprosa*.[6] The tight focus on the biblical text (the sermon is a tissue of biblical allusions) and the fusion of humanist and typological-allegorical exegesis are likewise hallmarks of Andrewes' style.

Cosin throughout emphasizes the universality of salvation: the lavish outpouring of grace to all peoples—to the gentiles, to beggars and outcasts sheltering under Palestinian hedgerows, to all sinners. As the contrast with Calvin's reading of Isaiah 60:3 (to which Cosin alludes and which I have therefore included as an appendix to the sermon) implies, this emphasis sets itself against any version of Christianity that confines the glad tidings to some few elect. That Cosin links the gentiles with England's hedge-dwellers—and thus the Epiphany with mercy shown to this vagrant riffraff—corroborates Jeffrey Knapp's reciprocal intuition that the rogues, gypsies, and vagabonds populating the early Stuart stage evoke an inclusive vision of the Church that has "room yet at supper for them."[7] To be sure, like a number of playwrights, Cosin has trouble finding room for puritans, yet one notes with some surprise how very close his view that the secular and sensual Christmas festivity "we commonly use . . . will end with weeping and gnashing of teeth" is to the puritan position on holiday pastimes.[8]

[6] The classic study of the latter is to be found in volume 2 of Eduard Norden's *Die antike Kunstprosa vom VI. Jahrhundert v. chr. bis in die Zeit der Renaissance* (Leipzig, 1898). See also Morris Croll, *"Attic" and Baroque Prose Style*, ed. J. Max Patrick and. Robert Evans with John Wallace (Princeton UP, 1966); Debora Shuger, *Sacred rhetoric* (Princeton UP, 1988); Marc Fumaroli, *L'âge de l'éloquence* (Geneva, 1984).

[7] Jeffrey Knapp, *Shakespeare's tribe: Church, nation, and theater in Renaissance England* (Chicago UP, 2002), 77.

[8] A view shared by other godly writers, e.g., Dod and Bayly <*vide supra*>, but one also finds similar sentiments in the sermons of Lancelot Andrewes and among the members of the Little Gidding community: see, e.g., the conclusion of the former's 1613 Nativity sermon and the latter's dialogue "On the austere life," in *Conversations at Little Gidding*, ed. A. M. Williams (Cambridge UP, 1970), 157–315.

Sources: *ODNB*; Brian Armstrong, *Calvinism and the Amyraut heresy* (U Wisconsin P, 1969); John Cosin, *The works of . . . John Cosin*, ed. J. Sansom, 5 vols., Library of Anglo-Catholic Theology (1843–55); John Cosin, *The correspondence of John Cosin, D.D.*, ed. and intro. George Ornsby, 2 vols. (Durham, 1869); Martin Klauber, *Between reformed scholasticism and pan-Protestantism: Jean-Alphonse Turretin (1671–1737) and enlightened orthodoxy at the Academy of Geneva* (Associated UP, 1994); Graham Parry, *The arts of the Anglican Counter-Reformation: glory, laud and honor* (Woodbridge, 2006); Timothy Schmeling, "Lutheran orthodoxy under fire: an exploratory study of the syncretistic controversy," www.blts.edu/wp-content/uploads/2011/06/TRS-Consensus-Repetitus.pdf (accessed June 6, 2012).

JOHN COSIN

Sermon I: Preached at St. Edward's in Cambridge, January the 6th, A.D. MDCXXI,
and at Coton[1] on the second Sunday after Epiphany

January, 1621

Now when Jesus was born in Bethlehem of Judea in the days of Herod the King, behold,
there came Wise Men from the East to Jerusalem, saying, where is he that is born King of the Jews?
for we have seen his star in the east, and are come to worship him.
Matt. 2:1-2

I chose my text for the time, the celebration of this day, that we may keep Solomon's rule, *verbum diei in die suo*;[2] and therefore before I come to the text I will say a little of the day, this Epiphany, this manifestation of our Lord and Savior.

We are still at the feast of Christmas, and this is the last and great day of the feast, as St. John said of another. A feast of joy it has been all this while, but this day was given us that our joy might be full. They were tidings of joy that the angels brought, a while since, to the shepherds, Jews, hard at hand; but when the glad tidings of the Gospel came abroad once to all the people, as this day they came so, then were they no more tidings of ordinary, but of great joy. "Behold, I bring you tidings," saith the angel, but not to you alone; though to you, yet others as well as you, "which shall be to all people."[3] Hitherto, then, it was *evangelizo vobis, vobis Judaeis*, but to-day it was *omni populo*: that now a Savior was born unto us all, which was Christ the Lord. And indeed this is our Christmas-day that were gentiles; for though Christ was born twelve days since in Jewry, yet he came not abroad the world while {until} now, and to us he seemed as yet unborn (being but like a rich treasure in a man's field, at this time not known to be so), till he was this day manifested unto us in the persons of these Wise Men, the first fruits of the gentiles.

---

[1] {Coton is a village near Cambridge. The minister of the parish church in 1621 was John Hayward, a nephew of Bishop Overall.}

[2] {The reference would seem to be to the Vulgate's 1 Esdras 3:4 (i.e., Ezra 3:4), *"opus diei in die suo* [the work of the day on its day]." The same wording also appears in Lancelot Andrewes 1620 Easter sermon.}

[3] {Since Cosin's sermons were not printed during the early modern period, I will follow their 19th-century editor in using quotation marks rather than italics.}

There were many Epiphanies before this, for it was made manifest many times before. To the Blessed Virgin first, for she knew it nine months before, and then to John Baptist before he was born himself, for he could seem in the womb to point at him, when his mother came, *Ecce Agnus Dei, qui tollit peccata mundi.*[4] And after he was born, the shepherds had tidings of the Lamb of God too. But all these were the Epiphanies of some few persons only, and the new Morning Star was seen but a little way, as far as Mary's family, or a field hard by, and no farther. Now to-day his lightnings gave shine unto the world, and at his Epiphany not a few persons at home or near at hand, but the nations abroad, even at the ends of the earth, had news brought them of it from heaven; and now this day not Jewry only (that was too strait for him who must have the heathen given him for his inheritance), but the whole world was the better for Christ's nativity. A true Christmas-day this, and Christmas rejoicing right, when all fare the better for it. Before, the heathen were about the hedges, shut quite out of doors; but to-day the gates were set open for them, as well as for the Jews. Which community was well figured, as the common note is, in the place that Christ would have his nativity happen in, even in a common inn, where every one might come, the gentile as welcome as the Jew; and because perhaps they would not be together in one chamber (for we read that the Jews meddle not with the Samaritans, nor keep their company), therefore Christ would be born in the stable, where there is no distinction made, but all put together in one room. . . . And we have heard with our ears, O God, and our fathers have told us of old, how thou hast not driven out the heathen, as David there speaks, but planted them in, fetched them home that were gone astray before, fetch[ed] them to thy blessed flock, that we might be all one fold under that great Shepherd that would give his life for his flock.

This then is the day which the Lord hath made, made it and made us with it too; indeed he had made us before, but we had marred his workmanship; now to-day we came to be made again, and our second making made us for ever, we were now become his workmanship in Christ Jesus, as St. Paul calls it. This is the day that the Lord hath made for us, and therefore this should be the day that we should make for him too; rejoice and be glad in it, as it follows there in the Psalm [118:24], and as it follows here in the Gospel too; for St. Matthew says, a little after the text, that when they saw the star they rejoiced exceedingly, and so they proved the angel's words true, tidings of great joy. And now I know there is no question but that most of us will rejoice too; nay, the world shall know that we do not mean to pass this day away without that. But such joy we commonly use as, God knows, will end with weeping and gnashing of teeth; our mouth shall be filled with laughter, if ye will, and we will be like them that dream, as the Prophet speaks, but not for the turning of our captivity this day from bondage, a worse than that in Babylon, from the bondage of sin and hell itself. "Sing we merrily unto God our strength," saith the Psalm. No, "Sing merrily" an ye will, so far we go; but if we come to "God our strength" then our voice is quite gone, we have no skill in such songs, and yet this must be our rejoicing, or else all our Christmas sport is but spoiled. It is true these are all days of joy indeed, of great joy; joy as much as ye will, even as they joy in harvest, saith Isaiah; but be sure ye take that along to make your joy sweet which the holy Virgin taught us at the very

---

[4] {Behold the Lamb of God who taketh away the sins of the world.}

first news of all of any Christmas rewards, at the Annunciation, "My soul doth magnify the Lord, and my spirit hath rejoiced in God my Savior."

And this day became God the savior of the gentiles, when we might see the star tell us, as Christ afterward told the publican: this day was salvation come unto us. Even this last day of all the solemnity it came, to make it greater than the rest, the greatest of all the twelve, as the Catholic Church hath ever accounted it; the great and proper feast of the gentiles, such as we were before it, and the last day was always the greatest day of the feast, as you may see in the Gospel. So I did not amiss to call this day at first, the great and last day of our Christmas solemnity. Last. (I'll warrant you every tradesman will tell you [specially if he has got a twang in his head[5]] that all these observations of times are but popish customs; they will not celebrate ye a day longer; nay, not so long neither, but for the law; the day of the gentiles' calling, what is that to them? They have a tribe and a calling by themselves, that was marked out for heaven sure long before either Jews or gentiles were stirring.) And "great" too, for the great and wide world was blessed this day with the day-star from on high, with the glad tidings of the Gospel, the tidings of the great Shepherd and the great King, the great King above all gods. . . .

And well may it be called thus, a day of many Epiphanies, were it but for the gentiles' coming only; for if ever many things were opened at once that were hid before, shadows of things to come, it was surely this day. For though there was no such matter thought on before, yet now it is made manifest what was figured by these same *exploratores*, the spies that went out beforehand to see the Land of Promise. And now ye may perceive plainly what it was that Solomon's Temple must have the wood from Lebanon amongst the gentiles, as well as stones at home among the Jews; and that Hiram, King of Tyre, must help to build God's house as well as {Solomon} himself, King of Jerusalem, and afterwards have twenty cities given him for the Jews and gentiles to dwell together in. And now it is plain what is meant that not Gideon's fleece alone, but the whole earth must be spread over with the morning dew; and that Moses had married a woman of Ethiopia; and that Samson must leave the daughters of his brethren, and first marry an uncircumcised Philistine, and then fall in love with the harlot Dalilah: which manifests likewise what we were, for before this day we went a whoring after our own inventions. And therefore it was well figured again in that, that God would have Hosea go and take unto him a wife of fornications; and that a woman in captivity must be married to Ahasuerus the King; and that Moses the servant of God must be adopted the son of Pharaoh's daughter; and that Isaac must have the inheritance, though Ismael were the eldest; and Jacob have the birth-right, though Esau were the first-born (which is St. Paul's application to the very honor of this day); and so that Ephraim must be put at the right hand of Jacob, though Manasses were the elder son, howsoever it displeased Joseph; and that Joseph himself must be sold for a bond-slave into Egypt, as we were before, and afterwards exalted to the golden chain and the best chariot that Pharaoh had, to the height of his kingdom, as we are now, for thus were we this day exalted; and lastly, that his father Jacob must have children by Leah that was blear-eyed, as well as by Rachel, that was beautiful and fair.

I hope by this time, it is clear why this day should be called the Epiphany; there were so many things made known in it, that lay under a cloud before; for these were all shadows

5 {an anti-puritan slur}

yet. But now when this star arose, it enlightened them all, made them manifest what they all figured, even this day's calling of the gentiles. Take but any of them; the blear-eyed Leah will tell us how blind we were before, as blind as men that grope in the dark, in the darkness of ignorance, darkness as black as that of Egypt; and that therefore this star, this day-spring from on high, did appear to-day to give light to them that sit in darkness and in the shadow of death, and to guide our feet into the way of peace; of peace right, for before we were at mighty variance with heaven. Before, we could hear of nothing but, to execute vengeance upon the heathen, and to bind their kings in chains; but to-day the heathen are come into God's inheritance, and without complaint too; no more indignation now to be poured upon them, as it follows there in the Psalm, but God now reigneth over the heathen, and the princes of the people are gathered unto the people of the God of Abraham; and though the gentiles did rage before, and the kings of the earth did band themselves against the Lord's Anointed, yet to-day they grew wise and took David's counsel, "Be wise now therefore, O ye kings"; they came and joined themselves together for a better purpose, to worship the Lord's Anointed, Christ the Lord. Before this time God was known in Jewry only, and his name was great in Israel alone, but now there is neither speech nor language but his voice hath been heard among them; and since the heavens have declared his glory, as this day they did, his sound is gone even unto the ends of the world, as far as the Magi of the East. Yea, though we were dogs before, and must not have the children's bread given us, as Christ bespake the woman, yet now he hath given us power to be the sons of God, as St. John speaks.

It was David's prayer that God would think upon his inheritance, and whensoever he thought upon it, to-day we are sure he did, and it was time to think and have mercy upon her, yea O Lord, the time was come, for it pitied thee to see us in the dust. And therefore as soon as Christ did but ask of him, as the Psalmist speaks, he gave him the heathen for his inheritance, and the uttermost parts of the earth for his possession [Ps. 2:8].

. . .

So then, for a conclusion, as God hath made this our day's deliverance like theirs, as we see in all points, what have we to do but to make the day, as they made it too, a day of joy and thanksgiving, a day of a solemn and set service. Moses with a song and Miriam with a timbrel in her hands that day. Woe to us if we had been still constrained to dwell in Mesech, or to have had our habitation among the tents of Kedar; then we might indeed have sat like unto them that mourn and have hanged our harps upon the willows. But since we are brought out of darkness, and now sit no more in the shadow of death, but have our feet guided by the light of his star, our hearts made glad with the tidings of the Gospel, now bring hither the tabret and harp, and blow up the trumpet of praise, for this is our solemn feast day.

And so I have done with the feast, and from the day I come to *opus diei*, from the time to the text, though I have not been far from it all this while.

"Now when Jesus was born in Bethlem." And now when I begin to read my text, methinks it is not *opus diei*, it doth not agree with the time, for Christ was not born in Bethlem to-day, and indeed unless we go on it will not be *verbum in die suo*, Solomon's rule. And therefore to make it so, it follows, "Behold Wise Men came from the East to Jerusalem, saying, where is he that is born King of the Jews, for we have seen," &c.

The text would do well to have no division to-day, because it is a day of union, wherein they that were divided before were made one under Christ; and therefore I might only call it the Epiphany, one general head, and so away. But because we have been long enough about that, and for order's sake too, you may observe these parts.

1. A peregrination, "Behold there came from the East to Jerusalem"; the first point.
2. "There came"—not poor pilgrims or beggars that had nothing else to do, but the great ones, the sages of the land, *Ecce, Magi venerunt*; and that is the second point, the persons that came.
3. And they came, not like men that had no comfort or company in their journey, that they knew not; but a gladsome director they had to go along with them, a star in the firmament; and that is the third.
4. Then for the fourth have you the end of their journey; the Kings of the East came just as the Queen of the South did, to see the King of the Jews, and therefore they ask, Where is the King of the Jews? Yet here they differed; for she came to hear and see, and they came to worship, and we are come to worship him.
5. And the last point of all is, the present occasion of their coming; which was Christ's being then newly born at Bethlehem—"When Jesus" &c.—And here the Kings' coming differed from the Queen's again, for she came to see Solomon in his full strength, and these to worship Christ in the beginning of his age; she to behold him in all his royalty, in his royal throne, in his kingly city; these to behold Christ in all his poverty, his robes being but the poor swaddling-clouts that his mother's mantle could make him, his attendants not lords of the chamber but beasts of the field, and his throne not of six fair steps or a great throne of ivory covered over with gold, but a rude manger covered perhaps with dust; or at the best, his mother's arms. This was the magnificence that they came to see, and this the King that they took all this pains to search and come from the East this day to worship.

1. I will handle the occasion first, because that lays first in the text, and so I will deal with all the rest. When Jesus was (1) born at (2) Bethlem, in the (3) days of (4) Herod the King; that is the occasion; and I will not handle it neither, I will but even touch it and so away; because, as I said before, it is not proper to the day. But somewhat we will make of it though, and because it stands in our way to the star, we will make a ladder of it, to bring us up thither, and we will go up apace too, for the time is short, and we have much to do when we come there.

There be but four steps in it, and the first step hits right; for it is fit to be the lowest of all, it is Christ's humility. *Cum natus esset Jesus*, when he was born, that Jesus who was the Son of the living God, as St. Mark begins his Gospel, should come to be the son of Joseph, as St. Matthew begins his; that the immortal God himself should come to be a mortal man, the Lord of Life come and subject himself to the state of dying men—this is beyond all degrees of lowliness. It had been humility enough, sure, had it been only *cum Jesus esset in Bethlem*, and *natus* left out, to have been there at all, for the Son of God to have visited the sons of men in what majesty best befitted him; but to be born, *cum natus esset*, that was too much for him: man that is born of a woman, saith David, is a thing of nought. Nay, *factus* then had been far less, for so he might have had a perfect body framed him, and "made" in the vigor of his age, as Adam was, and so have escaped the diseases of childhood; but now, not to be "made" but to be "born," that is to endure many more miseries, misery within the womb and misery without it, the age next the birth is full of them. Yet for all this, *Jesus natus est*, he did not abhor the Virgin's womb (a thing we may see by that to be abhorred), but was even content to be "born" for us, as all miserable men are. This is the first step.

2. But the second step is more lowliness yet, it comes a degree higher. (A strange virtue this humility hath, that the lower it goes the higher it riseth.)

Not "born" only, but "born in Bethlem"; the place where Jesus was born, in Bethlem. Why, if Jesus, the Son of God, must needs be born, a man would think he would have had a place fit for his birth; the glorious heaven would not have been amiss for this purpose, and therefore if Mary had been assumed into it beforehand, as they say she was afterwards, there to have brought him forth, it had been somewhat like himself. Or if not there, because he must have come down upon the earth howsoever, yet the city of the great King, the city of David, would have done well; for we use to say that the place doth not a little dignify the birth; and therefore St. Paul knew how well it would do to say that he was born at Tarsus, a famous and a noble city in Cilicia. But now in little Bethlem, one of the out and despised cities, was Christ content to be born in; and there, not in a palace, or any house of his own, or his mother's either, but in an inn among the common people. In an inn? No, I was mistaken, there was no room for him there; it was in the stable among the common beasts, and no soft couch spread for him there neither. It was even in a cold hard cratch,[6] in a very corner of the stable too. . . . him whom the heaven of heavens could not contain before, to be thus pent up: this was humility, lowliness to the height.

And now we are come to the top of the ladder. For besides his immortality and immensity, which ye see these two, "born" and "born at Bethlem," have humbled well enough, he had other attributes to be brought low too: his eternity first, and then his power.

3. So we make the third step to be "in the days": when Jesus was born at Bethlem in the days. . . . yet it was in the night time, and in the winter time besides. For the winter, our yearly observation of the feast will tell us it was so; and for the night, St. Luke saith, it was when the shepherds were keeping their flocks by night, as you may read in his Gospel. Now the day time might have afforded some comfort, or the summer time at least might have helped the nakedness of his tender body; but in a cold winter night to be born, there his charity was hot, that was fervent love indeed.

4. But it is not *in diebus* only, but *in diebus Herodis*, in the days of Herod the King, and that is a degree further, the fourth step: to have his power made subject to a tyrant. He that was the head of all, it was strange to have him live under any power, or if under any, yet not under a wicked and a cruel tyrant. If he must needs have a king over him, it would have been good to have had such a one as Pharaoh was to Joseph, or Ahasuerus to Esther, or Darius to Daniel; but to have another Pharaoh arise, that knew him not, and in his time to be born, and to have a Herod that would make a howling over all Rama but he would kill him, and then to come, this was more strange than all the rest. And yet, now I think of it, *in diebus Herodis* was a very fit time for him; it was time he should come, for the scepter was gone from Judah, and Christ must come to the Jews. As long as

[6] {feeding trough for animals}

it tarried there, God's prophets were enough to be sent; but when it came under strangers once, and under Herod, a cruel and wicked king, when the law of God was held in unrighteousness, then it was a just time for the Just One, the Son of God, to come; none could recover the kingdom but he, and he went a strange way about it. If he had not told us that his kingdom was not of this world, we might have wondered at it, and so we do still, to go no further than the text; for who would have been born in Jewry at such a time as he must presently run into Egypt before he could go alone. This was to add misery upon misery, one degree upon another, till he came to the highest pitch of humility. Count we: immortality itself made a mortal man, *natus*, the first step; immortality confined within a cratch, *natus in Bethlem*, the second; eternity measured by time, *in diebus*, the third; power made subject to tyranny, *in diebus Herodis regis*, the fourth. By this time we are come to the very top of the ladder.

Where we may stand and see, not the angels descending, as Jacob did, but the Son of God himself descending from the bosom of his Father to the womb of his mother, from heaven to earth, and this was the ladder he made for us to go up to heaven by; for unless he had come down, we should never have gone up. Whither he came with all his lowliness but to lead us up again, and to tell us that here was nothing to be looked for, here below; for if there had, the Wise Men today lost their labor in seeking him out for a king. And therefore he lifts up their eyes to heaven, to the bright star there; which, for all his lowliness here, gave them to understand that he had a kingdom in a better world. And thus we see how this ladder hath brought us from earth to heaven. But yet before we meddle with the star, because *Ecce Magi* stands first in the text, we will come to them first, and that shall be my order in the rest, howsoever the division went;[7] and now we are at *opus diei*, the proper text of the day. I have made a preparation, you see, to it, as St. Matthew did, that we might all account it the more solemn.

And first of all, we cannot but take notice of this same *Ecce*, Behold. It is a word set up for the nonce, a mark set up in our journey to Jerusalem, and it hath two faces, two uses in the text, one to make us look backwards, and another to make us look forwards; backwards to a word, if ye mark it, that we have left out all this while, *Cum*, "When" Christ was born; and forwards to all the rest, "Behold, when he was born there came Wise Men from the East to Jerusalem." Then, and not before, that is the first; and again, though not before, yet then, that is the second. So it hath two fingers, we see, to point backwards, first, *cum natus*, "when he was born" "they came," *venerunt*, and not before; for as long as there was nothing to be heard of but wrath and indignation upon the heathen, there was no coming to God, but like children that had heavily offended their father, were naturally fearful to come near so long; nay, as long as Peter considers himself a sinful man, Christ must not come near him neither; and Adam must hide himself in the bushes. Men with all their sins about them cannot endure to come near God; and therefore while he sent his Son to be born, that should save men from their sins, there was no encouragement to come. But now, *cum natus*, once, the second thing, then, *Ecce Magi*, Behold, the Wise Men came presently. Now, saith your new translation, instantly upon his birth they came, and go we and celebrate the day so. And so the publicans in the Gospel; they knew not,

---

[7] {This changing of course mid-stream, plus the occasional syntactic looseness, suggests that the text is based on a shorthand transcript of the sermon as preached.}

poor men, what they should think of themselves as long as the Pharisees were accounted the *ipses* of the age, and they but *iste publicanus* and *haec mulier*. But when they saw Christ keep company with them, and send into the hedges and contemned places for the halt and the heathen, then they began to take heart; then, saith St. Luke, drew near unto him all the publicans and sinners. So, though we were afraid before, yet when we hear God say once, "As I live, I will not the death of a sinner," and Christ, that there is room yet at supper for them which sat at the land's end in corners and hedges, that breeds some comfort. And so when God spake to us by the Law, the thunder and lightning was so big as we durst not come near the mountain; but since in these last days he hath spoken to us by his Son, since the lightning was turned into a bright star that told us a Savior was born to-day, *cum natus esset Jesus*, then we come from the East, from the world's end to seek him. And so much for the first use of this *Ecce*, which sent us two ways backwards by the relation it had with the word "when."

But the chief use of it is to make us look forwards, for there we have most to behold. "Behold, Wise Men came from the East to Jerusalem." *Ecce*, as if he should tell us that it was no ordinary matter, but a thing well worth our marking, more than we commonly take it for. . . . *Ecce Magi*. Indeed no small matter, that the Magi of the East, the gentiles, should come to Christ, and that the star should enlighten them that sit in darkness. For what hath light to do with darkness, saith the Apostle, *aut quae participatio est justitae cum iniquitate?*[8] What, should holy things be cast unto dogs? Or what should soothsayers do amongst the prophets, and profane diviners with the holy divinity of Christ? Sure this is a strange mystery, worth the attending and listening to, worth the going out to see. *Ecce Magi*, behold the magicians of the East. It was nothing such a wonder that the angels came down from heaven to worship him; they were always used to it before; and though it was a strange thing that the rude, ignorant shepherds should come and acknowledge God come in the flesh, yet much more marvelous was it that such men as these Magi, *sacrilegi et malifeci*, as St. Austin calls them, and tutored by the devil, as St. Hierome speaks, *cultores idolorum et divini nominis hostes*,[9] as St. Basil, St. Ambrose, and some other of the Fathers make them; for them to come and acknowledge the Son of God, as poorly as he lay, this was beyond an ordinary miracle. Or whether these Magi were such kind of men or no, or but only so called for their admirable wisdom and learning, or their account above other people, as the *philosophi* were among the Grecians, and the *sapientes* and *doctores* among the Latins, which is St. Chrysostom's and Anselm's and Bede's opinion, besides many other both of ancient and modern writers, and which is the fairest sense for us to follow, seeing our own Church hath gone before us in it, and translated it so, "Behold, Wise Men," I say if they were but thus, yet gentiles they were, remote from God's covenant, even as far as the ends of the earth were from Jerusalem, the east from the west; and therefore St. Matthew might well set an *Ecce* upon it, and bid us wonder how they should come thither. *Ecce venerunt Magi*.

I will not now trouble myself and you both, as many do, to tell you how many of these Magi there were, three, or more; or to tell you a tale out of Petrus de Palude[10] how,

---

[8] {what relation has justice to iniquity}

[9] {worshipers of idols and enemies to the divine name}

[10] {Early 14th-century Dominican theologian. The reference is to his *Sermones thesauri novi de sanctis* which went through many editions.}

being kings at first, they left that office for St. Thomas to make them all archbishops in their country . . . and what their names were besides all this. These kind of speculations will do us little stead, which way soever they go. Yet for their number, as I would not be too curious to search, so I would not be too boisterous to condemn and think everything popery that we read not in the text. It hath been a very ancient tradition (Leo hath it in his sermons), and perhaps at the first they had better reason for it than we know of now. And for their dignity, whether they were kings or no, I cannot tell; yet Tertullian says (and Tully likewise before him) they would have no other kings there but magi, such as these were; and it hath been an old custom of the Church (howsoever our new masters deride it) to apply that saying in the Psalms, "The kings of Tharsis and of the isles shall bring gifts" [Ps. 72:10] and that in Isaiah, "The gentiles shall walk in thy light, and kings at the brightness of thy rising up" [Is. 60:3]—to these Wise Men.[11] Kings! Why doth not St. Matthew call them so then? There may be reason for that. It more concerns us and God too, to have Christ acknowledged by the wise than by any king whatsoever; and perhaps he would teach us by it that the greatest honor we can have is to be wise men (it is a good use for us to make of it, at least):

> Regem non faciunt opes . . . .
> Rex est qui posuit metus
> Et diri mala pectoris.[12]
> > [Seneca, *Thyestes*, Chorus in Act 2]

Herod indeed, he might afford him the name of a king well enough, it was the only thing he had to stand upon; but for them that had wisdom to commend them, and came to worship him that had no kingdom of this world, it was no great matter to tell of their kingdoms. Herod, we know, made so much of his crown that rather than it should off he would murder all the coasts about him; whereas they contemned theirs so much (if they had any) that they took them off themselves and threw them at Christ's feet. So that they might be kings, for all St. Matthew calls them not so; or if not kings, as the tradition and some authority goes, yet all stories will make them the nobles and great ones of their country, men of no small account, as likely to be kings, such as they had in these parts, as any else.

And here now we may set up the *Ecce* again. *Ecce Magi*. Not men of mean condition, the outcasts of the people, or poor pilgrims that had little else to do, but men of authority and rule where they were, men famous besides for their knowledge, whose books to look on were as large as the heavens. *Reguli*[13] at least, if not *reges*, came from the East to Jerusalem, great men, the unlikeliest of any to take so much pains for devotion; more ready, a man would think, as these times go, to take their pleasure at home than to go upon pilgrimage abroad; to attend the world than to go and worship him that had nothing of it. And yet, great ones as they were, they came for all that, to tell us, first, who should come after, how the only way to be great is to be little, lowly before God the only way to be

---

[11] {Calvin's commentary on Isaiah 60:2-3 (*vide* the appendix following this sermon) vividly illustrates the difference between Cosin's theology and that of the "new masters."}

[12] {Riches do not make one a king. . . . He is a king who has put fear aside, and the evils of a cruel heart.}

[13] {princes, petty kings}

accounted kings, to be servants, to come and worship God; which we acknowledge every day in our Church service, *cui servire regnare est*, as the old collect goes, "whose service is perfect freedom," that is a kingdom right. And then to watch besides, that godliness and greatness would do well together, the king's house and God's house joined close to one another, for the more honor of both. The great ones of our age take journeys too, but it is for another purpose, not for religion's sake. Yes, saith St. John, I saw him riding upon a brave horse, but Death and Hell were his companions. Be we then what we will be, rich, or wise, or great, we had need take care where we go, for fear of such companions by the way. The best way will be to follow those Magi, even in their way to Christ; and then we shall not have darkness and death, but God's Spirit and a star in heaven go along with us.

But before we can go any further in the pilgrimage, there is a stop by the way, and that is one that asks us why these gentiles come so late? Why not they, learned and quick men, as soon as the ignorant and dull shepherds? We might say that the East was further off a great deal than the next field; but howsoever, sure I am that the Jews were nearer to God than the gentiles; we were all strangers to the covenant, *et ergo* (says one) *qui remotiores erant a foedere tardius accesserunt*;[14] and the Gospel ought first to come to you, saith St. Paul to the Jews. Therefore came the Magi last. And then (because there are more questions) Christ was not manifested to the learned, but the ignorant Jews; nor to the religious and just men of the time, but to the sinful gentiles; *nec doctis, nec justis* (saith St. Austin) *quippe qui venerat stulta eligere ut confunderet sapientes*,[15] and not to call the righteous but sinners to repentance. Therefore came the Magi, sinful men. And lastly: he was made known to the Jews in the persons of shepherds, and to the gentiles in the persons of great men, that we might know how the chief pastors and ministers of Christ's Church should come from the Jews, as St. Peter and the rest of the apostles; but the chief defenders of it, kings and princes, they should come out of the gentiles, as indeed they did. Therefore came the Magi, great men.

And now the way is clear, I go on. *Ecce Magi venerunt*. "Came." So the persons we have done with all, and now we are at their full pilgrimage. "Came from the East." And here we will go apace, for we have a great way yet to Christ, the end of their journey and of my text. I am afraid it will grow late before I shall get half way.

. . .

"From the East." Not from the next door, or a town hard by, but *à longe*, even from far, even as the Ethiopian in the Acts (whom some think they sent afterwards) came from the ends of the earth to worship at Jerusalem. A hard journey sure they had, saith St. Chrysostom,[16] for besides the long way there were huge mountains and horrid deserts, great floods and rivers to pass, wild beasts and (what is more) beastly and wild men to pass by. And yet by all these difficulties they came, even from the East to Jerusalem.

---

[14] {And therefore . . . those who were more distant from the covenant arrived later.}

[15] {nor, to be sure, to the learned or to the just . . . who came to choose the foolish and to confound the wise}

[16] {The similarities between Cosin's sermon and Lancelot Andrewes' famous sermon on the coming of the Magi, preached eleven months later (unless the 1621 date of this sermon is Old Style, in which case the sermon was preached in 1622, just a month after Andrews' sermon on the journey of the Magi) bespeak their shared debt to Chrysostom's sixth homily on Matthew (see /www.ccel.org/ccel/schaff/npnf110 .VI_1.html).}

Now what a shame was it for the Jews which were round about him, that the gentiles from the East should come to seek Christ, and they sit secure and idle at home, never enquiring after him. Or rather what a far worse shame is it for us, which be Christians now . . . yet we stir but at our leisure; the least business, if it be but a little more desire of sleep, will hinder us; and if we be seated but a little way off once, why then Jeroboam's counsel is very good, it is too much to go up to Jerusalem. These Wise Men here shall not have our company by the mountains and deserts, we are more tenderly brought up. By them? No! Not through a shower of rain. (Nay, if it rains we will not go to church.) Our ordinary sleep or the beams of the sun will keep some of us in, so dainty we are that we cannot endure it truly; and if no body else will go, Christ may comfort himself with his mother's arms, for we have neither worship, nor gold, nor frankincense, nothing for him. A greater offence, sure, than we use to make of it. These men of the East shall rise up in judgment, nay many more shall come from the East, and from the West, and sit with Christ one day, to tell us as much. But as we go along, there is another yet that meets us, to ask, why from the East? There were gentiles in the North and South too, why not from them as well, but from the East alone? Marry, best of all from hence, it suits well to make even with Eve in Paradise, that as from the East came the first news of sin, so from thence should come the first news of saving us from sin; and to make even with Balaam too, that as he came *a montibus Orientis*,[17] to curse God's people, so these Magi (that some say were his scholars far removed) should come *ab Oriente* too, to bless all the generations of the gentiles after them. And indeed, from whence should they come but from the East? *Omnes qui veniunt ad Christum*, saith Remigius, must come *ab Ipso*, from him first; now he is the true day-spring—*Oriens nomen ejus* &c.—as Zecharias speaks.

Then this was the beginning of our bliss, the very morning of our happiness; and therefore, as the morning and day begin, so began that, *ab Oriente*, from the East both; and then because the sun follows the day in the East too, it was most fit that such as brought us news of the Sun of Righteousness, the light that lightens every man which cometh into the world, should come from thence too. And if ye mark it, it was the most glorious sun that arose here of the two—the sun in the firmament being but a created body; this, he that made that so; that to lighten the body, and this to illuminate the mind. And now since we have begun to compare him with the sun, we will make it good every way; for as he rose here in the East among the gentiles, so he set in the West among the Jews. . . . And by this time we are come to Jerusalem.

"Behold there came Wise Men from the East to Jerusalem"; so their coming was like the sun's too, from east to west, and west was Jerusalem right, for it was full of darkness, they had almost lost their light, it was even a-going out, and *ergo* time for a Sun to rise out of the East, which might give light to them that were sitting in the dark West, the shadow of death.

But to let pass the allegory (which indeed should never be strained too far), they came to Jerusalem; but why thither? Christ was at Bethlehem. Oh, but this was the great city, "the city of the great King," and most like they should find the king they sought for there. Yet there he was not, and I told you the reason before. Then why came they? Marry, for

---

[17] {from the mountains of the East}

many reasons; there was first the Law and the Prophets, and God will have them looked in, even in the very search of his Son—to let us know the true way to him, and to eternal life (as Christ himself speaks) was by the Scriptures. . . . And then again here were the *Ipses* of the time, the Scribes and Pharisees and masters of the Law, that would have scorned to have been told of their new-born king by a company of silly shepherds, or to have searched the Prophets for them {*sic*}. And therefore it was fit the princes and great men of the East, since they were now a-coming, should go by the way to Jerusalem to bring these master-Jews[18] the news of their king; for how contemptible soever the shepherds' relation would have been, yet when such men came as the world admired for their wisdom and greatness, and came from far too, from the East, not likely to come in vain, it was like they would receive their testimony. But whatsoever a man would think, yet we see that they believed nothing, not one of them would go to Bethlehem to worship with the Magi. . . . But yet, as ill as they were, God would have the Magi to come that way, for to teach us one lesson more, and that is that, *omnia non manifestantur omnibus*,[19] and therefore they must come this way to ask what they knew not, where Christ was born. In the search of holy things we stand in need of great help, and since we cannot know all of ourselves, we must learn one of another: the Jews of the Magi, that there was a King born, and they of the Jews where he should be born. And last of all, to shew that this was the time when the Jew and gentile should come together, and be no longer parted; but since the King of Peace was come, that they should enter into peace too, teach one another the way to Christ. And therefore this was the right way they took, the way of peace, the way that Christ would have them, who is the Way himself; so they came from the East to Jerusalem, the "city of peace" too, and this was right to guide their feet in the way of peace.

And now we have followed them thus far, and are come along with them to Jerusalem; fain would we see what they do there, and so go along with them to Bethlehem too. But it is even fallen out as I told you I feared before, it is grown late before we can go any further, and therefore best staying here, for if we should go on, there be so many steps to be taken in the way that the night would overtake us ere we should get to the text's end. But all the day must not be spent in preaching; and therefore since we are at Jerusalem, the city of peace, crying "Glory be to God on high, and peace on earth," let us take the peace of God along with us and so depart for this time.

Now the peace of God which passeth all understanding, keep our hearts and minds in the knowledge and love of God, and of his Son Jesus Christ our Lord, that was this day made known unto us, and the blessing of God Almighty, the Father, the Son, and the Holy Ghost, be among us, and remain with us always. Amen.

TEXT: *The works of the Right Reverend Father in God, John Cosin*, vol. 1 (Oxford: John Henry Parker, 1842), 1–23.

[18] {The phrase seems to pick up the earlier references to "our new [Calvinist] masters" and to the godly tradesmen who "have a tribe and a calling by themselves"—the hostile portrait of puritan-as-Judaizer best known from Jonson's Rabbi Busy.}

[19] {all things are not disclosed to all persons}

APPENDIX
Calvin on Isaiah 60:2-3

60:2 *For, behold, darkness shall cover the earth.* He now exhibits in a stronger light, by means of comparison, that grace which he formerly mentioned, that we may form some idea how much God loves his elect, and how extraordinary is the privilege which he bestows upon them. The amount of what he says is that, while we are weighed down by innumerable afflictions and while the whole world, as it were, sinks under them, God will take care of his people in order to enrich them with various benefits. He shews, therefore, that the light of grace and favor which he mentioned will not be indiscriminately enjoyed by all, but will be peculiar to the people of God. . . .

Secondly, it ought to be observed that the Church alone, that is, the elect of God, are partakers of this brightness. Hence it follows that it is not a common or natural gift, but a gift by which the Lord relieves us from an ordinary defect of human nature. Thus also we perceive that there is no light or brightness but in the Church; for the rest of men, though they think that they enjoy light and brightness, are overwhelmed by darkness, from which they cannot be extricated in any other way than by the light of the Gospel.

And his glory shall be seen upon thee. He adds the word "glory" because, after having embraced us by his favor, the Lord continues more and more to increase his acts of kindness toward us.

60:3 *And the gentiles shall walk.* He confirms what we have already said, that there is no other light of men but when the Lord shines on them by his word. All indeed acknowledge this, but they do not set so high a value as they ought on this benefit, and imagine it to be something of an ordinary kind which naturally belongs to all men. But he shews that this grace is supernatural, and therefore it ought to be distinguished from nature, which is clearly shewn by the repetition of the words *upon thee* in the preceding verse.

First, then, we ought to believe that this benefit comes from God alone; and secondly, that all are not indiscriminately partakers of it, but only the elect, on whom the Lord shines by undeserved favor, so as to take them out of the ordinary rank of men. This is done by Christ, who is called "the Sun of Righteousness" because we are enlightened as if by his rays (Mal. 4:2). Besides, the Prophet declares that this favor shall be spread far and wide by the Jews; which is also intimated by the words of the covenant, "In thy seed shall all nations be blessed" (Gen. 22:18).

TEXT: John Calvin, *Commentary on the Book of the Prophet Isaiah*, trans. William Pringle (Edinburgh, 1854).

JOHN PRESTON
(1587–1628)

The son of a Northamptonshire farmer, Preston owed his early education to the generosity a wealthy uncle. He entered King's College, Cambridge, in 1604, intending to study music; within two years, however, he had migrated to Queen's and natural philosophy. He received his BA in 1608, a fellowship in 1609, and his MA in 1611. His conversion took place ca. 1611–12 during a sermon preached by John Cotton (then of Emmanuel, later of New England).[1] Preston's studies shifted to divinity, and he was ordained in 1614. His first minute of fame came in 1615 when, before the King and assembled University, he argued the famous disputation on whether dogs can make syllogisms. Despite offers of court preferment, he remained at Cambridge, although almost losing his fellowship in 1620 (the same year he took his BD) on charges of non-conformity. Preston, however, averted catastrophe by preaching in defense of the Prayer Book. His rise to prominence began shortly thereafter. A sermon preached before James in 1621 (the *Plenitudo fontis* reprinted below) garnered royal approbation for its intertwined defense of Calvinism, set prayer, and individual responsibility. He also won Buckingham's patronage and the post of chaplain-in-ordinary to Prince Charles. In the same year, Ussher sought to have Preston come to Dublin as Trinity's professor of theological controversies, but this he declined. A year later, however, he took John Donne's place as preacher to Lincoln's Inn, whose chapel was in the process of being refurbished with glorious stained-glass windows. Neither Preston nor anyone else seems to have disapproved.[2] His moderate puritan credentials remained unquestioned, and a few months after taking up the Lincoln's Inn post, he was also appointed master of Cambridge's unswervingly Calvinist Emmanuel College. Preston continued to enjoy Buckingham's support, especially since both men now backed military intervention in the Palatinate crisis. James, however, may have begun to have reservations about his son's chaplain, since in 1624 he apparently tried to block Preston's appointment as lecturer at Holy Trinity, Cambridge. Nonetheless, in 1625 Joseph Mede

---

[1] On Cotton, see the introduction to the 1619 Sanderson sermon <*supra*>.
[2] The chapel was consecrated Ascension Day, 1623, Donne preaching.

describes Preston as enjoying the King's "special favor." Under Charles, Preston's influence at court rapidly waned. At the York House Conference of 1626, where Preston defended the Calvinist position against Montagu and Cosin, it became evident that Buckingham favored the other side.[3] Shortly thereafter Preston helped organize the feoffees for impropriations, which, had it not been dissolved, would have supported a Calvinist preaching ministry largely beyond ecclesiastical control. By 1627 Preston's health was failing. He died in 1628 at the age of forty-one, the venerable old puritan, John Dod, ministering to him in his final illness.

After Preston's death, volume after volume of his sermons poured from the press (see Moore 230–55).[4] I have allotted considerable space to these sermons on the grounds of both literary merit and historical significance, reprinting not only the 1621 sermon that launched his public career but also three undated sermons that almost certainly belong to the mid-1620s.[5] Preston was an extraordinary preacher. Many on both sides of the Atlantic credited their spiritual awakening to his sermons, whose attention to "the inward motions of the human heart . . . [was] critical in establishing a new spiritual genre of protestant devotional publications" (*ODNB*). Their doctrine-and-use format and avoidance of mannerism or conspicuous artifice belong to the puritan plain style, yet they are scarcely low-keyed, but rather vivid, dramatic, and affective—heirs of the Augustine's powerful and passionate *sermo humilis*.

Moreover, Preston stood at the intersection of multiple circles of power, patronage, and piety. His closeness to Buckingham throughout the early 1620s has already been noted. As his role in the York House Conference suggests, he was the perceived spokesman for the puritan party at court. His aristocratic friends compose a "nominal roll of the Puritan opposition": the earls of Warwick, Lincoln, Pembroke, Bedford; his executor, Lord Saye and Seal; the second Lord Brooke, Sir Henry Mildmay, Henry Lawrence, and Lady Vere. As preacher to Lincoln's Inn, Preston also had ties to leading common lawyers; Prynne, a Lincoln's Inn man, was his disciple and, for some of the sermon collections, his editor. The Inns of Court were, of course, the usual training ground for MPs, and Christopher Hill notes that "the leadership of Parliament in the early sixteen-forties was largely in the hands of . . . the Preston group" (221). Along with these ties to court and city, Preston had extensive Cambridge connections—he was master of Emmanuel from 1622 until his death—connections that included old-school moderate puritans like Chaderton but also champions of the "softer" Calvinism espoused by the British delegation at Dort. Yet, despite Preston's multi-pronged institutional grounding, some of his deepest personal and spiritual bonds lay with non-conformist and semi-conformist godly ministers on the fringes of the established Church like Dod, Cotton, and Hildersham.

Preston spoke to and shaped the Calvinism of the court, the Inns, Parliament, and the universities. The "effectual leader of moderate puritanism" (Ford 43), he binds together,

---

[3] On the York House Conference, see Moore 141–69; Barbara Donagan, "The York House Conference revisited: laymen, Calvinism and Arminianism," *Bulletin of Historical Research* 64/155 (1991): 312–31.

[4] In response to a specific request, Preston sometimes wrote out one of his sermons, but the manuscripts seem to have been mostly stenographic transcripts (Moore 231).

[5] For the purposes of this volume, these undated sermons have been allocated to the gray area between 1624 and 1625.

both in his personal ties and theological positioning, the conformist and pastoral mainstream of early Stuart Calvinism with its more radical and politicized currents.

The sermons themselves interweave the dominant motifs characterizing the several strands of English Reformed spirituality. One finds in them the standard topoi of high Calvinist theology: the stress on God's glory and sovereignty, the distinction between the revealed and secret divine will, the irresistibility of grace, and the possibility—even "absolute necessity"—of reaching assurance of one's election.[6] Preston's conviction that our principal duty in this world is "to make our calling and election sure" (Moore 21n) locates him more specifically within the experimental predestinarian framework that Perkins inherited from Beza. Although he will echo Calvin's insistence that we are to look to Christ crucified for our assurance, Preston generally adopts the experimentalists' call to reflexivity, grounding assurance of redemption on the evidence of regeneration. Those on whom the Spirit has bestowed saving faith can and do "infallibly" know, by the very existence of such faith within their hearts, that God has loved them from all eternity <*Riches* 426>.[7] Indeed, Preston adds, by affirming the infallibility of assurance, Reformed teaching proves its superiority to Romish doctrine, which denies that one can ever be certain of God's favor and thus inculcates doubt and anxiety rather than joyous comfort of the Protestant elect. One notes that this infallible certainty granted true believers performs a role similar to the infallibility with which Tridentine theology invests the Church (*vide* Carier <*supra*> and Digby <*infra*>). Both wings of the Reformation divide, that is, rest on the claim to have anchored faith to truth by some unbreakable chain. The distinctiveness of "high-church" theology from Hooker through the Restoration lies precisely in its denial of any infallible certainties, individual or institutional, underwriting belief.[8]

In listing the signs of election, Preston puts charity and outward works at the bottom <*Riches*>. We are not to look to our actions for the workings of grace, but within: to our purity of motive, strength of faith, sincerity of repentance, humbling before the Law, and zeal for God's glory. Like so much else, Preston inherits this focus on affective interiority, together with his delicate and probing spiritual psychology, from Elizabethan puritanism; his friend and colleague, Laurence Chaderton, had been part of the Cambridge brotherhood that created its language of pastoral divinity—the language of Preston's colloquy with the "poor soul in the midst of his fear, temptations and troubles of mind" <*Riches* 421>.[9]

As the foregoing indicates, the continuities binding Preston to Elizabethan puritanism run deep (and to those mentioned, one might also add the Law-to-Gospel patterning of spiritual life and his contempt for the prayer-book piety of "common Christians"). Yet, his sermons also exemplify Calvinism's new and softer cutting-edge. This modification

---

[6] See Moore 72–78. All these motifs are multiply exemplified in the sermons that follow, although only page numbers of direct quotations will be given.

[7] (Except for *Plenitudo*, which follows this introduction, Preston's sermons are postponed to their 1624–25 approximate date.)

[8] See the introduction to Laud <*infra*>; Krook xii, 9; Shuger, "Faith and assurance."

[9] See Peter Ivor Kaufman, *Prayer, despair, and drama: Elizabethan introspection* (U Illinois P, 1996); Kenneth Parker and Eric Carlson, *Practical divinity: the works and life of Revd Richard Greenham* (Ashgate, 1998); Richard Greenham, *Two treatises of the comforting of an afflicted conscience* (London, 1598); and Richard Greenham, William Perkins, et al., *A garden of spiritual flowers* (London, 1625). Preston shares this focus on affective interiority with his fellow-minister at the Inns of Court, Richard Sibbes <*infra*>.

of predestinarian theology in response to anti-Calvinist objections <*vide* Hoard *infra*>, which Preston shares with Ussher, Davenant, and the British delegation at Dort, abandons the limited Atonement of Elizabethan Calvinism (the claim that Christ died only for the elect) in favor of the hypothetical universalist position that Christ died for all, but only those few whom God in his mercy elects out of the justly condemned mass of humankind receive the irresistible quickening grace that enables them to accept this universally-offered redemption. This is the single predestination of the Thirty-nine Articles (and Aquinas); there is only one divine decree: that which predestines some for eternal life. Those not chosen are simply left to continue in their wickedness and unbelief.

This hypothetical universalism provides the framework for Preston's massively influential covenant theology, which proposed a double covenant of grace, one covenant being general and conditional (if you believe, you shall be saved), the other particular and absolute, in which God promises his elect the ability to believe. The effect, and almost certainly the point, of covenant theology was to stress moral effort and responsibility, thus rebutting charges that Calvinism promoted an antinomian fatalism (*vide* Hoard <736, 760>, Dow <885–86>). The non-elect end up in hell not because of any decree but because they fail to perform the terms of the conditional covenant; without grace, they of course cannot perform them, but they cannot because they will not. The elect, conversely, are those who, enabled by grace, love and labor for the things of God.

Preston's double covenant also has ecclesiological implications. Preston himself seems to have been a full conformist. *Plenitudo fontis* defends the Church's authority with respect to outward worship. Yet Preston also makes the Church strangely irrelevant. All the baptized, reprobates included, are within the general covenant, allowing Preston to describe baptism as spousal union with Christ, even though his "evangelical theology tells him that this is not truly the case with most Englishmen" (Moore 135–36). For Preston, baptism cannot impart remission of sins, for the sins of reprobates are not remitted, nor can any of the Church's sacraments convey effectual grace, since reprobates do not receive such grace. Preaching retains a crucial function as the principal means God uses to draw his elect to himself, but the sacraments and ceremonies of the Church—and even the Church itself—pertain only to the general covenant. As far as salvation is concerned, they seem a fifth wheel.

Preston binds together the central concerns and claims of the English Reformed tradition, but he binds them not into a theological system but into sermons. The genre matters, for sermons function rhetorically; the point is to move one's hearers: to cast down and raise up, threaten and console, terrify and comfort. They are not lectures but catalysts of grace—like rain that, if it falls "upon valleys and fruitful places," germinates new life <*Plenitudo* 283>; like the rain that falls on Herbert's flower, alternately "killing and quick'ning, bringing down to hell / And up to heaven in an hour." Those who attain true faith must first experience "the curse of the Law and condemnation" <*Riches* 426>, but for those cast down, there is promise of infinite treasure, "arms-full and laps-full and baskets-full" <*Plenitudo* 285>.[10] The sermons thus interlace promise and consolation with urgent

---

[10] See Susan Snyder, "The left hand of God: despair in medieval and Renaissance tradition," *Studies in the Renaissance* 12 (1965): 18–59, esp. 23–31.

warnings to repent, to seize the moment of grace, to "hear how the damned souls in hell that neglected and refused grace do roar, yell and howl, that now would give worlds if they had them, to enjoy the time that the Lord affords thee to repent" *<Riches* 431>. The passages of comfort tend to be sweepingly inclusive hymns of wonder at the liberality of grace and Christ's love for poor sinners, whose glorious pictures of unearned mercy offered freely to all comers make one see why this sort of evangelical Protestantism proved so compelling. The passages of terror, insofar as they address individual congregants, are (or were meant to be) likewise compelling, the stick, no less than the carrot, having conversion for its end. Yet insofar as they address the congregation qua group, they enforce division and exclusion. "Triumphing faith," Preston informs them, "is so far from being a common gift to all that but few indeed have it" *<Riches* 425>. Those parishioners who neglect the preacher's offer of grace, which all but the elect invariably do, betray themselves to be, not imperfect fellow-Christians, but "reprobates that live in the Church," whose punishment for spurning mercy "shall exceed [that of] the devils in hell" (*<Riches* 443>, see also Moore 136n).

There is nothing singular about any of this. The divisive edge to godly preaching has long been noted. That Preston insists that the fault is ours if we refuse the mercy available to all, while simultaneously holding that grace is irresistible and for the elect alone, registers a tension suffusing late Jacobean Calvinism. Indeed, the tension may go back to the Elizabethan glory days of high Calvinism; the sermons of puritan icons like Chaderton, Perkins, and Whitaker hardly mention reprobation, but instead speak as though people could act differently, and if they did so, God's response would alter accordingly (Lake 151–53). The rhetorical dynamics and opposing pulls that characterize Preston's preaching embody tensions informing Reformed divinity since the mid-sixteenth century.

In part, these are tensions specific to Calvinism, yet to cordon off the Reformed tradition from other forms of early modern Christianity can be misleading. The Arminian Samuel Hoard also mingles celebrations of divine mercy with rhetorical terror tactics <757, 761–62>.[11] Other unresolved tensions in Preston's sermons likewise trace fault lines cutting across the early Stuart Church, particularly regarding what might be called perfectionism or rigorism: whether, for example, the *condition* for our forgiveness is that we first make "our hearts perfect to God in all things" *<Plenitudo* 280>. At times Preston sets the bar extraordinarily high; the sermons reprinted in this volume maintain (at one point or another) that, in the truly regenerate, grace replaces nature; and hence the elect, free from self-interest and by-ends, serve God for his glory's sake alone and with a pure heart; they have assurance of their salvation; they are transformed into wholly new creatures.[12] Yet the same sermons elsewhere present mixed motives, imperfect faith, and "selfness" as inseparable from the human condition; we are urged to seek Christ "in regard of the wages which are to come," and told that no one ever seeks unless persuaded that Christ will provide better for him then he can for himself *<Riches* 433>. Similar ambivalences suffuse the writings of Joseph Hall, another moderate Calvinist, but they also surface in

---

[11] As, often, does John Donne (see Debora Shuger, *Habits of thought* [U California P, 1991], 159–217); Jean Delumeau finds much the same in Catholic France in his *Sin and fear: the emergence of a Western guilt culture, 13th–18th centuries*, trans. Eric Nicholson (St. Martin's Press, 1990).

[12] Such passages, one notes, sound much like John Everard's antinomian perfectionism *<vide infra>*.

the anti-Calvinists Hales and Shelford <*vide infra*> and in seventeenth-century French Catholicism. They register an emergent discomfort with classical eudemonism, harbinger of the shift from virtue-ethics to rule-based morality, both Kantian and fundamentalist.[13] The tensions and ambivalences regarding perfectionism also, however, register a more unexpected discomfort with classic Augustinianism. Augustine opposed Pelagianism, as he had earlier opposed Donatism, *because* of its perfectionist implications; as Peter Brown writes in his magisterial *Augustine of Hippo*, Pelagius' message was "simple and terrifying: since perfection is possible for man, it is obligatory"; the Pelagian true Church is a communion of saints, with no second tier for the "conventional 'good Christian'" (342, 346). Augustine, however, "was in no mood to tolerate the *coteries* of 'perfect' Christians, that had sprung up . . . under Pelagian influence. For this reason, the victory of Augustine over Pelagius was also a victory for the average good Catholic layman . . . over an austere, reforming ideal" (348). For all their intense hostility to Pelagianism, numerous Calvinists, Preston included, apparently had serious misgivings about Augustine's victory in this instance.[14]

Plenitudo fontis was the sermon preached before James in 1621 that brought Preston to the attention of the court. It is the only one of Preston's sermons with obvious textual problems. The early printed editions (1639, 1640) lack the anti-Arminianism passages that first appear in 1644, and then again in the 1645 text reprinted below. Since the sermon predates the 1622 proclamation against handling the deep points of predestination, there seems no reason to doubt that the passages were part of the original sermon. The 1645 preface claims they were removed by Caroline censors, although John Strafford, for whom all four editions were printed, later blamed the cuts on the printer of the 1639 version (Moore 238–39). The preface to the 1640 edition raises a third possibility: that an individual copyist had redacted the sermon according to his own theological lights. However the changes occurred, they involve only cuts, not additions, a distinction that becomes significant in light of the 1645 preface's charge that the redacted text turned Preston into an Arminian. The charge is not without merit. The sermon's emphasis on the necessity of our labor, its promise that mercy is there for all who will receive it, the exhortations to seize the offer of grace could bespeak Arminianism (although "mere Christianity" might be a better label). The passages restored in 1644 are obviously and explicitly Calvinist, but they also proved to be surprisingly detachable.

---

[13] See Burnaby 272–97, who traces the discomfort back to Scotus; also Alastair McIntyre, *After virtue: a study in moral theory* (U Notre Dame P, 1981).

[14] George Gifford's 1582 *Country divinity* and Arthur Dent's 1601 *Plain-man's pathway* center on a godly minister proving to a good, conventional Protestant layman that his religion is worthless. Arminius' commentary on Romans 7, however, also betrays perfectionist tendencies, see the introduction to Michael Sparke's *Crumbs*, n. 4 <*infra*>; and John Bossy observes similar leanings in the Catholic Reformation, inspired by the austere reforming ideals of Carlo Borromeo (*Peace in the post-Reformation* 1–71). English high churchmen, on the whole, do not; at least I see no trace of it in Hooker, Andrewes, or Laud.

SOURCES: *ODNB*; Eric Auerbach, "Sermo humilis," in *Literary language and its public in late Latin antiquity and in the Middle Ages*, trans. Ralph Mannheim (Pantheon, 1958), chap. 1; Peter Brown, *Augustine of Hippo: a biography* (U California P, 1967); John Burnaby, *Amor Dei: a study of the religion of St. Augustine* (1938; rpt. Wipf & Stock, 2007); Alan Ford, *James Ussher: theology, history, and politics in early-modern Ireland and England* (Oxford UP, 2007); Christopher Hill, "The political sermons of John Preston," in *Puritanism and revolution: studies in interpretation of the English revolution of the 17th century* (1958; rpt. St Martin's, 1997), 216–47; Kendall, *Calvin and English Calvinism*; Dorothea Krook, *John Sergeant and his circle: a study of three seventeenth-century English Aristotelians*, ed. and intro. Beverley Southgate (Brill, 1993); Peter Lake, *Moderate puritans*; John Mayor, "King James I on the reasoning faculty in dogs," *Classical Review* 12.103 (1898): 93–96; McGee, *Godly man*; Milton, *Catholic and Reformed*; Moore, *English hypothetical universalism*; Shuger, "Faith and assurance"; and "Literature and the Church, 1603–1641," in *The Cambridge history of early modern English literature*, ed. Janel Mueller and David Loewenstein, 512–43 (Cambridge UP, 2002).

JOHN PRESTON

Plenitudo fontis, or, Christ's fullness and man's emptiness[1]
1621, published 1639 (rev. ed. 1644)

To the Anti-Arminian: or, to every good Christian reader.

Good Reader,

Pliny, the great naturalist, taxeth some of the Greek and Latin writers in his time of folly at the least for sending abroad their empty and worthless pamphlets with an over-praise in the title, promising much at the first sight, but utterly deceiving the reader in his further search; but he that shall with judgment read this sermon will find somewhat more than a naked title to commend it. Sometimes the workman graceth the work; sometimes the work, the workman; but behold in this treatise they kiss each other, and are joined together as a white rose & a red rose in one sweet posy. But, that both have been abused in the first impression {printing} hereof, it appeareth as clearly (by the manuscript) as the splendant sun within earth's spangled canopy: for all those passages which will make the Arminians to stumble and (without doubt) to fall in some measure are (by the imprima-turist[2]) deleted [2 leaves in some places], as if Arminianism were England's true doctrine. But now for thy comfort (dear Christian) thou hast the author's sermon as it was preached before King James, without the least diminution. And I send it out with that prayer or benediction that Jacob sent with his sons into Egypt: *God Almighty give thee mercy in the sight of the man*—in the sight of the great man, that thou mayst make him humble; of the poor man, that thou mayst make him content; of the stubborn man, that thou mayst hammer and supple him; of the penitent man, that thou mayst bind up his wounds & sores. Of every man, that thou mayst touch his conscience, and wound his soul. Amen.

Thine in the Lord Jesus, P. B.

Of his fullness we have all received grace for grace
John 1:16

---

[1] {For the sermon's date and publication history, see the preceding introduction.}
[2] {press licenser, censor}

Saint Augustine in his book *De civitate Dei* seems to stand amazed at the majesty which appears in this first of John, above all other passages of Holy Writ. And Calvin saith, he doth in this chap{ter} *detonare ab alto*,[3] giving it the chiefest instance wherein a divine stupendous authority appears beyond all the writing of men. Junius[4] saith that he was never strucken with an apprehension of the Deity till he read this first chapter, affirming it to be the first and chiefest cause of his conversion from atheism to a sincere embracing of Christianity (you may see it in his life written by himself). And in all this chapter, I find not a richer and fuller sentence than this which describes to us the *fullness* of Christ.

The parts of it are three:

First, here is a fullness attributed to Christ.

Secondly, this is not a respective but a diffusive fullness; that is, fullness not shut up in its own banks, but running over for our benefit and use. *Of his fullness we have all received*: that is, all that ever had any grace took it from this heap, drew it from this fountain.

Thirdly, these receipts are amplified by the variety of them, *grace for grace*. That is, Christ hath given to us, for all the graces which he received of his Father for us, graces answerable; as the seal is said to give to the wax print for print, character for character; or as a father is said to give to the son limb for limb, member for member, though not of the same bigness and measure. In the same sense Christ is said to give to us *grace for grace*. So that now you see here a full shop, many buyers or receivers, choice of wares; or rather, to use the Scriptures' similitude, a full table, many guests, variety of dishes. *Of his fullness we have all received grace for grace*.[5]

We begin with the first. This fullness is attributed to Christ in 4 respects. 1. In regard of his person. So he was full 1) with an increate fullness, for, as the glory of God filled the Temple that Moses could not enter in,[6] so the humanity of Christ, which answered to that type, was filled not only with the effects of the Deity, as then, but with the Deity itself, which is therefore said to dwell in him corporally or essentially. 2) He was moreover filled with a *created fullness*, and so he was said to be full of all divine good things, which John reduces to two heads, grace and truth: truth, which comprehendeth all the virtues of understanding; and grace, which compriseth all beauties and perfections of the will.

Secondly, this fullness is attributed to Christ in regard of his offices: 1) as a prophet; he was full of all the treasures of wisdom and knowledge, so that all the light which the world ever had came from him as a prophet.

All the revelations which Adam, Abraham, and Noah ever had; all the visions which Isaiah, Jeremy, and the rest of the prophets ever saw; all the mysteries which ever were declared to Paul and John, came from him; they all received their light from this Sun, which from the first morning of time shone to the dark world. . . .

Thirdly, this fullness is attributed unto Christ in regard of righteousness . . . whence we have these benefits following: 1) That he, who was so full himself, is able to make us full if we want faith or love or any other grace. 2) By this we know what a Mediator we

---

[3] {thunder from on high}

[4] {Franciscus Junius (1545–1602), Huguenot theologian; along with Emmanuel Tremellius, translator of the standard Protestant Latin Bible (1579–90)}

[5] {Preston here and throughout follows Calvin's treatment of this verse in his *Commentary on the Gospel according to John*.}

[6] {Exod. 40:30; the "Temple" was, of course, the tabernacle housing the ark of the covenant.}

have to deal withal, even with one full of love, full of patience, full of tender compassion which may invite us to come to him. Lastly, we have this comfort that, though our righteousness be very weak and small, yet in him we are complete (Coloss. 2).

. . .

If we would know the reasons, it is partly in regard of Christ himself. He was the corner stone; therefore there is reason he should be the fairest in all the building. . . .

But chiefly it was in regard of us and our emptiness, that with his fullness he might replenish our vacuity, otherwise we could neither have seen him nor received of him. Not have seen him, for the glorious beauty of his Godhead was too bright for our eyes to behold. It was therefore reason that it should be put into the lantern, or veil, of Christ's humanity, that in that we might behold it. Nor could we have received of it, for the Deity is an inaccessible fountain. It was reason therefore that Christ's humanity should be the cistern or conduit-head to receive it for our model and use.

. . .

What shall we now deduce hence for application to ourselves?

First, that which is also the scope of the Evangelist in this place: this should invite us to come to Christ and to take of this full heap. This incentive Paul often uses to inflame the desires of the gentiles to come to Christ, even the riches of that fullness which is in him, which in the fullness of time began to be exposed to all comers, as he saith: hidden before but now fully revealed; seen before but in types and shadows, now with open face; before preached but to a few, now to every creature under heaven; before the Spirit was given but by drops, but now *he that hath ascended on high and led captivity captive* hath so given gifts to men that he hath filled all things.

Let us therefore be exhorted, when we hear of such a *fullness*, not to take the *grace of God in vain*, but labor we to have our part in it, that as those Corinthians, we may be *made rich in Christ, filled with all knowledge and every grace*. Content not yourselves therefore to know this only, for that is our common fault: to content ourselves with the notions of such things, without practice.

But go to Christ as bees to a meadow that is full of flowers, as merchants to the Indies that have full mines, that you may experimentally find yourselves returning from him full-fraught with the treasures of truth and grace.

. . .

Secondly, if there be a fullness in Christ, we should answer it with fullness of affection on our parts: fully believe and trust in him, fully love and adore him, fully delight in him; for it is reason the affection should be answerable to the object. . . . All the excellency in the creature in comparison of this is but as a drop to the ocean, and a spark to the whole element of fire. . . . It is true indeed, that as men hide treasure from thieves under straw or baser covering, so God hides this full excellency from the world under a base outside, that his secret ones only might find it out; and others seeing, might not see, but stumble at it. Thus he hid Christ himself under a carpenter's son; so he hides divine mysteries under the mean elements of bread and wine; so the wisdom of God is hidden under the foolishness of preaching; and under sheepskins and goatskins, as the Apostle speaks, were hidden and such as the world is not worthy of {Heb. 11:37}, yet there is such a fullness of excellency notwithstanding; for if ever we saw beauty in sun, moon, stars, men, women, &c . . . all must needs be more abundantly in God, who is the author, maker, & giver of all these. . . . As the worth of many pieces of silver is comprised in one piece of gold, so all the petty excellencies which are scattered abroad in the creatures are all united in God; yea, the whole volume of perfections which is spread through heaven and earth is epitomized in him. Why do we not then with Paul trample upon the pomp and glory of the world, for the excellent knowledge of Christ? Why do we not with David turn away our eyes, hearts, and affections from beholding vanity, and pitch them all on him . . . in whom is the fullness of all excellency, beauty, and perfection?

Thirdly, if there be a fullness in Christ, then let us be content with him, having our hearts filled and satisfied with him.

. . . Let us be *content with him alone*, for he is our fullness. . . . Hence the hearts of men are not satisfied with the world, but, as the prophet speaks, *they eat and are not filled, they drink and behold their soul is empty*, because the creature is now but as the husk without the grain, the shell without the kernel, full of nothing but emptiness; and being empty in itself, cannot give us satisfaction; But Christ, the second Adam, hath filled all things again; Ephes. 1, last verse: *he fills all in all things*; that is, not only the hearts of men, but the things also. . . . Hence we may observe that many find a want in the midst of plenty; their hearts find no rest or satisfaction in all they enjoy; but with the holy regenerate man it is much otherwise. Though he have but a little wealth, a little food and raiment, yet there is a secret fullness put into that little which makes it fit to give him satisfaction . . .

If there be a fullness in Christ, then, what though there be a fullness of sin and guilt in us, yet there is a fullness of grace in him able to remove it and take it away. . . . So Christ, by reason of that vast fullness of grace which is in him, is as able, yea as forward and willing, to forgive the greatest sins as well as the least. I say as forward and willing, for mercy, though it be a quality in us, yet it is a nature in God. Now what is natural, there is no unwillingness or weariness in doing that: as the eye is not weary with seeing, nor the ear weary with hearing. Therefore, though our sins be never so great and many, yet if this condition be observed—that we lie in no known sin, that we have a full and resolute purpose, God bearing witness to our consciences, not to do the least evil nor omit the least good; in a word, that we make our hearts perfect to God in all things (for without this condition there is no remission of sins)—but if this condition be observed, I say that, although our sins be never so great and many, yet they are not gone beyond the price which hath been paid for them nor beyond the grace of him with whom we have to do, for there is a fullness in him.

Now, I beseech you, take not this exhortation in vain, for there is nothing more effectual to heal a rebellious disposition, to instill saving grace, to cause a sinner to change his course, than to be fully persuaded that he shall be received to mercy and that his sins shall be forgiven in Christ. Even as the thief, while the hue and cry is after him, never returns willingly; rebels and pirates, whiles the proclamation of rebellion is out against them, never come in; but if there be a proclamation of pardon—yea, and of some great advancement—if that be believed once, that and nothing else causeth them to come in, and to become faithful and loyal subjects. Therefore let this fullness of mercy in Christ be an effectual motive to us all to come in, to lay down the arms of rebellion, to choose God for our good, and to give up ourselves wholly to him, to serve him with perfect hearts & willing minds all our days.

So much for the first part.

The second part I will as briefly dispatch, and not meddle with the third, lest I be tedious.

Of his fullness we have all received

Whence the second point is *that all grace is received.* For as all stars shine in the light of the sun, so do all the saints through grace received. What else distinguished John from Judas, Simon Peter from Simon Magus, but only Christ, who shone upon one and not upon another when they sat both alike in darkness and in the shadow of death?

The Scripture is evident for this: Phil. 2:13, the deed is wrought in us by God; and not the deed only, but the will also which produces that deed; nor that only, but the thought also which begat that will. *For we are not able so much as to think a good thought of ourselves* (2 Cor. 3:5).[7] So that all grace, yea, all preparation to grace and ability to accept grace, are all from God (contrary to what Arminius affirmeth[8]) and not of ourselves; and that for these reasons.

Because nothing can work beyond the sphere of its own reach; the effect exceedeth not the cause. Therefore it is impossible for corrupt nature either to beget supernatural grace or to do any action preparing or bending or inclining the will to it. For as the water cannot heat (which is an action above the nature of it) until an higher principle of heat be first infused into it, no more can mere nature do anything tending to saving grace, having no principle in itself whence it can raise it.

And if it be objected (as it is by the Arminians) that though grace do all, yet to accept or reject it, to will or nil it, is natural to man as a free agent; I answer[9] that to will is natural, but to will well is supernatural and must rise from a higher well-head than nature is. For as an hatchet will cut when handled but with a common hand, but not make a chair or stool or any artificial thing except it have *influentiam artificis quatenus artifex*, the influence of an artificer as he is an artificer; so, though to will be natural, yet to will well, to do a supernatural work in a supernatural and holy manner, it cannot, except it have the influence of a supernatural agent to direct and guide it.[10]

If a man might accept grace or refuse it as he would, God were no God, because he might be crossed by his creature, and his own will should not absolutely bear rule, especially in that great matter of believing and not believing and in putting difference betwixt man and man in the matter of salvation and damnation: for according to Arminius, though God did heartily desire the conversion of such a man and offered him all the means of grace that could be, yet it is still in the free choice of his will to convert or not to convert. Their only answer here is that, seeing God hath made a decree that man shall be a free agent, though he do most earnestly desire the conversion of such and such men, yet because he cannot disannul his decree, he doth and must leave it to the liberty of the creature to do contrary to even that himself desires. But what is this else but to put God into such straits as Darius was in, who would fain have saved Daniel but because of his

---

[7] {This is the translation of 2 Cor. 3:5 given in the "Homily of repentance" (from the *Second book of homilies*), not the King James or Geneva bibles.}

[8] {The 1640 parenthesis reads "whatsoever men dream."}

[9] {In 1640 the paragraph begins at this point, preserving the theological point but omitting any mention of Arminius.}

[10] {The paragraphs that follow, up to "Hence 2 corollaries," do not appear in the 1639 and 1640 versions.}

decree he could not? And if grief in spirits and angels be but . . . a reluctancy of the will, as the Schoolmen affirm, what is this else but to attribute grief unto God, and so to detract from his blessedness?

Thirdly, if all grace be not received, but a man may accept it or reject it as he will, how can it be solved but that a man must rejoice and boast partly in himself, contrary to Paul's rule, and not *wholly in the Lord*? For ask the question of all that are saved, what is the reason that you are saved rather than another, their answer must needs be, I out of the liberty of my own will did receive and use well the grace offered, when another did not. So that, according to Arminius, the saints in heaven are not a jot more beholding to God than the damned in hell, for the offering of grace on God's part was alike common to both; only he that is in heaven may thank his own will that he chose it, when another refused it.

They have nothing here to answer but only that the means of grace are dispensed by God with some disparity. But what is that when they maintain such freedom of will that he who hath the greatest means may reject grace, and he who hath the least, may accept it?

Other reasons there are, but that I hasten: as that grace is not grace without being received, no more than . . . a gift can be a gift without being given; for no less doth it imply contradiction to suppose it to be a grace, & yet not to be freely bestowed by God and received by us.

Secondly, bowing of the will is an effect of grace, and grace is an effect of the Spirit. Now the Spirit breathes when, where, & in what measure it listeth. . . .

Hence 2 corollaries: one to rectify our judgment, the other to direct our practice.

The first shews us the errors of Arminius, who hath but refined the old Pelagianism, a dangerous error. For Arianism[11] was like a land-flood that overflowed the whole world but soon dried up again because it had not a spring to maintain it; but the best ages of the Church had in them . . . *multas fibras virulentiae Pelagianae*,[12] because it is an error agreeable to nature & reason, so that we have a spring within our own breast to nourish and maintain it. But now, to keep close to the point in hand, this point sheweth the error of Arminius and Pelagius, who ascribe the beginning, preparations, and ability of accepting grace to our own free will, although the complement to God. Whereas you see by what hath been said that not only the fuller streams, but every drop of grace is received from his fullness. This error proceeds from their not distinguishing aright betwixt acquisite habits and infused.[13] Indeed, in the acquisite, the acts go before the habits and prepare for them, but with infused habits it is clean contrary. It is with them as it is with the natural powers of the soul: we have first the faculty of seeing before we do see and the faculty of hearing before we do hear; so it is in infused habits, we have first the habits before we exercise the operations of them. For even as the wheel doth not run that it may be made round, but it is first made round that it may run, so the heart doth not first do the actions whereby it is put into a right frame, but it is first fashioned and made a new creature by grace, and then it doth actions and brings forth fruits worthy amendment of life . . . for nothing can prepare for grace but grace.

---

[11] {An early Christian heresy that made the Son subordinate to the Father.}

[12] {many strands of toxic Pelagianism}

[13] {The distinction between infused and acquired habits goes back to medieval scholasticism.}

And if it be objected, as Arminius doth in his book upon the 7 to the Romans,[14] that such as Seneca and Socrates were much enlightened, did approve the law of God according to the inward man, and had a kind of universal common grace, I answer that this privilege cannot be denied to many among the heathen, that, as alchemists, though they miss the end, yet they find many excellent things by the way; so though they failed of the right end, the glory of God, yet they were not destitute of many excellent common gifts, wherein, though one did go far beyond another, as Seneca beyond Nero . . . {yet} were they all alike destitute of original righteousness . . . alike dead in sins, though some (as dead bodies) more corrupted and putrefied than others.

And if it be objected, as it is by Arminius, to what end then are exhortations and threatenings, the propounding of punishments and rewards, if it be not in our power to accept grace & refuse it as we will; I answer that, as the rain, although it fall as well upon rocks and heaths as upon valleys and fruitful places, yet no man asketh to what end is the first and latter rain; so exhortations & admonitions, though they fall as well upon the reprobates and those that are desperately wicked as upon those that are docible and capable of better things, it is to {sic} no less folly to ask to what end they are, seeing, as the rain, so they are to many beneficial and useful.

So much for the first corollary, which serves to rectify judgments.

The next is for practice. If all grace be received, then defer not repentance, for no repentance is accepted but what proceeds from a sanctifying grace, and that, as you see, is received: that is given by God as he will. *It is not in him that willeth, nor in him that runneth, but he hath compassion on whom he will have compassion, and whom he will, he hardeneth* (Rom. 9:15). As I said before, the Spirit breatheth where and when it listeth. Therefore we should as millers and mariners are wont to do, who take the gale when it cometh, because they know the winds are not at their command. . . . So, if the Spirit shall breath into our hearts good motions of turning to God unfeignedly in our youth, at 16, 17, or whenever, it is the greatest wisdom in the world to take the opportunity and not to put it off. Who knoweth whether they will be had again or no. How many thousand are now in hell who thought to have repented and did not, because they neglected those breathings of the Spirit where they were offered? For there are certain acceptable times, after which God offers grace no more. Happy he that *knows that day of his visitation*, and as our Savior speaketh, *the things which belong to his peace*, in that his day. Which Jerusalem did not, which made Christ to weep over it; and which Saul did not, and the Jews in Jeremiah's time did not when God forbad Jeremy to pray for them. For as there were certain times when the angel moved the waters in the pool of Bethesda, and he that then stepped in was healed, so there are certain acceptable times wherein God troubles the hearts of men by his Spirit. Happy is he who then steps into a good course that he may be healed to salvation. I say there are certain times wherein God doth (as it were) thaw and soften the frozen hearts of men. And it is wisdom then with the husbandman to put in the plow while the ground is soft; for the heart in such a case is like iron in the furnace, easily fashioned; but stay till it be cold, and it will not be wrought upon. . . .

---

[14] {i.e., Arminius' *Dissertation on the true and genuine sense of the seventh chapter of the Epistle to the Romans*, in *The works of James Arminius: the London edition*, 3 vols., trans. James Nichols, intro. Carl Bangs (1825–75; rpt. Baker Book House, 1986), 2:471–683.}

. . . But if we would not have, with the merchant, *fortunam rudentibus aptam*,[15] that is, an estate hanging upon ropes and depending upon uncertainties, [how much less should a man have his salvation depending upon uncertainties,] especially seeing grace whence repentance proceedeth is, as you see, received, and not in our power.[16] But we mistake repentance, and that is the cause we defer it. It is not, as it is commonly thought, a sorrow for our sins only, nor a mere leaving of sins out of fear of hell and desire to be saved, which a man may do out of the strength of natural wisdom, providing for his own safety, but it is a much different thing, viz. putting life into a dead man (Eph. 2:1), making a man a new creature (2 Cor. 5:17); a change of the whole frame of the heart, as if another soul dwelt in the same body: as he saith, *Ego non ego*.[17] In a word, when a man is clean another man than he was, serving of God out of an inward propenseness and having the whole bent of his disposition turned to delight in the Law of God without these by-respects. And that this may yet be made clearer and put out of all doubt, I would ask but this question: that repentance which men take up in age or in times of extremity, whence proceedeth it? If from self-love, as it usually doth in such cases, because the soul is then strongly possessed with an apprehension of death and hell and another life, then there is no more than nature in it, for the stream riseth not higher than the fountain. A beast would do as much, which sinking into danger would struggle to save itself. But if it proceed from love to God, why was it not done sooner, why not in the flower of our youth? Yea, when it is done soonest, would we not be heartily sorry that it was not done sooner, if it proceeded out of love to him? And if it thus proceed out of an holy love to God, it cannot arise but from his Holy Spirit—the breathings of which Spirit as they are most free, so are they most precious. Therefore, when such a spark is kindled in our hearts, let us be careful to put fuel to it and not suffer it to go out again.

All the creatures in heaven and earth cannot help us again to them; yea the best ordinances are but as pens without ink or empty conduit-pipes which give not a drop of true grace, except Christ who is the fountain please to convey it by them. You know the famous story of Francis Spira, what bitter cries he used upon his death bed: *O that I had but one drop of faith, one of the motions which I have been wont to have*; but yet could not have them! but died with those desperate words in his mouth, *I am damned*.[18]

Therefore let us take heed how we let such motions rise up like bubbles in us and break again or go out like sparks upon wet tinder, lest often checking and snibbing and *quenching the Spirit*, in the end we be guilty of *resisting the Holy Ghost*, and *God shall swear in his wrath that we shall not enter into his rest*. (Where, by the way, observe that this doctrine teacheth us not to be idle and leave all to God, as they slander it), but as Paul maketh the consequence: because *God worketh in you both the will and the deed, therefore work out your salvation with fear and trembling*. Arminius contrarily, ourselves work in ourselves the will and the deed; therefore we need not work out our salvation with any such fear and solicitude, since we may do it at our own pleasure and leisure.

---

[15] {The Latin, which Preston translates, is from Cicero, *Tusculan disputations* 5.14.}
[16] {Bracketed clause added from 1640 version, p. 18. The 1645 text is defective.}
[17] {Gal 2:20: "I live, yet not I, but Christ liveth in me . . ."}
[18] {An Italian Protestant who, threatened by the Inquisition, recanted in 1548.}

But it will be said this is a hard case: although a man would repent, yet he cannot? though he desire to serve God, yet it is impossible? Therefore, to take away this scruple, we must know that God is exceeding free and open-handed in giving grace (if it may be taken in time); and if we will not believe it, John cometh here and telleth you, *I have received of his fullness*, and not only I, but all we have received; that is, all other saints that either are or have been—and since John's time, many thousand thousands. And shall not such a cloud of witnesses persuade us? If a beggar do but hear of an open-house kept, or a great dole, it affects him and invites him to go; but when he sees many come from it with arms-full and laps-full and baskets-full, then he is confident; that addeth wings to him. . . . So doth John here, *All we have received of his fullness*; like a bird that hath found out a full heap and calls his fellows to it. Say not, therefore, oh my sins are so great and my wants are so many. But rather think thus with yourselves: if there was grace enough for so many, there is surely enough for me. Only you must receive when it is offered *in the acceptable time*, lest often grieving the Spirit, God suffers *his Spirit to strive no longer*, but (as I said before) *swear in his wrath that you shall not enter into his rest* (Gen. 6:3).

2. If all grace be received, then let us be affected as receivers: 1) In thankfulness towards God; the most gracious are the most grateful. 2) In humility towards men: *for what have we that we have not received?* . . .

3. Let us be affected as receivers in begging grace at God's hands by prayer. . . . Now prayer is either private or public. Private is that wherein we express our private and particular occasions to God every day; wherein we renew repentance & covenants with God of abstaining from the sins we are most prone to and of doing the duties to which we are most unapt: in a word, that wherein we do every day set our hearts straight before God in all things. This is the very life of religion. . . . The next is public prayer: of which, because it is more questioned and not received by all with that reverence it should, I will add a word or two of it, and conclude.

That a set form of prayer is lawful, much need not to be said; the very newness of the contrary opinion is enough to shew the vanity and falseness of it, it being contrary to the judgment of approved Councils, learned Fathers, and the continual practice of the Church.

. . .

But, as I said before, of the lawfulness there is little question. That which is chiefly to be reprehended is of a secret disesteem of public prayers. By reason of which, many neglect to come to them, and they which do, do it in a perfunctory and overly[19] manner, which is an extreme fault. Better were it that men would come to this disjunction: either it is lawful to use them or not; if not, why do they not wholly abstain; and if they be lawful, why do they not use them constantly, and in a reverent and holy manner? One thing there is which, if it were well considered, would breed in the hearts of men another esteem of our public prayers than there is: and that is, that besides the end of obtaining the things we want (wherein yet public prayer hath the promise), there is another end in praying, and that is to worship God and to perform a service to him. . . .

Besides, how strait is that which is objected against the lawfulness of it, as that the Spirit is stinted when we are fettered with words appointed.

---

[19] {superficial}

Answ. The freedom of the Spirit stands not so much in the extent of the words as the intenseness of the zeal wherewith they are uttered. Besides, if this argument were good, it would swell against conceived[20] prayer, for if he that heareth hath a larger spirit than he that prayeth, there is to him the same stinting or restraint.[21]

Again, it is objected that we cannot pray for occasional necessities. Therefore we bind not only to a set form, but men may and ought to use besides, private prayer. . . . And if they be more public, there are prayers before and after sermon wherein the minister is left at more liberty. . . . But there needs not much be said to convince the judgment . . . especially seeing our public prayers be holy and good (and which should be a greater inducement), the Church hath commanded them. And if the Church be to be obeyed in indifferent things, as it is, much more in appointing of God's own ordinances.

And if a set form of prayer be lawful, then the Lord's Prayer must needs excel,[22] being dedicated by Christ himself, and is therefore to be more frequently used and with all reverence both in mind and gesture. Nor doth this want the practice and approbation of the Ancient. It is Cyprian's speech: *Quanto efficacius impetramus quod petimus Christi nomine si ipsius oratione petamus.*[23] And Saint Augustine: *Disce et retinete orationem Dominicam, et inter omnes sanctos consono ore proferatis.*[24] Thus if we shall shew ourselves affected as receivers, in using both public and private prayer, we shall find that success which John and the rest found, who of his *fullness received grace for grace.*

FINIS.

Text: EEBO (Wing / P3304A)

John Preston, *Plenitudo fontis: or, Christ's fullness, and man's emptiness. A sermon preached by John Preston* (London: Printed for John Stafford, 1645).

Corrected against John Preston, *The fullness of Christ for us. A sermon preached at the Court before King James of blessed memory* (London: J. Okes for John Stafford, 1640) (STC [2nd ed.] / 20225).

[20] {i.e., extempore}

[21] {On these puritan-presbyterian objections to set prayer, see Ramie Targoff, *Common prayer: the language of public devotion in early modern England* (Chicago UP, 2001), 36ff.; Lori Branch, *Rituals of spontaneity: sentiment and secularism from free prayer to Wordsworth* (Baylor UP, 2006).}

[22] {For the debate over the liturgical use of the Lord's Prayer, see Hooker, *Laws* 5.36.}

[23] {Translated in the 1640 version as "by how much the more effectually do we obtain that which we ask in Christ's name, if we do ask it in his own prayer" (20).}

[24] {Translated in the 1640 versions as "Learn ye and hold without book the Lord's Prayer, and with all the saints utter it with one same-sounding voice" (20).}

HUMPHREY SYDENHAM
(1591–ca. 1650)

A year after Sydenham's birth, his father found himself having to explain to the Somerset magistrates why he had disrupted church services by "causing the bells to be rung and diverse bagpipes to be blown, to the great dishonor of Almighty God" (Cannon), so young Humphrey apparently did not have a devout upbringing. He left for Oxford at fifteen, receiving his BA from Exeter in 1611. Two years later he took up a fellowship at Wadham, which had been founded in 1610 by the recusant gentlewoman, Dorothy Wadham; later the same year, he became the first Wadham fellow to graduate MA. Ordained in 1621, he remained at Wadham until resigning his fellowship in 1628, having received a Somerset vicarage in 1627, probably through the good offices of Laud, then bishop of Bath and Wells (see the dedicatory epistle prefacing *Sermons upon solemn occasions*). While still at Wadham, several of his sermons had appeared in print, including, in 1626, the unwaveringly Calvinist 1622 Paul's Cross sermon "Jacob and Esau"; these he then collected into a single volume, the *Five sermons preached upon several occasions*, which went through five editions between 1627 and 1637. In the 1630s, however, Sydenham's sermons modulate into a Laudian register: firmly supportive of established Church and monarchy, mistrustful of puritanism, and committed to the beauty of holiness. In 1645 the Parliamentary commissioners turned him out of his livings; he died about five years later in the Somerset parish where he had been born.

❧

The remainder of this introduction takes up not only the sermon which follows, the 1622 *Jacob and Esau*, but also the 1633 *Jehovah-Jirah* reprinted below, since their relation is itself of considerable interest. The former, preached only four years after Dort, is a defense of Calvinist orthodoxy, but one that articulates with unusual clarity the voluntarist core of the Reformed position: the voluntarism informing Sydenham's claim that God does not will something because it is good but rather something is good because God wills it. In Sydenham, as in other Reformed theologians, this voluntarist theology goes hand-in-glove with an overwhelming emphasis on the divine will—on its sheer omnipotence,

287

not its essential goodness. Moreover, Sydenham also downplays the role of human moral goodness; his argument that the sins of the elect are simply "dispensed with" borders on the antinomianism that Laudians detected lurking in Calvinist soteriology.[1]

Sydenham's presentation of the standard medieval/Catholic position, for which he makes Hugh of St. Victor spokesman, deserves mention on two counts. First, it makes the resistibility, or irresistibility, of grace the doctrinal cornerstone on which all else rests. Second, it suggests that Catholic and Reformed teachings diverge only with regard to the grace of conversion; once effectual grace has released the soul from its bondage, Sydenham has no real difficulty with Hugh's language of works, merit, and cooperation with grace. In conversion, however, grace does all, but only for a "narrow tribe," the rest being left to perish in their sins, because that is how God wills it.

Sydenham's 1633 *Jehovah-Jirah*, published four years later in a volume dedicated to Archbishop Laud, seems, at least initially, to belong to another world. Its theology is not Calvinist, nor even anti-Calvinist; the whole conceptual framework of the Reformation controversies over grace, free will, and election has vanished. Yet one's first impression of doctrinal volte-face gives way to intimations of more significant continuity. Both sermons center on the mystery of divine omnipotence: *Jacob and Esau* on God's absolute will, *Jehovah-Jirah* on his infinite power. Both seek to awaken fear, reverence, and trembling wonder as the proper response to God's terrifying and transcendent grandeur. If Reformed soteriology was "created to engender in the believer a feeling of awed powerlessness" (Dixon 181), then *both* sermons are versions of Calvinism. Yet something has changed, for the "awed powerlessness" of *Jehovah-Jirah* is the response demanded not by the moral incomprehensibility of the divine will but by, to use Sydenham's term, the "sublimity" of God's power, a power that seems less like sovereign authority (*potestas*, ἐξουσία, the power to hurt) than spectacular energy (*vis*, δύναμις).

One is right to be surprised by "sublimity"; the earliest witness in the *OED* comes from 1759.[2] Moreover, Sydenham uses the word in something very close to its Burkean sense: the mix of dread, exaltation, and awe in face of the *mysterium tremendum*, of transcendent power, both creative and destructive. If some passages of *Jehovah-Jirah* evoke Michelangelo's *Last Judgment*, others feel closer to the tempest and avalanche landscapes of J. M. W. Turner. As these analogies suggest (and as Sydenham's vividly sensuous prose-poetry confirms), the numinous awe that the sermon seeks to elicit is an *aesthetic* response; the sublime is an aesthetic category. This too is proto-Romantic, and yet recent scholarship has noted the same stress on sacred mystery and the aesthetic response to sacred mystery in Laudian spirituality.[3] Sydenham's sermons thus seem to push the evolution of a Calvinist theology of divine omnipotence into a proto-Romantic aesthetics of the natural sublime back to the Caroline period, and to raise the possibility that the Laudian emphases on the mystery and beauty of holiness functioned as the transformer.

---

[1] See the conclusion to the Christopher Dow reading <*infra*>, as well as the bibliography listed at the end of the Everard introduction <*infra*>, especially the studies by David Como and T. D. Bozeman.

[2] See, however, Shuger, *Sacred rhetoric* (Princeton UP, 1988), on the presence of the Longinian sublime in the Christian rhetorics of the *early* seventeenth century.

[3] See Cunningham's study of Ussher and Bramhall. This Laudian sublime also informs Thomas Laurence's 1634/5 sermon <*infra*>.

SOURCES: *ODNB*; Meyer Abrams, *Natural supernaturalism* (Norton, 1971); R. D. Cannon, "The bagpipe in Northern England," *Folk Music Journal* 2 (1971): 127–47; Jack Cunningham, *James Ussher and John Bramhall: the theology and politics of two Irish ecclesiastics of the seventeenth century* (Ashgate, 2007); Leif Dixon, "Calvinist theology and pastoral reality in the reign of King James I: the perspective of Thomas Wilson," *Seventeenth Century* 23:2 (2008): 173–97; David Frost, "Shakespeare in the seventeenth century," *SQ* 16 (1965): 81–89; Rudolph Otto, *The idea of the holy* (Oxford UP, 1923).

HUMPHREY SYDENHAM

Jacob and Esau: election, reprobation, opened and discussed
by way of sermon at Paul's Cross, March 4, 1622
published 1626

He will have mercy on whom he will have mercy; and whom he will, he hardeneth
Rom. 9:18

The text holds some analogy with the times we live in, fraught with no less subtlety than danger. . . . In sacred riddles, what we cannot resolve, give us leave to contemplate; and what not comprehend, admire . . . and when our reason is once nonplussed, we are hushed in a contented wonder. Where we may behold the Almighty (in a full shower) pouring down his blessings upon some, scarce dewing or sprinkling them on others; softening this wax and hardening that clay with one and the self-same sun (his will), and yet that will not clouded with injustice. Here is that will not only stagger but entrance a carnal apprehension: not a circumstance which is not equally loaded with doubt and amazement. . . .

   . . .

Part I.
He will

That the will of God is the principal efficient cause of all those works which he doth externally from himself, so that there is no superior or precedent cause moving and impelling it, shines to us no less from the eternity of his will than the omnipotency. . . . In his eternal decree, why are some marked out as inheritors of his Zion, others again expulsed and banished those blessed territories? They as vessels of mercy, for the manifestation of his goodness; these of fury, for the promulgation of his justice? Doubtless, the will & the *bene-placitum* of the Almighty. . . .

   . . .

   . . . In matters therefore of election, we acknowledge not a cause more classic[1] than the *cuius vult* here specified: *he will have mercy on whom he will*. Insomuch that in the parable of the householder (Matt. 20), I find but a *sic volo* as a sufficient and just cause

---

[1] {of the highest importance}

of his designs: *I will* give to this last as much as to thee; & yet this will so clothed with a divine justice that God is not said to will a thing to be done because it is good, but rather to make it good because God would have it to be done. For proof whereof, a sweet singer of our Israel instances in those wonderful passages of Creation, where 'tis first said that *Deus creavit*, God created all things, and the *valde bonum* comes aloof,[2] he saw that they were all good. And the moral portends but this, that every thing is therefore good because it was created, and not therefore created because it was good; which doth wash and purge the will of the Almighty from any stain or tincture of injustice. . . .

. . .

To inquire then the cause of God's will were an act of lunacy, not of judgment; for every efficient cause is greater than the effect; now, there's nothing greater than the will of God, and therefore no cause thereof. For if there were, there should something preoccupate[3] that will, which to conceive were sinful, to believe blasphemous. If any then (suggested by a vainglorious inquiry) should ask why God did elect this man and not that, we have not only to resolve, but to forestall so beaten an objection: because he would. But why would God do it? Here's a question as guilty of reproof as the author, who seeks a cause of that, beyond or without which there is no cause found, where the apprehension wheels and reason runs giddy in a doubtful gyre. . . . Here a scrupulous and human rashness should be hushed, and not search for that which is not, lest it find not that which is. For as the same Father {Augustine saith} . . . Let him that can, descry the wonders of the Lord in this great deep, but let him take heed he sink not. . . . Why God doth to this man so, and to that not so, who dare to expostulate? And why to this man, thus; to that, otherwise? Far be it that we should think it in the judgment of the clay, but of the potter. Down then with this aspiring thought, this ambitious desire of hidden knowledge, and make not curiosity the picklock of divine secrets. Know that such mysteries are doubly barred up in the coffers of the Almighty, which thou mayst strive to violate, not open. And therefore if thou wilt needs trespass upon Deity, dig not in its bosom; a more humble adventure suits better with the condition of a worm, scarce a man, or if so, exposed to frailty.

'Tis a fit task and employment for mortality to contemplate God's works, not sift his mysteries; and admire his goodness, not blur his justice. . . . And yet notwithstanding, though the will of God be the independent prime cause of all things, so that beyond it there is no other cause and without it there is no reason of God's actions, yet it is not the sole and particular cause, for there are many secondary concurring with the first, by the mediation whereof the will of God brings his intendments to an issue. As in matters of our salvation, the will and working of man shakes hands with that of God; for though without him we find a *Nil potestis facere* (Job 15:52), Ye can do nothing; yet assisted by his will and the powerful and effectual operations of his grace, our will cooperates with God's. Else how could David pray to him to be his helper, unless he himself did endeavor something? Or how could God command us to do his will, except the will of man did work in the performance of it? . . . To will and to believe is ours, but to give the faculty of operation to them that will and believe is God's. . . . He that hath created thee without thyself will not save thee without thyself. And therefore those whom God from all eternity hath destined

---

[2] {at a distance}
[3] {influence, preempt}

to salvation, he hath in a like privilege destined to the means. But why those means not communicable to all, many a busy endeavor hath struggled for a reason, not compassed it. Out of more than a double jury of interpreters . . . Hugo de Sancto Victore gives thus his verdict: God's grace is indifferently exhibited to all men—to the elect and reprobate—but all do not equally lay hold on it.[4] Some no less neglect than repulse God's grace, and when its comfortable beams shall shine upon them, they shut their eyes against it and will not behold it, and God in justice withdraws his grace from these men because they withdraw themselves from his grace. *Est enim in gratia quemadmodum in solis radio* (saith he), there is a proportion betwixt the rays of the sun and the eye, and betwixt the soul of man and the grace of God. The eye is ordained by nature to be the organ of the sight, and yet the eye cannot see except the sun enlighten it; neither can the sun make anything else see but the eye in man, for it may shine upon our hand or foot, nevertheless the hand or foot shall see nothing; so the soul hath a possibility to merit by her natural abilities, but that possibility shall be vain and fruitless unless it be quickened by the powerful operation of God's grace, which grace, if it shall once actuate it, then the soul will be able to attain to that double life of grace here, of glory hereafter. *Unde totum est ex gratia sic tamen ut non excludatur meritum*; whence he would have all to hang on grace, yet so that we exclude not merit.[5] But this inference is many stories above my reach, and in the greenness of my judgment, there is little truth in the consequence and palpable contradiction in the consequent. For how can the merits of man challenge anything, if all flow from the grace of God? Yes (saith Hugo), even as a weak child, which cannot yet go alone, should be led by the nurse; a man cannot say that the child goeth of himself, but by the assistance of the nurse, and yet the nurse could not make the child go unless he were naturally inclined to that motion.[6] So the soul of man is said to merit by the aid of grace and by her own natural inbred ability, but all the glory of the merit must be ascribed to God, because the soul can do nothing without the support and grace of God. Whence we can gather no truth but this, that . . . a man only may be saved without apparent contradiction; no unreasonable creature is capable of that everlasting blessedness and beatifical vision. . . . For man only hath a passive power to salvation, and man before his conversion hath a passive power only. And therefore the similes afore proposed, if they be referred to the soul before the conversion, are false and bear no proportion, for then the soul is stark blind and dead in trespass, and cannot look on the grace offered or move one jot in the course of Christianity. But after the conversion, when God speaks *Ephata* to the soul, be opened; when the understanding is illuminated and scales of error once drop from the eyes, then it may hold some correspondency with truth. As therefore in matters of our conversion, so of election too, all hangs on grace, and this grace in a holy reservation limited to a narrow tribe, for the *cuius vult* here insinuates no more, and *He will have mercy on whom he will* sounds in a direct equivalence with this, *He will have mercy* only on some—of which "some" there

---

[4] {Seventeenth-century Calvinists tend to label this position "Arminian" (e.g., Preston's *Plenitudo fontis* <*supra*>), but as Sydenham rightly notes, it is far older.}

[5] {Sydenham passes in silence over the fact that this is Augustine's position: see, e.g., *Ep.* 154, 5.16 ("*Quod est ergo meritum hominis ante gratiam, quo merito percipiat gratiam, cum omne bonum meritum nostrum non in nobis faciat nisi gratia, et cum Deus coronat merita nostra, nihil aliud coronet quam munera sua?*"), also *De grat. et lib. arbit.* 6.15, *Tract. in Ioan.* 3.10.}

[6] {Erasmus uses the same image in defending free will against Luther.}

is a definite and set number, uncapable of augmentation or diminution, however those new sprung sectaries,[7] out of a turbulent brain and thirst of cavillation, blaspheme the eternity of God's decree, making our election mutable, incomplete, conditionate, subject to change and revocation. . . .

We conclude then that the external grace which the creature affordeth us is not limited to a private number but to all; yet we deny the power and virtue of salvation in it. We allow a sufficiency of redargution[8] for convicting the heathen who, when they knew God, worshipped him not as God, and therefore are both desperate and inexcusable. Moreover, the grace which the Scripture affordeth us, as it is not universal, so nor of absolute sufficiency for salvation, but only in *genere mediorum externorum* (as the Schools speak), because it doth prescribe us the means *how* we may be saved, but it doth not apply the means *that* we are saved. Again, that grace of illumination is more peculiarly confined, and if by the beams of that glorious sun which enlighteneth every man that comes into the world we attain to the knowledge of the Scripture, yet the bare knowledge doth not save us, but the application. But the grace of regeneration is not only a sufficient, but an effectual grace, and as 'tis more powerful, so 'tis more restrained; they only partake of this blessedness whom God hath no less enlightened than sanctified, and pointed out than sealed: men invested in white robes of sincerity, whose delinquencies, though sometimes of a deep tincture, are now both dispensed with & obliterated, not because they were not sinful, but because not imputed: so involucrous and hidden are God's eternal projects that in those he relinquisheth or saves, his reason is his will; yet that as far discoasted {distant} from tyranny as injustice. The *quare* {wherefore} we may contemplate, not scan, lest our misprision {misunderstanding} grow equal with our wonder. And here in a double ambush dangerously lurk the Romanist and the Arminian, men equally swollen with rancor of malice and position {*sic*}, and with no less violence of reason than importunity press the virtue of Christ's death for the whole world. Alas, we combat not the price and worth of Christ's death, but acknowledge that an able ransom of a thousand worlds, but the ground of our duel tends to this, whether Christ dying proposed to himself the salvation of the whole world. . . . The main and chief cause that impelled Christ to die was his love (John 15). But Christ loved not all, but his own (Eph. 5). Therefore Christ died not for all, but for his own.

<hr />

TEXT: EEBO (STC [2nd ed.] / 23567)

Jacob and Esau: Election, reprobation opened and discussed by way of sermon at Paul's Cross, March 4, 1622. By Humphry Sydenham, Mr. of Arts, and fellow of Wadham College in Oxford (London: Printed [by Eliot's Court Press] for John Parker, 1626), 1–3, 7–8, 10–11, 13–16, 18–19.

[7] [Arminians]
[8] {reproof, refutation}

MICHAEL SPARKE
(ca. 1586–1653)

The son of an Oxfordshire husbandman, Sparke probably attended a local grammar school, since he could read Latin. From 1603, when he was apprenticed to a London stationer, Sparke made his living as a bookseller and printer. A staunch puritan and, from 1626 on, Prynne's invariable publisher, Sparke's life and work, in the words of the *ODNB*, reveal a "maniacal devotion to the Protestant religion." Some of his run-ins with the authorities (leading to several stints in prison) concerned copyright violations, but he also got into trouble for unlicensed printing of predestinarian tracts and, most famously, for publishing Prynne's *Histriomastix*. Although lionized by the Long Parliament, Sparke became bitterly critical of the unfolding godly revolution, whose proliferating sects and *politique* compromises he detested. The bitterness of his final years comes through in his will, which excluded members of the Stationers' Company and all women (other than his immediate kin) from his funeral, further mandating that those who did attend be given devotional books instead of the usual refreshments.

Little in Sparke's curriculum vitae bespeaks devotional inwardness, yet his demotic-Calvinist *Crumbs of comfort* became perhaps the "best-selling prayer book of the century," running through forty-two editions between 1623 and 1656 (Johns 185; Walsham 246n). Such gatherings of prayers constituted a common type of early Stuart devotional literature; like *Crumbs*, these were usually "less formal, more detailed for specific occasions, more particular in every way than the official book, more homely, and often more intimate" (White 159).

The selections that follow are interesting, and unexpected, in several respects. One notes that Sparke affirms what is usually seen as a Laudian claim that outward bodily gesture should "express the affections of the heart" <298>; that, with the exception of the brief midnight soliloquy, all the prayers address the Father rather than either the Son or the Triune God; and that the language of the prayers is surprisingly unscriptural.[1]

In fact, the language of the three prayers given below presents further puzzles. The prayers are quite different from one another. The morning prayer is a model of rhetorical and doctrinal propriety; the prose is quite formal and the theology overtly Calvinist, the core of the prayer being thanksgiving for one's election—for one's assurance of that election, which is what Calvinists mean by faith: the inner certainty that Christ died for *me*. The midnight soliloquy belongs to the devotional genre Sparke terms "ejaculation," an ancient type of prayer but rarely found in post-Reformation England; Helen White's survey of English devotional prose from 1600 to 1640 cites no one besides Sparke.[2] It is one of the very few prayers addressed to Jesus, and its agonized-erotic emotionalism and fierce yearning for sensuous contact contrasts sharply with the formality, guilt, and dread that characterize Sparke's prayers to the Father. The latter two qualities dominate the concluding "godly prayer." The title raises obvious questions since the prayer betrays not assurance but, seemingly at least, its opposite: abjection, failure, and guilt. Given the experimental predestinarian tendencies of Sparke's brand of Calvinism, one would have expected a godly prayer to express joyful assurance springing from the discovery in oneself of signs betokening elect status.[3] This prayer expresses the opposite, so why does Sparke describe it as "godly"?

The answer would seem to be that the sense of radical sinfulness it articulates was itself understood as a sign of election. So the British delegates at Dort concluded that the elect can differentiate themselves from reprobates because reprobates "never seriously repent; they are never affected with hearty sorrow for this cause, they have offended God by sinning; nor do they come to any humble contrition of heart." Such agonized self-accusation and "earnest desire of reconciliation" is precisely "the peculiar of the elect" <*Collegiate suffrage* Va.4, *supra*>.[4] The same paradoxical reading of felt desolation and spiritual failure as evidence of sainthood shows up in puritan diarists like Ralph Josselin and Nehemiah Wallington. Josselin thus confesses that "I desire to loathe myself, but yet I attain not to an inward spiritual frame." Wallington records his sins, "hoping by that means so 'to break' his 'proud heart' that he would come in humility to recognize his utter need for a savior and his complete dependence on Jesus Christ," for, he writes, "I glorify God by self-examination and judgment of myself" (Durston and Eales 12–13; Seaver 35). These passages suggest that the vast swaths of puritan devotional writing that resemble Sparke's godly prayer should not be taken as evidence of Calvinist meltdown

---

[1] By contrast, the language of Cosin's Laudian *Collection of private devotions* (1627) is heavily biblical (and liturgical). I decided not to include it precisely because about 95 percent of its material comes from either Scripture (especially the Psalms) or the Prayer Book—and it is available in a fine 1967 Oxford edition, with notes and commentary by P. G. Stanwood.

[2] George Herbert, of course, borrows the term for the subtitle of *The Temple*. Cosin also uses "pious ejaculations" for short prayers to be committed to memory; the examples he gives, however, bear no resemblance to Sparke's gushing effusions (Cosin, *A collection of private devotions* 65ff.).

[3] As, e.g., Simonds D'Ewes' "evidence of marks and signs, for my assurance of a better life," including "signs drawn from obedience to God and the magistrate, and from mercy or good works" (1:353, 363).

[4] Samuel Hoard attributes a similar view to the hard-line Calvinist Johannes Piscator (d. 1625); see *God's love to mankind* <762>.

and depression bordering on despair; rather, these torments of conscience and spiritual unsuccess seem, at least in some cases, to have been desired as signs of election. As Jennifer Herdt points out, puritan self-examination often sought evidence not of gradual sanctification but of desperate weakness and corruption "to stimulate a vivid awareness of one's need for grace, and ultimately to provide reassurance that no trace of self-confidence remained to suggest that one was not, after all, truly converted and among the elect." To the extent that Protestant teaching "requires that we abandon our own efforts and rely wholly on God's grace," it renders "the project of acquiring virtue . . . a false and fruitless assertion of human moral agency. . . . Honest confession of our own failure to attain virtue becomes in effect our sole 'virtue'" (Herdt 1, 206).[5]

✻✦✻

SOURCES: *ODNB*; Simonds D'Ewes, *The autobiography and correspondence*, ed. J. O. Halliwell, 2 vols. (London, 1845); Christopher Durston and Jacqueline Eales, "Introduction: the puritan ethos, 1560–1700," in *The culture of English puritanism, 1560–1700* (Macmillan 1996), 1–31; Jennifer Herdt, *Putting on virtue: the legacy of the splendid vices* (Chicago UP, 2008); Adrian Johns, *The nature of the book* (Chicago UP, 1998); Paul Seaver, *Wallington's world: a puritan artisan in seventeenth-century London* (Stanford UP, 1985); Alexandra Walsham, *Providence in early modern England* (Oxford UP, 1999); Helen White, *English devotional literature (prose), 1600–1640* (U Wisconsin P, 1931).

[5] Arminius' *Dissertation on the true and genuine sense of the seventh chapter of the Epistle to the Romans* mounts an extended critique of this position, arguing that it is not he "who is affected with a painful sense of sin, is oppressed with its burden, and who sorrows after a godly sort" that is regenerate, but rather he who "actually fights against sin, and, having obtained the victory over it, no longer does those things which are pleasing to the flesh and to unlawful desires, but does those which are grateful to God; that is, he actually desists from evil and does good" (*The works of James Arminius*, 3 vols., ed. Carl Bangs, trans. James Nichols, 2:471–683 [London, 1825–75; rept. Baker Book House, 1986], 2.497–98, also 539–44, 588). For the antinomian critique of Sparke-style godliness, see the introduction to Everarde <*infra*>.

MICHAEL SPARKE

Crumbs of comfort, the valley of tears, and the hill of joy
1623

To the Christian reader,
zeal in prayer through Christ.

Having known and found by some of my good friends the just want of a prayer book of this volume, I resolved for the glory of God and the good of his people to fit this for thee howsoever, which no doubt (but thou fitting thyself for it) will make thee a fit member to inherit eternal life. Go on in God's name, prepare thyself and soul to prayer, 1. with tears (Matt. 5), 2. with watching (Luke 4), 3. with alms (Acts 10), 4. with fasting, as the Ninevites (Jonah 3), as David did (2 Kings). For repentance, fasting, and prayer are the only means to bring thee to salvation; easy it is to pray, but to pray aright is difficult. Here are prayers prepared for thee; prepare thee for them, and Christ hath prepared thee a kingdom: to which kingdom, God grant we all may come.

Thine in the Lord,
T. S.

What prayer is

Prayer is a familiar speech with God, in the name of Christ; in which we either crave for needful things or give thanks for things received.[1]

What times are appointed for prayer

We ought always to pray at least three times a day: in the morning, at noon, at night. There is {sic} 3 special occasions for it: the entrance upon the day's calling in the morning, the receiving of God's creatures at noon, the going to rest at night. . . .

---

[1] {The Laudian Henry Isaacson gives a similar definition in his 1630 *Institutiones piae*: "Prayer . . . is a familiar conference with God. . . . [whereby we] have daily so free and easy admittance to his presence, to manifest our necessities to him, and to crave his supply and succor" (quoted in White 153).}

. . .

How to prepare ourselves
before prayer

If thou art to come before a king or great person, thou wilt order thyself in behavior, apparel, and words; & frame thyself to all dutiful reverence & seemliness; much more order thyself to come before thy glorious Creator, the King of kings (Eccl. 5:1). *Be not rash with thy mouth, nor let thy heart be hasty to utter a thing before GOD. For God is in the heavens, & thou art on the earth; therefore let thy words be few.*

What gesture we are to use in prayer

The most decent & fitting gesture is kneeling and looking up to heaven when we desire blessings upon us and pardon for our sins; groveling and looking downward unto the earth when we remember and bewail our sinful life passed (Acts 7:60). *Yet any decent gesture may be used in prayer. We may pray either in,*

1. *Going*
2. *Standing*
3. *Lying,* or
4. *Sitting*

So it be comely to express the affections of the heart, either by voice or silence.

The manner how we ought to conceive
of God in prayer

Man cannot see God face to face in prayer; but as a man may see another man's face in a glass that stands behind him,[2] so may man see God. A man may see the sea, but not the depth or bottom of the sea. The heavens, but not what they contain. The sun, moon, and stars, but not the excellency of their glory. So we may see God in his works, words, and deeds; but may not see him in his substance. So we must pray to him in his glory, but not in shape.

. . .

What our ejaculations are

Ejaculations are short and pithy prayers, as the lifting up of the heart into heaven, secretly and suddenly; & this short kind of prayer ought to be used as any occasion offers itself, every hour in the day.

‡

A morning prayer

O most gracious God and loving Father, we heartily thank thee for all thy loving kindness so abundantly shewed upon us: for our election, creation, redemption, merciful vocation, justification, sanctification, & continual preservation, and for the same assured and most

---

[2] {I.e., using a mirror, a man can see someone who is standing behind him.}

comfortable hope, which thou hast given us, of our glorification in the world to come. We praise thy gracious goodness for so mercifully preserving us this present night and delivering us from all dangers both of soul and body; for that thou hast given us so sweet and comfortable rest, and hast now presently brought us to the beginning of this day. And as thou hast safely preserved us unto this present hour from all dangers of this life, so we beseech thee to continue this thy favor towards us this day and the whole course of our life. Suffer us not by vain allurements of this world to be drawn away unto sin and wickedness; assist us with thy grace and Holy Spirit that we spend not our time vainly or idly, but that we may always be diligently exercised in the duties of our calling, to the benefit of our brethren and discharge of our conscience. Grant that in all our consolations, words, and works we may ever have thee present before our eyes: through Jesus Christ our Lord, *Amen.*

‡

A trance or soliloquy[3] at midnight

Lift up my heart (O Lord) unto thee; pluck down my haughty looks and humble me, and make me but one of thy number. O come Lord God, come sweet Christ; let me find comfort; let me feel some taste; let me feel some touch; let my heart be prepared; touch my heart, that good may enter into me; keep my soul now and ever from danger of sin, I humbly beseech thee O Lord in that prayer which thou hast taught me.[4]

‡

A godly prayer

O Lord God, heavenly Father, I am ashamed to come before thee and thy glorious throne, I am so sinful; yet hear me, good God, and grant my requests. By my rebellious nature I have offended. I confess myself unworthy of the name of thy child. I have despised thy love, forsaken thy ways, made slight of thy words, scorned thy chastisements, which thou hast laid upon me, without thinking what I do deserve; I have not felt the affliction of my brethren; I have not mourned with them; I fear not thy judgments nor dread thy threatnings. What shall I say more? I regarded not thy mercies; curses and punishments have I deserved, having so vilely, so willfully, and so obstinately despised thy favors. I rock myself in the cradle of security. I run after sin as swine after filth. I delight in evil; I apply myself to ungodliness; I tread the steps of the profane and wicked; I incline to lying, deceit, and cozenage, lust, perjury, and all wickedness. I go slyly away with my transgressions; I wink at great sins and I make small sins no sin at all. I promise amendment but still continue obstinate. I am prone and apt to all badness, dull and heavy to all goodness; my thoughts wicked, my deeds damnable, my life impious, my sayings deceitful, my heart hollow. I say one thing and do another; I run from sin to sin, from drunkenness to lust, from lust to greater sins, from one bad deed to another, from one ill

---

[3] {On the soliloquy (a term coined by St. Augustine), see Julia Staykova, "The Augustinian soliloquies of an early modern reader," *Literature and Theology* 23.2 (2009): 121–41.}

[4] {i.e., the Our Father}

thought to another. I am stained with pollution, stuffed with covetousness, desirous of the world, ambitious of honor. I never look back how wicked I have been, but continue as though there were no hell to swallow me, no devils to torment me, no conscience to accuse me, no judgment to terrify me. I regard not hell nor look after heaven; I become loathsome unto thee. Yet most glorious Lord God, once, once again, look back, I beseech thee; behold and pity me, poor condemned wretch; seal me a pardon. Help, O help me, dear Father. Open the fountains of thy mercies; let down the showers of thy grace upon me; distill tears from my eyes, sighs and sobs from my heart, sorrow for my sins, & grant unto me speedy courses of amending of my sinful life, and a steadfast and sure confidence in thee, for Jesus Christ his sake, *Amen.*

Text: EEBO (STC [2nd ed.] / 23015.7)

[Michael Sparke], *Crumms of comfort, the valley of tears, and the hill of joy . . . Perused and penned for every sinful soul*, 6th ed. (London, Printed for Michael Sparke, 1627), A2r–A4v, A5r–A7v, B2r–B3r, C11v–C11r, F7r–F8v.

JOHN DONNE
(1572–1631)

Born into a Roman Catholic family, Donne matriculated from Hart Hall, Oxford, in 1584, when he was only twelve, probably in the hope that he could finish his BA before turning sixteen, when he would have to take the Oath of Supremacy. In the event, he left Oxford without taking a degree, perhaps to travel abroad. In 1592 he was admitted to Lincoln's Inn; it was probably during his years as a law student that Donne began studying "the body of divinity as it was then controverted betwixt the Reformed and Roman Church" (Walton 19).[1] Around the same time, his brother Henry was thrown in prison for concealing a Jesuit. Henry died in prison in 1594; the Jesuit was drawn and quartered.

Donne had left Lincoln's Inn by early 1596 when he joined Essex's successful Cadiz expedition. He also took part in the bungled follow-up expedition, returning to England in October 1597. Shortly thereafter, Sir Thomas Edgerton, the Lord Keeper, made Donne his secretary, which strongly suggests that by this point, Donne had conformed to the Church of England. As is well known, Donne fell in love with Lady Edgerton's young niece, Anne More, whose secret marriage to Donne in 1601 got him briefly arrested and permanently dismissed from Edgerton's service. For years thereafter, the Donnes survived on the kindness of a few friends and relatives. It was during this period that most of Donne's religious poetry (*La Corona*, "A Litany," "Good Friday: Riding Westward," and many of the *Holy Sonnets*) was written, as well as his treatises on suicide (*Biathanatos* [1607–8]) and whether Catholics might take the oath of allegiance (*Pseudo-Martyr* [1610]), plus the anti-Jesuit satire, *Ignatius his conclave* (1611). Donne's two *Anniversaries*, commemorating the death of Elizabeth Drury, likewise date from 1610–11. Donne spent most of 1612 traveling with the Druries on the Continent. Upon their return, Sir Robert Drury provided Donne and his large family with a house, where they lived until 1621.

---

[1] It may be unnecessary to add that a good deal of his best-known poetry also dates from this period.

Donne had been an MP in the Parliament of 1601; he was elected again in 1614, but the session (known as the Addled Parliament) was a disaster, and James dissolved it after two months. Soon thereafter, Donne finally abandoned his efforts to find secular employment and, in January 1615, was ordained both deacon and priest, with John King, Bishop of London, officiating. Later the same year James made him a royal chaplain—in which capacity he preached the Lenten sermon below; the King also, against considerable opposition, pressured Cambridge into granting a DD to this new priest sans BA. In 1616 he received two benefices and, far more significant, the readership in divinity at Lincoln's Inn. The next year he preached his first Paul's Cross sermon.

From 1619 to 1620, Donne served as Viscount Doncaster's chaplain in James' eleventh-hour embassy to avert the war threatening to engulf Europe. (His "Hymn to Christ, at the author's last going into Germany" concerns this journey.) At the Hague, Donne received a medal commemorating the Synod of Dort, but the Doncaster mission was a failure.

Donne returned to his readership at Lincoln's Inn for almost a year, exchanging it in November of 1621 for the deanship of St. Paul's, where, according to Walton, he at once began "to repair and beautify the chapel" (48). In 1622, as the Protestant armies suffered defeat after defeat, the London pulpits grew increasingly fierce in their calls for a holy war; the King responded with directives forbidding ministers to "meddle" with matters of state and the "deep points of predestination" or to use "indecent railing speeches against the persons of either papists or puritans"—and picked Donne to defend the new rules in a Paul's Cross sermon. Modern scholarship on this sermon has sought to find a resistant or at least ambivalent subtext to its defense of censorship, but James was pleased and had the sermon printed at once.

The rebuilding of Lincoln's Inn chapel, with its glorious stained glass windows, had begun during Donne's tenure there, and he returned to preach the consecration sermon on Ascension, 1623.[2] Donne's theological position to this point has proven hard to pin down; however, his *Devotions upon emergent occasions*, written following a grave illness in the winter of 1623, defends the role of ceremony and sacrament along lines that clearly align him with the high-church wing of the Jacobean Church (Strier), and under Charles he equally "clearly retained the royal favor he had enjoyed under James" (*ODNB*).[3] By 1630 he had been short-listed for the next vacant bishopric, but by that time he was dying of stomach cancer. He preached his last sermon, *Death's duel*, at Whitehall in February of 1631; a month later he was dead.

One hundred and sixty of Donne's sermons survive. Almost all repay reading, although only one has been reproduced below. I chose the Whitehall Lenten sermon for 1623

[2] On the revival of the consecration rite in Jacobean England among Calvinist as well as high-church divines, see John Wordsworth, *On the rite of consecration of churches especially in the Church of England* (1898; rpt. Boughton Press, 2008), 8, 17.

[3] Charles' brief displeasure with Donne, based on the misreporting of a sermon, has been variously interpreted; the most plausible explanation is that given by Potter and Simpson in their introduction to vol. 7 of *The sermons of John Donne*, 41.

because it interweaves the body-soul issues that lie at the heart of Donne's thought with questions about the relation of the dead to the living that lie at the heart of the Reformation. The sermon grapples with the drastic remotion of the dead in the wake of the Protestant disavowals of purgatory and intercessory prayer—the remotion informing the extraordinary passage on why we weep for those who have died if their souls now rejoice in heaven; Donne's answer starts from the absolute gulf separating those on earth from their beloved dead and goes on to confront the possibility that even when they meet in heaven, their disembodied souls may not recognize each other, that the bonds of family and friendship end forever at death.

On further inspection, the sermon proved interesting in additional respects: above all, its unusually positive view of the emotions, a reassessment not without theological import. The distinctiveness of Donne's view becomes apparent if one contrasts his exegesis of John 11:35 ("Jesus wept") with his two principal contemporary sources:[4] *Commentaria in Scripturam Sacram* of the Flemish Jesuit Cornelius à Lapide (1567–1637) and Calvin's *Commentaries on John*. Like Donne, both à Lapide and Calvin affirm (against some currents of patristic opinion) the human reality of Christ's emotions. However, à Lapide focuses not on the tears of John 11:35, but on Christ's groaning (*fremitus*) mentioned two verses before, which, according to à Lapide, wells up from Jesus' heroic indignation at the injury Death has inflicted on Lazarus: like a soldier, Christ is rousing his emotions in preparation for battle (16:492–93). Donne omits all this, concerned only with Christ's grief and compassion, with his tears in response to human death, suffering, and sin—and, by extension, with the tears of pity and penitence that characterize true Christian manhood.

Calvin's reading of John 11:33 is closer to Donne's sermon—he underscores Christ's sympathy for Lazarus' sisters in their grief and his compassion for "the general misery of the whole human race," but Calvin averts his gaze from the tears; there is no commentary on verse 35. Instead, the discussion of 11:33 concludes by emphasizing that Christ's emotions were always "adjusted and regulated in obedience to God," never going beyond "proper bounds." Calvin then skips to verse 38, interpreting Christ's groans before entering the tomb as (like à Lapide re verse 33) those of a soldier preparing for combat against "the violent tyranny of death."

In Donne, the reality of Christ's compassion repeatedly grounds exhortations to fellow-feeling and responsiveness to others' needs (including a young heir's need for a decent allowance). But the sermon also uses Christ's compassion to ground an explicit denial of double (supralapsarian) predestination—if the Son had decreed the fall of Jerusalem absolutely, without respect to sin, he would not have wept over its destruction—and, more tentatively, to question the sublapsarian single-predestination upheld at Dort. One seems to hear such questions between the lines in Donne's urging Christ's example to argue that friends, even those whose misconduct makes them stink in our nostrils, ought "not be derelicted, abandoned to themselves,"[5] and again in his declaration that Christ's weeping over the impending fall of Jerusalem shows "he had rather it were not so," "had rather

---

[4] Donne cites neither; like most divines during this period, he names his patristic sources, since these are authorities, but only rarely modern theologians.

[5] On God's electing some from the condemned mass of fallen humanity, and simply passing over the rest (preterition, dereliction), see *Collegiate suffrage* Ib.1 <*supra*>.

her [Jerusalem's] own tears had averted and washed away those judgments." The passages on Jerusalem (which come right after the explicit denial of the supralapsarian position) imply that human choices can frustrate God's will,[6] and that, in matters relating to their salvation, people can do otherwise than they actually do: the city's inhabitants *could have* repented. As both the *Collegiate suffrage <supra>* and Hoard's Arminian *God's love to mankind <infra>* underscore, neither position is compatible with Calvinism of any sort—nor is the possibility Donne allows at the sermon's conclusion, that all baptized infants might be saved.

SOURCES: *ODNB*; John Calvin, *Commentary on John*, trans. William Pringle (Grand Rapids, Mich.: Christian Classics Ethereal Library, www.ccel.org/ccel/calvin/calcom34.html (accessed October 21, 2010); *Directions concerning preachers*, http://history.hanover.edu/texts/engref/er90.html (accessed August 3, 2010); Marjory Lange, *Telling tears in the English Renaissance* (Brill, 1996); Cornelius à Lapide, *Commentaria in Scripturam Sacram*, 23 vols. (Paris, 1868–80); Peter Marshall, *Beliefs and the dead in Reformation England* (Oxford UP, 2002); G. R. Potter and E. M. Simpson, eds. *The sermons of John Donne*, 10 vols. (U California P, 1953–62); Richard Strier, "Donne and the politics of devotion," in *Religion, literature, & politics in post-Reformation England, 1540–1688*, ed. Donna Hamilton and Richard Strier, 93–114 (Cambridge UP, 1996); Ramie Targoff, *John Donne, body and soul* (Chicago UP, 2008); Izaak Walton, *Lives* (London, 1888).

---

[6] A possibility Preston explicitly denies *<Plenitudo 281>*.

JOHN DONNE

Sermon preached at Whitehall, the first Friday in Lent
1623, published 1640

Jesus wept.
John 11:35

I am now but upon the compassion of Christ. There is much difference between his compassion and his Passion, as much as between the men that are to handle them here.[1] But *lacryma passionis Christi est vicaria*:[2] a great personage may speak of his Passion, of his blood; my vicarage is to speak of his compassion and his tears. Let me chafe the wax, and melt your souls in a bath of his tears now; let him set to the great seal of his effectual Passion, in his blood, then. It is a common place, I know, to speak of tears; I would you knew as well, it were a common practice to shed them. Though it be not so, yet bring St. Bernard's patience, *Libenter audiam, qui non sibi plausum, sed mihi planctum moveat*; be willing to hear him, that seeks not your acclamation to himself, but your humiliation to his and your God; not to make you praise with them that praise, but to make you weep with them that weep, *And Jesus wept.*

The Masorites (the Masorites are the critics upon the Hebrew Bible, the Old Testament) cannot tell us who divided the chapters of the Old Testament into verses; neither can any other tell us who did it in the New Testament. Whoever did it seems to have stopped in an amazement in this text, and by making an entire verse of these two words, *Jesus wept*, and no more, to intimate that there needs no more for the exalting of our devotion to a competent height than to consider how, and where, and when, and why *Jesus wept*. There is not a shorter verse in the Bible, nor a larger text. There is another as short: *semper gaudete, rejoice evermore*, and of that holy joy I may have leave to speak here-after more seasonably, in a more festival time, by my ordinary service. This is the season of general compunction, of general mortification, and no man privileged, for *Jesus wept*.

---

[1] {John Williams, Bishop of Lincoln, preached on Good Friday, 1623; as Lord Keeper, Williams would have borne the Great Seal.}

[2] {"A tear serves in place of (vicariously for) Christ's passion"; from St. Augustine's *Sermo ad fratres xi*, PL 40:1254.}

In that letter which Lentulus is said to have written to the Senate of Rome, in which he gives some characters of Christ, he says that Christ was never seen to laugh, but to weep often.[3] Now in what number he limits his *often*, or upon what testimony he grounds his number, we know not. We take knowledge that he wept thrice. He wept here, when he mourned with them that mourned for Lazarus; he wept again, when he drew near to Jerusalem and looked upon that city; and he wept a third time in his Passion. There is but one evangelist, but this, St. John, that tells us of these first tears; the rest say nothing of them. There is but one evangelist, St. Luke, that tells us of his second tears; the rest speak not of those. There is no evangelist, but there is an apostle that tells us of his third tears; St. Paul says, *that in the days of his flesh, he offered up prayers with strong cries and tears* {Hebr. 5:7}; and those tears, expositors of all sides refer to his Passion, though some to his Agony in the Garden, some to his Passion on the Cross; and these, in my opinion, most fitly: because those words of St. Paul belong to the declaration of the priesthood and of the sacrifice of Christ; and for that function of his, the Cross was the altar; and therefore to the Cross we fix those third tears.[4] The first were human[5] tears, the second were prophetical, the third were pontifical, appertaining to the sacrifice. The first were shed in a condolency of a human and natural calamity fallen upon one family: Lazarus was dead; the second were shed in contemplation of future calamities upon a nation: Jerusalem was to be destroyed; the third, in contemplation of sin, and the everlasting punishments due to sin, and to such sinners as would make no benefit of that sacrifice which he offered in offering himself. His friend was dead, and then Jesus wept; he justified natural affections, and such offices of piety. Jerusalem was to be destroyed, and then Jesus wept; he commiserated public and national calamities, though a private person. His very giving of himself for sin was to become to a great many ineffectual; and then Jesus wept; he declared how indelible the natural stain of sin is, that not such sweat as his, such tears, such blood as his could absolutely wash it out of man's nature. The tears of the text are as a spring, a well, belonging to one household, the sisters of Lazarus; the tears over Jerusalem are as a river, belonging to a whole country; the tears upon the Cross are as the sea, belonging to all the world; and though literally there fall no more into our text than the spring, yet because the spring flows into the river and the river into the sea, and that wheresoever we find that Jesus wept, we find our text (for our text is but that, *Jesus wept*), therefore, by the leave and light of his blessed Spirit, we shall look upon those lovely, those heavenly eyes, through this glass of his own tears, in all these three lines: as he wept here over Lazarus, as he wept there over Jerusalem, as he wept upon the Cross over all of us. For so often Jesus wept.

First then, Jesus wept *humanitus*; he took a necessary occasion to show that he was true man. He was now in hand with the greatest miracle that ever he did, the raising of Lazarus, so long dead. Could we but do so in our spiritual raising, what a blessed harvest

---

[3] {A letter by an imaginary governor of Judea, predecessor of Pontius Pilate, to the Roman Senate purportedly describing an amazing young prophet, with long nut-brown hair and beard, who goes by the name Jesus.}

[4] {See à Lapide, *Commentaria* 16:494}

[5] {Prior to the 18th century, "human" and "humane" are not differentiated; Donne uses the word in both senses throughout the sermon; I have spelled the word without the "e" except when the sense absolutely demanded it.}

were that? What a comfort to find one man here today raised from his spiritual death this day twelvemonth? Christ did it every year, and every year he improved his miracle. In the first year, he raised the governor's daughter; she was newly dead, and as yet in the house. In the beginning of sin, and whilst in the house, in the house of God, in the Church, in a glad obedience to God's ordinances and institutions there for the reparation and resuscitation of dead souls, the work is not so hard. In his second year, Christ raised the widow's son, and him he found without, ready to be buried. In a man grown cold and stiff in sin, impenetrable, inflexible by denouncing the judgments of God, almost buried in a stupidity and insensibleness of his being dead, there is more difficulty. But in his third year, Christ raised this Lazarus; he had been long dead, and buried, and in probability putrefied after four days.

This miracle Christ meant to make a pregnant proof of the resurrection, which was his principal intention therein. For the greatest arguments against the resurrection being for the most part of this kind: when a fish eats a man, and another man eats that fish, or when one man eats another, how shall both these men rise again? when a body is resolved in the grave to the first principles or is passed into other substances, the case is somewhat near the same; and therefore Christ would work upon a body near that state, a body putrefied. And truly, in our spiritual raising of the dead, to raise a sinner putrefied in his own earth, resolved in his own dung, especially that hath passed many transformations, from shape to shape, from sin to sin (he hath been a salamander and lived in the fire, in the fire successively—in the fire of lust in his youth, and in his age in the fire of ambition—and then he hath been a serpent, a fish, and lived in the waters, in the water successively—in the troubled water of sedition in his youth, and in his age in the cold waters of indevotion), how shall we raise this salamander and this serpent, when this serpent and this salamander is all one person, and must have contrary music to charm him, contrary physic to cure him? To raise a man resolved into divers substances, scattered into divers forms of several sins, is the greatest work. And therefore this miracle (which implied that) St. Basil calls *miraculum in miraculo*, A pregnant, a double miracle. For here is *mortuus redivivus*, a dead man lives; that had been done before; but *alligatus ambulat*, says Basil, he that is fettered and manacled and tied with many difficulties, he walks.

And therefore, as this miracle raised him most estimation, so (for they ever accompany one another) it raised him most envy: envy that extended beyond him, to Lazarus himself, who had done nothing; and yet *the chief priests consulted how they might put Lazarus to death, because by reason of him, many believed in Jesus.* A disease, a distemper, a danger which no time shall ever be free from; that wheresoever there is a coldness, a disaffection to God's cause, those who are any way occasionally instruments of God's glory shall find cold affections. If they killed Lazarus, had not Christ done enough to let them see that he could raise him again? For *caeca saevitia, si aliud videtur mortuus, aliud occisus*; it was a blind malice, if they thought that Christ could raise a man naturally dead, and could not if he were violently killed. This then being his greatest miracle, preparing the hardest article of the Creed, the resurrection of the body, as the miracle itself declared sufficiently his divinity, that nature, so in this declaration that he was God, he would declare that he was man too, and therefore *Jesus wept.*

He wept as man doth weep, and he wept as a man may weep; for these tears were *testes naturae, non indices diffidentiae*; they declared him to be true man, but no distrustful, no inordinate man. In Job there is a question asked of God, *Hast thou eyes of flesh, and dost thou see as man sees?* Let this question be directed to God manifested in Christ, and Christ will weep out an answer to that question: I have eyes of flesh, and I do weep as man weeps. Not as sinful man, not as a man that had let fall his bridle by which he should turn his horse, not as a man that were cast from the rudder by which he should steer his ship, not as a man that had lost his interest and power in his affections and passions; Christ wept not so. Christ might go farther that way than any other man; Christ might ungirt himself, and give more scope and liberty to his passions than any other man, both because he had no original sin within to drive him, no inordinate love without to draw him when his affections were moved; which all other men have.

God says to the Jews, *that they had wept in his ears.* God had heard them weep, but for what, and how? *they wept for flesh.* There was a tincture, there was a deep dye of murmuring in their tears. Christ goes as far in the Passion, in his agony, and he comes to a passionate deprecation, in his *tristis anima*, and in the *si possibile*, and in the *transeat calix.*[6] But as all these passions were sanctified in the root, from which no bitter leaf, no crooked twig could spring, so they were instantly washed with his *veruntamen*, a present and a full submitting of all to God's pleasure, *Yet not my will, O Father, but thine be done.* It will not be safe for any man to come so near an excess of passions as he may find some good men in the Scriptures to have done: that because he hears Moses say to God, *Dele me, Blot my name out of the book of life*, therefore he may say, "God damn me," or "I renounce God." It is not safe for a man to expose himself to a temptation because he hath seen another pass through it. Every man may know his own bias, and to what sin that diverts him: the beauty of the person, the opportunity of the place, the importunity of the party, being his mistress, could not shake Joseph's constancy. There is one such example of one that resisted a strong temptation; but then there are, in one place, two men together that sinned upon their own bodies, Her and Onan, then when no temptation was offered, nay when a remedy against temptation was ministered to them.

Some man may be chaster in the stews than another in the church; and some man will sin more in his dreams than another in his discourse. Every man must know how much water his own vessel draws, and not to think to sail over wheresoever he hath seen another (he knows not with how much labor) shove over; no, nor to adventure so far as he may have reason to be confident in his own strength, for though he may be safe in himself, yet he may sin in another, if by his indiscreet and improvident example, another be scandalized. Christ was always safe; *he was led of the Spirit*; of what spirit? his own Spirit. *Led* willingly *into the wilderness, to be tempted of the devil.* No other man might do that but he who was able to say to the sun, *Siste sol*, was able to say to Satan, *Siste Lucifer.* Christ in another place gave such scope to his affections, and to others' interpretations of his actions, that his friends and kinfolks thought him mad, besides himself. But all this while, Christ had his own actions, and passions, and their interpretations in his own power; he could do what he would. Here in our text, Jesus was troubled, and he groaned; and vehemently, and often, his affections were stirred; but as in a clean glass, if water be stirred and troubled, though it may conceive a little light froth, yet it contracts no foulness

---

[6] {The Latin quotes piecemeal from Matt 26:38-39.}

in that clean glass[7]—the affections of Christ were moved but so; in that holy vessel they would contract no foulness, no declination towards inordinateness. But then every Christian is not a Christ; and therefore, as he that would fast forty days, as Christ did, might starve; and he that would whip merchants out of the Temple, as Christ did, might be knocked down in the Temple; so he knowing his own inclinations, or but the general ill inclination of all mankind as he is infected with original sin, that should converse so much with publicans and sinners, might participate of their sins. The rule is, we must avoid inordinateness of affections; but when we come to examples of that rule, ourselves, well understood by ourselves, must be our own examples; for it is not always good to go so far as some good men have gone before.

Now though Christ were far from both, yet he came nearer to an excess of passion than to an indolency, to a senselessness, to a privation of natural affections. Inordinateness of affections may sometimes make some men like some beasts; but indolency, absence, emptiness, privation of affections makes any man at all times like stones, like dirt. *In novissimis*, saith St. Peter, in the last, that is, in the worst days, in the dregs and lees and tartar of sin, then shall come men, lovers of themselves; and that is ill enough in man; for that is an affection peculiar to God, to love himself. *Non speciale vitium, sed radix omnium vitiorum*, says the School in the mouth of Aquinas: self-love cannot be called a distinct sin, but the root of all sins. It is true that Justin Martyr says, *philosophandi finis est Deo assimilari*, the end of Christian philosophy is to be wise like God; but not in this, to love ourselves; for the greatest sin that ever was, and that upon which even the blood of Christ Jesus hath not wrought, the sin of angels, was that: *similis ero Altissimo*, to be like God. To love ourselves, to be satisfied in ourselves, to find an omni-sufficiency in ourselves, is an intrusion, an usurpation upon God; and even God himself, who had that omni-sufficiency in himself, conceived a conveniency for his glory, to draw a circumference about that center, creatures about himself, and to shed forth lines of love upon all them, and not to love himself alone. Self-love in man sinks deep; but yet, you see, the Apostle in his order casts the other sin lower, that is, into a worse place, *to be without natural affections.*

St. Augustine extends these natural affections to religious affections, because they are natural to a supernatural man, to a regenerate man, who naturally loves those that are of the household of the faithful, that profess the same truth of religion; and not to be affected with their distresses, when religion itself is distressed in them, is impiety. He extends these affections to moral affections: the love of eminent and heroical virtues in any man; we ought to be affected with the fall of such men. And he extends them to civil affections, the love of friends; not to be moved in their behalf is argument enough that we do not much love them.

For our case in the text, these men whom Jesus found weeping, and wept with them, were none of his kindred; they were neighbors, and Christ had had a conversation, and contracted a friendship in that family: *he loved Martha, and her sister, and Lazarus*, says the story; and he would let the world see that he loved them: for so the Jews argued that saw him weep, *Behold how he loved them.* Without outward declarations, who can conclude an inward love? to assure that, *Jesus wept.*

---

[7] {See Calvin, *Commentary on John*, re: 11:33: "if you compare his [Christ's] passions with ours, they will differ not less than pure and clear water, flowing in a gentle course, differs from dirty and muddy foam."}

To an inordinateness of affections it never came; to a natural tenderness it did, and so far as to tears; and then who needs be ashamed of weeping? *Look away far from me, for I will weep bitterly*, says Jerusalem in Esay. But *look upon me*, says Christ in the Lamentations, *Behold and see if ever there were any sorrow, any tears, like mine*: not like his in value; but in the root, as they proceeded from natural affection, they were tears of imitation; and we may, we must weep tears like his tears. They scourged him, they crowned him, they nailed him, they pierced him, and then blood came; but he shed tears voluntarily, and without violence;[8] the blood came from their ill, but the tears from his own good nature; the blood was drawn, the tears were given. We call it a childish thing to weep, and a womanish; and perchance we mean worse in that than in the childish, for therein we may mean falsehood to be mingled with weakness. Christ made it an argument of his being man to weep, for though the lineaments of man's body—eyes and ears, hands and feet—be ascribed to God in the Scriptures, though the affections of man's mind be ascribed to him (even sorrow, nay repentance itself, is attributed to God), I do not remember that ever God is said to have wept. It is for man. And when God shall come to that last act in the glorifying of man, when he promises *to wipe all tears from his eyes*, what shall God have to do with that eye that never wept?

He wept out of a natural tenderness in general, and he wept now out of a particular occasion. What was that? *Quia mortuus*, because Lazarus was dead. We stride over many steps at once, waive many such considerable circumstances as these: Lazarus his friend was dead, therefore he wept; Lazarus, the staff and sustentation of that family was dead, he upon whom his sisters relied was dead, therefore he wept. But I stop only upon this one step, *quia mortuus*, that he was dead. Now a good man is not the worse for dying: that is true and capable of a good sense, because he is established in a better world; but yet when he is gone out of this world he is none of us; he is no longer a man. The stronger opinion in the School is that Christ himself, when he lay dead in the grave, was no man.[9] Though the Godhead never departed from the carcass (there was no divorce of that hypostatical union), yet because the human soul was departed from it, he was no man. Hugo de S. Victor, who thinks otherwise, that Christ was a man then, thinks so upon a weak ground: he thinks that because the soul is the form of man, the soul is man; and that therefore, the soul remaining, the man remains. But it is not the soul, but the union of the soul,[10] that makes the man. The Master of the Sentences, Peter Lombard, that thinks so too, that Christ was then a man, thinks so upon as weak a ground: he thinks that it is enough to constitute a man that there be a soul and body, though that soul and body be not united; but still it is the union that makes the man; and therefore when he is disunited, dead, he is none of us, he is no man; and therefore we weep, how well soever he be. Abraham was

---

[8] {Donne is probably echoing à Lapide's "*in Christo hae passiones et affectus non erant involuntarii et violenti, sed voluntarii et libre assumpti*" (*Commentaria* 492), but the meaning of "voluntary" has shifted. In à Lapide, Christ's emotions (and, since the Fall, his alone) are voluntary in the sense that Christ's will, following the dictates of right reason, freely chooses its emotional states. For Donne, Christ's tears are voluntary not because he wills them but because they flow "from his own good nature." (The *OED* recognizes both meanings.)}

[9] {See Carolyn Bynum, *The resurrection of the body in western Christianity, 200–1336* (Columbia UP, 1995), 256–57.}

[10] {i.e., the union of the soul and body}

loath to let go his wife though the King had her; a man hath a natural loathness to let go his friend, though God take him to him.

St. Augustine says that he knew well enough that his mother was in heaven; and St. Ambrose, that he knew well enough that his master Theodosius the emperor was in heaven, but because they saw not in what state they were, they thought that something might be asked at God's hands in their behalf; and so out of a human and pious officiousness,[11] in a devotion perchance indigested, unconcoted, and retaining yet some crudities, some irresolutions, they strayed into prayers for them after they were dead. Lazarus his sisters made no doubt of their brother's salvation; they believed his soul to be in a good estate; and for his body, they told Christ, *Lord we know that he shall rise at the last day,* and yet they wept.

Here in this world, we who stay lack those who are gone out of it: we know they shall never come to us; and when we shall go to them, whether we shall know them or no, we dispute. They who think that it conduces to the perfection of happiness in heaven that we should know one another, think piously if they think we shall. For as, for the maintenance of public peace, states and Churches may think diversely in points of religion that are not fundamental, and yet both be true and orthodoxal Churches; so for the exaltation of private devotion, in points that are not fundamental, divers men may think diversely and both be equally good Christians. Whether we shall know them there, or no, is problematical and equal;[12] that we shall not till then, is dogmatical and certain: therefore we weep. I know there are philosophers that will not let us weep nor lament the death of any; and I know that in the Scriptures there are rules, and that there are instructions conveyed in that example: that David left mourning as soon as the child was dead; and I know that there are authors of a middle nature, above the philosophers and below the Scriptures, the Apocryphal books, and I know it is said there,[13] Comfort thyself, for thou shalt do him no good that is dead—*Et teipsum pessimabis* (as the Vulgate reads it); thou shalt make thyself worse and worse, in the worst degree. But yet all this is but of inordinate lamentation; for in the same place, the same wise man says, My son, let thy tears fall down over the dead; weep bitterly and make great moan, as he is worthy. When our Savior Christ had uttered his *consummatum est,* all was finished, and their rage could do him no more harm, when he had uttered his *In manus tuas,* he had delivered and God had received his soul, yet how did the whole frame of nature mourn in eclipses, and tremble in earthquakes, and dissolve and shed in pieces in the opening of the Temple, *quia mortuus,* because he was dead.

Truly, to see the hand of a great and mighty monarch, that hand that hath governed the civil sword, the sword of justice at home, and drawn and sheathed the foreign sword, the sword of war abroad, to see that hand lie dead and not be able to nip or fillip away one of his own worms (and then *Quis homo,* What man, though he be one of those men of whom God hath said, *Ye are gods,* yet *Quis homo, What man is there that lives, and shall not see death?*), to see the brain of a great and religious counselor (and God bless all from making, all from calling any "great" that is not religious), to see that brain that produced means to becalm gusts at council tables, storms in parliaments, tempests in popular

---

[11] {readiness in doing good offices; dutifulness}
[12] {evenly balanced}
[13] {The biblical allusions in next few sentences concern Sirah 38.}

commotions, to see that brain produce nothing but swarms of worms, and no proclamation to disperse them; to see a reverend prelate that hath resisted heretics and schismatics all his life, fall like one of them by death, and perchance be called one of them when he is dead;[14] to re-collect all, to see great men made no men, to be sure that they shall never come to us, not to be sure that we shall know them when we come to them; to see the lieutenants and images of God, kings; the sinews of the state, religious counselors; the spirit of the Church, zealous prelates; and then to see vulgar, ignorant, wicked, and facinorous men thrown all by one hand of death into one cart, into one common tide-boat, one hospital, one almshouse, one prison, the grave, in whose dust no man can say, "this is the king, this is the slave, this is the bishop, this is the heretic, this is the counselor, this is the fool"; even this miserable equality of so unequal persons, by so foul a hand, is the subject of this lamentation; even *quia mortuus*, because Lazarus was dead, *Jesus wept*.

He wept even in that respect, *quia mortuus*, and he wept in this respect too, *quia non adhibita media*: because those means, which in appearance might have saved his life, by his default were not used. for when he came to the house, one sister, Martha, says to him, *Lord if thou hadst been here, my brother had not died*; and then the other sister, Mary, says so too, *Lord if thou hadst been here, my brother had not died*. They all cry out that he who only, only by coming, might have saved his life, would not come. Our Savior knew in himself that he abstained to better purpose and to the further glory of God: for when he heard of his death, he said to his disciples, *I am glad for your sakes that I was not there*. Christ had certain reserved purposes which conduced to a better establishing of their faith and to a better advancing of God's kingdom: the working of that miracle. But yet because others were able to say to him, "it was in you to have saved him," and he did not, even this *quia non adhibita media*, affected him; and *Jesus wept*.

He wept, *etsi quatriduanus*, though they said unto him, *he hath been four days dead, and stinks*. Christ doth not say, "there is no such matter, he doth not stink," but "though he do, my friend shall not lack my help." Good friends, useful friends, though they may commit some errors, and though for some misbehaviors they may stink in our nostrils, must not be derelicted, abandoned to themselves. Many a son, many a good heir, finds an ill air from his father; his father's life stinks in the nostrils of all the world, and he hears everywhere exclamations upon his father's usury and extortion and oppression, yet it becomes him by a better life, and by all other means, to rectify and redeem his father's fame. *Quatriduanus est* is no plea for my negligence in my family: to say, my son or my servant hath proceeded so far in ill courses, that now it is to no purpose to go about to reform him because *quatriduanus est*. *Quatriduanus est* is no plea in my pastoral charge: to say that seducers and practicers and persuaders and solicitors for superstition enter so boldly into every family, that now it is to no purpose to preach religious wariness, religious discretion, religious constancy. *Quatriduanus est* is no plea for my usury, for my simony: to say, I do but as all the world doth and hath used to do a long time. To preach there where reprehension of growing sin is acceptable is to preach in season; where it is not acceptable, it is out of season; but yet we must preach in season, and out of season too. And when men

---

[14] {A probable allusion to John King, the Calvinist bishop of London and Donne's friend, after whose death in 1621 the Catholic rumor-mill circulated (apparently baseless) reports of an eleventh-hour conversion.}

are so refractory as that they forbear to hear, or hear and resist our preaching, we must pray; and where they despise or forbid our praying, we must lament them, we must weep. *Quatriduanus erat*, Lazarus was far spent, yet *Jesus wept.*

He wept, *etsi suscitandus*, though he knew that Lazarus were to be restored and raised to life again: for as he meant to declare a great good will to him at last, so he would utter some by the way; he would do a great miracle for him as he was a mighty God, but he would weep for him too as he was a good-natured man. Truly it is no very charitable disposition if I give all at my death to others, if I keep all all my life to myself. For how many families have we seen shaked, ruined by this distemper, that though the father mean to alien nothing of the inheritance from the son at his death, yet because he affords him not a competent maintenance in his life, he submits his son to an encumbering of his fame with ignominious shiftings, and an encumbering of the estate with irrecoverable debts. I may mean to feast a man plentifully at Christmas, and that man may starve before in Lent; great persons may think it in their power to give life to persons and actions by their benefits when they will, and before that will be up and ready, both may become incapable of their benefits. Jesus would not give this family, whom he pretended[15] to love, occasion of jealousy, of suspicion that he neglected them; and therefore, though he came not presently to that great work which he intended at last, yet he left them not comfortless by the way: *Jesus wept.*

And so (that we may reserve some minutes for the rest) we end this part, applying to every man that blessed exclamation of St. Ambrose, *ad monumentum hoc digneris accedere Domine Jesu*, Lord Jesus be pleased to come to this grave, to weep over this dead Lazarus, this soul in this body; and though I come not to a present rising, a present deliverance from the power of all sin, yet if I can feel the dew of thy tears upon me, if I can discern the eye of thy compassion bent towards me, I have comfort all the way, and that comfort will flow into an infallibility in the end.

And be this the end of this part, to which we are come by these steps: *Jesus wept*, that, as he showed himself to be God, he might appear to be man too; he wept not inordinately, but he came nearer excess than indolency; he wept because he was dead, and because all means for life had not been used; he wept, though he were far spent; and he wept, though he meant to raise him again.

We pass now from his human to his prophetical tears, from Jesus weeping in contemplation of a natural calamity fallen upon one family, Lazarus was dead, to his weeping in contemplation of a national calamity foreseen upon a whole people—Jerusalem was to be destroyed. His former tears had some of the spirit of prophecy in them; for therefore, says Epiphanius, Christ wept there, because he foresaw how little use the Jews would make of that miracle; his human tears were prophetical, and his prophetical tears are humane too, they rise from good affections to that people. And therefore the same author says, That because they thought it an uncomely thing for Christ to weep for any temporal thing, some men have expunged and removed that verse out of St. Luke's Gospel, that Jesus, when he saw that city, wept. But he is willing to be proposed, and to stand forever for an example of weeping in contemplation of public calamities;[16] therefore *Jesus wept.*

[15] {claimed, professed}

[16] {The year 1622 had seen one public calamity after another: the Jamestown massacre in Virginia; a series of major losses for the Protestant forces on the Continent, culminating in the fall of Heidelberg that September; the resumption of hostilities between Spain and the Netherlands.}

He wept first, *inter acclamationes*, in the midst of the congratulations and acclamations of the people; then when the whole multitude of his disciples cried out, *Vivat rex, Blessed be the king that comes in the name of the Lord*, Jesus wept. When Herod took to himself the name of the Lord, when he admitted that gross flattery, *It is a God and not a man that speaks*, it was no wonder that present occasion of lamentation fell upon him. But in the best times, and under the best princes (first, such is the natural mutability of all worldly things; and then—and that especially—such is the infiniteness and enormousness of our rebellious sin), then is ever just occasion of fear of worse, and so of tears.[17] Every man is but a sponge, and but a sponge filled with tears: and whether you lay your right hand or your left upon a full sponge, it will weep. Whether God lay his left hand, temporal calamities, or his right hand, temporal prosperity—even that temporal prosperity comes always accompanied with so much anxiety in ourselves, so much uncertainty in itself, and so much envy in others, as that that man who abounds most, that sponge shall weep.

Jesus wept, *inter acclamationes*, when all went well enough with him, to show the slipperiness of worldly happiness; and then he wept *inter judicia*; then when himself was in the act of denouncing judgments upon them, Jesus wept, to show with how ill a will he inflicted those judgments, and that themselves, and not he, had drawn those judgments upon them. How often do the prophets repeat that phrase, *onus visionis*, O the burden of the judgments that I have seen upon this and this people! It was a burden that pressed tears from the prophet Esay, *I will water thee with my tears, O Heshbon*; when he must pronounce judgments upon her, he could not but weep over her. No prophet so tender as Christ, nor so compassionate; and therefore he never takes rod into his hand but with tears in his eyes. Alas, did God lack a footstool, that he should make man only to tread and trample upon? Did God lack glory, and could have it no other way, but by creating man therefore, to afflict him temporally here and eternally hereafter? whatsoever Christ weeps for in the way of his mercy, it is likely he was displeased with it in the way of his justice? If he weep for it, he had rather it were not so. If then those judgments upon Jerusalem were only from his own primary and positive and absolute decree, without any respect to their sins, could he be displeased with his own act, or weep and lament that which only himself had done? Would God ask that question of Israel, *Quare moriemini domus Israel?* why will you die O house of Israel? if God lay open to that answer, We die therefore, because you have killed us? Jerusalem would not judge herself; therefore Christ judged her. Jerusalem would not weep for herself, and therefore Jesus wept; but in those tears of his, he showed that he had rather her own tears had averted and washed away those judgments.

He wept *cum appropinquavit*, says the text there, *when Jesus came near the city and saw it, then he wept*; not till then. If we will not come near the miseries of our brethren, if we will not see them, we will never weep over them, never be affected towards them. It was *cum ille*, not *cum illi*, when Christ himself, not when his disciples, his followers, who could do Jerusalem no good, took knowledge of it. It was not *cum illi*, nor it was not *cum illa*, not when those judgments drew near; it is not said so; neither is there any time limited in the text when those judgments were to fall upon Jerusalem; it is only said generally,

---

[17] {That Charles and Buckingham had arrived safely in Madrid eleven days previously was not yet widely known, and it was widely feared that they would never be allowed to return safely.}

indefinitely, these days shall come upon her. And yet Christ did not ease himself upon that, that those calamities were remote and far off, but though they were so, and not to fall till after his death, yet he lamented future calamities then; then Jesus wept. Many such little brooks as these fall into this river, the consideration of Christ's prophetical tears, but let it be enough to have sprinkled these drops out of the river: that Jesus, though a private person, wept in contemplation of public calamities; that he wept in the best times, foreseeing worse; that he wept in their miseries, because he was no author of them; that he wept not till he took their miseries into his consideration; and he did weep a good time before those miseries fell upon them. There remain yet his third tears, his pontifical tears, which accompany his sacrifice; those tears we called the sea, but a sea which must now be bounded with a very little sand.[18]

To sail apace through this sea: these tears, the tears of his Cross, were expressed by that inestimable weight, the sins of all the world. If all the body were eye, argues the Apostle in another place—why, here all the body was eye; every pore of his body made an eye by tears of blood, and every inch of his body made an eye by their bloody scourges. And if Christ's looking upon Peter made Peter weep, shall not his looking upon us here, with tears in his eyes, such tears in such eyes, springs of tears, rivers of tears, seas of tears, make us weep too? Peter, who wept under the weight of his particular sin, wept bitterly; how bitterly wept Christ under the weight of all the sins of all the world? In the first tears, Christ's human tears (those we called a spring), we fetched water at one house, we condoled a private calamity in another; Lazarus was dead. In his second tears, his prophetical tears, we went to the condoling of a whole nation; and those we called a river. In these third tears, his pontifical tears, tears for sin, for all sins (those we call a sea), here is *mare liberum*, a sea free and open to all; every man may sail home, home to himself, and lament his own sins there.

I am far from concluding all to be impenitent that do not actually weep and shed tears. I know there are constitutions, complexions, that do not afford them. And yet the worst epithet which the best poet could fix upon Pluto himself, was to call him *illachrymabilis*, a person that could not weep.[19] But to weep for other things, and not to weep for sin; or if not to tears, yet not to come to that tenderness, to that melting, to that thawing, that resolving of the bowels which good souls feel: this is a sponge (I said before, every man is a sponge), this is a sponge dried up into a pumice stone; the lightness, the hollowness of a sponge is there still, but (as the pumice is) dried in the Ætnas of lust, of ambition, of other flames in this world.

I have but three words to say of these tears, of this weeping. What it is, what it is for, what it does: the nature, the use, the benefit of these tears is all. And in the first, I forbear to insist upon St. Basil's metaphor, *lachrymae sudor animi male sani*;[20] sin is my sickness, the blood of Christ Jesus is my bezoar;[21] tears is the sweat that that produceth. I forbear Gregory Nyssen's metaphor too, *lachryma sanguis cordis defoecatus*; tears are our best blood, so agitated, so ventilated, so purified, so rarified into spirits, as that thereby

---

[18] {the sand being that in the preacher's hourglass}
[19] {Horace, *Odes* 4.9.26}
[20] {Literally, "tears are the sweat of a sick soul."}
[21] {antidote, medicine}

I become *idem spiritus*, one spirit with my God. That is large enough, and embraces all, which St. Gregory says, That man weeps truly, that soul sheds true tears, that considers seriously, first, *ubi fuit in innocentia*, the blessed state which man was in, in his integrity at first, *ubi fuit*; and then considers, *ubi est in tentationibus*, the weak estate that man is in now, in the midst of temptations, where, if he had no more, himself were temptation too much, *ubi est*; and yet considers farther, *ubi erit in gehenna*, the insupportable, and for all that, the inevitable; the irreparable, and for all that, undeterminable torments of hell, *ubi erit*; and lastly, *ubi non erit, in coelis*, the inexpressible joy and glory which he loses in heaven, *ubi non erit*, where he shall never be. These four to consider seriously, where man was, where he is, where he shall be, where he shall never be, are four such rivers, as constitute a paradise. And as a ground may be a weeping ground, though it have no running river, no constant spring, no gathering of waters in it; so a soul that can pour out itself into these religious considerations may be a weeping soul, though it have a dry eye. This weeping then is but a true sorrow (that was our first); and then, what this true sorrow is given us for, and that is our next consideration.

As water is in nature a thing indifferent—it may give life (so the first living things that were, were in the water) and it may destroy life (so all things living upon the earth were destroyed in the water)—but yet, though water may, though it have done good and bad, yet water does now one good office which no ill quality that is in it can equal: it washes our souls in baptism. So though there be good tears and bad tears, tears that wash away sin and tears that are sin, yet all tears have this degree of good in them, that they are all some kind of argument of good nature, of a tender heart; and the Holy Ghost loves to work in wax, and not in marble. I hope that is but merely poetical which the poet[22] says, *Discunt lachrymare decenter*, that some study to weep with a good grace; *Quoque volunt plorant tempore, quoque modo*, they make use and advantage of their tears, and weep when they will. But of those who weep not when they would, but when they would not, do half employ their tears upon that for which God hath given them that sacrifice, upon sin? God made the firmament, which he called heaven after it had divided the waters; after we have distinguished our tears, natural from spiritual, worldly from heavenly, then there is a firmament established in us, then there is a heaven opened to us: and truly, to cast pearls before swine will scarce be better resembled than to shed tears (which resemble pearls) for worldly losses.

Are there examples of men passionately enamored upon age? or, if upon age, upon deformity? If there be examples of that, are they not examples of scorn too? do not all others laugh at their tears? and yet such is our passionate doting upon this world. *Mundi facies*, says St. Augustine (and even St. Augustine himself hath scarce said anything more pathetically), *tanta rerum labe contrita, ut etiam speciam seductionis amiserit*; the face of the whole world is so defaced, so wrinkled, so ruined, so deformed, as that man might be trusted with this world, and there is no jealousy, no suspicion that this world should be able to minister any occasion of temptation to man: *speciem seductionis amisit*. And yet, *qui in seipso aruit, in nobis floret*, says St. Gregory, as wittily as St. Augustine (as it is easy to be witty, easy to extend an epigram to a satire, and a satire to an invective, in declaiming against this world): that world which finds itself truly in an autumn, in itself, finds itself

---

[22] {Ovid, *De arte amandi* lib. 3}

in a spring, in our imaginations. *Labenti haeremus*, says that Father, *et cum labentem sistere non possumus, cum ipso labimur*; the world passes away, and yet we cleave to it; and when we cannot stay it from passing away, we pass away with it.

To mourn passionately for the love of this world, which is decrepit and upon the deathbed, or immoderately for the death of any that is passed out of this world, is not the right use of tears. That hath good use which Chrysologus notes: that when Christ was told of Lazarus' death, he said he was glad; when he came to raise him to life, then he wept; for though his disciples gained by it (they were confirmed by a miracle), though the family gained by it (they had their Lazarus again), yet Lazarus himself lost by it, by being re-imprisoned, re-committed, re-submitted to the manifold incommodities of this world. When our Savior Christ forbad the women to weep for him, it was because there was nothing in him for tears to work upon; no sin. *Ordinem flendi docuit*, says St. Bernard, Christ did not absolutely forbid tears, but regulate and order their tears, that they might weep in the right place: first, for sin. David wept for Absalom: he might imagine that he died in sin; he wept not for the child by Bathsheba: he could not suspect so much danger in that. *Exitus aquarum*, says David, *rivers of waters ran down from mine eyes*. Why? *Quia illi, Because they* . . . Who are they? not other men, as it is ordinarily taken; but *Quia illi, Because mine own eyes* (so Hilary and Ambrose and Augustine take it) *have not kept thy laws*. As the calamities of others, so the sins of others may, but our own sins must, be the object of our sorrow. *Thou shalt offer to me*, says God, *the first of thy ripe fruits, and of thy liquors*, as our translation hath it. The word in the original is *vedingnacha, lachrymarum*— and of thy tears. Thy first tears must be to God for sin; the second and third may be to nature and civility and such secular offices. But *liquore ad lippitudinem apto quisquamne ad pedes lavandus abutetur?* It is St. Chrysostom's exclamation and admiration: *will any wash his feet in water for sore eyes?* Will any man embalm the carcass of the world, which he treads under foot, with those tears which should embalm his soul? Did Joseph of Arimathea bestow any of his perfumes (though he brought a superfluous quantity, a hundred pound weight for one body), yet did he bestow any upon the body of either of the thieves? Tears are true sorrow, that you heard before; true sorrow is for sin, that you have heard now; all that remains is how this sorrow works, what it does.

The Fathers have infinitely delighted themselves in this descant, the blessed effect of holy tears. He amongst them that remembers us that in the Old Law all sacrifices were washed, he means that our best sacrifice, even prayer itself, receives an improvement, a dignity, by being washed in tears. He that remembers us that if any room of our house be on fire we run for water, means that in all temptations we should have recourse to tears. He that tells us that money being put into a basin is seen at a farther distance, if there be water in the basin, than if it be empty, means also that our most precious devotions receive an addition, a multiplication by holy tears. St. Bernard means all that they all mean in that, *cor lacrymas nesciens durum, impurum*,[23] a hard heart is a foul heart. Would you shut up the devil in his own channel, his channel of brimstone, and make that worse? St. Hierome tells the way, *Plus tua lachryma, &c.* Thy tears torment him more than the fires of hell. Will you needs have holy water? truly, true tears are the holiest water. And for

---

[23] {"A heart that does not know how to cry is hard, unclean."}

purgatory, it is liberally confessed by a Jesuit, *Non minus efficax, &c.* One tear will do thee as much good as all the flames of purgatory. We have said more than once that man is a sponge; and *in codice scripta*, all our sins are written in God's book, says St. Chrysostom; if there I can fill my sponge with tears, and so wipe out all my sins out of that book, it is a blessed use of the sponge.[24]

I might stand upon this, the manifold benefits of godly tears, long—so long, as till you wept, and wept for sin; and that might be very long. I contract all to this one, which is all: to how many blessednesses must these tears, this godly sorrow reach by the way, when as it reaches to the very extreme, to that which is opposed to it, to joy? for godly sorrow is joy. The words in Job are, in the Vulgate, *Dimitte me ut plangam dolorem meum, Lord spare me awhile that I may lament my lamentable estate*; and so ordinarily the expositors that follow that translation make their use of them. But yet it is in the original, *Lord spare me awhile, that I may take comfort*: that which one calls *lamenting*, the other calls *rejoicing*; to conceive true sorrow and true joy are things not only contiguous, but continual; they do not only touch and follow one another in a certain succession, joy assuredly after sorrow, but they consist together, they are all one, joy and sorrow. *My tears have been my meat day and night*, says David; not that he had no other meat, but that none relished so well. It is a grammatical note of a Jesuit (I do not tell you it is true—I have almost told you that it is not true by telling you whose it is—but that it is but a grammatical note), that when it is said, *tempus cantus, the time of singing is come*, it might as well be rendered out of the Hebrew, *tempus plorationis, the time of weeping is come*; and when it is said, *nomini tuo cantabo, Lord I will sing unto thy name*, it might be as well rendered out of the Hebrew, *plorabo, I will weep, I will sacrifice my tears unto thy name*. So equal, so indifferent a thing is it, when we come to godly sorrow, whether we call it sorrow or joy, weeping or singing.

To end all: to weep for sin is not a damp of melancholy, to sigh for sin is not a vapor of the spleen, but as Monica's confessor said still unto her in the behalf of her son St. Augustine, *filius istarum lachrymarum*, the son of these tears cannot perish. So wash thyself in these three exemplar baths of Christ's tears—in his humane tears, and be tenderly affected with human accidents; in his prophetical tears, and avert as much as in thee lieth the calamities imminent upon others; but especially in his pontifical tears, tears for sin—and I am thy confessor, *non ego, sed Dominus*; not I, but the Spirit of God himself is thy confessor, and he absolves thee. *Filius istarum lachrymarum*, the soul bathed in these tears cannot perish, for this is *trina immersio*, that threefold dipping which was used in the primitive Church in baptism. And in this baptism thou takest a new Christian name; thou who wast but a Christian, art now a regenerate Christian; and as Naaman the leper came cleaner out of Jordan than he was before his leprosy (for his flesh came as the flesh of a child), so there shall be better evidence in this baptism of thy repentance than in thy first baptism: better in thyself, for then thou hadst no sense of thy own estate, in this thou hast; and thou shalt have better evidence from others too, for howsoever some others will dispute whether all children which die after baptism be certainly saved or no, it never fell into doubt or disputation whether all that die truly repentant be saved or no. Weep these tears truly, and God shall perform to thee, first that promise which he makes in Esay, *The*

---

[24] {Donne is thinking of wax writing-tables, commonly used during the period, which were erased by using a damp sponge or cloth.}

Lord shall wipe all tears from thy face, all that are fallen by any occasion of calamity here, in the militant Church; and he shall perform that promise which he makes in the Revelation, *The Lord shall wipe all tears from thine eyes*, that is, dry up the fountain of tears, remove all occasion of tears hereafter, in the triumphant Church.

TEXT: *The works of John Donne, D.D., Dean of Saint Paul's, 1621–1631*, 6 vols., ed. Henry Alford (London, 1839), 1:251–72.[25]

> Corrected against *The sermons of John Donne*, 10 vols., ed. G. R. Potter and E. M. Simpson (U California P, 1953–62), vol. 4, sermon 13.

[25] The sermon was first published in Donne's *LXXX sermons* (London, 1640).

LANCELOT ANDREWES

Easter sermon
1623

The introduction to Andrewes' life and works is to be found prefacing his 1604 Good Friday sermon *<supra>*. The Easter 1623 sermon follows the dominant patristic reading of Isaiah 63:1-3 as a prophetic vision of Christ victorious over death and hell.[1] Calvin's commentary on the same passage, however, provides an illuminating contrast:

> **[63:]1.** *Who is this that cometh from Edom?* This chapter has been violently distorted by Christians, as if what is said here related to Christ, whereas the Prophet speaks simply of God himself; and they have imagined that here Christ is red because he was wet with his own blood which he shed on the Cross. But the Prophet meant nothing of that sort. The obvious meaning is that the Lord comes forth with red garments in the view of his people, that all may know that he is their protector and avenger; for when the people were weighed down by innumerable evils, and at the same time the Edomites and other enemies, as if they had been placed beyond the reach of all danger, freely indulged in wickedness which remained unpunished, a dangerous temptation might arise, as if these things happened by chance, or as if God did not care for his people, or chastised them too severely. If the Jews were punished for despising God, much more the Edomites, and other avowed enemies of the name of God, ought to have been punished.
>
> . . .
>
> **3.** *Alone have I pressed the wine-press.* The Prophet now explains the vision, and the reason why the Lord was stained with blood. It is because he will take vengeance on the Edomites and other enemies who treated his people cruelly. It would be absurd to say that these things relate to Christ because he alone and

---

[1] On its *Christus victor* theology of the Atonement, see Gustav Aulen, *Christus victor: an historical study of the three main types of the idea of Atonement*, trans. A. G. Herbert (SPCK, 1931).

without human aid redeemed us; for it means that God will punish the Edomites in such a manner that he will have no need of the assistance of men, because he will be sufficiently able to destroy them.[2]

---

[2] *Isaiah, part IV: Calvin's commentaries*, vol. 16, trans. John King (1847–50), Internet Sacred Text Archive: Calvin, www.sacred-texts.com/chr/calvin/index.htm.

LANCELOT ANDREWES

A sermon preached before the King's Majesty at Whitehall, on the xiii of April,
A.D. MCDXXIII, being Easter Day
1623, published 1629

Quis est iste qui venit de Edom &c.

Who is this that cometh from Edom, with red garments from Bozrah? He is glorious in his apparel and walketh in great strength; I speak in righteousness, and am mighty to save.

Wherefore is thine apparel red, and thy garments like him that treadeth in the winepress?

I have trodden the winepress alone, and of all the people there was none with me, for I will tread them in mine anger, and tread them under foot in my wrath, and their blood shall be sprinkled upon my garments, and I will stain all my raiment.

{Isaiah 63:1-3, Geneva trans.}

Ever when we read or hear read any text or passage out of this prophet, the Prophet Esay, it brings to our mind the nobleman that sitting in his chariot read another like passage out of this same Prophet. Brings him to mind, and with him his question, *Of whom doth the Prophet speak this? of himself or of some other?* Not of himself, that's once;[1] it cannot be himself. It is he that asks the question. Some other then it must needs be of whom it is, and we to ask who that other was.

The tenor of Scripture that nobleman then read was out of the 53rd chapter, and this of ours out of the 63rd, ten chapters between. But if St. Philip had found him reading of this here, as he did of that, he would likewise have begun at this same Scripture as at that he did, and preached to him Christ—only with this difference: out of that, Christ's Passion, out of this, his Resurrection. For he that was led *as a sheep to be slain*, and so was slain there [Isa. 53:7], he it is and no other that rises and comes here back like a lion *from Bozrah*, imbrued with blood, the blood of his enemies.

I have before I was aware disclosed who this party is. It was not amiss I so should; not to hold you long in suspense, but to give you a little light at the first whom it would fall on. CHRIST it is. Two things there are that make it can be no other but he. One is

[1] {that's certain}

without the text, in the end of the chapter next before. There is a proclamation, *Behold, here comes your Savior,* and immediately he that comes is this party here from Edom. He is our Savior, and besides him there is none. Even Christ the Lord. The other is in the text itself, in these words: *Torcular calcavi solus,* I have trod the winepress alone. Words so proper to Christ, so everywhere ascribed to him, and to him only, as you shall not read them any where applied to any other; no, not by the Jews themselves. So as, if there were no more but these two, they shew it plainly enough it is, it can be none but Christ.

And Christ when? Even this day of all days. His coming here from Edom will fall out to be his rising from the dead. His return from Bozrah, nothing but his vanquishing of hell. (We may use his words in applying it, *Thou hast not left my soul in hell, but brought me back from the deep of the earth again* [Ps. 16:10, 71:20].) Nothing but the act of his rising again. So that this very morning was this Scripture *fulfilled in our ears.*

I. The whole text entire is a dialogue between two, 1. the Prophet, and 2. Christ. There are in it two questions; and to the two questions, two answers. The Prophet's first question is touching the party himself, who he is, in these words, *Who is this?* To which the party himself answers in the same verse, these words, *that am I, one that,* &c.

II. The Prophet's second question is about his colors, why he was *all in red* (in the second verse), *Wherefore then is thy apparel,* &c. The answer to that is (in the third verse) in these: *I have trodden, &c. For I will tread them down.*

Of Christ: of his rising or coming back, of his colors, of the winepress that gave him this tincture, or rather of the two winepresses: 1. the winepress of redemption first; 2. and then of the other winepress of vengeance.

⤞⌇⤝

I. The prophets use to speak of things to come as if they saw them present before their eyes. That makes their prophecies be called visions. In his vision here, the Prophet being taken up in spirit sees one coming. Coming, whence? From the land or country of Idumaea or Edom. From what place there? From Bozrah, the chief city in the land, the place of greatest strength. *Who will lead me into the strong city?* That is Bozrah. *Who will bring me into Edom?* He that can do the first, can do the latter. Win Bozrah, and Edom is won.

There was a cry in the end of the chapter before: *Behold, here comes your Savior.* He looked, and saw one coming. Two things he descries in this party: 1. One, his habit, that he was *formosus in stolâ,* very richly arrayed; 2. The other, his gait, that he *came stoutly marching,* or pacing the ground very strongly. Two good familiar notes to descry a stranger by: his apparel, whether rich or mean, which the world most commonly takes notice of men by; his gait, for weak men have but a feeble gait. Valiant strong men tread upon the ground so, as by it you may discern their strength.

Now this party, he came so goodly in his apparel, so stately in his march, as if by all likelihood he had made some conquest in Edom, the place he came from; had had a victory in Bozrah, the city where he had been. And the truth is, so he had. He saith it in the third verse: *He had trodden down his enemies,* had trampled upon them, made the blood even start out of them, which blood of theirs had all to-stained his garments. This was no evil news for Esay's countrymen, the people of God; Edom was their {*sic*} worst enemy they had.

With joy then, but not without admiration, such a party sees the Prophet come toward him. Sees him, but knows him not; thinks him worthy the knowing; so thinking, and not knowing, is desirous to be instructed concerning him. Out of this desire asks, *Quis est?* Not of himself, he durst not be so bold, "Who are you?" but of some stander-by, "Whom have we here? Can you tell *who this might be?*" The first question.

But before we come to the question, a word or two of the place where he had been, and whence he came. *Edom* and *Bozrah*, what is meant by them? For if this party be Christ, Christ was in Egypt a child, but never in Edom that we read, never at Bozrah in all his life; so as here we are to leave the letter. Some other it might be the letter might mean; we will not much stand to look after him. For however possibly some such there was, yet it will plainly appear by the sequel, that *the testimony of Jesus*, as it is of each other, so it *is the spirit of this prophecy* [Apoc. 9:10].

Go we then to the kernel, and let the husk lie; let go the dead letter, and take we to us the spiritual meaning that hath some life in it. For what care we for the literal Edom or Bozrah, what became of them; what are they to us? Let us compare spiritual things with spiritual things, that is it must do us good.

I will give you a key to this, and such like Scriptures. Familiar it is with the prophets, nothing more, than to speak to their people in their own language; than to express their ghostly enemies, the both mortal and immortal enemies of their souls, under the titles and terms of those nations and cities as were the known sworn enemies of the commonwealth of Israel. As of *Egypt*, where they were in bondage; as of *Babylon*, where in captivity; elsewhere, as of *Edom* here, who maliced them more than both those. If the Angel tell us right, Revelation 11, there is *a spiritual Sodom and Egypt where our Lord was crucified*; and if they, why not a spiritual Edom too whence our Lord rose again? Put all three together, Egypt, Babel, Edom, all their enmities, all are nothing to the hatred that hell bears us. But yet, if you ask, of the three which was the worst? That was Edom. To shew the Prophet here made good choice of his place: Edom upon earth comes nearest to the kingdom of darkness in hell, of all the rest. And that, in these respects:

First, they were the wickedest people under the sun. If there were any devils upon earth, it was they. If the devil, of any country, he would choose to be an Edomite. No place on earth that resembled hell nearer; next to hell on earth was Edom for all that naught was. Malachi calls Edom, *the border of all wickedness, a people with whom God was angry forever.* In which very points, no enemies so fitly express the enemies of our souls, against whom the anger of God is eternal, and *the smoke of whose torments shall ascend forever.* Hell, for all that naught is. That if the power of darkness, and hell itself, if they be to be expressed by any place on earth, they cannot be better expressed than in these, *Edom* and *Bozrah*.

I will give you another. The Edomites were the posterity of Esau; *the same is Edom.* So they were nearest of kin to the Jews of all nations; so should have been their best friends. The Jews and they came of two brethren. Edom was the elder, and that was the grief, that the people of Israel, coming of Jacob, the younger brother, had enlarged their border, got them a better seat and country by far than they, the Edomites, had. Hence grew envy, and an enemy out of envy is ever the worst. So were they, the most cankered

324

enemies that Israel had. The case is so between us and the evil spirits. Angels they were, we know, and so in a sort elder brethren to us. Of the two intellectual natures, they the first created. Our case now, Christ be thanked, is much better than theirs; which is that enrageth them against us, as much and more than ever any Edomite against Israel. Hell, for rancor and envy.

Yet one more. They were ready to do God's people all the mischief they were able, and when they were not able of themselves, they shewed their good-wills though, set on others. And when they had won Jerusalem, cried *Down with it, down with it, even to the ground*; no less would serve. And when it was on the ground, insulted and rejoiced above measure: *remember the children of Edom*. This is right the devil's property, *quarto modo*.[2] He that hath but the heart of a man will even rue to see his enemy lying in extreme misery. None but very devils, or devils incarnate, will do so: corrupt their compassion, cast off all pity; rejoice, insult, take delight at one's destruction. Hell for their ἐπέχαιρε κακία, insulting over men in misery.

But will ye go even to the letter? none did ever so much mischief to David, as did Doeg; he was an Edomite. Nor none so much to the Son of David, Christ, none bore more malice to him first and last than did Herod; and he was an Edomite. So, which way soever we take it, next the kingdom of darkness was Edom upon earth. And Christ coming from thence, may well be said to come from Edom.

But what say you to Bozrah? This: that if the country of Edom do well set before us the whole kingdom of darkness or region of death, Bozrah may well stand for hell itself. Bozrah was the strongest hold of that kingdom; hell is so of this. The whole country of Idumea was called and known by the name of Uz, that is, of *strength*; and what of such strength as death? all the sons of men stoop to him. Bozrah was called *the strong city*; hell is strong as it every way. They write, it was environed with huge high rocks on all sides, one only cleft to come to it by. And when you were in, there must you perish; no getting out again. For all the world like to hell, as Abraham describes it to him that was in it: *they that would go from this place to you cannot possibly, neither can they come from thence to us*; the gulf is so great, no getting out. No *habeas corpus*, from death; no *habeas animam* out of hell; you must *let that alone for ever* [Ps 49:8].

Now then have we the Prophet's true Edom, his very Bozrah indeed. By this we understand what they mean: *Edom*, the *kingdom of darkness and death*; *Bozrah*, the seat of the prince of darkness, that is, hell itself. From both which Christ this day returned. *His soul was not left in hell*; *his flesh saw not* (but *rose from*) *corruption*.

For over *Edom*, *strong* as it was, yet David *cast his shoe over it* (that is, after the Hebrew phrase), *set his foot upon it* and trod it down. And Bozrah, as impregnable a hold as it was holden, yet David won it, was led *into the strong city*, led into it, and came thence again. So did the Son of David this day from his Edom, death, how strong soever, yet *swallowed up in victory*, this day. And from hell, his Bozrah, how hard soever it held (as he that was in it found there was no getting thence), Christ is got forth, we see. How many souls soever were there left, his was not left there.

---

[2] {a fallacious, or at least dubious, syllogistic figure}

And when did he this? when *solutus doloribus inferni; he loosed the pains of hell, trod upon the serpent's head*, and all to-bruised it; took from *death his sting*, from *hell his victory*—that is, his standard, alluding to the Roman standard that had in it the image of the goddess Victory; seized upon the *chirographum contra nos*, the *ragman roll[3] that made so strong against us*; took it, rent it, and so rent, *nailed it to his Cross*; made his banner of it, of the law cancelled, hanging at it banner-wise. And having thus *spoiled Principalities and Powers, he made an open show of them, triumphed over them in semetipso*, in his own person (all three are in Colos. 2), and triumphantly came thence with the keys of Edom and Bozrah both, of hell and of death, both at his girdle, as he shews himself, Apoc. 1. And when was this? if ever, on this very day. On which, having made a full and perfect conquest of death, *and of him that hath the power of death, that is the devil* (Heb. 2), he rose and returned thence, this morning, as a mighty conqueror, saying as Debora did in her song, *O my soul, thou hast trodden down strength, thou hast marched valiantly!*

And coming back thus, from the debellation of the spiritual Edom, and the breaking up of the true Bozrah indeed, it is wondered *who* it should be. Note this: that nobody knew Christ at his rising, neither Mary Magdalene, nor they that went to Emmaus. No more doth the Prophet here.

Now there was reason to ask this question, for none would ever think it to be Christ. There is great odds, it cannot be he. 1. Not he; he was put to death, and put into his grave, and a great stone upon him, not three days since. This party is alive and alives-like. His ghost it cannot be: he glides not (as ghosts, they say, do), but paces the ground very strongly.

2. Not he; he had his *apparel shared amongst the soldiers*, was left all naked. This party hath gotten him on *glorious apparel*, rich scarlet.

3. Not he; for if he come, he must come in white, in the linen he was lapped in, and laid in his grave. This party comes in quite another color, all in *red*. So the colors suit not.

4. To be short, not he: for he was put to a foil, to a foul foil as ever was any; *they did to him even what they listed*; scorned, insulted upon him. It was then *the hour and power of darkness*. This party, whatsoever he is, hath gotten the upper hand, won the field; marches stately, conqueror-like. His the day, sure.

Well, yet Christ it is. His answer gives him for no other. To his answer then. The party, it seems, overheard the Prophet's asking, and is pleased to give an answer to it himself. We are much bound to him for it. No man can tell so well as he himself, who he is. Some other might mistake him, and misinform us of him; now we are sure we are right. No *error personae*.

His name, indeed, he tells not, but describes himself by two such notes as can agree to none properly but to Christ. Of none can these two be so affirmed, as of him they may. That by these two we know this is Christ, as plainly as if his name had been spelled to us. 1. *Speaking righteousness*; and righteousness, referred to speech, signifieth *truth* ever. *No guile to be found in his mouth*; and *omnis homo* is—you know what [1 Pet. 2:22]. 2. *Mighty*

---

[3] {a statute dealing with complaints of injuries; letters containing self-accusations of crimes against the state}

to save; and *vana salus hominis*, vain is the help of man. *Who ever spake so right* as he spake? Or who ever was so *mighty to save* as he? And this is his answer to *quis est iste.*[4]

That, am I. One *that speak righteousness*, and am *mighty to save. Righteous* in *speaking, mighty* in *saving*, whose word is *truth*, whose work is *salvation.* Just and true of my word and promise; powerful and mighty in performance of both. The best description, say I, that can be of any man; by his word and deed both.

And see how well they fit. *Speaking* is most proper; that refers to him as the Word—*in the beginning was the Word*—to his divine nature.[5] *Saving*, that refers to his very name Jesus, given him by the angel, as man, for that *he should save his people from their sins*, from which none had ever power to save but he. There have you his two natures.

Speaking refers to his office of priest: the *priest's lips to preserve knowledge*, the *law of righteousness* to be *required at his mouth. Saving*, and that mightily, pertains to him as a king; is the office, as Daniel calls him, of *Messias the Captain.* Righteousness he *spake*, by his preaching. *Saving*, that belongs first to his miraculous suffering; it being far a greater miracle for the Deity to suffer any the least injury than to create a new world, yea many. But secondly, which is proper to the text and time, in his mighty subduing and treading down hell and death, and all the power of Satan. *Prophetiza nobis*, they said at his Passion, *speak, who hit you* there; and *Ave Rex*[6] they said too—both in scorn, but most true both.

You may refer these two, if you please, to his two main benefits redounding to us from these two. Two things there are that undo us, error and sin. From his speaking, we receive knowledge of his truth, against error. From his saving, we receive the power of grace against sin, and so are saved from sin's sequel, Edom and Bozrah both. This is his description, and this is enough. A full description of his person, in his natures, offices, benefits; in word and in deed. He it is, and can be none but he. To reflect a little on these two.

You will observe that his speaking is set down simply, but in his saving he is said to be *mighty*, or as the word is, *multus ad servandum.* So, mark where the *multus* is. He is not *multus ad loquendum*, one that saith much, and *paucus ad servandum*, and then does little, as the manner of the world is. *Multus* is not there at his speech. It is put to *servandum*; there he is much, and his might much: *much of might to save.*

That his might is not put in treading down or destroying. No, but *multus ad igno-scendum*, in the fifty-five chapter before; and *multus ad servandum*, here. *Mighty* to shew mercy, and to save. Yet *mighty* he is too, to destroy and tread down; else had he not achieved this victory in the text. *Mighty to save* implieth ever *mighty to subdue*: to subdue them whom he saves us from. Yet of the twain he chooseth rather the term of *saving*, though both be true, because saving is with him *primae intentionis.* So of the twain, in that he would have his might appear rather. *Mighty to destroy* he will not have mentioned or come in his style; but *mighty to save*, that is his title; that, the quality he takes delight in: delights to describe himself, and to be described by.

[4] {Who is this?}

[5] {"Speaking" befits Christ's divine nature as the eternal Word (Logos), of John 1:1 ("In the beginning was the Word.").}

[6] {Hail, King}

You will yet mark also, as the coupling of these two in the description of Christ (for not either of these alone will serve, but between them both they make it up), so that they go together, these two ever. He saves not any but those he teaches. And note the order of them too. For that that stands first, he doth first; first teaches. *Mighty to save* he is, but whom to save? whom he *speaks righteousness* to, and they hear him, and *return not again to their former folly.* There is no fancying to ourselves we can dispense with one of these, never care whether we deal with the former or no, whether we hear him speak at all, but take hold of the latter, and be saved with a good will. No; you cannot but if you hear him speak first. He saith so, and sets them so himself.

And put this to it, and I have done this point. That such as is himself, such, if we hear him, will he make us to be. And the more true and soothfast any of us is of his word, the more given to do good and save, the liker to him, and the liker to have our parts in his rising. We know *quis est iste*, now. This for the first part.

II. Now, the Prophet hearing him answer so gently, takes to him a little courage to ask him one question more, about his colors; he was a little troubled with them. If you be so *mighty to save*, as you say, how comes it then, what ails your *garments* to be so *red*? and adds what kind of red; and he cannot tell what to liken them better to than as if he had newly come out of some winepress, had been treading grapes, and pressing out wine there. He calls it wine, but the truth is it was no wine. It was very blood. New wine in show; blood indeed, that upon his garments. So much appeareth in the next verse following, where he saith himself plainly that *blood it was that was sprinkled upon his clothes, and had stained them all over.* We know well, our reason leads us, there could be no vintage at this time of the year; the season serves not. Blood it was.

But because the Prophet made mention of a *winepress*, had hit on that simile, taking occasion upon the naming it, he shapes him an answer according: that indeed he had been in a *winepress*. And so he had. The truth is, he had been in one. Nay, in two then. In one he had been before this here. A double winepress (we lose nothing by this) we find; Christ was in both. We cannot well take notice of the one, but we must needs touch upon the other. But thus they are distinguished. In that former, it was *in torculari calcatus sum solus*; in this latter it is, *torcular calcavi solus*. In the former, he was himself trodden and pressed; he was the grapes and clusters himself. In this latter here, he that was trodden on before, gets up again, and doth here tread upon and tread down, *calcare* and *conculcare* (both words are in the verse) upon some others (as it might be the Edomites). The press he was trodden in was his Cross and Passion. This, which he came out of this day, was in his Descent and Resurrection, both proper to this feast; one to Good-Friday, the other to Easter-day.

To pursue this of the winepress a little. The press, the treading in it, is to make wine. *Calcatus sum* is properly of grapes, the fruit of the vine. Christ is the *true vine*; he saith it himself. To make wine of him, he and the clusters he bare must be pressed. So he was. Three shrewd strains they gave him. One, in Gethsemane, that made him sweat blood; the wine, or blood (all is one), came forth at all parts of him. Another, in the Judgment Hall, Gabbatha, which made the blood run forth at his head, with the thorns; out of his whole body, with the scourges; out of his hands and feet, with the nails. The last strain at

Golgotha, where he was so pressed that they pressed the very soul out of his body, and out ran blood and water both. *Haec sunt Ecclesiae gemina sacramenta*, saith St. Augustine, out came both sacraments, the *twin sacraments of the Church*.

Out of these pressures ran the blood of the grapes of the true vine, the fruit whereof (as it is said in Judg. 9) *cheereth both God and man*. God, as a *libamen* or drink-offering to him; man, as *the cup of salvation* to them. But, to make this wine, his clusters were to be cut; cut, and cast in; cast in and trodden on; trodden and pressed out; all these, before he came to be wine in the cup. As likewise, when he calls himself *granum frumenti*, the *wheat-corn* [Job. 12:24], these four, the sickle, the flail, the millstone, the oven, he passed through. All went over him before he was made bread; the *shew-bread* to God, to us *the Bread of life*.

But, to return to the winepress, to tell you the occasion or reason, why thus it behoved to be. It was not idly done. What need then was there of it, this first pressing? We find (1 Cor. 10) *calix daemoniorum*; the devil hath a cup. Adam must needs be sipping of it; *eritis sicut Dii*[7] went down sweetly, but poisoned him, turned his nature quite. For Adam was by God planted a natural vine, a true root, but thereby, by that cup, degenerated into a wild strange vine, which, instead of good grapes, brought forth *labruscas, wild grapes, grapes of gall, bitter clusters*. Moses calls them *coloquintida*; the Prophet, *mors in olla* and *mors in calice*;[8] by which is meant, the deadly fruit of our deadly sins.

But (as it is in the fifth chapter of this prophecy), where God planted this vine first, he made a winepress in it; so the grapes that came of this strange vine were cut and cast into the press; thereof came a deadly wine, of which, saith the Psalmist, *in the hand of the Lord there is a cup; the wine is red, it is full mixed, and he pours out of it; and the sinners of the earth are to drink it, dregs and all* [Psal. 75:8]. Those sinners were our fathers, and we. It came to *bibite ex hoc omnes* [Mat.26:27]; they and we were to drink of it all, one after another round. Good reason, to drink as we had brewed, to drink the fruit of our own inventions, our own words and works we had brought forth.

About, the cup went; all strained at it. At last, to Christ it came. He was none of the sinners, but was *found among them*. By his good will, he would have had it pass; *transeat a me calix iste*,—you know who that was. Yet, rather than we, than any of us should take it—it would be our bane, he knew—he took it; off it went, dregs and all. Alas, the myrrh they gave him at the beginning, the vinegar at the ending of his Passion, were but poor resemblances of this cup, such as they were. That, another manner draught. We see it cast him into so unnatural a sweat of blood all over, as, if he had been wrung and crushed in a winepress, it could not have been more. This lo, was the first winepress, and Christ in it three days ago; and, what with the scourges, nails, and spears, besides, so pressed as forth it ran (blood or wine, call it what you will) in such, so great quantity, as never ran it more plenteously out of any winepress of them all. Here is *Christus in torculari*, Christ's *calcatus sum*.

Of which wine so pressed then out of him, came our cup, the cup of this day, the *cup of the New Testament in his blood*, represented by the blood of the grape. Wherein long before, old Jacob foretold Shiloh should *wash his robe*, as full well he might have done,

---

[7] {Ye shall be as gods (Gen 3:5).}

[8] {death in the pot and death in the cup (2 Kgs 4:40)}

there came enough to have washed it over and over again. So, you see now, how the case stands. That former, our cup due to us and no way to him, he drank for us that it might pass from us, and we not drink it. Ours did he drink, that we might drink of his. He, *the cup of wrath*, that we, *the cup of blessing*, set first before God as a *libamen*, at the sight or scent whereof he smelleth a savor of rest, and is appeased. After, reached to us, as a sovereign restorative to recover us of the devil's poison, for we also have been sipping at *calix daemoniorum* more or less, woe to us for it! and no way but this to cure us of it.

By this time you see the need of the first press, and of his being in it. Into which he was content to be thrown and there trodden on; all, to satisfy his Father, out of his justice requiring the drinking up of that cup, by us, or by some for us; and it came to his lot. And never was there lamb so meek before the shearer, nor worm so easy to be trodden on; never cluster lay so quiet and still to be bruised, as did Christ in the press of his Passion. Ever be he blessed for it.

Now come we to the other of this day in the text. This is not that we have touched, but another. Wherein the style is altered: no more *calcatus sum*, but *calcavi* and *conculcavi* too. Up (it seems) he gat, and down went they, and upon them he trode. His enemies of Edom lay like so many clusters under his feet; and *he cast his shoe over* them, set his foot on them, and pashed them to pieces.

If it had meant his Passion, it had been his own blood; but this was none of his now, but the blood of his enemies. For when the *year of redemption* was past, then came the *day of vengeance*; then came the time for that, and not before.

For after the *consummatum est* of his own pressure, *sic oportuit impleri omnem justitiam*, and that all the righteousness he spake had been fulfilled; then *rise up, rise up thou arm of the Lord*, saith the Prophet, and *shew thyself mightily to save*. He took him to his second attribute, to be avenged of those that had been the ruin of us all, the ruin everlasting, but for him. To Edom, the kingdom of death, he went, whither we were to be led captives; yea, even to Bozrah, to hell itself, and there *brake the gates of brass, and made the iron-bars fly in sunder*. He that was weak to suffer, became *mighty to save*. Of *calcatus*, he became *Calcator*. He that was throwen himself, threw them now another while, into the press, trod them down, trampled upon them, as upon grapes in a fat {vat}, till he made the blood spring out of them, and all *to-sprinkle his garments*, as if he had come forth of a winepress indeed. And we, before, mercifully rather than mightily, by his Passion, now mightily also saved, by his glorious Resurrection.

Thus have you two several vines, the natural and the strange vine, the sweet and the wild; two presses, that in Jewry, that in Edom; two cups, the cursed cup, and the cup of blessing; of wine or blood. His own, his enemies' blood: one, *sanguis Agni*, the blood of the *Lamb slain*; the other, *sanguis draconis*, the blood of the dragon, *the red dragon* (Apoc. 12) trode upon; one of his Passion, three days since; the other of his victory, as today. Between his burial and his rising, some doing there had been; somewhat had been done; somewhere he had been: in some new winepress, in Bozrah, that had given a new tincture of red to his raiment all over.

Both these shall you find together set down in one and the same chapter, in two verses standing close one to the other, Apoc. 5: Christ represented first as a lamb, *a Lamb slain*, dyed in his own blood: this is the first press. And immediately, in the very next verse, straight represented again in a new shape, as a *lion*, all be-bloody with the blood of his prey—*a Lion of the tribe of Judah*; which comes home to this here. For Judah, it is said he should *wash his robe in the blood of the grape* (Gen. 44:9). And so much for *torcular calcavi*.

We must not leave out *solus* in any wise: that both these he did *alone*, so *alone* as not any man in the world with him in either.

Not in the first; there pressed he was *alone*. All *forsook him*; his disciples first; *alone* for them. Yet then he was not *alone*, his Father was still with him; but after, Father and all, as appeared by his cry, *Why hast thou forsaken me?* Then was he all *alone* indeed.

Not in the second neither. The very next verse, he complains how that *he looked about him round, and could not see any would once offer to help him.* Out of Bozrah he got *alone*; from death he rose, conquered, triumphed in *semetipso*, himself *alone*. The angel indeed *rolled away the stone*; but he was risen first, and the stone rolled away after.

Accordingly, we to reckon of him, that since in both these presses he was for us, he and none but he; that his, and none but his be the glory of both. That, seeing neither we for ourselves, nor any for us, could bring this to pass, but he and he only; he and he only might have the whole honor of both, have no partner in that which is only his due, and no creature's else at all, either in heaven or earth.

And is Christ come from Bozrah? then, be sure of this, that he returning thus in triumph (as it is in the 68 Psalm, the Psalm of the Resurrection), he will not leave us behind, for whom he did all this, but *his own will he bring again as he did from Basan*; as from Basan, so from Bozrah; as *from the deep pit of the sea*, so from the deep pit of hell. He that *raised* Jesus, shall by Jesus *raise us up also* from the Adama of Edom,[9] the red mould of the earth, the power of the grave; and from the Bozrah of hell too, the gulf whence there is no scaping out. Will make us in him, saith the Apostle, *more than conquerors, and tread down Satan under our feet.*

You see how Christ's garments came to be *red*. Of the winepress that made them so, we have spoken, but not of the color itself. A word of that too. It was his color at his Passion. They put him in purple; then it was his weed[10] in derision, and so was it in earnest. Both *red* it was itself, and so he made it more with the dye of his own blood. And the same color he is now in again, at his rising. Not with his own now, but with the blood of the wounded Edomites, whom treading under his feet, their blood bestained him and his apparel. So one and the same color at both; dying and rising in *red*; but with difference, as much as is between his own and his enemies' blood.

The spouse in the Canticles, asked of her beloved's colors, saith of him, *my beloved is white and red. White*, of his own proper: so he was when he shewed himself in kind, transfigured in the Mount; his apparel then so white, *no fuller[11] in the earth could come near it. White* of himself; how comes he *red* then? Not of himself that, but for us. That is our natural color, we are born *polluted in our own blood* [Lam. 4:14]. It is sin's color that, for shame is the color of sin. *Our sins*, saith Esay, *are as crimson, of as deep dye as any purple.*

---

[9] {"Edom" and "Adam" both come from the root meaning red: *adama* in Hebrew means field; *adom* is the "red stuff" or pottage for which Esau sold his birthright (Gen 25:30).}

[10] {standard Renaissance word for clothing}

[11] {i.e., fuller's earth, a whitening agent}

This, the true tincture of our sins, the Edomites' color right, for Edom is *red*. The tincture, I say, first of our sin original, dyed in the wool; and then again of our sins actual, dyed in the cloth too. Twice dyed; so was Christ twice. Once in his own, again in his enemies': right *dibaphus*, a perfect full color, a true purple, of a double dye, his too. So was it meet for crimson sinners to have a crimson Savior; a Savior of such a color it behoved us to have. Coming then to save us, off went his white, on went our red; laid by his own righteousness, to be clothed with our sin. He, to wear our colors; that we, his; he, in our red; that we, in his white. So we find (Apoc. 7) our robes are not only washed clean, but dyed a pure white in the blood of the Lamb. Yea, he died and rose again both, in our colors; that we might die and rise too, in his. We fall now again upon the same point in the colors we did before in the cups. He to drink the *sour vinegar* of our *wild grapes*, that we might drink his sweet in the *cup of blessing*. *O cup of blessing*, may we say of this cup! *O stolam formosam*, of that color! *Illi gloriosam, nobis fructuosam*; glorious to him, no less fruitful to us. He, in Mount Golgotha, like to us; that we, in Mount Tabor, like to him. This is the substance of our rejoicing in this color.

One more: how well this color fits him, in respect of his two titles, *loquens justitiam* and *multus ad servandum*. *Loquens justitiam* is to wear red; *potens ad servandum* is so too. The first. To whom is this color given? Scarlet is allowed the degree of Doctors.[12] Why? for their *speaking righteousness* to us, the righteousness of God, that which Christ spake. Nay, even they which speak but the righteousness of man's law, they are honored with it too.[13] But Christ *spake so as never man spake*, and so *call ye none on earth "Doctor" but one*; none in comparison of him. So of all, he to wear it. This ye shall observe: in the Revelation, at the first appearing of the Lamb, there was *a book with seven seals*. No man would meddle with it; the Lamb took it, opened the seals, read it, read out of it a lecture of righteousness to the whole world; the righteousness of God, that shall make us so before him. Let him be arrayed in scarlet; it is his due, his Doctor's weed.

This is no new thing. The heathen king propounded it for a reward to any that could read *the hand-writing on the wall*. Daniel did it, and had it. *Sed ecce major Daniele hic.*[14] Thus was it in the Law. This color was the ground of the Ephod, a principal ingredient into the priest's vesture. Why? For, *his lips were to preserve knowledge*, all *to require the law from his mouth*. And indeed, the very lips themselves, that we speak righteousness with, are of the same color. In the Canticles it is said, *his lips are like a scarlet thread*. And the fruit of the lips hath God created peace, and the fruit of peace is sown in righteousness; and till that be sown and spoken, never any hope of true peace.

Enough for *speaking*. What say you to the other, *potens ad servandum*, which of the twain seems the more proper to this time and place? I say, that way, it fits him too, this color. Men of war, great captains, *mighty to save* us from the enemies, they take it to themselves, and their color it is, of right. A plain text for it, Nahum 2, *Their valiant men*, or captains, *are in scarlet*. And I told you Christ, by Daniel, is called *Captain Messias*, and

---

[12] {i.e., Doctors of Divinity, virtually the only doctoral degree conferred by 17th-century English universities}

[13] {Sergeants-at-law wore distinctive red robes}

[14] {But a greater than Daniel is here.}

so well might. So in his late conflict with Edom, he shewed himself—fought for us, even to blood. Many a bloody wound it cost him, but returned with the spoil of his enemies, stained with their blood; and whoso is able so to do, is worthy to wear it. So in this respect also, so in both; his colors become him well.

Shall I put you in mind, that there is in these two, in either of them, a kind of wine-press? In *mighty to save*, it is evident. Trodden in one press, treading in another. Not so evident in *the speaking of righteousness*. Yet, even in that also, there is a *press* going. For when we read, what do we but gather grapes here and there; and when we study what we have gathered, then are we even *in torculari*, and press them we do, and press out of them that which daily you taste of. I know, there is great odds in the liquors so pressed, and that *a cluster of Ephraim is worth a whole vintage of Abiezer*; but, for that, every man as he may. Nay, it may be further said, and that truly, that even this great title, *mighty to save*, comes under *loquens justitiam*. There is in the word of righteousness a saving power. *Take the word*, saith St. James, *graft it in you, it is able to save your souls*; even that, wherein we of this calling, in a sort, participate with Christ, while *by attending to reading and doctrine we save both ourselves and them that hear us*; we tread down sin, and save sinners from *seeking death in the error of their life*.

But, though there be in the *word* a saving power, yet is not all saving power in that, nor in that only; there is a *press* beside. For this press is going continually among us, but there is another that goes but at times. But, in that, it goes at such times as it falls in fit with the winepress here. Nay, falls in most fit of all the rest. For of it comes very wine indeed, the blood of the grapes of the true Vine, which in the blessed sacrament is reached to us; and with it, is given us that, for which it was given, even *remission of sins*. Not only represented therein, but even exhibited to us. Both which when we partake, then have we a full and perfect communion with Christ this day: of his *speaking righteousness* in the word preached, of his *power to save* in the holy Eucharist ministered. Both *presses* run for us, and we to partake them both.

I may not end till I tell you there remaineth yet another, a third *winepress*, that you may take heed of it. I will but point you to it; it may serve as *sour herbs* to eat our Paschal lamb with. The sun, they say, danced this morning at Christ's resurrection; the earth trembled then, I am sure; there was an earthquake at Christ's rising. So, there is trembling to our joy; *exultate in tremore*, as the Psalmist wills us. The vintage of the earth, when the time of that is come, and when the grapes be ripe and ready for it, *one there is, that crieth to him with the sharp sickle in his hand* (Apoc. 14) to *thrust it in, cut off the clusters, and cast them into the great winepress of the wrath of God*. A dismal day that; a pitiful slaughter then. It is there said, *the blood shall come up to the horse-bridles by the space of a thousand six hundred furlongs*. Keep you out; take heed of coming in that *press*.

We have a kind *item*[15] given us of this, here in the text, in the last verse. There be two acts of Christ: one of being trodden, the other of treading down. The first is for his chosen; the other against his enemies. One is called *the year of redemption*; the other, *the day of vengeance*. The *year of redemption* is already come, and is now; we are in it; during which time, the two former winepresses run, of the word and sacrament. The *day of vengeance* is

---

[15] {admonition or intimation}

not yet come; it is *but in his heart*—so the text is—that is, but in his purpose and intent yet. But certainly, come it will, that day; and with that day, comes the last winepress with the blood to the bridles; ere it come, and during our *year of redemption*, that year's allowance, we are to endeavor to keep ourselves out of it; for that is *the day of vengeance*, of *ira ventura*, God's wrath for ever. So as all we have to study is, how we may be in at the first two, out at the last press; and the due Christian use of the first, will keep us from the last.

While then it is with us *the year of redemption*, and before that day come; while it is yet time of *speaking righteousness*, that is, *today if ye will hear his voice*; while *the cup of blessing* is held out, if we will take it, lay hold on both. That so, we may be accounted worthy to escape in that day, from that day and the vengeance of it; and may feel the fullness of his saving power in *the word engrafted, which is able to save our souls*; and in *the cup of salvation* which is joined with it, and that to our endless joy. *The year of redemption* is last in the verse; with that the Prophet ends. With that let us end also; and to that end, may all that hath been spoken arrive and bring us.

TEXT: EEBO (STC [2nd ed.] / 606)
XCVI sermons by the right honorable and reverend father in God, Lancelot Andrewes, late Lord Bishop of Winchester (London: Printed by George Miller for Richard Badger, 1629), 566–76.

WILLIAM DRUMMOND OF HAWTHORNDEN
(1585–1649)

Born at Hawthornden Castle on the outskirts of Edinburgh, William Drummond was the eldest son of Sir John Drummond, laird of Hawthornden and gentleman usher to James VI (later England's James I), to whom the Drummonds were distantly related. Drummond entered the University of Edinburgh in 1600, graduating MA five years later. In 1606 he made the first of his two brief trips to London, this on his way to France, where he spent at least some time studying civil law at Bourges; however, of the 399 books he brought back to Scotland on his return in 1608, only fourteen concerned law, the rest being mostly contemporary literature in French, Italian, Spanish, and English, along with some philosophy and theology. He returned to London in 1610, but that sojourn was cut short by his father's death, which left Drummond the laird of Hawthornden, with sufficient landed income to allow him to spend the rest of his life cultivating the muses in Scotland.

His first published volume of poems, *Tears on the death of Meliades* (1613), was an elegaic tribute to Prince Henry (d. 1612). A volume of lyric poetry, including some religious verse, followed in 1616. A year later, Drummond's verses celebrating King James' visit to Scotland brought him to the attention of London literary circles. He and Michael Drayton corresponded regularly thereafter, and in the winter of 1618–19, Ben Jonson spent three weeks at Hawthorndon. (Jonson's conversations with Drummond, as recorded by the latter, were discovered and printed in 1842.) Also in 1619, *A midnight trance*, published under the initials W. D., came out in London, perhaps without the author's permission; only one copy of the work is known to survive, and it was not until 1949 that this was identified as an early version of *A cypress grove*. The revised version, bearing the familiar title, came out in 1623, appended to Drummond's *Flowers of Sion*, a slim volume of religious poetry, centering, like *A cypress grove*, on mortality and transience, although there is also a handful of lyrics on the major feasts of the liturgical year.[1]

---

[1] The Ascension hymn, "Bright portals of the sky," may have been a model for Milton's "Nativity ode."

335

By the late 1620s, Drummond had gained the reputation of Scotland's greatest living poet. It was his verse that was chosen to celebrate King Charles' 1633 visit to Edinburgh, an occasion that also marked the end of Drummond's literary career. The farewell to poetry, however, may have had more to do with his marriage in 1632 and the nine children that followed than with the royal visit; or perhaps it was the King's visit that inspired Drummond to begin writing a history of Scotland from the mid-fifteenth to the mid-sixteenth century, a project he completed ca. 1644, although publication waited until 1655. From 1635 on, Drummond also wrote a series of political pieces betraying a love of peace and intense dislike of presbyterian theocracy. Despite his overtly monarchist stance, he continued to live unmolested at Hawthornden, where he died in December of 1649.

❧❧❧

A cypress grove, like Sir Thomas Browne's *Urn-burial* (1658), which here and there borrows from it, is a layman's *meditatio mortis*. As the scholarship on Drummond's piece repeatedly observes, *A cypress grove* weaves a richly ornamented fabric of Christian and neoplatonic commonplaces that "sum up the basic seventeenth-century attitudes towards death" (Hurtig 225; see also McDiarmid 22; Ellrodt 228; Stannard 1310). Yet this cannot be wholly right, since the work is untouched by fear of hell—or, for that matter, by hope of salvation; it never mentions sin or grace or faith or good works or the Cross. It affirms the will's absolute freedom and refers to pity as a vice. Apart from a single passing reference to the Trinity, the only specifically Christian doctrine affirmed is the resurrection of the body.[2] Yet the work (as its reception attests) "feels" traditional rather than post-Christian. Its reflections on the vanity of this life, the soul's immortality, and the joys of the life to come were staples of *ars moriendi* literature, and the curious omissions may bespeak only the overwhelmingly secular character of the university arts curriculum. Drummond's library included some theology (including Aquinas, Calvin, Bale, and Loyola), but his religious outlook does not really fit the categories that early modern divines used to interpret existence. One suspects that the same would hold for the religious outlook of many early modern laypersons.

The dead man who figures in the work's concluding dream vision is almost certainly Prince Henry. The same unnamed figure appears in the *Midnight trance*, which may have been written close to the time of the Prince's death and simply not published until 1619. The dream vision encounter with one of the illustrious dead is, of course, literary artifice,[3]

It doesn't appear in print until the 1630 *Flowers of Sion*, but Milton might have read it in manuscript (see Thomas Corns and Gordon Campbell, *John Milton: life, thought, and work* [Oxford UP, 2008], 52).

[2] The *Dialoghi della vita et della morte* (1550) of Innocentio Ringheri, which is Drummond's principal source for *A cypress grove* (Kastner 2:344–45), has multiple chapters on hell (e.g., "*Scielerati puniti nello inferno*") and salvation ("*Che i Christiani si confidano di conseguir l'immortalita per Christo*"), http://books.google.com/books?id=-Wo7AAAAcAAJ&printsec=frontcover&dq=%22Innocenzio+Ringhieri%22&source=bl&ots=js27umoQ3I&sig=wwWFJr3UY-GzqBf-zefbSfPoxvI&hl=en&ei=fepkTPiDO4zWtQOH-t24DQ&sa=X&oi=book_result&ct=result&resnum=2&ved=0CBcQ6AEwATge#v=onepage&q&f=false (accessed August 12, 2010).

[3] Drummond's dream-journey above the spheres, his vision of the insignificance of earth and earthly glory, his meeting with the heroic soul who urges the dreamer to turn from earthly aspiration to heavenly glory all derive from Cicero's *Somnum Scipionis*.

yet it does affirm at least the possibility (a possibility Donne <*supra*> and a good deal of Protestant theology denied) that the dead still care about the living, that they have not wholly departed.

SOURCES: *ODNB*; R. Ellrodt. "An earlier version (1619) of William Drummond's *Cypresse Grove*" 1949, 228–31, http://english.oxfordjournals.org/content/7/41/228.full.pdf (accessed June 6, 2012); Judith Hurtig, "Seventeenth-century shroud tombs: classical revival and Anglican context," *The Art Bulletin* 64.2 (1982): 217–28; L. E. Kastner, ed., *The poetical works of William Drummond of Hawthornden, with "A Cypresse grove,"* 2 vols. (Manchester UP, 1913); Matthew McDiarmid, "The Spanish plunder of William Drummond of Hawthornden," *Modern Language Review* 44 (1949):17–25; David Stannard, "Death and dying in puritan New England," *American Historical Review* 78.5 (1973): 1305–30.

WILLIAM DRUMMOND OF HAWTHORNDEN
A Cypress Grove
1623

A CYPRESS GROVE[1]

Though it hath been doubted if there be in the soul such imperious and superexcellent power as that it can, by the vehement & earnest working of it, deliver knowledge to another without bodily organs, & by the only conceptions and ideas of it produce real effects; yet it hath been ever and of all held as infallible and most certain, that it often (either by outward inspiration or some secret motion in itself) is augur of its own misfortunes and hath shadows of approaching dangers presented unto it before they fall forth. Hence so many strange apparitions and signs, true visions, uncouth heaviness, and causeless uncomfortable languishings—of which to seek a reason, unless from the sparkling of GOD in the soul or from the God-like sparkles of the soul, were to make reason unreasonable by reasoning of things transcending her reach.

Having often and diverse times, when I had given myself to rest in the quiet solitariness of the night, found my imagination troubled with a confused fear—no, sorrow, or horror—which, interrupting sleep, did astonish my senses and rouse me all appalled and transported in a sudden agony and amazedness; of such an unaccustomed perturbation, not knowing nor being able to dive into any apparent cause, carried away with the stream of my (then doubting) thoughts, I began to ascribe it to that secret fore-knowledge and presaging power of the prophetic mind, and to interpret such an agony to be to the spirit as a faintness and universal weariness useth to be to the body, a sign of following sickness; or as winter lightnings or earthquakes are to commonwealths and great cities, harbingers of more wretched events.

Hereupon not thinking it strange if whatsoever is human should befall me . . . I began to turn over in my remembrance all that could afflict miserable mortality and to

---

[1] {L. E. Kastner's edition of *Cypress grove* reveals that the work is a tissue of borrowings from Montaigne, Pierre Charron's *De la sagesse*, and, in particular, Innocenzio Ringhieri's *Dialoghi della vita et della morte* (1550); the notes that follow indicate only borrowings not found in Kastner.}

forecast every thing that with a mask of horror could show itself to human eyes, till in the end . . . I was brought to think, and with amazement, on the last of human terrors, or (as one termed it) the last of all dreadful and terrible evils: death. For to easy censure it would appear that the soul, if it foresee that divorcement which it is to have from the body, should not without great reason be thus over-grieved and plunged in inconsolable and unaccustomed sorrow: considering their near union, long familiarity and love, with the great change, pain, ugliness which are apprehended to be the inseparable attendants of death.

They had their being together, parts they are of one reasonable creature; the harming of the one is the weakening of the working of the other. What sweet contentments doth the soul enjoy by the senses? They are the gates and windows of its knowledge, the organs of its delight. If it be tedious to an excellent player on the lute to abide but a few months the want of one, how much more must the being without such noble tools and engines be plaintful to the soul? And if two pilgrims which have wandered some few miles together have a hearts-grief when they are near to part, what must the sorrow be at the parting of two so loving friends and never-loathing lovers as are the body and soul?

Death is the violent estranger of acquaintance, the eternal divorcer of marriage, the ravisher of the children from the parents, the stealer of parents from their children, the interrer of fame, the sole cause of forgetfulness, by which the living talk of those gone away as of so many shadows or age-worn stories; all strength by it is enfeebled, beauty turned into deformity & rottenness, honor in contempt, glory into baseness. It is the reasonless breaker-off of all actions, by which we enjoy no more the sweet pleasures of earth nor gaze upon the stately revolutions of the heavens; sun perpetually setteth, stars never rise unto us. It in one moment robbeth us of what with so great toil and care in many years we have heaped together. . . . By death we are exiled from this fair city of the world; it is no more a world unto us, nor we any more people into it. The ruins of fanes, palaces, and other magnificent frames yield a sad prospect to the soul, and how should it without horror view the wrack of such a wonderful masterpiece as is the body?

That death naturally is horrible and to be abhorred, it cannot well and altogether be denied, it being a privation of life, and a not-being; and every privation being abhorred of Nature, and evil in itself, the fear of it too being ingenerate universally in all creatures; yet I have often thought that even naturally to a mind by only Nature resolved and prepared, it is more terrible in conceit than in verity, and at the first glance than when well pried into; and that rather by the weakness of our fantasy than by what is in it; and that the marble colors of obsequies, weeping, and funeral pomp (which we ourselves cast over it) did add much more ghastliness unto it than otherways it hath. To aver which conclusion, when I had gathered my wandering thoughts, I began thus with myself.

If on the great theater of this earth, amongst the numberless number of men, *to die* were only proper to thee and thine, then undoubtedly thou hadst reason to repine at so severe and partial a law.[2] But since it is a necessity from the which never an age by-past hath been exempted, and unto which they which be, and so many as are to come, are

---

[2] {The first half of this paragraph owes more than a little to Claudius' speech on the universality of death in *Hamlet* act 1, scene 2.}

thralled (no consequent of life being more common and familiar), why shouldst thou with unprofitable and nought-availing stubbornness oppose to so unevitable and necessary a condition? This is the high-way of mortality, our general home; behold what millions have trod it before thee, what multitudes shall after thee, with them which at that same instant run. In so universal a calamity (if death be one) private complaints cannot be heard; with so many royal palaces, it is no loss to see thy poor cabin burn. Shall the heavens stay their ever-rolling wheels (for what is the motion of them but the motion of a swift and ever-whirling wheel which twineth forth and again up-rolleth our life?) and hold still time to prolong thy miserable days, as if the highest of their working were to do homage unto thee? Thy death is a piece of the order of this *All*, a part of the life of this world; for while the world is the world, some creatures must die & others take life. . . . Death no less than life doth here act a part, the taking away of what is old being the making a way for what is young. [This earth is as a table book, and men are the notes: the first are washen out that the new may be written in.][3] They which fore-went us did leave a room for us, and should we grieve to do the same to those which should come after us? Who, being suffered to see the exquisite rarities of an antiquary's cabinet, is grieved that the curtain be drawn & to give place to new pilgrims? And when the Lord of this universe hath shewed us the amazing wonders of his various frame, should we take it to heart when he thinketh time to dislodge? This is his unalterable and unevitable decree: as we had no part of our will in our entrance into this life, we should not presume of any in our leaving it, but soberly learn to will that which he wills, whose very willing giveth being to all that it wills; and reverencing the Orderer, not repine at the order and laws. . . .

. . . The violets have their time though they empurple not the winter; and the roses keep their season though they disclose not their beauty in the spring.

Empires, states, kingdoms have by the doom of the supreme providence their fatal periods; great cities lie sadly buried in their dust; arts and sciences have not only their eclipses but their wanings and deaths; the ghastly wonders of the world raised by the ambition of ages are over-thrown and trampled; some lights above, not idly entitled stars, are loosed and never more seen of us;[4] the excellent fabric of this universe itself shall one day suffer ruin, or a change like a ruin, and poor earthlings thus to be handled complain?

But is this life so great a good that the loss of it should be so dear unto man? If it be, the meanest creatures of Nature thus be happy, for they live no less than he. If it be so great a felicity, how is it esteemed of man himself at so small a rate that for so poor gains—nay, one disgraceful word—he will not stand {hesitate} to lose it? What excellency is there in it for the which he should desire it perpetual, and repine to be at rest and return to his old grandmother dust? Of what moment are the labors and actions of it that the interruption and leaving off of them should be to him so distasteful and with such grudging lamentations received?

. . .

---

[3] {This sentence, which first appears in the 1630 edition, alludes to the wax-covered writing tablets that early modern persons used as notebooks.}

[4] {Presumably a reference to the comet of 1618.}

Are the actions of the most part of men much differing from the exercise of the spider, that pitcheth toils {snares} and is tapist {hidden} to prey on the smaller creatures, and for the weaving of a scornful web eviscerateth itself many days, which, when with much industry finished, a tempestuous puff of wind carrieth away both the work and the worker?[5] Or are they not like the plays of children? Or (to hold them at their highest rate) as is a may-game, or what is more earnest, some study at chess? . . .

. . .

The air, the sea, the fire, the beasts be cruel executioners of man; yet beasts, fire, sea, and air are pitiful to man in comparison of man, for mo men are destroyed by men than by them all. What scorns, wrongs, contumelies, imprisonments, torments, poisons receiveth man of man? What engines and new works of death are daily found forth by man against man?[6] What laws to thrall his liberty? Fantasies and scare-bugs to inveigle his reason? Amongst the beasts is there any that hath so servile a lot in another's behalf as man? Yet neither is content: nor he who reigneth nor he who serveth.

The half of our life is spent in sleep,[7] which hath such a resemblance to death that often it separates, as it were, the soul from the body, and teacheth it a sort of being above it, making it soar beyond the sphere of sensual delights and attain knowledge unto which, while the body did awake, it could scarce aspire. And who would not, rather than abide chained in this loathsome galley of the world, sleep ever (that is die); having all things at one stay, be free from those vexations, misadventures, contempts, indignities, and many many anguishes unto which this life is invassaled and subdued? And well looked unto, our greatest contentment and happiness here seemeth rather to consist in the being released from misery than in the enjoying of any great good.

What have the most eminent of mortals to glory in? Is it greatness? Who can be great on so small a round as is this earth, and bounded with so short a course of time? How like is that to castles or imaginary cities raised in the sky by chance-meeting clouds? Or to giants modeled (for a sport) of snow, which at the hotter looks of the sun melt away and lie drowned in their own moisture? such an impetuous vicissitude towseth[8] the estates of this world. Is it knowledge? But we have not yet attained to a perfect understanding of the smallest flower, and why the grass should rather be green than red. The element of fire is quite put out;[9] the air is but water rarified; the earth moveth and is no more the center of the universe, is turned into a magnes {magnet}; stars are not fixed but swim in the ethereal spaces; comets are mounted above the planets; some affirm there is an other world of

---

[5] {The spider comparison is taken from Fra Luis de Granada's *Oración y consideración* (see Matthew McDiarmid, "The Spanish plunder of William Drummond of Hawthornden," *Modern Language Review* 44 [1949]: 24).}

[6] {The first portion of this paragraph is taken from de Granada's *Oración y consideración* (see McDiarmid 24).}

[7] {At this point, the 1619 version continues with more *Hamlet*: "which (sith it is a release of care, the balm of woe, an indifferent arbiter unto all) must be the best, and yet is but the shadow of Death; and who would not rather than suffer the slings and arrows of outrageous fortune, the whips and scorns of time, the oppressor's wrongs, the proud man's contumelies, sleep ever (this is, die) and end the heartache and the thousand natural shocks that flesh is heir to?" (*A midnight trance* [London, 1619], 31–32).}

[8] {tousle, pull out of joint, disorder}

[9] {an echo of Donne's *Second anniversary*}

men and creatures, with cities and towers, in the moon; the sun is lost, for it is but a cleft in the lower heavens through which the light of the highest shines. Thus sciences, by the diverse motions of this globe of the brain of man, are become opinions. What is all we know compared with what we know not? We have not yet agreed about the chief good and felicity. . . .

If death be good, why should it be feared? And if it be the work of nature, how should it not be good? For nature is an ordinance and rule which GOD hath established in the creating this universe (as is the law of a king), which can not err. For how should the Maker of that ordinance err? . . . He worketh powerfully, bounteously, wisely, and maketh (his artificial organ) nature do the same. How is not death of nature? Sith what is naturally generate is subject to corruption, and such an harmony (which is life) rising from the mixture of the four elements, which are the ingredients of our body, cannot ever endure, the contrariety of their qualities (as a consuming rust in the baser metals) being an inward cause of a necessary dissolution. Again, how is not death good? Sith it is the thaw of all those vanities which the frost of life bindeth together. If there be a satiety in life, then must there {not} be a sweetness in death? The earth were not ample enough to contain her offspring if none died: in two or three ages (without death) what an unpleasant and lamentable spectacle were the most flourishing cities? For what should there be to be seen in them save bodies languishing and courbing {bending} again into the earth? Pale disfigured faces, skeletons instead of men? And what to be heard but the exclamations of the young, complaints of the old, with the pitiful cries of sick and pining persons? There is almost no infirmity worse than age.

. . . What great pain then can there be in death, which is but a continued swooning, and a never again returning to the works and dolorous felicity of life?

Now although death were an extreme pain, sith it is in an instant, what can it be? Why should we fear it? For while we are, it cometh not; and it being come, we are no more. Nay, though it were most painful, long-continuing, and terrible-ugly, why should we fear it? Sith fear is a foolish passion but where it may preserve; but it cannot preserve us from death—yea rather, the fear of it, banishing the comforts of present content-ments, makes death to advance and approach the more near unto us. That is ever terrible which is unknown; so do little children fear to go in the dark, and their fear is increased with tales.[10]

But that (perhaps) which anguisheth thee most is to have this glorious pageant of the world removed from thee in the spring and most delicious season of thy life; for, though to die be usual, to die young may appear extraordinary. . . . Who will behold, and with the eyes of advice behold, the many changes depending on human affairs, with the after-claps of fortune, shall never lament to die young. Who knows what alterations and sudden disasters, in outward estate or inward contentments, in this wilderness of the world might have befallen him who dieth young, if he had lived to be old? Heaven, fore-knowing imminent harms, taketh those which it loves to itself before they fall forth. . . .

Though not for life itself, yet that to after-worlds thou mightst leave some monu-ment that once thou wast, haply in the clear light of reason it would appear that life

---

[10] {Francis Bacon, "Of death," *Essays*.}

were earnestly to be desired: for sith it is denied us to live ever (said one), let us leave some worthy remembrance of our once here being, and draw out this span of life to the greatest length and so far as is possible. O poor ambition! To what, I pray thee, mayst thou concredit {entrust} it? Arches and stately temples, which one age doth raise, doth not another raze? Tombs and adopted[11] pillars lie buried with those which were in them buried. Hath not avarice defaced what religion did make glorious?[12] All that the hand of man can up-rear is either overturned by the hand of man, or at length, by standing & continuing, consumed, as if there were a secret opposition in fate (the unevitable decree of the Eternal) to control our industry & counter-check all our devices & proposing. Possessions are not enduring; children lose their name—families glorying (like marigolds in the sun) on the highest top of wealth and honor (no better than they which are not yet born) leaving off to be: so doth heaven confound what we endeavor by labor and art to distinguish. That renown by papers, which is thought to make men immortal and which nearest doth approach the life of these eternal bodies above, how slender it is, the very word of *paper* doth import; and what is it when obtained but a multitude of words, which coming times may scorn. How many millions never hear the names of the most famous writers, and amongst them to whom they are known, how few turn over their pages. . . . Desert and virtue for the most part want monuments and memory, seldom are recorded in the volumes of admiration, while statues & trophies are erected to those whose names should have been buried in their dust and folded up in the darkest clouds of oblivion; so do the rank weeds in this garden of the world choke and over-run the sweetest flowers.[13] Applause, whilst thou livest, serveth but to make thee that fair mark against which envy and malice direct their arrows; at the best is like that Syracusian's sphere of crystal,[14] as frail as fair; and born after thy death, it may as well be ascribed to some of those were in the Trojan horse, or to such as are yet to be born an hundred years hereafter, as to thee who nothing knows and is of all unknown. What can it avail thee to be talked of whilst thou art not? Consider in what bounds our fame is confined, how narrow the lists are of human glory, and the furthest she can stretch her wings. This globe of the earth, which seemeth huge to us, in respect of the universe & compared with that wide wide pavilion of heaven, is less than little—of no sensible quantity, and but as a point; for the horizon which boundeth our sight divideth the heaven as in two halves, having always six of the zodiac signs above, and as many under it, which, if the earth had any quantity compared to it, it could not do.[15] More, if the earth were not as a point, the stars could not still in all parts of it appear to us of a like greatness; for where the earth raised itself in mountains, we being more near to heaven, they would appear to us of a greater quantity; and where it is humbled in valleys, we being further distant, they would seem unto us less: but the stars in all parts of the earth appearing of a like greatness, and to every part of it the heaven imparting to our sight the half of its inside, we must avouch it to be but as a point.

---

[11] {chosen as one's own—so, presumably, pillars one chose to serve as one's grave marker}

[12] {a rather hostile allusion to the despoliation of the abbeys for their lead and brass at the Reformation}

[13] {another echo of *Hamlet* act 1, scene 2 ("'tis an unweeded garden . . . things rank and gross in nature / Possess it merely")}

[14] {the sphere of Archimedes}

[15] {The sentence comes from de Granada's *Guía de pecadores* (McDairmid 24).}

Well did one compare it to an ant-hill, and men (the inhabitants) to so many pismires and grasshoppers in the toil and variety of their diversified studies. Now of this small indivisible thing, thus compared, how much is covered with waters? How much not at all discovered? How much unhabited and desert? And how many millions of millions are they which share the remnant amongst them, in languages, customs, divine rites differing, and all almost to others unknown? . . .

But (my soul) what ails thee to be thus backward and astonished at the remembrance of death, sith it doth not reach thee, more than darkness doth those far-shining lamps above? Rouse thyself, for shame. Why shouldst thou fear to be without a body, sith thy Maker and the spiritual and supercelestial inhabitants have no bodies? Hast thou ever seen any prisoner who, when the jail gates were broken up & he enfranchised & set loose, would rather plaine and sit still on his fetters than seek his freedom? Or any mariner who, in the midst of storms arriving near the shore, would launch forth again unto the main rather than strike sail and joyfully enter the lees of a safe harbor? If thou rightly know thyself, thou hast but small cause of anguish; for if there be any resemblance of that which is infinite in what is finite (which yet by an infinite imperfection is from it distant), if thou be not an image, thou art a shadow of that unsearchable Trinity in thy three essential powers, understanding, will, memory; which, though three, are in thee but one; and abiding one, are distinctly three. But in nothing more comest thou near that sovereign good than by thy perpetuity, which who strive to improve {disprove}, by that same do it prove—like those that, by arguing themselves to be without all reason, by the very arguing shew how they have some. For how can what is wholly mortal more know what is immortal than the eye can know sounds or the ear question about colors? If none had eyes, who would ever descant of light or shadow? To thee nothing in this visible world is comparable: thou art so wonderful a beauty and so beautiful a wonder, that if but once thou couldst be gazed upon by bodily eyes, every heart would be inflamed with thy love and ravished from all servile baseness and earthly desires. Thy being depends not on matter; hence, by thine understanding dost thou dive into the being of every other thing. And therein art so pregnant that nothing by place, similitude, subject, time is so conjoined, which thou canst not separate; as what neither is nor any ways can exist, thou canst feign and give an abstract being unto.[16] Thou seemest a world in thyself, containing heaven, stars, seas, earth, floods, mountains, forests, and all that liveth. Yet rests thou not satiate with what is in thyself, nor with all in the wide universe, until thou raise thyself to the contemplation of that first illuminating intelligence, far above time and even reaching eternity itself, into which thou art transformed; for, by receiving, thou (beyond all other things) art made that which thou receivest. The more thou knowest, the more apt thou art to know, not being amated with any object that excelleth in predominance, as sense by objects sensible.[17] Thy will is uncompellable, resisting force, daunting necessity, despising danger, triumphing over affliction, unmoved by pity,[18] and not constrained by all the toils

---

[16] {The imagination, that is, decomposes (and reconjoins) extant things to produce, for example, a sphinx or centaur; but it also has the capacity to make-up things that neither do nor could exist.}

[17] {I.e., the most excellent sensible objects overwhelm our senses—one cannot look directly at the sun.}

[18] {In stoic ethics, pity (*misericordia*) was a vice, as were all emotions; see Seneca, *De clementia* 2.5.4. By way of contrast, see Donne's 1623 Lenten sermon <*supra*>.}

and disasters of life. What the Arts-master[19] of this universe is in governing this universe, thou art in the body; and as he is wholly in every part of it, so art thou wholly in every part of the body. By thee man is that hymen {marriage} of eternal and mortal things, that chain together binding unbodied and bodily substances, without which the goodly fabric of this world were unperfect. Thou hast not thy beginning from the fecundity, power, nor action of the elemental qualities, being an immediate master-piece of that great Maker. Hence hast thou the forms and figures of all things imprinted in thee from thy first original. Thou only at once art capable of contraries; of the three parts of time, thou makest but one.[20] Thou knowest thyself so separate, absolute, and diverse an essence from thy body, that thou disposest of it as it pleaseth thee: for in thee there is no passion so weak which mastereth not the fear of leaving it. Thou shouldst be so far from repining at this separation, that it should be the chief of thy desires, sith it is the passage and means to attain thy perfection and happiness. Thou art here but as in an infected and leprous inn, plunged in a flood of humors, oppressed with cares, suppressed with ignorance, defiled and destained with vice, retrograde in the course of virtue; small things seem here great unto thee, and great things small; folly appeareth wisdom, and wisdom folly. Freed of thy fleshly care, thou shalt rightly discern the beauty of thyself and have perfect fruition of that all-sufficient and all-sufficing happiness, which is GOD himself. To whom thou owest thy being, to him thou owest thy well being: he and happiness are the same. For if God had not happiness, he were not God, because happiness is the highest and greatest good.[21] . . .

Why shouldst thou be fear-stroken and discomforted for thy parting from this mortal bride thy body, sith it is but for a time, and such a time as she shall not care for nor feel anything in, nor thou have much need of her? Nay, sith thou shalt receive her again more goodly and beautiful than when in her fullest perfection thou enjoyed her, being by her absence made like unto that Indian crystal, which after some revolutions of ages, is turned into purest diamond. If the soul be the form of the body, and the form separated from the matter of it cannot ever so continue but is inclined and disposed to be reunited thereinto, what can let and hinder this desire but that some time it be accomplished, and obtaining the expected end, rejoin itself again unto the body?[22] . . . If the body shall not arise, how can the only & sovereign good be perfectly and infinitely good? For how shall he be just—nay, have so much justice as man—if he suffer the evil and vicious to have a more prosperous and happy life than the followers of religion and virtue, which ordinarily useth to fall forth in this life? For the most wicked are lords and gods of this earth, sleeping in the lea port of honor, as if the spacious habitation of the world had been made only for them; and the virtuous and good are but forlorn castaways, floating in the surges of distress, seeming here either of the eye of providence not pitied or not regarded: being subject to all dishonors, wrongs, wracks; in their best estate, passing away their days (like the daisies in the field) in silence and contempt. Sith then he is most good, most just, of necessity there must be appointed by him another time and place of retribution, in the

[19] {i.e., Master of Arts, an unusual degree for God}
[20] {One can think of both past and future in the present.}
[21] {from de Granada's *Guía de pecadores* (McDairmid 23)}
[22] {See Caroline Bynum, *The resurrection of the body* (Columbia UP, 1995), 256–58.}

which there shall be a reward for living well and a punishment for doing evil, with a life whereinto *both* shall receive their due—and not only in their souls divested; for sith both the parts of man did act a part in the right or wrong, it carrieth great reason with it that they both be arraigned before that high justice to receive their own. Man is not a soul only, but a soul and body, to which either guerdon or punishment is due. This seemeth to be the voice of Nature in almost all the religions of the world; this is that general testimony, charactered in the minds of the most barbarous and savage people; for all have had some roving guesses at ages to come and a dim duskish light of another life, all appealing to one general judgment throne. To what else could serve so many expiations, sacrifices, prayers, solemnities, and mystical ceremonies? To what such sumptuous temples and care of the dead? To what all religion, if not to show that they expected a more excellent manner of being after the navigation of this life did take an end. And who doth deny it, must deny that there is a providence, a GOD; confess that his worship, and all study and reason of virtue, are vain; and not believe that there is a world, are creatures; and that he himself is not what he is.

But it is not of death (perhaps) that we complain, but of time, under the fatal shadow of whose wings all things decay and wither. This is that tyrant, which executing against us his diamantine laws, altereth the harmonious constitution of our bodies; benumbing the organs of our knowledge, turneth our best senses senseless; makes us loathsome to others and a burthen to ourselves—of which evils, death relieveth us. So that if we could be transported (O happy colony!) to a place exempted from the laws and conditions of time, where neither change, motion, nor other affection of material and corruptible things were, but an immortal, unchangeable, impassible, all-sufficient kind of life, it were the last of things wishable, the term {end} and center of all our desires. Death maketh this transplantation; for the last instant of corruption, or leaving off of anything to be what it was, is the first of generation or being of that which succeedeth. Death, then, being the end of this miserable transitory life, of necessity must be the beginning of that other all excellent and eternal, and so causelessly of a virtuous soul it is either feared or complained on.

As those images were portrayed in my mind (the morning star now almost arising in the East), I found my thoughts in a mild and quiet calm; and not long after my senses, one by one forgetting their uses, began to give themselves over to rest, leaving me in a still and peaceable sleep, if sleep it may be called, where the mind awaking is carried with free wings from out fleshly bondage.[23] For heavy lids had not long covered their lights, when I thought, nay, sure I was where I might discern all in this great *All*: the large compass of the rolling circles; the brightness and continual motion of those rubies of the night, which (by their distance) here below cannot be perceived; the silver countenance of the wandering moon, shining by another's light; the hanging of the earth, as environed with a girdle of crystal; the sun enthronized in the midst of the planets, eye of the heavens, gem of this precious ring the world. But whilst with wonder and amazement I gazed on those celestial splendors and the beaming lamps of that glorious temple (like a poor countryman brought from his solitary mountains and flocks to behold the magnificence of some

---

[23] {From this point on, until the final promise of the body's resurrection, Drummond's meditation echoes Cicero's *Dream of Scipio* (*Somnum Scipionis*).}

great city), there was presented to my sight a man, as in the spring of his years, with that self-same grace, comely feature, majestic look which the late _____[24] was wont to have; on whom I had no sooner set mine eyes, when (like one planet-stroken) I became amazed. But he, with a mild demeanor and voice surpassing all human sweetness, appeared (me thought) to say,

What is it doth thus anguish and trouble thee? Is it the remembrance of death, the last period of wretchedness and entry to these happy places, the lantern which lightneth men to see the mystery of the blessedness of spirits and that glory which transcendeth the curtain of things visible? Is thy fortune below on that dark globe (which scarce by the smallness of it appeareth here) so great that thou art heart-broken and dejected to leave it? . . . Fools, which think that this fair and admirable frame, so variously disposed, so rightly marshaled, so strongly maintained, enriched with so many excellencies, not only for necessity but for ornament and delight, was by that Supreme Wisdom brought forth that all things in a circulary course should be and not be, arise and dissolve, and thus continue, as if they were so many shadows cast out and caused by the encountering of these superior celestial bodies, changing only their fashion and shape, or fantastical imageries, or prints of faces into crystal.[25] No, no. The Eternal Wisdom hath made man an excellent creature, though he fain would unmake himself and return to nothing. And though he seek his felicity among the reasonless wights, he hath fixed it above. Look how some prince or great king on the earth, when he hath raised any stately city, the work being achieved, is wont to set his image in the midst of it to be admired and gazed upon; no otherwise did the Sovereign of this *All*, the fabric of it perfected, place man (a great miracle), formed to his own pattern, in the midst of this spacious and admirable city. . . .

But alas! (said I) had it not been better that, for the good of his native country, a _____ endued with so many peerless gifts had yet lived? How long will ye (replied he), like the ants, think there are no fairer palaces than their hills; or like to purblind moles, no greater light than that little which they shun? As if the master of a camp knew when to remove a sentinel, and he who placeth man on the earth knew not how long he had need of him? Every one cometh there to act his part of this tragicomedy called Life, which done, the curtain is drawn, and he removing is said to die. That providence which prescriveth causes to every event hath not only determined a definite and certain number of days, but of actions, to all men, which they cannot go beyond.

Most _____, then (answered I) death is not such an evil and pain, as it is of the vulgar esteemed? Death (said he) nor painful is, nor evil (except in contemplation of the cause[26]), being of itself as indifferent as birth. Yet can it not be denied but amidst those dreams of earthly pleasures, the uncouthness of it, with the wrong apprehension of what is unknown in it, are noisome; but the soul sustained by its Maker, resolved and calmly retired in itself, doth find that death (sith it is in a moment of time) is but a short, nay,

---

[24] {A prince? See the Drummond introduction *<supra>*.}

[25] {The reflection of faces in water? At this point, the 1630 text of *A cypress grove* adds "But more they which believe that he doth no other-ways regard this his work than as a theater raised for bloody sword-players, wrestlers, chasers of timorous and combaters of terrible beasts, delighting in the daily torments, sorrows, distress, and misery of mankind."}

[26] {original sin?}

sweet sigh; and is not worthy the remembrance compared with the smallest dram of the infinite felicity of this place. . . . Here doth that earnest appetite of the understanding content itself, not seeking to know any more. For it seeth before it, in the vision of the divine essence (a mirror in the which not images or shadows, but the true and perfect essence of everything created is more clear and conspicuous than in itself), all that may be known or understood. Here doth the will pause itself, as in the center of its eternal rest, glowing with a fiery affection of that infinite and all-sufficient good, which being fully known, cannot (for the infinite motives and causes of love which are in him) but be fully and perfectly loved. . . . But, although this bliss of souls be great and their joys many, yet shall they admit addition, and be more full and perfect at that long-wished and general meeting with their bodies.

Amongst all the wonders of the great Creator, not one appeareth to be more wonderful (replied I) than that our bodies should arise, having suffered so many changes, and nature denying a return from privation to a habit.

Such power (said he) being above all that the understanding of man can conceive, may well work such wonders; for if man's understanding could comprehend all the secrets and counsels of that eternal Majesty, it must of necessity be equal unto it. The Author of Nature is not thralled to the laws of Nature, but worketh with them, or contrary to them, as it pleaseth him. What he hath a will to do, he hath a power to perform. . . . This world is as a cabinet[27] to GOD, in which the small things (however to us hid and secret) are nothing less kept than the great. For as he was wise and powerful to create, so doth his knowledge comprehend his own creation: yea, every change and variety in it, of which it is the very source. Not any atom of the scattered dust of mankind, though daily flowing under new forms, is to him unknown; and his knowledge doth distinguish and discern what once[28] his power shall waken and raise up. Why may not the Arts-master of the world, like a molder, what he hath framed in diverse shapes, confound in one mass, and then severally fashion them out of the same? Can the spargirick[29] by his art restore for a space to the dry and withered rose, the natural purple and blush; and cannot the Almighty raise and refine the body of man after never so many alterations on the earth? Reason herself finds it more possible for infinite power to cast out from itself a finite world, and restore anything in it, though decayed and dissolved, to what it was first, than for man, a finite piece of reasonable misery, to change the form of matter made to his hand. The power of GOD never brought forth all that it can, for then were it bounded, and no more infinite. That time doth approach (O haste ye times away) in which the dead shall live and the living be changed; and of all actions the guerdon is at hand. Then shall there be an end without an end; time shall finish, and place shall be altered, motion yielding unto rest, and another world of an age eternal and unchangeable shall arise. Which when he had said (me thought), he vanished, and I all astonished did awake.

---

[27] {A case for the safe custody of jewels, or other valuables, letters, documents, etc.; and thus, a repository or case, often itself forming an ornamental piece of furniture, fitted with compartments, drawers, shelves, etc., for the proper preservation and display of a collection of specimens (*OED*).}

[28] {at some future time, one day}

[29] {follower of Paracelsus; chemist}

⤙⤚

TEXT: EEBO (STC [2nd ed.] / 7247)

Flowers of Sion. By William Drummond of Hawthorne-denne. To which is adjoined his Cypress Grove (Edinburgh: printed by the heirs of Andro Hart, 1623), 45–54, 56–77.

> Corrected with reference to *The poetical works of William Drummond of Hawthornden, with "A Cypresse Grove,"* 2 vols., ed. L. E. Kastner (Manchester UP, 1913), 2:67–112.

GEORGE WITHER
1588–1667

The oscillating pattern of Wither's career established itself early on. The eldest of ten children in a prosperous Hampshire family, Wither entered Magdalen College, Oxford, in 1604, only to depart a year later due to financial difficulties at home. He seems to have moved to London shortly thereafter, probably first entering one of the Inns of Chancery and then in 1615 the Middle Temple. His literary career started conventionally enough in 1612 with elegies on the death of Prince Henry, but quickly veered into dangerous waters with the 1613 publication of *Abuses stript and whipt*, which ran through eight editions by 1617 but also landed Wither in prison for five months, probably on a libel complaint brought by the Earl of Northampton. He seems to have won his freedom by the unusual hair-of-the-dog tactic of writing another satire—and sending it to the King (published in 1615 as *A satire: dedicated to his most excellent Majesty*). It was also while in the Marshalsea that Wither began his much-praised pastoral eclogues—and his association with the literary circle of Jacobean Spenserians that included Donne's friend, Christopher Brooke. These early poems were celebrated enough by 1620 to provoke a surreptitious edition, pretentiously called *The works of Master George Wither of Lincoln's Inn, gentleman*; two years later, Wither published an authorized edition under the more modest title of *Juvenilia*.

Soon after his release from prison, Wither started work on a new metrical translation of the Psalms to replace the lamentable Sternhold-Hopkins version that for a half-century had provided the only text for congregational singing. In 1619 he published a theoretical prolegomena (*A preparation to the Psalter*), followed by *Exercises upon the first Psalm* (1620) and *Songs of the Old Testament* (1621). In 1621, however, he also published *Wither's motto*, a satire similar to *Abuses* and meeting a similar fate: after being questioned by the House of Lords, Wither was imprisoned, this time for nearly a year. Since the Lords did not normally deal with censorship cases, and since the *Motto* includes nothing flagrantly offensive, all one can say with any certainty is that the work was felt to be gravely objectionable for reasons having to do with something other than its surface meaning.[1]

Whatever the grounds of his imprisonment, Wither regained his freedom in March of 1622. Then followed an astonishing reversal of fortune, for in 1623 King James granted Wither a fifty-one year royal patent for his forthcoming *Hymns and songs of the Church* and the right to have it bound with every future copy of the endlessly-reprinted Sternhold-Hopkins Psalter: an unprecedented privilege that could have given Wither a comfortable income for life, but instead, alas, led to a decade of futile conflict with the Stationers' Company, which refused to honor James' patent or to print anything Wither wrote.

Wither's output over the next ten years is therefore rather slim: his 1625 account of the conflict, *The scholar's purgatory*, which includes a very early defense of intellectual copyright, and the 1628 *Britain's remembrancer*, which Wither apparently had to print by hand. Having made peace with the Stationers ca. 1634, he went on to publish *A collection of emblems, ancient and modern*—its several books dedicated to Charles, Henrietta Maria, and other members of the royal family and nobility—and a translation of the late fourth-century Greek theologian Nemesius, this dedicated to Selden. Neither work prepares one for Wither's decision, implicit in the dedicatory epistle prefacing his 1641 *Hallelujah*, to cast his lot with Parliament when the war broke out in 1642.

Wither's subsequent career continued its uneven path. It also betrays a process of increasing radicalization: in the mid-1640s he forged ties with Lilburne; after the regicide, he played a significant role in the making of the republican settlement; later he wrote pangyrics on Cromwell. The *DNB* describes his post-1642 œuvre as "garrulous and tedious," frequently sinking to "imbecile doggrel"; David Norbrook's more generous estimate locates the value of these later works in the way they "break down the barriers between prophecy, autobiography, satire, journalism, political philosophy, and lyricism, in response to a political crisis" (220). Wither's radicalism survived the Restoration, and the last seven years of his life were spent in poverty and, often, prison. He was 78 when he died, and the author of over a hundred books.

Hymns and songs of the Church, from which the following selections come, would have been—had not the Stationers dug in their heels—the first Anglican hymnal. Instead, after going through four, quite different, editions in 1623, it was forced into oblivion because James' grant of something close to modern authorial copyright posed an obvious threat to the Stationers, in whom copyright was normally vested. Although the Privy Council twice upheld the validity of the patent, booksellers refused to bind Wither's text with the metrical Psalter or even to sell it as a separate volume. However, in the early twentieth century, the exquisite settings that Orlando Gibbons wrote for the volume were rediscovered—several of them incorporated (with different texts) into modern Anglican hymnals.

Given Wither's early satires and later radicalism, one might have expected *Hymns and songs* to take an oppositional posture, yet the lyrics ignore hallmark Calvinist doctrines and eschew the apocalyptic language of militant Protestantism; insofar as Wither addresses

---

[1] See the *ODNB*, Salzman, and French for conjectures as to the nature of Wither's trespass.

the Bohemian crisis at all, it is to reject the possibility that armed violence can bring about God's peace <hymn 83, st. 23>. James' warm support for the work would be inconceivable had it espoused the polarizing confessional politics he was struggling to contain. Nor, conversely, does Wither's inclusion of Marian and saints' day hymns necessarily signal a short-lived burst of high churchmanship. The hymns are keyed to the Prayer Book—to the saints' days and liturgical feasts it retained; as Wither himself states in the preface, he hoped the book would "become a means of increasing . . . Christian conformity" within the realm. Unlike the Laudian Cosin's 1628 *Private devotions*, with its extensive debt to medieval books of hours, the *Hymns and songs* knows only the Elizabethan Settlement, and is content with that. If a label must be given Wither's ecclesio-political stance in this volume, Judith Maltby's "Prayer Book Protestant" seems unquestionably the best fit.[2]

The 1623 hymns are scarcely great poems, but they are of considerable historical interest, not least because Wither published a massively revised version, *Hallelujah: or Britains' second remembrancer*, in 1641, a year before taking up a commission in the Parliamentary army. I have included portions of this later work at the end of this volume, thus transgressing its chronological boundaries, because the changes Wither introduces between 1623 and 1641 trace the radicalization of a mainline Jacobean Protestant; taken together, the volumes provide "a sensitive register to the perplexities and shifts of emotion" that so many individuals experienced during this period of "unprecedented political change" (Norbrook 220).

The changes Wither introduces in 1641 are unexpectedly nuanced and tentative, especially given the near-total collapse of censorship at the time. The 1623 hymns have undergone extensive revision, but most of them, including those for the liturgical feasts and saints' days, remain—and the revisions often seem poetically rather than politically motivated. Like the 1623 volume, that of 1641 has remarkably little in the way of anti-popery, apocalyptic foreboding, and Calvinist talking points. Yet, for all its carry-over from 1623, *Hallelujah* is not the work of a Prayer Book Protestant. Some liturgical hymns remain, but these are now confined to one subdivision of one of the volume's three principal sections: the Christmas carols are "temporary" (i.e., temporal) hymns, but so are those for Wednesday and winter. The other two sections—"occasional" and "personal" hymns—have no liturgical bearing. Their hymns do, however, resemble the similarly non-liturgical devotions one finds in Michael Sparke's puritan-populist *Crumbs of comfort* <supra>, with its "Prayer to be said when we wash in the morning," and in Joseph Hall's *Occasional meditations* (1630), whose entries bear such titles as "On the sight of a well-fleeced sheep," "On occasion of a red-breast coming into his chamber and singing," and "On the barking of a dog." By contrast, for all Wither's acknowledged debt to Herbert, *Hallelujah* includes nothing on altars, church windows, the priesthood, or the British Church. What takes their place are the hymns on washing, Wednesday, and housewarmings; for those in companionate marriages, for the disabled, for members of Parliament, and for men thankful to be men. It is precisely this sanctification of ordinary life—and concomitant sidelining of the institutional, liturgical, and material *Ecclesia*—that locates *Hallelujah* within the tents of the godly.

---

[2] Judith Maltby, *Prayer book and people* (Cambridge UP, 1998).

Wither's sanctification of ordinary life implicitly presents itself as an alternative to the beauty of holiness, but only implicitly. The 1641 hymns are not overtly anti-Laudian, nor are they overtly anti-anything. The one for those migrating to New England, rather than denounce prelatical tyranny at home, urges the exiles not to "defame/ Church, prince, or people here" <part III, hymn 61>. The volume as a whole makes it possible to imagine that not all those who took up arms against the King were principally motivated by fear and hatred (something one would not guess from reading Prynne); nor were they necessarily opposed to ceremonies, tradition, and festivity. *Hallelujah* defiantly retains its Christmas carols. Even in 1645, although politically Wither had moved considerably left, he grieves over the abolition of Christmas: he does not call for its reinstatement, but he sees its loss as punishment for England's sins, as the loss of something precious and sacred, not discarding a popish rag (*Vox pacifica* 7–8).

SOURCES: *DNB*; *ODNB*; Edward Farr, intro. to *Hymns and songs of the Church* (London, 1856); J. Milton French, "George Wither in prison," *PMLA* 45 (1930): 959–66; Kimberley Hackett, "Politics and the 'Heavenly Sonnets': George Wither's religious verse, 1619–1625," *History* 94 (2009): 360–77; David Norbrook, "Levelling poetry: George Wither and the English Revolution, 1642–1649," *ELR* 21.3 (1991): 217–56; Paul Salzman, *Literary culture in Jacobean England: reading 1621* (Palgrave, 2002); Paul Vining, "Wither and Gibbons: a prelude to the first English hymn book," *The Musical Times* 120 (1979): 245–46; George Wither, *Vox pacifica: a voice tending to the pacification of God's wrath* (London, 1645).

GEORGE WITHER

The hymns and songs of the Church
1623

To the high and mighty prince, James, by grace of God, King of Great Britain . . .
mercy and peace, through Jesus Christ our Lord.

These hymns, dread Sovereign, having divers ways received life from your Majesty, as well as that approbation which the Church alloweth, are now imprinted according to your royal privilege, to come abroad under your gracious protection. And what I delivered unto your princely view at several times, I here present again, incorporated into one volume. The first part whereof comprehends those canonical hymns which were written and left for our instruction by the Holy Ghost. . . . And (if the conjecture of many good and learned men deceive them not) the latter part, containing spiritual songs appropriated to the several times and occasions observable in the Church of England (together with brief arguments declaring the purpose of those observations) shall become a means both of increasing knowledge and Christian conformity within your dominions—which, no doubt, your Majesty wisely foresaw when you pleased to grant and command that these hymns should be annexed to all Psalm books in English meter[1]. . . .

And now (maugre their malice, who labor to disparage and suppress these helps to devotion) they shall, I trust, have free scope to work that effect which is desired and to which end I was encouraged to translate and compose them. For, how meanly soever some men may think of this endeavor, I trust the success shall make it appear that the Spirit of God was the first mover of the work, wherein, as I have endeavored to make my expressions such as may not be contemptible to men of best understandings, so I have also labored to suit them to the nature of the subject and the common people's capacities, without regard of catching the vain blasts of opinion. The same also hath been the aim of Master Orlando Gibbons (your Majesty's servant and one of the Gentlemen of your

---

[1] {I.e., the Sternhold-Hopkins metrical psalter, which was at the time the only work authorized for congregational singing in the English Church. For the militant Protestantism of its translations, see Beth Quitslund, *The Reformation in rhyme* (Ashgate, 2008).}

honorable Chapel) in fitting them with tunes: for he hath chosen to make his music agreeable to the matter and what the common apprehension can best admit, rather than to the curious fancies of the time, which path both of us could more easily have trodden. Not caring, therefore, what any of those shall censure, who are more apt to control {censure} than to consider, I commit this to God's blessing and your favorable protection, humbly beseeching your Majesty to accept of these our endeavors and praying God to sanctify both us and this work to his glory . . . .

Your Majesty's most loyal subject,

GEORGE WITHER

‡

CHRISTMAS DAY

This day is worthily dedicated to be observed in remembrance of the blessed Nativity of our Redeemer Jesus Christ, at which time it pleased the Almighty Father to send his only begotten Son into the world for our sakes, and by an unspeakable union to join in one person God and Man, without confusion of natures or possibility of separation. To express, therefore, our thankfulness and the joy we ought to have in this love of God, there hath been anciently, and is yet continued in England (above other countries), a neighborly and plentiful hospitality in inviting and (without invitation) receiving unto our well-furnished tables, our tenants, neighbors, friends, and strangers, to the honor of our nation and increase of amity and free-hearted kindness among us—but, most of all, to the refreshing of the bowels of the poor, being the most Christian use of such festivals. Which charitable and good English custom hath of late been seasonably re-advanced by his Majesty's gracious care, in commanding our nobility and gentry to repair (especially at such times) to their country mansions.[2]

SONG XLVI[3]

1.

As on the night before this blessed morn
A troop of angels unto shepherds told,
Where in a stable he was poorly born,
Whom nor the earth nor Heaven of Heavens can hold,
Through Bethlehem rung,
This news at their return;
Yea, angels sung,
That GOD WITH US was born,
And they made mirth because we should not mourn.

---

[2] {The 1641 *Hallelujah* makes no mention of these Christmas festivities; however, it retains (and merges) the following carols as #26 of part II.}

[3] {The "ed" ending in Wither is always a separate syllable. Thus, e.g., "moved" is a two-syllable word; if the meter requires one syllable, it is spelled "mov'd."}

Chorus

Their angel-carol sing we then,
To God on high all glory be;
For peace on earth bestoweth he,
And sheweth favor unto men.

2.

This favor Christ vouchsafeth for our sake:
To buy us thrones, he in a manger lay;
Our weakness took, that we his strength might take;
And was disrob'd, that he might us array:
Our flesh he wore,
Our sin to wear away.
Our curse he bore,
That we escape it may;
And wept for us, that we might sing for aye.

With angels therefore sing again,
To God on high all glory be;
For peace on earth bestoweth he,
And sheweth favor unto men.

SONG XLVII
ANOTHER FOR CHRISTMAS-DAY

1.

A song of joy unto the Lord we sing,
And publish forth the favors he hath shown;
We sing his praise, from whom all joy doth spring,
And tell abroad the wonders he hath done;
For such were never since the world begun.

His love, therefore, oh! let us all confess;
And to the sons of men his works express.

2.

As on this day the Son of God was born,
The blessed Word was then incarnate made;
The Lord to be a servant held no scorn;
The Godhead was with human nature clad,
And flesh a throne above all angels had.
His love, therefore, &c.

3.

Our sin and sorrows on himself he took,
On us his bliss and goodness to bestow;

To visit earth, he Heaven awhile forsook,
And to advance us high, descended low;
But with the sinful angels dealt not so.
His love, therefore, &c.

4.

A maid conceiv'd, whom man had never known;
The fleece was moistened, where no rain had been;
A virgin she remains that had a son;
The bush did flame that still remained green;
And this befell, when God with us was seen.
His love, therefore, &c.

5.

For sinful men all this to pass was brought,
As, long before, the prophets had forespoke;
So he, that first our shame and ruin wrought,
Once bruis'd our heel, but now his head is broke;
And he hath made us whole, who gave that stroke.
His love, therefore, &c.

6.

The Lamb hath play'd devouring wolves among,
The morning star of Jacob doth appear.
From Jesse's root our tree of life is sprung,
And all God's works (in him) fulfilled are;
Yet we are slack his praises to declare.
His love, therefore, &c.

THE CIRCUMCISION,
OR NEW YEAR'S DAY

The Church solemnizeth this day, commonly called New Year's Day, in memorial of our Savior's circumcision, that remembering how, when he was but eight days old, he began to smart and shed his blood for us, we might praise him for the same; and that with due thankfulness, considering how easy a sacrament he hath left us (instead of that bloody one, which the law enjoined), we might be provoked to bring forth the fruits of regeneration.

SONG XLVIII[4]
Sing this as the forty-fourth song[5]

1.

This day thy flesh, oh Christ, did bleed,
Mark'd by the circumcision-knife;

---

[4] {retained in 1641 with minor changes as #28 of part II}
[5] {See the musical settings by Gibbons at the end of this selection.}

Because the law, for man's misdeed,
Requir'd that earnest of thy life:
Those drops divin'd that shower of blood,
Which in thine agony began;
And that great shower foreshew'd the flood,
Which from thy side the next day ran.

2.

Then, through that milder sacrament,
Succeeding this, thy grace inspire;
Yea, let thy smart make us repent,
And circumcised hearts desire.
For he that either is baptiz'd
Or circumcis'd in flesh alone,
Is but as an uncircumcis'd,
Or as an unbaptized one.

3.

The year anew we now begin,
And outward gifts receiv'd have we;
Renew us also, Lord, within,
And make us new year's gifts for thee:
Yea, let us, with the passed year,
Our old affections cast away;
That we new creatures may appear,
And to redeem the time assay.

THE PURIFICATION OF ST. MARY THE VIRGIN[6]

According to the time appointed in the law of Moses, the blessed Virgin St. Mary reckoned the days of purification which were to be observed after the birth of a male child; and then, as the Law commanded, presented both her son and her appointed offering in the Temple. Partly, therefore, in commemoration of that her true obedience to the Law, and partly to memorize that presentation of our Redeemer (which was performed by his blessed mother at her purification), this anniversary is worthily observed.

SONG L
Sing this as the ninth song[7]

1.

No doubt but she that had the grace,
Thee in her womb, oh Christ, to bear,
And did all womankind surpass,
Was hallow'd by thy being there;

---

[6] {retained in 1641 with minor changes as #30 of part II}
[7] {See the settings by Gibbons at the end of this selection.}

And where the fruit so holy was,
The birth could no pollution cause.

2.

Yet in obedience to thy law
Her purifying rites were done,
That we might learn to stand in awe,
How from thine ordinance we run;
For if we disobedient be,
Unpurified souls have we.

3.

Oh keep us, Lord, from thinking vain,
What by thy word thou shalt command;
Let us be sparing to complain
On what we do not understand;
And guide thy Church, that she may still
Command according to thy will.

4.

Vouchsafe that with one joint consent
We may thy praises ever sing,
Preserve thy seamless robe unrent,
For which so many lots do fling;
And grant that, being purified
From sin, we may in love abide.

5.

Moreover, as thy mother went
(That holy and thrice blessed maid)
Thee in thy Temple to present,
With perfect human flesh array'd;
So let us, offer'd up to thee,
Replenish'd with thy Spirit be.

6.

Yea, let thy Church, our mother dear
(Within whose womb new-born we be),
Before thee at her time appear,
To give her children up to thee;
And take, for purified things,
Her, and that offering which she brings.

FOR THE COMMUNION

We have a custom among us that, during the time of administering the blessed sacrament of the Lord's Supper, there is some psalm or hymn sung, the better to keep the thoughts of the communicants from wandering after vain objects. This song, therefore (expressing a true thankfulness, together with what ought to be our faith concerning that mystery, in such manner as the vulgar capacity may be capable thereof), is offered up to their devotion who shall please to receive it.

SONG LXXXIII

1.

That favor, Lord, which of thy grace
We do receive today,
Is greater than our merit was,
And more than praise we may.
For, of all things that can be told,
That which least comfort hath
Is more than e'er deserve we could,
Except it were by wrath.

2.

Yet we not only have obtain'd
This world's best gifts of thee,
But thou thy flesh hast also deign'd
Our food of life to be;
For which, since we no mends can make
(And thou requir'st no more),
The cup of saving health we take,
And praise thy name therefore.

3.

Oh teach us rightly to receive
What thou dost here bestow,
And learn us truly to conceive
What we are bound to know;
That such as cannot wade the deep
Of thy unfathom'd Word,
May, by thy grace, safe courses keep
Along the shallow ford.

4.

This mystery, we must confess,
Our reach doth far exceed,
And some of our weak faiths are less
Than grains of mustard seed.

Oh, therefore, Lord, increase it so
We fruit may bear to thee,
And that implicit faith may grow
Explicit faith to be.

5.

With hands we see not as with eyes;
Eyes think not as the heart;
But each retains what doth suffice
To act his proper part;
And in the body, while it bides,
The meanest member shares
That bliss, which to the best betides,
And as the same it fares;

6.[8]

So, if in union unto thee
United we remain,
The faith of those that stronger be,
The weaker shall sustain;
Our Christian love shall that supply
Which we in knowledge miss,
And humble thoughts shall mount us high,
E'en to eternal bliss.

7.

Oh, pardon all those heinous crimes
Whereof we guilty are;
To serve thee more in future times,
Our hearts do thou prepare;
And make thou gracious in thy sight
Both us, and this we do,
That thou therein mayst take delight,
And we have love thereto.

8.

No new oblation we devise
For sins proferr'd to be;
Propitiatory sacrifice
Was made at full by thee;
The sacrifice of thanks is that,
And all that thou dost crave,

---

[8] {The 1641 communion hymn has nothing corresponding to this stanza; see, however, Sidney Godolphin's poem, "Lord, when wise men" <*infra*>.}

And we ourselves are part of what
We sacrificed have.[9]

9.

We do no gross realities
Of flesh in this conceive,
Or that their proper qualities
The bread or wine do leave;
Yet in this holy Eucharist
We (by a means divine)
Know we are fed with thee, oh Christ,
Receiving bread and wine.

10.

And though the outward elements
For signs acknowledg'd be,
We cannot say thy sacraments
Things only signal be,
Because, whoe'er thereof partakes,
In those this power it hath:
It either them thy members makes,
Or slaves of sin and death.

11.

Nor unto those do we incline
(But from them are estrang'd),
Who yield the form of bread and wine,
Yet think the substance chang'd:
For we believe each element
Is what it seems indeed,
Although that in thy sacrament
Therewith on thee we feed.

12.

Thy real presence we avow,
And know it so divine,
That carnal reason knows not how
That presence to define:
For when thy flesh we feed on thus
(Though strange it do appear),
Both we in thee, and thou in us,
E'en at one instant are.

[9] {This stanza draws on the prayer of consecration and post-Communion prayer from the 1559 Book of Common Prayer.}

13.

No marvel many troubled were
This secret to unfold,[10]
For mysteries faith's objects are,
Not things at pleasure told.
And he that would by reason sound
What faith's deep reach conceives,
May both himself and them confound,
To whom his rules he leaves.

14.

Let us, therefore, our faith erect
On what thy word doth say,
And hold their knowledge in suspect,
That new foundations lay:
For such full many a grievous rent
Within thy Church have left;
And by thy peaceful sacrament
The world of peace bereft.

15.

Yea, what thy pledge and seal of love
Was first ordain'd to be,
Doth great and hateful quarrels move
Where wrangling spirits be;
And many men have lost their blood
(Who did thy name profess),
Because they hardly understood
What others would express.

16.

Oh, let us not hereafter so
About mere words contend,
The while our crafty common foe
Procures on us his end;
But if in essence we agree,
Let all with love assay
A help unto the weak to be,
And for each other pray.

17.[11]

Love is that blessed cément, Lord,
Which must us reunite;
In bitter speeches, fire and sword,

---

[10] {See John 6:47-66.}

[11] {For the stanzas corresponding to 17–25 in the 1641 version of this poem, see Wither's *Hallelujah: or Britain's second remembrancer*, part I, hymn 53, st. 12–19 *<infra>*.}

It never took delight:
The weapons those of malice are,
And they themselves beguile,
Who dream that such ordained were
Thy Church to reconcile.

18.

Love brought us hither, and that love
Persuades us to implore
That thou all Christian hearts wouldst move
To seek it more and more;
And that self-will no more bewitch
Our minds with foul debate,
Nor fill us with that malice which
Disturbs a quiet state.

19.

But this especially we crave,
That perfect peace may be
'Mong those that disagreed have
In show of love to thee;
That they with us, and we with them,
May Christian peace retain,
And both in New Jerusalem
With thee for ever reign.

20.

No longer let ambitious ends,
Blind zeal, or cankered spite,
Those Churches keep from being friends,
Whom love should fast unite;
But let thy glory shine among
Those candlesticks, we pray,
We may behold what hath so long
Exil'd thy peace away:

21.[12]

That those, who, heeding not thy word,
Expect an earthly power,
And vainly think some temporal sword
Shall Antichrist devour;
That those may know thy weapons are
No such as they do feign,
And that it is no carnal war
Which we must entertain.

---

[12] {This and the following stanzas almost certainly refer to the ongoing conflict now known as the Thirty Years War, and they do not bespeak Protestant militancy.}

22.

Confessors, martyrs, preachers strike
The blows that gain this field;
Thanks, prayer, instructions, and the like,
Those weapons are they wield;
Long-suffering, patience, prudent care,
Must be the court-of-guard;
And faith and innocency are
Instead of walls prepar'd.

23.

For these (no question) may as well
Great Babel overthrow,
As Jericho's large bulwarks fell
When men did ram's-horns blow;
Which, could we credit, we should cease
All bloody plots to lay,
And to suppose God's holy peace
Should come the devil's way.

24.

Lord, let that flesh and blood of thine,
Which fed us hath to day,
Our hearts to thy true-love incline,
And drive ill thoughts away;
Let us remember what thou hast
For our mere love endur'd,
E'en when of us despis'd thou wast,
And we thy death procur'd.

25.

And with each other, for thy sake,
So truly let us bear,
Our patience may us dearer make,
When reconcil'd we are;
So when our courses finish'd be,
We shall ascend above
Sun, moon, and stars, to live with thee,
That art the God of Love.

HERE ENDETH THE HYMNS AND SONGS OF THE CHURCH.

{THE TUNES TO WITHER'S SONGS, COMPOSED BY ORLANDO GIBBONS}

Song 9. (p. 41.)

Song 13. (p. 53.)

(3)

Song 44. (p. 168.)

Wither's Songs.] (7)

TEXT: George Wither, *Hymns and songs of the Church*, ed. and intro. Edward Farr (London, 1856). Checked against the several version of *The hymns and songs of the Church, divided into two parts* (London, 1623).

WILLIAM LAUD
(1573–1645)[1]

The son of a prosperous Reading merchant and nephew to one of London's lord mayors, Laud matriculated at St. John's, Oxford, in 1589; he would remain there until his late forties. His theological views probably owe a good deal to his beloved tutor, John Buckeridge, with whom he formed a life-long friendship. Laud took his BA in 1594, his MA in 1598. Three years later, he was ordained by Young of Rochester and elected senior fellow by his college. By the first years of James' reign, Laud's thought had already assumed its distinctive cast: a 1602 lecture upheld the perpetual visibility of the true Church; his 1604 BD thesis argued for the necessity of baptism; his 1608 DD thesis defended divine right episcopacy. During these years (as for the remainder of his life), Laud repeatedly found himself accused of popery (and/or Arminianism) by colleagues baffled at his "failure to observe the standard lines of attack and defense in the conflict between Rome and protestantism" (*ODNB*). However, his annotations to Bellarmine's *Disputationes*, which date from this period, side with Calvin on key issues, including the final perseverance of the elect.[2] Laud was a high churchman, not an Arminian; when offered an Arminian tract in 1630, Laud replied that he probably wouldn't have time to read it and, if he did, doubted it would change his longstanding view that "something about these controversies [re predestination] is unmasterable in this life" (*Works* 6:292).

In 1608 Laud became chaplain to Richard Neile and, together with Buckeridge and Cosin, part of Neile's Durham House circle. Three years later, he was appointed royal chaplain and chosen president of St. John's. George Abbot had opposed this latter promotion, and in 1615 Abbot's brother Robert publicly accused Laud of crypto-Catholicism,

---

[1] Laud has been a controversial figure for four centuries, and much of the scholarship dealing even with basic biographical facts is partisan and suspect, a noble exception being Anthony Milton's *ODNB* entry, to which this introduction is much indebted.

[2] This was also Richard Hooker's position in "Of the certainty and perpetuity of faith in the elect," the sermon that the puritan Walter Travers denounced and, by so doing, brought Hooker to Whitgift's attention (see Shuger, "Faith and assurance").

368

leveling similar charges against John Howson *<vide supra>*; the King, who heard the case, ended up supporting Laud, whom in 1616 he appointed dean of Gloucester, and then in 1621 bishop of St. David's, a poor and remote Welsh see, which Laud only visited on a few occasions.

The following year, James requested that Laud debate with the Jesuit John Fisher in the presence of the Countess of Buckingham and her son, the all-powerful royal favorite. Laud's friendship with Buckingham—and his consequent political ascent—date from this meeting, to which we will return, since it lies behind the selections from Laud's writings included below.

During the great Montagu dust-up of 1624–29, Laud wrote Buckingham on the embattled priest's behalf (see the introduction to the Montagu readings *<infra>*), but it is clear from Montagu's own letters that the two men were not particularly close.

Shortly after Charles' accession, Laud became dean of the Chapel Royal, as well as (in swift succession) bishop of Bath and Wells (1626–28), London (1628–33), and archbishop of Canterbury (1633–45). Charles appointed him to the Privy Council in 1627. In 1630, to both Laud's and Charles' surprise (since they were supporting a different candidate), a group of Oxford dons successfully urged Laud's election as University chancellor, in which capacity he brought order and intelligibility to the University statutes, founded the lectureship in Arabic, and donated over a thousand manuscripts to the library.

The dedicatory epistle to Charles reprinted below, which prefaces the 1639 version of the *Conference with Fisher*, gives some sense of Laud's own ideals and endeavors as archbishop. Prynne's *News from Ipswich <infra>* may stand for the epistle's "wasps, or . . . hornets rather," menacing the Laudian *renovatio*—in the end, successfully. The collapse of the Caroline regime, which Laud's policies helped precipitate, took him down with it. Impeached by the Commons in December 1640 for high treason, he spent the next four years in the Tower; his prison diaries, the *History of the troubles and trial of William Laud*, together with its concluding scaffold speech, are among the unknown masterpieces of English literature.[3] As for the trial itself, which began in 1644, this "was a travesty of justice," Laud being "manifestly innocent of the charges of treason and the advancement of popery that were leveled against him" (*ODNB*). That he had not violated any of the treason statutes was manifest even to the Commons; as with Strafford, they therefore proceeded by bill of attainder. Under threats of mob violence, the Lords (with only nineteen peers present) ratified the bill on 4 January 1645. Laud was executed six days later. Given his age, he asked permission to read (rather than recite from memory) his scaffold address, whose grandeur and pathos movingly contrasts with the austere plain style of the trial narrative.

The *Conference with Fisher* reports Laud's version of an actual conference with the Jesuit Fisher held in May of 1622 at James' request in order to reclaim, if possible, the Countess of Buckingham from the Roman Church, which she had newly embraced or was on the verge of embracing, and—a matter of far more importance—to counteract the concerted

---

[3] William Lamont has shown conclusively that they are, unlike Prynne's competing account of Laud's trial, a reasonably accurate reconstruction of what transpired (*Marginal Prynne* 120).

efforts of both Fisher and the Countess to win Buckingham himself for Rome.[4] Earlier that year, Francis White had twice debated Fisher in the presence of the Countess and Duke (then Marquis). White's statements regarding the perpetual visibility and infallibility of the Church apparently failed to satisfy the Countess, so James asked Laud to take over for White in a third conference that would focus on this issue. Although both sides had been sworn to silence, Fisher's manuscript version of the debates was soon in wide circulation. In 1624 White and Laud jointly published their reply: the latter's *An answer to Mr. Fisher's relation of a third conference* appearing as a 74-page appendix to White's 600-page *Reply to Jesuit Fisher's answer*. Laud's contribution dealt with the Countess' question about the Church and also with Fisher's "Disputation touching the rule of faith, Scripture, and tradition," which gave the Jesuit's answer to questions that King James himself posed during the second debate between Fisher and White.

Fisher (alias A. C.) then responded to Laud's *An answer* in his 1626 *True relations of sundry conferences*, printed at St. Omer. Laud did not hear about this piece for some time, and when he did, his more pressing responsibilities delayed a reply until 1639, when he published an expanded, although not fundamentally altered, version of his 1624 tract, this time under his own name, and retitled *A relation of the conference between William Laud . . . and Mr. Fisher the Jesuit* (a.k.a. *Conference with Fisher*).[5] Although the work is a *seriatim* response to Fisher's arguments and its publication driven by the need to rebut the charges of popery that had always dogged Laud and by 1639 were poised to destroy him, it is as much spiritual apologia as *pièce d'circonstance*: this would seem to be the implication of Laud's will, which leaves £100 for its translation into Latin that "the Christian world may see and judge of my religion."

The epistle prefacing the 1639 edition is particularly notable for Laud's attempt to explain why ceremonies and external worship matter: why he held these things worth insisting on. The *Conference* that follows offers considerably more than "a moderate and legalistic defense of the separation from Rome" (*ODNB*). The passages reprinted below defend an "Erasmian" doctrinal latitude that (in dramatic contrast to Bayly's *Practice of piety <supra>*) makes only those tenets on which all Christians agree *fundamental*, that is, ordinarily necessary for salvation. Like so much else in the *Conference*, this creedal minimalism follows a path blazed by Richard Hooker—the sermons as well as the *Laws*.[6] Laud's efforts to show that authority may be merely human without being thereby illegitimate—and, conversely, divinely inspired without being thereby infallible—likewise echo Hooker; not surprisingly, its closest analog in this volume comes in *Of the Church <supra>* by Hooker's friend, Richard Field.

The heart of the Laudian case, however, concerns the grounds of religious belief. Although building on Hooker, Laud's argument here is his own, and perhaps the most thoughtful and penetrating account of faith that Stuart England produced. The

[4] Laud's 1639 dedicatory epistle *<infra>* lays out the circumstances leading to the conference and the subsequent publications.

[5] In the interim, Laud intervened to save Fisher's life when the Jesuit was captured and facing a death sentence in 1635 (see William Scott's introduction to the *Conference* in vol. 2 of Laud's *Works*).

[6] Nor is Laud's position far from the liberal rationalism of Chillingworth's *The religion of Protestants*, a work whose publication Laud had overseen just a year before *<vide infra>*.

discussion responds to the question regularly posed by Roman controversialists: if Protestants ground their faith on Scripture *as* the word of God, on what do they ground their faith that Scripture *is* the word of God? For belief to be more than opinion, it needs an infallible basis, and while Roman Catholics have an infallible Church to testify to the revealed truth of Scripture, Protestants have only the book, and this cannot bear witness to itself. Like Hooker (as also both Hales and Chillingworth), Laud rejects the premise: the visible Church is not infallible, nor is there any infallible magisterium in this world. The denial of infallibility does not, however, equalize all claims into an anarchy of mere opinion and private spirits. In Hales and Chillingworth, the scales of belief rely almost exclusively on reason for their counterweight. Laud's answer is less modern (i.e., less individualist, less rationalist) and more complex—more alert to the epistemic and experiential complexity of belief. That people in fact come to believe Scripture is the word of God, Laud avers, and that they are justified in so believing has to do with the interplay among multiple factors—not just evidence and arguments, but also supernatural illumination, affective disposition, cultural authority, institutional witness, and the testimony of tradition.[7] None of these, for Laud, constitutes proof (some of them, taken singly, have no epistemic weight whatsoever); yet taken together, they create a certainty sufficient both to enable and authorize the will's final leap of faith.[8]

NOTE: *A relation of the conference with Fisher* (or *An answer to Mr. Fisher's relation*, as the work was initially titled) belongs both to 1624 and 1639. The dedicatory epistle dates from the fuller version of 1639, as do a few passages in the selection reprinted below; yet since the actual debate between Laud and Fisher dates from 1622 and Laud's central ideas and arguments are already legible in the 1624 version, it seemed both more illuminating and more accurate to place the *Conference* under the date of its initial publication. One might, however, come back to its dedicatory epistle at the close of this volume.

SOURCES: *ODNB*; Laud, *The works*, 7 vols. in 5, ed. James Bliss and William Scott (Oxford: John Henry Parker, 1857; rpt. Georg Olms, 1977); William Lamont, *Puritanism and the English Revolution*, vol. 1: *Marginal Prynne* (Routledge, 1963; rpt. Aldershot: Gregg Revivals, 1991); Shuger, "Faith and assurance."

---

[7] Compare Hooker, *Laws* 3.8.13–17.

[8] See Shuger, "Faith and assurance" and, in this volume, the introduction to the Chillingworth section <*infra*> for a more detailed treatment of this Laudian epistemology.

WILLIAM LAUD

A relation of the conference between William Laud . . . and Mr. Fisher, the Jesuit[1]
1624 (rev. ed. 1639)

To
His Most Sacred Majesty,
Charles,
By the Grace of God,
King of Great Britain, France, and Ireland,
Defender of the Faith, &c.

Dread Sovereign,

This tract will need patronage, as great as may be had, that is yours. Yet when I first printed part of it, I presumed not to ask any, but thrust it out at the end of another's labors, that it might seem at least to have the same patron, your royal father of blessed memory, as the other work, on which this attended, had. But now I humbly beg for it your Majesty's patronage, and leave withal, that I may declare to your most excellent Majesty the cause why this tract was then written; why it stayed so long before it looked upon the light . . . why it comes now forth both with alteration and addition; and why this addition made not more haste to the press than it hath done.

The cause why this discourse was written was this: I was, at the time of these conferences with Master Fisher, Bishop of S. David's; and not only directed, but commanded, by my blessed master, King James, to this conference with him. He, when we met, began with a great protestation of seeking the truth only, and that for itself. And certainly, truth, especially in religion, is so to be sought, or not to be found. . . . After the conference ended, I went whither my duty called me, to my diocese, not suspecting anything should be made public that was both commanded and acted in private. . . . In my absence from London, M. Fisher . . . spread abroad papers of this conference, full enough of partiality

---

[1] {Following the dedicatory epistle, which Laud added in 1639, material appearing in the 1639 version but not in 1624 will be either underlined (unless the changes seem too minor to be worth noting) or, for the longer passages, inset.}

to his cause, and more full of calumny against me. Hereupon I was in a manner forced to give M. Fisher's *Relation of the conference*, an answer, and to publish it. . . .

There was a cause also why, at the first, the discourse upon this conference stayed so long before it could endure to be pressed. For the conference was in May 1622. And M. Fisher's paper was scattered and made common, so common that a copy was brought to me, being none of his special friends, before Michaelmas. And yet this discourse was not printed till April, 1624. . . . And this was caused partly by my own backwardness to deal with these men, whom I have ever observed to be great pretenders for truth and unity, but yet such as will admit neither, unless they and their faction may prevail in all; as if no reformation had been necessary. And partly because there were, about the same time, three conferences held with Fisher. Of these, this was the third, and could not therefore conveniently come abroad into the world till the two former were ready to lead the way, which till that time they were not.

. . .

There is a cause also why it looks now abroad again with alteration and addition. And it is fit I should give your Majesty an account of that too. This tract was first printed in the year 1624. And in the year 1626, another Jesuit (or the same), under the name of A. C., printed a relation of this conference, and therein took exceptions to some particulars and endeavored to confute some things delivered therein by me. Now being in years, and unwilling to die in the Jesuit's debt, I have in this second edition done as much for him, and somewhat more. For he did but skip up and down, and labor to pick a hole here and there, where he thought he might fasten; and where it was too hard for him, let it alone. But I have gone thorough with him, and (I hope) given him a full confutation; or at least such a bone to gnaw as may shake his teeth if he look not to it. And of my addition to this discourse, this is the cause; but of my alteration of some things in it, this: A. C. his curiosity to winnow me made me in a more curious manner fall to sifting of myself and that which had formerly passed my pen. And though (I bless God for it) I found no cause to alter anything that belonged either to the substance or course of the *Conference*, yet somewhat I did find which needed better and clearer expression, and that I have altered, well knowing I must expect curious observers on all hands.

. . .

Now, if it be M. Fisher himself under the name of A. C., then what needs these words: *The Jesuit could be content to let pass the chaplain's censure as one of his ordinary persecutions for the Catholic faith, but A. C. thought it necessary for the common cause to defend the sincerity and truth of his relation, and the truth of some of the chief heads contained in it?* In which speech, give me leave to observe to your sacred Majesty how grievously you suffer him and his fellows to be persecuted for the Catholic faith, when your poor subject and servant cannot set out a true copy of a conference held with the Jesuit, *jussu superiorum*[2] but by and by the man is *persecuted*. God forbid I should ever offer to persuade a persecution in any kind, or practice it in the least: for, to my remembrance, I have not given him or his so much as coarse language. But, on the other side, God forbid, too that your Majesty should let both laws and discipline sleep for fear of the name of persecution, and in the meantime

---

[2] {by command of his superiors}

let M. Fisher and his fellows angle in all parts of your dominions for your subjects. If in your grace and goodness you will spare their persons, yet I humbly beseech you see to it that they be not suffered to lay either their wheels[3] or bait their hooks or cast their nets in every stream, lest that tentation grow both too general and too strong. I know they have many devices to work their ends; but if they will needs be fishing, let them use none but lawful nets. Let us have no dissolving of oaths of allegiance; no deposing, no killing of kings; no blowing up of states to settle *quod volumus*, that which fain they would have in the Church, with many other nets as dangerous as these; for if their profession of religion were as good as they pretend it is, if they cannot compass it by good means, I am sure they ought not to attempt it by bad; for if they will *do evil that good may come thereof*, the Apostle tells me *their damnation is just* (Rom. 3).

Now, as I would humbly beseech your Majesty to keep a serious watch upon these fishermen, which pretend S. Peter, but fish not with his net; so would I not have you neglect another sort of anglers in a shallower water, for they have some ill nets too, and if they may spread them when and where they will, God knows what may become of it. These have not so strong a back abroad as the Romanists have, but that is no argument to suffer them to increase. They may grow to equal strength with number; and factious people at home, of what sect or fond opinion soever they be, are not to be neglected, partly because they are so near—and it is ever a dangerous fire that begins in the bed-straw—and partly because all those domestic evils which threaten a rent in Church or state are with far more safety prevented by wisdom than punished by justice. And would men consider it right, they are far more beholding to that man that keeps them from falling than to him that takes them up, though it be to set the arm or the leg that is broken in the fall.

In this discourse I have no aim to displease any, nor any hope to please all. If I can help on to truth in the Church and the peace of the Church together, I shall be glad, be it in any measure. Nor shall I spare to speak necessary truth out of too much love of peace; nor thrust on unnecessary truth to the breach of that peace which, once broken, is not so easily soldered again. And if for necessary truth's sake only, any man will be offended, nay take, nay snatch at that offence which is not given, I know no fence for that. It is truth, and I must tell it; it is the Gospel, and I must preach it (1 Cor. 9). And far safer it is in this case to bear anger from men than a *woe* from God. And where the foundations of faith are shaken, be it by superstition or profaneness, he that puts not to his hand[4] as firmly as he can to support them is too wary and hath more care of himself than of the cause of Christ; and it is a wariness that brings more danger in the end than it shuns, for the angel of the Lord issued out a curse against the inhabitants of Meroz *because they came not to help the Lord, to help the Lord against the mighty* (Judg. 5). I know it is a great ease to let everything be as it will, and every man believe and do as he list; but whether governors in state or Church do their duty therewhile is easily seen, since this is an effect of *no king in Israel* (Judg. 17).[5]

---

[3] {Laud refers to a fish-wheel, a device for catching fish.}

[4] {"to put to one's hand" means to exert oneself, to endeavor}

[5] {*Vide* Augustine, *City of God* 2.20. I am not sure anyone in Caroline England would have taken issue with Laud's profoundly unmodern position here. See the Thomas Adams' reading <*supra*>, n. 11.}

The Church of Christ upon earth may be compared to a hive of bees, and that can be nowhere so steadily placed in this world but it will be in some danger; and men that care neither for the hive nor the bees have yet a great mind to the honey; and having once tasted the sweet of the Church's maintenance, swallow that for honey which one day will be more bitter than gall in their bowels. Now, the king and the priest more than any other are bound to look to the integrity of the Church in doctrine and manners, and that in the first place; for that is by far the best honey in the hive. But, in the second place, they must be careful of the Church's maintenance too, else the bees shall make honey for others and have none left for their own necessary sustenance, and then all is lost; for we see it in daily and common use that the honey is not taken from the bees but they are destroyed first. Now, in this great and busy work, the king and the priest must not fear to put their hands to the hive, though they be sure to be stung—and stung by the bees whose hive and house they preserve. It was King David's case; God grant it be never yours. *They came about me* (saith the Psalm 118) *like bees.* This was hard usage enough, yet some profit, some honey might thus be gotten in the end. And that is the king's case. But when it comes to the priest, the case is altered: they come about him like wasps, or like hornets rather—all sting and no honey there—and all this many times for no offence, nay sometimes for service done them, would they see it. But you know who said *Behold I come shortly, and my reward is with me to give to every man according as his works shall be* (Revel. 22). And he himself is so *exceeding great a reward* as that the manifold stings which are in the world, howsoever they smart here, are nothing when they are pressed out with that *exceeding weight of glory which shall be revealed* (Rom. 8).

Now, one thing more let me be bold to observe to your Majesty in particular concerning your great charge, the Church of England. It is in a hard condition. She professes the ancient Catholic faith, and yet the Romanist condemns her of novelty in her doctrine; she practices Church government as it hath been in use in all ages and all places where the Church of Christ hath taken any rooting, both in and ever since the apostles' times, and yet the separatist condemns her for anti-christianism in her discipline. The plain truth is, she is between these two factions as between two millstones, and unless your Majesty look to it, to whose trust she is committed, she will be ground to powder, to an irreparable both dishonor and loss to this kingdom. And it is very remarkable that while both these press hard upon the Church of England, both of them cry out upon persecution; like froward children, which scratch and kick and bite, and yet cry out all the while as if themselves were killed. Now to the Romanist, I shall say this: the errors of the Church of Rome are grown now, many of them, very old; and when errors are grown by age and continuance to strength, they which speak for the truth, though it be far older, are ordinarily challenged for the bringers in of new opinions. And there is no greater absurdity stirring this day in Christendom than that the reformation of an old corrupted Church, will we, nill we, must be taken for the building of a new. And were not this so, we should never be troubled with that idle and impertinent question of theirs: *where was your Church before Luther?* for it was just there where theirs is now. One and the same Church still, no doubt of that; one in substance, but not one in condition of state and purity: their part of the same Church remaining in corruption and our part of the same Church under reformation. . . . And for the separatist and him that lays his grounds for separation or change of discipline, though all he says (or can say) be, in truth of divinity and among learned men, little better than ridiculous, yet since these fond opinions have gained some ground among your people, to such among them as are willfully set to *follow their blind guides through thick and thin, till they fall into the ditch together*, I shall say nothing. But for so many of them as mean well and are only misled by artifice and cunning, concerning them I shall say thus much only: they are bells of passing good metal, and tuneable enough of themselves and in their own disposition; and a world of pity it is that they are rung so miserably out of tune as they are by them which have gotten power in and over their consciences. And for this there is yet remedy enough; but how long there will be, I know not.

Much talking there is—bragging, your Majesty may call it—on both sides; and when they are in their ruff, they both exceed all moderation and truth too—so far till both lips and pens open for all the world like a purse without money; nothing comes out of this, and that which is worth nothing out of them. And yet this nothing is made so great, as if the salvation of souls—that great work of the Redeemer of the world, the Son of God— could not be effected without it. And while the one faction cries up the Church above the Scripture and the other the Scripture to the neglect and contempt of the Church, which the Scripture itself teaches men both to honor and obey, they have so far endangered the belief of the one and the authority of the other as that neither hath its due from a great part of men. Whereas, according to Christ's institution, the Scripture, where it is plain, should guide the Church; and the Church, where there is doubt or difficulty, should expound the Scripture; yet so, as neither the Scripture should be forced nor the Church so bound up as that, upon just and further evidence, she may not revise that which in any case hath slipped by her. What success this great distemper, caused by the collision of two such factions, may have, I know not. . . . And though I cannot prophesy, yet I fear that atheism and irreligion gather strength while the truth is thus weakened by an unworthy way of contending for it. . . .

. . . And this I have observed further, that no one thing hath made conscientious men more wavering in their own minds, or more apt and easy to be drawn aside from the sincerity of religion professed in the Church of England, than the want of uniform and decent order in too many churches of the kingdom; and the Romanists have been apt to say, The houses of God could not be suffered to lie so nastily, as in some places they have done, were the true worship of God observed in them or did the people think that such it were. It is true, the inward worship of the heart is the great service of God, and no service acceptable without it; but the external worship of God in his Church is the great witness to the world that our heart stands right in that service of God. Take this away or bring it into contempt, and *what light is there left to shine before men, that they may see our devotion and glorify our Father which is in heaven?* And to deal clearly with your Majesty, these thoughts are they, and no other, which have made me labor so much as I have done for decency and an orderly settlement of the external worship of God in the Church—for of that which is inward, there can be no witness among men nor no example for men. Now, no external action in the world can be uniform without some ceremonies; and these in religion, the ancienter they be, the better, so they may fit time and place. Too many overburden the service of God and too few leave it naked. And scarce any thing hath hurt religion more in these broken times than an opinion in too many men that because Rome had thrust some unnecessary and many superstitious ceremonies upon the Church, therefore the Reforma- tion must have none at all; not considering therewhile that ceremonies are the hedge that fence the substance of religion from all the indignities which profaneness and sacrilege too commonly put upon it. And a great weakness it is, not to see the strength which ceremonies—things weak enough in themselves, God knows—add even to religion itself; but a far greater, to see it and yet to cry them down all and without choice. . . .

I have been too bold to detain your Majesty so long, but my grief to see Christendom bleeding in dissension and, which is worse, triumphing in her own blood and most angry with them that would study her peace hath thus transported me; for truly it cannot but grieve any man that hath bowels to see *all men seeking*, but as S. Paul foretold (Phil. 2), *their own things, and not the things which are Jesus Christ's* . . . and to see religion—so much, so zealously pretended and called upon—made but the stalking-horse to shoot at other fowl upon which their aim is set; in the meantime, as if all were truth and holiness itself, no salvation must be possible, did it lie at their mercy, but in the communion of the one and in the conventicles of the other, as if either of these now were, as the Donatists of old reputed themselves, the only men in whom Christ at his coming to judgment should find faith. *No*, saith S. Augustine, and so I say with him, *Da veniam, non credimus*, Pardon us, I pray, we cannot believe it. The Catholic Church of Christ is neither Rome nor a conventicle. Out of that there is no salvation, I easily confess it. But out of Rome there is, and out of a conventicle too; salvation is not shut up into such a narrow conclave. In this ensuing discourse, therefore, I have endeavored to lay open those wider gates of the Catholic Church, confined to no age, time, or place; nor knowing any bounds but *that faith which was once* (and but once for all) *delivered to the saints* (Jude 3). And in my pursuit of this way, I have searched after, and delivered with a single heart, that truth which I profess. In the publishing whereof I have obeyed your Majesty, discharged my duty to my power to the Church of England, *given account of the hope that is in me*, and so testified to the world that faith in which I have lived, and by God's blessing and favor purpose to die; but, till death, shall most unfeignedly remain

Your Majesty's most faithful subject,
and most humble and obliged servant,

W. Cant.

A Relation of the Conference

F{isher}. The occasion of this conference was. . . .

B{ishop}. The occasion of this third conference you should know sufficiently. You were an actor in it, as well as in two other. Whether you have related the two former truly appears by Doctor White, the late Reverend Lord Bishop of Ely, his relation or exposition of them. I was present at none but this third, of which I here give the Church an account. But of this third, whether that were the cause which you allege, I cannot tell. You say,

> **F.** It was observed that in the second conference {with D. White}, all the speech was about particular matters; little or none about a continual, infallible, visible Church, which was the chief and only point in which a certain lady required satisfaction, as having formerly settled in her mind that it was not for her, or any other unlearned persons, to take upon them to judge of particulars, without depending upon the judgment of the true Church.

B. The opinion of that honorable person in this was never opened to me. And it is very fit the people should look to the judgment of the Church before they be too busy with particulars. But yet neither Scripture nor any good authority denies them some moderate use of their own understanding and judgment, especially in things familiar and evident which even ordinary capacities may as easily understand as read. And therefore some particulars a Christian may judge without depending.

> **F.** This lady, therefore, having heard it granted in the first conference that there must be a continual, visible company ever since Christ, teaching unchanged doctrine in all fundamental points (that is, points necessary to salvation), desired to hear this confirmed and proof brought {to show} which was that continual, infallible, visible Church, in which one may, and out of which one cannot, attain salvation. And, therefore, having appointed a time of meeting between a [certain] B. and me . . . before the B. came, the lady and a friend of hers came first to the room where I was and debated before me the aforesaid question, and not doubting of the first part, to wit, *that there must be a continual visible Church*, as they had heard granted by D. White, and L. K .,[6] &c.

B. What D. White and L. K. granted, I heard not; but I think both granted a *continual* and a *visible* Church; neither of them an *infallible*, at least in your sense. And yourself, in this relation, speak distractedly; for, in these few lines from the beginning hither, twice you add *infallible* between *continual* and *visible*, and twice you leave it out. But this concerns Dr. W., and he hath answered it.

> Here A. C.[7] steps in, and says, *The Jesuit did not speak distractedly, but most advisedly. For* (saith he), *where he relates what D. White or L. K. granted, he leaves out the word "infallible" because they granted it not; but where he speaks of the lady, there he adds it, because the Jesuit knew it was an infallible Church which she sought to rely upon.* . . .

‡

It ought to be no easy thing to condemn a man of heresy in foundation of faith, much less a Church; least of all, so ample and large a Church as the Greek, especially so as to make them no Church. Heaven gates were not so easily shut against multitudes when S. Peter wore the keys at his own girdle. And it is good counsel which Alphonsus a Castro,[8] one of your own, gives: *Let them consider that pronounce easily of heresy, how easy it is for themselves to err.* Or if you will pronounce, consider what it is that separates from the Church simply, and not in part only. I must needs profess that I wish heartily, as well as others, that those distressed men (whose cross is heavy already[9]) had been more plainly

---

[6] {i.e., the Lord Keeper, Bishop Williams}

[7] {A. C. is Fisher's pseudonym in his 1626 tract against Laud; see the introduction to this section.}

[8] {Alphonsus de Castro, Franciscan theologian and jurist, author of *Adversos omnes haereses libri xiv* (1534) and *De iusta hereticorum punitione libri iii* (1547).}

[9] {The "cross" referred to is the subjugation of Constantinople—and much of Orthodox Christendom—to the Ottoman Empire. The Roman Church considered Orthodox Christians, no less than Protestants, heretics.}

and moderately dealt withal, though they think a diverse thing from us, than they have been by the Church of Rome. . . .

. . .

For the first: *that all points defined by the Church are fundamental.* It was not the least means by which Rome grew to her greatness, to blast every opposer she had with the name of heretic or schismatic; for this served to shrivel the credit of the persons; and the persons once brought into contempt and ignominy, all the good they desired in the Church fell to dust for want of creditable persons to back and support it. . . .

But since these men distinguish not, nor you, between the Church in general and a general council, which is but her representation for determinations of the faith; though I be very slow in sifting or opposing what is concluded by lawful, general, and consenting authority; though I give as much as can justly be given to the definitions of councils truly general; nay, suppose I should grant, which I do not, that general councils cannot err; yet this cannot down with me, that all points even so defined are fundamental. For deductions are not prime and native principles; nor are superstructures foundations. That which is a foundation for all cannot be one and another to different Christians in regard of itself; for then it could be no common rule for any, nor could the souls of men rest upon a shaking foundation. No: if it be a true foundation, it must be common to all, and firm under all—in which sense the articles[10] of Christian faith are fundamental. And Irenaeus lays this for a ground, that the whole Church, howsoever dispersed in place, speaks this with one mouth: *he which among the guides of the Church is best able to speak, utters no more than this; and less than this, the most simple doth not utter.* Therefore the Creed, of which he speaks, is a common, is a constant foundation. And an explicit faith must be of this (in them which have the use of reason), for both guides and simple people—all the Church—utter this.

Now, many things are defined by the Church which are but deductions out of this, which, suppose them deduced right, move far from the foundation—without which deductions explicitly believed, many millions of Christians go to heaven—and cannot therefore be fundamental in the faith. True deductions from the article may require necessary belief in them which are able and do go along with them from the principle to the conclusion. But I do not see either that the learned do make them necessary to all or any reason why they should. Therefore they cannot be fundamental; <u>and yet to some men's salvation they are necessary</u>.

. . .

. . . For, first, no man denies but the Church is a foundation, that things defined by it are founded upon it, and yet hence it cannot follow that the thing that is so founded is fundamental in the faith: for things may be founded upon human authority and be very certain, yet not fundamental in the faith. . . . For full Church authority (always the time that included the holy apostles being passed by and not comprehended in it) is but Church authority; and Church authority, when it is at full sea, is not simply divine; therefore, the sentence of it not fundamental in the faith. And yet no erring disputer may be endured to shake the foundation which the Church in council lays. But plain Scripture with evident

[10] {"Articles," in this sense, are the several items of a summary of faith; Laud seems usually to identify them with the affirmations of the Apostles' Creed.}

sense, or a full demonstrative argument, must have room, where a wrangling and erring disputer may not be allowed it. And there is neither of these but may convince[11] the definition of the Council, if it be ill founded. And the articles of the faith may easily prove it is not fundamental, if indeed and verily it be not so.

‡

F. I asked how he {Laud} knew Scripture to be Scripture, and in particular Genesis, Exodus, &c. These are believed to be Scripture, yet not proved out of any place of Scripture. The B. said that the books of Scripture are principles to be supposed, and needed not to be proved.

B. I did never love too curious a search into that which might put a man into a wheel and circle him so long between proving Scripture by tradition and tradition by Scripture, till the devil find a means to dispute him into infidelity and make him believe neither. I hope this is no part of your meaning. Yet I doubt {suspect} this question, *How do you know Scripture to be Scripture*, hath done more harm than you will be ever able to help by tradition. But I must follow that way which you draw me. And because it is so much insisted upon by you, and is in itself a matter of such consequence, I will sift it a little further.

Many men laboring to settle this great principle in divinity have used divers means to prove it. All have not gone the same way, nor all the right way. You cannot be right, that resolve faith of the Scriptures being the word of God, into *only* tradition. For *only* and *no other* proof are equal.[12] To prove the Scripture, therefore (so called by way of excellence[13]), to be the word of God, there are several offers at divers proofs. For first, some fly to the testimony and witness of the Church and her tradition which constantly believes and unanimously delivers it. Secondly, some to the light and the testimony which the Scripture gives to itself, with other internal proofs which are observed in it and to be found in no other writing whatsoever. Thirdly, some to the testimony of the Holy Ghost, which clears up the light that is in Scripture and seals this faith to the souls of men, that it is God's word. Fourthly, all that have not imbrutished themselves and sunk below their species and order of nature give even natural reason leave to come in and make some proof and give some approbation upon the weighing and the consideration of other arguments; and this must be admitted, if it be but for pagans and infidels, who either consider not or value not any one of the other three, yet must some way or other be converted or *left without excuse* (Rom. 1), and that is done by this very evidence.

For the first: *the tradition of the Church*, which is your way. That taken and considered alone, it is so far from being the only, that it cannot be a sufficient proof to believe by divine faith that Scripture is the word of God. For that which is a full and sufficient proof is able of itself to settle the soul of man concerning it. Now, the tradition of the Church is not able to do this. For it may be further asked why we should believe the Church's tradition? And if it be answered, *we may believe because the Church is infallibly governed*

---

[11] {refute}

[12] {I.e., to say that tradition is the *only* ground for believing that Scripture is the word of God is equivalent to saying that there are *no other* grounds.}

[13] {as being preëminently entitled to the designation given (*OED*)}

by the Holy Ghost, it may yet be demanded of you, how that may appear? And if this be demanded, either you must say you have it by special revelation, which is the *private spirit* you object to other men, or else you must attempt to prove it by Scripture—as all of you do. And that very offer, to prove it out of Scripture, is a sufficient acknowledgment that the Scripture is a higher proof than the Church's tradition, which, in your own grounds, is or may be questionable till you come thither. <u>Besides, this is an inviolable ground of reason: *That the principles of any conclusion must be of more credit than the conclusion itself.* Therefore if the articles of faith—the Trinity, the Resurrection, and the rest—be the conclusions, and the principles by which they are proved be only ecclesiastical tradition, it must needs follow that the tradition of the Church is more infallible than the articles of the faith, if the faith which we have of the articles should be finally resolved into the veracity of the Church's testimony. But this your learned and wary men deny, and therefore I hope yourself dare not affirm.</u>

Again, if the voice of the Church saying *the books of Scripture commonly received are the word of God* be the formal object of faith upon which alone absolutely I may resolve myself, then every man not only may but ought to resolve his faith into the voice or tradition of the Church, for every man is bound to rest upon the proper and formal object of the faith. But nothing can be more evident than this, that a man ought not to resolve his faith of this principle into the *sole* testimony of the Church. Therefore, neither is that testimony or tradition, *alone*, the formal object of faith. The learned of your own part grant this: *Although in that article of the Creed* (I believe the Catholic Church) *peradventure all this be contained* (I believe those things which the Church teacheth), *yet this is not necessarily understood, that I believe the Church teaching as an infallible witness.*[14] And if they did not confess this, it were no hard thing to prove.

> But here is the cunning of this device. All the authorities of Fathers, Councils, nay of Scripture too, though this be contrary to their own doctrine, must be finally resolved into the authority of the present Roman Church; and though they would seem to have us believe the Fathers and the Church of old, yet they will not have us take their doctrine from their own writings or the decrees of Councils, because, as they say, we cannot know by reading them what their meaning was but from the infallible testimony of the present Roman Church teaching by tradition. Now, by this, two things are evident. First, that they ascribe as great authority (if not greater) to a part of the Catholic Church as they do to the whole which we believe in our Creed and which is the society of all Christians. And this is full of absurdity in nature, in reason, in all things, that any part should be of equal worth, power, credit, or authority with the whole. Secondly, that in their doctrine concerning the infallibility of their Church, their proceeding is most unreasonable. For if you ask them why they believe their whole doctrine to be the sole true Catholic faith, their answer is, *because it is agreeable to the word of God and the doctrine and tradition of the ancient Church.* If you ask them how they know that to be so, they will then produce testimonies of Scripture, Councils, and Fathers. But if you ask a third time, by what means they are assured that these testimonies

---

[14] [Stapleton, *Relect.* (*Scholast. Princip. fid. doct.*), lib. ii. cap. 20, pp. 754–55.]

do indeed make for them and their cause, they will not then have recourse to text of Scripture or exposition of Fathers, or phrase and propriety of language in which either of them were first written, or to the scope of the author, or the causes of the thing uttered, or the conference with like places, or the antecedents and consequents of the same places, or the exposition of the dark and doubtful places of Scripture by the undoubted and manifest, with divers other rules given for the true knowledge and understanding of Scripture, which do frequently occur in S. Augustine. No, none of these or the like helps: that, with them, were to admit a *private spirit*, or to make way for it. But their final answer is: *They know it to be so because the present Roman Church witnesseth it, according to tradition.* So arguing *primo ad ultimum*, from first to last, the present Church of Rome and her followers believe her own doctrine and tradition to be true and Catholic because she professes it to be such. And if this be not to prove *idem per idem*, the same by the same, I know not what is: which, though it be most absurd in all kind of learning, yet out of this I see not how it is possible to wind themselves, so long as the last resolution of their faith must rest, as they teach, upon the tradition of the present Church only.

It seems therefore to me very necessary that we be able to prove the books of Scripture to be the word of God by some authority that is absolutely divine. For if they be warranted unto us by any authority less than divine, then all things contained in them (which have no greater assurance than the Scripture, in which they are read) are not objects of divine belief. And that once granted will enforce us to yield that all the articles of Christian belief have no greater assurance than human or moral faith[15] or credulity can afford. An authority, then, simply divine, must make good the Scripture's infallibility, <u>at least in the last resolution of our faith in that point</u>. This authority cannot be any testimony or voice of the Church alone.[16]

> For the Church consists of men subject to error; and no one of them since the apostles' times hath been assisted with so plentiful a measure of the blessed Spirit as to secure him from being deceived. And all the parts being all liable to mistaking and fallible, the whole cannot possibly be infallible in and of itself, and privileged from being deceived in some things or other. And even in those fundamental things in which the whole universal Church neither doth nor can err, yet even there her authority is not divine, because she delivers those supernatural truths by promise of assistance yet tied to means, and not by any special immediate revelation, which is necessarily required to the very least degree of divine authority.

And therefore our worthies do not only say but prove *that all the Church's constitutions are of the nature of human law*.[17] And some among you not unworthy for their learning prove it at large, *that all the Church's testimony, or voice, or sentence*—call it what you will—*is*

---

[15] {On "moral faith," or "moral certainty," see the introduction to Chillingworth *<infra>*. See also the brief essay on this epistemic sense of the term in the *OED* under "moral" (adj), def. 7.}

[16] {1624 has "of the present Church alone."}

[17] [Hooker, *Eccl. Polit.*, book iii. chap. ix]

but suo modo *or* aliquo modo, *not simply, but in a manner divine.*[18] <u>Yea, and A. C. himself, after all his debate, comes to that, and no further, *That the tradition of the Church is, at least in some sort, divine and infallible.*</u> Now that which is divine but in a sort or manner, be it the Church's manner, is *aliquo modo non divina*, in a sort not divine. But this great principle of faith, the ground and proof of whatsoever else is of faith, cannot stand firm upon a proof that is and is not—in a manner and not in a manner—divine: as it must if we have no other anchor than the external tradition of the Church <u>to lodge it upon and hold it steady in the midst of those waves which daily beat upon it.</u>

> Now here A. C. confesses expressly, *that to prove the books of Scripture to be divine, we must be warranted by that which is infallible.* He confesses further, *that there can be no sufficient infallible proof of this but God's word, written or unwritten.* And he gives his reason for it: *because if the proof be merely human and fallible, the science or faith which is built upon it can be no better.* So then this is agreed on by me (yet leaving other men to travel by their own way, so be they can come to make Scripture thereby infallible), that Scripture must be known to be Scripture by a sufficient, infallible, divine proof. And that such proof can be nothing but the word of God is agreed on also by me. Yea, and agreed on for me it shall be likewise, that God's word may be written and unwritten. For Cardinal Bellarmine tells us truly, that it is not the writing or printing that makes Scripture the word of God, but it is the prime unerring essential truth, God himself, uttering and revealing it to his Church, that makes it *verbum Dei*, the word of God. And this word of God is uttered to men either immediately by God himself . . . and so it was to the prophets and apostles; or mediately, either by angels to whom God had spoken first—and so the law was given, and so also the message was delivered to the Blessed Virgin—or by the prophets and apostles, and so the Scriptures were delivered to the Church. But their being written gave them no authority at all in regard of themselves: written or unwritten, the word was the same. But it was written that it might be the better preserved and continued with the more integrity to the use of the Church and the more faithfully in our memories. And you have been often enough told (were truth, and not the maintaining of a party, the thing you seek for) that if you will show us any such unwritten word of God delivered by his prophets and apostles, we will acknowledge it to be divine and infallible. So, written or unwritten, that shall not stumble us. But then A. C. must not tell us, at least not think we shall swallow it into our belief, that everything which he says is the unwritten word of God, is so indeed.
>
> . . .
>
> . . . A. C. must not think that because the tradition of the Church tells me these books are *verbum Dei*, God's word, and that I do both honor and believe this tradition, that therefore this tradition itself is God's word too, and so absolutely sufficient and infallible to work this belief in me. Therefore, for aught A. C. hath yet added, we must on with our inquiry after this great business and most necessary truth.

[18] [Stapl. *Relect. Controv.* ix. Quest. iii. Art. 1.2]

For the second way of proving that Scripture should be fully and sufficiently known—as by divine and infallible testimony *lumine proprio*,[19] by the independency[20] of that light which it hath in itself only, and by the witness that it can so give to itself—I could never yet see cause to allow. For as there is no place in Scripture that tells us, such books, containing such and such particulars, are the canon, and infallible will and word of God; so, if there were any such place, that were no sufficient proof. For a man may justly ask another book to bear witness of that; and again, of that, another; and wherever it were written in Scripture, that must be a part of the whole; and no created thing can alone give witness to itself and make it evident; nor one part testify for another, and satisfy where reason will but offer to contest—except those principles only of natural knowledge which appear manifest by intuitive light of understanding, without any discourse; and yet they also to the weaker sort require induction preceding. Now this inbred light of Scripture is a thing coincident with Scripture itself, and so the principles and the conclusion in this kind of proof should be entirely the same, which cannot be.[21] Besides, if this inward light were so clear, how could there have been any variety among the ancient believers touching the authority of S. James' and S. Jude's epistles, and the Apocalypse, with other books which were not received for divers years after the rest of the New Testament? For certainly the light which is in the Scripture was the same then which now it is. And how could the Gospel of S. Bartholomew, of S. Thomas, and other counterfeit pieces obtain so much credit with some as to be received into the Canon, if the evidence of this light were either universal or infallible of and by itself? And this,[22] though I cannot approve, yet methinks you may, and upon probable grounds at least. For I hope no Romanist will deny but that there is as much light in Scripture to manifest and make ostension of itself to be infallibly the written word of God, as there is in any tradition of the Church that it is divine and infallibly the unwritten word of God. And the Scriptures, saying from the mouths of the prophets, *Thus saith the Lord*, and from the mouths of the apostles, that *the Holy Ghost spake by them*, are at least as able and as fit to bear witness to their own verity as the Church is to bear witness to her own traditions by bare saying they come from the apostles. And yourselves would never go to the Scripture to prove that there are traditions, as you do, if you do not think the Scripture as easy to be discovered by inbred light in itself as traditions by their light. And if this be so, then it is as probable at the least (which some of ours affirm) *that Scripture may be known to be the word of God by the light and luster which it hath in itself*, as it is (which you affirm) that *a tradition may be known to be such by the light which it hath in itself*, which is an excellent proposition to make sport withal, were this an argument to be handled merrily.

For the third opinion and way of proving: either some think that there is no sufficient warrant for this[23] unless they fetch it from the testimony of the Holy Ghost, and so look in

---

[19] {by its own intrinsic light . . . . This is the Calvinist position.}

[20] {self-sufficiency}

[21] {Instead of the underlined passage, the 1624 has "Besides, if it were so clear by native and in-given light, what should hinder but that all which hear it and do but understand the terms should presently assent unto it, as men use to do to principles evident in themselves? which daily experience teacheth us, they do not."}

[22] {"This" being the second way of proving Scripture the infallible word of God.}

[23] {i.e., for this belief that Scripture is the word of God}

vain after special revelations, and make themselves, by this very conceit {notion}, obnoxious {liable} and easy to be led by all the whisperings of a *seducing private spirit*—or else you would fain have them think so. For your side, both upon this and other occasions, do often challenge *that we resolve all our faith into the dictates of a private spirit*—from which we shall ever prove ourselves as free, if not freer than you. To the question in hand then: suppose it agreed upon that there must be a divine faith . . . under which can rest no possible error that the books of Scripture are the written word of God. If they which go to the testimony of the Holy Ghost for proof of this do mean by faith, *objectum fidei*, the object of faith that is to be believed, then, no question, they are out of the ordinary way; for God never sent us, by any word or warrant of his, to look for any such special and private testimony to prove which that book is that we must believe. But if by *faith* they mean the habit or act of divine infused faith, by which virtue they do believe the credible object and thing to be believed, then their speech is true, and confessed by all divines of all sorts. For faith is the *gift of God*, of God alone; and an infused habit, in respect whereof the soul is merely recipient;[24] and therefore the sole infuser, the Holy Ghost, must not be excluded from that work which none can do but he. For the Holy Ghost, as he first dictated the Scripture to the apostles, *so did he not leave the Church in general, nor the true members of it in particular, without grace to believe what himself had revealed and made credible.* So that faith, as it is taken for the virtue of faith, whether it be of this or any other article, though *it receive a kind of preparation or occasion of beginning from the testimony of the Church as it proposeth and induceth to the faith, yet it ends in God revealing within and teaching within that which the Church preached without.*[25] For till the Spirit of God move the heart of man, he cannot believe, be the object never so credible. The speech is true then, but quite out of the state of this question, which inquires only after a sufficient means to make this object credible and fit to be believed (against all impeachment of folly and temerity in belief), whether men do actually believe it or not. For which,[26] no man may expect inward private revelation without the external means of the Church, unless perhaps the case of necessity be excepted, when a man lives in such a time and place as excludes him from all ordinary means; in which I dare not offer to shut up God from the souls of men, nor to tie him to those ordinary ways and means to which yet in great wisdom and providence he had tied and bound all mankind.

Private revelation, then, hath nothing ordinarily to do to make the object credible in this, that Scripture is the word of God, or in any other article. For the question is of such outward and evident means as other men may take notice of, as well as ourselves. By which, if there arise any doubting or infirmity in the faith, others may strengthen us, or we afford means to support them; whereas the testimony of the Spirit, and all private revelation, is within, nor felt nor seen of any but him that hath it. So that hence can be drawn no proof to others. And miracles are not sufficient alone to prove it, unless both they, and the revelation too, agree with the rule of Scripture, which is now an unalterable rule by man or angel.[27] . . .

---

[24] {On infused habits, see Preston, *Plenitudo* <282>.]

[25] [Stapleton, *Relect. Controv.* Op. tom. 1, p. 755; Hooker, *Eccl. Polit.* book iii. ch. viii]

[26] {"Which" refers to "sufficient means."}

[27] {i.e., a rule that neither men nor angels may alter}

The last way, which gives reason leave to come in and prove what it can, may not justly be denied by any reasonable man.[28] For though reason without grace cannot see the way to heaven, nor believe this book in which God hath written the way, yet grace is never placed but in a reasonable creature, and proves, by the very seat which it hath taken up, that the end it hath is to be spiritual eye-water to make reason see what by nature only it cannot, but never to blemish reason in that which it can comprehend. Now the use of reason is very general; and man, do what he can, is still apt to search and seek for a reason why he will believe; though after he once believes, his faith grows stronger than either his reason or his knowledge. And great reason for this, because it goes higher, and so upon a safer principle, than either of the other[29] can in this life.

In this particular the books called the Scripture are commonly and constantly reputed to be the word of God; and so, infallible verity to the least point of them. Doth any man doubt this? The world cannot keep him from going to weigh it at the balance of reason whether it be the word of God or not. To the same weights he brings the tradition of the Church, the inward motives in Scripture itself, all testimonies within which seem to bear witness to it; and in all this there is no harm. The danger is when a man will use no other scale but reason, <u>or prefer reason before any other scale.</u> For the word of God and the book containing it refuse not to be weighed by reason.[30] But the scale is not large enough to contain, nor the weights to measure out, the true virtue and full force of either. Reason, then, can give no supernatural ground into which a man may resolve his faith that Scripture is the word of God infallibly; yet reason can go so high as it can prove that Christian religion, which rests upon the authority of this book, stands upon surer grounds of nature, reason, common equity, and justice than anything in the world which any infidel or mere naturalist hath done, doth, or can adhere unto against it, in that which he makes, accounts, or assumes as religion to himself.

The ancient Fathers relied upon the Scriptures—no Christians more; and having to do with philosophers (men very well seen in all the subtleties which natural reason could teach or learn), they were often put to it, and did as often make it good, that they had sufficient warrant to rely so much as they did upon Scripture. In all which disputes, because they were to deal with infidels, they did labor to make good the authority of the book of God by such arguments as unbelievers themselves could not but think reasonable, if they weighed them with indifferency. <u>For though I set the mysteries of faith above reason, which is their proper place, yet I would have no man think they contradict reason or the principles thereof. No sure. For reason by her own light can discover how firmly the principles of religion are true; but all the light she hath will never be able to find them false. Nor may any man think that the principles of religion—even this, *that Scriptures are the word of God*—are so indifferent to a natural eye that it may with as just cause lean to one part of the contradiction as to the other.</u>[31] For though this truth, that Scripture is

---

[28] [Thom Aquin. *Summ.* par. 1. Quest. i. Art. 8 ad secundum; S. Augustin. *de vera relig.* cap. xxvi; Thom. Aquin. Second. Secund. Quaest. ii. Art. 3. respons. ad tertium]

[29] {i.e., reason or nature}

[30] [Justin Martyr. *Apolog.* Prim. cap. ii; Tertull. *lib de Carne Christi*, cap. xvii. C; Henry. a Gand. *Summ.* tom. i. Art. ix. Quaest. 3]

[31] {I.e., although the claim that Scriptures are the word of God cannot be proven, there is more evidence in its favor than for the contradictory claim that Scriptures are not the word of God.}

the word of God, is not so demonstratively evident *a priori* as to enforce assent, yet it is strengthened so abundantly with probable arguments, both from the light of nature itself and human testimony, that he must be very willful and self-conceited that shall dare to suspect it.

Nay, yet farther. It is not altogether impossible to prove it, even by reason, a truth infallible, or else to make them deny some apparent principle of their own. . . .

Besides, whereas all other written laws have scarce had the honor to be duly observed or constantly allowed worthy approbation in the particular places where they have been established for laws, this law of Christ and this canon of Scripture (the container of it) is or hath been received in almost all nations under heaven; and wheresoever it hath been received, it hath been both approved for unchangeable good and believed for infallible verity. This persuasion could not have been wrought in men of all sorts but by working upon their reason, unless we shall think all the world unreasonable that received it. And certainly God did not give this admirable faculty of reasoning to the soul of man for any cause more prime than this: to discover, or to judge and allow, within the sphere of its own activity, and not presuming further, of the way to himself, when and howsoever it should be discovered.

One great thing that troubled rational men was that which stumbled the Manichee (an heresy it was, but more than half pagan): namely, that somewhat must be believed before much could be known. Wise men use not to believe but what they know; and the Manichee scorned the orthodox Christian as light of belief, promising to lead no disciple after him but upon evident knowledge. This stumbles many; but yet the principle that somewhat must be believed before much can be known stands firm in reason still. For, if in all sciences there be some principles which cannot be proved; if reason be able to see this and confess it; if almost all artists {scholars} have granted it; if in the mathematics, where are the exactest demonstrations, there be *quaedam postulata*, some things to be first demanded and granted, before the demonstration can proceed; who can justly deny that to divinity, a science of the highest object, God himself, which he easily and reasonably grants to inferior sciences which are more within his reach? And as all sciences suppose some principles without proving, so have they almost all some text, some authority, upon which they rely in some measure; and it is reason they should. For though these sciences make not their texts infallible, as divinity doth, yet full consent and prudent examination and long continuance have won reputation to them and settled reputation upon them very deservedly. And were these texts more void of truth than they are, yet it were fit and reasonable to uphold their credit, that novices and young beginners in a science, which are not able to work strongly upon reason, nor reason upon them, may have authority to believe till they can learn to conclude from principles, and so to know. Is this also reasonable in other sciences, and shall it not be so in theology: to have a text, a scripture, a rule, which novices may be taught first to believe, that so they may after come to the knowledge of those things which out of this rich principle and treasure are deducible? I yet see not how right reason can deny these grounds; and if it cannot, then a mere natural man may be thus far convinced, that the text of God is a very credible text.

Well, these are the four ways . . . men offer to prove the Scripture to be the word of God as by a divine and infallible warrant. And, it seems, no one of these doth it alone. (1) The tradition of the present Church is too weak, because that is not absolutely divine.

(2) The light which is in Scripture itself is not bright enough; it cannot bear sufficient witness to itself. (3) The testimony of the Holy Ghost, that is most infallible, but ordinarily is not so much as considerable in this question, which is not how or by what means we believe, but how the Scripture may be proposed as a credible object, fit for belief. (4) And for reason, no man expects that that should prove it; it doth service enough if it enable us to disprove that which misguided men conceive against it. If none of these, then, be an absolute and sufficient means to prove it, either we must find out another or see what can be more wrought out of these. <u>And to all this again, A. C. says nothing.</u>

For the tradition of the Church, then, certain it is we must distinguish the Church before we can judge right of the validity of the tradition. For if the speech be of the prime Christian Church—the apostles, disciples, and such as had immediate revelation from heaven—no question but the voice and tradition of this Church is divine, not *aliquo modo*, in a sort, but simply; and the word of God from them is of like validity written or delivered.[32] And against this tradition—of which kind this, that the books of Scripture are the word of God, is the most general and uniform—the Church of England never excepted.[33] And when S. Augustine said, *I would not believe the Gospel unless the authority of the Catholic Church moved me*, which place you urged at the conference, though you are now content to slide by it, some of your own will not endure it should be understood save of the Church in the time of the apostles only; and some, of the Church in general, not excluding after ages, but sure to include Christ and his apostles. And the certainty is there, <u>abundance of certainty in itself—but how far that is evident to us, shall after appear.</u>

But this will not serve your turn. The tradition of the present Church must be as infallible as that of the primitive. But the contrary to this is proved before, because this voice of the present Church is not simply divine. To what end, then, serves any tradition of the present Church? To what? Why, to a very good end. For, first, it serves, by a full consent, to work upon the minds of unbelievers, to move them to read and to consider the Scripture, which they hear by so many wise, learned, and devout men is of no meaner esteem than the word of God. And, secondly, it serves among novices, weaklings, and doubters in the faith to instruct and confirm them till they may acquaint themselves with and understand the Scripture which the Church delivers as the word of God. And thus, again, some of your own understand the fore-cited place of S. Augustine, *I would not believe the Gospel*, &c. For he speaks it either of novices or doubters in the faith, or else of such as were in part infidels. You, at the conference, though you omit it here, would needs have it that S. Augustine spake even of the faithful, which I cannot yet think; for he speaks to the Manichees, and they had a great part of the infidel in them. And the words immediately before these are, *If thou shouldst find one* qui Evangelio nondum credit, *which did not yet believe the Gospel, what wouldst thou do to make him believe?* Ego vero non, *Truly I would not*, &c. So to these two ends it serves, and there need be no question between us. But, then, everything that is the first inducer to believe is not by and by either the principal motive or the chief and last object of belief, upon which a man may rest his

---

[32] {See Chillingworth on "universal tradition" <*infra*>.}

[33] {Here 1624 adds, "And then here's the voice of God, of which no Christian may doubt, to confirm his word. For the Apostles had their authority from Christ, and they proved that they had it by apparent miracles, which were beyond exception."}

faith. <u>Unless we shall be of Jacobus Almain's opinion that we are *per prius et magis*, first and more bound to believe the Church than the Gospel. Which your own learned men, as you may see by Mel[chior] Canus, reject as extreme foul; and so indeed it is.</u> The first knowledge, then (after the *quid nominis* is known by grammar), that helps to open a man's understanding and prepares him to be able to demonstrate a truth and make it evident is his logic;[34] but when he hath made a demonstration, he resolves the knowledge of his conclusion not into his grammatical or logical principles, but into the immediate principles out of which it is deduced. So in this particular, a man is probably led by the authority of the present Church, as by the first informing, inducing, persuading means, to believe the Scripture to be the word of God; but when he hath studied, considered, and compared this word with itself and with other writings, with the help of ordinary grace and a mind morally induced and reasonably persuaded by the voice of the Church, the Scripture then gives greater and higher reasons of credibility to itself than tradition alone could give. And then he that believes resolves his last and full assent, *that Scripture is of divine authority*, into internal arguments found in the letter itself, though found by the help and direction of tradition without and grace within. And the resolution that is rightly grounded may not endure to pitch and rest itself upon the helps, but upon that divine light which the Scripture, no question, hath in itself, but is not kindled till these helps come. *Thy word is a light*: so David. A light? Therefore it is as much *manifestativum sui*, as *alterius*; a manifestation to itself, as to other things which it shows—but still, not till the candle be lighted, not till there hath been a preparing instruction what light it is. Children call the sun and moon candles—God's candles; they see the light as well as men but cannot distinguish between them till some tradition and education hath informed their reason. And *animalis homo*, the natural man, sees some light of moral counsel and instruction in Scripture as well as believers; but he takes all that glorious luster for candlelight, and cannot distinguish between the sun and twelve to the pound[35] till tradition of the Church and God's grace put to it have cleared his understanding. So tradition of the present Church is the first moral motive to belief. But the belief itself that the Scripture is the word of God, rests upon the Scripture, when a man finds it to answer and exceed all that which the Church gave in testimony, as will after appear. And as in the voice of the primitive and apostolical Church there was simply divine authority delivering the Scripture as God's word, so, after tradition of the present Church hath taught and informed the soul, the voice of God is plainly heard in Scripture itself. And then here is double authority, and both divine, that confirms Scripture to be the word of God: tradition of the apostles delivering it, and the internal worth and argument in the Scripture obvious[36] to a soul prepared by the present Church's tradition and God's grace.

The difficulties which are pretended against this are not many, and they will easily vanish. For, first, you pretend we go to private revelations for light to know Scripture. No, we do not; you see it is excluded out of the very state of the question. And we go to the

---

[34] {The 1624 text differs slightly at this point.}

[35] {Candles were typically sold by the pound in bundles of eight, ten, or twelve. See www.expressive candles.com/history.php (accessed June 6, 2012).}

[36] {The word has a somewhat weaker sense in the seventeenth century than it does now: perhaps "visible" would be the modern equivalent.}

tradition of the present Church, and by it, as well as you. Here we differ: we use the tradition of the present Church as the first motive, not as the last resolution, of our faith. We resolve only into prime tradition apostolical and Scripture itself.

Secondly, you pretend we do not nor cannot know the prime apostolical tradition but by the tradition of the present Church; and that, therefore, if the tradition of the present Church be not God's unwritten word and divine, we cannot yet know Scripture to be Scripture by a divine authority. Well, suppose I could not know the prime tradition to be divine but by the present Church; yet it doth not follow that therefore I cannot know Scripture to be the word of God by a divine authority, because divine tradition is not the sole and only means to prove it. For suppose I had not, nor could have, full assurance of apostolical tradition divine; yet the moral persuasion, reason, and force of the present Church is ground enough to move any reasonable man that it is fit he should read the Scripture and esteem very reverently and highly of it. And this once done, the Scripture hath then in and home arguments enough to put a soul, that hath but ordinary grace, out of doubt that Scripture is the word of God, infallible and divine.[37]

Thirdly, you pretend that we make the Scripture absolutely and fully to be known *lumine suo*, by the light and testimony which it hath in and gives to itself. Against this, you give reason for yourselves and proof from us. Your reason is, *If there be sufficient light in Scripture to show itself, then every man that can and doth but read it may know it presently to be the divine word of God, which we see by daily experience men neither do nor can.* First, it is not absolutely nor universally true, "there is sufficient light; therefore every man may see it." Blind men are men, and cannot see it; and *sensual men*, in the Apostle's judgment, are such. Nor may we deny and put out this light as insufficient because blind eyes cannot and perverse eyes will not see it, no more than we may deny meat to be sufficient for nourishment though men that are heart-sick cannot eat it. Next, we do not say that there is such a full light in Scripture as that every man upon the first sight must yield to it—such light as is found in prime principles, *every whole is greater than a part of the same*, and this, *the same thing cannot be and not be at the same time and in the same respect.* These carry a natural light with them, and evident; for the terms are no sooner understood than the principles themselves are fully known to the convincing of man's understanding; and so they are the beginning of knowledge, which, where it is perfect, dwells in full light. But such a full light we do neither say is nor require to be in Scripture; and if any particular man do, let him answer for himself. The question is only of such a light in Scripture as is of force to breed faith that it is the word of God, not to make a perfect knowledge. Now faith, of whatsoever it is, this or other principle, is an evidence, as well as knowledge. And the belief is firmer than any knowledge can be[38] because it rests upon divine authority which cannot deceive; whereas knowledge, or at least he that thinks he knows, is not ever certain in deductions from principles. But the evidence is not so clear, for it is of *things not seen* in regard of the object; and in regard of the subject that sees, it is *in aenigmate*, in a glass or dark speaking.[39] Now God doth not require a full demonstrative knowledge in us that the

---

[37] {1624 adds a half-paragraph of rather convoluted argument at this point to the effect that "the present tradition" may indeed help "prove the very prime tradition."}

[38] {1624 reads instead "and a firmer and surer evidence than any knowledge can have."}

[39] {For the epistemic background to Laud's claims here, see Shuger, "Faith and assurance," and Aquinas, *Summa theologiae* 2.2.1.1–4.}

Scripture is his word, and therefore in his providence hath kindled in it no light for that; but he requires our faith of it, and such a certain demonstration as may fit that. And for that he hath left sufficient light in Scripture to reason and grace meeting, where the soul is morally prepared by the tradition of the Church, unless you be of Bellarmine's opinion, *that to believe there are any divine Scriptures is not* omninò {wholly} *necessary to salvation.*

The authority which you pretend against this is out of Hooker: *Of things necessary, the very chiefest is to know what books we are bound to esteem holy; which point is confessed impossible for the Scripture itself to teach.* Of this, Brereley[40] . . . tells us that Hooker gives a very sensible demonstration: *It is not the word of God which doth, or possibly can, assure us that we do well to think it is his word; for if any one book of Scripture did give testimony to all, yet still that Scripture, which giveth credit to the rest, would require another [Scripture] to give credit unto it; neither could we ever come unto any pause to rest our assurance this way; so that unless, beside Scripture, there were something which might assure, &c.*[41] And *this he acknowledged* (saith Brereley) *is the authority of God's Church.* Certainly Hooker gives a true and sensible demonstration, but Brereley wants fidelity and integrity in citing him. . . . for, folding up all that Hooker says in these words, *This* (other means to assure us besides Scripture) *is the authority of God's Church,* he wrinkles that worthy author desperately, and shrinks up his meaning. For in the former place abused by Brereley, no man can set a better state of the question between Scripture and tradition than Hooker doth. His words are these: *The Scripture is the ground of our belief; the authority of man* (that is the name he gives to tradition) *is the key which openeth the door of entrance into the knowledge of the Scripture.* I ask now, when a man is entered and hath viewed a house, and upon viewing likes it, and upon liking resolves unchangeably to dwell there, doth he set up his resolution upon the key that let him in? No sure! but upon the goodness and commodiousness which he sees in the house. And this is all the difference that I know between us in this point: in which, do you grant, as you ought to do, that we resolve our faith into Scripture as the ground, and we will never deny that tradition is the key that lets us in. In the latter place, Hooker is as plain, as constant to himself and truth. His words are: *The first outward motive leading men so to esteem of the Scripture is the authority of God's Church, &c. But afterwards, the more we bestow our labor in reading or hearing the mysteries thereof, the more we find that the thing itself doth answer our received opinion concerning it; so that the former inducement, prevailing somewhat with us before, doth now much more prevail when the very thing hath ministered farther reason.* Here then again, in his judgment, tradition is the first inducement, but the farther reason and ground is the Scripture. And resolution of faith ever settles upon the farthest reason it can, not upon the first inducement. So that the state of this question is firm and yet plain enough to him that will not shut his eyes.

Now here, after a long silence, A. C. thrusts himself in again and tells me, *That if I would consider the tradition of the Church not only as it is the tradition of a company of fallible men*—in which sense the authority of it, as himself confesses, *is but human and fallible, &c.*—*but as the tradition of a company of men assisted by Christ and his Holy Spirit: in that sense I might easily find it more than an introduction,*

---

[40] {a Roman Catholic controversialist}
[41] [{Hooker}, *Eccl. Polit.* book ii, ch. iv. sect. 2; book ii, ch. vii, sect. 3]

indeed as much as would amount to an infallible motive. Well, I have considered the tradition of the present Church both these ways; and I find that A. C. confesses that, in the first sense, the tradition of the Church is mere human authority, and no more; and therefore, in this sense, it may serve for an introduction to this belief, but no more. And in the second sense, as it is not the tradition of a company of men only but of men assisted by Christ and his Spirit, in this second sense I cannot find that the tradition of the present Church is of divine and infallible authority till A. C. can prove that this company of men (the Roman prelates and their clergy he means) are so fully, so clearly, so permanently assisted by Christ and his Spirit as may reach to infallibility, much less to a divine infallibility, in this or any other principle which they teach. For every assistance of Christ and the blessed Spirit is not enough to make the authority of any company of men divine and infallible, but such and so great an assistance only as is purposely given to that effect. Such an assistance the prophets under the Old Testament and the apostles under the New had, but neither the high priest with his clergy in the Old, nor any company of prelates or priests in the New since the apostles ever had it. And therefore, though at the entreaty of A. C. I have *considered* this very well, yet I cannot, no not in this assisted sense, think the tradition of the present Church divine and infallible, or such company of men to be worthy of divine and infallible credit and sufficient to breed in us divine and infallible faith. Which I am sorry A. C. should affirm so boldly as he doth. What! That company of men, the Roman bishop and his clergy, of divine and infallible credit and sufficient to breed in us divine and infallible faith! Good God! Whither will these men go? Surely they are *wise in their generation*, but that makes them never a whit the more *the children of light. . . .*

But A. C. would have me consider again that it is as easy to take the tradition of the present Church in the two fore-named senses as the present Scriptures printed and approved by men of this age. For in the first sense, the very Scriptures, saith he, considered as printed and approved by men of this age, can be no more than of human credit. But in the second sense, as printed and approved by men assisted by God's Spirit for true copies of that which was first written, then we may give infallible credit to them. Well, I have considered this too; and I can take the printing and approving the copies of Holy Writ in these two senses; and I can and do make a difference between copies printed and approved by mere moral men and men assisted by God's Spirit; and yet for the printing only, a skillful and an able moral man may do better service to the Church than an illiterate man, though assisted in other things by God's Spirit. But when I have considered all this, what then? The Scripture, being put in writing, is a thing visibly existent; and if any error be in the print, it is easily corrigible by former copies. Tradition is not so easily observed nor so safely kept.

‡

. . . And you cannot shew an ordinary consent of Fathers—nay, can you, or any of your quarter, shew any one Father of the Church, Greek or Latin, that ever said we are to resolve our faith that Scripture is the word of God into the tradition of the present Church? And again, when the Fathers say we are to rely upon Scripture only, they are never to be understood with exclusion of tradition, in what causes soever it may be had. Not but that the Scripture is abundantly sufficient in and to itself for all things, but because it is deep and may be drawn into different senses <u>and so be mistaken, if any man will presume upon his own strength and go single without the Church</u>.

To gather up whatsoever may seem scattered in this long discourse to prove that Scripture is the word of God, I shall now, in the last place, put all together, that so the whole state of the question may the better appear.

First, then, I shall desire the reader to consider that every rational science requires some principles quite without its own limits, which are not proved in that science but presupposed. Thus rhetoric presupposes grammar; and music, arithmetic. Therefore it is most reasonable that theology should be allowed to have some principles also which she proves not but presupposes. And the chiefest of these is *that the Scriptures are of divine authority*.

Secondly, that there is a great deal of difference in the manner of confirming the principles of divinity and those of any other art or science whatsoever.

For the principles of all other sciences do finally resolve either into the conclusions of some higher science or into those principles which are *per se nota*, known by their own light, and are the grounds and principles of all science. And this is it which properly makes them sciences: because they proceed with such strength of demonstration as forces reason to yield unto them. But the principles of divinity resolve not into the grounds of natural reason—for then there would be no room for faith, but all would be either knowledge or vision—but into the maxims of divine knowledge supernatural. And of this we have just so much light, and no more, than God hath revealed unto us in the Scripture.

Thirdly, that though the evidence of these supernatural truths which divinity teaches appears not so manifest as that of the natural, yet they are in themselves much more sure and infallible than they. For they proceed immediately from God, that heavenly wisdom, which, being the foundation of ours, must needs infinitely precede ours both in nature and excellence. *He that teacheth man knowledge, shall not He know?* (Psal. 94). And therefore, though we reach not the order of their deductions nor can in this life come to the vision of them, yet we yield as full and firm assent, not only to the articles, but to all the things rightly deduced from them, as we do to the most evident principles of natural reason. This assent is called *faith*; and faith, being *of things not seen* (Heb. 11), would quite lose its honor, nay itself, if it met with sufficient grounds in natural reason whereon to stay itself. For faith is a mixed act of the will and the understanding; and the will inclines the understanding to yield full approbation to that whereof it sees not full proof.[42] Not but that there is most full proof of them, but because the main

---

[42] [Cardinal. Tolet. in S. Johan. xvi. Annot. 13; Stapleton, *Triplicat. adversus Whitaker*, cap. vi &c; Thom. Aquin. Second. Secund. Q. iv. A. 1. in conclus.; Jac. Almain in III. Sent. D. xxiv. Conclus. 6. Dub. 4. fol lxxxix; S. Augustine, Tractat. lii. in S. Johan.; Gabr. Biel in III. Sentent. D. xxv. Q. unic. Art. i]

grounds which prove them are concealed from our view and folded up in the unrevealed counsel of God—God in Christ resolving to bring mankind to their last happiness by faith and not by knowledge, that so the weakest among men may have their way to blessedness open. And certain it is, that many weak men believe themselves into heaven, and many over-knowing Christians lose their way thither while they will believe no more than they can clearly know. In which pride and vanity of theirs they are left, and have these things *hid from them* (Matth. 11).[43]

Fourthly, that the credit of the Scripture, the book in which the principles of faith are written, as of other writings also, depends not upon the subservient inducing cause that leads us to the first knowledge of the author, which leader here is the Church, but upon the author himself and the opinion we have of his sufficiency, which here is the Holy Spirit of God, whose penmen the prophets and apostles were. And therefore the mysteries of divinity contained in this book, as the incarnation of our Savior, the resurrection of the dead, and the like, cannot finally be resolved into the sole testimony of the Church, who is but a subservient cause to lead to the knowledge of the author, but into the wisdom and sufficiency of the author, who, being omnipotent and omniscient, must needs be infallible.

Fifthly, that the assurance we have of the penmen of the Scriptures, the holy prophets and apostles, is as great as any can be had of any human authors of like antiquity. For it is morally as evident to any pagan that S. Matthew and S. Paul writ the Gospel and Epistles which bear their names as that Cicero or Seneca wrote theirs. But that the apostles were divinely inspired whilst they writ them and that they are the very word of God expressed by them, this hath ever been a matter of faith in the Church, and was so even while the apostles themselves lived, and was never a matter of evidence and knowledge, at least as knowledge is opposed to faith. Nor could it at any time then be more demonstratively proved than now. I say, not *scientifice*, not demonstratively, for, were the apostles living and should they tell us that they spake and writ the very oracles of God, yet this were but their own testimony of themselves, and so not alone able to enforce belief on others. And for their miracles, though they were very great inducements of belief, yet were neither they evident and convincing proofs alone and of themselves, both because there may be counterfeit miracles and because true ones are neither infallible nor inseparable marks of truth in doctrine. Not infallible, for they may be marks of false doctrine in the highest degree. Not proper and inseparable, for all which wrote by inspiration did not confirm their doctrine by miracles. For we do not find that David or Solomon, with some other of the prophets, did any; neither were any wrought by S. John the Baptist (Joh. 10). So, as credible signs, they were and are still of as much force to us as it is possible for things on the credit of relation to be: for the witnesses are many, and such as spent their lives in making good the truth which they saw. But that the workers of them were divinely and infallibly inspired in that which they preached and

---

[43] {See Godolphin's poem "Lord, when wise men" <*infra*>.}

writ was still to the hearers a matter of faith, and no more evident by the light of human reason to men that lived in those days than to us now. For had that been demonstrated or been clear, as prime principles are, in its own light, both they and we had apprehended all the mysteries of divinity by knowledge, not by faith. But this is most apparent was not. For had the prophets or apostles been ordered by God to make this demonstratively or intuitively, by discourse or vision, appear as clear to their auditors as to themselves it did, that whatsoever they taught was divine and infallible truth, all men which had the true use of reason must have been forced to yield to their doctrine. Esay could never have been at *Domine quis? Lord, who hath believed our report?* (Esay 53). Nor Jeremy at *Domine, factus sum, Lord, I am in derision daily* (Jer. 20). Nor could any of S. Paul's auditors have *mocked at him* (Act. 17), as some of them did, for *preaching the resurrection*, if they had had as full a view as S. Paul himself had in *the assurance which God gave of it in and by the resurrection of Christ.* But the way of knowledge was not that which God thought fittest for man's salvation. For man having sinned by pride, God thought fittest to humble him at the very root of the tree of knowledge, and make him deny his understanding and submit to faith, or hazard his happiness. The credible object all the while—that is, the mysteries of religion and the Scripture which contain them—is divine and infallible, and so are the penmen of them by revelation. But we and all our forefathers, the hearers and readers of them, have neither knowledge nor vision of the prime principles in or about them, but faith only. And the revelation which was clear to them is not so to us, nor therefore the prime tradition itself delivered by them.

Sixthly, that hence it may be gathered that the assent which we yield to this main principle of divinity, *that the Scripture is the word of God*, is grounded upon no compelling or demonstrative ratiocination, but relies upon the strength of faith more than any other principle whatsoever. For all other necessary points of divinity may by undeniable discourse be inferred out of Scripture itself, once admitted; but this concerning the authority of Scripture, not possibly, but must either be proved by revelation, which is not now to be expected, or presupposed and granted as manifest in itself like the principles of natural knowledge, which reason alone will never grant; or by tradition of the Church both prime and present, with all other rational helps preceding or accompanying the internal light in Scripture itself, which though it give light enough for faith to believe, yet light enough it gives not to be a convincing reason and proof for knowledge. And this is it which makes the very entrance into divinity inaccessible to those men who, standing high in the opinion of their own wisdom, will believe nothing but that which is irrefragably proved from rational principles. For as Christ requires *a denial of a man's self that he may be able to follow him* (Luke 9), so as great a part as any of this denial of his whole self (for so it must be) is the denial of his understanding, and the composing of the unquiet search of this grand inquisitor into the secrets of him that made it, and the overruling the doubtfulness of it by the fervency of the will.

Seventhly, that the knowledge of the supreme cause of all, which is God, is most remote and the most difficult thing reason can have to do with. The *quod sit*, that there is a God, blear-eyed reason can see; but the *quid sit*, what that God is, is infinitely beyond all the fathoms of reason. He is a light indeed, but such as no man's reason can come at for the brightness (1 Tim. 6). If anything, therefore, be attainable in this kind, it must be by revelation, and that must be from himself; for none can reveal but he that comprehends, and none doth or can comprehend God but himself. And when he doth reveal, yet he is no farther discernible than himself pleases. Now, since reason teaches that the soul of man is immortal and capable of felicity; and since that felicity consists in the contemplation of the highest cause, which again is God himself; and since Christ therein confirms that dictate, that man's eternal happiness is to know God and him whom he hath sent (John 17); and since nothing can put us into the way of attaining to that contemplation but some revelation of himself, and of the way to himself; I say, since all this is so, it cannot reasonably be thought by any prudent man that the all-wise God should create man with a desire of felicity and then leave him utterly destitute of all instrumental helps to make the attainment possible, since *God and nature do nothing but for an end*; and help there can be none sufficient but by revelation; and once grant me that revelation is necessary, and then I will appeal to reason itself, and that shall prove abundantly one of these two: that either there was never any such revelation of this kind from the world's beginning to this day—and that will put the *frustra* {in vain} upon God in point of man's felicity—or that the Scriptures which we now embrace as the word of God is that revelation. And that is it we Christians labor to make good against all atheism, profaneness, and infidelity.

Last of all, to prove that the book of God which we honor as his word is this necessary revelation of God and his truth—which must and is alone able to lead us in the way to our eternal blessedness, or else the world hath none—comes in a cloud of witnesses:[44] some for the infidel and some for the believer, some for the weak in faith and some for the strong, and some for all. For then first comes in the tradition of the Church, the present Church; so it is no heretical or schismatical belief. Then the testimony of former ages; so it is no new belief. Then the consent of times; so it is no divided or partial belief. Then the harmony of the prophets, and them fulfilled; so it is not a devised but a forespoken belief. Then the success of the doctrine contained in this book; so it is not a belief stifled in the cradle, but it hath spread through the world in despite of what the world could do against it, and increased from weak and unlikely beginnings to incredible greatness. Then the constancy of this truth; so it is no moon-belief, for in the midst of the world's changes, it hath preserved its creed entire through many generations. Then, that there is nothing carnal in the doctrine; so it is a chaste belief. And all along it hath gained, kept, and exercised more power upon the minds of men, both learned and unlearned, in the increase of virtue and repression of vice, than any moral philosophy or legal policy that ever was. Then comes the inward light and excellency of the text itself, and so it is no dark or dazzling belief. And it is an excellent text. For see the riches of natural knowledge which

[44] {"Cloud of witnesses" is the subject of "comes in."}

are stored up there, as well as supernatural. Consider how things quite above reason consent with things reasonable. Weigh it well, what majesty lies there hid under humility; what depth there is with a perspicuity inimitable; what delight it works in the soul that is devoutly exercised in it; how the sublimest wits find in it enough to amaze them, while the simplest want not enough to direct them; and then we shall not wonder if—with the assistance of God's Spirit, who alone works faith and belief of the Scriptures and their divine authority, as well as other articles—we grow up into a most infallible assurance, such an assurance as hath made many lay down their lives for this truth, such as that *though an angel from heaven should preach unto us another Gospel*, we would not believe him or it.[45] No, though we should see as great and as many miracles done over again to dissuade us from it as were at first to win the world to it. To which firmness of assent, by the operation of God's Spirit, the will confers as much or more strength than the understanding, clearness; the whole assent being an act of faith and not of knowledge.[46] And therefore the question should not have been asked of me by F. *How I knew?* but *Upon what motives I did believe Scripture to be the word of God?*

TEXT: *Conference with Fisher*, in vol. 2 of *The works of the most reverend father in God, William Laud, D.D., some-time lord archbishop of Canterbury*, 6 vols. (Oxford: John Henry Parker, 1849), iii–xviii, 1–4, 29–33, 41, 70–106, 116–31.

Corrected against *A relation of the conference between William Lawd . . . and Mr. Fisher the Jesuit, by the command of King James of ever blessed memory, with an answer to such exceptions as A.C. takes against it* (London: Printed by Richard Badger, 1639).

And compared with *An answer to Mr. Fisher's relation of a third conference between a certain B. (as he styles him) and himself . . . which is here given by R.B., chaplain to the B. that was employed in the conference*, appended to Francis White's *A reply to Jesuit Fisher's answer to certain questions* (London, 1624).

---

[45] {Note that here, as throughout *A relation*, "assurance" does not have its usual Reformed sense of "certainty of *one's own* salvation."}

[46] {For the relevant background in Hooker and St. Thomas, see Shuger, "Faith and assurance."}

RICHARD MONTAGU
(ca. 1575–1641)

The son of a Buckinghamshire clergyman, Montagu studied at Eton from 1590–94 before proceeding to King's College, Cambridge, where he took his BA in 1598 and his MA in 1602. He was ordained two years later, after which he left Cambridge, but returned to take his BD in 1609. During this period he was assisting Henry Savile on his monumental edition of Chrysostom (1610–12) and completing his own edition of Gregory of Nazianzen's invectives against Julian (1610), one possible model for the oft-noted pugnacity of Montagu's prose. In 1613 he received from King James the rectory of Stanford Rivers, Essex, and two years later became a royal chaplain. In 1617 he was made a canon of Windsor, and then in 1623 rector of Petworth, Sussex. In these years he was also at work on both a critique[1] of Baronius' massive Roman Catholic church history (the *Annales ecclesiastici* [1588–1607]) and also on his 1621 treatise defending the divine right basis of tithes against John Selden's claim that these had always been a matter of positive law and custom. This appears to have been an amicable controversy, since a 1626 letter of Montagu's describes Selden as a close and trusted friend (Cosin 1:92–93).

In 1624 Montagu, then forty-nine and a respected priest, patristic scholar, and antiquarian, knowingly ignited a theological firestorm by publishing, first, a qualified defense of the invocation of saints, followed by an ostensibly anti-Catholic treatise (the *New gag*) whose argument hinged on the proposition that the Calvinist doctrines condemned by papal controversialists were not, as these controversialists had assumed, doctrines held by the Church of England.[2] Several outraged Calvinist divines replied to Montagu in print, but two took a further step and informed against him to the Commons, whose members found Montagu's book deeply offensive. The King, however, did not. According to Montagu's testimony before the House on July 6, 1625, "after the informations exhibited

---

[1] The critique was published in 1622 as *Analecta ecclesiasticarum exercitationum.*

[2] Montagu's *New gag* responds to the 1623 *The gag of the reformed Gospel* by Matthew Kellison (whom Montagu refers to as "the Gagger"), the then-president of the English College at Douai.

in Parliament, the King sent for him, and spoke to him . . . these words: 'If thou be a Papist, I am a Papist;' giving him leave to print somewhat in his own defense," although requiring Francis White, the Dean of Carlisle, to vet the work to make sure nothing contradicted the doctrine and discipline of the English Church, which Montagu, as an ordained minister, was sworn to uphold. Montagu published the said defense of his *New gag* in 1625 under the title *Appello Caesarem*, but White's imprimatur did nothing to abate the furious reaction of the Commons, whose Committee on Religion, headed by John Pym, strove repeatedly over the next four years—until Charles shut down Parliament in 1629—to have the book burned and Montagu himself declared a traitor. Two conferences were held in early 1626—the second, the York House Conference, involving Cosin, Buckeridge, and Preston—in an unsuccessful attempt to sort out the theological issues. In June of the same year Charles issued a proclamation silencing both sides.[3] The Commons, however, refused to let go of the matter until, in 1628, Charles took it out of their hands by appointing Montagu bishop of Chichester and thus liable only to the judgment of his peers in the House of Lords. Montagu served at Chichester until 1638 and then at Norwich until his death three years later; in both dioceses, he proved to be a tolerant, moderate, and even-handed ecclesiastical governor. He continued his patristic and antiquarian researches during these last years, apparently spending most of his income on rare books and manuscripts. He died, according to the *ODNB*'s laconic report, "very poor."

The theology of the *New gag* and *Appello Casearem* cannot, on its own, account for the apoplectic reaction they triggered. Donne's 1623 *Devotions upon emergent occasions*, which stands in the same theological tradition, provoked no such outcry (Strier). The abrasive scuffing and scoffing of Montagu's style (see, for example, the epistle prefacing *Appello*) was surely a factor, but the ferocity of the Commons' response may also have drawn pent-up force from the unbroken sequence of military disasters, including Buckingham's fiascos at Cadiz and Ré, that befell the Protestant cause between 1624 and 1629. These disasters stirred widespread fears of popish plots, and, in particular, of "Arminians" as crypto-papist double-agents working to undermine Protestantism from within.[4] (In 1619 the Dutch statesman Johan van Oldenbarnevelt had been executed on trumped-up charges involving precisely such an alleged Arminian plot.) It is also worth noting that the *New gag* came out only five years after the Synod of Dort, whose canons the British delegation had signed; in 1624 English Calvinists would have had reason to believe that the question of their Church's doctrinal position had been settled, and that victory was theirs. Montagu's revisionist picture presented a most unwelcome challenge to that newly won confidence.

At stake in both the *New gag* and *Appello Caesarem* is thus the theological identity of the English Church: whether or not the Calvinism upheld at Dort constituted its official teaching. Both at the time and thereafter, Montagu's own position was regularly termed (principally by its enemies) Arminian; that, however, it is not. Few Stuart divines

---

[3] This was the course recommended by Joseph Hall in his *Via media* <see introduction to Hall readings, n. 2, *infra*>.

[4] See *The spy* and *The locusts* <*infra*>.

adopted Arminius' distinctive stance on predestination. Montagu takes the distinctly un-Arminian view that mortal reason cannot explicate the workings of divine predestination, before whose mystery we are rather to fall silent and adore with the reverent wonder of Paul's *o altitudo*. Yet he also thinks it perfectly permissible for individuals to attempt explanations and to defend their conclusions in the usual academic venues, provided they do not confuse their private opinions with either official doctrine or revealed truth. In their August 1625 letter on Montagu's behalf, Laud, Buckeridge, and Howson similarly urged that technical points of school-divinity not be made official doctrine but "left at more liberty for learned men to abound in their own sense, so they keep themselves peaceable and distract not the Church" (Laud, *Works* 6:244–45). This anti-dogmatic stance, at once skeptical and conservative, but not Arminian, represents the typical "Laudian" view of the matter.[5]

The selections from the *New gag* and *Appello Caesarem* reprinted below center on whether the elect can fall, either totally or finally, from grace.[6] As the controversy over this issue at the 1604 Hampton Court Conference makes clear,[7] it was a point of long-standing tension between Calvinist divines and the "bishops' party." The latter's concern that the Calvinist claim—that all who once received justifying faith could never fall away—encouraged moral laxity might seem rather needless: Calvinists were not often lax in this respect. However, it is conceivable that their position created pastoral difficulties, since parish miscreants may have found this sort of godly talking point useful for brushing off clerical reproof.[8] Yet, at least for Montagu, closing moral loopholes does not seem to have been the main issue. He homes in on the issue of falling from grace because it represents the weak link in the Reformed *ordo salutatis* connecting regeneration, justification, sanctification, and perseverance together in an "inseparable and unbreakable 'golden chain'" (Hughes 245). As Montagu is at pains to show, on the question of falling from grace (i.e., final perseverance), the official formularies of the English Church did not support the Calvinist side. And if the elect can fall from grace, then it follows, as he likewise points out, that no one can be assured of his own salvation, that grace is not irresistible, and that there are no absolute decrees. To allow falling from grace takes down with it the entire edifice of Reformed spirituality. Conversely, Montagu further notes, the possibility of falling from grace underwrites a high sacramentalism; in particular, it supports viewing baptism as *imparting*, rather than merely signifying or sealing, the grace of regeneration, and as imparting it to *all* baptized persons, not just the tiny subgroup of the elect.[9]

---

[5] In 1624–25 Laud was not yet the public face of anti-Calvinism; in the 1620s, people spoke of "Montagutians" (Birch, *Charles* 1:105; the word is not in the *OED*).

[6] Note, however, that *A new gag* and *Appello Caesarem* treat a broad range of controversial topics (papal primacy, meritorious works, purgatory, celibacy, etc.).

[7] Reprinted in the appendix following *Appello Caesarem* <infra>.

[8] Carier, indeed, says as much <2.12>. Moreover, by the 1620s, antinomian preachers, who did hold that the elect were no longer bound by the moral law, were active in London, Sussex, and Essex, i.e., within possible earshot of Montagu. See Como, *Blown by the Spirit*, especially the sections dealing with John Eaton and John Eachard.

[9] If baptism imparts justifying grace, then, unless one wants to claim that all baptized persons are ipso facto saved, one has to allow for the possibility of falling from grace totally and finally.

Richard Montagu

SOURCES: *ODNB*; Thomas Birch, *The court and times of Charles the First*, 2 vols. (London, 1848); *Debates in the House of Commons in 1625*, ed. S. R. Gardiner, Camden Society n.s. 6 (Westminster, 1874); John Cosin, *The correspondence of John Cosin*, 2 vols. (Durham, 1869–72); Sean Hughes, "The problem of 'Calvinism': English theologies of predestination c. 1580–1630," in *Belief and practice in Reformation England*, ed. Susan Wabuda and Caroline Litzenberger (Ashgate, 1998), 229–49; Shuger, *Censorship*, chap ix.; Richard Strier, "Donne and the politics of devotion" in *Religion, literature, and politics in post-Reformation England, 1540–1688*, ed. R. Strier and D. Hamilton (Cambridge UP, 1996), 93–114.

RICHARD MONTAGU

A gag for the new Gospel? No, A NEW GAG for an old goose
1624

XVI

That by the fall of Adam, we have lost all our free-will, and that it is not in our own power either to choose good or evil

A question of obscurity, which better might have been over-passed in silence, fitting rather Schools than popular ears: especially the differences hanging on such niceties, and the controverted particulars of no great moment in fine {finally}, upon due examination. For it is confessed that free-will is a power of the reasonable soul and peculiar, under heaven, to man, which is endued with freedom to do or not to do, whereby they make choice of one end rather than of another and of some means rather than of other, upon advice and deliberation of the understanding, chief councillor to the will.

This power was conferred upon man at first, in the day of his creation, when he was made a living soul. In state of nature entire,[1] a natural faculty, not any supernatural endowment at all; whereby most freely and absolutely he was lord of his own actions and could do or not do what he pleased and would. That liberty was much impaired by sin, not extinct or abolished in corrupted nature such as now it is. The Council of Trent rightly so defineth it . . . and we profess, *non amissimus naturam sed gratiam* {we have not lost nature but grace}. As rightly is it by that Council determined, *liberum arbitrium non quidem extinctum esse, sed viribus attenuatum* {free-will is not indeed extinguished but its powers weakened}. The question is all of these *vires* {powers} remaining, and *quatenus attenuatum liberum arbitrium* {to what extent free-will has been weakened}. The Church of England, Artic. 10., concludeth thus: *The condition of man after the fall of Adam is such that he cannot turn nor prepare himself by his own natural strength and good works to faith and calling upon God; wherefore we have no power to do good works, pleasant and acceptable unto God,*

---

[1] {i.e., in the state of unfallen nature}

402

without the grace of God by Christ preventing[2] us that we may have a good will, and working with us when we have that good will. Man is here considered in a two-fold state, of nature depraved and restored. In that,[3] free-will is denied unto man for works of righteousness before conversion, not for works of nature or of morality. In the second, free-will is granted unto man: *When we have that good will, what is it else?* and *By our free-will, assisted by grace, work out our salvation unto the end.* This is not that opinion condemned in the Council of Trent . . . which taketh away free-will from man, after preventing grace, in cooperation unto increase of grace; for it is said that grace, infused first and had, *worketh together with our good will.*

So it is not denied but free-will is in us subsisting, not in title only. It is not said that by the fall of Adam we have utterly lost all of us our free-will, as if the soul were clean defeated and disfurnished of that power. So that this blunderer {the Gagger} stumbleth at a straw and impudently belieth our profession. What some have thought or taught is nothing to us. No Church is to be charged with private opinions. Man in state of corruption hath freedom of will in actions natural and civil. Secondly, man in state of corruption hath free-will in matters moral. Thirdly, man hath free-will in actions of piety and such as belong unto his salvation, but *quatenus* and *quale* {to what extent and of what sort} is the question as much amongst yourselves[4] as with us. For the concurrence of grace assisting with free-will, the correspondency of free-will with prescience, providence, and predestination, is much debated in your own Schools. Intricate disputes are hereupon inferred, questions almost inextricable. . . . We resolve thus far. First, with Saint Augustine . . . *Doth any of us affirm that free-will is perished utterly from man by the fall of Adam? Freedom is perished, I grant, by sin: but that freedom which was in Paradise, of having righteousness with immortality.* Again, we confess with the same Saint Augustine, Man is not merely passive in all works of grace to glory; for *qui creauit te sine te, non saluabit te sine te. He that made thee alone without thy help, will not save thee alone without thy concurrence.* Man is to work, that will have reward.[5]

In conclusion, the condition of man since the fall of Adam is such that he cannot turn nor prepare himself to God *by* or *through* his own natural or human power and strength. This is the doctrine of the Church of England. Prevented by grace and assisted therewith, he then putteth to his hand to procure augmentation of that grace and continuance unto the end. No man *cometh* to God but he is *drawn*. *Drawn*, he *runneth* or *walketh*, as his assistance is, and his own agility and disposition to the end. This is enough. And the wisdom of the Church hath not ventured far, to put a tie of obedience upon men's belief in points of inextricable obscurity almost, of the concordance in working of grace and predestination with free-will. Moderate spirits would well and wisely sit them down by temperate courses and not clamor with outrage where is no cause; nor delight to set the peace of the Church on hurres[6] only for faction and some private sinister indirect ends of their own. . . .

---

[2] {literally, "coming-before," acting in advance of}

[3] {i.e., in the state of fallen or depraved nature}

[4] {The "you" throughout *A new gag* is the Roman Catholic "Gagger" to whom Montagu is responding.}

[5] {For the analogous point, see Bayly, *The practice of piety* <127>.}

[6] {"To hur" can mean to snarl, to thunder, or to buzz; the noun, for which the *OED* gives no instances after 1500, refers to a child's game involving a piece of wood whirled about in the air.}

That of Deuter. 30:19 is more to purpose: *I call heaven and earth this day to record against you, that I have set before you life and death, blessing and cursing; therefore choose life, that both thou and thy seed may live.* For this is directly in point of piety and performance of duty immediate unto God. Neither was it spoken to men according to general notion of them and their general state in case of alienation from God, in state of nature only, and natural endowments—of which it is consented, I think, *they cannot choose life*—but to men prevented by grace, called to life, assisted with much and many concurrences of grace. This is not contrary to our tenet, as is plain in the Article before alleged.

That of Joshua 24:15 is to the same purpose, almost in the very same words: one answer will serve to both. The Article denieth free-will *quoad* {with respect to} points of piety to mere natural men only, in the state of depravation; but avoucheth it in state of grace, with concurrence of assistance. Ecclesiasticus 15:14 is not to purpose. The wise man speaketh of what was, not what is; in the state of innocency before the Fall; not of depravation, being fallen: *God from the beginning made man, and left him in the hand of his own counsel.* In 2 Sam. 12 I find not for free-will, but only this verse 17, that David would not eat meat, but refused it; which place, if ignorantly alleged, proveth this fellow, as he hath been discovered often, a plain blunderer; if with advise, a shameless slanderer, that would impute unto Protestants such a senseless assertion, that man had not free-will to eat if he would, for such is the inference upon that allegation.

In Matth. 23:37 there is an opposition of man's *willfulness* unto God's *will.* God would have called Judah; Judah would not. Therefore freely men renounce the calling of grace and freely run themselves, without any absolute irreversible decree, upon perdition; which I grant, being the purpose and intent of those succeeding texts of Scripture, with many moe to purpose in God's book. How this is done, how far it extendeth, I list not to dispute. It is for Schools, not for pulpits; searching wits are at stand therein; common capacities must not be surcharged with it. It is willfulness, or more, to deny free-will; and it is wisdom and truth to deny free-will. To deny the *being*, is so.[7] And I wish with Scotus . . . that a man so willful were well cudgeled until he confessed it stood in man's power to desist from beating him. But to give such an absolute sway to free-will, as many do, is little less than flat impiety against God; against Saint Paul, I am sure: *It is not of him that willeth, or him that runneth.* Truth is in the middle betwixt two extremes, evermore, and here also.

‡

XX

That faith once had cannot be lost

There is no such conclusion or Article tendered unto the Church of England or resolved of unto us as of faith. Opinions have varied and may keep at large, each one contenting himself with his own private, so be it he disturb not the peace of the Church nor impose his private judgment to be held of all. It is held by some, I grant, that justifying faith, that

---

7 {i.e., to deny the existence of free-will is willfulness, or worse}

excellent gift of God, is not conferred unto any but to the elect and predestinated unto life. The wicked that perish eternally from God, as they never were in the state of grace, so never were they endued with true faith. Secondly, as consequent hereunto, that faith once had cannot be lost or shaken out or off wholly from man, but continueth inextinguible, indefeasible. And therefore, thirdly, those that once have been endowed with that transcendent gift are sure to be saved eternally, nor cease to be and stand justified before God. These are opinions, and defended, but not of all Protestants, not of the Church of England; but opposed and refelled at home, abroad—as this fellow cannot but know, if he know anything in these points, which for the major part are fitter for Schools than popular discourses, and may be held or not held without heresy either way.

That faith once had (the propounded conclusion) *cannot be lost* may be interpreted, and is, moe ways than one: whether not lost at all, whether totally or finally lost. Men are divided in this tenet. Some suppose neither totally nor finally; some totally, but not finally; some both totally and finally. Which is indeed the assertion of antiquity and your School. Some perceiving the current of judgments for the loss thereof totally and finally— and considering also at least probability of Scripture consenting—put in a new distinction, of God and man, of the first and second causes of faith and justification. In regard of man his weakness, insufficiency, and opposition against him—in respect of second causes concurring in this action—faith once had may be lost, they say. But in regard of God, considering his counsel and purpose unchangeable, reflecting on his absolute decree irreversible, faith once had cannot totally or finally be lost, nor they perish eternally that were endowed therewith. Now, which of all these ways will you understand the position, *faith had may be lost?* For my part, I know your meaning well enough, but you should have explained it and not have covertly rested in ambiguities. You mean, it may be lost totally and finally in regard of God, who made no such absolute irreversible decree; as also in respect of second causes in man, both without him, and about him, and against him. I determine nothing in this question positively, which the Church of England leaveth at liberty unto us, though the learnedst in the Church of England assent unto antiquity in their tenet, which the Protestants of Germany maintain at this day, having assented therein unto the Church of Rome, in the Diet at Ratisborn . . . upon these grounds. First, Ezech. 18:24, 26: *If the righteous turn away from his righteousness and commit iniquity, and do according unto all the abominations that the wicked man doth, shall he live? all his righteousness that he hath done shall not be remembered, but in his transgression that he hath committed and in his sin that he hath sinned, in them shall he die. . . .* Again, Ezech. 33:12: *The righteousness of the righteous shall not deliver him in the day of his transgression.* And again, *The wickedness of the wicked shall not cause him to fall, in the day that he returneth from his wickedness; neither shall the righteous live for his righteousness in the day that he sinneth.* And verse 13: *If he commit iniquity, all his righteousness shall be no more remembered, but for his iniquity that he hath committed, he shall die for the same. . . .* Therefore the righteous may lose his righteousness, abandon his faith, die in his sins; and receive the reward of his transgressions in his aversion from God, hell fire.

. . .

Again, Rom. 11:20-21: *Thou standest by faith, be not high-minded, but fear;* and fear is not but where change may be. Here change may be, or why doth it follow, *Take heed least he also spare not thee?* The reason is, any man may have that which another had. Now

1 Timoth. 6:20: *Some have erred concerning faith.* And 1 Timoth. 1:18-19: *holding faith and a good conscience, which some having put away concerning faith have made shipwrack.* Nor was it only for those times, but foretold of succeeding ages. 1 Timoth. 4:1: *In the latter days some shall depart from the faith.* Gal. 5:4, Saint Paul spake not upon supposition of impossibility: *Ye are abolished from Christ, whosoever are justified by the Law, ye are fallen from grace.* For many were so, that having believed and being baptized, did evacuate Christ by their own righteousness in the Law. Of whom Saint Paul complaineth in all that Epistle to the Galatians and elsewhere. Nor in point of only heresy was faith by them lost, but also of good living and conversation. 2 Pet. 2:20: Where those that *had escaped the filthiness of the world*—therefore washed and made clean *through the knowledge of our Lord and Savior Jesus Christ*—therefore justified truly by faith—are yet *entangled again therein, and overcome.* Therefore lapsed from faith, as is expressed vers. 21 and 22 ensuing.

Infinite are the testimonies of Scriptures to this purpose insisted upon by the avouchers. I add but one of them. Heb. 6:4: *It is impossible that they which were once enlightened, and have tasted of the heavenly gift, and were made partakers of the Holy Ghost, and have tasted of the good word of God and of the power of the world to come* (if these were not justified, they know not who were; if these had not faith, where was it to be found), *if they fall away, should be renewed again by repentance, seeing they crucify again the Son of God unto themselves and make a mock of him.*

Thus Scripture speaketh plain. Their reasons from Scripture are evident. Man is not likely in state of grace to be of an higher alloy than angels were in state of glory, than Adam was in state of innocency, for grace is but a conformity thereto, and no conformity exceedeth the archetype; at most it is but an equality thereto, and equals are of the same proportion. Now if Adam in paradise and Lucifer in heaven did fall and lose their original state, the one totally, the other eternally, what greater assurance hath any man in state of proficiency, not of consummation?

Again, faith must needs be lost where it cannot consist.[8] It cannot consist where God will not abide. God will not abide where he is disobeyed; he is disobeyed where mortal sin is committed. The most righteous man living upon the face of the earth continually doth or may in this sort transgress: *Who can tell how oft he offendeth? Cleanse thy servant from presumptuous sins. Thou wilt have no fellowship at all with the deceitful; nor shall any evil dwell with thee.*

Saul was at first the child of God, called according to the election of grace, not only temporal for the kingdom of Israel, but also eternal for the heavenly kingdom. In opinion of antiquity thus he was; and yet afterward he fell, it is confessed. Totally, all say. Eternally, these say that maintain justifying faith cannot be lost. But if Saul were not of God's children in grace, endued with faith and the Holy Spirit, yet Solomon was; there is no question with them, because he was a writer of holy writ, and wrote as he was inspired by God. If they did not grant it, the Scripture would evict it. For 2 Samuel 7:{14}, God speaketh of him literally (though of Christ Jesus, intentionally): *I will be his father, and he shall be my son.* . . . Yet Solomon fell, as Saint Augustine and Saint Chrysostom are clear for it: at least temporally, and totally too, when he went and served other gods. If Solomon were

---

[8] {Here "consist" means to be capable of existing along with, to be compatible with (*OED*).}

never the child of God, yet David was without contradiction, and Saint Peter without nay. Yet David fell foul in that act of murder and adultery, and lost his faith and present state of grace. If David had perished in that his sin, what had become of his soul forever? It was not possible he should, in regard of the purpose of grace; but had it been so, where had he been? Surely he that desired a *new heart to be created* had not that heart which he had before his fall, for creation is production from *not being unto being*. Saint Peter was a chosen vessel of Christ Jesus, and if ever was any, the child of God. Yet he denied Jesus Christ with an oath, which was *peccatum lethale* {deadly sin}, as Saint Augustine proveth in his 66th Tractat. upon Saint John. Christ prayed for him that his faith might not fail. But his prayer was for the end, not the act: that he might not fall finally, and he did not; but not that not totally, for so he did. His infirmity appeared in his fall. God's mercy was seen in his restoration.

. . .

XXI

That God, by his will & inevitable decree, hath ordained from all eternity who shall be damned and who saved

Damned and *saved* divide mankind. Not any hath come forth of the loins of Adam but, as this Gaggler will himself confess, is necessarily ranged in one of these ranks: either with the damned or the saved, sheep or goats, upon the left hand or the right.

But he, whosoever, that is . . . finally and eternally *damned* or *saved*, as one day actively all shall be, is so damned or saved not without God's will, according to the purpose of his decree (at least consequent, though not antecedent), *who doth whatsoever he will in heaven and earth; who worketh all things according to the counsel of his will*, the highest rule, supremest law—nothing beyond it, against it, without it. So damned or saved are so ordained by God.

Whatsoever God willeth, cometh to pass; and whatsoever cometh to pass, cometh so to pass because God hath said, *so and not otherwise, it shall come to pass*—either positively, by disposing it, or else permissively, by giving way and suffering it so to come to pass as it doth come to pass. This his will, as nor himself, began not in time; it is and was eternal, as he is: ever, *I am*; not, *I will be* or *have been*. Whatsoever is done in process of time was so seen, so disposed of and ordered, before all time; for he is not measured but by eternity, which is *tota simul & perfecta possessio sui, the total and perfect possession of itself*.

If then there be *damned* and *saved*, as there are, God's eternal *will* did so determine of them & their final estate from all eternity; and after that determination of God, they are *damned* or *saved* inevitably; not only according unto prescience, but also according to predestination, say the Roman schools[9]. . . .

What then? Why, surely the poor man[10] meant well to the Catholic cause, and would say somewhat, though no matter what, which he did not understand nor could utter.

---

[9] {I.e., this version of predestination is one taught by Roman Catholic theologians—primarily, I suspect, Dominicans; the Gagger failed to differentiate this Roman Catholic position from the Calvinist one, which Montagu supplies in italics below.}

[10] {The Gagger; Montagu is being sarcastic.}

He thought well, though he could not handsomely tell his tale, which should have been marshaled thus:

> *That God, by his sole will and absolute decree, hath irrespectively resolved and inevitably decreed, some to be saved, some to be damned, from all Eternity.*

Man, in curiosity, hath presumed far upon and waded deep into the hidden secrets of the Almighty; nowhere more or with greater presumption than where that grand Apostle stood at gaze, with *O the depth!* and in consideration cried out, *How unsearchable are his ways!* {Rom. 11:33}, who yet was admitted into council of state and rapt up into the third heaven.

In the point of election for life and reprobation unto death, Protestants and Papists are many ways at odds in opposition, and each divided at home amongst themselves; not for the *thing*, which all resolve, but for the *manner*, in which they differ; agreeing in the main that *it is so*; disagreeing on the by *how it cometh so*, as if God meant to reserve no secrets unto himself, but impart them all to men; as if it were not enough to save some and cast others off, but he must give account of doing so.

Some Protestants, and no moe but some, have considered God, for this effect of his will, in reference to Peter and Judas, thus: that Peter was saved because that God would have him saved absolutely, and resolved to save him necessarily because he would so, and no further; that Judas was damned as necessarily because that God—as absolute to decree, as omnipotent to effect—did primarily so resolve concerning him and so determine touching him, without respect of anything but his own will: insomuch that Peter could not perish, though he would; nor Judas be saved, do what he could.

This is not the doctrine of the Protestants. The Lutherans in Germany detest and abhor it. It is the private fancy of some men, I grant; but what are opinions unto decisions? Private opinions, unto received and decided doctrines? The Church of England hath not taught it, doth not believe it, hath opposed it, wisely contenting herself with this *quoúsque* and limitation, Art. 17. *We must receive God's promises in such wise {quoúsque} as they be generally set forth to us in Holy Scripture* and not presuming to determine of *when, how, wherefore,* or *whom*—secrets reserved to God alone.

⟩⟨⟩⟨

Text: EEBO (STC [2nd ed.] / 18038)

Richard Montagu, *A gag for the new Gospel? No: A NEW GAG for an old goose. Who would needs undertake to stop all Protestants' mouths for ever with 276 places out of their own English Bibles. Or an answer to a late abridger of controversies, and beliar of the Protestants' doctrine* (London: printed by Thomas Snodham for Matthew Lownes and William Barret, 1624), 107–12, 157–63, 177–79.

RICHARD MONTAGU

Appello Caesarem: a just appeal from two unjust informers
1625[1]

To his most sacred Majesty.[2]

Most gracious and dread sovereign,

By a missive, from a papist I am sure, and I suppose from a priest,[3] I was not long since forced upon the controversies of these times between the Protestant and Romish confessionists. And because it hath been ever truly counted a readier way for the advancement of piety rather to lessen and abate than to multiply the number of many needless contentions in the Church, therefore when I first undertook to answer that very worthless author, *the GAGGER of all Protestants' mouths forever,* I did it with a firmed purpose to leave all private opinions and particular positions or oppositions whatsoever unto their own authors or abettors, either to stand or fall of themselves; and not to suffer the Church of England to be charged with the maintenance of any doctrine which was none of her own, publicly and universally resolved on. For we are at a great disadvantage with our adversaries, to have those tenets put and pressed evermore upon us for the general doctrine established in our Church, which are but either the problematical opinions of private doctors, to be held or not held either way; or else the fancies, many of them of factious men, disclaimed and censured by the Church, not to be held any way. Such disadvantages hath this Church too long endured, and out of just indignation against this Gagger and his fellows, I could not but so much the more labor to vindicate her freedom *ex professo*, and to assert[4] her (as far as I was able) unto her own proper, true, and ancient tenets, such as be without any doubt or question legitimate and genuine, such as she will both acknowledge and maintain for her own. My direct dealing herein, most dread sovereign, so reasonable, so necessary (as I supposed), hath very much and highly

---

[1] {For the overview of Montagu's life and works, see the introduction to *A gag <supra>*.}

[2] {King Charles; James had died while *Appello* was being printed.}

[3] {See *A new gag*, n. 2 <*supra*>.}

[4] {liberate}

409

discontented some private divines, who desire to have those opinions which are controverted among ourselves to be taken and defended for the common and public doctrine of the Church; but more especially hath it incensed those classical[5] puritans, who were wont to pass all their strange determinations, Sabbatarian paradoxes, and apocalyptical frenzies under the name and covert of *the true professors of Protestant doctrine*, supposing, as it should seem, that in this case we were all liable to the statute:[6] that is, bound to keep and foster their conceits as our own doctrines because they have cast them upon us and upon our Church like bastards upon the parish where they were born or vagabonds on the town where they last dwelt or were suffered to pass without due correction. Such urchins it was necessary to disband and send them away to shift for themselves, that our Mother the Church might no more be troubled with them. And yet for this cause have some informers articled against me and traduced me to the world for a Papist and an Arminian; though the world and themselves know I flatly defied and opposed the one; and God in heaven knoweth that I never so much as yet read word in the other. It was my happiness, most gracious sovereign, that so mean a vassal as my poor self was sufficiently known to be nor so nor so unto him[7] (who, if ever any of the royal rank, was indeed *sicut angelus Domini* to discern), my late most sacred lord and master of ever blessed memory, unto whom that information should have been represented;[8] by whom, in his most able and impartial judgment, I had my *quietus est* and discharge. But in regard their clamors were so impetuous and accusations so divulged, it pleased his Majesty, out of that goodness which was ever eminent in his most blessed disposition, not only to grant me leave humbly to *Appeal* from my defamers unto his most sacred cognizance in public and to represent my just defense against their slanders and false surmises unto the world; but also to give express order unto Doct. White, the Reverend Dean of Carlisle, for the authorizing and publishing thereof after it had been duly read over and approved by him to contain nothing in it but what was agreeable to the doctrine and discipline established in the Church of England, whereof his Majesty was most tender. It was read, approved, and sent to the press accordingly. Since which time, it hath pleased the King of kings to call him unto himself, and to crown him with glory and immortality in heaven, before I could return the book into his royal hands. But blessed forever be the Lord God of heaven that hath preserved your Majesty and set you upon his throne as king in stead of him, to go in and out before his people in his place, and to execute judgment in your father's room. What was then intended unto him, according to his own most gracious and royal direct appointment, I humbly crave leave upon my bended knees to present unto your most excellent and sacred self; and in all lowly wise, I cast both it and myself, and the best service I shall be able to do in God's Church, at your Majesty's feet, desiring

---

[5] {i.e., favoring a presbyterian-style church government}

[6] {The statute of 7 Jac. 1 c. 4 dealing with bastards, rogues, and vagabonds. The point of the allusion (implicit in the following clause) being that as a parish is by law liable for bastards born there and for vagabonds whom it fails to punish, so Calvinists hold that the Church of England now "owns" the predestinarian theology they foisted on it.}

[7] {i.e., King James knew Montagu was neither a Roman Catholic nor Arminian.}

[8] {The complaint was made not to James but to Parliament.}

no longer to live than I shall be and continue a most conformable and true member of this Church, and

Your Majesty's most loyal and faithful subject and servant,

Richard Montagu

‡

CHAP. IV

Of FALLING FROM GRACE: The tenet of antiquity therein. The doctrine of the Church of England in the 16th Article, the Conference at Hampton Court, the Book of Homilies, and the public liturgy

INFORMERS.[9] *And again: Some hold that faith may be lost totally and finally, which is indeed the assertion of antiquity. The learnedst in the Church of England assent unto antiquity in that tenet, which the Protestants in Germany maintain at this day, having assented unto the Church of Rome.*

MONTAGU. *Antiquum obtinent* {they uphold antiquity}. These men are still the same—calumniators—and run still along with all one indirect dealing. Their information in direct terms standeth thus: to make report, and no more but[10] to make report, of Arminianism (if yet it be Arminianism which is reported) is, in point of opinion, to be an Arminian. . . . for M. Montagu in this case hath done no more. The very suggestion, as it is by themselves here rendered, howsoever patched up of shreds cut out from several parts and laid together again for most advantage to their calumniation, will yet speak no further but only to this purpose, for themselves set it down in style not of position {affirmation} but of bare narration, with these terms of "some hold"; "it is the assertion," "the learnedst assent unto," &c. So that admit the points related were pure-pure Arminianism, yet so long as the relator passeth no consent upon them (I appeal unto your own, though never so much cheverellized[11] consciences, my good calumniators), can there be inferred a just accusation? If so, upon as good ground, in these terms, I can inform against the most precisest puritan in the kingdom for as good popery as any Bellarmine hath. . . . I demand, can you find any assent of mine annexed? nay, find you not rather assent denied? Have you not read in that passage these words, which any honest plain man would have cast into the information but yourselves: *I determine nothing in the question positively*? If you did not see nor read them, your eyes were not your own. If you read them, but marked them not, your wits went on wool-gathering at that instant. If you read and marked them, and yet did conceal them, what became of your honesty in the interim? You foully abused the world with false informations. . . . For he that professeth *he doth not determine*, as Mr. Montagu in express and precise words doth, in my logic cannot be said to consent nor concur in opinion for himself, but merely suspendeth his judgment in the case, and leaveth it indifferent and as he found it.

---

[9] {The informants quote the allegedly objectionable passages in Montagu's *A new gag*.}

[10] {Montagu often uses "but" where we would use "than."}

[11] {stretched, capable of stretching}

. . .

The Romish Gagger, whosoever he was, laid down his proposition—as he would have it conceived, against the approved and established doctrine of the Church of England, not against any either private fancy or more public opinion of any faction on foot or sect prevailing in the Church of England. Yet that he might play fast and loose (a fashion ordinary with those of his party), he proposeth the imputation in ambiguous & involved terms. In my answer, because I would draw the question unto an issue[12] and rightly state it, I was to difference opinions confounded by the Gagger (which in and touching this subject are not a few) concerning the loss of and falling away from faith; and therefore in the conclusion came home to distinguish them thus: *some suppose that faith cannot be lost either totally or finally; some, that totally, but not finally; some, that both totally and finally; which is indeed the opinion of antiquity and of your Schools. Some, perceiving the current of judgments for the loss thereof both totally and finally, and withal considering the, at least, probability of Scriptures therefore, put in a new distinction of God and man, of first and second causes of justification.* Having reported these distinct and several opinions of elder and modern divines . . . I demand of the Gagger, who in ambiguities lurketh *post aulaea* {behind the curtains}, *Which of all these ways will you have the proposition to be understood, that faith may be lost, &c?* and so come up unto him thus: *you mean, it may be lost both totally and finally in regard of* God, *who made no such absolute irrespective decree; as also in respect of second causes, in man, without man, about him, against him.* All this is there, as any man may perceive, by way of bare narration. And then, for my own opinion, I conclude thus: *I determine nothing in this question positively.* . . . resolving upon this, not to go beyond my bounds: the consented, resolved, and subscribed Articles of the Church of England. . . .

And concerning the particulars: wherein? whom have I misreported? If I can be convicted, I will reverse it. They will not contest for the Roman Schools, I know; as little for the Lutherans, I suppose. It is confessed on all hands that they hold falling from grace and losing of faith had, and detest the contrary opinion as heretical. For the tenet of antiquity, I cannot be challenged. S. Augustine, and after him S. Prosper, affirm more than M^r. Montagu hitherto hath done. . . . But the greatest question will be concerning the *learnedst in the Church of England*, said to *consent unto antiquity* in this case of *falling away from grace*. Where first I will not deny but that *many* in the *Church of England*, reputed *learned*, are of that opinion that *faith had cannot be lost*. But if it shall appear that the contrary tenet is the public doctrine of the Church of England, then I have not wronged private men in making this comparison between them and those whom themselves will acknowledge to be their superiors both in learning and authority. Now, to give them all due satisfaction which may think themselves wronged by my comparative speech, I argue as followeth.

> They *were the* learnedst *in the Church of England, that drew, composed, and agreed the* Articles *in* {15}52 *and* 62, *that ratified them in* 71, *that confirmed them again in* 1604, *that justified and maintained them against the puritans at Hampton Court;*

---

[12] {In English law, the issue is the point in question, at the conclusion of the pleadings between contending parties in a lawsuit, when one side affirms and the other denies (*OED*). Once the parties have pled to the issue, the case then goes to trial, where the parties argue the issue before a jury.}

that have read and subscribed them at their induction unto benefices and consecration unto bishoprics; that penned the Homilies *read in churches.*

But *all these have and all such do* assent unto antiquity *in this tenet, and subscribe it truly or in hypocrisy.*

Therefore *I may justly avouch it*: the learnedst in the Church of England assent therein to antiquity.[13]

The major, I suppose, no man will question. The informers themselves are peradventure within that pale. The minor I make good particularly, and will prove it accordingly *obsignatis tabulis*.[14] In the forenamed xvi Article we read and subscribe this: *After that we have received the Holy Ghost, we may depart away from grace, and fall into sin, and by the grace of God we may rise again and amend our lives.* Now let me ask the question: have you subscribed this Article, or have you not? If you be beneficed men, you have read it and subscribed it, professed your assent and consent thereto, before God and his Church, or else by Act of Parliament you have *forfeited your spiritual promotions* and are *deprived* ipso facto *within two months*. If so, then have you subscribed that "Arminianism" which you impute as an error unto me. Haply you will be of his mind, one of your tribe, who when he was told what he had subscribed (for, poor ignorant man, he understood it not) protested he would tear his subscription if he could come by it, and so would have lost his benefice; which few of you will do, if it be a good one, for conscience sake; marry for a poor one, you will not stick. Haply you will quarrel the sense of the Articles, but then you must remember that the plain words sound to the meaning for which I have produced them, and that until the Church itself expound otherwise, it is as free for me to take it according to the letter as for you to devise a figure. The Article insisteth upon men *justified*, speaketh of them *after grace received*; plainly avoucheth, *they may fall away, depart from that state which once they had*; they *may by God's grace rise again* and become new men—possible, but not certain or necessary. But the meaning by you assigned cannot be good, being allied unto the stock you are: for by your tribe, the true meaning of the Article . . . was upon this very point challenged as unsound because against the current of their *Institutions*.[15] And had Arminianism then been a nickname, the challenge without doubt had fastened there; but challenged it was in this sense as unsound at the Conference of Hampton Court by those that were petitioners against the doctrine and discipline established in the Church of England. And being so challenged before his sacred Majesty, was then and there defended, maintained, avowed, averred for true, ancient, justifiable, good, and catholic by the greatest bishops and learnedst divines then living in this Church, against that absolute, irrespective, necessitating and fatal decree of your new predestination, styled by you the doctrine of *your divines*, commonly called Calvinists. As indeed it is *yours*, being never heard of in the world but of late; but styled then and there by the Lord Bishop of London, Dr. Bancroft—in public audience, with much vehemency, without any check, dislike, distaste, dissent (for we read of none)—*a desperate doctrine of predestination*. At what time also that reverend prelate and most accomplished divine

---

[13] {The argument is presented in the syllogistic format of a university disputation.}

[14] {Proverbial. Literally, "with sealed writings," meaning in strict legal form and with proper documentation.}

[15] {i.e., Calvin's *Institutes*}

(whose memory shall ever be precious with all good and learned men) the late Bishop of Norwich then Dean of Paul's, D'. Overall, upon some touch[16] by occasion of mentioning the Articles of Lambeth,[17] did relate unto his most sacred Majesty those concertations {conflicts} which himself had sometimes had in Cambridge with some doctors there about this very point of falling from grace; and that it was his tenet, and had been, *That a justified man might fall away from grace, and so* ipso facto *incur God's wrath; and was in state of wrath and damnation until he did recover again and was renewed after his fall.* At which time, that doctrine of the Church of England—then quarreled, now styled Arminianism, accused of novelty, slandered as pernicious by these informers and their brethren—was resolved of and avowed for true, catholic, ancient, and orthodox by that royal, reverend, honorable and learned Synod. The book is extant (published by warrant and republished by command this present year) of the proceedings at that Conference, which will aver all that I say for truth against you here. See the book.[18]

And for explication of that authorized and subscribed doctrine, there is an homily in the Book of Homilies, first composed and published in King Edward's time, approved and justified in Parliament in Queen Elizabeth's days, and authorized again of late to be read in churches, entitled "Of falling away from God." Which very title is sufficient warrant for the doctrine or error in this point imputed to M. Montagu. But that which is delivered in the homily will justify him unto the full, for the homily doth thoroughly and wholly insist upon the affirmation, that *faith once had may again be lost.* Out of the first part of that homily, you may take this (my good informers) for your edification: *Whereas God hath shewed unto all them that truly do believe his Gospel his face of mercy in Christ Jesus, which doth so enlighten their hearts that they be transformed into his image, be made partakers of the heavenly light and of his Holy Spirit, be fashioned unto him in all goodness requisite unto the child of God; so if they do afterward neglect the same, if they be unthankful unto him, if they order not their lives according to his doctrine and example and to the setting forth of his glory, he will take from them his holy word, his kingdom whereby he should reign in them, because they bring not forth the fruit that he looked for.* Can your learning and understanding make any other construction of these words than that *a man may fall away from grace, become no child of God at all?* If you can, advance and teach me that which passeth my poor apprehension. They were *truly called*, that did *truly believe* . . . that *beheld the face of God's mercy in Christ.* . . . If these be not attributes of justified men, good Sirs, teach us some new divinity. Yet in the doctrine of the Church of England expounded in this homily, these men may prove unthankful, negligent, and lose the interest they had in that his kingdom of grace by his holy word. And yet further, in the second part of this homily, we are sent unto a conclusion more *ad oppositum*,[19] not only of total lapse for a time, but also of final separation and forever. Which is also according to the doctrine expressed in the Articles, for he that saith, *A man may fall away and may recover*, implieth withal that

[16] {rebuke, criticism, affront; words that "touch" a person's dignity}

[17] {A stridently predestinarian manifesto drawn up at Cambridge in 1595, the authors intending that it should be taken as a clarification of the English Church's official doctrinal. See Lake, *Moderate puritans*; Shuger, "Protesting." The Lambeth Articles themselves are available online.

[18] {The relevant passages from William Barlow's account of the Hampton Court Conference, to which Montagu here refers, can be found in an appendix following this selection.}

[19] {on the opposing side}

some men may fall away and may not recover; which the homily declareth thus: *they shall be no longer governed by God's Holy Spirit . . . they shall be deprived of the heavenly light and life which they had in Christ while that they abode in him.* They that thus fall away unto the state of damnation were *truly* justified, for it is said, *they were in Christ*; *they continued sometime in Christ*, for they *abode in him.* But yet this is not all, for it followeth, *They shall be given up unto the power of the devil, who beareth rule in all that are castaways from God, as he did in Saul and Judas.* I suppose this is plain and home enough.

If you be acquainted with the liturgy and public religious service of our Church (as to your shame few of you and your divines are or will be, unless it be to oppose and cavil at it), there you shall find also as much as *falling from grace* cometh to. In the form of holy baptism we are taught (otherwise than your masters teach) that *every child which is duly baptized, being before born in original sin and in the wrath of God, is now by that laver of regeneration received into the number of the children of God and heirs of everlasting life. For our Lord Jesus Christ doth not deny his grace and mercy unto such infants, &c.* So here they be put into the state of grace. And lest it should be left to men's charity (as you use to tell the world), we are there taught *earnestly to believe that Christ hath favorably received these infants that are baptized, that he hath embraced them with the arms of his mercy, that he hath given unto them the blessing of eternal life*; and out of that belief and persuasion, we are to *give thanks faithfully and devoutly for it, &c.* To make which doctrine the more sure against all novelists {innovators}, it is again repeated in the catechism, to the end that children might likewise be nursed up in it and taught that *in their baptism they were made the members of Christ and the children of God*, &c; and that *it is certainly true by the word of God that children being baptized have all things necessary for their salvation; and if they die before actual sin, shall be undoubtedly saved.* According whereunto all antiquity hath also taught us. Now let this be acknowledged to be the doctrine of our Church, that children duly baptized are put into the state of grace and salvation (which, you see, you cannot, you must not deny), and both your and my experience will shew that many so baptized children, when they come to age, by a wicked and lewd life do fall away from God and from that state of grace and salvation wherein he had set them, to a worse state wherein they shall never be saved. If you grant not this, you must hold that all men that are baptized are saved, which I know you will never do.

To make an end then. In my judgment this is the doctrine of the Church of England, not delivered according unto private opinions in ordinary tracts and lectures, but delivered publicly, positively, and declaratorily in authentical records. And you cannot be ignorant (for it is still extant upon record) that your prime leaders have understood the tenet of the Church of England to be as I have reported it, and accordingly they have complained against it (as you have against me), and objected it as one of their reasons why they refused to subscribe. Let there then be added express Scripture (Ezechiel 18:24) and a common unanimous consent of the most learned and ancient Fathers expounding that and other places of Scripture (which consent our Church doth by open profession maintain in these canons which she set forth to be subscribed unto, together with the XXXIX Articles *anno* MDLXXI), and I see no reason wherefore I might not have been as confident in maintaining *falling away from grace*, as you and your divines are, upon weaker grounds, in defending the contrary. But I have ever been solicitous to preserve peace and to give as little occasion of disturbance thereof unto distempered humors as was possible.

Salus Ecclesiae non vertitur in istis {the well-being of the Church does not hinge on these things}; and therefore I thought it not *tanti* {of such importance}; and being not urged upon necessity in my answer to the Gagger to handle this question otherwise than I did, I suspended mine own judgment and lay off aloof in a kind of neutrality. Neither do I now say more than I am urged to do by the plain and express words of our Articles and doctrine publicly professed and established in our Church; which I hope yourselves will give me leave to do, the rather because I know you have subscribed the same with your hands, though what became of your hearts in the mean time, I cannot tell.

TEXT: EEBO (STC [2nd ed.] / 18031)
Richard Montagu, *Appello Caesarem: a just appeal from two unjust informers* (Printed by H. L. for Matthew Lownes, 1625), Ep. Ded. and pp. 21–37.

APPENDIX

{*The discussion of falling from grace at the 1604 Hampton Court Conference, according to William Barlow's summary of the proceedings*}

. . .

For the first, he {Dr. Reinolds} moved his Majesty that the Book of Articles of Religion concluded 1562 might be explained in places obscure, and enlarged where some things were defective. For example, whereas Art. 16 the words are these: *After we have received the Holy Ghost, we may depart from grace*; notwithstanding the meaning be sound, yet he desired that, because they may seem to be contrary to the doctrine of God's predestination & election in the 17 Article, both those words might be explained with this or the like addition, *yet neither totally nor finally*. . . .

. . .

Upon the first motion concerning falling from grace, the Bishop of London {Bancroft} took occasion to signify to his Majesty how very many in these days, neglecting holiness of life, presumed too much of persisting in grace, laying all their religion upon predestination, *if I shall be saved, I shall be saved*; which he termed a desperate doctrine, shewing it to be contrary to good divinity and the true doctrine of predestination, wherein we should reason rather *ascendendo* than *descendendo*, thus: *I live in obedience to God, in love with my neighbor; I follow my vocation*, &c.; *therefore I trust that God hath elected me & predestinated me to salvation*; not thus, which is the usual course of argument: *God hath predestinated and chosen me to life, therefore, though I sin never so grievously, yet I shall not be damned, for whom he once loveth, he loveth to the end.* Whereupon he shewed his Majesty out of the next Article, what was the doctrine of the Church of England touching predestination, in the very last paragraph, *scilicet: We must receive God's promises in such wise as they be generally set forth to us in Holy Scripture; and in our doings, that will of God is to be followed which we have expressly declared unto us in the word of God*: which part of the said Article, his Majesty very well approved, and after he had, after his manner, very singularly discoursed upon that place of Paul, *work out your salvation with fear and trembling*, he left it to be considered whether anything were meet to be added for the clearing of the Doctor his doubt, by putting in the word *often*, or the like, as thus: *we may often depart from grace*, but, in the meantime wished that the doctrine of predestination might be very tenderly handled and with great discretion, lest on the one side, God's omnipotency might be called in question by impeaching the doctrine of his eternal predestination; or on the other, a desperate presumption might be arreared by inferring the necessary certainty of standing and persisting in grace.

‡

Upon this the Dean of Paul's {Overall}, kneeling down, humbly desired leave to speak, signifying unto his Majesty that this matter somewhat more nearly concerned him, by reason of controversy between him and some other in Cambridge upon a proposition which he had delivered there: namely, that whosoever (though before justified) did commit any grievous sin, as adultery, murder, treason, or the like, did become *ipso facto* subject to God's wrath and guilty of damnation, or were in state of damnation (*quoad praesentem statum*[1]) until they did repent; adding hereunto, that those which were called and justified according to the purpose of God's election, howsoever they might, and did, sometime fall into grievous sins and thereby into the present state of wrath and damnation, yet did never fall either *totally* from all the graces of God to be *utterly* destitute of all the parts and seed thereof, nor *finally* from justification, but were in time renewed by God's Spirit unto a lively faith and repentance, and so justified from those sins and the wrath, curse, and guilt annexed thereunto, whereinto they were fallen and wherein they lay so long as they were without true repentance for the same. Against which doctrine, he said that some had opposed, teaching that all such persons as were once truly justified, though after they fell into never so grievous sins, yet remained still just or in the state of justification before they actually repented of those sins; yea, and though they never repented of them, through forgetfulness or sudden death, yet they should be justified and saved without repentance. In utter dislike of this doctrine, his Majesty entered into a longer speech of predestination and reprobation than before, and of the necessary conjoining repentance and holiness of life with true faith, concluding that it was hypocrisy, and not true justifying faith, which was severed from them; for although predestination and election dependeth not upon any qualities, actions, or works of man, which be mutable, but upon God his eternal and immutable decree and purpose: yet such is the necessity of repentance after known sins committed, as that without it there could not be either reconciliation with God or remission of those sins.

TEXT: William Barlow, *The sum and substance of the Conference, which it pleased his excellent Majesty to have with the lords, bishops, and other of his clergy, (at which the most of the Lords of the Council were present) in his Majesty's privy chamber at Hampton Court, January 14, 1603* (Printed by John Windet for Matthew Law, 1604), 24, 28–30, 41–43.

[1] {with respect to their present state}

JOHN PRESTON[1]

Riches of mercy to men in misery; or, certain excellent treatises
concerning the dignity and duty of God's children
ca. 1625, published 1658[2]

The Buckler of a Believer

Who shall condemn? It is Christ that is dead, yea rather which is risen again,
who is also at the right hand of God, and maketh request also for us.
Rom. 8. Verse 34

In this most sweet and comfortable Scripture, I mean the eighth chapter, our blessed apostle Saint Paul shews at large the happy and safe estate of every true believer that hath his part in Christ, where he proves at large that there is nothing can hinder and disannul that estate, but that he must enjoy it according to his faith; shewing withal that if anything could hinder it, it must come either from sin or from the cross, the punishment of sin. Now he shews this, and proves it strongly against all the enemies of salvation, that neither sin nor the cross can do it, and therefore not anything.

Sin cannot do it (verse 1) because there is no condemnation (that is, for sin) to them. The cross cannot do it because (as vers. 28) *all afflictions, they shall work to good for them.* Therefore, once in Christ, nothing can hinder them from eternal salvation. And one would think this were sufficient proof; yet as if all this were nothing, therefore that he may raise the true believer to the highest pitch of sound and lasting comfort, he goes further and would have him to insult[3] and victoriously triumph (verse 33, 34) and rise to the highest pitch of holy confidence, speaking here in a kind of defiance, and saying: if any man dare be so bold as to accuse one that believes, yet where is he that can condemn him? as if he had said, There is none at all that can. So that briefly in these words

---

[1] {For the introduction to Preston's life and works, see his 1621 sermon, *Plenitudo fontis <supra>*.}

[2] {The volume is posthumous; the sermons date from ca. 1625. Although entered in the Stationers' Register in 1640, *Riches* is the last of Preston's sermon collections to see print. Jonathan Moore speculates that Sibbes may have lent the manuscript to Lord Saye, who failed to return it in a timely manner (*English hypothetical universalism* 239n).}

[3] {to exult proudly; to vaunt, glory}

contained in the text is laid down every holy believer's challenge, which he may take up against the face of all enemies whatsoever.

Wherein observe two parts:

First, a true believer's challenge in these words, *Who shall condemn?* Secondly, the person in whose name the challenge is made, which is Christ's: *It is Christ that is dead*, &c. For though the believer is weak in himself, yet in the rock, Christ, strong and invincible.

For the first, viz., the true believer's challenge, it is the more to be noted because it is laid down by way of interrogation, for that hath with it a strong confidence and a kind of victorious triumph, as if he said: there is none at all that can condemn though they may go about it. It is not *interrogatio rogantis* or *dubitantis*, but *instantis et triumphantis*; it is not a question of one asking by way of doubt, but of one earnest in affirming and triumphing. So that the point then is this:

> *There is not any one in heaven, earth, nor anywhere else that can bring in anything to condemn a true believer in the sight of God.* Or
> *There is not anything in this world, nor in the world to come, to hinder the salvation of a true believer.*

Where we are to consider,

First, what it is to condemn.

Secondly, that all and every one of us before we believe are in the estate of condemnation, and therefore easily to be condemned because under the curse of the Law and the guilt of sin.

Thirdly, that when we come truly to believe in Christ, even then we are not to think to be free from all that will assay and seek to condemn us and bring us to perdition and destruction.

Fourthly, that though there be many, as the devil and all his instruments, that aim and endeavor by many means to spoil us of our faith and hinder our salvation and so bring us to destruction, yet shall none ever be able to do it.

Lastly, we will make application of all to ourselves.

For the first, namely, what it is to condemn: it is taken diversely, either *in foro publico* (as in our courts), when one is guilty of some offence against the law and so is bound over by sentence of condemnation to suffer for it. Or else in *foro conscientiae*, in the court of conscience, as here before God, and it is nothing else but to have a conscience guilty of sin, and for that to be judged of God to eternal punishment—even to be separated from the love of God in Christ for ever and ever; and all this presupposeth a guiltiness for sin that justifies the judgment of God in regard of the just sentence of condemnation. Now who shall make the true believer guilty before God, being once in Christ? The answer is made by the Apostle: there is not one that can.

Now for the second thing observed: namely that those which come to believe, while they were in a state of nature and under the curse of the Law were in an estate of condemnation. . . . Of this their own conscience is witness against them. The Law of God is the bill of indictment, God the judge, the devil the executioner, and hell the prison, from whence it is impossible to escape until they come soundly to believe in the Lord Jesus.

For the third: when a man hath this blessed grace of faith and begins to lay hold on Christ, he is not to think himself safe and that he is secured from all that will seek his condemnation. For the devil will do what he can still to winnow all goodness and grace received out of him that nothing may remain but chaff; and therefore it is we are taught in the Lord's Prayer, after forgiveness of sins, to pray against temptations. Though thy sins be pardoned by the blood of Christ upon thy believing, yet there is one that seeks to break the force of thy faith and so to bring thee to destruction; and therefore it is he is called the *accuser* and *destroyer* (Rev. 12:10). So that thou must look that, though thou hast got out of his paws, yet he hath many ways whereby he will labor what he can to bring thee back, to condemn and destroy thee.

As first, he will lay unto thee the wrath of God to drive thee to despair, as he would have done Job, who was brought to sore trials, discovered in passionate speeches.

2. The curse of the Law is enforced against thee to make thee think thy obedience to be so poor as God will not accept thee.

3. Want of faith is another of his suggestions, and for this he will allege the condition of the Gospel, and tell thee that thou dost not believe and so art not only under the curse of the Law, but the Gospel also.

4. The sins of thy conscience, that he will buffet thee with, persuading thee that such a sin is not pardoned, or pardonable.

5. He will muster up the world, where he hath many troops following him, to choke the word and quench the grace of God that is in thee.

Lastly, he will fear thee with the grim and dismal look of that last enemy, death, and put thee under fears of never being able to undergo it.

Now for the fourth circumstance: that though with all his power, cruelty and subtlety, as before, he doth assail, yet a true believer he shall never be able to prevail against; and that first, because a true believer, his debt is paid by the death of Christ. *Who shall condemn?* saith the Apostle; Christ is mighty and strong. None, for faith hath a hand that lays hold on Christ, so that if Christ perish, he may; else not. And that,

First, even because Christ hath died for him; and the strength of the Apostle's reason stands thus: a man in debt, if his debt be paid, he is not in danger of the law to be condemned for it; so there is not one farthing that God can in his justice demand at a believer's hands, for it is paid by Christ. . . .

. . .

Ay, but the devil is crafty, may some poor soul say; it may be he hath some bill or bond yet undischarged that I know not of, which he may demand at my hands.

No, saith the Gospel, he hath *blotted out the handwriting that was against us* (Col. 2:14). All is crossed and cancelled, and this God hath spoken and sworn to. Therefore let him do what he can, only believe thou. Every writing is cancelled; there is not a whit to shew in the sight of God. A poor man is indebted a great sum of money to a mighty king, and knows not what to do, having nothing to pay it withal; whereupon he is convicted, condemned, cast into prison. Now it pleaseth the king's only son to undertake the debt; his father is content; and in process of time he pays it and satisfieth his father. Who then, I pray you, can condemn that man? Even so is it with the poor believer: he ought {owed} both body and soul, and was to be put into the prison of hell forever for breaking God's Law and incurring his displeasure, but the Lord Jesus, out of his love and free favor, undertakes for the poor believer and pays his debt. Who then can condemn this poor believer?

Now further, by way of gradation and ascent, to make us raise up our thoughts in assurance of this, the Apostle useth a second reason: that is, because Christ our surety[4] is not only dead for us and so hath paid our debt, but also is risen again to make the poor believer more sure he hath paid the debt. And the strength of the argument is thus: if Christ had not risen again but been still in the power of the grave and kept under by the enemy of our salvation, the poor believer might have been justly afraid his debt had not been paid; but Christ being risen and out of hold, he is out of doubt. As when the debtor sees the king's son that was his surety at liberty and in the king's court, he fears not but his debt is paid; so when the poor believer sees Christ set free from the power of the grave, &c., he knows God hath accepted the payment he hath made as sufficient for him. . . .

. . .

In the fourth place, add unto all this that Christ doth not only sit at God's right hand, but so as that he also maketh intercession for every true believer, having not only power but even the same good will and mind that ever he had to do them good. Consider this well, whether thou, believing, needest to fear the face of any enemy whatsoever. The poor man that was indebted to the great king, for whom the king's son was pleased to undertake and satisfy, when he sees him come out of prison, set at liberty in his father's court, in greater honor, and not only so, but highly favored of the king his father and continually requesting him for that poor man: what needs he now care for all his enemies? He need not be afraid to look all officers in the face, &c.

Is this the secure and happy estate of every true believer, out of himself, in Christ? Then see the necessity of using all those means (and that constantly) whereby Christ our blessed Redeemer is pleased to communicate himself and this his grace unto us. Faith is a special gift and grace, and comes from God in Christ, and Christ he comes only in the means, which are channels and conduit-pipes. Therefore if thou wouldest have this grace, and be strengthened and increased therein, even as thou wouldest have thy soul thus dignified, use carefully all the means. As,

The word which is the scepter of Christ's kingdom, submit thy soul to it. If thou wilt have an excellent spirit, such a one as Joshua had, pray to God for it, and take heed of grieving the Spirit of God by continuing in the practice of any known sin, which is as water that quenches the fire; but rather cherish thy faith and put fuel unto it by constant & conscionable hearing, reading, prayer, meditation, receiving the sacrament, holy conference, and watching over thy heart. For if thou put fuel to thy faith, and keep away that which may quench it, thou shalt clearly see this blessed truth and find the power of faith in this that hath been said. Therefore as thou wouldest have this confidence and comfort in thy heart and soul, use the means for it. The diligent hand becomes rich in God's ordinary providence, and so mayest thou in this grace, if thou use diligence; there is no way else. Therefore whilst thou hast time, use the means: give attendance to the word and all those heavenly means before mentioned.

It's true indeed Christ hath freed himself by dying, rising again, and being at the right hand of God; and this I believe, saith the poor soul in the midst of his fears, temptations,

---

[4] {One who makes himself liable for the default or miscarriage of another, or for the performance of some act on his part (e.g. payment of a debt); one who pledges himself for another (*OED*).}

and troubles of mind; but how should I be comforted in knowing that I am freed from all that danger and condemnation which my sins do deserve?

Yes, upon this ground every believing soul, and so thou, if thou dost believe, mayst be sure to be freed as Christ himself is freed, and that even because Christ undertook and did all this for the poor believing soul, and he had not done it but for him. Esai. 9:6, *To us a child is born, to us a Son is given*; all he did was for us and for our salvation, so that if Christ hath any happiness, thou, believing in him, mayest be assured of it as Christ himself. All God's intentions towards thee are founded in love, else how should that be true, John 3:16, *God so loved the world, &c.* Christ also took all upon him for our sake, even to redeem and save us; he needed not have done it for himself, for he was God in glory, *&c.* Lift up therefore thy heart by faith and believe this, and thou shalt find it true; though we miserable wretches are unworthy of any such mercies, yet is God worthy to be believed. Look on Christ and consider who he is, and reflect it upon thyself, and if thou canst, believe the Lord Jesus hath done all this for thy sake, to help and strengthen thee to this.

First, consider Christ did it for us that believe as a surety. We were all bankrupts in the Law of God for want of obedience thereunto. Now Christ, the surety of mankind, comes and undertakes for us and hath done it: Hebrews 7:22, *He was made surety of a better testament.*

Therefore think on him always as thy surety in glory; Christ there is said to be a surety of better things than the legal rites were, even of the New Testament, wherein whatsoever is contained, it is for us and there it is treasured up; *ask and thou shalt have, seek and thou shalt find.* All he did, he did as my surety; all the evil he took away and all the good he purchased, it was for me.

. . .

Now to handle this point as it is contrary to the erroneous doctrine of the Church of Rome.

Who can condemn? None. This is the speech of the Apostle in the person of every true believer, as well as those to whom he then wrote at Rome. Only, those that have but a weak faith, the weaker assurance; yet all shall find the truth hereof if they believe, both weak & strong. This then may serve in the next place against that tormenting and racking doctrine of doubting so much maintained by Bellarmine. 'Tis true indeed, saith he, we doubt not of God's mercy and the merit of Christ, nor of the efficacy of the sacrament, &c., but in regard of our own indisposition, infirmities, unworthiness, and sins; in respect of these we ought to doubt and fear. And so by a Council hath the Romish Church accursed all such as say they are assured of their salvation,[5] though here every believer is enjoined to believe it assuredly. But, as the Psalmist saith, *he that loves cursing, it shall enter into his own bowels.*

But what are Bellarmine's reasons against assurance?

First, saith he, because of our unworthiness.

But to this I answer, to what purpose should the Apostle speak that which he doth here if our own unworthiness or sins could condemn? But if they stand upon unworthiness, we will say as much of ourselves as they can possible. But seeing Christ hath

---

[5] {*The canons and decrees of the sacred and oecumenical Council of Trent*, sixth session (1547), chap. ix, http://history.hanover.edu/texts/trent/ct06.html.}

undertook as our surety in our stead, and God through his grace gives power to believe, he takes away our unworthiness and gives us Christ's righteousness to go out and in as he hath done; and so we make all our challenge in Christ's name, not in ourselves; and so our unworthiness obliges us more strongly to rest ourselves upon Christ. In which case we resemble the vine that goes up & lays hold on that which is stronger than itself; so we, in ourselves weak, close with Christ, in whom God looks on us not as we are in ourselves, but in him in whom he is well pleased. So we stand not upon nor look unto our righteousness, but to God in Christ by whom our sins are washed away in his blood and our persons covered with his righteousness.

Ay but, saith he, the promises of salvation are made conditionally, if we repent and believe; now in regard of ourselves, we cannot believe, and therefore we are to doubt.

To this the Apostle shall answer: though the promise of salvation be conditional, yet everyone that truly believeth, his faith hath from God a light in it that makes him believe and repent, 1 Cor. 2:12, *We have received*, saith the Apostle, *not the spirit of the world but the spirit which is of God, that we might know the things that are freely given us of God.* So that the true believer hath received such a light from the word which letteth him see and know in some measure that he hath faith and repentance. Then what can hinder him from believing in Christ that hath done all this for him. He may know he is chosen in that he is effectually called; he may know he is effectually called in that he hath true repentance and faith in the Lord Jesus; and therefore he may be assured of his salvation.

Ay, but who can tell, saith he, that he hath sufficient faith and sufficient repentance?

Our assurance depends not upon the sufficiency, that is upon the measure, but the truth of our faith and repentance. As our faith is true and strong, so is our assurance; though it be but as smoking flax, yet if it be true, Christ will not quench it. It stands not upon this, how much or how little we believe, but how truly. Acts 16:31, *Believe in the Lord Jesus and thou shalt be saved.* They said not, believe thus much.

Ay, but, saith he, a true believer hath many secret sins; how can he then be assured?

The true believer, though he do fall into sin, yet if he be in Christ, and Christ reign over him, then sin reigns not over him. . . . Assurance may stand with secret sins that a man confesseth and humbles himself for; but if a man be given up to any sin, he cannot be assured; else he may, howsoever sin may trouble him much.

Lastly, he saith we must doubt in regard of ourselves, because all we have is but natural assurance. A man may hope well, that he grants, but he cannot be certainly assured.

Romans 5, verse 5: he that hath sound hope is assured. That I soundly hope I know, for I truly believe—which shews what the Doctors of the Romish Church are: though greatly learned, yet fearfully given over to delusion. For all true hope is grounded upon present faith, so that if a man's hope be sound, his faith is sound; and therefore the true believer may have assurance. A true Christian, he looks not on himself but upon Christ what he hath done for him, utterly disclaiming his own merits.

Now we have heard this great Doctor's reasons and confuted him by Scripture, let us hear the instances he brings out of Scripture to maintain doubting. There are three examples Bellarmine brings of holy and righteous men in Scripture, that, saith he, durst not stand upon assurance; where is then that man, saith he, that dare presume of his assurance?

The first is Job 27:6 where he saith, *my heart shall not reprove me all my days*; I have lived so as in the main I have had a care to please God; therefore, let my friends say what they will, I will never forsake my righteousness.

Now, saith Bellarmine, if a man can say thus and yet fear as he doth (Job 9:20), saying *if I would justify myself, my own mouth shall condemn me; if I would be perfect, he shall judge me wicked; though I were perfect, yet I know not my soul*, who then dares stand upon assurance? For answer hereunto we must understand and know that justification is double: first, from faith; secondly, from the fruits of faith: namely, that righteousness we receive by his grace. The imputative righteousness that is by faith in Christ, that Job there speaks not of; so that we go not about to free ourselves by our own righteousness, or anything that we can do, but by Christ. So that though he durst not justify himself in his own righteousness and integrity of life, yet did not this hinder from the assurance of his salvation before God in Christ: for Job 19:25-26, *I am sure, saith he, my redeemer liveth &c. whom I myself shall see, and mine eyes shall behold, and no other for me*. So that though he stood not upon the righteousness of works for himself, yet he was assured in Christ of eternal salvation.

The second example he brings is of David, Psalm 26:1, who saith, *Judge me, O Lord, for I have walked in mine innocency*, to show what a holy and righteous man he was; and yet, saith Bellarmine, for all that he doubts of his salvation, as appears Psal. 19:12, where he saith, *Lord, who can understand his errors? cleanse me from secret faults*. Now if he had secret sins that he feared might hinder him, how then could he have assurance?

We deny that. Because he that truly believes and repents, all his sins both secret and open are pardoned; known and unknown, he confesses and repents of all, and therefore they are forgiven. . . .

Ay, but he was afraid he might be blinded in them; and so he might doubt, saith he.

We deny not but he might fear; for we say none can be assured of salvation but he that fears to offend, as a good child fears to offend his father. Now his fear hinders not his father's love; fear of God's favor indeed may hinder assurance, but not fear to offend him; fear of sinning against God keeps him that his assurance is the stronger. The child of God that falls into sin when he casts off his fear and trembling lest he should offend against God, dashes and weakens the strength of his assurance; and the more a man fears to sin, the more it keeps him in the favor of God. . . .

. . .

Fourthly, Solomon. Bellarmine holds that he perished, yet he saith that he was a man beloved of God (2 Sam. 12:25).

Therefore, say we, he fell not totally and finally; he lost not all grace, because he had still so much grace as kept him from falling finally, as we may see by his book of repentance {Ecclesiastes}.

Fifthly, David. Bellarmine saith he fell totally.

But that is not so. He lost not all when he fell into sin, as appeareth Psalm 51:12. Though the operation of his faith ceased, yet lost he not the substance and habit thereof, for there was a spirit of prayer and repentance still left; he had a conflict within that made him so earnestly pray, *restore me to the joy of thy salvation, &c.*—where note, he prays not simply for salvation, for that he was assured of, but for the comfort of it; and his prayers, we know, were the prayers of faith, for they brought him joy and comfort. So that then he had not lost all his faith.

. . .

The use of this in the third place is for trial: namely that we should examine ourselves to find if we have this insulting and triumphing faith whereby we may be able to look up to God in the day of trial and hold out. If a man have base and counterfeit coin in his purse, he cannot abide to let it be tried; but if it be sound and good, he is not afraid to bring it to the touchstone. God in this case will take nothing for current but what hath his own stamp upon it. The word of God hath that in it that will try us. Let us therefore, every one, deal sincerely with our own hearts as in the sight and presence of Almighty God, that so we may know whether we have this blessed grace of faith or no. But before we come to this, let us consider these grounds.

First, that all that live under the Gospel have it not, though it be called the word of faith and be the very means to beget faith. For this, look 2 Thess. 3:2, where it is given as a reason why those that truly receive the Gospel are so reproached and hardly dealt withal by the world: even because all men have not faith; for if all had faith, then could all be of the same mind; and holiness, righteousness and love would be their delight.

Secondly, that this triumphing faith which upholds a man and opens his mouth to speak upon grounds of faith is so far from being a common gift to all that but few indeed have it. It is a special and peculiar grace that makes a man triumph over condemnation. That this was hard to be found, the Prophet complains in his days, Isa. 53:1, *Lord, who hath believed our report?* And that not among the heathen only, but even among the people of God.

The like complaint Christ takes up in the very words of the Prophet (John 12:38; Rom. 10:16). He admires at the paucity of true believers. So now the sound of the Gospel hath come to all of us, but who shews this faith of God's elect in them? This also we may see in the parable of the sower, wherein is set forth the estate of the visible Church, where there is but one sort of the four kinds of hearers that bring{s} forth this fruit. Three sorts come to hear: some but for fashion sake or compelled thereunto, some to get knowledge only, some to carp, scoff, or catch somewhat to run to rulers with or to judge that which shall judge them one day. This triumphing faith it ariseth from an immortal seed of God's word alone.

Thirdly, that though there be but few that have this faith, yet not the poorest and meanest of God's children, if they have any true hope of God's mercy, but in his time shall come to it: Act. 13:48, *As many as were ordained to eternal life believed.* Whosoever is God's child shall have this faith, and therefore (Titus 1:1) it is set out to be a peculiar grace and gift of God that only belongeth to the elect: Gal. 3:6, all are said by faith in Christ to be God's sons. John 10, our Savior shews, as none will, so none can believe but such as are God's sheep; that is, his elect, even those that are chosen in Christ to eternal life.

The fourth thing we are to consider as a matter to be believed is that those that have this faith that will save their souls, they may know they have it. Which is against Bellarmine's reasons of diffidence and doubting.

First, they may know it to themselves for their comfort, and next they may make it known to others by the fruits thereof: 1 Cor. 2:12, *That we may know*, saith the Apostle, *the things which are given us of God in Christ*, which is spoken in common to all that truly believe, and not only to any special person. The true believer hath such a light going along with his faith that he comes to know, though not perfectly, yet truly and infallibly, that God hath chosen, adopted, and sanctified him, &c. He takes hold of the promise of salvation upon God's commandment. . . . John 15:10, *he that believes in the Son of God hath the witness in himself.* So that thou needest not have others tell thee that thou dost believe, for if thou hast faith indeed, 'tis not so hid and buried in thy heart but that thou mayest know it.

Secondly, others also may know it as it manifests itself in the fruits. Rom. 1:8, their *faith was spoken of* far and near which was known by their wonderful change. They were become new creatures, such as were now of a holy life and conversation, for which Paul thanks God and desires to be with them to be comforted with their faith and his own.

Next to this, consider that this triumphing faith, wheresoever it is kindled, it will endure the trial, even the fire of God's spirit; it will endure also the fiery trial of affliction (1 Cor. 3:13). It is not a chaffy or counterfeit faith. That, all the troubles or temptations can blow away. But being begotten by the word, it pacifies the conscience and stablishes the heart in the blood of Christ, and purges the heart to make it fit for the Holy Ghost to dwell in. Also it works by love and makes a man not churlish and froward but loving, and that even to his very enemies, for Christ sake. Thy heart will tell thee thus much, and make thee say, I thank God I have this faith in me.

Lastly, seeing it is thus: namely, that it is the duty of all & everyone that lives under the Gospel to prove his heart and search it to the bottom: 2 Cor. 13:5, *examine your selves whether you be in the faith.* This shews that it is not a thing to be taken as granted that we have this faith, except we find that we have it indeed; but to search and try ourselves for it, because else we are in a great danger, even in the state of reprobates. Therefore examine thyself, and if thou hast it, bless God that ever thou wert born to be brought to such a blessed state wherein thou mayst thus triumph.

Now for the notes whereby thou mayest try thyself, they may be these.

The first is taken out of Rom. 8:15, *ye have not received the spirit of bondage to fear again, but the spirit of adoption whereby we cry Abba, Father.* Thou hast found thyself before to have been in an estate of bondage, as those believing Romans there who were accepted in an estate of fear and bondage under the curse of the Law and condemnation, even in despair of themselves; the spirit of bondage for that time shews us the Law that condemns us, and makes it to triumph over a man so long as it lasts. Try therefore if thou hast felt thy conscience set on thee and found thyself to be condemned for thy sins. Thus all God's children truly converted indeed have felt, though some more, some less, and lain under it some a longer, some a shorter time. If thy soul have drooped, been afraid to be utterly cast away, if thou hast found thyself in a lost estate, then is thy case good, for this goes always before that insulting faith that triumphs against all condemnation. If thou hast not found this, but hast gotten faith without it, then dost thou speak peace to thyself before God speaks it, and it is all one as if the Israelites should have looked up to the brazen serpent before they had been bitten with the fiery serpent in the wilderness—who had been never the better, not finding indeed the need thereof, as those that are stung and troubled with sin do. Many are driven to believe because they are convinced thereof in their judgment, and the example of others they think would shame them else. But that is not enough. Thou must find thyself thoroughly awakened for thy sins and feel thyself lying under the wrath of God and lost, as it were, in thyself, before thou canst truly see the need of a Savior and look up to him effectually.

Secondly, if thou hast obtained this absolving, quitting {acquitting}, and triumphing faith, then, after this spirit of bondage, thou hast found the spirit of adoption spoken of in the same place (Rom. 8:15); for before thou hast been bitten with thy sins, the devil, and thine own conscience, thou canst not receive any true comfort. But when thou once findest in thee nothing but matter of condemnation & art driven quite out of thyself, then the Spirit with the Gospel opens thy heart and enlargeth it to rejoice and draw stronger consolation from the Gospel than the Law could bring condemnation. So that if thou hast found the spirit of grace and comfort calming thy mind and purging thy conscience, and so sealing thy heart and giving thee some assurance that thy sins are forgiven thee, then is thy estate good. Assure thyself, nothing in the world could do this but the Spirit of God. . . .

Thirdly, if thou hast this faith, then art thou united unto Christ and hast fellowship with him; thou art then knit to Christ as a man to his wife in a marriage bond, for thou must know that Christ is the believer in a spiritual and mystical manner (Rom. 8:1). We first are in Christ—that is, when we once come to believe—and then Christ is in us (as it is vers. 10), when his death kills the body of sin in us. And John 17:21, 23, *I in them*, saith Christ, *and they in me*: which shew, as in divers other places in like manner, that there is then an union, which is an infallible note that floweth immediately from the grace of faith once begotten & wrought in any poor soul. . . . Let every one therefore examine if he have such a faith in him, by which he may know whether he find Christ in him or himself in Christ, and so a blessed fellowship between them; and this thou mayest know, if thou findest not the world and sin working and reigning in thee, but the spirit of Christ having the rule and dominion in thee. . . . O blessed man that hast this. O blessed habitation, to dwell in Christ, to be engrafted and have an happy being and fellowship with Christ.

This discovers abundance of false faith in most men in the world, that dream and think to be saved by Christ's death on the Cross, now ascended and being in heaven, &c. But if this be all, the wickedest heart in the world that knows of this may say as much; but here is the defense that cuts the thread: the sound believer hath further the spirit of Christ to kill sin in him; he hath also Christ's blood in him—that is, the worth and merit thereof—taking away the guilt of sin and purifying his conscience, which he finds by the peace of it. . . .

Fourthly, if thou hast this insulting and triumphing faith, then thou art a devoted and consecrated man to God and Christ, to serve God in righteousness and true holiness all thy days; hence all believers are said to be saints: that is, sanctified and set apart to God; dealing with worldly things, not with hearts set upon them, but using them as if they used them not, even with holy affections and hearts consecrated to God and Christ; hence also is it, that they are called temples to God, set apart to their Redeemer by baptism and profession. But do those that think they have this faith thus carry themselves? this belongs to every man and woman; we must not be devoted to the pleasures of this world, but keep our hearts as men devoted to God and Christ, even in our recreations. We must have a special care we destroy not this temple by prostrating ourselves to base lusts. Try thyself for this, and though none can do this as they should, yet are all to labor and endeavor it.

. . .

Sixthly, if a man have this, then is he the most forward unto and fruitfulness {*sic*} and abounding in good works above all others in the world. For this faith, it transplants and sets us (being by nature wild olives) into Christ the true vine, who is no barren root, but fruitful; 2 Cor. 9, this we may see in the believing Corinthians' charity he speaks of there, and in the woman that cast all that she had into the Treasury, and in Zaccheus that gave half his goods to the poor; faith opened his heart that before was niggardly; and so John 12, how did Mary pour out the ointment . . . so also Acts 2:4, they were now content all should be for Christ. Now these examples, with many more, are all set down for our learning and imitation, if we will find indeed such a faith as will save our souls another day.

. . .

A second impediment that keeps men from seeking this faith is a conceit that it is impossible ever to get it, and this sticks too much in our unbelieving hearts and is strongly rooted in our ignorant Protestants that give themselves to other books but not to the careful and conscionable reading of God's book, where there is nothing so beaten upon, both in Old and New Testament, as that we should trust in God and not upon ourselves; and that this, which belongs to every child of God that shall be saved, is no conceit of impossibility; but this faith belongs to every child of God. . . .

. . .

A fourth let or hindrance is a conceit that it is either needless, or at least not of such absolute necessity, but that a man may do well enough though he come not to such assurance and confidence in his faith as to insult and triumph therein. And this is a conceit that hinders those that are more forward in profession than others, and in the performing of some duties more careful, yet go not home to God so thoroughly as they should, but keep their souls aloof, as it were, from God. But without this faith it is impossible for them to know whether they be elect or reprobates, hypocrites or the true children of God indeed. And therefore let such know it is of absolute necessity: 2 Cor. 13:5, *know ye not that they* {*sic; lege ye*} *are in the faith*, saith the Apostle, *except ye be as reprobates?* Let not therefore any such conceit still possess thee; but seeing this faith is of absolute necessity, as the truth of God's word shews, pluck up thy heart and go to God for it.

A fifth impediment is a conceit that this is the only way to open a gap to all licentiousness. But who are they that say thus? surely none but atheists that fear neither God nor man, or else Papists that are blinded themselves and would blind others. Oh that such learned men as many of them be should be so grossly ignorant of God's truth. Indeed they that have not this faith may open a gap to all licentiousness, but no true believer that hath found this conquering and insulting faith; for he is the most fearful man of all other to commit sin; and before this a man never makes conscience of sin. . . . When this once comes, it opens his eyes and makes him pry into his own heart to see what a dunghill it is, and so makes him labor to cast out all his filthy affections and sinful lusts, and to endeavor after holiness and righteousness. So far is this from making a man licentious: for it is the very root from whence all holiness of heart and life flows; and therefore let no man suffer this conceit to hinder him from seeking this faith.

We shall be kept to the possession of that salvation we once believed and hoped for. If we could quite lose it again, then must there be something stronger than the power of God; but we know that cannot be, for God only hath power to consume all things from the earth in a moment with the breath of his nostrils; and therefore there is nothing above his power. O then in how blessed an estate are they above all the world whom the Lord hath pleased to set in such an estate as once to be assured of this faith and walk in it? . . .

Now come we to consider the means which God hath appointed to work this faith and increase it in ourselves: which be indeed abundant, but the main means of all is the lifting up of the standard, the preaching of the Gospel of Jesus Christ. . . . It is that which opens the heart and so lets in Christ, who by his spirit doth enable us from an inward light and power to say, *Lord, I believe*, and therefore am assured of my salvation. . . . and is no conceit or bare imagination gotten by contemplation, but a settled persuasion arising from God's word, even the root of all good works that can possibly be accepted in God's sight.

And the first means whereby to come to such a faith is to see, consider, and take to heart what estate we are in without believing in Christ. . . .

. . .

A second means is when a man . . . resolveth to cast away that sin he sees in himself. A man may come to consider his estate deeply and yet go on in wicked courses. But when he can desire with all his heart to be rid of all his sin and cast it off, it is a special means and a further step to this faith, at least to the manifestation of it to us. Repent and believe is the voice of the Gospel. No man can believe except he repent and cast off sin; so no man can repent except he believe and have some hope that his sins may be pardoned. Many see their sins yet cast them not away, and therefore the conscience beats them off and will not let them believe. It tells them that Christ and such a soul cannot stand together. . . . So that the soul hath a second step to believe when a man truly repents of all his sins (2 Cor. 6:17, 18). Then God offers himself as a father to a man when he casts off such as are limbs, as it were, of Satan and of the fellowship of darkness: that is when a man casts off his evil company and all sin that may defile his soul and make him unworthy to be God's child. And therefore when a man casts off sin and the instruments of sin, then is he fit to believe, and God will be ready to shew himself unto him not a judge but a father (Rev 3:19). . . .

A third means is when a man renounces as well his own righteousness as his sins. It is Christ's righteousness that must make us righteous before God; that is our justification to eternal life. There is (to say the truth) no righteousness before a man comes to be in Christ—only 'tis call'd an outward righteousness, and is so taken before men. And therefore, if thou wilt come to this faith, thou must cast off all, not conceit of righteousness, but thine own righteousness indeed, for that cannot further thee in this point, as thine own sins cannot hinder thee. What hindered the Jews and Papists, and thousands of Protestants at this day, from faith that should uphold their souls but a conceit of their own righteousness? . . . We lost all in Adam and recover all again in Christ. Many ignorant Protestants, and some that have knowledge also, will not stick to say that if a man have a good meaning, dealing righteously and serving God, he shall be accepted—all which is nothing without Christ.[6] For the more a man goes on in good intentions before he be in Christ by faith, all his performances are but cursed abominations and so further off from

---

[6] {For a similarly dismissive assessment of such "ignorant Protestants," see Arthur Dent's massively influential *Plaine mans path-way to heaven* (London, 1601), 27. On the widespread resistance to the rigors of godly religion, see Christopher Haigh, *Pathways to heaven* (Oxford UP, 2007), 79–82, 206, and his *English Reformations* (Oxford UP, 1993), 281, 286.}

faith, and that which God hath most severely punished, as he did Saul his good intention without obedience unto him.[7]

But may some say, if it be so, then it is better to sin and not do good works at all.

Not so, for then thou increasest thy punishment. Thy sin is the less if thou hast a good meaning, because thou thinkest that thou doest that which is good. If thou knewest and thoughtest otherwise, thy condemnation should be the deeper. Yet know this, till thou art in Christ, all is abominable before God, and but lost labor. . . . So must we cast away all our own righteousness and goodness, and fetch all from God, and serve God according to his will and not after our own phantasies or the prescripts of man, dealing also truly with everyone we have to do withal. 'Tis not our own righteousness, but the relying on it, that hinders and keeps a man from faith, without which all is but abominable; even our eating, drinking, and whatsoever we do is odious before God until we come to get this true faith, to triumph over condemnation. A man when he is naked in himself is then the fitter to be clothed with Christ's robe; every thing is then sweet to him, and so he comes to desire and say, *come, Lord Jesus.*

A fourth means is a poor spirit and beggarly; that is, such a one as hath neither comfort within nor without; when nothing will now so comfort him as the thinking of his present estate will humble him. And this will make a man poor indeed, though he be never so rich, and bring him with David to say, *I am poor and needy, Lord help me* (Psal. 70:5). This will let him see that he is a poor lazar, begging at the gates of God, who is rich in mercy. And it is a further degree to bring him to Christ, and make Christ to enrich him. That which hinders many from coming to Christ is that they are full enough; these, whatsoever they say in words, they indeed cast off Christ's righteousness because their spirits are not cast down to beg at God's hand—if they have children, honor, wealth and professions. Tell them of condemnation; they are proud, and think themselves well enough; they will tell you that they hope to be saved as well as the best. But let such know, *all fullness dwells in Christ,* none at all in us, in the matter of salvation. Get Christ first to reign in thee, that thou mayst after come to reign with him in glory.

A fifth means is the fair, free, large, and great offer of grace made in the Gospel. . . . John 3:16, *God so loved the world,* &c. Here is a means to bring thee to believe indeed: a strange thing that the judge and party offended should thus offer, to every soul to whom the Gospel comes, his Son. That God himself should offer a pardon, who would not strive with himself and sigh and groan, yea even burst his heart in pieces to believe? This is one of the specialest means of all to bring a man to believe: that God himself, the party offended, should come and say, here is my Son, take him unto thee. Labor therefore to get him, lay fast hold on him, and he will bless and comfort thee forever. If thou dost open thy heart and let him in, he offers his Son to thee to believe in. And why? Is it because thou art such a beautiful and great person? &c. No, it comes from the love of his own heart, and therefore it is free. As thy righteousness cannot further it, so thy sins cannot hinder it, if thou lay but hold on it. The offer is not only to noble, rich, young, &c., but to all; whosoever believes, though never so mean, poor, old, may take him, go away with him,

---

[7] {Behind this is one of the most contentious Reformed theses, and one of the most often handled in the Oxford commencement disputations: whether, without faith, all acts, however seemingly good, are sins. See Shuger, "St. Mary the Virgin and the birth of the public sphere," *HLQ* 72.3 (2009): 13.}

and live with him forever. Many think they should have something of their own. No, God looks at his own love, and so do thou, that his love, mercy, & grace may be magnified in thee. Let us therefore stir up ourselves and look and seek to God. He will give his Spirit to all his at one time or another.

A sixth means is to know that there is not only a free offer, but also a commandment to enjoin us not to refuse and neglect God's offer that is the greatest blessing that can be: to have him come unto thee, to reign over thee, and subdue thy sin. It is the Spirit of God that would draw thy heart to believe; open therefore and receive it. Consider for this 1 Joh. 3:23, *This is his commandment that we should believe on the name of his Son Jesus Christ.* . . . God commands thee to believe, and therefore it is not indifferent whether thou hast it or no, or to think only that thou hast it. And this is a further means, and that which leaves us without all excuse if we obey not. A man oft times will do a thing upon command that else he would not do.

A seventh means is to remember the fearful threatenings: John 3:18, he that believeth not is condemned, because he hath not believed in the name of the only begotten Son of God. . . . Now to encourage thee hereunto, know this, that God hath promised that, though thou canst not do it, yet if thou seek to him, he will help thee. Go to God therefore upon his promise, if thou wouldst not have thy portion with the condemned devils. He that will not believe hath nothing to uphold him against the guilt of conscience, than the which there needs no more. He that hath the wrath of an infinite God to wrestle withal cannot but be condemned; the care of this therefore ought to be above all other care for wife, children, or any thing else in the world whatsoever.

But you are very strict and hard, may some possibly say.

If thou think strange of this, think strange of God, for here is nothing spoken but from God.

An eighth and a chief means is the word preached: Rom. 10:17, *faith cometh by hearing, and hearing by the word of God.* Therefore be careful to come as thou oughtest to the word, and bring others under the sound of the Gospel which is the word of faith. Submit thyself to it, and God will not fail thee. This do, and it shall come, it will come, yea it must needs come, because God is faithful and unchangeable. Stumble not therefore at anything that is said by the faithful ministers of God's word; if any weakness pass, bear with it, and take all in the best part. If thou get this faith, thou shalt eat and drink and sleep and trade and live in the world with more comfort than ever thou didst, and after live with the Lord Jesus forever.

The last means is prayer, which serveth as bellows to blow up all. Pray that thou mayest see, consider, and take to heart thy woeful and lamentable estate by nature; then will thy sighs and groans be strong and powerful with God. Pray withal that God will be pleased to humble thee and enable thee to do all as aforesaid. To stir thee up to this, lay thine ear and hear how the damned souls in hell that neglected and refused grace do roar, yell, and howl; that now would give worlds, if they had them, to enjoy the time that the Lord affords thee to repent in. Consider these things wisely, and the Lord give thee understanding in all things.

‡

Self-Seeking Opposite to Christ's Interest

For all men seek their own, and not the things that are Jesus Christ's.
Philip. 2:21

The occasion of these words you shall see in the two verses going before them. The Apostle tells the Philippians to whom he wrote that he would send Timothy to them, which (saith he) will be much for your advantage; and he gives them this reason of it: for, saith he in the words before, he will be very diligent to do you any good, to take care of your matters, which he sets out comparatively: saith he, *I have no man like minded, who will naturally, or faithfully, take care to your things.* Now he gives a reason why he saith he had no man like minded to Timothy that would faithfully and naturally take care for their matters: for, saith he, this is the condition of men, this I have found by experience, *every man seeks his own things and not the things of Jesus Christ.*

. . .

The words are so plain that I need not to analyze, or open them, or stand long upon the exposition. These three things, you shall see, may very easily be observed out of them.

First, whereas the Apostle complains of it as a great fault and a sin that men seek their own things and not the things of Jesus Christ, one conclusion hence then is that *it is every man's duty, or every man ought, to seek the things of Jesus Christ and not his own.*

. . .

. . . There is scarce any man but seeks his own things; therefore you need not wonder why all the world is ready to go in a wrong way; a man in this business hath so few to keep him company. It is a thing that always hath been: every man is apt to seek his own things. Therefore let not a man be discouraged with it; it is no more than hath been; it is no more than you are to look for: for the most seek themselves and their own things. Those that will seek the things of Jesus Christ, the world accounts them busybodies because they are occupied about things that the world likes not of. It hath been the custom of all times to seek their own things, and it is in every man's nature thus to do. He that doth best and doth deny himself, yet he hath the same nature with the rest. So then that is the second observation, that every man doth it, he seeks his own things.

And lastly from this opposition—every man seeks his own things and not the things of Jesus Christ—there is this third conclusion: that for the most part our own things and the things that tend to Jesus Christ and his advantage, they are contrary and opposite one to the other. For our natures are contrary; there is an enmity between Christ and us; that which we do for Christ must needs be contrary to ourselves; that which is for the advantage of Christ, for the most part is for our disadvantage. And the reason is, I say, because of the contrariety between our natures and the nature of Jesus Christ and his ways. Now we will begin with the first, that

It is the duty of every man not to seek his own things, but the things of Jesus Christ. . . .

There is this reason from yourselves why you should seek the things of Jesus Christ: because God hath commanded you so to do. You know this is the command, *Thou shalt love the Lord above all and thy neighbor as thyself.* Christ is to be loved above all, above yourselves. Now for the most part when we hear such a command as this, we look upon it as a legal precept which only shews a man his sin, and to be as a schoolmaster, a precept that no man can keep. But you must know that it is not so: for every command is to be kept by every regenerate man. It is said that *not the least tittle of the Law shall perish; heaven and earth shall pass away first.* The meaning is not that no man can be saved, nor no man is in Christ but he that keeps every jot and tittle of the Law, but we must endeavor to keep even the very least tittle of God's commands with all our might.

If God will not suffer the least command to pass, but you must bend yourselves with all your strength to keep it, then this which is a main command, to *love God above all*, you must think you are bound to keep it; and every regenerate man doth keep it in some measure: he keeps it in sincerity and truth with an upright heart, though he cannot rise to that degree and height as he should do.

Now, I say, it is not only a command, but it is best for every man to deny himself and not to seek his own things, partly because his good is contained in God more than in himself; and so he shall provide better for himself in self-denial, by seeking God, than by looking directly to his own matters. . . . Mark it, the commands of God are given for our advantage. Whensoever a man is a loser by keeping any command, though it appear so, he is not so indeed, for every command is for our wealth. So I say it is best for us partly because our good is contained in God.

And partly also because God is the end of every creature. Now you know the perfection of every creature stands in obtaining its end. Whatsoever the end of anything is, when it hath gotten that end, it is brought into a perfect condition. For there are certain rules that God hath given to every creature to walk by to attain its end, that in attaining thereof it might attain perfection; so he hath given to the fire and to the water, *&c.* When they kept close to that rule there is the perfection of them. So he hath given a rule to the reasonable creatures to walk by: that is, to walk in his commands. Now in keeping close to them, that creature attains his happiness, he puts himself into a happy condition. Now God is not bound to this, because he is the utmost end, the utmost cause; there is nothing beyond him, and therefore he may do all for himself. But if the creature do all things for himself, he destroys himself, because there is a cause, an end, beyond him. Now as there is this reason for the duty why we should do it: in regard of ourselves.

So also in regard of Christ—partly in respect of his love and goodness he hath already shewed to us. You know when a man hath done much for one, he hath reason to respect him. When Christ hath done so much for us, if there were nothing to come, there is reason and justice and equity to seek him, to do whatsoever may be for his advantage, that we should seek not our own things but the things of Jesus Christ. And partly also why we should seek the things of Jesus Christ is in regard of the wages which are to come: they are so large that he is not worthy to have them, he is not worthy to be saved by him, that will not do something for him, that will not deny himself and neglect his own things for his sake. So you see what reason there is for this duty why we should do {it}.

Now to make use of it: if this be a duty that lies upon every man, not to seek his own things but the things of Jesus Christ, what remains but that you consider how you have kept this; and if you be failing in it, that you stir up yourselves to do it in a better manner than you have done formerly. Let every man therefore ask this question with himself: have I sought the things of Jesus Christ? have I not many times sat still for my own ease, for my own safety, for my credit and profit, when if I had stirred I might have done something for the advantage of Jesus Christ? And consider that our behaving of ourselves after this manner is not only sinful, but it is very unreasonable and disadvantageous for ourselves: for the more we lose for Christ, the more we gain; he that will be content to be nobody in the flesh, he shall be the more in the spirit. For that rule holds true, *he that will lose his life shall save it.* I say it holds true in everything else: he that will lose his credit, shall gain his credit; he that will be content to let go his friends or profits or advantages, he shall be a gainer by it. So that he that is most prodigal of all these things to spend them for Christ's advantage, he that is most forward to suffer imprisonment and loss of goods, to endure infamy and disgrace for Christ's sake, he is the wisest man, the happiest man; he provides best for himself.

For alas (my brethren), *what is it that we have of all our labors under the sun?* but only the riches of good works; those only go with us. . . .

All other things that you have in this life are of a contingent nature; but your good works, the things you do for God, your seeking after the things of Christ, they are of a sure nature and will not fail you. Therefore let us consider what we do in this case, when we come to any business wherein we are to deny ourselves, and let us think thus with ourselves: what are these things that I call mine own? The truth is, there is no man that hath any thing that is his own; therefore, when there is an occasion offered you to speak anything, you ought to say, this is not my credit, this is not my wealth, this is not my strength, these are not my friends, this is not my estate, but they are the Lord's; and shall I withhold them from him when he stands in need of them? This is to rob God of his due; it is sacrilege. This consideration will make a man think that it is reasonable for him to do it: when he considers that it is none of his, but it is God's.

. . .

But you will say, what are these things of Jesus Christ which I ought to seek?

I answer, that you may know it distinctly, the meaning of it is this . . . when any matter of your own, any advantage of your own, anything that tends to your own profit or credit shall come in competition with anything that is Christ's, now to let that go: this is to seek his things, and not your own.

. . .

But the chief thing to be considered is, what it is to seek? for in the duty there are but two things; the *object*, the things you are to seek; and the *act*, what it is to seek. To seek a man's own things, or the things that are Jesus Christ's, that is to do it with all intention, to do it with all earnestness; so the word signifieth: to do things as a man would do them for himself. . . . So to seek the things of Jesus Christ is to do them after that manner, and that consists in these three things:

	1.	Willingly
To do it	2.	Diligently
	3.	Faithfully

First, a man must do it willingly. As you know, when a man hath anything to do for himself, he doth it with willingness. This the Lord requires at our hands: to be willing to do them, which is much more than to do them. . . . It is a greater matter to do things with an inward willingness and an inward propenseness of mind than to do the things themselves.

Therefore that condition is required; Jude 3, we are exhorted to *contend earnestly*; that is, that you do it with much intention of mind; to contend earnestly, as a man that is in an argument contendeth, or as a man that is wrestling; after this manner you must contend for the common faith. For you must know that it is not enough for a man simply to do a thing, but he must do it with such an intention as is required. . . . An example of this we have in the Apostle Paul (2 Cor. 11:18); you shall there have an expression of his own mind in taking care for the things of Jesus Christ: *I am cumbred daily* (saith he) *and have the care of all the Churches.* The word in the original is, it lies upon me as a continual burden. It is not a thing that I take up now and then by fits, but it is a thing that lies upon me always. . . . And then he saith, *who is offended, and I burn not?* that is, when there is any disadvantage to the Church, when I see any man stumble, it is not a thing that I look lightly upon, but I take it to heart, I am burned with grief; that is, it takes a deep impression in me. Therefore you must not think when you come to do anything for Jesus Christ to do it as of necessity; but you must think and plot with yourselves as about your own business; you must seek for occasions; and when you see a door opened, to go in at it; for to have abilities and not to use them, to have opportunities and not to employ them, it is another manner of matter than we think it is: for not only thorns and briars, but unfruitful trees are appointed for burning; and cowardliness in doing duties deserves a curse as well as the not doing them. . . .

. . .

And again, it requires not only that you put all your strength to it, but that you be constant in doing it; for if a man hold not out, this man is not diligent but negligent. It is a usual thing for men in doing the Lord's business to be weary in well-doing, to give over well-doing; therefore you must add that also to it, that if you will do it diligently, you must do it constantly. . . .

Thirdly and lastly, as to do it willingly and diligently, so to do it faithfully. Many a man may be willing to do something for Christ, and to be diligent too for the time; but to do it faithfully—that is, without any respect to himself, not for his own ends, but to do it for the Lord and for his sake—that is that which is required. . . . So that for a man when he comes to do the things of Jesus Christ to have an eye to himself, to be considering what will make for my advantage, what profit shall I have by it? and so to be put on by that motive, this is to do the work of Christ unfaithfully. And herein our hearts for the most part are exceeding deceitful; when we have to do any thing for Christ, the flesh in us is ready to have the first and the chief hand in any such business: that is, self-respects and self-aims are ready to mingle themselves with the best actions we do, unless we have a narrow eye to them.

You know Jehu did the work of the Lord very diligently, but not faithfully, for his zeal was not for the Lord, but for himself.[8] They that followed Christ, many of them followed him far; but it was not for him, but for the loaves, because they were fed with them and *were filled.* . . . So I say, a man may do the things of Christ diligently, and yet not faithfully. Two servants may both be very diligent in their master's work, and yet there may be a broad difference between them: the one hath indeed an eye to his master's profit, the other to his own.

[8] {2 Kgs. 9–10}

This is all in all therefore to consider whether the talents that we use, we use them for our Master's advantage or our own. Thou mayst do very much, thou mayst use thy talent as diligently as any man; yet if thou examine thy heart and deal strictly with thyself, thou mayst find that these are used for thyself and not for thy Master, which is the greatest folly in the world. For, my brethren, what do we gain when we take a great deal of pains for Christ? surely there is nothing ours but the sincerity we do it withal. It is for other men's advantage, the most glorious and specious works we perform. The greater they are, the more may be the profit and benefit of the Church by them; but there is nothing thine own but thy faithfulness and sincerity in doing them.

Therefore consider this, whether when we do any thing for Christ, we do it faithfully or no, for in this our hearts are apt to deceive us. How many are there that pass {care} not much for the doing of the thing, so themselves may have their end? Diotrophes was willing to work with the Apostle, but it was to have the preeminence.[9] How many great actions are overthrown for want of this faithfulness: that men do not simply do that which they do, but out of contention and vainglory they do it? How many great actions, I say, are overthrown? So that when two men are both of them alike set to do a thing, both are willing to do the work, yet because one may not have the praise of it, the glory of it, because he may not be first and chief in the business, therefore he lets it go.

I cannot better compare it than to two men that are to carry a beam in at a narrow door. Both would be first in, and when they do so, we see they carry it across and in a thwart manner and so they cannot do it. If one would be first and another second, it might be done with ease. So when the business of Christ is to be done, we go crossly about it, and the work is left undone because every one seeks for his own particular preeminence.

But, you will say, if it be a thing wherein the heart is so exceeding deceitful, how shall I find whether I do that I do faithfully with a single sincere heart or no?

Consider what thou doest when thy own case and Christ's are severed: if thou find that when thy own credit and profit and advantage is involved in Christ's business, then thou art willing and forward in the work of Christ, and not otherwise, thou mayest suspect thyself. When one servant follows two masters that go before, while they go together it is difficult to know to whom he belongs, but when they part, you know who the master is by the servant's following of him. . . . Moreover consider what thou doest when thou hast to do with people that are ill deserving: for if thou do what thou doest for Christ, though men do not answer thy pains but carry themselves in a contrary manner to thee, yet if it be done for Christ, thou wilt continue to do it. That was the trial of Saint Paul's faithfulness, when the Jews set themselves against him and would have pulled him in pieces, yet he continued in the same faithfulness in his service of Christ and the Church.

If you shall give over because men use you ill, it is an argument that you did what you did not simply for Christ. If you do what you do to get the love and credit and applause of men, when you miss of that, you will then give over, and that is a sign of insincerity.

. . .

But you will say, this is a hard and difficult thing for a man to seek the things of Jesus Christ after this manner. Who is able thus to do them? so to do them in sincerity and with diligence and faithfulness as not to mingle any self-respect or aim at his own ends?

---

[9] {3 John 1:9}

I answer, it is true; and the holiest men that are have some such tincture in their best actions, but they are not to be discouraged, so it be not the chief; but they are to be humbled and to strive against it. And this use (by the way) you may make of it: that a man may see how little cause he hath to be puffed up or to be conceited for his best actions if he consider how unfaithfully he hath done them, how unwillingly, how negligently. But, I say, though these things be in us, we are not to think that the things we do are presently done in hypocrisy. The thing that we are to look to is that those aims and respects to ourselves that are mingled with our best actions do not prevail, that we do not allow them in ourselves.

But, you will say, how shall we bring our hearts to this, not to seek our own things but the things of Jesus Christ?

In a word, this you must do, you must give your own selves to Christ; when a man hath once given himself to Christ, he will be ready to give all that is his. . . . Therefore no natural man can do it because he makes himself the end; he sets himself up for his end because he hath not given himself to Christ. But a regenerate man is able to give all to Christ because he hath already given himself to Christ.

But, you will say, what is it to give a man's self to Christ?

When a man is persuaded of this, that Christ will take care of him and provide better for him than he can himself, he is willing to submit to Christ and give himself to Christ. A man will never go off of his own bottom till he be assured of a better foundation.

And partly also it is done by changing a man's opinion of himself, for every unregenerate man hath a different opinion of himself to that which he hath when he is regenerate. One man thinks that that which consists in his private and outward happiness and safety, and therefore his profit or credit, or whatsoever may make up that, that he reckons himself and that he will build upon. But when a man is in Christ his opinion is changed: there is a new part, a regenerate part in him, and where that is in a man, that he reckons to be himself. What a man hath an opinion to be himself, whatsoever makes up that self, that he will draw to himself. When a man reckons the regenerate part to be himself, he is willing to be a loser by all other things, so that that self may be a gainer, because he knows that all this while {he} is no loser in himself so long as he grows in grace and keeps a good conscience. So long as he knows and is persuaded that God will take care of him far better than himself can do, so long the building up of himself goes forward, and he takes care for nothing else besides. This is for a man to give up himself to Christ.

. . .

Now when a man seeks his own things, it is natural for a man, and that a man doth easily; but to seek the things of Jesus Christ, that is above nature, and then there must be much intention;[10] a man must have something in him to move him to mind it most and above all other things. When a boat goes against the stream and against the wind, you know there must be much labor to drive it on. So, to seek the things of Christ, it being above the stream of nature, there must be an intention from above; you must beseech God to keep it in the intention of your hearts.

Now again to these two—when a man hath given up himself to Christ, and when he doth mind it and intend it and pray for it—you must add to this faith, without which no

---

[10] {effort, mental application, volition}

man can do it. For this objection presently cometh: what, must I seek the things of Jesus Christ and not mine own? what will then become of me? how shall I provide for myself, or for my family and those that depend upon me? Now there must be faith to give this answer: the Lord will provide for thee. For till a man think that there is another that hath will and power to take care for him and to provide for him, it is impossible that he should seek the things of that other; but believe this once, that God will take care for thee, and then thou wilt be content to deny thyself. As if a master should say to his servant, be you diligent in my service; I will take care for your meat and drink and clothing, and when your apprenticeship is out, I will give you sufficient to live upon. If the servant believe this, he will be willing to neglect all other things and to seek his master's profit and to intend his master's business. So here we should seek the things of Jesus Christ, for, saith he, I will provide for you; I will take care for you; you shall want nothing in this present life; you shall have all things necessary, and when your apprenticeship is at an end, I will provide an inheritance for you. If you will believe these things and these promises, you will then seek the things of Jesus Christ, and not your own things.

. . .

Now fourthly, we must add to our faith, love; for love enableth a man to seek the things of Jesus Christ. Therefore, 1 Cor. 13, it is said that *love seeketh not her own things.* If you would bring your hearts not to seek your own things but the things of Christ, get love. That is, you must know that self-love seeks its own things . . . but the love of another makes a man seek the things of another; it makes a man bountiful: as Saint Paul saith, *I am ready to be bestowed for your sakes.* And therefore you have that saying that *love edifieth*; that is, it makes the magistrate to take care for the good of the people, the minister for his charge, &c.

The mother and the nurse, where they love, you see what pains they take, what neglect they express of themselves and all, that they may do good to the child: for that is the nature of love. And therefore, when we do not seek the things of Christ, it is an argument that we want the love of Christ and the love of God. You see the Apostle Paul, 2 Cor. 5, he gives this reason why he sought the things of Christ with the neglect of himself: *The love of Christ constraineth me.* . . . Now how came he to this love of Christ? *why thus we judge* (saith he) *that if Christ died for us, &c.* So that if you would bring your hearts not to seek your own things but the things of Jesus Christ, you must labor to have your hearts enflamed with the love of Christ, and that you may do so, use the means that Saint Paul layeth down: he died for me, he is worthy of it, he deserves it of me, he hath done this and this for me; therefore there is reason I should no longer live to myself; therefore there is reason I should seek his things, that I should do his work. Thus to stir up our hearts to love the Lord Jesus is the means to prepare us to seek him. And so you see the business we have to do: we are to seek the things of the Lord Jesus willingly, diligently, and faithfully. And also what it is that prepares and disposeth the heart so to do:

First, to give up ourselves to Christ.
Secondly, to labor to have it kept in the purpose of our hearts.
Thirdly, to have faith in the promises and providence of God.
Lastly, to have love to the Lord Jesus. And so much for this point, and for this time.

‡

Free Grace Magnified

Let him that is a thirst come; and whosoever will, let him take of the waters of life freely.
Revel. 22:17

. . .

The point we will deliver is not a point of controversy, which we rather decline, but a point of singular and great comfort, and that is that glorious Gospel which Paul did so much magnify, that mystery the angels did so much labor to pry into, that secret that was so much kept from the Jews and revealed in due time to the gentiles: and that is the offer of Christ to all men in the world that would take him, without all exceptions of persons or sins. God doth not only or merely offer Christ, but he sendeth out his ministers and ambassadors *beseeching* us to be *reconciled*; he doth not only tell us that there is a marriage of his Son, and that whosoever will come may come, but he sendeth messengers to beseech and to use an holy violence and earnest persuasion; yea, and not only thus, but he commandeth men and chargeth them upon their allegiance to come, *this is his commandment*, saith the Apostle, *that ye believe on him whom he hath sent.* Yea, he chargeth us upon death and damnation to come: *If you believe you shall be saved. If you believe not you shall not be damned.*

The first reason of this is because God would not have the death of his Son to be of none effect; he would not have the blood of his Son spilt in vain; and therefore he doth not make a bare offer of Christ, but he beseecheth and compelleth men to come and believe on him. . . .

The second reason is to shew forth the riches of God's mercy and the abundance of his love to mankind; the same motives he had to give Christ, the same motives he hath to entreat men to believe: and this is his love, and this he sheweth to the elect, that they might know the greatness and largeness of his love to them; and to the wicked, that the glory of his justice might appear in their damnation when they shall see that they have displeased and despised so gracious an offer.

The third reason is because it is acceptable to God that the Gospel should be obeyed: that is, that men should believe that they might live and not die. And therefore he saith he desireth not the death of a sinner, and so are many speeches scattered in the Scripture: *Oh that my people would hearken, why will ye die O ye house of Israel?* These and many more sheweth that it is a thing very pleasing to God that men should not perish, but that they come in and believe and live for ever.

But here may objections arise, for when you hear that it is a thing pleasing to God that all men should believe, here it may be objected: how can these two stand together, that God desires that men should believe and live, and he it is that must give them ability to believe, and yet doth not; he hath it in his power to make them to believe and yet will not, notwithstanding he expresseth in the forenamed places of Scripture such an earnest desire to have men live and not die?

To this I answer that the scope of all places in Scripture is to shew that if men will come in, there shall be no impedient upon God's part; and they shew that he is full of mercy and compassion; the fault shall be in their own stubbornness and contempt. And these declare that it is more acceptable to God to save them than to condemn them, and that he is full of mercy and ready to forgive, that he hath such a disposition as was in the father of the Prodigal. This, I say, is the main scope of those and such like places of Scripture. But there is a double consideration of the will of God: it is either simply considered, and so to believe and repent and obey, all these are pleasing to him. . . . but then there is a secret will of God by which he dispenseth to man an ability to believe, and this he giveth to some and not to others for reasons best known to himself;[11] and in this consideration all those places of Scripture are to be taken and considered: that *he will have mercy on whom he will, and whom he will he hardeneth*, and that *it is not in him that runneth, but in God that sheweth mercy*. So that according to the first consideration we must understand that it is acceptable to God to have men to believe.

It may be objected: is it possible that the same will should be carried upon the same object in different respects, as if God should will the damnation and salvation of Judas both at one time?

To this I answer that it is most possible for a man to will and nill one and the same thing upon the same object if it be in different respects; as for example, a man may will his friend's departure from him and yet not will it; he wills his departure out of a desire he hath of his friend's good, and yet will{s} it not out of a love he hath of his friend's company. And so God here, he willeth that all men should be saved, and therefore he beseecheth men to believe because it is agreeing to him, and it is so; neither can it be otherwise because of the conformity the thing itself hath with his will; yet he will not use all means to bring this to pass. A father will not have his son drunk; if he will tie him up in a chamber, he will not be drunk; yet he will not take such a course, though he hath a will his son should not be drunk. So God, though he do will that men should believe and repent and be saved, yet he will not be said to use all means for the effecting of it in all men because he will glorify his justice as well his as mercy.

It may be here objected that when God offereth Christ to all, and beseecheth them and persuadeth them, and commandeth men to come in and believe, and yet knoweth beforehand that man of himself hath no ability to believe, it may seem that God hath some collusion and deceit in this, in that notwithstanding he knoweth men cannot believe of themselves, yet he offereth Christ and persuadeth and commandeth men to lay hold on him by faith.[12]

To this I answer, first, that God may seriously offer and give a thing, and yet know aforehand that the party to whom it is offered will not receive it out of the stubbornness and refractoriness of his own will. A prince may offer and give a pardon to a rebel, and yet know aforehand that the rebel, to whom it is offered, out of pride and contempt will not receive it. So, I say, when God offereth Christ, he offereth him in good earnest; here is no deceit; what he promiseth, he will perform; he offereth him to the reprobate. To this I will add two similitudes: the one by St. Ambrose on those words, *the sun shineth upon the just and unjust*: now (saith he) if any, but of neglect or carelessness of it, hides himself in a place to keep the sun off from him, the fault is not in the sun but in him. And another useth this similitude: the death of Christ is like a medicine that hath efficacy enough to heal all mankind, if they will apply it; now if men will not take it and

[11] {See Hoard <749> for the Arminian critique of this distinction.}
[12] {Prynne's *God no impostor* <*infra*> deals with this objection at length.}

receive it, it is not out of a defect in the thing itself but out of the contempt and stubbornness of their own will.

It may be further objected here: God doth command and beseech men to believe and to be saved, which seemeth to be an unreasonable thing when as it is impossible for them to do so of themselves—as if a man should beseech & command a man to escape out of prison when he is enthralled and bound with chains, or for a man to command or entreat a man to come out of a well when it is so deep that he cannot.

To this I answer, first, that there is an end in speaking to a man in spiritual bonds, to desire and command him to escape, for the very words do put life into such a man; such is the word we preach: it hath power going along with it to put life into those that hear it; as Christ when he spake to the sick man to arise, it was to some purpose. Such, I say, is the word we do preach.

Secondly, I answer that these similitudes hold not because it is very difficult to exhort and command a man to do a thing when there is an extreme {*sic*; *lege* external} impediment, as it is with a man in a well and in prison. But that is not the case here, for if a man hath but the will to come to Christ, there is no external impediment; and therefore if we exhort and command men to come to Christ, and they come not, we cannot only say that they cannot come, but rather that they will not come; here then is reason enough for our exhortations in this kind.

It may be objected that men cannot will to come; there is an impossibility, though no external impediment, because they cannot will.[13]

To this I answer, first, that it is false that men cannot will. In two cases indeed it is true: either when the thing is not revealed to a man . . . and therefore those that never heard of Christ cannot will Christ, and therefore they shall not be condemned for not receiving of Christ. Secondly, if the thing be revealed to a man, yet if it be revealed as a thing impossible, in this case also a man cannot will; it is against the order of nature for a man to will that which he conceiveth to be impossible to be attained; for he must look upon it as a thing possible to be had afore it can be said that he can will it. But Christ is revealed to men in the Church, and so propounded not as a thing impossible, but as a thing possible. Now it cannot be said only that they cannot will, but that they will not will; and therefore when as men complain that it is impossible to will, here is the glory of God's justice made manifest, because there is a freedom in the manner of refusing: they might have had Christ if they would.

It is objected that the covenant that is made by God seemeth to be made with the elect only, and therefore the condition belongeth only to them. How can Christ belong to all, seeing the exhortation and commandment must not exceed the covenant, for the benefit is propounded to the elect, and the condition to be required of none but of such as are within the covenant?

To this I answer that there is a covenant of grace, and that is double: either a general covenant propounded without exception: *Let whosoever will come and believe in Christ, he shall be saved*; here is none excluded, and that none are excluded out of this general covenant this reason will shew. Baptism, the seal of the covenant, is to be administered to all within the Church—to infants though afterwards they do not actually and visibly

---

[13] {For the Arminian response to Preston's argument here, see Hoard <744–45>.}

believe. Now God would not appoint that the seal of the covenant should be given to those to whom it doth not generally belong. But secondly, there is another covenant of grace which belongeth peculiarly to the elect: for in this God doth not only promise to give salvation if men believe, but he promiseth to give them ability to believe, as may be seen, Jer. 31:33, Ezekiel 36. In the first place, God promiseth that he will *put his law in their inward parts*, and that *they shall not teach any more every man his neighbor, but they shall all know me from the least to the greatest*, and so the like in other places where God promiseth the thing and ability of performing of it, which belongeth only to the elect, But the other general covenant belongeth to all without exception.

Lastly it is here objected that the prayer which Christ made before his death was but only for some: *I pray not for the world but for those that thou hast given me out of the world*, and therefore the death of Christ belongeth to such only as he made intercession for.

To this I answer that the intercession and prayer of Christ doth not fall upon his death, to make that belong to some and not to others, for that is not mentioned in the intercession; but the prayer falleth upon the persons to whom his death is effectual, and therefore he prayeth that some may have ability to come (that they may believe and be saved), though others have not: I pray for them, I pray not for the rest that belong not to my election. Therefore where you find any other intercession of Christ in any other place, you must understand that it falleth not on the act of his redemption, but on such to whom his death is made effectual; for Christ is made the second Adam, and by his death he hath set open the gates of heaven to all that believe, but to some he giveth ability to come and to others he denieth it.

So much for the clearing of this point; the use of it followeth.

And first, if Christ be offered to all freely without exception, and also seeing God hath commanded and beseech{eth} men to come and receive him, then let us take good heed of refusing of it, for if there be no greater mercy than the offer of Christ, so then there is no greater curse followeth than if it be refused. For the clearing of this point we are to know that we are all by nature enemies to God, and this enmity we increase by our personal rebellions, and so we are become liable to the curse. Man now being in this condition, God sendeth forth his messengers to beseech men to be reconciled, assuring them that the pardon is general, no matter what they are or have been; but if they thirst after Christ, he is for them; but indeed you must take whole Christ, as well as priest or prophet, as a king to rule over all your affections. Hereupon some take him and others will not; they think the condition too hard, and therefore they will not forgo their profits and pleasures and their liberties falsely so called; and therefore, notwithstanding this year of Jubilee, they love their old master still—that is, the lust that they serve—and they would rather be bored in the ear to serve them perpetually; they love the flesh-pots of Egypt and loathe this spiritual manna, notwithstanding it is the most precious and excellent that ever was offered to mankind. Now this, I say, of all the sins that can be committed—original sins, all our personal rebellion provoke not God so much to anger as the rejection of his Son for this contempt of the Gospel. . . . To this end, consider that when Christ is offered, it is not such an offer as when a man offereth a thing, if it be not taken the party offering looseth nothing; but it is such an offer as when the thing offered is spilt and lost if it be not received and taken; not as when a man inviteth another to a feast and he cannot come, the master is at no charge; but when the promise is made and the dinner prepared, and then the guests not to come, it is loss. So it is in this offer of Christ: all is ready; Christ is slain, and his blood is poured out. If you do not come and take it, you put away from you the blood of Christ, and so, in as much as in you lieth, you make the death of Christ of none effect, and so by consequence you shall be guilty of the blood of Christ. . . .

. . .

Secondly, consider that the Gospel which you refuse aggrevateth the sin, for the Gospel disobeyed hath much more terror than the Law disobeyed. . . . For the clearer understanding of this, you are to know that the Gospel hath two parts. Not only if you believe you shall be saved, but also *if you believe not you shall be damned*, which sheweth that the Gospel broken is more terrible than the Law, and therefore John Baptist, the first preacher of the Gospel, came with more terror and severity than the prophets did; he came in a coarse habit and severe in his doctrine, and therefore when he came to preach the Gospel, he saith, *Now is the axe laid to the root of the tree, and those that* are found *chaff* shall be *cast into the fire*, and what was the reason? because the Gospel was preached. Therefore if it be refused and this pardon rejected, God will now sooner lay the axe to the root than aforetime, and so indeed they found it by experience afterwards; for if we observe the Scripture, from the time that the Jews became a nation, for all their transgressions, he gave them not a full bill of divorcement till Christ was preached unto them and they refused to receive him; then those natural branches were broken off and the wild olive engrafted in. Till that time, I say, the Jews were not rejected. By this, therefore, we may see the danger of refusing the Gospel. . . .

. . .

. . . When the Law was broken there was but one breach to God; but in rejecting of the Gospel there is a is a double law transgrest, for when we had cast ourselves into a desperate condition with Adam, God offered us an help and means of recovery; now the refusing of this makes sin the greater by how much the more the mercy is the greater. . . . and therefore the reprobates that live in the Church shall exceed the devils in hell in judgment because they have had more mercy tendered to them than ever the devils had; and therefore in this respect God will exercise on them a more severe kind of justice. Let all these things teach you how dangerous it is to disobey the Gospel and to refuse Christ.

Thirdly, you are to consider that Christ who is offered unto you is the chiefest of all God's works, the utmost end that God propounded to himself in making of mankind; it is he that is the top of his Father's glory, in whom the glory of God most shineth. Therefore be assured, God will not lose his chiefest glory. He will not lose one jot of his glory, much less the principal part of it; and therefore he that refuseth Christ, contemneth the chiefest of God's works and layeth the chiefest of his glory in the dust, and therefore God will not suffer that to be done without great judgment.

Whatsoever God is known by, that is his Name. Whatsoever he makes himself more known by, that is his special Name; and his Name he will not suffer to be taken in vain. And therefore he saith, *he will not hold him guiltless that taketh his Name in vain*; and certainly this will bring the heaviest condemnation—the offer of Christ being the greatest mercy that was ever shewed to any creature either in heaven or in earth, and therefore the refusing of this mercy must needs produce the greatest judgment. . . . If we had been guilty of Adam's sin only, we should have had the judgment that Adam had upon breach of the condition. But we are offered Christ and to be heirs of heaven upon condition of

443

obedience to the law of faith; answerable therefore to the greatness of this mercy shall be the greatness of this condemnation if we refuse it. Let all these things stir us up most affectionately to embrace Christ, and consider what an injury and offence it is against God to refuse Christ. Remember those compassionate terms that he useth, *Come unto me, and why will ye die O house of Israel? And I delight not in the death of a sinner*, and many such like places. Take heed of refusing when God offereth his Son; rather *kiss the Son lest he be angry and ye perish*. And remember not only to take him, but take him in time; *now* God calleth upon you, and if you will not hear, beware lest when you call he will not hear. When the day of sickness and extremity cometh, then you will find that Christ is Christ indeed, and that faith is faith indeed, and that the feet of the messenger are beautiful, but then you shall not see them; for this is God's judgment: if they will not receive it in time of peace, he either offereth it no more, or else giveth them no hearts to receive it. Therefore defer not the taking of his offer. Take heed least God *swear in his wrath you shall not enter into his rest*, if you refuse this excellent gift. Remember that, though it be true that the whole time of this life be a time of grace, yet there is an opportunity in which God offereth grace, and after that offer, it is no more. And therefore he would offer Jerusalem no more peace, because *she knew not the time of her visitation*, and afterwards God either offered her none at all, or gave her not an heart to take it.

If God beseech and entreat men to believe, then it followeth that faith is a thing very pleasing and acceptable to God. If you therefore make the query of the Jews, *What shall we do to work the works of God?* I answer with Christ, *Believe on him whom he hath sent.* So also, if you ask what is the great commandment, I answer *that you believe in the only begotten Son of God.* You can do nothing so acceptable to God *as to believe on his Son*, for faith is the very life of a Christian, that which distinguisheth him from all other men. But what is this faith? It is not a small matter to believe (as our adversaries affirm), which {error} riseth out of the mistaking of the nature of faith, for it is not only to give assent unto a proposition that it is true, but this justifying faith *taketh* and *layeth* hold on Christ. Now in taking there are two things to be understood:

First, you must let go all that is in your hands before.

Secondly, you must lay hold on the thing offered. So in faith, first, there is an emptying quality whereby a man is made empty of all that is in himself; he must forgo father and mother and pleasures and profits and all to receive Christ. Secondly, there is an apprehending quality to lay hold on Christ, a forsaking of anything that is precious, and a receiving of him and a resting on him with a purpose to serve him only with a perfect heart and a willing mind. It is true, there is much excellency and necessity in works; but faith is the wellhead from whence all the streams of good works arise; and therefore faith exceedeth them as much as the cause doth the effect, for faith is the spring of good works; the more faith, the more works; where there is more oil, there is the greater flame. Faith then being the cause of works, it must needs follow that the stream cannot rise higher than the fountain.

Again, all the good works that we do give not so much glory to God as faith. Now nothing is so dear unto God as his glory, and therefore faith is most acceptable to God. . . . Further, in this doth the true worship of God principally consist. Now God delighteth in his worship, and the worship of God consisteth not only in the bowing of the knee, but it mainly consisteth in the inward persuasion of the heart, when a man is persuaded that God is a most holy, a most wise, just, and merciful God; and out of this he worshippeth and obeyeth him, and this is an act of faith. Remember, therefore, that faith is that which God doth principally call for, and therefore faith goeth far before works, inasmuch as *without faith it is impossible to please God.* Let us therefore be exhorted to labor to believe, seeing it is a thing so acceptable to God. And that this exhortation be not in vain, it is needful for men to know whether they believe or no; to this end therefore I will give you two or three signs of faith:

First, if you would know whether you truly believe, whether you are within the number of those that are within the compass of regeneration, consider whether you be soundly humbled, for that is a preparation that goeth before faith and without which no man is made ever partaker of Christ, for the direction of Christ is made to those that mourn in Zion. . . .

The murderer will not seek to the city of refuge before the revenger of blood follow him; and this must not be done slightly, but your conscience must be awakened to apprehend sin fully; and this prepareth you for Christ, for in these three things stands the sound conversion of a sinner to God: *first*, humiliation, *secondly*, the taking of Christ as the chiefest good, *thirdly*, when you will not forsake for him any worldly thing. . . . If you would therefore know whether you have taken Christ in good earnest or no (for many think they have Christ when they have him not), I ask you this question: do you grow in Christ and wax green in Christ? are you changed into the same nature with him? If you find these things, it is a sure sign you have taken Christ; but if you find not this new life in you, it is a sign you never received him; and this is not a light change but a great and manifest change, as apparent as the difference is betwixt a dead man and a living man; because when a man takes the Son, he hath the spirit of the Son within him, and if he hath the spirit he hath the disposition of the Son, the same life that the Son hath; for the spirit is to the soul as the soul is to the body; and therefore if you find no life, it is a sign you have no part in Christ.

Lastly, consider whether you be broken off from the old stock upon which you did grow, from whence you did take sap and bring forth fruit. Those therefore deceive themselves that think they can take Christ and yet follow their pleasures and covetousness; this crosseth their commixtures, and, I assure you, they make the way too broad, for whosoever will receive Christ must part with all things else, though they be never so dear to him.

FINIS

⤞⤝

Text: EEBO (Wing / P3306)

Riches of mercy to men in misery; or, certain excellent treatises concerning the dignity and duty of God's children. By the late Reverend and Faithfull Minister of Jesus Christ, John Preston, Doctor of Divinity and Chaplain in Ordinary to his Majesty, Master of Emmanuel College in Cambridge and sometime Preacher of Lincolns Inn (London, 1658), 143–66, 168–79, 373–80, 382–92, 394–96, 419, 421–36.

PHINEAS FLETCHER
(1582–1650)

The son of a Kentish diplomat, cousin to the dramatist John Fletcher, and older brother of the poet Giles Fletcher, Phineas Fletcher studied at Eton, leaving for King's College, Cambridge, in 1600. He took his BA in 1604, his MA four years later, and a BD some time thereafter. He entered holy orders in 1611, the same year he received a fellowship at King's. He left Cambridge in 1615 to serve as chaplain to Sir Henry Willoughby, who in 1621 presented him with the living of Hilgay in Norfolk, where Fletcher served until his death (except for a brief period when he was suspended by Bishop Wren for "the omission of some ceremonies") and in whose churchyard he is buried.

During his years in the ministry, Fletcher wrote a devotional treatise, posthumously published under the title *A father's testament* (1670). Virtually all his poetry dates from his years at Cambridge, although it was not published until over a decade after his departure. *The locusts* (1627) and *The purple island, or, the Isle of Man* (1633) are his best-known works. The latter, an astonishingly detailed anatomical allegory, in which the inner workings of the human body represent the structures of moral and political existence,[1] came out in an expensive and lavishly illustrated Cambridge edition, the printing costs underwritten by Fletcher's wealthy friend, patron, and disciple, Edward Benlowes.

The locusts, Fletcher's first published poem, appeared in a single volume with his neo-Latin brief epic on the same subject, the *Locustae, vel, pietas Jesuitica*. The two works are closely related, although it is not known whether the English constitutes an expanded version of the Latin or the Latin a condensed version of the English. No manuscripts for *The locusts* survive, but there are three for *Locustae*, the earliest dating from 1611. The manuscripts have dedications to Prince Henry and Prince Charles; the 1627 printed *Locustae*, however, is dedicated to Sir Roger Townshend, with a separate dedication of its English twin to

---

[1] The elaborate image of the Tritons enforcing the one-way flow of blood from heart to liver in *The locusts* 1.9 is quintessential *Purple island*.

446

his wife, Mary Townshend, née Vere. The Vere-connection is significant. Sir Horace and Lady Mary Vere were puritan grandees and ardent champions of the international Calvinist cause: the former, the commander of the English volunteer forces in the Palatinate; the latter, patron of such eminent puritan ministers as John Dod, John Preston, and William Ames. Their daughters' husbands are a roll-call of the opposition leadership: John Holles, Oliver St. John, Thomas Fairfax.[2] Roger Townshend, although not a major player, sat in the Parliaments of 1621–22 and 1628–29, and seems also to have been "a noted Puritan" (E. J. Lines 75). *The locusts* affirms the politics of its dedicatee but, unlike *The spy <infra>*, has an imaginative power that pushes beyond the demands of ideology.

The Gunpowder Plot inspired several neo-Latin brief epics, including both the *Locustae* and Milton's *In quintum Novembris*. *The locusts*, however, would seem to be the sole vernacular exemplar. Its Spenserian lineage is evident throughout, as are its anticipations of Milton, who repeatedly draws on Fletcher's poem in the first two books of *Paradise Lost*. Indeed, as this genealogy suggests, *The locusts*, although admittedly more for an age than all time, has some claim to be the quintessential English Protestant epic of that age. Its reading of post-Reformation history through the lens of Revelations draws on ancient topoi of Protestant self-understanding; yet, however conventional (or, perhaps, because of its deep cultural rootedness), Fletcher's vision of the supernatural agencies at work behind the veil of mortal unknowing has a kind of mytho-poetic grandeur, an almost archaic sense of the proximity of the invisible realms. The poem evokes the late antique *cosmos plena deorum—et daemonum*, where men, as Paul writes the Ephesians, "wrestle not against flesh and blood, but against principalities, against powers, against the rulers of the darkness of this world" (6:12). So as Aeneas races back to the burning citadel of Troy, his goddess mother checks his desperate efforts to save the doomed city by

> tear[ing] away all the mist that now, shrouding your sight,
> dims your mortal vision . . .
> [for] here, where you see shattered heaps of stone
> torn from stone, and smoke billowing mixed with dust,
> Neptune is shaking the walls, and the foundations stirred
> by his mighty trident, and tearing the whole city up by it roots.
> There, Juno, the fiercest, is first to take the Scaean Gate, and,
> sword at her side, calls on her troops from the ships, in rage.
> Now, see, Tritonian Pallas, standing on the highest towers,
> sending lightning from the storm-cloud, and her grim Gorgon
> breastplate. . . .
>   She spoke, and hid herself
> in the dense shadows of night. Dreadful shapes appeared,
> and the vast powers of gods opposed to Troy. (*Aeneid* 2.604–23)

The locusts of Fletcher's title are the mist-shrouded "dreadful shapes" whose malice turns cities to rubble and ashes.

---

[2] Mary, however, broke ranks when, after Sir Roger's death, she married the royalist peer and poet Mildmay Fane.

The poem interleaves its darkly powerful scenes from the infernal city with glorious evocations of a sacral cosmos <5.19–28>, of heaven's endless joy <1.35>, and the ancient paradoxes of the Incarnation <1.11>. Its subject is the Gunpowder Plot; the world of the poem is early Stuart England, and yet shot through with supernatural presences—"the traffic of Jacob's ladder/ Pitched betwixt Heaven and Charing Cross" (as well as the heavier traffic coming up from the other direction).[3] The poem knows nothing of the Protestant remotion of the divine or the silence of infinite space. It is innocent of *Entzauberung*.[4]

Yet Fletcher's mythic and visionary renderings of history alternate jarringly with passages of anti-Catholic paranoia, conspiracy fantasies, and jingoistic militarism. The juxtapositions probably feel more disturbing now, but it seems hard to imagine that even at the time the Catholic-as-cannibal imagery that threads through the stanzas would not have lent a queasy resonance to the concluding plea that godly magistrates will "strip, eat, and burn" the Romish whore's "flesh in fire" <5.37>. So too Fletcher's *laudatio* of the Reformation—and of Jacobean England—as fostering a Messianic-Augustan age of peace, where "men plow with swords" <1.23>, further unsettles the poem's unsettling call to revive Britain's "martial fame" by repeating Charles V's 1527 sack of Rome <5.38>. Given that this is a poem about demons plotting to do something along these lines to London, Fletcher's enthusiasm for civic destruction seems quite staggering.[5]

It is hard to know what to make of these very unresolved tensions. The most extreme may result from the work's *longue durée* composition. Up to the final stanzas, David Norbrook's anodyne summary of its politics—Fletcher celebrates James as the "ideal Protestant poet-king, defending the faith with pen rather than the sword," and yet recognizes "that the sword has to be held in reserve" to deal with the Jesuit menace (80)—seems basically accurate. Only at the end does the poem start howling for blood—the same stanzas that address the newly crowned Charles.[6] Their sudden embrace of apocalyptic violence may register the political mood of the new regime, for in 1625–27, when these final stanzas were written, Charles was pushing for war with Spain and a return to the militant Protestantism of the Elizabethan glory days. The ending of *The locusts* suggests that Charles had little trouble conjuring up this Calvinist fighting spirit. It would prove harder to lay.

SOURCES: *ODNB*; Reid Barbour, *Literature and religious culture in seventeenth-century England* (Cambridge UP, 2002); Estelle Haan, ed. and trans., *Phineas Fletcher: "Locustae vel pietas Iesuitica,"* Supplementa Humanistica Lovaniensia IX (Leuven UP, 1996); Eliza J. Lines, *Marks-Platt Ancestry* (n.p., 1902); David Norbrook, *Poetry and politics in the English Renaissance* (Routledge, 1984; rpt. Oxford UP, 2002); David Quint, "Milton, Fletcher and the Gunpowder Plot," *JWCI* 54 (1991): 261–68.

[3] The quotation is from the concluding lines of "The Kingdom of God" by Francis Thompson (d. 1907).

[4] The same is true for Lancelot Andrewes' quite extraordinary sermons on the Gunpowder Plot.

[5] And, one might add, an exceptionally literal instance of demonic othering.

[6] There's no counterpart in the Latin, which ends praising James for overthrowing Rome with the weapons of the Muses.

PHINEAS FLETCHER

The locusts, or Apollyonists
1627

THE
LOCUSTS,
OR
APOLLYONISTS[1]

CANTO I[2]

1

Of men, nay beasts; worse, monsters; worst of all,
Incarnate fiends, English Italianate;
Of priests, O no, Mass-priests, priests-cannibal,†   †a conventional swipe at
Who make their Maker; chew, grind, feed, grow fat   transubstantiation
With flesh divine; of that great City's fall,
Which born, nurs't, grown with blood, th' Earth's Empress sat,
Cleansed, spoused to Christ, yet back to whoredom fell,
None can enough, something I fain would tell.
How black are quenched lights! Fall'n Heaven's a double Hell.

2

Great Lord, who grasp'st all creatures in thy hand,
Who in thy lap lay'st down proud Thetis' head,
And bind'st her white curled locks in cauls† of sand;   †coifs

---

[1] {"Apollyon," the Greek equivalent of the Hebrew "Abaddon," means "the Destroyer" (or place of destruction); in Rev. 9:1-11 the figure is the king of the bottomless pit with monstrous locusts.}
[2] {Side notes marked with † are editorial additions; the rest are Fletcher's.}

Who gather'st in thy fist and lay'st in bed
The sturdy winds; who ground'st the floating land
On fleeting seas, and over all hast spread
Heaven's brooding wings to foster all below;
Who mak'st the Sun without all fire to glow,
The spring of heat and light; the moon to ebb and flow:

3

Thou world's sole pilot, who in this poor Isle
(So small a bottom†) hast embark't thy light,   †ship
And glorious self;[3] and steer'st it safe, the while
Hoarse drumming seas and winds' loud trumpets fight;
Who causest stormy Heavens here only smile:
Steer me, poor ship-boy, steer my course aright.
Breathe gracious Spirit, breathe gently on these lays,
Be thou my compass, needle to my ways;
Thy glorious work's my fraught†, my haven is thy praise.   †freight, contents

4

Thou purple Whore, mounted on scarlet Beast,   Revel. 17:2-4, 6
Gorged with the flesh, drunk with the blood of Saints,
Whose amorous golden Cup and charmed feast
All earthly kings, all earthly men attaints:
See thy live pictures, see thine own, thy best,
Thy dearest sons, and cheer thy heart that faints.
Hark thou saved Island, hark, and never cease
To praise that hand which held thy head in peace.
Else had'st thou swum as deep in blood, as now in seas.

5

The cloudy Night came whirling up the sky;
And scatt'ring round the dews, which first she drew
From milky poppies, loads the drowsy eye;
The wat'ry Moon, cold Vesper, and his crew
Light up their tapers; to the Sun they fly,
And at his blazing flame their sparks renew.
Oh why should earthly lights then scorn to tine†   †light
Their lamps alone at that first Sun divine?
Hence as false falling stars,[4] as rotten wood they shine.

---

[3] {On the "little England" topos, see Jeffrey Knapp, *An empire nowhere: England, America, and literature from Utopia to The Tempest* (U California P, 1992).}

[4] {See Isaiah 14.}

6

Her sable mantle was embroidered gay
With silver beams, with spangles round beset;
Four steeds her chariot drew: the first was gray,
The second blue, third brown, fourth black as jet.
The hollowing owl, her post, prepares the way,
And winged dreams (as gnat-swarms) flutt'ring, let†   †hinder
Sad sleep, who fain his eyes in rest would steep.
Why then at death do weary mortals weep?
Sleep's but a shorter death, death's but a longer sleep.

7

And now the world, & dreams themselves, were drowned
In deadly sleep; the laborer snorteth fast,
His brawny arms unbent, his limbs unbound
As dead, forget all toil to come, or past.
Only sad Guilt, and troubled Greatness crowned
With heavy gold and care, no rest can taste.
Go then, vain man, go pill the live and dead,
Buy, sell, fawn, flatter, rise, then couch thy head
In proud but dangerous gold, in silk but restless bed.

8

When lo a sudden noise breaks th' empty air:
A dreadful noise, which every creature daunts,
Frights home the blood, shoots up the limber hair;
For through the silent Heaven, Hell's pursuivants
Cutting their way, command foul spirits repair
With haste to Pluto, who their counsel wants.
Their hoarse bass-horns like fenny bittours sound;
Th' Earth shakes, dogs howl, & Heaven itself astound
Shuts all his eyes; the Stars in clouds their candles drowned.

9

Meantime Hell's iron gates by fiends beneath
Are open flung; which framed with wondrous art
To every guilty soul yields entrance eath†;   †easily
But never wight but He could thence depart,
Who dying once was death to endless death:
So where the liver's channel to the heart
Pays purple tribute, with their three-fork't mace
Three Tritons stand and speed his flowing race,
But stop the ebbing stream if once it back would pace.

10

The porter to th' infernal gate is Sin,
A shapeless shape, a foul deformed thing,
Nor nothing, nor a substance: as those thin
And empty forms which through the aïr fling
Their wand'ring shapes, at length they'r fast'ned in
The crystal sight.[5] It serves, yet reigns as King;
It lives, yet's death: it pleases, full of pain:
Monster! ah who, who can thy being feign?
Thou shapeless shape, live death, pain pleasing, servile reign.

11

Of that first woman and th' old serpent bred,
By lust and custom nurst; whom, when her mother
Saw so deformed, how fain would she have fled
Her birth and self? But she her dam† would smother,   †Eve, the "mother" of sin
And all her brood, had not He rescued
Who was His mother's sire, His children's brother:
Eternity, who yet was born and died;
His own Creator, Earth's scorn, Heaven's pride,
Who th' Deity inflesht, and man's flesh deified.

12

Her former parts her mother seems resemble,
Yet only seems to flesh and weaker sight;
For she with art and paint could fine dissemble
Her loathsome face; her back parts (black as night)
Like to her horrid Sire would force to tremble
The boldest heart; to th' eye that meets her right
She seems a lovely sweet, of beauty rare;
But at the parting, he that shall compare,
Hell will more lovely deem, the Devil's self more fair.

13

Her rosy cheek, quick eye, her naked breast,
And whatsoe'er loose fancy might entice,
She bare exposed to sight, all lovely drest
In beauty's livery and quaint devise;
Thus she bewitches many a boy unblest,
Who drench't in Hell, dreams all of Paradise:

[5] {The forms or *species* are the ghostly images conveyed from an object to the eye (the "crystal sight"); they thus enable the eye to see things at a distance.}

Her breasts his spheres, her arms his circling sky;
Her pleasures heav'n, her love eternity:
For her he longs to live, with her he longs to die.

14

But he that gave a stone[6] power to descry
'Twixt natures hid and check that metal's pride
That dares aspire to gold's fair purity,
Hath left a touch-stone erring eyes to guide,
Which clears their sight and strips hypocrisy;
They see, they loathe, they curse her painted hide;
Her, as a crawling carrion, they esteem:
Her worst of ills, and worse than that, they deem;
Yet know her worse than they can think or she can seem.

15

Close by her sat Despair, sad ghastly sprite,
With staring looks, unmoved, fast nailed to Sin;
Her body all of earth, her soul of fright,
About her thousand deaths, but more within:
Pale, pined cheeks; black hair, torn, rudely dight†; †arrayed
Short breath, long nails, dull eyes, sharp-pointed chin:
Light, life, Heaven, Earth, her self, and all she fled.
Fain would she die, but could not; yet half dead,
A breathing corpse she seemed, wrap't up in living lead.

16

In th' entrance Sickness and faint Languor dwelt,
Who with sad groans toll out their passing knell;
Late Fear, Fright, Horror that already felt
The torturer's claws preventing† Death and Hell. †prefiguring
Within loud Grief and roaring Pangs (that swelt
In sulfur flames) did weep and howl and yell.
And thousand souls in endless dolors lie,
Who burn, fry, hizz, and never cease to cry,
Oh that I ne'er had lived, Oh that I once could die!

17

And now th' Infernal Powers, through th' air driving,
For speed their leather pinions broad display;

---

[6] {A touchstone is a small tablet of dark stone such as fieldstone, slate, or lydite, used for assaying precious metal alloys. It has a finely grained surface on which soft metals leave a visible trace, http://en.wikipedia.org/wiki/Touchstone_%28assaying_tool%29 (accessed June 7, 2012).}

Now at eternal Death's wide gate arriving,
Sin gives them passage; still they cut their way,
Till to the bottom of Hell's palace diving,
They enter Dis'† deep Conclave. There they stay,   †Satan's
Waiting the rest; and now they all are met,
A full foul Senate; now they all are set,
The horrid Court, big swol'n with th' hideous Council, sweat.

18

The mid'st, but lowest (in Hell's heraldry
The deepest is the highest room) in state
Sat lordly Lucifer: his fiery eye,
Much swol'n with pride but more with rage and hate,
As censor mustered all his company,
Who round about with awful silence sat.
This do, this let rebellious Spirits gain:
Change God for Satan, Heaven's for Hell's Sov'reign:
O let him serve in Hell, who scorns in Heaven to reign!

19

Ah wretch, who with ambitious cares opprest,
Long'st still for future, feel'st no present good;
Despising to be better, would'st be best,
Good never; who wilt serve thy lusting mood,
Yet all command—not he who raised his crest,
But pulled it down, hath high and firmly stood.
Fool, serve thy tow'ring lusts, grow still, still crave,
Rule, reign: this comfort from thy greatness have,
Now at thy top, thou art a great commanding slave.

20

Thus fell this Prince of Darkness, once a bright
And glorious star; he willful turned away
His borrowed globe from that eternal light.
Himself he sought, so lost himself; his ray
Vanish't to smoke, his morning sunk in night,
And never more shall see the springing day.
To be in Heaven the second he disdains;
So now the first in Hell and flames he reigns,
Crowned once with joy and light; crowned now with fire and pains.

21

As, where the warlike Dane the scepter sways,
They crown usurpers with a wreath of lead

And with hot steel; while loud the traitor brays,
They melt and drop it down into his head.
Crowned he would live, and crowned he ends his days:
All so in Heaven's courts this traitor sped.
Who now (when he had overlook't his train),
Rising upon his throne, with bitter strain
Thus 'gan to whet their rage & chide their frustrate pain.

22

See, see you Spirits (I know not whether more
Hated or hating Heaven), ah, see the Earth
Smiling in quiet peace and plenteous store.
Men fearless live in ease, in love and mirth;
Where arms did rage, the drum & cannon roar,
Where hate, strife, envy reigned, and meager dearth,
Now lutes and viols charm the ravish't ear.
Men plow with swords; horse heels their armors wear.
Ah, shortly scarce they'll know what war & armors were.

23

Under their sprouting vines they sporting sit.
Th' old tell of evils past; youth laugh and play,
And to their wanton heads sweet garlands fit,
Roses with lilies, myrtles weaved with bay:
The world's at rest. Erinnys,[7] forc't to quit
Her strongest holds, from Earth is driven away.
Even Turks forget their Empire to increase.
War's self is slain, and whips of Furies cease.
We, we ourselves, I fear, will shortly live in peace.

24

Meantime (I burn, I broil, I burst with spite)
In midst of peace, that sharp two-edged sword
Cuts through our darkness, cleaves the misty night,
Discovers all our snares; that sacred word
(Lock't up by Rome) breaks prison, spreads the light,
Speaks every tongue, paints and points out the Lord:
His birth, life, death, and cross. Our gilded stocks,
Our laymen's books, the boy and woman mocks;
They laugh, they fleer, and say, Blocks teach and worship Blocks.

---

[7] {In classical mythology, the Erinnys are the Furies; here, as in Spenser's *Faerie Queene* 2.2.29, Erinnys is a personification of discord.}

25

Spring-tides of light divine the air surround
And bring down Heaven to Earth. Deaf Ignorance,
Vext with the day, her head in Hell hath drowned;
Fond† Superstition, frighted with the glance   †foolish
Of sudden beams, in vain hath crossed her round.[8]
Truth and Religion everywhere advance
Their conqu'ring standards; Error's lost and fled.
Earth burns in love to Heaven; Heaven yields her bed
To Earth, and common grown, smiles to be ravished.

26

That little swimming Isle above the rest,
Spite of our spite and all our plots, remains
And grows in happiness: but late our nest,
Where we and Rome and blood and all our trains—
Monks, nuns, dead and live idols—safe did rest;
Now there (next th' Oath of God) that Wrastler reigns,[9]
Who fills the land and world with peace; his spear
Is but a pen, with which he down doth bear
Blind Ignorance, false gods, and superstitious fear.

27

There God hath framed another Paradise:
Fat olives dropping peace, victorious palms;
Nor in the midst, but everywhere doth rise
That hated tree of life, whose precious balms
Cure every sinful wound: give light to th' eyes,
Unlock the ear, recover fainting qualms.
There richly grows what makes a people blest:
A garden planted by Himself and drest,
Where He Himself doth walk, where He Himself doth rest.

28

There every star sheds his sweet influence
And radiant beams: great, little, old, and new
Their glittering rays and frequent confluence
The milky path to God's high palace strew:
Th' unwearied Pastors with steeled confidence
Conquered, and conquering fresh their fight renew.

---

[8] {i.e., repeatedly makes the sign of the cross—a superstitious charm to ward off evil}
[9] {ca. 1340, Hampole, *Psalter* xiii.11: For iacob is als mykill at say as wrestlere or supplantere of syn (*OED*, q.v. "wrestler"). "James" is the equivalent of Hampole's "Iacob."}

Our strongest holds that thund'ring ordinance†   †preaching (lit. cannon)
Beats down, and makes our proudest turrets dance,
Yoking men's iron necks in His sweet governance.

29

Nor can th' Old World content ambitious Light:
Virginia, our soil, our seat and throne
(To which so long possession gives us right—
As long as Hell's), Virginia's self is gone;
That stormy Isle, which th' Isle of Devils hight,[10]
Peopled with faith, truth, grace, religion.
What's next but Hell? That now alone remains,
And that subdued, even here He rules and reigns,
And mortals gin to dream of long but endless pains.[11]

30

While we (good harmless creatures) sleep or play,
Forget our former loss and following pain;
Earth sweats for Heaven, but Hell keeps holy-day.
Shall we repent, good souls? or shall we plain?
Shall we groan, sigh, weep, mourn, for mercy pray?
Lay down our spite, wash out our sinful stain?
May be He'll yield, forget, and use us well,
Forgive, join hands, restore us whence we fell;
May be He'll yield us Heaven, and fall Himself to Hell.

31

But me, oh never let me, Spirits, forget
That glorious day, when I your standard bore,
And scorning in the second place to sit,
With you assaulted Heaven, His yoke forswore.
My dauntless heart yet longs to bleed and sweat
In such a fray; the more I burn, the more
I hate. Should He yet offer grace and ease,
If subject we our arms and spite surcease,
Such offer should I hate, and scorn so base a peace.

32

Where are those Spirits? Where that haughty rage,
That durst with me invade eternal Light?

---

[10] {An early name for the island now called Bermuda, where the Virginia Company built a settlement in 1612.}

[11] {This final line seems defective.}

457

What? Are our hearts fall'n too? Droop we with age?
Can we yet fall from Hell and hellish spite?
Can smart our wrath, can grief our hate assuage?
Dare we with Heaven, and not with Earth to fight?
Your arms, allies, yourselves as strong as ever;
Your foes, their weapons, numbers weaker never.
For shame tread down this Earth. What wants but your endeavor?

33

Now by your selves, and thunder-daunted arms,
But never daunted hate, I you implore,
Command, adjure: reinforce your fierce alarms;
Kindle, I pray, who never prayed before,
Kindle your darts; treble repay our harms.
Oh our short time, too short, stands at the door.
Double your rage. If now we do not ply,
We 'lone in Hell, without due company,
And worse, without desert, without revenge shall lie.

34

He, Spirits (ah that, that's our main torment), He
Can feel no wounds, laughs at the sword and dart,
Himself from grief, from suff'ring wholly free;
His simple nature cannot taste of smart—
Yet in His members we Him grievèd see;
For and in them He suffers; where His heart
Lies bare and nak't, there dart your fiery steel;
Cut, wound, burn, scare, if not the head, the heel.
Let Him in every part some pain and torment feel.

35

That Light comes posting on, that cursed Light,
When they, as He, all glorious, all divine
(Their flesh clothed with the sun and much more bright,
Yet brighter spirits) shall in His image shine,
And see Him as He is. There no despite,
No force, no art their state can undermine:
Full of unmeasured bliss, yet still receiving,
Their souls still childing joy, yet still conceiving,
Delights beyond the wish, beyond quick thoughts' perceiving.

36

But we fast pinioned with dark fiery chains
Shall suffer every ill, but do no more.

The guilty spirit there feels extremest pains,
Yet fears worse than it feels; and finding store
Of present deaths, Death's absence sore complains:
Oceans of ills without or ebb or shore,
A life that ever dies, a death that lives,
And, worst of all, God's absent presence gives
A thousand living woes, a thousand dying griefs.

37

But when he sums his time, and turns his eye
First to the past, then future pangs, past days
(And every day's an age of misery)
In torment spent by thousands down he lays,
Future by millions, yet eternity
Grows nothing less; nor past, to come allays.
Through every pang and grief he wild doth run,
And challenge coward Death; doth nothing shun
That he may nothing be; does all to be undone.

38

O let our work equal our wages. Let
Our Judge fall short, and when His plagues are spent,
Owe more than He hath paid, live in our debt.
Let Heaven want vengeance, Hell want punishment
To give our dues. When we with flames beset
Still dying live in endless languishment,
This be our comfort: we did get and win
The fires and tortures we are whelmed in;
We have kept pace, outrun His justice with our sin.

39

And now you States of Hell, give your advise,
And to these ruins lend your helping hand.
This said, and ceas't, straight humming murmurs rise;
Some chafe, some fret, some sad and thoughtful stand,
Some chat, and some new stratagems devise,
And everyone Heaven's stronger powers banned†,   †cursed
And tear for madness their uncombed snakes,
And everyone his fiery weapon shakes,
And everyone expects who first the answer makes.

40

So when the falling Sun hangs o'er the main,
Ready to drop into the western wave

By yellow Cam, where all the Muses reign
And with their towers his reedy head embrave†,   †adorn
The warlike gnat their flutt'ring armies train;
All have sharp spears and all shrill trumpets have;
Their files they double, loud their cornets sound,
Now march at length, their troops now gather round;
The banks, the broken noise, and turrets fair, rebound.

. . .

CANTO II

1

What care, what watch need guard that tot'ring State
Which mighty foes besiege, false friends betray,
Where enemies strong and subtle, swol'n with hate,
Catch all occasions,[12] wake, watch night and day?
The town divided, e'en the wall and gate
Prove traitors, and the Council self takes pay
Of foreign States; the Prince is overswayed
By underminers, puts off friendly aid,
His wit by will, his strength by weakeness over-laid.

2

Thus men. The never seen, quick-seeing fiends—
Fierce, crafty, strong—and world conspire our fall;
And we (worse foes) unto ourselves false friends:
Our flesh and sense a trait'rous gate and wall;
The spirit and flesh man in two factions rends;
The inward senses are corrupted all;
The soul weak, willful, swayed with flatteries,
Seeks not His help, who works by contraries,
By folly makes him wise, strong by infirmities.

3

See drowsy soul, thy foe ne'er shuts his eyes.
See, careless soul, thy foe in council sits.
Thou prayer restrain'st; thy sin for vengeance cries;
Thou laugh'st, vain soul, while justice vengeance fits.
Wake by His light, with Wisdom's self advise:
What rigorous Justice damns, sweet Mercy quits.
Watch, pray. He in one instant helps and hears;
Let Him not see thy sins but through thy tears;
Let Him not hear their cries but through thy groaning fears.

---

[12] {take advantage of every opportunity}

4

As when the angry winds with seas conspire,
The white-plumed hills, marching in set array,
Invade the Earth and seem with rage on fire,
While waves with thun'dring drums whet on the fray,
And blasts with whistling fifes new rage inspire;
Yet soon as breathless airs their spite allay,
A silent calm ensues: the hilly main
Sinks in itself, and drums unbrac't refrain
Their thund'ring noise, while seas sleep on the even plain.

5

All so the raging storm of cursed fiends,
Blown up with sharp reproach and bitter spite,
First rose in loud uproar, then falling, ends,
And ebbs in silence; when a wily sprite
To give an answer for the rest intends:
Once Proteus, now Equivocus he hight†,   †is called
Father of cheaters, spring of cunning lies,
Of sly deceit, and refined perjuries,
That hardly Hell itself can trust his forgeries.

6

To every shape his changing shape is drest,
Oft seems a lamb and bleats, a wolf and howls;
Now like a dove appears with candid breast,
Then like a falcon preys on weaker fowls,
A badger neat that flies his 'filed nest,
But most a fox, with stink his cabin fouls:
A courtier, priest, transformed to thousand fashions,
His matter framed of slight equivocations,
His very form was formed of mental reservations.

7

And now more practick grown with use and art,
Oft times in heavenly shapes he fools the sight,
So that his scholars selves have learn't his part:
Though worms, to glow in dark, like Angels bright.
To sinful slime such gloss can they impart,
That, like the Virgin Mother, crowned in light,
They glitter fair in glorious purity
And rays divine; mean time the cheated eye
Is finely mock't into an heavenly ecstasy.

8

Now is he General of those new stamp't Friars,
Which have their root in that lame soldier-saint,
Who takes his ominous name from Strife and Fires.*   *Ignatius*
Themselves with idle vaunt that name attaint
Which all the world adores: these master-liars
With truth, Abaddonists with Jesus paint
Their lying title.† Fools, who think with light   †*Jesu-it*
To hide their filth; thus lie they naked quite;
That who loves Jesus most, most hates the Jesuite.

9

Soon as this Spirit (in Hell, Apollyon,
On Earth, Equivocus) stood singled out—
Their Speaker there, but here their Champion,
Whom lesser States and all the vulgar rout
In dangerous times admire and gaze upon—
The silly Commons circle him about,
And first with loud applause they usher in
Their Orator, then hushing all their din,
With silence they attend, and woo him to begin.

10

Great Monarch, Air's, Earth's, Hell's Sovereign,
True, ah too true, you plain, and we lament:
In vain our labor, all our art's in vain;
Our care, watch, darts, assaults are all misspent.
He, whose command we hate, detest, disdain,
Works all our thoughts and works to His intent:
Our spite His pleasure makes, our ill His good,
Light out of night He brings, peace out of blood:
What fell which He upheld? what stood which He withstood?

11

As when from moors some fiery constellation
Draws up wet clouds with strong attractive ray,
The captived seas, forc't from their seat and nation,
Begin to mutiny, put out the day,
And pris'ning close the hot dry exhalation,
Threat Earth and Heaven, and steal the sun away;
Till th' angry captive (fired with fetters cold)
With thundring cannons tears the limber mold,
And down in fruitful tears the broken vapor's rolled.

12

So our rebellion, so our spiteful threat
All molten falls; He (which my heart disdains)
Waters Heaven's plants with our hell-flaming heat,
Husbands His graces with our sinful pains:
When most against Him, for Him most we sweat;
We in our Kingdom serve, He in it reigns.
Oh blame us not; we strive, mine, wrastle, fight.
He breaks our troops; yet thus we still delight,
Though all our spite's in vain, in vain to shew our spite.

13

Our fogs lie scatt'red by His piercing light,
Our subtilties His wisdom oversways,
His gracious love weighs down our ranc'rous spite,
His Word our sleights, His truth our lies displays;
Our ill confined, His goodness infinite,
Our greatest strength His weakness overlays.
He will, and oh He must, be Emperor.
That Heaven and Earth's unconquered at this hour,
Nor let Him thank, nor do you blame our will, but pow'r.

14

Nay, earthly gods that wont in luxury,
In masques and dalliance, spend their peaceful days,
Or else invade their neighbor's liberty
And swim through Christian blood to heathen praise,
Subdue our arms with peace; us bold defy,
Armed all with letters, crowned with learned bays;
With them whole swarms of Muses take the field,
And by Heaven's aid enforce us way to yield;
The goose lends them a spear; and every rag, a shield.[13]

15

But are our hearts fall'n too? shall we repent,
Sue, pray, with tears wash out our sinful spot?
Or can our rage with grief and smart relent?
Shall we lay down our arms? Ah, fear us not;
Not such thou found'st us, when with thee we bent
Our arms 'gainst Heaven, when scorning that fair lot
Of glorious bliss (when we might still have reigned)
With Him in borrowed light and joys unstained,
We hated subject crowns and guiltless bliss disdained.

---

[13] {Early modern paper was made from rags.}

16

Nor are we changelings. Find, oh find but one,
But one in all thy troops, whose lofty pride
Begins to stoop with opposition:
But as when stubborn winds with Earth rallied†   †combine forces
(Their Mother Earth), she, aided by her son,
Confronts the seas, beats off the angry tide,
The more with curled-head waves, the furious main
Renews his spite and swells with high disdain,
Oft broke and chased, as oft turns & makes head again;

17

So rise we by our fall. That divine science[14]
Planted below, grafted in human stock,
Heavens with frail Earth combines in strong alliance;
While He, their Lion, leads that sheepish flock,
Each sheep, each lamb dares give us bold defiance;
But yet our forces broken 'gainst the rock
We strongly reinforce, and every man,
Though cannot what he wills, wills what he can,
And where we cannot hurt, there we can curse and ban.

18

See here in broken force, a heart unbroke,
Which neither Hell can daunt nor Heaven appease;
See here a heart, which scorns that gentle yoke,
And with it life and light and peace and ease:
A heart not cooled, but fired with thundring stroke,
Which Heaven itself, but conquered, cannot please.
To draw one blessed soul from's heavenly cell,
Let me in thousand pains and tortures dwell:
Heaven without guilt to me is worse than guilty Hell.

19

Fear then no change. Such I, such are we all:
Flaming in vengeance more than Stygian fire.
When He shall leave His throne and starry hall,
Forsake His dear-bought Saints and Angels' quire,
When He from Heaven into our Hell shall fall,
Our nature take, and for our life expire:
Then we perhaps (as man) may waver light,
Our hatred turn to peace, to love our spite,
Then Heaven shall turn to Hell, and day shall change to night.

[14] {a pun on "scion"—i.e., a graft}

20

But if with forces new to take the field
Thou long'st, look here, we prest and ready stand:
See all that power and wiles that Hell can yield
Expect no watchword but thy first command;
Which given, without or fear or sword or shield,
We'll fly in Heaven's face; I and my band
Will draw whole worlds, leave here no room to dwell.
Stale arts we scorn, our plots become black Hell,
Which no heart will believe nor any tongue dare tell.

21

Nor shall I need to spur the lazy monk,
Who never sweats but in his meal or bed,
Whose forward paunch ushers his useless trunk,
He barrels darkness in his empty head:
To eat, drink, void what he hath eat and drunk,
Then purge his reins†: thus these Saints merited;   †kidneys
They fast with holy fish and flowing wine—
Not common, but (which fits such Saints) divine*:   *Hence called
Poor souls, they dare not soil their hands with precious mine!   *vinum theologicum*

22

While th' Earth with night and mists was overswayed
And all the world in clouds was laid a-steep,
Their sluggish trade did lend us friendly aid;
They rock't and hush't the world in deadly sleep:
Cloist'red the Sun, the Moon they overlaid,
And prisoned every Star in dungeon deep.
And when the Light put forth his morning ray,
My famous Dominic took the light away,
And let in seas of blood to quench the early day.

23

But oh, that recreant Friar,† who long in night   †Luther
Had slept, his oath to me his Captain brake,
Uncloist'red, with himself, the hated Light;
Those piercing beams forc't drowsy Earth awake.
Nor could we all resist: our flatt'ry, spite,
Arts, arms, his victory more famous make.
Down cloisters fall; the monks chased from their sty
Lie ope, and all their loathsome company:
Hypocrisy, rape, blood, theft, whoredom, sodomy.

24

Those troops I soon disband, now useless quite;
And with new musters fill my companies,
And press the crafty wrangling Jesuite.
Nor train I him as monks; his squinted eyes
Take in and view askance the hateful Light;
So stores his head with shifts and subtilties.
Thus being armed with arts, his turning brains
All overturn. Oh with what easy pains
Light he confounds with light, and truth with truth distains.

25

The world is rent in doubt: some gazing stay,
Few step aright, but most go with the crowd.
So when the golden Sun with sparkling ray
Imprints his stamp upon an adverse cloud,
The wat'ry glass so shines that's hard to say
Which is the true, which is the falser proud.
The silly people gape, and whisp'ring cry
That some strange innovation is nigh,
And fearful wizard sings of parted tyranny.

26

These have I trained to scorn their contraries,
Out-face the Truth, out-stare the open Light;
And what with seeming truths and cunning lies
Confute they cannot, with a scoff to slight.
Then after loss to crow their victories,
And get by forging what they lost by fight.
And now so well they ply them, that by heart
They all have got my counterfeiting part,
That to my scholars I turn scholar in mine art.

27

Followed by these brave spirits, I nothing fear
To conquer Earth, or Heaven itself assail;
To shake the stars as thick from fixed sphere,
As when a rustic arm with stubborn flail
Beats out his harvest from the swelling ear;
T' eclipse the Moon, and Sun himself injail.
Had all our army such another band,
Nor Earth nor Heaven could long unconquered stand,
But Hell should Heaven, and they, I fear, would Hell command.

28

What country, city, town, what family,
In which they have not some intelligence
And party, some that love their company?
Courts, councils, hearts of kings find no defense,
No guard to bar them out: by flattery
They worm and screw into their conscience;
Or with steel, poison, dags dislodge the sprite.
If any quench or damp this orient Light,
Or foil great Jesus' name, it is the Jesuite.

29

When late our Whore of Rome was disarrayed,
Strip't of her pall and scarlet ornaments,
And all her hidden filth lay broad displayed,
Her putrid pendant bags, her mouth that scents
As this of Hell, her hands with scabs arrayed,
Her pust'led skin with ulcered excrements;
Her friends fall off; and those that loved her best
Grow sick to think of such a stinking beast,
And her, and every limb that touch't her, much detest.

30

Who help't us then? Who then her case did rue?
These, onely these, their care and art applied
To hide her shame with tires† and dressing new;   †attire
They blew her bags, they blanch't her leprous hide,
And on her face a lovely picture drew.
But most the Head they pranck't† in all his pride   †adorned
With borrowed plumes, stol'n from Antiquity:
Him with blasphemous names they dignify;
Him they enthrone, adore, they crown, they deify.

31

As when an image gnawn with worms hath lost
His beauty, form, respect, and lofty place,
Some cunning hand new trims the rotten post,
Fills up the worm-holes, paints the soiled face
With choicest colors, spares no art or cost
With precious robes the putrid trunk to grace;
Circles the head with golden beams that shine
Like rising sun: the Vulgar low incline,
And give away their souls unto the block divine.

32

So do these Daedal workmen plaster over
And smooth that stale† with labored polishing;   †decoy
So her defects with art they finely cover,
Clothe her, dress, paint with curious coloring;
So every friend again, and every lover
Returns, and doats through their neat pandaring;
They fill her cup, on knees drink healths to th' Whore;
The drunken nations pledge it o'er and o'er;
So spew, and spewing fall, and falling rise no more.

33

Had not these troops with their new forged arms
Strook in, even air, earth too, and all were lost.
Their fresh assaults and importune alarms
Have Truth repelled, and her full conquest crossed:
Or these or none must recompense our harms.
If they had failed we must have sought a coast
I' th' Moon (the Florentine's new world) to dwell,
And, as from Heaven, from Earth should now have fell
To Hell confined, nor could we safe abide in Hell.

34

Nor shall that little Isle (our envy, spite,
His paradise) escape; even there they long
Have shrouded close their heads from dang'rous Light;
But now more free dare press in open throng;
Nor then were idle, but with practick sleight
Crept into houses great; their sugared tongue
Made easy way into the lapsed breast
Of weaker sex; where lust had built her nest,
There laid they cuckoo eggs, and hatch't their brood unblest.

35

There sow they traitrous seed with wicked hand
'Gainst God and man; well thinks their silly son
To merit Heaven by breaking God's command,
To be a patriot by rebellion.
And when his hopes are lost, his life and land
And he and wife and child are all undone,
Then calls for Heaven and Angels—in step I,
And waft him quick to Hell; thus thousands die,
Yet still their children doat: so fine their forgery.

36

But now that stormy season's laid; their spring
And warmer suns call them from wintry cell.
These better times will fruits much better bring,
Their labors soon will fill the barns of Hell
With plenteous store. Serpents, if warmed, will sting;
And even now they meet and hiss and swell.
Think not of falling, in the name of all
This dare I promise, and make good I shall,
While they thus firmly stand, we cannot wholly fall.

37

And shall these mortals creep, fawn, flatter, lie,
Coin into thousand arts their fruitful brain,
Venter life, limb, through earth and water fly
To win us proselytes? Scorn ease and pain,
To purchase grace in their whore-mistress eye?
Shall they spend, spill their dearest blood to stain
Rome's Calendar,[15] and paint their glorious name
In hers and our saint-rubric? Get them fame,
Where saints are fiends, gain loss, grace disgrace, glory shame?

38

And shall we, Spirits, shall we (whose life and death
Are both immortal), shall we, can we fail?
Great Prince o' th' lower world, in vain we breath
Our spite in Council: free us this our jail.
We do but lose our little time beneath.
All to their charge. Why sit we here to wail?
Kindle your darts and rage. Renew your fight.
We are dismist. Break out upon the Light.
Fill th' Earth with sin and blood, Heaven with storms and fright.

39

With that the bold black Spirit invades the day,
And Heav'n and Light, and Lord of both defies.
All Hell run out, and sooty flags display,
A foul deformed rout. Heav'n shuts his eyes;
The stars look pale, and early morning's ray
Lays down her head again and dares not rise.
A second night of Spirits the air possest;

---

[15] {Liturgical calendars use red ink to designate feasts of martyrs.}

The wakeful cock that late forsook his nest,
Mazed how he was deceived, flies to his roost and rest.

40

So when the South (dipping his sable wings
In humid seas) sweeps with his dropping beard
The air, earth, and ocean; down he flings
The laden trees; the plowman's hopes new-eared
Swim on the plain; his lips' loud thunderings
And flashing eyes make all the world afeard;
Light with dark clouds, waters with fires are met;
The Sun but now is rising, now is set,
And finds West-shades in East, and seas in aïrs wet.

CANTO IIII[16]

. . .

16

So said,[17] and ceased: while all the priestly round
In sullen grief and stupid silence sat:
This bit his lip, that nailed his eye to th' ground,
Some cloud their flaming eyes with scarlet hat,
Some gnash't their spiteful teeth, some loured and frowned,
Till (grief and care driv'n out by spite and hate)
Soft murmurs first gan creep along the crowd;
At length they stormed and chaf't & thundered loud,
And all sad vengeance swore, and all dire mischief vowed.

17

So when a sable cloud with swelling sail
Comes swimming through calm skies, the silent air
(While fierce winds sleep in Æol's rocky jail),
With spangled beams embroid'red, glitters fair;
But soon 'gins lour and groan; straight clatt'ring hail
Fills all with noise, Light hides his golden hair,
Earth with untimely winter's silvered.
Then Loyol's eldest Son lifts up his head,
Whom all with great applause and silence ushered.

---

[16] {In Canto III the devils and Jesuits foment war and civil strife throughout Europe; Equivocus heads to papal Rome, whose corruption is described at length. At the opening of Canto IIII he enters the breast of Pope Paul V, who, gripped by satanic *furor*, summons a conclave charged with reversing the decline of papal power.}

[17] {The subject here is the Pope, who has just finished addressing the demonic conclave.}

18

Most holy Father, priests', kings' Sovereign,
Who equal'st th' highest, makest lesser Gods,
Though Dominic and Loyola now sustain
The Lateran Church, with age it stoops and nods.[18]
Nor have we cause to rest or time to plain:
Rebellious Earth (with Heaven itself to odds)
Conspires to ruin our high envied state.
Yet may we by those arts prolong our date,
Whereby we stand; and if not change, yet stay our fate.

19

When captains strive a fort or town to win,
They lay their batt'ry to the weakest side;
Not where the wall and guard stands thick, but thin;
So that wise Serpent his assault applied,
And with the weaker vessel would begin:
He first the woman with distrust and pride,
Then she the man subdues with flatt'ring lies;
So in one battle gets two victories.
Our foe will teach us fight, our fall will teach us rise.

20

Our Chief, who every sleight and engine knows,   *Bellarmine*
While on th' old troops he spent his restless pains,
With equal arms assaulting equal foes,
What hath he got, or we? What fruit, what gains
Ensued? we bear the loss, and he the blows;
And while each part their wit and learning strains,
The breach repairs, and (foiled) new force assumes;
Their hard encounters and hot angry fumes
Strike out the sparkling fire, which lights them, us consumes.

21

Instead of heavy arms, hence use we slight;
Trade we with those, which trained in ignorance
Have small acquaintance with that heavenly Light:
Those who disgrac't by some misgovernance
(Their own, or others') swell with grief or spite.
But nothing more our Kingdom must advance
Or further our designs, than to comply

---

[18] Pope Innocent the 3 dreamed that the Lateran church at Rome was falling, but that Saint Dominic, setting to his shoulders, underpropt it, whereupon he confirmed his order.

With that weak sex, and by fine forgery
To worm in women's hearts, chiefly the rich and high.[19]

22

Nor let the stronger scorn these weaker powers;
The labor's less with them, the harvest more:
They easier yield and win; so fewer hours
Are spent; for women sooner drink our lore,
Men sooner sip it from their lips than ours;
Sweetly they learn and sweetly teach, with store
Of tears, smiles, kisses, and ten thousand arts
They lay close batt'ry to men's frailer parts;
So finely steal themselves, and us, into their hearts.

23

That strongest Champion, who with naked hands
A lion tore, who all unarmed and bound
Heap't mounts of armed foes on bloody sands,
By woman's art, without or force or wound
Subdued, now in a mill, blind, grinding stands.
That sun of wisdom, which the Preacher crowned
Great King of arts, bewitch't with women's smiles,
Fell deep in seas of folly by their wiles.
Wit, strength, and grace itself yield to their flatt'ring guiles.

24

This be our skirmish; for the main, release
The Spanish forces, free strong Belgia
From fear of war, let arms and armies cease.
What got our Alva, John of Austria?
Our captain, Guile; our weapons, Ease and Peace—
These more prevail than Parma, Spinola.
The Dutch shall yield us arms and men; there dwell
Arminians, who from Heaven half-way fell:
A doubtful sect, which hang 'tween truth, lies, Heaven and Hell.

25

These Epicenes have sown their subtle brain
With thorny difference and neat illusion;
Proud, fierce; the adverse part they much disdain.
These must be handled soft with fine collusion:

[19] {Probably a reference to the *Monita secreta*, allegedly a secret Jesuit tract giving rules for increasing the wealth and power of the Order; flattering the wives of the powerful was highly recommended. The manuscript was discovered in 1612 and first published in 1614, with 22 further editions by 1700.}

For Calvin's hate, to side with Rome and Spain,
To work their own and their own home's confusion.
And by large sums, more hopes, we must bring in
Wise Barnevelt to lay our plotted gin:
So where the lion fails, the fox shall eas'ly win.

. . .

29

All this a prologue to our Tragedy.
My head's in travail of an hideous
And fearful birth, such as may fright the sky,
Turn back the sun: help, help Ignatius.
And in this act prove thy new Deity.
I have a plot worthy of Rome and us,
Which with amazement Heaven and Earth shall fill.
Nor care I whether right, wrong, good, or ill:
Church-profit is our law; our only rule, thy will.

30

That blessed Isle, so often curst in vain,
Triumphing in our loss and idle spite,
Of force shall shortly stoop to Rome and Spain.
I'll take a way ne'er known to man or sprite.
To kill a King is stale, and I disdain;
That fits a Secular, not a Jesuite.
Kings, Nobles, Clergy, Commons, high and low,
The Flower of England in one hour I'll mow,
And head† all th' Isle with one unseen, unfenced blow.   †behead

31

A goodly frame, raised high with carved stones,
Leaning his lofty head on marble stands
Close by that Temple, where the honored bones
Of Britain Kings and many princely Grands
Adorned rest with golden scutcheons,
Garnish't with curious work of daedal hands.
Low at his base the swelling Thamis falls,
And sliding down along those stately halls,
Doth that chief City wash, and fence with liquid walls.

32

Here all the States in full assembly meet,
And every order rank't in fit array,
Clothed with rich robes fill up the crowded street.
Next 'fore the King, his Heïr leads the way,

Glitt'ring with gems and royal coronet—
So golden Phosphor† ushers in the day—   †the morning star
And all the while the trumpets triumphs sound,
And all the while the people's votes resound:
Their shouts and tramplings shake the air and dancing ground.

33

There in Astrea's balance do they weigh
The right and wrong, reward and punishment;
And rigor with soft equity allay,
Curb lawless lust and stablish government;
There Rome itself, and us, they dare affray
With bloody laws and threat'nings violent:
Hence all our suff'rings, torments exquisite,[20]
Varied in thousand forms, applied to fright
The harmless yet (alas!) and spotless Jesuite.

34

But cellars large and caverns vaulted deep
With bending arches borne and columns strong,
Under that stately building slyly creep:
Here Bacchus lies, concealed from Juno's wrong,[21]
Whom those cold vaults from hot-breathed airs keep.
In place of these we'll other barrels throng,
Stuf't with those fiery sands and black dry mould,
Which from blue Phlegeton's shores that Friar[22] bold
Stole with dire hand, and yet Hell's force and color hold.

35

And when with numbers just the house gins swell,
And every State hath filled his statiön,
When now the King, mounted on lofty sell†,   †seat
With honeyed speech and combed oratiön
Charms every ear, midst of that sugared spell
I'll tear the walls, blow up the natiön,
Bullet to Heaven the stones with thunders loud,
Equal to th' Earth the courts and turrets proud,
And fire the shaking town, & quench't with royal blood.

[20] The printed lies concerning the torments of their Roman martyrs, which I saw in the study of that learned knight, Sir Thomas Hutchinson, privileged by the pope, are for their monstrous impudency incredible.

[21] {The gunpowder was stored in a wine cellar.}

[22] {Fletcher may be referring to the 13th-century Franciscan, Roger Bacon, whose *Opus maior* contains the first known recipe for gunpowder in the West; more likely, however, the allusion is to the mythical monk Berthold Schwartz, whom a late 14th-century legend credits with gunpowder's invention.}

36

Oh how my dancing heart leaps in my breast
But to fore-think that noble tragedy!
I thirst, I long for that blood-royal feast.
See where their laws, see, Holy Father, see
Where laws and makers, and above the rest
Kings marshal'd in due place through th' aïr flee:
There goes the heart, there th' head, there singed bones.
Hark, Father, hark; hear'st not those music tones?
Some roar, some howl, some shriek; Earth, Hell, and Aïr groans.

37

Thus sang, and down he sat, while all the Choir
Attune their echoing voices to his lays;
Some Jesuit piety and zealous fire,
Some his deep reaching wit and judgment praise;
And all the plot commend, and all admire,
But most great Paul† himself; a while he stays, †Pope Paul V, 1605–21
Then sudden rising, with embraces long
He hugs his son, while yet the passion strong
Wanting due vent, makes tears his words, and eyes his tongue.

. . .

CANTO V

1

Look as a wayward child would something have,
Yet flings away, wralls,† spurns, his nurse abuses; †squirms
So froward man, what most his longings crave
(Likeness to God), proffered by God refuses;
But will be rather Sin's base drudge and slave.
The shade by Satan promised greed'ly chooses,
And with it Death and Hell. Oh wretched state,
Where not the eyes, but feet direct the gait!
So miss what most we wish, and have what most we hate.

2

Thus will this Man of Sin† be like to Christ: †The pope,
A king, yet not in Heaven, but Earth that reigns;   imagined as anti-Christ
That murthers, saves not Christians; th' highest Priest,
Yet not to wait his course (that he disdains)
But to advance aloft his mitred crest,
That Christ himself may wait upon his trains.
Strange Priest, oft Heaven he sells, but never buys;

Strange Doctor, hating truth, enforcing lies:
Thus Satan is indeed, and Christ by contraries.

3

And such his Ministers all glist'ring bright
In night and shades, and yet but rotten wood
And fleshly Devils; such this Jesuit,
Who (Loyol's Ensign) thirsts for English blood.
He culls choice souls (souls vowed to th' Prince of night,
And Priest of Rome), swears them (an English brood,
But hatch't in Rome for Spain) close to conceal,
And execute what he should then reveal;
Binds them to Hell in sin, & makes Heaven's Lord the seal.[23]

4

Now are they met: this armed with a spade,
That with a mattock, void of shame and fear.
The earth (their Grandam Earth) they fierce invade,
And all her bowels search and rent and tear;
Then by her ruins flesh't, much bolder made,
They ply their work; and now near Hell, they hear
Soft voices, murmurs, doubtful whisperings:
The fearful conscience, prick't with guilty stings,
A thousand hellish forms into their fancy brings.

5

This like a statue stands; cold fright congeals
His marble limbs; to th' earth another falling,
Creeping behind a barrel softly steals;
A third into an empty hogshead crawling
Locks up his eyes, draws in his straggling heels;
A fourth, in vain for succor loudly calling,
Flies through the air as swift as gliding star;
Pale, ghastly, like infernal sprites afar
Each to his fellow seems; and so, or worse, they are.

6

So when in sleep's soft grave dead senses rest,
An earthly vapor clamb'ring up the brain
Brings in a meagre ghost, whose launched breast
Showers down his naked corps a bloody rain;
A dull-blue-burning torch about his crest
He ghastly waves. Half dead with frightful pain

---

[23] {The conspirators took an oath on the Blessed Sacrament.}

The leaden foot fain would, but cannot fly;
The gaping mouth fain would, but cannot cry;
And now awake still dreams, nor trusts his open eye;

7

At length those streams of life, which ebbing low
Were all retired into the frighted heart,
Back to their wonted channels gan to flow.
So peeping out, yet trembling every part,
And list'ning now with better heed, they know
Those next adjoining rooms hollowed by art
To lie for cellerage: which glad they hire,
And cram with powder and unkindled fire.[24]
Slack aged Time with plaints and prayers they daily tire.

8

Slow Time, which every hour grow'st old and young,
Which every minute die'st, and liv'st again;
Which mak'st the strong man weak, the weak man strong;
Sad time which fly'st in joy, but creep'st in pain,
Thy steps uneven are still too short or long.
Devouring Time, who bear'st a fruitful train,
And eat'st what e're thou bear'st, why dost not flee,
Why dost not post to view a tragedy,
Which never Time yet saw, which never Time shall see?

9

Among them all, none so impatient
Of stay as fiery Faux, whose grisly feature
Adorned with colors of Hell's regiment
(Soot black and fiery red) betrayed his nature.
His frighted mother, when her time she went,
Oft dreamt she bore a strange & monstrous creature,
A brand of Hell swelt'ring in fire and smoke,
Who all, and 's mother's self would burn and choke.
So dreamt she in her sleep, so found she when she woke.

10

Rome was his Nurse, and Spain his Tutor; she
With wolvish milk flesh't him in deadly lies,
In hate of Truth, and stubborn error; he
Fats him with human blood, inures his eyes

---

[24] {When the conspirators' attempt to dig a tunnel failed, they rented the cellar underneath the Parliament.}

Dash't brains, torn guts, and trembling hearts to see,
And tuned his ear with groans and shrieking cries.
Thus nurst, bred, grown a cannibal! Now prest
To be the leader of this troop, he blest
His bloody maw with thought of such a royal feast.

11

Meantime the Eye which needs no light to see,
That wakeful Eye, which never winks or sleeps,
That purest Eye, which hates iniquity,
That careful Eye, which safe his Israel keeps,
From which no word or thought can hidden be,
Looks from his Heaven, and piercing through the deeps,
With hate and scorn views the dire Jesuit
Weary his hand and quintessential wit
To weave himself a snare and dig himself a pit.

12

That mounting Eagle, which beneath his throne,
His sapphire throne, fixed on crystal base,
Broadly dispreads his heaven-wide pinion,
On whom, when sinful Earth he strikes with 'maze,
He wide displays his black pavilion,
And thund'ring, fires high towers with flashing blaze,
Dark waters draw their sable curtains o'er him,
With flaming wings the burning Angels shore him,
The clouds & guilty heavens for fear fly fast before him:

13

That mounting Eagle forth he sudden calls:
Fly, winged Herald, to that City fly,
Whose towers my Love, Truth, Wisdom builds and walls;
There to the Council this foul plot descry;
And while thy doubtful writ their wit appalls,
That great Peace-maker's sense I'll open; I
Will clear his mind, and plain those riddling folds.
So said, so done. No place or time withholds
His instant course: the town he thinks, he sees, and holds.

14

There in another shape to that wise Peer†   †Robert Cecil
(That wisest Peer) he gives a darksome spell;
He was the State's Treasure and Treasurer,
Spain's fear, but England's earthly oracle;
He patron to my Mother Cambridge, where

Thousand sweet Muses, thousand Graces dwell.
But neither he nor human wit could find
The riddle's sense, till that learned royal mind,
Lighted from Heaven, soon the knot and plot untwined.

15

And now the fatal morn approached near;
The Sun and every Star had quench't their light,
Loathing so black a deed: the Artic Bear,
Enjoined to stay, trembling at such a sight,
Though drench't in airy seas, yet wink't for fear.
But hellish Faux laughed at blind Heaven's affright.
What? Such a deed not seen? In vain (saith he)
You drown your lights; if Heaven envious be,
I'll bring hell-fires for light, that all the world may see.

16

So ent'ring in, reviews th' infernal mines;
Marshals his casks anew, and ord'ring right
The tragic scene, his hellish work refines;
And now returned, booted and drest for flight,
A watchful swain the miner undermines,
Holds, binds, brings out the Plot to view the light:
The world amazed, Hell yawned, Earth gaped, Heaven stared,
Rome howled to see long hopes so sudden marred:
The net was set, the fowl escap't, the fowler snared.

17

Oh thou great Shepherd—Earth's, Heaven's Sovereign—
Whom we thy pasture-sheep admire, adore:
See all thy flocks prostrate on Britain plain,
Pluck't from the slaughter, fill their mouths with store
Of incens't praise; oh see, see every swain
'Mazed with thy works, much 'mazed but ravish't more,
Pour out their hearts thy glorious name to raise.
Fire thou our zealous lips with thankful lays;
Make this saved Isle to burn in love, to smoke in praise.

18

Teach me thy groom, here dulled in fenny mire,
In these sweet lays, oh teach me bear a part;
Oh thou dread Spirit, shed thy heavenly fire,
Thy holy flame into this frozen heart;
Teach thou my creeping Muse to Heaven aspire;
Learn my rude breast, learn me that sacred art,

Which once thou taught'st thy Israel's shepherd-King;
O raise my soft vein to high thundering;
Tune thou my lofty song, thy glory would I sing.

19

Thou liv'dst before, beyond, without all time;
Art held in none, yet fillest every place.
Ah, how (alas!) how then shall mortal slime
With sinful eyes view that eternal space
Or comprehend thy name in measured rhyme?
To see forth-right the eye was set i' th' face;
Hence infinite to come I well descry;
Past infinite no creature sees with eye;
Only th' Eternal's self measures eternity.

20

And yet by thee, to thee all live and move;
Thou without place or time giv'st times and places.
The Heavens (thy throne) thou liftest all above,
Which, folded in their mixt but pure embraces,
Teach us in their conjunctions chastest love.
Next to the Earth, the Moon performs her races;
Then Mercury; beyond, the Phosphor bright:
These with their friendly heat and kindly might
Warm pallid Cynthia's cold and drain her wat'ry light.

21

Far thou remov'st slow Saturn's frosty drythe,†   †dryness, drought
And thaw'st his ice with Mars his flaming ire;
Betwixt them Jove by thy appointment fly'th,
Who parts and tempers well his son and sire;
His moist flames dull the edge of Saturn's scythe,
And airy moisture softens Mars his fire.
The Heart of Heaven midst of Heaven's body rides,[25]
From whose full sea of light and springing tides
The lesser streams of light fill up their empty sides.

22

The Virgin Earth, all in green-silken weed
(Embroidered fair with thousand flowers) arrayed,
Whose womb untilled knew yet nor plow nor seed,
Nor midwifry of man, nor heaven's aid,

---

[25] {This sounds like heliocentrism, but the following lines, which imply that the stars take their light from the sun, bespeak a pre-scientific cosmology.}

Amazed to see her num'rous virgin breed,
Her fruit even fruitful, yet her self a maid;
The Earth of all the low'st, yet middle lies;
Nor sinks, though loosely hanged in liquid skies:
For rising were her fall, and falling were her rise.

23

Next Earth, the Sea a testy neighbor raves,
Which, casting mounts and many a churlish hill,
Discharges 'gainst her walls his thund'ring waves,
Which all the shores with noise and tumult fill;
But all in vain: thou beat'st down all his braves;
When thee he hears commanding, *Peace, be still*,
Down straight he lowly falls, disbands his trains,
Sinks in himself, and all his mountains plains;
Soft peace in all the shores, and quiet stillness reigns.

24

Thou mad'st the circling air aloft to fly
And all this Round enfold at thy command;
So thin, it never could be seen with eye;
So gross, it may be felt with every hand.
Next to the hornèd Moon and neighbor sky,
The fire thou highest bad'st, but farthest stand.
Strangely thou temper'st their adverse affection;
Though still they hate and fight, by thy direction
Their strife maintains their own and all the world's perfection.

25

For Earth's cold arm cold Winter friendly holds,
But with his dry the other's wet defies;
The Air's warmth detests the Water's colds;
But both a common moisture jointly ties;
Warm Air with mutual love hot Fire enfolds,
As moist, his drythe abhors; drythe Earth allies
To Fire, but heats with cold new wars address:
Thus by their peaceful fight and fighting peace
All creatures grow, and die, and dying still increase.

26

Above them all thou sit'st, who gav'st all being,
All everywhere, in all, and over all;
Thou, their great Umpire, all their strife agreeing,
Bend'st their stiff natures to thy sovereign call.
Thine eye their law; their steps by overseeing

Thou overrul'st and keep'st from slipp'ry fall.
Oh if thy steady hand should not maintain
What first it made, all straight would fall again,
And nothing of this All, save nothing, would remain.

27

Thou bid'st the Sun piece out the ling'ring day,
Glitt'ring in golden fleece. The lovely Spring
Comes dancing on; the Primrose strews her way,
And satin Violet; lambs wantoning
Bound o'er the hillocks in their sportful play;
The wood-musicians chant and cheerily sing;
The World seems new, yet old by youth's accruing.
Ah wretched men, so wretched world pursuing,
Which still grows worse with age, and older by renewing!

28

At thy command th' Earth travails of her fruit;
The Sun yields longer labor, shorter sleep;
Out-runs the Lion in his hot pursuit;
Then of the golden Crab learns back to creep.
Thou Autumn bid'st (drest in straw-yellow suit)
To press, tun, hide his grapes in cellars deep;
Thou cloth'st the Earth with freeze[26] instead of grass,
While keen-breathed Winter steels her furrowed face,
And vials rivers up, and seas, in crystal glass.

29

What but thy love and thou which feel no change?
Seas fill and want; their waters fall and grow.
The windy air each hour can wildly range.
Earth lives and dies; Heaven's lights can ebb and flow:
Thy Spouse herself†, while yet a Pilgrim strange,   †the Church
Treading this weary world (like Cynthia's bow),
Now full of glorious beams and sparkling light,
Then soon opposed, eclipsed with earthly spite,
Seems drowned in sable clouds, buried in endless night.

30

See, Lord, ah see thy rancorous enemies
Blown up with envious spite, but more with hate,
Like boisterous winds and seas high-working, rise;

---

[26] {pun on "frieze," a coarse, woolen cloth}

So earthly fires, wrapt up in wat'ry night,
With dire approach invade the glist'ring skies,
And bid the Sun put out his sparkling light;
See, Lord, unless thy right hand even steers,
Oh if thou anchor not these threat'ning fears,
Thy Ark will sail as deep in blood, as now in tears.

31

That cursed Beast (which with thy princely horns,
With all thy styles and high prerogatives
His carrion corpse and serpent's head adorns)
His croaking Frogs to every quarter drives;
See how the key of that deep pit he turns,
And clucks his Locusts from their smoky hives;
See how they rise, and with their numerous swarms
Filling the world with fogs and fierce alarms,
Bury the Earth with bloodless corpse and bloody arms.

32

The bastard Son of that old Dragon (red
With blood of Saints) and all his petty States;
That triple monster, Geryon,† who bred,   †Spain
Nurs't, flesh't in blood, thy servants deadly hates;[27]
And that seducèd Prince† who hath his head   †Presumably Louis XIII
Eyes, ears, and tongue all in the Jesuit pates: of France
All these, and hundred kings and nations, drunk
With whorish Cup of that dire witch and punk,
Have sworn to see thy Church in death for ever sunk.

33

Now from those hell-hounds turn thy glorious eyes;
See, see thy fainting Spouse swim, sink in tears.
Hear, Lord, oh hear her groans and shrieking cries.
Those eyes long wait for thee. Lord, to thine ears
She brings heart, lips, a turtle-sacrifice.†   †the biblical sacrifice of a
Thy cursed foe that pro-Christ trophies rears:[28]   turtle-dove
How long (just Lord), how long wilt thou delay
That drunken Whore with blood and fire to pay?
Thy Saints, thy Truth, thy Name's blasphemed: how canst thou stay?

[27] {"Thy servants" is the object of "hates."}
[28] {This line seems corrupt.}

34

Oh is not this the time, when mounted high
Upon thy Pegasus of heavenly breed,
With bloody arms, white armies, flaming eye,
Thou vow'st in blood to swim thy snowy steed,
And stain thy bridle with a purple dye?
This, this thy time; come then, oh come with speed,
Such as thy Israel saw thee, when the main
Piled up his waves on heaps; the liquid plain
Ran up, and with his hill safe walled that wand'ring train.

Revel. 19:11-14; Revel. 14:20

35

Such as we saw thee late, when Spanish braves
(Preventing fight with printed victory),
Full fraught with brands, whips, gyves for English slaves,
Blest by their Lord God Pope, thine enemy,
Turned seas to woods. Thou armed with fires, winds, waves,
Frownd'st on their pride. They fear, they faint, they fly;
Some sink in drinking seas or drunken sand,
Some yield, some dash on rocks; the Spanish Grand†
Banquets the fish in seas, or fowls and dogs on land.

†grandees

36

Oh when wilt thou unlock the seeled eyes
Of those ten horns; and Kings, which with the Beast
(Yet by thy hand[29]) 'gan first to swell and rise,
How long shall they (charmed with her drunken feast)
Give her their crowns? Bewitch't with painted lies,
They dream thy Spirit breathes from her sugared breast,
Thy Sun burns with her eye-reflected beams,
From her life, light, all grace and glory streams.
Wake these enchanted sleeps, shake out these hellish dreams.

Revel. 17:12-13, 16

37

Wake, lesser Gods, you sacred Deputies
Of Heaven's King, awake: see, see the Light
Bares that foul Whore, dispels her sorceries:
Blanch't skin, dead lips, sour breath, splay foot, owl-sight.
Ah, can you dote on such deformities?
While you will serve in crowns, and beg your right,
Pray, give, fill up her never filled desire,
You her white sons: else knives, dags, death your hire.
Scorn this base yoke: strip, eat, and burn her flesh in fire.

Revel. 17:16

[29] {I.e., all royal power comes from God's hand.}

38

But thou, Great Prince, in whose successful reign,
Thy Britains 'gin renew their martial fame,
Our Sovereign Lord, our joy more sovereign,
Our only Charles, under whose ominous name
Rome wounded first, still pines in ling'ring pain;[30]
Thou who hast seen and loathed Rome's whorish shame:
Rouse those brave sparks which in thy bosom swell,
Cast down this second Lucifer to Hell;
So shalt thou all thy sires, so shalt thy self excel.

39

'Tis not in vain that Christ hath girt thy head
With three fair peaceful Crowns; 'tis not in vain
That in thy Realms such spirits are daily bred
Which thirst and long to tug with Rome and Spain.
Thy royal Sire to Kings this lecture read;
This, this deserved his pen and learned vein.
Here, noble Charles, enter thy chivalry;
The Eagle scorns at lesser game to fly:
Only this war's a match worthy thy realms & thee.[31]

40

Ah happy man, that lives to see that day!
Ah happy man, who in that war shall bleed!
Happy who bears the standard in that fray!
Happy who quells that rising Babel seed!
Thrice happy who that Whore shall doubly pay!
This (royal Charles), this be thy happy meed.
Mayst thou that triple diadem trample down;
This shall thy name in Earth and Heaven renown,
And add to these three here, there a thrice triple crown.

TEXT: *The locusts, or Apollyonists*, in *Giles and Phineas Fletcher: poetical works*, 2 vols., ed. Frederick Boas (Cambridge UP, 1908), 1:128–86.

Checked against Phineas Fletcher, *The locusts, or Apollyonists* (Printed by Thomas Bucks and John Bucks, printers to the University of Cambridge, 1627)[32] (STC [2nd ed.] / 11081).

[30] {an allusion to Charles V's sack of Rome in 1527}

[31] {Between 1626 and 1628, Charles did, catastrophically, declare war on the Catholic powers of Spain and France.}

[32] {The title page of the volume as a whole mentions only the *Locustae, vel pietas Jesuitica*. *The locusts*, which follows the Latin mini-epic, gets its own title page and dedication, but the pagination is continuous throughout.}

J.R.

The spy: discovering the danger of Arminian heresy and Spanish treachery
(1628)

.

Despite some awkward dislocations of word order, this is a neoclassical verse satire of not negligible poetic merit. It is also a seditious libel, representative of the kind of religio-political writing that precipitated the crisis of trust that became the English Civil War. *The spy* seeks, quite overtly, to foment suspicion of England's clerical and political leadership. The first half, the part that concerns religion, argues that numerous high-ranking churchmen only seem to be loyal Protestants, but are in fact a fifth-column working on behalf of Spain and the papacy to carry out a plan concocted in hell, which seeks to overthrow Protestantism by a divide-and-conquer strategy: the diabolic Arminius will infect Protestant lands—above all, England—with popish-pelagian doctrines, breeding doubt and discord that will prepare the way for a Spanish-papist take-over.

The basic outlines of this conspiracy derive from Dutch Calvinist pamphlets of ca. 1618 that invented the link between Arminius and the Catholic powers in order to justify the execution of the Arminian statesman, Johan van Oldenbarneveldt <see *The spy*, l. 659>, but the motif soon crossed the Channel, where it informs the final scene of Thomas Scott's 1620 *Vox populi* and Francis Rous' 1629 Parliamentary rant about how "an Arminian is the spawn of Papist."[2]

The overarching ideological framework, however, is the apocalyptic reading of history as "an endless bloody war that never yet / Cessation, truce, or peace did once admit" <ll. 104–5> between Satan's followers and God's elect. "Bloody" is crucial. Augustinian historiography, although hinging on the structural opposition between the city of God and city of man, imagined the actual relation between these two cities in this life not as war but coexistence, since, although the citizens of the two cities pursue different ultimate ends, they share common temporal goals; for both, peace, justice, concord, prosperity are

---

[1] {The poem is often attributed to one John Russell (d. 1688), the author of several poems praising Gustavus Adolphus.}

[2] See the introduction to the *Collegiate suffrage* <*supra*, n. 3>; also Shuger, *Censorship*, 40–45; Trevor-Roper, 124–30.

real and legitimate goods. For *The spy*, written during the final terrible decades of nearly a century of pan-European confessional wars, the history of God's Church is written in blood.[3] At points, the poem implies that the blood will always be that of the saints: suffering is the sign of the true Church, persecuting the badge of antichrist <ll. 198–200, 134–35>. Yet the allure of godly militancy rather compromises this martyrological paradigm; the call to heroic Christian warfare against the Hapsburgs <ll. 25–41> and the concluding plea that deviations from Reformed orthodoxy meet swift punishment indicate a willingness to play persecutor (under another name).

An anti-papist, apocalyptic militancy characterizes swathes of English Protestantism from the mid-Elizabethan period. The radicalism of *The spy* comes from its insistence that the real danger is the enemy within: above all, the Arminian quislings in the English Church, who "under name of Truth's stout'st champions, work / Her ruin" <ll. 448–52>. Even if they themselves are not Spanish-Romish operatives (although the poem seems to think this likely), their questioning of Reformed orthodoxy threatens both the Protestant cause and England itself, because religion constitutes the principle bond holding together mystical bodies like churches and nations. The devil and his allies conscripted Arminius precisely in order to foment religious division within Protestantism, for

> None's hurt but by himself. To Christ none is
> A foe so mortal as he that seems his.
> Schisms in the Church are like, i'th'soul, a wound:
> To cure't no Aesculapius can be found.
>
> <ll. 580–84>

Hence, despite the opening complaints about censorship, *The spy* views toleration even of small doctrinal differences as catastrophic—a sure way to turn the Church's "happy peace to bloody war" <l. 629>—and recommends shutting down any nascent public sphere, since allowing religion to be debated "in public print" breeds nothing but doubt and suspicion "'mongst the vulgar sort" <ll. 664–76>.[4]

The selection printed below is the first half of the poem; the second half concerns the sins and crimes of the Duke of Buckingham, particularly his responsibility for England's recent military catastrophes.

Sources: Alastair Bellany, *The politics of court scandal in early modern England* (Cambridge UP, 2002); "The murder of John Lambe" *P&P* 200 (2008): 37–76, and his "Railing rhymes revisited: libels, scandal, and early Stuart politics," *History Compass* 5.4 (2007): 1136–79; Cyndia Clegg, *Press censorship in Caroline England* (Cambridge UP, 2008); David Colclough, *Freedom of speech in early Stuart England* (Cambridge

[3] This martyrological-militarist view of history is already implicit in Calvin's reading of Isa. 63:1-3 (quoted in the introduction to Andrewes' 1623 Easter sermon <*supra*>), which breaks with the traditional exegesis of the passage precisely by seeing it as prophetic of the military victory of the saints over their enemies rather than of Christ's spiritual victory over death and hell.

[4] On *The spy*'s refusal of free speech to ideological opponents, see Norbrook 52, and, for the opposing view, Colclough 118.

UP, 2005); Wilhelmina Frijlinck, ed. and intro., *The tragedy of Sir John van Olden Barnavelt* (Amsterdam: H. G. van Dorssen, 1922); Andrew McRae, *Literature, satire and the early Stuart state* (Cambridge UP, 2004); McRae, ed., *Railing rhymes: politics and poetry in early Stuart England*, special issue of *HLQ* 69.1 (2006); David Norbrook, *Writing the English Republic* (Cambridge UP, 1999); Kevin Sharpe, *The personal rule of Charles I* (Yale UP, 1992); Shuger, *Censorship*; Hugh Trevor-Roper, *The crisis of the seventeenth-century* [1967], Online Library of Liberty, http://files.libertyfund.org/files/719/0098_LFeBk.pdf (accessed June 7, 2012).

J.R.

The spy: discovering the danger of Arminian heresy and Spanish treachery[1]
1628

Possibile est satyras non scribere?[2]

TO all zealous Professors and true hearted Patriots in Great Britain:

My blushing disabilities have at length adventured to pass the pikes of censure—unprovided of any other arms or ornaments than sincere loyalty, devoted to my king and country's service—rather than my king and country should be (for want of a timely discovery of those dangers, wherein they have been cunningly and intricately entangled) thrust blindfold upon the pikes of foreign enemies or the poniards of domestic traitors. Sooner had these naked raptures visited the world had this age afforded but an Egyptian midwife to forward them. Fain would they have fluttered abroad the last Parliament, but the supercilious looks of over-awing greatness had so daunted these degenerous times, that none durst adventure to give wings to their desire. Howsoever, I hope, their flight home from a foreign country will not now be unseasonable. . . .

Strasbourg, Aug. 23. sty. vet.

Your affectionate though afflicted servant and countryman, J. R.

THE SPY[3]

MVST I turn mad like Solon and write rhymes,
When Philippics would better fit the times?
Yes, yes, I must. For whatsoe'er they be,
In press or pulpit, dare of speech be free

---

[1] {The title page gives Strasbourg as the place of publication but the work was probably printed in Amsterdam. On the printing of radical puritan materials in Amsterdam, often with a false title page, see Keith Sprunger, *Trumpets from the tower: English puritan printing in the Netherlands, 1600–1640* (Brill, 1994).}

[2] {An echo of Juvenal's "*difficile est saturam non scribere*" (1.30).}

[3] {Marginal glosses marked by † are editorial. Those marked with a * were in the original.}

In Truth's behalf and vent their grieved mind
In phrase more serious or some graver kind
(Though at the common good they only aim,
And be as strictly careful to shun blame
As wisdom can devise), they cannot 'scape
The malice of the age. Some mouths must gape   10
(Whose guilty conscience tells them, this was penned
To lash at us) their sland'rous breath to spend
In their disgrace, and bring them into hate
As movers of sedition in the state—
As if Truth's friend must needs be England's foe.
These rhymes, I hope, shall not be censur'd so.
Councels[4] of old encourag'd such men still
(Till those made councilors did curb their will)
Who boldly would, for public safety, utter
What now the best, in private, dare not mutter   20
Under the Fleet's† damnation. Nay 'tis fear'd,   †Fleet prison
That their advice in Council is not heard
Who pass their cues enjoin'd, or else come short.[5]
Nor is this strange, for we have precedents for't.
Our fathers dead, their sons their courage lost;
Many of blood, of spirit few can boast.
Where now is Essex, Norris, Raleigh, Drake
(At whose remembrance yet proud Spain doth quake)?
Where's Burleigh, Cecil, all those axletrees
Of state, that brought our foes upon their knees?   30
Where are such fearless, peerless Peers become?
All silenc'd? What, is all the world turned dumb?
Oh how hath treach'rous coward fear enchanted
This plying† temporizing age, and danted   †spineless
Our noblest spirits? what dull heavy fate
Hath lull'd asleep and stupifi'd our state
That few will see, at least none dare disclose,
Those plots our foreign and domestic foes
Have laid to ruin us? Shall th'Austrian brood†   †the Hapsburgs
Abroad be gorg'd and glutted with the blood   40
Of our allies and friends? nay shall they here
At home a Babel of confusion rear,
And none speak to prevent it? is there not
Unslaughter'd or unpoison'd left one Scot
Dares tell the blindfold state it headlong reels

---

[4] {both "councils" (as in "Privy Council") and "counsels"}
[5] {who disregard their proper role or else show up late (?)}

To Spanish thralldom upon Spanish wheels?[6]
And that those pillars may be justly fear'd
Will fall on us, that we ourselves have rear'd?

    Then give him leave (for Sion's sake) to speak,
Whose heart with grief, had it no vent, would break.   50
Thou therefore, sacred Mother, Christ's dear wife†   †the Church
(From whose pure breasts, I suck'd the food of life),
And thou, dear country (in whose peaceful lap
First to receive my breath 'twas my blest hap),
Vouchsafe t'accept and graciously peruse
Th'abortive offspring of an unripe Muse;
And suffer not weak insufficiency
To counterpoise his heart's true loyalty
In your affections, who, to do you good,
Would think th'exhausion of his dearest blood   60
Great happiness; and want of liberty,
Large freedom; nay, could ev'n contented be
Or for your safety to be sacrific'd
Or your salvation anathematiz'd.†   †Rom. 9:3

    Nor fear I censure, though strict Cato read,
Whil'st in the well-known path of Truth I tread,
And travail in her cause. The subject's weight
Repels the breath of ev'ry vain conceit.
And for Spain's agents and time's flatt'ring minions,
I neither pass[7] their persons nor opinions.
For God, that doth the hearts of all men see,
Knows my intentions just and honest be.
'Tis no vainglorious humor makes me do it,
Nor doth malicious envy force me to it,   75
But hate of Spanish treason and true zeal
Unto the good of Church and Commonweal.
Why, therefore, arméd with so just a cause,
Should I the censure fear of rightful laws?
Or once suspect a check or prohibition
From any but a popish-pack'd Commisssion?†   †High Commission
Nor can the Council take such subjects ill
As to true patriots have been welcome still.
What ever yet did merit condemnation,

[6] {The "Scot" is Thomas Scot, author of the anti-Arminian/anti-Spanish *Vox populi* (1624). "Unpoison'd" alludes to the widespread rumor that Buckingham was responsible for poisoning both the Scottish Marquis of Hamilton and King James; see Shuger, *Censorship*, 35–40; Tom Cogswell, "John Felton, popular political culture, and the assassination of the Duke of Buckingham," *Historical Journal* 49 (2006): 357–85; Alastair Bellany, "The poisoning of legitimacy? Court scandal, news culture, and politics in England 1603–1660." Diss. Princeton, 1995.}

[7] {"pass" can mean "sit in judgment on" or "approve of"}

Tending alone to public preservation?
Mistake me not (you props of state), I pray: 85
Such bold presumption never yet bare sway
In my acknowledg'd weakness, as to go
About t'inform your well-tri'd judgments. No,
I but persuade and not prescribe, incite
And not instruct your wisdoms, to what's right.
Those then of malice shall traduce my name,
By being guilty, bring themselves to shame;
Should such squint, Lamian,[8] envious eyes reflect
On their own breasts, they would themselves correct
Before they would censure others. But such spite
Shall never mount my Muse's lowest flight.
So high this world I prize not as to close
With falsehood's fautours† and God's favor lose.   †flatterers
If friends by flatt'ry be procur'd alone,
Befriend me Heav'n, on earth I'll look for none.   100
Grant therefore, God of Truth, into his hands
I never fall that holy Truth withstands.

The Explanation of the Table Prefixed.[9]

AN endless bloody war that never yet
Cessation, truce, or peace did once admit,
From the world's cradle to[10] its hoary age
Hath still been wag'd with unappeased rage
By cursed Satan and his damned bands
Of reprobates against Christ's Church. Like sands
Her foes in number are; no station's free   110
From fierce assaults and furious battery.
When time began this malice first began,
Nor will it end but with the latest man
Time shall produce. Thus justice hath decreed:
Those shall be crown'd in Heav'n, on earth must bleed.
To exercise the Church's patience, hope,
And faith, God hath ordain'd a Turk or Pope
To persecute her saints: her sins to scourge,
And from her purer gold the dross to purge
Of vain corruption; oft He tries in flames   120

---

[8] {The Lamia-myth has many variants; according to some versions, she eats children out of envy of their mothers; according to others, she is unable to close her eyes to block out the images of the dead children. See http://en.wikipedia.org/wiki/Lamia_(mythology) (accessed June 7, 2012).}

[9] {The EEBO text lacks any table (i.e., picture); it is conceivable that "table" here means "synopsis," referring to lines 1–102, but I suspect that the poem had (or was intended to have) a prefatory woodcut.}

[10] {The original reads "so."}

Her glorious martyrs; and sometimes He tames
Her self-admiring, and -applauding pride
(That on presumption of His love doth ride
Into that high conceit the Jews have told her:
Since God hath chose her, He is bound t'uphold her)
By[11] drawing from her His supporting grace:
That seeing in what a weak and wretched case
She is without His help; how soon she'd fall
(If grace be not her leader general)
To heresy or any other snare   130
The tempter, to entrap her, shall prepare,
She may rely upon His power alone
Who is the Rock of her salvation.

     To be exposéd thus to Satan's spleen,
Of Christ's true Church, a true mark still hath been.
The church malignant, whose prodigious head
The Devil is himself, we see hath led
The captive world in triumph, liv'd at rest,
And most of nations with subjection prest.
No streams of martyrs' blood her temples dyed,   140
Nor did she persecution e'er abide.
His cruelty, not to his friends, but foes,
The Prince of Darkness here in this world shows.
Whom but th'apostles did he sift like wheat?
And whom, like Paul, did he desire to beat
Without, with Jewish scourges, and within,
With buffets of his flesh-assaulting sin?
Such barb'rous tortures, who did e'er endure
(Without all pity) as the saints most pure?
This bold adventurous foe, his fiery darts   150
Directs, with matchless cunning, at the hearts
Of them that are the best of saints. And where
He sees the richest graces shine most clear,
There he his strongest engines doth erect:
(If possible) ev'n to subvert th'elect.
Thus have we seen in heat of war's alarms
(Where bloody fields are pav'd with broken arms),
The foes redouble all their force and might
To break the battles where the gen'rals fight.
Such was the Syrian monarch's charge:* to bring   *1 Kings 22:31
Captive or kill none else but Israel's King.
So Cæsar thought those soldiers worthiest grace,
Whose points still level'd at their foemen's face.

[11] [neither totally nor fully, but in the sensibility of operation]

Thus strong temptations, forcibly applied,
Have made the best of God's own children slide.   165
Lot, Noah, David, Peter foully fell
Because their gifts did all men's else excel.[12]
Adam, in Paradise, no safety found;
Nay, He that of all safety is the ground
Escap'd not unassaulted: of whose fare,
Good reason, all His servants should have share.
     Stand forth then, Roman strumpet, wipe thine eyes,
Pull off thy scales of blindness, yet be wise—
Ere 't be too late. Then shalt thou clearly see
Who the erroneous, who the true Church be.
I will not (nor is't fitting) here discuss
Those points of doctrine wherein you from us
Are in diameter opposed as far
As bright truth from dark falsehood: such a war
Requires a larger and more spacious field   180
Than this restrained strain can aptly yield.
Wherefore in freer method, more solute,
I leave your tenets for the Schools' dispute.
And yet how easy were't to make you know
Human traditions are (alas) too low
To mate[13] God's sacred word, nor may the vain
Inventions of an erring mortal brain
Brave th'oracle of Truth. If th'ark to check
Dagon presume, Dagon shall break his neck.
How easy were't to prove that saving grace,   190
Of our corrupted nature, must take place?
Error hath champions: 'tis not my intent
That antichristian Council, which from Trent
Takes its denomination, to refell,
Since those blasphemous canons now do smell
O'er all the world, and you yourselves are fain
Many (for shame) back to revoke again.
No (were there no mark else the Church to know),
Our truth, your falsehood, this would clearly show
To prove us Christ's, and aggravate your sin: 200
We have the patients, you the agents been
In all massacres, treasons, persecutions,
Close murthers, cruel bloodshed, and dirutions†   †overthrowings

---

[12] {The lines defend the Calvinist doctrine of perseverance—that the elect, whatever their sins, never totally or finally fall from grace—and the corollary that "sainthood," being one of God's elect, need not be accompanied by sanctity of life.}

[13] {probably with the sense of "contend or couple with," but also "defeat"}

Of cities, kingdoms' woeful devastations,
Rebellions, powder-plots, and wrong invasions,
Perform'd to force men's consciences, and make
Inconstant souls with error part to take.
These are the bloody glosses of your text,
Which, you well hoped, we should interpret next.
And if your projects be not timely crossed   210
Our freedom and religion both are lost.
For, that our safety might be undermin'd,
You have not only all your powers combin'd
Abroad, but ev'n at home prepar'd such way,
That we ourselves should our own selves betray.
To what end else did you (in time of danger),
You introduce, we entertain a stranger
T'our reform'd doctrine? was't for conscience sake
To bring us to the truth? or was't to make
Entrance for Spanish wasps to th'English hive,   220
While we, for conscience, with ourselves should strive?
Thus simple Truth hath by your cunning been
Assailed without, falsely betrayed within.
And when religion's bond's once broke asunder,
No marvel foreign atheism bring us under.
Which, that the Church may better take to heart,
And yet prevent that for which else she'll smart,
Her dangers here appear: that when you view them
You better may advise which way t'eschew them.
        Truth's Fortress[14]—whose foundation's laid upon   230
Th'apostles, prophets, and that Corner-stone
Whereon they build; mortar'd and cemented
With blood of martyrs (for the Gospel shed),
Then by degrees rais'd to the present frame
By such of ancient and of later fame,
Whose works and words, lives, lines, hearts, hands have made
Truth flourish, error vanish, falsehood fade,
And shak'd proud Babel—stands beleagured here
On all sides by her foes. Two ports appear
'Gainst which th'assailants (armed with fury, rage,   240
And hellish spleen that nothing can assuage
But blood and ruin) all their engines plant
And forces bend; here is, of plots, no want,
Or cunning projects: for their brains are filled
With all the stratagems that hell can yield.
Religion's port's beleaguer'd by the whore

---

[14] {The missing table may have depicted an assault on Truth's Fortress, i.e., England.}

Of erring Babel's cursed paramour,*   *the Pope
Whose right hand's armed with the fulmination
Of kingdoms-blasting excommunication,
To send to hell, or some such place, all those   250
His jurisdiction or his laws oppose.
His bull's his buckler, wherewith he defends
(As he makes credulous souls believe) his friends,
Pardons their sins, pulls such from Satan's paws
As damn themselves for his unhallowed cause.
     Next him, the Cardinals march in pompous sort,
Wh'would rather the defendants of the port
Corrupt than force by conquest. This implies
They shall not want for earthly dignities
And temp'ral honors, that with Rome will side   260
Gainst Heav'n: in worldly triumph those shall ride;
And he, for Babel's whore, will spend a soul,
Shall quaff in fornication's golden bowl.
Be it so, Lord. Such their reward have here,
And plagues hereafter; but thy children dear
Now suffer, that they may be after crown'd,
When they† shall, in thy cup of wrath, be drowned.   †God's enemies
     A squadron of fat bishops marcheth next,
Whose arms are pickaxes instead of text.
Truth, by the spirit, can sustain no harm;   270
Therefore they'd batter't with the flesh's arm.
     The last (though not the least in force) consists
Of a whole legion of Ignatius' priests,
Who (having learned the undermining art
From him that taught it first to Berthold Schwart†)   †thought to be the inventor
Doubt not to make Truth's strongest hold to fly,   of firearms
With powder-barrels, up into the sky.
When lying, forging, and equivocation
Too weak, they found, to batter Truth's foundation,
And that the seeming'st reasons they could rack   280
From their sublimest brains reflected back
Upon themselves with shame and with disgrace
(For falsehood must, at last, to truth give place
Though ne'er so nearly varnish'd), they betook
Themselves to treasons, and their books forsook
(As Julius[15] did his keys); with fire and sword,
Instead of zeal and the spiritual word,
They take the field, not only to enthrall

---

[15] {The note is illegible, but presumably the early sixteenth-century Pope Julius II, whose nickname was the warrior pope.}

Men's consciences, but liberty and all.
Thus arguments for arms they have refused,   290
And treasons base for their best reasons used;
Thus have they chose, for Pallas' powerful charms,
Mars his more harsh and forcible alarms.
And not prevailing by far-strain'd conclusions,
Would put down Truth by lawless wrong confusions.
This Germany too sensibly hath felt
And smarted for. (Whose soul can choose but melt
To think on't? where the title to the crown
Of that unhappy kingdom tumbled down
Truth's best professors.) For the plot was laid,   300
Before th'election of the Palzgrave† made,   †the Elector Palatine
How to defeat him. This was only done
To make him on his own confusion run,
And that they might the eyes of justice blind
With some pretence of equity, and bind
Our hands that were engaged to support
So just a cause. How grossly did they sport
With thy† mild nature? thou, whose sacred name   †James I
The title of the Prince of Peace may claim.
How was thy soul abus'd with false relations   310
And hopes of ne'er-meant reconciliations?
How did that damned Don† and's agents here,   †Gondomar the Spanish
That were, of all thy subjects, plac'd most near   ambassador
Thy naught-suspecting heart, infatuate
The wisest prince on earth? and captivate
That judgment, whereat all the world did gaze?
Sure he that screw'd thee into such a maze
Of error was no Spaniard, but a devil
Sent up from hell to work the Church such evil.
How couldst thou else with patience sit and see   320
Truth's fall and thine own children's misery?
While (as 'tis thought) there was more treasure spent
In fruitless embassades and compliment
Than would not only have the Paltz secur'd
But in its bounds the Austrian pride immur'd.
Wer't not for this (blest King) and th'old one's plaster,[16]
Thou migh'st (perchance) have yet been Britain's master.
    Now Germany lies drown'd in her own blood,
And all that for Religion's quarrel stood
Have suffer'd martyrdom; and France's King   330

---

[16] {Another allusion to the widely circulated libel alleging that Buckingham killed King James with a poisoned plaster. See note 6 to this poem <*supra*>.}

Is set a-work the Huguenots to bring
Into subjection. Yet one sore doth lie
In th'eye o'th'Pope and 's Catholic Majesty,†   †Philip IV of Spain
Which needs must be remov'd before the rest:
And that's our land, *heretics' the nest* *   **nido d'heretici*
(As they please term it). How they this may do,
Spain's council, and the Roman conclave too,
With Beelzebub, that sits as president,
At council table have a long time spent.
With foreign forces to invade a land   340
So rich, so well appointed, so well manned
With high resolvéd spirits that ever bore
Themselves, in wars, victorious heretofore,
And made good proof of perfect valor (till
Base treachery against the valiant's will
Did generally mislead them now of late,
And the whole world may admire all thereat)—
T'invade so stout a people needs must be
A dang'rous action, full of jeopardy.
Besides the very thought of eighty eight   350
Daunts them, and quells such resolutions straight.
Wherefore 'tis safest in such case to fly
From open war to secret treachery.
He that intends to bring a country under,
Either he must, before he lighten, thunder;
Or else raise up and nourish in't a faction,
May make him entrance through their own distraction.[17]
In eighty eight, the former they assay'd,
Then treating peace, when th'had their anchors weigh'd
To sail to our destruction. But (be blest   360
You Heav'ns) their sword was turn'd on their own breast.
Now of the second project they make trial
(And Spanish gold, alas, finds rare denial):
From Spain's exchequer some, some from the Pope's,*   **of pardons &c.*
Are fed with gold, but more with golden hopes.
This th'have attempted long; and how too true
'Tis th'have prevail'd (I fear) too late we rue.
First, seeing religion is the strongest chain
To tie men's hearts together, and 'tis vain
To hope for conquest whiles that concord's band   370
Environs (like a wall of brass) our land,
His Holiness hath learn'd of Machiavel

---

[17] {In crochets in the original, probably to distinguish these Machiavellian maxims from the authorial voice.}

(In whom all popes have ever been read well)

T'advise his standard bearer* to divide   *the devil

Truth's chiefest followers, that while they do side

In factions 'mongst themselves, he may with ease

Destroy them all, ev'n as himself shall please,

By taking part with th'one. Which to effect

Satan his writs doth readily direct

To all the peers of darkness. Who being met,

And (capering to the council-table) set,†   †seated

In comes the devil's duke,† great Lucifer;   †a swipe at the Duke of

When all to make obeisance quickly stir,   Buckingham

Scraping their cloven feet and lowly bending,

Because their honors are from him depending.   385

Straight Beelzebub, the chosen president,

After a hem (that all in pieces rent

The walls of Limbo), an oration roar'd

To all the Luciferians, amply stor'd

With threatnings. What he said, I did not hear.

If needs you'll know the cause: I was not there.[18]

But, by the sequel, I perchance may guess

That solemnly his hate he did profess

To Truth and all her foll'wers, and 's desire

T'enlarge his empire and to bring it nigher

To universal greatness. But there lay

(To curb his great designs) a rub i'th'way:

Truth's Fortress, whence he often had sustained

Loss irrecov'rable and seldom gained

Ought else but shameful falls, disgraceful foils,   400

Or strong repulses. Therefore all their wiles

Of hellish policy they now must prove,

This let of their ambition to remove.

All spend their censure,† that, since force prevails not,   †give their opinion

Treason must do't; that too too often fails not.

Wherefore with general voices they conclude

That fiends in shew of friends must Truth delude,

And so betray her. To this cursed end,

In human shape Arminius they send;

Got by Pelagius, and in Rome nurst up,   410

Whence, drunk with superstitious error's cup,

---

[18] {Probably a gently mocking allusion to Thomas Scott's *Vox populi* (1620), which pretends to be an eyewitness account of a Spanish Council meeting during which the grandees formulate a plot, involving an Arminian fifth-column, to subject England to Spanish-papal control, thus removing the last serious obstacle to their goal of world domination—i.e., a plot very much like the one being proposed by the "peers of darkness" here.}

He's sent to Leiden by the Pope's direction
To blast the world with 's heresies' infection.
Nor rests th'ambiguous crafty monster there,
But spews the poison of 's false doctrine here;
Comes, like a Protestant in shew before,
And vows he hates the antichristian whore;
Disclaims her tenets. Nay, none seems to be
More zealous in the Gospel's cause than he.
(Oh that false tongues were ever made so smooth,   420
Or lying lips should have the power to soothe.)
Tell him the doctrine of the pope is true
Concerning merits, he will censure you
For error straight. Say that we may attain
By nature, power salvation to gain,
By working it ourselves, he will reply
These doctrines are condemned for heresy.
And yet (what positively he thus denies)
By necessary consequence implies.
So that, observe him well, within you'll find   430
A friar's heart, as here his cowl behind.
Behold now, Satan's masterpiece, t'ov'rspread
The Church with popery so long banishéd.
Had he, in public, these his tenets held
And justified, he should have been expell'd
From all reforméd Churches; and confuted,
Had he such theses in the schools disputed.
Therefore with Truth dissembling to take part,[19]
He (Joab-like) doth closely wound her heart;
And silly souls, entangled by him, lie   440
In nets of errors that they cannot spy.
Yet though Arminius, Holland had infected,
Since we his poisonous doctrine had detected,
And that blest King most learnedly refell'd
Those false positions seduc'd Vorstius[20] held.
What madness was't for us to foster here
Those errors that our Church condemnéd there?†   †at the Synod of Dort
Had Satan's instruments been all without,
The danger were not great: we need not doubt
So much our safety. But within they lurk,   450
That, under name of Truth's stout'st champions, work
Her ruin; and to back her making show,

---

[19] {i.e., therefore pretending to be on Truth's side}

[20] {A Dutch Arminian (with, in the eyes of some, Socinian leanings) whose works James ordered publicly burned in 1612.}

Betray her, and conspire her overthrow.
No sooner comes Arminius to untwine
The bond of concord and to undermine
Religion with condemn'd Pelagianism
(To make way for the pope), but factious schism
With senseless atheism, cold neutrality,
Loose Epicurism, and damned policy
Are ready t'entertain him; and declare   460
Themselves (perfidious wretches as they are)
For him, 'gainst truth receiv'd. Wherefore in haste,
As he is foremost by the Devil plac't,
With schism's wildfire, Religion's port to set
In a combustion, he is straightway met
By messengers sent to salute him. Who
They are, I scarce can yet precisely know.
But bishops' chaplains they should be, I deem,
For by their stately port no less they seem.
And such is he, whose purblind *couzning*† eye   †i.e., John Cosin
Its objects (as't appears) doth multiply,
And make two sacraments seem sev'n.[21] Like him
(But that his carriage something is more grim)
Is he, that takes upon him to suppress
All books against his Leiden friend, unless   475
His sense of feeling be a little fee'd.[22]
(Were I his judge) it should be so indeed.
But him that welcomes first this heretic,
His very looks proclaim a schismatic.
He hath commission, with a false forg'd key,
To let this monster in,[23] and so make way
For all the rest of that accursed crew
In Truth's chief martyrs' blood their hands t'mbrue.
These, these, not those at Clerkenwell we took,[24]
The strong foundation of our Church have shook,
And made Religion reel. Our foes we shun;
But these false feignéd friends have Truth undone.
Oh vipers most unnatural, thus to tear

[21] {See Cosin's *A collection of private devotions* (London, 1627), 54.}

[22] {Probably a reference to Thomas Worrall, the Bishop of London's chaplain, and accused in 1628 by a radical puritan printer of demanding illegal fees from those seeking a license. See *Commons debates: 1628*, 4 vols., ed. Robert Johnson, Mary Frear Keeler, Maija Jansson Cole, and William Bidwell (Yale UP, 1977–78), 3:151.}

[23] {Probably Richard Montagu, whom writers at the time describe as unusually unattractive (see his biography in the *ODNB*).}

[24] {For the Clerkenwell incident (March 1628), which ended with ten Jesuits being imprisoned, see Martin Havran, *The Catholics in Caroline England* (Stanford UP, 1962), 55, 67–68, 124.}

The bowels of that mother, held you dear.
Alas, alas, too true it is, I see,   490
All men are for themselves; few, Christ, for thee.
Error prevails, and while thy shepherds sleep,
Wolves in sheep's clothing worry all thy sheep.
Who, almost, cares which way Religion bends,
So they may compass their ambitious ends?
How soon do those that should firm *mountains* be[25]
For truth to build on, lean to popery,
Laud Romish laws, and to disgrace endeavor
In truth's profession such as would persever.
So they may rise, they make their betters fall.   500
Thus do they shipwrack faith, love, soul, and all.
Yet (blest be God) Truth ne'er was so distrest
But she had still some champions (those the best)
T'abet her quarrel. See the faith's defender,[26]
With 's brandish'd sword, is ready aid to lend her;
And thousands more of soldiers stout there be,
Which never yet to error bow'd their knee;
For truth's sake would, in midst of faggots dance:
Yea, *bishops* some. But see a luckless chance
Befalls one prelate: hast'ning to repel   510
Arminius and 's adherents back to hell
For fear of faction, he himself is ta'en
By proud ambition (that is still the bane
Of all religious acts, the root of evil,
The character and darling of the Devil)
And violently (I know not why) 's thrown down,
Unable to resist—ev'n by a frown.†   †probably John Williams, Bishop
Methinks 'tis pity, for a cause unjust,   of Lincoln
That godly gravity should lie i'th'dust.
But, though he fall, himself (he says) shall rise,   520
And he shall fall when none shall wet their eyes.
How speed the rest? their well-meant labor 's lost,
A bald apparitor† hath their journey crossed: †an official in the ecclesiastical
Who muzz'ling them, by virtue of his box,   court
Extorts the Spirit's sword from th'orthodox.
Nor do these flattr'ing prelates cease to bring
Such men in hatred daily with their King,

[25] {Alluding to John Howson, Bishop of Oxford, and George Montaigne, Bishop of London; "*Laud*" in the next line refers, rather unsubtly, to William Laud, in 1627 Bishop of Bath and Wells. In the original "*How soon*" is spelled "*Howsone*."}

[26] {"Defender of the faith" was one of the king's titles, so this may be a (somewhat perfunctory) loyalist gesture.}

And falsely, that th'are Calvinists, report,
Only to make them odious in the Court.
Nor is 't unlike, some hope, by pleasing so   530
The kingdom's secret bane and Church's foe,
They may, in this golden corrupted state,
Bishoprics purchase at an easier rate
Then the chief-justice-ship.[27] Thus Error bears
Herself aloft; while Truth (bedew'd with tears
To think upon the woeful sad events
Schisms ever bring upon the Church) laments.
For, if the monuments of former ages
We search and studiously turn o'er the pages
Of all historians, they will shew us plain,   540
No state or kingdom ever did sustain
Such fatal downfalls, gen'ral devastations,
Final subversions, and depopulations,
By open foes (though ne'er so fiercely bent)
As by intestine civil broils. How went
The Grecian monarchy to nothing? why
Lost Rome her greatness? wherefore doth she lie
Buried in her own ruins (who was once
The glory of the East), an heap of stones?
But ask Antiquity how these did fall,   550
'T will answer, discord hath o'erthrown them all.
Enquire of Carthage, and her rubbish towers
Will cry, *would Hannos' house had ne'er been ours.*
Ask how the Thracian empire's stately seat
Became a slave to Mahomet the great,
How we lost all those countries in the East,
And how that land our Savior's presence blest?
Truth must reply, dissension was their fall,
And Christian princes' discord lost them all.
This was spied wisely by a grave bashaw,   560
And as a strong persuasion us'd to draw
Great Solyman to Rhodes. For *while* (quoth he)
The Christian princes thus divided be,
They hasten their destruction. 'Twas too true.†   †Rhodes fell to Suleiman II in 1522
This counsel Rhodes and Hungary did rue.
Civil dissentions are most mortal ever;
But when religion breeds them, then they sever
The very souls of men. This nature makes
Become unnatural; it no notice takes

---

[27] {On November 28, 1626, Thomas Richardson became Chief Justice of the Common Pleas, an advancement that was said to have cost him £17,000.}

Of father, brother, friend: but all doth use   570
With like contempt, with equal hate pursues.
Which Satan (th'enemy of human peace,
The Gospel's glory, and the truth's increase)
Perceiving; and by long experience knowing
That nothing keeps religion more from growing
Than Church contentions; as the surest way
To raise up error and make Truth decay,
He hath suborned in all ages those
That under Christ's own name should Christ oppose.
None's hurt but by himself. To Christ none is   580
A foe so mortal as he that seems his.
Schisms in the church are like, i'th'soul, a wound:
To cure't no Aesculapius can be found.
Th'are like Elias' cloud: though small at first,
Yet still increasing, and being daily nurst
With malcontented humors, at the length
They (by degrees) attain to so much strength,
Truth's sun is by them overshadowed quite,
And, like a tempest, on the Church they light,
O'erwhelming with a bloody inundation   590
Cities and kingdoms, ev'n to desolation.
Such sad proceedings had the Arian error,
Which, first contemn'd, prov'd afterwards a terror
To all the world. That spark, whence once it brake
To flames, made Europe, Asia, Afrike quake;
And so obscur'd the Church's glory over,
She never could her luster yet recover.
So was th'Arabian* in Heraclius' days   *Mahomet
(Whom Satan did another agent raise
Truth to disturb), when he began to broach   600
His damnéd dogmas, fitter of reproach
And scorn reputed than represt to be
By force or council's censure. And thus he
(Though an unread barbarian) after came,
By this connivance, to attain such fame
For false-supposed truth (since no man could
Gainsay as it was thought, because none would,
This new-sprung doctrine) that it quickly grew
Through force and juggling of this pagan Jew
To such an height of greatness and of power,   610
That from that age unto this present hour,
His barb'rous proud successors still have been
The executioners of Satan's spleen,
And heaviest scourges for the Gospel's side

That ever Christendom did yet abide.
So fatal 'tis (oh then what state would do't?)
To let an error in the Church take root.
If later times' examples better take,
And in men's minds deeper impression make:
What frequent streams of blood of Christians drew   620
The mad, fantastic, giddy-headed crew
Of German Anabaptists? to maintain
Whose gross erroneous tenets there were slain
Thrice fifty thousand souls, who lost their breath
In that false quarrel by a timeless death.
If then th'obtrusion of new dogmatics
Upon th'abused Church so deeply pricks
Her grieved heart, if it her quiet mar
And turn her happy peace to bloody war,
What Belial's brats, or Bichri's sons† could find   †2 Samuel 20:2
In heart to be s'unnatural and unkind
As, to that mother, ill for good to render,
Who hath been ever of their welfare tender?
Oh that such dang'rous serpents e'er should rest
I'th'choicest mansions of a kingdom's breast,   635
Would suck her heart blood out; it were too much
In monster-molding Africk to find such.
Who then would e'er suspect a monstrous seed
And more prodigious Africk e'er did breed
Should spawn in England? in so cold an air
Where matter of corruption should be rare?
That, then, that doth this mishap'd births create
Is not the sun of zeal, but fire of hate
And slime of pride and treason: these they be
That turn a man into a prodigy.
And such there are too many, who do hope
And strongly labor to reduce† the pope,   †bring back
Usher'd by Arminius, that themselves in time
To th'honor of a Cardinal's cap may climb.
First let them break their necks. And let that hand   650
Be ever mark'd with th'ignominions brand
Of infamous sedition, whose *appeal*,†   †Montagu's *Appello Caesarem*
For Spanish-English favor, not for zeal
To God or truth, did hither first transfer
The Belgian heretic,† to make us err.   †Arminius
Did we not see, of late, what sad effect
This doctrine wrought in that pernicious sect?
Had not the States like, to their cost, t'have felt
(By th'treacherous designs of Barnevelt,

His sons, and others) what religious fruits   660
We might expect from such seditious bruits?
If the same danger we had meant to shun,
Why the same hazard did we rashly run?
Nor were these tenets in the Schools discussed
(Fit places where such paradoxes must
Be controverted) but in public print[28]
(To make unlearnéd vulgar eyes to squint
From truth on falsehood); all the land about
These dang'rous books are cast, to make men doubt
The truth receiv'd; and not resolving where   670
Safely to stand or to what side t'adhere,
To fall as fast to Rome or atheism
As those in Arius' time to gentilism.†   †paganism
Better discretion from the heathens' laws
Might be observ'd. For no religious cause
With them was handled 'mongst the vulgar sort.
And with the Turks, his life he forfeits for 't
Dares question any. Learnéd Varro shut
Such books in schools and private closets. But
'Bove all th'apostles and the Fathers were   680
Herein most chary. For whenever there
Sprung any diff'rence 'twixt them, they ne'er made
Saucy appeals to temp'ral kings to shade
Or bolster up their fancies.[29] None did write
Bitter invectives 'gainst his opposite,
Nor clamorous bills in any prince's Court
Put up; but lovingly they did resort
I'th'fear of God together; there propose
Their doubts, allege their reasons, confirm those,
And then determine from God's sacred word   690
What must be follow'd, what must be ahorr'd.[30]
Good shepherds lead their flocks to feeding nigh
Those pleasing rivers that stream quietly
And not in whirlpools. Those of highest place
Shall have fruition in th'Almighty's grace
That draw most souls unto Him. Where shall they
Become that fright unstable souls away?

[28] {a curious objection under the circumstances}

[29] {An extraordinary departure from the classic Reformation view that from the time of Constantine this had been precisely the role of Christian princes, a role later usurped by the papacy.}

[30] {On London godly ministers' preference for such private clerical conferences rather than more official forums to resolve theological disputes, see Lake, *Boxmaker's revenge*, 226–54; David Como and Peter Lake, "'Orthodoxy' and its discontents: dispute settlement and the production of 'consensus' in the London (Puritan) 'underground,'" *JBS* 39 (2000): 34–70.}

Consider this, all you whose hot desire
Of worldly honor far surmounts the fire
Of your cold zeal. And fix in Heav'n your mind,   700
Where only, lasting honor you shall find.
So shall our Church be happy in her seed;
So shall she be from present dangers freed;
So shall the Gospel 'mongst us ever flourish;
So shall our state the true professors nourish;
So shall the God of Truth your labors bless
And your endeavors crown with wish'd success

. . .

Text: EEBO (STC [2nd ed.] / 20577)
The spy. Discovering the danger of Arminian heresy and Spanish treachery. Written by I. R. (Printed at Strasburgh, 1628).

JOHN EARLE
(ca. 1600–1665)

Born in York, he may have been the John Earle who matriculated from Christ Church, Oxford, in June 1619, as well as the John Earle who graduated BA from Merton College that July, becoming a fellow there soon afterward and proceeding MA in 1624, DD in 1640. However, there seems no doubt whatsoever that John Earle wrote the anonymous Theophrastean character sketches entitled *Microcosmography*, first published in 1628 and reaching a sixth edition by 1630.[1] In 1632 Earle was made rector of St. Mary's, Gamlingay, a Cambridgeshire parish in the gift of Merton. During the 1630s, Earle was a frequent visitor to Great Tew, "no man's company . . . [being] more desired and more loved," where he taught Greek to Lord Falkland and claimed to have received in turn "more useful learning by his [Falkland's] conversation than he had at Oxford."[2] At some point during the 1630s, Earle also became chaplain to Philip Herbert, fourth earl of Pembroke, who presented him to the rectory of Bishopston, Wiltshire, in 1639.[3] It was probably via Pembroke that Earle came to the notice of the King, who was sufficiently impressed to appoint him tutor to the future Charles II, when in 1641 the Prince's former tutor, Brian Duppa, became bishop of Salisbury. Pembroke, although Charles' lord chamberlain and a lover of painting, hunting, and literature (Shakespeare's first folio is dedicated to him), sided with Parliament, which is probably why in 1643 Earle was nominated to the Westminster Assembly. He declined, and in 1644 was deprived as a malignant both his Bishopston rectory and chancellorship of Salisbury Cathedral, to which he had just been appointed. Soon thereafter Earle went into exile. From 1651–60 he was with the English

[1] All the twelve 17th-century editions were anonymous, although the 1628 entry in the Stationer's Register calls the work "Earles Characters" and contemporaries seem never to have doubted the attribution; Earle's name first appears on the title page in 1732 (McIver).

[2] So Clarendon, himself a member of Falkland's circle, writes; for more on Great Tew, see the introduction to William Chillingworth *<infra>*.

[3] Both the *ODNB* and *DNB* follow Bliss' 1811 edition of *Microcosmography* in claiming that Earle became Philip Herbert's chaplain ca. 1630, when Herbert was chancellor of Oxford. Philip Herbert, however, *lost* the election for chancellorship in 1630—he lost it to Laud.

court in Paris, serving as Charles II's chaplain and clerk of the closet—and producing Latin translations of Richard Hooker's *Laws of ecclesiastical polity*[4] and the *Eikon basilike*, the latter published in 1649. These were difficult years for Earle, the King being often unable to pay his chaplains, but the Restoration brought abundant recompense with preferment to the deanery of Westminster in 1660, the see of Worcester in 1662, and that of Salisbury in 1663. All surviving testimonies depict Earle as a lovely human being: "universally beloved," as John Evelyn wrote, "for his gentle & sweet disposition" (*ODNB*); the non-conformist Richard Baxter noted in the margin of a letter Earle had written him, "O that they were all such" (*ODNB*). According to Gilbert Burnet, Charles II, who had a generally low opinion of clerics, valued Earle "beyond all the men of his order" (*DNB*). He died at Oxford in 1665 and was buried with considerable fanfare near the Merton chapel high altar.

>·····•···••·····✦

It is important not to read Earle's "characters" as sociology, although one suspects that they had some empirical basis. Yet even if his sketches render in part a world he perceived, in part half-created,[5] we generally have no way of telling which parts belong to which half. We cannot, therefore, view *Microcosmography* as a mirror held up to nature; as a lamp, however, it proves quite, as it were, illuminating; that is, it sheds light on the religious views, visions, and nightmares of its author and his textual community.

Prior to the 1640s, when a side had to be taken, Earle's stance eludes our customary labels (not godly, not Laudian, not Calvinist conformist, not even particularly avantgarde). In the 1630s, the Earl of Pembroke took him in, as did Great Tew; the former ended up siding with Parliament; those associated with the latter followed the King; both parties making their opposed choices with considerable ambivalence and repeated attempts at mediation. The invitation to join the Westminster Assembly suggests that as late as 1643 Earle's own commitments were not obvious, and perhaps quite different from those informing *Microcosmography*, which was written in the late 1620s.

The theological import of Earle's portraits—the location of their views, visions, and nightmares in the Caroline confessional landscape—comes into clearer focus if one sets them in relation to his English models for the Theophrastan character: the *Characters of virtues and vices* (1608) by the Calvinist divine Joseph Hall *<vide infra>* and the immensely popular volume of characters by multiple hands, most of them gentleman wits and dramatists (including Webster, Donne, and Dekker), published together with Sir Thomas Overbury's "A wife" and thence known as the Overburian characters or simply "Overbury."[6]

Earle's rendering of his various religious stock-figures has much in common with Overbury, far more than with Hall, yet suggestive differences remain. In Overbury, the

[4] The manuscript, long believed lost, may well be the Latin translation of Hooker's treatise that recently surfaced in the Folger Shakespeare Library.

[5] Wordsworth, *Tintern Abbey*, 105–7 (misappropriated).

[6] The volume went through sixteen editions between 1614 and 1638, the later printings containing many more characters than the twenty-two of the first edition. On the Theophrastan character in early modern England, see Benjamin Boyce, *The Theophrastan character in England to 1642* (Harvard UP, 1947) and J. W. Smeed, *The Theophrastan character* (Oxford UP, 1985).

godly are truly dangerous troublemakers: the puritan "murmurs at . . . anything that the law allows but marriage and March beer . . . what it disallows and holds dangerous, makes him a discipline. . . . His greatest care is to contemn obedience; his last care to serve God handsomely and cleanly" (Morley 49). The clerical hypocrite "carrieth a burden that no cords of authority, spiritual nor temporal, should bind if it might have the full swing," and the lay-hypocrite, his disciple, "will not acknowledge the tithe of any subjection to any mitre, no, not to any scepter, that he will do to the hook and crook of his zeal-blind shepherd." The Overburian precisian, who "is so sure of his salvation that he will not change places in heaven with the Virgin Mary," can "better afford you ten lies than one oath, and dare commit any sin gilded with a pretense of sanctity," holding it "lawful [to steal], so it be from the wicked and Egyptians" (Morley 58–61). Earle's puritans lack this seditious *libido dominandi* and oppositional rage. His young raw preacher is a deeply conventional soul, absurdly proud of his Oxford degree, whose sermons, despite their histrionic emotionalism, are cribbed from notes taken at University. Earle clearly finds his little learning a tedious thing, but he also thinks him more likely to marry a chambermaid than threaten the Elizabethan settlement. Earle's other godly character, the she precise hypocrite, is a comic masterpiece: an astonishing cross between the classic stage puritan (e.g., her sermon-gadding, predilection for Old Testament names, and phobia about oaths [Collinson 224]) and Chaucer's Wife of Bath, who also, one recalls, liked to quote Scripture.

Earle's grave divine, who has no counterpart in Overbury, provides the positive foil to his raw young preacher. The portrait betrays Senecan commitments with regards to style and anticipates Laud's distaste for cudgeling "popish errors" with "barren invectives," but in general Earle's portrait would appear studiously to eschew sectarian markings; Bliss' 1811 edition of *Microcosmography* underscores its mere Christianity by invoking Chaucer's "povre persoun of a toun." Yet if one turns to Hall's portrait of ideal Christian manhood, its staggering contrast with Earle suggests that his grave divine does not embody a timeless, consensual understanding of true holiness but a deeply contested one. The eyes of Hall's faithful man

> have no other objects but absent and invisible, which they see so clearly as that to them sense is blind. . . . He walks every day with his Maker, and talks with him familiarly, and lives ever in heaven, and sees all earthly things beneath him. When he goes in to converse with God, he wears not his own clothes, but takes them still out of the rich wardrobe of his Redeemer, and then dares boldly press in and challenge a blessing. The celestial spirits do not scorn his company; yea, his service. . . . Without a written warrant he dare do nothing; and with it, anything. His war is perpetual, without truce, without intermission, and his victory certain; he meets with the infernal powers, and tramples them under feet. . . . His faults are few; and those he hath, God will not see. He is allied so high that he dare call God *father*, his Savior *brother*, heaven *his patrimony*, and thinks it no presumption to trust to the attendance of angels. His understanding is enlightened with the beams of divine truth. God hath acquainted him with his will; and what he knows he dare confess: there is not more love in his heart than liberty in his tongue. If torments stand betwixt him and Christ, if death, he contemns them;

and if his own parents lie in his way to God, his holy carelessness makes them his footsteps. His experiments have drawn forth rules of confidence, which he dares oppose against all the fears of distrust. . . . He is not so sure he shall die as that he shall be restored, and outfaceth his death with resurrection. Finally, he is rich in works, busy in obedience, cheerful and unmoved in expectation, better with evils; in common opinion miserable, but in true judgment more than a man." (Morley 114–16)

David Como's work has taught us to associate this sort of high-flying perfectionism with antinomian radicals, but Hall was an impeccably mainstream Calvinist. Earle knew Hall's *Characters* (McIver 221), making it hard not to see his own rationalist and charitable divine as a total, albeit implicit, condemnation of such appalling sanctity.[7]

Hall's "Character of the hypocrite," by contrast, satirizes godly formalism and "preciseness" along much the same lines as Earle and the Overburians:

At church he will ever sit where he may be seen best, and in the midst of the sermon pulls out his tables[8] in haste, as if he feared to lose that note; when he writes either his forgotten errand or nothing. Then he turns his Bible with a noise to seek an omitted quotation, and folds the leaf as if he had found it. . . . He turneth all gnats into camels, and cares not to undo the world for a circumstance.

Yet what follows this final sentence redirects the critique from puritan to high-church hypocrisy: "flesh on a Friday is more abomination to him than his neighbor's bed; he more abhors not to uncover at the name of Jesus than to swear by the name of God" (Morley 130–32). The phrasing parallels oaths with adultery; for Hall, swearing is a sin, not, like removing one's hat at the mention of Jesus' name, a mere formality. Earle shows no inclination to defend hat-doffing, but neither does he seem particularly horrified by oaths; we are not meant to be impressed by the she-hypocrite's censure of "by my truly." In *Microcosmography* and the Overburian characters, hypocrisy, despite Hall's best efforts to spread the guilt, is a decidedly puritan affliction. Yet, although they disagree as to whose religion consists of external shows, all three texts share an obsession with the dangers of formalism. Nor was the issue peculiar to character-writers; most post-Reformation disputes concerned forms of religious observance: vestments, kneeling, the Sabbath, altar rails. As J. C. Davis observes, "the challenge of true reformation had always been to get beyond outward conformity, formality, to inner conviction, the reformation of the heart, mind and will, and thence to conscientious action," rendering formality "a cancer more insidious and potentially destructive than outward enemies." Moreover, this "crisis of formalism" involved not only "a struggle *against* formality but also *for* the forms of godly order," whether that of puritan Terling[9] or Laudian Oxford (Davis 269–72).

Hypocrites and formalists are the stock in trade of early Stuart character-literature. Earle's religious skeptic is a less common figure. He is not a classical skeptic, who suspends

---

[7] The concluding paragraphs of Montaigne's "Of experience" mount an explicit condemnation of the Roman Catholic counterpart.

[8] i.e., wax writing-tablets

[9] On Terling, see Keith Wrightson and David Levine, *Poverty and piety in an English village: Terling, 1525–1700* (Clarendon, 1995).

belief on principle; he does, however, resemble both of the final two portraits of false religion in Donne's late Elizabethan "Satire III":

> . . . . Careless Phrygius doth abhor
> All, because all cannot be good, as one
> Knowing some women whores, dares marry none.
> Graccus loves all as one, and thinks that so
> As women do in divers countries go
> In divers habits, yet are still one kind,
> So doth, so is Religion. (ll. 62–68)

Unlike Graccus, Earle's skeptic does not believe everything, but he half-believes everything, and so, like Phrygius, ends up believing nothing. He is, obviously, a casualty of the fragmentation of Christendom; but his portrait's final sentence, by invoking the terminology of university disputation, suggests that he is also a casualty of the educational system, which required that every controverted doctrine, every cherished belief and sacred cow, be argued *in utramque partem*, and for each student defending orthodoxy, there were three classmates opposing (Shuger). Perhaps for this reason, Earle has mercy on his skeptic, and, unlike Donne,[10] grants the possibility at least of his salvation.

SOURCES: *ODNB*; *DNB*; Patrick Collinson, *Elizabethans* (Cambridge UP, 2003); Como, *Blown by the Spirit*; J. C. Davis, "Against formality: one aspect of the English revolution," *Transactions of the Royal Historical Society*, 6th series, 3 (1993): 265–88; Bruce McIver, "John Earle: The unwillingly willing author of *Microcosmography*," *English Studies* 3 (1991): 219–29; Henry Morley, ed., *Character writings of the seventeenth century* (London, 1891); Debora Shuger, "St. Mary the Virgin and the birth of the public sphere," *HLQ* 72.3 (2010): 313–46.

---

[10] Donne follows these portraits by condemning both stances: "thou / Of force must one, and forc'd, but one allow, / And the right." Some critics, however, find the condemnation suspiciously pro forma; see Richard Strier, *Resistant structures* (U California P, 1995), 139–43.

JOHN EARLE

Microcosmography: or, a piece of the world discovered, in essays and characters
1628

II
A YOUNG RAW PREACHER

Is a bird not yet fledged, that hath hopped out of his nest to be chirping on a hedge, and will be straggling abroad at what peril soever. His backwardness in the university hath set him thus forward; for had he not truanted there, he had not been so hasty a divine. His small standing, and time, hath made him a proficient only in boldness, out of which, and his table-book,[1] he is furnished for a preacher. His collections of study are the notes of sermons, which, taken up at St. Mary's,[2] he utters in the country; and if he write brachigraphy,[3] his stock is so much the better. His writing is more than his reading, for he reads only what he gets without book.[4] Thus accomplished, he comes down to his friends, and his first salutation is grace and peace out of the pulpit. His prayer is conceited,[5] and no man remembers his college more at large.[6] The pace of his sermon is a full career, and he runs wildly over hill and dale, till the clock stop him. The labor of it is chiefly in his lungs; and the only thing he has made in it himself is the faces. He takes on against the pope without mercy and has a jest still in lavender[7] for Bellarmine; yet he preaches heresy if it comes in his way—though with a mind, I must needs say, very orthodox. His action[8] is all passion, and his speech interjections. He has an excellent faculty in bemoaning the

---

[1] {writing tablets, notebook}

[2] {Oxford's university church}

[3] {shorthand}

[4] {He copies out other preachers' sermons more than he reads, and he reads only what he then memorizes, presumably to recycle in his own sermons.}

[5] {witty, rhetorically striking, and elaborate}

[6] [It is customary in all sermons delivered before the university, to use an introductory prayer for the founder of, and principal benefactors to, the preacher's individual college, as well as for the officers and members of the university in general. This, however, would appear very ridiculous when "*he comes down to his friends*," or, in other words, preaches before a country congregation {Bliss' note}.]

[7] {in reserve, stored up}

people, and spits with a very good grace. [His style is compounded of twenty several men's; only his body imitates some one extraordinary.[9]] He will not draw his handkercher out of his place, nor blow his nose without discretion. His commendation is that he never looks upon book; and indeed he was never used to it. He preaches but once a year, though twice on Sunday, for the stuff is still the same, only the dressing a little altered; he has more tricks with a sermon than a tailor with an old cloak, to turn it and piece it and at last quite disguise it with a new preface. If he have waded farther in his profession and would shew reading of his own, his authors are postils,[10] and his school-divinity a catechism. His fashion and demure habit gets him in with some town precisian, and makes him a guest on Friday nights. You shall know him by his narrow velvet cape and serge facing; and his ruff, next his hair, the shortest thing about him. The companion of his walk is some zealous tradesman, whom he astonishes with strange points, which they both understand alike. His friends and much painfulness[11] may prefer him to thirty pounds a year; and this, means to a chambermaid, with whom we leave him now in the bonds of wedlock—next Sunday you shall have him again.

III
A GRAVE DIVINE

Is one that knows the burthen of his calling and hath studied to make his shoulders sufficient; for which he hath not been hasty to launch forth of his port, the university, but expected[12] the ballast of learning and the wind of opportunity. Divinity is not the beginning but the end of his studies, to which he takes the ordinary stair and makes the arts[13] his way. He counts it not profaneness to be polished with human reading or to smooth his way by Aristotle to school-divinity. He has sounded both religions and anchored in the best, and is a Protestant out of judgment, not faction; not because his country, but his reason is on this side. The ministry is his choice, not refuge, and yet the pulpit not his itch, but fear. His discourse is substance, not all rhetoric, and he utters more things than words. His speech is not helped with enforced action, but the matter acts itself. He shoots all his meditations at one butt; and beats upon his text, not the cushion, making his hearers, not the pulpit groan. In citing of popish errors, he cuts them with arguments, not cudgels them with barren invectives; and labors more to shew the truth of his cause than the spleen. His sermon is limited by the method, not the hour-glass; and his devotion goes along with him out of the pulpit. He comes not up thrice a week, because he would not be idle;[14] nor talks three hours together, because he would not talk nothing; but his tongue preaches at fit times, and his conversation is the everyday's exercise. In matters of ceremony he is not ceremonious, but thinks he owes that reverence to the Church to bow his judgment to it,

---

[8] {his bodily gestures while delivering his sermon}

[9] {not in 1628 ed.}

[10] {biblical glosses, brief running commentary on a biblical text}

[11] {pains-taking}

[12] {awaited}

[13] {the bachelor's and master's degrees in arts—the standard university prerequisites for the study of divinity}

[14] {I.e., he doesn't preach three times a week, because he would not waste his congregation's time with empty words.}

and make more conscience of schism than a surplice. He esteems the church hierarchy as the Church's glory; and however we jar with Rome, would not have our confusion distinguish us. In simoniacal purchases he thinks his soul goes in the bargain, and is loath to come by promotion so dear; yet his worth at length advances him, and the price of his own merit buys him a living. He is no base grater of his tithes and will not wrangle for the odd egg. The lawyer is the only man he hinders, by whom he is spited for taking up[15] quarrels. He is a main pillar of our Church though not yet dean or canon, and his life our religion's best apology.[16] His death is the last sermon, where, in the pulpit of his bed, he instructs men to die by his example.

X
A CHURCH-PAPIST[17]

Is one that parts his religion betwixt his conscience and his purse, and comes to church not to serve God but the king. The face of the law makes him wear the mask of the gospel, which he uses not as a means to save his soul, but charges. He loves popery well, but is loath to lose by it; and though he be something scared with the bulls of Rome, yet they are far off, and he is struck with more terror at the apparitor.[18] Once a month he presents himself at the church to keep off the church-warden, and brings in his body to save his bail. He kneels with the congregation, but prays by himself, and asks God forgiveness for coming thither. If he be forced to stay out a sermon, he pulls his hat over his eyes and frowns out the hour; and when he comes home, thinks to make amends for this fault by abusing the preacher. His main policy is to shift off the Communion, for which he is never unfurnished of a quarrel and will be sure to be out of charity at Easter;[19] and indeed he lies not, for he has a quarrel to the sacrament. He would make a bad martyr and good traveler, for his conscience is so large he could never wander out of it, and in Constantinople would be circumcised with a reservation.[20] His wife is more zealous and therefore more costly, and he bates her in tires[21] what she stands him in religion. But we leave him hatching plots against the state, and expecting Spinola.[22]

[15] {settling, patching up; on the *theological* importance of such dispute resolution, see John Bossy, *Peace in the post-Reformation* (Cambridge UP, 1998).}

[16] {from the Latin *apologia*, a reasoned defense}

[17] {On the polemical and historiographic deployment of this category, see Alexandra Walsham, *Church papists: Catholicism, conformity and confessional polemic in early modern England* (Woodbridge, 1999); Michael Questier, "Conformity, Catholicism, and the law," in *Conformity and orthodoxy in the English Church, c. 1560–1660*, ed. Peter Lake and Michael Questier (Woodbridge, 2000), 237–61; Peter Lake, "Religious identities in Shakespeare's England," in *A Companion to Shakespeare*, ed. David Scott Kastan (Oxford UP, 1999), 65–72.}

[18] {officer of an ecclesiastical court}

[19] {The preface to the Communion liturgy in the 1559 Book of Common Prayer states that the curate is to restrain those "*betwixt whome he perceyveth malice and hatred to raigne, not suffering them to be partakers of the Lordes table untyll he know them to be reconciled.*"}

[20] {i.e., the controversial 17th-century Roman Catholic practice of mental reservation (or equivocation): a silent qualification tacitly added in making a statement, taking an oath, etc., when it was thought inadvisable to express open dissent (*OED*)}

[21] {he subtracts from her clothing-allowance}

[22] {awaiting an invasion by the Spanish general, Ambrose Spinola (1569–1630)}

XXXIV
A SHE PRECISE HYPOCRITE

Is one in whom good women suffer, and have their truth misinterpreted by her folly. She is one, she knows not what herself if you ask her, but she is indeed one that has taken a toy at the fashion of religion and is enamored of the new fangle. She is a nonconformist in a close stomacher and ruff of Geneva print,[23] and her purity consists much in her linen. She has heard of the rag of Rome and thinks it a very sluttish religion, and rails at the whore of Babylon for a very naughty woman. She has left her virginity as a relic of popery and marries in her tribe without a ring.[24] Her devotion at the church is much in the turning up of her eye and turning down of the leaf in her book when she hears named chapter and verse. When she comes home, she commends the sermon for the Scripture, and two hours. She loves preaching better then praying, and of preachers, lecturers;[25] and thinks the weekday's exercise far more edifying than the Sunday's. Her oftest gossipings[26] are sabbath-day's journeys, where (though an enemy to superstition) she will go in pilgrimage five mile to a silenced minister, when there is a better sermon in her own parish. She doubts of the Virgin Mary's salvation and dares not saint her, but knows her own place in heaven as perfectly as the pew she has a key to. She is so taken up with faith she has no room for charity, and understands no good works but what are wrought on the sampler. She accounts nothing vices but superstition and an oath, and thinks adultery a less sin than to swear *by my truly.* She rails at other women by the names of Jezebel and Delilah; and calls her own daughters Rebecca and Abigail, and not Ann but Hannah. She suffers them not to learn on the virginals because of their affinity with organs, but is reconciled to the bells for the chimes' sake since they were reformed to the tune of a psalm. She overflows so with the Bible that she spills it upon every occasion, and will not cudgel her maids without Scripture. It is a question whether she is more troubled with the devil or the devil with her: she is always challenging and daring him, and her weapon is *The practice of piety.*[27] Nothing angers her so much as that women cannot preach, and in this point only thinks the Brownist erroneous; but what she cannot at the church she does at the table, where she prattles more than any against sense and Antichrist, 'till a capon's wing silence her. She expounds the priests of Baal, reading ministers;[28] and thinks the salvation of that parish as desperate as the Turks. She is a main derider to her capacity of those that are not

[23] {Geneva Bibles typically used a very small typeface, here compared to the small ruffs preferred by puritan ladies.}

[24] {Puritans objected to the ring in marriage as unbiblical.}

[25] {Lecturers, who were often chosen by the parish and supported by voluntary contributions, preached the afternoon or evening sermons (lectures), but, although ordained, were not parochial clergy and did not conduct Prayer Book worship; godly ministers who had scruples about ceremonial conformity and were far more comfortable in the pulpit than at the altar found lectureships an attractive option.}

[26] {meeting with friends and acquaintances; on puritan forms of sacred sociability, see Patrick Collinson, "Elizabethan and Jacobean puritanism as forms of popular religious culture," in *The culture of English puritanism, 1560–1700,* ed. C. Durston and J. Eales (St. Martin's Press, 1996), 32–57.}

[27] {For Bayly's *The practice of piety* <*vide supra*>. This clause was not in the first edition, where the sentence instead ended, "her weapons are spells no less potent than different, as being the sage sentences of some of her own sectaries."}

[28] {On the puritan disallowance of reading (as opposed to preaching) ministers, see Bradshaw, chap. III, sect. 9 <*supra*>.}

her preachers, and censures all sermons but bad ones. If her husband be a tradesman, she helps him to customers, howsoever to good cheer, and they are a most faithful couple at these meetings, for they never fail. Her conscience is like others' lust, never satisfied, and you might better answer Scotus than her scruples. She is one that thinks she performs all her duties to God in hearing, and shews the fruits of it in talking. She is more fiery against the may-pole than her husband, and thinks she might do a Phineas' act to break the pate of the fiddler. She is an everlasting argument,[29] but I am weary of her.

XXXV
A SKEPTIC IN RELIGION

Is one that hangs in the balance with all sorts of opinions, whereof not one but stirs him and none sways him. A man guiltier of credulity than he is taken to be, for it is out of his belief of everything that he fully believes nothing. Each religion scares him from its contrary; none persuades him to itself. He would be wholly a Christian but that he is something of an atheist, and wholly an atheist but that he is partly a Christian, and a perfect heretic but that there are so many to distract him. He finds reason in all opinions, truth in none: indeed the least reason perplexes him and the best will not satisfy him. He is at most a confused and wild Christian, not specialized by any form,[30] but capable of all. He uses the land's religion because it is next him, yet he sees not why he may not take the other, but he chooses this, not as better, but because there is not a pin to choose.[31] He finds doubts and scruples better than resolves them, and is always too hard for himself. His learning is too much for his brain, and his judgment too little for his learning, and his over-opinion of both spoils all. Pity it was his mischance of being a scholar, for it does only distract and irregulate him, and the world by him. He hammers much in general upon our opinion's uncertainty, and the possibility of erring makes him not venture on what is true. He is troubled at this naturalness of religion to countries: that protestantism should be born so in England and popery abroad, and that fortune and the stars should so much share in it. He likes not this connection of the common-weal and divinity, and fears it may be an arch-practice of state. In our differences with Rome he is strangely unfixed, and a new man every new day, as his last discourse-book's meditations transport him. He could like the gray hairs of popery did not some dotages there stagger him; he would come to us sooner, but our new name affrights him. He is taken with their miracles, but doubts an imposture; he conceives of our doctrine better, but it seems too empty and naked. He cannot drive into his fancy the circumscription of truth to our corner, and is as hardly persuaded to think their old legends true. He approves well of our faith, and more of their works, and is sometimes much affected at the zeal of Amsterdam. His conscience interposes itself betwixt duelers, and whilst it would part both is by both wounded. He will sometimes propend[32] much to us upon the reading a good writer, and at Bellarmine recoils as far back again; and the Fathers jostle him from one side to another. Now Socinus

---

[29] {"theme," with a punning secondary sense of "debate"}

[30] {A somewhat metaphysical way of saying that he does not embrace any particular branch of Christianity.}

[31] {because he can see no real difference between them}

[32] {incline}

and Vorstius[33] afresh torture him, and he agrees with none worse than himself. He puts his foot into heresies tenderly as a cat in the water, and pulls it out again, and still something unanswered delays him; yet he bears away some parcel of each, and you may sooner pick all religions out of him than one. He cannot think so many wise men should be in error nor so many honest men out of the way, and his wonder is double when he sees these oppose one another. He hates authority as the tyrant of reason, and you cannot anger him worse than with a Father's *dixit*, and yet that many are not persuaded with reason shall authorize his doubt. In sum, his whole life is a question, and his salvation a greater, which death only concludes,[34] and then he is resolved.

TEXT: John Earle, D. D., *Microcosmography; or, a piece of the world discovered; in essays and characters: a reprint of Dr. Bliss' edition of 1811*, preface by S. T. Irwin (Bristol, 1897).[35]

[33] {Faustus Socinus (1539–1604) was an anti-Trinitarian. Conrad Vorstius (d. 1622), a Dutch Arminian, was thought by many, including King James, to hold equally unsound views regarding the Godhead.}

[34] {"decides" or "settles," as well as "ends"}

[35] Irwin's preface notes that Bliss used the 1732 edition as a base text, collating it against the edition of 1628 (xlv).

WILLIAM PRYNNE

God no imposter
(1629)

The biographical sketch of this incendiary puritan common lawyer and anti-Laudian polemicist is postponed to the introduction prefacing his 1637 *News from Ipswich*, since the pamphlet's significance is inseparable from its biographical and historical contexts. The tract reprinted below, one of Prynne's earliest works, seemed worth including on two grounds: first, as an expression of the theological convictions held by those spearheading the opposition to the Caroline regime; and second, as an example of what Anthony Milton terms the "uncertain and sometimes incoherent progress" of the "moderate English Calvinism" espoused by British delegation at Dort and by John Preston, Prynne's own minister at Lincoln's Inn (422).

Except in one respect, there is nothing extraordinary about *God no impostor*; many Protestant divines in the 1620s found themselves thrown on the defensive re justifying the ways of Calvin's God. Already in the late sixteenth century, Perkins had grappled with the objection that double predestination left the Gospels' seemingly universal offer of salvation looking like a cheat. Preston, the divinity reader at Lincoln's Inn and a major influence on Prynne's theological formation, repeatedly comes back to this question of whether God is mocking the reprobate by inviting them to believe and be saved while at the same time denying the grace needed to do either.[1] Moreover, in February of 1626 when the Duke of Buckingham and several Calvinist peers brought together Richard Montagu's supporters and opponents to debate their differences, Preston apparently had some difficulty explaining how his denial that Christ died equally for all men did not impeach God's veracity. In writing *God no impostor*, Prynne was, among other things, defending his revered preacher against the negative fallout from York House.

Preston *had* tried to address Arminian objections by proposing (like the British delegates at Dort) a "new and much softer brand of Calvinism" that apparently dismayed some of the old-style predestinarians at York House. Although Prynne partially mutes

[1] See Preston's "Free grace magnified" <*supra*>.

this (he avoids the whole question of for whom Christ died), his insistence that the reprobates cannot respond to the Gospel's invitation because they will not—and not because of any fatal divine decree—is characteristic of early Stuart endeavors to secure the moral intelligibility of Calvinism. Prynne's attempt to justify the ways of God to the reprobate by appealing to the graces and illumination experienced by the non-elect <525–26> thus echoes not only Perkins, whom Prynne cites, but also the canons proposed by the British at Dort (see *Collegiate suffrage* Ib.4, Va.1–3 <*supra*>).

However, Prynne's main argument, several times repeated, is distinctive—its distinctiveness related to the fact Prynne is virtually the only (and the "virtually" may be unnecessary) layman publishing on controversial divinity in early Stuart England. All the rest are clergymen. Prynne, however, was a lawyer, which explains his initially puzzling thesis that, since no one on this side of eternity can know that he is a reprobate, no one "can say God deals falsely with him in desiring his conversion when as he {God} never did intend it" <523>, and this clears God of being an impostor or deluder. Prynne never disputes that most people are reprobates; what matters for him is that no individual can say that *he* is a reprobate. This matters because common-law tort actions require a plaintiff; the action can only be brought by the specific person (or persons) allegedly harmed as the result of the defendant's actions.[2] Since the only persons who would be harmed by God's deceit are reprobates, the fact that no one knows whether he is a reprobate—and therefore whether he has been injured by the alleged deception—means that no one has legal standing to bring charges; and since there's no plaintiff, the case against God is dismissed.

NOTE: a revised and enlarged edition of *God no impostor* was reprinted in 1629 and again in 1630. The base text for the selection that follows is the shorter, and presumably earlier, 1629 edition. However, the subsequent editions add an extraordinary final section on the politics of divine sovereignty and possessive individualism—its relation both to the liberties of freeborn Englishmen and to the royal prerogative—which is reprinted here at the conclusion of the sermon.

SOURCES: Barbara Donagan, "The York House Conference revisited," *Historical Research* 64 (1991): 312–30; Kendall, *Calvin and English Calvinism*; Moore, *English hypothetical universalism*; Milton, *Catholic and Reformed*.

---

[2] In Star Chamber and the ecclesiastical courts, which did not use common law procedure, the court could move against wrongs without waiting for a plaintiff to bring charges; that is, they could act ex officio to give relief to a group of persons injured by another's actions, even if none of the victims brought charges and even if the court did not know, at the time of handing down its verdict, who in particular the victims were (see S. R. Gardiner, ed., *Reports of cases in the courts of Star Chamber and High Commission* [London, 1886], 46–48).

WILLIAM PRYNNE

God no imposter nor deluder
1629 (rev. ed. 1630)

It is a common demand which the patrons of universal grace and free will use to make, how God can be excused from hypocrisy, collusion, and deceit, if he hath not seriously purposed and determined to convert and call all such to whom the Gospel is preached, but only to {*sic*} the elect?

To give a full, a clear and satisfactory answer unto this demand, which stumbles many, we must consider in the first place that the glad tidings and promises of the Gospel are proper and peculiar to the elect and chosen saints of God, and not common to the elect and reprobates as the Law is, which binds all men alike. Hence is it, that the elect only are said *to be the children of the promise, the seed of Abraham; and the promise of faith by Jesus Christ* is said *to be given only to them which believe. The voice of Christ is proper only to the sheep of Christ,* who are the elect—whence the faith of the Gospel is styled *the faith of God's elect,* as being proper and peculiar unto them alone. Christ Jesus hath *bequeathed his Gospel as a peculiar legacy to his saints and chosen ones, and delivered and committed it to them.* Wherefore the apostles did always dedicate and direct their *epistles to the elect, the chosen and faithful in Christ Jesus; to the saints, the sanctified, called and preserved in Christ Jesus, and to no others*: to signify that the Gospel is proper and peculiar unto them. Secondly, you must observe that, though the ministers of the Gospel are to *preach the Gospel to every creature,* yet it is not with an intent to convert all those that hear it unto God, but only the elect. Paul did preach and *endure all things* not for all those to whom he preached, but *only for the elect's sake.* . . . The preachers of the Gospel, who are styled *angels,* are sent out only *to gather the elect* (not all men) *from the four winds.* . . . Thirdly, you must take notice, that though the Gospel be to be preached unto every creature, yet it is not with an intent to convert & save all those that hear it preached, but only true believers: this is evident by that commission which Christ gave unto his apostles: *Go ye* (saith he) *into all the world, and preach the Gospel to every creature; he that believeth and is baptized shall be saved, but he that believeth not shall be damned.* By which conditional clause and limitation, it is most apparent that God did never intend that his Gospel should convert and save all such as hear it preached . . . but only such as should believe and embrace it in their hearts. Now these are only the elect, and no others; for *they only do believe.* Therefore the Gospel is intended unto them alone.

If this then be granted and yielded unto me, that the promises and glad tidings of the Gospel are proper and peculiar to the elect alone; that the ministers of the Gospel are sent out only to call and gather together the elect; and that the preaching of the Gospel unto every creature is not with an intent to convert and save all such as hear it but only such as do believe it, who are always the lesser number and only such as are elected; then it follows inevitably that there is no repugnancy nor contradiction between the secret and the revealed will of God; and that God deludes and cozens none to whom the Gospel is preached, though they are not converted, because he did never intend to convert all those that should be the hearers, but only such as are the true embracers and believers of his Gospel, who are only the elect, in whom alone he works this grace of faith.

Yea, but you will now object that God doth seriously exhort and entreat even reprobates and wicked men to repent and believe, though he hath determined to give no faith nor yet repentance to them. Therefore, if they cannot repent and believe of themselves (as we affirm), God cannot but mock and dissemble with them, because he exhorts them unto that which they of themselves (without God's aid) can never do and which himself hath decreed irrevocably that they shall never do.

To this I answer that it is true that if God himself, who knows the hearts and estates of all men, should tell any man from heaven that he was a reprobate and that he had irrevocably decreed it that he would never work any faith or repentance in him; and should come to such a man in particular and seriously exhort him to believe and repent that so he might be saved, that then there were some shew of mockery, falsehood, and double-dealing in God, and this objection might stand good. But here the case stands otherwise. For though God doth oft times seriously exhort and entreat even such to believe and repent as he hath reprobated and forever rejected in his secret purpose and decree, yet here is no delusion nor deceit at all. First, because the minister, who is God's agent and ambassador unto this reprobate, can never determine whether he be a reprobate, yea or no; so that he tenders grace and mercy to him, not as to a reprobate or cast away, but as to a chosen saint of God—for ought he knows. Secondly, because this reprobate, to whom this exhortation and tender of grace is made, can never fully satisfy nor yet resolve himself that he is a reprobate, because he was never privy to God's counsel and because his whole life is a time of grace to him—for ought he knows. Since then it is neither revealed to the minister that offers grace, nor yet to him to whom this grace is tendered, that he is a reprobate and that God hath determined to bestow no grace upon him, neither the minister nor yet himself can truly say that God doth mock him or delude him; because that unto them, and to all other men, there is a possibility, yea and a probability, that this very reprobate may be saved, because he is no reprobate as unto them nor yet as to himself.

Yea, but you will object that God himself doth certainly know that this very reprobate neither will nor can repent . . . therefore God must needs delude and mock him, though man cannot discern it.

To this I answer that if man cannot discern that God deludes men in this his dealing, then how doth it come to pass that you who prosecute this objection can charge God with delusion and cozenage in his dealing, when as man cannot discern it? what, are you now translated into gods or angels, that you can fathom and find out this mystery, which all the saints and reprobates in the world cannot espy? Doubtless if there be never a reprobate in the world that can say God deals falsely with him in desiring his conversion when as he never did intend it—because he could not satisfy himself whether he were a reprobate yea or no—then it is certain that you who make this mystical and strange objection must cease to charge God with collusion and double dealing. . . . Secondly, though God doth certainly know that reprobates neither can nor will repent, yet he doth not mock nor delude them by inviting, exhorting, and persuading them to repent, because that, as God doth not invite them to faith and repentance as they are reprobates, so his decree of reprobation is not the immediate cause of their infidelity and impenitency, but their own corrupt and sinful natures, which God is not bound to heal and cure. Indeed if God himself should purposely bind them hand and foot in the chains and fetters of sin, and then should bid them go or walk and run on towards him in a serious and earnest manner, he might then be thought for to delude them: but this God doth not do. He casts no rubs nor blocks into our way, but what we cast ourselves. If we come not in when as he invites us, it is not because God himself doth not enable us, but because we have ensnared ourselves in sins and trespasses, and disabled ourselves to come unto him as we ought, so that here we must accuse ourselves, not God.[1] Thirdly, when God doth offer grace unto us, we must know that he doth not immediately infuse this grace into us, but he works it in us by the use of means. Now God, when as he offers grace to reprobates, they always slight, neglect, and vilify the means by which God offers and conveys his grace; so that if they miss of grace (as they always do) they cannot lay the blame on God or say that he did not intend for to convert them, but they must take the blame upon themselves; because if they had used the means with care and conscience as they ought and done that which was requisite on their parts, God would have wrought effectually by his Spirit in their hearts—for ought that they could tell or think to the contrary. Fourthly, when God doth seriously and earnestly invite us to repentance and true saving faith, he doth not always promise and resolve to work this faith and repentance in our hearts (for then they should be always wrought effectually in us, because God's purposed and resolved will is *always executed, and cannot be resisted*), but he doth only seriously declare what things he doth approve and require in us. A king may seriously wish and desire that such a subject of his were a rich, a great and honorable person, but yet he may not purpose and resolve to make him such a one. God doth earnestly command and desire that all men (but especially his saints) should not offend nor sin against him, but yet he doth not purpose to cause them not to sin: for *in many things we offend all; and there is no man that liveth, and sinneth not*. God may desire something in his revealed will, which he hath not purposed nor decreed to effect and work in his secret will. He *desires not the death of a sinner*, and yet sinners always die in sin, without repentance.[2] Since therefore God may desire and require something in his revealed will, which he hath not purposed nor decreed to effect in his secret will,[3] it follows not that God doth therefore intend and purpose to work effectually by his

---

[1] {Prynne's standpoint here, and throughout the tract, seems unequivocally Infralapsarian.}

[2] {i.e., sinners, unless they repent, die in sin}

[3] {It is precisely this distinction between God's revealed and secret will that Donne rejects in a 1628 sermon preached in St. Paul's: "as the Law is our Judge, and the Judge does but declare what is Law, so the

grace in hypocrites and reprobates when as he offers grace and mercy by his word—and so he mocks them not. Fifthly, the Gospel, in which God offers grace to men, though it be propounded in a common and universal manner in respect of the hearing of it, from which none are excluded; yet it is always propounded distributively, restrictively, and conditionally in respect of the benefit and comfort of it: not to men as they are men . . . but to all those, and to those only, that shall believe it, embrace it, and obey it in the sincerity of their hearts. If then the Gospel be thus preached and propounded to a whole congregation, can any man say that God deludes him? If he will believe and apply the Gospel, he shall be sure to reap the fruit and comfort of it. . . . If he believe and receive it not at all, he cannot say that God deludes him . . . because he propounded it with this proviso, *if he would believe and apply it to his own eternal good*: which proviso and condition he hath not yet fulfilled; and therefore he cannot blame the Lord, who did not promise to fulfill it for him.

Yea, but, say you, a reprobate may thus object: I cannot receive nor believe the Gospel unless God give me an heart and will to do it, which heart and will he hath not determined to give me; therefore he doth but delude and cozen me in proffering grace unto me upon such impossible terms and conditions as these, which I cannot perform. I answer, that it is true that God must give men hearts to embrace and use the means of grace in an effectual manner, or else they cannot do it; yet this I say withal: that even reprobates themselves might have done more than now they do, and been more diligent in the outward means had they put their whole might and strength unto it, and prayed earnestly to God for his assistance; so that they cannot truly say that God was wanting unto them in altering of their hearts, but that they were wanting to themselves in being negligent in the use of means and in blocking up their hearts against the Lord by daily sins. Secondly, that inability to believe and use the means of grace which is in reprobates, proceeds not from any decree or act of God, but from reprobates themselves. God made man able at the first to do his will and to use the means of grace, which liberty mankind hath wholly and justly lost in Adam's fall. Since therefore that impotency and impossibility of getting and receiving grace which is in reprobates proceeds not from any fatal or necessitating decree of God, but only from that original depravation and natural imbecility which is in them, from which God is not pleased for to free them,[4] these reprobates cannot say that God deludes and mocks them in tendering grace unto them, though he denies them hearts and wills for to embrace it—which he is not bound in justice for to give them; but they must rather magnify his mercy towards them in offering grace unto them, when as they have made themselves unworthy of it and unable to receive it. Thirdly, what reprobate is there that, when God doth offer grace unto him by his ministers, can truly say that God hath positively resolved not to give him an heart or will for to embrace it? Is any reprobate privy unto God's decrees, to know what he hath purposed concerning

---

Scripture is our Judge, and God proceeds with us according to those promises and Judgments. . . . [Hence,] if I come to think that God will call me in question for my life, for my eternal life, by any way that hath not the Nature of a *Law*, (And, by the way, it is of the Nature and Essence of a Law, before it come to bind, that it be *published*) if I think that God will condemn me by any *unrevealed will* . . . this is to reproach God" (*Sermons*, 8:281–82). See also Hoard, *God's mercies* <749>.}

 [4] {Compare *Collegiate Suffrage* Ib.1 <*supra*>; the position seems very close to that of Aquinas (*Summa theologiae* 1a.23.3).}

him? . . . for ought he knows, he may belong to God's election; and if so, then God will surely change his heart and give him power to embrace his grace. Fourthly, if God should offer grace to reprobates in a serious manner, yet he should not delude them, though he gives them no power to receive it, because there is in reprobates such a love of sin . . . that they would be *utterly unwilling to receive this grace upon those terms that God doth offer it, although they had power to embrace it.* Reprobates, though they might have grace for the very taking of it, yet they would not take it, though they might, upon God's conditions. Therefore God doth not delude them in tendering grace unto them, though they cannot take it; because they would not take it though they might. Fifthly, God doth not mock nor yet delude these reprobates in offering grace unto them by the ministry of the Gospel . . . because they have many privileges, benefits, and advantages by the Gospel, though their hearts are not converted nor reformed by it. For first, by this proffer of the Gospel to them, they have always something to support their souls from sinking in despair; they have always a possibility, a hope and probability, of their true conversion and salvation, which those who are deprived of the Gospel want, whence they are said to be *aliens from the commonwealth of Israel, strangers from the covenant of promise, having no hope.* Reprobates who live under the Gospel have always hope till their dying day, because they know not whether they are reprobates, yea or no, till then. . . . Secondly, reprobates who enjoy the Gospel have a more clear, distinct, and full apprehension of God . . . yea, they *taste a sweetness in the word and promises, and in the powers of the world to come*; they know more then all the world besides, which is deprived of the Gospel. Now the very knowledge of God and Christ . . . and of all those things which the Scriptures do reveal unto reprobates is an invaluable and matchless blessing; it is a greater good and happiness than man by all the light of art and nature (without the Scriptures) can attain unto; therefore no reprobates can say that God deals hardly or falsely with them, though his word doth not convert them. Thirdly, reprobates, though they are not converted by the Gospel, have always as *great (nay sometimes a greater) share and portion in those outward blessings and privileges* which the Gospel brings (which are great and many) as the saints themselves. The Gospel commonly brings peace and plenty, health and safety, and all outward happiness and tranquility with it; it is always accompanied with many great and excellent blessings, of which reprobates drink as deep as any others. Therefore it is not altogether in vain unto them, though it convert them not. Fourthly, reprobates, though they are not truly sanctified nor called by the Gospel, yet many of them have oft times many moral, outward, and commendable virtues, gifts, and graces wrought within them by it. Again, many of them are oft times civilized, curbed, rectified, and reformed by it, so that they run not into the same excess of sin and wickedness as else they would; by which it comes to pass that their eternal torments in hell fire are much extenuated and abated. Therefore they cannot truly say that the Gospel is ineffectual and fruitless to them, because their very souls reap much advantage by it. Fifthly, reprobates have oft times many sudden, transitory, and flashy joys, and many good motions, purposes, and resolutions wrought within them by the word. Yea the word of God is sometimes so prevalent and powerful in their souls that it makes them to do many things for God, and to go very far in the outward practice and profession of religion; insomuch that they seem to many to be the elect of God and the undoubted members of Jesus Christ [see Mr. Perkins how far a reprobate may go]: so that the Gospel is not altogether in vain unto them.[5] . . . Sixthly, reprobates . . . do enjoy the society and company of God's elect and chosen saints, by means of whom their souls and bodies do oft times fare the better. . . . It is common in the Scriptures and ordinary in experience that God sometimes blesseth reprobates and keeps off judgments from them for the godly men's sake that live among them; wherefore, though the Gospel doth not convert them to the Lord, yet it is not in vain unto them even in this respect. Seventhly, reprobates who live under the Gospel are sometimes made the instruments and means of good to others, and the furtherers of God's glory, though they do no good to themselves. Kings, ministers, magistrates, scholars of all sorts, artificers, and the like, though they are such as God hath rejected, are oft times made the instruments of much good unto the saints. . . . which brings much joy and comfort to them for the present, and gains respect and honor to them in the sight of men. Since therefore reprobates enjoy so many blessings, privileges, and comforts by the Gospel as these here mentioned, they have no cause to say that God deludes and mocks them when as he sends the Gospel to them, because . . . he derives many outward blessings, comforts, privileges, and favors to them by it, for which their souls and bodies fare the better.

If you now object that the Gospel aggravates the sins of reprobates and makes their condemnation greater because it leaves them without excuse—therefore they are no gainers but losers by the Gospel—I answer that it is true that it had been better for some reprobates—yea, for all those reprobates that go on in sinful and rebellious courses without restraint—that they had never enjoyed the Gospel by reason of their disobedience to it; but as for others who are reclaimed by it, though it aggravates their condemnation one way, in adding to the greatness of their sins; yet it extenuates it another way, in detracting from the multitude and number of their sins, which they would have doubled and trebled had not the ministry and preaching of the word restrained them: so that they are far greater gainers in this last respect than losers by the first. All reprobates fare the better for the Gospel here, in regard of those many outward blessings and privileges that accompany it; many of them speed the better for it not only here but hereafter too. Those that fare the worser for it, it is from their own defaults. . . . Lastly, though God doth not give men power to believe and receive his Gospel, yet he doth not delude them though he offers it unto them with a desire that they should receive it: for as God doth not delude men in enjoining them not to sin and to observe his law in every point, though he gives them no power nor strength to do it and though it be *impossible for them to fulfill it*, no more can he be said to delude or mock men in offering grace unto them by the Gospel though he gives them no power to receive it: because he commands them no more than they had strength at first to do, which strength and power they lost through their own defaults; and because the end of this command is to no other purpose but to cause men for to see their own disability and so to fly to him for strength, for grace and mercy.

. . .

. . . If the ministers could discern between the elect and reprobates . . . they might then propound the Gospel to the elect alone; but because they know not who are chosen

[5] {On William Perkins' doctrine of temporary faith and its role in English experimental predestinarianism, see Kendall, *Calvin and English Calvinism*.}

and elected, nor who are reprobated, therefore they must preach the Gospel unto all, that so those who are elected may be effectually called and converted out of all. Thirdly, the Gospel must be thus propounded, because else it would be vain and ineffectual unto all; for if the Gospel should be pronounced to the elect alone (as he that is elected shall be saved), then no man could apply it to his own soul; for before a man's conversion unto God, he can never truly say that he is elected: yea, the very elect themselves can never say that they are elected till they find the blessed fruits of election in their hearts, which are wrought by the preaching of the word. . . . therefore it is propounded generally unto all, that so men might be able to apply it. Fourthly, the Gospel must be thus propounded, that so no man whiles he liveth here might have cause to despair of God's mercy. If God should cull out his elect from among the reprobates, and make an open division and separation of them here, preaching the Gospel unto them alone, then all these reprobates must needs despair of his grace and run into some desperate course, knowing that they are designed and marked out for hell. . . . Fifthly, the Gospel is thus generally preached unto all, that so reprobates who willfully disobey, reject, and slight it may be left without excuse, laying all the blame upon themselves and not on God, who was not wanting to them in the means. Sixthly, the Gospel is thus generally propounded unto all, though it becomes not effectual unto all, because the saints of God who are converted by it may have greater cause to love, to bless and praise the Lord for making it effectual unto them, when as he hath not made it so to others. Seventhly, it is thus propounded unto all, because it is a *rule of life* to reprobates as well as others, though it be no salve nor plaster to them for to heal their souls. The Gospel, though it works not grace in all, yet it is a square and rule of life to all that hear it; and it is that by which they shall *be judged at the last*. . . . Eighthly, it is thus propounded unto all, that so the riches of God's love and mercy to mankind in Jesus Christ . . . might be more publicly known, manifested, and revealed to the sons of men, to the glory and praise of God. The more the Gospel is spread abroad, the more God and Christ are glorified, though it converts not all, because it doth more propagate and divulge those great, those glorious attributes & treasures of goodness which are in them, and wins them a greater, a more awful and commanding reverence and adoration in the hearts of men. Therefore it is thus preached unto all. Ninthly, it is propounded unto all because it works effectually on many reprobates, though not to turn them wholly and fully to the Lord, yet to convert them from their atheism, their paganism, idolatries, profane and dissolute courses, and from many other sins into which they would have plunged themselves had not the Gospel pulled them back. We know it by experience that the Gospel works very far on many reprobates; it makes them *do much, and part with many sins*. . . . If the Gospel had been preached to the elect alone, then many who profess the Gospel, acknowledging the deity of God and Christ, and the truth and holiness of the Gospel,[6] had lain still in darkness and in their heathenish rites and superstitious worshipping of devils, stocks, stones, and other creatures for gods, and embracing fabulous, blasphemous, absurd, and idle poems and histories of their idol-gods for sound

---

[6] {Note that the logic of the sentence requires that the "many" who "profess the Gospel" are reprobates, and therefore, by definition, without faith. Accepting the truth of Christian teaching is not what Prynne (or most evangelical Protestants) means by faith. On what does count as saving faith in this tradition, see Preston, "The buckler of a believer" *<supra>*; also, Kendall, *Calvin and English Calvinism*; Shuger, "Faith and assurance."}

divinity; by which the glory of God and Christ . . . should have been much eclipsed. God therefore commands the Gospel to be propounded unto all, and not to the elect alone, that so all *men might come to the acknowledgement of his truth* and deity, for the greater manifestation of his glory. Twelfthly, the Gospel is thus propounded unto all, that so reprobates as well as others might be *convinced* of their own weakness, wretchedness, and perverseness in God's sight, and acknowledge that he deals justly in rejecting them and in inflicting vengeance on them for their sins. When a reprobate . . . shall discover by the brightness of the word, the greatness, bulk, and infinite multitude of his sins, then he is even forced *to confess* that God deals justly with him; then his conscience stops his mouth . . . so that he hath nothing to reply against God, but willingly submits unto his doom as being scarce proportionable to his sin. So that there is great reason why the Gospel should be thus propounded unto all, though it converts not all that hear it. Thirteenthly, the sacraments are administered unto all, to reprobates as well as to the elect; reprobates are baptized and receive the sacrament of the Lord's Supper as well as any of God's chosen ones. It is fit therefore that the Gospel should be extended unto all as well as the sacraments, because they are both of the same extent and latitude, and go hand in hand together, like twins that cannot be divided. Lastly, the Gospel is thus propounded unto all, because it hath a several effect in all—though not to save & convert all those that hear it. To the elect, it is the *power of God to salvation*. . . . to the wicked *it is the savor of death unto death*, the rule of life and judgment, the declaration of God's will and pleasure, the *cause oft times of their obduration & greater condemnation* by reason of their contempt and neglect of it. Since therefore the Gospel hath a work in reprobates as well as in the elect, it is propounded to them both: yet not as unto elect and reprobates . . . but as to men who are capable of grace & salvation if they repent & believe that Gospel which is preached to them, and of damnation if they do reject it. And thus you see this grand objection cleared: that God is no deluder nor impostor, though he hath not purposed nor decreed to convert and call all such to whom the Gospel is preached.

FINIS.

‡

And if you now demand of me why God doth thus convert and call home one man by his word, and not another; or why he converts not all, *since there is no respect of persons with him?*[7]

I answer: that no other reason can be rendered of it but that *it is his good will and pleasure thus to do.* All the reason why God shews mercy to any man, or to this man more than to another, is only this: because he will have mercy, and because it is his pleasure thus to do. This is all the ground and reason which God himself, or the Scriptures for him, render; and why should we curiously inquire after any other, which God himself hath not revealed? We all confess that we were in a desperate and lost condition, and that God might have suffered us all to perish without any injury or injustice to us. If God therefore be so exceeding gracious and compassionate to save some whom he thinks good to save, and so just and righteous as to suffer others for to perish, shall *we potter's clay be so*

---

[7] {For the Arminian critique of the view Prynne here defends, see Hoard's *God's love to mankind* <*infra*>.}

presumptuous as to interrogate him, why he doth it? Certainly, if we consider but that absolute and sovereign right that God hath in us as we are his creatures, how we are wholly and solely his, and not our own; how we are in his hands as the clay in the potter's to fashion and frame us, yea to crush us in pieces at his pleasure, though we had no sin at all within us—yet then if God should cast us all into hell, we might justly lay our hands upon our mouths and not so much as dare to ask of him a reason why he doth use us thus. Alas, which of us could then say unto God, what doest thou? or why hast thou made or rejected me thus? Is it not lawful for God to do what he will with his own? And may he not then dispose of us at his pleasure, without any injury or injustice?[8] Do not weak and mortal men, who are but tenants at will or sufferance of all their earthly goods and possessions, argue thus: that they may dispose of them at their will and pleasure, without control or check, *because they are their own*—when as in truth they are not theirs but God's? and shall we then deny that liberty to God in that which is truly his, which we all do take unto ourselves in that which is none of ours but only at God's pleasure?

We see that potters and glass-men cast the selfsame metal into diverse different shapes and forms, and oft times dash and mar their work, because it is their pleasure. . . . Do not nobles and gentlemen pull down such a house, repair and build another? Do they not design such a room or plot of ground to one use, such a one to another? Do they not demolish, alter, or transplant their orchards, gardens, parks, or walks? Do they not kill such a stag or buck or fowl or hare, and spare another, because it is their pleasure? Yet no man dares control them for it, because they are their own. We see earthly monarchs do oft dispense and cast their honors, favors, and disfavors upon men, advancing this man and displacing that, upon no other grounds at all but that *it is their pleasure*. Yet who may say unto them, what doest thou? We know that masters, landlords, fathers dispose of their slaves and vassals, lands and tenements, sons and daughters, goods and chattels, at their pleasure, to whom, or how they please, yet no man questions nor controls them for it, because they are their own. And shall we poor dust and ashes, who take such liberty to ourselves in all that we conceive to be our own (though in truth the right and property of it be in God himself and not in us), so limit and confine the boundless prerogative and absolute sovereignty of the omnipotent and supreme commander, proprietor, king, and God of heaven and earth, *in whom, from whom, for whom all creatures live and move and have their being, and for whose only will and pleasure they are and were created*, as to deny him liberty to do what he will with his own, to elect and reprobate, reject or choose, what men he please? . . .

TEXT: EEBO (STC [2nd ed.] / 20459.3)

God, no impostor nor deluder, or, An answer to a popish and Arminian cavil, in the defense of free-will, and universal grace wherein God's tender of grace by the outward ministry of the gospel, to reprobates who neither do, nor can receive it, is vindicated from those aspersions of equivocation, falsity, and collusion, which some by way of objection, cast upon it / by William Prynne . . . (London [?], 1629).

The final passage comes from Prynne's *God no impostor nor deluder* (S.I.: A. Mathewes, 1630?), 20–23.[9] (STC [2nd ed.] / 20459.7)

[8] [August. *De praedest. & gratia* c. 16.]

[9] From 1626 through 1640, publishing on the controverted points of predestination was illegal; hence the vagueness regarding actual place and date of publication.

JOSEPH HALL
(1574–1656)

Hall's early theological formation took place under the guidance of Anthony Gilby, a close family friend, incumbent at Hall's childhood parish of Ashby-de-la-Zouch, Leicestershire, and noted puritan controversialist. Gilby's son Nathaniel helped make it possible for Hall to attend Emmanuel, Cambridge's newly established puritan seminary, where he matriculated in 1589 together with his grammar school classmate, William Bradshaw <vide supra>. He took his BA in 1593 and then, through a complicated sequence of accidents, usurped Nathaniel Gilby's fellowship, which allowed him to stay on for his MA (1596) and a two-year lectureship in rhetoric. Between 1597 and 1610 he published several groundbreaking literary works, including the first English collection of formal verse satires and the first Theophrastean characters. During the same years he also published the first Protestant adaptations of continental contemplative literature: the *Meditations and vows, divine and moral* (1605) and *Art of divine meditation* (1606).

Ordained in 1600 (BD 1603; DD 1610), Hall was appointed one of Prince Henry's chaplains in 1607 and quickly became a celebrated preacher. In 1617 he accompanied James to Scotland; in 1618 he went to Dort as a member of the British delegation (although he had to drop out due to a severe illness). Having been made dean of Worcester in 1616, in 1627 he was consecrated bishop of Exeter, in 1641 translated to Norwich. During these years he produced an extensive body of controversial writings against Rome, against Arminianism, and, most famously, in support of divine right episcopacy—this latter ranging him against Milton and his fellow Smectymnuans. In his autobiographical *Heart measure* (1647), Hall vividly describes the catastrophic effects of the Civil War both for his family and his diocese. Driven out of his episcopal residence in 1647, Hall spent the remainder of the Interregnum in rural Suffolk, where he continued his ministry (including ordination) and his devotional writing.

What follows is a portion of a Gray's Inn sermon preached in the late 1620s, selected for its relation to Sibbes' *Bruised reed*, which grew out of sermons also preached at Gray's Inn during the same years.

Given Hall's stature and voluminous output, this extract seems meager. Hall does not anthologize well. He consistently strove to mediate between all parties—at least all parties within the Church of England—to any dispute (his episcopal seal at Norwich showed Noah's ark on the waters, a dove bearing an olive branch above, with the inscription DA PACEM NOBIS[1]), but the result tends to be endless backpedaling, waffling, and inconsistency. His claim in *The old religion* (1628) that Rome was "a true visible Church in respect of outward profession of Christianity" but "an heretical apostatical, anti-Christian Synagogue in respect of doctrine and practice" is classic Hall in its suspension between murkiness and self-contradiction. Similar fudging characterizes Hall's *Via media* (ca. 1624–26), which attempts to resolve the conflict between Calvinist and Arminian teaching on predestination by denying that any significant disagreement exists:

> For the first: both parts hold there is no other impulsive cause of God's decree of election or reprobation than the free will and pleasure of the Almighty. ¶ Only, the one part holds that God's decree looks at faith and infidelity as conditions in those who are to be chosen or refused; the other easily grants that no man is elect but the believer, no man reprobate but the rebellious and unbeliever, although they will not put these as fore-required conditions into the act of God's decree. ¶ Why should the mere supposal of a condition be worth their quarrel, since it is yielded on all hands that in God's decree of our justification he looks at our faith as a necessary condition required thereunto, without any derogation to the perfect freedom of that his gracious decree? If faith may be granted not to be in our own power, but that it is the gift of God, there can no main inconvenience follow upon this tenet, that God, in our election, had an eye to our qualification with that faith which he would give us.[2]

While the sermon reprinted below itself betrays no such contradictions, other of Hall's works warmly oppose the moralist perfectionism it so warmly defends.[3] One has some sympathy with Hall's desire to have it both ways, given that when Laud finally forced him to take a coherent and consistent position in *Episcopacy by divine right* (1641), Milton bit his head off.[4] Hall's sermons and tracts often provide invaluable insight into the array of issues, large and small, roiling the Church of England at any particular time (e.g., "Abraham's Purchase" re church burial), since he will lay out the various positions and the reasoning behind them; yet he also tends to affirm each *seriatim* over the course of a single work.

Sources: *ODNB*; W. K. Riland, *The blazon of episcopacy* (Clarendon, 1897); P. Wynter, ed., *The works of the Right Reverend Joseph Hall*, 10 vols., rev. ed. (Oxford UP, 1863).

[1] Give us peace.

[2] Hall's conclusion in *Via media*, however, is that "there is no possible redress {of the predestinarian debate} but in a severe edict of restraint, to charm all tongues and pens upon the sharpest punishment from passing those moderate bounds which the Church of England, guided by the Scriptures, hath expressly set; or which on both sides are fully accorded on"—a conclusion that Charles also reached, his 1626 proclamation forbidding further publication on the controverted issues snaring *Via media* in its net; the work was not printed until 1660.

[3] See, e.g., Hall's *Heaven upon earth*, 3rd ed. (London, 1607), 40–53.

[4] See Milton's 1642 "Apology against a pamphlet call'd a modest confutation of a sclanderous and scurrilous libell, entituled 'Animadversions upon the Remonstrants defense against Smectymnus.'"

JOSEPH HALL

The estate of a Christian laid forth in a sermon preached at Gray's Inn
on Candlemas Day

late 1620s

But be ye changed (or transformed) by the renewing of your minds.
Romans 12:2

The true method of Christian practice is first destructive, then astructive: according to the Prophet, *cease to do evil, learn to do good.* This our Apostle observes, who first unteacheth us ill fashions and then teacheth good.

We have done with the negative duty of a Christian, what he must not do: hear now the affirmative, what he must do: wherein our speech, treading in the steps of the blessed Apostle, shall pass through these four heads: first, that here must be a change; secondly, that this change must be by transformation; thirdly, that this transformation must be by renewing; fourthly, that this renewing must be of the mind: *But be ye changed*, or *transformed, by the renewing of your minds.* All of them points of high and singular importance, and such as do therefore call for your best and carefullest attention.

Nothing is more changing than the fashion of the world: *Mundus transit, The world passeth away*, saith St. John [1 John 2:17]. Yet here, that we may not fashion ourselves to the world, we must be changed: we must be changed from these changeable fashions of the world to a constant estate of regeneration. As there must be once a perfect change of this mortal to immortality, so must there be, onwards, of this sinful to gracious; and as holy Job resolves to *wait all the days of his appointed time* for that *changing*; so this change contrarily waits for us, and may not be put off one day.

. . .

. . . We, that are naturally in the way to that damnation, have reason to desire a change: worse we cannot be upon earth than in a state of sin. Be changed therefore, if ye wish well to your own souls; that it may be said of you, in St. Paul's words, *such ye were.* What an enemy would upbraid by way of reproach is the greatest praise that can be: faults that *were.* O happy men, that can hear, "Ye were profane, unclean, idolatrous, oppressive, riotous!" Their very sins honor them, as the very devils that Mary Magdalen had are mentioned for her glory, since we do not hear of them but when they were cast out.

. . . Away with this frippery of our nature. *Old things are passed*: if ever we look to have any party {part} in God, in heaven, we must be changed.

But, secondly, every change will not serve the turn. The word is not ἀλλοίσις, alteration, nor μεταβολή, but metamorphosis: a word whose sound we are better acquainted with than the sense; the meaning is, there must be a change in our very form.

. . .

. . . there are changes that reach to the very forms whence all actions arise: as when of evil, we are made good; of carnal, spiritual. This is the metamorphosis that is here called for. Indeed it hath been a not more ancient than true observation, that the change of some things makes all things seem changed: as when a man comes into a house wherein the partitions are pulled down, the roof raised up, the floor paved, bay-windows set out, the outside rough-cast; he shall think all the frame new; and yet the old foundation, beams, studs, roof stand still. So it is here. The very substance of the soul holds still, but the dispositions and qualities and the very cast of it are altered; as when a round piece of paste is formed into a square; or, which is the highest of all patterns, as our Blessed Savior was transformed in the Mount Tabor. His Deity was the same, his humanity the same, the same soul, the same body; yet he was μεταμορφωθείς (it is the very word that the Holy Ghost uses both there and here) in that the Deity did put a glorious splendor upon his human body which before it had not. Thus it must be in our transformation onwards: the Spirit of God doth thus alter us through grace, while we are yet for essence the same.

. . .

Our mythologists tell us of many strange metamorphoses: of men turned into beasts, birds, trees—wherein, doubtless, they had moral allusions. Let me tell you of a metamorphosis as strange as theirs, and as true as theirs fabulous. They tell us of men turned into swine by Circe; I tell you of swine turned into men: when drunkards and obscene persons turn sober and well governed. . . . They tell us of a self-loving man turned to a flower; I tell you of a fading transitory creature changed into the image of the Son of God. They tell us of a Proteus turned into all forms; I tell you of a man of all hours, all companies, all religions, turned into a constant confessor and martyr for the name of Christ. They tell us, lastly, of their Jupiter and other deities turned into the shape of beasts for the advantage of their lust; I tell of men, naturally of a bestial disposition, made the sons of God, *partakers of the divine nature*, as the Apostle speaketh.

These changes are not imaginary, as in the case of lycanthropy and delusions of juggling sorcerers, but real and unfeigned: truly wrought by God, truly felt by us, truly seen by others. Not that we can always judge of these things by the mere outsides, for *even Satan himself is transformed into an angel of light*; neither do any faces look fairer than the painted. But *ex fructibus* is the rule of our Savior; that will try out the truth of all our transformations. Let us not flatter ourselves, honorable and beloved; we are all born wolves, bears, tigers, swine, one beast or other. It must needs be a notable change, if of beasts we become men; of men, saints. Thus it must be; else we are not transformed.

Neither is this transformation real only, but total; not resting in the parts, but enlarged to the whole person: and therefore the charge is . . . *Be ye transformed*; not some pieces of you, but the whole. . . . God be merciful to us! the world is full of such monsters of hypocrisy, who care only for an appearing change of some eminent and noted part, neglecting the whole: as some sorry tap-house white-limes and glazes the front towards the street, and sets out a painted sign; when there is nothing in the inward parts but sticks and clay and ruins and cold earthen floors and sluttery. This is to no purpose. If any piece of us be unchanged, we are still our old selves: odious to God, obnoxious to death.

. . .

That, whereinto we must be transformed, is the image of God (2 Cor. 3:18), consisting in holiness and righteousness (Eph. 4:24). That image we once had and lost, and now must recover by our transformation. O blessed change, that of the sons of men, we become the children of the ever-living God; of the firebrands of hell (such we are naturally), we become the heirs of heaven! That, as the eternal Son of God, having the form of God, did yet graciously change this glorious habit for the form of a servant, so we, that are the sons of men, should change the servile form of our wretched nature into the divine form of the Son of God!

. . .

There is nothing more wretched than a mere man. We may brag what we will how noble a creature man is above all the rest, how he is the lord of the world, a world within himself, the mirror of majesty, the visible model of his Maker; but, let me tell you, if we be but men, it had been a thousand times better for us to have been the worst of beasts.

Let it not seem to savor of any misanthropy to say that as all those things which are perfections in creatures are eminently in God, so all the vicious dispositions of the creature are eminently in man, in that debauched and abused reason is the quintessence of all bestiality. What speak I of these silly brutes? In this strait triangle of man's heart there is a full conclave of cardinal wickednesses, an incorporation of cheaters, a gaol of malefactors, yea a legion of devils.

Seest thou then the most loathsome toad that crawls upon the earth or the most despised dog that creeps under thy feet? thou shalt once envy their condition, if thou be not more than a man. Thou seest the worst of them; thou canst not conceive the worst of thine own. *For flesh and blood cannot inherit the kingdom of God*; and *foris canis, without shall be dogs* (Rev. 22:15). When they shall be vanished into their first nothing, thou shalt be ever dying in those unquenchable flames, which shall torment thee so much the more, as thou hadst more wit and reason without grace.

. . .

. . . True sorrow and contrition of heart must begin the work, and then an unmoved constancy of endeavor must finish it. Whosoever thou art therefore, if thy heart have not been touched, yea, torn and rent in pieces with a sound humiliation for thy sins, the old slough[1] is still upon thy back; thou art not yet come within the ken of true renovation. Or, if thou be gone so far as that the skin begins to reave up a little in a serious grief for thy sins, yet if thy resolutions be not steadily settled and thine endeavors bent to go through with that holy work, thou comest short of thy renewing; thine old loose film of corruption shall so encumber thee that thou shalt never be able to pass on smoothly in the ways of God.

But because now we have a conceit, that man, as we say of fish, unless he be new, is naught, every man is ready to challenge this honor of being renewed: and, certainly, there may be much deceit this way. We have seen plate or other vessels that have looked like

---

[1] {the outer skin periodically shed by a snake}

new when they have been but new gilded or burnished; we have seen old faces that have counterfeited a youthly smoothness and vigorous complexion; we have seen hypocrites act every part of renovation as if they had fallen from heaven. Let us therefore take a trial by those proofs of examination that cannot fail us; and they shall be fetched from those three ways of our renewing which we have formerly specified.

If we be renewed by creation, here must be a clean heart. *Cor mundum crea*, saith the Psalmist (Psalm 51:10). For as, at the first, God looked on all his works and found them very good, so still, no work of his can be other than like himself, holy and perfect. If thy heart therefore be still full of unclean thoughts, wanton desires, covetousness, ambition, profaneness, it is thine old heart of Satan's marring; it is no new heart of God's making, for nothing but clean can come from under his hands. . . .

. . .

For us, as we bear the face of Christians, and profess to have received both souls and bodies from the same hand, and look that both bodies and souls shall once meet in the same glory, let it be the top of all our care that we may *be transformed in the renewing of our minds*; and let the renewing of our minds bewray itself in the renewing of our bodies. Wherefore have we had the powerful Gospel of our Lord Jesus Christ so long amongst us if we be still ourselves? What hath it wrought upon us if we be not changed?

Never tell me of a popish transubstantiation of men: of an invisible, insensible, unfeasible change of the person, while the *species* of his outward life and carriage are still the same. These are but false, hypocritical jugglings to mock fools withal. If we be transformed and renewed, let it be so done, that not only our own eyes and hands may see and feel it, but others too: that the bystanders may say, "How is this man changed from himself! he was a blasphemous swearer, a profane scoffer at goodness; now he speaks with an awful reverence of God and holy things. He was a luxurious wanton; now he possesseth his vessel in holiness and honor. . . . He was a devil; now he is a saint."

Oh, let this day, if we have so long deferred it, be the day of the renovation, of the purification of our souls! And let us begin with a sound humiliation and true sorrow for our former and present wickednesses.

It hath been an old (I say not how true) note that hath been wont to be set on this day,[2] that, if it be clear and sun-shiny, it portends a hard weather to come; if cloudy and louring, a mild and gentle season ensuing. Let me apply this to a spiritual use, and assure every hearer that if we overcast this day with the clouds of our sorrow and the rain of our penitent tears, we shall find a sweet and hopeful season all our life after.

Oh, let us renew our covenants with God that we will now be *renewed in our minds*. The comfort and gain of this change shall be our own, while the honor of it is God's and the Gospel's: for this gracious change shall be followed with a glorious.

Onwards, this only shall give us true peace of conscience; only upon this shall the Prince of this World find nothing in us. How should he, when we are changed from ourselves? And when we shall come to the last change of all things, even when the heavens and elements shall be on a flame and shall melt about our ears, the conscience of this change shall lift up our heads with joy and shall give our renewed souls a happy entry

---

[2] {The Feast of the Purification is February 2, now also known as Groundhog Day.}

into that new heaven. Or when we shall come to our own last change in the dissolution of these earthly tabernacles, it shall bless our souls with the assurance of unchangeable happiness, and shall bid our renewed bodies lie down in peace and in a sweet expectation of *being changed to the likeness of the glorious body of our Lord Jesus Christ* and of an eternal participation of his infinite glory. Whereto, he who ordained us, graciously bring us, even for the merits of his Son, our Savior Jesus Christ the Just: to whom, with the Father and the Holy Ghost, be all praise, honor, and glory now and for ever. Amen.

TEXT: Joseph Hall, *The works of the Right Reverend Joseph Hall*, 10 vols., ed. Philip Wynter (Oxford UP, 1863), 5:300–313. The sermon seems to have been first published in Josiah Pratt's 10 volume *The works of . . . Joseph Hall* (London, 1808), where it appears in vol. 5, pp. 288–99.

JOHN EVERARD
(ca. 1584–1640/41)

Among the most important scholarly developments in recent years has been the excavation of England's pre-1640 antinomian underground, whose far-flung circles provided the seedbed for the radical religion of the Interregnum and whose conflict with mainstream Protestantism in the late 1620s served as the prequel to the better known antinomian controversies that roiled the Massachusetts Bay Colony in the late 1630s.[1] In early Stuart England, antinomianism seems often to have emerged within a godly milieu as a fierce protest against the "devotional and disciplinary grind that . . . lay at the heart of the puritan practice of piety" (Bozeman 640). However, its teachings go back to the anti-materialist spirituality of late medieval mysticism—Meister Eckhard, Tauler, and, above all, the *Theologia Germanica* (Packhull 219)—and to the spiritualist movements of the Reformation era, both Catholic and Protestant, whose unifying feature was an emphasis on the Spirit's real and immediate presence within the faithful—an inner divine light that rendered all external mediation (whether by institutions, sermons, or sacraments) peripheral, if not irrelevant.

For many leading English antinomians of the early seventeenth century, little remains besides court records; however, major works by John Eaton and John Everard attained posthumous publication after 1641. Since T. D. Bozeman has written extensively on Eaton,[2] this entry will focus on Everard, whom Nigel Smith describes as the central figure in Anglicizing and disseminating the "mystical anthropology of Medieval German spiritualism as it had been interpreted by the sixteenth-century German spiritualist and Anabaptist Movement" (136). The two sermons reprinted below come from *The Gospel*

---

[1] The principal figures in this rediscovery are T. D. Bozeman and David Como. The whole of this introduction draws extensively on their work.

[2] Along with his article listed in "Sources," see Bozeman's *The precisianist strain: disciplinary religion and antinomian backlash in puritanism to 1638* (U North Carolina P, 2004).

treasury opened, a collection of his sermons preached between 1625 and 1636, published with an introduction by his friend and disciple, Rapha Harford, in 1653.[3]

The specifics of Everard's biography are rendered somewhat conjectural by the existence of more than one person of that name born at approximately the same time and sharing outwardly similar life histories.[4] The antinomian Everard seems to have been the eldest son of a Northamptonshire minister and to have matriculated at Clare Hall, Cambridge, in the late 1590s, receiving his BA in 1601, his MA in 1607. He may have been the John Everard ordained in Peterborough in 1609, but it is also possible that he remained in Cambridge studying for his BD, which he received in 1619, his DD shortly thereafter. Sometime between 1616 and 1618 he arrived in London, where he soon became the lecturer at St. Martin's-in-the-Fields, a post allotted to puritan clergy and dependent on the free-will contributions of godly parishioners. Everard did not disappoint. From 1618 through 1623 he was regularly in trouble and repeatedly in prison for sermons denouncing the Spanish Match, only winning release when influential friends, perhaps including Francis Bacon, intervened on his behalf. Throughout this period, Everard's views seem to have differed from the godly mainstream only in their stridency. His conversion to antinomianism came shortly after 1623, when he became chaplain to Henry Rich, Earl of Holland. In 1626 he was questioned about the perfectionist import of a St. Martin's sermon in which he denied that Christians should pray for temporal blessings. Ordered to recant, he compounded the offense in a second sermon that distinguished "perfect men," who cared only about spiritual things, from the weak who still cared about material "gewgaws." Having reaffirmed rather than recanted his position, Everard soon found himself barred from St. Martin's pulpit. However, by 1628, through Holland's good offices, he had received a lectureship at the equally upscale parish church in Kensington, just west of the City. From the mid-1620s through the mid-1630s, Everard was a renowned London preacher, "drawing a very wide auditory from all sections of society" (*ODNB*).[5] During the same period, Everard and the Earls of Holland and Mulgrave formed some sort of spiritual brotherhood; it was for Holland that Everard translated the *Theologia Germanica* in the mid-1630s. In 1637 the Privy Council somehow found Everard on its radar and ordered his home searched for such papers "as may concern the State" (*ODNB*). Whatever they were hunting for, they apparently did not find it. In 1638, however, one Giles Creech approached Laud with "wild tales" about London's antinomian community; the ensuing investigation led to Everard's arrest and trial before the High Commission on doctrinal charges that included pantheism, denying the resurrection of the body, and making God

---

[3] The syntax in these sermons is often so rough that I suspect they derive from shorthand transcripts of Everard's preaching; the constructions morph in mid-sentence in a manner characteristic of oral delivery.

[4] E.g., one John Everard entered Clare Hall in 1597, another in 1603. For Everard's life, I am relying mostly on Como's *Blown by the Spirit,* but supplemented and/or corrected by the *ODNB* entry when it sounds very sure of its facts.

[5] Of the over twenty-two sermons in *The Gospel treasure,* fourteen (not counting the two synopses of "several" public sermons) were preached in public venues (presumably the parish church) in Kensington, Islington, Highgate, and London; eight were preached privately (presumably in antinomian conventicles) in Kensington and London.

the author of sin. In July of 1639 the court found him guilty, imposing a heavy sentence that included both fines and deprivation, but holding out the possibility of reprieve if Everard recanted. Eleven months later, he knelt before the court and abjured his errors. In return, Everard was restored to his ministry, but by March of 1641 death had imposed a more permanent silencing.

⤛⤜

In the words of David Como, Everard's theology "challenged almost all the assumptions of early Stuart Christian piety" (224). Like other early Stuart antinomians, Everard held that those whom Christ adorns "with his own graces . . . need no law, no light; for they are a law to themselves; and there is a light within them" <539>. He defends the authority of this indwelling "private spirit," affirming that each person must "seek for the anointing, for the Spirit promised by Christ *that may lead us into all truth*" <550>.[6] As the final clause implies, Everard affirms a vision of progressive illumination, denouncing with withering scorn the orthodox divines, who, trapped in their dwarfish dogmas, "cannot endure to grow taller nor hear of new light or a new birth or that any should know more than they" <551>. At moments, Everard's theology betrays an almost gnostic fascination with "the secrets of the Almighty" <553>, but far more often the promise held out is not knowledge but feeling: comfort, strength, joy, rapture. As this suggests, what matters to Everard is the individual's affective experience of God within. The two sermons reprinted below include only a single reference to the collective body of Christ, the Church, which for Everard is not a site or channel of divine presence; his God dwells within persons, not parishes.

These particular sermons do not exhibit the bitter animus against Calvinist practical divinity—the repudiation of godly discipline as mere works-righteousness and of Calvinism's voluntarist ethics[7] as slavish bondage to the letter—characteristic of much early Stuart antinomianism, although Everard's position is implicit in the first sermon's dismissal of the controversies tearing apart the Caroline church as children's quarrels "about trifles and things of no great worth" <552>. Instead, the sermons turn their wrath against Calvinism's literal-historical approach to Scripture.[8] For Everard, "this sticking in the letter is that which hath been the bane of all growth in religion" <552>. A literal understanding of Scripture "maketh a man not one hair's breadth the better before God," but "true understanding is that of the Spirit . . . the mind and inside of the Scriptures," whose narratives are not mere reports of long-ago events but allegories of spiritual inwardness <547>. Christ's life and death matter not because they happened but because they "shew and represent to our senses, by external actions, what he is still doing in the souls of men" <560>. Whereas the faithful traditionally sought to enter imaginatively into the sacred drama on Calvary, for Everard, it is the Passion narrative that enters the faithful; the historical events are types of inner realities, for "to believe only in an external Christ is no better than a faith of devils" <548>.

---

[6] On the controversies relating to the private spirit and its authority, see the selections from Laud <*supra*>, Chillingworth <*infra*>.

[7] A voluntarist ethics is one that defines moral goodness as obedience to God's will (revealed in Scripture) and moral evil as disobedience thereto. ("Will" in Latin is *voluntas*.)

[8] See, e.g., Calvin's exegesis of Isa. 63:1-3, quoted in the introduction to Andrewes' 1623 Easter sermon <*supra*>.

So too, Everard discards as a childish fable belief in an external, "material," heaven: a place of harping angels and pearly gates beyond the stars.[9] Heaven, he insists, is not "up there" nor hereafter, but heaven is "where God is: that is, everywhere, for . . . he is not only in every place, but in every place alike" <547>[10]—a vision of radical divine immanence that contests both the Calvinist emphasis on divine transcendence and Laudian claims for the special sacrality of the altar and its environs. Or alternatively, and this the alternative on which Everard dwells, heaven is "in our souls," and we are "in heaven" when God "manifests his presence in us and to us . . . when we see him there in the beauty of holiness" <557>.

This relocation of rapture from *Jenseits* to *Diesseits*, from the life to come to this present world, marks all strains of early Stuart antinomianism. Everard, however, drawing on the *Theologia Germanica*'s picture of selfhood as separation from God,[11] reconceives the *visio Dei* as something close to deification attained via ego-death—a becoming nothing in order to become God. As Everard explains in the haunting allegory that concludes the second sermon, as a drop of water that falls into the ocean ceases to exist qua drop because it is now part of the ocean, so too "if we can be content to die & forsake our selves . . . we shall return into him who is Almighty, we shall be dissolved into him who is infinitely vaster than ten thousand seas or oceans" <564>.

In contemporary nomenclature, antinomianism, together with all forms of spiritualist or illuminationist Christianity, falls within the category of radical religion, where "radical" has sociopolitical as well as theological import. It is not hard to see the radical import of Everard's antinomianism. Its anti-legalism and anti-literalism drain sacraments, ceremonies, and Sabbaths, together with ecclesiastical disciplines and reformations of manners, of their divine authority and salvific value. It opens the door to private spirits and the privatization of religion. Yet the sermons reprinted below do not fit a worm-in-the-cheese model of early modern radicalism; they are the opposite of materialist, and their author, like most English antinomians before 1641, was neither a miller nor a box-maker but a university divine.

Moreover, if being thrown in prison for one's views is a mark of radicalism, then Everard's "radical" period predates his antinomian conversion. He was, as noted above, locked up a half-dozen times between 1618 and 1623; thereafter, although once or twice called on the carpet, he remained a free man and a London preacher of considerable renown until 1638. Nor was his patron, the Earl of Holland, an aristocratic revolutionary;

---

[9] For the conventional Calvinist view, see Debora Shuger, "The Laudian idiot," in *The world proposed: Thomas Browne quatercentenary essays*, ed. Reid Barbour and Claire Preston (Oxford UP, 2008), 52.

[10] Everard elsewhere asserts that if God exists wholly everywhere, then he exists in toads, flies, and "the damnedest devil in hell, no less than in angels" (Como 254)—a position which, if not quite Spinozan pantheism, remains deeply foreign to Christian tradition, which prefers to keep good and evil distinct. As Como notes, the High Commission was perfectly justified in suspecting that Everard's view of radical divine immanence made God the author of sin (257).

[11] According to the *Theologia Germanica*, "The self, the I, the me and the like all belong to the evil spirit. . . . The I, the me, and the mine, nature, selfhood, the Devil, sin, are all one and the same thing" (Jones xxvi).

he did side with Parliament in 1641, but crossed to the royalists in the second Civil War and was executed by the army in same year as the King.

Our sense of antinomianism as radical religion confronts a further challenge, one that takes us back to Cambridge's Clare Hall, Everard's alma mater. During the same period when Everard was preaching the sermons reprinted below, another Clare graduate translated one of the classic texts of sixteenth-century antinomian spirituality, Juan de Valdés or Valdesso's *The hundred and ten considerations* (*Ciento i Diez Consideraciones*), a work treasured by Familists and later by Quakers. The translator, however, was neither. He was, rather, the saintly Anglican founder of Little Gidding, Nicholas Ferrar,[12] and his translation, although blocked by Cambridge censors, came out in 1638 at Oxford, where Laud was chancellor, with notes by George Herbert and an imprimatur from the Arminian high churchman Thomas Jackson. It is possible that Everard and Ferrar overlapped at Cambridge, but the Clare Hall connection may be significant regardless, since the college apparently had an antinomian mystic in residence during the late Elizabethan period, whose memory, and library, an undergraduate arriving in 1597, or even 1610, would have encountered (Como 227n). Indeed, Ferrar may well have first read Valdès at Clare, since his tutor, Augustine Lindsell (the future Laudian bishop of Peterborough), owned a 1563 French translation; Lindsell must have known that Ferrar prized Valdès' work since he left the volume to his former student in his will.

None of the above *were* antinomians. Herbert, Ferrar, and Jackson all acknowledge that Valdès' book has things at which a weak reader may stumble and even a "wise and charitable reader may justly blame" (Valdès *2r). Yet, Herbert, although objecting to a handful of the work's 110 "considerations," calls Valdès "a true servant of God," praising his "observation of God's kingdom within us, and the working thereof" (Valdès ****4r, A1v). This praise strikes one recent scholar as "fairly surprising in view of Valdesso's radical doctrine of inspiration" (Clarke 359), while another expresses equally justified surprise that Valdès' spiritualist mysticism "attracted not only Ferrar but also several of his friends, most of whom were numbered among the Laudians in the Caroline church" (Ransome 6).[13]

What attracted Ferrar was, in his own words, Valdès' "many very worthy discourses of experimental and practical divinity" (Valdès *2r). "Experimental" is a term usually associated with godly self-scrutiny for assurance of election—the "experimental predestinarianism" of R. Kendall's *Calvin and English Calvinism*. However Ferrar also uses the word not only to characterize Valdès but also in an uncharacteristically personal passage on the transcendent joy possible in this life, describing the "wealth, glory, & delight" that fill "the banks of the soul & spirit brim-full" with "spiritual raptures" that can only be "apprehended" by "experiment" (Blackstone 105). Ferrar is not an antinomian, but his experimental divinity has more in common with Everard's "heaven . . . in our souls" <557> than the anguished penitential inwardness in Sparke's *Crumbs of comfort <supra>*.[14]

---

[12] See the introduction to *The Little Gidding story books <infra>*.

[13] Her observation is consistent with Christopher Marsh's finding that that high-church divines seem, particularly in comparison to their godly counterparts, remarkably untroubled by Familism, even though not particularly attracted to it. See Marsh's *The Family of Love in English society, 1550–1630* (Cambridge UP, 1993), 36, 282–83.

[14] See also the *Collegiate suffrage* Va.4 <supra>.

Antinomianism clearly was often radical, and often perceived as such by both Calvinists and Laudians. The foregoing has, however, tried to inject a note of confusion, or at least complexity, to which a final example of theological border-crossing may contribute. The year 1573 saw the first English printing of the *Beneficio di Christo*, the most influential work of sixteenth-century Italian spiritualism, a work theologically akin to Valdès' *Considerations* and partly written by one of his followers (MacCulloch 255; Ransome 18).[15] The translator of this antinomian classic was William Golding, whose other translations include a long list of Calvin's works (and key treatises by the anti-Calvinist Niels Hemmingsen), as well as Ovid's *Metamorphosis*—the one piece for which Golding is remembered.

Sources: *ODNB*; Roland Bainton, review of Domingo Ricart, *Juan de Valdès y el pensamiento religioso europeo en los siglos xvi & xvii*, in *Renaissance News* 13.2 (1960): 153–54; B. Blackstone, ed. *The Ferrar papers* (Cambridge UP, 1938); T. D. Bozeman, "The glory of the 'Third Time': John Eaton as contra-puritan," *Journal of Ecclesiastical History* 47.4 (1996): 638–54; Elizabeth Clarke, "Silent, performative words: the language of God in Valdesso and George Herbert," *Journal of Literature & Theology* 5.4 (1991): 355–74; Como, *Blown by the Spirit*; R. M. Jones, *Spiritual reformers in the 16th and 17th centuries* (Beacon Press, 1914); Diarmaid MacCulloch, *The Reformation: a history* (Penguin, 2004); Julia Merritt, *The social world of early modern Westminster* (Manchester UP, 2005); Werner Packull, "An introduction to Anabaptist theology," in *The Cambridge companion to Reformation theology*, ed. David Bagchi and David Steinmetz (Cambridge UP, 2004), 194–219; Joyce Ransome, "George Herbert, Nicholas Ferrar, and the 'pious works' of Little Gidding," *George Herbert Journal* 31 (2007): 1–19; Nigel Smith, *Perfection proclaimed* (Oxford UP, 1989); Juan de Valdès, *The hundred and ten considerations of Segnior John Valdesso*, trans. Nicholas Ferrar, with notes by George Herbert (Oxford UP, 1638).

[15] The volume went through two further printings over the next decade; a fourth came out in 1633, printed by a cousin of Ferrar, followed by a fifth printing in 1638, the same year as Ferrar's translation of Valdès.

JOHN EVERARD

The Gospel treasury opened
ca. 1625–36, published 1653

Christian Reader,

As there were many causes of delay in publishing these sermons, so there are also in bringing them to light now: the time when they were preached was in the days of the last bishops, who endeavored the strangling of many truths in the birth, as Pharaoh the children of Israel, lest they should increase and multiply to discover and suppress their deeds of darkness; to that end high-commissioning many precious and bright-shining lights, whereof this author was in the number . . . as if they were guilty of foul doctrine or foul life or both; and though they could prove nothing against them, yet keeping them in their courts, if possible, to awe and vex them, if they could not suppress them.

The author hereof being spotless in either, especially since God in a special and extraordinary manner appeared to him, in him, in his latter days; for he confessed, with the Apostle Paul (Eph. 4:17, 18), that in the days of his former ignorance and vanity, he walked *as other gentiles*, and as men *living without God in the world, in the vanity of his mind, having his understanding darkened, being alienated from the life of God, because of the blindness of his heart*; which no doubt our merciful and ready-pardoning God had forgiven, though men could not or would not forget, which he regarded not much, God speaking peace and pardon to his soul.

But afterward he desired nothing more than to bring in others to see what he saw and to enjoy what he enjoyed, and to clear truth to them in either respect; he oftentimes averring—as to others, so to the publisher hereof—that his trouble was not for self-sufferings, but that truth should be any way obstructed or defamed through him.

. . .

. . . For as truth is strongest, so God had wonderfully come into him and declared himself by him, in his late years, and made him (as it were) a Sampson against the numerous Philistines and a David against the huge and mighty Goliaths of those times. . . . yet as he was a man of presence and princely behavior and deportment, and fit to accompany such, so he was also familiar even with the meanest, and if willing to be taught, he was as willing to instruct and teach them; and they were (upon this account) more welcome to him than lords or princes, imitating the humble carriage of his Lord and Master; he not thinking it any disparagement to accompany with the worst and lowest of men, so he might do them good; for (he knew) he was not sent to call the righteous but the sinners, nor to heal the whole but the sick; not the justiciaries[1] and those who, though they may be large in confession of sin, yet really see but little in themselves, and less to repent of.

Insomuch, that those who were about him, either in sickness or health, would often say they gat more good instruction from him in discourse than by many sermons of other men's, he being still forward, if they were backward, to take occasions to communicate some divine truths, so that he won their attention to hearken to him, as Christ did Mary's, who *chose that better part* [Luke 10:42] *which should never be taken from her.* . . . He was also a man of a choice, courageous, and discerning spirit, endowed with skill and depth of learning, judgment, and experience to manage what God had (though but of late) revealed to him (as he often would say), affirming he was now ashamed of his former knowledge, expressions, and preachings, even since he commenced Dr. in Divinity; although he was known to be a very great scholar and as good a philosopher, few or none exceeding him; yet when he came to know himself and his own heart, and also to know Jesus Christ & the Scriptures more than grammatically, literally, or academically, viz. experimentally, he then counted all those things (even all his acquired parts and human abilities) *loss and dung, for the excellency of the knowledge of Jesus Christ and him crucified* [Phil. 3:8] not only externally but particularly, buried and risen again in himself; and for that blessed sight, to see how the Scriptures were daily fulfilling in himself and others—they concerning as much all times, all men, and all ages, as those of whom they were the history—wherein lies (as in these sermons he sheweth) the chief excellency, fatness, and marrow of the Scriptures, and without which the word is of so little use to us that to us it is not the word of God, which the Apostle saith (Heb. 4) *is quick and powerful, and mighty in operation, sharper than a two-edged sword, and piercing between even the joints and marrow*, as he also largely in several parts of this book sheweth. And this was the alone knowledge whereby he was crucified *to the world and to himself* [Gal. 6:14].

And thereby his depth in learning and philosophy being sanctified, they so much the more confirmed and centered his spirit; they brought him to his heaven, home, and rest, even into that ever blessed union and communion with God, which before was but skin-deep learning and philosophy (as he termed it). And the courageousness of his spirit was such, when he was but a bare, literal, University preacher (as he afterward still called himself), that he was the only man that opposed, preached against, and held it out to the utmost against the late King's matching with the Infanta of Spain. When others durst but whisper their consciences and thoughts, he chose texts on purpose to shew the unlawfulness and the great sin of matching with idolaters, being often committed to prison for it when he was preacher at Martin's-in-the-Fields; and then by the next Sabbath day one Lord or other would beg his liberty of the King, and presently, no sooner out, but he would go on and manage the same thing more fully, notwithstanding all the power of the bishops; being committed again and again; being, as I heard him say, six or seven times

---

[1] {One who administers justice, but also a term used by Protestants from the Reformation through the early 18th century for those who boast of their own righteousness and think to be saved by it.}

in prison; insomuch, they coming so oft to King James about him, he began to take more notice of him, asking, *What is this Dr. Ever-out? His name* (saith he) *shall be Dr. Never-out.*

Then began the bishops for this to be his deadly adversaries, fetching him up into their High Commission, and never left prosecuting him until they had took from him his benefice, being four hundred pounds a year. And at his second convening thither, spoken of before, Canterbury threatened him, *he would bring him to a morsel of bread*, and all because he could not have his will of him, to make him stoop and bow to him. And where is the man that hath adventured (for all their forward and great professions) so far as he hath done in discharge of duty and conscience, because he thought he was bound thereto by command from God! And yet for all this (as he said of himself), this he did by a mere power of self, from natural abilities, and from the power of the old man suggesting and working in him, and carrying it out with much boldness, magnanimity, and true zeal (as to man's judgment). Oh, what great things may men do this way, externally, and have no principle of grace or true fear of God! yea not only to the loss of means and liberty, but to the loss of their heads and lives, and merely out of vainglory or some such self-interest, and herein truly is little or no difference at all between them and *sufferers as evil-doers* [1 Pet. 4:15].

. . .

And yet in all this we have said commendatory of the author, Christian friends, do not think that we have gone about to praise or lift up man, or that we would have you fasten your eyes on any creature whatever. No, no, God forbid; far, far be any such thing from our thoughts. For *what is man? or wherein is he to be accounted of?* [Isa. 2:22]. Neither was it the author's practice at all to lift up man, neither do we here present him as a perfect man; but with Elijah, as the Apostle saith of him (James 5:17), *He was a man subject to like passions as we are*, and with Lot, Abraham, David, Paul, and Peter, he had his infirmities; but he could say also with Paul, *in me, that is in my flesh, dwelleth no good thing; but I delight in the Law of God after the inward man; now if I do that I would not, it is no more I that do it, but sin that dwelleth in me* [Rom. 7:18]; neither did he ascribe any good, either graces or gifts, to himself, but all to God; he would not set that crown upon his own head or upon the head of any creature, but with Paul confessed (Gal. 2:20), *I am crucified with Christ; nevertheless I live; yet not I, but Christ liveth in me.* And when God had rapt[2] up his spirit in preaching even, as it were, to behold himself in the third heaven, yet he had that prick in the flesh, which would cause him often to say, even in public: Beloved, if at any time you find any good by me, or see any truth more than you did before, or find your souls raised from death to life, or the cripple from his mother's womb healed and cured within you; or if you see any grace, any gift in me, as Peter to the Jews, *Ye men of Israel, why look ye on us so earnestly, as though by our own power or holiness we had made this man walk* [Acts 3:12]; if you see in me any good, know that is none of mine; I dare not claim it; neither can any creature claim it. But if you see in me or yourselves any sin, any evil, that is most properly mine and yours; and *yet it is not I that do it, but sin that dwelleth in me* [Rom. 7:20], but all good is God's; whatever it be that comes under the notion of Good, under what name soever, it is God's, and his only. So that we have only hereby labored to set and fix your eye on him from whom all excellencies flow, to see and behold

---

[2] {The 1657 edition reads "wrapt."}

the excellencies and virtues (not of man) but *of him who calleth from darkness to light* [Acts 26:18], *from the power of Satan to God*; and that you should wonder and be amazed that the Almighty should stoop so low as to work in men, and to communicate of his own nature, and put forth his mighty workings in and through such poor nothings as men are. And in this respect let no man fear to speak to the utmost freely and fully of the virtues, excellencies, and workings of the Lord in the hearts of his people; for in them he displays his glories; they are his Sanctuary, his Temple; in them he rests, as in his holy hill, where *every one speaks of his glory*; and although these motions and mighty miracles be wrought in man, yet they are not of man, or by man. Therefore let men . . . but keep to this rule, and fix their eye on him to whom all glory and praise is due, and then let them set forth freely and fully whatever virtues or whatever is praise-worthy in any of the sons of men, thus far made the sons of God; then they need never fear to be charged with flattery or hope of rewards from men. . . .

. . .

So we commit thee and them to him who is not tied to man's teachings, but is able to teach without him (and it is only he that teacheth by him), according to his most gracious promise in the new covenant, *I will be their God, and they shall be my sons and daughters* [Jer. 31: 33-34], *and they shall not teach every man his brother, saying, Know the Lord; for they shall all know me, from the least to the greatest.*

Farewell.
Yours, desiring if by any means he might serve you in the Gospel,
and help you on to perfection.
R. H.

‡

Of Milk for Babes; and of Meat for Strong Men

And the child grew, and waxed strong in spirit, filled with wisdom,
and the grace of God was upon him.
Luke 2:40

Preached at Kensington public meeting-place

As it is said of John (Luk. 2 *ult*), *That the child grew & waxed strong in spirit, & was in the deserts till the day of his shewing unto Israel*, so likewise here the same is said of Jesus Christ; yet with this exception and difference: John hath an ἀκμὴ, or set time, after which he decreaseth and grows less (John 3:30), *He must increase, but I must decrease.* And so it is with believers: they must grow less and less, and come to nothing, that so Jesus Christ may become *all in all*, according to that in Dan. 2:34-35, *that stone cut out of the mountain without hands, which smote the image and break it to pieces, and it became a great mountain and filled the whole earth.* This stone is Jesus Christ, which breaks to pieces all things; that is, that all worships and religions, and whatever is mixt with iron and clay, and whatever is of man, may decrease, that himself may increase and grow great and fill the whole earth with the knowledge and manifestation of himself, he being *all in all*.

But I must forbear, for I prevent[3] myself.

The text contains:

    1. A History.

    2. A Mystery.

And this, as I was speaking before, comes under the second part: *viz.* the mystery.

For the history, that is brief and shews only the truth of his human nature, which though hypostatically united to the divinity even from the instance of his conception, as it followeth in the text, *that he was filled with wisdom, and the grace of God was upon him . . . that he increased in wisdom and stature and in favor with God and man*; which cannot be meant in regard of his divine nature, as if there could be any access or increase of or to that which is infinite, but only in the expression and manifestation thereof, in those organs which the God of order had therefore ordained and co-apted.

So that if any shall ask, how that which is full and perfect can be said to increase?

I answer as before: not in augmentation but in manifestation. God cannot grow greater or lesser, be more or less excellent or glorious; but his greatness, power, and glory is further manifested, more spread and made known, according to that promise, Numb. 14:21 and Isa. 6:3: *All the earth shall be filled with the glory of the Lord.* Our great and infinite God filleth the whole earth and the heavens, yea, and the heavens of heavens, with his majesty and glory, at all times and in every place alike; but then he is said to fill the earth or heavens with his glory and greatness when he is manifested more to men or angels, and when he enlargeth the knowledge of himself and of his power and greatness.

. . . Know this, that the fountain of all good is always with us, nigh at hand, if we could but see him; and we need never fear, nor never despond and doubt so as we do: For as Moses saith concerning the command (Deut. 30:14), *It is not hidden from thee, neither is it far off thee: not in heaven, nor beyond the sea, but nigh unto thee, in thy mouth and in thy heart*; so the Apostle (Rom. 10:6-7), he applies that Scripture to Jesus Christ, who is (Col. 1:16) *the first begotten of all creatures, by whom all things consist, and in whom they live, move, and have their being.*

But the second part is the mystery of the text.

That which is more *material* is the *mystery.* Though all Scripture be written for *instruction*, yet know, the Scripture is a mystery, of μύεω, which, as Eustathius saith, comes from μὺω, *claudo*, because it is kept secret, sacred, and shut up; because in all mysteries tis necessary to keep close the mind and not to shew the things which are to be concealed, as one saith. For as St. Paul saith concerning circumcision (Rom. 2:28-29), *He is not a Jew which is one outwardly; neither is that circumcision which is that of the flesh; but he is a Jew which is one inwardly; and circumcision is that of the heart, in the spirit and not in the letter, whose praise is not of men but of God*; so say I of saving knowledge. He that sees the mystery of the Scripture, he hath the true knowledge of the Scripture. He is not taught of God that knows only the letter and the flesh of the Scripture; but true understanding is that of the Spirit and not of the letter; and though men may cry up and praise literal knowledge, yet God only esteems of inward knowledge, & the mind and inside of the Scriptures. All other knowledge is vain and maketh a man not one hair's breadth the better before God.

---

[3] {anticipate}

. . .

But you will say to me, *How doth the letter kill?*

I answer, by resting therein and not seeking for the marrow, the food, and the life, but contenting ourselves with the knowledge of the history and outside. But because I have at other times unfolded this unto you, I shall here pass it by, and come to the spirit and mystery of our text in hand.

So then, it resteth . . . that we may safely conclude even thus much: that as our Savior was typified by others who went before him (he was the substance of all those shadows, both of persons and things), even so Christ Jesus himself, he is the resemblance and type of himself: his outward, temporal, and visible actions in the flesh were a type of his inward and internal actions in the souls of all believers, he being their life and resurrection; they being before but dead men in trespasses and sins, until his actions be their life and regeneration. So likewise, as his life was typical and resembled himself, so in regard of his death and crucifying: whatever he suffered externally in the flesh, it shews how he is internally crucified daily, even to the end of the world (Heb. 6:6): *Seeing they crucify to themselves the Son of God afresh, and put him to an open shame.* So likewise for all his other actions and passages related of him: as his nativity, it held out our spiritual birth, and Christ his being born in the soul; as the Apostle expresseth it (Gal. 4:19), *My beloved of whom I travail in birth, till Christ be formed, or brought forth in you.* So also in his circumcision is held forth our spiritual circumcision, as in that of Col. 2:11: *Ye are complete in him, in whom also ye are circumcised with the circumcision made without hands, in putting off the body of the sins of the flesh, by the circumcision of Christ, &c.* So also for holiness of life: Christ's holiness shew us what holiness shall be in them that are his children and people (Mat. 5:16), *Let your light so shine before men, that they may see your good works and glorify your Father which is in heaven.*

So also for his outward teaching, it represents to us that all his people should be *taught of God* . . . And Christ himself cites these places, John 6:45, *It is written in the prophets, And they shall all be taught of God; every man therefore that hath heard and learned of the Father cometh unto me. . . .*

. . . So also of his Resurrection: *If ye be risen with Christ, seek those things which are above* (Col. 3:2). And so of his Ascension, and all other his actions and miracles, to see all these things held forth and typified in the person, actions, and miracles of our Savior.

These are all saving actions, wrought in us, and we thereby partake of the excellency and virtue thereof; the other, though wrought for us, yet if we are not quickened, vivified, and put into act by these, we receive no benefit by them. An outward dead faith, to believe only in an external Christ, is no better than a faith of devils.[4] . . .

Now then as all the other actions and passions of Christ were not only meritorious in themselves but also typical and significant, so is this growth of Jesus Christ. He grows up in us in *wisdom and stature*, and he in us *waxeth strong in spirit, being filled with wisdom and understanding.* He teacheth us the true wisdom; he in us chooseth *that good thing which shall never be taken away*; he is the grace of God in us: *I live*, saith the Apostle, *yet not I, but it is Christ his life in me* [Gal. 2:20]. From him cometh all growth in grace, not from ourselves; the work is his, none of ours. From him cometh faith, hope, charity,

---

[4] {See, contra, Laud <379>, Dow <860>.}

strength, virtue, &c. If any of these come from man, from the power, industry, or strength of man, they are false and good for nought. Yet how ready are most men to assume these to themselves? or at least to think that by their power or wisdom or industry they have attained them?. . . .

When Jesus Christ doth once begin to display and declare the glory of himself in the soul and to adorn the soul with himself, what a palace, what a kingdom, what a temple is that soul? Well might David say, *Glorious things are spoken of thee, O thou city and temple of God* (Psal. 82:3), more glorious than the Temple spoken of {in} Rev. 21; and saith our Savior, *The kingdom of heaven is within you.* All that description there at large setteth out the glory and light of that Temple, which was like jasper most precious, and clear as crystal, and the wall high and stately, wherein were twelve gates, & the gates kept by twelve angels, and the walls of jasper, and the city pure gold, and the very foundation garnished with precious stones: a jasper, a sapphire, a chalcedony, an emerald, a sardonyx, a sardius, a chrysolite, a beryl, a topaz, a chrysophrasus, a jacinth, an amethyst.

I say all these things are accomplished in a great measure—in some less, in some more—in all those where Jesus Christ is pleased to display his glories, and in that soul where he is pleased to adorn it with his own graces and with the fruits of the Spirit, as faith, hope, charity, strength, virtue, love, joy, peace, long-suffering, gentleness, goodness, meekness, temperance, &c. Those that are thus qualified, enriched, and adorned, let me tell you, they need no law, no light; for they are a law to themselves; and there is a light within them, like that city (Rev. 21:23) that had *no need of the sun, neither of the moon to shine in it, for the glory of God did lighten it, and the Lamb is the light thereof.* Nay, I may say, and say truly (as I may say), they are gotten above Law, above Letter, in this regard: for they have the Gospel and the life within them.[5] Yet for all this, do not think that I speak against law or letter or ordinances. Use them (as I say), but *rest not in them.* And know this also, that while the soul is rapt up in the glory, sight, and beholding of Jesus Christ, he knows this, that he enjoys that which is the substance and that which is as far above the other as the substance is above the shadow, and the life above the letter, and the spirit above the flesh. Yet he will not slight nor cast away these means or ordinances, because God hath often appeared in them and by them to him, as I have shewed more at large upon other Scriptures.

But I say, let us look to find that in us which Christ affirms: that *the kingdom of God is within us.* . . .

. . .

Beloved, I hope and I know there are some that hear me which know and see and feel these things to be true, yea (as you say), as true as Gospel; yea, so true as nothing is nor can be more true. And some others I know there be, which will believe none of all these things, but they will dwell in the letter, and think all the things spoken thereof are some visible and ocular glories; as the disciples, while they were weak and but babes, they pleased themselves with apprehensions of their master his being a temporal king, and that he should sit upon his throne & they all should sit about him; and Zebedee's children, nothing would serve them but *that the one might sit at his right hand and the other at his left.* And such childish apprehensions have many, yea most men; they please their fancies,

---

[5] {contrast Bayly <131>}

hopes, and imaginations with these things: viz. that the glory of heaven shall be only hereafter; and that glory to consist in thrones and crowns and scepters, in music, harps, and viols, and such like carnal and poor things compared to that glory; and though they talk and prattle that *grace is glory begun* and *glory is grace perfected*, yet how far wide are they in this practice? and how harsh and uncouth is this doctrine to such men? but it is the rejoicing of my soul that I speak to some that have seen and felt far, far more than my tongue is able to express; for these things are known not so much by man's teaching as by feeling and enjoying them, and by the teachings of God.

But indeed and in truth, there is so much literalness, even among great professors and most teachers, that they are always but at the very beginning of the principles of the doctrine of Christ [Heb. 6:1-2]. And if those that profess and think themselves able teachers do stick here and go no further, how can they be a means to bring others on toward perfection? I tell you, beloved, this dwelling in the letter is that which hath been the occasion of so many errors, rents, and differences as hath been in the Church. The truth is known by none but by those that can come to the truth: *In thy light we shall see light.* You that are of the truth, you have received *the anointing*, and that *anointing teacheth you all things* [1 Joh. 2:27]. Not as if any individual man knoweth all things, but ye, ye the Church, ye the Body, ye know all things, as I have shewed you at large upon that text. Take the complete Body of Christ, both past, present, and to come, & add to them the Head, & then we may not only say, *Thou art all fair my Love, there is no spot in thee* [Cant. 4:7], but thou art altogether amiable, and ye know all things.

Beloved, one runs away with one interpretation, and another with another; as the Apostle saith, *Every one of you hath a doctrine, a psalm, an interpretation, a tongue, a revelation*; but let us mind this *anointing*, what that teacheth us; let us labor to see that we must be *all taught of God*, that we may come to have the mystery and the living sense; and this will instruct, guide, lead, and conduct us aright and safely, that we shall not only see these hidden things, but we shall know, yea know undoubtedly, that they are *the Truth, the Life, & the Way*, as Christ saith of himself. Did men but see things, and were led by the Spirit and by the Truth, they would not run away with such poor, weak, carnal and empty notions and interpretations as they do. . . .

Not that I would have men neglect preaching the letter, or whatever can be found out externally to be fulfilled; but let us not rest there, but seek for the anointing, for the Spirit promised by Christ *that may lead us into all truth.* . . .

He that is taught these things hath the mysteries of the kingdom of God; he hath even this Scripture fulfilled in him: *And the child grew and waxed strong in spirit, filled with wisdom, and the grace of God was upon him.* Here you may see the reason, and what Christ meant when he said (Mat. 19:14), *Suffer little children to come unto me, and forbid them not, for of such is the kingdom of God.* And yet Lev. 21:20, there tis forbid that any dwarf of the tribe of Levi should approach to offer sacrifice to God. How shall we reconcile God's commandment and Christ his practice? Truly thus: I suppose Christ in that saying holds forth by little children such as are in an humble, meek, lowly, and in a growing condition, and coming on to perfection; for, saith he, *He that receiveth not the kingdom of God as a little child, he shall not enter therein.* But for dwarfs, whose growth is stinted, they are at their highest and will never grow taller; I mean such who profess themselves tall Christians, but are not so much as little children; nor cannot endure to grow taller nor hear of new light or a new birth or that any should know more than they; this is hateful to them, for they think they have been brought up with the Scriptures, they have been at the university, sat at the feet of Gamaliel, exercised in the Holy Scriptures from a child, studied all points in divinity . . . and shall we tell these men of new light? they cry *new lights are old errors.* Do you think that these men are true disciples? or fit to be Christ's disciples, by him to be led into all truth? Is this voice the voice of the Spouse? which continually looking upon her own ignorances and infirmities, cryeth, *Oh thou whom my soul loveth, tell me, teach me, where thou feedest, & where thou restest at noon?* [Cant. 1:7]. But you know what the Holy Ghost saith, *He that is wise in his own conceit, there is more hope of a fool than of that man* [Pro. 26:12].

. . . Those fat and full things of God's house, though they talk of them, yet they never reach them. And those that do speak of them, give them an offence and get their hatred and hard sentence: *he must be a Familist or a Sectary or an Antinomian or some such like.* And to say the truth in few words, they censure others and applaud themselves; and though they have been long teachers, yet they themselves had need be taught the very lowest things in Christianity; and children they find their auditors, and children they leave them.

. . . And again, when Paul saw that they began to rest upon baptism, he slighted it and undervalues it. When men begin to make the shadow the substance, or the image the Truth, he undervalues them; although being rightly used, he practiced and used them himself—so they be but used as means and schoolmasters and tutors to bring us to Christ. But if they, instead of bringing us to him, keep and bar us from him, away with them. If we begin to admire them and cry up them, and make our duties—and the sacraments themselves, though appointed by Christ himself—to be our saviors, we are to slight them and disesteem them in that regard, as Paul did the holy law itself in that Epistle to the Galatians and elsewhere. For all these ordinances are for no other use but that they may be as steps to him & as guides to him who is the truth and the substance. Nay Paul went so high that he not only undervalued the law or ordinances or duties if they hindered from Christ, but he attempted to draw aside and undervalued and slighted the very person and body of Jesus Christ in that case. If men rest in any outward privilege or enjoyment, they keep us from Christ.

Beloved, be not offended. See what himself saith (2 Cor. 5:16) when some slighted him, who it may be knew or heard Christ personally, and began to prefer the shadow before the substance: he undervaluing all *but a new creature,* he bursts out in an holy defiance of all things else besides it; let it be Moses, or Christ Jesus himself in regard of his body and external presence or knowledge: *Henceforth know we no man after the flesh.* One would think he had spoke there generally and inclusively enough, but he boldly adds, *Yea, although we have known Christ after the flesh, yet henceforth know we him no more,* as if he should say, tell not me of outward privileges or ordinances; I seek a proof of Christ in you; shew me the *new birth,* the new CREATURE. Is Christ formed in you? This is that only *that I travail in birth for,* and for nothing else.

And so likewise to instance in baptism, which some think is come in the room of circumcision. Well let it be so, we will not contend about that, Christ removing that burthensome and legal ordinance; but for Christ the substance we ought and must contend for to the utmost. Yet some there are that would have baptism administered after such manner that it is as burthensome, yea more burthensome to some, than circumcision. You know what I mean: as to instance, the unseasonableness of weather sometimes, & the weakness and sickness of some bodies; besides, that of circumcision was only for the males & not for females, as the ordinance of baptism is, with many other reasons too long to stand upon; therefore more burthensome than circumcision; they speak of plunging over head and ears as if it were an absolute injunction; because the Apostle saith (Rom. 6:4) *buried with him in baptism*, therefore they must be plunged.

Truly, there is a great deal of stir more than need, for baptism is but a type and shadow of the true baptism; and I conceive (and to me it's clear) that the Apostle there sets the shadow against the substance, one to set out the other: for Christ's baptism was his humbling himself and emptying himself and submitting to his Father's will in his whole passions and sufferings, which is the thing baptism holds forth. . . .

. . .

Truly, my friends, this sticking in the letter is that which hath been the bane of all growth in religion and an occasion of so many disputes and differences therein; which I do not wonder at, for children can do no other than quarrel about trifles and things of no great worth. Not that the soul should slight or undervalue ordinances, or any other duty. Beloved, I am fain to use this caution the oftener, because ye are so subject to catch and carp. I say, let all those things have their due time, place, and esteem; but to rest in these is the worm, the gourd. But this I say, when the soul by these ordinances . . . shall come to see and enjoy God, her portion; when she is in the pursuit of her beloved, she undervalues and leaves all things of this nature behind, and *presseth after the mark, the price of the high calling of God in Jesus Christ.* And to this soul in this condition I may boldly say, what's duties? what's ordinances? what's Christ in the flesh? I beseech you give me leave: what are all these, when the soul embraces the truth of all these things? Can that soul at that time leave its Beloved's arms, and prize the shadows, the handmaids, above or equal to him?[6] But I grant that those that never came to these embraces, these swallowings up, these overcomings, this spiritual drunkenness, may censure and revile a soul that may say indeed and in truth, he is above these. What do you think Paul thought of these things, when he was *caught up into the third heaven?* [2 Cor. 12:4]. I grant also, beloved, that the most elevated, triumphing, and most raised soul lives not always in this condition. These things and these raptures and these embraces come but seldom; and the soul comes to fall lower and have more use of ordinances; but she uses them as handmaids so as to conduct her to her Beloved.

Beloved, I would have you ponder these things well. If ye set up ordinances, &c. so as to build and rest in them, ye do make idols of them; or at the best, you play the babes and the children with them, by resting always on such crutches and go-bies, and never come to be young men, much less as fathers in Christ. Paul and Peter, James and John, they

---

[6] {See the penultimate paragraph of Sir Thomas Browne's *Urn burial*: "Pious spirits who passed their dayes in raptures of futurity, made little more of this world, then the world that was before it, while they lay obscure in the Chaos of pre-ordination, and night of their fore-beings. And if any have been so happy as truly to understand Christian annihilation, extasis, exolution, liquefaction, transformation, the kisse of the Spouse, gustation of God, and ingression into the divine shadow, they have already had an handsome anticipation of heaven; the glory of the world is surely over, and the earth in ashes unto them," http://penelope .uchicago.edu/hydrionoframes/hydrio5.html (accessed June 7, 2012).}

would have always enjoyed those raptures: Paul in the third heaven and the others in the Transfiguration. But the one had a *prick in the flesh* and the others came *down again from the Moun*t; and in these declinations and lower enjoyments, I would not for a world forbid men to use means, not only in regard of themselves but of others who may (by those) come to have the same enjoyments, making them no more but means, and not the end.

And so much more I will say to satisfy you: that I have great cause to mistrust those spirits, whether they come the right way to God or into such raptures, that leap into them on a sudden without use of means or ordinances, but out of a blind and profane condition come suddenly into these enjoyments; for God doth usually make use of these means. Yet I may not limit nor direct nor circumscribe the sovereign Almighty; yet usually *faith cometh by hearing, and hearing by the word preached*. But herein lies the general abuse of these truths and of these enjoyments: that because some may and do come thus to enjoy God—and forsake ordinances at a season, at the very time of such enjoyments—therefore some, having gotten this in notion, have presumptuously affirmed that they are above these, and so far abuse themselves and shew an ill example to others that they have quite *forsaken the assemblies* and the use of any ordinances [2 Cor. 8].

Beloved, all these things are an offence, and hereby many a soul by this delusion of Satan drowns itself in perdition. . . .

. . .

And as it is in things of this nature, so it is in the general estate of all Christians. First they are servants and under the yoke before they come to be sons; but when once the true heir comes to age, then cast out the bond-woman and her son, as the Apostle alledgeth that of Abraham for this very purpose: not that they do cast away obedience according to the Law, but that they do it upon another account, even from love. Then tis no longer a yoke, but according to that promise (Jer 31:33), I will write my law in their heart; and so they obey out of love and not for fear. . . .

. . . And Christ himself saith (John 8:35), *The servant abideth not in the house forever, but the son abideth forever*. But what is it to be a servant? and what a son? Christ answers it himself (John 15:15), *Henceforth I call you not servants, for the servant knoweth not what his Lord doth; but I have called you friends; for all things which I have heard of my Father, I have made known unto you; and ye are my friends, if ye do whatsoever I have commanded you*. Servants, you know, are kept at a distance and know not the secrets of their master; but if you be friends or sons (it's all one), you shall *abide in the house forever*. The inheritance is yours; the secrets of the Almighty are yours; you shall not only have the external and outward command, but shall see the excellency, the glory, the pleasure and delight of those commands: that is, you shall not only have the letter but the life, and shall know whatever the Lord doth. You shall not always be servants but shall grow up to be sons; and if ye grow not, you may well question yourselves, whether ye shall ever come to the inheritance or no. But I say, look to yourselves therefore in the name of Jesus Christ; for I affirm boldly in his name that faith which is not a growing faith is not a true faith; if your faith and light be the same as it was many years ago, that you have only an external faith, and your faith is taught only by the precepts of men, and Christ is not your teacher and that he grows not in you; this is but a dangerous and dead faith. . . . saith Christ, *Considerate lilia quomodo crescunt, Consider the lilies, how that they grow*; and *a grain of mustard seed, which is the least of all seed*, yet it grows the tallest. Then flatter not yourselves, beloved; that faith that grows not is not true faith; and that light that increaseth not is not true light; that Christ that grows not in you, dwells not in you. Beloved, look about you, this doctrine falls heavy as lead upon abundance of professors.

‡

All Power Given to Jesus Christ, in Heaven and in Earth

All power is given unto me in heaven and in earth, &c.
Mat. 28:18-20

In one sermon, preached at a private meeting in Old Street.

Augustine and others with him reckon this to be the ninth and last time of our Savior's appearing to his disciples after his resurrection; and that for this end he appeared so often: to manifest the truth of his resurrection; and yet for all this *some still doubted*, as you read in the foregoing verse. And they had great cause, for though he had appeared to so many, and so many times, as this being the ninth time; and it is also said, *He was seen of more than five hundred brethren at once*, yet for all this *some doubted*. And although the disciples were particularly appointed by Jesus to come *at this time into this mountain, and when they saw him, they fell down and worshipped him*, yet *some* for all this *doubted*. They knew they had seen him in great and extreme sorrow and anguish of soul, even to the utmost that the malice of men and devils could invent; they saw him *yield up the ghost*, and they thought they had done their last office for him, accompanying him to his execution and death, and so to his grave and sepulcher. But here he, after many appearings to them to confirm their faith, appears this once more; and it seems to be very probably the last time of his appearing, immediately before his ascension. And now he gives them a commission and command *to go and teach all nations* (as it follows in the 19 and 20 verses), *baptizing them in the name of the Father &c. and teaching them to observe all things that I have commanded you: for lo I am with you always, even to the end of the world.* And because they should be able to shew their authority and warrant, if any should ask who sent them, he tells them, He that is I AM hath sent you; I AM is with you; and further tells them that their power they shall derive from him: *For all power is given to me in heaven and earth.* And these words, however they be few in number, yet there is in them an abyss of matter; there is a mighty power and a vast length and breadth, height and depth in all his words, for his words are always full of sense, spoken to the highest pitch that our capacity can conceive or reach. . . . Others, it may be, writ they knew not what themselves (as I may so speak), even the penmen of the Holy Scriptures, for they wrote things beyond their own comprehension, they being directed by another Spirit. . . . and latter and after-times shall make known that which they themselves which wrote them knew not, for they spake as inspired by God. But Christ's words are always absolute and perfect truth. He knew and saw very well what he said; there is nothing useless in his words; there is no tautologies (as we call them), no vain repetitions. When Christ speaks, they are words of weight, words of power; they carry virtue with them. As for instance, if ever the winds blow and the storms arise in thy soul, then thou shalt find experimentally and feelingly that one word from Christ's mouth will do thee more good than all the words and all the power of men *to still those winds* and *storms*. Those who have experience hereof know it full well; as we see when the ship was like to be overcome by the winds and storms, and Christ was asleep: you may see there how one word from him ceased them [Mar. 4:39]; no more but *peace and be still*; and tis the same in the soul. And Psal. 107:29: *He maketh the storm a calm, so that the waves thereof are still.*

These words we have now read, *All power is given to me in heaven and earth.* They signify that Christ is God equal with the Father; but there seems to be a great difficulty in the words, in that Christ never said, before he was ready to leave the earth, *All power is given unto me in heaven and earth.*

The question is, what power had Christ now committed to him that he had not before? what new power received he, that when he was to leave the earth, and had given his disciples a commission, and it was to be sealed at the day of Pentecost, that he should say now and never before, *All power is given me in heaven and earth?* what addition of power had he now, which he had not before, if he be God equal with his Father? and he saith many times, *the Father hath committed all judgment to the Son*; and again, *Before Abraham was, I am*, and many such like words; which shews he is God, and of equal power and authority with his Father; and yet he saith in the 14 of John, *The Father is greater than I.* Can God receive any new access of power?

No, certainly. But these words are so hard and difficult to reconcile that in the days of Arius it filled the Church full of errors and heresies. The Church fell much at odds, for many from hence denied the divinity of Christ because they could not reconcile these Scriptures. And (by the way) if he be Lord of all power, then he leaves none for man to claim to himself.

But that I may answer this doubt and make it clear, I will lay down two grounds.

First, although God receive no new power in himself, yet he doth receive power by being made further known unto man. And secondly, by man's being made further known unto him.

First, by his being made further known unto man: the revealing and discovering of God unto man, making himself more known; the manifestation of this is said to add power to him; but not that anything can be added to him who is infinite. If there could, he were not infinite, and he were not God.

But know this, whatever attribute God hath ascribed to him, it is in regard of his creatures, not in regard of himself; for there are no such things in God, neither in regard of his incommunicable or communicable attributes, as eternity, infiniteness, omnipotency, immenseness, &c., or in regard of his communicable, as wisdom, justice, and mercy, and patience, &c., as if these were several things in God; for God is one, and cannot be more. For when he is said to be any of these, just or good or severe or the like, these are all one and the same thing in him; they are but attributed to him that we may conceive of him; it is but spoken of him according to the several workings of God on the creatures.

As for instance, the sun makes the rose to smell sweet and pleasant, and it makes the nettle to sting; it makes the fields to grow and cast a pleasant savor, but it makes the carrion and the dunghill to stink; and all this variety is by one and the self-same sun: the same light and heat doth divers things, causes divers effects in the subjects. Says the rose, it makes me fragrant and sweet; and says the dung-hill, but it makes me stink and be unsavory. Says the wax, it makes me soft and pliable; but says the clay, it makes me hard and obdurate; yet the sun doth not do one thing to one and another thing to another. Even so, beloved, it is with our God: one man, he finds God a comfort and a rejoicing to his heart; another, he finds God a terror and an amazement to him. One he finds God a sweet guide and direction to him, and thereby and therefore he draws nearer to God, loveth and embraceth him. Another apprehends God an enemy to him, and this makes him run away from God. Is God therefore thus various? No no; he is the self-same God to the one and to the other; and the self-same action in him is to the one and to the other. He that is a hammer to the hard heart, he is also mollifying and softening oil to the penitent soul. He that is a *comfort to the fatherless and widow* [Ps. 146:9], he is as an enemy, a revenger, and a consuming fire to the obstinate and rebellious. And yet for all this, our God is always the same; he is not nor cannot be changed; in *him is no shadow of change* [Jam. 1:7]. And therefore we cannot imagine that he can grow greater or less in regard of himself, but as to us he doth: that is, if he manifest himself more to us, more within us, in our souls, then he is said to be greater; and if he lessen the knowledge of himself as to us, then he is said to grow less. And in this sense also he is said *to come nearer to us* and *go further from us*. As also he is said so to do, when he expresses, as to us, more or less, some act of justice or mercy or any other attribute. Then, I say, he is only said to be so, in regard of us to grow greater or less, to come nearer or depart further; but he in himself is forever blessed and perfect, unchangeable, immoveable, always the same. We can no way touch him or alter him; but it is only we, the creature, is altered, and he is altered to us, as to our feeling, to our sight, to our apprehension and comprehension, but not at all in himself.

We cannot honor him, no, nor dishonor him, as to himself; he is infinitely far above our praises or dispraises; neither toucheth him; as David saith, *My goodness extendeth not to him*; and *Job, if I sin, it toucheth not him*. He is neither better or worse by all our works, either by sin or righteousness. Beloved, be sure of this: we can neither diminish nor increase his praise in himself, though in regard of us we do; for though we hold our tongues, though we run upon our own destruction, yet all (as creatures) praise him. If he be not glorified by us in his mercy, he is and will be in his justice.

It is said in Phil. 2 *that he emptied himself of all his glory*; that is, he (as it were) drew a curtain between our eyes and his glory, not between his own eyes and his glory; for he was the same in himself. But as to men, he drew a curtain or veil before his glory; for he honored himself most in that he emptied himself; and therefore he saith here, *All power is given unto me in heaven and in earth*: not but that he had the same power before, but now, *All power is given me*; that is, now men shall see it, how in this very thing I honored myself; how in this very thing, I manifested myself to be the Savior of the world. And though he seemed to unclothe and disrobe himself of all power and glory, yet men shall now see and acknowledge that he still, at that very instant, retained it as much as ever; yea manifested it more: to them I seemed to lay it down, and now to them I will be seen to take it up again, and they shall see that it never departed from me, nor I from it.

But now it may be you will say to me, We see you have partly cleared it and made it appear in what sense it is to be understood that *all power is given to him in earth*; but how is *all power* given him *in heaven*? do the angels add anything to him, or is anything added to them? Yea, certainly, for by the Church these things are more made known unto them; for they were not created in such an estate but they may be made better; nor are they so perfect, but that they desire an increase in their perfection. For it is said (1 Pet. 1:12), *The angels do stoop down to pry into these mysteries*; therefore their knowledge and perfection is increasing. And indeed it is certain they see their imperfections more than man because of the great light they have; they are nearer to God, who is light, and therefore see their darkness and imperfection more than we; for we are more dark and further off the light. But alas, vain men think they see a great deal; and because of their blindness, they think themselves such excellent creatures; being thereby puffed up in themselves, looking on themselves as lords of all: everything was made for him, and that Christ was sent merely to redeem him, to save him. God overlooked (as he conceives) all creatures, both above him and below him, and had respect to none but to him: as proud Haman said, *I only am in the king's favor*. O poor creatures! you are deceived; think not so. This is only a fruit of your ignorance, of your blindness. Limit not God's Church to so narrow a scantling. The dominions of his Church reach infinitely further than you are aware of; but we must not now enter upon that.

But hereby you may see that *things in heaven* have a revelation and manifestation of Christ unto them; and his power *is given unto him there*, as well as on earth—if so it be that you do take heaven according to our general and common notion of taking heaven, which we vulgarly conceive to be above the circumference of the sun, and God to be present more especially there; but this also is a limiting the bounds of his Church and kingdom. His kingdom (as I conceive) is everywhere, and heaven is where he is, for he is everywhere.

Yet I remember I was taught, when I was a child, either by my nurse or my mother or schoolmaster, that God Almighty was above in heaven, viz. above the sun, moon and stars; and I thought of a long time afterwards that there was his court and his chamber of presence; and I thought it a great height to come to this knowledge. But I assure you, I had more to do to unlearn this principle than ever I had to learn it; and I am afraid too many of us are gone no further than this childish principle, whereupon follow many errors.

But it is more safe taking *heaven* in the largest sense; either as God filling all places and all things, as well above the sun as below, and below as above; and so heaven to be where God is: that is, everywhere, for he cannot be excluded from any place; but he is not only in every place, but in every place alike.

Or else to take *heaven* in that sense the Prodigal doth (Luk. 15:18), *Father, I have sinned against heaven and before thee*; to take heaven to be in our souls. When God comes into our souls and dwells there—that is, when he manifests his presence in us and to us—then he is said to dwell there: not but that he dwelt there in regard of himself as much before, but then he is there as in his Temple, as in his glory, to us-ward; then we see him there in the beauty of holiness; then he is compassed about with our praises, as it is exprest in that 68 Psalm, *It is well seen, O God, how thou goest; how thou my God goest, when thou art in thy sanctuary; the singers go before and the minstrels follow after; in the midst are the damsels with timbrels, &c.* When God is not only in us as he is in all creatures, but when he is there sensibly to us that we feel him and see him and rejoice to behold his presence and glory and so we come thereby to glorify him more.

Whenever we come to this sight, then are we come into a degree of the kingdom of heaven, into God's chamber of presence. There we shall see all creatures, all angels and saints, and the whole creation compassing him round about with glories and hallelujahs.

Then (as to us) is he set upon his throne. And till then he is as crucified, as upon the Cross, as buffeted, as spit upon, as emptied, as disrobed, as slighted, trod upon, as upon the dunghill, as separate from his glory: but all this is but as to men, not as to himself, as I said before.

For to him *all angels cry aloud, the heavens and the earth and all the powers therein, and all creatures cry continually, Holy, holy, holy, Lord God of Sabbaths; heaven and earth are full of the majesty of thy glory* [Isa. 6:3]. And he knows his own glory and praise infinitely beyond our apprehensions; but, as I said, he is more praised and glorified, as to us and by us. And in this sense are our Savior's words here, that he hath now All power given him in heaven and in earth, in regard there is a great deal more light come to us, and he is revealed unto more; for Christ, as he saith, Joh. 1:9, *He is the true light that enlightneth every man that comes in to the world*

. . .

And Christ began his miracles and preached first at Jerusalem, and from thence sent out his disciples into all the world. From which observation we may apply thus much to ourselves, that whensoever Christ teacheth any man to salvation, that when he preacheth healthfully and savingly in the soul, he preacheth first to the heart: begins there, sets that right, and from thence his word is derived and sent forth to all the members of the body. Christ and his disciples first began at Jerusalem, and then afterward their commission was to go into all the world. He tied himself very strictly to the Jews before ever he would suffer them to go to the gentiles. This truth I would commend to you as a stable maxim of truth: *All faith and holiness is first to be preached to the heart before we go about to rectify the members and the actions*, which in this regard may well be called Jews and gentiles.

Religion, if it begin not at the heart, is nothing worth; it is but a folly to preach to the eyes and to the ears, to the hands and to the feet, before we preach to the heart. We must observe Christ's rule, first begin at Jerusalem and then go into all the world; first preach to the Jews, afterward to the gentiles. God only speaks to the heart and teacheth that. To begin with the outward man that so they may teach the heart is the way of man, not of God. *Great is thy God in the midst of thee*, in thy heart; do but rectify that, and the actions cannot be amiss; make the tree good, and there will follow good fruit. Can you expect figs of thorns, or grapes of thistles? nay, can you, by all your manuring, watching and dressing or forcing them, cause them to bear such [Mat 7:16]? Certainly no: therefore see the folly of many men in our days; they think by their pains and by their discipline to force men into religion, into faith & good works and spiritual actions. When thereby they have only restrained the outward man. And with them, they pass for excellent Christians. Alas, alas! *either* (saith our Savior) *make the tree good and his fruit good; or else make the tree evil and his fruit evil*. Whatever fair pretences their actions may have, and though they seem good to men, if the heart be not reformed, they are but golden vices, rotten nutmegs and rotten apples gilded over; gilded sepulchers; they neither have a good root nor tend to a right end: fair without, but false, rotten, and stinking within; they are carried on by Self to base, carnal, & fleshly ends. Self is both the rise and end of their actions, and they no better than thorns and thistles, and fit for nothing but to be burnt up. As the Apostle saith, *the fire shall try every man's work of what sort it is* [1 Cor. 3:13-14].

. . .

. . . Ye restrain your hands and your feet from evil because you would not come under the penalty of men's laws, and you do escape them; *verily herein you have your reward*. And you do your good works for the praise of men, and you have it: *Verily I say unto you, you have your reward.*

And though you may think highly of such works, and of yourselves for them, yet there is nothing of God in them; and to him they are no better sacrifice than cutting off a dog's neck or the offering up of swine's blood, as the Prophet Isaiah saith [66:3]. This is nothing but one sin casting out another for self-advantage . . . for it is nothing but the old man working within his own sphere, and to his own advantage: ye do it that ye may be counted honest among men, and ye are accounted so; ye would be and are esteemed great professors, verily you have your reward. Many such like ends you have, and so many such rewards. This is nothing but the devil's preaching and the devil's learning within thee. It's no better than the devil's work, and thou canst expect no other but the devil's wages.[7] . . .

. . . Take up the cross; expect reproaches, persecutions, and death from the world. This preaching is of God. Let thy life be in forsaking the glory of the world; though thou livest in the world, yet let thy heart, thy affections dwell and abide with me: *Use the world as if thou usedst it not* [1 Cor. 7:30 &c.]. Count nothing in the world thine own; be thou but as a steward in whatever thou hast, always ready to give an account of all. This preaching is from God, from heaven. . . .

Even as the life in the body by the blood flows from the heart to all the members— if not, those members are dead—so the life of true grace flows from the heart as from the fountain. For if either fear or law or heaven or hell, reward, or any hopes or by-ends urge the heart to goodness, these are but *dead works*; and you shall know it by this: do but take away these respects and by-ends, and these works cease. Take away hope of reward and fear of punishment, and this body is dead; he works no more. Why? Because there is no life, no heat within to move him. Tell him—I mean he whose heart is set right for God, reformed by him—tell him he must deny, forsake the world, he must be emptied of all the glory of the world, of all self-seeking, self-glorying, self-praising; why herein is his life, his peace, his glory. But to the other who hath been only taught by such precepts as come from men, from Self, this preaching is death to him; but his life and peace and joy is to hear how he shall be advanced, esteemed, honored &c.; how he shall be made rich and great. Therefore you may easily hence distinguish what preaching and practice is from God, and what from Satan and Self.

Thus much may serve for the first thing, to open unto you the meaning of these words, *All power is given unto me in heaven and in earth*. To me it seems very plain and clear, and I hope to you also, that that which before seemed obscure, now is made manifest.

The second ground: Christ also, as he is man, hath *all power given unto him* as being united to God, so also to man: and this definition, as being united to God, is very large and deep, as the river at the entrance into the Sanctuary, which at the first entrance took a

---

[7] {The threat of hell here, as likewise the rewards glowingly detailed on <552>, suggest that for all Everard's depreciation of "fear or law or heaven or hell, reward or any hopes or by-ends" <559> as motives, his theology retains the eudemonist identification of the good with that which makes for true happiness. I do not know of an early Stuart Christian thinker who finally discards this premise, although some seem at moments to have been troubled by it.}

man but up to the ankles, and then a little further up to the knees, and then to the middle, and at last it would quite drown and swallow up all; it grew into a vast sea [Ezek. 47:4-5]. The meaning of the words in this sense we are not able to comprehend or understand, but the more we wade into them the more we are drowned and swallowed up.

Jesus Christ, he had the same glory in himself when he was upon earth as he had with his Father before all worlds, and he is *his well-beloved Son, in whom only he is well-pleased* [Mat. 3:17]. But as he is man, he to us-ward emptied himself of all his glory and came in the form of a servant; he was subject to the like passions and infirmities as we are except sinful; and hereby man came to be further made known unto him. That is, in regard of his human nature, he was hungry and thirsty and weary and suffered death and the like; and yet in regard of his divine nature, he held his glory and union with his Father. And it was necessary it should be so in both regards: for had it not been so, he could not have complied so with the creatures, and felt their wants and necessities; and had he not retained his unity with his Father . . . he could not have complied so perfectly with his Father for the salvation of mankind. For as he was in the bosom of his Father, he was unknowable to any creature; he was known only to himself; he was inexplicable, not to be unfolded; and in this regard, the more ye enter into darkness and unknowing, the more ye know of him: for he is nothing that we can comprehend or understand, as we are creatures, until we come to be one with him, and swallowed up into him.

But let us observe that Christ never made this boast of himself, that *all power is given unto me in heaven and in earth*, till he was ready to leave the earth; never till he had been crucified, dead, and buried, and rose again. It is remarkable, he never all the while he was on earth ever appropriated *all power* to be his, till he was ready to depart out of the earth. And beloved, this is for our imitation: Christ was no boaster, though none might boast more; but he was *meek and lowly*; he became *a servant to all* when he might have been advanced and made a king [John 6:15]. . . . He was far of another spirit than is now in the world and always was in the world among the men of the world; and no greater sign of a carnal, earthly, low, base spirit than to be always seeking the great things of the world; to be tickled and itching after the praises of men, to lift up our selves to be some-body in the world, to desire to sit above and to trample upon their brethren, to have the cap and the knee:[8] and yet how many of such men forsooth must be the only gracious and religious men of this age. But you see these are far from the life of Christ, as far as the East from the West. . . . Are these the men that brag of power and wisdom and holiness, and yet are thus swallowed up in the world, love the praise of men and greetings in the market and *the highest seats in the synagogues and the uppermost rooms at feasts* [Luke 20:46]? Their phylacteries must be broad and long, viz. to be known from other men, that they may be bowed to and reverenced of all men. Are these the doctors and teachers of all others? Are these the disciples and ministers Christ hath sent out to preach to us the life of Christ by their doctrine and example? Judge ye.

Beloved, ye must know, that all Christ's actions which were imitable, while he was here upon earth, they were symbolical; they shew that he is *yesterday, and to day, and the same for ever* [Heb. 13:8]; for whatever he did then, he did but shew and represent to our senses, by external actions, what he is still doing in the souls of men, and will be to the end of the world.

---

[8] {Removing one's hat and bowing were gestures of respect shown to a superior.}

. . .

Those actions of his he did then upon the bodies of men do but shew what he doth upon their souls: for he then cast out but some devils, not all; he healed and cured but some of their diseases, not all; for that was not the end of his coming. For had it been so, he would have cast out all devils as well as some, and cured all diseases as well as some; but he only by them did teach our dull capacities, which else could not conceive what he did in the soul but by representing the same thing outwardly, even by those things which were most equivalent to them.

Did he resist the temptations of Satan and so made him depart from him? it was to shew that he doth the same in those that are his, even by himself, in his own person and through his own power in them. For whatever actions he did, they were done by him only for a resemblance of his internal workings. Did he pray whole nights? it doth but shew that his Spirit in us makes continual requests and expressions, *even with sighs and groans which cannot be expressed* [Rom. 8:26]. Did he come before Pontius Pilate, and was accused, arraigned, whipped, buffered {*sic*}, mocked, and crowned with thorns? yea, he was; and this was to shew how our carnal judgments arraign him, and how we whip him and pierce him by our sins, mock and *grieve his blessed Spirit* [Eph. 4:30]. Was he nailed to the Cross? did he die? and was he put to death by the Jews? and was he buried, and a stone rolled upon him, never to rise again? they did so; and in these and other his actions lies all our hope and our faith; this is our anchor-hold and our trust, and whoever shall deny it, let his tongue cleave to the roof of his mouth. Yet these were but symbols and representations of our killing of him, crucifying and burying of him daily in our souls by our sins, by following our own wills, and by our arrogance, pride, and selfness; and thereby his life is crucified. And also it is to shew how we have daily quenched the motions of his blessed Spirit so that it lives not in us, but the *old Adam*, the old man, is alive; and Christ, the *new man*, is dead within us. And so likewise in the rest of his actions.

Did he rise again the third day and triumph over hell and death? it shews how this mighty Lion of the tribe of Judah hath and will raise up himself and overcome all his enemies, and hath and will put them all *under his feet* in our souls. . . . As you know, it is the nature of fire to draw all things, to ascend upward to its own center: so if Christ be risen and ascended in us, he will so display his own glories and beauties in us that he will draw all our affections up to him, so that we cannot but eagerly and vehemently desire to be like him: to draw all our love to the love of him, and all our hatred to hate that which he hateth; and all our love to love that which he loveth; our hate and love, joy and grief, and all our other affections to be like his. Even as fire also endeavors vehemently to make everything like itself, so doth Christ wherever he comes with his life, light, and glory.

Thus you see, that what Christ did for a time in the history, the same he still also doth as truly, as really, and as constantly in the mystery. He did some things visibly to shew that he doth the same things as truly invisibly; he did so much as was enough to manifest himself to be *Emmanuel*, and that he was *God manifested in the flesh*.

And as I said, when Christ was ready to leave the earth, then he made this boast of himself; and never before did he ascribe this power to himself. Even so, till we are made one with him, till we are made like him, and till we can sit so loose to the earth that we are with him ready, willingly and freely, to leave the earth, we can never claim this power. Till thou art dead to every creature, thou canst never make this boast. Beloved, if you would have power *to remove mountains and to offer violence to the kingdom of heaven* [Mat. 11:12], then you are to be thus qualified: that thou hast experimentally seen and felt in thy own soul how that thy sins have *plowed* and made *long furrows upon his back*, as David saith [Ps. 129:3]; and how you by your sins have quenched the light that is in you; and how in thee he is crucified, dead, and buried; and how thou hast drawn grave-stones of custom over him; and how you have buried his light, resisted and grieved his Spirit in you; and that you have found him arise in your own souls; that you have really seen and felt all these things actually done within you: his birth, his life, his death, his resurrection; that as his enemies have overcome and crucified him within you, so you have found him arise gloriously and triumphantly within you; and that he hath *put down all his enemies under his feet in thee* [Ps. 110:1], insomuch that thou hast heard him and seen him, and felt him crying within thy soul, Isa. 1:24, *Ha, ha, I will now arise, I will avenge me on my adversaries*: now I that was crucified am now risen again, so that you see his glory and the love of him triumphing in you; so that now thou canst truly say with David, Psal. 27:4, Now I am so far gotten from and forsaken the world, and my self, that now *I desire but one thing, and that will I seek after*: even that thou wouldest give me thy self, unite me and make me one with thine own life, *that I may dwell in the house of the Lord all the days of my life, and visit his Temple.*

You being once come to this pass really in experience, then you also may say, *All power is given to me in heaven and earth*, for then you are (as I may say) within an inch of being swallowed up into God; and then are you ready to leave the earth and all things therein; for this man he is become *one spirit with the Lord.* And if we be one spirit, as Christ's prayer hath purchased, Joh. 17:21, *that they may be one, as thou and I are one; that thou mayest be in me, and I in them, and they in me, that the world may believe that thou hast sent me*; if it be so, then Christ himself lives in us, and all our words are the words of Christ; we have no thoughts but the thoughts of Christ; we have no life, but Christ lives in us; as the Apostle saith, *I live, yet not I, but Christ liveth in me.* And then also, as the Apostle again saith, and so may you say, *All is yours*, and not before: *whether Paul or Apollos or Cephas or things present or things to come, all are yours, and you are Christ's, and Christ is God's.* You being come to this, as you may claim a right to all things, so you may claim a power over all things; for you are already set down in heavenly places with Christ himself in the very glory of God the Father, who is blessed forever.

. . .

For when a man is come to that life we formerly spake of, then he is made Lord of the earth and hath then real dominion over all the creatures: *And made little lower then the angels*, as it is exprest in Psal. 8. Then thou belongest to and art one with him who is *King of kings, and Lord of lords*, though you see it not.

A supposition of two drops reasoning together

As suppose two drops apart from the sea should reason together, and the one should say to the other,

Whence are we? canst thou conceive whence we are? either whence we come or to whom we belong or whither we shall go? Something we are, but what will in a short time become of us, canst thou tell? And the other drop should answer:

Alas, poor fellow-drop, be assured we are nothing; for the sun may arise and draw us up and scatter us, and so bring us to nothing.

Says the other again, suppose it do; for all that, yet we are; we have a being, we are something.

Why, what are we? saith the other.

Why, Brother Drop, dost thou not know? we, even we, as small & contemptible as we are in ourselves, yet we are members of the sea? Poor drops though we be, yet let us not be discouraged: we belong to the vast ocean.

How? saith the other, we belong to the sea, to the ocean? how can that be? We have heard of the mighty greatness of the ocean; we have heard, that there is the huge Leviathan that sports himself there, who is so great and terrible he feareth none; whose heart is as firm as a stone and as hard as a piece of the nether millstone; the mighty are afraid before him, who feareth not the spear nor the dart nor the habergeon; who esteemeth iron as straw, and brass as rotten wood . . . who maketh the deeps to boil like a pot and maketh the sea like a pot of ointment, so that he maketh a hoary path to shine after him, and upon earth there is not his like. What? that we are of the sea? how can it be? We have heard the sea is great and wide, Wherein also are things creeping innumerable, both small and great beasts: there is that Leviathan who is made to play and sport therein; and they that go down into the sea in ships *and do their business in great waters, they see the wonders of the Lord in the deeps: there are the huge & roaring waves that mount them up to heaven, and suddenly they fall down into the depths, and their souls melt because of trouble; and those great waves make them roll to and fro and stagger like a drunken man, so that they are at their wit's end* [Ps. 104, 107]. In the sea also we hear there be those huge and mighty rocks, whose foundations are unmoveable. Thou sayest that we are of the sea and we belong to the ocean: where is any such vastness in us? where is any of all those wonderful and mighty things in us? therefore we cannot be of the ocean.

No, tis true, saith the other, for the present we are not of the ocean, because we are not yet joined to the ocean, and except we perish and be dissolved as it were to nothing, we are nothing; but if the sun draws us up and dissolve us to nothing, that we are not seen to be {as} much as drops, then are we like to be something; for then we shall return into the ocean, to which we belong. Then we are those that have in us *those rocks and those ships and those Leviathans, and fish innumerable, both small and great; and they have room to play and sport themselves in us*: Then we may claim and appropriate to ourselves whatever may be appropriated to the sea or to the ocean as well as any other drop, for we are united and made one with the ocean.

The application by way of dialogue

So, just so in like manner, suppose two mortal men reasoning together, the one in jealousy and the other in revelation.

What are we? says the one.

We are nothing, says the other: we are but a shadow, *a dream* [Ps. 73:20], a bibble; not so much as *the drop of a bucket* or as the *dust of the balance*; we are but *as stubble before the fire* [Isa. 40:15 & 47:14] and as *smoke before the wind* [Hos. 13:3], ready to be consumed, scattered, and dissolved into nothing.

Oh, says the other, though in ourselves we are poor drops; and as thou sayest, we are no more than a drop, a bubble, soon up and soon down: we have no power, the least and weakest of all things imaginable; yet we are; we have a being; nay, we are more than thou canst imagine.

Why what are we?

Why, I'll tell thee what we are: we are members of the very body of Jesus Christ. We are (as I may say) flesh of his flesh and bone of his bone. And we are to be made *one spirit* with him [1 Cor. 6:17]. And therefore be contented; though we in ourselves are poor and contemptible, and apart from him nothing; yea, worse then nothing; yet *by the grace of God we are what we are* [1 Cor. 15:10]. We in ourselves cannot say, I am, or I live; we cannot call ourselves "I." *I live, yet not I, but Christ liveth in me*; and in time I shall see myself to live in him; and then I may and thou mayst claim the same life, the same power with him. For we shall return into him who is Almighty, we shall be dissolved into him who is infinitely vaster than[9] ten thousand seas or oceans.

Ah brother! saith the other, how can these things be? we have heard that Jesus Christ is God equal with his Father . . . that he hath *all power given him in heaven and in earth*; that he rules over all his enemies and treads them all under his feet; that he *rules them with a rod of iron and crushes them in pieces like a potter's vessel* [Ps. 2:9]; and he is set upon his throne, and triumphs in glory and majesty, and is set down in holy and heavenly places with his Father, in his throne and full authority. In us, behold, there is none of these things: we are poor drops and weak creatures; as little as we are, we are full of nothing but sin and corruption; we are empty and vile and despicable, not only because of our smallness and nothingness but by reason of our sinfulness and impureness.

We have none of our enemies at command; we are empty and changeable, and no stability in us; all our actions declare and render us to be always in a dying, perishing condition; but Jesus Christ, to whom (thou sayest) we belong, he is glorious and blessed, and lives for ever. And therefore I will not, I cannot believe. Wilt thou make me believe I am a part of him? it can never be.

Oh! saith the other, be contented: *Corn cannot bring forth fruit except it die* [1 Cor. 15:36], neither can a drop return to the ocean except it be dissolved in itself and from its own proper being. So, even so, we poor drops in ourselves, we are nothing: empty, poor, despised Nothings, less then Nothings, apart from the immense ocean. But if we can be content to die & forsake our selves, then should we return and be made one with that immense ocean. Could we but be contented to annihilate our selves, to be brought to nothing, we should be made Something. If that sun of righteousness would but arise and dissolve us, and draw us up into himself, then we, even we, as poor as we be, should be united and made one with the Almighty. Beloved, beloved,

The only reason why we remain such empty drops is because we esteem our selves to be somewhat, when indeed we are nothing. While we set such a great price upon our selves, and look on our selves as good, holy, and pure, and take notice of our selves what a progress in religion we have made, and despise others: this keeps us from being united to him. . . .

---

[9] {The 1657 text reads "then then."}

My eye can never be united to the sun till I behold and look upon it. Then those beams that come from it draw my eye in a direct line to be joined to it; so thou art never united to Christ till the Lord himself, by the eye of faith, which is as a beam that comes from him, unites and draws up thy soul in a direct line to him again. As long as thou art Something in thyself, so long thou art Nothing; and when thou beginnest to be nothing in thy own esteem, then thou beginnest to be really something: then is Jesus Christ beginning to arise and to exalt himself in thee. Then, as I said before, hast thou a right to all things, and thou mayest claim all those great things spoken of before to thyself to be thine: though not to thyself individual and as separated, but as united to him to whom *all power is given both in heaven and in earth*. But till this work be done, Christ is kept under, and thy self is exalted, and it rules thee & governs thee & terminates all thy actions; however they seem to thee and to other men . . . never so glorious and beautiful, yet Christ is crucified and Self is alive and set in the throne.

. . .

These things, brethren, we ought still to find in our own experience—not only to hear and read the history of them as done in and by others, but to see and feel how they are really accomplished in ourselves; for except we see this fighting and resisting accomplished in us, except we have found *the strong man* bound in us [Mat. 12:29] and felt *those fightings* and resistings that he makes till he be bound and overcome, we are yet in our sins. . . .

And if we have not found these things in ourselves, we have not been so much as in the way to union with Jesus Christ. But having found it, we have cause infinitely to rejoice: for then those masters and lords that formerly commanded thee, now thou shalt command them, and they shall obey. Then thou shalt find *that he hath* in thee *broken the gates of brass and cut the bars of iron in sunder* (Ps. 107:16). Thou (through him) shalt have power now to rectify thy understanding, thy will, thy affections, to rule and govern them as a king, because Christ is exalted as king in thy soul. . . . In ourselves indeed, and in our own strength, we can do nothing, but by the power of Christ and by his strength in us, we shall *be more than conquerors*; and we shall find these words true to ourselves that our Savior here saith, *All power is given to me in heaven and in earth.* . . . Then you shall come *to see such things as never eye saw, nor ear heard, nor ever entered into the heart of man* [1 Cor. 2:9], *things unutterable* [2 Cor. 12:4]. For till this comes to pass within you, you shall never see *the new heavens and the new earth* so often promised in the Scriptures; not till then shall we ever see the day that *old things shall pass away, and all things shall become new*, as it is exprest, Rev. 21:4. Then is the day come *that God shall wipe away all tears from our eyes.* And thou shalt hear Christ himself in thee proclaiming, *Behold, I make all things new.* . . .

. . . I'll tell thee, such a pass thou art now come to, that as thou stinkest to the world, so the world stinks to thee. As all things are ready to forsake thee, so thou art as ready to forsake them; so that thou beginnest to see no excellency in anything the world presents to thee: no, not in *propriety* {ownership}, which the whole world, yea generally all esteem so highly of and are of all things lothest to forgo. I say, to this man, even propriety begins to die to him, and he to it. . . .

This man is as a man dead and clean cast out of sight, as David saith, clean out of mind; he is as a bubble that nobody sets by. But yet be contented: happy, yea thrice happy are those men that are come to this, to be *dead men.* You know, dead men are not affected with any thing; dead men lay no claim to any thing; dead men cannot so much as say, *This is I.* They esteem not of themselves; they boast not of themselves; praise and dispraise is all one to them; they can let men do what they will with them, they are all at one pass; they claim no interest, no propriety in anything: let them be merry while he lies by, or let them be sad, all is one to him. Let them be sharers of his goods, one will have one part, and another another part; let them make merry and spend lavishly of his goods: he is not moved. Why? The reason is because he hath lost all his senses; in this world his life is gone; he is a dead man.[10]

Beloved, this was the condition the blessed apostles and disciples were brought to. Oh, but where are such disciples now? where are your great doctors and your learned men? Are they doctors in this school of the Cross of Christ? No, no, nothing less. Are they dead men? Are they come to this, to let others rejoice in the heaping up riches, and adding land to land, and making themselves and their posterity great in the world? These things should not concern dead men. And saith David again, *I am as a broken pitcher that can hold no water.* Just so is this man; he is a broken pitcher that can hold nothing. Pour riches into him, health, wealth, praise, honor, or the contrary: whatever ye give to him or take from him, he is all one. If ye t*ake his cloak* from him, he will *give you his coat*; if ye *strike him on the one cheek*, he cannot revenge, *he will rather turn the other.* Curse him, and *he will pray for you.* And all this he learns of his dear Savior JESUS CHRIST. And all this he hath attained by being united and by being made one with him, whose practice and command, you know, it was so to do; and whose nature and life he partakes of, knowing assuredly by experience that there is no other way to find rest to his soul but by forsaking his own will and living free in the world, and dead unto it and to his own proper will and affections.

Oh beloved, how happy and how free doth such a soul live? how at liberty and free from those chains that most men are fettered with? as love of money and honors and houses and lands; distracted with hopes on one hand and fears on the other, and are never at rest, but are like the troubled sea, tumbled this way and that way, rolling to and again, and never quiet. But this man is delivered, set free, from all such things. What a comfort is it for a man to be made willingly to leave the love of the world? to live free, and above all hopes and fears. What a comfort is it not to fear death (for this man dies daily)? not to fear to *answer all our enemies in the gate* [Ps. 127:5]? to look boldly and undauntedly on death, on Satan, as knowing them overcome and brought under? what a comfort is it to find, see, and feel the life of Christ in us? and that we are in some measure, and every day more and more, made conformable to our Head? And that we shall now forever overcome and be at rest, and sit down with him upon his throne, even as he is *set down upon his Father's throne* [Rev. 3:21]? what a comfort is it to feel and see our graces, faith, hope, and patience, and the rest, to revive, to live and flourish, which in former times flagged and died? What a comfort is this? To see that when either the north wind or the south wind blow, let him be in any kind of condition, yet his garden prospers, his soul flourishes, and the spices thereof flow out; and Christ and he *to eat the pleasant fruits thereof* {Cant. 4:12-16}. To this man,

---

[10] {From the Middle Ages on, the common law described monks, nuns, and anchorites as having undergone "civil death"; they were, i.e., dead in the eyes of the law, and hence incapable of holding property, which passed to their heirs the moment they took their vows.}

nothing is a rod to him, nothing a judgment. Let God do what he will with him, he can see no anger, no frowns in anything, but all that comes is to him mercy and loving kindness. This is the soul that lives with God and lives in God: this soul is at rest, and none else but this soul: for he hath, in part, possession of the kingdom of heaven, and the kingdom of heaven possession of him, even while he is in the body—which possession he knows he shall never be deprived of, but shall have the FULL possession and enjoyment thereof for ever and ever, in his Father's due time.

O my dear friends, to what a blessed tranquility and sereneness of spirit is this soul attained. These are to him BLESSED and HALCYON DAYS.

Here end the sermons of John Everard and all that can be of his expected.

Text: EEBO (Wing / E3531)

The Gospel treasury opened, or, The holiest of all unveiling discovering yet more the riches of grace and glory to the vessels of mercy unto whom only it is given to know the mysteries of that kingdom and the excellency of spirit, power, truth above letter, forms, shadows / in several sermons preached at Kensington & elsewhere by John Everard ; whereunto is added the mystical divinity of Dionysius the Areopagite spoken of Acts 17:34 with collections out of other divine authors translated by Dr. Everard, never before printed in English (London, printed by John Owsley for Rapha Harford, 1657), A7r–B1r, B5v–B6v, 186–210, 214–16, 375–413.

RICHARD SIBBES
(ca. 1577–1635)

Son of a wheelwright with a dim view of higher education, Sibbes entered St. John's, Cambridge, as a work-study student (a subsizar) in 1595 when he was eighteen, seventeen at the youngest. He remained at St. John's for the next twenty-one years, taking his BA in 1599, his MA in 1602, his BD in 1610. (His Cambridge doctorate came only in 1633.) He had been appointed fellow in 1601 and then elected senior fellow in 1619. Sometime around 1601 "it pleased God to convert him" and to call him to the ministry. Ordained in 1608, he was in quick succession made college preacher (1609) and chosen to give the public Sunday afternoon lecture at Holy Trinity, where his preaching drew so numerous a congregation that the church had to be enlarged. The Canons of 1604 required all clergy to subscribe to Whitgift's three articles, and hence to bear witness that they found nothing in the Prayer Book to be contrary to the word of God; like many godly ministers, Sibbes hesitated, principally troubled by the baptismal rubric mandating the sign of the cross. Yet, although he feared the rite could mislead simple souls, he did not consider it per se sinful; thus, after a brief hesitation, Sibbes subscribed in December of 1616. Two months later, he was appointed preacher of Grey's Inn, where his sermons once again necessitated architectural upgrades to accommodate the multitude that came to hear him. He retained his fellowship at St. John's until 1626, when he was appointed Master of St. Catharine's, a post he held, together with that at Grey's Inn, until his death.

In the dissenting hagiographies of the late seventeenth century, Sibbes had been an early non-conformist hero: one who had refused to subscribe and for that refusal been "deprived, censured, and silenced" and thereafter "constantly troubled by William Laud." This remained the dominant view of Sibbes until Mark Dever's 2000 study showed beyond question that Sibbes had conformed, and was neither deprived, censured, nor silenced. On two occasions, however, he was troubled by William Laud. In 1625 Sibbes became one of the Feoffees for Impropriations: a group of leading puritans who sought to buy back tithes and other Church revenues that had fallen into lay hands (i.e., been impropriated), with the aim of using the reclaimed income to support godly ministers and lecturers across England. Laud was also passionately committed to restoring impropriations—but for the Church, to be distributed by its bishops for its parish clergy. Laud viewed the Feoffees' attempt to gain control of those revenues in order to endow a ministry operating outside ecclesiastical structures as a serious threat, and in 1633 the Court of the Exchequer dissolved the group on a technicality. The second clash occurred in 1627, when Laud reproved some godly ministers, Sibbes among them, for unauthorized fundraising on behalf of their counterparts in the Palatine. Neither clash brought Sibbes any lasting harm. The same year the Feoffees were dissolved, the Crown presented him to the perpetual curacy of Holy Trinity. On a Sunday afternoon in June two years later, he fell ill shortly after leaving his Grey's Inn pulpit; a week later, he was dead.

A bruised reed, which came out in 1630, is, a handful of prefaces apart, Sibbes' first published work. *The saints' cordials* had appeared under his name the year before, but this gives every appearance of being sermon-notes taken by one of Sibbes' auditors and printed without his knowledge. As its preface indicates, Sibbes had *A bruised reed* published to forestall the like "bad quarto" edition of the sermons on which it is based. By 1632 the work was in its fourth edition, at which point Sibbes took up this new ministry of print and started entering titles of his revised sermon collections in the Stationers Register. Of these, only one came out during his lifetime (*The saints' safety* [1633]); after his death, however, they poured from the London presses: twenty-four separate works between 1635 and 1641, many in multiple editions; forty-five in toto over six years.

A bruised reed, like all Sibbes' work, belongs to a lineage of puritan piety going back to Greenham and those divines Baxter termed "affectionate practical English writers" (922), whose plain and spiritual preaching sought to comfort wounded consciences rather than quarrel over adiaphora. The genre was not restricted to the godly: Hooker's "Of the certainty of faith" belongs here, as (in its complex and compassionate inwardness) does the poetry of Herbert's *Temple*, as well as the Jesuit Robert Southwell's rendering of the Magdalen's heart-broken faith[1] and Cosin's Epiphany sermon *<supra>*. The extraordinary impact of *A bruised reed*, however, almost certainly derives from the directness and intensity of its grappling with the spiritual perfectionism and ethical rigorism to which all forms of early modern Christianity seem to have felt a fatal attraction, but English Calvinism above all, since the godly's assurance of election required finding within themselves a faith and sanctity far surpassing that of ordinary Christians: the rigorism and perfectionism of Bayly's *Practice of piety* and Hall's "The estate of a Christian" *<vide supra>*.

SOURCES: *ODNB*; Richard Baxter, *A Christian directory* (1673); Patrick Collinson, *The Elizabethan puritan movement* (U California P, 1967); Mark Dever, *Richard Sibbes: puritanism and Calvinism in late Elizabethan and early Stuart England* (Mercer UP, 2000); Alexander Grosart, ed. *The complete works of Richard Sibbes*, 7 vols. (Edinburgh, 1862–64); Kendall, *Calvin and English Calvinism*; Richard Strier, *Love known: theology and experience in George Herbert's poetry* (Chicago UP, 1983).

---

[1] Robert Southwell, *Mary Magdalen's funeral tears* (1591); see Debora Shuger, *The Renaissance Bible* (U California P, 1994; rpt. Baylor UP, 2010), 167–91.

RICHARD SIBBES

The bruised reed and smoking flax
1630

To the Christian reader,

To prevent a further inconvenience, I was drawn to let these notes pass with some review: considering there was an intendment of publishing them by some who had not perfectly taken them. And these first, as being next at hand, and having had occasion lately of some fresh thoughts concerning this argument, by dealing with some, the chief ground of whose trouble was the want of considering of the gracious nature and office of Christ. The right conceit of which is the spring of all service to Christ and comfort from him. God hath laid up all grace and comfort in Christ for us, and planted a wonderful sweetness of pity and love in his heart towards us. As God his Father *hath fitted him with a body*, so with a heart to be a merciful Redeemer [Heb. 10:7]. What doth the Scriptures speak but Christ's love and tender care over those that are humbled; and besides the mercy that resteth in his own breast, he works the like impression in his ministers and others *to comfort the feeble-minded and to bear with the weak.* Ministers by their calling are friends of the Bride, and to bring Christ and his Spouse together, and therefore ought upon all good occasions to lay open all the excellencies of Christ, and amongst others, as that he is highly born, mighty, one in whom all the treasures of wisdom are hid, &c., so likewise gentle and of a good nature and of a gracious disposition. It cannot but cheer the heart of the Spouse to consider in all her infirmities and miseries she is subject unto that she hath a Husband of a kind disposition, that knows how to give the honor of mild usage to the weaker vessel. That will be so far from rejecting her because she is weak, that he will pity her the more. And as he is kind at all times, so especially when it is most seasonable, he will speak to her heart, *especially in the wilderness.* The more glory to God and the more comfort to a Christian soul ariseth from the belief and application of these things, the more the enemy of God's glory & man's comfort labors to breed mispersuasions of them, that if he cannot keep men from heaven and bring them into that cursed condition he is in himself, yet he may trouble them in their passage. Some, and none of the worst, Satan prevails withal so far as to neglect the means, upon fear they should (being so sinful) dishonor God and increase their sins; & so they lie smothering under this temptation,

570

as it were bound hand and foot by Satan, not daring to make out to Christ, and yet are secretly upheld by a spirit of faith, shewing itself in hidden sighs and groans unto God. These are abused by false representations of Christ, all whose ways to such being ways of mercy; and all his thoughts, thoughts of love. The more Satan is malicious in keeping the soul in darkness, the more care is to be had of establishing the soul upon that which will stay it. Amongst other grounds to build our faith on, as the free offer of grace to all that will receive it; the gracious invitation of all that are weary and heavy laden . . . this is one infusing vigor and strength into all the rest: that they proceed from Christ, a person authorized, and from those bowels that moved him not only to become a man, but a curse for us—hence it is, *that he will not quench the smoking wick or flax.* It adds strength to faith, to consider that all expressions of love issue from nature in Christ, which is constant. God knows that, as we are prone to sin, so when conscience is thoroughly awaked, we are as prone to despair for sin; and therefore he would have us know that he setteth himself in the covenant of grace to triumph in Christ over the greatest evils and enemies we fear, and that his thoughts are not as our thoughts are, that he is God and not man, that there is heights and depths and breadths of mercy in him above all the depths of our sin and misery; that we should never be in such a forlorn condition wherein there should be ground of despair, considering our sins be the sins of men, his mercy the mercy of an infinite God. But though it be a truth clearer than the sunbeams that a broken-hearted sinner ought to embrace mercy so strongly enforced, yet there is no truth that the heart shutteth itself more against than this, especially in sense of misery, when the soul is fittest for mercy, until the Holy Spirit sprinkleth the conscience with the blood of Christ and sheddeth his love into the heart, that so the blood of Christ in the conscience may cry louder than the guilt of sin. For only God's Spirit can raise the conscience with comfort above guilt, because he is only greater than the conscience. Men may speak comfort, but it is Christ's spirit that can only comfort. Peace is the *fruit of the lips*, but yet *created* to be so. No creature can take off wrath from the conscience but he that set it on, though all the prevailing arguments be used that can be brought forth, till the Holy Ghost effectually persuadeth by a divine kind of rhetoric, which ought to raise up our hearts to him who is the comforter of his people, that he would seal them[1] to our souls. Now God dealing with men as understanding creatures, the manner which he useth in this powerful work upon their consciences is by way of friendly intercourse, as entreaty and persuasion and discovery of his love in Christ and Christ's gracious inclination thus even to the weakest and lowest of men. [*Loquitur Deus ad modum nostrum, agit ad modum suum.*[2]] And therefore because he is pleased by such like motives to enter into the heart and settle a peace there, we ought with reverence to regard all such sanctified helps; and among the rest, this of making use of this comfortable description of Christ by God the Father, in going boldly in all necessities to the throne of grace. But we must know this comfort is only the portion of those that give up themselves to Christ's government, that are willing in all things to be disposed of by him. For here we see in this Scripture both joined together: mercy to bruised reeds, and yet government prevailing by degrees over corruptions. Christ so favoreth weak ones as that he frameth their souls to a better condition than they are

---

[1] {the arguments}

[2] {God speaks according to our capacities, but acts according to his own.}

in. Neither can it be otherwise but that a soul looking for mercy should submit itself at the same time to be guided. Those relations of husband, head, shepherd, &c. imply not only meekness and mercy, but government likewise. When we become Christians to purpose, we live not exempt from all service, but only we change our Lord. Therefore if any in an ill course of life snatch comforts before they are reached out unto them, let them know they do it at their own perils. It is as if some ignorant man should come into an apothecary's shop stored with variety of medicines of all sorts & should take what comes next to hand, poison perhaps instead of physic. There is no word of comfort in the whole book of God intended for such *as regard iniquity in their hearts*, though they do not act it in their lives. Their only comfort is that the sentence of damnation is not executed, and thereupon there is yet opportunity of safer thoughts and resolutions; otherwise they stand not only convicted but condemned by the word, and Christ *that rideth on the white horse* will spend all his arrows upon them and wound them to death. If any shall bless himself in an ill way, God's wrath shall burn to hell against such. There is no more comfort to be expected from Christ than there is care to please him. Otherwise, to make him an abettor of a lawless and loose life is to transform him into a fancy; nay, into the likeness of him whose works he came to destroy, which is the most detestable idolatry of all. One way whereby the Spirit of Christ prevaileth in his is to preserve them from such thoughts; yet we see people will frame a divinity to themselves, pleasing to the flesh, suitable to their own ends, which, being vain in the substance, will prove likewise vain in the fruit, and as a building upon the sand.

The main scope of all is to allure us to the entertainment of Christ's mild, safe, wise, victorious government, and to leave men naked of all pretences why they will not have Christ to rule over them, when we see salvation not only strongly wrought but sweetly dispensed by him. His government is not for his own pleasure but for our good. We are saved by a way of love, that love might be kindled by this way in us to God again, because this affection melteth the soul, and mouldeth it to all duty and acceptable manner of performance of duty. It is love in duties that God regards more than duties themselves. This is the true and evangelical disposition arising from Christ's love to us and our love to him again; and not to fear to come to him as if we were to take an elephant by the tooth. It is almost a fundamental mistake to think that God delights in slavish fears, when as the fruits of Christ's kingdom are peace and joy in the Holy Ghost, for from this mistake come weak, slavish, superstitious conceits.

Two things trouble the peace of Christians very much: [1] their weaknesses hanging upon them, and [2] fear of holding out for time to come. A remedy against both is in this text, for Christ is set out here as a mild Savior to weak ones; and for time to come, his powerful care and love is never interrupted until he bring forth judgment to victory. And thereupon it is that both the means of salvation and grace wrought by means—and glory, the perfection of grace—come all under one name of the Kingdom of God so oft; because whom by means he brings to grace, he will by grace bring to glory.

This maketh the thoughts of the latter Judgment comfortable unto us, that he who is then to be our Judge cannot but judge for them who have been ruled by him here; for whom he guides by his counsel, those he brings to glory. If our faith were but as firm as our state in Christ is secure and glorious, what manner of men should we be?

If I had gone about to affect writing in a high strain, I should have missed of mine end and crossed the argument in hand. For shall we that are servants quench those weak sparks which our Lord himself is pleased to cherish? I had rather hazard the censure of some than hinder the good of others; which if it be any ways furthered by these few observations, I have what I aimed at. I intended not a treatise but opening of a text; what I shall be drawn to do in this kind must be by degrees, as leisure in the midst of many interruptions will permit. The Lord guide our hearts, tongues, and pens for his glory and the good of his people.

R. Sibbes

The Bruised Reed and Smoking Flax

A bruised reed shall be not break, and smoking flax shall he not quench,
till he send forth judgment into victory.
Matt. 12:20

The prophet Esay, being lifted up and carried with the wing of prophetical spirit, passeth over all the time between him and the appearing of Jesus Christ in the flesh, and seeth with the eye of prophesy and with the eye of faith, Christ as present, and presenteth him in the name of God to the spiritual eye of others in these words, *Behold my servant whom I have chosen, &c.* which place is alleged by Saint Matthew as fulfilled now in Christ.[3] Wherein is propounded,

First, the calling of Christ to his office;

Secondly, the execution of it.

[1] For his calling: God styleth him here his *righteous servant, &c.* Christ was God's servant in the greatest piece of service that ever was, a chosen and a choice servant; he did and suffered all by commission from the Father. Wherein we may see the sweet love of God to us, that counts the work of our salvation by Christ his greatest service. And that he will put his only beloved Son to that service. He might well prefix, *Behold,* to raise up our thoughts to the highest pitch of attention and admiration. In time of temptation, misgiving consciences look so much to the present trouble they are in that they need be roused up to behold him in whom they may find rest for their distressed souls. In temptations it is safest to behold nothing but Christ, the true *brazen Serpent, the true Lamb of God that taketh away the sins of the world*; this saving object hath a special influence of comfort into the soul, especially if we look not only on Christ, but upon the Father's authority and love in him. For in all that Christ did and suffered as Mediator, we must see God *in him reconciling the world unto himself.*

What a support to our faith is this, that God the Father, the party offended by our sins, is so well pleased with the work of redemption? And what a comfort is this, that, seeing God's love resteth on Christ as well pleased in him, we may gather that he is as well pleased with us, if we be in Christ. For his love resteth in whole Christ, in Christ mystical,

---

[3] {Isa. 41:1; Matt. 12:18. For a similar understanding of biblical prophecy, see Andrewes' 1623 Easter sermon *<supra>*.}

as well as Christ natural, because he loveth him and us with one love. Let us therefore embrace Christ, and in him, God's love, and build our faith safely on such a Savior that is furnished with so high a commission.

See here (for our comfort) a sweet agreement of all three persons: the Father giveth a commission to Christ; the Spirit furnisheth and sanctifieth to it; Christ himself executeth the office of a mediator. Our redemption is founded upon the joint agreement of all three persons of the Trinity.

[2] For the execution of this his calling, it is set down here to be modest, without making a noise or raising dust by any pompous coming, as princes use to do. *His voice shall not be heard*: his voice indeed was heard, but what voice? *Come unto me all ye that are weary and heavy laden* &c. He cried, but how? *Ho, every one that thirsteth, come* &c. And as his coming was modest, so it was mild, which is set down in these words: *the bruised reed shall he not break*, &c., wherein we may observe these three things:

First, the condition of those that Christ had to deal withal. 1. They were *bruised reeds.* 2. *smoking flax.*

Secondly, Christ's carriage towards them: he *brake not* the bruised reed nor *quenched* the smoking flax—where more is meant than spoken; for he will not only not break the bruised reed, nor quench &c. But he will cherish them.

Thirdly, the constancy and progress of this his tender care *until judgment come to victory*; that is, until the sanctified frame of grace begun in their hearts be brought to that perfection, that it prevaileth over all opposite corruption. For the first, the condition of men whom he was to deal withal is that they were bruised reeds and smoking flax; not trees, but reeds; and not whole, but bruised reeds. The Church is compared to weak things: to a *dove* amongst the fowls; to a *vine* amongst the plants; to *sheep* amongst the beasts; to a *woman*, which is the *weaker vessel*; and here God's children are compared to *bruised reed* and *smoking flax*. And first we will speak of them as they are bruised reeds, and then as smoking flax.

They are bruised reeds before their conversion, and often times after. Before conversion all (except such as being bred up in the Church, God hath delighted to shew himself gracious unto from their childhood), yet in different degrees, as God seeth meet; and as difference is in regard of temper, parts, manner of life, &c., so God's intendment of employment for the time to come: for usually he empties such of themselves, and makes them nothing, before he will use them in any great services.

[1] This bruised reed is a man that for the most part is in some misery, as those were, that came to Christ for help, and [2] by misery brought to see sin the cause of it; for whatsoever pretences sin maketh, yet bruising or breaking is the end of it. [3] He is sensible of sin and misery, even unto bruising, and [4] seeing no help in himself, is carried with restless desire to have supply from another, with some hope, which a little raiseth him out of himself to Christ, though he dareth not claim any present interest of mercy. This spark of hope being opposed by doubtings and fears rising from corruption maketh him as smoking flax, so that both these together, a bruised reed and smoking flax, make up the state of a poor distressed man, such an one our Savior Christ termeth *poor in spirit* (Math. 5), who seeth a want, & withal seeth himself indebted to divine justice, & no means of supply from himself or the creature, and thereupon mourns; and upon some hope of mercy from the promise, & examples of those that have obtained mercy, is stirred up to hunger & thirst after it.

This bruising is required before conversion that so the Spirit may make way for itself into the heart by *leveling all proud high thoughts*, and that we may understand ourselves to be what indeed we are by nature: we love to wander from ourselves and to be strangers at home, till GOD bruiseth us by one cross or other, and then we bethink ourselves and come home to ourselves with the prodigal. A marvelous hard thing it is to bring a dull and a shifting heart to cry with feeling for mercy. Our hearts (like malefactors), until they be beaten from all shifts, never cry for the mercy of the judge. Again, this bruising maketh us set a high price upon Christ; the Gospel is the Gospel indeed then; then the fig-leaves of morality will do us no good; and it maketh us more thankful, and from thankfulness more fruitful in our lives. For what maketh many so cold and barren but that bruising for sin never endeared God's grace unto them. Likewise this dealing of God doth establish us the more in his ways, having had knocks and bruisings in our own ways. This is the cause oft of relapses & apostasies, because men never smarted for sin at the first; they were not long enough under the lash of the Law. Hence this inferior work of the Spirit in *bringing down high thoughts* is necessary before conversion. And for the most part, the Holy Spirit, to further the work of conviction, joineth some affliction, which sanctified, hath a healing, purging power.

Nay, after conversion we need bruising, that reeds may know themselves to be reeds, & not oaks. Even reeds need bruising by reason of the remainder of pride in our nature, and to let us see that we live by mercy; and that weaker Christians may not be too much discouraged, when they see stronger shaken and bruised. Thus Peter was bruised when he *wept bitterly*. This reed, till he met with this bruise, had more wind in him than pith. *Though all forsake thee, I will not, &c.*

The people of God cannot be without these examples. The heroical deeds of those great worthies comfort the Church not so much as their falls and bruises do. Thus David was bruised until he came to a free confession without guile of spirit; nay, his sorrows did rise in his own feeling unto the exquisite pain of *breaking of bones* (Psalm 51). Thus Hezekiah complains that God had *broken his bones as a lion*. Thus the chosen vessel S. Paul needed the messenger of Satan to buffet him, lest he should be lifted up above measure.

Hence we learn that we must not pass too harsh judgment upon ourselves, or others, when God doth exercise us with bruising upon bruising. There must be a conformity to our head, Christ, who was bruised for us, that we may know how much we are bound unto him. Profane spirits, ignorant of God's ways in bringing his children to heaven, censure broken-hearted Christians for desperate persons, when as God is about a gracious good work with them. It is no easy matter to bring a man from nature to grace and from grace to glory, so unyielding and untractable are our hearts.

The second point is *that Christ will not break the bruised reed*. Physicians, though they put their patients to much pain, yet they will not destroy nature but raise it up by degrees; surgeons will lance and cut, but not dismember. A mother that hath a sick and froward child will not therefore cast it away. And shall there be more mercy in the stream than in the spring? Shall we think there is more mercy in ourselves than in God, who planteth the affection of mercy in us? But for further declaration of Christ's mercy to all bruised reeds: consider the comfortable relations he hath taken upon him of *husband, shepherd, brother,* &c., which he will discharge to the utmost. For shall others by his grace fulfill what he calleth them unto, and not he that out of his love hath taken upon him these relations, so thoroughly founded upon his Father's assignment and his own voluntary undertaking?

Consider his borrowed names from the mildest creatures, as *lamb, hen,* &c., to shew his tender care. Consider his very name *Jesus,* a *Savior,* given him by God himself. Consider his office, answerable to his name, which is that he should *heal the broken-hearted* (Esay. 61:1). At his baptism the Holy Ghost sat on him in the shape of a dove to shew that he should be a dovelike gentle mediator. See the gracious manner of executing his offices: as a prophet, he came with blessing in his mouth, *Blessed be the poor in spirit,* &c., and invited those to come to him whose hearts suggested most exceptions against themselves, *Come unto me, all ye that are weary and heavy laden.* How did his bowels yearn when *he saw the people as sheep without a shepherd?* He never turned any back again that came unto him, though some went away of themselves. He came to die as a priest for his enemies. In the days of his flesh he dictated a form of prayer unto his disciples, and put petitions unto GOD into their mouths and his Spirit to intercede in their hearts, and now makes intercession in heaven for weak Christians, standing between God's anger and them; and shed tears for those that shed his blood. So he is a meek king; he will admit mourners into his presence, a king of poor and afflicted persons. As he hath beams of majesty, so he hath bowels of mercies & compassion: a *prince of peace.* Why was *he tempted* but *that he might succor those that are tempted?* What mercy may we not expect from so gracious a Mediator, that took our nature upon him that he might be gracious. He is a physician, good at all diseases, especially at the binding up of a broken heart, that he might heal our souls with a plaster of his own blood and by that death save us which we were the procurers of ourselves, by our own sins; and hath he not the same bowels in heaven? *Saul, Saul, why persecutest thou me,* cried the head in heaven, when the foot was trodden on, on earth. His advancement hath not made him forget his own flesh; though it hath freed him from passion, yet not from compassion towards us. The Lion of the tribe of Judah will only tear in pieces those that *will not have him rule over them.* He will not shew his strength against those that prostrate themselves before him.

What should we learn from hence but *to come boldly to the throne of grace* in all our grievances? Shall our sins discourage us, when he appears there only for sinners? Art thou bruised? Be of good comfort, he calleth thee; conceal not thy wounds, open all before him, keep not Satan's counsel. Go to Christ, though trembling (as the poor woman); if we can but *touch the hem of his garment,* we shall be healed and have a gracious answer. *Go boldly to God* in our flesh. For this end, that we might go boldly to him, he is *flesh of our flesh and bone of our bone.* Never fear to go to God, since we have such a Mediator with him that is not only our friend, but our brother and husband. Well might the angels proclaim from heaven, *Behold, we bring you tidings of joy;* well might the Apostle stir us up to *rejoice in the Lord again and again.* He was well advised upon what grounds he did it; peace and joy are two main fruits of his kingdom. Let the world be as it will; if we cannot rejoice in the world, yet we may rejoice in the Lord. His presence maketh any condition comfortable. *Be not afraid* (saith he to his disciples when they were afraid as if they had seen a ghost); *it is I*—as if there were no cause of fear where he is present.

Let this stay us when we feel ourselves bruised: Christ his course is first to wound, then to heal. No sound whole soul shall ever enter into heaven. Think in temptation, Christ was tempted for me; according to my trials will be my graces and comforts. If Christ be so merciful as not to break me, I will not break myself by despair, nor yield myself over to the roaring lion Satan to break me in pieces.

Thirdly, see the contrary disposition of Christ and Satan and his instruments. Satan setteth upon us when we are weakest, as Simeon and Levi upon the Shechemites *when they were sore.* But Christ will make up in us all the breaches sin and Satan have made; he *binds up the broken-hearted,* and as a mother tendereth most the most diseased and weakest child, so doth Christ most mercifully incline to the weakest; and likewise putteth an instinct into the weakest things to rely upon something stronger than themselves for support. The vine stayeth itself upon the elm, and the weakest creatures have oft the strongest shelters. The consciousness of the Church's weakness makes her willing to lean on her Beloved and to hide herself under his wing.

[Object.] But how shall we know whether we are such as those that may expect mercy?

[Answ.] 1. By *bruising* here is not meant those that are brought low only by crosses, but such as by them are brought to see their sin, which bruiseth most of all. When conscience is under the guilt of sin, then every judgment brings a report of God's anger to the soul, and all lesser troubles run into this great trouble of conscience for sin. As all corrupt humors run to the diseased and bruised part of the body; and as every creditor falls upon the debtor when he is once arrested; so when conscience is once awaked, all former sins and present crosses join together to make the bruise the more painful. Now he that is thus bruised will be content with nothing but with mercy from him that hath bruised him; *he hath wounded, and he must heal.* 2. Again, a man truly bruised judgeth sin the greatest evil, and the favor of God the greatest good. 3. He had rather hear of mercy than of a kingdom. 4. He hath mean conceits of himself and thinketh he is not worth the earth he treads on. 5. Towards others he is not censorious, as being taken up at home, but is full of sympathy and compassion to those that are under God's hand. 6. He thinketh those that walk in the comforts of God's Spirit the happiest men of the world. 7. He *trembleth at the word of God* and honoreth the very *feet of those* blessed instruments *that bring peace* unto him. 8. He is more taken up with the inward exercises of a broken heart than with formality, and yet careful to use all sanctified means to convey comfort.

[Quest.] But how shall we come to have this temper?

[Ans.] First, we must conceive of bruising either as a state into which God bringeth us or as a duty to be performed by us. Both are here meant; we must join with GOD in bruising of ourselves; when he humbles us, let us humble ourselves and not stand out against him, for then he will redouble his strokes; and let us justify Christ in all his chastisements, knowing that all his dealing towards us is to cause us to return into our own hearts; his work in bruising tendeth to our work in bruising ourselves. Let us lament our own untowardness, and say, Lord, what an heart have I, that needs all this, that none of this could be spared? We must lay siege to the hardness of our own hearts, and aggravate sin all we can. We must look on Christ, who was bruised for us, look on him whom we have pierced with our sins. But all directions will not prevail unless God by his Spirit convinceth us deeply, setting our sins before us and driving us to a stand. Then we will make out for mercy. Conviction will breed contrition; and this, humiliation. Therefore desire God that he would bring a clear and a strong light into all the corners of our souls and accompany it with a spirit of power to lay our hearts low.

A set measure of bruising ourselves cannot be prescribed, yet it must be so far as we may prize Christ above all and see that a Savior must be had; and secondly, until we reform that which is amiss, though it be to the cutting off our right hand or pulling out our right eye. There is a dangerous slighting of the work of humiliation, some alleging this for a pretence for their overly {superficial} dealing with their own hearts that *Christ will not break the bruised reed.* But such must know that every sudden terror and short grief is not that which makes us bruised reeds: not a little hanging down our heads like a bulrush, but a working our hearts to such a grief as will make sin more odious unto us than punishment, until we offer an holy violence against it. Else, favoring ourselves, we make work for God to bruise us, and for sharp repentance afterwards. It is dangerous (I confess) in some cases with some spirits to press too much and too long this bruising, because they may die under the wound and burthen before they be raised up again. Therefore it is good in mixt assemblies to mingle comforts, that every soul may have its due portion. But if we lay this for a ground, that there is more mercy in Christ than sin in us, there can be no danger in thorough dealing. It is better to go bruised to heaven than sound to hell. Therefore let us not take off ourselves too soon, nor pull off the plaster before the cure be wrought, but keep ourselves under this work till sin be the sourest and Christ the sweetest of all things. And when God's hand is upon us in any kind, it is good to divert our sorrow for other things to the root of all, which is sin; let our grief run most in that channel, that as sin bred grief, so grief may consume sin.

[Quest.] But are we not bruised unless we grieve more for sin than we do for punishment?

[Ans.] Sometimes our grief from outward grievances may lie heavier upon the soul than grief for God's displeasure; because in such cases the grief works upon the whole man, both outward and inward, and hath nothing to stay it but a little spark of faith, which, by reason of the violent impression of the grievance, is suspended in the exercises of it; and this is most felt in sudden distresses which come upon the soul as a torrent or land flood, and especially in bodily distempers, which, by reason of the sympathy between the soul and the body, work upon the soul so far as they hinder not only the spiritual but often the natural acts. Hereupon S. James wisheth in affliction to pray ourselves, but in case of sickness to *send for the Elders*, that may, as those in the Gospel, offer up the sick person to God in their prayers, being unable to present their own case. Hereupon God admitteth of such a plea from the sharpness and bitterness of the grievance, as in David, Psal. 6 &c. *the Lord knoweth whereof we are made.* Psal. 103, *he remembreth we are but dust*, that our strength is not the strength of steel. It is a branch of his faithfulness unto us as his creatures, whence he is called *a faithful Creator; God is faithful, who will not suffer us to be tempted above that we are able.* There were certain commandments which the Jews called the hedges of the Law: as to fence men off from cruelty, he commanded they should not take the dam with the young, nor seethe the kid in the mother's milk, nor muzzle the mouth of the ox. Hath God care of beasts and not of his more noble creature? and therefore we ought to judge charitably of the complaints of God's people which are wrung from them in such cases. Job had the esteem with God of a patient man, notwithstanding those passionate complaints. Faith overborne for the present will get ground again; and grief for sin, although it come short of grief for misery in violence, yet it goeth beyond it in constancy, as a running stream fed with a spring holdeth out when a sudden swelling brook faileth.

For the concluding of this point, and our encouragement to a thorough work of bruising, and patience under God's bruising of us, let all know that none are fitter for comfort than those that think themselves furthest off. Men (for the most part) are not lost enough in their own feeling, for a Savior. A holy despair in ourselves is the ground of true hope. In God, the fatherless find mercy; if men were more fatherless, they should feel more God's fatherly affection from heaven. For God that *dwelleth in highest heavens*, dwelleth likewise in the lowest soul. Christ's sheep are weak sheep, and wanting in something or other; he therefore applyeth himself to the necessities of every sheep. Ezek. 34:16, he seeks that which was lost, and brings again that which was driven out of the way, and binds up that which was broken, and strengthens the weak; his tenderest care is over the weakest. The lambs he carrieth in his bosom. *Peter, feed my lambs.* He was most familiar and open to the troubled souls. How careful was he that Peter & the rest of the apostles should not be too much dejected after his Resurrection: *Go tell the disciples, and tell Peter.* Christ knew that guilt of their unkindness in leaving of him had dejected their spirits. How gently did he endure Thomas his unbelief? & stooped so far into his weakness as to suffer him to thrust his hand into his side.

‡

So in the censures of the Church, it is more suitable to the spirit of Christ to incline to the milder part, and not to kill a fly on the forehead with a beetle {mallet} nor shut men out of heaven for a trifle. The very snuffers of the Tabernacle were made of pure gold to shew the purity of those censures whereby the light of the Church is kept bright. That power that is given to the Church is given for edification, not destruction. How careful was Saint Paul that the *incestuous Corinthian* repenting should not be swallowed up with too much grief?

As for civil magistrates, they for civil exigencies and reasons of state must let the law have its course; yet thus far they should imitate this mild King, as not to mingle bitterness and passion with authority derived from God. Authority is a beam of God's majesty and prevaileth most where there is least mixture of that which is man's. It requireth more than ordinary wisdom to manage it aright. This string must not be too much strained up nor too much let loose. Justice is an harmonical thing. Herbs hot or cold beyond a certain degree kill. We see even contrary elements preserved in one body by a wise contemperation. Justice in rigor is oft extreme injustice, where some considerable circumstances should incline to moderation, and the reckoning will be easier for bending rather to moderation than rigor.

Insolent carriage toward miserable persons, if humbled, is unseemly in any who look for mercy themselves. Misery should be a lodestone of mercy, not a footstool for pride to trample on.

Sometimes it falleth out that those that are under the government of others are most injurious by waywardness and harsh censures, herein disparaging and discouraging the endeavors of superiors for public good. In so great weakness of man's nature, and especially in this crazy age of the world, we ought to take in good part any moderate happiness we enjoy by government, and not be altogether as a nail in the wound, exasperating things by misconstruction. Here love should have a mantle to cast upon lesser errors of those above us. Oft-times the poor man is the oppressor by unjust clamors; we should labor to give the best interpretations to the actions of governors that the nature of the actions will possibly bear.

In the last place, there is something for private Christians, even for all of us in our common relations, to take notice of: we are debtors to the weak in many things.

1. Let us be watchful in the use of our liberty, and labor to be inoffensive in our carriage, that our example compel them not. There is a commanding force in an example, as Peter, Gal. 2. A looseness of life is cruelty to ourselves and to the souls of others; though we cannot keep them from perishing which will perish in regard of the event,[4] yet if we do that which is apt of itself to destroy the souls of others, their ruin is imputable to us.

2. Let men take heed of taking up Satan's office in depraving the good actions of others as he did Job's: *Doth he serve God for nought?* or slandering their persons, judging of them according to the wickedness that is in their own hearts. The devil getteth more by such discouragements and these reproaches that are cast upon religion than by fire and faggot. These (as unseasonable frosts) nip all gracious offers in the bud, and, as much as in them lieth, with Herod labor to kill Christ in young professors. A Christian is a hallowed and a sacred thing, Christ's temple; and he that destroyeth his temple, him will Christ destroy.

3. Amongst the things that are to be taken heed of, there is amongst private Christians a bold usurpation of censure, not considering their temptations. Some will unchurch & unbrother in a passion. But distempers do not alter true relations; though the child in a fit should disclaim the mother, yet the mother will not disclaim the child.

There is therefore in these judging times good ground of S. James his caveat that there should not *be too many masters*; that we should not smite one another by hasty censures, especially in things of an indifferent nature. Some things are as the mind of him is that doth them or doth them not; for both may be unto the Lord.

A holy aim in things of a middle nature makes the judgments of men, although seemingly contrary, yet not so much blamable. Christ, for the good aims he seeth in us, overlooketh any ill in them so far as not to lay it to our charge.[5]

Men must not be too curious in prying into the weaknesses of others.[6] We should labor rather to see what they have that is *for eternity*, to incline our heart to love them, than into that weakness which the Spirit of God will in time consume, to estrange us. Some think it strength of grace to endure nothing in the weaker, where as the strongest are readiest to bear with the infirmities of the weak. Where most holiness is, there is most moderation (where it may be without prejudice of piety to God and the good of others). We see in Christ a marvelous temper {blend} of absolute holiness with great moderation, in this text. What had become of our salvation if he had stood upon terms and not stooped thus low unto us! We need not affect to be more holy than Christ; it is no flattery to do as he doth, so it be to edification.

The Holy Ghost is content to dwell in smoky offensive souls. Oh that that Spirit would breath into our spirits the like merciful disposition! We endure the bitterness of wormwood and other distasteful plants & herbs only because we have some experience of some wholesome quality in them; and why should we reject men of useful parts and

---

[4] {i.e., outcome: our conduct cannot alter divine predestination}
[5] {Note that Sibbes here approaches Chillingworth's position <897>.}
[6] [*Nemo curiosus qui non malevolus.* {No one is curious who is not also malicious.}]

graces only for some harshness of disposition, which, as it is offensive to us, so grieveth themselves?

Grace, whilest we live here, is in souls, which as they are unperfectly renewed, so they dwell in bodies subject to several humors, which will incline the soul sometimes to excess in one passion, sometimes to excess in another.

Bucer was a deep, and a moderate divine. Upon long experience {he} resolved to refuse none in whom he saw *aliquid Christi*, something of Christ.

The best Christians in this state of imperfection are like gold that is a little too light, which needs some grains of allowance to make it pass. You must grant the best their allowance. We must supply out of our love & mercy that which we see wanting in them.

The Church of Christ is a common hospital, wherein all are in some measure sick of some spiritual disease or other, that we should all have ground of exercising mutually the spirit of wisdom and meekness.

This, that we may the better do, let us put upon ourselves the spirit of Christ. . . . That great physician, as he had a quick eye and a healing tongue, so had he a gentle hand and a tender heart.

And secondly, put upon us the condition of him whom we deal withal; we are, or have been, or may be such; make the case our own, and withal consider in what near relation a Christian standeth unto us, even as a brother, a fellow-member, heir of the same salvation. And therefore let us take upon ourselves a tender care of them every way: and especially in cherishing the peace of their consciences. Conscience is a tender and delicate thing, and so must be used. It is like a lock—if the wards be troubled, it will be troublesome to open.

For trial, to let us see whether we be this smoking flax which Christ will not quench. In this trial remember these rules:

1. We must have two eyes: one to see imperfections in ourselves and others; the other to see what is good. *I am black*, saith the Church, *but yet comely*. Those ever want comfort that are much in quarrelling with themselves and through their infirmities are prone to feed upon such bitter things as will most nourish that distemper they are sick of. These delight to be looking on the dark side of the cloud only.

2. We must not judge of ourselves always according to present feeling, for in temptations we shall see nothing but smoke of distrustful thoughts. Fire may be raked up in the ashes, though not seen; life in the winter is hid in the root.

3. Take heed of false reasoning: as, because our fire doth not blaze out as others, therefore we have no fire at all; and by false conclusions come to sin against the Commandment in *bearing false witness* against ourselves. The prodigal would not say he was no son, but that he was not worthy to be *called a son*. We must neither trust to false evidence nor deny true; for so we should dishonor the work of God's Spirit in us and lose the help of that evidence which would cherish our love to Christ and arm us against Satan's discouragements. Some are so faulty this way, as if they had been hired by Satan, the *accuser of the brethren*, to plead for him in accusing themselves.

4. Know (for a ground of this) that in the covenant of grace, God requires the truth of grace, not any certain measure; and a spark of fire is fire as well as the whole element. Therefore we must look to grace in the spark as well as in the flame. All have not the like strong, yet the like precious faith, whereby they lay hold & put on the perfect righteousness of Christ. A weak hand may receive a rich jewel; a few grapes will shew that the plant

is a vine and not a thorn. It is one thing to be wanting in grace, and another thing to want grace altogether. God knoweth we have nothing of ourselves; therefore in the covenant of grace he requireth no more than he giveth, and giveth what he requireth, and accepteth what he giveth: *He that hath not a lamb may bring a pair of turtledoves.* What is the Gospel itself but a merciful moderation, in which Christ's obedience is esteemed ours, and our sins laid upon him; and wherein God of a judge becometh a father, pardoning our sins and accepting our obedience, though feeble and blemished. We are now brought to heaven under the covenant of grace, by a way of love and mercy.

It will prove a special help to know distinctly the difference between the *covenant of works* and the *covenant of grace*, between Moses and Christ. Moses without all mercy *breaketh all bruised reeds* and *quencheth* all *smoking flax*. For the Law requireth 1. personal, 2. perpetual, 3. perfect obedience, 4. and from a perfect heart—and that under a most terrible curse—and giveth no strength; a severe taskmaster, like pharaoh's, requireth the whole tale {amount} and yet giveth no straw. Christ cometh with blessing after blessing, even upon those whom Moses had cursed, and with healing balm for those wounds which Moses had made.

The same duties are required in both covenants: as *to love the Lord with all our hearts, with all our souls, &c.* In this covenant of works, this must be taken in the rigor; but under the covenant of grace, as it is a sincere endeavor proportionable to grace received—and so it must be understood of Josiah and others, when it is said they *loved God with all their hearts, &c.* It must have an evangelical mitigation.

The Law is sweetened by the Gospel and becometh delightful to *the inner man.* Under this gracious covenant, sincerity is perfection. This is the *death in the pot* in the Roman religion, that they confound two covenants; and it deads the comfort of drooping ones, that they cannot distinguish them. And thus they suffer themselves to be *held under bondage*, when Christ hath set them free; and stay themselves *in the prison*, when Christ hath set open the doors before them.

5. Grace sometimes is so little as is indiscernible to us; the Spirit sometimes hath secret operations in us which we know not for the present; but Christ knoweth. Sometimes in bitterness of temptation, when the spirit struggles with sense of God's anger, we are apt to think God an enemy; and a troubled soul is like troubled waters—we can see nothing in it; and so far as it is not cleansed, it will *cast up mire and dirt.* It is full of objections against itself. Yet for the most part we may discern something of this hidden life and of these smothered sparks.

In a gloomy day there is so much light whereby we may know it to be day and not night; so there is something in a Christian under a cloud whereby he may be discerned to be a true believer and not an hypocrite. There is no mere darkness in the state of grace, but some beam of light, whereby the *kingdom of darkness* wholly prevaileth not.

These things premised, let us know for a trial:

First, if there be any holy fire in us, it is kindled from heaven by the *Father of lights,* who *commanded light to shine out of darkness.* As it is kindled in the use of means, so it is fed. The light in us and the light in the word spring one from the other, and both from one Holy Spirit; and therefore those that regard not the word, it is because there *is no light in them.* Heavenly truths must have a heavenly light to discern them. Natural men see heavenly things, but not in their own proper light, but by an inferior light. God in every converted man putteth a light into the eye of his soul proportionable to the light of truths revealed unto them. A carnal eye will never see spiritual things.

Secondly, the least divine light hath heat with it in some measure. Light in the understanding breedeth heat of love in the affections. In what measure the sanctified understanding seeth a thing to be true or good, in that measure the will embraces it. Weak light breeds weak inclinations; a strong light, strong inclinations. A little spiritual light is of strength enough to answer strong objections of flesh and blood, and to look through all earthly allurements and all opposing hindrances, presenting them as far inferior to those heavenly objects it eyeth.

All light that is not spiritual, because it wanteth the strength of sanctifying grace, it yieldeth to every little temptation, especially when it is fitted and suited to personal inclinations. This is the reason why Christians that have light little for quantity, but yet heavenly for quality, hold out, when men of larger apprehensions sink.

This prevailing of light in the soul is because, together with the spirit of illumination, there goeth in the godly a *spirit of power* to subdue the heart to truth revealed, and to put a taste and relish into the will, suitable to the sweetness of the truths; else a mere natural will will rise against supernatural truths as having an antipathy and enmity against them. In the godly, holy truths are conveyed by way of a taste: gracious men have a spiritual palate as well as a spiritual eye. Grace altereth the relish.

Thirdly, where this heavenly light is kindled, it directeth in the right way. For it is given for that use, to shew us the best way and to guide in the particular passages of life; if otherwise, it is but common light, given only for the good of others. Some have light of knowledge, yet follow not that light, but are guided by carnal reason and policy—such as the Prophet speaks of: *All you that kindle fire, walk in the light of your own fire, and in the sparks that you have kindled, but this you shall have of mine hand, ye shall lie down in sorrow.* God delights to confound carnal wisdom as enmity to him and robbing him of his prerogative, who is God only wise. We must therefore walk by his light and not the blaze of our own fire. *God must light our candle* (Psal. 18:28) or else we are like *to abide in darkness*. . . .

The light that some men have, it is like lightning, which after a sudden flash leaveth them more in darkness. They can love the light as it shines, but hate it as it discovers and directs. A little holy light will enable to keep the word and not to betray religion & deny Christ's name, as Christ speaketh of the Church of Philadelphia (Rev. 3:8).

Fourthly, where this fire is, it will sever things of divers natures & shew a difference between things, as gold and dross. It will sever between flesh and spirit, and shew this is of nature, this of grace. All is not ill in a bad action, or good in a good action. There is gold in ore, which God and his Spirit in us can distinguish. A carnal man's heart is like a dungeon, wherein is nothing to be seen but horror and confusion; this light maketh us judicious, and humble, upon clearer sight of God's purity and our own uncleanness; and maketh us able to discern of the work of the Spirit in another.

Fifthly, so far as a man is spiritual, so far is light delightful unto him, as willing to see anything amiss, that he may reform; and any further service discovered, that he may perform, because he truly hateth ill and loveth good. If he goeth against light discovered, he will soon be reclaimed, because light hath a friendly party within him.

. . .

. . . Spiritual light is distinct; it seeth spiritual good with application to ourselves; but common light is confused, and lets sin lie quiet. Where fire is in any degree, it will fight against the contrary matter. God hath put irreconcilable hatred between *light* and *darkness* at first, so between good and ill, *flesh* and *spirit*. Grace will never join with sin, no more than fire with water. Fire will mingle with no contrary, but preserveth its own purity and is never corrupted as other elements are. Therefore those that plead and plot for liberties of the flesh shew themselves strangers from the life of God. Upon this strife gracious men oft complain that they have no grace, but they contradict themselves in their complaints—as if a man that seeth, should complain he cannot see, or complain that he is asleep—when the very complaint, springing from a displeasure against sin, sheweth that there is something in him opposite to sin. Can a dead man complain? Some things, though bad in themselves, yet discover good, as smoke discovers some fire. Breaking out in the body shews strength of nature. Some infirmities discover more good than some seeming beautiful actions; excess of passion in opposing evil (though not to be justified) yet sheweth a better spirit than a calm temper when there is just cause of being moved. Better it is that the water should run something muddily than not at all. Job had more grace in his distempers than his friends in their seeming wise carriage. Actions soiled with some weaknesses are more accepted than complemental performances.

Fire, where it is in the least measure, is in some degree active; so the least measure of grace is working, as springing from the Spirit of God, which from the working nature of it is compared to fire. Nay, in sins, when there seemeth nothing active but corruption, yet there is a contrary principle, which breaks the force of sin so that it is not *out of measure sinful*, as in those that are carnal. . . .

. . .

Fire turneth all, as much as it can, to fire; so grace maketh a gracious use even of natural and civil things, & doth spiritualize them. What another man doth only civilly, a gracious man will do holily.

Sparks by nature fly upwards; so the spirit of grace carrieth the soul heaven-ward, and setteth before us holy and heavenly aims; as it was kindled from heaven, so it carries us back to heaven. The part followeth the whole. Fire mounteth upward, so every spark to its own element. Where the aim and bent of the soul is God-wards, there is grace, though opposed. The least measure of it is holy desires springing from faith and love, for we cannot desire anything which we do not believe first to be; and the desire of it issues from love. Hence desires are counted a part of the thing desired in some measure: but then they must be, first, constant, for constancy shews that they are supernaturally natural, and not enforced. Secondly, they must be carried to spiritual things, as to believe, to love God, &c., not out of a special exigent (because if now they had grace, they think they might escape some danger), but as a loving heart is carried to the thing loved for some excellency in itself. And thirdly, with desire there is grief when it is hindered, which stirs up to prayer: *Oh that my ways were so directed, that I might keep thy statutes* (Psal. 119:5). *O miserable man that I am, who shall deliver? &c.* [Rom. 7:24]. Fourthly, desires put us onward still, O that I might serve God with more liberty; O that I were more free from these offensive, unsavory, noisome lusts.

Fire worketh itself (if it hath any matter to feed on) into a larger compass and mounteth higher and higher, and the higher it riseth, the purer is the flame. So where true grace is, it groweth in measure and purity. Smoking flax will grow to a flame, and as it increaseth, so it worketh out the contrary and refineth itself more & more. Therefore it argueth a false heart to set ourselves a measure in grace, and to rest in beginnings, alleging that Christ will not quench the smoking flax. But this merciful disposition in Christ is joined with perfect holiness, shewed in perfect hatred to sin; for rather than sin should not have its deserved punishment, himself became a sacrifice for sin, wherein his Father's holiness and his own most of all shined. And besides this, in the work of sanctification, though he favors his work in us, yet favors he not sin in us; for he will never take his hand from his work until he hath taken away sin, even in its very being, from our natures. The same Spirit that purified that blessed mass whereof he was made, cleanseth us by degrees to be suitable to so holy a head, and frameth the judgment and affection of all to whom he sheweth mercy to concur with his own, in laboring to further his ends in abolishing of sin out of our nature.

From the meditations of these rules and signs, much comfort may be brought into the souls of the weakest; which that it may be in the more abundance, let me add something for the helping them over some few ordinary objections and secret thoughts against themselves, which getting within the heart oftentimes keepeth them under.

Some think they have no faith at all because they have no full assurance, when as the fairest fire that can be will have some smoke. The best actions will smell of the smoke. The mortar wherein garlic hath been stamped will always smell of it. So all our actions will savor something of the old man.

. . .

Some again are haunted with hideous representations to their fantasies, and with vile and unworthy thoughts of God, of Christ, of the word, &c., which as busy flies disquiet and molest their peace; these are cast in like wildfire by Satan, as may be discerned by the 1) strangeness, 2) strength and violence, 3) horribleness of them even unto nature corrupt. A pious soul is no more guilty of them than Benjamin of Joseph's cup put into his sack. . . . Shall every sin and blasphemy of man be forgiven, and not these blasphemous thoughts, which have the devil for their father? when Christ himself was therefore molested in this kind, that he might succor all poor souls in the like case?

Some think when they begin once to be troubled with the smoke of corruption more than they were before, therefore they are worse than they were. It is true that corruptions appear now more than before, but they are less. For first, sin, the more it is seen, the more it is hated, and thereupon is the less. Motes are in a room before the sun shines, but they then only appear.

Secondly, contraries, the nearer they are one to another, the sharper is the conflict betwixt them; now of all enemies, the spirit and the flesh are nearest one to another, being both in the soul of a regenerate man, and in all faculties of the soul, and in every action that springeth from those faculties; and therefore it is no marvel the soul (the seat of this battle), thus divided in itself, be as smoking flax.

Thirdly, the more grace, the more spiritual life, and the more spiritual life, the more antipathy to the contrary; whence none are so sensible of corruption as those that have the most living souls.

And fourthly, when men give themselves to carnal liberties, their corruptions trouble them not, as not being bounded and tied up. But when once grace suppresseth their extravagant and licentious excesses, then the flesh boileth (as disdaining to be confined), yet they are better now than they were before. That matter which yields smoke was in the torch before it was lighted, but it is not offensive till the torch begins to burn. Let such know that if the smoke be once offensive to them, it is a sign that there is light. It is better to enjoy the benefit of light, though with smoke, than to be altogether in the dark.

Neither is smoke so offensive, as light is comfortable to us, it yielding an evidence of truth of grace in the heart. Therefore though it be cumbersome in the conflict, yet it is comfortable in the evidence. It is better corruption should offend us now than, by giving way to it, to redeem a little peace with loss of comfort afterwards. Let such therefore as are at variance and odds with their corruptions look upon this text as their portion of comfort.

‡

Since Christ is thus comfortably set out unto us, let us not believe Satan's representations of him. When we are troubled in conscience for our sins, his manner is then to present him to the afflicted soul as a most severe judge armed with justice against us. But then let us present him to our souls as thus offered to our view by God himself, as holding out a scepter of mercy and spreading his arms to receive us. When we think of Joseph, Daniel, John the Evangelist, &c., we frame conceits of them with delight as of mild & sweet persons. Much more when we think of Christ, we should conceive of him as a mirror of all meekness. If the sweetness of all flowers were in one, how sweet must that flower needs be? In Christ all perfections of mercy and love meet; how great then must that mercy be that lodgeth in so gracious a heart? Whatsoever tenderness is scattered in husband, father, brother, head, all is but a beam from him; it is in him in the most eminent manner. We are weak, but we are his; we are deformed, but yet carry his image upon us. A father looks not so much at the blemishes of his child as at his own nature in him; so Christ finds matter of love from that which is his own in us. He sees his own nature in us. We are diseased, but yet his members. Who ever neglected his own members because they were sick or weak? None ever hated his own flesh. Can the head forget the members? Can Christ forget himself? We are his fullness, as he is ours. He was Love itself clothed with man's nature, which he united so near to himself that he might communicate his goodness the more freely unto us. And took not our nature when it was at the best, but when it was abased, with all natural and common infirmities it was subject unto. Let us therefore abhor all suspicious thoughts as either cast in or cherished by that damned spirit, who as he labored to divide between the Father and the Son by jealousies (*If thou beest the Son of God, &c.*), so his daily study is to divide betwixt the Son and us by breeding mispersuasions in us of Christ, as if there were not such tender love in him to such as we are. It was his art from the beginning to discredit God with man by calling God's love into question with our first father, Adam; his success then makes him ready at that weapon still.

[Object.] But for all this, I feel not Christ so to me (saith the smoking flax) but rather the clean contrary: he seemeth to be an enemy unto me. I see and feel evidences of his just displeasure.

[Answ.] Christ may act the part of an enemy a little while, as Joseph did, but it is to make way for acting his own part of mercy in a more seasonable time. He cannot hold in his bowels long; he seemeth to wrastle with us, as with Jacob, but he supplies us with hidden strength at length to get the better. Faith pulls off the vizard from his face and sees a loving heart under contrary appearances. At first he answers the woman of Canaan crying after him, not a word; 2) then gives her a denial; 3) gives an answer tending to her reproach, calling her dog, as being without the covenant; yet she would not be so beaten off, for she considered the end of his coming. As his Father was never nearer him in strength to support him than when he was furthest off in sense of favor to comfort him, so Christ is never nearer us in power to uphold us than when he seemeth most to hide his presence from us. The influence of the sun of righteousness pierceth deeper than his light. In such cases, whatsoever Christ's present carriage is towards us, let us oppose his nature and office against it: he cannot deny himself, he cannot but discharge the office his Father hath laid upon him. We see here the Father hath undertaken that he shall not *quench the smoking flax*, and Christ again undertaken for us to the Father, appearing before him for us, until he presents us blameless before him. The Father hath given us to Christ, and Christ giveth us back again to the Father.

[Object.] This were good comfort if I were but as smoking flax.

[Answ.] It is well that thy objection pincheth upon thyself and not upon Christ; it is well thou givest him the honor of his mercy towards others, though not to thyself; but yet do not wrong the work of his Spirit in thy heart. Satan, as he slandereth Christ to us, so he slandereth us to ourselves. If thou beest not so much as smoking flax, then why dost thou not renounce thy interest in Christ and disclaim the covenant of grace? This thou darest not do. Why dost thou not give up thyself wholly to other contents? This thy spirit will not suffer thee. Whence comes these restless groanings and complaints? Lay this thy present estate together with this office of Christ to such, and do not despise the consolation of the Almighty, nor refuse thy own mercy. Cast thy self into the arms of Christ, and if thou perishest, perish there. If thou dost not, thou art sure to perish. If mercy be to be found anywhere, it is there.

Herein appears Christ's care to thee, that he hath given thee a heart in some degree sensible. He might have given thee up to hardness, security, and profaneness of heart—of all spiritual judgments the greatest. He that died for his enemies; will he refuse those, the desire of whose soul is towards him? He that by his messengers desires us to be reconciled, will he put us off when we earnestly seek it at his hand? No, doubtless. When he prevents us by kindling holy desires in us, he is ready to meet us in his own ways. When the prodigal set himself to return to his father, his father stays not for him but meets him in the way. *When he prepares the heart to seek, he will cause his ear to hear* [Psal. 10:17]. He cannot find in his heart to hide himself long from us. If God should bring us into such a dark condition as that we should see no light from himself or the creature, then let us remember what he saith by the prophet Esay: *He that is in darkness and seeth no light, no light of comfort, no light of God's countenance, yet let him trust in the name of the Lord.* We can never be in such a condition wherein there will be just cause of utter despair; therefore let us do as mariners do: cast anchor in the dark. Christ knows how to pity us in this case. Look what comfort he felt from his Father in his breakings; the like we shall feel from himself in our bruising.

The sighs of a bruised heart carry in them some report, as of our affection to Christ, so of his care to us. The eyes of our souls cannot be towards him but that he hath cast a gracious look upon us first. The least love we have to him is but a reflection of his love first shining upon us. As Christ did in his example whatsoever he gives us in charge to do, so he suffered in his own person whatsoever he calleth us to suffer, that he might the better learn to relieve and pity us in our sufferings. In his desertion in the Garden and upon the Cross, he was content to want that unspeakable solace in the presence of his Father, both to bear the wrath of the Lord for a time for us and likewise to know the better how to comfort us in our greatest extremities. God seeth it fit we should taste of that cup of which his Son drank so deep, that we should feel a little what sin is, and what his Son's love was; but our comfort is that Christ drank the dregs of the cup for us, and will succor us, that our spirits utterly fail not under that little taste of his displeasure which we may feel. He became not only a man, but a curse, a man of sorrows for us. He was broken, that we should not be broken; he was troubled, that we should not be desperately troubled; he became a curse, that we should not be accursed. Whatsoever may be wished for in an all-sufficient Comforter is all to be found in Christ: 1) authority—from the Father all power was given him; 2) strength in himself, as having his name the mighty God; 3) wisdom, and that from his own experience how and when to help; 4) willingness, as being flesh of our flesh & bone of our bone. . . .

‡

And so for the Church in general, by Christ it will have its victory. Christ is that *little stone cut out of the mountain without hands, that breaketh in pieces that goodly image*—that is, all opposite government—until it become *a great mountain and filleth the whole earth* [Dan. 2:35]. So that the stone that was cut out of the mountain becomes a mountain itself at length. Who art thou then, O mountain, that thinkest to stand up against this mountain: all shall lie flat and level before it. He will bring down all mountainous high-exalted thoughts and lay the pride of all flesh low. When chaff strives against the wind, stubble against the fire, when the heel kicks against the pricks,[7] when the potsherd strives with the potter, when man strives against God, it is easy to know on which side the victory will go. The winds may toss the ship wherein Christ is, but not overturn it. The waves may dash against the rock, but they do but break themselves against it.

[Object.] If this be so, why is it thus with the Church of God and with many a gracious Christian? The victory seemeth to go with the enemy.

[Answ.] For answer, remember, 1. God's children usually in their troubles overcome by suffering . . . that herein they may be conformable to Christ, who conquered most when he suffered most. Together with Christ's kingdom of patience, there was a kingdom of power.

2. This victory is by degrees, and therefore they are too hasty-spirited that would conquer so soon as they strike the first stroke, and be at the end of their race at the first setting forth. The Israelites were sure of victory in their voyage to Canaan, yet they must fight it out. God would not have us presently forget what cruel enemies Christ hath overcome for us . . . that so by the experience of that annoyance {harm} we have by them, we might be kept in fear to come under the power of them.

---

[7] {A goad for driving cattle; chiefly in figurative context with allusion to Acts 9:5, *to kick against the pricks* (*OED*).}

3. That God often worketh by contraries: when he means to give victory, he will suffer us to be foiled first; when he means to comfort, he will terrify first; when he means to justify, he will condemn us first; whom he means to make glorious, he will abase first. A Christian conquers even when he is conquered: when he is conquered by some sins, he gets victory over others more dangerous, as spiritual pride, security, &c.

4. That Christ's work both in the Church and in the hearts of Christians often goeth backward that it may go the better forward. As seed rots in the ground in the winter time but after comes better up, and the harder the winter, the more flourishing the spring; so we learn to stand by falls, and get strength by weakness discovered. We take deeper root by shaking, and, as torches, flame brighter by moving. Thus it pleaseth Christ out of his freedom, in this manner to maintain his government in us. Let us herein labor to exercise our faith that it may answer Christ's manner of carriage towards us: when we are foiled, let us believe we shall overcome; when we are fallen, let us believe we shall rise again. Jacob, after he had a *blow upon which he halted,* yet *would not give over wrastling* till he had gotten the blessing; so let us never give over, but in our thoughts knit the beginning, progress, and end together, and then we shall see ourselves in heaven, out of the reach of all enemies. Let us assure ourselves that God's grace, even in this imperfect estate, is stronger than man's free will in the state of first perfection, and it is founded now in Christ, who as he is the author, so will be *the finisher of our faith.* We are under a more gracious covenant.

Hereupon it followeth that weakness may stand with the assurance of salvation. The disciples, notwithstanding all their weaknesses, are bidden to *rejoice* that their names are written in heaven. Failings (with conflict) in sanctification should not weaken the peace of our justification and assurance of salvation. It mattereth not so much what ill is in us, as what good; not what corruptions, but how we stand affected to them; not what our particular failings be, so much as what is the thread and tenor of our lives: for Christ's mislike of that which is amiss in us redounds not to the hatred of our person but to the victorious subduing of all our infirmities.

Some have after conflict wondered at the goodness of God, that so little and shaking faith should have upheld them in so great combats, when Satan had almost catched them. And indeed it is to be wondered, how much a little grace will prevail with God for acceptance, and over our enemies for victory, if the heart be upright. Such is the goodness of our sweet Savior, that he delighteth still to shew his strength in our weakness.

><>~<>~<><

TEXT: EEBO (STC [2nd ed.] / 22479)

Richard Sibbes, *The bruised reed, and smoking flax. Some sermons contracted out of the 12. of Matth. 20. At the desire, and for the good of weaker Christians* (London: Printed [by M. Flesher] for R. Dawlman, 1630), 1–45, 76–108, 113–30, 160–75, 248–56.

THE LITTLE GIDDING STORY[1] BOOKS
Christmastide, 1631

Little Gidding was a religious community, an experimental fusion of manor house and monastery, founded in 1625 when an elderly widow, Mary Ferrar, along with her daughter and two sons, their spouses, and a dozen or so children, moved into an abandoned rural estate in Huntingdonshire and set about repairing the chapel, which had last been used as a pigsty. The sons, John and Nicholas, had both been MPs and key players in the Virginia Company. The latter is by far the best-known member of the Little Gidding community, in part because we have John's biographical sketch of his brilliant and saintly younger brother. A graduate (BA 1610) and fellow of Clare Hall, where he formed a life-long friendship with his tutor Augustine Lindsell, the future Laudian bishop of Peterborough, Nicholas left Cambridge for the Continent in 1613, spending the next four years travelling and studying in Italy, France, Germany, and Spain. In 1617 he returned to his parents' home, where his niece Mary Collett was already living. Turning down a geometry professorship at Gresham College, Nicholas joined John on the board of the Virginia Company during the tumultuous years leading to its dissolution in 1624. The proto-republican opposition leader, Sir Edwin Sandys, was another major player in the Company, and a close friend (he later donated a silver flagon to the Little Gidding chapel); he and Nicholas jointly led the Commons' drive against the royal minister, Lionel Cranfield, in the 1624 Parliament. The next year Nicholas retired from public life to the remote manor he purchased with his mother's dower, the rest of the family soon following. In order to serve the community's liturgical and spiritual needs,[2] in early 1626 Nicholas was ordained deacon in Westminster Abbey; William Laud, then bishop of St. David's, officiated, with Lindsell in attendance.

From 1625 until his death in 1637, Nicholas oversaw the quasi-monastic rule of life at Little Gidding, a rule that he himself had largely crafted. Together with John, he also

---

[1] "Story" here (and in early modern English generally) means history or narrative, not fiction.

[2] A deacon could lead morning and evening prayer; a layman could not.

worked hand-in-glove with George Herbert to restore the nearby parish church of Leighton Bromswold. At his death, Herbert entrusted Nicholas with the manuscript of *The Temple* to publish or burn at his discretion. Having chosen the former option, Nicholas successfully battled the press licenser, who initially denied permission to print unless a single line, which he found suspect, were changed or cut. The manuscript was printed without alteration.

Although John Ferrar's life of Nicholas foregrounds his brother's role in ordering and guiding the Little Gidding community, contemporary observers (particularly the hostile ones) tended to comment on its female government. A 1641 puritan libel terms it an "Arminian nunnery," and Thomas Fuller notes that many viewed the place as an "embryo nunnery, suspecting that there was a pope Joan therein" (Mayor 76n). Writing from a more sympathetic vantage point, a visitor to Little Gidding described how "the 9 or 10 young women, most of them daughters of John and Susanna Collett, always wore black stuff, all of one grave fashion, always the same, with comely veils on their heads. They were curious at their needles, and they made their scissors to serve the altar or the poor. They were fine surgeons, and they kept by them all manner of salves, oils, and balsams . . . None of them were nice of[3] dressing with their own hands poor people's wounds, were they never so offensive. . . . And together with helps for the body the virgins were expert and ready to administer good counsels, prayers, and comforts to their patients for their souls' health" (Sharland xxvi).

The Little Gidding women make up five of the six principals in the dialogues reprinted below: Susanna Collett (1581–1657), Nicholas' sister and senior by nearly two decades, plus four of her daughters: Hester and Margaret, who were probably in their late teens, and their older sisters Mary (1601–80) and Anna (1603–38), whom Maycock, writing in 1963, considered "two of the most saintly women who have ever adorned the Church of England" (178). Their relationship with Nicholas was particularly close: his dying words addressed "his most dearly beloved nieces, Mary and Anna, whom he most entirely loved" (Muir and White 117 ¶203); an old family friend noted that Nicholas held "the framing of his virgin nieces" to have been his life's "masterpiece" (Muir and White 39). Nicholas' letters to Anna begin, "My daughter in the best and dearest of fatherhood" and "Mine own dear child"; he salutes Mary as "Sister of my soul," and she replies "My most faithful friend and dear father"; "Father of my soul, faithful friend" (Blackstone 249, 258, 271–74).

The community, with its female majority, numbered about thirty persons: the extended Ferrar-Collett family; schoolteachers for Latin, mathematics, "writing fair hands," and music; four poor women for whom a suite of rooms in the manor house had been set aside; and miscellaneous young people there for an education. Between 50 and 100 children came every Sunday for church, a free dinner, and to receive a penny for each Psalm memorized. The main house included the Concordance Room, where Nicholas and the elder Collett sisters created and bound exquisitely designed and illustrated biblical harmonies. These were originally designed for use within the community, but their fame spread quickly, the King requesting one for himself, with others going to Prince Charles,

---

[3] squeamish about

Herbert, and Laud. In another part of the house, an infirmary served the community as well as the family. Three times a week twenty gallons of gruel were distributed to the hungry, and each weekday morning poor persons could come to request assistance. There were other sorts of visitors as well. Richard Crashaw, a regular guest, was particularly close to Mary Collett, whom he viewed as his spiritual mother. Twice, King Charles came, the last time as a fugitive. Izaak Walton described the community as resembling an Oxbridge college, but it also bore the impress of the Catholic foundations Nicholas had encountered in Italy—of his desire to adapt these "to adorn our Protestant religion, by a right renouncing the world with all its profits and honors, in a true crucifying the flesh, with all its pleasures, by continued temperance, fasting, and watching unto prayers" (Muir and White 96 ¶145). It is for the prayers and watching that Little Gidding is best known: the thrice-daily Prayer Book services in the chapel—beautifully and simply adorned with flowers, herbs, candles, the communion table covered with "carpets of blue silk embroidered with gold"—the brief hourly daytime prayers in the Great Chamber, the night watches where, at opposite ends of the house, two men and two women each night knelt and prayed through the Psalter, either reciting it antiphon-style or softly singing to an organ.

✣

The Collett daughters (the "maiden sisters"), their mother Susanna, and their uncles John and Nicholas made up the "Little Academy": the group that met in the Sisters' Chamber between early 1631 and 1634 to discuss medieval and modern history, Christian ethics, and theology. These colloquies were taken down in shorthand and later written up in exquisite manuscripts known in the family as the Story Books. The sheer intelligence of these colloquies, plus their proto-feminist "quilting-party" format, make them candidates for the single most important corpus of women's literature in English from ca. 1400 to 1650. Feminist scholarship, however—indeed (with one exception) recent scholarship *tout court*—has wholly ignored this material.[4] They ignored it because from the late seventeenth century through the mid-twentieth, most accounts of the Story Books credit them to Nicholas: an early manuscript terms them "ascetic conversations . . . [spoken] by the seven virgin ladies . . . first drawn up for their use by their *Visitor*, the pious Mr. Nicholas Ferrar" (Mayor 294); Samuel Jebb, writing in the eighteenth century, seems to have viewed the Story Books as play-scripts, which Nicholas "compiled and wrote . . . to be transcribed by the actors that had parts in them" (Mayor 275). Sharland, who edited the first printed volume (1899), describes the colloquies as "discourses in the Platonic way" (xli), that is, as *fictional* dialogues; the introduction to the second printed volume of the Story Books (1938) treats Nicholas under the subhead, "The Writer."[5]

Nicholas probably translated the stories (e.g., the narratives concerning Gennadius, Ficino, and Agaton reprinted below), although Mary seems to have known Latin, and perhaps the other women did as well. (The community had a Latin master in 1625, when the only boys at Little Gidding were under six.) Since Nicholas was famously good at shorthand and, although often referred to as present, says nothing, it seems reasonable to

---

[4] The exception is the opening chapter of Barbour's *Literature and religious culture*, which is where I learned of the volumes' existence.

[5] Sharland xli; Blackstone xi; see also Muir and White 5, 17; Mayor 275.

assume that he served as the regular note-taker.[6] He clearly contributes the Story Books' opening mission-statement *<infra>*, as well as the occasional aside. Yet every shred of evidence points to the Story Books having a collaborative, and largely female, authorship. First, as Muir and White observed in 1996, "the best reason for believing his [Nicholas'] contribution" to have been fairly limited "is the total absence of any reference to the Little Academy" in John Ferrar's life of his brother. Given John's lovingly detailed picture of "Nicholas' arrangements for the well-being and education of the different members of the community, it seems impossible he should have omitted such an important matter if it had been primarily Nicholas' idea or if he had indeed composed the stories or directed the conversation" (18).

The family letters mentioning the Story Books likewise never imply that Nicholas is the sole or primary author. On February 2, 1632, Anna and Mary presented their grand-mother with a manuscript of the first year's colloquies prefaced by their cover-letter, which calls the volume "the first fruits of our labors." The two young women thank Mrs. Ferrar for the loan of her best room "for the performance of this" (where "this" refers both to the spoken colloquies and the written transcript) and gratefully acknowledge that to her they owe "even the very abilities themselves that are in us towards the performance of this or any other good thing." When Mrs. Ferrar writes back to Mary and Anna, she thanks them for "your book." On the same day, Mary and Anna also write to their married sister, Susanna Maplethorp, submitting the manuscript to the judgment of her minister-husband, "beseeching him to give us notice of what he there shall find amiss," a request that would be inconceivable were Nicholas the real author. That he was not, Nicholas' own letter to Susanna makes clear, for he tells his eldest niece that he gladly gives her his part, "as your sisters have done theirs of this book" (Sharland li-lv). The manuscript, like the colloquies themselves, was a collaborative endeavor, although, as "our labors" and "your book" imply, primarily the work of the maiden sisters. Indeed, their role seems to have been common knowledge at the time. In October of 1631, several months before the let-ters just mentioned, Arthur Woodnoth—a Ferrar relative and close family friend—wrote Nicholas that if each of his cousins (i.e., the maiden sisters) would send Mrs. Herbert "one of their stories, I conceive it would be received with very great acceptation; this I have all but promised, and it was the last thing Mr. Herbert put me in mind of" (Blackstone 268–69). Arthur's "their stories," like Mrs. Ferrar's "your book," assign the intellectual property rights in the Story Books to the maiden sisters—an assignment implicit in the fact that the stories, although requested by George Herbert, were to be sent to Jane.

The selections from the Story Books that follow include Nicholas' preface, dated Feb-ruary 2, 1631; a fragment from the December 29, 1631, meeting of the Little Academy on whether disembodied souls, which lack sense-organs, are capable of perception; and a longer extract from a later session that same Christmastide dealing with patience. All

---

[6] He does speak in the 1634 colloquies, where it would seem that the four participants take turns as scribes (each "portion" of the conversation involves at most three speakers; one person is always silent, and when he or she rejoins the discussion, another member drops out). The writing-master may also have filled in during times when Nicholas was away from Little Gidding.

three passages come from the first of the five extant Story Book manuscripts, the manuscript given Mrs. Ferrar on February 2, 1632.

Both Christmastide sessions follow the Little Academy's usual format: a mix of narrative and conversation on a set theme, with one of the participants guiding the discussion. The stories told in these two sessions are likewise characteristic: the Agaton narrative comes from Heribert Rosweyde's 1615 *Vitæ patrum, sive, historiæ eremiticæ libri decem*, "one of the best-read books in the library at Little Gidding" (Maycock 219); the dream of Gennadius from Augustine's Epistle 159;[7] the Ficino-anecdote probably from Baronius.[8] Most of the Little Academy's stories come from the desert fathers of Egypt and Syria, medieval histories, and post-Reformation Catholic writers (J. A. de Thou, François de Sales), but a story about Zwingli presents him as a champion of Christian orthodoxy (Blackstone 134–35).[9] One would not know from the Story Books that the Reformation had occurred, nor the Great Schism.

The discussions have an unusual reflective intensity: the topic of future "rewards and punishments" announced at the outset of the December 29th session leads instantly to epistemic considerations: "how it can be that there should be any sensible apprehension of things when the senses are dissolved with the body's corruption in the grave." The session on patience grapples with the limits of rational ethics, with the morality of discipline and punishment, with the possibility that "either God knows not, or cared not, for the things done on earth." Equally striking is the participants' skepticism regarding cultural codes, traditional practices, and the conventional norms of their own social class: their suspicion of most of what they "received by tradition from our fathers" and their determination to weigh "those opinions and practices which the world recommends or disallows" in the scales of right reason and Scripture. We tend to associate such views with Milton's *Areopagitica* and Civil War radicalism, not pious Laudian ladies; the Little Academy's stance—which, moreover, has much in common with Hales' "Of inquiry and private judgment in religion" <*infra*>—suggests a rather more complex picture.

Although the Little Academy seems untouched by the Reformation, the ongoing religious warfare on the Continent exerts a steady, if unspoken, pressure on their discussions. The celebration of patience as true Christian fortitude—another Miltonic parallel, although the classification of patience under fortitude goes back at least to Aquinas—belongs to the rethinking of heroism that Reid Barbour sees as at once the leitmotif of the Story Books and the defining cultural project of the 1630s, both responding to the catastrophe and carnage of the Thirty Years War. The celebration of patience also targets the aristocratic honor code and its attendant violence.[10] Moreover, the harshness of the

---

[7] www.newadvent.org/fathers/1102159.htm (accessed September 24, 2010).

[8] Hugh James Rose, et al., *A new general biographical dictionary*, 12 vols. (London, 1850–57), 7:366.

[9] Foxe's *Acts and monuments* was the favorite book of Mrs. Ferrar; a portion was read aloud at Little Gidding each Sunday evening.

[10] Prior to 1620, James' sole censorship edict was a proclamation outlawing reports of duels because these, the King maintained, merely served to continue the quarrel; Charles sought to stop gentlemen from killing each other by resurrecting the Court of Chivalry, which turned out to be a very costly mistake. See Jennifer Low, *Manhood and the duel: masculinity in early modern drama and culture* (Palgrave Macmillan, 2003); Mark Peltonen, *The duel in early modern England* (Cambridge UP, 2003); George Squibb, *The High Court of Chivalry: a study of the civil law in England* (Clarendon, 1959); Charles Mackay, *Extraordinary popular delusions and the madness of crowds* (1841; rpt. Templeton Foundation Press, 1999), 658–81.

Little Academy's critique—the condemnation of chivalric romance, as well as its equally dour take on lapdogs, alehouses, Christmas feasts, and ladies-in-waiting—has a distinctly puritan ring, as does its conviction that early Stuart England was not, in any meaningful sense, a Christian culture, so that the pursuit of holiness entailed breaking with prevailing customs, conventions, and pastimes. Yet, although the difference is at most one of degree, the Little Academy tends to construe moral goodness less as honoring God by obeying his commandments than as seeking the good of others and oneself. The Little Academy does not object to literature on the grounds of paganism, idolatry, or sensuality; it denounces *The Faerie Queene* and *La Gerusalemme liberata* for using a patina of Christianity to gild their inculcation of revenge. Moreover, despite the participants' commitment to the specifically Christian virtues of forbearance, humility, and patient suffering, their basic framework remains that of classical virtue-ethics, eudemonism, and the care of the self:[11] one strives for patience because it affords "excellency both of strength and happiness." So too, the extraordinary discussion of women's work with which the session on patience concludes centers on the question of whether early modern England affords women any role not "utterly unworthy the dignity of man's nature[12] . . . [and] those noble faculties of the will and reason that were made for contemplations and pursuit of heavenly affairs."

Two final, and related, points deserve mention. First, John Ferrar's attempt to explain his sudden recognition that toleration may be a bad thing—that it is our duty (often a hideously difficult duty) to reprehend sin, especially the sins of those for whom we are accountable—captures quite forcefully a basic premise of Laudian rule. Second, his observation that most of his contemporaries preferred a live-and-let-live toleration of "all manner of impiety that is not to their own prejudice," finding "zeal" as objectionable as the wrong-doing it sought to correct, would seem to imply that by the 1630s most Englishpersons were already Millian liberals, happy to extend laissez-faire toleration to the self-regarding conduct of their neighbors.[13] To the extent that John's assessment is accurate, the modern position seems less a novel insight than the triumph of the secular values of the average seventeenth-century gentleman over the Christian idealism of the priest and puritan.

Sources: *ODNB*; Reid Barbour, *Literature and religious culture in seventeenth-century England* (Cambridge UP, 2002); A. L. Maycock, *Nicholas Ferrar of Little Gidding* (SPCK, 1963); J. E. B. Mayor, ed., *Cambridge in the seventeenth century*, part 1: *Nicholas Ferrar: two lives by his brother John and by Doctor Jebb* (Cambridge UP, 1855); Lynette Muir and John White, eds., *Materials for the life of Nicholas Ferrar* (Leeds Philosophical and Literary Society, 1996).

The manuscript Little Gidding Story Books appeared in print between 1899 and 1970 in three volumes: 1) E. Cruwys Sharland, ed. *The Story Books of Little Gidding: being the religious dialogues recited in the Great Room, 1631–32* (New York: Dutton, 1899); 2) *The Ferrar papers*, ed. B. Blackstone (Cambridge UP, 1938); and 3) A. M. Williams, ed., *Conversations at Little Gidding . . . dialogues by members of the Ferrar family* (Cambridge UP, 1970).

[11] Alasdair MacIntyre, *After virtue: a study in moral theory* (Notre Dame UP, 1981); Michel Foucault, *The care of the self*, trans. Robert Hurley (Vintage, 1990).

[12] I.e., human nature—as the context makes clear.

[13] See John Stuart Mill, "On liberty" (1859). See www.constitution.org/jsm/liberty.htm (accessed June 7, 2012).

THE LITTLE GIDDING STORY BOOKS

The story books of Little Gidding: being the religious dialogues recited in the Great Room[1]
1631–32

BOOK I
THE FEAST OF THE PURIFICATION,
1631

Formation and design of the Little Academy.

It was the same day wherein the Church celebrates that great Festival of the Purification that the Maiden Sisters, longing to be imitators of those glorious Saints by whose names they were called (for all bare Saints' names, and she that was elected CHIEF, that of the Blessed Virgin Mary), having entered into a joint covenant between themselves and some others of nearest blood (which according to their several relations they styled FOUNDER, GUARDIAN, and VISITOR) for the performance of divers religious exercises, lest, as sweet liquors are oftentimes corrupted by the sourness of the vessels wherein they are infused, there should arise in their hearts a distaste or abuse of those excellent things which they purposed, they therefore resolved, together with the practice of devotion, to

---

[1] The Participants in the 1631 Christmastide Dialogues

Mary Ferrar
(1550–1634)
Mother, Founder, Grandmother

Susanna Collet (1581–1637)	John Ferrar (1590–1657)	Nicholas Ferrar (1592–1637)
Moderator	*Guardian*	*Visitor*
Mary Collet (1601–80)		
Chief		
Anna Collet (1603–38)		
Patient		
Hester Collet (m. 1635)		
Cheerful		
Margaret Collet (m. 1636)		
Affectionate		

intermingle the study of wisdom, searching and enquiring diligently into the knowledge of those things which appertain to their condition and sex.

Finding in themselves, and observing in others that do sincerely pursue virtue, that the greatest bar of perfection was ignorance of the truth, whereby through misapprehension many prejudicial things were embraced, and many most behoveful to their ends and most delightful in performance were not only neglected but abhorred; which, having by many particulars experimented[2] in themselves, doubting[3] that they were alike abused in most of those things which we have received by Tradition from our Fathers, they determined with firm promises each to other to make a particular survey of those opinions and practices which the world recommends or disallows, weighing them not in the scales of common judgment, but of true and right reason according to the weights and by the standard of the Scripture; wherein being excellently versed, so as they were able to repeat by heart both the book of Psalms and most part of the New Testament, they found that there was neither action nor opinion that could be propounded but might receive a clear solution and direction from that book.

Wherefore, not upon presumption of their own abilities, but on confidence of God's gracious assistance to their humble and diligent endeavors, they agreed every day at a set hour to confer together of some such subject as should tend either to the information of the understanding or to the exciting of the affections, to the more ready and fervent prosecution of virtues and better performance of all such duties as in their present or other course of life hereafter should be required of them.

‡

VII
CHRISTMASTIDE, 1631, DECEMBER 29th

Though earthly things (said the Chief) to them that are unexperienced seem full of happiness, yet to those that have made any small trial they are found so full of insufficiency that most men perhaps would be easily persuaded to call back their affections if they knew where else to place them; but now because love cannot but work, and desire pursue something, there seems to most men a kind of necessity imposed on them to follow that which they see here below, because those things that are above, being far removed out of sight, they can scarce be persuaded that they are at all. The inevidency of the things after this life breeds a doubt in most men's minds of the certainty whether they be or no.[4] And the affections, that, like the conclusion, follow the weaker part, thinking it ground enough to be cold in the love of what they have not known and in the fear of what they have not seen, spend all their strength in the embracing or avoiding of the good or evil that falls under their senses. Further than they reach few men will adventure, holding it great folly to leave the hold of what we have in our hands for the apprehension of that which is represented unto us in hope.

---

[2] {experienced}

[3] {suspecting}

[4] {On the certainty of evidence, or lack thereof, regarding spiritual realities, see Laud <388, 390–91>; also Shuger, "Faith and assurance."}

It will be, therefore, in my opinion, sweet companions, most profitable to carry up our thoughts, that are amated[5] with the wretchedness of this world, to the meditation of those better things in heaven by the recompting of some such story as may tend to the confirmation of our mutual vows touching the despising of all which the world tenders unto us now for the love of that which faith promiseth us hereafter to enjoy.

What an absurdity seems it to flesh and blood to put a man's self to certain pain here in expectation of future joy or to defy present for the dread of after torment.

To take away this perplexity there's nothing more effectual than the remembrance of those proofs which GOD hath sometimes extraordinarily given of the certainty and largeness both of the rewards and punishments that shall crown good or evil actions. I pray, therefore, let this day's stories be to this effect. But let them be such as may suit with the excellency and dignity of our former discourses. And because that all men's minds, when they enter into these meditations, do first stumble at the very entrance of the other world—that is, how it can be that there should be any sensible apprehension of things when the senses are dissolved with the body's corruption in the grave—I pray you, dear PATIENT, to remove this block by the recompting of that admirable passage which our VISITOR lately told us out of St. Augustine, if I mistake not.

You mistake not at all (replied the PATIENT), for it was St. Augustine that recounts it in a certain letter which he wrote to one Evodius. This particular I afterwards learned, for the excellency of the matter made me curious to inform myself more fully of it.

You did therein (replied the AFFECTIONATE) answerably to that good discretion which you use in all other matters. The knowledge of these circumstances not only gives much satisfaction to the hearers, but adds authority to the relation itself. But, I pray you, proceed, for our desires brook no delay. You shall have it (said the PATIENT), neither of mine, nor of any other's composing, but in the very words of St. Augustine himself, for so did our VISITOR, giving me the story in writing, advise, if ever occasion were, I should recompt it.[6]

Our brother Gennadius, famous amongst all and very dear to us, that now lives a physician at Carthage and was highly esteemed for his skill at Rome, is, as thou knowest, a very devout man, most bountiful in the free disposition of his mind and of unwearied mercifulness touching the care of the poor. Nevertheless, as himself lately related, when he was a young man and very fervent in those kind of alms-deeds, he fell into a doubtfulness whether there were indeed any other life after death. Now GOD, no way purposing to desert this mind of his and these works of mercy, there appeared unto him in sleep a young man very conspicuous and regardful, and said unto him: "Follow me." Whom whilest Gennadius followed, he came unto a certain city from the right hand part whereof he began to hear the sound of music most delectable beyond all usual or known sweetness. And whilest he was musing what it might be, the other told him that they were the hymns of blessed men and saints. What he reported to have seen on the left hand, I now remember not. In the end Gennadius awaketh and his dream

[5] {cast down}

[6] {What follows is a translation of Augustine's letter 159, written ca. 415; a modern translation can be found at www.newadvent.org/fathers/1102159.htm. I have added the quotation marks.}

departed, and he thought no more of the person than of the dream. But behold another night the same young man comes to him again and demands whether he knew him. Gennadius made answer, he knew him full well. The other asked him where he had known him. Gennadius his memory was not wanting what to answer, but with as great facility as things freshly done, remembered both all the vision and those hymns of the saints which he came to the hearing by his guidance. Whereupon the other asked whether he had seen those things which he now related in sleep or waking. Gennadius answered, "In sleep." "You say right," replied the other; "you saw them in your sleep; but know that what thou now seest thou likewise seest in thy sleep." Gennadius hearing this believed it to be so, and by his acknowledgement confirmed it. Then he that taught the man added further, saying, "Where is now thy body?" "In my chamber," said he. "And dost thou know," replied the other, "that those eyes in thy body are now bound up, shut and silent, and thou seest nothing at all with them?" To which Gennadius, not knowing what to answer, became mute. Whereupon the other, in this perplexity, took the hint to open unto him that which he had intended to reach by these former questions, and immediately said: "And those eyes of thy flesh are now altogether still in this sleep on thy bed without any manner of operation, and yet, nevertheless, are the selfsame with which thou now lookest on me and usest in this vision. So likewise, when thou shall be dead, the eyes of thy flesh ceasing from all work, there shall yet remain a life to thee whereby thou shall live, and a sense by which thou shall be sensible. Take heed, therefore, that thou doubt no more whether there be any life after death." By this means, that faithful man affirms, his doubtfulness was removed.

Who, instructing him about the providence and mercy of God (for he was so taught by a natural instance), yet his mind being illuminated by the brightness of heavenly grace, he was changed, as the Apostle speaketh, from glory to glory, even as by the Spirit of the Lord.[7]

The Patient having finished her story, the Cheerful began.—

‡

The company was about to dissolve, when the Guardian staying them with the sign of his hand, spake thus. . . . There's no surfeiting in this kind of feast. Let us therefore, I beseech you, sit down again, and receive those further dainties which the Chief's bounty intendeth to the perfecting of this day's work, that it may every ways be a complete piece.

I understand (said the Chief), most honored Guardian, and hope to satisfy your desires. You expect that, according to the wise householder's practice in the Gospel, bringing out both new and old things out of his treasure, these elder miracles should be confirmed and set forth by some further examples of later times.

You so well know my thoughts, dearest Chief (said the Guardian), that you have much better expressed them than I myself could have done.

---

[7] {The first part of this sentence paraphrases the conclusion of Augustine's telling of Gennadius' dream: "By whom was he taught this but by the merciful, providential care of God?"}

The proof of having taken so right aim (said the CHIEF) at your intention makes me the rather hope to hit the mark which you desire. If you do but believe it true, you cannot esteem it less wonderful than any you have yet heard. And that you may believe it to be true, you shall know that it is not only confidently written in serious works of most famous men, but hath been often by very discreet and religious persons delivered in the pulpits of Italy as an undoubted truth received at first from the relation of those whose fidelity and wisdom was above all suspicion either of deceiving others or being deceived themselves.[8]

Marsilius Ficinius, the oracle of his times for learning, had a dear friend and companion in the selfsame studies of philosophy, named Michael Mercatus, to whom, amongst his works, there is extant an epistle full of excellent matter touching the eternity of GOD and the immortality of men's souls. One time, amongst their philosophical discourses happening to fall upon the consideration of those things which follow after the determination of this life, finding a greater perplexity according to the principles of philosophy (though they both followed that which is far the best, Plato's school) than they could well explicate—and perhaps even in this regard the rather by God's just award entangled in this labyrinth of human reason, because they had attributed too much thereunto—they in the end grew to a covenant, and confirmed it with solemn oath, that he that first should die of them two would, if it might be, give the other notice of his estate.

A long time passed after this, and a large separation by distance of place between them. But in the end, as Michael Mercatus one morning very early was deep in his philosophical speculations, he hears afar off the noise of a horse running very swiftly, and at last, upon a stopping under his window, the well-known voice of friend Marsilius calling out aloud, Oh Michael, Michael, those things are true, they are true indeed! At this, with much astonishment, Michael starts up, but his speed was far slower than Marsilius, who before the other could thrust his head out of the window, had turned about his horse and was now upon a swift pace departing. But though he saw not his face, yet by that which he saw, he knew him perfectly to be the man whose voice he heard, only his habit was far different, all white, and of the same color was his horse. Michael followed him with his voice, doubling the name of Marsilius. But he answered not. He followed him with his eyes, but those were immediately likewise disappointed by the other's vanishing. When wonderment had given way to other thoughts, he gave present order to enquire touching Marsilius, whom in the end he understood the very selfsame hour that he appeared unto him to have departed this life at Florence.[9] You desire to know; I'll tell you what followed, and with that, as it will be to the confirmation of the truth of this fact, so it may be to the impression of the like affections and resolutions in our minds.

---

[8] {The same episode is recounted in chapter 3 of Wolfgang Eder's *Die andere Welt: das ist dass nach disem zeitlichen ein anderes, und zwar ewiges, immerwehrendes Leben seye* (Munich, 1694), which cites Baronius as its source. Nicholas Ferrar, however, had been in Italy ca. 1614–16 and so could have heard "very discreet and religious persons" recounting the story there.}

[9] {See Field <81>, whose distinction between the state of souls at the moment of death and once adjudged to heaven or hell leaves room for this apparition of the (presumably) heaven-bound Marsilius within a Protestant framework (which, of course, does not generally allow for ghostly sightings, since ghosts traditionally were purgatorial spirits, and Protestants denied the existence of purgatory.}

Though Michael was a man of that goodness which, because we cannot find in our present times, we attribute to the old world, though he had led a life not only full of innocency, but of much benefit to others, as a true philosopher should do, yet from that day, sending a bill of divorce to all his former studies of learning, he applied himself only to learn Christ Jesus crucified; and the remainder of his days was altogether spent in the preparation for that better life which is to succeed the short and miserable ages on earth, and he dies more famous for devotion than he lived ever honored for learning, and yet therein, by the common vote of this world, he was not second to any.

This was the conclusion of this day's stories . . .

‡

CHRISTMASTIDE, 1631

The next day falling to the Patient's turn, the absence of the Master[10] and the removal of the provisions necessary for the music giving notice that it was not that day to be expected, she began to the excuse thereof in this manner:

The want of your wonted music—whilst I am so poor not only in skill but in good hap as I cannot find a song any ways answerable to your present action—gives you opportunity (most honored Grandmother and worthy Company) by the gentle passing over this wrongful disappointment of your justly expected pleasure through my defect, to exercise that virtue of patience which falls to be the matter of this day's consideration.

The happy agreement of your practice in this thing to your name, dear Patient (said the Chief), causeth sweeter melody than any voice or instrument could do. We want not music therefore, though we have it not in the ear, that have so much delight in our hearts through the harmony that is made by the sweet concent[11] of your disposition and actions to that which is the subject of our intended discourse. Yourself are an example of that patience which you are to speak of. This is the noblest music that can sound in mine, and I am sure in all others' opinions.

What I am (said the Patient) in this respect is God's grace; and what I want (and that is infinitely more than what I have attained touching this virtue) is my own fault.

Well (said the Guardian), in the country of the blind he that hath but half an eye is king. Our general imperfections make us all think you are proceeded far in the grace, for which we as truly bless God as we heartily desire to be partakers of the same. But I hope, that though you are not furnished with music, yet you have in supply thereof provided some other kind of antepast for us. If we cannot have a song, let us have (as the old proverb is) some good saying, I pray, to begin with, touching this matter of patience, in knowledge whereof I confess myself to be a stranger, as well as in the practice, having all my life long till of late been persuaded that patience was not a virtue to be sought for, but only for necessity to be accepted when a man could not choose; not to be desired when a man might shift it.

---

[10] {presumably the music master, one of the three instructors resident at Little Gidding}
[11] {harmony, concord}

You say very true (said the CHIEF), that's the world's doctrine and language: when a man cannot put away sufferings in any kind, then he is advised to put on patience.[12] You must be content to have patience, say the wise friends of this world. But to be so in love with patience as a man should gladly undergo grief and evil when it comes, for the exercise thereof, is an argument of a crazed brain and of a cowardly heart in most men's judgments, and yet is the plain and constant doctrine of the Blessed LORD by whose name we are honored,[13] and of all his holy apostles, that there is more excellency both of strength and happiness in patient enduring of evil than in the prosperous enjoyment of all the good things in the world. And therefore St. James wills to count it when we fall into divers temptations, only for this reason, because it works patience, which, if it may have its free and full operation, will work us perfect and complete both in grace and glory, so that there shall be nothing wanting either in body or in soul even in this life on earth, not only in that which is to come in Heaven. Let patience have her perfect work, that ye may be perfect and entire, wanting nothing {James 1:4}.

Oh, the wretched mistake of my blind affections, that in the pursuit of virtue and happiness have ever avoided and impugned that which would have given the greatest furtherance to what they pretended unto!

I thought the exercise of patience a burden that would tire out my strength, a block that encumbered the way and made me stumble, and made me fall; and therefore thought even impatience itself, in removing of that which was offensive, to have been a piece of wisdom, a practice of goodness. That nobody should cross me, that nothing should be contrary to my mind, was that which I supposed most just to desire, most profitable to endeavor. I see mine error, I feel my loss. I thank my GOD, that hath given me this timely warning. By his grace, henceforward patience shall be my study, the attainment of it in my prayers, the exercise of it my joy, mine honor, and my happiness. Say, LORD, Amen to these purposes, to these protestations, which thou hast now put into my mouth and heart.

We second you with our prayers (said the CHEERFUL) and hope we shall second you with the like resolutions and endeavor not to seek so much for an uncontrolled satisfaction of our desires, as for a patient sufferance of what shall happen contrary to them. The last is far the more easy condition to be attained, and surely the more excellent, the patient man being every way better and more happy than the prosperous—a mystery which, I confess with you, to have been long ignorant of, and now with you coming to the knowledge, I hope I shall, by God's assistance, with you proceed in the careful practice thereof, the great offences which my erring judgment had conceived against this heavenly grace having been by God's mercy not only removed out of my mind, but turned into so many arguments of love. Now, by your love to it and me, I beseech you, dear CHEERFUL, to let us understand the particular more fully (said the CHIEF).

You have so put on your request (said the CHEERFUL) as it would not be only unkindness but sin to deny you. Though it be therefore to my shame, I will freely confess that, I know not how—whether by false information from the world or false apprehension in mine own mind or both, inward corruption being attracted by outward infection—I was grown to a strong and manifold prejudice against the divine virtue of patience as an

---

[12] {See, e.g., the ending of Chaucer's *Knight's tale* on making a virtue of necessity (ll. 3041–44).}

[13] {I.e., we bear the honorable title of Christians.}

effect of weakness, the mother of contempt, and an invitation to further injuries. And thus and no otherwise it appeared to me a feeble disposition, always disrespected, many times oppressed. Evil affections instantly followed wrong opinions. Methought it was unlovely, uncomely, prejudicial in others; in myself it should be most odious, disgraceful, dangerous.

It's no small happiness, beloved Cheerful (said the Guardian), that you have so good an opportunity of making amends for so great errors, and you improve it wisely by making so large and clear a declaration of them. The searching of a wound to the quick, though it be painful, yet it is a sure preparation to the cure; in which regard I should perhaps envy you but that I hope I may become a partner of the benefit by application of the selfsame remedy, appeaching myself to be guilty of all that you have made confession of, and much more in regard of the bad effects which have. . . .[14]

{Cheerful} Well had it been with me had I stayed there. Many a mischief had been avoided, and many a good business had been accomplished which hath chiefly {been} ruined by my want of patience. And I had not, it may be, wanted it, if I had known it so well as I have done of late. I had all your mistake in opinions, and I had more. I persuaded myself there was a strong taint of injustice in patience: that a man did wrong when he did not right himself, and that he was cruel to himself in being in such a manner gentle to others. I went further in the misapprehension, and the evil consequences have been much worse on my part. But I doubt not but by God's mercy all is cancelled. What is past is past. How to be sincere, constant, and perfect in the exercise of patience, wherein I have been hitherto so unsound, unstable, and defective, is now all my care. Let us therefore know, I pray, what it was that helped you, which cannot surely but do us good. The remedy must needs be proper since the disease is common.

Penance always follows confession, you know (said the Moderator to the Cheerful). Let it not therefore trouble you to be put now to little pains for so many friends' sake in a matter of such consequence.

Good resolutions, except they be confirmed in the mind by good reason, run more hazard of extinguishing the {than?} lights set in open plains without coverts. The weightiest ships float with every puft of wind if they be not well [anchored].[15] And the firmest inventions of man's heart for good are easily shaken if they be not stabilised by good arguments.

However fair the world seem to comply in most things with the letter, yet surely it bears deadly feud to the spirit and power of religion in all points; in none more than in this matter of patience, which, as it is one of the greatest buttresses of Christian faith, so it is mainly and maliciously, however subtly, undermined by the world, even when it seems most to promote and set it forth. Since it is certain, therefore, that we shall meet with much and violent opposition, I would be glad that everyone might be furnished with some solid arguments both to maintain the truth and to convince gainsayers.

I beseech you, most honored Moderator (said the Chief), that you would make us understand this mystery a little plainlier touching the world's proceedings with such semblance of love, and yet with such effects of hatred, to this virtue of patience, which, I

---

[14] {There is a lacuna in the manuscript at this point.}

[15] {The material in square brackets are editorial additions from the 1899 first printing.}

am persuaded, will rather give light and furtherance than be of diversion to that which we hope to learn from the Cheerful.

Why, verily (said the Moderator), if you well observe, the wisdom of this world gives no allowance, much less applause, to patience, but only in two cases: the first of necessity, which you before observed; the second of advantage, when either honors or some other gain is to be made by the exercise thereof, in this last case making it but a matter of merchandise; in the first giving it but the honor of a stupifying medicine, but on the selfsame ground hating the true and perfect for which they give approbation to this imperfect and counterfeit patience of their own devising. This kind and degree of patience, because it gives furtherance to carnal affections in the abatements of griefs and procurement of gain and honor, hath a free and commendable entertainment. But true and Christian patience, which voluntarily undergoes sufferings and makes damage and disgrace the subject of her embracements, dissolving the whole frame of their content, which lies altogether in fleshly and worldly satisfaction, suits only in their judgment to the condition of an ass—on this ground become the vilest of all other beasts, for otherwise, undoubtedly, if we make the comparison by shape or serviceableness, there are very few creatures to be preferred before the ass.

But the proportionableness of his natural temper to that disposition and those affections which patience causeth is the misery that hath made him the scorn and byword of mankind; and yet for this very cause did the Lord of Glory single him out for his own use amongst all other creatures. Think not that it was for contempt's sake, for neither was an ass in those times and places contemptible, and it was act of triumph which was intended, to which a contemptible carriage had been altogether dissonant. But it was in regard that an ass is an emblem of meekness and patience, that our blessed Savior made choice to ride upon an ass, a colt, the foal of an ass, when he went to shew himself the King of Israel, to comfort the daughter of Sion {Matt. 21:5}.

And, undoubtedly, as it then passed, so it still fares in these days; and with us he hath not changed his bodily residence. Our blessed Lord sits not as a king in any man's soul, nor ministers the saving comforts of his grace and spirit in any great measure or sweetness but to them which by their love and exercise of patience are become in the world's opinion very asses.

Christ, for the resemblance that an ass' nature hath with meekness and patience, gave him the preeminence of honor amongst all beasts; and man, for the same cause, gives his name as the highest title of infamy to them that are truly patient.

A patient man is an ass by the common vote of the world. He that for wisdom, as perhaps many do, forbears to express this conceit of others, yet by enforcement of truth cannot forbear to instance it in himself if he be put hard to it. Do you think me an ass? or, Would you have me an ass? Is the last refuge which the wisest of this world betake themselves unto when they purpose to shut off patience. But God forefend that such a word of death should be found henceforward amongst us. To which intent I have been willing to give you a taste of the malignity that this kind of language contains. As for the contradiction it bears to Christian religion, you may read it, as it were, in text letters,[16] and yet is this but the least and weakest of many engines wherewith the world batters the fort

---

[16] {i.e., in Holy Scripture}

of true patience. That generally received opinion, that impatiency is an effect, at least a consequence, of great spirits and great fortunes, is a far more strong and more pernicious argument of error in this matter.

The profession of valor and the ostentation of dignity in the common judgment of this world are by no means thought possible to be set better off than by an absolute kind of impatiency in all kinds.

. . .

He that takes an injury patiently. . . . he that makes himself a worm shall be trod on, he that makes himself a sheep the wolf will eat him, are main articles of the world's creed, and hold {*sic*} invincible arguments to prove the damage and danger of patience. That's the third slander whereby the world manifesteth the cankered malice that it bears against patience, as well as the contradiction of its own doctrine to that which Christ hath taught in this matter.

You have made it evident beyond exception (said the GUARDIAN) that the world is no friend, much less a good master to teach patience. We therefore so much the more desire to understand by whose recommendation and instruction our CHEERFUL is become so enamored of it that these horrible maims and deformities with which the wise masters of the earth have set forth patience are turned into matters of beauty and loveliness in her eyes. Sure there must be some great sorcery on the world's part, or some extreme blindness in men's eyes, that they should be thus deluded.

There's both (said the CHEERFUL), as I have woefully proved in myself. The world hath made false spectacles, and men that have a mind to be deceived gladly put them on.

Corrupt affections and purblind reason, with which the world hath made false views of this matter, are those deceitful glasses which cause this monstrous transformation that straight is made crooked, white is made black, and that which is great appears little. So it fares in this particular. Take it into the true light of God's word, and you shall see (whatever the world says to the contrary) that there is nothing more strong, more honorable, more beneficial, more just, and in a word, more excellent than true patience is.

The Word of GOD indeed (said the GUARDIAN) is a clear and certain light, whereby all impostures are discovered.

True (said the CHEERFUL). As metals are tried in the fining pot, so are all things manifested by the Scriptures of what nature and worth they be. But patience is one of those things which a man cannot come to the knowledge of by any other means than by the Scriptures. Depraved reason leads clean away. That which is most rectified falls so short of the truth that it rather confounds the understanding than persuades the heart to the love and exercise of true patience.

Undoubtedly it is so (said the GUARDIAN), and a manifest proof hereof is the Stoics' failing in this attempt, who are justly taxed by other philosophers not only to root up all affections, but to dam up the very senses, whilst they go about to introduce, by force of reason, patience.

A stupid senselessness or a wretched carelessness may perhaps (said the CHEERFUL) be wrought by arguments and exercise, by long custom and by firm resolution. But these dispositions are but the carcasses of patience; and, like men's bodies deprived of life, are not only unprofitable, but offensive to reason and to sense.

True patience is a most powerful, active virtue, full of sweet fruits of comfort in itself, of benefit to others, and the knowledge of it so proper to the Scripture as St. Paul makes it one of the chief: *Whatsoever things were written aforetime were written for our learning, that we through patience and comfort in the Scriptures might have hope* {Rom 15:4}.

You have brought us to the school door and to the mine (said the AFFECTIONATE). If we go not away rich in this learning it is our own default.

But for our better encouragement and direction by assay taken and pattern given how we ought to proceed in this search, we desire you should shew unto us some of those veins wherein the rich ore lies most easy and abundantly, by telling us some of those main and most effectual arguments whereby the Scriptures have informed and convinced your erring judgment.

That which of all others, in my apprehension, carries the greatest weight in this business (said the CHEERFUL) is that patience is one of those attributes which the Scripture gives to the Divine Majesty. St. Paul calls GOD the GOD of patience, and joins it with consolation; to which add what David saith, GOD is a righteous Judge, strong and patient, and you have at once the utter overthrow of all the world's cavillous opposition against patience.

It is an honor to GOD, and that as he is a judge. It flows from his might—he is strong and patient—and is unseparably matcht with consolation. And how then can it be matter of disgrace to weakness, or injustice, or an occasion of grief in man?

It cannot possibly (said the GUARDIAN) be thought, much less spoken, without blasphemy either of preferring man before GOD or in denying that patience is in GOD, which not only the Scriptures but experience teacheth, and all men, as I suppose, naturally agree unto. Then is my natural disposition most reprobate of all others (said the CHIEF), for till I was instructed by God's word, I could by no means believe that patience was in God. Your natural disposition must have been better than all others had you thought otherwise (said the MODERATOR). That all the world partakes of the same error is evident by the heathens' fashioning their gods, both in their conceits and in their writings, full of all manner of impatiency—of which temper even our Christian poets in these times feign the blessed saints and angels of Heaven to be, when in their compositions they bring them on the stage of this world. Such an unanswerable contradiction is there in man's apprehension between meekness and greatness, long-suffering and power, patience and happiness. Your skill in these studies makes you an absolute judge (said the GUARDIAN).

My many precious hours wasted in these vanities (replied the MODERATOR) have given me too much and too certain a knowledge of this malignous error in poets which, had not my affections and opinions complied with, I could never with such delight and approbation have continued in the reading of them.

The inference which you intend is plain (said the GUARDIAN) and undeniable. The universal applause that these conceits are entertained with shew that they are really believed in the world, how ever not so willingly perhaps confessed as by you. But though I was in the wrong touching this particular, yet surely not in that other, which yet the CHIEF seems equally to oppose by a precise limiting of her credence touching God's patience to the authority of the Scriptures, with the rejecting of all other means. Doth not experience itself convince that there must needs be an infinite patience in GOD, whilst he daily comports[17] such a numberless, measureless world of offences and impieties as are daily committed?

They that looked upon this matter by the light of reason in elder times extract a far more different conclusion than you do (said the CHIEF). This is the very ground which brought over divers philosophers absolutely to deny God's providence, and the wisest of them, as I have heard, to speak very doubtfully of it. That either GOD knows not, or cared not, for the things done on earth are inferences so necessary, in the eye of reason, upon the observation of God's forbearance of presumptuous sinners, as the best and holiest men in the world have been strongly tempted this way. David confesseth of himself that he could not by any means find the solution of this matter until he went into the Sanctuary; then he understood what before and otherwise was too hard for him {Psalm 73}. I am no whit, therefore, discouraged at my natural uncapableness wherein I have so great partners. But I bless GOD for the revelation of this mystery and my assent unto it.

That there is an infinite patience in GOD, and that this patience hath man's salvation for its end, and repentance for the means to lead him unto it, is a truth which, by the authority of the Scripture and the operation of the Holy Spirit, I believe; but, through the violence of the devil and the frailty of human reason, do continually labor under the defense and maintenance thereof. I tell you my weakness that you may help me with your prayers. There's no temptation that I am sorer pressed with by the enemy of our souls, upon the remembrance and refreshment[18] of my sins, than to interpret the long-suffering and patience of GOD to me-ward, that most wretched of all sinners, but a treasuring up of wrath against the day of vengeance: wherein reason for the most part, although it be infinitely to our prejudice, takes part against me. I cannot, therefore, be persuaded to attribute anything to reason touching my knowledge or belief of this saving truth. A saving truth, I call it, in regard that the hope of salvation fails not in any man till his assent thereunto be overthrown. He that feels the loving effects of God's patience in the continuance of this life on earth and the affording of means for attainment of heaven can never give entrance to despair till he have inverted this truth as the devil persuades— construing, with the devil, that the long-suffering of GOD is for the increase of sin and torment, whereas, in truth, as St. Peter teacheth, we ought to account it salvation.

I cannot but rejoice in mine error, at least in the manifestation (said the GUARDIAN), that hath given occasion to come to the knowledge of so important a truth as this is, whereby I not only understand the sovereign excellency of God's patience but the conditions that we must have if we desire it should be perfect as God's is:

That patience is often the example of God's which sincerely intends the benefit of him to whom it is exercised; and that forbearance in error which works to amendment is conformable to that long-suffering which GOD useth. But patience that emboldens to sin or that dissembles a while only to repay double vengeance at the last, as they are contrary both in their intentions and effects to God's long-sufferings and patience, so must they needs proceed from a contrary spirit. And yet the last of these is counted a piece of singular wisdom, the first a point of great goodness; and in the practice thereof lies all the evidence that the world can produce for its love to patience. They can willingly comport

---

[17] {endures, tolerates}
[18] {remembering}

all manner of impiety that is not to their own prejudice. To this end they think patience to be necessary, and in this way the exercise of it to be holy; otherwise it's sin and folly. Tell a man that he should have patience when his goods are wasted or his good name impaired, and he will turn with great anger and tell you that a man neither can nor ought to have patience in such cases; and yet the selfsame person will tell another, when he sees him angry against sin in those who are so under his charge as he shall give an accompt for them, that he must have patience; and if he make answer, as he ought to do, that he neither can nor ought to have patience in this case, they persuade themselves, and others too, that there's as great a fault in his zeal as in the wickedness which he reprehends and goes about to punish. But let the world say and judge what it please; since I now, by God's mercy, have attained the true copy of patience, I'll follow it, by his blessed assistance, as near as I may. There's no suffering in temporal respects that I will not endeavor to bear patiently. There shall be no sin, especially in those whom I must answer for, which I will not redress. As long as patience works to this effect, I shall esteem it a virtue, and further not. Where long-suffering mends not, chastisement must follow, and is a part of charity as well as of necessity. No man shall henceforth persuade me that that patience which, by abetting or occasioning of obstinacy in evil [leads] to destruction, can be a branch of God's patience, which by inducement of repentance, leads on to salvation.

Your conclusion seems so right and necessary in my judgment (said the CHIEF), as I cannot but earnestly beseech GOD that I may be your partner in the execution as well as I now am in the assent thereunto.

And now, I pray you, dear CHEERFUL, to proceed, the richness of this vein having increased our desires to the further opening of this mine.

The second great proof of the excellency of patience (said the CHEERFUL) is the Scriptures instancing it as a virtue and honor in all the saints of GOD. . . .

. . .

. . . And verily, set charity aside, which is not one, but the perfection of all virtues and graces, and there is not anything whatsoever whereby our conformity to CHRIST and his doctrine is so absolutely evinced and made manifest as by long-suffering and patience. It's the prime lesson that CHRIST set us if we desire to become like him: *Learn of me, I am meek and lowly*; and our careful taking out is the best testimony that we can have ourselves, or give others, to be really his scholars. Other virtues may be learned by his ushers, but patience is that which our great Master reserves to his own teaching. *Learn of me* directs us not only to the perfect, but to the only master of this profession.

. . .

This is that second argument that enforced me to the love and admiration of patience: that our LORD gave it, and all his saints have accepted it, as the proper arms of Christian religion. Not only the distinction, but the honor of God's children lies in it. He that refuseth to bear patience for his coat must pass over into some other family. He may be a gallant, a martial man, a great man of this world; a saint of Heaven, a good Christian he cannot be. True patience is ever the inseparable consort of Christian religion when it is sincerely professed; and Christian religion is the only profession that gives admittance to true patience.

Verily (said the GUARDIAN) it must needs be as you say; and now I see the reason why not only Virgil and Homer, but Ariosto and Spenser and all other books of chivalry bring in their feigned worthies so defective in patience. Man's wit can well enough, I perceive, fit all other weapons of Christian religion to serve the world's turns even against religion, but only patience; that's too weighty to be put on a counterfeit. He must be a Christian in earnest and not in appearance that wears this piece of armor, which, because these famous devices[19] want, however complete in the height of all other virtues they be made, I cannot allow them to pass for good examples of virtue amongst Christians.

Your censure is very favorable (said the CHIEF) in comparison of his that is of opinion that Orlando and the rest of those renowned paladins, through the recompting of their worthy action, have been made the destroyers of more Christian souls than ever they killed pagan bodies, and yet he doubts not (as he saith) of that battle wherein above three hundred thousand Moors are, by good and authentical historians, reported to have been slain by Orlando in one day. The full proof of this charge I shall leave to be made at the light of that bonfire which is resolved, as soon as conveniency permits, to be made of all these kinds of books by our VISITOR.[20] But that which is proper to this subject we are on, and perhaps not of so common observation though of much greater consequence to the disclosing of that mystery of iniquity which lies wrapped up in them, I should do wrong, me thinks, to overpass.

You should, indeed (said the GUARDIAN), both to the matter we have in hand and to the company, some of whom, it may be, through an habituated delight in these vanities from their cradle almost, have need of all the antidotes that can be ministered to keep them from relapse into a tolerable opinion at least of that which they have so clearly loved and prized.

That, then (said the CHIEF), which I have by way of minister to present unto you, is that the world and the devil owe to these histories of chivalry the making of that match between Christianity and revenge, which could never, though diligently labored from the very first, be brought to pass till these last and perilous times of ours.

If I were not a Christian I would strike thee again, said the invincible Christopher when he received a blow in the face from the President of Samos; but because I am a Christian I put it up without repayment. Antiquity knew not how, though, in the representation of an Hercules, to feign a composition between Christian profession and requital of evil, though it were but one for another. Whence, then, comes it now, that a sevenfold return of injuries passeth for an honor amongst them that not only prize themselves, but are honored by others with the name of good Christian professors of the Gospel?

Undoubtedly, from the lying patterns of Orlando and Rogero, from the counterfeit approbation of Carloman and Gotgride[21] touching these practices. There lies the spring-head of these poisonous [histories], and thence are those wretched opinions first taken, which afterwards, by fond reason and ungodly examples of eminent personages, take eternal rooting in carnal minds.

---

[19] {A "device" is a heraldic figure or motto, thus picking up on the armor-image of the previous clause; but it also can refer more generally to fanciful or witty writing.}

[20] {Shortly before his death in 1637, Nicholas Ferrar did in fact incinerate his considerable library of secular literature.}

[21] {Carloman I (d. 771), King of the Franks and brother of Charlemagne; "Gotgride" is perhaps Godfrey of Bulloigne, leader of the First Crusade, the subject of Tasso's *Gerusalemme liberata*.}

There's nothing, questionless, more pleasing to man's corrupt nature than revenge. The allowance that Mahomet's religion gives hereunto is one of the great inducements which procured him at the first, and still maintains him, so many followers.

False Christians, loath to turn open Turks and yet as eagerly bent to the prosecution of this affection, have at last found the salve of this by coining such new patterns as might serve their own turn. Champions in the faith are produced complete in all manner of virtues, patience excepted. That which is left out in the example is that which is chiefly intended for imitation. All the rest is but a flourish, and serves only to make this deformity the more lovely whilest it is accompanied with such abundance of excellencies. But painted fire warms not, however lively it be set forth; nor was ever any man made truly better by means of these devises. Who dare truly say that either temperance, justice, charity, or any other virtue ever took rise or heat in his mind or desires from Orlando his examples, or any of the rest of those chimeras? And who can truly deny but that, on the contrary, through the fair appearances and encouragements of such uncontrolled precedents as they are made, the impatiency of offences, the requital of injuries, the shedding of blood as if it were but shedding of water, have been bred and nourished in his heart as dispositions necessary and comely in worldly respects, tolerable enough with Christian religion? The plausible entertainment of these opinions in the world is that which chiefly is intended in these books—if not in the authors' designs, yet certainly in the devil's application, without the assistance of whose spirit they are never contentedly read: and what hand may we think he had in the composing of them! Let no man be deceived by the fair, goodly portraitures of the virtue which appeareth engraven to the life in them. They are but like the matron dress and modest behavior wherewith wicked strumpets enflame evil affections.

In the removal of patience they sap the groundwork, and manifest to them that well observe, that all their pretence of building up the walls is but the more [designed] to color their undermining the foundation of Christian religion—the life and power whereof, in many wise and good men's judgments, hath in these last times been [more endangered] by these kind of books than by any other engine of hell whatsoever, insomuch as the allowing of them in a family professing God's service is, by men very great both in learning and devotion, thought and written to be sin enough to cause the burning of the house, or the unnatural death of the heir, or any other such grievous calamity; and they think it may justly be imputed to this when other guiltiness appears not evidently to have drawn them on.

. . .

Since we have your assurance, dearest CHIEF (said the GUARDIAN), that this ere long shall come not only to fuller handling but final determination,[22] I think it just for the present to restrain my desires, though they be very earnest. Only one thing, which I know not whether I shall have the like opportunity for, I pray now make me understand a little better. That patience is a greater gift than miracles I have often heard from many, and believe; and that it is a greater proof of God's grace than miracles seems undeniable, St. Paul making it plainly the first and main proof of our dependence on CHRIST as servants: in all

---

[22] {In university disputations, the "determination" was the concluding and definitive resolution of the question being debated.}

things approving ourselves as the ministers of GOD, in much patience and in afflictions {2 Cor. 6:4}; but that it should be a miracle itself, as you say, I do not so well [comprehend].

I shall tell you (said the CHIEF) a short story out of Cassianus,[23] which will perhaps better satisfy you touching this matter than a long discourse of mine own.—

A venerable old man walking the streets of Alexandria in time of persecution, upon notice given that he was a Christian, is suddenly enclosed by an unruly multitude of idolaters, who, after all manner of despiteful usage, both in words and deeds, began jointly with much scorn to demand of him what great miracles hath this CHRIST of thine done, whom thou makest to be GOD? to which the blessed Saint cheerfully made answer, That I can patiently endure all those wrongs which you do me, and more and greater if need be, without any disquiet in myself or offence towards you.

Oh, now I perceive my former dullness (said the GUARDIAN). The fire burns not the body either more naturally or more fiercely than injuries do the mind. It must, therefore, be alike miraculous to comport wrong without offence as to walk through the flame without scorching; and now, there being no more to be expected touching this point, I desire you, dear CHEERFUL, to go on to the next.

The wonderful gain that accrues by patience is the third argument which, me thinks, ought to compel everyone, as it did me, to the pursuit thereof above all other things. The time would fail to recount all. I will only therefore instance three benefits proper to patience, and exceeding all others in my apprehension.

First, it resettles a man in the possession of himself, from whence sin and other passions have ejected him. In your {*sic*} patience (saith our Savior to his disciples) possess your souls {Luke 21:19}.

Secondly, it entitles him to the kingdom of heaven. Blessed are the poor in spirit, and blessed are those that suffer persecution, for theirs is the kingdom of heaven.

And thirdly, it invests him in the fruition of all the good things of this life. The meek-spirited shall possess the earth and shall be refreshed in the multitude of peace. Other virtues regain by little and little, one parcel after another, what we have lost, but patience makes an entire, absolute re-entry at once into heaven, earth, and ourselves. And what thing then can we find answerable to patience for advantage and beneficialness?

That patience makes a man owner of himself (said the GUARDIAN), the world cannot well deny, seeing it is one of the first prayers that men commonly make upon any great distress: that GOD would give them patience to keep themselves in their right wits; and, on the other side, of impatient men they say they are out of their wits and beside themselves. As for the kingdom of heaven, they will not much contend but that the interest that patience hath thereunto may be as great as CHRIST promiseth. But that it should be such a seed of content here on earth and such a way to purchase honor and happiness in this life, they will never be brought to believe, how many texts of Scripture soever be brought in proof thereof.

. . .

. . . I pray, therefore, tell me whether you so conceive that true patience ever works to ease of the sufferings and return of comfort.

---

[23] {5th-century monk and theologian, John Cassian}

Always (said the PATIENT) at the last to them that desire ease and deliverance. Many examples, I doubt not, in all ages may be brought of longsome sufferings in good men, and some, perchance, which a little impatiency would have much speedlier rid them of than patience did; but none can be brought, as I suppose, where patience wrought not deliverance in the end, and that of a far better kind than impaciency could have done if they had followed the persuasions thereof.

If David had took away Saul's life upon those fair opportunities which were offered him, he might have been the sooner free perchance from that dread and anguish wherein he lived by Saul's persecution, but assuredly he had never come to that glory and happiness whereunto in the end he attained. The workings of patience are oftimes slow, but they are ever sure and abundant. The delay is manifoldly repaid by the plenty of the retribution[24] which patience brings to them that desire retribution in this life, which many have refused, as St. Paul testifieth, to the intent they might be partakers of a greater reward in heaven. . . .

. . .

Well then, I pray (said the GUARDIAN), what may that be which . . . you have learned so much to the matter we are now in hand with?

That impatiency is the cause of all the imperfections in men's works and actions (said the AFFECTIONATE), and that, on the other side, patience is the nurse, if not the mother, of all perfection, not only in divine but also in human respects and things of this world.

Indeed (said the GUARDIAN) this is a transcendent exaltation of folly on impatiency's behalf, as on the contrary it must needs enforce a great preeminence of wisdom belonging to patience if it be such a main cause of perfection. But how can you make proof of these things by Scripture?

What need we seek for proof in Scripture (said the AFFECTIONATE) of that which daily experience gives evident demonstration of in all things? Look well and you shall see that all that bungling in trades, that unskillfulness in arts, that error in sciences, and, in a word, all that insufficiency in professions which deforms and ruins the world proceeds mainly from impatiency, either in learning or in practicing their several works. Natural abilities in most men serve well enough; fitting instruments and all other opportunities abound to know all things aright and to do them well. Only patience is wanting, and that mars all.

. . .

. . . A right simple wit by patience and perseverance overcomes all manner of difficulties, and brings forth whatever it undertakes complete; whereas the most excellent abilities with all the helps that can be, if patience be away, foil themselves instantly in their own apprehension of things, in the expression of them to others, and in the performance of that which comes to execution. Their conceits run clean away; their words are now short, now over, never hitting the mark; their actions always full of error and incongruity, all merely through impatiency, that in contemplation hastens them away before they fully understand the matter, that in deliberation puts them on to speak before they well know what, and, when they come to put things in execution, makes them give over or turn to other means when they find any rub in that way which they have begun. These are the

---

[24] {recompense, repayment}

fruits of impatiency—and the predominancy of it and them in our weaker sex, the only ground of the flightiness and insufficiency wherewith not only all women's words and works, but even their natural constitution, is taxed. I say not but there be some few things perhaps whereunto neither the capacity of women's minds nor the abilities of their bodies do generally serve, such as are the depth of learning and the labors of war. But that in all things, aye, even in those things which seem properly our own, we should be so far outrun by men when they set themselves to vie with us cannot proceed from anything but from the impatiency of our minds, which suffers us not to be seriously intentive to that which we desire to learn nor steadily employed in that we undertake to perform. So that we both know and say and do all good things but by halves at the best, which questionless might be thoroughly in all perfection accomplished, if we would let patience have her perfect working. . . . And this is one of those things that I was taught by those words: He that is impatient exalteth folly {Prov. 14:29}.

Why if it be but one (said the GUARDIAN), it is not all; and therefore you may not here make an end, for both your promise and our expectation is that you should teach all that yourself is taught in this matter.

I shall gladly do it (said she) because I conceive it to be neither less true nor less profitable than the former. The second thing was, therefore, that all the high prized follies in the world have been chiefly set up and are maintained in honor and esteem by and for impatiency, that it may have the freer bent, and pass without control.

What (said the GUARDIAN smilingly), will you persuade us that all your womanly niceties of rubbing floors till you may see your faces shine in them, of whiting linen till it pass the driven snow, of conserving, preserving, and all those other busy curiosities for which you so magnify yourselves, have their credit chiefly for the better inducement and support of impatiency?

Ay, verily (said she), and all those other more boisterous and more pernicious vanities you men are carried with of building, of hunting, of keeping company, and the like proceed from the same ground and tends to the same end, is that which I would persuade and am confident to make proof of. But why, I pray, do you instance our womanly affairs with such contempt?

Because (said the GUARDIAN) they be utterly unworthy the dignity of man's nature to take any pleasure or delight in them, and much more to glory of them. Judge in yourselves what a debasement it must needs be of those noble faculties of the will and reason, that were made for contemplations and pursuit of heavenly affairs, to pour out themselves in the love and prosecution of such abject matters.

Why, something we must needs do (said the AFFECTIONATE). Man's soul cannot be without employment; and since you have taken away great matters from us, you ought not to vilify these so much wherein the mind, in regard of its own working, is nobly busied, however the subject be but mean. There's exercise of invention, of composition, of order, and of all the other excellent operations of the soul, and the beauty and pleasure and other good effects that arise from these employments. And herein lies our delight, not in the things themselves, as you seem to conceive.

That cannot possibly be (said the GUARDIAN). For then, by how much it is more excellent to have the minds of your families well composed than the rooms of your house curiously dressed, your children well fed than your table daintily furnished, by so much would your care {have} been greater in these matters than in the other.

You would have us then (said the Affectionate) spend all our time and care upon our servants and children, instructing their understandings and framing their manners, still watching over them to exact an orderliness and perfection in virtue and knowledge as we bring our houses to the height of beauty and conveniency? And so we must become absolute school-mistresses instead of good housewives?

I would have you both (said the Guardian) careful guides of your house and diligent teachers of your children; the neglect and disesteem of which office and employment seems to me one of the sovereign follies of this world, there being no duty which parents so much owe their children, nor anything wherein themselves can be more nobly exercised, than in teaching their children and instructing them in virtue and learning. But are we not wandered from the point?

Not at all (said the Affectionate), if you will but tell us whence the withdrawing of parents from this duty proceeds. Is it perhaps through ignorance of the worth thereof, or through want of love to their children?

All wise parents (said the Guardian) give instruction the prize of all other benefits which their children receive by their means.

And why, then, since it is the best portion, are they not desirous to bestow it by their own hands and mouths rather than by others' mercenary paps and care (said the Affectionate)? Do they want love to perform it?

No, no (said the Guardian). Now I perceive the cause; they want patience. That's the common and the only answer which they will stand by. And now I understand whereat you aim, and must needs yield unto it as an evident truth. It's impatiency only that hath suffered this painful education of our children {to be considered} as too mean a matter for persons of better rank and spirit. And it can be nothing else but impatiency that hath set up on high those other vain employments which come in place thereof. What you have brought me to see in one particular is true in all the rest. The impatiency of enduring that pains and care which belongs to government makes our gentry and nobility cast up their own and their country's business, and betake themselves to hunting, hawking, and the like riots. And these they magnify as noble employment, not because themselves are so persuaded (for their own consciences tell them they be but unworthy vanities), but because by the appearance of bodily labor they have a fair color for the idleness of their minds, and in the independancy that these kind of actions have to any others, a freedom for their inconstant affections and humors to revel as they please. And now to make a proof whether I rightly and fully understand this matter, give me leave, dear Affection-ate, to make the conclusion according to mine own apprehension, wherein, if I any ways fail, make you the amends by addition and correction of what shall be needful. This, then, me thinks, seem to be plain: that everyone that through impatiency deserts his own proper work; first endeavors, by slighting it, to find excuse for what he leaves undone; and next, by amplifying the worth of that which he set himself about, to have a pretence for his continuance therein. Thus far you go very rightly (said Affectionate). . . .

‡

The reference that my story hath to the most of these things which have been hitherto spoken of (said the CHEERFUL) will, I doubt not, persuade you it hath not been unfitly kept to the last.

Agaton having by long continuance in all manner of godly conversation gained the reputation of a saint, certain strangers, desirous to prove the sincerity of his so far renowned holiness, told him that as the great report of his virtues had induced them to come from far to visit him, so the strange accusations of many, and those no mean persons, did much distract and perplex their minds; for they tell us, said the strangers, that out of a haughty mind thou takest upon thee to teach many new and unusual doctrines, and that thou seemest little to regard the authority and reasons that are contrary to thee, as though thyself wert only wise and good.

They affirm likewise that thou dost presumptuously censure divers actions and practices approved by those that are much thy betters; yet thou art a bold and a continual reprover of others' faults, thereby to persuade men that thou art an enemy to vice. In a word, they lay to thy charge that all thy appearing holiness is but hypocrisy, and that thou seemest to despise worldly pleasures and to contemn wealth because thou canst not compass them; or rather, by a more commodious way hast found the satisfaction of ambition and other evil affections under the pretence of religion than other men do.

Agaton, having without any shew of distaste heard them, sighing deeply, made answer that all was true that he was accused of. But do you, dear brethren, shedding many tears, pray GOD for the pardon of my sins, the creating of a new and right spirit within me, that in heart I may be such as I appear outwardly to men.

The strangers, much edified in the evidence of his humility and patience, proceeded further, saying, Some likewise tell us that thou art an heretic and dost hold naughty and idolatrous opinions. But then Agaton cried out aloud, GOD forbid. Herein they do me wrong. However wretched man that I am, confessing myself guilty of divers other crimes, yet surely, by the mercies of GOD, I am clear from the taints of superstition and heresy. The good men, sorry to see him offended, besought him to pass by that which was only spoken to make proof of his virtue, and out of abundance of charity to tell them why he so readily confessed those former crimes, of which they well saw he was not guilty, and seemed so much troubled at the imputation of heresy. He, constrained by their importunity, replied, My sons, there is indeed so much of all those evil affections in my heart of which you at first laid to my charge, and though by the goodness of GOD they do not rule or sway either to do or undo anything, but all that I do is upon better grounds and to better ends, yet because they do forcibly intermingle themselves with my best actions, it is not fit for me to deny, especially when the confession of my weakness and imperfection may more advance God's glory and edify my brethren than I should do by the defense of mine own innocency, which is not mine own but the gift and grace of GOD. And herein I follow our LORD and SAVIOR, who did no sin, neither was guilt found in him, and yet, notwithstanding, patiently endured the contradiction of sinners, not answering again when he was reviled, leaving us an example that we should follow his steps. But as for heresy and false belief in religion, that makes an absolute partition between the soul of man and GOD. I may not, therefore, endure the imputation of that which cast me altogether from the communion of CHRIST, that desirously undergo all other manner of reproaches and injuries that I may be made the more like unto him, both in the conformity of a patient and humble mind.

There is no truer proof of a good heart than the ready confession of its own badness. He that justifies himself for the inward knows not himself; the more we grow to perfection, the more do we discover our corruptions. He is in a safe and a good way that's only bad in his own eyes; but he that justifies himself by the good intention and disposition of his heart when his outward actions condemn him is yet in the snares of the devil.

This (said the GUARDIAN), GOD be thanked, is happily brought about, and the want of our music have been occasion of greater pleasure than I could have thought. Now it remains that, calling upon GOD, we faithfully endeavor to act what we have learned and put in execution what we have promised, both touching our own selves and our living together, whilest we do live, cheerfully going on by humility and patience unto the perfection of love. That's the end of all virtues and the beginning of happiness. . . .

TEXT: *The story books of Little Gidding: being the religious dialogues recited in the Great Room, 1631–2*, ed. E. Cruwys Sharland (New York: Dutton, 1899), 1–2, 73–76, 86–88, 103–24, 126–27, 130–38, 149–51.

FRANCIS QUARLES
(1592–1644)

Born into the Essex gentry, the younger son of a high-ranking Elizabethan civil servant and puritan mother, Quarles took his BA at Christ's College, Cambridge, in 1609, departing the next year for Lincoln's Inn to get a gentleman's acquaintance with the law. After Princess Elizabeth's marriage to the Elector Frederick in 1613, Quarles joined the noble company escorting the couple to Heidelberg. It was on this trip that he probably met Robert Sidney, later Earl of Leicester, to whom he dedicated his earliest published work, a paraphrase of Jonah entitled *A feast for worms* (1620)—the first of several biblical paraphrases published during the 1620s. By 1620 he had married (the couple had eighteen children) and moved to London to pursue "the life of a cultivated gentleman of scholarly and literary interests" (*ODNB*). Between 1626 and ca. 1630, Quarles was in Ireland as secretary to Archbishop Ussher, whose royalism, loyalty to the established Church, and (presumably) Calvinism he shared. The two men remained friends, but by 1632 Quarles was back in Essex where he enjoyed a period of creative energy and literary fame—and the friendship of two other Cambridge poets, Edward Benlowes and Phineas Fletcher, who, like Quarles, were experimenting with new allegorical forms of devotional poetry. Quarles' *Divine fancies* came out in 1632, his *Emblems* in 1635. The first of his topical religio-political pastorals, *The shepherd's oracles*, probably dates from the same years, although the work was heavily revised in the early 1640s and only posthumously published in 1646. He was appointed city chronologer in 1640, the same year he published his very popular *Enchiridion*, a collection of royalist political maxims, most near-verbatim pilferings from Bacon and Machiavelli. The work was later translated into Latin, Dutch, Danish, Swedish, and German—and, in 1650, re-plagiarized under the title *Regales aphorismi* and attributed to King James. During the last four years of his life, he wrote a series of prose tracts defending the royalist cause and his one attempt at drama: an allegorical political comedy entitled *The virgin widow*. His anguish over the political crisis of the early 1640s was exacerbated by personal calamities in the form of increasingly dire financial straits and malicious allegations of crypto-Catholicism.

617

Quarles, Christopher Hill remarks, may have been "the most popular English poet in the seventeenth century" ("Francis Quarles" 188). His *Emblems* was undoubtedly "the most important and most successful English emblem book," perhaps "the most popular book of English verse of its century." No other English emblem book had a second edition; Quarles' went through over fifty. In its own day, *Divine fancies* was yet more popular, going through eleven editions between 1632 and 1676, compared to *Emblems'* eight.[1] While some of his poems have considerable merit, aesthetics alone cannot explain Quarles' astonishing popularity, which must rather have something to do with his success "in gauging the protestant religious feeling of Englishmen at large"; as Hill observes in connection with Quarles, "minor poets are even more useful to the social historian than major poets: for the virtues and vices of the small man are apt to be those of his age" ("Benlowes" 143). Quarles' wife said much the same, although without the condescension, describing her husband's religion as that of "a true son of the Church of England" (Liston xviii). If Hill and Mrs. Quarles are right in viewing Quarles as representative of the "protestant religious feeling" of Caroline "Englishmen at large," his sacred poetry is of considerable historical interest, especially with regard to the vexed question of what constituted early Stuart "mainstream" religion.[2]

For Anthony Wood, Quarles was a "puritanical poet." Modern scholars generally find the term inconsistent with Quarles' warm royalism, preferring to describe him as "a staunch middle-of-the-road Calvinist Anglican" (Hill, "Francis Quarles" 190) or, less informatively, a "moderate Protestant" (*ODNB*). In truth, there is virtually no scholarship on the *Divine fancies*, perhaps because the poems create problems for doctrinal labels. Many of the poems deal with issues central to Calvinist teaching, yet the poems themselves are unmarked by Calvinism. They are not Arminian, not even anti-Calvinist, just un-Calvinist. Thus the first poem <1.1> deals with the relation between divine grace and human agency, the second <1.2> with predestination, but in the former the bellows of God's organ apparently blow equally for all, and it is up to us, the organists, whether the music is played well or ill; the latter gives Boethius' classic answer to the problem of future contingents, affirming the autonomy of secondary causes and hence the possibility of free will (see *Paradise Lost*, but also Hoard's 1633 Arminian *God's love* <infra>). The next poem <1.3>, moreover, apparently takes Cosin's controversial "Laudian" position that, although there are only two dominical sacraments, five other rites are also sacraments in some sense (Cosin 54); indeed Quarles implies that all seven may be conduits of grace.[3] The theologically oddest poem, however, is 1.30, whose anti-eudemonist position (that seeking God in order to enjoy him forever is sin) was extremely rare in early seventeenth-century England except (maybe) among antinomians.[4] Augustine, Aquinas, and Calvin

---

[1] Höltgen, "Aspects" 31; Haight 188; Liston xv.

[2] The question has an extensive bibliography, much of it engaging, whether pro or con, with Nicholas Tyacke's *Anti-Calvinists*, but see also Collinson, *Religion of Protestants*. A recent overview of the scholarship can be found in Shuger, "Protesting," 587–630.

[3] Poems 1.9, 1.34, and 2.79 seem likewise impossible to square with anything approaching Calvinist orthodoxy. See the notes to the individual poems <infra>.

[4] See the introduction to Everard <supra>; also Como, *Blown by the Spirit* 194–95, 244–45.

take for granted that all persons seek happiness as their final end; indeed, the Reformed emphasis on personal assurance does not forbid but rather foregrounds concern for one's own salvation. The theological ethics of Duns Scotus (d. 1308) are anti-eudemonist, as are those of the Jansenists, whose writings postdate Quarles by at least a decade.[5]

SOURCES: *ODNB*; John Cosin, *A collection of private devotions* (London, 1627); Gordon Haight, "The sources of Quarles's Emblems," *Transactions of the Bibliographic Society: The Library* 16 (1935): 188–209; Jennifer Herdt, *Putting on virtue* (Chicago UP, 2008); Christopher Hill, "Francis Quarles and Edward Benlowes," *Writing and revolution in 17th-century England: collected essays*, vol. 1 (U Massachusetts P, 1985), 188–206; and "Benlowes and his times," *Essays in Criticism* 3 (1953): 143–41; Karl Josef Höltgen, *Aspects of the emblem: studies in the English emblem tradition and the European context*, foreword by Roy Strong (Kassel: Edition Reichenberger, 1986); William Liston, ed. *Francis Quarles' "Divine fancies": a critical edition* (Garland, 1992).

---

[5] Herdt 2–3, 50–53, 94, 226; *Stanford encyclopedia of philosophy* (q.v. "religion and morality"); Calvin, *Institutes* 3.25.1–2. Note that Quarles' *Emblems* 5.5 <*infra*> is flagrantly eudemonist; what the speaker desires is precisely the ecstatic experience of the divine whose pleasure exceeds that of the most intense erotic delights.

FRANCIS QUARLES

Divine fancies: digested into epigrams, meditations, and observations
1632

{Book I}

1. *On the music of organs*

Observe this organ; mark but how it goes:
'Tis not the hand of him alone that blows
The unseen bellows, nor the hand that plays
Upon th'apparent note-dividing kays,
That makes these well-composed airs appear
Before the high tribunal of thine ear.
They both concur; each acts his several part:
Th'one gives it breath, the other lends it art.
Man is this organ: to whose every action
Heav'n gives a breath (a breath without coaction),
Without which blast we cannot act at all,
Without which breath the universe must fall
To the first nothing it was made of, seeing
In him we live, we move, we have our being.
Thus fill'd with his diviner breath, and back't
With his first power, we touch the kays and act;
He blows the bellows; as we thrive in skill,
Our actions prove, like music, *good* or *ill*.

2. *On the contingency of actions*

I saw him dead; I saw his body fall
Before Death's dart, whom tears must not recall.
Yet is he not so dead but that his day
Might have been lengthen'd, had th'untrodden way

To life been found. He might have rose again,
If something had or something had not been.
What mine sees past, Heav'n's eye foresaw to come.
He saw, how that contingent act should sum
The total of his days; his knowing eye
(As mine doth see him dead) saw he should die
That very fatal hour; yet saw his death
Not so so necessary, but his breath
Might been enlarg'd unto a longer date,
Had he neglected *this* or taken *that*.
All times to Heav'n are *now*, both first and last;
He sees things *present* as we see them past.

3. *On the sacraments*

The *loaves of bread* were five, the *fishes* two,
    Whereof the multitude was made partaker.
Who made the *fishes?* God. But tell me, who
Gave being to the *loaves* of bread? the *baker*.
      Ev'n so these sacraments, which some call seven,
      Five were ordain'd by *man*, and two by *Heaven*.

4. *On the infancy of our Savior*

Hail blessed Virgin, full of heavenly grace,
Blest above all that sprang from human race,
Whose Heav'n-saluted womb brought forth in one,
A blessed Savior and a blessed Son:
O! what a ravishment 'thad been, to see
Thy little Savior perking[1] on thy knee!
To see him nuzzle in thy virgin breast!
His milk-white body all unclad, undrest;
To see thy busy fingers clothe and wrap
His spradling[2] limbs in thy indulgent lap!
To see his desp'rate eyes, with childish grace,
Smiling upon his smiling mother's face!
And, when his forward strength began to bloom,
To see him diddle[3] up and down the room!
O, who would think so sweet a babe as this
Should ere be slain by a false-hearted kiss!
Had I a rag, if sure thy body wore it,
Pardon sweet babe, I think I should adore it;

---

[1] {perching (as a bird); also showing delight, lifting one's head inquisitively}
[2] {sprawled}
[3] {toddle}

Till then, O grant this boon (a boon far dearer),
The weed not being, I may adore the wearer.

6. *On the life and death of man*[4]

The world's a theater; the earth, a stage
Plac'd in the midst, whereon both prince and page,
Both rich and poor, fool, wise-man, base and high,
All act their parts in life's short tragedy.
Our life's a tragedy. Those secret rooms
Wherein we tire[5] us are our mothers' wombs;
The music ush'ring in the play is mirth
To see a man-child brought upon the earth;
That fainting gasp of breath which first we vent
Is a dumb-shew, presents the argument;
Our new-born cries that new-born griefs bewray
Is the sad prologue of th'ensuing play;
False hopes, true fears, vain joys, and fierce distracts
Are like the music that divides the acts;
Time holds the glass, and when the hour's out-run,
Death strikes the epilogue, and the play is done.

9. *Of light and heat*

Mark but the sun-beams, when they shine most bright,
They lend this lower world both heat & light;
They both are children of the self-same mother,
Twins, not subsisting one without the other;
They both conspire unto the common good,
When in their proper places understood.
Is't not rebellion against sense to say,
Light helps to quicken; or, the beams of day
May lend a heat, and yet no light at all?
'Tis true, some obvious[6] shade may chance to fall
Upon the quickened plant, yet not so great
To quench the operation of the heat.
The heat cannot be parted from the light,
Nor yet the light from heat. They neither might
Be mingled in the act, nor found asunder.
Distinguish now, fond man, or stay and wonder.
      Know then,
Their virtues differ though themselves agree:

---

[4] {A reworking of the famous lyric "What is our life? A play of passion," ascribed to Raleigh, first published in Orlando Gibbons' *First set of madrigals*, 1612.}

[5] {attire}

[6] {situated in the way; positioned in front of or opposite to something; facing (*OED*)}

Heat vivifies; light gives man power to see
The thing so vivified. No light, no heat.
And where the heat's but small, the light's not great;
They are inseparable and sworn lovers,
Yet differing thus: *that* quickens; *this* discovers.
Within these lines a sacred myst'ry lurks:
The *heat* resembles *faith*; the light, *good works.*[7]

30. *On Servio*

Servio serves God. Servio has bare relation
(Not to God's glory) but his own salvation.
Servio serves God for life. Servio, tis well:
Servio may find the cooler place in hell.

31. *A soliloquy*[8]

Where shall I find my God! O where, O where
Shall I direct my steps to find him there?
Shall I make search in swelling bags of coin?
Ah no, for *God* and *Mammon* cannot join.
Do beds of down contain this heavenly stranger?
No, no, he's rather cradled in some manger.
Dwells he in wisdom? Is he gone that road?
No, no, man's wisdom's foolishness with God.
Or hath some new plantation, yet unknown,
Made him their king, adorn'd him with their crown?
No, no, the kingdoms of the earth think scorn
T'adorn his brows with any crown but thorn.
Where shall I trace, or where shall I go wind him?
My Lord is gone, and O! I cannot find him.
I'll ransack the dark dungeons; I'll enquire
Into the furnace, after the sev'nth fire.
I'll seek in Daniel's den and in Paul's prison;
I'll search his grave, and see if he be risen;
I'll go to th'house of mourning, and I'll call
At every alms-abused hospital.
I'll go and ask the widow that's opprest,

---

[7] {Luther uses the same analogy in the preface to Romans in his 1522 New Testament translation. The faith/works contrast alludes to James 2:18: "Yea, a man may say, Thou hast faith, and I have works: shew me thy faith without thy works, and I will shew thee my faith by my works."}

[8] {On "soliloquy," see Julia Staykova, "The Augustinian soliloquies of an early modern reader," *Literature & Theology* 23.2 (2009): 121–41; in early modern usage, "soliloquy" almost always refers to an inner or private speaking to God (*vide* Sparke's *Crumbs of comfort <supra>*). Quarles' poem is perhaps the earliest instance in which the word means speaking to oneself, or to no one in particular, although the usual meaning still hovers in the background.}

The heavy-laden that enquires rest;
I'll search the corners of all broken hearts,
The wounded conscience, and the soul that smarts,
The contrite spirit fill'd with filial fear:
Ay, there he is, and no where else but there.[9]
Spare not to scourge thy pleasure, O my God,
So I may find thy presence with thy rod.

23 {misprint for 33}. *On those that deserve it*

O, when our clergy at the dreadful Day
Shall make their audit; when the Judge shall say,
Give your accompts[10]: what, have my lambs been fed?
Say, do they all stand sound? Is there none dead
By your defaults? come shepherds, bring them forth
That I may crown your labors in their worth:
O what an answer will be given by some![11]
We have been silenc'd; canons struck us dumb;
The great ones would not let us feed thy flock,
Unless we play'd the fools and wore a frock;
We were forbid unless we'd yield to sign
And cross their brows (they *say, a mark of thine).*
To say the truth, great Judge, they were not fed;
Lord, here they be; but, Lord, they be all dead.
Ah cruel shepherds! Could your conscience serve
Not to be fools, and yet to let them sterve?
What if your fiery spirits had been bound
To antic habits or your heads been crowned
With peacock's plumes? had ye been forc'd to feed
Your Savior's dear-bought flock in a fool's weed?
He that was scorn'd, revil'd, endur'd the curse
Of a base death in your behalfs; nay worse,
Swallow'd the cup of wrath charg'd up to th' brim—
Durst ye not stoop to play the fools for him?

34. *Do this and live*

Do this and live? Tis true, great God, then who
Can hope for life? for who hath power to do?
Art thou not able? Is thy task too great?
Canst thou desire help? Canst thou entreat

---

[9] {See Sparke's "Godly prayer" in *Crumbs of comfort <supra>.*}

[10] {account books}

[11] {The "some," as the following lines make clear, are the non-conformists who left their ministry rather than make the sign of the cross or wear a surplice as required by the canons, etc. See, in this volume, Bradshaw, *English puritanism*, and Sanderson's 1619 sermon on conformity <supra>.}

Aid from a stronger arm? Canst thou conceive
Thy *helper* strong enough? Canst thou *believe*
The suff'rings of thy dying Lord can give
Thy drooping shoulders rest? *Do this and live.*[12]

40. *On the Day of Judgment*

O when shall that time come, when the loud trump
Shall wake my sleeping ashes from the dump
Of their sad urn! That blessed Day, wherein
My glorifi'd, my metamorphiz'd skin
Shall circumplex and terminate that fresh
And new refined substance of this flesh!
When my transparent flesh, dischargd from groans
And pains, shall hang upon new polisht bones!
When as my body shall re-entertain
Her cleansed soul, and never part again!
When as my soul shall, by a new indenture,
Possess her new-built house, come down and enter!
When as my body and my soul shall plight
Inviolable faith, and never fight
Nor wrangle more nor altercate again
About that strife-begetting question, sin!
When soul and body shall receive their doom
Of *o ye blessed of my Father, come!*
When Death shall be exil'd, and damn'd to dwell
Within her proper and true center, Hell!
Where that old Tempter shall be bound in chains
And overwhelm'd with everlasting pains;
Whilst I shall sit and, in full glory, sing
Perpetual anthems to my Judge, my King.

The second Book

5. *On Jesus and Sampson*[13]

An angel did to Manoah's wife appear
And brought the news her barren womb should bear.
Did not another angel, if not he,
Thrice blessed Virgin, bring the same to thee?
The wife of Manoah (nine months being run)

---

[12] {See Herbert's "The Holdfast," published a year later, which handles the same issue, but with greater (Augustinian) theological complexity.}

[13] {On the typological parallels between Samson and Christ, see Michael Krouse, *Milton's Samson and the Christian tradition* (Princeton UP, 1949); David Gunn, *Judges through the centuries*, Blackwell Bible Commentaries (Blackwell, 2005), 170–82.}

Her Heav'n-saluted womb brought forth a son;
To thee, sweet Virgin, full of grace and Heaven,
A child was born, to us a Son was given.
The name of hers was Sampson, born to fight
For captiv'd Israel, and a Nazarite;
Thine was a Naz'rite too, and born to ease us
From Satan's burthens, and his name is Jesus.
Sampson espous'd and took in marriage her
That was the child of an idolater;
Our Jesus took a wife that bow'd the knee
And worshipt unknown gods, as well as she.
Assaulted, Sampson met and had to do
With a fierce lion; foil'd and slew him too.
Our conquering Jesus purchas'd higher fame;
His arm encountered Death, and overcame.
Victorious Sampson stept aside, and drew
Pure honey from the carcass that he slew;
When our triumphing Jesus sought and found
A greater sweetness in his lion's wound.
Uxorious Sampson pleases to divide
His purchas'd honey to his fairest bride.
But what! Is Sampson singular in this?
Did not our Jesus do the like to his?
Sampson propounds a riddle, and does hide
The folded myst'ry in his faithless bride;
Our blessed Jesus propounds riddles, too,
Too hard for man, his bride unsought, t'undo.
The bride forsakes her Sampson, do's betroth her
To a new love, and falsely weds another;
And did not the adult'rous Jews forgo
Their first love Jesus, and forsake him too?
Displeased Sampson had the choice to wed
The younger sister in the elder's stead;
Displeased Jesus had espous'd the younger—
God send her fairer, and affections stronger.
Sampson sent foxes on his fiery errant
Among their corn, & made their crimes his warrant;
Offended Jesus shews as able signs
Of wrath: his foxes have destroy'd their vines.[14]
Our Sampson's love to Delilah was such
That for her sake poor Sampson suffer'd much;
Our Jesus had his Delilah; for her
His soul became so great a sufferer.

[14] {Cant. 2:15}

Sampson was subject to their scorn and shame;
And was not Jesus even the very same?
Sampson's betray'd to the Philistine's hands,
Was bound a while, but quickly brake his bands;
Jesus the first and second day could be
The grave's close pris'ner, but the third was free.
In this they differ'd: Jesus' dying breath
Cry'd out for *life*, but Sampson's call'd for *death*.
Father forgive them, did our Jesus cry;
But Sampson, *let me be reveng'd and die*.
Since then, sweet Savior, tis thy death must ease us,
We fly from Sampson, and appeal to Jesus.

29. *On beggars*

No wonder that such swarms of beggars lurk
In every street: 'tis a worse trade to work
Than beg. Yet some, if they can make but shift
To live, will think it scorn to thrive by gift.
'Tis a brave mind, but yet no wise fore-cast;
It is but pride, and pride will stoop at last.
We all are beggars—should be so, at least.
Alas! we cannot work; the very best
Our hands can do will not maintain to live;
We can but hold them up, whilst others give.
No shame for helpless man to pray in aid;
Great Sol'mon scorned not to be free o' th' trade;
He begg'd an alms and blusht not, for the boon
He got was treble fairer then his crown.
No wonder that he thriv'd by begging so;
He was both beggar and a chooser too.
O who would trust to work that may obtain
The suit he begs without or sweat or pain?
O what a privilege, great God, have we,
That have the honor but to beg on thee!
Thou dost not fright us with the tort'ring whips
Of bedels;[15] nor dost answer our faint lips
With churlish language. Lord, thou dost not praise
The stricter statute of last Henry's days;[16]
Thou dost not damp us with the empty voice
Of *nothing for ye*; if our clam'rous noise
Should chance t'importune, turn'st thy gracious eye

---

[15] {The beadle was a minor parish officer responsible for keeping order in church and punish petty offenders, including beggars and vagrants.}

[16] {Presumably the 1547 statute authorizing the branding of vagrants, repealed a few years later.}

Upon our wants, and mak'st a quick supply.
Thou dost not brand us with th'opprobrious name
Of idle vagabonds. Thou know'st w'are lame,
And cannot work. Thou dost not, pharoah-like,
Deny us straw, and yet require brick.
Thou canst not hear us groan beneath our task,
But freely giv'st what we have faith to ask:
The most for which my large desire shall plead
To serve the present's but a loaf of bread,
Or but a token (ev'n as beggars use):[17]
That of thy love will fill my slender cruse.
Lord, during life, I'll beg no greater boon,
If at my death thou'lt give me but a crown.

70. *On Cain and David*

Their sins were equal, equal was their guilt.
They both committed homicide, both spilt
Their brother's guiltless blood. Nay, of the twain,
The first occasion was less foul in Cain.
'Twas likely Cain's murther was in heat
Of blood; there was no former grudge, no threat.
But David's was a plot. He took the life
Of poor Uriah to enjoy his wife.
Was justice equal? Was her balance even?
Cain was punisht; David was forgiven.
Both came to trial; but good David did
Confess that sin, which cursed Cain hid.
Cain bewailed the punishment wherein
His sin had plung'd him; David wails his sin.
If I lament my sins, Thou wilt forbear
To punish, Lord, or give me strength to bear.

TEXT: EEBO (STC [2nd ed.] / 20530)

Francis Quarles, *Divine fancies: digested into epigrams, meditations, and observations* (London: Printed by M. F. for John Marriot, 1633).

Checked against *Francis Quarles' "Divine Fancies": a critical edition*, ed. William Liston (Garland, 1992).

[17] {Those licensed to beg were given a badge; at least in Scotland, these often seem to have been made from communion tokens; that this was the case in England as well seems implied by the poem's eucharistic allusions to the bread and cruse: see William Carroll, "Semiotic slippage: identity and authority in the English renaissance, *The European legacy* 2.2 (1997): 213–14; R. Kerr, "Scottish beggars' badges," 297, http://ads .ahds.ac.uk/catalogue/adsdata/arch-352-1/dissemination/pdf/vol_095/95_291_299.pdf (accessed June 7, 2012); see also www.coinlibrary.com/wpns/club_wpns_pr_communion.htm#USE (accessed June 7, 2012).}

JOHN COSIN

Sermons preached at Brancepath, 1632–33[1]

Among Cosin's twenty-three surviving sermons are five dealing with the First and Fourth Commandments, all preached at his Brancepath parish outside Durham in 1632 and 1633. The second of these (Sermon X) censures the Roman Catholic veneration of saints along wholly conventional lines and then mounts a considerably more interesting attack on witchcraft, which Cosin clearly regards as mere superstition—providing those who have suffered misfortune with a scapegoat on whom to vent their rage—but also as a sin: not the sin of falsely accusing old women, however, but of "a whoring after strange gods." A skeptical modernity regarding the reality of witchcraft dovetails with a classically Protestant stress on God's sole and absolute sovereignty. Neither figures in most pictures of Laudianism.

Yet Cosin's unquestionably Laudian sermons often strike a classically Protestant note; numerous passages sound very much like such godly Calvinist authors as Dod and Bayly. Then again, the French Catholics quoted in Jean Delumeau's *Guilt and fear in the West* not infrequently sound like puritan caricatures. In its basic principles, Cosin's view of the Fourth Commandment seems indistinguishable from Bayly's Sabbatarianism.[2] They diverge only over some details: for example, Bayly understands the Commandment as pertaining to the Lord's Day alone; Cosin, to all days set apart for the worship of God, including Sundays, but also including the feasts and fasts of the liturgical year. In practice, of course, this disagreement over the scope of the Commandment underwrote sharply contrasting styles of worship.[3] The devil is in the details. Yet on the more fundamental

---

[1] For the synopsis of Cosin's life and labors, see the introduction prefacing his 1621 Epiphany sermon *<supra>*.

[2] Cosin's sermons on the Fourth Commandment date from 1633, shortly before or after the October 1633 proclamation reissuing the Book of Sports. Although Cosin does not explicitly contest its allowing of secular pastimes following the afternoon service, his insistence on a "whole day" spent in God's service suggests that he shared Bayly's reservations.

[3] On the puritan Sabbath with its Psalm-singing, fasting, and sermon-gadding, see Patrick Collinson, "Elizabethan and Jacobean puritanism as forms of popular religious culture," *The culture of English*

issues of whether the Fourth Commandment remains binding on Christians, whether it is a precept of natural law, whether it has anything like the moral weight of the other Commandments, whether it forbids both ordinary labor and secular recreations, Cosin and Bayly stand together.

The similarities between Cosin's ninth sermon and Dod's *Exposition of the Ten Commandments* point to a deeper congruence. For both, true religion hinges on submission to God's will and hence on abjuring both one's own sense of good and bad and one's own natural desires for freedom and pleasure. Religion is, in Cosin's words, a "yoke," "subjection," "law." If nothing else, these texts help us grasp why *Paradise Lost* makes obedience, which is now primarily valued in dogs, the central virtue for men and angels alike. Cosin's sermon also sheds considerable light on Laudian rule—on the now-profoundly-alien assumptions that motivated it and made it intelligible: the moral recoil from a polity where men are not "forced nor bound to anything but what they are willing to do of themselves," coupled with the recognition that this is precisely the sort of government "the world labors for"; the understanding of authority—of its *proper* use—as resisting the will of the people; as compelling often resentful subjects to act for the common good, for their souls' eternal welfare, and for the greater glory of God.[4]

---

puritanism, 1560–1700, ed. Christopher Durston and Jacqueline Eales (Palgrave Macmillan, 1996), 32–57, esp. 46–57. See also Dow's account of godly fast days <888>.

[4] See, in this volume, Laud <374>, Buckeridge <63>, and Adams <148–49>.

JOHN COSIN
Sermons preached at Brancepath
1632–33

Sermon IX: Preached at Brancepath, July 8, 1632

Non habebis deos alienos coram Me.
Thou shalt have no other gods before my face, or, no other gods but me.
Exodus 20:3

‡

Erewhiles I compared the Law of God to a building; in a building the foundation must be first laid, and this is the foundation here of all that follows, the first proposition, that we must have a God; wherein I doubt not but we shall all agree with the Psalmist to condemn him for a fool that says, *There is no God.* The very heathen themselves would not say it; and if any did, says Tully, there was a fire made to make him away.[1] But then, if there be one, and in the mean while we have him not, we are never a whit the nearer. The duty here is to "have" him. What is that? To know him, to acknowledge and love him, to recognize his supreme dominion over us, to give him worship and honor, to yield him fear and obedience, to be ruled by his will, to live by his laws: this is to have a God.

Indeed this to have him, that we have not ourselves and become our own gods; for our own gods we become when we be not guided by him. If there be not a superior will over us to rule and control ours, or if our wills be our own, and (as the devil told the woman) if we may judge of good and evil as we like best ourselves, according to the mind we have or have not towards it, in any duty that belongs us; then are we the gods ourselves, and a God above us acknowledge we none. Therefore *eritis dii* struck right here, and the devil said true in that sense, that *they should be gods*; for they did their own will, and not his; and in that very respect were gods to themselves.

[1] {See Cicero, *De natura deorum* 1.23.}

The duty then enjoined, ye see, that the will of God be our will; that his law be our rule and guide, and then we have him.

The sin opposed and forbidden, other men call atheism; but because we all confess a God, whether we have him or no, we will call this sin profaneness: when though there be a God, we will have none for all that: no god nor no law to control our own liking; but every man will be a god and a law to himself, to do that only which seems good in his own eyes, like the sons of Belial in the Book of Judges, that did everyone what they had a lust to do themselves, when there was no king in Israel to rule them. It is that the world labors for, and every man studies with himself how to bring it to pass, even at this day: not to be in subjection under any commandments whatsoever, not to have a yoke upon them, nor to be forced nor bound to anything but what they are willing to do of themselves, and then, they say, it would be a merry world. A merry, or a miserable? for then the first thing they did, they would surely raze out this First Commandment, they would have no director, no lawgiver, no commander, no God at all; or if they had, he should be such a one as would take care to provide only for their ease, and not for his own honor; and that would exact no service from their hands, nor no works from their hands, but specially and above all, no tribute from their purses; one that would fill their bellies and clothe their bodies, and not be too curious about their souls or their religion howsoever; in sum, one that would command them nothing which is unpleasing, nor forbid them anything which they have a mind to follow. But be it far from the just to harbor these thoughts or to follow the gross and bestial conceits of these ungodly men.

. . .

Sermon X: Preached at Brancepath, 1632

Non habebis deos alienos coram Me.
Thou shalt have no other gods but me.

‡

But one thing I would have you heed: it was for want of knowledge that this impiety got head; they were not diligent to find out the true God and the right way to worship him, and therefore they were content with any, the next that came to hand.

In hac fide natus sum, in hac moriar, as Auxentius[2] was wont to say: so did his elders before him, and there was all the care he took. This was their case, and it is to be feared lest the devil should make some of your cases alike, while they among you that are ignorant will be ignorant still, and take no thought (so they may live and like) either what god they serve or what religion they profess.

(2.) We come to another impiety, that hath been the offspring and issue of this: the impiety of some Christians (I mean the Papists) that are ready to persuade some of you to their own errors, and say that this is none of God's commandments; and that I know not what or how many saints may be worshipped and prayed to, as well as he. . . .

. . .

---

[2] {Arian bishop of Milan (d. 374). In this faith I was born, in this I shall die.}

When they would not have their corn hurt by tempest, they hold up and fall down to St. John the Evangelist; when they fear burning by fire, St. Agatha is their goddess; and when they fear the plague, they run to St. Sebastian for mercy and pity to be shewn upon them; when they are troubled with a fever, they call upon St. Petronelle; and when their teeth pain them, they bemoan themselves to St. Apoline. St. Felicity is called upon for children; St. Margaret, for a safe delivery; and St. Barbara, for a good departure out of the world. It were infinite to number up all. But I trow this is sufficient to shew their vanity, their impiety, their manifest contempt and breach of this precept, when they have so many gods to run to, so many helpers to trust to besides One; and let no man deceive you: they that hold of this religion, they hold of a wrong one, and one that will deceive them all at last.

. . . They say to the blessed Virgin, *O holy Mother of God, vouchsafe to keep us, we worship thy name, and that world without end; let thy mercy lighten upon us, as our trust is in thee.* And again, *In thee only* (and what can be said more to God?), *in thee only have I trusted, let me never be confounded.* This to her; and to others, *Tu dona coelum, Tu perduc ad gloriam, pestem fuge, solve a peccatis,*[3] in direct and plain terms, so absolute that I know not what can be more; and sure I am that we have no more for God and for Christ himself. Insomuch that we may be bold to conclude and to assure you all that whoever they be that practice themselves or persuade any other to use this kind of religion, they do it by some other precept, for precept of God have they none. Nay this precept, this command of his, is directly set up against them; and though the memory of the saints be precious among us, and ought so to be, though we honor their glorified persons, though we sing and praise and magnify their virtues, though we teach all generations to call them blessed, yet for all this, the commandment of God and the glory of God, of their God and ours, is precious to us above them all, and so let it be for ever; and let all the people say *Amen.*

I have done with the impiety,[4] the breach of this Commandment, abroad, and now I am loath, nay I am sorry to find any at home; but even amongst ourselves this precept is also torn in pieces, and religion suffers violence from many of our people, as well as it does from others, even in this very point of *me* and *non alium*; for what shall we say other, what shall we otherwise conceive of them, who when they have neither faith, hope, nor trust in God, know not his power, know not his providence, nor have any care to learn them neither (as it was Pharaoh's case and Saul's after him), run to the soothsayers and the woman witch of Endor to ask help of the devil and so make a god of him. I trow this is as bad as popery, if it be not worse; and yet, as if it were good lawful Christianity among us, we run to a wizard, that they may ask the devil counsel for us, as readily, nay and a great deal more readily too, many of us, than we run hither to God.

Two sorts of miscreant and wicked people we have: the first challenging and taking to themselves, the second attributing and giving unto others, that power which only appertaineth unto God.

For there are who if any grief or sickness befalls them, if they happen to have any loss of children or corn or cattle or other goods whatsoever, are by and by exclaiming and crying out that they are bewitched, that such a woman has done them harm, that such

---

[3] {Give thou us heaven; lead us to glory, banish plague, absolve from sin.}

[4] {i.e., the impiety with respect to this Commandment shown by Roman Catholics abroad}

another can do them good; therefore to the one they seek for help, of the other they seek revenge. And all this while, God's Commandment is not so much as thought of; but to other helpers they run, as if there were no God in Israel that ordereth all things according to his will, in whose hands are life and death, sickness and health, wealth and woe, and who hath therefore commanded us in all our necessities to resort unto him.

And what a scandal is it to the Gospel of Christ, to the profession of our faith, that the glory and power of God should be so abridged and abated as to be thrust into the hands or lips or medicines or charms of a lewd old woman, woman or man, or whosoever; that the power of the Creator should be attributed unto any creature at all; that there should be such gross and reckless presumption, either in the one or the other, as to take Christ's office from him, as to take upon them to heal and cure diseases, to foretell things to come, to tell the secrets of the mind, whereby he was specially known and made known to be God;[5] that if any happen to be somewhat strangely afflicted with diseases or torments or losses, such as are described in the New Testament, we fly from trusting in the Son and power of God to trusting in a witch. . . . And if anything happen well, presently it must be attributed to that kind of skill; but if all fail, they are yet ready to think they came rather an hour too late than went a mile too far; and truly if this be not to go a whoring after strange gods, I know not what is.

Sure I am it is the cunning and illusion of the devil thus to infatuate and besot the minds of gross and ignorant people to the distrust of God and to the destruction of their souls. . . .

. . .

Now besides this wicked distrust in God, and seeking after other remedies, there be other vain and silly observations whereby men also transgress this First Commandment, and forget the power and providence of him that made it.

Those they be, that by casting of fortunes, by chattering of birds, by viewing the lines of the hands, and other such unlawful and superstitious observations, take upon them to judge of men's acts and lives and of other things to come; for what is this, saith the prophet Isaiah, but to make more gods than one; *Annunciate nobis quae ventura sunt in futurum, et sciemus quia dii estis*, "Take upon you to tell us beforehand what things shall come after, and we shall say ye be gods." It is God's office to do this, and none of yours.

And though it be common, yet it is a common sin among the rest of them that are transgressors against this Commandment, to be superstitious and fearful or distrustful of God, upon fond and idle observations: as at the crossing of the hare and the stumbling at the threshold to turn back and give over their journey. A number of such other vanities there are—which argue men's fear and distrust in God's providence, and therefore their contempt and breach of this law—whatever they say their fore-elders have taught them to the contrary. For they that trust to their own fancies, to old and foolish fables, more than they trust to God and his sayings, sure I am they are out here at *habebis me*, they have him not as they should have him. . . .

And if there be any among you that are given this way, God give them grace to repent and amend; for both they that use it and they that seek after it or resort unto it will in

---

[5] {Only God knows the secrets of the mind and heart; and one way Christ made known his divinity was his knowledge of such secrets.}

the end find themselves where they would be full loath to be found, even in the power of him upon whose power they depended here. Whereas they that trust not in him here shall stand in no fear of him hereafter, but having God for their strength and relying upon his will and providence alone, according to this his precept, shall at last be satisfied with the abundance of his mercies and goodness in his eternal kingdom of glory, which Christ, the King of glory, grant unto us; to whom, with the Father, &c.

Sermon XI: Brancepath, 1633

Memento, ut diem Sabbathi sanctifices, &c.
Remember that thou keep holy the Sabbath day; six days shalt thou labor, &c.
Exodus 20:8

This is the Fourth Commandment; there are three before it that took order for the worship of God himself, and for the honor of his name; this takes order for the public form of his worship and the solemnity of his honor: that it be not only done, but done at a set time and upon the days appointed for it, when nothing else may be done; and done in a solemn assembly and a full meeting of the people together, when they shall do it so much the better.

It is a commandment whereupon God hath bestowed some cost, urged it more fully, given more reasons for it, spent more words upon it, than upon any of the rest. And I trow, this is a sign that his heart is set upon it, that he will never endure the neglect of it; and therefore that whatever we do, we should be sure to remember and regard this as one of his most special commandments; for which purpose he begins it with a *memento* too, so as he doth none of the other.

. . .

I. *Remember thou keep,* &c. We begin with the *memento,* which word, that the better notice might be taken of it, is emphatically delivered in the original, and doubled over for fear it should be forgotten or neglected by any. *Recordando recordere,* "remember; and while you are remembering, remember still," that is, remember so that at no time it may slip out of your memory, but that at all times you be careful and diligent to keep it; to keep it in mind, that you may the better observe it in practice.

It is a vehement *epiphonema*[6] this, like that of our Savior in the Gospel, *Let him that heareth hear,* to stir up the dullness of the ear, even while it was a-hearing; or like those frequent repetitions in our public service here in the Church, *Let us pray,* and again praying, *let us pray,* that while we are at it, we be mindful of it (as many of us are not), and in doing of it, we do it indeed; this is *recordando recordare.*

A word and an item (as I said), of all the Ten Commandments set only at the beginning of this; as if God had made his choice, his special choice, of this above all the rest, to put his *memento* here, which he would have them that have forgotten it to call back into their remembrance well; and they that do remember it, never to forget it again.

Of God's choice to set it here I will shew you some reasons, and then proceed to that which follows.

[6] {exclamation}

1. There is not in all the Commandments a duty that we are more hardly brought unto than so to attend God's service as wholly to neglect our own for it; no law we grudge, no commandment that we murmur and repine at so much as to leave all our own occasions, and come a mile or twain, or spend a whole day or two in a week, to attend his; for that this is the duty of this precept, we will prove hereafter. In the meanwhile, we are naturally averse from it; so given to our own ways, to our profit, to our pleasures, or to our ease that we are ever ready to neglect, always willing to forget, what God would have us remember about it. This is one reason that God hath set his *memento* upon it.

2. Another is for that this precept is the very life of all the Decalogue, by due observance whereof we come both to learn and to put in practice all the rest of God's commandments the better; and without which, in a short time, they would come all to nothing. For therefore is this time set apart, that people, among other ends, might meet together to hear the whole Law of God, and by hearing what it is, learn to observe and do every duty that belongs unto it. But let it be as the world would have it, sit at home barely and take your ease; look to your own, and remember God's affairs that list; hear not of the Law and the Prophets but when ye are at leisure; listen not to the duties of a Christian above once or twice a quarter, as the lewd custom among a great many of you is, and see what your Christianity will come to, or what will become of all the duties of the Law, of all the sermons of the Prophets, and of all the service and worship of God in a short time. Certain it is, that through the neglect of this, all the rest of the Commandments come to be neglected too, many duties of them not so much as known; and sure I am, most of them not so well put in practice as otherwise we might have hoped they would be. Remember this therefore, and the benefit of it will be that it will bring all the rest of the Commandments into your remembrance. So the *memento* set here, which is the life and the practice of all, is as much as if it had been set upon them all, upon every Commandment by itself. And be this the second reason.

3. Ye shall have a third, and so we will leave it. There was at this time of giving the Law, throughout the world a more general neglect of this Commandment than of all the rest; other things they remembered, this they forgot, and therefore it was high time to put them in mind of it with a *memento*; they found time for everything but for the public and solemn service of God; every day of the week they took to be their own, this day and all, and had quite obliterated, razed out of their hearts, that which the law of nature had written there from the beginning: that some time of the revolution, and a full sufficient time too, such as this is, was to be reserved and set apart for God himself, not to be spent in any other service than his own. Which being now at the giving of the Law determined to the seventh day, the Jews kept it after their manner very strictly; but being since (at the time of the Gospel) changed to the first day, and that upon good ground too (as afterwards ye shall hear), in these latter days we observe it as loosely; insomuch as, if ever, it is full time now to renew and set the *memento* upon it again, *remember* that we keep it holy; for by our doings we seem, most of us, to have forgotten it full profanely. . . . And this for the *memento*.

II. Follows what we are to remember, *diem Sabbathi*, "Remember to keep the Sabbath day." And a Sabbath day is nothing else in signification but a day of rest; always provided . . . that it be no idle rest, but a rest from common affairs that holy and sacred actions may be the better attended.

In this sense every festival, lawfully appointed and made sacred, is a Sabbath; and by the moral virtue of this precept, even from this very word *Sabbathum*, we are bound to keep them every one. So were the Jews—all the rest of their feasts (which were called Sabbaths too) besides their *dies septimus*, the day that is hereafter mentioned. . . .

And from hence we fetch the morality of this precept, that which the law of nature taught every man, even from the word *Sabbathum*, that there are days of rest and sanctity to be kept holy to the Lord, and that unto what day soever the *Sabbathum* is applied, upon any day that a holy rest is lawfully instituted and appointed, that day, so far as the institution goes and so long as the appointment lasts, is to be kept sacred and holy to God. So the Jews were to keep their Sabbaths, and we our festivals, every one according to the laws and institutions that were made for them by God and the Church.

For as for the *dies septimus* here, the seventh day, whereunto the name of the Sabbath was afterwards given by way of eminence, we have nothing now to do with it, it expired with the Jews' synagogue. . . .

. . .

Remember then that you keep the festivals appointed, is a good paraphrase upon this text, neither can I give you a better; for the Jews' Sabbaths are all gone, gone like shadows; and in sign that they are gone indeed, the very name of a Sabbath in regard of our festivals is gone away with them too; for ye shall not read in all the ancient writers for 1500 years together that ever any Christians would use that name (though in a few late writers, I know not why, it be again taken up), but in place of their Sabbaths, the apostles and their successors have instituted Christian festivals, of which the Lord's day is the chief, succeeding in the room of that which was also more eminently styled the Jewish Sabbath.

By this time then ye know what ye are to remember and what to understand by the Sabbath day.

III. Follows the end of remembering it: *memento ut sanctifices*, remember it to keep it holy. And then we only keep it holy when we apply it unto holy uses.

For ye must know that God hath dealt with this day, and other days made holy, as he hath done with men and other creatures: sanctifying some of them and destinating them to a more reserved and higher use than that which is common. By nature all men are alike, so are all days; but yet for all that, there be some men separated from the vulgar sort and exalted above the rest, as magistrates and kings are, as priests and ministers of God are; we must not use them at our pleasure, as we would use one of our own servants.[7] It is alike with these days, which above all other days are made holy to God; the rest are like our own servants, we may employ them about our own affairs; but these holy days we may not be so bold with; they are set apart for holy uses, for God's service; they are none of ours, nor may they be employed about our own business. . . . As the water in baptism, as the bread and wine in the Eucharist, so is this day consecrate and set apart by the Church for holy and divine uses.

[7] {On kings differing from other men only with respect to their "use," see *The political works of James I*, intro. Charles McIlwain (Harvard UP, 1918), 41. That holy things differ from ordinary not by any intrinsic sanctity but by being appointed to a "higher use" is a commonplace of Tudor-Stuart *eucharistic* theology; that Cosin goes on to enlarge this principle to "everything which is hallowed" (i.e., everything used in God's service) adds a Laudian spin (see Peter Lake, "The Laudian style," *The early Stuart Church, 1603–1642*, ed. Kenneth Fincham [Stanford UP, 1993], 164–65). See also, Field, *Of the Church*, bk 4 chap. 31 <*supra*>.}

And what God hath made holy let no man make common, by applying or spending that time at his pleasure which God hath consecrated and dedicated and marked out for his service. It is of the nature of every thing which is hallowed, not to be used as other common things are [Levit. 27-29]; every thing separate from the common use must be holy to the Lord; not so much but the very fire-forks and the flesh-hooks, the meanest instruments that belonged unto the sacrifice, but they were forbidden to be put to any other use; the very snuffers of the temple not to touch another lamp, nothing that is sanctified to be profaned, that is, to be used as other common things are. . . . And take it for your rule, ye may as well profane and use this house of God at your pleasure—make it your workshop, make it your barn—as ye may take the liberty which ye do to profane and use at your pleasure these holy days of God; the sins are both of one nature, and therefore hath God also joined the duties together: ye shall reverence my sanctuary and observe my Sabbaths.

. . .

The keeping of these days holy in manner as we ought respects both our public and our private duties.

The public first, enjoined and commanded under the name of *convocatio sancta* in the twenty-third chapter of Leviticus and third verse: "But in the day of rest" (that is, as is there expressed, upon every festival) "shall be an holy convocation to the Lord"; that is, a meeting and a gathering together of all the people in the public place of God's worship, which is the church, there to do him open homage and service, and (as we tell you here, before we begin the service) "to render thanks for the great benefits we have received at his hands, to set forth his most worthy praise, to hear his most holy word, and to ask those things that are requisite and necessary, as well for the body as the soul." This is the public duty of every day that is made holy.

For a private holiness at home will not serve, will not satisfy this Commandment of God. . . . *Aperite mihi portas*, "Open me," saith he, "the gates of righteousness," that is, the church doors. His own house, as holy as it was, would not hold him; but open the doors of the tabernacle of the Temple; thither will I go in and shew in the congregation; in the great congregation will I praise and give thanks unto the Lord. A congregation, I say, and a great one, not when half the church is empty, but so great that it may *constituere diem solennem in condensis usque ad cornua altaris* [Ps.118.27], as in the Psalm he goes on, that the people may stand so thick in the church, as to fill it up from the entrance of the door to the very edge of the altar; that is, from the very lowest to the very highest place of the church. This is that which God enjoins, *convocatio sancta*.

. . .

. . . And ye shall see the reason of this public assembling together to set forth the service of God.

1. God shall have the more honor by it, more by a full congregation than by a few. . . .

2. It makes more for the good of the Church; the prayers are the stronger for it, they are carried up the higher, they pierce the clouds when they are sent up with a full cry of all the people together; whereas they languish, like the congregation itself, when they want half their company to help them.

3. Every private Christian is the better for it; he does his service with more cheerfulness when he has all his companions and fellow-servants to join with him in it; the worse

a great deal if he wants them; dull and heavy at his work, ever ready to sleep, besides the evil example that he takes to be as negligent as he sees others be, and otherwhiles also to take the same liberty, and tarry away himself, which toy takes a many; I fear it will take them all together at once, one time or other (as many holy days it does), and so we shall have a goodly solemnity to celebrate God's festivals. . . . The truth is, all are ill disposed or else they would never make such poor pretences as they usually do. The rawness of the weather, the hardness of the way, the length of the journey, the least indisposition of the body are, with most of you, now thought to be reasons sufficient enough to affront this law and commandment of God; and yet your own affairs, your own pleasures and customs, they shall not affront. The day before was a day for your market; perhaps the weather worse, the journey longer, yet that you could bear. This day is a market for your souls; and this place, hither you cannot come, could not, no by no means; you had endangered your health, and yet you would venture it for a less matter by far. So comes God's church, his market-place, to be the emptiest always of the two, to the shame of your pretended religion. Indeed he said well, if the people will not come, *satis unus, satis nullus*,[8] let the priest serve God by himself rather than God should have no service done him at all; the brooks must run on in their channels whether the beasts will come and drink of them or no; and God must have his honor done him, whether the people be pleased to assist at it or not. "Well if one," says the heathen man; but better a great deal if many, if all the people come together.

Better for the reasons we have given already, and for these besides. 1. In regard of the Church's uniformity, that they may all be known to be of one and the same mind, of one and the same religion, that they keep one profession of their faith; and therefore it is said of the very first Christians of all, as a true note of their holiness and religion, that they were all together with one accord in one place.

2. Then in regard of the commonwealth, whose blessing it is when God maketh men to be of one mind in this house; whose strength and stay it is, when God is duly honored, as well as when the king is duly served and obeyed by all the people together.

3. And lastly, in regard of each private man; that here, hence, as from a store-house, he may fetch food for his soul . . . give praise and honor and obedience unto God, who, in exchange, will give him knowledge to enlighten his understanding and grace to reform his will and assistance in plenty to resist the temptations of this wicked world. Which he grant unto us for his mercy's sake; for I cannot now, the time will not suffer me, to go any further. To God, &c., &c.

Sermon XIII: Preached at Brancepath in 1633

But the seventh day is the Sabbath of the Lord thy God; in it thou shalt do no manner of work
thou and thy son and thy daughter, thy man-servant and thy maid-servant, thy cattle
and the stranger that is within thy gates, &c.
Exodus 20:10

‡

---

[8] {one [reader] would suffice, or none (Pyrrho)}

And this is that which the Psalmist speaks, *vacate et videte*; first *vacate*, rest from your bodily labor, to distinguish the day; and then *videte*, come hither to behold God's presence in holiness, to sanctify the day; so that in keeping of all holy days, there is still a *cessate*, a rest from bodily and servile labor. For ordinary labors are both in themselves painful, and base also in comparison of festival services done to God; in regard whereof the very natural difference between them must needs enforce that the one should submit and give way to the other, because neither of them can concur and be done together. And besides of rest for this purpose, all that ever made trial what it was to have the soul busied in high matters will certainly say, as the philosopher said truly, *postulandis esse secessum ut melius intendamus*; we must give over other cares, if we mean to intend these here as we should do.

By all which ye see here that we take not rest for idleness. They are idle who to avoid painfulness will not use the labor whereunto God and nature hath bound them; they rest which either cease from their work when they have done it and made it perfect, or else give over a meaner labor because a worthier and a better is to be undertaken. And of this latter sort is the rest that we speak of, and is requisite for the better keeping and sanctifying the holy days and festivals of God. So have you the two first, sanctity and rest.

We come to the other two properties, joy and bounty. For the days which are chosen out to serve as public memorials of God's mercies to us ought to be clothed with those outward robes of festivity, whereby their difference from other days may be made sensible.

3. And that joy and gladness is one of these, we have express Scripture for it, from the mouth of the prophet David, "This is the day which the Lord hath made, let us rejoice and be glad in it"; and from the mouth of God himself, "In your solemn feasts ye shall take of the goodly fruits, and branches of the trees, and you shall eat your bread with joy, and rejoice before the Lord."

According to the rule of which general directions taken from the law of God, the practice of the Church hath ever been guided; that is, in regard of the natural fitness and decency of the thing itself, and not with reference to any Jewish ceremonies, such as were properly theirs, and are not by us expedient to be continued.

But this of joy is so expedient and natural for a festival solemnity that without it, it seems no feast at all, seems rather one of those black and dismal days, wherein well may we be humbled with sorrow and fasting for some punishment that justly befell us upon the day, but acknowledge no benefit or great work of Christ, such as was done for us upon this day.

Fasting then, and sitting all day pensive and still upon Sundays, as the use of some is, is no good Christianity, is unnatural and no way suitable to the honor of the day, nor no way decent in itself neither; because, while the mind hath just occasion to adorn and deck herself with gladness, as upon the apprehension and meditation of Christ's benefits this day it hath, the need of sorrow and pensiveness becometh her not.

(4.) To joy and cheerfulness we add bounty and liberality, which is required in them that abound, partly as a sign of their own joy and thankfulness to God, expressed by any oblation to him, and partly as a means whereby to refresh the poor and needy; who being, especially at these times, made partakers of relaxation and joy with others, do the more religiously bless God with us and the more contentedly endure the burden of that hard estate wherein they continue. Neither did the old Christians, that were any ways able, think any Lord's day, or other holy day, rightly observed by them, wherein they brought not their offering to the Church in sign of thankfulness to God, and gave not their alms to the poor besides, in sign of amity and love to their brethren. . . .

III. And now by these things that are commanded ye may easily collect both what is forbidden and what is permitted.

1. Forbidden first, profaneness, unholiness, the opposite to sanctity; all sin and wickedness in private, all careless and reckless attendance of God's holy service in public. . . .

. . .

And they in special, that regarding neither the holiness of this day nor the holiness of this place, come not at it to do their bounden duty and service to God, but pass their time either in idleness or riot or other vain and idle pastimes. St. Austin said well of them, these people keep not *Sabbathum Jehovae* but *Sabbatum Satanae*; they keep holy day for the devil and not for God; and should be better employed, says he, laboring and plowing in their fields than so to spend the day in idleness and vanity; and women should better bestow their time in spinning of wool (*lanam et linam* are his words) than upon the Lord's day to lose their time leaping and dancing, and other such wantonness. . . . for following idleness and sport and lewd pastimes, he calls it *Sabbatum vituli aurei*; they that skipped about the golden calf kept as good a holy day as these.

2. The next thing forbidden, which I can but name now, is servile and bodily labor, our worldly employments, though other days never so lawful. . . .

. . . And truly, the voluntary, scandalous contempt, such as otherwhiles we see among some of our people, of the rest from labor by means whereof God is publicly served upon this day, cannot too severely be corrected and bridled. Nehemiah protested against them, and so do we, and so hath the Church of God, and the Christian superiors and governors of God's people ever done, pleading for the honor of Christ and for this day of his Resurrection in their sermons, in their laws, in their edicts, everywhere most fully and religiously. I thought to have produced them now, but I think I have said enough for once, and the next time, by God's help, I shall end all.

To which God, the Father, Son, and Holy Ghost, ascribe we, &c.

TEXT: John Cosin, *The works of the Right Reverend Father in God, John Cosin*, vol. 1 (Oxford, 1842).[9]

---

[9] This was the first edition; on the printing history of Cosin's sermons, see <255>.

RICHARD CORBETT[1]

Upon Fairford windows
ca. 1632–33

Upon Fairford windows[2]

TELL me, you anti-saints, why glass
With you is longer-lived than brass?[3]
And why the saints have scap't their falls
Better from windows than from walls?
Is it because the brethren's fires
Maintain a glass-house at Blackfriars?[4]
Next which the church stands north and south,[5]
And east and west the preacher's mouth.
Or is't because such painted ware
Resembles something what you are:
So pied,[6] so seeming, so unsound

---

[1] {The introductory biography for Corbett can be found on <100>, prefacing his "An elegy on the death of Dr. Ravis."}

[2] [Are much admired, says the provincial historian of Gloucestershire, for their excellent painted glass. There are twenty-eight large windows, which are curiously painted with the stories of the Old and New Testament: the middle windows in the choir, and on the west side of the church, are larger than the rest; those in the choir represent the history of our Savior's Crucifixion; the window at the west end represents hell and damnation; those on the side of the church and over the body represent the figures in length of the prophets, apostles, fathers, martyrs and confessors, and also the persecutors of the church. . . . {Gilchrist's note; for further discussion of these windows, see the introduction to William Strode's poem on the same subject <*infra*>}.]

[3] {Referring to the Reformation destruction of brass funeral monuments on the grounds that their inscriptions seeking prayers for the souls of the dead encouraged superstition.}

[4] {On the godly parish of St. Anne's, Blackfriars, see *Survey of London* <689>.}

[5] {Churches were traditionally oriented on an east-west axis, a custom the godly disdained.}

[6] {inconstant, flawed; "spotted" in both the literal and metaphoric sense}

In manners and in doctrine found,
That, out of emblematic wit,
You spare yourselves in sparing it?
If it be so, then, Fairford, boast
Thy church hath kept what all have lost,
And is preservéd from the bane
Of either war or puritan,
Whose life is color'd in thy paint:
The inside dross, the outside saint.

TEXT: *The poems of Richard Corbet, late Bishop of Oxford and of Norwich*, 4th ed., ed. Octavius Gilchrist (London, 1807).

Checked against J. A. W. Bennett & Hugh Trevor-Roper, *The poems of Richard Corbett* (Clarendon, 1955).

WILLIAM STRODE
(ca. 1601–1645)

His father died when Strode was just a child, but the generosity of relatives enabled him to attend Westminster School and, in 1617, to enter Christ's Church, Oxford, from whence only death did him depart. He took his BA in 1621, his MA in 1624. The majority of his secular poems probably date from the 1620s. These were wildly popular; mid-seventeenth-century commonplace books and manuscript miscellanies transcribe more Strode lyrics than any other poet's work, including that of Jonson, Donne, and Carew. His "On Chloris walking in the snow" was perhaps the most popular poem of the century, excepting only Herrick's "Gather ye rosebuds." A German traveling in Persia heard a Farsi version at the court of Shah Sefi I, and Swedenborg translated it into Latin.

In 1628, however, Strode entered the priesthood, soon after becoming chaplain to Richard Corbett, the newly installed Bishop of Oxford. The year following, he became university orator—his letters and speeches on behalf of the University betraying a taste for florid compliment that later caused trouble both for himself and Laud (on whom many of Strode's high-flying titles were bestowed), although Strode's answers apparently satisfied the Parliamentary inquisitors.[1] Some time around 1628, he also started writing sacred poetry.

Strode, who had taken his BD in 1631, remained at Oxford following Corbett's translation to Norwich a year later. For the royal visit of 1636, two months after Convocation had adopted the Laudian statutes, the Archbishop, who was also Oxford's chancellor, sought to mark the occasion with splendid entertainments embodying the spirit of the reforms (Smyth 461). To this end, he commissioned Strode's sole play, *The floating island*, which was staged with scenery by Inigo Jones and the music of Henry Lawes. An intelligent, prophetic, and spectacularly undramatic psycho-political allegory of rebellion and restoration, the performance flopped. (Despite its defects as theater, however, the work more than repays reading.) Strode returned to his studies, taking his DD in 1638, and, through Laud's good offices, receiving a canonry at Christ's Church.

[1] Laud, *Works* 4:157–60.

When the war broke out, Strode remained at Oxford, preaching but also editing and revising his poetry for publication. Death, however, arrived before Strode had time even to make a will, and the poetry manuscript vanished. A poorly printed *Floating island* came out in 1655, but Strode's celebrated lyrics sunk into quick oblivion. An attempt was made to rescue them in 1907 when Bertram Dobell printed an edition based on commonplace-book and miscellany versions, but their multiplicity of variant readings and contradictory ascriptions of authorship left Dobell's text too conjectural for comfort. And then in 1952 Margaret Crum discovered Strode's lost manuscript in the Corpus Christi archives. A scholarly edition of Strode's poetry based on this manuscript is currently being prepared by Margaret Forey.

Of the four poems reprinted here, two can be dated with some confidence. Mary Prideaux, the child commemorated in Strode's elegy and the daughter of John Prideaux—the eminent Calvinist rector of Exeter College and Oxford's regius professor of divinity—died in December 1624, just two months shy of her eighth birthday.[2] "On Fairford windows" is one of several poems (including one by Corbett *<vide supra>*) on the wondrously preserved medieval stained glass of a Cotswold parish church, all which poems probably respond to Henry Sherfield's unauthorized 1630 assault on Salisbury's medieval windows and the resulting Star Chamber trial of 1632–33. The remaining two poems provide no hints as to their possible date; and, in truth, since Strode frequently revised his own poems, often substantially, trying to assign a specific lyric to a specific date might be thought both fruitless and misleading.

Whenever their composition, they are extraordinary poems. Like much of Strode's verse, "On Fairford windows" meditates on "the inadequacy of language" (Smyth 445).[3] It is also a sustained engagement with Protestant iconoclasm, which begins by admitting the iconoclasts' premise that images of such vividness do strike us as "real." Those who over the years have viewed the two caged doves Mary brings to her purification half-believe that the pair may have hatched some little ones that subsequently flew out the window <ll. 29–32>. The blurring of the line between representation and presence dominates the second half of the poem, which focuses on the interplay between the images and the viewer's imagination that makes it seem as though the ghosts in the Last Judgment window are rising from the dead, and the saints bending downward "past the glass"—past the window's edge to the living Christians beneath <ll. 45–46>. In the lines that follow, the viewers start to respond in terror and grief to the painted scenes of Crucifixion and Deposition as if witnessing the events. Yet this is not idolatry; the viewers do not adore the windows or confuse glass with God. The windows have a spiritual and emotional power inseparable from the vivid realism of their images, the power to make us see Christ "as in a glass" <ll. 27–28>,[4] where "glass," in its double sense of window and mirror, evokes Paul's description of human knowing "through a glass darkly." The windows, that is, function like the

---

[2] My heartfelt thanks to Margaret Forey for providing this information.

[3] On the windows themselves, see Sarah Brown and Lindsay MacDonald, *Life, death and art: the medieval stained glass of Fairford parish church* (Sutton, 1997).

[4] Note that Milton attributes a very similar power to song in "At a solemn music."

compositio loci of Ignatian meditation: they do not draw us to worship their images but to glaze—to "anneal," as Herbert says in his "Church windows"—their sacred story on our hearts <ll. 68–70>, thus (quoting Herbert once again) "making Thy life to shine within."

"On the Bible" might be thought of as a companion piece to "On Fairford windows"—contrapuntal celebrations of image and word, where "word" shifts between (and at moments conflates) Scriptural text, the eternal Logos that "spake" in Creation, and the incarnate Christ.

The image of the paper-wrapped Scriptures as the swaddled infant Christ of a Nativity scene with which the poem concludes seems an implicit reproach to the Reformed tendency to divorce the written from the incarnate word. The theology of Strode's "Justification," however, is fully Protestant. Luther's *Turmerlebnis* centered on the realization that, despite our personal unrighteousness, God accepts us because Christ's alien righteousness covers our sins so that we are pleasing in his sight; by virtue of Christ's "imputed justice" (his justice, imputed to us), the "clay" of fallen nature "seems fair, well-spoke, smooth, sweet, each way" <ll. 7–8>. If the poem does not sound quite like standard Protestant doctrine, it is because Strode transposes the concept of imputation, which typically has forensic overtones, into an aesthetic register, describing how various things become pleasing, not because they themselves undergo change, but by being scented, smoothed, sweetened with an alien loveliness.

The transposition is witty, but not subversive; the poem affirms, even as it aestheticizes, a Protestant understanding of justification. The complex, rather than merely oppositional, relation of a dyed-in-the-wool Laudian like Strode to the Reformed wing of the English Church likewise makes itself felt, although along different lines, in the elegy commemorating the little daughter of Oxford's most distinguished Calvinist theologian. Recent scholarship (e.g., the 2004 *ODNB* entry on John Prideaux) depicts his relation to Laud and Laudian Oxford as so unremittingly antagonistic and unhappy that one cannot conceive of a priest like Strode being present at his dying child's bedside or seeking to console the bereaved parents. Yet the *ODNB* entry also notes that "Prideaux had a pedagogue's penchant for punning and wordplay," one contemporary even remarking his "becoming festivity," which sounds very Strode-like; and the fact that he remained a royal chaplain throughout Charles' reign, with Laud apparently intervening more than once on his behalf, suggests the existence of bonds that could at least partially override soteriological differences.

The poem itself is the only early modern elegy I have read that conveys something of what it must have been like to watch one's child die. Dobell said that had Strode "written nothing else, this poem would alone suffice to place him in the front rank of elegiac poets" (xxxii). It is not "a thing done perfectly"—the consolatory section has frigid patches and a few lines make no sense, although the problem here may be textual corruption rather than Homer nodding—but, overall, Dobell's praise does not seem misplaced.

Sources: *ODNB*; Bertram Dobell, intro. and ed., *The poetical works of William Strode* (London, 1907); Laud, *Works*; Adam Smyth, "'Art reflexive': the poetry, sermons, and drama of William Strode (1601?–1645)," *Studies in Philology* 103.4 (2006): 436–64.

WILLIAM STRODE[1]

Sacred Poems
ca. 1625–45

On Fairford windows

I know no paint of poetry
Can mend such colored imag'ry
In sullen ink; yet, Fairford, I
May relish thy fair memory.
    Such is the echo's fainter sound,   5
Such is the light when sun is drown'd;
So did the fancy look upon
The work before it was begun;
Yet when those shews are out of sight,
My weaker colors may delight.   10
    Those images so faithfully
Report true feature to the eye
As you may think each picture was
Some visage in a looking-glass,
Not a glass-window face; unless   15
Such as Cheapside hath, where a press
Of painted gallants looking out
Bedeck the casement round about.
But these have holy phis'nomy:
Each pane instructs the laity   20

---

[1] {My deepest gratitude to Margaret Forey for her help with textual emendations based on Strode's rediscovered manuscript <vide introduction supra>, which I have silently substituted for the Dobell readings whenever the manuscript version seemed clearly superior.}

With silent eloquence, for here
Devotion leads the eye, not ear,
To note the catechizing paint,
Whose easy phrase doth so acquaint
Our sense with Gospel, that the Creed,   25
In such a hand,[2] the weak may read.
Such types, even yet, of virtue be;[3]
And Christ, as in a glass, we see.
    Behold two turtles in one cage,
With such a lovely equipage,[4]   30
As they who knew them long may doubt
Some young ones have been stolen out.
    When, with a fishing rod, the clark
Saint Peter's draught of fish doth mark,
Such is the scale, the eye, the fin,   35
You'd think they strive and leap within;
But if the net which holds them break,
He with his angle some would take.
    But would you walk a turn in Paul's?
Look up; one little pane enrolls   40
A fairer temple: fling a stone,
The church is out o' the windows thrown.
    Consider, but not ask your eyes,[5]
And ghosts at midday seem to rise;
The saints there, striving to descend,   45
Are past the glass, and downward bend.
    Look there! The devil! all would cry
Did they not see that Christ was by.
See where he suffers for thee. See
His body taken from the tree: 50
Had ever death such life before?
The limber corpse, besullied o'er
With meager paleness, doth display
A middle state twixt flesh and clay;
His arms and legs, his head and crown,   55
Like a true lambskin dangling down.
Who can forbear, the grave being nigh,
To bring fresh ointment in his eye?
    The wondrous art hath equal[6] fate,

---

[2] {in such handwriting, i.e., the language of images}

[3] {I.e., they still retain their power or efficacy (a standard early meaning of "virtue").}

[4] {attire, "get up"—here presumably the turtledoves' feathers}

[5] {The Corpus Christi manuscript reads "Consider not, but ask your Eyes"—a significant variant.}

[6] {The fate of the windows—the fact that, although unprotected, they have remained unharmed—is a wonder equal to that of their art (with thanks to Margaret Forey for this gloss).}

Unfenc'd and yet unviolate.   60
The puritans were sure deceiv'd,
And thought those shadows mov'd and heav'd,
So held from stoning Christ; the wind
And bois'trous tempests were so kind
As on his image not to prey,   65
Whom both the winds and seas obey.
    At Momus' wish[7] be not amaz'd;
For if each Christian heart were glaz'd
With such a window, then each breast
Might be his own evangelist.

On the Bible

Behold this little volume here enroll'd:[8]
'Tis the Almighty's present to the world.
Hearken, earth, earth; each senseless thing can hear
His Maker's thunder, though it want an ear.
God's word is senior to his works; nay, rather,   5
If rightly weigh'd, the world may call it father:
God spake, 'twas done; this great foundation
Is the Creator's exhalation
Breath'd out in speaking. The best work of man
Is better than his word; but if we scan   10
God's word aright, his works far short do fall:
The Word is God; the works are creatures all.
The sundry pieces of this general frame
Are dimmer letters, all which spell the same
Eternal word; but these cannot express   15
His greatness with such easy readiness,
And therefore yield. The heavens shall pass away,
The sun and moon and stars shall all obey
To light one general bonfire; but his word,
His builder-up, his all-destroying sword,   20
That still survives; no jot of that can die;
Each tittle measures immortality.
    The Word's own mother, on whose breast did hang
The world's upholder drawn into a span,
She, she was not so blest because she bare him   25
As 'cause herself was new-born, and did hear him.
Before she had brought forth, she heard her Son

---

[7] {Momus, the ancient god of satire, wished that people had windows in their breasts so that each might see what others really felt.}

[8] {both "wrapped up" and hence "swaddled," but also rolled up, as a scroll}

First speaking in th'Annunciatïon;
And then, even then, before she brought forth child,
By name of *Blessed* she herself instyl'd.   30
      Once more this mighty word his people greets,
Thus lapt and thus swath'd up in paper sheets;[9]
Read here God's image with a zealous eye,
The legible and written Deity.

Justification

See how the rainbow in the sky
Seems gaudy through the sun's bright eye;
Hark how an echo answer makes;
Feel how a board is smooth'd with wax;
Smell how a glove puts on perfume;   5
Taste how their sweetness pills assume:
So by imputed justice, clay
Seems fair, well-spoke, smooth, sweet, each way.
      The eye doth gaze on robes appearing,
      The prompted echo takes our hearing,   10
      The board our touch, the scent our smell,
      The pill our taste: man, God as well.

On the same M. M. P.†[10]   †Mistress Mary Prideaux

Sleep pretty one, oh sleep, while I
Sing thee thy latest lullaby;
And may my song be but as she,
Ne'er was sweeter harmony.
Thou wert all music: all thy limbs   5
Were but so many well set hymns
To praise thy Maker. In thy brow
I read thy soul, and know not how
To tell which whiter was, or smoother,
Or more spotless, one or th'other.   10
No jar, no harshness in thee; all
Thy passions were at peace; no gall,
No rough behavior, but even such
In disposition as in touch.
Yet Heaven, poor soul, was harsh to thee;

---

[9] {All early modern paper was made from cloth rags.}

[10] {Some manuscripts attribute the first two parts of this poem to Strode, but doubts arise because Strode did write another poem on Mary Prideaux's death, and so this one may have been attributed to him by mistake. Margaret Forey, however, notes that Strode sometimes wrote two poems on the same subject. He did not include it in the manuscript he was working on at the time of his death.}

Death used thee not half orderly.
If thou must needs go, must thy way
Needs be by torture? must thy day
End in the morning? and thy night
Come with such horror and affright?   20
Death might have seiz'd thee gentlier, and
Embrac't thee with a softer hand.
Thou wert not, sure, so loath to go
That thou needst be dragged so;
For thou wert all obedience, and hadst wit
To do Heaven's will and not dispute with it.
Yet 'twere a hard heart, a dead eye
That sighless, tearless, could stand by
Whiles thy poor mother felt each groan
As much as ere she did her own   30
When she groan'd for thee; and thy cries
Marr'd not our ears more than her eyes.
Yet if thou tookst some truce with pain,
Then was she melted more again
To hear thy sweet words, while thy breath
Faintly did strive to sweeten death,
Calldst for the music of thy knell,
And crydst 'twas it must make thee well.
Thus whilst your prayers were at strife,
Thine for thy death, hers for thy life,   40
Thine did prevail, and on their wings
Mounted thy soul; where now it sings,
And never shall complain no more
But for not being there before.

Consolatorium, ad parentes

Let her parents then confess
That they believe her happiness,
Which their tears question. Think as you
Lent her the world, Heaven lent her you;
And is it just then to complain
When each hath but his own again?   50
Then think what both your glories are
In her preferment: for tis far
Nobler to get a saint and bear
A child to Heaven than an heir
To a large empire. Think beside
She died not young, but liv'd a bride.
Your best wishes for her good
Were but to see her well bestow'd;

Was she not so? She married to
The heir of all things, who did owe   60
Her infant soul, and bought it too.
Nor was she barren: markt you not
Those pretty little graces, that
Play'd round about her sick bed? Three:
Th'eldest, Faith; Hope & Charity.
Th'were pretty big ones, and the same
That cried so on their Father's name.
The youngest is gone with her; the two
Eldest stay to comfort you;
And little though they be, they can   70
Master the biggest foes of man.
Lastly think that her abode
With you was some few years' board
After her marriage. Now she's gone
Home, royally attended on;
And if you had Elisha's sight
To see the number of her bright
Attendants thither, or Paul's rapt sprite
To see her welcome there, why then,
Wish if you could her here again.   80
I'm sure you could not, but all passion
Would lose itself in admiration,
And strong longings to be there
Where, cause she is, you mourn for her.

Her epitaph[11]

Happy grave, thou dost enshrine
That which makes thee a rich mine;
Remember yet, 'tis but a loan,
And we must have it back: her own,
The very same. Mark me: the same.   90
Thou canst not cheat us with a lame
Deformed carcass. She was fair,
Fresh as morning, soft as air;
Purer than other flesh as far
As other souls than bodies are.
And that thou mayst the better see
To find her out: two stars there be,
Eclipsed now; uncloud but those

[11] {Margaret Forey regards this final section as probably the work of George Morley (1598–1684), graduate of Westminster School and Christ's Church, Oxford, member of Great Tew circle, and at the time of his death, bishop of Winchester.}

And they will point thee to the rose
That dyed each cheek, now pale and wan,   100
But will be when she wakes again
Fresher than ever. And howe'er
Her long sleep may alter her,
Her soul will know her body straight;
'Twas made so fit for't, no deceit
Can suit another to it, none
Clothe it so neatly as its own.

TEXT: *The poetical works of William Strode (1600–1645): now first collected from manuscript and printed sources*, ed. Bertram Dobell (London: privately printed, 1907).

Corrected against the Corpus Christi manuscript readings kindly provided by Margaret Forey.

HUMPHREY SYDENHAM[1]

Jehovah-Jireh. God in his providence and omnipotence discovered:
a sermon preached ad magistratum *at Chard in Somerset, 1633*
published 1637

To the most reverend Father in God, my very good lord, William, Lord Archbishop of Canterbury his grace, Primate of all England, and Metropolitan and Chancellor of the University of Oxford

Most Reverend,

In matters of bounty or benefit received, *he that speaks thanks* commonly *speaks all* [Seneca, *De Ben.* 2]. The divine not so. His profession requires as well devotion as gratitude, and what is only acknowledgment in others should be prayer in him. These have made way for this ambition of mine (for so it will be censured) in seeking your Grace's patronage, to which, by your former great favors and encouragements, I have met with a double stair: the one, in my first admission to spiritual preferment; the other, in settling it when it was disturbed. Both these here bound up by a thankful and zealous obligation in this tender of my poor endeavors—which, though I fear will scarce hold weight in the scale of your stricter judgment, yet in that of your charity they may pass . . . and so vindicate me from the imputation of that loose and lazy ignorance, which the very spirit of ignorance would put upon me, where vociferation is cried up for industry; and faction, for holiness; and a bitter and unbridled zeal, for sound knowledge. But notwithstanding the foaming of those muddy waters, springs may run clear, and I doubt not but mine shall, if they find a current in your Grace's protection, with whom, though in the most critical and envious eye, all things are clear and pure, without the least taint or tincture of corruption (like waters in their own source and fountain). Yet the waters of Marah have been round about you, and no doubt but your Grace hath had a taste (no less than others of that hierarchy) of their gall of bitterness. Witness their divine tragedies and impudent

---

[1] {The introduction to Sydenham will be found prefacing his 1622 sermon, *Jacob and Esau <supra>*. Note that, although the sermon was preached in 1633, the preface, with its crisis-mentality and histrionics, dates from 1637.}

appeals, their late corantos and legends of Ipswich[2] . . . in which they have not so much wounded the particular honors of eminent and learned men as struck through the sides of religion itself in blemishing the outward face of the Church—not only by obtruding to her her former spots and moles (as what Church was ever yet without them?) but overspreading it with a kind of leprosy. And so, instead of being *black like the tents of Kedar,* they would make her ugly *like the tent of Korah,* thereby exposing her to the scornful eyes of her enemies abroad and (if possible) of her own sons at home. Now, if bold men dare thus play with the very beard of Aaron, what will they do to the skirts of his raiment. . . . However, in despite of the envious basilisk, this poison of the asp and gall of the viper, the spears and arrows and sharp swords of these holy libelers (o blessed forever be the God of heaven, and under him here, his god of earth, a most gracious sovereign!), Ezra is in high favor and *the king hath granted him all his requests according to the hand of the Lord his God upon him* [Ezra 7:6]. So that your Grace is still above danger and shot-free of their power, though not of their envy. . . .

Pardon this digression, most reverend father. Obscure men may, without offence, deplore the miseries they cannot redress. Those that are more eminent may do both. A general harmony, as well in doctrine as in discipline, is yet wanting in the public practice of our Church, though not in the principles thereof—which is the main anvil most of my sermons hammer on. . . .

> Your Grace's most obliged
>> honorer and servant,

> > > > > > > Hum. Sydenham

‡

I will sing of thy power, and sing aloud of thy mercy
Psal. 59:16

I think it not unseasonable, nor besides my errand, to sing of the power and mercy of one God in the presence of another. Greatness is a kind of deity, God himself affording rulers & nobles no lower title than his own: of gods—but gods by office or deputation, not by essence; and yet so gods by office that they personate that God by essence. Power they have, a mighty one, and mercy too, or should have, and both these the people sing of. Only mortality puts the distance and divides between *civil* and *sacred.* . . . *I say ye are gods, gods* with a *moriemini,* mortal gods; there is a *but* annexed to the deity: *But ye shall die, die like men, and fall as one of the princes* (Psal. 82:6).[3]

And now, that I may not beguile time nor you with any curiosity of preface, the text being only a parcel of a Psalm . . . I shall dwell for the present only in the expression of *divine power.* A subject (I confess) like the ocean, wide and deep, and not without some danger to him that shall either steer or sound it. But that God who was a staff to his patriarch to pass over Jordan will be a pilot to his disciple in the sea too, that he sink and perish not (this vast and troubled sea of his Omnipotence) where some learned wits have been overwhelmed, either by a bold curiosity, venturing too far to shoot the strait and gulf they

---

[2] {i.e., Prynne's *News from Ipswich <infra>*}

[3] {The authorities whom Sydenham addresses are the Somerset magistrates.}

should not, or else by a vainglorious conceit of their own tenets have proudly borne a sail against wind and tide, the main drift of Scripture and current of the true faith, and so at length have run themselves on the shelves of heresy or blasphemy, or both. Against both which I shall ever pray in the language of the disciples in the great storm: *Master, save me lest I perish.* And thus by thee in safety, I shall daily *sing* of thy *power*, and *sing aloud of thy mercy*, because thou hast been my defense and refuge in the day of my trouble.

 I will sing of thy power.

This word *power* in respect of God is *homonymon*[4] and of various signification in sacred story. Sometimes it is taken only for Christ; so by Saint Paul: *unto the Jews and Greeks . . . we preach Christ,* θεοῦ δύναμιν, *the Power of God* (1 Cor 1:24). Sometimes for the Gospel of Christ. . . . Sometimes neither for Christ nor his Gospel, but the enemies of both. . . . But here we take *power* for that essential property of God, by which he is able and doth effect all in all, and all in every thing. . . . this active power being in him principal and most eminent, and indeed the very mint and forge where all things had their first stamp and hammering.

Now this power of God is not only infinite in its own nature . . . but in respect of objects to which it is extended, and of effects which it can produce, and of action too by which it doth or can work miraculously: which action is never so valid {strong} and intense (for so Polanus[5] words it) but it may be set to a higher pin and screw, and wound up even to infiniteness; and therefore it is not only called power . . . but omnipotence. . . .

And as this power is always, so it is only active . . . [and] so worketh in us that no power of any creature can hinder that operation, for *the throne of it is a fiery flame, and the wheels of it a burning fire* (Dan. 7:9).

 . . .

Seeing, then, the essence of God is infinite, his power of necessity must be infinite too. Now, because to be thus infinite is to be but one, there is but one omnipotence, as there is but one essence; and yet, for the diversities of respects, divines have cut it into a double file, an actual and absolute omnipotence.[6] The absolute omnipotence of God is that by which he can perfectly do anything that is possible to be done; and it is called absolute because it is not limited by the universal law of nature, as if divinity were necessarily pinned to the order of secondary causes and that God could not do anything besides or above that law; and this the schools call . . . God's extraordinary power, because by that he can work besides the trodden and accustomed course of nature. . . . This omnipotence is simply essential, by which God can absolutely and simply do all things which are possible to be done: to wit, such as do not repugn the will or nature of God, though they do sometimes the course of nature. . . . What natural power calls impossibility is without dispute possible to omnipotence; and therefore there is nothing that hath but a capability of being that comes not within the verge of God's absolute power—of his power, though sometimes not of his will or wisdom; for God can do many things which these think neither convenient nor necessary to be done. . . . God can of stones raise up

---

 [4] {homonymous, i.e., denoting different things by the same term}
 [5] {Amandus Polanus (1561–1610), Reformed theologian}
 [6] {On this distinction, see William Courtenay, "The dialectic of divine omnipotence," in his *Covenant and causality in medieval thought* (London: Variorum Reprints, 1984).}

children unto Abraham, but he never did, nor I think will. . . . God could have sent twelve legions of angels to fight against those Jews that apprehended Christ, *sed noluit*, saith Lombard. . . . God raised Lazarus in body, and could he not Judas in spirit also? *potuit quidem, sed noluit,*[7] saith S. Augustine.

Thus antiquity, you hear, still pleads for God's *potuit*, his infinite power . . . And doubtless he can do more things than he doth do, if he *would* do them, but he will not: not that there is any defect in his will or power, but because in wisdom he doth not think it meet.

God's *actual omnipotence* is that by which he is not only able to do whatsoever he willed or decreed to be done, but also really doth it . . . at a beck or command, without difficulty or delay, with a mere *dixit & factum est*, he speaks only, and he does it. . . . And this hath respect to the particular law of nature, and to a special order bequeathed things by that law through which he at first created all things and still either conserves or moderates or destroys them.

. . .

Thus, at length, the atheist and infidel we have hushed and all their cavils examined and refuted. Let's now hear the Christian speak, what dialect he uses, how he sings of the power of his Creator. He inquires not so much what God can do as admires what he hath done, and still doth. In divine mysteries, he thinks it safer to believe than to discuss, and to exercise the solidity and vigor of his faith than any acumen and pregnancy of his reason. And here is enough to employ all his faculties, embark the whole man, set all the engines and wheels both of soul and spirit running, and turn them in endless speculations. Whatsoever is above him or below him, without him or within him, is a fit object of God's power, and his own wonder. *When I consider* (saith our Prophet) *the heavens, the work of thy fingers, the moon and stars which thou hast ordained, Lord, what is man?* (Psal. 8). What is man? Nay, *how* is he? Surely like one in a slumber or a dream; for as he that dreameth hath his fancy sometimes disturbed with strange objects, which are rather represented than judged of, so in the view of those celestial bodies, the contemplative man stands (as it were) planet-strucken in his intellectuals; whilst he considers the heavens, he loses them; and that moon and those stars which should enlighten, dazzle him. The finger of God in them he doth acknowledge, but not discover. He made them by his power, he confesses; he ordained them. But how he ordained or made them so, his apprehension is at a stand or bay; and transported beyond measure, cries out with that afflicted penitent, *tonitru potentiae ejus quis intelligat?*[8] The thunder of his power, who can understand? Canst thou by searching find out God? Canst thou find out the Almighty to perfection? It is high as heaven, what canst thou do? Deeper than hell, what canst thou know? If he cut off or shut up or gather together, who can hinder him? (Job 11:9-10).

If we lift up our eyes from the foot-stool to the throne of God, and thus lifted up, cast them back again; could they make an exact and uncontrolled discovery of both globes, see all the wonders and secrets that nature hath there locked up in her vast storehouse, we should find in each cranny thereof the sway of his powerful scepter. Water, fire, earth, air limit not his commands, but through the territories of heaven and hell, the bonds of his

---

[7] {Indeed, he could, but would not.}

[8] [Job 26:14] {This is the Latin of the 16th-century Protestant Junius-Tremellius translation.}

power obtain a jurisdiction. Will you hear his own secretaries speak? The registers and pen-men of divine story? How they sing of his power! How they blazon his omnipotence! *Lo, he metes out heaven with a span,*[9] *measureth the waters in the hollow of his hand, comprehends the dust of the earth in a measure, weigheth the mountains in scales, and the hills in a balance* (Isa. 40:12). Here is the whole world circled in one verse, and yet not his whole power in that circle. His power is his Godhead, and God himself hath been called a circle. *It is he that sitteth upon the circle of the earth, and the inhabitants thereof are as grasshoppers before him.* Mark, *he sits* there. He is not contained there. There? No, that were above miracle, the greater circle contained in the less. The heathens themselves could tell us *God was an intelligible sphere* [Empedocles], without dimensions; a circle whose center was everywhere, nowhere his circumference. Nowhere, not in the whole world, not in the earth, not in the waters, not in the heavens that circle both. The waters (you hear) he measures in the hollow of his hand, the earth in the same measure, the heavens that contain these in a span. Here is but a span and handful of his power; and yet this handful grasps the universe. This made our Prophet often sing, and in his song close as he began, *how wonderful is thy name in all the world! How wonderful in all the world!* A double wonder indeed in respect of man; though of God, not so. God could not be so wonderfully great if man had ability to express him; and therefore, having none, he[10] expresses himself by himself; or, at least, by his prophets, to whom himself he dictates; who, like men infused and entranced, *speak aloft* in sacred allegories such as beseem the majesty and greatness as well of the penman as inspirer.

And here, what sublimity both of power and language![11] He clothes himself with light as with a garment, stretcheth out the heavens like a curtain, and spreadeth them as a tent to dwell in.[12] By his Spirit hath he garnished the sky and fashioned it like a molten looking-glass. In them hath he set a tabernacle for the sun, which as a bridegroom cometh out of his chamber, and rejoiceth as a giant to run his course. He, he hath appointed also the moon for seasons, and at his pleasure sealeth up the stars. He binds the sweet influences of the Pleiades and looses the bonds of Orion, brings forth Mazaroth in his season and guides Arcturus with his sons. Here all human eloquence is befooled: *non vox hominum sonat; o Dei, certe.*[13] Such an expression of God none could frame but God himself; and this made our Prophet sing again, *O Lord of hosts, how wonderful are thy works. In wisdom hast thou made them all; who is a strong Lord like unto thee, or to thy power and faithfulness round about thee?* (Psal. 89:8).

Let us now leave the firmament, and (the Lord bowing the heavens and coming down) see what empire and dominion he hath in the regions of the air. There he layeth

---

[9] {The distance from the tip of the thumb to the tip of the little finger, or sometimes to the tip of the forefinger, when the hand is fully extended; the space equivalent to this taken as a measure of length, averaging nine inches (*OED*).}

[10] {i.e., God}

[11] {The *OED* gives 1779 as the earliest use of "sublimity" to designate "that quality in external objects which awakens feelings of awe, reverence, lofty emotion, a sense of power, or the like," a date which this sermon moves back nearly a century and a half.}

[12] {Much of the sermon from this point on is a tissue of biblical allusions so woven into the text that they are neither identified nor italicized in the original.}

[13] {The voice is not that of a human; surely it is God's—a Christianizing of *Aeneid* 1.328.}

the beams of his chamber in the waters, maketh the clouds his chariot, and rideth upon the wings of the wind. Through the brightness of his presence are coals of fire kindled, lightnings and hot thunderbolts. There he hath made a decree for the rain, the balancings of the clouds (as Job styles them), and there hath he begotten the drops of dew. Thence he giveth snow like wool, and scattereth the hoar frost like ashes, & casteth out his ice like morsels. There he maketh weight for the winds; he bindeth up the waters in a cloud as in a bottle, and the cloud is not rent under them. This made our Prophet sing aloft, *Praise the Lord in the heights, praise him fire and hail, snow and vapors, stormy wind fulfilling his word* (Psal. 108:1, 8).

Let us descend once more, and amongst those heaps of earth which seem to lift their heads even to the very stars, observe what sway his power carries there, or rather what terror. He shall thresh the mountains and beat them small, and make the hills as chaff. He shall fan them, and with his whirlwind shall he scatter them and shall overturn them by the roots. If he be angry, Lebanon is not enough for incense nor the beasts thereof for a burnt sacrifice. The foundations of the round world are discovered at his chiding, at the blasting of the breath of his displeasure. This made our Prophet sing again, *The Lord is a great God, and a great king above all gods; in his hands are all the corners of the earth, and the strength of the hills is his also* (Psal. 95:3-4).

Shall we yet stoop lower and, descending this mount, see how he is a Lord of the valleys and the inhabitants thereof. Lo, the foundation of the earth he hath wonderfully set, and laid the cornerstone thereof; at his pleasure again he shaketh it out of her hinges, and the pillars tremble. He turns the hard rock into a standing water, and the flint-stone into a springing well. The nations before him are less than nothing; they are accounted as the drops of a bucket and as the small dust of the balance. He bindeth kings in chains and nobles in fetters of iron. He gives his enemies as dust to the sword and as driven stubble to his bow. He shall rise up as in Mount Perazim; he shall be wroth as in the Valley of Gibeon, that he may do his work, his great work, and bring to pass his act, his great act. This made our Prophet sing again, *The earth is the Lord's, and all that therein is; the compass of the whole world, and all that dwell therein; for he hath founded it upon the seas, and prepared it upon the floods* (Psal. 24:1-2).

Shall we now leave the earth and those that sojourn there, and see the wonders of the Lord in the great deep? There he gathereth the waters of the sea together, and lays them up in storehouses. At his command, the floods lift up their voice, the waves begin to swell, and he makes them boil like a pot of ointment. Again, he ruleth the raging of the sea, and the waters thereof he stilleth at his pleasure. He bindeth the floods from overflowing; shuts up the sea with doors when it breaks forth as if it issued out of the womb; makes the cloud a garment thereof and thick darkness a swaddling band; breaks up for it his decreed place,[14] and sets bars and gates, and says, *Hitherto shalt thou come, no farther; and here shall thy proud waves be stayed* (Job 38:9-10).

Shall we yet step a stair lower, and, opening the jaws of the bottomless pit, see how powerfully he displays his banners in the dreadful dungeon below? *Behold, hell is naked*

---

[14] {This is close to the King James translation of Job 38:10; other translations read "And prescribed bounds for it," or words to like effect, following the Septuagint. A lucid discussion of the underlying Hebrew can be found at http://bible.cc/job/38-10.htm (accessed June 7, 2012).}

before him, and destruction hath no covering. This made our Prophet sing more generally, *The Lord is above all gods; whatsoever pleased him, that did he, in heaven and earth and in the sea and in all deep places* (Psal. 135:6).

Thus, you hear, God is in the world as the soul is in the body: life and government. And as the soul is in every part of the body, so is God in every part of the world. No quarter-master nor vice-gerent he, but universal monarch and commander: *totus in toto, & totus in qualibet parte*; a God everywhere, wholly a God, and yet one God everywhere, only One. . . . alone to be blessed, honored and adored by all for evermore.

And is God the Lord indeed? Is he chief sovereign of the whole world? Hath his power so large a jurisdiction? Doth it circuit and lift {*sic*} in water, earth, air, fire; nay, the vaster territories of heaven and hell too? How then doth this frail arm of flesh dare lift itself against Omnipotence? Why doth it oppose (or at least incite) the dreadful armies of him who is the great Lord of hosts? Why do we muster up our troops of sins as if we would set them in battle array against the Almighty? Scarce a place where he displays the ensigns of his power but man seems to hang out his flag of defiance, or at least of provocation; and though he hath no strength to conquer, yet he hath a will to affront. If he cannot batter his fort, he will be playing[15] his trenches; anger his God, though not wound him. In the earth, he meets him by his groveling sins of avarice, oppression, violence, rapine, sacrilege, and others of that style and dunghill. In the water, by his flowing sins of drunkenness, riots, surfeits, vomitings, and what else of that frothy tide and inundation. . . . But wretched man that thou art, who shall deliver thee from the horror of this death? *When the Lord shall reveal himself from heaven with his mighty angels in flaming fire, taking vengeance on them that fear him not,* what cave shall hide or what rock cover them? At his rebuke, the foundations of the world are discovered, even at the blast of the breath of his displeasure. Out of his mouth cometh a devouring flame, and if he do but touch these mountains, they shall smoke; if he but once lift up his iron rod, he rends and shivers and breaketh in pieces like a potter's vessel. He heweth asunder the snares of the ungodly, and his enemies he shall consume like the fat of lambs. O then let all the earth fear the Lord; let all the inhabitants of the world stand in awe of him. Let kings throw down their scepters at his feet, and the people their knees and hearts at those scepters. From the cedar of Libanus and the oak of Basan to the shrub of the valley and the humble hyssop on the wall, let all bow and tremble; princes and all judges of the earth, both young men and maidens, old men and children; let them all fear; and in fearing, praise; and in praising, sing of the name and power of the Lord God, for his name only is excellent, and his power and glory above heaven and earth.

On the other side, is the Lord omnipotent indeed? Hath his power so wide a province and extent? Is the glory of his mighty acts thus made known to the sons of men? Is his kingdom not only a great, but an everlasting kingdom? His dominion through and beyond all generations? Doth he plant and root up? prune and graft at his own pleasure? Doth he raise the humble and meek, and bring the ungodly down to the ground? Is he with his Joseph in the prison, with Elijah in the cave, with Shadrach in the furnace, with Daniel in the den? . . . Doth he clothe the lilies of the field? Have lions (roaring after their

---

[15] {i.e., firing his artillery (or gun) at}

prey) their food from him? Doth he give fodder unto the cattle? quench the wild asses' thirst? . . . Abate the edge of the sword, shake the very powers of the grave, and all for the rescue and preservation of his servants? his faithful, his beloved servants? Why art thou then so sad, o my soul; why so sad and why so disquieted within thee? Trust in God; he healeth those that are broken in heart and giveth medicine to heal their sickness. Though thy afflictions be many, thy adversaries mighty, thy temptations unresistable, thy grievances unwieldy, thy sins numberless, their weight intolerable, yet there is a God above in his provident watch-tower, a God that can both protect and pardon, infinite as well in mercy as in power. Are thy wounds grievous? There is balm in Gilead. . . . Doubtless he that watcheth his Israel will neither slumber nor sleep, but preserveth his children as tenderly as the apple of that eye that watched them. He is their staff and crutch and supportation in all their weakness; he erects them if they fall, directs them if they err, succors them if they want, refresheth them in the heat of their persecutions, mitigates the tempests of their sorrows, moderates the waves of their bitter passions, smiteth their enemies upon the cheek-bone, breaks the teeth of those that rage and grin so furiously upon them. . . .

This should arm us with resolution against that triple assault of the world, flesh, and devil, and make us buckle on our harness as that good king of Israel did: *I will not be afraid* (saith he) *for ten thousands which should compass me round about* (Psal. 3:6). Afraid? No, for ten thousand of men and dangers. If calamities hover over me, God is my tower. . . . Then put not your trust in princes nor in any child of man, for there is no help in them. Blessed is he that hath the God of Jacob for his help and whose hope is in the Lord his God, which made heaven and earth, the sea and all that therein is, which keepeth his promise forever. This made our Prophet awake his harp and lute, and cheerfully sing that *Magnificat* of his: *Praise the Lord, o my soul, praise the Lord; yea as long as I have any being, I will sing praises unto my God. I will be like a green olive tree in the house of my God; my trust shall be in the tender mercy of God forever and ever* (Psal. 52:9).

Once more, and but once: is God thus indeed a God of power? Questionless. And only a God of power? No. The text tells us he is a God of mercy too; his goodness keeps pace with his greatness, his sanctity with his fortitude. *He that is mighty* (saith the blessed Virgin) *hath done great things for me, and holy is his name.* Upon which place, Stella had an *adverte lector,*[16] a note (it seems) worth observation: Mary there to God's name joining both sanctity and power[17] . . . {because}, saith he, command not seasoned with holiness is but tyranny. Let Nebuchadnezzar and Pharoah stand for instance, whose wickedness got them the nickname of tyrants, which by their power otherwise had the title of gods. Empire, therefore, must acknowledge itself indebted to religion, godliness being the chiefest top and wellspring of all true virtues, even as God is of all good things. So natural is the union of true religion with power that we may boldly deem, there neither is truly, where both are not. . . . Power and sanctity conjoined proclaim a god; power without sanctity, sometimes a devil. Mistake me not. I come not here to school the gray hair, to cast dirt in the face of the magistrate. No, I remember well what Elihu said unto Job, *Is it fit to say to princes, ye are ungodly?* (Job 34:18). By no means. I leave such reproofs to

---

[16] {hearken, reader [{Didacus} Stella in I. Lucae v. 49]}

[17] {In the *Magnificat*, the Virgin joins both sanctity ("and holy is his name") and power ("he that is mighty") to God's name.}

those saucy and pragmatic spirits, which will undertake to catechize a god, teach divinity what it hath to do; for whom the reply of Job to Zophar shall pass for a counter-check: *O that you would altogether hold your peace, and it should be counted your greater wisdom* (Job 13:5). My drift and purpose in this point is only to shew you how prone and headlong those dispositions are to all manner of depravedness which project rather to be great than good. And this an instance or two from antiquity shall clear, in which the relation only shall be mine; the application (as you bring it home to your own breasts), yours.

It was but an itch of ambition and a thirst of greatness not rectified as it ought, that was the ground-work and first stair of Julian's apostasy. His fiercest enemies did acknowledge that he was once a man of rare dexterity and forwardness both in wit & virtue, and these not without their salt and seasoning of true religion . . . {But} his love of empire, and a little curiosity to boot, blew off his devotions from Christianity to paganism. . . .

What projects will not ungodly men set on foot, first for the advancement of their name, and then the perpetuity; but such a perpetuity is not without a kind of rottenness. 'Tis a curse the Spirit of God breathes against the wicked, that *their memory shall rot*, nothing shall remain of them but their vices, and they sometimes of that stench and loathsomeness that the scent of them is quick,[18] though unsavory, in the nostrils of posterity. What lives there of Herod (besides his lust and cruelty) but the manner of his death? which was no less a prodigy than his life: the story of the one being written by the blood of innocents; of the other, by the fury of worms. And yet how cautelous this monster was to propagate his honor to after-ages, who, doubting the baseness of his parentage should in future be discovered, burns the genealogies of the Jews that he might be thought to have had his descent as royal as the rest of his predecessors. And this is the customary plea of the aspirer (the gourd and mushroom in commonwealth): he cares not whose name be obliterate, so his own flourish, causing other families to vanish in a snuff, whilest his own must shine like a light in a watch-tower. . . . nothing stands up with the greatness of their spirit or design but a general devastation, laying house to house and field to field, like ravens of the valley pecking out the very eyes and heart-blood of those that come under the tyranny of their bill. And thus *they gather stones for other men's burial*, in which they inter both their[19] fortunes and their names; not only scarify {wound} them alive but torment them when they are dead also: strip them of their monumental rites (the solemn pomp and trophies of the grave), ravish their sepulchers, deface those ensigns and inscriptions which should remark them to succeeding times—a barbarism or rather sacrilege abhorred amongst the heathens as a capital injury and violence to their *Manes* and infernal gods, the profaneness whereof they threatened with the torture of all the furies.

O consider this, all you whom God hath advanced either in title or blood above others; think it not enough to be great or fortunate, but to be good also, that men may as well sing of your mercy as your power; rather magnify your compassion than murmur at your rigor. You are exalted to protect the innocent, not to oppress them. The lazar and widow and orphan should proclaim your care and pity, not your insultation, acknowledge your power rather by their love than fear. Remember, the greater you are in place, the nearer

[18] {alive, fresh, keen}

[19] {i.e., the fortunes and names of other men, those whose tombs puritan zealots have defaced (perhaps in order to reuse the brass and stone for their own manors and monuments)}

you are unto God; and he that is near unto God hath a greatness as well of mercy as of power. And as of these you sing unto God, so the afflicted must sing unto you; and as in their calamities you have been a strength and refuge for them, so in all your troubles, God will be a sanctuary for you. And then you may boldly rejoice in the words of our Prophet here: *I will sing of thy power, and I will sing aloud of thy mercy in the morning, because thou hast been my defense and refuge in the day of my trouble.*

Gloria in excelsis Deo.
Amen

✨～✨

Source: EEBO (STC [2nd ed.] / 23573)

Humphrey Sydenham, *Sermons upon solemn occasions: preached in several auditories* (London: Printed by John Beale for Humphrey Robinson, 1637), A2–A3, 119–27, 133–49.

ANTHONY MUNDAY (ca. 1560–1633)

and the

1633 *Survey of London*

The final portion of the 1633 *Survey of London*, written by Anthony Munday, details the reparation and beautification of over a hundred churches in and around London. The original 1598 *Survey of London*, however, came from the pen of John Stow (1526–1605), whose descriptions of the Elizabethan ecclesiastical cityscape record a post-Reformation legacy of neglect, vandalism, and sacrilege. Stow, whose patrons included the Archbishop of Canterbury, conformed to the new church order, but his picture of it bears nostalgic witness to the losses entailed.

The 1633 additions reveal a different scenario. Munday began his update of Stow's *Survey* shortly after the latter's death, publishing his first revised edition in 1618; the second, which includes the chapters reprinted below documenting the massive ecclesiastical renovation projects of the previous two decades, came out just months after Munday's own death in 1633—the same year that saw the posthumous publication of Herbert's *Temple*, Greville's *Caelica*, and Donne's *Songs and Sonnets*.

Particularly in comparison to the clerics who populate most of this volume, Munday had a checkered and precarious career. A Londoner by birth and orphaned young, he trained as a printer, eventually gaining the freedom of both the Drapers' and Merchant-Taylors' Companies. During a 1578 trip to the Continent, he entered the Jesuit-run English College in Rome, an experience that became the basis for his 1582 exposé, *The English Roman life*—one of several violently anti-Catholic tracts Munday wrote during this period—as well as for Munday's testimony at the 1581 treason trials of various Jesuits (including Campion) who had left the safety of Rome for England. Thereafter Munday was regularly employed by the government in tracking down both clandestine priests and radical puritans. By the early 1580s, however, Munday had also become an actor; and throughout the rest of Elizabeth's reign, he worked as a writer and translator of romances, and as a staff playwright at the Rose, usually in a collaborative capacity. He had a hand in *The Book of Sir Thomas More* (ca. 1593), as well as plays on Robin Hood, Oldcastle, and other staples of English popular history. For reasons unknown, he left the stage in 1602 and began writing civic pageants; almost all Jacobean lord mayor's shows are his either wholly or in part. However, the work for which he hoped to be remembered—the work his tombstone proclaims—was the revised *Survey of London*. Shortly before his death, Stow had given Munday the materials he had gathered for a revised edition in the hope that Munday might "proceed in the perfecting" of it (Epist. ded. to the 1618 ed.). Some time thereafter, the Bishop of London, John King, asked Munday to report on the rebuilding of churches and refurbishing of altars taking place throughout London, a major undertaking that required surveying the repairs, monuments, inscriptions, and ornaments of over a hundred parishes. Munday was unable to finish this task in time for the 1618 edition, but for the 1633 edition he updated the information he had previously gathered, so that the final chapters of the 1633 text, although focusing on the latest round of improvements, note changes going back to the early years of James' reign.

These chapters afford the quite startling revelation that the renovation and beautification of the ecclesiastical fabric, at least in London, predated the Laudian ascendancy by more than a decade. (Its beginnings seem rather to coincide with *Abbot*'s archiepiscopate.) Indeed, the single most un-Protestant item in Munday's survey bears the date 1617: the stained glass depiction of Jehovah at St. Giles-in-the-Fields. Admittedly, St. Giles, where Roger Manwaring[1] had been rector since 1616, seems to have been the *sole* clearly high-church parish in London.[2] Yet two unmistakably puritan parishes—St. Antholine's and St. Mildred's, Breadstreet—also have their full complement of memorials and adornment, including pictorial stained glass; the subjects and style differ widely from those at St. Giles, but by the 1620s the visual anorexia of the Reformation decades has released its hold.[3] In the vast majority of the parishes Munday describes, however, the renovations proclaim neither Anglo-Catholic nor political-puritan commitments. Churches get clocks, galleries, pews, pulpit and altar cloths, a churchyard, a steeple, and new paving far more often than carved angels or Armada memorials. Individual bequests likewise resist categorization: the same people who leave money for lectures donate communion vessels; testators who fund quarterly sermons specify that they are to be given on saints' days or Marian feasts. Even at St. Giles-in-the-Fields, the mottos under the stained glass windows include Pauline affirmations of justification by faith. What Munday's survey emphatically does not show is a Church splitting apart into hostile factions, each new-modeling its parochial strongholds in a show of liturgical identity politics.[4] Munday himself seems to

---

[1] Manwaring is best known for a 1627 sermon that seemed to defend absolutism (i.e., the king's right to impose taxes, with or without Parliamentary approval).

[2] Although the statuary Paul Pinder contributes to St. Paul's also bespeak high-church predilections <675>.

[3] See Lake's *Boxmaker's revenge* for the even more spectacular refurbishment of a godly parish in the 1630s. On the "visual anorexia" of the Tudor period, see Patrick Collinson, *Birthpangs of Protestant England* (Macmillan, 1988), 99.

[4] I have omitted all mention of the Queen Elizabeth monuments, largely because there were so many of them, yet it seemed misleading to include some and omit others. It is possible that the erection of a Queen Elizabeth monument signals a parish's political-puritan commitments, but the differences among the various monuments suggest that their semiotics are considerably more complicated. For more on these

be as impressed by the militantly Protestant iconography of St. Mildred's, Breadstreet, as by the high-church baroque of St. Giles. He tends, in fact, to be most impressed by the *cost* of a renovation, betraying a distinctly unmodern sense of money as the spiritual-symbolic measure of a gift's piety, charity, even beauty.

It is certainly possible that the harmonious picture presented by the *Survey* results from Munday's deliberate erasure of conflict, but that cannot be the whole story since the inscriptions he transcribes likewise avoid clear theological positioning. None asks passers-by to pray for the deceased's soul—a standard feature of pre-Reformation tombs—so in that respect they are clearly Protestant,[5] but most eschew further specificity. Instead the inscriptions on tombs and tables point to the survival of traditional religion—by which I do not mean vestigial Catholicism but rather the values and practices that the Reformation left fundamentally unchanged: above all, relieving the material wants of the poor, ransoming prisoners, funding needy students, supporting the clergy.[6] The great majority of inscriptions dwell upon these; very few mention someone's faith or assurance, and I found none that praised a person for Sabbath-observance or zealous sermon-going.

Both Munday's 1633 survey of London's churches and the inscriptions his text preserves are memorials honoring the dead for their generosity to the poor and the parish—and holding up their example for imitation. These benefactors, their charity written in stone and on paper for all posterity to admire, represent a surprisingly wide socioeconomic swathe. Pride of place in Munday's "Remains" (the first chapter of this concluding section) goes to Edward Alleyne, a wealthy entrepreneur but also a former actor. Many of those commemorated for their "noble and charitable deeds" are knights, esquires, and gentlemen. Many, however, are not. The London churches of the early seventeenth century turn out to have been filled with inscriptions memorializing the generosity of very ordinary people. A table of benefactors to the poor erected in the Savoy lists a tailor's £6 gift and the 40 shillings per annum bestowed by a vinter from his tavern rents, as well as a lord chief baron's £20 donation. Some of the proto-Laudian ornaments adorning St. Giles come from a noblewoman, a prominent lawyer, a founding member of the Virginia Company; others from a cloth-worker, a fishmonger, and a baker's widow. The window depicting the Crucifixion was the gift of a cook. The intermingling of gentry, citizens, and laboring folk in these sacred "theaters of memory" (Archer 90) so conflicts with our assumption about early modern class stratification that most studies of 1633 *Survey* pass over the phenomenon in silence.

Two additional features of these inscriptions deserve comment. First, the burial groupings raise fascinating questions about the early modern family. None of the tombs Munday describes contains the same-sex couples Alan Bray studied in his brilliant *The friend*; one, however holds sisters who chose to be buried together rather than with their respective spouses. In another, married children lie with their parents. Of particular interest, given the scorn and disgust remarriage, especially female remarriage, elicit on the

---

poorly understood (and now vanished) memorials, see Merritt, "Puritans, Laudians," 953; Everard Home Coleman, "Queen Elizabeth's Monuments," *Notes and Queries*, 7th series, 8 (December 14, 1889): 461–63.

[5] Yet although the post-Reformation tomb inscriptions do not request prayers for the person buried beneath, many express hope for reunion with him or her at the resurrection, thus preserving, albeit reconfigured, a sense of connectedness, of relationships continued, across the boundary of death.

[6] See Hamilton 175, 182.

Jacobean stage, are those memorializing three or more persons joined by marriage: either a husband with his successive wives or a wife with her successive husbands.

Second, many tombs include poems: most, like those of Donne, Greville, and Herbert, written long prior to print publication; all, again like those of Donne, Greville, and Herbert, first printed, posthumously, in 1633. The verse epitaphs comprise a more motley crew than the devotional lyrics of the other 1633 volumes; they are anonymous public poetry, often (judging from the not-infrequent metrical lapses) truly the work of "forced fingers rude." Yet they are surprisingly un-formulaic, surprisingly individuated; their sociological range allows us to hear voices not elsewhere audible; and some do have considerable merit. The most powerful are often those mourning a young woman, but there is also a striking auto-epitaph in which a wife speaks to her husband from the dead. Almost all this verse is religious—or at least ends with some sort of supernatural consolation—with the exception of the three epitaphs for writers (Drayton, Spenser, and Munday himself), which care more about the immortality of art.

Sources: *ODNB*; Ian Archer, "The arts and acts of memorialization in early modern London," in *Imagining early modern London: perceptions and portrayals of the City from Stow to Strype*, ed. J. F. Merritt (Cambridge UP, 2001), 89–113; Donna Hamilton, *Anthony Munday and the Catholics, 1550–1633* (Ashgate, 2005); Julia Merritt, "Puritans, Laudians, and the phenomenon of church-building in Jacobean London," *Historical Journal* 41 (1998): 935–60, and her "The reshaping of Stow's *Survey*: Munday, Strype, and the Protestant City," in *Imagining early modern London*, 52–88; John Parton, *Some account of the hospital and parish of St. Giles in the Fields, Middlesex* (London, 1822).

ANTHONY MUNDAY

The survey of London
1633

THE REMAINS[1]
OR
REMNANTS
OF DIVERS WORTHY THINGS,

which should have had their due place and honor in this work, if promising friends had kept their words.

But they failing, and part of them coming to my hands by other good means, they are here inserted, to accompany my perambulation four miles about London

The College of Gods-Gift at Dulwich, in the county of Surry: founded, raised, and builded at the cost and charges of Master *Edward Alleyne*,[2] esquire, in *anno Dom.* 1614

The thirteenth day of September, being Monday, *anno* 1619, the College of Gods-gift in Dulwich, consisting of one master, one warden, and four fellows: three of which are persons ecclesiastical and the fourth a skilful organist; moreover, twelve aged poor people and twelve poor children; Master *Edward Alleyne*, publicly and audibly, in the chapel of the said College, did read and publish one writing quadrupartite in parchment, bearing date the day and year forementioned; whereby he did make, create, erect, found, and establish the said College, according to the power and liberty given him by his Majesty's letters patents under his Great Seal, bearing date at Westminster the 21 of June in the year abovesaid. When he had read and published the said writing, he subscribed it with

---

[1] {I will use ellipses to indicate a gap *within* a memorial, but not for those between either parishes or memorials.}

[2] {The renowned Elizabethan actor, whose signature roles included Faustus and Tamburlaine. Also the husband of John Donne's daughter.}

his name and then fixed his seal to every part of the quadrupartite writing in the presence and hearing of these witnesses:

Francis {Bacon} Lord Verulam, Lord Chancellor of England, and one of his Majesty's Privy Council,

Thomas Earl of Arundel, Knight of the Garter, Earl Marshal of England, and one of his Majesty's Privy Council,

Sir *Edward Cecil*, knight, *alias* General Cecil, second son to Thomas, {Earl of} Exeter,

Sir *John Howland*, knight, and High Sheriff of the counties of Sussex and Surry,

Sir *Edmund Bowyer* of Cammerwell, knight,

Sir *Tho. Grymes* of Peckham, knight,

Sir *John Bodly* of Stretham, knight,

Sir *John Tonstal* of Cashaulten, knight,

And divers other persons of great and worthy respect. The four quadrupartite writings forenamed were ordered to four several parishes,

viz.

Saint Botolph's without Bishopsgate,

Saint Giles without Cripplegate,

Saint Saviour's in Southwarke,

And the parish of Cammerwell.

A brief recital of the particulars

. . .

The Master and Warden to be unmarried, &c.

The Master and Warden to be one and twenty years of age at the least.

Of what degrees the Fellows ought to be.

Of what condition the poor Brothers and Sisters ought to be.

Of what condition the poor scholars ought to be.

Of what parishes ought the assistants to be.

Of what parishes the poor are to be taken, and members of the College.

The form of their election.

The Warden to supply, when the Master's place is void.

The election of the Warden.

The Warden to be bound by recognizance.

The Warden to provide a dinner at his election of his own charges.

The manner of investing the Fellows.

The manner of electing the scholars.

Election of the poor of Cammerwell.

The Master and Warden's oath.

The Fellows' oath.

The poor Brothers' & Sisters' oath.

The assistants' oath.

The pronunciation of admission.

The Master's office.

The Warden's office.

The Fellows' office.

The poor Brothers' & Sisters' office.

The Matron of the poor scholars.

The porter's office.

The office of the thirty members.

Of residency.

Orders for the poor and their goods.

Of obedience.

Orders for the chapel and burial.

Orders for the school and scholars, and placing of poor scholars forth.

Order of diet.

The scholars' surplices and coats.

Time for viewing expenses.

Public audit and private sitting days.

Audit and treasure chamber.

Of lodgings.

Orders for the lands and woods.

The Master and Warden allowed diet for one man apiece; and what servants for the College, and their wages.

. . .

A brief remembrance of such noble and charitable deeds as have been done by the late right honorable Baptist Lord Hicks, Viscount Campden, as well in his life as at his death: recorded to the glory of God, his own honor, and good example of others.

Good deeds done to the town of Campden, in the county of Gloucester

He built an alms-house or hospital for six poor men and six poor women, which cost 1000 li.[3]

Since the year of the foundation of the said alms-house, to wit 1612, he hath allowed the said twelve poor people weekly maintenance to the value of 1300 li.

And at his death he hath settled 140 li. *per annum* (forever) upon the said alms-house, allowing to each of the said poor pensioners three shillings four pence weekly; and yearly, a gown, a hat, and a tun of coals.

He built a commodious market-house in the said town, which cost 90 li.

By his last will, he gave to the said town, for the setting of the poor to work, a stock of 500 li.

[3] {The abbreviation "li." means "pound," the standard unit of English currency, now denoted by "£." On its purchasing power in the early seventeenth century, see www.measuringworth.com/calculators/ppower uk/ (accessed June 7, 2012).}

To the church of Campden

He gave a bell which cost threescore and six pounds.

He caused a pulpit to be made, and gave a cloth and cushion thereto, which cost two and twenty pounds.

He built a gallery there, which cost eight pounds.

He made a window, which cost thirteen pounds.

He gave a brass falcon, which cost six and twenty pounds.

He gave two communion cups, which cost one and twenty pounds.

He built the roof of the chancel and new leaded it, which cost 200 li.

He repaired the chapel by the said chancel, supplied and new cast the leads, which cost 20 li.

He round walled the church-yard, which cost 150 li.

Within the county of Middlesex

He built a sessions house for the Justices of Middlesex to keep their sessions in, which cost 600 li.

He repaired and adorned the chapel of Hampsted, which cost threescore and sixteen pounds.

He caused a window to be set up in the chancel of Kensington, and beautified it, which cost 30 li.

He hath given by his last will to the said town of Kensington, to be employed for the benefit of the poor, the sum of 200 li.

In the City of London

He hath given by his last will to Saint Bartholomew's Hospital, 100 li.

To Christ's Church Hospital, 50 li.

To Newgate, Ludgate, and the two other prisons of the Counters, 40 li.

He erected a window in Saint Laurence church in the Old Jewry, and gave a pulpit cloth, and a cushion also, which cost 30 li.

Impropriations purchased, and bestowed upon the Church

One in Pembrokeshire, to be given to the town of Tewkesbury in Gloucestershire, whereof one moiety goeth to the preacher and the other moiety to the poor, which cost 460 li.

Another in Northumberland, whereof one moiety is to be given towards the maintenance of an able preacher in Hampsted, the other moiety to Saint Paul's School in London towards the maintenance of certain scholars in Trinity College in Cambridge, which cost 760 li.

One in the bishopric of Durham to be bestowed on such churches as shall have most need thereof, according to the disposition of the supervisors, which cost 366 li.

Another in Dorsetshire to be bestowed in the like manner, which cost 760 li.

Certain chantry lands also in Lincolnshire, which cost 240 li.

He hath also given to two ministers, to be chosen out of Jesus College in Oxford, to serve in their several places, 40 li. each man *per annum*, which cost 80 li.

He hath bequeathed legacies to several ministers, the sum of 140 li.

He hath given to Master A. E. during his life, yearly the sum of 100 li.
He hath given among his household servants the sum of 30 li.

An epitaph made in his memorial

> Reader, know, who-e'er thou be,
> Here lies Faith, Hope, and Charity,
> Faith *true*, Hope *firm*, Charity *free*,
> Baptist, *Lord* Campden was these three.
> *Faith* in God, *Charity* to brother,
> *Hope* for himself, what ought he other?
> *Faith* is no more, *Charity* is crown'd,
> 'Tis only *Hope* is under ground.

Upon a tomb in the Temple Church in London:

Here lieth the body of *Anne Littleton*, wife of *Edward Littleton* of the Inner Temple, esquire, son and heir of Sir *Edward Littleton* of Henley in the county of Salop, knight; daughter of *John Littleton* of Franckley in the county of Worcester, esquire, by *Muriel*, the daughter of Sir *Thomas Bromley*, knight, Lord Chancellor of England. She died the vi day of February 1623, on whom was made this epitaph:

> Here she lies, whose spotless fame
> Invites a stone to learn her name.
> The rigid Spartan, that deny'd
> An epitaph to all that died,
> Unless for war or chastity,
> Would here vouchsafe an elegy.
> She died a wife, but yet her mind
> (Beyond virginity refined)
> From lawless fire remain'd as free
> As now from heat her ashes be.
> Her husband (yet without a sin)
> Was not a stranger but her kin,
> That her chaste love might seem no other
> Unto a husband than a brother.
> Keep well this pawn, thou marble chest;
> Till it be call'd for, let it rest:
> For while this jewel here is set,
> The grave is but a cabinet.

Upon a tomb in the chancel in Saint Botolph's Aldersgate

She died a virgin on Whitsunday, *anno Domini* 1622, about eighteen years of age, and having at her death a spiritual combat with Satan about her salvation, wherein she prevailing, most cheerfully departed from earth to heaven, to be married to Christ Jesus, the Lord of both.

At the bottom:

The monument of Mistress *Judith Plat*, the only daughter of Sir *Hugh Plat*, knight, with the matches of her ancestors and near allies on her father and mother's side; as also her lineal descent from the ancient earls of Surry, Huntingdon, Arundel, and Chester, and her spiritual conquest at her death against Satan.

This tomb is in Saint Bride's church:

Here resteth the body of Sir *George Curzon* of Croxall in the county of Derby, descended from ancient gentry, and of long continuance in that place; who, like the race from whence he came, was a man of upright life, religious and hospitable; he took to wife *Mary*, the daughter of Sir *Richard Leveson* of Lelleshull in the county of Salop, knight, by whom he had *Walter*, who died young, and *Mary*, then his only daughter and heir, who was married to *Edward Sackville*, Earl of Dorset, Knight of the Honorable Order of the Garter; which lady caused this monument to be here infixed to the sacred memory of her dear father. He departed this life the 17 of November 1622.

This tomb stands in Saint Giles Cripplegate church:

Memoriae Sacrum.

Here lieth the body of *Matthew Palmer*, esquire, who died the 18 of May, 1605, together with *Anne* his wife, who died the last day of June, 1630, by whom he had four sons and one daughter, *viz. Thomas Palmer*, his eldest son, deceased the fifth of May, 1631, and here also buried; *Elizabeth, Edward, Andrew*, and *Ralfe*, who whenas it so pleaseth God, desire this place for the custody of their bodies likewise, till their assured and glorious resurrection.

This tomb was made 1631 and stands near the south door in Westminster.

Michael Drayton, esquire, a memorable poet of this age, exchanged his laurel for a crown of glory, *anno Dom.* 1631.

> Do, pious marble, let thy readers know
> What they and what their children owe
> To *Drayton's* name, whose sacred dust
> We recommend unto thy trust:
> Protect his memory and preserve his story;
> Remain a lasting monument of his glory;
> And when thy ruins shall disclaim

To be the treasurer of his name,
His name that cannot fade shall be
An everlasting monument to thee.

On a tomb in the south wall of Saint Botolph's church without Aldersgate, London:

Near to this place lyeth buried the body of *Pierce Edgcombe*, in the county of Devon, gentleman, who deceased the 8 day of July 1628 in assured hope of a joyful resurrection.

> Behold the end of dust and clay,
> O thou which livest, with living eye.
> Yet doth his soul for ever reign
> With Christ, which he by faith did gain.
> In learning he his time did spend,
> And virtue was the only end;
> So long before his glass was run,
> With world and vanity he had done.
>   *A. E.* frater ejus.[4]

In Saint Botolph's Church, on a tomb there:

Here lyeth the body of *Christopher Tamworth* of Grays-Inn in Holborn in the county of Middlesex, esquire, third son of *Christopher Tamworth* of Halsted in the county of Leicester, esquire, who died the 19 of September 1624, being of the age of threescore and ten years.

He having dealt kindly and liberally with his wife and many of his kindred & friends, and to the poor of divers parishes, hath also by his will given xx li. of current money of England to the dean and prebends of the College[5] of Saint Peter's of the City of Westminster in the county of Middlesex to be employed by them about the reparations of the said college church of Saint Peter's.

And 400 marks, to the intent that with that money there should be twenty marks worth of lands of inheritance of yearly rent to be purchased, whereby there may be one in holy orders maintained to say divine service such as the Church of England shall allow of every work day in the year, twice perpetually, viz. at or about nine of the clock in the morning and at or about three of the clock in the afternoon, in the parish church of Saint Botolph's without Aldersgate, London.

And 400 li. to the end and intent that there should be 20 li. of lands of annual revenue of inheritance by the year bought with it, to allow perpetually to six poor men and four poor widows past labor, dwelling and inhabiting within the parish of Saint Botolph aforesaid, 40 shillings a year apiece, to be paid quarterly, with this limitation, that the said poor people shall be bound to repair every work day

---

[4] {A. E., his brother}

[5] {A community or corporation of clergy living together on a foundation for religious service (*OED*).}

in the year twice a day to hear divine service in the parish church aforesaid, at the hours and terms aforesaid.

And 200 marks more to purchase lands of inheritance of the annual value by the year of 6 li. 3 s. 4 d. for the maintenance of one within holy orders to say divine service as aforesaid, every work day in the week twice, through the whole year perpetually, in the parish church of Saint Martin's in Leicester in the county of Leicester aforesaid, at the hours and times aforementioned.

All which said sums of money he willed should be actually and really delivered into the hands and possession of the dean and prebends of Westminster aforesaid within xx days next immediately after his death, for the performance and use aforementioned within the space and time of two years at the uttermost after his death.

And having made *Audrey*, one of the daughters of *Charles Allayne* of the Mote in the county of Kent, esquire, son and heir of Sir *Christopher Allayne*, knight, his dear and loving wife, his full executrix, she faithfully performed the same according to the trust reposed on her by her husband's will; and in remembrance of him hath at her own cost and charges erected this monument.

The gift of Sir Paul Pinder to Saint Paul's church in London:

Sir *Paul Pinder*, knight, in the time of King *James*, his Majesty's ambassador, many years resident at Constantinople with the great Turk, hath of late, to the glory of God, to the delight and content of all good Protestants, and for the better expression of his love and zeal to true religion, beautifully and bountifully, with great costs and charges, repaired the old decayed stonework of the west front of the chancel in Saint Paul's church in London, adorning the outside thereof with many fair polished pillers of black marble, and with curious carved statues of kings and bishops, the first founders and benefactors of the whole fabric; and also graced the inside thereof with divers angels and other ornaments; he hath likewise amended and repaired all the decays and defects of the wainscot work of the choir, and hath further beautified the same with a fair rail of wainscot and a great number of cherubins artificially carved: all which work he hath caused to be sumptuously gilded and painted with rich colors in oil; he hath also magnificently clothed the whole choir and the upper part of the presbytery with fair and chargeable tapestry-hangings: whose godly and pious example will (I hope) excite and stir up other religious and well-minded gentlemen and citizens to perform some acts of piety and bounty towards the reparation of the same church.

A brief collection how the Court of Request, commonly called the Court of Conscience, in London, hath been established and continued for many years past, for the relief of poor debtors in London and the liberties thereof, *viz.*

First, I find that *primo* February, *anno* 9, H. 8, an Act of Common Council was made that the lord mayor and aldermen of the same city for the time being should monthly assign and appoint two aldermen and four discreet commoners to be commissioners to sit in the same court twice a week, viz. Wednesday, and Saturday, there to hear and determine all matters brought before them between party and party (being citizens and freemen of London) in all cases where the due debt or damage did not exceed forty shillings.

This Act was to continue but for two years then next ensuing, but being found charitable and profitable for the relief of such poor debtors as were not able to make present payment of their debts, and to restrain malicious persons from proceeding in their wilfull suits, and also to be a great ease and help to such poor persons as had small debts owing to them and were not able to prosecute suits in law for the same elsewhere, the same Act hath sithence been continued by divers other Acts of Common Council; and hereby (besides the said two aldermen monthly assigned) the number of commissioners were increased from four to twelve. And so by that authority, the same court continued till the end of the reign of Queen *Elizabeth*, &c.

And then divers people, being citizens and freemen of London (contrary to their oaths formerly taken), repining at the authority of the same court; and not regarding the expense of any charges how great soever so they might have their desires upon their poor debtors, and being often animated thereunto by divers attorneys and solicitors (for their own particular gain), did daily commence suits for such petty debts and causes against poor men (citizens and freemen of London) in the high courts at Westminster or elsewhere out of the said Court of Requests, to avoid the jurisdiction of the same court and to bar the said commissioners from staying such suits and examining the said causes, and thereby caused the said poor men many times to pay six times as much charges as their principal debts or damage did amount unto, to the undoing of such poor men, their wives and children, and also to the filling of the prisons with the poor so sued, where otherwise they might have got their debts in the said Court of Requests for very small charge and little trouble.

For remedy whereof & for the strengthening & establishing the said court, an Act of Parliament was then made in *anno primo Iacobi Regis* that every citizen and freeman of London that had or should have any debts owing to him, not amounting to forty shillings, by any debtors (citizens and free men of London) inhabiting in London or the liberties thereof, should or might cause such debtors to be warned to appear before the commissioners of the said court; and that the said commissioner, or the greater number of them, should from time to time set down such orders between such parties, plantiff and defendant, creditor and debtor, touching such debts not exceeding forty shillings, as they should find to stand with equity and good conscience.

But sithence the making of that Act, divers persons (intending to subvert the good and charitable intent of the same) have taken hold of some doubtful and ambiguous words therein and have wrested the same for their own lucre and gain, to the avoiding the jurisdiction of the same court, contrary to the godly meaning of the said Act.

For remedy whereof, and to the intent that some more full and ample provision might be made for the further establishing and strengthening of the said court, and for the better relief of such poor debtors, another Act of Parliament was made *anno 3 Iac.*, whereby the authority of the said commissioners were much enlarged. . . . And by this last Act, the said Court of Requests is established & continued to this day; and God grant it may so long continue to the relief of the poor, &c.

In the same church {St. Margaret's Westminster} is a new monument lately erected in the north aisle, and this inscription on it:

In expectation of a joyful resurrection, near this place resteth the body of *Robert Golding*, gentleman, born in this City of Westminster and sometime chief burgess thereof; his honesty and charitable life gained good esteem; his age, due and deserved respect of all. And in the house where he took beginning in his infancy, he most peaceably and piously ended his days on the 22 of November 1629, being always careful of his ways, charitable to the poor, and very judicious and ready in discharging of all offices incident to the civil governement of this city, wherein he fully proceeded {prospered} long before his death. He lived to see the change of four kings and queens; and yet in assured hope of never-changing bliss by the meritorious Passion of his only mediator, Christ Jesus, he never altered or changed from the now truly professed religion, wherein he most constantly died in the 78 of his age, leaving behind him two sons and three daughters.

To whose pious memory *William Golding*, his eldest son and sole executor, hath at his own charge erected this monument, June 1631.

This monument stands in Westminster Abbey, and hath this inscription:

Here lies, expecting the Second Coming of our Lord Jesus Christ, the body of *Edmund Spenser*, the prince of poets in his time, whose divine spirit needs no other witness than the works which he left behind him: he was born in London in the year {1552} and died in the year 1596.

In the south side of the choir of Saint Paul's church stands a white marble statue on an urn, with this inscription over it:

Ioannes Donne
Sac. Theol. profess.
Post varia studia, Quibus
ab annis Tenerrimis Fideliter,
nec infaeliciter incubuit,
Instinctu, & Impulsu Spir. Sancti,
Monitu, & Hortatu Regis Iacobi,
Ordines sacros amplexus
Anno sui Iesu, 1614 & suae aetat. 42.
Decanatu hujus Eccles. indutus
27 Novemb. 1621
Exutus morte ultimo die
Martii. an. 1631
Hic licet in Occiduo cinere,

Aspicit eum
Cujus Nomen, est Oriens.[6]

Over against the little north door in the same aisle, under a fair marble stone without any inscription upon it, lyeth buried the body of Doctor *Howson*, late Bishop of Durham.

Another monument on the south side of the choir {in St. Giles Cripplegate}, with this inscription:

To the Memory

Of *Constance Whitney*, eldest daughter to Sir *Robert Whitney* of Whitney, the proper possession of him and his ancestors in Herefordshire for above 500 years past. Her mother was the fourth daughter of Sir *Thomas Lucy* of Charlecoite in Warwickshire, by *Constance Kingsmell*, daughter and heir of *Richard Kingsmell*, Surveyor of the Court of Wards. This Lady *Lucy*, her grandmother, so bred her since she was eight years old.

Thus far written upon the figure or resemblance of a coffin:

As she excel'd in all noble qualities becoming a virgin of so sweet proportion of beauty and harmony of parts, she had all sweetness of manners answerable:

A delightful sharpness of wit;

An offenceless modesty of conversation;

A singular respect and piety to her parents; but religious even to example.

She departed this life most Christianly at seventeen; dying, the grief of all; but to her grandmother an unrecoverable loss, save in her expectation she shall not stay long after her, and the comfort of knowing whose she is and where in the resurrection to meet her.

This table is on the south side of the choir in Saint Sepulcher's, with this inscription:

To the living memory of his deceased friend, Captain *John Smith*, who departed this mortal life on the 21 day of June, 1631; with his arms and this motto,

Accordamus, vincere est vivere.[7]

Here lies one conquer'd that hath conquer'd kings,
Subdu'd large territories, and done things
Which to the world impossible would seem

---

[6] {John Donne, who professed sacred theology after various studies which from his early years he pursued not without success; and by the instinct and impulse of the Holy Spirit as by counsel and urging of King James, took holy orders in the year of his Savior 1614, when 42 years of age. He was invested with the deanery of this church on November 27, 1621, and divested by death on the last day of March 1631. Although sunk into dust, he beholds him whose name is Rising.}

[7] {Let us agree, to conquer is to live.}

But that the truth is held in more esteem.
Shall I report his former service done
In honor of his God and Christendom?

How that he did divide from pagans three,
Their heads and lives, types of his chivalry,
For which great service in that climate done,
Brave *Sigismundus* (King of Hungarion)
Did give him as a coat of arms to wear,
Those conquer'd heads got by his sword and spear?
Or shall I tell of his adventures since
Done in Virginia, that large continence?[8]
How that he subdu'd kings unto his yoke,
And made those heathen fly as wind doth smoke;
And made their land, being of so large a station,
A habitation for our Christian nation,
Where God is glorifi'd, their wants suppli'd,
Which else for necessaries might have died?
But what avails his conquest, now he lies
Inter'd in earth, a prey for worms and flies?
O may his soul in sweet Elizium sleep,
Until the Keeper that all souls doth keep
Return to Judgment, and that after thence,
With angels he may have his recompence.

Captain *John Smith*, sometime Governor of Virginia and Admiral of New England.

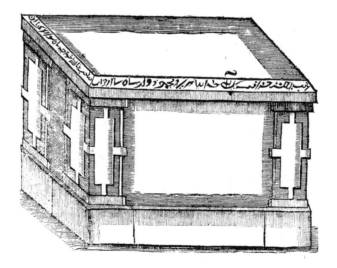

---

[8] {presumably, "continent"}

Coya Shawsware.

This monument <above>, or that of which this is a shadow, with their characters engraven about it, stands in Petty France, at the west end of the lower churchyard of Saint Botolph's Bishopsgate (not within, but without the walls, the bounds of our consecrated ground), and was erected to the memory of one *Coya Shawsware*, a Persian merchant and a principal servant and secretary to the Persian ambassador, with whom he and his son came over. He was aged 44 and buried the tenth of August 1626—the ambassador himself, young *Shawsware* his son, and many other Persians (with many expressions of their infinite love and sorrow) following him to the ground between eight and nine of the clock in the morning. The rites and ceremonies that (with them) are due to the dead were chiefly performed by his son, who sitting crosslegged at the north end of the grave (for his tomb stands north and south), did one while read, another while sing, his reading and singing intermixt with sighing and weeping. And this, with other things that were done in the grave in private (to prevent with the sight the relation[9]), continued about half an hour.

But this was but this day's business: for, as this had not been enough to perform to their friend departed, to this place and to this end (that is, prayer, and other funeral devotions) some of them came every morning and evening at six and six for the space of a month together. And had come (as it was then imagined) the whole time of their abode here in England, had not the rudeness of our people disturbed and prevented their purpose.

A PERAMBVLATION
OR,
CIRCUIT-WALK

four miles about LONDON:
And what memorable matters and monuments we
have found and met withal in our journey.

. . .

In the church at Putney are these ensuing monuments.

Marito dilectissimo, *Maria Lusher* conjux moestissima, in perpetuum amoris testimonium, hoc monumentum plorans posuit.[10]

Mary (by her first match, *Lusher*), daughter of *George Scot*, esquire, descended from *John Scot*, Lord Chief Justice of *England* in the reign of King *Edward* the third; and after wife to *Thomas Knivet*, descended from *John Knivet*, knight, Lord Chief Justice in the same King's reign and Lord Chancellor of England.

To Thomas Knivet

That you have laid my body here,
By that first side I lov'd so dear,

---

[9] {I.e., to prevent people from seeing, and hence from reporting on, what was done.}

[10] {His most sorrowful wife, Maria Lusher, weeping erected this monument to her beloved husband as an eternal witness of her love.}

I thank you, husband; that the poor
Are still your care, I thank you more.
These last I charg'd you with alive;
Being done, I rest, while you survive.
But yet I have another boon,
When Fate shall come (as come full soon
It will, and will not be deni'd),
That you would close my other side.
Y'ave thought it worthy to be read
You once were second to my bed;
Why may you not like title have,
To this my second bed, the grave?
This stone will cover us all three,
And under it we shall be free
From love or hate or least distrust
Of jealousy to vex our dust;
For here our bodies do but wait
The summons for their glorious state.

On the same monument is this inscription:

Quam diu, Domine.
Siste
Siste Hospes:
Quod reliqui est lectissimae foeminae
Te rogitat,
Etiam ego, superstes maritus,
superstes ipse funeri meo.
Nam in conjuge, conjunx vixi,
et cum illa elatus sum.
Maria, mea Maria,
Dulcissima Maria
Hic sita est.
Cor gratiarum, flos venustatis merus,
Sedes amorum, castitatis exemplar
Tanti erga me affectus
Talisque.
Morum ac vitae perpetuae sanctimoniae,
ut vivens, moriensque,
Singulari praeluxerit face
omnibus
Vel ordinis sui, vel sexus.
Heu qualem amisi
Ex puerperio raptam?
Et cum ea, spem posteritatis.
Sic me relinquis? Sic terras deseris?

O Christianae perfectionis imago,
Injuriarum contemptrix facilis,
Doloribus ferendis fortis:
Omnes in te certabant virtutes
sed vicit Pietas.
Fulges etiam in ipsa mortis umbra,
Divini amoris, dum vixisti, flamma,
Et postquam vixisti, astrum.
Vale, Vale, Maria:
Nullum de te dolorem
Nisi ex acerbissima tua morte
Accepi.[11]

. . .

In the church at Lambeth are these ensuing monuments.

Over against the other in the same aisle lieth the body of *Elizabeth Bayly*, late wife of *John Bayly*. Obijt 24 of June, aetatis suae 25.

Reader tread soft, under thy foot doth lie
A mother buried with her progeny:
Two females and a male, the last a son,
Who with his life, his mother's thread hath spun;
His breath her death procur'd (unhappy sin,
That thus our joy with sorrow ushers in).
Yet he being loth to leave so kind a mother,
Changes this life to meet her in another.
The daughters first were rob'd of vital breath;
The mother next in strength of years met death;
The father's only joy, a hopeful son,
Did lose his life when life was scarce begun.
If harmless innocence, if loyal truth
Found in a constant wife, combin'd with youth,
If a kind husband's prayers or father's tears
Could have prevail'd, they had liv'd many years.

[11] {How long, O Lord . . . Stranger, halt, halt. That which remains of a most excellent woman beseeches you, even I, her surviving husband, the survivor of my own funeral; for I, a spouse, lived in my spouse, and with her have been buried. Maria, my Maria, sweetest Maria, lieth here. A heart of all graces, the pure flower of beauty, the seat of love, the paradigm of chastity, whose love for me was so great and so prized. Of such holiness of conduct and life that, living and dying, she outshone all others of her rank and sex. Alas, what have I lost, snatched away in childbirth? And with her, the hope of posterity. Will you leave me thus? Thus depart this earth? O image of Christian perfection, who easily contemned all affronts and bore suffering with fortitude: all the virtues contested [for supremacy] in you, but piety triumphed. You illumine even the shadows of death—you who in life were the light of divine love, and thereafter its star. Farewell, farewell, Maria. No grief on your account did I experience, except from your most bitter death. . . .}

But these all failing, here, rak'd up in dust,
They wait the resurrection of the just.
A husband's love, a father's piety
Dedicates this unto their memory:
And when he hath his debt to Nature paid,
In the same grave himself will then be laid,
That altogether, when the trump shall sound,
Husband, wife, children may in Christ be found.

In Saint George's church in Southwarke, on the north side, are these monuments thus written on.

Lo, Master *William Evans*, he whose body lieth here,
Bequeathed hath by his last will, forever by the year,
Ten pound eight shillings to the poor, which is a blessed stay,
And must be given them in bread, on every Sabbath day:
One half to Crekederus' poor, his native soil so dear,
The other moiety to the poor of this our parish here.
See now, all ye that love the poor, how God did guide his ways;
Tenscore & eight are serv'd with bread, in two and fifty days,
More than many would have done, to yielded any share.
Praise God, ye poor, who gave to him so provident a care.[12]

He was of the right worshipful Company of the Merchant-Taylors, and deceased the 29 of July, *anno* 1590 in the 32 year of the most prosperous reign of our Sovereign Lady, Queen *Elizabeth, aetatis suae* 67.

At the upper end of that chancel {at Wansworth}, is thus written:

Here lyeth the body of *Henry Smith*, esquire, sometime citizen and alderman of London, who departed this life the 30 day of January, *an. Dom.* 1627, being then near the age of 79 years, who while he lived gave unto these several towns in Surry following one thousand pounds a piece to buy lands for perpetuity for the relief and setting the poor people on work in the said towns. . . . And by his last will and testament did further give and devise to buy lands for perpetuity for the relief and setting their poor on work, unto the town of Reigate one thousand pounds. And unto this town of Wandsworth, wherein he was born, the sum of 500 pounds, for the same uses as before. And did further will and bequeath one thousand pounds to buy land for perpetuity to redeem poor captives and prisoners from the Turkish tyranny. And not here stinting his charity and bounty, did also give and bequeath the most part of his estate, being to a great value, for the purchasing lands of inheritance forever for the relief of the poor and setting them on work.

---

[12] {On the custom of distributing bread to the poor, often a highly ritualized event centering on the communion table, see Archer, "The arts and acts" 106.}

A pattern worthy the imitation of those whom God hath blessed with the abundance of the goods of this life to follow him herein.

At the upper end of this chancel is this inscription:

Susanna Powell, late of Wandsworth, widow, daughter of *Thomas Hayward* of Wandsworth, Yeoman of the Guard unto King *Henry* the 8, King *Edward* the 6, to Queen *Mary*, and to Queen *Elizabeth* (of ever precious memory), and wife unto *John Powell* of Wandsworth, gentleman, who was servant to Queen *Elizabeth*. This *Susanna Powell* was a gracious benefactor unto this town of Wandsworth. She lived a widow the space (almost) of twenty years, deceased the 19 day of February 1630, & at her death bequeathed by her will unto 24 poor widows of this town of Wandsworth forever four pence in bread and four pence in money to be distributed every Lord's Day, 12 on one Sabbath and 12 another, forever, at the north door of the church at Wandsworth.

She also bequeathed 40 shillings every year forever to put forth a poor man child an apprentice, with divers other loving remembrances unto her good friends and neighbors. These foresaid donations are to issue out of the benefits and profits of the rectory of Wandsworth.

This was desired to be recorded that God might be glorified, the memorial of the just might be blessed, and the living stirred up to such like good works of piety and compassion.

More:

To this church, for the communion table, two flagon pots of silver, price xx li. and upwards.

To release poor prisoners out of prison on the day of her burial, xx li.

To the poor of the parish of Putney, long before she deceased, 50 li.

To the poor housholders of Wandsworth, for many years before her death, toward payment of their rent, *per annum*, 5 li.

A monument in the south aisle {at Islington}, with this inscription:

To the sacred memory of *Anne*, late wife of *Henry Chitting*, esquire, Chester Herald at Arms; eldest daughter of *William Bennet*, gentleman, by *Joyce*, widow of *Richard Joselin* of Newhall *Joselins* in Essex, esquire, and daughter of *Robert Atkinson* of Stowell in the county of Glocester, esquire; she had four children, whereof three are living, *Thomas*, *Joyce*, and *Henry*, of which last she died in childbed the 8 of May 1632, in the 27 of her age, and 4 year of her marriage.

Mors mihi vita.[13]

---

[13] {Death to me is life.}

Life is Death's road,
    and Death Heaven's gate must be,
Heaven is Christ's Throne,
    and Christ is life to me.
The angels of the Lord protect
    All those that are his own Elect.

Vivit post funera virtus.[14]

Another monument there also {in Saint Giles church in the Fields}, with this inscription:

Here lieth the body of *Thomas Fouler*, esquire, born in Wicam in the county of Lancaster, who was controller and paymaster of the works to Queen *Mary* and to our Sovereign Lady, Queen *Elizabeth*, by the space of ten years. He was very charitable to the poor in his lifetime, and at his death he gave by will out of his dwelling house a perpetual annuity of 40 s. by the year, to be given to 20 poor householders of this parish at Christmas forever. He had in marriage three wives, *Ellen*, *Margaret*, and *Elizabeth*, which also lyeth here entombed. He surviving them, having no child at his death, made three of his old servants, namely *Henry Bludder*, *Matthew Switzer*, and *William Humphrey*, his executors, who in remembrance of him have caused this monument to be made.

On the same wall {in Saint Margaret's church, Westminster} in a table, is this epitaph:

In memory of the late deceased virgin, Mistress *Elizabeth Hereicke*:[15]

Sweet Virgin, that I do not set
Thy grave-verse up in mournful jet
Or dapl'd marble, let thy shade
Not wrathful seem or fright the maid
Who hither at her weeping hours
Shall come to strew thy earth with flowers:
No, know blest soul, when there's not one
Remainder left of brass or stone,
Thy living epitaph shall be,
Though lost in them, yet found in me.
Dear, in thy bed of roses then,
Till this world shall dissolve (as men),
Sleep, while we hide thee from the light,
Drawing thy curtains round—Good night.

[14] {Goodness lives after one's death.}
[15] {A kinswoman of Robert Herrick, who composed the epitaph.}

A RETURN
TO
LONDON,

In which most of the parish churches have of late
years been rebuilded, repaired, or at least beautified.

A catalogue whereof here followeth, wherein not only the year in which but the means
likewise by which each work was perfected are set down, as also all the monuments of
Queen *Elizabeth*, as they are in every church.

S. Alban's Woodstreet

I am sorry that, but now beginning to speak of building, repairing, and beautifying
of all the parish churches in this famous City of London, I must in the very front of the
alphabet (for that is the rule I go by) speak of the pulling down, demolishment, and ruins
of a church, and one of the most ancient among them: Saint Alban's in Woodstreet.

This church, being wonderfully decayed and perished, was by these gentlemen, Sir
Henry Spiller, Inigo Jones, esquire, Captain *Leake*, and Captain *Williams*, surveyed to see
what repair might help it. But by these gentlemen, and workmen appointed with them,
it was found to be too far gone for repair; neither would any workman put himself into
hazard upon it: affirming it to be in every part of it so spent, decayed, and enfeebled that
they must suddenly pluck it down or it would suddenly prevent that labor and fall to the
ground of itself, which the fallings every day increasing (and more and more growing and
appearing) did most evidently seem to threaten.

For this cause, many of the parishoners refused to go to it; many that went, went
unwillingly, but all with much fear, where they sat with more, their danger all the time
much troubling and disturbing their devotion.

This great necessity enforcing, it was the last year 1632 betwixt Easter and Midsummer pull'd down, and yet July 1633 (a sad object) so lies in its pitiful ruins.

Many of the ablest sort of this parish, to shew they would do what they could towards
the recovery of this great loss, have joined certain moneys (their free and voluntary gifts)
together, which they have again disbursed in stone and some other materials. But this
many, being but few to the number of those that in this kind can do little or nothing, and
their good wills falling extremely short of that great sum that must begin and finish so
great a work as this, they were constrained to petition his Highness for his letters patents
for the help of a collection for it.

Their petition graciously received, his Majesty was pleased (as a cause of all other his
piety especially favors) to send his letter to the Lord Bishop of London for the forwarding
and effecting their desires.

Yet notwithstanding this fair degree to their wish, they are for a time put off, by
reason (as I am informed) of the great collection for the repair of the famous cathedral
church of Saint Paul; but they hope it will not be long.

In which hope they have many partners, as also in their prayers for all the good means
that may be to the speedy rebuilding of it; till which time, the church appointed unto

them for the Sabbath exercises, marriage, burying, churching, and the sacraments is the parish church of Saint Alphage near Cripplegate. And thus much of this church, Saint Alban's.

Alhallows Barking

This church was repaired and beautified in the year of our Lord God 1613, and within some few years before and after (in their several times) other wants were supplied and furnished, *viz.*

A very fair new pulpit set up, many fair pews, a fair communion table with other graceful ornaments to it. This table was the gift of one Master *John Burnell*; all the rest, the charge of the parish. Also, in the south aisle, over the entry into the church, in the year of our Lord 1627 there was a very handsome gallery erected, at the cost and charge of the parish.

Thomas Covell
John Shaw, churchwardens.

In the south wall is a monument with this inscription:
In the aisle against this place lyeth the body of *Francis Covell*, citizen and skinner of London; he lived in this parish 52 years, was married to his wife *Margery* 42 years, had issue by her *Thomas* his only son. He had borne office in his Company and this ward with good reputation; was in his life religious, peaceable, and charitable; and at his death gave clothing to the poor of this parish yearly forever. He lived 69 years, and rendred his soul in peace to God, September 7, 1625.

All-hallows Breadstreet

This church, in the many decayed places of it, was repaired and in every part of it richly and very worthily beautified, at the proper cost and charges of the parishioners, in the year of our Lord God 1625,

Samuel Tucker

William Hunt, churchwardens.
On the south side of the chancel, in a little part of this church called The Salters' Chapel, is a very fair window with the portraiture or figure of him that gave it very curiously wrought upon it, with this inscription:

Thomas Beaumont, salter, the founder of this chapel and a worthy benefactor to
the Company of the Salters, 1629. This window being then erected.
In the midst of this little chapel, in a fair marble tomb, this man with his two wives lies interred. . . .

To the sacred memory

Of that worthy and faithful minister of Christ, Master *Richard Stocke*, who, after 32 years spent in the ministry, wherein, by his learned labors joined with wisdom and a most holy life, God's glory was much advanced, his church edified, piety increased, and the true honor of a pastor's place maintained, deceased April 20, 1626; some of his loving parishoners have consecrated this monument of their never-dying love, Jan. 28, 1628:

. . .

Thy lifeless trunk
    (O Reverend *Stocke*)
Like Aaron's rod
    sprouts out again,
And after two
    full winters past,
Yields blossoms
    and ripe fruit amain.

For why[16] this work of piety,
Performed by some of thy flock
To thy dead corps and sacred urn,
Is but the fruit of this old *Stocke*.

A fair new monument in the south aisle, on the wall, almost at the upper end:

This monument was erected at the cost of this parish in memorial of Master *John Dunster*, citizen and clothworker of London, who lieth buried near this place, and gave amongst other charitable gifts, 200 pounds towards the late building of this church, and 200 pounds which hath purchased 12 pounds a year forever towards the reparation of the same. He departed this life the 14 of October, 1625, being of the age of 58 years.

S. Alphage

This church (the decays in divers parts of it calling upon the parishioners for it) began to be repaired in the year of our Lord God 1624, the repair continuing 25 and 26, in which time the masons' work amounted to 400 pounds. The further repair in 27 and 28, in the last of which it was beautifully finished, arising to 100 pounds more: the sole cost and charge of the parish. . . .

On another fair stone in the same aisle:

In Christ alone I only trust,
To rise in number of the just.

Here under lyeth buried the body of *Katharine Edwards*, sometime beloved wife of *John Edwards*, of this parish of Saint Alphage. She departed this transitory life

---

[16] {because}

on the sixth day of January 1628 and in the 45 year of her age, having had issue by her said husband five sons and seven daughters.

My body here in dust doth rest,
Sin caus'd that earth claims it as due,
My soul's in heaven forever blest,
Yet both in one Christ will renew.

Andrew Undershaft

This church was repaired and laudably trimmed and beautified at the cost and charge of the parishioners, in the year of our Lord God 1627
William Bargins
Simon Farewell, churchwardens.

Then (I say) trimmed and beautified, although for some few years before and since, to this present year 1633, the care and cost of the parishioners have been still employed in the supplying and furnishing of it with such things as either for necessity or beauty their love to God's house should find wanting. Among other things these, *viz.*

They have new raised their chancel, adding to that cost a communion table with a very fair frame[17] about it; they have made many new pews, a fair alabaster font, and a clock: a necessary thing that in the memory of man this parish hath not had, nor the eldest parishioner ever heard of.

They have also in this church (much commending the founders & continuers of it) at the lower end of the north aisle, a fair wainscot press {cupboard} full of good books, the works of many learned and reverend divines, offering (at seasonable and convenient times) the benefit of reading to any that shall be as ready to embrace it as they and their maintainers to impart it.

Anne Blackfriars

The ancient church belonging to the Blackfriars, London, was (before the dissolution of religious houses by Henry the 8) one of the most spacious and fair churches in London; but the friars being put out, the church (together with other fair buildings) was utterly demolished. Therefore the inhabitants of the said Blackfriars, London, fitted an upper room of 50 foot in length and 30 foot in breadth for a public place of divine worship. The charges of purchasing and fitting the said room for a church appeareth not in any record that we can find.

In *anno* 1597 when the church was empty and nobody in it, a great part of the roof thereof fell down, whereupon the then inhabitants, being about to repair their said church, obtained of Sir *George Moore*, knight, so much ground as enlarged their church with an aisle on the west 50 foot in length and 15 foot in breadth; for which ground they built at their own cost a fair warehouse under the said aisle for the use of Sir *Jerome Bows*,

---

[17] {altar rails, on which parishioners would kneel to take Communion; see Edwin Freshfield, *On the parish books of St. Margaret-Lothbury . . . in the City of London* (London, 1876), 20.}

knight, who then had the said ground in lease, and also gave him 133 li. The new building of their said church and aisle (beside the foresaid 133 li. given to Sir *Jerome Bows*) cost 300 li. 18 shillings.

In June 1607 the inhabitants of the said Blackfriars paid 120 li. to Sir George Moore for the purchase of their preacher's house, their churchyard, their church, and the porch appertaining thereunto, together with the right of patronage of, in, and to the said church.[18]

In *anno* 1613 the inhabitants of the said Blackfriars purchased on the south of their church, so much housing as enlarged their church aforesaid 36 foot in length and 54 foot in breadth, the purchase whereof, together with the vault for burying, and other rooms under that part of the church, and the new building of all, and making new pews and pulpit, cost 1546 li. 6 shillings.

In anno 1632 the inhabitants of the said Blackfriars purchased the rooms directly under the above mentioned upper room converted to a church, which said under rooms they purchased to repair the foundation & walls whereon the church stood, which walls were very much decayed. The purchase whereof, and repair of decays, cost 500 li.

The sum of all bestowed upon Blackfriars church since the reformation of religion in England amounteth to 2600 pounds, 4 shillings.

S. Antholine's

This church was repaired and beautified in the year of our Lord 1616, towards which the gentlemen here under named were free and very bounteous benefactors. . . .

To this was added a very rich and beautiful gallery, every pane or division of it (the number of them 52) filled with the arms of kings, queens, and princes of this kingdom, beginning with *Edward the Confessor* and ending with the badge or symbol of *Frederick*, Count Palatine of the Rhine, Duke of Bavaria, and Prince Elector, &c.[19]

Begun in the year 1623 . . .

S. Austin

This church was in part rebuilded, leaded, and in every part of it richly and very worthily beautified at the proper cost and charge of the parishioners in the years of our Lord God 1630 and 1631,

> Ralph Tonstell
> Daniel Hallingworth
> Samuel Langham, churchwardens.

The charge of this great and costly repair amounting to the sum of 1200 pounds.

---

[18] {It was most unusual for a congregation to own either the church buildings or the living; the latter was normally in the gift of the bishop, the archbishop, the Crown, or a lay patron.}

[19] {That these images of English royalty end with the Palzgrave Frederick (the Protestant holy warrior, whose overreaching triggered the Thirty Years War) signals the parish's godly commitments.}

Bartholomew Exchange

This church was repaired and beautified, at the proper cost and charge of the parishioners, in the year of our Lord 1620. . . .

Monument in the south side of the chancel thus written on:

Here lieth *Richard Crashawe*, sometimes Master of the Company of Goldsmiths and deputy of this ward. He was very liberal to the poor, and in the time of the great plague 1625, neglecting of his own safety, he abode constantly in this City to provide for their relief; he did many charitable acts in his time, and by his will he left above 4000 li. to the maintaining of lectures, relief of the poor, and other pious uses. He dwelt in this parish 31 years, and being 70 years old, he died the 2 of June 1621.

In the same church and the same aisle, upon a fair stone, is this inscription:

Here lieth interred the body of *William Drew*, citizen and grocer of London, who departed this life the 29 day of August 1631, being of the age of 56 years, expecting a blessed and joyful resurrection at the coming of Christ.

Bennet Grace-Church

There hath been bestowed on this parish church within the passage of 20 years several charges, amounting to the sum of 700 pounds. But the greatest part of this in the last repair, which was in the year of our Lord 1630, in which, as it was very carefully repaired, so richly and very worthily beautified.

Some useful, necessary, and most needful things in (and since added to) this worthy repair were these: a new clock, a new dial, new chimes, and now 1633 a very fair turret for the steeple.

S. Faith

We cannot in this place keep our ordinary course in speaking of decays and repairing, for (as it is anciently said of this church)

This church needs no repair at all,

Saint Faith's defended by Saint Paul.

And for beauty, it hath sufficient, being still supplied and furnished with whatsoever the virtuous and religious guardians of it know fit either for use or ornament. Which while we speak of, we cannot forget that especial addition of beauty, light: that light, that by pulling down those houses that stood before it, is plenteously descended into it; nor (with that) the cost of the parishioners (having gained such a long-wanted benefit) in trimming and new glazing their windows.[20]

---

[20] {The pulling-down of the houses crowding St. Paul's (and St. Faith's) became one of the charges against Laud at his trial, although most of the specific allegations date from 1634; see Laud, *Works* 4:92–96.}

At that time also, 1632, they purchased at the lower end of the south aisle (going up through the entry into Paul's) a convenient place for a vestry, upon which (having none before) they have bestowed a great deal of cost and beauty. . . .

A very fair marble stone in the chancel under the communion table, with these words about it:

> Under this stone lie buried the bodies of *John* and *Francis Astley*, the sons of Sir *John Astley* of Allington Castle in the county of Kent, Master of the Revels, and a Gentleman of the Privy Chamber in ordinary to *Charles* the first.

Upon it:

> In obitum immaturum Ioh. & Fr. Astley, filiorum domini Ioh. Astley, Equitis Aurati, quorum hic undecem, alter duo de viginti annos natus, ad superos migravit. Utrique vero sub eodem marmore tumulantur.

> Sic rebar, solum spes tanta
> invida Fata
> Ostendisse viris, &
> Rapuisse simul.
> Aut pater omnipotens,
> & qui dedit, abstulit, aptes
> Vidit quippe astris,
> asseruitque sibi.
> Illi autem humanis exempti
> Rebus, Olympum
> Nunc habitant, ubi pax,
> & sine fine quies.
> Vno hoc felices; quod cum
> unus venter utrosque
> Foverat, una etiam
> nunc capit urna duos.[21]

A fair monument on the north side of the chancel, with this inscripion:

M. S.

Hic juxta situs est Richardus Ironside, vir summa prudentia, industria, vitaeque integritate, una cum 2 lectiss. uxorib. Quarum posteriorem, morum suavitate,

---

[21] {In memory of the early death of *John* and *Francis Astley*, sons of *John Astley*, knight, of whom one, at the age of eleven, the other at the age of eighteen passed to the company above, but both are buried under the same monument.

Thus was I reflecting that such hope is showed to men by envious fates only to be at once snatched away. But the Almighty Father (he who gave and has taken away) saw indeed that they were fit for heaven, and claimed them for himself. But they, released from human cares, inhabit the heights where is peace and endless rest. Happy in this alone, that as one womb had cherished them both, so now one urn holds the two.}

elegantia, & amore conjunctam, Fato sibi raptam, non ita multo post sequutus est. Quibus hoc monumentum in opprobrium mortis, quae has tam pias animas eripuit à 13 liberis, qui se ipsos poene quaerunt in illarum desiderio, consecravit

E. I. filius & haeres.[22] 1627.

A fair monument at the upper end of the chancel, with this inscription:

Here lieth buried the body *Katherine* (third daughter of *Edward* Lord *Nevill*, Baron of Abergaveny), wife of Sir *Stephen Lessieur* of Chiswicke in the county of Middlesex, knight. She was brought from her said house to this parish in hope to recover her bodily health by the help of God and physicians. But the same God, knowing and having ordained that which was best for her pious soul, hath been pleased to take her from the miseries of this vain world, and to receive her soul with his saints in heaven. As she did profess in all the time that she lived in the state of a maid and of a wife to be a true and obedient child of God, even so she did behave herself in her sickness, bearing her affliction with a true Christian patience, much delighting to read or to hear the word of God read unto her, hoping and trusting to be saved by the only merits and Passion of our Savior Jesus Christ, and recommending her spirit into the hands of Almighty God, she exchanged her mortal life for the immortal, the 4 of August 1630.

Revel. 14:13

Blessed are the dead that die in the Lord, yea saith the Spirit, that they rest from their labors, and their works follow them.

Quid aliud est mors vitae hujus mortalis, quam finis mortis hujus vitalis, & janua vitae immortalis?

Ergo

Vive diu, sed vive Deo, nam vivere mundo mortis opus: viva est vivere vita Deo.[23]

A very fair table hanging about the middle of the south aisle of Saint Faith's church, *anno Dom.* 1630:
Benefactors, and their gifts to the poor of this parish

Years	Names	Gifts
1586	*David Smith*, embroiderer, gave 20 shillings a year forever.	
1592	The Lady *Allington* gave 5 pounds to be distributed.	

---

[22] {Close by is buried Richard Ironside, a man of great wisdom, industry, and probity; together with his two beloved wives, the latter of whom—knit to him by sweetness of bearing, refinement, and love—having been snatched away by fate, he soon after followed. To these—and in defiance of the death that snatched three such pious souls from thirteen children, who seem almost to be seeking themselves in their longing for them—, his son and heir, E. I., consecrated this monument.}

[23] {What is the death of this mortal life other than the end of this living death and the door to life immortal? Therefore, live long, but live to the Lord; for to live to the world is the work of death; a living life is lived in God.}

1598	*John Payne*, esquire, gave 12 pence a week in bread forever.
1600	*Justinian Kidd*, gentleman, gave 10 pounds to be employed forever.
1605	*Francis Lamplow*, clothworker, gave 10 pounds to be employed forever.
1610	*George Bishop*, stationer, alderman, gave 10 pounds to be distributed.
1611	*William Evans*, tallow-chandler, gave 40 pound to be employed forever.
1612	*John Norton*, stationer, alderman, gave 150 pounds for 12 poor people to receive three pence a piece every Wednesday weekly forever.
1613	*Mary Bishop*, the wife of *George Bishop*, gave 10 pounds to be distributed.
1614	*John Law*, proctor of the Arches, gave 10 pounds to be employed.
1620	*Thomas Adams*, stationer, gave 10 pounds to be distributed.
1623	*Jasper Underwood*, vintner, gave 10 pounds to be distributed.
1624	*John Sanderson*, draper, gave 150 pounds for 12 poor men to receive three pence a week, every Sunday weekly, forever.
1625	*Elizabeth Underwood*, widow, gave 10 pounds to be distributed, and 60 pounds towards a lecture forever.
1626	*John Beliall*, silk-man, gave 10 pounds to be distributed.
1628	*Ally Mercer*, gave 5 pounds to be distributed.
1629	*John Speed*, merchant-taylor, gave 5 pounds to be distributed.

Ex dono Iacobi Trussell.

Katherine Cree-Church

The foundation of this now famously finished house of God was begun to be laid upon the 23 day of June in the year of our Lord God 1628.[24] The first brick, as also the first stone in this foundation, was laid by Master *Martin Bond* of this parish, alderman's deputy of the ward, and one of our city captains. The brick was laid (as is aforesaid) the 23 of June, and the stone (a principal cornerstone) the 28 of July following. Many of the parishioners (following this worthy leader) laid every man his stone—with which they laid something else, which the workmen took up very thankfully.

On the backside of the north wall of the old church was a cloister, the breadth of it seven foot and above, which cloister, by the taking down of that wall, being taken into the church, gave it all its breadth to enlarge it. In digging under this wall there was found the figure of half the face of a man cast in lead . . . upon it this word, *Comes* {Count}. Digging under the south row of pillars, they found the skull of a man, the thickness of which was three-quarters of an inch and better, measured by many, and admired by all that have seen it.

At the west end of this church, adjoining to the steeple, stands a pillar of the old church as it stood and was there erected. This pillar . . . being eighteen foot high, and but three to be seen above ground, shews the measure or height to which the floor of this new church hath been raised above that of the old, which is the hidden part of the pillar, or the 15 foot of it buried.

---

[24] {On the renovation and consecration of St. Katherine Cree, see Peter Lake's splendid account in *The Boxmaker's revenge*.}

This structure, not of brick but built from the ground with the choicest freestone might be got, without, within, and in every part of it supplied, furnished, and enriched with whatsoever might add to its greatest grace and lustre, was finished in the year of our Lord God 1630. In this year (accounting from March to March) upon the 16 day of January, it was consecrated by the right Reverend Father in God, *Wil.{Laud}*, Lord Bishop of London, and upon the same day (as on such it is usual with us) were the sacraments of the Lord's Supper and the sacrament of baptism administered. In this church the pulpit and communion table are pure cedar and (both) the gift of Master *John Dyke*, a merchant living in this parish.

A very fair gate built at the east end of the south wall was the gift of *William Avenen*, citizen and goldsmith of London, who died in December 1631.

Lawrence Pountney

The steeple of this church was new leaded, five new bells were hung, and the frames they hang in new made, all the aisles were new raised and levelled, and the whole church within and without worthily repaired and beautified, at the cost and charge of the parish, in the years of our Lord God 1631 and 1632,

> George Downes
> Robert Meade, churchwardens.

A monument at upper end of the north aisle, with this inscription:

> Hoc est nescire, sine Christo
> plurima scire;
> Si Christum bene scis,
> satis est, si caetera nescis.[25]

This monument was erected *anno Dom.* 1620 by the Lady *Anne Bromley*, late wife unto Sir *Henry Bromley* of Holt in the county of Worcester, knight; daughter of *William Beswicke* of London, alderman; in remembrance of her first husband, *William Offley*, of London, merchant, who being free of the Merchant-Taylors, fined[26] both for sheriff and alderman. He had issue by the said *Anne* 15 children, whereof five are living, *viz. William, Elizabeth, Margaret, Robert*, and *Mary*; the rest died infants.

Michael Cornhill

Here a repair follows a repair so close that, while I speak of the one, I must not forget the other; the former being in the years of our Lord God 1618, 1619, and 1620; at the finishing,

---

[25] {To be ignorant is to know many things and yet to be without Christ. If you know Christ well, it is enough, even if you are ignorant of other things.}

[26] {I.e., he had been selected for these posts but paid a fine rather than serve.}

William Stannard

George Hill

Francis Mosse, churchwardens.

Of the beauty, conceive by the cost—the charge of it amounting to 644 li.

The other in this present year of our Lord, 1633, in which the roof over the chancel was new trim'd, the chancel likewise enriched with a fair and very curious table of the Commandments, the windows about it were new glazed, the stones through the whole body of the church taken up, new layed and levelled, and in a word, every part of it, at the cost and charge of the parishioners, was well and very worthily beautified,

John Collison

Richard Norton

Francis Middleton, churchwardens.

The charge of this arising to 300 li. and upward.

A very fair monument on the wall in the north aisle, with this inscription:

Memoriae sacrum

Laurentio & Mariae Caldwall conjugibus, sacro foedare iunctis, & duodenae prolis parentibus; quorum uxor & mater Maria obiit Octobris xx anno Dom. 1621. Maritus & pater Laurentius, Novemb. xxj 1625, septuagenariis utrisque. Liberalibus & suis, & de suis. Hoc sepulcrum posuere, parentalis haeredes bonitatis, filii eorum observantissimi, quos defunctos, & Deus habet, & pauperes carendo lugent.[27]

As it were in a scroll, held by an angel:

Omnia ossa justi custodit Dominus.[28]

Under this upon the figure of a tomb:

Here is lodg'd a loving pair;

Sleeping, rest they free from care;

Though their journey, from their birth,

Hath been tedious long on earth,

He that freed them from their sin,

Sent them to this holy inn,

Joyful requiems for to sing,

Hallelujahs to their King,

Till the summons, till the day,

Till the trump sound, *Rise, Away.*

---

[27] {Sacred to the memory of Lawrence and Mary Caldwall, joined in holy matrimony and parents of twelve children. Mary, wife and mother, died October 20, 1621. Lawrence, husband and father, on November 21, 1625—both in their seventies. Generous both to their own and of their own. The heirs of this parental goodness, their most loving sons, erected this tomb for the departed, whom God now has and whose loss the poor mourn.}

[28] {The Lord guardeth all the bones of the just.}

Michael Querne

This church was repaired, and with all things either for use or beauty richly supplied and furnished, at the sole cost and charge of the parishioners, in the year of our Lord 1617.

A fair monument in the north aisle, with this inscription:

John Bankes, mercer and esquire, whose body lyeth here interred, the son of *Thomas Bankes*, free of the Barber-Surgeons; this *John* was aged 59 and expired the ninth of September, *anno* 1630

His first wife was *Martha*, a widow, by whom he had one only son, deceased; his second wife was *Anne Hasell*, who left unto him one daughter and heir, called *Anna*, since married unto *Edmond Wallers* of Berkensfield in Buckinghamshire, esquire. He gave by his last will and testament (written with his own hand) to unbeneficed ministers; to decayed housekeepers; to the poor of many parishes; to all (or the most) of the prisons, bridewells, and hospitals in and about London; to young beginners to set up their trades; to the Artillery Garden and towards the maintenance thereof forever, very bountifully; to his own Company, both in lands and money; to his friends, in tokens of remembrance; to divers of his kindred; and to other charitable and pious uses, the sum of 6000 li., notwithstanding noble and sufficient dower to his daughter reserved. And all these several legacies by his careful executor *Robert Tichbourne* and his overseers punctually observed and fully discharged.

Inbalm'd in pious arts, wrapt in a shroud
Of white innocuous charity, who vow'd,
Having enough, the world should understand
No deed of mercy might escape his hand,
Bankes here is laid to sleep; this place did breed him,
A precedent to all that shall succeed him.
Note both his life and immitable end,
Know he th'unrighteous Mammon made his friend,
Expressing by his talents' rich increase
Service that gain'd him praise and lasting peace.
Much was to him committed, much he gave,
Ent'ring his treasure there, whence all shall have
Return with use[29]: what to the poor is given
Claims a just promise of reward in heaven.
Even such a bank, *Bankes* left behind at last,
Riches stor'd up, which age nor time can waste.

---

[29] {usury, interest}

Mildred Breadstreet

This church was repaired and very worthily beautified in the year of our Lord 1628. The greatest part of the north wall was new built, the arches in the middle of the church, four fair windows over them, and a very fair gallery, at the cost and charge of the parish. . . .

This for a general charge; somewhat of particular bounties:
At the upper end of this church on the south side is a fair window with this inscription:

> This window was glazed at the charge of *Hester Crispe*, late wife of *Ellis Crispe*, citizen and alderman of London, who lieth fixt in a vault at the bottom of this window, 1629.

At the upper end of the church on the north side, another with this inscription:

> This window was glazed at the charge of *Samuel Crispe*, citizen and salter of London, 1630.

Between these two, at the upper end of the chancel, is a fair window full of cost and beauty, which being divided into five parts, carries in the first of them a very artful and curious representation of the Spaniards' great Armado and the battle in 1588. In the second, of the monument of Queen *Elizabeth*. In the third, of the Gunpowder Plot. In the fourth, of the lamentable time of infection, 1625. And in the fifth and last, the view and lively portraitures of that worthy gentleman, Captain *Nicholas Crispe*, at whose sole cost (among other) this beautiful piece of work was erected, as also the figures of his virtuous wife and children, with the arms belonging unto them: The verses to every story are these:

The Story of Eighty-eight
Star-gazing Wizards sat upon this year,
Matter of wonder, and did threaten fear
Towards us, in so much that *Rome* and *Spain*
This land accounted their assured gain.
But mark how God did quite their hopes confound,
Both ships and men we did see flee and drown'd.

Queen Elizabeth's Monument
Marvel not why we do erect this shrine,
Since dedicated tis to worth divine:
Religion, arts, with policy and arms,
Did all concur in her most happy reign,
To keep God's Church and us from plotted harms
Contriv'd by Romish wits and force of *Spain*.

The Powder Plot 1605
When force could not prevail nor plots abroad
Could have success, sin now invents new fraud:
Guy Vaux is sent Ambassador to *Styx*,
And thence returning, furnisheth with tricks

His damned crew, who forth withal conclude
To blow up King, the State, and Multitude.

The Great Plague 1625

The stories past, God's blessings to the State
Do clearly shew. But sure we were ingrate;
For now, behold, instead of sweet protection,
Thousands are swept away by foul infection.
But mark God's mercy: in midst of greatest cries,
He sheath'd his sword, and wip't tears from our eyes.

The Founder's Figure, with his Wife, Children, and their Arms

These ensigns which you see, and monument,
Are not so much to represent
The founder's person, as his zealous care
T'express God's love and mercies rare
To this his vineyard; for to that sole end
Did he these stories thus commend
To after ages, that in their distress,
They might God's goodness still express.

With this, this gentleman gave towards the repair of this church, among the parishioners, above his share as a parishioner, 75 li.

Also for the communion table, two great flagon pots to the value of 57 li.

Also very fair font, in which a child of his own was first christened.

His brother, Master *Samuel Crispe*, beside his window, above his ordinary share as a parishioner, gave to this fair reparation 25 li.

The mother of these worthy gentlemen, the aforenamed *Hester Crispe*, the late wife of *Ellis Crispe*, citizen and alderman of London, now (by a second and thrice-happy nuptials) the Lady *Pie*, beside her window, gave to this fair reparation 20 li., though at that time out of the parish and removed from thence to Christ-Church.

Nicholas Acons

This church was repaired and beautified in the year of our Lord God 1615 at the cost and charge of the parishioners. . . .

A handsome monument on the south side of the chancel, with this inscription:

This picture is for others, not for me,
For in my breast I wear thy memory.
It is here plac'd, that passengers may know,
Within thy ground no weeds, but corn did grow;
That there did flow within thy vital blood,
All that could make one honest, just, and good.
Here is no elbow room to write of more;

An epitaph yields taste, but seldom store.
Thy troop of virtues grac'd thee amongst men,
And now attend thee at the Court in Heav'n.
Thy worth, sweet *Charles*, deserves the rarest wit;
Thy *Jane* for such a task is most unfit.

Corpus Caroli Haukins, civis & aromatarii Londinensis, in hoc tumulo depositum est. Erat Deo devotus, charitatis plenus & virtutis; adeo studiosus, ut vitam laudabilem, finemque optimum peregerit. Jana, uxor ejus, filia Johannis Reeve Armigeri natu minima, postea nupta fuit Iohanni Suckling Equiti Aurato, Regiae Majestati à supplicum libellis, praedicti Caroli & Ianae insignes dotes tanti aestimavit, ut monumentum hoc, sumptibus propriis, in honorem defuncti pie posuerit, anno Dom. 1621.[30]

Over these lines, as in a book in the hands of this gentleman, these words:

Beatus vir, cui Dominus non imputavit peccatum, & in cujus spiritu, non est dolus.[31]

A monument on the north side the chancel, with this inscription:

In God is all my hope.
All men are born to die.
In Christ is my redemption.

John Hall, draper, of the age of 90 years, a housholder in this parish 58 years, and in that time, by the providence of God, the father of 27 children, all born here. These great mercies, I do confess in my heart, not to be of my deserts but of God his good grace only, shewed unto me more abundantly than unto many thousands in my time; wherefore with heart and tongue, I yield all honor and praise unto thee, O God.

Here under lyeth interred the body of *John Hall*, once Master of the worshipful Company of the Drapers, and 25 years one of the bridgemasters of the City of London, who deceased the 19 day of November 1618, aged 93 years. And also the body of *Anne Browne*, daughter of Master *John Browne*, gentleman, being his third wife, by whom he had 23 children: she died the 17 of December 1619, being aged 73 years.

---

[30] {The body of Charles Hawkins, citizen and spice-merchant, lies buried in this tomb. He was devoted to God, full of charity and goodness, of which he was so desirous that he enjoyed a praiseworthy life and best of all deaths. His wife Jane was the youngest daughter of John Reeve, knight, and afterward married John Suckling, knight, master of his Majesty's Court of Requests. He so valued the excellent endowments of the aforesaid Charles and Jane that he erected this monument at his own cost in honor of the deceased, in the year of our Lord, 1621.}

[31] {Blessed is the man to whom the Lord does not impute sin and in whose spirit there is no deceit (Ps. 31[32]:2).}

Peters Poor

There hath been in this church since the beginning of the year 1615 to the year 1630 many costly repairs and charges. In the year 1615, this church was on the west side enlarged in the breadth eight foot and better by the taking down of the north wall, and, over a slip of ground that formerly lay behind it so far outward, erecting another. Upon the foundation of the old wall were erected new pillars and arches, and from them to the new, a fair roof. This empty, useless, and rude piece of ground being turned to this use and beauty (with the very fair windows in it) at the sole cost and charge of Sir *William Garway*, knight, who at the east end of this wall, in a vault (made likewise at his own cost) lies under his fair monument interred. The charge of this aisle was 400 pounds.

In the year 1616, this new aisle and the whole church was new pewed, and the great window in the chancel enlarged.

In the year 1617, the roof, and the inside of the church throughout, was richly and very worthily beautified.

In the years 1629 and 1630, the steeple and a very costly gallery at the west end of the church were new built and beautified, and the bells new cast and hung.

The charge of all this amounting to the sum of 1587 pounds and upwards, all which, deducting the 400 pounds cost of the aisle, was the cost and charge of the parish.

A fair monument at the upper end of the chancel, with this inscription:

Anno 1624, aetatis 54, a memorial of the worshipful Master Robert Wadson, late citizen and merchant-taylor of London.

Epitaphium

So frail and brittle is the life of man,
That who lives longest liveth but a span;
In youth and age all die; God hath so doom'd,
That earth returns to earth to be entomb'd.
Wadson, who of that substance was compos'd,
Lies in his mother's center here enclos'd,
A sheet doth hide his face, but not his fame,
The grave contains his corpse, not his good name:
For his good name outlives (O blessed man)
When others' good names die before they can.
The sixth of January (that fatal day)
Sixteen hundred twenty four, he did pay
The debt to nature, which, all men do know,
He was no sooner born but he did owe.
If virtues could have stayed the hand of Death,
Then *Wadson* still had drawn his vital breath.

His soul above, his worths do here remain,
Till Christ shall come to raise him up again:

Thus he enjoys Heav'n's immortality
And, here on earth, earth's happy memory.
>   *Post varios vitae casus,*
>   *dabit urna quietem.*[32]

Steven's Colemanstreet

To the memory of that ancient servant to the City with his pen, in divers employments, especially the *Survey of London*, Master *Anthony Munday*, citizen and draper of London.

> He that hath many an ancient tombstone read
> (I'th'labor seeming more among the dead
> To live than with the living), that surveyed
> Abstruse antiquities and o'er them laid
> Such vive and beauteous colors with his pen
> That (spite of time) those old are new again,
> Under this marble lies inter'd: his tomb
> Claiming (as worthily it may) this room
> Among those many monuments his quill
> Has so reviv'd, helping now to fill
> A place (with those) in his *Survey*, in which
> He has a monument more fair, more rich,
> Than polished stones could make him; where he lies,
> Though dead, still living, and in that he ne'er dies.

Obiit anno aetatis suae 80; Domini 1633. Augusti 10.

A Review also of the Sixteen Parishes without the Walls of this City

---

Andrew Holborn

This church hath had no repair or cost bestowed upon it (worthy any record or memory) for the space of many years; indeed so many that the many decayed parts & places of it call rather for a rebuilding than a repairing—which is (as I am told) now providing for, the parishioners purposing very shortly to pull it all down and rebuild, enlarge, and enrich it with that beauty that becomes so great a work—and the house of the great God Almighty.

What I have heard, I relate, and believe, both for the truth and speed: which when it begins, in the progression and finishing, the blessing of God go with it.

A very comely monument upon a pillar in the south aisle, with this inscription:

Aspice, Respice, Prospice[33]

---

[32] {After the many accidents of this life, the urn will give rest.}
[33] {Look, Hearken, Await}

Near to this place lyeth buried the body of *Elizabeth Ade*, late the wife of *John Ade*, of Doddington in the county of Kent, gentleman; and eldest daughter of *Thomas Waller* of Beckonfield in the county of Buckingham, esquire, who in her time was the mirror of her sex, replete with all the gifts that grace or nature could afford: religious towards God and charitable towards men, loving and faithful to her husband, beloved of all, hated of none.

This world not worthy of her, she was translated to a better, the third of May 1619 and about the 32 year of her age, leaving by her death a most infortunate husband, three sons, *John*, *Edward*, and *Nicholas*, and four daughters, *Dorothy*, *Elizabeth*, *Mary* and *Francis*.

> Whosoever thou art, that passest by,
> Learn here to live, and here to die.

Upon a brass plate near the north door is this inscription:

> Here lies a maid, for heaven by her pure life
> So fit, she could not stay to be a wife;
> And with her, half a man lies buried,
> That is but half himself, now she is dead:
> His other half lives but in hope to be
> Enclosed in this urn as well as she.
> In losing her, the *Lovets* lost a gem,
> A *Margarite*,[34] too rich (indeed) for them,
> But not for Him, to whom she went from hence,
> Vsher'd by Faith, Hope, Love, and Innocence.
> Then you that are her friends, your grief forget;
> In Heaven your *Margarite* is richly set.

Obiit 4 die Februarii, anno Domini 1631.

Botolph Algate

This church was repaired and beautified in the year of our Lord God, 1621.

In the year of our Lord 1633, all the ground through the church was new laid and levelled. In the doing of which, where before from the lower end of the church to the upper end it was all but one even floor without any ascent or rising, they have made a fair ascent at the beginning of the chancel; and in that again, at the place where they give the Communion; further gracing and enriching it with a fair new table, and the whole chancel with new pews, very decently wrought and disposed.

---

[34] {"Margarite" comes from the Greek word for pearl.}

A fair monument upon a pillar on the south side of the chancel, over against the pulpit: the figure of the gentleman for whom it was erected leaning upon a death's-head.

> A memorial erected by the right worshipful, the Company of Merchant-Taylors, for *Robert Dove*, esquire, citizen, and merchant-taylor of London, Master of the same Company, and one of the Customers in the Port of London. Who gave in his lifetime 3528 li. 10 s. 8 d. to perform divers charitable deeds forever, to divers poor brethren of the same Company, and other uses for the said Company, *viz.*, to Christ's Hospital, to Saint Sepulcher's parish, to the two Compters,[35] to Ludgate and Newgate, to the poor of this parish, to Saint John Baptist's College in Oxford, and to Queen Elizabeth's Hospital at Bristol, 2958 li. 10 s. 8 d. . . .

He lived virtuously all his lifetime, and died in the true faith of our Lord Jesus the second day of May, *an. Dom.* 1612, being full of days, at the age of 90 years. His arms under him, *Three Doves.*

Upon a marble stone (in the middle of this church) under the figure of a death's-head is this inscription:

> Under this marble stone resteth, in hope of a joyful resurrection, the bodies of two sisters: *Elizabeth Roe*, wife to *John Roe*, mariner, who died the 16 day of July 1625.
> And *Sarah Stevens*, wife unto *John Stevens*, citizen and cook of London, who died the third of August in the same year of our Lord, 1625.

Dunstan's West

It is since this church was repaired 20 years, yet, though so long, it hath more of that beauty still, and still remains fresher and fairer than many other churches that half so much time hath not wrought upon. And yet, as I am informed (which is more to the business in hand), it is shortly again to be repaired richly and very worthily beautified.

A fair table in glass upon a pillar in the middle aisle, thus written on:

> The comfortable farewell of a young infant,
> sighed out in his dying sickness, to his mornful parents

Let not my father grieve, or mother moan,
That I this wretched world have soon forgone.
Better I die before I do amiss,
Than live to sin, and be bereft of bliss;
All I can now be charg'd with at the tribunal Throne
Is sin original, for actual I have none;
And that I know my Savior with his blood
Hath washt away, and made my badness good.

---

[35] {both debtors' prisons}

And cause I know (though knowledge I have small)
That Jesus Christ did die to save us all,
I pass with joy in heaven to meet my King,
With angels and archangels there to sing.
Then father mourn and mother weep no more;
I now die rich, that might have liv'd but poor;
For had I progress unto man's estate,
It is not certain what would be my fate:
Whether a cross or blessing I should prove,
Or merit parents' direful hate, or love.
For oft you see how youths' rebellious pranks
Make sons ingrate to those they owe most thanks.
And might not I have been amongst the number
Of those that do their parents' states encumber?
Yes, yes, I might perhaps have been a slave,
And kil'd your hearts with care, and dig'd your grave.
But now my silly[36] dove-like soul doth part
In peace of God and love of parents' heart;
Sweet Innocence, my shield, I bear in hand,
To guard me towards that most holy Land,
Where parents both, and sister, I shall see
In God's appointed time triumphantly.
Till when, adieu, sweet parents, Jehovah calls away,
My name is *Simon*, and I must obey.   [*Simon* signifies *obedience.*]

Epitaphium

Young *Simon* up to *Sion* is ascended,
His best life is begun, his worst being ended.

A fair monument in the south aisle, on the wall under the monument of one Cuthbert Fetherstone:

Before this pew door, next to the body of the above named *Cuthbert Fetherstone*, lyeth his beloved wife, *Katharine Fetherstone*, who as they piously lived in wedlock forty odd years together, so at their deaths they desired to be interred together, not doubting at the general resurrection, through Christ's merits, to rise together, and forever in heaven to live together.

Obiit Novemb. 1622, aetatis 85.

And this in part they do attain,
Who by their deaths new lives do gain.

[36] {innocent, pious}

Corpus moritur per poenam, resurgit per gloriam,
Anima moritur per culpam, resurgit per gratiam.[37]

A table with a fair coat-arms encompast with a wreath of laurel, upon a pillar in the chancel over against the vestry, thus inscribed:

In this fair, fragrant, maiden month of May,
When earth her flowery embroidery doth display,
Jane Watson, one of Virtue's flowers most fair,
For beauty, wit, and worth, a primrose rare,
Adorn'd this earth, changing earth's marriage bed
To join her virgin soul to Christ her head.

A fair monument over the vestry door in the chancel, with this inscription:

In memory of the honorable, and virtuous *Margaret Talbot*, widow, who deceased the 31 of March, 1620.

By this small statue (reader) is but shown,
That she was buried here; but hadst thou known
The piety and virtues of her mind,
Thou wouldst have said, Why was she not enshrin'd?
Both *Vere's* and *Windsor's* best blood fill'd her veins,
She matcht with *Talbot*, yet their noble strains
Were far below her virtue, in whose breast,
God had infus'd his graces 'bove the rest
Of all her sex, whose sacred course of life,
Both in the state of widow, maid, and wife—
For each she had been, though her latter days
Chaste widowhood crown'd, to her immortal praise—
Was so immaculate, she deserves to be
The crystal mirror to posterity.
More honor hast thou by her burial here,
Dunston, than to thee chanc'd this many a year;
Earth from her coffin heave thy ponderous stones,
And for thy sacredst relic keep her bones:
Since, spite of envy, it cannot be deni'd,
Saint-like she liv'd, and like a saint she died.

A table hanging upon a pillar in the middle row of pews, with this inscription:

On the death of the discreet and virtuous Mistress *Mary Davies*, daughter of *Thomas Croft* of Okley-Park in the county of Salop, esquire, and wife of *John Davies* of Hereford, she died on New Year's day, 1612.

---

[37] {The body dies as punishment; it arises in glory; the soul dies on account of guilt; it arises on account of grace.}

Here lies her dust, who in a span of life
Compast the virtue of the worthiest wife:
If odds there be (well measur'd) 'twill be found
She more acquir'd, so her bright stock renown'd,
And to those wives that glory most do gain
She was a mirror that no breath could stain.
Though she a female were, her judgement was
To truest masculines a truer glass:
For she by nature, grace, and wisdom too,
Shew'd by a woman, what best men should do
In their best actions, for she acted nought
That came not from a grave and gracious thought.
But Nature (though familiar, yet most strange,
Shewing how much she doth delight in change,
In thousand fashions doth herself array)
Permits nought here to stand at constant stay.
And Time and Death with her therein conspire,
Else had these ashes still held vital fire.
But these just lines, in Time and Death's despite,
Shall lead all times to do her virtue right.

A good name is better than a good ointment; and the day of death, than the day
that one is born, *Eccles.* 7:3.

Giles Cripplegate

How this church, any thing in or about it (either for necessity or beauty), hath from
time to time been kept, supplied, and maintained, all men that know it know—to the
perpetual credit and commends of those worthy gentlemen to whom, in their several
times and succession, the charge of it hath been committed.

. . .

In the year of our Lord 1629, the steeple, very much decayed, was repaired, all the
four spires (standing in four towers at the corners of it) taken down, with new and very
substantial timber-work re-built, and with the lead new-cast, new covered; every one of
these spires enlarged somewhat in the compass, a great deal in height, but most in their
stately, eminent, and graceful appearance. In the midst of these, where there was none
before (gracing and being graced by them), was a very fair turret erected, the head of it
(which much overpeers those spires) covered with lead, as also the props that support it:
this, and the spires, having every one a cross, with very fair vanes upon them.

The charge of all this I could not certainly get and would not uncertainly speak it,
but the greatness of the things speak the cost to be great, all being the sole charge of the
parishioners.

A very fair table with a rich coat-arms hanging upon a pillar in the middle aisle, about it this inscription:

> The sacred corps of *Sarah*, wife of *Henry Goodericke*, daughter of *William Bodenham*, knight, was interred at the south end of this seat, towards the pulpit.

Within it thus:

> Buried the 6 of June, *anno* 1616.

> The bearer's sorrow, sable lions shew,
> Like to that lion which did overthrow
> The man of God, and, charg'd alike, do stand
> Grand guardians here to check the upheav'd hand
> Unweeting wights, or ignorant, shall lay
> Upon her hallowed corps that here did pray.
> A sacred temple 'twas, wherein did shine
> Her Maker's glory, human and divine:
> Sweet commerce[38] sanctified with zeal mov'd there
> In beauty's fabric, its own proper sphere;
> For which it towers above the sight of eye.
> God's temples must lie low that tower so high.

Under two hands joined, one out of a cloud, the other out of a globe, these words:

> 'Till then, Farewell.

Upon a very fair marble stone in the south aisle is this inscription:

> Here lyeth buried the body of *Ellen Monyns*, who died the 29 of April, in the year of our Lord 1632.
> Here also lyeth buried the body of her sister, Mistress *Frances Monyns*, who died the 17 of June in the same year.
> They were the daughters of Sir *William Monyns* of Waldershaw in the county of Kent, Baronet, and of the Lady *Jane* his wife, the daughter of *Roger Twisden* of Roydon Hall in the same county, esquire.
> They lived religious and virtuous lives, and in their youths departed this life in the true faith of Jesus Christ.

Saviour's Southwarke

Upon this spacious and specious {beautiful} church (for well it deserves those epithets) we look backward twenty years or thereupon, at which time it was in many parts of it repaired and within throughout richly and very worthily beautified.

. . .

---

[38] {*Commerce* has its modern sense in the early 17th c., but can also mean "converse with God" (*OED*).}

Among many rich and beautiful things that have been added to this church at divers times . . . we here only remember that extraordinary fair and curious table of the Commandments and the screen at the west door set up in the year of our Lord God, 1618.

But passing all these, somewhat now of that part of this church above the chancel that in former times was called *Our Lady's Chapel.* It is now called, *the New Chapel,* and indeed, though very old, it now may be call'd a new one, because newly redeemed from such use and employment as—in respect of that it was built to, divine and religious duties—may very well be branded with the style of wretched, base, and unworthy; for that, that before this abuse was (and is now) a fair & beautiful chapel, by those that were then the Corporation (which is a body consisting of 30 vestrymen, six of those thirty, churchwardens) was leased and let out, and this house of God made a bake-house.

Two very fair doors that from the two side aisles of the chancel of this church, and two that through the head of the chancel (as at this day they do again) went into it, were lath't, daub'd, and dammed up; the fair pillars were ordinary posts, against which they piled billets and bavens. In this place they had their ovens; in that, a bolting-place; in that, their kneading-trough; in another (I have heard), a hogs-trough (for the words that were given me were these: this place have I known a hog-sty); in another, a storehouse to store up their horded meal; and in all of it, something of this sordid kind & condition. . . .

The time of the continuance of it in this kind, from the first letting of it to *Wyat* to the restoring of it again to the church, was threescore and some odd years in the year of our Lord God 1624; for in this year, the ruins and blasted estate that the old Corporation sold it to were by the Corporation of this time repaired, renewed, well and very worthily beautified: the charge of it for that year, with many things done to it since, arising to two hundred pounds.

. . .

In the same chapel and aisle, upon a gravestone is thus written:

Not twice ten years of age, a weary breath
Have I exchanged for a happy death;
My course so short, the longer is my rest;
God takes them soonest whom he loveth best:
For he that's born today and dies tomorrow
Loseth some days of rest, but more of sorrow.

Here lies buried the body of *John Buckland*, glover, 1625, who deceased the 16 of August.

Upon a fair stone close to this, under the Grocers' arms, is this inscription:

Garret, some call'd him, but that was too high,
His name is *Garrard*, who now here doth lie;
He in his youth was toss'd with many a wave,
But now at port arriv'd, rests in his grave.
The church he did frequent while he had breath,
And wisht to lie therein after his death.

Weep not for him, since he is gone before
To heaven, where grocers there are many more.

All these, with that rich and cosly monument of the Right Reverend Father in God, *Launcelot* {*Andrewes*,} Bishop of Winchester, are in this chapel.

A Review also of the Nine Out-Parishes
in Middlesex and Surrey

Clement Danes

The care of those that by an annual succession have the charge and oversight of this church hath continually been such, as upon the least defect or failing either in strength or beauty, it hath instantly been employed, both in repairs and adornment.

. . .

The sum of all these repairs, all being the sole cost of the parishioners, 1586 li.

A fair monument in the chancel on the north side at the upper end, with this incription . . .

Foeminae lectissimae, dilectissimaeque,
Conjugi charissimae castissimaeque,
Matri piissimae indulgentissimaeque,
xv annis in conjugio transactis,
vii post xii partum (quorum vii superstant) dies
immani febre correptae
(quod hoc saxum fari jussit,
ipse prae dolore infans)
Maritus (miserrimum dictu) olim charae charus
Cineribus cineres spondet suos,
Novo matrimonio (annuat Deus) hoc loco sociandos,
Ioannes Donne,
Sacr. Theolog. Profess.
Secessit,
Anno xxxiii aetat. suae & sui Iesu
CIƆ. DC. XVII.
Aug. XV.[39]

---

[39] {John Donne, D.D., to a most choice and cherished woman, a most beloved and chaste wife, a most careful and caring mother, who was, after fifteen years of marriage and seven days after the birth of their twelfth child (seven children yet surviving), snatched away by a terrible fever (which he commanded this stone to speak, he himself being speechless from grief), her husband formerly (alas) so dear to his dear one promises to join his ashes (God permitting) with hers in a new marriage in this place. She departed this life at age 33, in the year of her Savior 1617, on August 15.}

A fair monument on the south side of the chancel, with this inscription:

> By the churchwardens and feofees of this parish, this monument was set up the 20 of January 1603.

> Here lieth buried the bodies of *Richard Bedoe*, gentleman, and *Anne* his first wife, one of the ancientest of this parish and a feofee of the poor, who ended his life with a charitable disposition the first day of September 1603 . . . being, when he died, of the age of 56 years, and was born in the parish of Ricken in Salop: who of their charity have given so many of their tenements[40] within the Duke's Place in Cree-Church, alias Christ's-Church, near Algate, London, as do now go for 20 li. *per annum* to the maintenance and use of the poor of this parish forever. And also 110 *li.* to be lent gratis to 50 poor householders and young beginners of the same parish for two years a piece, putting in good security for the same: with condition that this stone, by the churchwardens and feofees of the same parish for the time being, shall from time to time forever be maintained; and four sermons yearly forever to be made on the feast days of *All-Saints*, the *Purification of our Lady*, the *Ascension of our Lord God*, and Saint *John Baptist*, to remember and give God thanks for the givers thereof. God increase charity unfeigned.

Margaret Bedoe, last wife of *Richard Bedoe*, gave by her last will, in the year 1633, the sum of twenty pounds to be added to her husband's gift of a hundred pounds, and so to be employed and disposed of as her husband's now is, the preacher four times a year mentioning her gift with his, according to her will, or else her gift to be void.

A handsome monument on the wall in the south aisle, with this inscription:

> Hereby lyeth buried the body of *Edward Price*, gentleman, and of *Edward* his only son, who for the space of 24 years lived in this parish, wherein God so blessed him, that of his good and charitable devotion he hath given three pounds a year forever out of his free land, called the Blew Lyon, in the said parish, to be bestowed in sea coals and to be distributed freely to the poor by the churchwardens. And also twenty pounds forever to be lent to two poor young householders gratis, from two years to two years, ten pounds apiece.

> He departed this life the 8 of March, 1605.

On the same tomb, under that above, is this written:

> This tomb was erected at the charge of *Elizabeth*, the wife of *Henry Baten*, esquire, one of his Majesty's Sergeants at Arms, and late wife of *Edward Price*, deceased, who of her godly disposition hath given 20 s. a year forever to the preacher of this parish, to be paid out of her house called the Three Cups, next adjoining on the west side of the same Blew Lyon, only that he shall make recital hereof at two several sermons yearly: one on the Sunday before Christmas Day, and the other

---

[40] {dwelling (with no perjorative connotation)}

on the Sunday before Midsummer Day. And the said *Elizabeth* also, of her godly love and zeal to the Church, hath given a flagon-pot, silver and gilt, weighing 38 ounces and an half, for the service of the communion table, to remain forever; and three pounds to the poor to be distributed at her funeral, and five pounds to the poor of Kniton in Derbyshire where she was born. She departed the 10 of November, *anno* 1616.

A very fair glass table hanging on a pillar in the south aisle, in which there is the figure of a gentlewoman all in black, with a gilt book in her hand, laid as upon her tomb; over her head an angel, over her at the feet, Death with a dart and hour-glass.

Giles in the Fields

Before I speak of this new church, I must briefly say of the old that indeed it was very old, and in the antiquity of it stood now still in danger of falling; that some part of it did fall, foretelling the rest to follow if not speedily prevented by pulling it down to re-build it, which after a diligent search, the necessity found, was done. For this new church, it began to be raised in the year of our Lord God 1623, was finished 1625, and encompast with a fair brick wall in the year 1631.[41]

Which take more amply in that absolute delivery of it that I find engraven over the door on the north side of this church; the words are these:

> Quod felix bonumque sit
> Posteris,
> Hoc Templum loco veteris ex annosâ
> vetustate
> Collapsi, mole & splendore auctum
> Multo paroecorum Charitas
> Instauravit,
> In quibus pientissimae heroinae
> D. Aliciae Duddeley
> Munificentia gratum marmoris hujus
> meretur eloquium.
> Huc etiam accessit aliorum quorundam
> pietas,
> Quibus provisae in Coelo sunt grates.
>
> . . .

---

[41] {For additional material on St. Giles during this period, see John Parton, *Some account of the hospital and parish of St. Giles in the Fields, Middlesex* (London, 1822), 194–201. Among Parton's discoveries was the fact that the "players of the Cockpit playhouse" were among the major contributors to the renovations, on which connection, see also G. E. Bentley, "Players in the parish of St. Giles in the Fields," *RES* 6 (1930): 149–66.}

Heus Viator, an effoetum est bonis operibus hoc seculum?[42]

To the raising, finishing, and (in every part of it) richly and very excellently beautifying of this great work there were many good and great benefactors. The names of all, with their particular gifts, my time gave not leave to compass; neither, for many of them, could any enquiry get them, they desiring to be concealed. . . .

For the rich and costly glazing of this church, the work and work-masters thus follow:

A very rich and beautiful window in the head of the chancel, of four several panes or parts: in the first, the figure of *Abraham* sacrificing his son; in the second, *Moses* with the table of the Commandments; in the third, the figure of the holy Prophet *David*; in the fourth and last, *Solomon*.

The inscription to the first is this:
Credidit Abraham Deo, & reputatum est illi ad justitiam.[43] anno Dom. 1628.

Of the second is this:
Erat vir Moyses mitissimus super omnes homines qui morabantur in terra.[44] 1628.

Of the third this:
Solum medium tutum.[45] 1627.

Of the fourth this:
Dum spiro spero.[46] 1628.

The first of these was the charge of *Abraham Speckart*, esquire.
The second, of *Hamo Claxton*, esquire.
The third, of Sir *John Fenner*, knight.
The fourth, of *Francis* Lord Mount-Norris.

A very fair window on the south side of the chancel.
At the top of it,
Jehovah

Under the figures in it,
Shelbery 1617. Shelbery and Wrothe.
Domine misere nostri.[47]

---

[42] {That it might be happy and good for posterity, the charity of parishioners erected this temple in place of the former one that had collapsed due to its great age, but has now been much increased both in size and splendor. In which [rebuilding], the generosity of the most religious noblewoman, Alice Duddeley, deserves the grateful eloquence of this marble. The piety of certain others, whose reward is in heaven, also added to this. . . . Hark, wayfarer, is this age incapable of good works?}

[43] {Abraham believed God, and it was counted unto him for righteousness (Rom. 4:3).}

[44] {Moses was the gentlest man of all those who dwelt upon earth (Num. 12:3).}

[45] {The middle way alone is safe.}

[46] {While I breathe, I hope.}

[47] {Lord, have mercy upon us.}

A very fair window on the north side of the chancel, two fair figures in it: the one of the Virgin Mary with Christ in her arms; the other of Mary Magdalen.

Under this window lyeth buried the body of *Mary Pill*, of this parish; which window was set up at the charges of *Mary Maudit*, her daughter and heir, 1629.

Under the first, these verses:
From *Mary's* tears to *Mary's* joy,
This *Mary* is translated;
And after threescore years' annoy,[48]
In heaven she is instated.
With this, she chose the better part,
Never to be repented;
And held her Savior in heart;
Thus are her joys augmented.

Under the other, these:
This sought her Savior at his tomb,
His feet with tears bedewed.
That bore our Savior in her womb,
Whereby our joy's renewed.
Then happy soul, thrice happy this,
Happily interessed,[49]
In *Mary's* tears, and *Mary's* bliss,
Rest thou forever blessed.

A very fair window with the King's arms in it over the entrance into the chancel.
Glazed at the charge of Sir *William Segar*, knight, *alias* Garter principal King of Arms, *anno Dom.* 1626.

A very fair window at the upper end of the south aisle,
Glazed at the charges of *Marmaduke Rawdon*, citizen and clothworker of London, *anno Dom.* 1625.

Another next to this downward,
Glazed at the charge of *Robert Rawdon*, citizen and fishmonger of London, *anno Dom.* 1625.

Another next to this downward, bearing the figure of a lion in the wilderness,
Glazed at the charge of M. *John Johnson*, innkeeper in High Holborn, 1625.

Another next to this downward, having the figures of Saint John, Saint Philip, and Saint Matthew,
Glazed at the cost and charges of *Philip Parker*.

---

[48] {tribulation, suffering}

[49] {"to interess" someone is to invest him/her with a right to or share in something; to admit to a privilege (*OED*).}

Next to this downward, a very fair window.
Glazed at the charges of *Katherine Best*, widow, late wife of *John Best*, deceased, who gave order in his lifetime for the glazing of this window and was buried there-under the 7 day of April 1625. And there lie also his son *James* and his daughter *Dorothy.*

Next to this downward, a very fair window,
Glazed at the charges of *Alice Hodges*, widow, late wife to *Thomas Hodges*, baker, deceased, who was buried under this window the 6 day of October 1625. And here lie also his three children.

A fair window next to this, the lowest in the south wall,
Glazed at the cost of *William Perkins* of London, merchant-tailor, 1626.

At the lower end of this aisle over the southwest door, a very fair window, bearing in it (very curiously done) the figure of our Savior. Over his head, as in a garland supported by two angels, these letters:
 I·H·S·
Round about him, clouds full of cherubins.

On one side of him, this,
 I am the door, by me if any man enter in, he shall be saved, *Joh.* 10:9.

On the other side,
 Come unto me all ye that labor and are heavy laden, and I will give you rest, *Matth.* 11:28.

Beckinghamus Boteler Armiger fieri fecis.
anno Domini 1627.[50]

Over the great west door is a fair window with the Carpenters' arms, and a fair coat-arms close by it. This window hath no name or other inscription. It was (as I was told) the gift of a stranger—one, that upon a day that they made a collection for it, being there, was (among the rest) desired to bestow his good will; he answered, he had no money, but if the glazing of a window, if they had any yet undisposed of, would be accepted of, he would be at the charge to do it. The collectors giving him thanks and shewing this window, he suddenly set a glazier on work, and what he had promised he performed.

A very fair window at the head of the north aisle bearing the figure of Christ crucified as also (one on the one side, the other on the other) of the two *Marys.*

On the right side of him, this,
 Woman, behold thy son.

On the left,
 Behold thy mother.

Glazed at the cost of *Thomas Esto,* cook, of this parish, *anno Dom.* 1625.

---

[50] {Beckingham Boteler, knight, had this made, in the year of our Lord 1627.}

. . .

A fair window over the door in the middle of the north aisle, bearing a worthy coat-arms, with these words: *Whitaker & Egerton.*

This window is divided into three parts; under the first, this,

Ego sum ostium, per me si quis introierit, servabitur, & ingredietur, & egredietur, & pascua inveniet.[51] Joh. 10:9.

Under the second thus:

In tuo lumine (Domine Iesu) lumen aeternum videre sperantes, vitreum hoc luminare fabricari fecerunt Laurentius & Margareta Whitaker, anno salutis humanae 1625.[52]

Under the third thus:

Eligo frequentare limen in domo Dei mei magis quam habitare in tentoriis improbitatis.[53] Psal. 84:10.

A fair window next to this downward, bearing a very fair coat-arms, with these words: *Cope & Aston.*
Glazed at the charges of the Lady *Katherine Cope,* widow, late wife to Sir *Ed. Cope,* of this parish, 1625.

A very rich window next downward, divided into three parts, bearing the curious figures of the three theological virtues; under them,

Fides, Spes, Charitas.[54]

Under Faith this:

Faith root, Hope stock, the branch is Charity;
Faith sees, Hope looks, for Charity is free.
Faith knits to God; to heaven, Hope; Love, to men;
Faith gets, Hope keeps, and Love pours out again. 1626

Mandatum novum do vobis, ut diligatis unus alium,[55] Joh. 13:34.

Under Hope this:

Tres Elohim: pater est primus qui procreat, inde
Filius est, ex his Spiritus almus adest.
Sunt Tria dona Dei: sit prima Fides pia Mater,
Filia Spes, ex his tertius ortus Amor.[56] 1626

---

[51] {I am the door: by me if any man enter in, he shall be saved, and shall go in and out, and find pasture (KJV).}

[52] {In your light, Lord Jesus, hoping to see light eternal, Lawrence and Margaret Whitaker had this window made, in the year of man's salvation 1625.}

[53] {I had rather be a doorkeeper in the house of my God, than to dwell in the tents of wickedness (KJV).}

[54] {Faith, Hope, and Charity}

[55] {A new commandment I give unto you, That ye love one another (KJV).}

[56] {Three Lords: the first, the Father who procreates; thence is the Son; from both, the life-giving Spirit.

Nam spe servati sumus; spes autem si cernatur non est spes: quod enim quis cernit, cur speret?[57] Rom. 8:24

Under Charity this:

Now remain these three, Faith, Hope, Charity, but the greatest of these is Charity,
    1 Cor. 13:13

Scriptum est, justus ex fide vivet,[58] Rom. 1:17.

Next unto this downward, the last of this north aisle, is a plain window without either color or inscription.

Upon a fair grave-stone in the middle aisle is this inscription:

Here lyeth buried the body of *Elizabeth*, late wife of *Richard Maunsell*, esquire, one of the daughters and heirs of *Roger Wingfield*, of Great Dunham in the county of Norfolk, esquire. She departed this life upon the sixth of October in the year of our Lord God 1620.

Upon a fair stone near to the other, is this inscription:

Inter'd, the corps of Baron *Birch* lies here,
Of Grey's Inn sometime; by degree, esquire;
In Chequer 18 years a judge he was,
Till soul from aged body his did pass.
Alive his wife *Eliza* doth remain,
Of Stydfolke stock; one son and daughters twain
She bare by him; the eldest in his life
He gave to *Thomas Boyer* for his wife.
His body sleeps till angels' trump shall sound.
God grant we all may ready then be found.

Iohannes Birch, obiit anno Dom. 1581, Maii 30, aetatis suae 66.

In the same aisle is a very fair stone, which hath been beautified with many fair figures in brass:[59] but much of it being gone, all we can see now of it is this:

Here lieth *George Carew*, the fourth son of Sir *Edmund Carew*, &c. 1583.

There are three gifts of God: let the first be faith, holy mother; the daughter, hope; from these arises the third, love.}

[57] {For we are saved by hope: but hope that is seen is not hope: for what a man seeth, why doth he yet hope for? (KJV)}

[58] {It is written, the just shall live by faith.}

[59] {On the destruction of brass funeral ornaments at the Reformation, see <343n12, 642n3>.}

In the south aisle

Lies buried the body of *Alexander Barnes*, vinter, sometime churchwarden of this parish, &c. He deceased the 4 of November, 1614, being of the age of 57 years.

Alexander Barnes here doth lie,
Glory be to God on high,
For he on earth hath finished his days,
And now liveth in heaven to give God praise.

And now having done with the church, we begin in the church-yard with this inscription, standing in the middle of the south wall:

Laus Deo.

In cujus, & Christianae sepulturae, honorem, nimis arcti olim coemeterii fines, novi hujus, 128 pedes longi, & 17 lati, donatione, Abrahamus Speckart, Arm. & Dorothea uxor ejus ampliarunt, anno Dom. 1630.[60]

A very fair tombstone in the church-yard, about it these verses:

Thornton of Thornton, in Yorkshire bred,
Where lives the fame of *Thorntons*, being dead;
Full south this stone four foot doth lie
His father *John*, and grandsire *Henry*.

Upon it:

Iohannes Thornton, in memoria charissimae uxoris Margaretae, filiae Georgii Collins, hujus parochiae Sancti Aegidii in Campis, hoc monumentum posuit.[61]

Under this sad marble sleeps
She, for whom even marble weeps;
Her praise lives still, though here she lies,
Seeming dead, that never dies:
Religion, love, in suffering breast,
Her charity, mildness, and the rest
Hath crown'd her soul; all mourn with Fame
Her husband's loss, and midwives' blame.
She died in childbed, seventy times blest and seven,
Her child and she deliver'd both in heaven.

Obiit octavo die Ianuarii, anno Dom. 1611, aetatis suae 16.[62]

---

[60] {Praise be to God, in whose honor, and in the honor of Christian burial, Abraham Speckart, knight, and his wife Dorothy enlarged the boundaries of this once too narrow cemetary by a gift of an additional 128' × 17' in the year of our Lord 1630.}

[61] {John Thornton erected this monument in memory of his beloved wife Margaret, daughter of George Collins and a parishioner of St. Giles-in-the-Fields.}

[62] {She died the 8th of January, 1611, at the age of 16.}

On a fair stone in the church-yard is this inscription:

I·H·S·

Hereunder lyeth buried the body of *Joane Barker*, late wife of *Richard Barker*, 17 years of this parish, who deceased the last day of July, *anno Dom.* 1626, whom the Lord send a joyful resurrection.

Expecta donec veniat.[63]

Upon it thus:

Honesta mors initium vitae.[64]

Turn again then unto thy rest, O my soul, for the Lord hath rewarded thee; and why? thou hast delivered my soul from death, mine eyes from tears, and my feet from falling.

I will walk before the Lord, in the land of the living. *Psal.* 116.

This stone was laid by her husband *Richard Barker*, one of the Yeomen of the Guard to Queen *Elizabeth* and King *James* 30 years, and now to King *Charles*. And was married to his late deceased wife 20 years and one month, and had seven children, whereof five live, *Horatio, Anne, Elizabeth, Katherine*, and *Mary*.

Martin's in the Fields

The enlargement of this church was begun in the year of our Lord God, 1607 . . . to the which enlargement, our said sovereign lord, King *James*, and our most noble Prince *Henry* were most gracious benefactors; the rest of the charges were borne by the inhabitants of this parish.

. . .

A very fair table fastened to a pillar near the pulpit, in which is curiously drawn the figure of an angel holding the coat of the gentry[65] of the living husband and dead wife for whom it was there set up; also of a death's-head with an hourglass upon it; the border of the table filled (excellent in proportion and colors) with death's-heads, branches of palm, and other fresh and beautiful flowers.

Nascendo Morimur.[66]

Quid Cranii sibi forma novi
vult ista? Quid Hora?
Quidque super Cranio,
lumen nova nata, segesque?
Nempe dies mortis,

---

[63] {Await until he comes.}

[64] {an honorable death, the beginning of life}

[65] {i.e., heraldic coat of arms}

[66] {In our birth, we die. (The English poem that follows the Latin is a free translation.)}

vitae fit origo perennis;
Quae moritur mundo,
Nascitur illa Deo.

What doth this skull? what doth this hourglass show?
The corn and palm that on the skull doth grow?
It meaneth this, that Death, the end of strife,
Is the beginning to eternal life.
Death is the door to immortality.
She's born to God that to the world doth die.
The burning taper to his end doth waste,
Whilst life and death to meet each other haste;
Then happy she that did her life apply
Here and above to live eternally.

To the permanent honor and remembrance of the pious and all-virtuous gentlewoman, Mistress *Susan Price*, daughter to the honorable Baronet, Sir *Paul Tracy* of Stanway in Glocester; and the late dearly beloved wife of the religious, learned, and truly virtuous gentleman, *William Price* of Winchester, esquire, one of his Majesty's most honorable Privy Chamber. She died the 13 of March 1632.

Ye holy angels and ye powers of light,
The glad enjoyers of God's glorious sight;
You that in faithful *Abraham's* bosom rest,
You have receiv'd your sanctified guest.
Fair *Susan Price* hath blessed heaven obtain'd,
And for her well-run race, God's glory gain'd;
Shining in robes of Immortality,
Contemns the earth and worldly vanity.
True Christian faith indued her constant mind,
And unto her the promise was assign'd.
Most honor'd be her memory, outwasting
All genealogies, and everlasting,
Whilst there be elements, stars, orbs, or spheres,
Day's sun, or night's moon, to direct the years.
The heavens possess her soul, the world her fame
And fair example, her virtues, worth, and name.
What nature, goodness, institution, fact
Could heap to a perfection, was her Act.
The angels sing her glory, who did call
Her sweet soul home to its original,
And now she's gone hence for to pass the time
She ought her husband, in a better clime.
There shall her harvest and her summer be,
Where she shall never any winter see.
Then *Price* grieve you no more; she lives in joy.
Wipe you your tears, her tears are wip'd away.

The Epitaph.

Stay ere you pass,
    lament, and fix your eyes
Upon a worthy
    Consort's obsequies.
Susan here lies, for beauty,
    worth, and life,
Admir'd; the worthy
    William Price's wife.
Never was after death
    one more desir'd,
Nor ever living
    was one more admir'd.
A file of lasting praises
    crowns her name;
Perpetual glories
    do attend her fame;
Rich in all joys, she
    now hath chang'd her bed,
Ioined in marriage
    unto Christ her head.
Come, whosoever would
    enjoy like state,
Endevor all her worth
    to imitate.

Over the figure of Death:

Ibimus omnes.[67]
    Ladies, when you your purest beauties see,
    Think them but tenants to mortality.
    There's no content on earth; joys soon are fled;
    Healthful today we live, tomorrow dead.
    I was as you are now, young, fair, and clear;
    And you shall once be as you see me here.

    Mors mihi lucrum.
    Moriendo nascimur.[68]

Upon her tombstone, at the foot of this monument:

Mistress *Susanna Price*, the wife of *William Price*, esquire, one of the grooms of his
    Majesty's most honorable Privy Chamber, daughter of Sir *Paul Tracy*, Baronet,

---

[67] {We will all go [there].}
[68] {Death to me is gain. By dying, we are born.}

departed this life the 13 of March 1632, before she had been married full 14 weeks.

She was so full of virtue and of goodness, few might compare with her, none could excel her.

Her body is here interred; here is her body; her soul is in heaven with her Savior.

Mary Whitechapel

This church, in the many (and greatly) decayed parts of it, was repaired; and within, without, and in every part of it richly and very worthily beautified at the cost and charge of the parishioners, in the year of our Lord God, 1633.

. . .

To shew the never-dying love of these parishioners to their deceased pastor, Master William Crashaw,[69] *take this inscription from a very fair gallery in the south aisle:*

To the honor of God, the advancement of religion, and in thankfulness to God for the safe return of our hopeful and gracious Prince *Charles* from the dangers of his Spanish journey, this gallery was erected at the charge of this parish, *anno* 1623 and the seventh year of Master *Crashaw's* residence.

His name, as in this, in many other places remembred.

. . .

Savoy Parish

We have not in the collection of all these churches looked so far back upon any repair as this: but as we find it, we present it.

The repairing and trimming of this church (which was at that time performed with great cost and beauty) was in the year of our Lord God 1600 at the sole cost and charge of the parishioners.

. . .

Next to the other is a very ancient monument, with this inscription:

Pray for the souls of Sir *Richard Rokeby*, knight, and Dame *Jane* his wife, whose bones rest here under this tomb, which Sir *Richard* deceased the 27 of April, 1523, and the said Dame *Jane* deceased the 15. On whose souls Jesu have mercy.

Over the vestry door in the chancel is a very fair tomb with these words:

Hîc jacet Alicia, Filia Simonis Steward, de la Kingheth, Suff. Obiit 18 Junii, humanae salutis, 1573.

Virtutis praemium virtus.[70]

---

[69] {Father of the poet, Richard Crashaw}

[70] {Here lies Alice, daughter of Simon Steward of Kingheth, Suff. She died on the 18th of June, in the year of man's salvation 1573. Goodness is the reward of goodness.}

In the wall on the west side of the church is this ancient memorial:

> The first sepulted in this place,
>> after they it sacrated,
> *Was Humphrey Summerset,*
>> Deacon, which here doth lie,
> Bachelor in the Arts,
>> whom cruel Death oppressed,
> The fifteen hundred & fifteenth year
>> of God Almighty,
> The fifteenth day of April,
>> which *Humphrey* doth call and cry
> With lamentable escrikes
>> and good devotion:
> *All devout Christen men*
>> *and women that pass hereby,*
> *Pray for my dolorous soul,*
>> *for Christ's bitter Passion.*

On an ancient place close to the former is this inscription:

Here by this wall side buried is *William Vevian*, son and heir unto *Michael Vevian* of Cornwall, esquire, which *William* was servant unto the right noble *Charles Somerset*, Earl of Worcester, the King's Chamberlain, and by misfortune drowned in the Thames on Passion Sunday at afternoon in the year of our Lord God 1520. For whose soul pray of your charity, as you would be prayed for.

In the body of the church, upon a brass plate on the ground, is this inscription:

Here lyeth *Humfrey Gosling*, of London, vintner of the White Hart of this parish, a neighbor of virtuous behavior, a very good archer, and of honest mirth, a good company-keeper,

So well inclin'd to poor and rich,
God send more *Goslings* to be sich.

He was servant to the Right Honorable, the Lord *Hunsden*, Lord Chamberlain, and deceased the 22 of July 1586.

A very fair stone, with a fair picture of the party buried wrought in brass, having these several inscriptions:

Over his head, two brass circles. In the one thus:

Credo quod Redemptor meus vivit, & in novissimo die, de terra surrecturus sum.[71]

In the other thus:

Et in carne mea videbo Deum salvatorem meum.[72]

In a circle upon his breast thus:

Reposita est haec spes mea, in sinu meo.[73]

Under him thus:

Situs hic est pietatis ac religionis cultor Ioannes Floid, Artis Musicae Bacchalaureus, qui dum vixit, Regis Henrici octavi in sacello cecinit, & Christi sepulcrum invisit Ierosolymis. Obiit Anno Dom. 1523, Mens. Aprilis die tertio.[74]

A table or memorial of all such benefactors as have given any sums of money or legacies, to the value of five pounds and upwards, to this parish of Saint *Mary Strand*, alias *Savoy*, for the use of the poor or to other pious uses within this parish, beginning from the year of our Lord God 1597. And as touching all other legacies and sums of money under five pounds given by benefactors in this kind since the time aforesaid, they are registered in a book kept for that purpose. Anno Dom. 1622.

    Richard Denham

    James Bradford, churchwardens.

Ralph Abnet, of this parish, died in the year of our Lord God 1597, and gave unto the use of the poor of this parish the sum of twenty pounds, and five pounds more for the advancement of 5 poor maidservants of this parish in marriage.

Richard Jacob, of the parish of Saint Clement Danes, vintner, died in the year of our Lord God 1612, and gave unto the poor of this parish, forty shillings *per annum* for 32 years, to be paid out of the rent of the Chequer Tavern in the parish aforesaid.

Meredith Thomas, of the parish of Saint Clement Danes, tailor, died in the year of our Lord God 1620, and gave the sum of six pounds to this parish forever, to be lent unto two poor men of this parish, either of them three pounds a piece for three years, without interest—they giving good security to the churchwardens for the time being to repay the said six pounds at the three years' end.

Francis Smith, of this parish, grocer, died in the year of our Lord God 1621, and gave the sum of twenty pounds, whereof ten pounds to the poor of this parish and the other ten pounds for the maintenance of a sermon to be yearly preached upon Midsummer Day in this church forever.

---

[71] {I believe that my redeemer lives, and that I shall be raised from the earth on the last day.}

[72] {And in my flesh I shall see God my Savior.}

[73] {This my hope is laid up in my breast. (This and the prior two quotations are from the Vulgate translation of Job 19:25-27.)}

[74] {Here lyeth John Floyd, a friend of piety and religion and bachelor of music, who, when he lived, sang in the chapel of Henry VIII and visited the sepulchre of Christ at Jerusalem. He died on the 3rd of April 1523.}

Dame *Margaret Walter*, wife of Sir *John Walter*, knight, of this parish, died in the year of
our Lord God 1622, and gave unto the poor of this parish the sum of five pounds.

John Bennet, baker, of this parish, died in the year of our Lord God 1625, and gave unto
the poor of this parish the sum of ten pounds forever.

Jane Lane, widow, daughter of *James Howson*, of this parish, died in the year of our Lord
God 1625, and gave unto the poor of this parish the sum of five pounds.

There is given unto this parish, the six and twentieth day of March 1628, by _____
the sum of five pounds, for the maintenance of two sermons to be preached yearly on Easter Monday and Whitson Monday by some sufficient and able minister.

A second memorial

_____ of this parish, widow, in the year 1629 gave unto this parish the
sum of six pounds to buy a second pulpit cloth, to remain to the church for ever.

Sir *John Walter*, knight, Lord Chief Baron, died in the year 1630 and gave to the use of
the poor of this parish forever the sum of twenty pounds.

James Howson the elder, of this parish, died in the year 1631 and gave unto the poor of this
parish the sum of five pounds.

To the Reader

We are here to give you notice (gentle Reader) that the monuments, epitaphs, and inscriptions that in this collection of churches (builded, repaired, and beautified) are here (with
their churches) inserted, are only such as have been raised, composed, and added since the
last imprinting of this book called *The Survey of London*—that impression being in the
year 1617. Those of greater times and antiquity are to be turned to as they stand before in
their several wards and parishes.

⌦⌫

TEXT: EEBO (STC [2nd ed.] / 23345.5)

John Stow, Anthony Munday et al., *The survey of London containing the original, increase, modern estate and
government of that city, methodically set down: with a memorial of those famouser acts of charity, which for public and
pious uses have been bestowed by many worshipfull citizens and benefactors: as also all the ancient and modern monuments erected in the churches, not only of those two famous cities, London and Westminster, but (now newly added) four
miles compass / begun first by the pains and industry of John Stow, in the year 1598 ; afterwards inlarged by the care
and diligence of A.M. in the year 1618 ; and now completely finished by the study & labor of A.M., H.D. and others,
this present year 1633; whereunto, besides many additions (as appears by the contents) are annexed divers alphabeti-
cal tables, especially two, the first, an index of things, the second, a concordance of names* (London: Printed for
Nicholas Bourn, 1633),[75] 759–67, 769–70, 773–74, 776, 778–81, 783–85, 791–95, 799–801, 812,
819–21, 823–28, 833–35, 839, 843, 856–60, 862–63, 867–69, 872–73, 878–81, 883–86, 889, 891,
893–99, 901–4, 906–9.

    Corrected against *An electronic edition of John Strype's "A survey of the cities of London and Westminster"*
{the 1720 update of Stow's *Survey of London* that includes much of the 1633 material added by Mun-
day}, www.hrionline.ac.uk/strype/index.jsp (accessed June 7, 2012).

---

[75] {On p. 758 of the *Survey*, the first page of "The remains or remnants," the printer is given as Elizabeth
Purslow.}

SAMUEL HOARD
(1599–1658/59)

Having entered All Souls, Oxford, as a chorister in 1614, Hoard transferred to St. Mary Hall shortly before receiving his BA in 1618. He graduated MA in 1621, and at about the same time began serving as a curate in a London parish. By 1625 he had become chaplain to Robert Rich, the puritan (and, later, Parliamentary) Earl of Warwick, who presented Hoard with the rectory of Moreton, Essex, where he spent his life's ministry. All the evidence indicates that until ca. 1630, when he took his BD, Hoard was a generic Calvinist conformist. Soon after, however, he began wrestling with questions that grew into doubts and then into objections, leading to the Arminian conversion defended in *God's love to mankind*, the first serious critique of predestinarian theology in English.[1] Perhaps to atone for this ideological defection, Hoard dedicated his next work, *The soul's misery and recovery* (1636), to Warwick. His only other publication is the 1637 *The Church's authority asserted* defending ceremonial conformity—the print version of a sermon Hoard preached at Laud's 1636 metropolitan visitation. Also in 1637 Hoard became a prebendary of St. Paul's, a post soon lost to the upheavals of the 1640s, although he retained the living at Moreton throughout the civil wars and Interregnum—presumably due to Warwick's good offices.

⤙⤚

According to their respective title pages, two printings of *God's love* came out in 1633, a third two years later, none of which name either author or publisher, presumably because the work contravened Charles' 1626 edict banning further public debate on predestination.[2] The title pages, however, may be misleading. In 1636 William Twisse (the future prolocutor of the Westminster Assembly) wrote a long and irate reply to *God's love*, entitled

---

[1] Harsnett's 1594 Paul's Cross sermon makes many of the same points but was not published until 1656 as a tailpiece to *Three sermons preached by the reverend and learned Dr. Richard Stuart*.

[2] There were two subsequent editions in 1656 and 1673; these, although still anonymous, indicated the publisher.

The riches of God's love unto the vessels of mercy consistent with his absolute hatred or reprobation of the vessels of wrath.[3] At the beginning of its second part, Twisse relates that in 1631 he was asked to confer with Hoard about his newfound difficulties over predestination. Twisse says that he requested Hoard to set down his views in writing. Hoard complied, delivering Twisse the manuscript around July of 1632. Seven months later Twisse sent back a lengthy reply that, in his opinion, should have resolved all doubts. He claims to have heard nothing further of the matter until 1635, when *God's love* "was but newly found creeping in corners." Twisse thinks the 1633 title-pages antedate the actual publication by two years in order to disguise the tract's outrageous failure even to acknowledge his reply. This seems a highly self-serving explanation. However, Twisse also hints at a somewhat more likely alternative scenario in remarking that it was rumored that Brian Duppa, while vice-chancellor, had disallowed the publication of Hoard's tract at Oxford. Duppa served as vice-chancellor from 1632 to 1634. The rumor, if true, suggests that the manuscript was finished or nearly so by the time Twisse sent Hoard his objections in early 1633, but it may well not have been printed until 1635.[4]

Twisse further complicates matters by alleging that the manuscript Hoard sent him was much shorter than the printed book, which leads Twisse to think that someone else wrote the additional material; he suspects Henry Mason, a London clergyman who had recently crossed over to the Arminians, adding that there was gossip Mason had written the entire piece. Given Twisse's sputtering rage over Hoard's failure to acknowledge him, one is inclined to view this questioning of Hoard's authorship as pay-back—especially since the only basis for Twisse's conjecture is that the summary of his views Hoard sent him in 1632 did not contain every point made in the 1633 (or 1635) book.

The same 1626 proclamation that (allegedly) led Duppa to stop the publication of *God's love* in 1633 also blocked rejoinders prior to the collapse of Caroline censorship in 1641, at which point John Davenant's *Animadversions* on Hoard's treatise appeared. Twisse's *Riches of God's love* did not see print until 1653, seven years after its author's death.

God's mercies is less a defense of Arminianism than a sustained critique of both the supralapsarian and infralapsarian strains of Reformed orthodoxy.[5] Although some of Hoard's claims lack plausibility (especially those that charge Calvinism with promoting *che será será* libertinage), on the whole the work is analytic, thoughtful, and free from the twitting sarcasm embittering (and enlivening) much post-Reformation controversy. Yet for all Hoard's quiet restraint, the clear implication of his argument is that Calvinism amounts

[3] For the 1636 date of composition (the work was not published until 1653), see the preface to the second part (from which all the following details come).

[4] Twisse also notes that Christopher Potter "check[ed] the Stationers for selling the copies of it." Since both Duppa and Potter were staunch Laudians, and presumably sympathetic to Hoard's position, their refusal to allow its publication strongly supports the view that the Laudian authorities enforced the 1626 proclamation with considerable even-handedness (see Kevin Sharpe, *The personal rule of Charles I* [Yale UP, 1992], 284–98; Sheila Lambert, "Richard Montagu, Arminianism and censorship," *Past and Present* 124 [1989]: 36–68; Julian Davies, *The Caroline captivity of the Church* [Oxford UP, 1992]).

[5] Hoard ignores Roman Catholic theologies of predestination, although Twisse regularly cites Aquinas as a fellow-infralapsarian.

to devil-worship. The supralapsarian God, as Hoard depicts him, resembles a man who has children so that he might later show his authority and power by torturing them <737>.[6] The notion that God creates persons who can do no other than sin and so necessarily perish strikes Hoard as monstrous; nor, Hoard notes, is he alone in this opinion. A revealing anecdote recounts how at the end of the Colloquy at Mompelgart, the Lutheran Count Frederick asked his clergy to shake hands with Beza's party, which request "they utterly refused," saying they could not give "the right hand of brotherhood" to men guilty of such "pestilent errors" <735>. The ministers do not object to the Calvinist view as mistaken, but recoil from it as evil. The anecdote starkly illustrates the threat to religious unity spring-loaded into the predestinarian debates. One *ought* not shake hands with men who make God the author of sin.

Most Calvinists, of course, denied making God responsible for evil. Moreover, mainstream Stuart Calvinism was acutely sensitive to this charge, as evidenced in the turn toward hypothetical universalism. In his 1641 response to Hoard, Davenant insists that he too holds that there is no "eternal decree" appointing men "unto damnation" without "respect unto the just desert of their sin" (Davenant 39; see also 7, 41–42). Indeed, Davenant often sounds remarkably like Hoard. The resemblance is misleading. At bottom they differ over the theoretical yet fundamental question of what constitutes freedom. For Hoard, freedom entails the possibility of doing otherwise; someone locked in a room is not there freely, even if he does not wish to leave <744, 754>. For Davenant, a person's acts are free insofar as they are voluntary; if a man willingly remains in a locked room, then he stays freely; that he could not have left had he wished to is irrelevant. The reprobate, on this Calvinist definition of freedom, sin of their own free will and are therefore justly damned, even though, lacking grace, they could not not-sin (Davenant 36–37). Hoard, however, argues that if God withholds effectual grace from the non-elect—without which grace they cannot do otherwise than sin—then he bears responsibility for their damnation for the same reason that a parent who withholds food from an infant is guilty of the child's death <754>.

Hoard's definition of freedom stands behind his insistence on God's universal saving will, on the possibility of resisting offered grace, and on the conditionality of the divine decrees. His arguments, however, also depend on a second premise: "that justice mercy, truth, and holiness in God are the same in nature with these virtues in men," so that "that which is just, upright and merciful in men is so in God too" <750>. Hoard's analogies between absolute reprobation and homicidal child abuse depend on seeing God and men as, in Cicero's wonderful phrasing, *consociati*, fellow-citizens of the city that is the universe, a city founded on the *communio iuris*, the shared notions of right and just binding heaven and earth (*De legibus* 1.22–25).[7] That this was not the standard Calvinist view can be seen from Twisse's reaction, which was one of astonished horror: "I conceived it, and do conceive it to be one of the absurdest positions that ever dropped from the pen of a School-divine" (*God's riches* 2.2).

---

[6] Prynne seems to hold something close to this view of God <528–29>; see also Como 281.

[7] Note the striking overlap between Hoard's theological principles and legal maxims, e.g., the discussion of causation, culpability, negligence, and accident on <751>.

The horror seems not wholly misplaced. Hoard's theology has, in some respects, more in common with Locke than Augustine. He has serious reservations about the doctrine of original sin <753>; he suggests that the gentiles have a chance at heaven <757>, from which it follows that salvation cannot be by faith alone; he has rather less to say about the wickedness of fallen nature than about human freedom and autonomy. Yet Hoard, like Arminius, Milton, and the Laudians, but in contrast to Locke (or, for that matter, Socinus, Castellio, and Edward Herbert[8]), embraces the supernatural mysteries of faith as a domain of revealed truth beyond and above the rationally apprehensible axioms of the moral law <755>. He is not a proto-deist.

Finally, like most early Stuart divines but few modern readers, Hoard views *cui bono* as an *ethical* question, and a central one; religion and morality demand self-discipline and self-denial, which flesh and blood will only endure in hope of reward or from fear of punishment <758–59>.

⟊⟋

Sources: *ODNB*; David Como, "Predestination and political conflict in Laud's London," *The Historical Journal* 46.2 (2003): 263–94; John Davenant, *Animadversions upon a treatise intitled, Gods love to mankind* (Cambridge UP, 1641); Barbara Donagan, "The clerical patronage of Robert Rich, Second Earl of Warwick, 1619–1642," *Proceedings of the American Philosophical Society* 120.5 (1976): 388–419; William Twisse, *The riches of God's love unto the vessels of mercy consistent with his absolute hatred or reprobation of the vessels of wrath, or, An answer unto a book entituled, Gods love unto mankind* (Oxford UP, 1653).

[8] See Ronald David Bedford, *The defense of truth: Herbert of Cherbury and the seventeenth century* (Manchester UP, 1979).

SAMUEL HOARD

God's love to mankind
1633 (1635?)

TO THE READER

The author of this treatise was persuaded to pen the reasons of his opinion against absolute reprobation that he might satisfy a worthy friend of his who required it. What satisfaction that learned gentleman his friend hath received by these reasons, I know not, but sure I am {that} they have given good content to some others who have read them and do still desire a copy of them for their further use, to ease whose pains in transcribing this treatise, it doth now appear in this form. If any contrary opinion shall undertake to answer or refute it, I wish he would set down his opinion and reasons with that perspicuity and modesty that our author set down his. Such a course of disputing will gain more credit to himself and his cause than voluminous vagaries about impertinent things. If any shall use railing speeches or unnecessary diversions from the cause, I shall ever interpret that to be a strong sign of a weak cause. Or, at least, I shall think it to be an argument of an obstinate mind, who neither knoweth how to yield to the truth nor to defend his error. I hope the reader who loves his own salvation will be a more indifferent judge in a question which concerneth him so nearly. And so I leave him to God's blessing.

GOD'S LOVE TO MANKIND[1]

Sir, I have sent you here the reasons which have moved me to change my opinion in some controversies of late debated between the Remonstrants and their opposites.[2]

. . .

In the delivery of my motives, I will proceed in this order:

1. I will state the opinion which I dislike.
2. I will lay down my reasons against it.

---

[1] {Hoard has a great many one-sentence paragraphs, some of which I have merged into a longer paragraph.}

[2] {On the terms "Remonstrants" and "Counter-Remonstrants," see the introduction to *Collegiate suffrage <supra>*.}

Touching the first, your Worship knows these two things very well:

1. That the main . . . question in these controversies, and that on which the rest do hang, is what the decrees of God are touching the everlasting condition of men and how they are ordered.

2. That the men who have disputed these things may be reduced to two sorts and sides.

The first side affirmeth that there is *an absolute and peremptory decree* proceeding from the alone pleasure of God, without any consideration of men's final impenitency and unbelief, by which God casteth men off from grace and glory and shutteth up the far greater part (even of those that are called by the preaching of the Gospel to repentance and salvation) under invincible and unavoidable sin and damnation.

The other side, disavowing any such decree, say that God's decree of casting men off forever is grounded upon the foresight of their continuance in sin and disbelief, both avoidable by grace and consequently inferring no man's damnation necessarily.

The first side is divided, for

1. Some of them present man to God in the decree of reprobation look't on out of or above the Fall,[3] and say that God, of his mere pleasure, antecedent to all sin in the creature, original and actual, did decree to glorify his sovereignty and justice in the eternal rejection and damnation of the greatest part of mankind as the end and in their unavoidable sin and impenitency as the means. And this way go Calvin, Beza, Zanchius, Piscator, Gomarus, and some of our own countrymen.[4]

2. The rest of that side, thinking to avoid the great inconveniences to which that supralapsarian way lieth open, fall down a little lower and present man to God in his decree of reprobation lying[5] in the Fall and under the guilt of original sin, saying that God, looking upon miserable mankind lying in Adam's sin, did decree the greatest number of men (even those men whom he calls to repentance and salvation by the preaching of the Gospel) to hell torments forever and without all remedy, for the declaration of his severe justice. This way went the Synod {of Dort}.

The difference between them is not much and even in their own account too small a discord to cause a breach. Notwithstanding this petty difference, therefore, they agree well enough together, as we may see in the Hague conference[6] and the Synod.

In the conference at Hague, the Contra-Remonstrants have these words: *as touching the diversity of opinions in this argument,* viz. *that God looked at man in this decree, not yet created, or created and fallen:*[7] *because this belongs not to the foundation of this doctrine, we do in Christian equity bear with one another.*

---

[3] {I.e., these theologians see the decree of reprobation as having been made either without reference to the Fall or causally prior to it.}

[4] {Theodore Beza (1519–1605), Calvin's successor at Geneva and early proponent of supralapsarianism; Jerome Zanchius (1516–90), Italian-born Protestant, author of *The doctrine of absolute predestination*; Johannes Piscator (1546–1625), German Reformed theologian, a rigid supralapsarian (although late in life embracing Arminianism); Franciscus Gomarus (1563–1641), Dutch Contra-Remonstrant and the leading supralapsarian at Dort.}

[5] {"lying" modifies "man" (Hoard sometimes forgets he is writing in English, not Latin.)}

[6] {A conference in the spring of 1611 between six Remonstrant and six Counter-Remonstrant theologians.}

[7] {"not yet . . . and fallen" modifies "man"}

After[8] this, in the Synod at Dort, they permitted Gomarus to set down his judgment in the upper way. And the delegates of South-Holland were very indifferent which way they took. For these are their words: *whether God in choosing considered men as fallen or else as not fallen*, they (the delegates of South-Holland) think it is not necessary to be determined, so it be held that God in choosing considered men in a like estate. Maccovius,[9] also professor of divinity at Franeker, a violent and stiff maintainer of the most unsavory speeches which have been uttered in this controversy, and one that undertook in the very Synod to make good against Lubbert,[10] his fellow professor, that God did *will sins, ordain men to sin, and would not at all that all men be saved*; and besides this, openly and peremptorily affirmed that *except these things were held and maintained by them*, they could not possibly keep their own ground but *must come over to the Remonstrants*—this man was not only not censured, but publicly declared in the Synod to be *pure* and *orthodox*, and dismissed with this kind and friendly admonition: *that he should hereafter take heed of such words as might give offense to tender ears and could not well down with those who are yet incapable of such mysteries.*

By these instances it appeareth that they of the first side can easily bear one with another in this difference. And (to say the truth) there is no reason why they should quarrel about circumstances, seeing they agree in the substance. For they both contend,

1. That the moving-cause of the reprobation is the alone will of God, and not the sin of man, original or actual.

2. That the final impenitency and damnation of reprobates are necessary and unavoidable, by God's absolute decree.

These two things are the *maxima gravamina*, principal grievances, that the other side stick at. So that these two paths meet at last in the same way.

Both these opinions of the first side I dislike. My reasons why are of two sorts:

1. Such as first made me to question the truth.
2. Such as convince me of their untruth.

My reasons of the first sort do indifferently respect and make against both, and I will set them down against both together. My second sort of reasons I will divide, delivering some of them against the upper and more rigid way, others against the lower and more moderate way. I begin with those reasons which first moved me to question the truth of absolute reprobation as it is taught both ways.

They are these four, which follow:

1. The novelty of this opinion. Absolute and inevitable reprobation hath little or no footing in antiquity. The upper way was never taught or approved by any of the Fathers (even the stoutest defenders of grace against the Pelagians) for the space of 600 (I may say 800) years after Christ. . . . They did generally agree upon the contrary conclusion and taught men in their times:

---

[8] {in accordance with}

[9] {Johannes Maccovius (1588–1644), Polish Reformed theologian, whose extreme supralapsarian position was allowed, although not endorsed, by the Synod of Dort.}

[10] {Sibrandus Lubbertus (1555–1625), Counter-Remonstrant, an infralapsarian, who challenged the orthodoxy of Maccovius' position at Dort.}

That it was possible for them to be saved which in the event were not saved, and to have repented which repented not, and that there was no decree of God which did lay a necessity of perishing upon any son of Adam. This that I saw, Mr. Calvin himself doth freely acknowledge, speaking of election and reprobation according to God's foreknowledge: *this commonly received opinion* (saith he) of a conditional and respective decree *is not the opinion only of the common people but hath had great authors in all ages.* Reverend Beza, likewise speaking of the same opinion, hath these words to the same purpose: *into which surely most foul error Origen hath driven many of the ancients, both Greek and Latin.* To the same effect also Prosper (St. Augustine's follower) hath a remarkable speech: *Almost all the ancients* (saith he) *did grant with one consent that God decreed men's end according to his foresight of their actions*, and not otherwise. . . .

The truth of this charge may further appear by a few particular instances.

Minucius Felix[11] brings in the pagans objecting to the Christians that they held the events of all things to be inevitable and did feign and frame to themselves an unjust God who did punish in men their unavoidable destinies, not their ill choices. . . . To this he answereth: *Christians hold no other fates than God decrees, who, fore-knowing all men and their actions, did accordingly determine their retributions.*

St. Hierom, an eager opposer of the Pelagians, in many places of his writings saith the same thing. . . . *The love and hatred of God ariseth either from the foresight of future things or from the works; otherwise we know that God loveth all things, nor doth he hate any thing that he hath made.* And in his book against Pelagius he saith: *eligit Deus quem bonum cernit, God chooseth whom he seeth to be good.*

. . .

In the disputation at Mompelgart {Montbéliard}, *anno* 1586,[12] held between Beza and Jacobus Andrea,[13] with some seconds on both sides, Beza and his company having disputed with the Lutherans about the person of Christ and the Lord's Supper, when they came to this point did decline the sifting of it, and gave this reason among others, that it could not then be publicly disputed of *without the great scandal and hurt of the ignorant and unacquainted with these higher mysteries.* The Contra-Remonstrants also in their conference with the opposite parties at the Hague in the year 1611 could not be drawn to dispute with them about this point. . . . In the synod likewise at Dort in the years 1618 and 1619, the Remonstrants were warned by the president of the synod *that they should rather dispute of the point of election than the odious point of reprobation.*

Can this doctrine be a truth and yet blush at the light which maketh all things manifest? Especially considering these things:

1. That reprobation is a principal head of divinity, by the well- or ill-stating the ordering of which, the glory of God and the good of religion is much promoted or hindered.

2. That there is such a necessary connection between the points of election and reprobation (both being parts of predestination) that the one cannot well be handled without the other.

---

[11] {One of the earliest Latin Christian thinkers (ca. 150–270) and author of the *Octavius*, a dialogue between a pagan and Christian.}

[12] {The Lutheran Count Frederick of Würtemberg arranged a conference at Montbéliard on March 21, 1586 in an attempt to bridge the sharp divide between the Lutherans and Calvinists.}

[13] {Jacobus Andreae (1528–90), Lutheran theologian}

3. That the doctrine of reprobation was the chief cause of all the uproars in the Church at that time.

4. That it was accused with open mouth and challenged of falsehood, and therefore bound in justice to purge itself of crimination.

5. That the Remonstrants did not at that time desire that it should be talked of among the common people, who might have stumbled at it, but disputed of among the judicious and learned who (as the threshing oxen which were to beat the corn out of the husk) are to bolt out those truths which are couched and hidden in the letter of the Scriptures.

That the doctrine which is loath to abide the trial even of learned men carrieth with it a shrewd suspicion of falsehood, the heathen orator shall witness for me, who, to Epicurus saying that he would not publish his opinion to the simple people—who might haply take offense at it—answereth thus: *declare thine opinion in the place of judgment, or if thou art afraid of the assembly there, declare in the Senate-house among those grave and judicious persons. Thou wilt never do it, and why? But because it is a foul and dishonest opinion.*[14]

This striving to lie close is (peradventure) no infallible argument of a bad cause, yet it is a very probable one. For true religion (as Vives saith) is not a thing *gilded over, but gold itself; the more that's scraped and discovered, the brighter and goodlier it is,* and so is the truth. *Disputations illustrate and set forth true opinions more than silence can; let's not fear, therefore* (saith he), *lest our faith when it is laid open appear filthy to the eyes of the beholders. Let false and superficial religions in which there is no soundness be afraid of this.*

The Jew is loath to reason with the Christian touching his Law, and the Turk is forbidden to dispute of his Alcoran, because their religions are brittle like glass, broken with the least touch. But the Christian who *is confident of the goodness of his faith feareth no examination, but rather as much as may be soliciteth and provoketh his adversary to combat.*[15]

Truth, whether it be in men or doctrines, is best when it is uncovered; it covets no corners, though error do, but is willing to abide the trial. . . .

3. The infamy of it. It is an opinion (especially as it is defended the upper way) odious to the Papists, opening their foul mouths against our Church and religion; abhorred (maintained either way) by all Lutherans, who for this very tenet call us damned Calvinists, think us unworthy to be above ground, and in their writings protest that they will rather unite themselves to the Papists than to us. And it is also distasteful to all the Greek churches, which are very many. Molin in his *Anatomy,*[16] speaking of the supralapsarian doctrine, saith *if it should be so that God hath reprobated men without the consideration of sin or hath ordained them to sin, yet it is the part of a wise man to conceal these things or not to know them rather than to utter them, because when they are taught and defended they fill men's heads with scruples and give occasion to the adversaries of defaming the true religion.* The same may as truly be said of the sublapsarian way. For (as I have said) they are in substance all one. And Sir Edwyn Sandys[17] is of the same mind too. For in his most excellent book called a *Survey of the state of religion in the western parts of the world,* speaking of the

---

[14] [Cicer. *de fin. bon. & malorum*]

[15] [{Juan Luis} Vives *de ver{itate} fidei*]

[16] {Pierre du Moulin (1568–1658), Huguenot minister, appointed prebendary at Canterbury Cathedral in 1615; author of *The Anatomy of Arminianism* (1619; Engl. trans. 1620).}

[17] {For Sandys, see the introduction to *The Little Gidding Story Books* <supra>.}

deadly division between the Lutherans and Calvinists in Germany, he hath these words, that *though the Palsgrave and Landsgrave have with great judgment and wisdom, to aslake those flames, imposed silence in that part to the ministers of their party, hoping the charity and discretion of the other party would have done the like, yet it falls out otherwise. For both the Lutheran preachers rail as bitterly against them in their pulpits as ever, and their princes and people have them in as great detestation, not forbearing to profess openly that they will return to the Papacy rather than ever admit that sacramentary and predestinary pestilence.*

For these two points are the ground of the quarrel, and the latter more scandalous at this day than the former. And in the same book, pg. 194 and 198, speaking of men whom he commendeth for *singular learning and piety* (whose judgment he so sets down as that he declareth it to be his own), he saith that they think *it were no blemish* for the Reformed doctors to *revise their doctrines and to abate the rigor of certain speculative opinions* (for so he is pleased to call them), *especially touching the eternal decrees of God, wherein some of their chief authors have run into such an extreme to all Romish doctrine as to have exceedingly scandalized all other Churches withal, yea and many of their own to rest very ill-satisfied.*

At the closing up of the conference at Mompelgart, when Frederick Earl of Würtemberg exhorted his divines to acknowledge Beza and his company for brethren and to declare it by giving them their hand, they utterly refused, saying they would pray to God to open their eyes and would do them any office of humanity and charity, but they would not give them the right hand of brotherhood because they were proved to be guilty . . . *of most pestilent errors*, among which they reckoned {this} for one.

Hemingius left his own side and joined with us in the point of the sacrament, but he would come no nearer, maintaining always a distance in this.[18]

And as for the Grecians, we learn also by Sir Edwin Sandys his relation that *they do mightily dissent from that doctrine touching the eternal counsels of God, which Calvin (as some conceive) first fully revealed or rather introduced into the Christian world . . . as thinking it very injurious to the goodness of God and directly and immediately opposite to his very nature. In regard of which, one of their bishops hath written a book against it, which hath been sent to Geneva and there received.*

It is a morsel which the greatest part of Christian Churches cannot swallow, and therefore (I think) it should not very easily without suspicion down with us.

And to say one thing more, besides this infamy of it among Christians, it is very probable that among too many scandals given to the Jews by the Christians among whom they dwell, this doctrine is not one of the least rubs in the way of their conversion. For *they think it a bad opinion* (says the same judicious and learned gentleman) *which some of great name have seemed to hold, that God in his everlasting and absolute pleasure should affect the extreme misery of any of his creatures for the showing of his justice and severity in tormenting them; or that the calamity, casting away, and damnation of some should absolutely and necessarily redound more to his glory than the felicity of them all, considering that his nature is mere goodness and happiness and hath no affinity with rigor or misery.* This is my third reason.

---

[18] {Niels Hemmingsen (1513–1600), Danish Lutheran theologian; his theological position was close to Melanchthon's, and some Lutherans viewed both men's sacramental theology as crypto-Calvinist. Hemmingsen was also a friend of the Cambridge proto-Arminian Peter Baro, and the former's Ephesians commentary played a key role in the formation of Elizabethan anti-Calvinism.}

The fourth, its affinity with the old exploded errors of the Stoics and Manichees.

The opinion of the Stoics was that all actions and events were unavoidable . . . all things being so put together from eternity that one thing must needs follow another as it doth; and the *prima materia* being so disposed that things cannot successively come to pass otherwise than they do, but must of necessity be as they are, even *invito Deo*, though God would have some things be otherwise than they are.

The Manichees held that all men's actions, good or evil, were determined too: good actions by a good god who was the author of all good things that were created and of all good actions that came to pass in the world; evil actions by an evil god who was . . . *the prime author of all evil things or actions* that were extant in the world.

The maintainers of the absolute decree do say one of these two things: either that all actions natural and moral, good and evil, and all events likewise, are absolutely necessary (so the supralapsarians), or that all men's ends (at least) are unalterable and indeterminable by the power of their wills (so the sublapsarians). And this is upon the matter all one with the former. For first, in vain is our freedom in the actions and means, if the end at which they drive be pitched and determined, sith all actions are for the ends' sake, that it might be obtained by them, which without them could not. And secondly, the determination of the end doth necessarily involve the means that precede that end: as if a man be fore-determined to damnation, he must unavoidably sin, else he could not be damned.

Now in these 3 opinions we may note two things:

1. The substance and formality of them, which is an unavoidableness of men's actions and ends whatsoever they be; in this all of them agree, all holding that in all things, at least in all men's ends, undeclinable fates and insuperable necessity do domineer.

    . . .

2. We may note the circumstance or the grounds of their opinions. The Stoics derive this necessity from the stars or the first matter; the Manichees from two . . . first principles of all things eternal and coeternal;[19] these last from the peremptory decree of Almighty God.

So that they differ in their grounds indeed, but in this difference the Stoics and the Manichees in some respects have the better. For it is better to derive this necessity of evil actions and unhappy events from an evil god or the course of nature than from the decree of that God who is infinitely good. The substance of their opinions is all one; the ground wherein they differ is but accidental to the error.

Which being so, for this very reason alone may this doctrine of absolute reprobation be suspected, because those dreams of the Stoics were exploded by the best philosophers of all sorts; and this of the Manichees was generally cried down by the Fathers not only as foolish but as impious and unworthy of entertainment in a Christian heart or Christian commonwealth, not so much for anything circumstantial in it as for the substance of the error, because it made all things and events to be necessary and so plucked up the roots of virtue, planted vice, and left no place for just rewards or punishments.

These are my reasons of the first sort.

---

[19] {"Eternal and coeternal" modifies "first principles."}

The reasons that have convinced me of the untruth of absolute reprobation now follow. And, first, of those that fight against the upper way.

They are drawn *ab incommodo*, from the great evils and inconveniences which issue from it naturally, which may be referred to two main heads:

1. The dishonor of God.
2. The overthrow of religion and government.

It dishonoreth God. For it chargeth him deeply with two things no ways agreeable to his nature:

1. Men's eternal torments in hell.
2. Their sins on earth.

First, it chargeth him with men's eternal torments in hell and maketh him to be the prime, principal, and invincible cause of the damnation of millions of miserable souls. The prime cause, because it reporteth him to have appointed them to destruction of his own voluntary disposition, antecedent to all deserts in them; and the principal and invincible cause, because it maketh the damnation of reprobates to be necessary and unavoidable through God's absolute and uncontrollable decree, and so necessary that they can no more escape it than poor Astyanax could avoid the breaking of his neck when the Grecians tumbled him down from the tower of Troy.[20]

Now this is a heavy charge, contrary to Scripture, God's nature, and sound reason.

1. To Scripture, which makes man the principal, nay the only cause (in opposition to God) of his own ruin: *Thy destruction is of thyself, O Israel, but in me is thy help* (Hos. 13:9). *As I live, saith the Lord, I wish not the death of the wicked,* &c. *Turn ye, turn ye, why will ye die* (Ezek. 33:11). *He doth not afflict willingly, nor grieve the children of men* (Lam. 3:33). To which speeches, for likeness' sake, I will join one of Prosper's: *God's predestination is to many the cause of standing; to none, of falling.*

2. It's contrary to God's nature, who sets forth himself to be *a God merciful, gracious, long suffering, abundant in goodness,* &c., and he is acknowledged to be so by King David: *Thou Lord art good and merciful and of great kindness to all them that call upon thee.* And by the Prophets Joel, Jonah, and Micah: *He is gracious and merciful, slow to anger and of great kindness,* saith Joel. *I know* (says Jonah) *that thou art a gracious God and merciful, slow to anger, and of great kindness.* And *who* (saith Micah) *is a God like unto thee, that taketh away iniquity?* &c. *He retaineth not his wrath forever because mercy pleaseth him.*

3. 'Tis contrary also to sound reason, which cannot but argue {accuse} such a decree of extreme cruelty, and consequently remove it from the Father of mercies.

We cannot in reason think that any man in the world can so far put off humanity and nature as to resolve with himself to marry and beget children, that, after they are born and have lived a while with him, he may hang them up by the tongues, tear their flesh with scourges, pull it from their bones with burning pincers, or put them to any cruel tortures, that by thus torturing them he may shew what his authority and power is over them. Much less can we believe without great violence to reason that the God of mercy can so far forget himself as out of his absolute pleasure to ordain such infinite multitudes

---

[20] {First-born son of Hector and Andromache; the account of his murder is given by Pausanius.}

of his children, made after his own image, to everlasting fire; and create them one after another that after the end of a short life here he might torment them without end hereafter to shew his power and sovereignty over them. If to destroy the righteous with the wicked temporally be such a piece of injustice that Abraham removeth it from God with an *absit*[21]—*Wilt thou destroy the righteous with the wicked? That be far from thee, O Lord. Shall not the judge of all the world do right?*—how deeply (may we think) would that good man have detested one single thought that God resolveth upon the destruction of many innocent souls eternally in hell fire?

But God, say some, is sovereign Lord of all creatures and men; they are truly and properly his own. Cannot he therefore dispose of them as he pleaseth and do with his own what he will?

The question is not what an almighty sovereignty and power can do to poor vassals, but what a power that is just and good may do. By the power of a lord, his absolute and naked power, he can cast away the whole mass of mankind, for it is not repugnant to omnipotency or sovereignty; but by the power of a judge—to wit, that actual power of his, which is always clothed with goodness and justice—he cannot. For it is not compatible with these properties in God to appoint men to hell of his mere will and pleasure, no fault at all of theirs preexisting in his eternal mind.[22]

1. It is not compatible with justice, which is a constant will of rendering to everyone his proper due: and that is, vengeance to whom vengeance belongeth, namely to the obstinate and impenitent. *God is good* (saith St. Austin) *and God is just; he may without any deserts free men from punishment, because he is good, but he cannot without evil deservings condemn any man, because he is just.* In another place also he saith, *if God be believed to damn any man that by sin deserveth it not, he is not believed to be free from injustice.*

2. Nor is it compatible with goodness, which is an inclination in God of communicating that good which is in himself to his creatures as far as he can without wronging his justice; and therefore if God be (as the Scripture reporteth him) *good to all*, it cannot be that he should of himself, without any motive in the reasonable creature, provide for it from everlasting the greatest of all miseries, and that before he thought of making it or bestowing any good at all upon it.

It is further objected that we do and may slaughter our beasts for our daily use without any cruelty or injustice, and therefore God may as well, nay much more, appoint as many of us as he pleaseth to the torments of hell for his glory and yet be just and good notwithstanding, for there is a greater disproportion between God and us than between us and beasts.

1. For answer to this we are first to premise thus much: namely, that our slaughtering of our beasts for our daily use is by God's ordinance and appointment. We had not this authority of ourselves, but God of his bounty towards us gave it us, as we may see, Gen. 9:2, 3, where we may observe, first, that God delivereth up all creatures—beasts, birds, and fishes—into the hands of men. Secondly, that the end why he doth so is that they might be meat for men, and consequently that they might be slain.

---

[21] {*"Absit"* is Latin for "let that not happen," i.e., "far be it from thee."}

[22] {On the distinction between God's absolute and actual power, see the opening of Sydenham's *Jehovah-Jirah* <infra> and the bibliography in Francis Oakley, *Politics and eternity* (Brill, 1999), 288–89.}

Which being so, our slaughtering of oxen, sheep, and other creatures for our daily use is to be accounted God's doing rather than ours. And therefore the objection should be made thus, God may without any breach of goodness or justice appoint brute creatures to be slain for man's use; therefore, he may ordain men to be cast into hell-torments forever for his own use, that is for the declaration of his sovereignty, &c.

This being premised, I answer further that this comparison holds not, for there is little proportion between the objects compared and less between the acts.

1. There is but small proportion between the objects, beasts and men, creatures of a different nature and made for a different end. Beasts are void of reason and liberty in their actions, creatures whose beings vanish with their breath, made only for the use and service of men upon earth; but men are reasonable and understanding creatures, able through the Creator's bounty to discern between good and evil, and according to their first principles, to choose the good and forsake the evil. They are the very image of God's purity and eternity, and were made for the service of God alone upon earth and his blessed and everlasting society in heaven.

So that, albeit there be a very great distance between God and men, yet nothing so great as between God and beasts. It followeth not therefore that if God may appoint beasts to be killed of his own free pleasure for man's use, he may with like equity and reason appoint men of his own will to destruction for his own use. We read that God required of his people many thousand beasts for sacrifices, but not one man.

The first born of other creatures he challenged for burnt offerings (except they were unclean beasts), but the first-born of men were to be redeemed, which sheweth that he put a wide difference between the blood of men and beasts. Besides, in the 9 of Gen., he giveth men power to kill and feed upon all living creatures, but he straitly forbids them to shed man's blood, and giveth this reason of the prohibition: *man is the image of God.* So that we may well conclude that there is but small proportion between the objects compared, men and beasts, in respect of this act of killing or slaughtering.

2. There is far less, or rather no proportion at all, between the acts compared, killing and eternal tormenting. A man may kill, but he cannot without barbarous injustice and cruelty torment his beast and prolong the life of it that he may daily vex and torture it to shew what power and sovereignty he hath over it; so I doubt not . . . but God may kill a man of his own free pleasure, yea and resolve him into nothing, without any cruelty or injustice, because in doing so he doth but take away what he had given him; but he cannot, without both these, antecedently decree to keep him alive forever in hell that he may there torment him without end to shew his sovereignty. For this is to inflict an infinite evil upon a guiltless creature to whom he had given but a finite good. And so is the comparison most unequal too in the acts compared and therefore proveth just nothing.

But it is replied by some (who will rather speak unreasonably and against common sense than lay down the conclusions which they have undertaken to maintain) that it is better and more eligible {preferable} to be tortured in hell than to want or lose a being: for he that wants a being enjoyeth no good, but he that is tormented in hell hath a being and by consequence something that is good. If therefore God may take away a man's being that is innocent and turn him into nothing for his pleasure, much more may he torment him in hell.

1. To the first part of this reply—namely that it is more desirable to be in hell than to be nothing—I oppose three things:

1. The speech of our Savior concerning Judas: *Woe be to that man by whom the Son of Man is betrayed; it had been good for that man if he had never been born*. . . . It is as much as if our Lord had said, Judas the traitor shall be damned, and therefore so woeful will his condition be that it had been good and happy for him if he had never received a being: good in earnest, as interpreters do generally expound it, not in the opinion and esteem of weak-minded, faint-hearted men only, as some few understand it. . . .

. . .

Secondly, I oppose common consent. Where shall we pick out a man but will say (if he speak from his heart) that he were better to vanish into a thousand nothings than to be cast into hell? What is the reason why men are so afraid of hell when they are touched to the quick with the conscience of their ungodly lives and the expectation of eternal vengeance, that with Job they curse their birth day and wish an hundred times over that they had never been or might cease to be that so they might not come into the place of torments, but because they judge a being there to be incomparably worse than no being anywhere? And why are men who are sensible of hell fire so strongly curbed and held in by the fear of feeling it, even from darling and beloved sins, but because they apprehend it to be the most terrible of all terribles! Fear of being annihilated can never do that which the fear of hell doth.

The third thing which I oppose is common sense, which judgeth pains when they are extreme to be worse than death. Hence it is that Job, being tormented in his body by the devil, cursed his birth day, magnified the condition of the dead, and wished himself in the grave, plainly preferring the loss of his being before that miserable being which he then had. And hence it is that men even of the stoutest and hardest spirits (as we see by daily experience) would (if they might enjoy their option) choose rather to have no bodies at all than bodies tormented with the stone or gout or any other sharp and sensible disease. It is a known saying grounded on this judgment of sense . . . *better it is to die once than to be always dying*. This the tyrant Tiberius knew very well, and therefore he would not suffer those towards whom he purposed to exercise his cruelty to be put to a speedy death but to lingering torments, as Suetonius reporteth of him in that chapter where he reckoneth up his barbarous and cruel practices.

. . .

Secondly, this opinion chargeth God with men's sins on earth and makes him the author not of the first sin only that entered by Adam into the world, but of all other sins that have been, are, or shall be committed to the world's end: no murders, robberies, rapes, adulteries, insurrections, treasons, blasphemies, heresies, persecutions, or any other abominations whatsoever fall out at any time or in any place but they are the necessary productions of God's almighty decree. The Scriptures, I am sure, teach us another lesson. *Thou are not a God* (saith David) *that hath pleasure in wickedness*. And the prophet Esay tells the people that when they did evil in the sight of the Lord, *they did choose the things which he would not. Let no man say when he is tempted, I am tempted of God, for God cannot be tempted with evils, neither tempteth he any man, but every man is tempted when he is drawn away with his own concupiscence*. . . . To which speeches let me add the speech of

Siracides, though not of the same authority: *Say not thou, it is through the Lord that I fell away; for thou oughtest not to do the things that he hateth. Say not thou, he hath caused me to err; for he hath no need of the sinful man* [Ecclus 15:12].

Pious antiquity hath constantly said the same, and pressed it with sundry reasons, some of which are these that follow. If God be the author of sin, then

1. He is worse than the devil, because the devil doth only tempt and persuade to sin, and his actions may be resisted; but God (by this opinion) doth will and procure it by a *powerful and effectual decree*, which cannot be resisted. This is Prosper's argument, who, to some objecting that by St. Austin's doctrine, when . . . men commit any horrible villainies, *it cometh to pass because God hath so decreed*, answereth that *if this were laid to the devil's charge, he might in some sort clear himself of the imputation, because, though he be delighted with men's sins, yet he doth not, he cannot, compel them to sin; what a madness therefore is it to impute that to God which cannot be justly fathered upon the devil?*

2. He cannot be a punisher of sin, for none can justly punish those offences of which they are the authors. This is Prosper's argument too: *it is against reason to say that he which is the damner of the devil would have any man to be the devil's servant.* This reason Fulgentius useth likewise . . . *God is the avenger of that {of} which he is not the author.* Tertullian also before them hath said, *he is not to be accounted the author of sin who is the forbidder, yea, and the condemner of it.*

3. He cannot be God because he should not be just nor holy nor the judge of the world, all properties essential to God. And this is St. Basil's reason, who hath written a whole homily against this wicked assertion. *It is all one* (saith he) *to say that God is the author of sin and to say he is not God.*

Upon these and the like considerations I may well conclude that the opinion which chargeth the holy God with the sins of men is neither good nor true.

But this opinion doth so. For albeit the writers that have defended it (Piscator and a few more of the blunter sort excepted) have never said directly and *in terminis* {explicitly} that God is the cause of sin, yet have they delivered those things from which it must needs follow by necessary consequence that he is so. For they say,

1. That as the decree of reprobation is absolute, so it is inevitable: those poor souls which lie under it must of necessity be damned. *It is* (saith Marlorat[23]) *a firm and stable truth that the man whom God in his eternal counsel hath rejected, though he do all the good works of the saints, cannot possibly be saved.*

2. That without sin this decree of reprobation cannot be justly executed. *God* (saith Piscator) *did create men for this very purpose, that they might indeed fall, for otherwise he could not have attained those his principal ends*: he meaneth the manifestation of his justice in the damnation of the reprobates and of his mercy in the salvation of the elect. Maccovius also saith the same: *if sin had not been, the manifestation of justice and mercy* (which is as much to say as the damnation of reprobates) *had never been.*

3. That therefore God decreed that reprobates should unavoidably sin, and sin unto death, that his eternal ordinance might be executed and they damned. *We grant* (saith Zanchius) *that reprobates are held so fast under God's almighty decree that they cannot but sin and perish.* . . .

---

[23] {Augustin Marlorat (1506–62), French Reformer and exegete}

Calvin also saith that reprobates obey not the word of God partly through the wickedness of their own hearts and partly because *they are raised up by the unsearchable judgment of God to illustrate his glory by their damnation.* I will end this with that speech of Piscator: *reprobates are precisely appointed to this double evil: to be punished everlastingly and to sin, and therefore to sin that they might be justly punished.*

4. That as he hath immutably decreed that reprobates shall live and die in sin, so he procures their sins in due time by his almighty hand, partly by withdrawing from them grace necessary for the avoiding of sin and partly by moving and inclining them by his irresistible and secret workings on their hearts to sinful actions. Calvin saith that devils and reprobate men are not only held fast in God's fetters so as they cannot do what they would, but are also urged and forced by God's bridle . . . *to do as he would have them.* And in the next chapter these are his words: *that men have nothing in agitation, that they bring nothing into action but what God by his secret direction hath ordered, is apparent by many and clear testimonies.* In the section following he saith, *and surely unless God did work inwardly in the minds of men, t'would not be rightly said that he taketh away wisdom from the wise,* &c. In those two chapters, that which he mainly driveth at is to shew that God doth not only behave himself privatively in procuring the sins of men, but doth also put forth powerful and positive acts in the bringing of them to pass. And in his second book and 4 chapter, after he had said that God may be said to harden men by forsaking them, he putteth in another way by which God hardeneth men, and that (he saith) cometh a great deal nearer to the propriety of the Scripture phrases: namely, by stirring up their wills; God doth not only harden men by leaving them to themselves but by *appointing their counsels, ordering their deliberations, stirring up their wills, confirming their purposes and endeavors by the minister of his anger, Satan,* and this he proveth by the work of God on Sihon, King of the Amorites (Deut. 2:30), and then insinuateth the end, too, why God thus hardens men in their wicked courses, which is that he might destroy them: *because God intended his ruin, he prepared him for it by his induration.*

. . .

That God is the author of men's salvation and conversion, all sides grant; and yet he doth no more in the procuring of them than these men report him to do in the reprobates' impenitency and damnation. The salvation and conversion of the elect (say they) he hath *absolutely* and *antecedently,* without the foresight of any deservings of theirs, resolved upon; and by irresistible means . . . draweth them to believe, repent, and endure to the end, that so they might be saved and his absolute decree accomplished. On the other side, the damnation, the sins, and the final impenitency of reprobates, he hath of his alone will and pleasure peremptorily decreed; this his decree he executeth in time, drawing them on by his unconquerable power and providence from sin to sin till they have made up their measure, and in the end have inflicted on them[24] that eternal vengeance which he had provided for them. What difference is here in the course which God taketh for the conversion and salvation of the elect and the obduration and damnation of reprobates? And therefore what hindereth but that God (by their grounds) may as truly be styled the prime cause and author of the sins of the one as of the conversion of the other?

---

[24] {The verb here is passive: men will have this inflicted upon them.}

The Fathers thought it a plain case, and therefore they did generally make sin an object of prescience, not {of} predestination, and bent the most of those arguments, by which they refuted this foul assertion, against an absolute, irresistible, and necessitating decree—as I could easily shew but that I fear to be overlong. Only I will cite some few of those authors' words whom the learned and reverend Bishop {Ussher} hath alleged in favor and for the defense of the predestinarians and the maintainers of Gotteschalk's opinion.[25]

The Church of Lyons, in their answer to the positions of Johannes Scotus[26] which he framed against Gotteschalk, hath these words: *whosoever saith that God hath laid a constraint or a necessity of sinning upon any man, he doth manifestly and fearfully blaspheme God, in as much as he maketh him, by affirming that of him, to be the very author of sin.* Remigius, archbishop of that Church[27] . . . hath these words to the same purpose: *God* (saith he) *by his prescience and predestination hath laid a necessity of being wicked upon no man; for if he had done this, he should have been the author of sins.*

And thus (in my judgment) doth it plainly appear that by absolute reprobation, as it is taught the upper way, God is made to be the true cause of men's sins.

Many distinctions are brought to free the supralapsarian way from this crimination, all which (me thinks) are no better than mere delusions of the simple and inconsiderate, and give no true satisfaction to the understanding.

There is (say they) a twofold decree:

1. An operative, by which God positively and efficaciously worketh a thing.
2. A permissive, by which he decreeth only to let it come to pass. If God should work sin by an operative decree, then he should be the author of sin, but not if he decree by a permissive decree to let it come to pass. And this only they say they maintain.

It is true that God hath decreed to suffer {permit} sin, for otherwise there would be none. Who can bring forth that which God will absolutely hinder? He suffered Adam to sin, leaving him in the hand of his own counsel (Ecclus. 15:14). He suffered the nations in times past to walk in their own ways, and daily doth he suffer both good and bad to fall into many sins. And this he doth, not because he stands in need of sin for the setting forth of his glory, for he hath no need of the sinful man (Ecclus. 15), but partly because he is *summus provisor*, supreme moderator of the world, and knoweth how to use that well which is ill done and to bring good out of evil, and especially for that reason which Tertullian presseth, namely, because man is made by God's own gracious constitution a free creature, undetermined in his actions till he determine himself, and therefore may not be hindered from sinning by omnipotency because God useth not to repeal his own ordinances.

2. It is true also that a permissive decree is no cause of sin, because it is merely extrinsical to the sinner and hath no influence at all upon the sin; it is an antecedent only, and

---

[25] {The reference is to Ussher's 1631 *History of Gottschalk*, the 9th-century monk who defended double predestination. Re Ussher's *History*, see Alan Ford, *James Ussher: theology, history, and politics in early-modern Ireland and England* (Oxford UP, 2007).}

[26] {Johannes Scotus Eriugena (815–77), Irish-born theologian, Greek scholar, and neoplatonist; author of *De divina praedestinatione*.}

[27] {Remigius (d. 875), archbishop of Lyon, defended Gotteschalk.}

such a one too, as being put, sin followeth not of necessity. And therefore it is fitly contradistinguished to an operative decree. And if that side would in good earnest impute no more in sinful events to the divine power than the word *permission* imports, their main conclusion would fall and the controversy between us end. But,

(1) Many of them reject this distinction utterly and will have God to decree sin *efficaciter*, with an energetic and working will. Witness that discourse of Beza wherein he averreth and laboreth to prove that God doth not only permit sin but will it also; and witness Calvin too, who hath a whole section against it, calling it a carnal distinction, invented by the flesh and . . . a mere evasion to shift off this seeming absurdity that that man is made blind *volente & jubente Deo, by God's will and commandment,* who must shortly after be punished for his blindness; he calleth it also *figmentum,* a *fiction,* and saith they do *ineptire, play the fools* that use it.

By many reasons also doth he endeavor to lay open the weakness of it, taxing those who understand such Scriptures as speak of God's smiting men with a *spirit of slumber* and giddiness, of blinding their minds, infatuating and hardening their hearts, &c., of a permission and suffering of men to be blinded and hardened: *nimis frivola est ista solutio,* saith he, *this {is} too frivolous a gloss.* In another place he blameth those that refer sin to God's prescience only—calling their speeches *argutiae, tricks and quirks,* which Scripture will not bear—and those likewise that ascribe it to God's permission, and saith, *what they bring touching the divine permission in this business will not hold water.*

2. They that admit the word *permissive* do willingly mistake it; and while (to keep off this blow) they use the word, they corrupt the meaning. For,

(1) Permission is an act of God's consequent and judiciary will, by which he punisheth men for abusing their freedom and committing such sins day by day as they might have avoided, and to which he proceedeth *lento gradu,* slowly and unwillingly, as we may see: Psal. 81:11, 12, *Israel would none of me, so I gave them up,* &c. . . . In these places and many more, we may see that persons left to themselves are sinners only—and not all sinners, but the obstinate and willful which will by no means be reclaimed. But the permission which they mean is an act of God's antecedent will, exercised about innocent men lying under no guilt at all in God's eternal consideration.

2. Permission, about whomsoever it is exercised, obstinate sinners or men considered without sin, is no more than a not-hindering of them from falling that are able to stand, and supposeth a possibility of sinning or not sinning in the parties permitted; but with them it is a withdrawing or withholding of grace needful for the avoiding of sin, and so includeth an absolute necessity of sinning; for from the withdrawing of such grace, sin must needs follow, as the fall of Dagon's house followed Samson's plucking away the pillars that were necessary for the upholding of it. Maccovius, in two disputations expounding this word "permission," circumscribes it within two acts, the first of which is a subtraction of divine assistance necessary to the preventing of sin and, having proved it by two arguments, that none may think he is alone in this, he saith that he is compassed about with a cloud of witnesses and produceth two: 1. The first of them is our reverend and learned Whitaker,[28] some of whose words alleged by him are these: *permission of sin*

---

[28] {William Whitaker (1548–95), Cambridge Calvinist theologian. See Peter Lake, *Moderate puritans and the Elizabethan Church* (Cambridge UP, 1982).}

is a privation of that aid which, being present, sin would have been hindered. The second is Pareus,[29] for saying that *that help* (which God withdrew from Adam), *being withdrawn, Adam could not so use his endowment as to persevere. And this doctrine* (saith he) *is defended by our men. . . .*

Their permission therefore of sin, being a subtraction of *necessary* grace, is equivalent to an actual, effectual procuring and working of it (for . . . *a deficient cause in things necessary is truly efficient*) and so is but a mere fig leaf to cover the foulness of their opinion.

. . .

The will is determined to an object two ways:

1. By compulsion, against the bent and inclination of it.
2. By necessity, according to the natural desire and liking of it.

God's predestination (say they) determineth the will to sin this last way, but not the first; it forceth no man to do that which he would not, but carrieth him towards that which he would. When men sin, it is true they cannot choose, and it is as true they will not choose. It followeth not, therefore, from the grounds of their doctrine that God's decree is the cause of men's sins, but their own wicked wills.

1. The ancients made no distinction between these two words, *necessity* and *compulsion*, but used them in this argument promiscuously and did deny that God did necessitate men to sin, lest they should grant him hereby to be the author of sin. . . .

. . .

2. That which necessitateth the will to sin is as truly the cause of sin as that which forceth it, because it maketh the sin to be inevitably committed which otherwise might be avoided; and therefore if the divine decree necessitates man's will to sin, it is as truly the cause of the sin as if it did enforce it.

3. That which necessitateth the will to sin is more truly the cause of sin than the will is, because it overruleth the will and beareth all the stroke, taketh from it its true liberty, by which it should be lord of itself and disposer of its own acts, and in respect of which it hath been usually called by philosophers and Fathers too . . . *a power which is under the insuperable check and control of no lord but itself.* It overruleth (I say) and maketh it become but a servile instrument, irresistibly subject to superior command and determination, and therefore is a truer cause of all such acts and sins as proceed from the will so determined than the will is. For when two causes concur to the producing of an effect, the one a principal overruling cause, the other but instrumental and wholly at the devotion of the principal, then is the effect in all reason to be imputed to the principal, which by the force of its influx and impression produceth it, rather than to the subordinate and instrumental, which is but a mere servant in the production of it. We shall find it ordinary in Scripture to ascribe the effect to the principal agent. *It is not ye that speak* (saith Christ) *but the spirit of my Father that speaketh in you* (Math. 10:20). *I labored more abundantly than they all, yet not I, but the grace of God which was in me* (Cor. 15:10). And *I live, yet not I, but Christ liveth in me,* saith St. Paul (Gal. 2:20).

[29] {David Pareus (1548–1622), Reformed theologian and Heidelberg professor, whose works James I ordered burned on political grounds.}

In these and many other places, the effect or work spoken of is taken from the instrument and given to the principal agent. Which being so, though man's will work with God's decree in the commission of sin and willeth the sin which it doth, yet seeing what the will doth, it doth by the commanding power of God's almighty decree, and so it doth that otherwise it cannot do, the sin committed cannot so rightly be ascribed to man's will, the inferior, as to God's necessitating decree, the superior cause.

4. That which maketh a man sin by way of necessity only, that is, with and not against his will, is the cause of his sin in a worse manner than that which constraineth him to sin against his will, as he which by powerful persuasions draweth a man to stab or hang or poison himself is in a grosser manner the cause of that evil and unnatural action than he that by force compelleth him, because he maketh him to consent to his own death. And so, if God's decree do not only make men sin, but sin willingly too, not only cause that they shall *malè agere, do evil*, but *malè velle, will evil*, it hath the deeper hand in the sin.

. . .

The second inconvenience is the overthrow of true religion and good government among men. To this, this opinion seemeth to tend, for these reasons:

1. Because it maketh sin to be no sin in deed, but only in opinion. We used to say *necessity hath no law*; creatures or actions in which necessity beareth sway are without law. Lions are not forbidden to prey . . . because their actions are natural and necessary; they cannot upon any admonition do otherwise. Among creatures imbued with reason and liberty, laws are given to none but such as can use their principles of reason and freedom; fools, mad men, and children are subject to no law because they have no liberty. To men that can use their liberty, laws are not given neither but in these actions which are voluntary. No man is forbidden to be hungry, thirsty, weary, sleepy, to weep, to laugh, to love, or to hate, because these actions and affections are natural and necessary; the will may govern them, but it cannot suppress them.

And so, if to deal justly, to exercise charity, &c., with their contraries, be absolutely and antecedently necessary too, whether this necessity flow from a principle within or a mover without, we are as lawless in these as in the other.

Now if necessity have no law, then actions in themselves evil, if under the dominion of absolute necessity, are transgressions of no law, and consequently no sins. For *sin is a transgression of the Law* (1 John 3:4).

This that I say hath been said long ago. For Justin Martyr, speaking against destiny, hath these words: *if it be by destiny* (that is, by absolute necessity, for that the Fathers do generally call by the name of destiny) *that men are good or bad, they are indeed neither good nor bad.* . . .

. . .

2. Because it taketh away the conscience of sin. Why should men be afraid of any sin that pleaseth or may profit them, if they must needs sin? Or what reason have they to weep and mourn when they have sinned, feeling they have not sinned truly because they sinned necessarily?

The Tragedian saith, when a man sinneth, *his destiny must bear the blame; necessity freeth him from all iniquity.*[30] Sins are either the faults of that *irresistible decree* that causeth them, or no faults at all. If either, then sorrow, fear, or any other act of repentance whatsoever may as well be spared as spent. This conceit being once drunk in, religion cannot long continue, for the affections have been the strongest planters and are the surest upholders of it in the world. *Primus in orbe deos fecit timor.*[31]

3. Because it taketh away the desert and guilt of sin. Offenses, if fatal, cannot be justly punished. The reason is because those deeds for which men are punished or rewarded must be their own, under their own power and sovereignty, but such are no fatal actions or events. Neither temporally nor eternally can sin be punished if it be absolutely necessary.

(1) Not *temporally*, as God himself hath given us to understand by that law which he prescribed to the Jews (Deut. 22:25), which was, that if a maid commit uncleanness by constraint, she should not be punished. . . . This particular law is of universal right: no just punishment can be inflicted for sin where there is no power in the party to avoid it. . . .

. . .

. . . All things whatsoever, though they seem to do somewhat, yet (by this opinion) they do indeed just nothing: the best laws restrain not one offender, the sweetest rewards promote not one virtue, the powerfulest sermons convert not one sinner, the humblest devotions divert not one calamity, the strongest endeavors in things of any nature whatsoever effect no more than would be done without them, but the necessitating, overruling decree of God doth all. And if laws do nothing, wherefore are they made? If rules of religion do nothing, why are they prescribed? If the wills of men do nothing, why are men encouraged to one thing, feared from another? . . . Who seeth not plainly whither these things tend: to nothing more than the subversion of piety and policy, religion and laws, society and government. This did the Romans see full well, and therefore they banished *mathematicos*, the teachers and abettors of destiny, out of Rome. These and the like inconveniences which come from the upper way did work so with Prosper as that he calls him no Catholic who is of this opinion: *whosoever saith that men are urged to sin and to be damned by the predestination of God, as by a fatal* (unavoidable) *necessity, he is no Catholic.*

. . .

Thus far of my reasons against the upper and more harsh and rigorous way.

The arguments by which for the present I stand convinced of the untruth even of the milder and lower way too, I will take from these five following heads: namely from

1. Pregnant testimonies of Scripture directly opposing it.
2. Some principal attributes of God not compatible with it.
3. The end of the word and sacraments, with other excellent gifts of God to men, quite thwarted by it.
4. Holy endeavors much hindered, if not wholly subverted by it.
5. Grounds of comfort (by which the conscience in distress should be relieved) which are all removed by it.

---

[30] {Seneca, *Oedipus* 1019.}

[31] {"Fear first created the gods in heaven," Lucretius, *De rerum natura* (where it is an argument for atheism).}

1. It is repugnant to plain and evident places of Scripture even *in terminis*, as will appear by these instances:

As I live, saith the Lord, I have no pleasure in the death of a sinner, but that the wicked learn from his ways and live [Ezek. 33:11].

And lest men should say, it is true God willeth not the death of a *repenting* sinner, the Lord in another place of the same prophet extendeth the proposition to them also that perish: *I have no pleasure in the death of him that dieth.*

. . .

Now if God delight not in the destruction of wicked men, certainly he never did out of his absolute pleasure seal up so many millions of men lying in the Fall under invincible damnation, for such a decreeing of men to eternal death is directly opposite to a delight in their repentance and everlasting life.

God hath shut up all in unbelief, that he might have mercy ever all [Rom 11:2]. In these the Apostle's words are two *All*s of equal extent, the one standing against the other. An *All* of unbelievers and an *All* of objects of mercy: look how many unbelievers there be, on so many hath God a will of shewing mercy. And therefore, if all men of all sorts and conditions, and every man in every sort, be an unbeliever, then is every man of every condition under mercy; and if every man be under mercy, then there is no precise antecedent will of God of shutting up some, and those the most, from all possibility of obtaining mercy. For these two . . . cannot stand together.

God so loved the world that he gave his only begotten Son, that whosoever believeth in him should not perish, &c [John 3:16]. *God loved the world,* saith the text, that is, the whole lump of mankind; therefore he did not absolutely hate the greatest part of men. Again, God loved it fallen into a gulf of sin and misery. For he so loved them as to send his Son to redeem them, and a savior presupposeth sin. He did not therefore hate the most of them lying in the Fall, for love and hatred are contrary acts in God and cannot be exercised about the same objects.

Many expositors (I know) do take *world* here in a restrained sense, and understand by it the company of the elect or the *world of believers* only, but they have little reason for it (in my opinion). For,

1. I think there can be no place of Scripture alleged wherein this word *world*, especially with the addition of *whole* . . . can be produced, where *world* doth signify only the elect or only believers, but it signifieth either all men, or at least the most men living in some certain place and at some certain time, but without distinction of good and bad; or if it be used anywhere more restrainedly, it is applied only to wicked and reprobate men, who in their affections are wedded to the world and its transitory delights, and therefore do most properly deserve this name.

. . .

. . . In the first verse there is a duty enjoined, *I will that prayers and supplications be made for all men,* and in this verse the motive is annexed, *God will have all to be saved,* as if he should have said, our charity must reach to all whom God extends his love to {1 Tim. 2:1-4}.

God out of his love will have all to be saved, and therefore in charity we must pray for all. Now in the duty, *all* signifieth every man, for no man, though wicked and profane, is to be excluded from our prayers.

Pray for them (saith our Savior) *that persecute you; and pray* (saith the Apostle here) *for kings and all that are in authority*—men in those days, though the greatest, yet the worst: the very lions, wolves, and bears of the Church. *Pray for them.* And if for them, then for any other. Thus in the duty it signifieth every man, and therefore it must have the same extent in the motive too, or else the motive doth not reach home nor is strong enough to enforce the duty.

The second answer is that God will have all to be saved with his revealed will, but millions to be damned with his secret will.[32]

But if this answer stand, then (in my apprehension) these inconveniences will follow:

1. That God's words (which are his revealed will) are not interpretations of his mind and meaning, and by consequence are not true; for the speech which is not the signification of the mind is a lie.

2. That there are two contrary wills in God, a secret will that many sons of Adam shall irrevocably be damned, and a revealed will that all the sons of Adam may be saved.

3. That one of God's wills must needs be bad, either the secret or the revealed will. For of contraries, if the one be good, the other is bad, and so of God's contrary wills. . . .

Not willing that any should perish, but that all should come to repentance, &c. [2 Pet. 3:9]. This Scripture. . . . speaketh that in plain terms which is contrary to absolute reprobation.

That which is usually replied is that the persons here spoken of are the elect only and such as truly believe: God is not willing that any of them should perish.

. . .

By all these and many other places that speak conditionally (for ought that I can see), it is clear that God forsaketh no man considered simply in the Fall till, by actual sins and continuance in them, he forsake God. Now if God reject no man from salvation in time and in deed till he cast off God, then surely he rejected no man in purpose and decree but such a one as he foresaw would reject and cast off him. For God's acts in time are regulated by his decrees before time. Ephes.1:11, *he worketh all things* (saith the Apostle) *according to the counsel of his own will,* and therefore there must be an exact conformity between them, as between . . . the rule and the thing squared thereby. By whatsoever therefore God doth in the world, we may know what he purposed to do before the world; and by his actual casting men off when they grow rebellious and impenitent, and not before, we may certainly gather that he decreed to cast them off for their foreseen rebellion and impenitency, and not before.

Besides, it is in substance all one to cast a man off indeed and to entertain a resolution to do it. Our *velle* {willing} and *facere* {doing} are all one in God's account, and the reason is because where there is a deliberate and settled will, the deed will follow if nothing hinder. Much more is God's will and deed all one, seeing his will is omnipotent and irresistible, and whatsoever he willeth directly and absolutely is certainly done when the time cometh.

Well, all these plain and express Scriptures, with the whole course and tenor of God's word, this opinion flatly contradicting[33] (though it do, perhaps, shroud itself in some dark and obscure speeches of Holy Writ), I take it to be an untruth. For what St. Austin saith

[32] {See Prynne, *God no impostor* <523>.}
[33] {"This opinion" is the subject.}

749

in another case, I may safely say in this: *shall we contradict plain places because we cannot comprehend the obscure? A few testimonies* (saith Tertullian) *must receive an exposition answerable to the current of Scripture, not contrary to it.*

This is my first reason.

Secondly, it crosseth some principal attributes of God; therefore it cannot be true. For God useth not to make decrees contrary to his own most glorious nature, and such as are incompatible with these excellent attributes by which he hath discovered part of himself to men. *Voluntas Dei semper sequitur naturam suam* is a rule among divines, *God's will always follows his nature.* The reason why is given by the Apostle (2 Tim. 2:13): *God cannot deny himself.*

Two things are here to be premised:

1. That God's chief attributes are those perfections in the manifestation of which, by acts conformable to them, God is most glorified: which are mercy, justice, truth, and holiness. For God is more honored by the exercise of these among men than by the putting forth of his unlimited power and sovereignty, as a king is more renowned among his subjects for his equity, candor, and clemency than for his dominion and authority or anything that is done only for the manifestation thereof. And there is good reason for it. For,

> (1) Power is no virtue, but holiness, mercy, justice, and truth are. Acts of power are not morally good in themselves, but are made good or evil by their concomitants. If they be accompanied with justice, mercy, &c., they are good; if otherwise, they are naught. . . .
>
> (2) Power and sovereignty may as well be shewed in barbarous and unjust actions as in their contraries. . . .

2. The second thing to be preconsidered is that justice, mercy, truth, and holiness in God are the same in nature with these virtues in men, though infinitely differing in degree (as light in the air and the sun are the same in nature, not degree), and that which is just, upright, and merciful in men is so in God too. . . .

. . .

II. Secondly, they {sublapsarians} say that God hath immutably decreed to leave the far greater part of mankind in this impotent condition irrecoverably and to afford them no power and ability sufficient to make them rise out of sin to newness of life, and this decree he executeth in time; and both these he doth out of his only will and pleasure.

. . .

1. God (say they) hath decreed to leave them without sufficient grace, and consequently under an everlasting necessity of sinning. This is the very Helen which they fight for, the main act of that absolute reprobation which with joint consent and endeavor they labor to maintain.

. . .

3. God both decreeth and executeth this leaving of men to themselves of his alone absolute will and pleasure. This is the third branch.

That they say so, witness the suffrage of our English divines:[34] *We affirm that this nonelection is founded in the most free pleasure of God.* And *that no man lying in the Fall is passed*

---

[34] [*Suffr. Brit. art.* I. *de reprob. explic. thes.* 1. {See *The collegiate suffrage* Ib.1 and Ib.error3 <*supra*>.}]

over by the mere will of God is numbered by the same divines among the heterodox positions. To this purpose also speak the ministers of the Palatinate: *the cause of reprobation is the most free and just will of God*; that God passeth over some and denieth them the grace of the Gospel, the cause is the same free pleasure of God.

God decreed to leave some in the Fall of his own good pleasure: thus the divines of Hessen. The proof of this they fetch from the execution of this decree in time: *God doth in time leave some of mankind fallen and doth not bestow upon them means necessary to believe,* &c. and *this out of his most free pleasure.* This they jointly affirm and prove it by this reason especially: all men were looked on as sinners; if sin therefore were the cause that moved God to reprobate, he should have reprobated or rejected all.

But he did not reprobate all; therefore for sin he reprobated none, but for his own pleasure, in which we must rest without seeking any other cause.

Now from these two things laid together, viz.

1. That God did bring men into a necessity of sinning,
2. That he hath left the reprobates under this necessity, it will follow that he is the author of the reprobates' sins.

1. Because . . . *the cause of a cause is the cause of its effect* (if there be a necessary subordination between the causes and the effect), whether it be a cause by acts negative or positive. But God is the chief or sole cause (by their doctrine) of that which is the necessary and immediate cause of the sins of reprobates, namely their impotency and want of supernatural grace; therefore he is (by the same doctrine) the true and proper cause of their sins.

2. Because . . . that which withdraweth or withholdeth a thing which, being present, would hinder an event, is the cause of that event; as for example he that cutteth a string in which a stone hangs is the cause of the falling of that stone, and he that withdraweth a pillar which, being put to, would uphold a house, is the true cause in men's accounts of the falling of that house. But God (by their opinion) withholdeth from reprobates that power which, being granted them, might keep them from falling into sin; therefore he becometh a true moral cause of their sins. *In whose power it is that a thing be not done, to him it is imputed when it is done*, saith Tertullian.

It will not suffice to say that God, by withholding grace from reprobates, becometh only an accidental, not a proper and direct, cause of their sins. For a cause is then only accidental in relation to the effect, when the effect is beside the intention and expectation of the cause. For example, digging in a field is then an accidental cause of the finding a bag of gold, when that event is neither expected nor intended by the husbandman in digging. But when the effect is looked for and aimed at, then the cause (though it be the cause only by withholding the impediment) is not accidental, as a pilot who withholdeth his care and skill from a ship in a storm, foreseeing that by his neglect the ship will be drowned, is not to be reputed an accidental but a direct and proper cause of the loss of this ship. This being so, it followeth that God, by this act and decree of removing and detaining grace necessary to the avoiding of sin from reprobates, not as one ignorant and careless what will or shall follow, but knowing infallibly what mischief will follow and determining precisely that which doth follow, namely, their impenitency and damnation, becometh the proper and direct cause of their sins.

Secondly, it opposeth God's mercy.

God is merciful; a part it is of his title. Exod. 34:6, *merciful and gracious*. He is mercy in the abstract; 1 Joh. 4:16, *God is love*; *a Father of mercies*, and *God of all consolations* (2 Cor.1:3), *a Savior of men* (1Tim. 4:10). And thus the Church hath always taken him to be. . . .

Two ways is God's mercy spoken of in Scripture, absolutely and comparatively.

(1) Absolutely, and so it is set out in high and stately terms. It is called *rich mercy* (Eph. 2:4), *great kindness* (Jonah 4:2), *absolute mercy* (1 Pet.1:2), *love without height or depth, length or breadth, or any dimensions,—love passing knowledge* (Eph. 3:18). So great it is that Jonah could not entreat him to punish the little, infant, harmless Ninivites with temporal death for the sins of their guilty parents (Jonah 4:11).

(2) Comparatively. With two things it is compared:
   1. His own justice,
   2. The love that dwelleth in the creature.

And is advanced above both.

1. With his own justice it is compared and advanced above it: not in its essence (for all God's excellencies are infinitely good, and one is not greater than another) but in its expressions and some things that have relation to it, particularly these:

(1) In its naturalness and dearness to God. It is said of *mercy*, it *pleaseth him* (Micah 7:18), but justice is called *his strange work, alienum a natura sua* (Esay 28:21). *He doth not afflict willingly nor grieve the children of men* (Lamentat. 3:33).

(2) In the frequent exercise of itself. He is said to be *slow to anger* but *abundant in goodness* (Exod. 34:6); mercies are bestowed every day; judgments are inflicted but now and then, sparingly, and after a long time of forbearance, when there is *no remedy* (2 Chron. 36:15). . . . God waits a great while for the conversion of sinners, as mariners do for their tide; and at last with much ado, if there be a necessity, he chideth and fighteth.

(3) In its amplitude or objects to whom it is extended, visiting the iniquities of the fathers upon the children *to the third and forth generation*, but shewing mercy *to thousands* (Exod. 20:5). In these words God implieth that his mercy reacheth farther than his justice, and that, look how much 3 or 4 come short of a thousand, so much doth his justice come short of his mercy in the exercise of it.

(4) In the occasions that move God to exercise them. It is a great matter that moveth God to punish, as we may see [Gen. 6:5-7, 12-13]: when the *wickedness of man was great in the earth, and all flesh had corrupted his way*, then God thinketh of a flood. . . .

   . . .

Thus is God's mercy advanced above his justice.

2. It is compared also with the affection of a father to his son, of a tender mother to her child, and of the most affectionate brutes to their brood, and set above them all. It goeth beyond a father's to his son (Mat. 7:11): *If you that are evil can give good gifts to your children, how much more will your heavenly Father give good things to them that ask him?* What doth this *"quanto magis"* imply but that God's love outstrips a father's! And so it doth a mother's too (Esay 49:15): *Can a woman forget her sucking child that she should not have compassion upon the son of her womb? Yea, they may forget, yet I will not forget thee.*

Women are compassionate toward their children because they are the fruit of their wombs and a part of themselves, but most indulgent are they toward those children to whom they are nurses as well as mothers, to their sucking children. And yet mothers may forget even their sucking children, but as for God, he can never forget his children

. . .

With this inviolable justice of God cannot absolute reprobation (of such especially as are commanded to believe and are called to salvation) be reconciled.

My reasons are these:

1. Because it maketh God to punish the righteous with the wicked. The supralapsarians[35] say directly in plain terms that God decreed to destruction men considered without sin, and therefore yet righteous. And the sublapsarians say as much in effect, for they say two things:

> (1) That God did lay a necessity upon every man of being born in original sin (as I have noted before).
>
> (2) That he hath determined for that sin to cast away the greatest part of mankind forever. And so they make God to do that by two acts, the one accompanying the other, which the other say he did by one.

This is so clear a case that Calvin with some others have not stickt to say that God may with as much justice determine men to hell the first way as the latter. See *Instit.* l.3.c.23.c.7, where, against those who deny that Adam fell by God's decree, he reasoneth thus: all men are made guilty of Adam's sin by God's absolute decree alone; Adam therefore sinned by this only decree. *What lets {hinders} them to grant that of one man, which they must grant of all men?* And a little after he saith: *it is too absurd that these kind patrons of God's justice should thus stumble at a straw and leap over a block.* God may with as much justice decree Adam's sin and men's damnation out of his only will and pleasure as, out of that will and pleasure, the involving of men in the guilt of the first sin and their damnation for it. That is the substance of his reasoning. . . . To these consenteth Dr. Twisse[36] and saith: *if God may ordain men to hell for Adam's sin, which is derived unto them by God's only constitution, he may as well do it absolutely, without any such constitution.* And it is most true; it is all one in substance: simply to decree the misery of an innocent man, and to involve him in a sin that he may be brought to misery.

Neither of these decrees (I take it) are just.

2. The second reason why it is against God's justice is because it maketh him to require faith in Christ of those to whom he hath precisely in his absolute purpose denied both a power to believe and a Christ to believe in.

That God bindeth reprobates to believe as well as others is the constant doctrine of the divines. . . . Mr. Perkins[37] . . . [saith] *everyone in the Church, by virtue of this commandment*

---

[35] {The text says "sublapsarians," but that is clearly an error.}

[36] {William Twisse (1578–1646), Calvinist theologian of a pronounced supralapsarian stripe; later Prolocutor of the Westminster Assembly. The quotation is from his 1632 *Vindiciae gratia*. Twisse's 1653 *The riches of God's love* is a critique of Hoard.}

[37] {William Perkins (1558–1602), Cambridge divine and leading Calvinist theologian. Hoard's note cites his *Liber de predestinatione* (presumably the *De praedestinationis modo et ordine* of 1598). Preston's "Free grace magnified" <*supra*> makes much the same argument that Hoard attributes to Perkins.}

[believe the Gospel], *is bound to believe that he is redeemed by Christ, as well the reprobates as the elect, though for a different reason: the elect, that by believing he may be saved; the reprobate, that by not believing he may be without excuse, and this out of the very purpose of God.*

But now they cannot in justice be bound to believe, if they be absolute reprobates, for three causes:

(1) Because they have no power to believe; they want it and must want it forever. God hath decreed they shall never have any to their dying day. . . . No man can be justly tied to impossible performance. . . .

(2) Because it is not God's unfeigned will they shall believe. No man will say that it is God's serious will that such a man shall live, when it is his will that he shall never have the concourse of his providence and the act of preservation. Nor can we say that God doth in good earnest will that those men should believe whom he will not furnish with necessary power to believe. It may rather be said it is God's unfeigned will they shall not believe. For it is a maxim in logic . . . *He who willeth a thing in the cause, willeth the effect that necessarily floweth from that cause.* Now if it be the certain will of God that reprobates shall in no wise believe, he cannot with reason and equity tie them to believe. For then he tieth them to an act contrary to his determinate will.

(3) Because they have no object of faith, no Christ to believe in . . . he commandeth to believe and affordeth no object to believe in; this soundeth not well. . . . If a man should command his servant to eat, and punish him for not eating—and in the meantime, fully resolve that he shall have no meat to eat—would any reasonable man say that such a man were just in the command or punishment? Change but the name and the case is the same. Again, that Christ died for reprobates (by the doctrine of absolute reprobation) is a lie, and can God justly bind men to believe a lie?

This is the second reason.

3. The third reason why the absolute decree infringeth God's justice is because it will have him to punish men for omission of an act which is made impossible to them by his own decree: not by that decree alone by which he determined to give them no power to believe, having lost it, but by that decree also by which he purposed that we should partake with Adam in his sin and be stripped of all that supernatural power which we had by God's free grant bestowed upon us in Adam before he fell.

These are the reasons which move me to think that this absolute decree is repugnant to God's justice.

Three things are usually answered.

1. That God's ways may be very just and yet seem unjust to man's erring understanding, and so is this decree, though flesh and blood will not yield it to be so.

This answer I take to be false and the contradictory to it to be true: namely, that nothing is truly just which human understanding—purged from prejudice, corrupt affections and customs—hath in all ages, places, and persons judged to be unjust. The reason is because God hath—by the light of nature and those general impressions of good and evil, honest and dishonest, just and unjust made in the hearts of men—sufficiently instructed and enabled them to judge what is just and what is not. . . . That this power is engraft in men, God himself (who best knoweth with what endowments he hath beautified his creature) hath sufficiently signified in those Scriptures where he calleth on men to be judges of the equity of his ways. *Judge I pray you between me and my vineyard* (Esay 5). *Judge, O ye house of Israel, are not my ways equal and your ways unequal?* (Ezek. 18:25). God would never put them upon the trial of reason if he had not made it able to examine them. The incarnation of the Son of God, his birth of a virgin, his dying, the resurrection of the body, and such mysteries as are peculiar to the Gospel and the proper objects of the Christian faith, God hath not offered to the trial of our understandings, but rather derideth those that presume to judge of them by reason (1 Cor. 1:20): *where is the Scribe? Where is the wise? Where is the disputer of this world?* And the reason is because, these things being supernatural and therefore not discernible by natural power, man is no competent judge of them by his natural understanding nor may adventure upon the trial and judgment of them with less danger than Uzzah looks into the Ark. . . . But of this justice of his decrees and ways, he maketh him a judge because, the common notions of just and unjust being imprinted in nature, he is able by natural reason to apprehend what is just in divine acts, as well as in his own.

2. It is answered that these decrees are set down in Scripture to be the will of God, and therefore they must needs be just. For God's will is the rule of all righteousness.

To this answer, I have these things to reply.

(1) This rule in divinity is much abused by the maintainers of absolute reprobation, and may not be admitted in their sense and meaning. For God's will is not a *rule of justice* to himself, as if things were therefore just because he willeth them and worketh them, but his justice rather is a rule of his will and works, which are expressions of his will. . . . God doth not will a thing and so make it good, but willeth it because it is in itself good antecedently and before the act of God's will about it.

. . .

(3) Absolute reprobation can be no part of God's revealed will. The reason is because it is odious to right reason and begetteth absurdities. For . . . no truth begetteth absurdities. Diverse truths are revealed in Scripture which are above but not contrary to right reason, whether they be matters of faith or life. Faith and reason, nature and Scripture, are both God's excellent gifts, and therefore, though there may be a disproportion, yet there can be no repugnancy between them. The worship which God requireth is . . . *a reasonable service* (Rom. 12:2). . . .

. . .

3. Their third answer is that God is not bound to restore men power to believe, because they once had it and have lost it through their own fault, as a master is not bound to renew his servant's stock, if he have wasted it by bad husbandry.

This answer doth not satisfy me. For I grant that God is simply and absolutely bound to no man, because he is *agens liberrimum*, a most free dispenser of his own favors, where and what and to whom he will, and no man is aforehand with God. . . .

But yet he is conditionally bound, for he hath determined and tied himself 3 ways especially:

(1) *Decernendo*, by decreeing. The Almighty is eternally subject to his own ordinances, or else he should be mutable. And therefore what gifts soever he hath decreed to men, he is bound to give them by virtue of his own decree.

(2) *Promittendo*, by promising. We use to say *promise is debt*; it is justice to perform what it was free to promise. . . . If therefore God hath made a promise of any gift or grace to men, his promise bindeth him to performance, *nam semel emissum volat irrevocabile verbum*.

(3) *Legem ferendo,* by giving men a law to keep, which without supernatural grace they can no more keep than they can eat a rock. By such a law, the supreme lawgiver bindeth himself to his people to give them such power as may enable them to keep that law, or else he becometh (as the evil servant in the parable styled him) *a hard master, reaping where he sowed not,* and the very true and proper cause of the transgression of that law. We shall find God always giving strength when he giveth a command. When he commanded the creatures to *increase and multiply,* he gave them a multiplying virtue; when Christ bade the lame man *arise, take up his bed and walk,* he put into his limbs an ability of walking; when Adam had a spiritual law given to him to obey, which without spiritual strength he could not, God gave him strength answerable to the law, as divines agree, consenting to that noted speech of St. Austin that Adam had *posse non cadere* though he never had *non posse cadere;* a power and possibility, though no necessity, of continuing in obedience.

That I may bring this home to my purpose, I say that God is bound to restore unto men power to believe, supposing these things that follow:

1. That he hath vouchsafed to enter into a new covenant of peace with men, when he needed not.
2. That in that covenant, he requireth obedience at men's hands, even at theirs that perish.
3. That he promiseth eternal life to every man, if he obey and keep the covenant.
4. That he punisheth the disobedient with everlasting death.

These particulars supposed, the most free God, who is absolutely bound to none, is engaged to give ability of believing unto men; nor can he justly, without this gift, punish the disobedient any more than a magistrate, having put out a man's eyes for an offense, can command this man with justice to read a book, and because he readeth not, put him to death.[38] . . .

. . .

. . . And it is all one for a man that hath a daughter to bestow in marriage to tell her suitor, "I will give you my daughter, if you will span the earth or touch the heavens with your finger" and to tell him plainly, "set your heart at rest; I will never bestow her upon you." For the suitor speedeth both ways alike.

And it is in circumstance a great deal worse. For it is a denial under color of the contrary, a denial joined with a scoff, a derision. . . . If God have made a decree that such men shall never believe and yet offer them heaven on condition they will believe, it may most truly be said that God doth not only deny them heaven, but deny it with a bitter derision, which is far from that candor and goodness that dwelleth in him.

And thus have I shewed the contrariety of this opinion to four principal attributes of God, which is my second general reason against it.

Thirdly, it is contrary to the use and end of God's gifts bestowed upon men, which gifts are of two sorts:

---

[38] {Hoard refers here to benefit of clergy (reading the neck-verse); see http://en.wikipedia.org/wiki/Benefit_of_clergy (accessed June 7, 2012).}

(1) Gifts of nature: our creation, sustentation, preservation, together with health, strength, beauty, wisdom, &c.

(2) Gifts of grace, which have a more immediate relation to everlasting life, and are means either of purchasing salvation or of applying it. Means of purchasing it are the coming of Christ into the world and the sacrificing of himself on the Cross. Means of applying it are the ministry of the word and sacraments, the long suffering of God, the enlightening of men's understandings, the plantation of many excellent virtues in their hearts, with many more of the like sort.

Now of these endowments of nature and grace, what the true use and end is the Scripture doth plainly and particularly shew us.

First, for gifts of nature, we find them bestowed upon all that have them for the encouraging and enabling of them to serve God and save their souls. For the Apostle saith that God (even in those times in which he suffered the gentiles to walk in their own ways and withheld from them the light of his holy word) did give unto the people of the world *rain from heaven and fruitful seasons, filling their hearts with food and gladness*, and in so doing he left not himself among them *without witness*. This implieth that therefore he gave them these good things that he might make himself known unto them and so might draw them to glorify him according to the knowledge which they had of him.

Act. 17:26, the Apostle saith directly that therefore men are made and placed in this world and appointed to their several times and dwellings *that they might seek and find God*; that is, that they might serve him and save their souls. For what is it to seek God but to serve him? And what is it to find God but to enjoy his face and favor here and in heaven? To this purpose, Prosper: *therefore* (saith he) *is every creature made and ordained especially, that mankind, which is endowed with knowledge and ability to discourse, might by the sight of so many goodly sorts of creatures and the taste of so many blessings be drawn to the love and service of his and their Maker.* And a little after he saith in the same chapter: *look of what use the Law and Prophets were to the Israelites, of the same use were the gifts of creation and providence to the gentiles.* God never intended to deal with the gentiles (as the foul-mouthed Manichees said he dealt with the Jews) to feed and fat them up with outward and more common blessings, as so many hogs and swine with husks and acorns, but to draw them up by these to an expectation of better things and a careful endeavor to please God, that so they might obtain them.

The end then of all creatures and of all created gifts bestowed upon man is subordinate to the end of man. Man's end is to glorify God upon earth and enjoy perpetual society with him in heaven, and the end of those gifts is to direct and encourage men to achieve that high and excellent end to which his Creator had appointed him.

Now for the gifts of grace, they likewise are given to all them that enjoy them for the same use and end too.

For first, Christ came into the world, not that he might be a rock of offense at which the greater part of men should stumble and fall, but to shed his blood and by that blood to purchase salvation for all mankind, not only for those who are saved but for those also who through their willful unbelief and impenitency are not saved, as we may see, Joh. 3:17: *God sent his Son* (saith the Son) *into the world, not to condemn the world, but that the world through him might be saved.* In which words the end of his coming is set down.

. . .

2. The ministry of the word and sacraments is given also and appointed for the same end, and is, in its own proper nature and use, an instrument of conveying the Spirit of regeneration to those that live under it, and to all those.

. . .

Touching the sacraments, this is also the use and end for which they were ordained. . . . *All that have been baptized into Christ* (saith the Apostle) *have been baptized into his death. All ye that have been baptized into Christ have put on Christ.* The very phrases there used shew that baptism is in its original intention an instrument of uniting men to Christ and giving them communion with him in the benefits of his death. *Except a man be born again of water* (saith our Savior) *and of the Spirit, he cannot,* &c. In which words are these two things:

1. The necessity of regeneration: *Except a man be born again.*

2. The working cause of it: efficient, the Spirit; instrumental, the sacrament of baptism, there called *water* from the outward matter of it. Baptism therefore is appointed to be a means of regeneration to all those that are baptized, and doth effect it in all who do not put an obstacle in the way to hinder it. So much doth the Apostle ascribe to baptism, and for this cause doth dignify it with this title, *the laver of regeneration* (Tit. 3:5).

I will shut up this with Act. 2:38 where Peter saith, *Repent and be baptized every one of you for the remission of sins,* plainly implying that therefore is baptism ordained to be received, that those who do receive it might have their sins remitted.

This is also God's intent in the Lord's Supper. *This is my body* (saith Christ) *and this is my blood,* in those words teaching us that in the sacrament there is an exhibition of Christ and his benefits intended on God's part, and received of those by whom no obstacle is interposed, and therefore doth the Apostle call it in express words (1 Cor. 10:16), *the communion of the body and blood of Christ,*

. . .

My fourth general reason against this absolute reprobation is it is a hindrance to piety. It is a doctrine that serveth greatly to discourage holiness and encourage profaneness. It maketh ministers (by its natural importment) negligent in their preaching, praying, and other services which are ordained of God for the eternal good of their people. It maketh people careless in hearing, reading, praying, instructing their families, examining their consciences, fasting and mourning for their sins, and all other godly exercises. In a word, it cutteth asunder the very sinews of religion and pulleth away the strongest inducements to a holy life. Therefore it is no true and wholesome doctrine.

1. It taketh away hope and fear: hope of attaining any good by godliness, fear of sustaining any hurt by wickedness, and so it taketh away two principal props of religion.

This reason may be resolved into these two branches:

1. Hope and fear uphold godliness. Were it not for these, it would come to ruin; by these are men strongly led onto virtue and withheld from vice. Hope doth . . . stir men up to begin and . . . strengthen them in the doing of any good action begun. By this hope of heaven did our Savior stir up himself to *endure the cross and despise the shame* (Heb. 12:2). By this he heartened his disciples to do and to suffer for his sake. By this have all the godly in all ages encouraged themselves in well doing. . . . Abraham left his country and kindred at God's call *because he looked for a city whose builder and maker was God*; Moses left all the

pleasure and treasures of Egypt . . . *because he saw him that was invisible, and had respect to the recompense of reward*; the martyrs endured the racks, gibbets, lions, sword, fire, with a world of other torments because *they looked for a better resurrection*. Paul endeavoreth *always to keep a clear conscience* through the hope which he had of a blessed resurrection (Act. 24:15). All the noble and heroic acts of active and passive obedience have sprung from the hope of eternal glory. Soldiers, merchants, husbandmen, all are whetted on by hope to diligence in their callings, as daily experience sheweth us. Hope, saith Aquinas . . . *conduceth to action*, and he proveth it by a twofold reason: 1. From the nature of hope's object, which is . . . *some excellent good attainable by industry*. . . . 2. From the effect of hope, which is *delectatio*, an inward pleasure, which the party that liveth under hope is attracted with by his hope. There is not any man which hath an inward contentment and satisfaction of heart in the work he hath to do but goeth on merrily. The hope of heaven therefore is a great encouragement to piety.

The fear of hell also is a strong curb to hold men in from impiety, and therefore (saith one) God hath planted in men a fear of vengeance that by it, as the ship by the rudder, the soul may be presently turned aside from any rocks, gulfs, or quicksands of sin when it is near them and may steer its course another way. . . . Nor doth fear only hinder a bad action, but it promoteth a good. It hindereth a bad action (directly) because it is . . . a flying from that evil of misery which is annexed to the evil of sin, and it promoteth a good action (accidentally) because men think that they are never so safe from the mischief which they fear as when they are exercised in such employments as tend to the getting of a contrary state. *Work out your salvation* (saith the Apostle) *with fear and tremblings*. . . .

. . .

3. Men are not willing to be employed in fruitless actions, if they know it. *I so run* (saith St. Paul) *not as uncertainly; so fight I, not as one that beateth the air, but I keep under my body and bring it into subjection, lest that by any means, when I have preached to others, I myself should be a castaway*. The meaning is, I endeavor to keep God's commandments; I fight with the temptations of the devil, the allurements of the world, and mine own corruptions; I keep my body low by watchings and fastings and other severe exercises of holy discipline. But *cui bono*? Do I all this at random, uncertain whether I shall obtain any good or prevent any mischief hereby? No, but I do this as one that is sure that by so doing I shall attain everlasting life, and without so doing, I cannot avoid eternal death—intimating in these words the common disposition of men, which is to labor where some proportionable good is to be gotten or evil prevented, otherwise to spare their heads and hands too.

To be employed in fruitless affairs is both a folly and a misery.

(1) A folly for *no man useth deliberation about things necessary*, saith the Philosopher. . . .

(2) It is a misery in the opinions of all men, as the fable of Sisyphus implieth. . . . Men will rather be exercised in high and hard employments that produce proportionable ends than pick straws, play with feathers, or with Domitian spend their times in flapping and killing of flies, or do any other easy work which endeth in nothing but air and emptiness, except they be fools or self-tormenters. And therefore when Balaam once *saw that the Lord had fully determined to bless Israel* and that all his sorceries could not effect the contrary, he presently gave over and set no more enchantment. And reason teacheth every man to do

the like. . . . And were it evident that every commonwealth had *terminum magnitudinis*, a condition appointed for it which could not be altered and a fatal period which could not be avoided, then would the king call no parliaments, use no privy counselors, make no laws and ordinances for the preventing of a kingdom's ruin or the procuring of its prosperity and continuance . . . but would follow the poet's counsel:

> *Solvite mortales animos, curisque levate,*
> *Totque supervacuis animum deplete querelis:*
> *Fata regunt orbem, certa stant omnia lege.*[39]

From these three premises laid together it followeth directly that the doctrine of an absolute decree, which determineth men's ends precisely, is no friend at all to a godly life. . . .

. . .

I conclude therefore that by this opinion (which is taught for one of God's principal truths), religion either is or may be made a very great loser, which is my fourth general reason against it.

But there are three things which are usually answered to vindicate this opinion from this crimination.

First, that many of them which believe and defend this doctrine are holy and good men, and therefore of itself it openeth no way for liberty of life, but through the wickedness of men who use to pervert the sweetest and surest truths of Scripture to their own damnation. . . .

. . .

It cannot (I confess) be denied that many of this opinion are godly men, but it is no thanks to their opinion that they are so. . . .

Secondly, it is said that, albeit this doctrine teach that men are absolutely elected or absolutely reprobated, yet,

(1) It tells no man who in particular is elected, who rejected.

(2) It teacheth that men must get the knowledge of their election by good works, and so by consequent doth rather encourage than stifle holy and honest endeavors.

For answer to the first of these: the ignorance of a man's particular state (in my judgment) doth not alter the case a jot. For he that believeth in general that many, and they the greatest company without comparison, are inevitably ordained to destruction and a few others to salvation is able, out of these two general propositions, to make these particular conclusions and to reason thus with himself: either I am absolutely chosen to grace and glory or absolutely cast off from both. If I be chosen, I must of necessity believe and be saved; if I be cast off, I must as necessarily not believe and be damned. What need I therefore take thought either way about means or end? . . . I have my supersedeas;[40] I may take mine ease and so I will; enough it is for me to sit down and wait what God will do unto me. Thus (it is likely) did Tiberius reason with himself. For Suetonius reports of him

---

[39] {"O mortals, relax, banish your cares, and rid your mind of all this vain complaint! Fate rules the world, all things stand according to its immutable laws." (Manilius, *Astronomica*)}

[40] {Latin for "you shall desist," a writ by a higher court commanding a lower court not to enforce or proceed with a judgment or sentence.}

that he was *the more negligent in religion because he was fully persuaded that all things came to pass by destiny.* . . .

. . .

I come now to my last reason against it, drawn from the uncomfortableness of it: it is a doctrine full of desperation both to them which stand and to those that are fallen, to men out of temptation and to men in temptation.

It leadeth into {and} leaveth in temptation.

And therefore can be no doctrine of God's word, for that is ἐυαγγέλιον, good news to men, a storehouse of sweet consolations for us in our *turbidis & lucidis intervallis*, in our best and worse conditions and changes. *These things are written* (saith the Apostle) *that by patience and comfort of the Scriptures we might have hope*: implying that therefore was the word written and left to the Church, that by the comforts comprised in it those poor souls that look toward heaven might never want in any changes or chances of this mortal life a sweet gale of hope to refresh them and to carry-on their ship full merrily toward the haven.

1. First this doctrine leadeth men into temptation, and into such a one, too, as is as sharp and dangerous as any the tempter hath. The devil can easily persuade a man that maketh absolute reprobation a part of his creed that he is one of those absolute reprobates, because there are far more absolute reprobates (even a hundred for one) than absolute chosen ones, and a man hath a great deal more reason to think that he is one of the most than one of the fewest, one of the huge multitude of inevitable castaways than one of that little flock for whom God hath precisely prepared a kingdom. Such a man is not only capable of but framed and fashioned by his opinion for this suggestion, which is a very sore one, if we may believe Calvin, Bucer, and Zanchius. Calvin telleth us that the *devil cannot assault a believer with a temptation more dangerous*. And a little after he saith that it is so much the deadlier by how much commoner it is than any other.

So ordinary is this temptation that *he which is at all times free from it is a rare man* (we are to conceive that he speaketh of those who hold absolute reprobation); and so dangerous it is that if it get strength, he which is under it is either *miserably tormented or mightily astonished*. And a little after he saith again: *he that will not wrack his soul must avoid this rock.* . . .

. . .

But grounds convincing and satisfying, a minister that maintaineth absolute reprobation hath not in store. . . . All he can say is, be of good comfort; you are a believer, a truly repenting sinner; therefore no reprobate; for faith and repentance are infallible fruits of election, and arguments of a state contrary to what you fear. But this the tempted will deny. He will say that he is no believer, &c., and how will the minister convince him that he is? He must prove to him by the outward acts of faith and repentance (for they only are apparent to him) that he doth repent and believe.

But this proof is not demonstrative nor doth convince, because . . . the external acts of faith, repentance, or any other grace may be counterfeited. The devil may seem to be an angel of light. . . .

Which being so, I say that a minister cannot, by the outward acts and fruits of faith and repentance which he seeth come from him, make evident to the tempted (to the silencing of all replies) that he is without doubt a true believer and repenting sinner and consequently no reprobate. For still the tempted may say, you may be deceived in me, for you cannot see anything more in me than hath been seen in many a reprobate. And if this be all you can say to prove me to be none, I am not satisfied. I may be a reprobate. Nay, I am a reprobate, and you are but a miserable comforter, a physician of no value.

This that I say, Piscator doth confess ingenuously in *Disput. de Praed. contra Scharf-mann*, thes. 85, where he saith,

1. That no comfort can be possibly instilled into the souls of reprobates afflicted with this horrible temptation; from whence it followeth that the far greatest part of men, even an hundred for one, must bear their burden . . . as well as they can. The Gospel is not able to afford them any solid comfort.

2. That the elect being in this condition may indeed be comforted, but it must be by their sense of sin and their desire to be freed of it by Christ: which proofs are but probable to the best, and to a man in temptation no proofs at all; and consequently either no comforts or very small ones.

Text: EEBO (STC [2nd ed.] / 13534)

[Samuel Hoard], *Gods love to mankind manifested, by disproving his absolute decree for their damnation* (London, 1633), A3r–A4v, 1–5, 8–21, 24–27, 30–36, 38–40, 44–51, 55–61, 66–73, 79–82, 84–85, 91–92, 95–101, 109–10.

THOMAS LAURENCE
(1597/58–1657)

The son of a Dorset clergyman, Laurence matriculated at Balliol in 1615; two years later, he was elected a fellow of All Souls. He received his BA in 1618, his MA in 1621. In 1625, William Herbert—the Earl of Pembroke and also Chancellor of Oxford—made Laurence his chaplain. Laurence took his BD in 1629 and was appointed soon thereafter as a canon of Lichfield Cathedral and chaplain to Charles I. His Act-Sunday sermon of the same year drew down accusations of popery from John Prideaux, Oxford's staunchly Calvinist regius professor of divinity, for its claim that the clergy in Convocation alone had authority to define doctrine—a pointed, if implicit, critique of the Commons' campaign to impose Calvinism by statute.[1] In 1633 Laurence received his DD and, in the footsteps of George Herbert, the parsonage at Bemerton—a gift of Philip Herbert, the then Earl of Pembroke. Four years later, Laurence also took on the mastership of Balliol, in 1638 assuming the further post of Lady Margaret professor of divinity—both, in all likelihood, with Laud's support. A decade later, however, the case had altered. The new regime had no use for a high churchman like Laurence, but a parliamentary officer who owed his release from a royalist prison to Laurence's good offices got him the chaplaincy of Colne in Huntingdonshire, where he died in 1657.

During his years at Oxford, Laurence apparently did a good deal of scholarly writing, but only a list of titles survives. His published works amount to three sermons, all from the mid-1630s: among them, the Act-Sunday sermon reprinted below, preached to the gathered University and visiting dignitaries on the Sunday prior to the commencement solemnities. The sermon beautifully exemplifies Peter Lake's "Laudian style" in its hieratic

---

[1] On this campaign, see <399>; also Shuger, *Censorship* 264–72. There is, it should be noted, nothing *inherently* Laudian about this position; at Dort, it was the Calvinists who maintained that ecclesiastical synods had exclusive jurisdiction over doctrine, while the Arminians argued for the coordinate role of the civil magistrate (Hales 3:59, 73, 90).

sacerdotalism, its vision of the material church as the house of God and locus of divine presence, its Longinian aesthetics of sacral grandeur and numinous dread,[2] its insistence on "the mystery which sheathed and surrounded the divine will and the divine presence in the world," and the need to defend that mystery "from the codifying rationalism of puritan predestinarian speculation" (184). One might also note the characteristically Laudian focus on the majesty of God (in contrast to Calvinism's attention to the kinetics of personal salvation) and the equally Laudian privileging of simple moral goodness over conspicuous godliness. Laurence's critique of Protestant scholasticism bears the same ideological markings, although the point need not be a narrowly partisan one, given that Laurence is preaching to newly minted university graduates, many of whom would soon find themselves in a country parish. Celebrated Calvinist preachers like Adams and Sibbes knew as well as Laurence that God desired to save people, not puzzle them with "needless speculation" <771>. Laurence, in turn, seems to have known the allure of "cobweb divinity" as intimately as any Calvinist, the fatal attraction betrayed by his extraordinary, albeit brief, fascination with the theological implications of vomit.[3]

SOURCES: *ODNB*; *The works of John Hales*, 3 vols. (Glasgow, 1765); Peter Lake, "The Laudian style: order, uniformity, and the pursuit of the beauty of holiness in the 1630s," in *The early Stuart Church, 1603–1642*, ed. Kenneth Fincham (Stanford UP, 1993), 161–86.

[2] Note the similar aesthetics of Sydenham's 1633 sermon <*supra*>.
[3] No, I will not give the page number. Read the sermon.

THOMAS LAURENCE

The duty of the laity and privilege of the clergy. Two sermons.
The first preached at St. Mary's in Oxford, July 13, 1634, being Act-Sunday
Published 1635

And the people stood afar off, and Moses drew near unto the thick darkness, where God was.
Exod. 20:21

GOD made man, placed him in Eden, spake to him, in the second of Genesis, and man was not afraid. God came in a *walking voice* in the third of Genesis, and man was afraid, because he had not sinned in the second chapter and had sinned in the third. For where no sin is, there is no fear. *Perfect love,* saith S. John, *casteth out fear,* which therefore is not fit company for heaven because love is perfect there. The happiness of that place consists in the vision of God, *in whose presence is the fullness of joy,* saith David: which therefore *the souls under the altar,* as S. John, or *in their chambers,* as Esdras speaks, long to see, saying *when cometh the fruit of our reward?* . . . And who desires what he trembles at, or joys in that he fears? But tis otherwise here. In heaven we shall be ravished with God, not afraid of him. In earth, we are afraid of any messenger from heaven. An angel appeared to Gideon, and he was afraid; an angel appeared to Manoah, and he was afraid; an angel appeared to the shepherds, & these were afraid; an angel appeared to the Maries, and they were afraid. Afraid all of those angels, which brought the message of joy. For because, ever since an angel guarded Paradise with a drawn sword, we have deserved no good news from above. We conceive no other design of such messengers but to strike. And what shall Israel fear from God himself, if these imagined no less than death from the sight of an angel? That glorious just Lord cannot bespeak my damnable vileness but in thunder; and therefore, if Moses intend they shall live to keep the Law, Moses himself must deliver the Law; God must speak no more *lest they die* (v. 19). He comforted them indeed, and said *fear not* (v. 20), which is all one as if he should say, sin not; for while they were guilty of sin, they must be subject to fear. Bounds were defined, unto which they came not, and yet they came too near. God's command removes them far, and their own fear removes them farther: *And the people stood afar.*

The words represent the duty of the laity in Israel the people, and the privilege of the clergy in Moses their priest.[1] So the Holy Ghost esteemed him, *Moses and Aaron among*

---

[1] {On the partly sacerdotal character of the kingly office in Stuart political thought, see Debora Shuger,

the priests (Psal. 99:6) . . . so he esteemed himself: sanctifying the assembly, dedicating the tabernacles, hallowing the vessels, offering sacrifice, consecrating Aaron with his sons, and officiating both for the scepter and miter too, the prince and the priest, to shew that there is no natural repugnancy between the ephod and the maze {*sic, lege* mace?}, the tribunal and the altar, but that both thrive the better for the vicinity of each other, as the vine helps the elm and by this neighborhood climbs the higher.

The duty of the laity requires,

1. An obsequious attention to God: *the people stood.*
2. An humble distance from God: *the people stood afar off.*

The privilege of the clergy discovers,

1. The approximation[2] or immediateness of their access: *Moses drew near.*
2. The limitation of this approximation: *Moses drew near unto the thick darkness.*
3. The condition of this limitation: *Moses drew near unto the thick darkness where God was.*

1. *Vox vagina sensus*: language is the sheath of sense, saith the Cardinal, and words are the attire of the mind, saith the Orator. He therefore whose tongue is too big for his heart, that speaks more than he thinks, cases a needle in a scabbard and presents little David in great Goliath's armor, or, rather, arrays a child with the clothes of a giant and so invests him not with a suit but estates in a house. God is no friend to the hypocrisy of compliment, and therefore in Scripture ever means more than he speaks: *the words of the Lord are pure words, as silver tried seven times in the fire*, saith the Psalmist; calcined and sublimated from this dross. For he is a God of truths, not of varnishes; of realities, not of shadows. He hates that mouth which belies the mind, and likes men on earth best when they resemble the saints in heaven, where souls commerce *per verbum mentis*, without tongues; and thoughts are seen without the mediation of words. Tis so in my text, where a syllable of God's signifies more than a volume of man's, a word of his than a library of mine; and the people's standing here comprehends as much as the people should do, and much more indeed than they would.

First, standing is a posture of respect. We kneel and stand to our superiors. Kneel to shew our subjection, and stand to shew our obedience: that we are ready to execute what these are to command. *Seest thou a man diligent in his business; he shall stand before kings* (Prov. 22:29); and although *the angels turned their faces to Sodom, Abraham stood yet before the Lord* (Gen. 18:22). Standing and kneeling then become inferiors; sitting doth not. *The Lord said to my Lord, sit thou at my right hand*: there's an equality of nature betwixt the Father and the Son, and therefore one sits by the other (Psal. 110:11). *And when the son of man shall sit on the throne of his glory, then shall ye also sit upon twelve thrones, judging the twelve tribes of Israel*: there's an equality of grace or favor betwixt the judge and his assessors,[3] & therefore these have thrones together (Matt. 19:18). So that those

---

Political theologies in Shakespeare's England (Palgrave, 2001), 59–60; also the Buckeridge reading in this volume <*supra*>.}

[2] {proximity, nearness}

[3] {assessor (*OED*): One who sits as assistant or adviser to a judge or magistrate; *esp.* a skilled assistant competent to advise on technical points of law}

antipodes[4] which tread cross to the world, which fast at the birth of our Savior and feast at his Passion; which will not say "Christmas," and yet will call a Christian "Demas"; which sit at the altar because we kneel, say not with the Syro-phoenician, *Lord, I am not worthy to eat the crumbs under thy table*, but Lord, I am worth to sit at thy table; I am as good as thyself.

Standing then is a posture of respect, and respect is a preparative to attention, for no man listens to what he scorns. Lydia's affection must be warmed before she can attend; regard S. Paul she must, before she can hear him; *when God shall open her heart*, then will she open her ears (Act. 16:14). Nor wonder I, the conversions of this Apostle were so many, seeing his honors were so great. Like that Roman commander, he conquered as many nations as he saw; wheresoever he came, his Savior followed him, and therefore his stay was not so long anywhere, his travels more frequent and farther than those of others: *in labors more abundant he was, and in journeying often* (2 Cor. 11:23, 26). For God blessed him with such as would pull out their own eyes in his behalf: their own eyes, not his. Such as had humility enough to learn, had not pride enough to teach the apostle. Such as believed his eyes so much that they thought they had no use of their own (Galat. 4:15). *Hear therefore the word of the Lord, ye that tremble at this word* (Isa. 66:5), as if none were fit to hear but such; the rest not worth the looking after, as indeed they are not. For *to him will I look that trembleth at my word*: such I will look after, and I will not look after those that are not such. . . .

2. Standing is a posture of attention, the posture of hearers; *when Ezra opened the Law, all the people stood up* (Neh. 8:5). There is no duty oftener enjoined than this. . . . *give ear, and come unto me; hearken, and your soul shall live.* Heaven is the reward of your attention, hell of your scorn. . . . *Behold I stand at the door and knock; if any man hear my voice and open the door, I will come in.* "Behold," because he knocks not often; for he that stands is going away, especially if he stand at the door without a shelter, if he stand only to knock; and not to knock neither, after he is slighted; this were to awake the deaf or speak to the dumb (Apocal. 3:20).

But Lord, who hath believed our report, or to whom hath the arm of the Lord been revealed? Where are those throngs now, and presses upon Christ? Where is that early coming in the Gospel? how soon are we up to sport, and how late to pray? how small in many places is the gleaning of their churches to the vintage of their cities? how low is the ebb in those courts of the Lord, when tis full sea in their streets? how do we *look the priest in the face, and cast his words behind our backs*, as David complains? his ordinary entertainment resembling that of music, which serves only to fill our ears when discourse is done. Good women there were which consecrated their looking-glasses to the Tabernacle (Exod. 38:8), and will ye know how ye may do so now? By . . . coming hither with half a dress {rather} than losing half a prayer. Wherefore *libera {me} ab homine malo*, saith David; that is á *meipso*, saith S. Aug., deliver me from myself, ô God, that I may come hither . . . from my malicious self, when an injury heats my blood; and from my wanton self, when the assembly discloses a beauty, a well-attired piece of handsome clay; from my intemperate self, when the thought of Egypt brings on me a loathing of Canaan; and from my profane self, when some incarnate Satan assails my attention by whispering in his vanities at my ears and clothing his atheism with the Scripture.

---

[4] {The sense is "contrarian," although literally refers to inhabitants of the Southern Hemisphere, whom the ancients sometimes imagined as walking upside down. Laurence's *antipodes*, however, are puritans.}

3. Standing is a posture of action, the posture of servants: *Gehazi went in and stood before his master*, the readier therefore to come or go at his command (2 Reg. 5:25). Practice is the life of attention, and he that hears but does not is a monster in religion that hath two ears and no hands. The Jews were taught this by their meats, and the ceremonial law was but a shadow of the moral. What poisonous temper in the hare? What dangerous nourishment in the swine? Why might they not as freely feed on the rabbit as the sheep? Or what philosophy makes the goat more wholesome than the crab or the swan? *He shewed by this, O man, what is good, and what the Lord requires of thee*: thy effeminateness is forbidden in the hare, which changeth his sex, as Gesner writes, and is at several times both he and she; and thy laziness in the down of the swan. Thy oppression is interdicted in the eagle, and thy drunkenness in the swine. Thy gluttons prey on cormorants, and thy night-walkers on owls. For God instructed them what they should do by what they might eat, and every prohibited meat was a menace against sin. Or lest this light should seem too dim, he describes the same with the rays of the sun: *he that lifteth not his eyes to idols, defileth not his neighbor's wife, spoileth none by violence, gives not upon usury, restoreth the pledge, bestows his bread on the hungry, walketh in my statutes, he shall surely live*. He is not just that hath faith, unless he have works too, nor doth the Gospel save without the Law (Ezek. 18:6-8). 'Tis S. Aug{ustine's} speech of the ancient prophets: *illorum non tantum linguam, sed vitam fuisse propheticam*; that they prophesied as well by their lives as their writings, and their six days contain'd a commentary on the seventh. For if I cry *the Temple of the Lord*, but obey not the Lord of the Temple . . . if I am only sermon-sick while I am rocked in a church-tempest abroad and presently recover again as soon as I lie at hull at home; if *my voice be Jacob's*, but *my hands Esau's*, and I wear Elias' mantle without his spirit; if I acknowledge God with my tongue but deny him in my life; profess a Christian and live a pagan; go from church to a brothelhouse; join the spirit of chastity and the spirit of whoredoms together, the holy and unholy Ghost, Christ and Belial, *the Temple of God and the temple of devils*; if I run to heaven one day, to hell six, and contradict the truth of my sermons by the error of my life, what the prophet said to Amaziah, the priest may say to me: *I know that the Lord hath determined to destroy thee because thou hast done this thing, and has not hearkened to my counsel* (2 Chron. 25:16).

Nevertheless, when the *Son of man shall come, will he find faith on earth*, saith our Savior (Luc. 18:8)? Yes, faith enough, but no works. Faith that removes mountains, that pulls down churches, and clothes not the poor; faith that hates idols and loves sacrilege, a tun of faith for a dram of charity. *Shew me thy faith by thy works*, saith S. James. Not so, my works must be judged by my faith; *to the pure all things are pure*, and if God see my faith, he is not angry with my sins; my tree must be esteemed by the leaves, not by the fruit; and my watch must rule the sun. Heretics there were, styled by the Church *praedestinati*, which presumed upon a fatality of their election and would needs have heaven promised without the condition of works, for they dreamt of a conveyance without a proviso and thought themselves able to ascend Jacob's ladder without climbing by the rounds. But such as make themselves of God's council are usually none of his friends. He will profess himself a stranger to these intruders, and a friend to those which observed their distance. To those that said *we have eaten with thee, I know you not*; but such as said, *when saw we thee hungry and fed thee, or thirsty and gave thee drink? Come ye blessed of my Father, inherit a kingdom*. These which pretended least acquaintance were those only which observed him (Matt. 25:34). *Where is the wise? where is the scribe? where is the disputer of this world?* (1 Cor. 1:20). Surely neither in heaven, nor here. The fear of God was amongst these; this fear wrought respect; this respect, attention; this attention, obedience: and all this because they more observed what God said than searched what he was. They were near enough to receive his command, but not near enough to pry into his nature; near enough to obey, but not near enough to see him. God commanded them *to stand off*, and therefore *they stood afar off*—their humble distance from God, and my second general.

2. God was unwilling the people should forget themselves and therefore shadowed forth this duty so often: in Paradise, by permitting Adam the tree of life and interdicting the tree of knowledge to shew he rather desires to make us saints than rabbis or doctors. In the wilderness, Moses was hardly permitted a glimpse or dawning of his glory, & what Red Sea hast thou divided, what multitudes hast thou fed from heaven or water'd out of a rock that thou shouldst look as high as he? At the giving of the Law, that king-priest only entered the clouds. Aaron came almost to it, the Elders farther off, and at a remoter site, the people. Limits are defined, and if they transgress these, if they *break through to gaze on God, they must die.* . . . In the service of the tabernacle, who were conversant but the Levites? . . . In the disposal {arrangement} of the tabernacle, the laity had a distinct court from the priests; as anciently in the church, the chancel was appropriated to the clergy, the rest to the people. In the building of the Temple, the door into the oracle was but a fifth part of the wall . . . that into the Sanctum a fourth, to shew that more come into the church than unto the ark. Many tread the courts of the Lord that were never admitted to his council. . . . In the Law communicated to all; the Cabala . . . from God to Moses only, and from Moses only to the Seventy. For although Mirandula tell us that Sixtus IV procured the translation of this, and call God to witness that he read there the mysteries of our faith . . . yet we know from Esdras what a concealment this Cabala was. Under what hieroglyphics the Trinity and the Resurrection and the life to come and the Messiah lay buried under the Law. How general and implicit the faith of S. Peter and Martha and the Eunuch . . . which occasioned that hesitancy at Ephesus concerning the reality of the Holy Ghost . . . that irresolution of the apostles about the Passion and the Resurrection . . . that design of all upon the external glory of a temporal dominion, admitting no sovereignty of God unless he change his cross into a throne, his reed into a scepter. In the glory of our Savior on the Mount where Moses and Elias attended him, in his bloody sweat in the Garden where an angel comforted him—beyond the ken of the multitude. . . . In their diet, *milk, and not meat*: easy positive divinity. In their appellations, *lambs and sheep*, the inapprehensivest creatures of any. *Children and babes*, which move not a foot but by the direction of a hand, and sooner cry for what offends than what profits them. . . . In the essential measure of faith: no larger than a verse in S. Paul's creed: *if thou confess with thy mouth the Lord Jesus, and believe with thy heart that God raised him from the dead, thou shalt be saved.*[5] No larger than a verse in S. John's: *this is life eternal, that they might know thee, the only true God, and whom thou has sent, Jesus Christ.* Nor much larger in that of all the apostles,[6] being dilated thus in that *foundation of faith*, as Cyril of Jerusalem, Epiphanius, and S. Ambrose call it. *In futurae praedicationis normam*, saith S. Aug., as the

---

[5] {So too Laud in his *Conference with Fisher* (in *Works* 2:362, 402–3); for the contrary position, see Everard <*supra*>.}

[6] {i.e., in the Apostles' Creed}

compass and square of their sermons, that all might beat those paths to heaven easier by tracing the same steps; and teach but one, though they went several ways; for the Apostles' is but an exposition of S. Paul's and S. John's creed; the Nicene and Athanasian but a paraphrase on this. . . . the same faith in weight and substance, though not in bulk or size, as tis the same piece in a bullet and a sheet of gold: that being throng'd into a mold which, beaten and expanded by an artificer, may anon cover and gild all the leaves of my Bible.

But ô the unnatural chemistry of this age! how infinite are the extractions from this simple, this single breviary? What seas are derived from this drop? . . . How soon hath a vapor . . . raged into a cloud, and this cloud grown too big for heaven? How have some resolved . . . all those disputes which disquiet the world into this quintessence, this spirit of faith; and thence, as if that catechism in our liturgy were not long enough to reach from earth to heaven, have cast into the mint of the Church the dross of their own fancies, and lead their *catechumeni* through all the Roman and the Belgic controversies as disquisition of necessary belief, giving way to the saucy liberty of their tongues and pens against all our ecclesiastical hierarchies for interdicting such polemical discourses in popular assemblies (which yet is no more than Constantine in Eusebius did). . . . and forsaking the waters of Siloe that mildly and generally flow in the radical {fundamental} doctrines of our Church, *rejoice* only *in Rezin and Remaliah's son*, which always angle in the troubled waters of Jewry {Isa. 8:6}. . . . Nay, have they not charged her wisdom with sloth and apostasy too because she will not impose an absolute faith upon the airy projections of their distempered brains, because themselves cannot be believed in as well as God, because she thinks heaven was made for some besides; because she fears their clamorous zeal might at length importune such assemblies for the anathematization of *ego currit* and *tu currit*, like those at the end of Lombard,[7] if a synod should be called for such. But I must tell them that, as S. Paul saith, *there is but one God*, so he saith, *there is but one faith too.* . . . nor can there be any other way to heaven than what hath been trodden from the apostles: *neither circumcision, nor uncircumcision, but a new creature*, saith the Doctor of the gentiles. Neither controversy nor school-divinity, but a new life, say I. God intends not to lay traps for my soul in such niceties as these, nor will I make that yoke heavy which himself made easy & light. It will not be said at the last assize, *come ye blessed*, for ye have disputed, for ye have preached, for ye have understood well; but *I was naked, & ye clothed me; I was hungry, and ye fed me.* . . . I shall not be judged by my writings but by my works. Devotion will then turn the scale against learning; an ounce of goodness outweighs a pound of talk. And I must tell them again, if they direct to those happy regions, they have discovered a northwest passage thither, a passage concealed from the ancient, a passage our Savior and S. Paul knew not. . . . And when the Twelve demand, *Lord, wilt thou at this time restore the kingdom to Israel?* he returns no resolution, but a check: come you may to that kingdom above, and yet never come to such curiosity below. A saving voyage may be made by the merchandise of ivory and gold, without freighting your vessels thus with apes and peacocks. I will not tell you because *it is not for you to know* (Act. 1:7). But when the young

---

[7] {These trivial grammatical lapses (literally, "I runs" and "you runs") were condemned as heretical errors at Oxford in 1276 by Archbishop Robert Kilwarby. See J. M. H. Thijssen, "What really happened on 7 March 1277? Bishop Tempier's condemnation and its institutional context," in *Texts and contexts in ancient and medieval science*, ed. Edith Sylla and Michael McVaugh (Brill, 1997), 109.}

man enquired, *What shall I do that I may have eternal life* . . . how plain then, how gently doth he run? No clouds nor eclipse there, but he writes his mind with the light of the heavens: *if thou wilt enter into life, keep the commandments. He saith unto him, which? Jesus said unto him, these.* He answers to necessary queries; to impertinent he answers not: speaks nothing but mists and storms when their demands are curious, nothing but light & smiles when their demands are requisite. He that would not shew his disciples when they should be delivered will shew this stranger how he may be saved (Matt. 19:17-8). And when the Apostle is pressed with some cobweb divinity . . . he only controls {checks} their folly: ô man, who art thou that *repliest against God?* (Rom. 9:20); bids them be amazed and wonder: ô the depth of the wisdom and knowledge of *God.* . . . God requires more practice than most men have, less knowledge than most men brag of. . . . For his part, therefore, he'll not distract them with any needless speculations, his intent being not to puzzle but to *save them.* . . . I am content to be saved, and desire others should be so too, and therefore I say to my hearers, *turn from your evil ways, for why will ye die, ô ye house of Israel?* To myself, ô wretched man that I am, who shall deliver me from this body of sin? To priest and people, *come let us walk,* not let us discourse, *in the light of the Lord.* To God, for all: *turn us ô Lord, so shall we be turned.* . . . *draw us too, so shall we run after thee.* Do not lead us, do not follow our humors; bring us not that easy speculative way we like (for then we shall never come to thee), but draw us that hard, that narrow way, the way of obedience and practice. *Who is sufficient for these things,* saith S. Paul? . . . Why should my ignorance presume farther than Aaron did, or think to view the face of God, when Moses saw only his hinder parts; to gaze on this sun, when he saw nothing but a cloud? *And Moses drew near unto the thick darkness where God was.*

3. Moses as an extraordinary priest . . . discharged the parts of an agent, and did both carry and recarry betwixt earth and heaven. A Master of Requests[8] he was to God: the people's petitions were his lading up. An ambassador he was from God: the Lord's commands were his carriage down; as our Savior prayed on the Mount and preached in the villages of Jewry.

1. The approximation, therefore, or immediateness of the priests' access depends in the first place upon their employment upward. They have his ears before the rest because they are the mouths of the rest, and designed from God to commence the suits of the people. For, although *the eyes of the Lord are over the righteous . . . and his ears are open to their prayers* wheresoever those prayers are made—every faithful soul in the world being a priest, every angle of the world a temple & an altar—yet are his ears more open, his eyes more attent to the prayers here, & a collect from the priest's mouth goes further than a liturgy from the people's—as the blessing of any is good, but the blessing of my parents is better. . . . His presence is indeed everywhere, but his residence especially there; and though his essence be diffused through heaven and earth in Jeremy, his glory, in Exodus, is peculiar to the Tabernacle. The ladder which Jacob saw, that ascent & descent of angels, that thoroughfare betwixt earth and heaven, was at Bethel, the house of God; and in Jewry, the propitiatory or mercy-seat was only in the Temple, which occasioned that general concourse thither under any pressure or calamity—men using us, as fruit trees are used by us, which we cudgel in the sun and run to for shelter in a storm. *Pray for me,* saith

---

[8] {On the Court of Requests, see the 1633 *Survey of London* <supra>.}

Pharaoh to Moses. *Pray for me*, saith Simon Magus to the apostles. *Let them pray over him*, saith S. James. Though I may, and must, come by myself, my coming by these is more effectual, as my suit is less gracious to my prince from ordinary hands than his secretaries' because the way is by such mediators as best know how to bespeak the king, and when.

2. And as the approximation or immediateness of the priests' access depends, in the first place, upon their employment upwards, so doth it, in the second, upon their employment downwards, according to their double aspect on God and the people. They are his stewards. So S. Paul calls them in one place: stewards to discharge us of our service, to lock heaven against us; and stewards to admit us into service again, to unlock heaven for us: *the gates of hell shall not prevail against such as keep these keys of heaven . . .* and what need I a safer conduct, a surer warrant than this. They are his ambassadors,[9] so S. Paul calls them . . . and by whom may we expect the king's mind, if not by the king's ambassador? . . . They are his *friends*, so our Savior calls them . . . *the Lord doth nothing which he reveals not to such*, saith the Holy Ghost; that is, nothing which concerns them or others to know. Servants are strangers to their lord's actions, friends are not; servants must not interpret their counsels, friends may. I wish from my heart, as Moses did, *that all the Lord's people were prophets, and that the Lord would pour out his spirit upon them*. But I wish they would forbear prying into the ark with the Bethshemites till then; that all would not preach which can speak, and, because S. Paul calls every family a church, would not turn every table's end into a pulpit . . . that the clew[10] of predestination might not be reel'd up at the spindle nor the decrees of God unraveled at the loom. . . . that the people would not presume beyond their bounds *least the Lord break forth upon them. . . . Ye take too much upon you, ye sons of Reuben; wherefore get ye out of the Sanctuary, for ye have trespassed, neither shall it be for your honor from the Lord* (2 Chron. 26:18).

And if now any say of Jerusalem, as formerly Edom did, *down with it, down with it, even to the ground*, I must pray against this atheism as Moses did: *arise ô Lord, into thy resting place, thou and the ark of thy strength*. Thou hast said, *this shall be thy rest forever*, and, ô Lord, let it ever be so. Twas the sacrilegious zeal of those times: what use have we of churchmen now? who ever wore a cope for armor, or in a pitched field exchanged a headpiece for a miter? And my reply shall be that of Moses to the rebels: *seemeth it a small thing unto you, that the God of Israel hath separated these from the congregation of Israel to bring them near to himself*[11] . . . .There is use of these while there are prayers to be heard or sins to be pardoned or God to be served or men to be saved. . . . *My father, my father, the chariot of Israel and the horsemen thereof*, saith Elisha to Elijah. Lay devotions are the infantry, the foot; but the strength of the battle, the chariots & the horse, are the orisons of the clergy. The land was better secured by this man of peace than those men of war, nor was it Joshua's hand that overcame Amalek, but Moses' prayer: *the day of the Lord*, saith the Prophet, *is darkness*; all we see of him being evening and night—a perception only that we cannot see him. And who walks safely in the dark without guidance of a light? For

[9] {For the priest-as-ambassador trope, see Donne's "To Mr. Tilman after he had taken Orders."}

[10] {ball of yarn or thread}

[11] {Num. 16:1-35: the rebellion of Korah against the emergent sacerdotalism of Moses and Aaron, Korah protesting to the other two, "Ye take too much upon you, seeing all the congregation are holy, every one of them, and the Lord is among them: wherefore then lift ye up yourselves above the congregation of the Lord?" (AV).}

how gloomy a midnight is this to thee, that was a *thick darkness* to Moses? The limitation of his access, and my fourth general.

4. The Lord concealed not himself only from Moses in *thick darkness*, but threatened also in lightning and thunder; and although he climbed the Mount by especial command—and that to receive the Law by his appointment (and the Cabala or exposition, as the rabbis say), to dispense such fundamental truths on earth which might convey them to heaven, being entertained as an ambassador extraordinary by the joint commission of God and the people—rated {rebuked} him yet out of a tempest too, Moses being rapt out of himself by the assault of a sudden and impetuous wind, for nothing so much hinders the sight and apprehension as this. The Lord admits him not into his presence while he is himself, lest he should fall a-longing for his glory, as once he did; nor must he discourse with God, while he is Moses.

And all this to shew what Cato afterwards said, *rebus divinis magnam inesse caliginem*, that the nature & counsels of God are not only a *great depth*, as David calls them, but a thick darkness besides: deep and dark too. So to the best eyes: *his footsteps unknown* to the Psalmist, that continually traced them; *his ways unsearchable* to S. Paul, that was rapt into the third heaven; and to Moses, that talked with God. So in one aspect, and yet not so in another, for religion is *meat and milk*, saith the Apostle, and hath provision both for *men and babes*. There are *arcana Dei*, secret things that belong unto the Lord; and there are *revelata Dei*, revealed things that belong to us. Every faithful soul is a *building*, and every true Church, a *house*, saith the Holy Ghost. Wherefore, as in a house, so in the Church . . . some are necessary or essential parts, and some are like the imagery or sculpture . . . there ensues . . . no hazard to the soul on the ignorance of these. . . .

. . . For although we know as much as we must, because it were unreasonable to invite us to heaven without shewing the way; we know not as much as we may, because God is a voluntary glass and discloses himself no further than he will. Some he brings by the periphery or bow, others by the diameter or string; as the same period was but a few weeks' journey when Israel went for the necessary provision of bread; many years' pilgrimage when Israel lusted for the unnecessary curiosity of flesh, being thus led from Marah to Rephidim, from Rephidim to Meribah, from thence to Taberah, from the heat & bitterness of one contention to another, till at length after many discontented and wrangling steps, the children grew wiser by the misery of their fathers, and with the price of their blood purchased the inheritance of Canaan. For as every profession is a mystery, so is religion too; nor am I commanded to believe what I am able to know. The birth of God is a *mystery*, saith S. Paul here; and the death of God *a mystery*, saith the same apostle there; the sacrament *a mystery*, in a third place; and the resurrection *a mystery* in a fourth. Our election in Christ *a mystery* now, & our union with Christ *a mystery* then. God the Father *a mystery* in this place; and God the Son *a mystery* in another. And yet *I am the bright morning star*, saith our Savior, which all see but such as are asleep, and his coming brought the day with it. . . . *Behold I shew you a mystery*, saith S. Paul to the Corinthians: a mystery, and yet shewn. *Great is the mystery of godliness, God was manifested in the flesh*, saith S. Paul to Timothy. A mystery, and yet manifest too. . . . Mysteries all, in respect of the manner; & yet no mysteries in respect of the matter; how they were done is a mystery; that they were done, is none. . . . I believe the procession of the Holy Ghost from God, which is yet but one essence with God: that he came forth and yet is always there.

I believe two natures in one hypostasis: one, and yet another. I believe the omnipotency of God created all out of nothing, and that the same can resolve all into nothing again. I believe all received beginning from that God which is without beginning . . . that was not yesterday nor shall not be tomorrow; but yesterday and tomorrow, before the world and after the world, eternally *I am*. I believe this body shall live after it is dead. . . . I believe, though I bar my doors, I lock not my God in; though I close my windows, I shut not my God out. If I seek to lose him in a labyrinth by unchaste embraces, he wants no clew to find me there. If I flee into the wilderness by a solitary sin, he needs no perspective {telescope} to discover me here: that he is in my closet {study} when I exchange him for a bribe, and in my bed when I wish him out. That he is as essentially in that place where I provoke him by my drunkenness as I that am drunk, & the only reason why my surfeits bespatter him not is not because this wants pollution, but because he wants dimension; not because this falls where he is not, but because it falls where he is without a body. But how a son without a father, how a virgin & yet a mother; how the Creator of all was born, or God should die; how the Holy Ghost came from the Father and yet may not be called the son of the Father; how he descended thence and yet is always there. . . . *How the Father himself begat that which is himself, & yet God the Father begat God which is not the Father;* how *the Persons are the Trinity, and yet no Person is a part of the Trinity;* how *there is one essence of three Persons & three Persons of one essence, and yet not one God of three Persons or three Persons of one God.* How the Deity was united to the flesh by the mediation of the soul & yet was not divided from the flesh by the separation of the soul; how all the world together can but make something of something, & yet God made all the world of nothing; how this body of mine shall first be earth, & then grass, then digested by worms, & then incorporated into man; how I shall have my own flesh, & he that eats me shall have it too at the last day. How the Lord can be. . . . everywhere, and yet without expansion; of an infinite presence without an infinite place. Here I say with Lombard out of Hilary, *et si sensu non percipiam teneo conscientiâ*, I believe though I cannot see; and there, that they are *nimiae profunditatis altitudines, & insolubiles, sensumque superantes humanum*,[12] beyond my reason, though not against it. Tis enough for me *micas edere sub mensa domini, & indignum soluere corrigiam*.[13] . . . Say *I Am that I Am hath sent me*, saith God to Moses; or, if thy curiosity desire more, know tis beyond thy reach; do not venture thy wings about this flame. As my name is secret, so is my nature infinite. Thou canst not know that thou canst not; for *I am that I am*, no matter to thee (Exod. 3:14). *Credo quia impossibile*, saith Tertull. I believe it is so because it is impossible it should be so—and learn by reading to speak more timorously, but not more understandingly, of God.

Text: EEBO (STC [2nd ed.] / 15328)

Thomas Laurence, *Two sermons: the first preached at St. Mary's in Oxford, July 13, 1634, being Act-Sunday; the second, in the cathedral church of Sarum at the visitation of the Most Reverend Father in God, William, Archbishop of Canterbury, May 23, 1634* (Oxford: Printed by John Lichfield, 1635), 1–30 (the sermon itself goes on for another nine pages).

[12] {heights too steep, and unknowable, and beyond the reach of human perception}

[13] {To eat the crumbs under the table of the Lord, [as being] unworthy to unlace [his] shoe-lachet: alluding to Mark 7:28 (*via* Cranmer's prayer of humble access in the Communion liturgy) and John 1:27.}

FRANCIS QUARLES[1]

Emblems
1635

To the Reader

An *emblem* is but a silent parable. Let not the tender eye check to see the allusion to our blessed Savior figured in these types. In holy Scripture, he is sometimes called a sower, sometimes a fisher, sometimes a physician; and why not presented so as well to the eye as to the ear? Before the knowledge of letters, God was known by *hieroglyphics*, and, indeed, what are the heavens, the earth, nay every creature, but *hieroglyphics* and *emblems* of his glory? I have no more to say. I wish thee as much pleasure in the reading, as I had in the writing. Farewell, Reader.

By Fathers back'd, by Holy Writ led on,
Thou shew'st a way to heav'n by Helicon;
The Muses' font is consecrate by thee,
And poesie, baptiz'd divinity.
Blest soul, that here embark'st, thou sail'st apace,
'Tis hard to say mov'd more by wit or grace,
Each Muse so plies her oar; but O, the sail
Is fill'd from heav'n with a diviner gale.
When poets prove divines, why should not I
Approve in verse this divine poetry?
Let this suffice to license thee the press;
I must no more, nor could the Truth say less.

Sic approbavit RICH. LOVE,

Procan. *Cantabrigiensis*[2]

---

[1] {For an overview of Quarles' life and works, see the introduction to his 1632 *Divine fancies <supra>*. Marginal glosses marked with a † are editorial.}

[2] {The author of this extraordinary verse imprimatur, Richard Love, was appointed Master of Corpus

XIV.

Phosphore redde diem.

Wᴵˡˡ: *Marshall Sculpsit.*

Book I
Emblem XIV

Psal. 13:3

Lighten mine eyes, O Lord, lest I sleep the sleep of death.

Will't ne'r be morning? Will that promis'd light
    Ne'r break, and clear these clouds of night?
Sweet Phosphor,† bring the day,   † the morning star
    Whose conqu'ring ray
May chase these fogs: sweet Phospher, bring the day.

Christi by royal mandate in 1632, in 1633–34 serving as University vice-chancellor, in which capacity he licensed Quarles' book. Despite "staunchly defending Anglican doctrines and discipline" (*ODNB*), Love retained his mastership throughout the Civil Wars and Interregnum, the only Cambridge head to do so.}

How long! how long shall these benighted eyes
    Languish in shades, like feeble flies
Expecting spring! How long shall darkness soil
    The face of earth, and thus beguile
Our souls of rightful action? when will day
    Begin to dawn, whose new-born ray
May gild the weather-cocks of our devotion,
    And give our unsoul'd souls new motion?[3]
        Sweet Phospher, bring the day,
          Thy light will fray
These horrid mists; sweet Phospher, bring the day.

Let those have night that slyly love t'immure
    Their cloister'd crimes, and sin secure;
Let those have night that blush to let men know
    The baseness they ne'r blush to do;
Let those have night that love to take a nap
    And loll in Ignorance's lap;
Let those whose eyes, like owls, abhor the light,
    Let those have night that love the night:
        Sweet Phospher, bring the day;
          How sad[4] delay
Afflicts dull hopes! sweet Phospher, bring the day.

Alas! my light-in-vain-expecting eyes
    Can find no objects but what rise
From this poor mortal blaze, a dying spark
    Of Vulcan's forge, whose flames are dark
And dangerous, a dull blue-burning light,
    As melancholy as the night:
Here's all the suns that glister in the sphere
    Of earth. Ah me! what comfort's here?
        Sweet Phospher, bring the day;
          Haste, haste away
Heav'ns loit'ring lamp; sweet Phospher, bring the day.

Blow, Ignorance. O thou, whose idle knee
    Rocks earth into a lethargy,
And with thy sooty fingers hast bedight
    The world's fair cheeks, blow, blow thy spite;
Since thou hast puff't our greater taper, do
    Puff on, and out the lesser too.
If e'er that breath-exiléd flame return,

---

[3] {Aristotle defines the soul as an internal principle of motion.}
[4] {"sad" can mean dark, gloomy, somber-colored, as well as sorrowful}

Thou hast not blown, as it will burn:
> Sweet Phospher, bring the day;
> > Light will repay
The wrongs of night; sweet Phospher, bring the day.

S. AUGUST. in Joh. ser. 19

God is all to thee: if thou be hungry, he is bread; if thirsty, he is water; if in darkness, he is light; if naked, he is a robe of immortality.

ALANUS de conq. nat.[5]

God is a light that is never darkened, an unwearied life that cannot die, a fountain always flowing, a garden of life, a seminary of wisdom, a radical beginning of all goodness.

EPIG. 14

My Soul, if Ignorance puff out this light,
She'll do a favor that intends a spite:
'T seems dark abroad; but take this light away,
Thy windows will discover break of day.[6]

---

[5] {Alanus of Lille (12th c.), *The complaint of nature*}

[6] {"breake a day" in the original, but it seemed dreadful to end the poem with an awkward archaism.}

III.

Haue mercy on me o L.d for Jam weake
o L.d heals me for my bones are vexed
Ps: 6. 2.

Book III
Emblem III

Psalm 6:2

Have mercy, Lord, upon me, for I am weak;
O Lord, heal me, for my bones are vexed.

Soul   Jesus

Soul   Ah, Son of David, help. **Jes.** What sinful cry
      Implores the Son of David? **Soul.** It is I.

Jes.   Who art thou? **Soul.** Oh, a deeply wounded breast
      That's heavy laden, and would fain have rest.

Jes.   I have no scraps, and dogs must not be fed
      Like household children with the children's bread.

Soul True, Lord; yet tolerate a hungry whelp
To lick their crumbs: O Son of David, help.

Jes. Poor Soul, what ail'st thou? **Soul**. O I burn, I fry;
I cannot rest; I know not where to fly
To find some ease; I turn my blubber'd face
From man to man; I roll from place to place
T'avoid my tortures, to obtain relief,
But still am dogg'd and haunted with my grief:
My midnight torments call the sluggish light,
And when the morning's come, they woo the night.

Jes. Surcease thy tears, and speak thy free desires.

Soul Quench, quench my flames, & 'swage these scorching fires.

Jes. Canst thou believe my hand can cure thy grief?

Soul Lord, I believe; Lord, help my unbelief.

Jes. Hold forth thy arm, and let my fingers try
Thy pulse. Where (chiefly) doth thy torment lie?

Soul From head to foot; it reigns in ev'ry part,
But plays the self-law'd tyrant in my heart.

Jes. Canst thou digest? canst relish wholesome food?
How stands thy taste? **Soul**. To nothing that is good:
All sinful trash, and earth's unsav'ry stuff
I can digest and relish well enough.

Jes. Is not thy blood as cold as hot, by turns?

Soul Cold to what's good; to what is bad it burns.

Jes. How old's thy grief? **Soul**. I took it at the fall
With eating fruit. **Jes.** 'Tis epidemical;
Thy blood's infected, and th'infection sprung
From a bad liver; 'tis a fever strong
And full of death unless, with present speed,
A vein be op'ned; thou must die, or bleed.

Soul O I am faint and spent: that lance that shall
Let forth my blood, lets forth my life withal;
My soul wants cordials, and has greater need
Of blood than (being spent so far) to bleed.
I faint already. If I bleed, I die.

Jes. 'Tis either thou must bleed, sick soul, or I.
My blood's a cordial. He that sucks my veins,
Shall cleanse his own, and conquer greater pains
Than these. Cheer up; this precious blood of mine
Shall cure thy grief; my heart shall bleed for thine.
Believe, and view me with a faithful eye,
Thy soul shall neither languish, bleed, nor die.

S. AUGUST. lib. 10. Confess.

Lord, be merciful unto me. Ah me. Behold, I hide not my wounds. Thou art a physician, and I am sick; thou art merciful, and I am miserable.

S. GREG. in Pastoral.

O Wisdom, with how sweet an art does thy wine and oil restore health to my healthless soul! How powerfully merciful, how mercifully powerful art thou! Powerful for me, merciful to me!

EPIG. 3

Canst thou be sick, and such a doctor by?
Thou canst not live, unless thy doctor die!
Strange kind of grief, that finds no med'cine good
To 'swage her pains but the physician's blood!

V.

My Soule melted, when my beloved spake. Cant: 5.6.

Will: Simpson scul:

Book V
Emblem V

Canticles 5:6

My Soul melted whilst my Beloved spake.

Lord, has the feeble voice of flesh and blood
The pow'r to work thine ears into a flood
Of melted mercy? or the strength t'unlock
The gates of heav'n, and to dissolve a rock
Of marble clouds into a morning show'r?
Or has the breath of whining dust the pow'r
To stop or snatch a falling thunderbolt
From thy fierce hand, and make thy hand revolt†   †turn back

782

From resolute confusion,† and instead   †destruction
Of vials,† pour full blessings on our head?   †Rev. 16–18
Or shall the wants of famisht ravens cry,
And move thy mercy to a quick supply?†   †Ps. 147:9
Or shall the silent suits of drooping flow'rs
Woo thee for drops, and be refresh'd with show'rs?
Alas, what marvel then, great God, what wonder
If thy hell-rousing voice, that splits in sunder
The brazen portals of eternal death;
What wonder if that life-restoring breath
Which drag'd me from th'infernal shades of night,
Should melt my ravisht soul with o'er-delight?
O can my frozen gutters[7] choose but run,
That feel the warmth of such a glorious Sun?
Methinks his language, like a flaming arrow,
Doth pierce my bones, and melts their wounded marrow.
Thy flames, O Cupid (though the joyful heart
Feels neither tang of grief, nor fears the smart
Of jealous doubts, but drunk with full desires)
Are torments weigh'd with these celestial fires;
Pleasures that ravish in so high a measure
That, O, I languish in excess of pleasure.
What ravisht heart, that feels these melting joys,
Would not despise and loath the treach'rous toys
Of dunghill earth? what soul would not be proud
Of wry-mouth'd scorns, the worst that flesh and blood
Had rancor to devise? Who would not bear
The world's derision with a thankful ear?
What palate would refuse full bowls of spite,
To gain a minute's taste of such delight?
Great spring of light, in whom there is no shade
But what my interposéd sins have made,
Whose marrow-melting fires admit no screen[8]
But what my own rebellions put between
Their precious flames and my obdurate ear:
Disperse these plague-distilling clouds, and clear
My mungy† soul into a glorious day.   †dank, gloomy
Transplant this screen, remove this bar away;
Then, then my fluent soul shall feel the fires
Of thy sweet voice, and my dissolv'd desires
Shall turn a sov'reign balsam, to make whole
Those wounds my sins inflicted on thy soul.

---

[7] {a brook or stream; but also "a channel forming a receptacle for dirt or filth" (*OED*); or a channel on the roof to carry off rainwater}

[8] {Screens were used to protect those sitting by the fire from its heat.}

S. AUGUST. Soliloq. cap. 34.

What fire is this that so warms my heart! What light is this that so enlightens my soul! O fire that always burnest and never goest out, kindle me. O light which ever shinest and art never darkened, illuminate me. O that I had my heat from thee, most holy fire! How sweetly dost thou burn! How secretly dost thou shine! How desiderably dost thou inflame me!

BONAVENT. Stim. amoris cap. 8.

It makes God man; and man, God; things temporal, eternal; mortal, immortal; it makes an enemy a friend; a servant, a son; vile things, glorious; cold hearts fiery, and hard things liquid.

EPIG. 5.

My soul, thy gold is true, but full of dross;
Thy Savior's breath refines thee with some loss;
His gentle furnace makes thee pure as true;
Thou must be melted, ere th'art cast anew.

X.

Bring my foule out of Prifon that I may praif thy Name : Ps:142.7. will:fimpfon. faulpf

Book V
Emblem X

Psalm 142:7

Bring my soul out of prison, that I may praise thy name.

My soul is like a bird; my flesh, the cage
Wherein she wears her weary pilgrimage
Of hours as few as evil, daily fed
With sacred wine and sacramental bread;
The keys that locks {*sic*} her in and lets her out
Are birth and death; 'twixt both, she hops about
From perch to perch; from sense to reason, then
From higher reason down to sense again;
From sense she climbs to faith, where, for a season,
She sits and sings; then down again to reason;

From reason back to faith; and straight from thence
She rudely flutters to the perch of sense;
From sense to hope; then hops from hope to doubt
From doubt to dull despair; there, seeks about
For desp'rate freedom, and at ev'ry grate
She wildly thrusts, and begs th'untimely date
Of unexpired thralldom to release
Th'afflicted captive that can find no peace.
Thus am I coop'd within this fleshly cage;
I wear my youth, and waste my weary age,
Spending that breath, which was ordain'd to chant
Heav'ns praises forth, in sighs and sad complaint,
Whilst happier birds can spread their nimble wing
From shrubs to cedars, and there chirp and sing,
In choice of raptures, the harmonious story
Of man's redemption and his Maker's glory:
You glorious Martyrs, you illustrious troops
That once were cloister'd in your fleshly coops
As fast as I, what rhetoric had your tongues?
What dext'rous art had your elegiac songs?
What Paul-like pow'r had your admir'd devotion?
What shackle-breaking faith infus'd such motion
To your strong pray'rs, that could obtain the boon
To be inlarg'd, to be uncag'd so soon?
When I (poor I) can sing my daily tears,
Grown old in bondage, and can find no ears.
You great partakers of eternal glory,
That with your heav'n-prevailing oratory
Releas'd your souls from your terrestrial cage,
Permit the passion of my holy rage
To recommend my sorrows (dearly known
To you in days of old; and, once, your own)
To your best thoughts (but, oh, 't does not befit ye
To move our pray'rs; you love and joy, not pity).[9]
Great Lord of souls, to whom should pris'ners fly
But thee? Thou hadst thy cage, as well as I;
And, for my sake, thy pleasure was to know
The sorrows that it brought, and feltst them too.
O set me free, and I will spend those days,
Which now I waste in begging, in thy praise.

[9] {I.e., one cannot pray to the blessed souls in heaven, because they are now exempt from pity, knowing only love and joy. On the remotion of the living from the blessed dead, see Donne's sermon on John 11:35 <*infra*>.}

ANSELM in Protolog. Cap. I

O miserable condition of mankind, that has lost that for which he was created! Alas! What has he left? And what has he found? He has lost happiness for which he was made, and found misery for which he was not made. What is gone? and what is left? That thing is gone, without which, he is unhappy; that thing is left, by which he is miserable. O wretched man! From whence are we expell'd? To what are we impell'd? Whence are we thrown? And whither are we hurried? From our home into banishment; from the sight of God into our own blindness; from the pleasure of immortality to the bitterness of death: miserable change. From how great a good to how great an evil? Ah me. What have I enterpris'd? What have I done? Whither did I go? Whither am I come?

EPIG. 10

Paul's midnight voice prevail'd; his music's thunder
Unhing'd the prison doors, split bolts in sunder,
And sitst thou here? and hang'st the feeble wing?
And whin'st to be enlarg'd? Soul, learn to sing.

><><

Text: EEBO (STC [2nd ed.] / 20540)
Francis Quarles, *Emblemes* (London: Printed by G[eorge] M[iller], 1635).

ROBERT SHELFORD
(ca. 1563–1638/39)

Shelford was presumably a poor man's son, since he entered Peterhouse, Cambridge, as a sizar (in modern parlance, a work-study student), serving as Bible-clerk and amanuensis to Peterhouse's master, the proto–Anglo-Catholic Andrew Perne (1519–89).[1] He took his BA in 1584, proceeding MA in 1587, the same year he was ordained. In 1599 Sir Thomas Egerton granted him the rectory of Ringsfield in the northeast corner of Suffolk, where Shelford served for nearly four decades. His one publication other than the *Discourses* was a 1596 treatise on children's education (reprinted in 1602 and 1606). His memorial tablet in the Ringsfield church describes him as unmarried (*coelebs*).

Five learned and pious discourses was printed at Cambridge in 1635, with prefatory verses by Richard Crashaw. Its sustained critique of English Calvinist orthodoxies—in the sermon reprinted here, the glorification of preaching as the chief, if not sole, ordinary means of salvation—elicited Archbishop Ussher's outraged protest that "such rotten stuff" smacked of Perne's teaching (*ODNB*), a comment that casts interesting light on the Tudor prehistory of Laudianism.[2] For, as the portions of Shelford's book reprinted below (including Crashaw's verses) make evident, the *Discourses* is a Laudian work. Yet Shelford is Shakespeare's contemporary, and his book reminded Ussher of Perne, who grew up in pre-Reformation England, not of newfangled Caroline divinity. Moreover, although forty years his senior, Shelford at points sounds very much like Laud's godson, William Chillingworth, and the points at which Shelford anticipates Chillingworth are precisely those at which Chillingworth sounds very much like Milton's *Areopagitica*: the points at which Shelford upholds the authority of the individual conscience, argues for the spiritual and moral autonomy of the laity, and defends their capacity to understand the fundamental and essential parts of Scripture and their Christian liberty to read it for themselves. The

---

[1] See Collinson, "Perne."
[2] See Tyacke 53–56; MacCulloch 17; Shuger 608–9, 617–18; Collinson, "Perne").

obvious question then arises as to how such seemingly Miltonic moments can possibly cohere with Shelford's sacramentalism and sacerdotalism, his Caroline royalism, his Laudian churchmanship.

To grasp their coherence is to grasp Shelford's central claim: that the holy enters this world at *multiple* sites. The pulpit is not the only channel of grace, for God is present in nature, in families, in Scripture, in the public reading of common prayer and the private reading of printed sermons, in the sacraments, in the Christian social order of Stuart England, in its "godly governors," as also in the voice of the indwelling Spirit and the dictates of the individual conscience.[3] This multiplicity of sacral loci disallows the invidious contrast between Christ's little flock and the merely civil religion of the majority (or the sub-Christian religion of the village),[4] as it likewise disallows Milton's heroic individualism. Shelford urges the spiritual autonomy of laypersons vis-à-vis dogmatic preachers, not in relation to their neighbors or their culture or their families or their rulers, these being, no less than one's own conscience and reason, ordinary, although neither invariable nor infallible, ministers of the word—as are, on occasion, even one's servants.

SOURCES: *ODNB*; Patrick Collinson, "Perne the turncoat: an Elizabethan reputation," *Elizabethan essays* (London: Hambledon, 1994), 179–218; Diarmaid MacCulloch, "The myth of the English Reformation," *JBS* 30.1 (1991): 1–19; Shuger, "Protesting"; Tyacke, *Anti-Calvinists*.

[3] Note that this insistence on a plurality of sacral loci is formally akin to the argument of Laud's *Conference with Fisher* <*vide supra*> that our assurance that Scripture is the word of God rests not, contra both Catholic and Calvinist teaching, on some one infallible basis but instead on the conjoined witness of tradition, grace, authority, and reason.

[4] This contrast is endemic to godly Calvinism (*vide* the scholarship of Christopher Haigh on this point), but also, as the Everard selections <*supra*> indicate, to antinomianism. Two notorious antinomian ministers—Eaton at Wickham Market and Eachard at Darsham—had parishes within twenty miles of Shelford's Ringsfield.

ROBERT SHELFORD

Five pious and learned discourses
1635

Upon the ensuing treatises

Rise then, immortal maid! *Religion* rise!
Put on thyself in thine own looks; t' our eyes
Be what thy beauties, not our blots, have made thee,
Such as (ere our dark sins to dust betrayed thee)
Heav'n set thee down new dressed, when thy bright birth
Shot thee like lightning to th' astonisht earth.
From th' dawn of thy fair eyelids wipe away
Dull mists and melancholy clouds; take day
And thine own beams about thee; bring the best
Of whatsoe'er perfum'd thy *Eastern nest*.
Girt all thy glories to thee; then sit down,
Open this book, fair Queen, *and take thy crown.*
These learned leaves shall vindicate to thee
Thy holiest, humblest handmaid, Charity.
She'll dress thee like thyself, set thee on high
Where thou shalt reach all hearts, command each eye.
Lo where I see thy altars wake and rise
From the pale dust of that strange sacrifice
Which they themselves[1] were, each one putting on
A majesty that may beseem thy throne.
The holy youth of heav'n whose golden rings
Girt round thy awful altars, with bright wings
Fanning thy fair locks (which the world believes

[1] {i.e., the altars destroyed at the Reformation. See Kenneth Fincham and Nicholas Tyacke, *Altars restored: the changing face of English religious worship, 1547–c. 1700* (Oxford UP, 2008).}

As much as sees), shall with these sacred leaves
Trick their tall plumes, and in that garb shall go
If not more glorious, more conspicuous though.

       —Be it enacted then
By the fair laws of thy firm-pointed pen:
God's services no longer shall put on
Pure sluttishness for pure religion;
No longer shall our churches' frighted stones
Lie scatter'd like the burnt and martyr'd bones
Of dead Devotion, nor faint marbles weep
In their sad ruins, nor Religion keep
A melancholy mansion in those cold
Urns. Like God's sanctuaries they looked of old;
Now seem they temples consecrate to none,
Or to a new god, Desolation.
No more the hypocrite shall th' upright be
Because he's stiff and will confess no knee;
While others bend their knee, no more shalt thou,
Disdainful dust and ashes, bend thy brow,
Nor on God's altar cast two scorching eyes
Bak't in hot scorn for a burnt sacrifice;
But, for a lamb, thy tame and tender heart
New struck by love, still trembling on his dart;
Or, for two turtle doves, it shall suffice
To bring a pair of meek and humble eyes.
This shall from henceforth be the masculine theme
Pulpits and pens shall sweat in, to redeem
Virtue to action, that life-feeding flame
That keeps Religion warm; not swell a name
Of *Faith* (a mountain word made up of air)
With those dear spoils that wont to dress the fair
And fruitful Charity's full breasts of old,
Turning her out to tremble in the cold.
What can the poor hope from us, when we be
Uncharitable ev'n to Charity?[2]
Nor shall our zealous ones still have a fling
At that most horrible and horned thing—
Forsooth *the Pope*, by which black name they call
The Turk, the devil, furies, hell and all,
And something more. "O he is antichrist;
Doubt this, and doubt (say they) that Christ is Christ.
Why, tis a point of faith." What e'er it be,

---

[2] {The final ten lines were omitted in the version printed in Crashaw's *Steps to the Temple* (1646).}

I'm sure it is no point of charity.
In sum, no longer shall our people hope
To be a true Protestant's but to hate the pope.

Rich. Crashaw, Aul. Penb. A. B.

THE TEN PREACHERS,
or
a sermon preferring holy charity before faith, hope, & knowledge

Knowledge puffeth up, but charity edifieth.

There were a sort of Christians in the apostles' time which would not consort with their fellows because they understood more then they did. They would eat meat in the idols' temples with the idolaters because they had learned that an idol was nothing, and that all the creatures of God were good. The other, which knew less, durst not because they had neither warrant for it nor precedent. The like difference is at this day among our professors.[3] One sort will not sociate with the rest of their neighbors in the house of God because they have not every day a sermon to teach them more knowledge. Both these[4] the Apostle here reproveth in saying *knowledge puffeth up*—that is to say, makes men proud—*but charity edifieth.*

What the Apostle hath here put down in the general, I will proceed to prove in the particulars. And to begin with the pride of knowledge: in the Creation, God made his angels exceeding bright and glorious in understanding, and then propounded to them his Son to be their governor, to direct them in his service, according to that {in} Heb. 1:6, *Let all the angels of God worship him*, as if it were said, "let them follow his direction." But they, seeing themselves made in such perfection of knowledge, were so lifted up in pride that they refused a director and would serve him after their own understanding; for which their pride, they were thrown down from heaven to hell. After this, the angels perceiving that the pride of their knowledge had thrown them down, they set upon Adam and Eve, persuading them also to break their order in eating of the tree of knowledge. The serpent-angel told them that if they would eat of this tree, they should be as gods, knowing good and evil. This conceit of knowledge did so puff them up too that they broke God's commandment and were *ipso facto* thrown out of Paradise. After this, when man was ejected out of Paradise, so politic and proud grew they that they would make a tower to clamber up to heaven and to defend themselves against God's providence. God, seeing their pride, confounded their devices by changing their language, and then they were dispersed all the earth over like straying herds. The like pride hath nowadays puffed up our puritans that, being but very ignorant people, yet they will not be content to be accounted men of any mean knowledge or be satisfied with any settled estate, but they will run from church to church, from preacher to preacher, and from one opinion to another until they have lost and confounded themselves in the tower and Babel of their own fancies. . . .

---

[3] {persons of conspicuous piety; aka, the godly}

[4] {i.e., both those in the apostles' time who "would not consort with their fellows" and their modern counterparts}

"But," saith the puritan, "we have no sermons; we are without a preacher; we shall perish for want of knowledge."[5] I answer, it is not knowledge that shall save, because then all they that know the will of God and the mysteries of life must needs be saved. But so they shall not, because our Savior saith, *he that knows his master's will and doth it not shall be beaten with many stripes*; and S. Paul saith, *the hearers of the Law are not righteous before God; but the doers of the Law shall be justified.* Then knowledge without charity saveth not, but increaseth punishment and puffeth up. Besides, if knowledge were able to save, then the devils might be saved, because they know more than the best minister in the land. And whereas thou standest upon much knowledge (for we will yield thee that which is sufficient), I say more unto thee: that one may be saved without any knowledge at all." Know you what you say?" Yes. The child of three months old, when by God's providence it departeth, what knowledge hath that of salvation? Yet the Church in all ages hath taught that such shall go to the kingdom of heaven; and what should let? It is without original sin, because that is washt away in baptism; and actual sin it never committed any by reason it wanted the use of free-will. Besides, the infant after baptism is within the covenant and united to God by his grace; and God cannot deny either his grace or his covenant. Now if the poor infant shall be saved without any knowledge at all, why then shouldest thou think that thou canst not be saved with mean knowledge fit for thy estate? . . . The school tenet is *amentes, furiosi, & infantes non peccant*; that is, *fools, mad-men, and children sin not.* Therefore mad-men, though they kill a man, are not put to death for it. . . . And my charity teacheth me to hope that as the Savior of the world at his first coming had mercy on the gentiles, who before lived without faith and without God in the world, so at his second coming he likewise will shew favor to these want-wits and weak-wits, and then open the windows of their understanding to see God face to face, because they are within the covenant and are baptized Christians.

But to return to thy former challenge, "we have no sermons, we want a preacher, we shall die in our sins, we know not what to do." The Lord open thy eyes as he opened the eyes of Elisha his servant in the 6 chapter of the 2 book of Kings, and then thou shalt see a multitude of preachers. First, all God's creatures are thy preachers and daily teach thee. And to prove this, turn to the 19 Psalm 1-3: *The heavens declare the glory of God, and the firmament sheweth his handiwork. One day telleth another, and one night certifieth another. There is neither speech nor language, but their voices are heard among them.* Again, turn to the 12 of Job, 7-8, and there he will bid thee *ask the beasts, and they shall teach thee; and the fowls of heaven, and they shall tell thee. Or speak to the earth, and it shall shew thee; or the fishes of the sea, and they shall declare unto thee.* When thou travellest abroad and seest a good piece of ground, a good cow, or a good horse, thou wilt say, "I would my neighbor would sell me these for reasonable money." Canst thou see the goodness of the creature in these, and not see the goodness of the Creator? Canst thou learn in these books what is good for thy body, and not learn what is good for thy soul? Open thy eyes wider, and then thou shalt see that there could be no goodness in the creature, except God had made it; and that if the effect be good, then the cause of this good must needs be infinitely more

---

[5] {See Hooker, *Laws* 5.22 (plus the notes found in either the Keble or Folger Library editions) for the Elizabethan background to the puritan-conformist controversy over the relative importance of preaching.}

good; and therefore he above all things is to be sought of us. And this is so clear a lesson, that except a man will shut his eyes, he must see it and understand it, because the Apostle saith, Rom. 1:19-20, *That which may be known of God is manifest in them. For the invisible things of him, that is, his eternal power and Godhead, are seen by the creation of the world, being considered in his works, that they should be without excuse.* . . .

Secondly, God's word is thy preacher, and this is proved by the book of Solomon called Ecclesiastes, for that book, as the learned know, signifieth *a preacher*. Again, turn to Acts 15:21, and there the Holy Ghost will tell thee that Moses was preached every day in the synagogues while his words were read unto them. If thou saist that God's Scriptures are too high for thy capacity, then what sayest thou to the 19 Psalm, vers. 7, which teacheth that *the testimony of the Lord giveth wisdom to the simple*? And art thou so simple to think that when God gave his Scriptures to the Church, he gave them so darkly that men might not understand them?[6] Then he might as well not have given them. Thou wilt object that of the eunuch in Acts 8:30, 31, where, when Philip asked the eunuch whether he understood what he read, he answered, *How can I, except I had a guide?* And I answer thee again that there is a great difference between the eunuch and thee . . . for he was out of the Church, which is the house of light, and thou art in it. Again, that Scripture was to him a mystery, but to thee it is no mystery. For in Isaiah no name is exprest, but it is read, *He was led as a sheep to the slaughter*; but what *he* this was, the articles of our faith express to the simplest: that it was *Jesus Christ* the Messiah of the world, who was delivered by the Jews to Pontius Pilate to be slain for our redemption; and therefore this excuse of darkness is utterly taken from thee because the Gospel is the blazing of the Law, and there is nothing so dark in one place but in some other it is so bright that the very blear-eyed may see it. . . .

Thirdly, God's holy sacraments are our preachers while by visible and sensible signs they teach us what we are to believe, for which they are of the learned called *visibilia verba, words visible.* Therefore when we see the water in baptism, this bringeth to our remembrance the water and blood which came out of our Savior's side; and when we see the bread and wine, this preacheth to us that his body was broken and his blood shed for our sins, as the water signifieth the washing away of our transgressions. And these sacraments do that for us that all the preachers of the land cannot do: for they by their words can but only teach us and enlighten our understanding, but these preachers, the sacraments, besides the light which they give to our understanding, infuse, through Christ's power and effectual ordinance, grace into our souls and make us acceptable before God. . . . But oh the lamentation of our times! Who shall make our people to believe that Christ's sacraments bestow grace? They say they signify only, and that faith cometh by hearing only, yet when they have heard what they can and believe what they will, they shall never be saved without the grace of the sacraments, at least in desire. . . . Therefore the men which shut up all in the preaching of the word evacuate Christ's sacraments and do they know not what; for preaching is but a preparation for the sacraments, and there the principal grace lies hid. For this cause our Savior said to his apostles, Matt. 28:19, *Go teach all nations, baptizing them in the name of the Father and of the Son and of the Holy Ghost.* For people must first be taught that God bestoweth grace in the sacraments, or else they will not

[6] {A century earlier, Shelford's position regarding the Bible's clarity had been the *Protestant* stance.}

receive them. And the principal sacrament is baptism, because that only bestoweth new life, and the rest strengthen and preserve it.[7]

Fourthly, printed sermons are thy preachers. For as soon as there is any rare sermon preached, by and by it is put to print, and from the press it is disperst all the land over. There is scarce a house in any town but one or other in it by reading can repeat it to thee. Then how shouldest thou starve for want of preaching when the best preachers in the land, such as thou never sawest, nor they thee, yet by this means continually preach unto thee?

Fifthly, God's Spirit is thy preacher. And to prove this, see 1 John 2:27 where it is written, *But that anointing which ye have received of him dwelleth in you; and ye need not that any teach you, but, as the same anointing teacheth you of all things, &c.* This anointing is nothing else but God's Spirit and grace bestowed upon Christians in their baptism. And of this Spirit and grace speaketh S. Paul, 1 Cor. 2:10, *God hath revealed them to us by his Spirit, for the Spirit searcheth all things, yea the deep things of God.* Then if God's word be true, the Spirit of grace which he hath given to his children is another of thy preachers.

Sixthly, thy conscience is thy preacher. For as soon as thou hast done anything amiss or left anything undone that ought to be done, that will by and by tell thee of it. . . . Thus every man's conscience is his tutor to teach and govern him, not only after, but before he hath done amiss. "Wouldest thou be thus dealt withal?" will it say. Thou mayst bribe thy preacher with a gift and thou mayst stop the mouth of the parish-priest with a good tithe, but nothing will stop the mouth of thy conscience that is a continual preacher within thee. And of this preacher the prophet Isaiah saith further in his 30 chapter, vers. 21, *And thine ears shall hear a word behind thee saying, This is the way, walk ye in it, when thou turnest to the right hand and when thou turnest to the left.* This *word behind thee* is the word of thy conscience; thou canst turn thyself no way but that will speak unto thee. . . . But how comes thy conscience to preach thus to thee? From the law that is written in thine heart by the finger of God's own hand, as S. Paul teacheth, Rom. 2:15: *Which shew the effect of the law written in their hearts, their conscience bearing witness, and their thoughts accusing one another, or excusing.* If thou doest ill, thy conscience will preach nothing to thee but the Law & judgment; but if thou doest well, then nothing but the Gospel and mercy; then thy conscience will be to thee *a continual feast*, as Solomon saith. Besides, thy conscience hath another law to inform thee, and this is the new covenant of the Gospel, spoken of Jer. 31:33-34: *This shall be the covenant that I will make with the house of Israel: after those days, saith the Lord, I will put my law in their inward parts and write it in their hearts, and I will be their God, and they shall be my people. And they shall teach no more every man his neighbor, and every man his brother, saying, Know the Lord; for they shall all know me, from the least to the greatest, saith the Lord.* Is this word of God true? then how canst thou complain for want of teaching except thou wilt make God's word a liar? And here you shall further understand that there be two kinds of teaching: the one outward, the other inward. The outward is that which comes from the mouth of man; the inward is that which comes from the mouth of the conscience. And this inward teaching, because it is next to the heart, worketh far more strongly upon it than the outward doth. When men had more of this inward teaching and less of the outward, then was there far better living, for then they

---

[7] {On 17th-century English sacramental theology, see Bryan Spinks. *Sacraments, ceremonies, and the Stuart divines: sacramental theology and liturgy in England and Scotland, 1603–1662* (Ashgate, 2002).}

lived always in fear of offending, and as soon as they had done anything amiss, their conscience by and by gave them a nip and a *memento* for it. Then they confessed their sins to God and their minister, for spiritual comfort and counsel; then they endeavored to make the best temporal satisfaction they could by alms, prayer, and fasting, and other good works of humiliation; but now outward teaching, being not rightly understood, hath beaten away this. "Faith only justifieth," saith the vulgar preacher. Then, saith the solifidian[8] and loose liver, "what need I care how I live? no sin can hurt me so long as I believe." Thy preacher and thou are both in an error because God's word nowhere teacheth this, but the contrary: *Ye see*, saith S. James, *how a man is justified by works and not by faith only.* Thou wilt say, "The Fathers taught this doctrine, and our own Church too." But how, and in what sense? To shut out works before faith be come and to acknowledge faith to be the only beginning in the preparations of our justification. But our young preachers and hearers shut up all in faith only and stay at the beginning, and thus, *verbo tenus*,[9] they prove but half-Christians. Thine own conscience will preach better to thee, for that will exclude no virtue and admit no vice. And as for thee which art an hearer, though thy principles be good, yet thy apprehension cannot well digest them because they be somewhat above thy reach. Therefore the Church in all ages hath provided that the common people should be content with the *common faith*, as S. Paul calleth it, Titus 1:4, and that deep mysteries should be reserved for the learned, who have their wits *exercised to discern both good and evil* [Hebr. 5:14. Canon Apost. 48].

Seventhly, good life and conversation of Christians is thy preacher, by which very heathens may be won and converted to God. But you will say, "How prove you that?" Turn to 1 Pet. 3:1, where you shall find it thus written, *Let wives be subject to their husbands, that even they which obey not the word may without the word be won by the conversation of the wives, while they behold your pure conversation coupled with fear.* . . . . Good life, my brethren, is better than a good sermon, for that with many goes in at one ear and out at the other, but a good life is a sermon in print: it is always before thee to behold and it makes deep penetration when it speaks in alms-deeds or benefits. . . .

Eighthly, parents are preachers to their children and servants. The first world for more then two thousand years together, until the giving of the Law, had no other preachers. Then every private man's house was a church. . . . And this kind of preaching was commanded by God in the Law (Deut. 6:7): *And thou shalt rehearse them continually to thy children.* And Solomon, Prov. 1:8, thus beginneth his sermon to his son Rehoboam, *My son, hear thy father's instruction and forsake not thy mother's teaching.* . . . My father and mother were the first that converted me to God, by their example and teaching. And this kind of preaching was not only before the Law and after the Law, but it is continued also in the Gospel, as we read, Ephes. 6:4, *Ye fathers, provoke not your children to wrath, but bring them up in the nurture and admonition of the Lord.* And this kind of preaching is so needful that the Church hath derived it from the natural parents to the spiritual parents (who are God's ministers) in catechizing of youth. And this kind of preaching, as the most ancient and effectual, is so highly commended of King James before all other that in his second direction to the Archbishop of Canterbury, he giveth this charge *that those*

---

[8] {one who holds that faith alone, without works, is sufficient for justification (*OED*)}

[9] {convicted by their own words}

preachers be most encouraged and approved of, who spend the afternoon exercises in examining children in their catechism and in expounding the several heads thereof, which (saith he) *is the most ancient and laudable custom of teaching in the Church of England.* But how is this regarded? Preaching hath preached away catechizing, and the new preaching hath beat out the old. Nowadays every man's own wit is best, though it be the greenest and youngest.

A ninth kind of preachers are thy Christian neighbors, for they have not gone so long to church & to sermons but they have learned something to speak of the knowledge of God and his laws & in the way of good living. And this duty S. Paul requireth of all in Coloss. 3:16: *Let the word of Christ dwell in you plentifully in all wisdom, teaching and admonishing one another.* And thus sometime one neighbor admonisheth another of his faults, sometime ancient kindred instruct their younger in the fear of the Lord, and sometime servants give good advice to their masters and dames. . . .

Tenthly, God's minister is thy preacher, and the divine service in the Church-book is his sermon. In this service and in this sermon is contained whatsoever is necessary to salvation. But you will say, "How prove you that?" I say, thus: whatsoever is necessary to salvation is contained in these four points—in true faith, in good life, in prayer, and grace. True faith is contained in the three Creeds. . . . Good life is expressed in the Ten Commandments; prayer in the Lord's Prayer, the litany, and the rest; and grace in the sacraments. You will say, "We plain people cannot understand these without some to explain them." I answer, Canst thou tell me of one man that can make them more plain to thee by his words than God himself and his blessed apostles have done by their words? . . . But to come nearer to thee: when our commissioners of justice under the king send their warrants to our cities and villages, and they are read to thee by our under-officers, dost thou not understand them? dost thou not prepare thyself to perform them? Now canst thou understand & believe the warrants of men when they are read to thee, and canst thou not understand and believe the warrants of Almighty God when they are read by his ministers? Cannot God as significantly express himself unto thee as a lieutenant, a justice, or a chief constable? If thou takest exception at God's greatness and his high style, know thou that he spake to men. And though he once wrote his Law with his own finger and spake it with his own mouth, yet ever since he hath spoken all his divine precepts and written all his divine warrants by such men as we ourselves are and used too our own words and dialects. If thou objectest the deep revelations of S. John or the hard things of S. Paul, then I will tell thee of our Church-tenet against Papist and Puritan: that all things necessary to salvation are so plainly written and so easy of digestion that, as Fulgentius writeth, *there is abundantly both for men to eat and for children to suck.* Then, whosoever thou art, if thou canst not here be satisfied, the fault is thy own. For as the children of Israel loathed the heavenly bread of manna, so thou loathest the divine food of the soul because it is as common to thee as manna was to them. As our horse and kine in the spring, having tasted of the fresh grass, will eat no more hay, so our Puritans, after the taste of fresh sermons, will touch no more the common service but blow upon it, though there be the root and substance of all their sermons.

. . . But if God be a good teacher and a plain teacher, as may appear in the Articles of the faith, in the Ten Commandments, and the Lord's Prayer; and if all things necessary to salvation are manifest in the Scripture . . . then, for shame, gather thy wits together and understand. Wilt thou ever be a child? *Brethren* (saith S. Paul), *be not children in under-standing; in maliciousness be ye children, but in understanding be of a ripe age.* Understand-est thou these words? They are plain enough, and why canst thou not understand them when they are read to thee out of God's book? Wilt thou ever be like a young bird, fed out of the dam's bill? Canst thou not eat thy meat when it is before thee, except another put it into thy mouth or chew it for thee, as nurses do for young infants? Fie on this negligence!

. . .

But what doth this singularity work in thee but a contempt of government and a con-demning of all other save thyself? Government is contemned because they will not yield to it. Their own minister is contemned, else ask the woman of the next parish, who called her minister's preaching *bull's-beef*;[10] yet she paid for good ox-beef[11] before the commis-sary[12] left her. And what think they of their neighbors that follow them not? "Oh they are but civil men and women; they sit at home and starve their souls." Are not these puft up when they take upon them God's place and office? Do they starve their souls, which make to God a most humble confession of their sins, entreating him in Christ's name to forgive them? Are they but civil men and women which make a public profession of the Father, the Son, and the Holy Ghost? And do they starve their souls, who pray to God for grace and for all blessings spiritual and temporal? And are they but civil men who every Lord's Day lay up the law of God in their hearts and follow it in their lives all the week after? If thy neighbors be in the state of salvation, then why bearest thou not them company? But if thou condemnest thy neighbors and wilt be singular by thyself, then I will say unto thee as the good Emperor Constantine said once to the arch-puritan Novatus, *Scalam in coelum erigito, &c. Make thee a ladder and climb up from us into heaven alone.* But thou wilt say, "Oh but knowledge is a good thing; I would be glad to have more knowledge." So is honey a good thing too, and yet a man may eat too much of it. . . . For as the weak stomach cannot well digest much meat, so the common and plain people cannot gov-ern much knowledge . . . Then they wax proud and will contest with their ministers, as Miriam and Aaron did with Moses; then they will talk of antichrist; then they will soar into points of predestination and will be moderators between Papists and Protestants; and what will they not do? When they find their wings but spoon-feathered, they will offer to fly. Were the learned at this time my auditory, I would ask of them at what time most heresies were broached, and they would tell me that it was in the primitive Church when there was most preaching; therefore afterward they slacked it. And is it not so now too? Then ask the cobbler of Amsterdam. There every tradesman will be a professed preacher. Is not there the sink and drain of all false doctrine? This the ancient and learned Fathers foreseeing, inveighed what they could against it. First, S. Hierome in his epistle to Pau-linus hath, *Quod medicorum est, promittunt medici; tractant fabrilia fabri; sola scriptura-rum ars est quam sibi omnes passim vendicant. Scribimus indocti doctique poëmata passim.*[13]

---

[10] {a term of abuse}

[11] {perhaps a pun on the ancient Greek coin called "ox" from the image stamped on it; plus an allusion to the folk saying that ox-beef was better than bull's-beef (*OED*)}

[12] {an officer exercising spiritual or ecclesiastical jurisdiction as the representative of the bishop in parts of his diocese (*OED*)}

[13] {Horace, *Epist.* 2.1.117}

Hanc garrula anus, hanc delirus senex, hanc sophista verbosus, hanc universi praesumunt, lacerant, docent antequam discant. What belongs to physic, physicians profess; and tradesmen handle their tools; only the art of the Scriptures is that which all men challenge. Learned and unlearned write poems; so the prating old wife, the doting old man, the wrangling sophister, all presume upon the Scriptures, mangle them, and teach them others before they have learned them themselves. If plain men and women would profess what they know soberly, desire to learn what they do not know, and submit themselves to governors and live orderly, good leave should they have to shew themselves; but when they grow so proud that they will beard their governors, be wiser than canons, and control the learned, this is not sufferable.

. . . This proud knowledge maketh some of you to say that your minister is not worthy of his living because he preacheth not. Had they as much knowledge as they would seem to have, they would not say so, because S. Paul saith to the contrary, *If we have sown unto you spiritual things, is it a great matter if we reap your carnal things?* Yes, it is a great matter with some, who prize their corn and their calves and their pigs above God's service and his grace. "But," will they say, "what is the service you so much stand upon? the read service? I have a boy at home will read that as well as you."[14] Aye, but can thy boy read as a minister and administer the sacraments like a minister? Who called him to this? when did God commit unto him the word of reconciliation? when did God give him power to bless in his name? who laid his hands upon him? Away with thy boy; thou talkest like a profane fellow. Thou mayst as soon make a new god as make unto him new ordinances. The stranger in this place God threatened to be slain, as we read, Numb. 18. And Uzza, being a lay-man, was presently smitten of God by death for but touching the Ark with his hand to stay it up when it was like to fall. But to return to thy minister, who is God's officer: when he by his holy sacrament hath been the true mean to confer new life to thy child, to make him a member of Christ and an heir to the kingdom of heaven, in this one part of his office he hath performed a better work than all thy lands and goods are worth; and this no king, no nobleman, no monarch can do for thee, but only God's minister.[15]

. . .

But now besides the ten kinds of preaching of which I have already entreated and which are able to stop the mouths of all discontented and itching-ear'd professors, there is yet another kind of preaching, which is not fit for every minister but for extraordinary and excellent men called by God and the Church to reform errors and abuses or to promulge to the world new laws and canons. And as this kind is to be performed by extraordinary men, so it is not always so needful, but only when necessity requireth; for when things are settled, there needs no more settling but only preserving. We ought not to have many Moseses nor many evangelists nor many apostles. . . .

Lastly, when much needless and some unsound teaching by tract of time had sued {proceeded} into the ark of Christ's Church by the prelates and priests thereof, then in the 19 year of King Henry the 8 began licenses to be granted by the court of Star Chamber to preach against the corruptions of the time, like to that of King Jehoshaphat. But now, thanks be to God, the corruptions are removed, and the ancient and true doctrine of the

---

[14] {See Hooker, *Laws* 5.31 for the Elizabethan background.}

[15] {Here Shelford, rather surprisingly, seems to accept the distinctive Calvinist position that lay-baptism is invalid. See Hooker, *Laws* 5.61–62.}

primitive Church by settled articles is restored; therefore this extraordinary kind is not now so necessary, except it be upon some notorious crimes breaking in upon our people or some exorbitancies of green heads broaching the froth of their own brains, which will hardly be reformed until many of these be unfurnished of their licenses, and those that are permitted be restrained to certain times and seasons. . . . Many of these men, partly to serve the expectation of others and partly to seek their own applause, after they have been in the high place[16] and saluted after the descent, take it upon them, as though they were young prophets and new apostles, to preach a new gospel to the world, as our Puritans, Brownists, and other novelists have done. . . .

Having shewed this kind of preaching to be extraordinary—for special men, special times and occasions—it followeth that the preaching by reading, proved out of Acts 15 and other places of Scripture, is the ordinary preaching ordained by God himself in his Church. . . .

Now to conclude with thee which runnest after this extraordinary kind where thou thinkest best, I will shew the inconvenience. First, thou breakest the Church-canon, and when thou fallest on breaking of canons, then follows nothing but confusion & disorder. Secondly, thou discreditest thine own minister, though he hath better parts and gifts than the men that thou runnest after. Thirdly, thou troublest thy neighbors' seats in a strange church. Fourthly, thy servants and children will not come to catechizing because thou art absent: the hatchet flies one way and the helve another; thou gainest, and thy family loseth. Fifthly, when thou shouldest help thy neighbors in singing psalms to God's praise, then thy trumpet is abroad in another parish. Lastly, if all the rest should follow thee, some would fall short under hedges and there pray lewd parts.[17] The Lord open thine eyes to give thee more discretion, that thou mayst give a better example.

Knowledge puffeth up, but charity edifieth.

Having spoken of the first part of my text, now I must proceed to the second, in which I must as much extol charity as before I disabled unformed[18] knowledge. . . .

. . .

. . . Will you know then what charity is, which is thus advanced above knowledge? It is the most noble above all virtues, as our Apostle teacheth, 1 Cor. 13:13, *Now abideth faith, hope, and charity, but the greatest of these is charity.* He saith not, *shall be*, as Calvin and Beza offer to evacuate the Apostle's comparison & commendation, but "is now": *Now abideth faith, hope, and charity, but the greatest of these is charity.* This is the lust and desire of the spirit, as concupiscence is the lust and desire of the flesh; the one sanctifieth and justifieth, the other damnifieth and condemneth, Gal. 5:17. As concupiscence is the root of all vices, so this is the root of all virtues; it is the soul's sanctified appetite. . . .

. . .

To proceed, charity is the most excellent grace because it is the divine seed of a Christian [1 John 4:7] by which we are born of God and freed from mortal sin: 1 John 3:9,

---

[16] {i.e., the raised pulpit}

[17] {I.e., some of those who leave their parish church out of a thirst for sermons will not end up in another parish church but will be drawn aside to an illicit conventicle.}

[18] {i.e., not informed by charity}

Whosoever is born of God sinneth not, for his seed remaineth in him. This seed S. Hierome in his 2 book against Jovinian, and S. Austin in his 5 tract upon 1 John, calleth charity, for in it is contained the beginning of our conversion to God, which is a holy desire. For no man desireth anything until he loves it, but when he loves it, then he desires it; when he desires it, then he seeks it; after he hath sought it, then he finds it, according to that in the Gospel, *Seek and ye shall find, knock and it shall be opened*; and when a man hath found, because he loves it entirely, he will so cleave to it that he will not be removed from it. So is it between the regenerate heart and God. When God hath given a man a heart to love him, then he begins to desire him; when he desires him, then he seeks him, then he knocks at heaven gates by prayer and will not away till God open to him, because his seed remaineth in him. And after he hath found him, then he so cleaves to him by hope and hangs so fast upon him that he will die before he leave him, because faith hath persuaded him that God is his maker and redeemer, and that he is moreover *a rewarder of them that diligently seek him*, Heb. 11:6. And how will he reward him? not with gold and silver, which are corruptible, but with life everlasting and the joys of heaven. Oh, here is enough; we will seek no further.

. . . Faith converts the mind to God, but it is love and charity that converts the heart and will to God, which is the greatest and last conversion, because we never seek anything until we desire it. . . .

. . .

Further, that must be the most excellent grace which joineth the soul to God. . . . but charity above all virtues causeth a man to cleave to God because, as S. Bernard saith, by charity the soul is as it were married to God; and in marriage a man forsakes all other to cleave to his wife, and the wife forsakes all other to cleave to her husband. . . . So they that have charity will leave all things to cleave to God, to be one spirit with him. Yea so fast doth charity glue the good soul to God . . . that it will die before it leave him, as is to be seen in all the holy martyrs. Nothing may quench this fire, as Solomon singeth, *Set me as a seal upon thy heart and as a signet upon thy arm, for love is strong as death, jealousy is cruel as the grave; the coals thereof are fiery coals, yea, a vehement flame. Much water cannot quench love, neither can the floods drown it; if a man would give all the substance of his house for love, they would greatly contemn it.* For what is that which makes all the marriages in the world? Is it not love? If they did not love one another, they would never come together. Now this charity is nothing else but divine love; and this makes God and man one spirit, as natural love and marriage makes man and wife one flesh; and it is called *charity* to distinguish it from natural love. . . .

. . .

Lastly, there is yet another title of excellency belonging to charity, and this is *queen of virtues*, because it commandeth and governeth them all to right ends. . . . For every action, as the learned know, proceeds from election: election is in the will, and the principal power of the will is love and charity. Therefore look which way that goeth, that way go all thy actions of heart and mind. If thy love be natural, then it orders and carries all thy actions to a natural end, and that leadeth to hell; but if thy love be divine and spiritual, which my text calleth charity, then that like a queen regulates all thy actions to a supernatural end, which is to serve God and to gain his kingdom. . . .

The main tenet of the Scripture is that God will reward every man according to his works.[19] Therefore the more good works a Christian doth in the kingdom of grace, the greater shall be his crown in the kingdom of glory. For, as S. Paul saith, 1 Cor. 15:41-42, *As one star differeth from another in glory, so is the resurrection of the dead*: the body, with the more good works it riseth, the more it shall shine in heaven's glory. . . .

. . .

Charity edifieth. Lastly, as charity edifieth in a man's own self, so it edifieth in others also. If there be any infirmity in neighbors, it will bear with it and help to amend it. *Charity suffereth long, it boasteth not itself, it is not puffed up.* There is no pride in charity, but it submitteth itself to all good ordinances both in Church and commonwealth. . . . This will say, "Come neighbors, let us hold together; we must be subject to our governors for conscience sake; we may not do what we list; we may not be our own judges; we may not make ourselves equal with apostles and say in our own causes, 'It is better to please God than men,' and then please neither, for now it is not as it was in the apostles' days. Then were wicked governors; now we have godly governors." Thus charity edifieth in our own selves and others, but proud knowledge pulleth down and destroyeth. And in this predicament are they which make havoc of Church-discipline: they will not keep holy days though they be in honor of the Savior of the world; they will not observe saints' days though their examples in the liturgy be the glasses of our lives. To stand up in reverence when *Gloria Patri, Te Deum, Benedictus*, and the rest are said (wherein we speak to God) with them is a needless ceremony; confession and absolution is flat popery; and with such all is superstition save only a sermon from the spirit without premeditation and a prayer *ex tempore* or of their own framing without authority. Might these have their wills, there should be no face of religion among us. They profess themselves to be hearers, but if you talk with them, then they will be preachers. Not need but pride, not edifying but ambition makes them to amble about the country for choice hearing and precise fashions; but the true speakers and true hearers are always in charity, Ephes. 4:15. . . . I will conclude all with the saying of Hugo de S. Victore, lib. 6: *Dilectio supereminet scientiae; plus enim diligitur quàm intelligitur, & intrat dilectio ubi scientia foris est.*[20]

FINIS

Text: EEBO (STC [2nd ed.] / 22400)
Robert Shelford, *Five pious and learned discourses* . . . (Printed by [Thomas Buck and Roger Daniel] the printers to the University of Cambridge, 1635), 57–72, 74–77, 80–87, 89–96, 100–101, 105–7, 111–12, 114–16, 118–19.

[19] {Rom 2:6. Compare Calvin's rather more complex account of the relation between good works and heavenly reward in *Institutes* 3.18. Yet Lake notes that Elizabethan puritan sermons make Shelford-like claims about the reward accruing to good works (*Moderate puritans*, 152, 162).}

[7] {Love is greater than knowledge, for more is loved than is understood, and love enters where knowledge remains outside.}

ROBERT SANDERSON[1]

A sovereign antidote against Sabbatarian errors
1636

The 1636 *A sovereign antidote* complicates the *jus divinum* versus adiaphora framework of Sanderson's 1619 sermon by differentiating two types of divine law (or divine right— "*jus*" has both senses): one transcendent, absolute, and eternal (e.g., "thou shalt have no other gods before me"); the other capable of being modified or suspended, but only under exceptional circumstances. For something to be a matter of divine right in this second sense, God need not expressly command it, as long as it can be inferred from the inter-laced testimony of reason, Scripture, and tradition. By 1636, that is to say, Sanderson sounds less like Whitgift than like Hooker.

The point of recognizing a second broader category of *jus divinum* seems twofold: first, to find a way to soften Laudian claims for *divino jure* episcopacy so as not to unchurch the non-episcopal Protestant denominations of the Continent;[2] but also—as Sanderson's reference to infant baptism as *de jure divino* in this second sense implies—to limit the authority of the particular Churches of the post-Reformation to go their own way, with-out regard to "the continued practice of the Christian Church," as if its constitution, liturgy, calendar—everything but doctrinal formulae—were adiaphora and therefore matters that "every particular Church hath power in herself" to modify "at her pleasure." In 1619 Sanderson argues for the freedom of a particular Church to keep the old forms; in 1636 against its freedom to abandon them. At least by 1636, therefore, the overriding commitment is not to "the authority of the prince over things indifferent," but a distinc-tively "Anglican" (or Anglo-Catholic) vision of the Church.[3]

---

[1] For Sanderson's career, see the introduction prefacing his 1619 visitation sermon <*supra*>.

[2] See Milton, *Catholic and Reformed*, 454–94; Collinson, *Religion of Protestants*, 12–19.

[3] Peter Lake, "Serving God and the times: the Calvinist conformity of Robert Sanderson," *JBS* 27 (1988): 115.

ROBERT SANDERSON

A sovereign antidote against Sabbatarian errors
1636

To the Reader

It is a matter of great use and necessity to have now in remembrance the admonition of the Apostle and teacher of the gentiles, *Remember them which have the rule over you, obey them, and submit yourselves* (Hebr. 13:7, 17) . . . And it is not without reason, because in the house of God, which is the Church of the living God, they work the work of the Lord and they watch for our sake, as they that must give account . . . whose office is so honorable that God himself not only hath given a charge that *every man that will do presumptuously, and will not hearken to the priest,* the man shall be put away from Israel, but hath also severally this inobediency punished: *the wrath of the Lord arose against his people,* and gave them into the hands of the king of the Chaldees, *because they mocked the messenger of God and despised his words* and misused his prophets (Deut. 17:12; 2 Chron. 36:16). . . .

‡

Touching the observation of a weekly Sabbath, there are these three different opinions, viz.,

1. That it is *de jure naturali,* as a branch properly of the law of nature.[1]
2. That it is properly and directly *de jure divino positivo,* established by God's express positive ordinance in his word.
3. That it is merely *de jure humano & ecclesiastico,* introduced by authority, and established by the custom and consent of the Catholic Church.

Touching which three opinions, I leave it to the judicious to consider,

1. Whether the last of them might not hap to be of evil consequence, by leaving it in the power of every particular Church at her pleasure to change the old

[1] {The numbering of the various points in what follows is singularly unhelpful, but the argument seems clear enough.}

proportion of one in seven (which hath continued ever since Moses) into any other greater or less proportion of time.

2. Whether the two former opinions (though they indeed avoid that inconvenience) do not yet stand on such weak grounds otherwise, that they are by many degrees more improbable than the third.

3. Whether a fourth opinion going in the middle way might not be proposed with greater probability and entertained with better safety than any of the former three: viz., that the keeping holy of one day in seven is of divine positive right, taking *jus divinum* in a large signification, not for that which is primarily, properly, and directly such, according to the tenor of the second opinion, but including withal that which is secondarily, consequently, and analogically such.

For the better understanding whereof, we are to consider,

1. That those things are *de jure divino* in the first and strict sense, which either are enjoined by the express ordinance and command of God in his holy word or may be deduced therefrom by necessary, evident, and demonstrative illation {inference}. In which sense there are not very many things *de jure divino* in the New Testament.

2. That for a thing to be *de jure divino* in the latter and larger sense, it sufficeth that it may be by human discourse upon reasons of congruity probably deduced from the word of God as a thing most convenient to be observed by all such as desire unfeignedly to order their ways according to God's holy will.

3. This kind of *jus divinum* may be reasonably discerned by the concurrence of all or the chiefest of these four things following, viz.,

    1. A foundation of equity for the thing in general, either in the law of nature or by virtue of divine institution.

    2. An analogy held for the particular determination with such laws and directions as were given to the Jewish people in the Old Testament, so far as the reason of equity holds alike.

    3. Some probable insinuations thereof in the Scripture of the New Testament.

    4. The continued practice of the Christian Church so far as the condition of the times in the several ages thereof would permit, for *lex currit cum praxi*.[2]

Fourthly, that all these do in some measure concur for the observation of a weekly Sabbath, as upon examination of the several particulars will easily appear.

This distinction of *jus divinum* is to be observed the rather because it may be of very good use (if rightly understood and applied),

1. For cutting off the most material instances usually brought by the Romish party for maintenance of their unwritten traditions.

Secondly, for the clearing of some and silencing of other some controversies in the Church disputed *pro & con* with much heat, viz.,

---

[2] {Literally, "the law runs with practice," the sense being that continued practice provides a trustworthy guide as to what the scope and intent of the law actually is.}

1. The government of the Church by bishops.
2. The distinction of bishops, priests, and deacons.
3. The exercise of ecclesiastical censures, as suspension, excommunication, &c.
4. The building and consecrating of churches for divine service.
5. The assembly of synods upon needful occasions for maintenance of the truth and settling of Church-affairs.
6. Prohibition of marriages to be made within certain degrees of consanguinity and affinity.
7. Baptizing of infants born of Christian parents.
8. Maintenance of the clergy by tithes. And sundry other things.

Some of which have been doubted of in that prime and proper sense, but yet all or most of them, in my understanding, seem at least to be *de jure divino* in the latter and larger sense and signification.

Thirdly, for the right bounding of the Church's power, that she be neither denied her lawful liberty in some things, nor yet assume to herself a greater power than of right belongs to her in some other: for,

1. In things that are merely *de jure humano*, every particular Church hath power in herself from time to time to order and alter them at her pleasure, and may exercise that power when she thinks fit.
2. Things that are *de jure divino* in that first sense, the universal Church may not (much less any particular) at all take upon her to alter, but must observe them inviolably, whatever necessities or distresses she be put to.
3. Things that are *de jure divino* in the latter sense, every particular Church (but much more the universal) hath power to alter in case of necessity, but the exercise of that power is so limited to extraordinary cases that it may not be safe for her at all to exercise it, unless it be for the avoiding of mighty inconveniences not otherwise to be avoided.

Text: EEBO (STC [2nd ed.] / 679)

[Robert Sanderson,] *A sovereign antidote against Sabbatarian errors. Or, A decision of the chief doubts and difficulties touching the Sabbath* . . . (London: Printed by Thomas Harper for Benjamin Fisher, 1636), A3r–A4v, 13–19.

SIDNEY GODOLPHIN
(ca. 1610–43)

The son of a Cornish landed gentleman and mining engineer, Godolphin entered Exeter College, Oxford, in 1624. He may have studied at the Inns of Court in 1627; in the late 1620s he traveled on the Continent and was part of the Earl of Leicester's embassy to Denmark. He returned to London, twice serving as a Cornish MP (1628, 1640) and from 1634 to 1641 as a gentleman of the privy chamber extraordinary. He was part of the Great Tew circle, a friend of Falkland, Clarendon, Hobbes, and Waller. Elected to the Long Parliament, Godolphin was one of the last royalists to leave it; he withdrew after having voted against Strafford's attainder and opposed Pym's strategy to neutralize the Lords. He then joined the royalist forces in the west, where he proved an able soldier and strategist. In February 1643, he and his party were ambushed by Parliamentary soldiers; Godolphin fell from his horse, killed by a chance shot.

Edmund Gosse called him "the hope of a great house, a courtier, a scholar, and a poet as well as a brave soldier" (109), Clarendon adding that "there was never so great a mind and spirit contained . . . in so very small a body" (1:43). In his dedication to the *Leviathan*, Hobbes paid tribute to Godolphin as one in whose "generous constitution" there shone every "virtue that disposeth a man either to the service of God or the service of his country" (xiii).

❧

Godolphin's known oeuvre consists of about thirty lyrics plus a partial translation of the *Aeneid*'s fourth book. Most of the poems were first published in 1906, one not until 1997 (Norbrook). The majority are secular lyrics, remarkable for their early mastery of the Augustan couplet (Gosse 110–11). Except for a couple of psalm paraphrases, "Lord when wise men" is Godolphin's only sacred poem.[1] One's first instinct is to read it as a Caroline

---

[1] One can assume that it was written some time after Laud became archbishop in 1633, given the allusion in the fourth stanza to bowing at the altar, yet before the political crises of the late 1630s; I have therefore, somewhat arbitrarily but not unreasonably, assigned it the mid-point date of 1636.

defense of traditional religion against the sort of Calvinism that made a detailed grasp of the ordering of the divine decrees and the inner operations of the Trinity necessary for salvation. Yet, if the wise men are supposed to be Calvinist ministers, why are they tracing "Nature's laws" and bowing to the altar? Hobbes' research in the 1630s focused on natural science, and the clergy associated with Great Tew were mostly high churchmen (Sheldon, Hammond, Chillingworth). Godolphin's relation to these men—and the extraordinary gentleness of the poem's censure—suggests that Godolphin has in mind the position taken in Hales' sermon on private judgment and Chillingworth's *The religion of Protestants* that an unexamined religion is not worth believing.[2]

Sources: *ODNB*; Irene Coltman, *Private men and public causes: philosophy and politics in the English civil war* (Faber and Faber, 1962); Edmund Gosse, *From Shakespeare to Pope: an inquiry into the causes and phenomena of the rise of classical poetry in England* (Cambridge UP, 1885); Thomas Hobbes, *Leviathan*, ed. A. R. Waller (Cambridge UP, 1904); Edward Hyde, *The life of Edward Earl of Clarendon . . . written by himself*, 2 vols. (Oxford UP, 1957); David Norbrook, "An unpublished poem by Sidney Godolphin," *RES* 48 (1997): 498–500; Perez Zagorin, "Clarendon and Hobbes," *Journal of Modern History* 57.4 (1985): 593–616.

[2] Note that Chillingworth wrestles with this issue, at one point insisting that it is enough if person believes largely on the say-so of a priest whom he trusts <2.83>, although elsewhere inclined to think that God regards such blind faith as the "sacrifice of fools" <2.113>.

SIDNEY GODOLPHIN

"Lord, when the wise men"
ca. 1630–40

"Lord, when the wise men"

Lord, when the wise men came from far,
Led to thy cradle by a star,
Then did the shepherds too rejoice,
Instructed by thy angel's voice:
Blest were the wise men in their skill,
And shepherds in their harmless will.

Wise men in tracing Nature's laws
Ascend unto the highest cause;
Shepherds with humble fearfulness
Walk safely, though their light be less:
Though wise men better know the way
It seems no honest heart can stray.

There is no merit in the wise
But love (the shepherds' sacrifice).
Wise men, all ways of knowledge past,
To the shepherds' wonder come at last:
To know can only wonder breed,
And not to know is wonder's seed.

A wise man at the altar bows
And offers up his studied vows
And is received; may not the tears,
Which spring too from a shepherd's fears,

And sighs upon his frailty spent,
Though not distinct,[1] be eloquent?

'Tis true,[2] the object sanctifies
All passions which within us rise;
But since no creature comprehends
The cause of causes, end of ends,
He who himself vouchsafes to know
Best pleases his Creator so.

When then our sorrows we apply
To our own wants and poverty,
When we look up in all distress
And our own misery confess,
Sending both thanks and prayers above,
Then, though we do not know, we love.

TEXT: *Minor poets of the Caroline period*, 3 vols., ed. George Saintsbury (Clarendon, 1905–21), 2:246–47.[3]

[1] {clearly articulated}

[2] {The final stanzas hinge on the distinction implicit in the previous one between the prayers that the wise man "offers up" to God and the shepherd's fearful sense of his own "frailty."}

[3] {This is the first printed edition of Godolphin's poems.}

WILLIAM PRYNNE
(1600–1669)

Prynne, whose pamphleteering counts among the causes of the English Civil War, came from a prosperous farming family. He entered Oriel College, Oxford, in 1616, taking his BA in 1621, the same year he began studying law at Lincoln's Inn. Between 1626 and his death forty-three years later, Prynne published over 200 tracts, several the size of Shakespeare's first folio. His early publications defend Calvinist orthodoxy (see his 1629 *God no impostor* <*supra*>) and press for a puritan reformation of manners, denouncing long hair in men, short hair in women, drinking toasts, mixed dancing, maypoles, and stage plays. *Histriomastix*, his massive 1632 treatise against the latter, brought on a Star Chamber trial, and conviction, for seditious libel: that the book more-or-less called the Queen a whore did not help his case, but the principal offense was the more serious one of alienating the people's love for their King by arguing at endless length that dancing, plays, and the like were satanic, that those who engaged in such activities were damned, and that those who permitted them were snuffing the light of the Gospel in order to return England to paganism and popery. The court's sentence barked worse than it bit, so that within a year Prynne was out of jail and back to pamphleteering: primarily, at this point, against the Laudian bishops. In 1641, he came out against episcopacy itself; by 1643 he was writing in support of Parliamentary sovereignty; in 1643–44 he threw his legal and authorial energies into securing Laud's execution. However, he was no more receptive to presbyterian *divino iure* claims than he had been to the bishops', and liked the Independents even less. He vehemently condemned the regicide, and after 1649 his sympathies shifted back towards the royalists, a change of heart noted by the new Commonwealth, which held him in prison from 1650 to 1653. Upon his release, he worked behind the scenes on behalf of the royalist cause, and at the Restoration Charles II appointed him keeper of the Tower records, in which capacity he produced historical scholarship of lasting value.

No single label fits Prynne's ecclesio-political stance. He was a Calvinist, a puritan, but also, as William Lamont forcefully argues, an Erastian moderate, committed to the divine right of kings and royal supremacy. (One of his main charges against Laud was that his high-church episcopalianism threatened the king's prerogative.) Yet, however moderate his core beliefs and however exemplary the historical scholarship of his final years, from the early 1630s to the late 1640s, Prynne exploited to full effect (and with, I suspect, full consciousness of the likely effects) the rhetoric of a fire-breathing demagogue. He was a fervent conspiracy theorist who seems never to have met a popish plot he did not credit: *News from Ipswich* casts the bishops as masked papists; later tracts have Levellers and Quakers playing the same role. He readily denounced any practice or position of which he disapproved—a long list—in violent terms and with very little regard for either truth or consequences. His edition of Laud's diary, which was timed to come out on the final day of his treason trial, included the tidbit that Laud had been offered a Cardinal's hat if he would defect to Rome, omitting the next sentence, in which the Laud noted his refusal.

News from Ipswich, which led to Prynne's second Star Chamber conviction for seditious libel, gives a fairly accurate sense of his modus operandi. Writing to John Winthrop in New England, an anonymous correspondent describes it as "a book of extreme bitterness, & far enough off from the spirit of Christ, wherein the libeler (for so he is generally termed) speaks of the bishops that which the Archangel would not speak unto the devil" (*Collections* 447). Most of Prynne's allegations concern seemingly minor changes made to the 1636 fast book[1] read through the magnifying lens of an hermeneutic of suspicion. Prynne thus suggests the strong likelihood that, by omitting the prayer for seasonable weather found in earlier fast books, the prelates had brought on the recent tempests at sea.[2] Other accusations are similarly tendentious; even Gardiner, who thoroughly dislikes Laud, notes that his speech at Prynne's trial made mincemeat of the accusations *News from Ipswich* had made against him.[3] In all fairness, it should be added that Laud himself plays fast and loose with some factual details. In response to one of Prynne's main charges—that Laud dropped the words "who art the Father of thine elect and of their seed" from the prayer for the royal family in order to insinuate that its members "were all reprobates & none of the number of God's elect"—Laud explains that the words had been dropped by his predecessor at the beginning of Charles' reign, the new King at that time having neither wife nor children. This is technically true, but Laud fails to mention that after Charles became a father, the phrase was put back, only to disappear for good in 1634, shortly after Laud had succeeded Abbot at Canterbury. In the Laudian prayer books, the minister asks God to endue the royal family with "thy Holy Spirit, enrich them with thy heavenly grace, prosper them with all happiness, and bring them to thine everlasting kingdom, through Jesus Christ our Lord," rendering the absurdity and malice of Prynne's charge apparent. Laud was not consigning the royal family to hell; it seems reasonable to assume that he took out the phrase because of its heavy-handed Calvinism but chose not to ruffle feathers by stating this in open court.

---

[1] The fast books were special penitential liturgies issued at times of crisis and disaster.

[2] Both Prynne and Burton (see Dow, *Innovations <infra>*) lay claim to an extraordinary knowledge of divine semiotics.

[3] I have quoted fragments of Laud's speech, published under the title *A speech delivered in the Star Chamber . . . at the censure of John Bastwick, Henry Burton, & William Prynne* (1637), at relevant points in the notes to *News from Ipswich*.

As for the 1637 trial of Prynne and his co-defendants Burton and Bastwick, often seen as the moment when popular opinion tipped decisively against the Caroline regime, one can scarcely do better than Gardiner's magisterial account:

Prynne's style of writing had not grown less bitter since his exposure in the pillory in 1634. . . . ¶Burton was as outspoken as Prynne. On November 5, 1636, he preached two sermons which he afterwards published under the title of *For God and the King*. In these he attacked the tables turned into altars, the crucifixes set up, and the bowing towards the east, with a fierce relentlessness which was certain to tell on the popular mind. The inference which would be widely drawn was that these innovations being the work of the bishops, the sooner their office was abolished the better it would be for the nation.

The inference at which Burton arrived was the starting-point of Bastwick. Born in Essex, and brought up, like so many Essex men, in the straitest principles of puritanism, he had, after a short sojourn at Emmanuel College, the stronghold of puritanism at Cambridge, left England to serve as a soldier, probably in the Dutch army. He afterwards studied medicine at Padua, and returned home in 1623 to practice his profession at Colchester.

Ten years later he published his *Flagellum pontificis* in Holland. It was an argument in favor of presbyterianism. He was, in consequence, brought before the High Commission and sentenced to exclusion from the practice of medicine, and to an imprisonment which was to last till he saw fit to retract his opinions. . . . ¶The *Flagellum pontificis* was a staid production, unlikely to inflame the minds even of those who were able to read the Latin in which it was couched. . . . At last he flung off all restraint, and struck fiercely at his persecutors. *The Litany of John Bastwick* (1637) kept no quarter with the bishops. "From plague, pestilence, and famine," he prayed, "from bishops, priests, and deacons, good Lord, deliver us!" The prelates, he said, were the enemies of God and the king. They were the tail of the Beast. . . . The Church was "as full of ceremonies as a dog is full of fleas." . . . In Bastwick's eyes the ecclesiastical courts were altogether abominable. "I shall ever be of this opinion," he wrote, "that there is never a one of the prelates' courts but the wickedness of that alone and their vassals in it is able to bring a continual and perpetual plague upon the King's three dominions." . . . "Take notice," he wrote in conclusion, "so far am I from flying or fearing, as I resolve to make war against the Beast, and every limb of Antichrist, all the days of my life. . . . If I die in that battle, so much the sooner I shall be sent in a chariot of triumph to Heaven; and when I come there, I will, with those that are under the altar, cry, 'How long, Lord, holy and true, dost thou not judge and avenge our blood upon them that dwell upon the earth?'"

On June 14 the three assailants of the bishops appeared before the Star Chamber to answer to a charge of libel. Even men who were attached to the existing system of government long remembered with bitterness the scene which followed. When Prynne took his place at the bar, Finch called upon the usher of the court to hold back the locks with which he had done his best to cover the scars left by the execution of his former sentence. "I had thought," said the Chief

Justice with a sneer, "Mr. Prynne had no ears, but methinks he hath ears." The executioner had dealt mercifully with him three years before, and there was still a possibility of carrying out the sentence which Finch had made up his mind to inflict. The three cases were practically undefended. Burton's answer had been signed by his counsel but was rejected by the court as irrelevant. The answers of the other two were so violent that no lawyer could be induced to sign them. The three accused persons said what they could, but in the place in which they stood nothing that they could say was likely to avail them. . . .

The sentence was indeed a foregone conclusion. At Cottington's motion the three accused men were condemned to lose their ears, to be fined £5,000 apiece, and to be imprisoned for the remainder of their lives in the Castles of Carnarvon, Launceston, and Lancaster, where, it was fondly hoped, no breath of puritan sympathy would reach them more. Finch savagely added a wish that Prynne should be branded on the cheeks with the letters S. L., as a Seditious Libeller, and his suggestion was unanimously adopted.

The speech which Laud delivered in court was long and argumentative. The main charge which had been brought against him by the prisoners was that the ceremonies which he had enforced were innovations on established usage. His answer was in effect that they were not innovations on the established law. On many points of detail he had far the better of the argument . The removal of the communion-table to the east end he treated as a mere matter of convenience, for the sake of decency and order; and he quoted triumphantly an expression of the Calvinistic Bishop Davenant, "'Tis ignorance to think that the standing of the holy table there relishes of Popery." His own practice of bowing he defended. "For my own part," he said, "I take myself bound to worship with body as well as soul whenever I come where God is worshipped; and were this kingdom such as would allow no holy table standing in its proper place—and such places some there are—yet I would worship God when I came into His house." He flatly denied that he had compelled anyone to follow his example. . . .

To the question of the king's jurisdiction in ecclesiastical matters Laud answered with equal firmness. One of the charges brought against the Archbishop was that he was undermining the royal authority by laying claim to a divine right for his own order. On this point the speech was most emphatic. "Though our office," Laud said, "be from God and Christ immediately, yet may we not exercise that power, either of order or jurisdiction, but as God hath appointed us; that is, not in his Majesty's or any Christian king's kingdoms but by and under the power of the King given us so to do." So pleased was Charles with the language of the Archbishop that he ordered the immediate publication of his speech. He also referred to the judges the question whether the bishops had infringed on his prerogative by issuing processes in their own names, and the judges unanimously decided that they had not.

Whatever the judges might say they could not meet the rising feeling that the power of the Crown was being placed at the disposal of a single ecclesiastical party. Large numbers of Englishmen leapt to the conclusion that the object of that party was the restoration of papal authority. The three years which had just gone by . . . had effected a great change in the temper of the nation. In 1634, as far as any evidence has reached us, Prynne had suffered uncheered by any sign of sympathy. There was no lack of sympathy now. As he stepped forth, with Burton and Bastwick by his side, on his way to the place where the sentence of the Star Chamber was to be carried out, he found the path strewed with herbs and flowers. Bastwick was the first to mount the scaffold. He was quickly followed by his wife. She kissed him on his ears and mouth. The crowd set up an admiring shout. "Farewell, my dearest," said her husband as she turned to descend, "be of good comfort; I am nothing dismayed."

For two hours the three stood pilloried, conversing freely with the bystanders. . . . Prynne characteristically employed his time in explaining that his sentence was not warranted by precedent. The real cause of his coming there, he said, was his refusal to acknowledge that the prelates held their office by divine right. He was ready to argue the question against all comers, and, if he did not make his point good, to be "hanged at the Hall Gate." Once more the people shouted applaudingly. Burton followed, thanking God that he had enabled him thus to suffer. Even the rough men whose duty it was to superintend the execution were melted to pity, and sought to alleviate his suffering by placing a stone to ease the weight of the pillory on his neck. His wife sent him a message that "she was more cheerful of that day than of her wedding-day." "Sir," called out a woman in the crowd, "every Christian is not worthy of the honor which the Lord hath cast on you this day." "Alas!" replied Burton,"who is worthy of the least mercy? But it is his gracious favor and free gift to account us worthy in the behalf of Christ to suffer anything for his sake."

At last the time arrived for sharper suffering. . . . "The hangman," wrote one who recorded the scene, "burnt Prynne in both the cheeks, and, as I hear, because he burnt one cheek with a letter the wrong way, he burnt that again; presently a surgeon clapped on a plaster to take out the fire. The hangman hewed off Prynne's ears very scurvily, which put him to much pain." . . . A story got about which, whether it were true or false, was certain to be eagerly credited, that a Popish fellow told some of those which wept that, if so be they would turn Catholics, they need fear none of this punishment. On his way back to prison Prynne composed a Latin distich, in which he interpreted the S L which he now bore indelibly on his cheeks as *Stigmata Laudis*, the Scars of Laud.

Sources: *ODNB*; *Collections of the Massachusetts Historical Society*, vol. 6 (1863): 398–452; *A forme of common prayer together with an order of fasting: for the averting of God's heavie visitation upon many places of this kingdome* (1636); S. R. Gardiner, *History of England from the accession of James I to the outbreak of the Civil War*, 10 vols. (Longmans, Green, 1909), 8:228–32; William Lamont, *Puritanism and the English Revolution*, vol. 1: *Marginal Prynne, 1660–1669* (1963; repr. Aldershot: Gregg Revivals, 1991); Shuger, *Censorship*.

WILLIAM PRYNNE (alias Matthew White)

News from Ipswich
1636

Woe be unto the pastors that destroy and scatter
the sheep of my pasture, saith the Lord.
Jer. 23:1

Take heed therefore unto yourselves, and to all the flock over the which the Holy Ghost hath made you
bishops, to feed the Church of God, which he hath purchased with his own blood. For I know this,
that after my departing shall grievous wolves enter in among you, not sparing the flock.
Acts 20:28-29

Christian Reader, this is the deplorable news of our present age: that our presses formerly open only to *truth* and *piety* are closed up against them both of late, and patent for the most part to naught but *error, superstition, and profaneness.* Witness those *many profane erroneous, impious books,* printed within these 3 years by authority (pointblank against the established doctrine of the Church of *England* and his *Majesty's pious Declarations*) in defense of *Arminianism, popery, and popish ceremonies;*[1] and which is yet more impious and detestable, *against the very morality of the Sabbath and 4th Commandment:*[2] the divine institution, title, and entire religious sanctification of the Lord's-day SABBATH, and the

---

[1] [[Robert] *Shelford's 5 Treatises* {i.e., *Five pious and learned discourses* (1635)}; {Edmund} *Reeve, Communion book catechism expounded* {1636}; {Thomas} *Chounaeus, Collect{iones theologicarum quarundam conclusionum ex diversis authorum sententiis . . . excerptae* (1636)}; {Peter Heylyn,} *A coal from the altar* {1636}; {Anthony Stafford,} *The female glory* {1635}; {Peter} Studley, {*The looking-glasse of schisme* (1634)}; Dr. {Thomas} *Lawrence* and *Browne's* sermons, with others; {Richard Montagu,} *Apparatus ad hist. ecclesiast.* {i.e., *Apparatus ad origines ecclesiasticas* (1635)}.]

[2] [*The Treatise, History, Doctrine, and Discourse of the Sabbath* {i.e., Francis White, *A treatise of the Sabbath-day* (1635); Peter Heylyn, *A history of the Sabbath* (1636); John Prideaux, *The doctrine of the Sabbath* (1634); Christopher Dow, *A discourse of the Sabbath* (1636)}; {Robert Sanderson,} *A soveraigne antidote {against sabbatarian errours* (1636)}. Dr. {David} Primrose, {*A treatise of the Sabbath and the Lords-day* (1636)}; Reeve, Shelford, & Powel, in the life of King Iue {perhaps Robert Powell, *The life of Alfred, or Alured . . . together with a parallel of our soveraigne lord, K. Charles* (1634)}.]

necessity of frequent preaching (exceedingly pressed in our Homilies[3] and Book of Ordination[4]), which some of our unpreaching, domineering secular prelates (out of their arch-piety towards God and arch-charity to the people's souls, which they seek to murder) now so far detest that they not only give over preaching themselves, as no part of their function, & suppress most weekday lectures in divers countries; but have likewise lately shut up the mouths of sundry of our most godly, powerful, painful preachers (who have won more souls to God in a year than all the lord bishops in England or the world have done in divers ages) *out of mere malice to religion and the people's salvation*—contrary to the very laws of God and the realm—and strictly prohibited under pain of suspension, in sundry diocese, all afternoon sermons on the Lord's own day, that so the profane vulgar might have more time to dance, play, revel, drink, and profane God's Sabbaths, even in these days of plague and pestilence, *to draw down more plagues & judgments on us for this sin of Sabbath-breaking*. . . . Alas, what could Beelzebub the prince of devils, had he been an archbishop or lordly prelate here in England . . . have done more against the strict entire sanctification of the Christian Sabbath day to make it the devil's day instead of the Lord's Day and to advance his own kingdom and service on it, or against the frequent powerful preachers and preaching of God's word and salvation of the people's souls, than some Luciferian lord bishops have lately done, whose impiety in this kind transcends all precedents whatsoever in former ages? And yet these profane, atheistical, graceless persecutors of all holiness, piety, sincerity, godly ministers, and preaching of God's word (yea in these pestilential times, as means to spread the plague, though the Scripture and all former ages have prescribed fasting, preaching, and praying as the chief antidotes and cure against it) will needs be lord bishops *jure divino* by the *Holy Ghost's own institution* (who never yet instituted any unpreaching, rare-preaching prelates or persecutors and suppressors of preaching) and shame not to style themselves the godly holy Fathers of our Church and pillars of our faith, whenas their fruits and actions manifest them to be naught else but the very *step-fathers and caterpillars*, the very pests and plagues of both. Take but one fresh instance for an example: these desperate arch-agents for the devil and pope of Rome, and master-underminers of our religion, as they were the only instruments of delaying the present general fast in the beginning of the pestilence when it was most acceptable and requisite; so, to shew their inveterate malice against preaching (the thing that the devil wrestleth most against[5]—all whose study hath been to decay the office of preaching, which should not be diminished) they (contrary to his Majesty's pious intention, who hath so oft protested against all innovations) have cunningly caused all sermons (the very life and soul of a fast, as being the only means to humble men for their sins & bring them to repentance) to be prohibited on the fast-day, both in London and the suburbs, and in all other infected places, during the time of the infection in them.[6] In parishes not infected (as if preaching only of all God's ordinances were pestilential, & that on the fast-day, not

---

[3] [preface to them, Of the right use of the Church]

[4] [exhortation to those that are to be made Ministers]

[5] [Bp. Latimer's 4th & 6th Sermons before King Edw., which I would our prelates would now peruse, and his Sermon of the Plough]

[6] {In his Star Chamber speech responding to Prynne, Burton, and Bastwick's allegations against him, Laud notes that the prohibition "was no particular act of prelates; but the business was debated at the Council-table, being a matter of State as well as of religion" (Laud, *Works* 6:46).}

on others), contrary to the precedents of all former ages, & orders for the general fasts in the two last great plagues, which prescribed two sermons of one hour long apiece, forenoon and afternoon, every fast day, and that as well in parishes infected as others, even in the summer season when the infection was more contagious and raging than now. By which device they have not only made this fast distasteful to all sorts of men in infected places, who have little heart unto it; robbed the poor of much charitable relief; and deprived the people of the spiritual food & physic of their souls, when they need and desire it most, to their intolerable grief & discontent; but quite suppressed all settled Wednesday lectures in London and other infected towns as long as the infection shall continue in any one parish, though it should last these 7 years (the thing they principally aimed at); forced many ministers & people to fly out of infected places into the country to keep their fasts where there is preaching; brought in a *famine of God's word, the greatest plague of all others*, to the increasing & further spreading of the present pestilence *& drawing down of God's wrath upon us to the uttermost, by inhibiting ministers in the time of greatest need to preach unto the people that they may be saved.* O heavens, stand amazed at this unparalleled practice of impious popish prelates. But is this all? No, verily. For whereas his Majesty [see the proclamation] commanded that the book of common prayer for the fast, formerly set forth by his authority upon the like occasion, should be reprinted, these Romish inquisitors have miserably gelded it, after it was new printed, in sundry particulars. First, they have purged out the prayer for seasonable weather: one cause of the shipwrecks & tempestuous unseasonable weather ever since its publication.[7] Secondly, they have dashed *the Lady Elizabeth and her children* in the old collect quite out of the new;[8] as they have expunged both them, with our gracious King, Queen, and their children, out of the catalogue of God's elect, by blotting out this clause, *who art the Father of thine elect and of their seed*, out of the collect for them in this and all new common prayer books, as if they were all reprobates & none of the number of God's elect, either to a temporal or an eternal crown. O intolerable impiety, affront, and horrid treason. Thirdly, they have left out this collect: *It had been best for us &c.* in the new book (though the most effectual prayer of all) because it magnifies continual, often preaching of God's word and the Scriptures, and calls our powerful preachers *God's servants*: a sign these prelates have conspired together like so many execrable traitors to extirpate our frequent powerful preachers and continual preaching of God's word (as they have done in many places of late), though prescribed by God himself, & our Homilies. Fourthly, they have dashed this remarkable clause out of the first collect: *Thou hast delivered us from superstition and idolatry* (two grand causes both of many former, and our present plagues no doubt) *wherein we were utterly drowned, & hast brought us into the most clear and comfortable light of thy blessed word; by which we are taught how to serve and honor thee, and how to live orderly with our neighbors in truth and verity*[9]—the rest of the collect remaining as before. Now what can

---

[7] {Laud comments that "when this last book was set out, the weather was very seasonable" (*Works* 6:48).}

[8] {Laud observes that their names were removed from the collect "according to the course of the Church, which ordinarily names none in the prayer but the right line descending"; once Charles had a child, his sister and her children were no longer in the direct line of succession to the English crown (*Works* 6:49).}

[9] {Laud comments, "though God did deliver our forefathers out of 'Romish superstition,' yet (God be

be the cause of this strange purgation but a resolved professed conspiracy of these Romish prelates even now again utterly to drown us in popish superstition and idolatry[10] (which have now drowned us in God's judgments by their stupendous late increase among us) and to remove us out of *the most clear and comfortable light of God's word, by the which we are taught how to serve and honor him* (the true cause why they now suppress lectures, preaching, and suspend our powerfulest preachers everywhere), that so we may walk on in Romish hellish darkness, serving and honoring the pope and devil instead of God, *and live in all disorder, without truth or verity.* Fifthly, in the 6th order for the fast, they have pared away this passage—*to avoid the inconvenience that may grow by the abuse of fasting, some esteeming it a meritorious work; others a good work and of itself acceptable to God without due regard of the end*—only to gratify the Papists whose doctrine this is, and to place some merit in this present fast;[11] adding this clause to it—*in places where sermons are allowed by the Proclamation*—of purpose to put down Wednesday lectures, and preaching in London and other places where any parish is infected. If these prelates then be thus desperately wicked and popish, as to take advantage of God's judgments to suppress the preaching and preachers of his word when it is most necessary and useful, and to countenance, justify, and set up popery, superstition, idolatry, error, and disorder (the chief causes of our plagues), even in these days of pestilence, & that in the very fast-book to abuse and *mock God to his face*, to dishonor his Majesty and grieve his people's souls: how transcendently impious & popish will they prove when God shall stay this plague, if they be not now deservedly punished for these their notorious impieties? And is it not high time then for his Majesty to hang up such arch-traitors to our faith, Church, religion, & such true-bred sons to the Roman antichrist (from whom Dr. Pocklington boasts they are lineally descended), & to execute judgment on them for these strange purgations & other their Romish innovations, whereat the whole kingdom cry shame; which breed a general fear of a sudden alteration of our religion? Certainly till his Majesty shall see these purgations rectified, superstition & idolatry removed, God's Sabbaths duly sanctified, the suppressed preachers & preaching of God's word restored;[12] and hang up some of these Romish prelates & inquisitors before the Lord as the Gibeonites once did the 7 sons of Saul, we can never hope to abate any of God's plagues . . . which have strangely increased since this fast begun, contrary to all human reason and probability, whereas it much decreased before . . . a clear evidence that God is much offended with these purgations & the restraint of preaching on the fast day, against which some prelates are so mad that they have silenced & persecuted divers ministers since the fast proclaimed, there being now so many suspended in our Norwich diocese, only for not yielding to popish innovations, that in sundry churches *they have neither prayers, preaching, nor fasting*, which hath brought the plague among them and made the people at their wits' ends, many ministers & people

---

blessed for it) we were never in. And therefore that clause being unfittingly expressed, we thought fit to pass it over" (*Works* 6:49).}

[10] [Witness their altering of the Gunpowder-treason book, their pleading for the pope and Church of Rome, and setting up altars, images, crucifixes, and bowing to them in all cathedrals, and elsewhere, and in their own chapels]

[11] {Laud comments that it was left out "because in this age and kingdom there is little opinion of meriting by fasting" (*Works* 6:49).}

[12] [The honor and safety of the kingdom. 2 Chron. 17:7-10]

there having left the kingdom and thousands more being ready to depart the land, there being never such a persecution or havoc made among God's ministers since Q. Mary's days as a lecherous proud insolent prelate[13] hath there lately made, against all laws of God and man, to the astonishment of the whole realm. What then can we expect but plagues upon plagues, till such desperate persecutors be cut off & God's word and ministers restored unto their former liberty by our most gracious Sovereign—*persecution of God's ministers and people being one chief cause of plagues.* Wherefore O England, England, if ever thou wilt be free from pests and judgments, take notice of these thy antichristian prelates' desperate practices, innovations, & popish designs, to bewail, oppose, redress them with all thy force and power. O all ye English nobles, courtiers, and others, who have any love or spark of religion, piety, zeal, any tenderness of his Majesty's honor or care for the people's, the Church or kingdom's safety yet remaining within your generous breasts, put to your helping hands & prayers to rescue our religion and faithful ministers now suspended from the jaws of these *devouring wolves* and tyrannizing lordly prelates (raised from the dunghill) who make havoc of them both. O our most pious King Charles, as thou hast in two several Declarations protested *before God to all thy loving subjects, that thou wilt never give way to the licensing or authorizing of anything whereby* ANY INNOVATION IN THE LEAST DEGREE *may creep into our Church; nor ever connive at* ANY BACKSLIDING TO POPERY; *and that it is thy heart's desire to be found worthy of that title which thou esteemest the most glorious in all thy crown, Defender of the Faith*: to now behold these desperate innovations, purgations, and Romish practices of thy prelates, in open affront of these thy Declarations; & now or never shew thyself (as we all hope, believe, and pray thou wilt) a prince more worthy of this glorious title than any of thy royal progenitors, by rooting all popery, superstition, idolatry, errors, innovations out of this Church & kingdom, by restoring the preaching, the preachers of God's word, and purity of his worship, and *taking vengeance* on these perfidious prelates who have thus gelded thy fast-book (and intend to make an *Index expurgatorius* upon all other ancient English writers ere they be reprinted, a thing considerable), thus openly abused thy only sister and her children now present with thee, oppressed and grieved thy faithful subjects, dishonored thy God, betrayed thy religion, increased the plague among thy people, & as much as in them lieth, robbed thee both of thy God's and people's loves, & pulled thy crown off thy royal head to set it on their own traitorous ambitious pates by exercising all ecclesiastical power—yea papal jurisdiction—over thy subjects in their own names and rights alone; and by trampling all thy laws and subjects' liberties like cobwebs, thy subjects like dogs and dirt under their tyrannical papal feet. If thou thus *execute judgment on them* and ease thy people from their intolerable tyranny, no doubt *this plague shall be ceased* and this fast be pleasing to the Lord; else he will not accept it, but proceed to plague us more and more. O blessed sovereign, that thou didst but hear the several cries and outcries of thy people against these persecuting prelates in many places . . . the people cry for the bread of their souls, and their ministers are prohibited to give it them. This not only wounds but breaks their hearts and makes them amazed. O therefore gracious sovereign, help now and hear the petitions, cries, and tears of thy poor people, and hang up these popelings for these and other their

---

[13] {i.e., Matthew Wren, bishop of Norwich, 1633–38}

innumerable oppressions, extortions, innovations and harms, who suspend, imprison, and ruin others for mere toys and trifles, yea for defending your royal prerogative against their papal usurpations.

This is all the news I shall now impart in this coranto. The next week, God willing, you shall hear of Mr. Dade his excommunicating of Ferdinando Adams, a churchwarden in our town, for not blotting out this sentence of Scripture written on Mr. Ward's church wall over his bawdy thievish court:[14] *it is written my house shall be called an house of prayer, but ye have made it a den of thieves* [Matt. 21:13] . . . and of the strange proceedings at Colchester against Mr. Samuel Burrowes for indicting Parson Necoman for railing in the Communion table altar-wise and causing the communicants to come up to the rail to receive in a new unaccustomed manner, contrary to the statute of 1 Eliz. c. 2 and his Majesty's Declarations.[15] . . . In the meantime, I shall conclude my News with the words of Patrick Adamson Archbishop of St. Andrewes, in his *Public recantation in the Synod of Fife*, April 8, 1591:[16] *That the office of a diocesan bishop hath no authority at all to support it in the word of God; that it is only founded on the politic device of men; that the primacy of the pope or antichrist sprung from it, that it is worthily condemned; and that it hath been for 500 years and more the chief original and instrument of suppressing the preaching of God's word in all kingdoms, as all ecclesiastical historians testify.* I therefore shall close up all with the collect on S. Matthias' Day: *Almighty God, which in the place of the traitor Bishop[17] Judas, didst choose thy faithful servant Matthias, to be of the number of the 12 Apostles* [Acts 1:20]: *grant that thy Church, being always preserved from false Apostles, may be ordered and guided by faithful and true pastors, through Jesus Christ our Lord.* And with the collect on St. Peter's Day: Almighty God, which by thy Son Jesus Christ hath given to thy Apostle St. Peter many excellent gifts and commandedst him earnestly to feed thy flock: make (we beseech thee) all bishops and pastors diligently to preach thy holy word, and the people obediently to follow the same, that they may receive the crown of everlasting glory, through Jesus Christ our Lord,

Amen.

From Ipswich, November 12, 1636.
Thine in the Lord, *Matthew White.*

[14] {Note dated 1845 on back fly-leaf: "Mr. Ward was minister of St. Mary Tower, and the bawdy thievish court refers to the ecclesiastical court held in that church—called the Archdeacon's Court. It still exists at the east end of the South aisle."}

[15] {Prynne treats the Burrowes-Necoman clash at length in his *A quench-coale, or, a briefe disquisition and inquirie, in what place of the church or chancell the Lords-Table ought to be situated* (n.p., 1637), 351–58; see also John Walter, *Understanding popular violence in the English Revolution: the Colchester plunderers* (Cambridge UP, 1999), 173–84.}

[16] {This document is now widely suspected of having been a forgery.}

[17] {The word "Bishop" is Prynne's addition to the Prayer Book collect.}

TEXT: EEBO (STC [2nd ed.] / 20469.7)

News from Ipswich. Discovering certain late detestable practices of some domineering lordly prelates, to undermine the established doctrine and discipline of our Church, extirpate all orthodox sincere preachers and preaching of God's word, usher in popery, superstition and idolatry; with their late notorious purgations of the new fast-book, contrary to his Majesty's proclamation, and their intolerable affront therein offered to the most illustrious Lady Elizabeth, the King's only sister, and her children, (even whiles they are now royally entertained at Court) in blotting them out of the collect; and to his Majesty, his Queen and their royal progeny, in blotting them out of the number of God's Elect (Printed at Ipswich [i.e. London?]: [s.n.], 1636).

JOHN HALES
(1584–1656)

The son of a Somerset attorney, Hales entered Corpus Christi, Oxford, in 1597, receiving his BA in 1603, by which point—despite (or perhaps because of) this longer than usual time-to-degree—he had already won a reputation for scholarship. Shortly after graduation, Sir Thomas Bodley gave Hales a post in his newly erected library. Then in 1605, the same year Hales took holy orders, Sir Henry Savile offered him the Greek lectureship at Merton, where he joined the editorial team working on the magisterial Chrysostom edition (the eight-volume Greek text printed 1610–12 at Savile's own press at Eton), a team that included Richard Montagu. In 1613 Savile, who was the Eton provost as well as the warden of Merton, had both Hales and Montagu appointed to fellowships at Eton. From 1615 to 1619 Hales also served as Oxford's regius professor of Greek; in 1618–19 he attended the Synod of Dort as chaplain to Sir Dudley Carleton, the English ambassador at The Hague—his letters to Carleton recounting the proceedings were published in 1659 as part of Hales' posthumous *Golden remains*.

In 1657 Hales' close friend Anthony Farindon wrote that Hales had "often" told him that at Dort he "bid John Calvin good night." Recent scholarship has raised some questions about this celebrated adieu. Hales' letters to Carleton are on the whole more sympathetic to the Calvinist party than their opposites (Godfrey 173), yet his 1617 Oxford sermon (the *Abuses of hard places of Scripture*) already displays the Erasmian rationalism of Hales' post-Dort theology, and of the Great Tew circle.

Upon his return from the Netherlands, Hales returned to teach and occasionally preach at Eton, his retirement broken by visits to London and perhaps also to Great Tew. He, Falkland, Hyde, and Chillingworth were in contact during the 1630s, and Hales' *Tract concerning schism* (ca. 1636) may have been written for Chillingworth, who was then at work on his *The religion of Protestants*.[1]

---

[1] Elson 22–23; see also the introduction to the Chillingworth readings <*infra*>).

When the Civil War broke out, Hales quickly lost the canonry at Windsor he had received in 1639 under circumstances to be discussed below. However, he continued at Eton unmolested until 1650, when he refused to swear allegiance to the new Commonwealth and was in consequence expelled from his fellowship. For some years thereafter he served as tutor and chaplain in the household of Lady Salter, Bishop Duppa's sister. As a proclaimed "malignant," his presence exposed Lady Salter to government reprisal, and in November 1655 Hales, now seventy-one, returned to Eton, lodging with the widow of a former college servant. He died six months later. John Aubrey met the elderly Hales at Eton wearing a violet gown (rather than clerical black) and reading Thomas à Kempis' *Imitatio Christi*. On his deathbed he dictated an orthodox confession of faith (later printed as "Mr. Hales' confession of the Trinity") in an attempt to refute the persistent charges of Socinianism leveled against him (Butt 272).

Hales has not received the attention his importance deserves, primarily, I suspect, because most of his work is undated, and perhaps undatable.[2] His funeral oration on Bodley was published in 1613, his sermon on Scriptural exegesis in 1617, but the rest of the sermons could, in principle, have been preached at any time between 1613 and 1649. However, the *Tract concerning schism* can be placed ca. 1636. The two sermons by Hales that follow the *Tract* in this volume probably date from before the unraveling of Caroline rule in the late 1630s, but whether two years before or twenty is anyone's guess. I put them under 1636 because they had to go somewhere.

That the *Tract* disturbed Laud when it came to his attention some time around 1638 is scarcely surprising, given its radically individualist, anti-authoritarian, anti-clerical, and anti-Laudian argument (Elson 93–100). Yet in crucial respects, Hales' outlook (like Chillingworth's, for whom the *Tract* may have been written) resembles Laud's: all three share a core Erasmian conviction that very little in the way of explicit belief is necessary for salvation; that these saving truths are those about which virtually all Christians agree; and therefore with respect to controverted issues, individuals can be left to follow their own judgments (provided their disagreements do not trouble the peace of the Church). For Laud, however, such judgments should rest on multiple criteria: ecclesiastical authority, patristic testimony, the universal consensus of Christians, the determinations of an individual's own rational inquiry.[3] Hales dismisses the first three with contempt; the only admissible scales are those held by reason.[4] Moreover, unlike Laud (and most conformist churchmen), Hales refuses to confine his Erasmian minimalism to questions of doctrine. Laud was prepared to allow considerable latitude of belief, while insisting on liturgical conformity; Hales quite pointedly makes requiring Christians to profess suspect doctrines all one with requiring them to use suspect ceremonies, and holds that a Church that

---

[2] The one monograph on Hales (Elson) mentions only printed sources, as does the 2004 *ODNB* entry, but neither indicates that an attempt was ever made to locate Hales' papers, so it is conceivable that manuscripts survive that might shed light on the chronology.

[3] Laud's position is very close to that of the Erasmian Catholic, Georg Cassander (1513–66), a similarity noted by contemporaries.

[4] Hales' rationalism is thus more stringent than Chillingworth's, which accepts universal consensus, together with individual reason, as normative <*vide infra*>.

imposes either is *eo ipso* schismatic. His point may have been to legitimate England's break with Rome, but its topical applicability is too obvious to have been unintended, especially given Hales' explicit censure of the beauty-of-holiness project for driving Christians apart over gewgaws.[5]

Laud could scarcely have been pleased, so when word that the Archbishop had seen the *Tract* got back to Hales, he wrote Laud, attempting to explain his position but retracting nothing.[6] Laud then summoned Hales to Lambeth. Clarendon, who at the time knew both men well, reports the interview in some detail.

> Dr. Laud, who was a very rigid surveyor of all things which never so little bordered upon schism, and thought the Church could not be too vigilant against and jealous of such incursions . . . sent for Mr. Hales, whom, when they had both lived in the University of Oxford, he had known well, and told him that he had in truth believed him to be long since dead; and chid him very kindly for having never come to him, having been of his old acquaintance; then asked him whether he had lately writ a short discourse of schism and whether he was of that opinion which that discourse implied. He told him that he had, for the satisfaction of a private friend (who was not of his mind) a year or two before writ such a small tract, without any imagination that it would be communicated; and that he believed it did not contain any thing that was not agreeable to the judgment of the primitive Fathers; upon which the Archbishop debated with him upon some expressions of Irenaeus and the most ancient Fathers; and concluded with saying that the time was very apt to set new doctrines on foot, of which the wits of the age were too susceptible, and that there could not be too much care taken to preserve the peace and unity of the Church; and from thence asked him of his condition and whether he wanted anything, and the other answering that he had enough and wanted or desired no addition, so dismissed him with great courtesy.[7]

Clarendon's account cannot be too far off, since it is a matter of record that shortly after this conversation Laud preferred Hales to a canon of Windsor, a rich and honorable sinecure just across the river from Eton.[8] Only one further scrap of information about their relationship survives: it is said that when Hales heard of Laud's execution six years later, he "wished he had died in his place" (Elson 27).

---

[5] Hales and Montagu take opposing positions so consistently that one wonders whether the views of each took shape in response to the other during their collaboration on the Chrysostom edition; the key issues on which they differ—the authority of councils, of antiquity, of tradition, of the Fathers—would have come up repeatedly.

[6] The letter was first published in 1716, with no indication as to whether the original had been found among Hales' papers or Laud's; the prose is surely Hales', but it is conceivable that he never sent it (Lyte 239–40).

[7] *Life of the Earl of Clarendon*, reprinted in *The works of . . . Hales* 1:xiv. Peter Heylyn gives a somewhat different version in which Laud refutes all Hales' arguments, whereupon Hales decides to return to the folds of orthodoxy and the bosom of Mother Church, a version Heylyn attributes to Hales, whom he knew (Elson 25, quoting Heylyn's 1668 *Cyprianus Anglicus* 362).

[8] Lyte (240) says that Laud also made Hales one of his chaplains.

The sermon on Luke 16:25 (the parable of Dives and Lazarus), which follows the *Tract* and letter to Laud in this volume, has none of their proto-Enlightenment edge. It is also wholly characteristic of Hales' preaching on Christian ethics, both in its emphases on charity and self-denial and in its deep traditionalism.[9] Hales' teaching is that of the Greek Fathers, but also medieval poor law: the duty to bestow one's "superflux" on "poor naked wretches" that Lear intuits in the storm. The sermon challenges a congregation of upper-class boys with the Church's ancient social gospel.[10]

However, the final sermon, titled by eighteenth-century editors "Of inquiry and private judgment in religion," returns to the radicalism of the *Tract* (where "radical" connotes not simply opposition to dominant ideologies but opposition along lines that anticipate modernity), but this time not in a private communication to a fellow scholar but in a sermon preached to boys and townsfolk. It vigorously defends rationalism, individualism, anti-clericalism, and intellectual egalitarianism with respect to both class and gender: everyone is to think and judge for him- or herself; the laity are to take nothing on trust from their ministers; truth is not given in some normative past but discovered through on-going inquiry. The sermon's commitments are those of Milton's *Areopagitica*, but Hales is a Caroline churchman preaching to the sons of England's ruling elite from a pulpit virtually under the walls of Windsor Castle.[11]

How could Hales have been permitted to hold these views? Why did Laud prefer rather than punish him? The answer must have something to do with Hales' insistence in the letter to Laud that his true aim was "no more than that precept of the Apostle: *As far as is possible, have peace with all men. . . .* [and] there could be no great harm in the premises, where the conclusion was nothing but peace." The *Tract*, Clarendon points out, argued *against* "the frequent and uncharitable reproaches of heretic and schismatic too lightly thrown at each other amongst men who differ in their judgment" (Hales 1:xiii). Moreover—and here the crucial difference between Hales' stance and that of *Areopagitica* comes into focus—Hales decided against publication.[12] He did so, Clarendon explains, not because he feared for himself but rather because, "he would often say," although "his opinions, he was sure, did him no harm," yet "he was far from being confident that they might not do others harm who entertained them, and might entertain other results from them than he did; and therefore he was very reserved in communicating what he thought himself in those points in which he differed from what was received" (Hales 1:xi). What mattered to Hales was not rights and liberties. Like the rest of Great Tew circle—royalists to a man in the end—he sought to discern a way "whereby private judgment, Christian charity, and civil peace might be preserved" (Elson 2). Yet Hales was in many respects a

---

[9] See Brian Tierney, *Medieval poor law* (U California P, 1959), 34–37; Debora Shuger, "Subversive Fathers and Suffering Subjects: Shakespeare and Christianity," in *Religion, Literature, and Politics in Post-Reformation England, 1540–1688*, ed. Richard Strier and Donna Hamilton (Cambridge UP, 1995), 50–53.

[10] Yet Hales' decision to ignore the liturgical calendar by giving the sermon on Shrovetide sits oddly with its traditionalist ethics—an oddness compounded by the second part of the sermon, which, preached on Easter Sunday, shifts emphasis from charity to a neo-Stoic detachment from worldly goods.

[11] Eton and Windsor are less than a mile apart.

[12] Hales published nothing after 1617; there were three unauthorized printings of the *Tract* in 1642; everything else is posthumous.

radical thinker, as both he and Laud knew, and his existence calls in question the binaries that structure received accounts of Caroline religion and Caroline politics.

SOURCES: *ODNB*; John Butt, "Izaak Walton's collections for Fulman's *Life of John Hales*," *Modern Language Review* 29.3 (1934): 267–73; James Elson, *John Hales of Eton* (New York: King's Crown Press, 1948); W. Robert Godfrey, "John Hales' good-night to John Calvin," in *Protestant scholasticism: essays in reassessment*, ed. Carl Trueman and R. Scott Clark, 165–80 (Paternoster, 1999); John Hales, *The works of the ever-memorable Mr. John Hales*, 3 vols. (Glasgow, 1765); H. C. Maxwell Lyte, *A history of Eton College, 1440–1910*, 3rd ed. (Macmillan, 1899).

JOHN HALES

A tract concerning schism
ca. 1636, published 1642

Heresy and *schism* as they are in common use, are two theological μορμώς or scarecrows, which they who uphold a party in religion use to fright away such as, making inquiry into it, are ready to relinquish and oppose it, if it appear either erroneous or suspicious. For as Plutarch reports of a painter who, having unskillfully painted a cock, chased away all cocks and hens that so the imperfection of art might not appear by comparison with nature; so men willing, for ends, to admit of no fancy but their own, endeavor to hinder an inquiry into it by way of comparison of somewhat with it, peradventure truer, that so the deformity of their own might not appear. But howsoever in the common manage *heresy* and *schism* are but ridiculous terms, yet the things in themselves are of very considerable moment, the one offending against truth, the other against charity, and therefore both deadly—where they are not by imputation but in deed.

It is then a matter of no small importance truly to descry the nature of them, that so they may fear, who are guilty of them; and they, on the contrary, strengthen themselves, who through the iniquity of men and times are injuriously charged with them.

Schism (for of heresy we shall not now treat . . .), schism, I say, upon the very sound of the word, imports division; division is not but where communion is or ought to be. Now communion is the strength and ground of all society, whether sacred or civil. Whosoever therefore they be that offend against this common society and friendliness of men and cause separation and breach among them, if it be in civil occasions, are guilty of sedition or rebellion; if it be by occasion of ecclesiastical difference, they are guilty of schism: so that schism is an ecclesiastical sedition, as sedition is a lay-schism. Yet the great benefit of communion notwithstanding, in regard of divers distempers men are subject to, dissension and disunion are often necessary: for when either false or uncertain conclusions are obtruded for truth, and acts either unlawful or ministering just scruple are required of us to be perform'd, in these cases, consent were conspiracy, and open contestation is not faction or schism but due Christian animosity {courage}.

For the further opening therefore of the nature of schism something must be added by way of difference to distinguish it from necessary separation: and that is, that the causes

828

upon which division is attempted proceed . . . from well-weighed and necessary reasons; and that, when all other means having been tried, nothing will serve to save us from guilt of conscience but open separation. So that schism, if we would define it, is nothing else but an unnecessary separation of Christians from that part of the visible Church of which they were once members. Now as in mutinies and civil dissensions there are two attendants-in-ordinary belonging unto them—one, the choice of one elector or guide, in place of the general or ordinary governor, to rule and guide; the other, the appointing of some public place or rendezvous where public meetings must be celebrated—so in church-dissensions and quarrels, two appurtenances there are which serve to make a schism complete.

First, the choice of a bishop in opposition to the former (a thing very frequent amongst the ancients, and which many times was both the cause and effect of schism).

Secondly, the erecting of a new church and oratory for the dividing-party to meet in publicly. For till this be done, the schism is but yet in the womb.

In that late famous controversy in Holland *de praedestinatione & auxiliis*, as long as the disagreeing parties went no further than disputes and pen-combats, the schism was all that while unhatched; but as soon as one party swept an old cloister and by a pretty art suddenly made it a church by putting a new pulpit in it for the separating party there to meet, now what before was a controversy became a formal schism.[1] To know no more than this, if you take it to be true, had been enough to direct how you are to judge and what to think of schism and schismatics; yet because in the ancients (by whom many men are more affrighted than hurt) much is said and many fearful dooms are pronounced, in this case will we descend a little to consider of schisms, as it were by way of story {history}, and that partly further to open that which we have said in general by instancing in particulars; and partly to disabuse those who, reverencing antiquity more than needs, have suffered themselves to be scared with imputation of schism above due measure. For what the ancients spake by way of censure of schism in general is most true; for they saw (and it is no great matter to see so much) that unadvisedly and upon fancy to break the knot of union betwixt man and man (especially amongst Christians, upon whom, above all other kind of men, the tie of love and communion doth most especially rest) was a crime hardly pardonable, and that nothing absolves a man from the guilt of it but true and unpretended conscience; yet when they came to pronounce of schisms in particular (whether it were because of their own interests, or that they saw not the truth, or for what other cause God only doth know), their judgments many times (to speak most gently) are justly to be suspected: which that you may see, we will range all schism into two ranks.

For there is a schism in which only one party is the schismatic: for where cause of schism is necessary, there not he that separates but he that occasions the separation is the schismatic.

Secondly, there is a schism wherein both parties are the schismatics: for where the occasion of separation is unnecessary, neither side can be excused from the guilt of schism.

But, you will ask, who shall be the judge what is necessary? Indeed that is a question which hath been often made, but I think scarcely ever truly answered; not because it is a

---

[1] {Hales probably refers here to the Counter-Remonstrant minister Rosaeus, who in 1617 took over a cloister church at the Hague—the implication being that, for Hales, the Calvinist party were the schismatics.}

point of great depth or difficulty truly to assoil it, but because the true solution carries fire in the tail of it. For it bringeth with it a piece of doctrine which is seldom pleasing to superiors. To you for the present this shall suffice: if so be you be *animo defaecato*, if you have cleared yourself from froth and grounds; if neither sloth nor fears nor ambition nor any tempting spirits of that nature abuse you (for these, and such as these, are the true impediments why both that and other questions of the like danger are not truly answered), if all this be, and yet you see not how to frame your resolution and settle yourself for that doubt, I will say no more of you than was said of Papias, St. John's own scholar, you are of small judgment, your abilities are not so good as I presumed.

But to go on with what I intended and from which that interloping question diverted me: that you may the better judge of the nature of schisms by their occasions, you shall find that all schisms have crept into the Church by one of these three ways: either upon matter of fact, or matter of opinion, or point of ambition. For the first, I call that matter of fact when something is required to be done by us, which either we know or strongly suspect to be unlawful. So the first notable schism of which we read in the Church contained in it matter of fact; for it being upon error taken for necessary that an Easter must be kept; and upon worse than error, if I may so speak (for it was no less than a point of Judaism forced upon the Church), upon worse than error, I say, thought further necessary that the ground for the time of our keeping that feast must be the rule left by Moses to the Jews; there arose a stout question, whether we were to celebrate with the Jews on the 14th moon, or the Sunday following? This matter, though most unnecessary, most vain, yet caused as great a combustion as ever was in the Church, the West separating and refusing communion with the East for many years together. In this fantastical hurry {tumult}, I cannot see but all the world were schismatics; neither can anything excuse them from that imputation, excepting only this, that we charitably suppose that all parties out of conscience did what they did. . . . By the way, by this you may plainly see the danger of our appeal unto antiquity for resolution in controverted points of faith, and how small relief we are to expect from thence. For if the discretion of the chiefest guides and directors of the Church did in a point so trivial, so inconsiderable, so mainly fail them as not to see the truth in a subject wherein it is the greatest marvel how they could avoid the sight of it, can we, without imputation of extreme grossness and folly, think so poor-spirited persons competent judges of the questions now on foot betwixt the Churches? Pardon me; I know not what temptation drew that note from me.

   . . .

. . . yet you may safely upon your occasions communicate with either, so be you flatter neither in their schism. For why might it not be lawful to go to church with the Donatist or to celebrate Easter with the Quartodeciman, if occasion so require, since neither nature nor religion nor reason doth suggest anything to the contrary? For in all public meetings pretending[2] holiness, so there be nothing done but what true devotion and piety brook, why may not I be present in them and use communication with them? Nay, what if those to whose care the execution of the public service is committed do something either unseemly or suspicious, or peradventure unlawful? what if the garments they wear be censured as, nay indeed be, superstitious? what if the gesture of adoration be used at

---

[2] {laying claim to—with no connotation of hypocrisy}

the altar, as now we have learned to speak? What if the homilist or preacher deliver any doctrine of the truth of which we are not well persuaded (a thing which very often falls out): yet for all this we may not separate, except we be constrained personally to bear a part in them ourselves. The priests under Eli had so ill demeaned themselves about the daily sacrifice that the Scripture tells us they made it to stink, yet the people refused not to come to the tabernacle nor to bring their sacrifice to the priest. For in these schisms which concern fact, nothing can be a just cause of refusal of communion but only to require the execution of some unlawful or suspected act. For not only in reason but in religion too, that maxim admits of no release, *cautissimi cujusque praeceptum quod dubitas, ne feceris*.[3] Long it was ere the Church fell upon schism upon this occasion, though of late it hath had very many; for until the second Council of Nicaea (in which conciliabule[4] superstition and ignorance did conspire), I say, until that rout did set up image-worship, there was not any remarkable schism upon just occasion of fact. All the rest of schisms of that kind were but wantonness; this was truly serious. In this the schismatical party was the synod itself and such as conspired with it. For concerning the use of images in *sacris*: first, it is acknowledged by all that it is not a thing necessary; secondly, it is by most suspected; thirdly it is by many held utterly unlawful. Can then the enjoining of the practice of such a thing be ought else but abuse? Or can the refusal of communion here be thought any other thing than duty? Here, or upon the like occasion, to separate may peradventure bring personal trouble and danger (against which it concerns every honest man to have *pectus benè praeparatum*[5]); further harm it cannot do. So that in these cases, you cannot be to seek what to think or what you have to do.

Come we then to consider a little of the second sort of schism, arising upon occasion of variety of opinion. It hath been the common disease of Christians from the beginning not to content themselves with that measure of faith which God and Scriptures have expressly afforded us; but out of a vain desire to know more than is revealed, they have attempted to discuss things of which we can have no light, neither from reason nor revelation; neither have they rested here, but upon pretence of church-authority, which is none, or tradition, which for the most part is but figment, they have peremptorily concluded and confidently imposed upon others a necessity of entertaining conclusions of that nature; and to strengthen themselves, have broken out into divisions and factions, opposing man to man, synod to synod, till the peace of the Church vanished without all possibility of recall. Hence arose those ancient and many separations amongst Christians occasioned by Arianism . . . and many more both ancient and in our time—all which indeed are but names of schism, howsoever in the common language of the Fathers they were called heresies. For heresy is an act of the will, not of reason; and is indeed a lie, not a mistake, else how could that known speech of Augustine go for true, *errare possum, haereticus esse nolo?*[6] Indeed Manichaeism, Valentianism, Marcionism, Mahometanism, are truly and properly heresies, for we know that the authors of them received them not but minted them themselves, and so knew that which they taught to be a lie. But can any man avouch that Arius

---

[3] {The safest rule is, if you are in doubt, do not do it.}
[4] {technical term for a minor ecclesiastical council}
[5] {a breast well prepared}
[6] {I might be wrong; I do not want to be a heretic.}

and Nestorius and others that taught erroneously concerning the Trinity or the person of our Savior did maliciously invent what they taught and not rather fall upon it by error and mistake? Till that be done, and that upon good evidence, we will think no worse of all parties than needs we must, and take these rents in the Church to be at the worst but schisms upon matter of opinion. In which case what we are to do is not a point of any great depth of understanding to discover, so be distemper and partiality do not intervene. I do not yet see, that . . . men of different opinions in Christian religion may not hold communion *in sacris* and both go to one church. Why may I not go, if occasion require, to an Arian church, so there be no Arianism expressed in their liturgy? And were liturgies and public forms of service so framed as that they admitted not of particular and private fancies, but contained only such things as in which all Christians do agree, schisms on opinion were utterly vanished. For consider of all the liturgies that are or ever have been, and remove from them whatsoever is scandalous to any party and leave nothing but what all agree on, and the event shall be that the public service and honor of God shall no ways suffer; whereas to load our public forms with the private fancies upon which we differ is the most sovereign way to perpetuate schism unto the world's end. Prayer, confession, thanksgiving, reading of Scriptures, exposition of Scripture, administration of sacraments in the plainest and simplest manner were matter enough to furnish out a sufficient liturgy, though nothing either of private opinion or of church-pomp, of garments, of prescribed gestures, of imagery, of music, of matter concerning the dead, of many superfluities which creep into the churches under the name of order and decency, did interpose itself. For to charge churches' liturgies with things unnecessary was the first beginning of all superstition, and when scruples of conscience began to be made or pretended, then schisms began to break in. If the spiritual guides and fathers of the Church would be a little sparing of encumbering churches with superfluities, and not over-rigid either in reviving obsolete customs or imposing new, there were far less danger of schism or superstition; and all the inconvenience were likely to ensue would be but this: they should in so doing yield a little to the imbecilities of inferiors, a thing which St. Paul would never have refused to do. Meanwhile, wheresoever false or suspected opinions are made a piece of the church liturgy, he that separates is not the schismatic, for it is alike unlawful to make profession of known or suspected falsehoods as to put in practice unlawful or suspect actions.

The third thing I noted for matter of schism was ambition, I mean episcopal ambition, shewing itself especially in two heads: one concerning plurality of bishops in the same see; another, the superiority of bishops in divers sees. Aristotle tells us that necessity causeth but small faults, but avarice and ambition were the mothers of great crimes. Episcopal ambition hath made this true. For no occasion hath produced more frequent, more continuing, more sanguinary schisms than this hath done. . . .

. . .

But that other head of episcopal ambition, concerning supremacy of bishops in divers sees, one claiming superiority over another, as it hath been from time to time a great trespasser against the Church's peace, so it is now the final ruin of it: the East and the West, through the fury of the two prime bishops, being irremediably separated without all hope of reconcilement. And besides all this mischief, it is founded in a vice contrary to all Christian humility, without which no man shall see his Savior. For they do but abuse themselves and others that would persuade us that bishops, by Christ's institution, have any superiority over other men further than of reverence; or that any bishop is superior to another further than positive order agreed upon amongst Christians hath prescribed. For we have believed him that hath told us *that in Jesus Christ there is neither high nor low; and that in giving honor, every man should be ready to prefer another before himself;* which sayings cut off all claim most certainly to superiority by title of Christianity, except men can think that these things were spoken only to poor and private men. Nature and religion agree in this, that neither of them hath a hand in this heraldry of *secundum sub & supra;* all this comes from composition and agreement of men among themselves. . . .

Now concerning schism arising upon these heads, you cannot be for behavior much to seek, for you may safely communicate with all parties as occasion shall call you; and the schismatics here are all those who are heads of the faction, together with all those who foment it; for private and indifferent persons, they may be spectators of these contentions as securely, in regard of any peril of conscience (for of danger in purse or person, I keep no account), as at a cock fight. Where serpents fight, who cares who hath the better? The best wish is that both may perish in the fight.

Now for conventicles, of the nature of which you desire to be informed, thus much in general. It evidently appears that all meetings upon unnecessary occasions of separation are to be so styled, so that in this sense, a conventicle is nothing else but a congregation of schismatics. Yet time hath taken leave sometimes to fix this name upon good and honest meetings, and that perchance not altogether without good reason. . . .

. . .

But when it was espied that ill-affected persons abus'd private meetings, whether religious or civil, to evil ends, religiousness to gross impiety . . . both Church and state joined, and jointly gave order for forms, times, places of public concourse, whether for religious or civil ends; and all other meetings whatsoever, besides those of which both time and place were limited, they censured for routs and riots and unlawful assemblies in the state, and in the Church for conventicles.

So that it is not lawful, no not for prayer, for hearing, for conference, for any other religious office whatsoever, for people to assemble otherwise than by public order is allowed. Neither may we complain of this in times of incorruption—for why should men desire to do that suspiciously in private which warrantably may be performed in public? But in times of manifest corruptions and persecutions wherein religious assembling is dangerous, private meetings, howsoever besides public order, are not only lawful but they are of necessity and duty; else how shall we excuse the meetings of Christians for public service in time of danger and persecutions, and of ourselves in Queen Mary's days? And how will those of the Roman Church amongst us put off the imputation of conventicling, who are known amongst us privately to assemble for religious exercise against all established order both in state and Church? For indeed all pious assemblies in times of persecution and corruptions, howsoever practiced, are indeed, or rather alone, the lawful congregations; and public assemblies, though according to form of law, are indeed nothing else but riots and conventicles, if they be stained with corruption and superstition.

>━━◆

Text: EEBO (Wing [2nd ed.] / H268A)
Four tracts, By the ever memorable Mr. JOHN HALES of Eaton College . . . (London, 1677), 40–51, 53–56.

JOHN HALES

"Letter to Archbishop Laud upon occasion of the Tract concerning schism"[1]
ca. 1638, published 1716

May it please your Grace,

Whereas of late an abortive discourse indited by me for the use of a private friend hath, without lawful pass, wandered abroad, and mistaking its way, is arrived at your Grace's hands, I have taken the boldness to present myself before you in behalf of it, with this either apology or excuse indifferently, being resolved *in utramvis aleam*[2] to beg either your approbation or your pardon. For myself, I have much marveled whence a scribbled paper, dropt from so worthless and inconsiderable a hand as mine, should recover so much strength as to be able to give offence. But I confess it to be most true, that *bellum inchoant inertes, fortes finiunt*; and a weak hand often kindles that fire which the concourse of the whole vicinity cannot quench. If therefore any fire can arise out of so poor a spark (which I can hardly conceive), I am myself here at hand to pour on water to prevent a further mischief.

Whatsoever there is in that schedule[3] which may seem apt to give offence consists either in phrase and manner of expression, or in the conceits and things themselves there pressed and insisted upon. For the first. Whosoever hath the misfortune to read it, shall find in it, for style, some things over-familiar and subrustic,[4] some things more pleasant[5] than needed, some things more sour and satirical. For these, my apology is but this: that your Grace would be pleased to take in consideration, first, what the liberty of a letter might entice me to. Secondly, I am by genius open and uncautelous;[6] and therefore some pardon might be afforded to harmless freedom and gaiety of spirit, utterly devoid of all distemper and malignity. Thirdly, some part of the theme I was to touch upon was (or

---

[1] {First published in 1716 in *Several tracts by J. H.*}

[2] {however the die may fall}

[3] {scrap of paper, jottings, brief note}

[4] {somewhat clownish or boorish}

[5] {facetious, jocular}

[6] {"genius" here means temperament; "uncautelous," unsuspecting}

at least seemed to me) of so small and inconsiderable a moment and yet hath raised that noise and tumult in the Church, that I confess it drew from me that indignation which is there expressed. When Augustus the Emperor was asked what was become of his *Ajax* (for he made a tragedy upon the life and fortunes of that man), he answered, *Incubuit in spongiam.*[7] For all these things which I have above touched upon, my answer is, *Incumbant in spongiam.*[8] And I could heartily wish (for in the case I am, I have nothing but good wishes to help me) that they into whose hands that paper is unluckily fallen would favor me so much as to sponge them out.

Now concerning the things discussed in the pamphlet, I humbly beg leave, before I come to particulars, to speak for myself thus much in general. If they be errors which I have here vented (as perchance they are), yet my will hath no part in them, and they are but the issues of unfortunate inquiry. Galen, that great physician, speaks thus of himself, *I know not how,* says that worthy person, *even from my youth up, in a wonderful manner, whether by divine inspiration, or by fury and possession, or however you may please to style it, I have much contemned the opinion of the many; but truth and knowledge I have above measure affected, verily persuading myself that a fairer, more divine fortune could never befall a man.* Some title, some claim I may justly lay to the words of this excellent person, for the pursuit of truth hath been my only care ever since I first understood the meaning of the word. For this I have forsaken all hopes, all friends, all desires which might bias me and hinder me from driving right at what I aimed. For this I have spent my money, my means, my youth, my age, and all I have: that I might remove from myself that censure of Tertullian,—*Suo vitio quis quid ignorat?*[9] If with all this cost and pains, my purchase is but error, I may safely say, to err hath cost me more than it has many to find the truth; and truth itself shall give me this testimony at last, that if I have missed of her, it is not my fault, but my misfortune.

Having begged your Grace's pardon for this περιαυτολογία[10] (peradventure unseasonable), I will take liberty to consider of the things themselves discussed in the pamphlet.

And first, howsoever I have miscast some parcels of my account, yet I am most certain that the total sum is right, for it amounts to no more than that precept of the Apostle: *As far as it is possible, have peace with all men.* For this purpose, having summoned up sundry occasions of schism, and valuing them with the best judgment I could, I still ended with advice to all possible accommodation and communion, one only excepted. Now certainly there could be no great harm in the premises, where the conclusion was nothing else but peace.

One of the ancient grammarians, delivering the laws of a comedy somewhat scrupulously, thought *non posse ferrum nominari in comoedia, ne transeat in tragoediam,* that to name a sword in a comedy was enough to fright it into a tragedy.[11] The very theme I handled caused me to fall on words of dissension and noise and tumult and stir, yet I hope it is but an unnecessary fear that, the last scene being peace, the discourse will prove any other than comical.

---

[7] {It has been expunged.}

[8] {Let them be expunged.}

[9] {Is it not his own fault that he did not know it?}

[10] {self-absorption; talking about oneself}

[11] {Possibly alluded to in the mechanicals' perplexity about the sword in *A Midsummer Night's Dream,* act 3, scene 2.}

To touch upon every jarring string in it were too much to abuse your Grace's patience, of which once already you have been so extraordinary liberal unto me. All that may seem to lie open to exception, I will comprise under two heads, within compass of which all other petty and inferior matters will easily fall. The first concerns my carriage towards antiquity; the second towards authority: against both which I may be supposed to trespass. For the first, I am thought to have been too sharp in censuring antiquity, beyond that good respect which is due unto it. In this point, my error, if any be, sprang from this, that taking actions to be the fruit by which men are to be judged, I judged of the persons by their actions, and not of actions by the persons from whom they proceeded; for to judge of actions by persons and times, I have always taken it to be most unnatural. Hence it is, that having no good conceit (for I will speak the truth) of our rule by which we celebrate the feast of Easter (first, because it is borrowed of Moses, without any warrant, for ought I know; secondly, because it is of no use: for which way is the service of God or man any jot more advanced by making that feast wander betwixt day and day than by fixing it on one known day? thirdly, because it is obscure and intricate, few scholars acquainting themselves therewith, and there being nothing more ridiculous than *difficiles nugae*, useless intricacies and obscurities), I could not with patience speak gently of those who used so small and contemptible an occasion to the great disturbance and rending of the Churches, and in maintenance of a toy and simple ceremony which it is no way beneficial to preserve, to fall into that error than which, themselves everywhere tell us, there can scarcely any be more dangerous.

Whereas in one point, speaking of church-authority, I bluntly added "which is none," I must acknowledge it was incautiously spoken and, being taken in a generality, is false; though as it refers to the occasion which there I fell upon, it is (as I think I may safely say) most true. For church-authority (that is, authority residing in ecclesiastical persons) is either of jurisdiction in church-causes and matter of fact, or of decision in point of church-questions and disputable opinion. As for the first: in church-causes or matter of fact, ecclesiastical persons, in cases of their cognizance, have the same authority as any others have to whom power of jurisdiction is committed. Their consistories, their courts, their determinations stand upon as warrantable evidence as the decisions of other benches and courts do. I count {reckon}, in point of decision of church-questions, if I say of the authority of the Church that it was none, I know no adversary that I have, the Church of Rome only excepted. For this cannot be true except we make the Church judge of controversies—the contrary to which we generally maintain against that Church. Now it plainly appears that upon this occasion I spake it; for beginning to speak of schism arising by reason of ambiguous opinion, I brought in nakedly those words which gave occasion of offence, which if I had spoken with due qualification, I had not erred at all. Again, whereas I did too plainly deliver myself *de origine dominii*,[12] and denied it to be founded either in nature or in religion, I am very well content to put off the decision of this point till Elias comes. In the meantime, whether it be true or false, let it pass for my mistake, for it is but a point of mere speculation which we fall upon when we study Aristotle's *Politics*, and in common life and use hath no place at all. For authority is not wont to dispute, and it goes but lazily on when it must defend itself by arguments in the schools. Whether

---

[12] {concerning the origin of *dominium*, i.e., lordship, ownership, sovereignty}

dominion *in civilibus* or *in sacris*, be κτίσις,[13] &c. or comes in by divine right, it concerns them to look to who have dominion committed to them. To others, whose duty it is to obey (and to myself above all, who am best contented to live and die a poor and private man), it is a speculation merely useless. Our Savior questions not Herod's or Augustus' title, and confessed that Pilate had his power from above, which yet we know came but by delegation from Tiberius Caesar. Let titles of honor and dominion go as the providence of God will have, yet quiet and peaceable men will not fail of their obedience; no more will I of ought, so be that God and good conscience command not the contrary. A higher degree of duty I do not see how any man can demand at my hands; for whereas the exception of good conscience sounds not well with many men, because oft-times under that form pertinacy {pertinacity} and willfulness is suspected to couch itself, in this case it concerns every man sincerely to know the truth of his own heart and so accordingly to determine of his own way, whatsoever the judgment of his superiors be or whatsoever event befall him. For since, in case of conscience, many times there is a necessity to fall either into the hands of men or into the hands of God, of these two, whether is the best, I leave every particular man to judge—only I will add thus much: it is a fearful thing to trifle with conscience, for most assuredly according unto it a man shall stand or fall at the last.

One thorn more there is, which I would, if I might, pull out of the foot of him who shall tread upon that paper: for by reason of a passage there wherein I sharply taxed episcopal ambition, I have been suspected by some, into whose hands that schedule fell before ever it came to your Grace's view, that in my heart I did secretly lodge a malignity against the episcopal order; and that, under pretence of taxing the ancients, I secretly lashed at the present times. What obedience I owe unto episcopal jurisdiction, I have already plainly and sincerely opened unto your Grace; and my trust is, you do believe me: so that in that regard I intend to say no more; and the very consideration of the things themselves which there I speak of frees me from all suspicion of secret gliding {swiping} at the present. For I spake of schisms arising either out of plurality of bishops in one diocese or superiority of bishops in sundry dioceses: both these are strangers to ours, and proper to the ancient times; the first arising from the unruliness of the people, in whose hands in those times the nomination of bishops was; the other from somewhat (whether good or bad, I know not) in the princes then living, who left the bishops to themselves (among whom some there were no better than other men) and took no keep of the ancient canons of the Church by which the limits, orders, and preeminences of all dioceses and provinces were set. But our times have seen a prosperous change, for the nomination of bishops (which was sometimes in the people) is now most happily devolved into the prince's hand, together with the care of the preservation of the bounds of bishops' sees and ancient titles of precedency. So that now, since that happy change, for well near one hundred years we have had no experience of any such misorders, neither are we likely hereafter to fear any so long as so good, so moderate, so gracious a royal hand shall hold the stern: which God grant may be either in him or his, till times be no more.

TEXT: *Works of the ever memorable Mr. John Hales of Eaton, now first collected together, in three volumes* (Glasgow, 1765), 1:135–44.

[13] {established by men}

JOHN HALES

The danger of receiving our good things in this life[1]
ca. 1619–38, published 1660

Son, remember that thou in thy life-time receivedst thy good things
Luke 16:25

. . . That man of misery, whose woeful end occasioned this discourse in St. Luke, whence I have chosen out these few words as my subject to treat of at this time, much desires that one from the dead might be sent unto his brethren to give them warning that they come not into that place of torment in which himself was. May not I at this time justly seem to be that messenger? For methinks I come into the pulpit as young Polydore in the tragedy enters the stage, and may speak unto you as he did unto his auditors in another language, *I come from the pit of the dead, from the gates of utter darkness, where the devil hath his mansion far removed from God.*[2] First, the sadness of the message with which I come might easily tempt you to think so, as being very unwelcome to the ears of flesh and blood; for, *ubi mors non est*,[3] where shall we find rest, in what shall we joy, *if the good things of our life deceive us?* Certainly so disconsolate a piece of news could never come but from some place of extreme sadness. Secondly, the unfitness of the time might help on well to this conceit: there is μέγα χάσμα, saith Abraham in this Scripture, *there is a great gulf betwixt you and us.* Beloved, the difference betwixt those two places here mentioned is not much greater than is the distance betwixt my text and this time; for the time invites you to that from which my text affrights you: eating, drinking, merry-making, *totum choragium Epicureum*,[4] all the rest of this rich man's daily service, these are the subject of the time; but my text pulls you by the ear, and bids you beware lest even these good things (for so men

---

[1] {The title is an artifact of the 1765 Glasgow edition.}

[2] {The opening lines of Euripides' *Hecuba*}

[3] {Literally, "where death is not," probably from Rufinus' translation of Origen's *Peri archon* 3.6.5, "ut neque ultra triste sit aliquid, ubi mors non est [that there shall be no more sadness, where death is not]" (see C. A. Patrides, "The salvation of Satan," *JHI* 28.4 (1967): 468.}

[4] {the whole Epicurean scenario}

commonly call them) may be amongst those things, which, when time comes, may draw after them this *recordare*. Remember, you may be told, *remember you had your Shrovetide*; for what else, I beseech you, was the whole life of this miserable man here but in a manner a perpetual shroving?

But neither the sourness of the message, nor any pretended unseasonableness of the times, must hinder us from communicating unto you what the Spirit of God shall put into our hearts. Let it be unwelcome, what then? . . . Sick persons must not look for smoothing and much-making, but for that which fits their malady.

. . .

. . . So I return to resume the words again, and to consider a little more largely of them, *Cave ne recipias*, Take heed you receive not.

Quid audio? What is this I hear? Must I not receive the good things of this life? If either right of patrimony and inheritance devolve them to me, or some casual providence of God cast them upon me, or my labor and industry woo and win them, must I bid defiance, and shut the doors against them? Is this precept here like to the command of old *Euclio* in the comedy,[5] who wills his servant to keep his doors shut, and open to none, *ne si bona quidem fortuna venerit*; no, though good fortune herself should come and knock? Beloved, here I am *in bivio*.[6]

For answer to this question: it is reported of Aristippus, the famous philosopher, that travelling over some parts of Africk, with his servants overladen with gold, when they complained of their burthen and told him that they were so loaded they should never reach their journey's end, he bad them lay down their burthens, and take up so much as they thought themselves conveniently enabled to bear, and leave the rest *proximo occupanti*, to the next that came that way. From this example I draw my answer. Wouldst thou know whether thou shouldst receive the good things of the world? Try thy strength. Art thou able to confront occasions, to converse amongst men, to wrestle with temptations, and take no foil? In a word, art thou able, with the three in Daniel, to go through the fire and come out untoucht? Do as Aristippus' servants did: take up thy gold, receive the blessings that offer themselves, entertain them, welcome them. On the contrary, art thou weak, or suspectest thou thy strength? will fears or hopes or pleasures over-master thee? canst thou not touch pitch but thou must be defiled with it? Then do as Aristippus' servants did: leave thy gold behind thee; these goodly glittering things, refuse them, though they drop into thy lap. Briefly, two ways is this question answered: hast thou strength of mind? receive them. Hast thou not? refuse them. The first is the wisest way, the second is the safest. He that receives them not doth well, but he that receives them doth better. I will begin with the first: *receive them*. I know that this seems a riddle unto you, for my text seems to command you not to receive them; and I have told you that one way to put this precept in use is to receive them. This is true, receive them we may, but yet so as if we received them not. Many of the saints of God, yea Abraham himself, received large portions of the good of this world, and how then shall they, with Abraham himself, avoid this bitter exprobration of *recepisti, thou hast received*, but that some way or other even they that have received them may justly be said not to have received them? . . . For whatsoever

---

[5] {Euclio is the miser in Plautus' *Aulularia*.}

[6] {at a crossroads}

it be that thou hast received from God, thou art but in debt for it, thou art but entrusted with it. Look what it is thou hast, and say unto thyself . . . so much I have that I may have nothing. In debt, I say, thou art for all thou hast; and wilt thou know who are thy creditors? Even every man that needs thee. The hungry man begs at thy gate, he is thy creditor; thou art in debt to him for his dinner. The naked man in the streets, he is thy creditor; thou art in debt to him for his garment. The poor oppressed prisoner, he is thy creditor; thou art in debt to him for his relief. The wronged captive, he is thy creditor; thou art in debt to him for his redemption. Be then like the widow's oil in the Book of Kings: run as long as there is a vessel to receive thee; pay all these thy debts, and leave thyself nothing, and lo, thou hast found the wonderful art of receiving much at the hands of God, and yet receiving nothing. Had our rich man here done thus, he had never heard of *recepisti, thou hast received*; for to receive here is not to take that which God offers, but to impropriate, to enjoy alone the gifts of God, either by dispending them on thyself or thy vanities, or locking them up and neither enjoying them thyself nor suffering any other so to do; by making them *bona tua* {thy goods}, and placing thy felicity in them: this is to receive. Thou sittest at thy full table and crams thyself with meats and drinks, whilst Lazarus starves at thy gate, *recepisti*; thou cladst thyself with superfluous and gaudy apparel, whilst thy naked brother freezes in the street, *recepisti*; thou refreshest thyself with dainty restoring physic, whilst the sick indeed perisheth for want of care, *recepisti*. Take heed. Every vanity, every superfluity, every penny that thou hast misspent to the prejudice of him that wants, when the time comes, shall cry out unto thee, *recepisti, thou hast received*. On the contrary, *recepisse, sed non tibi*, to have received, but not unto thyself, to have spent thyself for others' good; he that doth thus, to him there can be no more objected a *recepisti* than there can unto the sun that he received his beams, which he hath communicated to the world; or to the fountain that it received its springs, wherewith it hath water'd the earth for which it was given.

Erewhile, when I considered the words in particular, I advised you to put a *cave* {beware} upon the word *thy: thy good things*. For indeed here is the πρῶτον ψεῦδος, here is the ground of all abuse and error, that we take upon us to think and call anything ours. For now we think, by and by we may infer, *May we not do with our own what we list?* we think we are ἀνυπέυθυνοι,[7] no action of account lies against us, we fear no *recepisti*. Beloved, there is more danger in the use of that word then you are aware of: *ours, mine*, is a gross, a crass, a secular term, easily taken up by wordlings; by better men not so easily. When Laban had overtaken Jacob and began to chide with him, *These daughters*, saith he, *are my daughters, these children are my children, these cattle are my cattle, and all that thou seest is mine.* Jacob had done enough to style them his; he had bargain'd, he had served, he had watcht, he had sweat, he had freezed for them; and yet he would not take up that word, nor count any thing his. Nabal, a man of the same letters and of the same garb and quality with Laban, when David sent unto him to require relief of him, speaks in the same *sibboleth: Shall I take*, saith he, *my bread and my water and my flesh, which I have killed for my shearers, and give it unto men whom I know not?* Neither is it any wonder that they thus speak; for this is the language which they learnt of their father, of their prince, of their god, even the prince which ruleth in the air, the god of this world, the devil; for he, setting

[7] {not liable for}

upon our Savior in the Gospel, courts him in the same manner; for, shewing him all the kingdoms of the earth, and the glory of them, he tells him, *All this is mine, and to whom I will I give it.* He lies, I doubt not, when he thus spake (but that's no marvel); yea, and all those who take up the dialect are no whit truer of their word. . . . But the sons of God in their better thoughts speak in another dialect. When David had with great providence, with great hazard of person, treasured up much for the use of the house of the Lord, and was now come to dedicate it and offer it up unto God, he dares not say, *mine,* but . . . *thine: out of thine own* we present unto thee. . . .

Yet that we may descend a little more particularly into this question of propriety, wouldst thou know indeed what it is *quod possis dicere jure, meum est,* of which thou mayst justly say unto thyself, it is *mine?* Examine thyself, find out thine own measure, so much as thou needest is *thine*; the rest thou art but entrusted withal for others' good. That part of the beam of light which shines in thine eye is thine; all the rest is another's; that which thou eatest to suffice thine hunger is thine; all the rest is thy neighbor's; that water which thou drinkest of thy well is thine; all the rest is *occupantis.*[8] If thy barns and store-houses, thy wardrobes, thy treasuries imprison and detain anything, thou art but a common enemy and offendest against a common profit. . . . It is the bread of the hungry that thou detainest, it is the garment of the naked which thou lockest up in thy wardrobe, it is the shoe of the barefoot that rots by thee, it is the poor's money and the talent of thy Lord which thou hidest under the ground. Look how many thou hast not furnisht, so many hast thou wronged.[9] It is well that the providence of God hath left in common the light, the heat, the influence of heaven, *& omnibus undamque auramque patentem*;[10] for if some men had their will, even these should suffer enclosure and restraint, neither should we freely enjoy the benefit of light and air. For I know not how it falls out that, whereas there are two pages, two parts of every account, the receipt and the expense, there is a reigning madness amongst men to increase their receipts, whilest in the meantime they are secure of their expense; whereas it is the expense that most concerns us; for what we shall receive is in the care and will of our master, but all our care and providence is seen in our expense. Now I know not how it comes to pass that many seem to lessen the reputation of thrift and good husbandry with God, and therefore they treasure and lock up their receipts, as if they thought to clear their accounts and save themselves from a *recepisti* by returning God his own again. But the account with God is in one circumstance very different from that with men; the steward that hath received his lord's money, when he comes to his audit, if he repay what he hath not expended, he hath his acquittance, and all is well. But in our great audit with God there is no refunding; all must be dispended. Could we pay back again our Lord's money which we have not laid out, yet still the account depends,[11] still we are in danger of a *recepisti*; for nothing clears our accounts with God but pariation of expenses with receipts. God's account must have no remain. Secular thrift is seen in saving, but divine thrift is best seen in spending: whether therefore thou spendest amiss, or whether thou savest amiss, thou art still liable to a *recepisti.*

---

[8] {for whomever makes use of it}
[9] {The sentence comes from St. Basil's homilies on Luke; I have omitted the Greek.}
[10] {and the water and air left free to all}
[11] {remains unsettled}

Text: EEBO (Wing / H274)

Sermons preach'd at Eton, by John Hales, late fellow of that College. Not till now published (London: Printed by J. G. for Richard Marriot, 1660), 15–16, 22–27.

JOHN HALES

Of inquiry and private judgment in religion[1]
ca. 1619–38, published 1660

Be not deceived, God is not mocked;
For whatsoever a man soweth, that shall he also reap.
Galat. 6:7

. . .

. . . This μὴ πλανᾶσθε, *be not deceived*, seems to be a precept of great weight; yea, so great, as it may be doubted whether it be fit to be given to men. He that will be sure to be deceived in nothing had need be omniscient and know all things, which is a property of God alone: for, as for men, first, it is most true which Columella observes, *quicunque sunt habiti mortalium saepientissimi, multa scisse dicuntur, non omnia*; the wisest of men that ever lived were never taken to know all things, but many things. And secondly, such things as they do know, they know but imperfectly and in part. Now either of these is enough to overthrow all possibility of this precept of not being deceived, for it cannot be but we should be deceived in what we know not. That it was a great precept the Apostle knew well and, as it seems to be, purposed that we should know it too. For, for this end, I may well think, hath he in this place almost parallel'd God and man, or as the Psalmist speaks in the 8 Psalm, *He hath made him little less than God*. For that μυκτηρισμὸς, that mockery, which here he denies can befall God, is nothing else but that deceit which here he teaches ought not to befall us. He might have changed the words without any wrong to the sense and placed them thus: be not you mocked, for God is not deceived. For whatsoever deceives a man, that may properly be said to mock and abuse him. So that one and the same thing is here averred both of God and of us; only there is this difference, in God it is a necessity: he cannot be mocked, he cannot be deceived; in man it is a duty: he ought not to be mocked, he ought not to be deceived. No exception therefore is it to the precept that it seems to be proper to God. When Rachel, repining that she bare no child,

---

[1] {Title given this sermon in the Glasgow 1765 edition. In the first printed edition, that of 1660, its only title is "The first sermon."}

843

came in a whining and discontented humor to Jacob, saying, *give me children, else I die*; he answered, *am I like God, who hath withheld from thee the fruit of the womb?* and with this answer he both reproved her and excused himself. But, beloved, if any man should reply upon our blessed Apostle and tell him, "Am I like God, that I should look not to be deceived?" this cannot excuse him. For behold, as if he had purposely meant to have taken this objection away, the Apostle joins together both God and us, and tells us, as God cannot, so we must not be deceived.

Now that we may the better see what is locked up in this precept, we will consider first, who they are to whom this precept of Christian infallibility is given, together with the means how we may attain it; for I will blend and mix them both together. And secondly, what things they are in which a Christian man may safely suppose (or rather know) himself to be infallible. For though the Apostle gives this precept of not being deceived only with relation to that one lesson which here he teaches, yet pertains it to as many more as every Christian is bound to learn. For the assurance that we have of our Christian doctrine, and every point of it, consists not in opinion, is not founded upon probabilities—like to the wind, subject to mutability and change; it must be a most certain, most infallible acknowledgment, which nothing in heaven, earth, and hell can any way infringe. First, therefore, of the persons unto whom this precept of infallibility is given, together with the way by which they may attain unto it.

Infallibility hath been for a long time past the subject of great dispute and quarrel in the Church; for since there was no other likelihood but, as amongst other men, so amongst Christians, doubts, debates, dissensions would arise, men always have thought it a thing very equitable that, by the providence of God, there should in some part of the Church or in some person reside a power of clearing such doubts and settling such scruples as many times possess the minds of most Christians. Now to appoint such a judge and not to give him infallibility in his decision, but to permit him to wander and mistake in his sentence, this peradventure were not to mend but only to change, and supplant one error by bringing in another. An infallibility therefore there must be, but men have marvelously wearied themselves in seeking to find out where it is. Some have sought it in general councils and have conceived that if it be not there to be found, it is for certainty fled out of the world. Some have tied it to the Church of Rome and to the bishop of that see. Every man finds it, or thinks he finds it, accordingly as that faction or part of the Church upon which he is fallen doth direct him. Thus, like the men of Sodom before Lot's door, men have wearied themselves and have gone far and near to find out that which is hard at hand. We see many times a kind of ridiculous and joculary forgetfulness of many men, seeking for that which they have in their hands; so fares it here with men who seek for infallibility in others, which either is, or ought to be, in themselves: as Saul sought his father's asses whilst they were now at home; or as Oedipus in the tragedy sent to the oracle to enquire the cause of the plague in Thebes, whereas himself was the man. For, beloved, infallibility is not a favor impropriated to any one man; it is a duty alike expected at the hands of all; all must have it. St. Paul, when he gives this precept, directs it not to councils, to bishops, to teachers and preachers, but to all of the Galatian churches; and in them, to all of all the churches in the world. Unto you, therefore, and to everyone, of what sex, of what rank or degree and place soever, from him that studies in his library to him that sweats at the plow-tail belongs this precept of S. Paul, *Be not deceived.*

Which command that you may the better conceive and drink in, let us see what it is that a man must do who resolves to obey the Apostle and not to be deceived. It is not much; I comprise it all in two words: *what* and *wherefore*. First, you must know *what* it is that is commanded you; secondly, *wherefore*: that is, upon what authority, upon what reason. . . . I know this is something an hard doctrine for the many to hear, neither is it usually taught by the common teachers. . . . One part you will be content to yield unto: namely, to take at our hands what it is you are to believe or do; but the other part you stiffly refuse: to know the grounds and reasons of what you do, or of what you believe. This you remit to us: *non vestrum onus, bos clitellas*;[2] To require this at your hands were as improper as if we should clap the saddle on the back of the ox. And for this you have your reasons too, as you think: you are men whose time is taken up in your trades and callings; you are unlearned, unread, of weak and shallow understandings;[3] it is therefore for you not only modesty, but even necessity, to submit yourselves to better judgment; and for enquiry into the reasons and causes of commands, this, as a little too speculative, you are content should lie upon your teachers: *felix qui potuit rerum cognoscere causas*;[4] they are men born under happier stars than ordinary who attain to the discovery of reasons and causes of things. Beloved, all this I know, yet I must still go on and require the performance of the Apostle's precept, *be not deceived*; which is a point of perfection which you shall never arrive at except you forgo these pretences. Saint Hierome tells us that it was a precept of Pythagoras, *oneratis superponendum opus, deponentibus non communicandum*; where you find a man laden, there to increase his burthen, and never to go about to ease him which would lay his burthen down. . . . the meaning, saith he, of that precept was, to men that go on in virtue and industry, you must still give and add new precepts, new commands; but idle persons must be forsaken.

Beloved, it falls me by lot this day to act Pythagoras his part. The burthen of this precept laid upon you by the blessed Apostle, I told you, consisted of two parts: *what* and *why*. That part of your burthen which contains *what*, I see you will willingly take up; but that other which comprehends *why*, that is either too hot or too heavy; you dare not meddle with it. But I must add that also to your burthen, or else I must leave you for idle persons. For without the knowledge of *why*, of the true grounds or reasons of things, there is no possibility of not being deceived. Your teachers and instructors whom you follow, they may be wise and learned, yet may they be deceived. But suppose they be not deceived, yet if you know not so much, you are not yet excused. Something there is which makes those men not to be deceived; if you will be sure not to be deceived, then know you that as well as they. Is it divine authority that preserves them from being deceived? you must know that as well as they. Is it strength of reason? you must know it as well as they. For still in following your teachers you may be deceived (for ought you know) till you know they are not deceived; which you can never know until you know the

---

[2] {Quintilian, *Institutes* 5.11.21 (translated in the following sentence)}

[3] {This passage implies that Hales was not preaching to Eton scholars, or at least not only to them. Eton's vice-provost at the time regularly preached in the surrounding parishes, and it is possible that Hales did the same (see Lyte, *A history of Eton College* 201). Yet the reference four paragraphs later to an early provost of Eaton as "one sometimes of this body" presupposes a collegiate setting, making it more likely that the congregation for the chapel services included villagers.}

[4] {Vergil, *Georgics* 2.490}

grounds and reasons upon which they stand: for there is no other means not to be deceived but to know things yourselves.

I will put on this doctrine further and convince you by your own reason. It is a question made by John Gerson, sometimes Chancellor of Paris . . . *Wherefore hath God given me the light of reason and conscience, if I must suffer myself to be led and governed by the reason and conscience of another man?* Will any of you befriend me so far as to assoil {answer} this question? For I must confess I cannot. It was the speech of a good husbandman, *Non satis est agrum possidere velle, si colere non possis*; it is but a folly to possess a piece of ground, except you till it. And how then can it stand with reason that a man should be possessor of so godly a piece of the Lord's pasture as is this light of understanding and reason, which he hath endued us with in the day of our creation, if he suffer it to lie untill'd or sow not in it the Lord's seed? Needs must our reason, if it be suffered thus to lie fallow, like the vineyard of the sluggard in the Proverbs quickly υλομανείν {become wild} and be overrun with briars and thorns. Think we that the neglect of these our faculties shall escape unpunished with God? Saint Basil tells us that the man that is utterly devoid of all education and hath nothing but his reason to be guided by . . . yet even such an one, if he doth offend, shall not escape unpunished, because he hath not used those common notions engrafted by God in his heart to that end for which they were given. How much severer then shall that man's punishment be, who in this great means of education, amidst so many, so plain, so easy ways of cultivation of our reasonable faculties, yet neglects all and lets them lie fallow, and is content another should have his wits in keeping?

It were a thing worth looking into, to know the reason why men are so generally willing in point of religion to cast themselves into other men's arms, and leaving their own reason, rely so much upon another man's. . . . I will not forbear to open unto you what I conceive to be the causes of this so general an error amongst men. First, peradventure the dregs of the Church of Rome are not yet sufficiently washed from the hearts of many men. We know it is the principal stay and supporter of that Church to suffer nothing to be inquired into which is once concluded by them. Look through Spain and Italy: *jumenta sunt, non homines*; they are not men, but beasts, and Issachar-like patiently couch down under every burthen their superiors lay upon them. Secondly, a fault or two may be in our own ministry. Thus to advise men (as I have done) to search into the reasons and grounds of religion opens a way to dispute and quarrel, and this might breed us some trouble and disquiet in our cures more than we are willing to undergo; therefore, to purchase our own quiet and to banish all contention, we are content to nourish this still humor in our hearers, as the Sybarites, to procure their ease, banished the smiths because their trade was full of noise. In the meantime, we do not see that peace which ariseth out of ignorance is but a kind of sloth or moral lethargy, seeming quiet because it hath no power to move. Again, may be the portion of knowledge in the minister himself is not over-great; it may be therefore good policy for him to suppress all busy inquiry in his auditory, that so increase of knowledge in them might not at length discover some ignorance in him. Last of all, the fault may be in the people themselves, who, because they are loath to take pains (and search into the grounds of knowledge is evermore painful {difficult}), are well content to take their ease, to gild their vice with goodly names, and call their sloth "modesty," and their neglect of inquiry, "filial obedience." These reasons, beloved, or some of kin to these, may be the motives unto this easiness of the people of entertaining their religion upon trust and of the neglect of inquiry into the grounds of it.

To return, therefore, and proceed in the refutation of this gross neglect in men of their own reason, and casting themselves upon others' wits. Hath God given you eyes to see and legs to support you that so yourselves might lie still or sleep and require the use of other men's eyes and legs? That faculty of reason which is in every one of you, even in the meanest that hears me this day, next to the help of God, is your eyes to direct you and your legs to support you in your course of integrity and sanctity. You may no more refuse or neglect the use of it, and rest yourselves upon the use of other men's reason, than neglect your own and call for the use of other men's eyes and legs. The man in the Gospel who had bought a farm excuses himself from going to the marriage-supper because himself would go and see it; but we have taken an easier course: we can buy our farm and go to supper too, and that only by saving our pains to see it. We profess ourselves to have made a great purchase of heavenly doctrine, yet we refuse to see it and survey it ourselves, but trust other men's eyes and our surveyors; and wot you to what end? I know not, except it be that so we may with the better leisure go to the marriage-supper. . . . that so we may the more freely betake ourselves to our pleasures, to our profits, to our trades, to our preferments and ambition. Never was there any business of weight so usually discharged by proxy and deputy as this sacred business hath been from time to time. Sleidan the historian {d. 1556} observes that it was grown a custom in his time for great persons to provide them chanteries and chaplains to celebrate their obits and to offer for their souls' health even in their lifetimes, whilest they themselves intended other matters; and thus they discharged the cure of their own souls by deputy. Not only in Germany, where Sleidan lived, but even in England, amongst us that custom had taken footing, and was sometimes practiced, even in this place, by one sometimes of this body.[5] Margaret of Valois {d. 1615}, not long since Queen of France, built her a chapel, provided her chaplains and large endowment for them, that so perpetually day and night, every hour successively without intermission, by some one or other there might intercession be made to God for her unto the world's end—a thing which herself had little care or thought of in her lifetime, as having other business to think on. So confident are we of the eternal good of our souls upon the knowledge, devotion, and industry of others, and so loath to take any pains ourselves in that behalf—and that in a business which doth so nearly concern us.

. . . We have a common saying . . . *many scholars prove far better than their masters.* Would you bear a part in this saying and prove better than we that are your teachers? Then make our knowledge yours—not . . . by imputation or by believing well of it, but by thoroughly perceiving and understanding it, and discovering the uttermost grounds on which it subsists. There is no way but this, and this David found by his own experience; *I am wiser than my teachers,* saith he in his 119 Psalm. Why? because he believed them? This could never have made him so wise, much less wiser. Why then? *for thy testimonies,* saith he, *are my studies.* Therefore is he wiser than his teachers, because that knowing all that they could teach him, he stayed not there, but by his own search and study he arrives at a degree of knowledge beyond his masters. St. Basil in his sermons upon some of the Psalms taxes a sort of men who thought it a sin to know more of God than the tradition of their

---

[5] R{oger} Lupton {Provost of Eton, 1504–35}

fathers would give them leave . . . and would not advance and improve the knowledge of the truth by any faculty or industry of their own. Beloved, there is not a more immediate way to fall into this reproof of St. Basil and to hinder all advancement and growth of Christian knowledge amongst the common sort of men than this easy and slothful resolution to rest themselves on others' wits.

Saint Hierome, in the preface to his comments on the Epistle to the Galatians, much commends Marcella, a gentlewoman of Rome, for this: that in her pursuit of Christian knowledge she would receive nothing from him *more Pythagorico*, upon trust, and upon his bare word and authority, but would so thoroughly sift and try all things of herself, *ut sentirem me* (saith he) *non tam discipulam habere quàm judicem*, that she seemed not so much to be my scholar and hearer as my judge. Beloved, what hinders but we should all, all of all sexes, ages, callings, be like to this Roman matron, and be not only hearers but judges too? *Nec protinus quicquid respondetur rectum putare*, neither to adore all things for gospel which our betters tell us, but to bring all things to the true test: to know the reasons, try the authorities, and never rest ourselves till we can take up that conclusion of the Psalmist, *As we have heard, so have we seen in the city of our God.*

Now to remove you yet a little farther from this fancy of casting yourself into the arms of others, and to conciliate you the more to God and your reason, I will open one thing further unto you, which is this: that you put off the care of your faith and religion from yourselves on other men sundry ways when you think you do nothing less. For when we plead for the truth of our profession, and appeal either to our education or breeding, *thus we have been brought up, thus we have been taught*; or to antiquity, *thus have our ancients delivered unto us*; or to universality, *this hath been the doctrine generally received*; or to synods, councils, and consent of Churches, *this is the doctrine established by ecclesiastical authority*: all these are nothing else but deceitful forms of shifting the account and reason of our faith and religion from ourselves and casting it upon the back of others. I will shew it you by the particular examination of every one of these, which I will the willinger do because I see these are the common hackney reasons which most men use in flattering themselves in their mistakes; for all this is nothing else but man's authority thrust upon us under divers shapes. For, first of all, education and breeding is nothing else but the authority of our teachers taken over our childhood. Now there is nothing which ought to be of less force with us or which we ought more to suspect: for childhood hath one thing natural to it which is a great enemy to truth and a great furtherer of deceit. What is that? Credulity. Nothing is more credulous than a child; and our daily experience shews how strangely they will believe either their ancients or one another in most incredible reports. For to be able to judge what persons, what reports are credible is a point of strength, of which that age is not capable. . . . Saith Epicharmus,[6] the chiefest sinews and strength of wisdom is not easily to believe. Have we not then great cause to call to better account and examine by better reason whatsoever we learnt in so credulous and easy an age, so apt, like the softest wax, to receive every impression? Yet notwithstanding this singular weakness, and this large and real exception which we have against education, I verily persuade myself that if the best and strongest ground of most men's religion were open'd, it would appear to be nothing else.

[6] {Early Greek dramatist, only fragments of whose work survive.}

Secondly, antiquity, what is it else (God only excepted) but man's authority born some ages afore us? Now for the truth of things, time makes no alteration; things are still the same they are, let the time be past, present, or to come. Those things which we reverence for antiquity, what were they at their first birth? Were they false? Time cannot make them true. Were they true? Time cannot make them more true. The circumstance therefore of time, in respect of truth and error, is merely impertinent. . . .

Thirdly, universality is such a proof of truth as truth itself is ashamed of; for universality is nothing but a quainter and a trimmer name to signify the multitude. Now human authority at the strongest is but weak, but the multitude is the weakest part of human authority; it is the great patron of error, most easily abused and most hardly disabused. The beginning of error may be, and mostly is, from private persons, but the maintainer and continuer of error is the multitude. *Ubi singulorum error fecerit publicum, singulorum errorem facit publicus.*[7] It is a thing which our common experience and practice acquaints us with, that when some private persons have gain'd authority with the multitude and infused some error into them and made it public, the public-ness of the error gains authority to it, and interchangeably prevails with private persons to entertain it. The most singular and strongest part of human authority is properly in the wisest and most virtuous; and these, I trow, are not the most universal. If truth and goodness go by universality and multitude, what mean then the prophets and holy men of God everywhere in Scripture so frequently, so bitterly, to complain of the small number of good men careful of God and truth? Neither is the complaint proper to Scripture. It is the common complaint of all that have left any records of antiquity behind them. Could wishing do any good, I could wish well to this kind of proof; *sed nunquam ita bene erit rebus humanis, ut plures sint meliores*, it will never go so well with mankind that the most shall be the best. The best that I can say of argument and reason drawn from universality and multitude is this: such reason may perchance well serve to *excuse an error*, but *it can never serve to warrant a truth*.

Fourthly, councils and synods and consent of Churches, these indeed may seem of some force; they are taken to be the strongest weapons which the Church had fought with; yet this is still human authority after another fashion. Let me add one thing: that the truth hath not been more relieved by these than it hath been distressed. At the Council at Nicaea met thirty-eight bishops to defend the divinity of the Son of God, but at Ariminum met well near six hundred bishops to deny it. I ask then, what gain'd the truth here by a synod? Certainly in the eye of reason it more endanger'd it; for it discovered the advantage that error had among the multitude above the truth, by which reason truth might have been greatly hazarded. I have read that the nobility of Rome, upon some fancy or other, thought fit that all servants should wear a kind of garment proper to them that so it might be known who were servants, who were free-men; but they were quickly weary of this conceit, for perceiving in what multitudes servants were in most places, they feared that the singularity of their garment might be an item to them to take notice of their multitude and to know their own strength, and so at length take advantage of it against their masters. This device of calling councils was but like that fancy of the Roman gentleman; for many times it might well have proved a great means to have endangered the truth by

---

[7] {Seneca, *Epist. mor.* 10.81.29}

making the enemies thereof to see their own strength and work upon that advantage; for it is a speedy way to make them to see that, which for the most part is very true, that there are more which run against the truth than with it.

TEXT: EEBO (Wing / H274)

Sermons preach'd at Eton, by John Hales, late fellow of that College. Not till now published (London: Printed by J. G. for Richard Marriot, 1660), 1, 3–14.

CHRISTOPHER DOW

(fl. 1613–38)

Dow barely surfaces in the archives. We know that he received his BA from Christ's College, Cambridge, in 1617, his MA in 1620. In 1621 he was incorporated MA at Oxford. He took his BD in 1627, at which point he left the University to become the vicar of Battle, Sussex, in 1629; and then in 1636, rector of All Saints, Hastings, in which year he also published *A discourse of the Sabbath and the Lord's Day*. His *Innovations unjustly charged* came out a year later. He was awarded the DD in 1638, and presumably died shortly thereafter.

Innovations is a confutation of Henry Burton's 1636 diatribe against the Laudian Church, *For God and the king*, published in Amsterdam—although Dow, rather confusingly, refers to the work under the title of another Burton tract from the same year, *An apology of an appeal*. (Dow was apparently working from a volume in which the tracts were bound together, although separately paginated, with the *Apology* placed first.) Dow, who had thought that *Innovations* would come out during Burton's Star Chamber trial, initially included critiques of both tracts, but the trial ended while the book was still in press, at which point Dow pulled his discussion of Burton's *Apology*, since it covered ground already handled by the judges in their verdict.[1]

Dow is clearly and professedly a Laudian (and may have owed the living at Hastings to Laud's patronage), Burton, equally clearly, a root-and-branch puritan. In setting forth their respective positions, *Innovations* provides a reasonably comprehensive overview of the religious disputes that precipitated the English Civil War—from a Laudian vantage point, to be sure, but Dow does not grossly misrepresent Burton's views (as, for example, Prynne distorts Laud's in *News from Ipswich*). The final chapter, which feels more tendentious, is explicitly marked off as "no accurate or elaborately methodical discourse" but merely "a

---

[1] On the 1637 Star Chamber trial of Burton, Bastwick, and Prynne, see the introduction to the Prynne's *News from Ipswich* <supra>.

851

rough draft" of such objections that occurred to him. I have chosen to include a longer than usual selection from Dow's apologia because it offers the best contemporary survey of the theological disputes fissuring the English Church in the 1630s.[2] Its chapters address whether predestination should be considered an abstruse school-doctrine or essential saving knowledge; whether God has ordained preaching the ordinary means of salvation; whether the sacraments are instruments of grace; whether unscripted prayer is preferable to a set liturgy; whether Calvinist teaching re assurance and perseverance sunders any meaningful link between the conduct of life and salvation; whether the pope is the antichrist and all Catholics rebellious heretics; whether the identity of the English Church is to be located in its continuity with the Church of the Fathers and the Schoolmen or rather in its solidarity with the continental Reformed Churches; whether the fourth Commandment forbids all Sunday recreations; whether ceremonies not mandated by Scripture are mere will-worship or whether the ancient traditions of the Church—including altars, altar rails, prayers for the dead, confession, standing for the *Gloria Patri*, kneeling for Communion—have a sacred authority; whether the English episcopate derives its authority from Christ or the king or both.

Moreover, Dow's account of these controversies suggests that underlying and informing the various specific disputes is a more fundamental disagreement about mediation and middle states. For Dow, God works through human institutions; tradition, the Church, kings, and bishops mediate divine grace, truth, authority, and justice. Yet Dow also accepts Burton's claim (and that of the Thirty-nine Articles) that Scripture alone is the word of God, that it alone is the source of those truths necessary for salvation. Human institutions mediate the sacred, but they do so partially, imperfectly. Royal authority comes from God, but it can also oppose God's law, and when it does, God is to be obeyed rather than man. So too the Church, although subordinate to Scripture, "received her power from the Holy Ghost." The bishops' authority is likewise *divino iure*, but depends for its exercise on royal permission, and even then does not reach to matters of faith (at least not to those truths necessary for salvation) but only to the ordering of outward worship and regulation of manners. For Dow, human institutions come from God and do his work in the world, and as such demand our respectful obedience; yet they are not infallible, not themselves the voice of God. This is, of course, the classic "Anglican" position.[3]

For Burton (as for Bradshaw and most radical puritans), authority is either divine or fraudulent; human institutions in particular are, for him, deeply suspect, since all "merely human" authority usurps the rightful authority of God. Puritan opposition to non-biblical ceremonies rests on this intuition, but it also shapes Burton's pervasive difficulty (as Dow presents it) with things of a middle nature. Burton thus seems to find it self-evident that if the bishops lay claim to a real authority, they are declaring themselves infallible. Moreover, the same considerations force Burton and those of his ilk to treat their own claims as having, if not infallibility per se, then prophetic authority; to present them as based on some immediate access to divine truth: hence Burton's (and Prynne's) vatic pronouncements attributing both plague and bad weather to God's displeasure with

---

[2] It also includes some quite striking descriptions of the Caroline culture of godly puritanism, e.g., the hidden-in-plain-sight London fast days described at the end of chapter 21 *<infra>*.

[3] See the selections from Field, Sanderson, Shelford, Chillingworth, and Laud in this volume.

the English Church; the elevation of sermons to "the word of God" and so, by implication, on a par with Scripture; the central role played by assurance—the certain knowledge, granted only to the elect, of one's own election—in puritan spirituality. To Dow, conversely, such claims seem either delusional or charlatanry.

A few more points deserve brief mention. Dow's authoritarianism is hard to overlook; whether it should be viewed as "Laudian" seems less clear. His insistence on deference to superiors, although whole-hearted, seeks to rebut Burton's charge that the bishops gave individuals *liberty* to observe or ignore the Sabbath as they chose; similarly, Dow's support for the authority of parents and masters responds to Burton's condemnation of the bishops for encouraging youthful disobedience. Authoritarianism was not a fault in the earlier seventeenth century, nor peculiar to any one party. Also worth noting is Dow's passing comment in his final chapter that puritans viewed hope of heavenly reward as a sub-Christian motive, which is striking only because it is exceedingly rare: most early Stuart Christians, of whatever theological stripe, seem not to have had proto-Kantian qualms about the self-interested, "mercenary" basis of a eudemonist ethics.[4] Finally, if one turns back to Bradshaw's *English puritanism*, it appears that Dow and Bradshaw alike hold that the clergy have only spiritual jurisdiction, with all coercive authority residing in the Crown;[5] they draw vastly different conclusions, however, because Dow takes as normative the existing English setup whereby the Crown authorizes the Church to exercise certain powers and functions, just as it authorizes the secular courts to exercise others; it is precisely this entanglement of spiritual and civil domains that Bradshaw resists.

Sources: Collinson, *Religion of Protestants*; Kenneth Fincham, "William Laud and the exercise of Caroline ecclesiastical patronage," *Journal of Ecclesiastical History* 51 (2000): 69–93; *Alumni Cantabrigienses*, part 1, vol. 2, ed. John and J. A. Venn (Cambridge UP, 1922); S. R. Gardiner, *History of England from the accession of James I to the outbreak of the Civil War*, 10 vols. (Longmans, Green, 1883–84), esp. vol. 8; Laud, "A speech delivered in the Star Chamber . . . at the censure of John Bastwick, Henry Burton, & William Prynne" (1637), rpt. in *Works* 6.1:35–70.

[4] Although antinomians (and some early Protestants) clearly had qualms, yet even they presuppose a fundamentally eudemonist moral and spiritual framework. see the Everard selection <*supra*>, as well as nn. 4 and 5 from the introduction to Quarles' *Divine fancies* <*supra*>.

[5] This turns out to be Tudor-Stuart orthodoxy, with roots in the medieval contest between Empire and Papacy (*vide* Marsilius of Padua, *Defensor pacis* [ca. 1325]; Laud, *Works* 3:406–7).

CHRISTOPHER DOW

Innovations unjustly charged upon the present Church and state
1637

Chap. I

An introduction to the ensuing discourse, containing the reasons
inducing the author to undertake it, and his aim in it

It is better (in the judgment of St. Cyprian) *by silence to condemn the ignorance of the erroneous than by speaking to provoke the fury of the enraged.* And for this judgment of his, he had the warrant (as he saith) of divine authority. And certainly, it must needs be a great point of folly to grapple with those who . . . *by the noise of clamorous words seek rather to get vent and passage for their own than patiently to hear the opinions of others; it being more easy to still the waves of the troubled sea than by any discourse to repress the madness of such men.* To undertake such a task therefore, is but a vain attempt and of no more effect than to hold a light to the blind, to speak to the deaf, or to instruct a stone. Foul-mouth'd railers and barking dogs are soonest still'd by passing on our way in silence, or by severe and due correction: yet notwithstanding, this rule is not without some exception, and therefore Solomon, who giveth this counsel, *not to answer a fool according to his folly*, adds in the next words (as it were) a cross-proverb to it, bidding us *answer a fool according to his folly, lest he be wise in his own conceit.* In that case, an answer to clamorous and slanderous railers . . . is not unfit or unseasonable. And there are (no doubt) other cases in which . . . a man may, yea and it is expedient that he should, make answer to the envenomed railings of embittered spirits. And if at any time, sure then, when such detractors are not only wise in their own conceits but, which is more, have inveigled many simple and (perhaps otherwise) well-meaning people and drawn them to an opinion of their wisdom, and belief and approbation of their false and wicked calumnies. Much more, when they level their poisoned arrows of detraction against the sovereign power and against the fathers of the Church; which, if they should prevail, would wound and endanger the settled government and peace of both Church and state. In such case, it cannot be accounted rashness for any true-hearted subject and son of the Church to break an otherwise resolved silence to prevent (what in him is) the growth of so great a mischief.

I will add one other particular: when men shall be so impiously presumptuous as to break into the secrets of the Almighty and peremptorily to pronounce of his inscrutable judgments (as if they had been his counselors) and to cast the causes of the present plague and all the evils that have lately threatened or befallen us upon those men to whom, next under God, we owe, and in duty ought to acknowledge, our preservation hitherto . . . it is high time then to speak, lest silence should be interpreted a confession of guilt and inability to wipe off such desperate and malicious slanders. And herein I have for my warrant the authority of the same Father {Cyprian}, who, having upon the grounds before mentioned long held his peace and with patience overcome the rage of his adversaries, at length he thus breaks forth: *Seeing thou sayst, many complain that it is to be imputed to us* [Christians] *that wars so often rise, that plague and famine to rage, and that we have such long droughts: we must no longer be silent, lest now it be not modesty but diffidence that we held our peace, and while we scorn to refute your criminations, we should seem to acknowledge the crime.* Upon these considerations, and in imitation of that holy Father and martyr, I have set upon this work (in a calm and compendious way) to endeavor the stopping of the mouth of detraction, and to shew the groundlessness and vanity of those suspicious jealousies and clamors which of late have been raised in many parts of this kingdom; and which Mr. B. (having first vented in the pulpit) did after send abroad (gathered into one bundle) in his book entitled *An apology of an Appeal, &c.* And though I know it to be most true that among the ruder sort and common people the loudest cry takes the most ears, and that audacious errors and bold calumnies find more free entertainment and welcome with light and weak judgments than peaceable and modest truth; and that there seem so great an indisposition and disaffection in the minds and hearts of some in these days either to the present authority or to the things by it either commended or enjoined, that important truths and wholesome orders, becoming once countenanced or pressed by authority, instead of credit and obedience, receive nothing but clamor and detraction; and that such as, according but as duty bindeth them, do undertake to plead in their just cause or speak in their defense shall from many, instead of thanks, gain nothing but odious and opprobrious names and contumelies, yet withal I know and am persuaded that the iniquity of the times is not such but that truth and a good cause many yet find equal judges, who, following the precept of our blessed Savior, *Judge not according to appearance, but judge righteous judgment.* . . .

Chap. II

A short relation, or description, of Mr. H. Burton his course and manner of life. Of the occasion of his discontent, his dismission from the Court. The ground of his dislike and hatred against the bishops, and betaking himself to the people. The course he hath since taken in his books and sermons to make himself plausible, and the bishops envied.
Of the book called A divine tragedy, &c.

. . . And he, thinking the times now come wherein he might come even with those whom he conceived to be his adversaries . . . he behaved himself in such sort that his Majesty dismissed him the Court and his service;[1] whence being cashier'd, and all his hopes of preferment dasht, he betakes himself to the people, as more patient of his criminations and more apt to side with him against the reverend bishops; and having, by the help of popular applause, advanced from the hatred of some bishops' persons to a total dislike of their order and of all their proceedings, he made their actions his continual theme, and his sermons and writings so many satires and bitter invectives, accusing them of Arminianism, popery, and whatsoever might make them odious and himself gracious with his new masters, the people, and proceeding in this course with strange violence . . . he sent forth a book called *A divine tragedy late acted, &c*, wherein he hath in a strangely presumptuous and daring manner perkt up into God's throne and taken upon him to read the dark and dim characters of the causes of his inscrutable judgments, and wrested many late accidents that have happened, to make them speak God's indignation against such as have used the liberty granted by his Majesty's late *Declaration for sports upon the Sundays and holy days*[2]—of which accidents, there are some which fail in the truth of story; others that are so common and ordinary that it is ridiculous to reckon them for memorable examples of God's judgments; others that though they may well be accounted such, yet have other causes of them that may with more probability be assigned than that for which he brings them; yea, there is not one of them that so clearly speaks that which he pretends that any man (without the just imputation of impious rashness) can say that they were inflicted for that cause only or principally; and (which is yet more), granting that they were all true, and so remarkable as he makes them, and that they did (in as plain language as is possible for them) speak God's indignation against the profanation of the Lord's Day, yet it will not follow that God did thereby confirm the Sunday-Sabbatarian doctrine. . . . For, without all question, whether the observation of the Lord's Day stand by virtue of God's immediate precept in the Fourth Commandment . . . or only by apostolical or ecclesiastical constitution, the profanation of that day must needs be a grievous sin and powerful attractive of divine vengeance, seeing it is acknowledged by all that in the profanation of that day both God's precept (so far as it is moral in the Fourth Commandment[3]) is violated and the authority which God hath commanded all Christians to obey is contemned; yea, and the public worship of God, without which there can be no true religion, neglected, vilified, and overthrown. . . .

Chap. IV

Of the sermons. The author's intention in the examination of them. A general view of their materials. Their dissonancy from the text in every part of it. Their principal argument: supposed innovations. The author's pitching upon them as containing the sum of all.

. . . what readier way can be devised to extirpate the fear of God and true religion and piety out of men's hearts than is here taken in these sermons? For example, to mock at the devout gestures and pious expressions of holy reverence in God's service: to call that

---

[1] {Burton had been Charles' clerk of the closet during his father's reign, but was dismissed shortly after Charles became king, probably for making unfounded accusations of popery.}

[2] {For an example of this sort of Sabbatarian providentialism, see Bayly <*supra*>, and, more generally, Alexandra Walsham, *Providence in early modern England* (Oxford UP, 2001).}

[3] {i.e., insofar as the Fourth Commandment is ethical rather than merely ceremonial}

due and lowly reverence which is done at the mention of that sweet and blessed name by which alone men can be saved, a *complemental crouch to Jesus*, and in a blasphemous jeer, *Jesu worship*; and that honor which is tendered to God toward that place where, of all others, he manifests himself most graciously, *altar worship, adoration of the altar-God, false shews, will-worship, a kind of courtship, a compliment,* etc.; to style the singing of praises to God *chanting*, and the music (which is used to allay distracting and disturbing thoughts, to raise our dull affections and to stir them up to a devout cheerfulness in praising of God) *piping*; yea, to deride the whole service of God (ever allowed and approved in our Church) under the name of *long Babylonish service*, and the solemn prayers of the Church appointed and used at the fast, *mocking of God to the face*, and the fast itself a *mock-fast*. What a dis-heartening must this needs be to men and what an allay to that little fervor which is in them to God's worship, when their best performances, both for matter and manner, shall be thus derided and scorned? . . .

What opprobrious language, what bitter terms and titles of reproach hath he used against those whom he conceives opposite to him in opinion, aiming principally at the r{everend} bishops and fathers of the Church, whose dignity he contemns, calling them *enemies and rebels to God, fogs and mists risen from the bottomless pit, frogs and unclean spirits crept out of the mouth of the Dragon, limbs of the Beast even of Antichrist.* . . . Neither hath he been contented to keep himself in generals, but hath shot out the poisoned shafts of his serpentine tongue against particular persons (a thing hateful and intolerable in a public sermon) as (not to speak of those of lower rank, of whom the meanest is far above him in every kind of worth) the L. Bishop of Norwich {Wren}, a man eminent for his learning and approved to his Sacred Majesty by his long and faithful service, upon whom he bestows these titles: *an usurper, a bringer in of foreign power, an innovator, oppressor, persecutor and troubler of the peace of the Church and kingdom.* The L. Bishop of Chichester {Montagu}, that mirror of learning, he calls a *tried champion for Rome*, and—joining him with that thrice-venerable the L. Bishop of Ely (whom in contempt he calls *Dr. White*)— saith, *They are men well affected to Rome*, when it is well known they have done more real (not railing) service to this Church against Rome than ever Mr. Burton or any or all his faction ever did or could. But I am beneath their worth thus to compare them.

But if ever he shewed himself his craft's-master in the art of reviling, lying, and slandering, it is against the most reverend Father in God, the Lord Archbishop of Cant. his Grace, against whom he hath with an impudent forehead framed such odious lies, endeavoring to load him with so many false and foul aspersions and using so insolently base and reproachful terms against his person, his chair, and dignity, that he may seem (to use a phrase of his own) to have *strained the veins of his conscience no less than of his brains* in the venting and inventing of them. . . . Yet further. It was wisely and truly observed by that worthy prelate and late glory of our Church, Bishop Andrewes . . . that *they that in the end prove to be seditious (mark them well), they be first detractors—ever, as at first it did, so doth it still begin in the gainsaying, in the contradiction of Korah. So began he: This Moses and this Aaron, they take too much upon them, do more than they may by law; they would have somewhat taken from them* {Numb. 16}. *So Absalom: Here is nobody to do any justice in the land* {2 Sam. 15:3}. *So Jeroboam: Lord, what a heavy yoke is this on the people's neck!* {1 Kings 12:4}. *Meddle not with these detractors.* So he. And indeed what more powerful detractive of obedience from the sovereign power can there be invented than to fill the people's heads with conceits of the *King's neglect of religion, his oaths and protestations*, to persuade them that (as if unable to rule) he suffers his *royal throne to be overtopped* by others, his *laws trampled on*, and *himself swayed to acts against justice and religion?* What greater incentive, what readier way to kindle the fire of sedition than to cast contempt and scorn upon those in authority under him, to make them hated as contemners of law, oppressors, persecutors, enemies of God and all goodness?

. . . And, whatever fair colors he puts upon it, the change he aims at is neither so agreeable to the word of God nor Christ's sweet yoke as is the present church-government, nor the presbytery (save in title) less lordly than the prelacy. Nay, there is no prelate, nor all of them together, that doth or will challenge that power and dominion which is exercised in that Discipline, to which not the people only but the king himself must be subject—yea, and deposed too, if he will not submit, as by their practice at Geneva, where it had its first beginning, is most apparent. . . .

Chap. V

Of the supposed innovations in doctrine. Of King James his order to the Universities for reading the Fathers, done long since; unjustly charged upon the present bishops. By whomsoever procured, upon just grounds. Not popish, but against popery. King James' other order for preaching of election &c. justified.

First, saith he, *they* (the prelates) *have labored to bring in a change of doctrine, as appeared by these instances. I. By procuring an order from King James of famous memory to the Universities, that young students should not read our modern learned writers, as Calvin, Beza, and others of the Reformed Churches, but the Fathers and Schoolmen.*[4]

This first crimination is far fetched, being (if I mistake not) a thing acted above twenty years ago; so that it seems he means to take him compass enough, the times present not affording him sufficient store; and, if he had gone back but twice as many more, he might have found the reading of Calvin and Beza accounted as great an innovation as now he holds the debarring of men from reading of them, and that by those that were as good Protestants as Mr. Burton, and as far from popery.

. . .

. . . And it is one thing to give the right hand of fellowship to a particular Church (which we willingly do to all the Reformed Churches beyond the seas) and another to like and approve every tenet that any man in that Church shall hold or deliver. I suppose Mr. Burton is not so uncharitable as to deny the Lutheran Churches the right hand of fellowship and to exclude them from being a true Church; and yet I believe he would be loath to agree with them in all opinions which they maintain, especially if he knew . . . that they held all those tenets about predestination, free will, and falling from grace, which he so much condemns in those whom he terms Arminians. . . .

Chap. VI

Of his Majesty's Declaration prefixed to the Articles of Religion. Mr. Burton's cunning trick to color his railing against his Majesty's actions, and the danger that may come of it. All truths not necessary

---

[4] {On this order, see the introduction to Digby's *A conference with a lady <infra>*.}

to be known or taught. The doctrine of predestination in Mr. Burton's sense best unknown.
he Gospel not overthrown but furthered by the want of it. An uncomfortable doctrine.

But leaving King James, he comes to our gracious sovereign that now is, and saith, *After that there is set forth a* Declaration *before the* Articles of Religion *in King Charles his name.*[5] And why in *King Charles his name*, and not *by him*? The title calls it *his Majesty's Declaration*, and the whole tenor if it runs in his Majesty's style. How then shall we know it was not his? This is but a cunning quirk to teach the people to decline obedience to his Majesty's commands. If they can be persuaded that his Majesty's declarations and proclamations which are sent out (if they concern things that cross their fancies) be none of his acts, then to what pass things in short time will grow it is easy for any man that is but half-witted to conjecture. If men may, at their liberty, father the king's acts upon the prelates or any other whom they favor not, and then rail at them at their pleasure and reject them as none of his, his Majesty will ere long be fain to stand to his subjects' courtesy for obedience to his royal commands. Or if men may say of such things as come out in the king's name, that *they tend to the public dishonor of God and his word, to the violation and annihilation of his commandments, the alteration of the doctrine of the Church of England, the destruction of the people's souls, and that they are contrary to his solemn royal protestations* (as Mr. B. speaks about the *Declaration for Sports . . .*) and therefore that they are not the king's acts, what doth he else but persuade the people, who (for all his gloss) believe them (as indeed who can believe otherwise) to be his, that his Majesty is (I tremble to speak it out) such as he makes them whom he entitles to[6] those acts? And then what may we expect to follow but the practice of that doctrine which is taught in many of his orthodox authors:[7] the withstanding and opposing of their commands and deposing of their persons. But this passage is better answered by the justice of authority than a scholar's pen. Let us see then what it is he finds fault with in this *Declaration*. First, he intimates that *God's truth*—that is, *the saving doctrines of election, predestination, effectual vocation, assurance, and perseverance—are thereby silenced and suppressed.* Be it so. Is it not better that some truth for a while be suppressed than the peace of the Church disturbed? St. Augustine saith, *It is profitable to keep in some truth, for their sakes that are incapable* [*de persev. Sanctorum*, c. 15], and surely we might truly say of the time when this *Declaration* was published by his Majesty, that men were incapable of these doctrines. When men begin once to strive about names, to quarrel about abstruse mysteries, to side one against the other, and to count each other anathema (as it was with our neighbors,[8] and began to be with us), was it not time to enjoin silence to both parties? All truths, we know, are

[5] {*His Majesty's Declaration* prefixed to the 1628 reprint of the Thirty-nine Articles ordered that, with respect to the predestinarian controversies, "all further curious search" was to be laid aside "and these disputes shut up in God's promises, as they be generally set forth to us in the Holy Scripture." The *Declaration* followed Charles' 1626 proclamation against writing, preaching, or printing on these controverted issues. There seems nothing peculiarly Caroline (or Laudian) about this response. Hales' *Tract* notes that it was tried in Germany <*supra*>. The conformist Calvinist Joseph Hall's *Via media* (ca. 1624) reaches the same conclusion. See the introduction to Hall, note 2 <*supra*>.}

[6] {i.e., to whom he ascribes}

[7] {On Calvinist resistance theory, see Quentin Skinner, *The foundations of modern political thought*, vol. 2: *The age of Reformation* (Cambridge UP, 1978).}

[8] {Dow is thinking about the Netherlands; see *Collegiate suffrage*, introduction and text <*supra*>.}

not of the same rank or of equal necessity; some things there are which must be preached in season and out of season, but those points he mentions come not within that number. . . . And though *the godly consideration of predestination and our election in Christ*[9] . . . may in some sense be called a saving doctrine, yet not so as the ignorance of it should exclude from salvation. However, taking it in the sense he intends—for those absolute and peremptory decisions, desperate positions, and high speculations, and such as are opposite to the *receiving of God's promises in such wise as they be generally set forth to us in the Holy Scripture*, and harping upon that will of God which is secret and not declared unto us in the word of God (which is the doctrine which he aims at)—we may count this doctrine among those things of which Prosper saith that *they profit being unknown*. And Mr. Burton is much deceived, and deceives the people, when he saith, *Thus the ministry of the Gospel is at once overthrown, and nothing but orations of morality must be taught the people*. Indeed Mr. Burton's gospel is thus overthrown, which consists in such daring speculations. But blessed be God, the Gospel of Christ by this means hath had a freer passage than it was like to have had if things might have been suffered to have gone on as they begun. And then is the Gospel in most vigor, when the people by it are instructed what it is that God hath commanded and what they ought to do, which in contempt he calls *orations of morality*. God doth not bring men to heaven by difficult questions; the way to eternity is plain and easy to be known: to believe that Jesus Christ was raised from the dead, to acknowledge him to be the Lord and Christ, and to live soberly, righteously, and religiously in this present world is the sum of saving doctrine and Christian religion; and this is left written for our learning in so plain characters that he that runs may read it.

. . . As for the comfortableness of that {predestinarian} doctrine as they teach it, let the poor tormented consciences speak, which have by it been affrighted and driven to desperation. I heard one once (an acquaintance of Mr. Burton's) {to one?} making this objection against his preaching about reprobation, that said, *It was very fit that therefore it should be taught, that men that found in themselves the marks of reprobation should be driven to horror and despair, and have hell fire kindled in them here in this life*. A most comfortable doctrine no question.

Chap. VII

Of the books that have been printed of late. Of Franciscus à S. Clara. Desire of peace warranted by St. Paul. We and they of Rome differ not in fundamentals. What are fundamentals in Mr. Burton's sense. The distinction, in fundamentalibus & circa fundamentalia justified. The Church of England not schismatical. How far separated and wherein yet united with the Romish Church. Good works necessary to salvation. Justification by works, by charity, in what sense no popery. Whether the pope be that Antichrist, disputable. Of confession. Of prayer for the dead. How maintained by our Church. Praying to saints justly condemned by Protestants.

For the books that he saith of late times have come abroad maintaining popery and Arminianism, my answer is that Mr. Burton knows well enough how to get books printed in spite of authority, and therefore he cannot lay the blame there, if any such have passed out without license. And for those that have been licensed, it passeth Mr. Burton's learning

---

[9] {This and the quotation that follows come from Article 17 of the Thirty-nine Articles.}

(yea, though Mr. Prynne should be of his counsel) to find anything in them which is not consonant to the doctrines of the Church of England, contained in the 39 Articles and the Book of Common Prayer.

. . .

. . . the Church of England did reform the errors and abuses of Rome without schism. And that though we have separated from them in those things which they hold not as the Church of Christ, but as the Roman and Pontifician, yet we remain still united both in the bond of charity and in those articles of faith which the Church yet hath from apostolical tradition; yea, and in those acts of God's worship which they yet practice according to divine prescript: that is, we and they profess one belief of the same Apostolic Creed as it is expounded by the four first General Councils; we approve with them the things which the ancient Church of Christ decreed against Pelagius; we and they worship and invocate the same God, in the name of the same Jesus Christ. And (whatsoever some turbulently uncharitable haply may do) we study to reduce them from their errors and pray for their salvation, accounting them not quite cut off, but to continue still members (though corrupt ones) of the same Catholic Church. . . .

To the third—that the pope is not Antichrist—I answer, that though many of the learned in our Church (especially at the beginning of the Reformation, when the greatest heat was stricken between us and Rome) have affirmed the pope to be Antichrist and his whole religion antichristian. . . . yet to them that calmly and seriously consider it, it may, not without good reason, be disputed as doubtful whether the pope—or any of them in his person, or the papal hierarchy—be that great Antichrist which is so much spoken of. And which way soever it be determined, it makes not the religion any whit the better, nor frees the practices of the popes and Court of Rome from being justly accounted and styled *antichristian*. . . .

. . .

. . . It cannot be denied but that the Church of England did ever allow the private confession of sins to the priest for the quieting of men's consciences burdened with sin and *that they may receive ghostly counsel, advice, and comfort, and the benefit of absolution* [BCP: exhortation before the Communion]. This is the public order prescribed in our Church. And it were very strange if our Church, ordaining priests and giving them power of absolution and prescribing the form to be used for the exercise of that power upon confession, should not also allow of such private confession. To "advise" then, and to urge the use and profit of private confession to the priest, is no popish innovation, but agreeable to the constant and resolved doctrine of this Church, and that which is requisite for the due execution of that ancient power of the keys which Christ bestowed upon his Church. And if any shall call it "auricular" because it is done in private and in the ear of the priest, I know not why he should therefore be condemned of popery. But if Mr. Burton by "auricular confession" mean that sacramental confession which the Council of Trent hath defined to be of absolute necessity by divine ordinance and that which exacts that (many times impossible) particular enumeration of every sin and the special circumstances of every sin, this we justly reject as neither required by God nor so practiced by the ancient Church. And if Mr. Burton knows any that hath preached or printed ought in defense of this new pick-lock and tyrannical sacramental confession, he may, if he please (with the Church's good leave), term them in that point popish innovators.

For the second point: simply to condemn all prayer for the dead is to run counter to the constant practice of the ancient Church of Christ.[10] *Prayer for the dead, it cannot be denied, it is ancient*, saith the late learned Bishop of Winchester {Andrewes}. That the ancient Church had commemorations, oblations, and prayers for the dead, the testimonies of the Fathers, ecclesiastical histories, and ancient liturgies, in which the forms of prayers used for that purpose are found, do put out of all question; and they that are acquainted with the canons and liturgy of our own Church cannot but say this doctrine hath been ever taught and maintained among us: that is, *we praise God for all those that are departed this life in the faith of Christ*, and pray that they *may have their perfect consummation in bliss both in body and soul*, &c. And thus far, prayer for the dead is no innovation, and much less popish. For we maintain no suffrages for the relief of souls in the fool's-fire of purgatory, which prayers and place we condemn as *fond things vainly invented and grounded upon no warranty of Scripture, but rather repugnant to the word of God* [Article 22]. So our church-article speaks, and in the same condemnation joins that other point of Mr. Burton's charge, invocation of saints, which doctrine, taken at the best and as the learned Papists defend it, deserves that censure; and as it is commonly practiced by the vulgar sort among them, is not foolish only but flatly idolatrous, and therefore justly exploded and condemned by all Protestants; and I dare boldly say, Mr. Burton cannot produce any one of those whom he endeavors to blemish that holds or teaches that doctrine.

Chap. VIII

Of the doctrine of obedience to superiors. How taught and maintained by the bishops. Wherein it must be blind, and how quick-sighted.

We have two changes in doctrine yet remaining. First, in the doctrine of obedience to superiors. Secondly, in the doctrine of the Sabbath or Lord's Day.

By the first (he saith) *man is so set in God's throne, as all obedience to man must be absolute, without regard to God and conscience.* I verily believe there is none of those he means that have raised obedience so high, but that Mr. B. would bring it down to as low a peg; and haply, considering how prone such as he are to debase it, it might not be thought ill policy to exact somewhat more than of strict right it can challenge. But where or by whom is this doctrine taught? Of that he saith nothing here, but tells us *he hath spoken of it sufficiently before.* And indeed, we find more than enough by him spoken about this point: for, speaking of the connection of the fear of the Lord and of the king, and from thence (rightly) observing that these two ought not to be separated, *but that God must be so honored, as we do also in the second place honor our superiors; and our superiors so honored, as that in the first place we honor God*, he comes to reprove those that separate these two, the second sort of whom he makes *those that separate the fear of the king from the fear of the Lord, by attributing to kings such an unlimited power as if he were God Almighty himself, so as hereby they would seem to ascribe that omnipotency to the king which the pope assumes and his parasites ascribe to his holiness. And this* (he saith) *these parasites and paramours of the king's courts do*, &c. All this is easily granted. The doctrine, there is no good Christian but will subscribe to—yea, and the use too—and think those . . . unworthy the name of

---

[10] {On prayers for the dead, see Field, *Of the Church* <*supra*>.}

Christians and to be accounted none of God's good subjects that shall go about by flattery or otherwise to advance the power of the king to the prejudice of God's supereminent sovereignty; or which, when the commands of the one and the other come in opposition, shall not (as the apostles) choose rather to obey God than man. . . .

. . .

. . . They {the bishops} hold and teach that it is more agreeable to Christian piety to be blind rather than thus quick-sighted in our obedience, and approve that of St. Gregory, *True obedience doth not discuss the intention of superiors nor make difference of precepts; he that hath learned perfectly to obey, knows not how to judge.* To be blind, so as not to see the imperfections and failings of superiors, nor to be less ready for these[11] to perform their commands, and to look only at him {God} whose place they {superiors} hold. . . . Lastly, they would have obedience to be better-sighted, and not so blind as Mr. Burton hath shewed himself. They would have obedience to have eyes to see what God commands as well as what the king, and to discern God to be the greater of the two and to be obeyed in the first place, but they would not have men mistake their own dreams and fancies for God's commands. And not this only, but to see what is commanded by their superiors, and who it is that commands, and to know them to be God's deputies to whom obedience is due as unto God himself. And they have learned of Solomon that *where the word of a king is, there is power; and who may say unto him, what doest thou?* [Eccles. 8:4]. This is no novel Jesuitical doctrine, but sound divinity and that which this Church ever taught and the law of the land ever approved—if it be good law which was long ago delivered by Bracton, with which I will shut up this point. *The king* (saith he) *is under none, but only God.* And, a little after, *If he do amiss (because no writ goes out against him), there is place for supplication that he would correct and amend his deed; which if he do not, it is enough punishment for him that the Lord will punish it. For no man must presume to enquire or discuss his actions, much less to go against them.*[12]

Chap. IX

Of the doctrine of the Sabbath and Lord's Day, falsely accused of novelty. The sum of what is held or denied in this point by those whom Mr. B. opposeth. The Church's power, and the obligation of her precepts. The maintainers of this doctrine have not strained their brains or conscience.

The last innovation in doctrine that he mentions is concerning the doctrine of the Sabbath or Lord's Day: wherein, he saith, *our novel doctors have gone about to remove the institution of it from the foundation of divine authority and so to settle it upon the ecclesiastical or human power.* Thus he. But in this (as in the rest), he betrays a most gross and palpable ignorance and malice. 1. In that he accuseth that doctrine of novelty which was ever (as hath been sufficiently demonstrated) the doctrine of the ancient Church and of the Church of England and of the Reformed Churches beyond the seas and the principal of the learned among them, as Calvin, Beza, &c. 2. In accusing those that teach this doctrine with removing the institution of the Lord's Day from the foundation of divine authority, which

---

[11] {i.e., despite such imperfections}

[12] Bracton, *de leg. & consuet. Ang.* c. 8 {Henry Bracton, *On the laws and customs of England*, trans. Samuel Thorne, 2 vols. (Harvard UP, 1968), 2:33}.

. . . is most false, for they acknowledge the appointment of set times and days to the public and solemn worship and service of God to be not only divine, but moral and perpetual, and that the common and natural equity of the Fourth Commandment obligeth all mankind to the end of the world.

Secondly, they affirm that the institution of the Lord's Day, and other set and definite days and times of God's worship, is also of divine authority, though not immediately, but by the Church, which received her power from the Holy Ghost; and that Christian people are to observe the days so ordained in obedience to the equity of the Fourth Commandment, to which those days are subordinate and their observation to be reduced.

Thirdly, they grant that the resting from labor on the Lord's Day and Christian holy days, in respect of the general, is both grounded upon the law of nature and the perpetual equity of the Fourth Commandment.

Fourthly, they grant a special sense of that Commandment of perpetual obligation: so that they have not absolutely removed the institution of the Lord's Day from the foundation of divine authority; nor is the Fourth Commandment wholly abolished, as he falsely and unjustly clamors. That which they deny in this doctrine and concerning the Fourth Commandment may be reduced under these heads:

They deny the Fourth Commandment to be wholly moral; so doth Mr. Burton.

Particularly, they deny the morality and perpetual obligation of that Commandment as it concerns the seventh day from the Creation, which is our Saturday. And this is the Apostle's doctrine, who calls it a shadow, which Mr. Burton also granteth.

They deny that the peculiar manner of the sanctification of the Jewish or seventh-day Sabbath in the observation of a strict and total rest and surcease from ordinary labors can, by virtue of that Commandment, be extended to the Lord's Day or Christian holy days, but that it (together with the day on which it was required) is expired and antiquated. And this also Mr. Burton must needs grant: 1. Because there is the same reason of the day and the rest required upon it, both being appointed for a memorial of God's rest from his work of Creation and other typical respects. 2. Because otherwise he will contradict his fellows and those that side with him in this argument, who generally allow some things to be lawfully done on the Lord's Day which on the Jewish Sabbath were not permitted.

. . .

That which they ascribe unto the Church in this argument is: 1. The institution of the Lord's Day and other holy days; that is, the determination of the time of God's public worship to those days.

2. The prescription of the manner of the observation of these days, both for the duties to be performed, and the time, manner, and other circumstances of their performance.

Concerning which, they affirm 2 things. First, that the Church hath liberty, power, and authority thus to do. Secondly, that Christians are in conscience bound to observe these precepts of the Church, and that they that transgress them sin against God, whose law requires that we must obey every lawful ordinance of the Church. And as St. Bernard speaks, *The obedience that is given to superiors* (he speaks of the prelates and governors in the Church) *is exhibited to God; wherefore whatsoever man in God's stead commands (if it be not for certain such as displease God) is no otherwise at all to be received than if God had commanded it. For what matters it whether God by himself or by his ministers, men or angels, make known his pleasure to us?* So he, and much more to that purpose in that place. So that they which maintain the institution of the Lord's Day to be from the Church do not thereby (as they are wrongly charged) discharge men from all tie of obedience and give them liberty to observe it or not at their own pleasure, which no man will affirm but those only who have learned to undervalue and despise the Church of God and her rightful authority.

. . .

Chap. X

Of his Majesty's Declaration for Sports,[13] *&c. Mr. Burton's scandalizing the memory of K. James about it. His wicked censure of his Majesty for reviving and republishing it. His abusive jeer upon my Lord's Grace of Cant. Five propositions opposed to his so many unjust criminations in this argument.*

This is all he saith of his supposed innovations in doctrine. But before I part with this last point, I must annex somewhat of his Majesty's *Declaration concerning lawful sports to be used upon Sundays,* as . . . being the great pretended grievance in this argument.

. . .

. . . The *Declaration* itself he hath used in the same manner that he hath done the authors of it: styling it by all the names he could devise to make it odious and to harden others in their obstinacy against it. For answer whereunto, I shall briefly oppose these five following propositions to his so many unjust criminations:

First, the *Declaration* is no inlet to profaneness or irreligion, or hindrance of the due sanctification of the Lord's Day.

2. That the sports permitted by it to be used are lawful and such as are not prohibited either by God's law or the law of the land.
3. That it is no means of breaking the Fifth Commandment, nor doth allow any contempt of parents' or masters' authority over their children and servants.
4. That the reading of it by ministers in their several congregations was enjoined and intended by his Majesty, and that it is a thing that may lawfully be done by them.
5. That such as refuse to publish it accordingly are justly punished, and their punishment no cruelty or unjust persecution.

Chap. XI

Of the 1. proposition: the Declaration no inlet to profaneness. His Majesty's respect to piety in it. Recreations only permitted, not imposed. Of the 2. proposition: the sports allowed are lawful on those days and in themselves not against the law of the land. Mr. Burton's seeming respect of the Fathers. Of reveling. Of mixt dancing: how unlawful and how condemned by the ancients and by the Imperial edicts. Of Calvin's judgment in this point. Of the 3. proposition: the book no means of violation of the 5 Commandment.

For the first, it is most evident to any impartial reader that shall peruse the *Declaration,* that his Majesty, intending only to take away that scandal which some rigid Sabbatarians had brought upon our religion to the hindering of the conversion of popish recusants, and

---

[13] {First issued by James in 1618; reissued by Charles in 1633, with the requirement that it be read in pulpits throughout England, creating a crisis of conscience for Sabbatarian clergy.}

to allow (especially to the meaner sort) such honest recreations as might serve for their refreshment and better enabling them to go through with their hard labors on other days, his Majesty (I say), in this his charitable intention, did not forget his wonted respect to piety and the service of God, or due sanctification of the Lord's Day.

For first, he doth straightly charge and command every person first to resort to his own parish church.

Secondly, he doth expressly provide that none shall have the benefit of the liberty granted that will not first come to the church and serve God, thereby excluding all recusants and idly profane persons who absent themselves from God's house and service.

Thirdly, he doth enjoin that they, to whom it belongeth in office, shall present and sharply punish all such as, in abuse of this his liberty, will use the exercises allowed before the ends of all divine services for that day. Which things rightly considered, if they be as well put in execution as they were piously intended by his Majesty, are so far from hindering, that they are a great furtherance of the due service of God upon that day; inasmuch as thereby many that otherwise would not may be allured and compelled to present themselves in the church at the public worship of God.

. . .

If then, by the *Declaration*, the public service of God be duly provided for, no recreations permitted to the hindrance thereof, no nor the pious affections of well-disposed Christians for the applying of themselves on that day to private duties of devotion and piety any way prohibited, then it cannot justly be accounted any inlet to profaneness or irreligion, or hindrance of the due sanctification of the Lord's Day, which was my first proposition.

. . .

2. For reveling, taking it in the usual sense for drunken and disorderly meetings, &c., we must subscribe to the Fathers and Councils, and not to them only, but to the sacred Scripture, where they are plainly condemned as works of the flesh; and say withal that it was one end that his Majesty aimed at in this *Declaration*, to hinder such revelings, which he condemns under the name of *filthy tippling and drunkenness*. But if Mr. Burton intend by it all those other sports mentioned in the *Declaration*, as wakes and Whitson-ales, &c., I say then that he is much wide in his conceit of them; they are no such things, especially in his Majesty's intention, who hath therefore given express charge for the preventing and punishing of all disorders in them.

Thirdly, that then which remains under the sentence of condemnation is only dancing, and, as I suppose, mixed dancing (as they use to call it) of men and women together, for single dancing is not by the strictest disallowed. As for mixed dancings, I know they may be abused and become unlawful by the immoderate and unseasonable use of them, and may otherwise (yea, and they do many times) become incentives unto lust, and that in two ways especially.

First, when there are used in them such immodest motions and gestures as have in them manifest tokens of a lascivious mind.

Secondly, when they are done *animo libidinoso*, with an intention to stir up the fire of lust. Where either of these are, they must needs become unlawful.

Now these, as they may be as well in single dancing, so they are not in all mixed dancings so as to make them all to be condemned. For what hinders but that men and women may together express their joy in such modest motions and with as chaste intentions as they may otherwise walk, talk, salute, and converse together? If any shall say there is a danger because of our frailty, which is prone to abuse these to wantonness, I say so there is in other conversings of men and women together, but that danger not such as to make either altogether unlawful.

Again, I would know fain why men and women (especially where the custom of the country allows it) may not as unblameably dance together, as for either sex to become spectators of other's dancing? David, we know, danced in the sight of women (2 Sam. 6) and Miriam (Exod. 15). And (if we grant that the women danced *seorsim à viris*[14]), yet it cannot be denied but that they danced in the sight of men. Why then may they not do it together? But they expressed a holy and religious joy, which our country-dancers are far from. What if they did? will that hinder the creeping of impure affections into the minds of the beholders? or must there be no dancing but in expression of spiritual joy? I suppose no wise man will be so straitlaced; and if not, then must they not condemn mixed dancing (which have in them only grave and modest motions) because men's corruptions may abuse them to lust and wantonness.

. . .

If any say that our morris-dancing and maypoles do also savor of heathenism . . . I answer that things are not therefore rightly called heathenish, unless there be something in them for which Christians might not use them. . . . Christianity doth not forbid men to do anything which the heathens did, but such only as were contrary unto the law of God and the law of right reason; neither doth it exact in all men a philosophical or Cato-like severity to which these delights may seem no better than folly: for grant that wise men esteem of them as Solomon of laughter and mirth (Eccl. 2:2), yet it will not follow that such as by reason of their mean education and parts hardly aspire to know the pleasure of other delights should not use such as they are capable of.

. . .

. . . We know there are many things prohibited by our statutes which are not unlawful but only inconvenient in regard of the time, place, or persons in which and to whom such things shall be so prohibited.

For example, no man can truly say that bowling or shove-groat or other exercises by statute forbidden to be used by artificers, husbandmen, servants, &c. are unlawful either in themselves or for those persons. Yet was that statute founded upon very good reason: namely, that such persons, restrained from those and suchlike exercises nothing profitable for themselves or the kingdom, might betake themselves to the too much (by means of those) neglected exercise of shooting in the long bow, that so they might at all times be ready to serve their country when occasion should require and, in the mean while, uphold the occupations of *bowers and fletchers, and keep them from settling in other countries to their comfort and the detriment of this realm*, as that statute speaks. So that in statutes and edicts of princes and states, always the end and other circumstances ought to be considered, as well as the bare letter of the law, if from thence we will judge of the lawfulness or unlawfulness of things by them commanded or forbidden. . . .

. . .

[14] {apart from the men}

It is a part of Mr. Burton's declamation against this *Declaration, That it is a trenching, or rather a violent inroad, upon the Fifth Commandment, which saith,* Honor thy father and thy mother, *&c.* . . . *and so cuts asunder the very sinews not only of religion but of all civil society at one blow.* . . . Sure it is an evil thing and worthy to be abolished that shall thus violate God's commandments by couples; and were it not that this charge is (as his others use to be) a little defective in one thing (which we call *truth*), I should (not so much as I do) dislike those men that refuse to publish it. Let us then consider his proofs. All that I find by him alleged (though there be more than enough of it) may well be resolved into his private opinion boldly vented and faced with certain interrogatives, which perhaps he mistook for good reasons in the pulpit, where no man would or durst contradict him. For I find him speaking (in many more words) after this manner: . . . *Alas! then what shall parents and ministers do, when their sons and servants will abroad and take their liberty of sports, at leastwise after evening prayer every Lord's Day, and will stay out as long as they please.* A heavy case, no doubt; and because the man (by the moan he makes) seems to be in some distress, I'll resolve his doubt and free him from his perplexity. *Alas! what shall they do?* Marry, give them such correction as befits such rebellious and disobedient sons and servants that shall dare to take upon them to be their own carvers in their liberty, with contempt of those whom the law of God and nature commands them to honor and obey. But this plaster seems too narrow for his sore; for he adds, *gladly would they restrain them, but they may not, they dare not, for fear of being brought to the Assizes, there to be punished.* No? may not? dare not? Surely a man by this may swear Mr. Burton never read the *Declaration*; or if he did, is very dull of understanding, or very willing to mistake. For I would demand, when ever Mr. Burton or any man else knew a father or master bound over or brought to the Assizes for restraining his son or servant? or where this danger is intimated? It saith indeed that *the Justices of Assize shall see that no man do trouble or molest any of his Majesty's loyal and dutiful people in or for their lawful recreation, having first done their duty to God, and continuing in obedience to his Majesty and his laws, &c.*

But what is all this to parents and masters? shall they lose their authority and government over their children and servants? God forbid. Were that true, then indeed farewell all obedience to superiors, whose first model and foundation is laid in private families. But, God be thanked, there is no such thing. Neither 1. in the book, wherein the names of servants or children are not once mentioned, but the persons for whom the liberty is granted supposed to be *sui iuris*. Nor 2. in the intention of it; for all that is spoken is of public hindrance and molestation by the public magistrate or officer, whose office ordinarily and in such cases is not exercised *inter privatos parietes*, within private walls, at least not without express order to that purpose. So that every man is still free and hath as full power to order his family and to prescribe bounds to his children and servants' liberty as before. Yea, they may, if they please (as too many use to do in this case) notwithstanding the *Declaration* prove tyrants in the exercise of their authority.

. . .

Chap. XII

Ministers commanded by his Majesty to read the book. They may and ought to obey. The matter of the book not unlawful. Things unlawfully commanded may sometimes be lawfully obeyed.

*What things are required to justify a subject's refusing a superior's command. Refusers to read
the book justly punished. The punishment inflicted, not exceeding the offence.
Not without good warrant.*

That the reading of the book by ministers in their several congregation was enjoined and intended by his Majesty, and that it is a thing that may lawfully be done by them: both these are denied by Mr. Burton, and the latter brought as a reason to the former thus: the thing is unlawful *as tending to the public dishonor of God* &c. Therefore *the King did not nor can any honest man imagine that he should ever intend to command it.*

This is a common fetch of his, and it is very pretty, to pass a false sentence upon his Majesty's just and pious actions and then to charge those actions upon others, that so he may the more freely vent his invectives against them and yet seem, in this midst of this his great-seeming zeal, to retain his dutiful and loyal respect of his Majesty's honor. . . .

. . .

. . . It must be *apertè*, manifestly known to be against the will of God, and past all doubt and peradventure. The subject may not deny his sovereign his obedience because he fears that which is commanded is not agreeable to God's will, or because he cannot see the words of God for it, or because some doubt of the lawfulness of it. He that will do nothing at the command of his superiors which is doubted of by any whether it be lawful or no, will pin up his obedience within very narrow bounds and prove but a bad subject. It is our own conscience, not another's, that must be our guide in matters of obedience to the powers ordained by God. In things left to our liberty, we may, yea, we must have respect to the conscience of another; that is St. Paul's doctrine: *For why* (saith he) *should my liberty be judged by another man's conscience?* [1 Cor. 10:29]. That is, why should I use my liberty so as to be condemned by the conscience of another? But St. Paul doth nowhere say, Why should my obedience be judged? That is no matter of liberty, but duty. If another man's conscience (mine own being resolved) shall condemn me for my obedience, they may, but to their own hurt, not mine, who do but my duty without offending against charity, which must never be extended to cross justice. To offend and wound mine own, for fear of offending another man's conscience, is not a well-grounded charity, but (to speak but right) sinful folly. Though a man must love and tender his neighbor as himself, yet he needs not, he must not in this case, love him more or before himself; but if it come to that, that the one must be neglected, here every man must think himself his nearest neighbor and prefer himself before all others.

2. Neither is it sufficient to excuse our disobedience to say, God hath not in his word commanded any such thing as man requires. For this were to deny all obedience to man, whose power is properly in those things which are left undefined in the word of God. It is sufficient warrant for us to know the things by human authority commanded, not to be forbidden by God in his word, and that they are not contrary to that which God commands: which everything which he hath not commanded cannot with reason be said to be.

. . .

It will follow then that they are justly punished, and their punishment no cruelty or unjust persecution, which is my fifth and last proposition. For they to whom God gives authority to command, they have also from the same hand of God a sword, an emblem of their power, not defensive only, but coercive also, to punish the disobedience

of such as resist their commanding power; and this vindicative power is as necessary as the other. Yea, it is that which supports and gives life to their commands. . . . But haply the punishment may exceed the nature of the offence and so become cruelty, and they justly termed cruel that execute it. For those Seneca calls cruel, *who have cause but no measure of punishing.* Indeed, Mr. B. would make men that know nothing of the case think there were strange severity, yea, *injustice; illegal, uncanonical proceedings, severe and wicked censures, persecution exercised against ministers in this cause.* But it is no new thing for men of his spirit to call their deserved punishment *unjust persecution,* when (to speak as St. Austin once did in the like case to his Donatists) *if the thing they suffer be compared with the deeds which they commit, who sees not which are rather to be called persecutors.* And whether these men suffering for their faults, or the Church and state suffering under their irregularity and turbulency, may most rightly be said to be in persecution is no hard question to determine. But to the point. They complain of two things: 1. the censure is too heavy. 2. without warrant. For 1, *will no less censure serve the turn than suspension, excommunication, deprivation, and the like*? I answer, No, especially for those that after admonition, instruction, and long forbearance remain not only refractory but add thereto many intolerable affronts to authority by public invectives, private whisperings, and false suggestions, buzzing into the people I know not what dangerous issues[15] (mere fictions of a pettish fancy) to follow; for these men, these censures are mild enough. And I dare appeal to that conscience which Mr. B. hath yet left him, whether, if he did erect his new discipline and godly government, he would not exercise as harsh censures upon them that not only willfully but thus turbulently oppose the commands of those in authority. And we may easily guess what he would do if he had once the upper ground, when being on the lower he can so severely censure those that are above him with deprivation not of living but of life, and turn suspension into (plain English) hanging [*Ips. News* {Prynne <820>}]. And that the Churches where that purer discipline is in place, for matters of lesser moment, hath inflicted as heavy censures, is better known than to need rehearsing.
. . .

Chap. XIII

Of the innovation (pretended to be) in discipline. The courts ecclesiastical have continued their wonted course of justice. St. Augustine's apology for the Church against the Donatists fitly serves ours. The cunning used by delinquents to make themselves pitied and justice taxed. Their practices to palliate and cover their faults. Mr. Burton's endeavor to excuse Ap-Evans. Mr. Burton's opposites not censorious. What they think of (those whom he calls) professors, and *the profession itself.[16] True piety approved and honored in all professions. The answer to his crimination summed up. The censured partial judges of their own censures. How offences are to be rated {rebuked} in their censures.*

. . . Was it ever known that any Church or any civil government did or could subsist without inflicting censures upon the willful violators of their orders and constitutions? Hath not ever the edge of discipline been justly sharpened against those that shall, to

---

[15] {outcomes}

[16] {"Profession" has the neutral sense of "religious denomination," but "professor" (i.e., one who truly professes Christianity) was primarily used among the godly as a label for their own.}

their disobedience, add contempt of the authority, and that with contumelious reproaches and slanders against the persons invested with it. If men for the maintenance of their self-willed humors, and for exalting of their private fancies against the public orders of the Church and the authority ecclesiastical shall *presume so far, how much more is it fit and behooves those who stand for the truth of peace and Christian unity . . . to endeavor with all earnestness and diligence, not only for the securing of those which are Catholics, but also for the correction of those that are not. For if stubbornness seek to get such strength, what ought constancy to have, which in that good which incessantly and unweariedly it doth, both knows that it pleaseth God and without doubt cannot displease wise men.*

So Saint Augustine once apologized for the Church in his days proceeding against the Donatists; and a fitter I cannot use for our Church at this day, nor need I add more in this case.

But this will not haply be contradicted by any that thus views things in their true notions. . . . But the cunning mask that is put upon it makes it pass current . . . when it shall be presented under the names of *persecution* and *unjust censures inflicted upon God's people and ministers*, and that for their *virtue* and *piety*. Who then can but pity and commiserate the sufferers, and condemn their persecutors of notorious injustice and horrible impiety? It is an old and a cunning stratagem used by some expert captains to march disguised and to bear the colors of those against whom they fight, that they may find the more easy passage. And this practice hath been long in use with the disturbers of the Church's peace, to usurp the name and privileges of the true Church and to appropriate that to themselves which of right belongs to those whom they oppugn. But never any were better artists in this kind than the Donatists in St. Augustine's time, who were wont to circumscribe the Church within the bounds of their party and to account all other Christians as pagan, and to call the repression of their turbulencies *persecution*, and boast of martyrdom. . . .

. . .

. . . I know that many among them follow their leaders . . . *in simplicity of their hearts, not knowing anything* [1 Sam. 15:11]. . . . I honor piety and the purity of religion in all professions, and while I condemn those that condemn others, I would be loath to make myself liable to the same condemnation. I judge not of religion by faction, but by facts; not by the leaves of profession, but by the fruits of righteousness that are *sown in peace of them which make peace* [Jam. 3:18]. My desire is that *mercy and truth may meet together, and righteousness and peace kiss each other* [Psal. 85:10]; that the *power of godliness* professed may shew itself in a due performance of the *service of God* [1 Pet. 2:17, 3:8], with all *holy reverence and devotion, in humility* and subjection to superiors, in charity and compassion one towards another, and keeping ourselves unspotted from the world [Jam. 1:27]. And whosoever they be (or of what profession soever) that *walk according to this rule, peace be on them, and mercy, and upon the Israel of God* [Gal. 6:16].

. . .

But haply the edge of censure is more sharp against them {godly ministers} than other men or than their crime deserves; which, if it be, they have good cause to cry out of an over-severity and injustice.

To this I answer: 1. that the censured are but ill and very partial judges of their own censures. There are but few that (though convict of a crime) would pass sentence upon themselves by the rule of justice, without some favor. . . . 2. In the censure of sins and offences, they are not altogether to be rated by the atrocity of the fact or by the law that is violated, but by other circumstances; whereby it comes to pass that a slight offence in itself considered and against a positive and human law or constitution, may sometimes (without violation of justice) be as deeply censured as sins of an higher nature and against the moral and eternal law of God. And this is approved for good justice by all commonwealths in cases of treason and the like, where sometimes a little aberration or word mis-placed is sentenced with death. Yea, God himself, who is the judge of all the world and must needs do right, did set this pattern of judicature in the first sentence that was pronounced in the world, sentencing Adam and all his posterity with death, not for the violation of any law of nature, but of the positive precept of eating the forbidden fruit; which . . . may seem but a small sin in comparison of those that are against the law of nature, yet inasmuch as by that sin man did as it were renounce his subjection and disclaim his obedience to his Maker, whereof that precept was given for a symbol or testification, God in this (as in all other his actions) must needs be justified. In like manner, if the violation of the orders of the Church, being in themselves matters of ceremony rather than of the substance of religion, receive as heavy censures, or perhaps more grievous, than the breach of the moral laws of God himself, yet is not authority presently unjust . . . or cruel, considering that these offences, when they come to be so censured, are heightened by willfulness and seconded by self-justification and contempt and condemnation of authority: which if it should not with all severity be repressed would induce in short time a mere anarchy and confusion in the Church—than which there can be no greater evil under the sun.

Chap. XIV

Of the supposed innovations in the worship of God. Ceremonies no substantial parts of God's worship.
The crimination, and a general answer. Of standing at Gloria Patri. *What will-worship is.*
Standing at the Gospel. Bowing at the name of Jesus. Of the name of altar, and what sacrifice is
admitted. Of the standing of the altar. Of communicants going up to the altar to receive.
Of the rails. Of bowing toward the altar and to the east, and turning that way when we pray.
Of reading the second service at the altar.

I come now to the third kind of innovations pretended to be made in the worship of God, which Mr. Burton saith they (the bishops) *go about to turn inside outward, placing the true worship, which is in spirit and truth, in a will-worship of man's devising*, &c. This is the crimination, which is set forth in most odious manner, but proved as weakly as the former; for whereas he pretendeth an innovation in the worship, he produceth nothing but certain ceremonies or usages, which cannot be accounted parts or anything of the substance of God's worship: such as are bowing at the name of Jesus. . . . These and some other like, mentioned by him in other places, are by him charged as 1. innovations lately brought in; 2. that they are made part of God's worship; 3. that they are will-worship and (as often elsewhere he calls them) superstitious and idolatrous. Lastly, he taxeth the rigor which is used in urging of these things, and punishing the refusers of them in the High Commission, &c. My answer shall be brief, yet such as may give some satisfaction to the ingenuous in all these. First, I cannot but wonder with what face he can accuse any of these things of novelty, when there is not one of the things he names which hath not been used in the primitive and purest ages of the Church; and though, by the disaffection of some and the carelessness and negligence of others, they have been in many places for some while too much neglected, were never wholly out of use in this Church of ours, but observed as religious customs derived from the ancient Church of Christ: and that not only in cathedrals and the royal chapel (though that might sufficiently clear them from these foul imputations) but in many parochial churches in this kingdom. . . .

. . . For the standing at *Gloria Patri* (which Cassianus, who lived 1200 years ago, saith was used in all the churches of France), why any man . . . should judge it either superstitious or unfit, is beyond my capacity. Surely no man can deny but that to rise up and stand is a more reverent gesture than to sit or lean; and if that be but granted, this solemn doxology may worthily challenge that that is the more reverent posture.[17] . . . Neither do any that I ever heard of make this gesture any part of the worship of God, which ought to be in spirit and truth. It is only an external ceremony (and ceremonies are not of the substance of God's worship, but necessary attendants of it), yet such as being well suited with the affection wherewith God's inward worship ought to be performed, may well be used; yea, and if commended to us by our superiors, ought not to be omitted.

Lastly, both this and the rest here questioned are most injuriously and ignorantly termed *will-worship of man's devising*. Everything of man's devising in the worship and service of God is not to be accounted will-worship. If that rule should hold, many things which they hold in high esteem would deserve that name. That only is will-worship which is so of man's devising that it is cross to God's will, or at least not subservient thereunto.
. . .

. . .

I come now to speak of that which (without any cause) hath made much speech in the world, and which our author seems much offended at. The name of altars, their standing, railing about of them, and the reverence which is done to God toward them, and the service which is there used.[18]

And here, 1. The very name, by reason of disuse among us of late and of some prejudice conceived against it, is grown with many very offensive, and yet the name is neither new nor savoring of any superstition. 1. Not new, as having been used from the beginning of Christianity and mentioned by the most approved authors that have written in the Church; and the blessed Eucharist, or sacrament of the Lord's Supper, called the *sacrament of the altar*. . . . And this is the relation that is between a sacrifice and an altar; grant the one, and I know not how the other can be denied. And who is there that will say that Christians have not their sacrifices? Nay, who is there that knows the nature of the sacrament of the Lord's Supper or the doctrine of antiquity concerning it but will confess it to be a true (and rightly so called) sacrifice?

2. Neither can all this be accused of superstition, for confessing a sacrifice and an altar, we intend not either the reviving of the Levitical bloody sacrifices of the Old Law nor the unbloody propitiatory sacrifice offered in the popish Mass for the quick and the dead; we hold (with the subscribed Articles) transubstantiation a bold and unwarranted

---

[17] {The text reads "that this is," which makes no sense.}

[18] {On this controversy, see Kenneth Fincham and Nicholas Tyacke, *Altars restored: the changing face of English religious worship, 1547–c. 1700* (Oxford UP, 2008).}

determination of Christ's presence in the sacrament, and think such sacrifices no better than *blasphemous fables and dangerous deceits*. We believe that our blessed Savior upon the Cross, *by his own oblation of himself once offered made a full, perfect, and sufficient sacrifice, oblation, and satisfaction for the sins of the whole world* [Communion Book], and that he *needeth not to be often offered* [Heb. 10], nor can without impiety and imposture be said to be made of bread by the priests and daily offered in the Mass.

The sacrifice which we admit is only 1. representative: to represent to us visibly in those elements the all-saving sacrifice of Christ's death, and to behold him crucified before our eyes, and his body broken in the bread, and in the wine his blood poured out. 2. It is spiritual: offered and participated by faith. 3. It is commemorative: done (according to our Savior's institution) in remembrance of him and of his death and passion. This is all the sacrifice we acknowledge, and we desire no other altar than what may suit with it and serve for the offering of such sacrifices. A spiritual altar for a spiritual sacrifice. It may be still, and must be, a Communion table, and yet nevertheless an altar: that properly, this mystically. A table it is for the Lord's Supper, and an altar for the memorial sacrifice of the Lord's death. And both a table and an altar it is, whatever the matter of it be, whether of stone, as sometimes and in some places they have been; or of wood, as among us in most places they usually now are.

Yet, and wheresoever they be placed . . . and with what site soever—whether it stand table-wise (as they call it) with the ends to the east and west; or altar-wise, with the ends from north and south; whether upon a plain level or mounted by steps—these are but accidents which alter not the nature and use of it; but that though these vary, yet still it remains both a table and an altar, in the sense that I have mentioned. And that it may be placed at the east end of the church, according to the ancient and most received fashion of the Christian world, Queen Elizabeth's injunction for that purpose is warrant sufficient, which appointeth it to be *set in the place where the altar stood, and not thence removed except at the time of the Communion, for more conveniency of hearing and communicating*. Which, if it may be as well there . . . as in any other part of the church or chancel, for ought that I can see, it may stand there still. And however, the placing of it . . . and the decision of all doubts about ceremonies is left to the discretion of the Ordinary[19]. . . .

. . .

I will add one thing more: that this place is of all others the most fit for the standing of the Lord's Table, because (as St. Justin Martyr saith) *those things which are the best and most excellent with us, we set apart for the service of God; and for that, in the opinion and judgment of men, that part where the sun riseth is the chief of all the parts of created nature, we look to the east when we pray, for that cause* [ad orthodox. quaest. 118[20]]. And as that part of the church hath been ever accounted the chiefest, so it is great reason that our best services should thence be tendered unto God, and that his table should have the highest place in his own house, and no man suffered to perk above it and him.

[19] {in ecclesiastical law, the person who has, of his or her own right and not by the appointment of another, immediate jurisdiction in ecclesiastical cases, such as the archbishop in a province, or the bishop or bishop's deputy in a diocese (*OED*)}

[20] {This work is no longer attributed to Justin Martyr.}

And if it may be there placed and (in case the Ordinary shall think that place convenient for ministration) there remain, then can it not (as some think and as the Ipswich libel glancingly intimates) be unlawful for the communicants to go up thither when they receive. As for the custom (which in too many places is late crept in) of the priests carrying the holy bread and cup to every person in their seats, it is both unseemly and derogatory to the majesty of those sacred mysteries, and, I am sure, beside the intention of our Church, expressly commanding all those that intend to communicate to *draw near*. . . .

But the rails also offend, as well as the site, and have afforded some matter of railing and calumniation; and Mr. Burton seems angry at them because they *insinuate into the people's minds an opinion of some extraordinary sanctity in the table, more than in other places of the church*, &c. But I wonder at him, and for my part think it very fit that that place be railed off and separated from common access and danger of profanation, as finding it practiced in ancient times; and 2. that such an opinion of sanctity should by all means be insinuated into the people's minds. What? sanctity and holiness in the table? Aye, in the table. But how? this holiness is not any internal, inherent quality infused, transforming the nature of it, but an external adherent quality which it hath by being consecrated to that most holy use and service, in relation to which it is truly holy. And this holiness, as it is only compatible to things of this nature, which are inanimate and not capable of higher, so it belongs to this table in the highest measure; so that (though all the church, and the things belonging it, be holy in their degree) this may be said to be most holy, as dedicated to the most august mystery of our religion, and being, as Optatus calls it, *the seat or place of the body and blood of Christ*, and where God (of all other places on earth) doth vouchsafe the most lively exhibition of his gracious presence, and so must needs make the greatest impression of holiness to that place—which no man can deny, unless he withal will grant either that God is less present to us under the Gospel in these mysteries than he was in those under the Law; or that, being there, he is less to be regarded, and the places where he is less worthy or less capable of the impression of holiness: as I suppose no understanding Christian will do.

. . . For though we do not (as Mr. B. slanders) *tie God to a fixed place*, yet we do (not without good cause and warrant from Scriptures) acknowledge different manners and degrees of his gracious presence. He is, we confess, truly present in all places, and, as the Prophet speaks, *fills heaven and earth* [Jer. 23:24], yet there is no man that understands anything in divinity but will say he is otherwise in heaven, otherwise in earth: there as in his throne; here as on his foot-stool; for which cause we are to direct our prayers to him not as by us or in us (though he be both) but as above us, and to say: *Our Father, which art in heaven*. . . .

‡

Chap. XVI

Of the altering of the prayer books. The putting in for at. The leaving out of Father of thine elect, &c. no treason. Mr. B. rather guilty. His pretty shift about it; and how he and some of his use the prayers of the Church. Of the prayers for the fifth of November altered. Those prayers not confirmed by Act of Parliament. The religion of the Church of Rome not rebellion. Of the alterations in the last fast-book. The restraint of preaching. Fasting days no Sabbaths.

The fifth innovation (he tells of) is in altering of prayer books set forth by public authority.[21] And this (out of the zeal he beareth to authority) much troubles him, so that he makes a great ado about both in his sermons, and so doth the author of the Ipswich libel. Let us briefly inquire what the matter may be that thus moves his patience. First, he tells us of alterations made in the Communion Book . . . as in the Epistle for the Sunday before Easter that *in the name of Jesus* is turned into *at the name of Jesus*. Surely a mighty alteration and which toucheth the substance of religion and worship of God, to read it in the Epistle as it is used to be read in the Lesson when that chapter is appointed: for so it is there turned both by (his friends) the Genevans and our last translators.[22] But he hath a matter of other-like moment than this: *In the collect for the Queen and royal progeny, they have put out "Father of thine elect and of their seed."* This he keeps a foul pudder about, and in the *Epitome* they cry out, *O intolerable impiety, affront, and horrid treason!* [{Prynne}, *News Ips.* p. 3], and puts it in the title-page to startle and amaze the readers at first dash and make them cry shame upon the bishops. . . . But, in good earnest, doth he think it treason? truly, I can hardly believe he doth; but if he or any other (seduced by his sermons and libels) should, I will, by asking a question or two, get them assoiled {absolved} from so heavy a charge. For how if this alteration were (as indeed it was, and for that cause altered) before the King's Majesty had any royal progeny? Sure then it could be no treason. . . .

The next book that (he saith) they {the bishops} have altered is that which is set forth for solemn thanksgiving for our deliverance from the Gunpowder treason. In the last edition whereof, instead of this passage—*root out that Babylonish and antichristian sect, which say of Jerusalem, down with it,* &c.—they read, *root out that Babylonish and antichristian sect of them which say* &c.; and little after, for *whose religion is rebellion, and faith faction,* they read, *who turn religion into rebellion, and faith into faction.* . . . His exception {objection} is that *they which made that alteration would turn off rebellion and faction from the Romish religion and faith to some persons, as if the religion itself were not rebellion and their faith faction.* But he craves leave *to prove it so to be, according to the judgment of our Church, grounded upon manifest and undeniable proofs,* and without expecting {waiting for} the grant of what he craves from any (but his good masters, the people), he sets upon it, but presently forgets his promised brevity, for he spends almost five leaves in that argument. And lest I forget my promise in the same kind, I'll sum him into a very narrow room: 1. Their religion is rebellion . . . because the Oath of Supremacy is refused by Jesuits, seminary priests, and Jesuited papists, and if any papist take it, he is excommunicated for it. But this reason concludes nothing against the religion, but against the practice of some of that religion, and some positions of a faction, rather than the generally received faith among them. It is well known that the French and Venetian States profess the Romish religion and faith, and live in communion with that Church; and yet they do not acknowledge that extravagant power over princes which some popes have challenged and

---

[21] {For the charges against the bishops handled in this section, see the notes to Prynne's *News from Ipswich* <supra>.}

[22] {The weekday lessons would have been read out of the Bible, which, in both the Geneva and King James translations, has, for Phil. 2:10, "at the name"; the Book of Common Prayer included the Scripture passages appointed for Sunday worship, but it normally used the Great Bible's translation ("in the name").}

their flatterers do ascribe to them. As is evident. . . . by the public decree made in France *anno* 1611 for expelling the Jesuits except they approved these four articles:

1. That the pope hath no power to depose kings.
2. That the Council is above the pope.
3. That the clergy ought to be subject to the civil magistrate.
4. That confession ought to be revealed if it touch the king's person.

{Additionally} by that memorable controversy that of late happened between Pope Paul the V and the state of Venice, where the just liberty of princes and states in their dominions, against that Pope's tyrannical interdict and sentence of excommunication, is defended by those who notwithstanding profess their union in religion and due obedience to the See of Rome.[23] By all these (I say), it is evident that (whatever the tenets of fiery-spirited Jesuits and other furious factionists of that religion be) the religion may be held, and yet due obedience to princes maintained and performed, which could not be if the *religion* were *rebellion*, and *faith faction*. . . . To make this clear by an instance wherein I am sure Mr. B. would be loath to admit this reasoning for true logic: some Genevans (and some of ours that learn'd it from them) allow the deposition of tyrannical and idolatrous princes and rulers and the people's rising against them . . . and, in a word, go as far in this kind as the boldest and bloodiest among the Jesuits—and are in this worse than they, in that the Jesuits allege their obedience therein and zeal to an higher authority pretended to be in the pope; but these hold the right of sovereignty to be in the people and allow them to be their own carvers of their liberty. If any man should hereupon conclude that the Genevan *religion* were *rebellion*, and *faith faction*, I suppose Master B. would—and for my part (though I detest and abhor these principles as most wicked and unchristian), I should—think they said more than they proved, and so I think Master B. hath here done against the Papists.

. . .

But I pass to his other exception—the restraint of preaching upon the fast days— which was thought fit for the avoiding of the danger of contagion that might grow by the concourse of people, when, being fasting, they were most apt to take the infection, which by wiser than he was thought to have been a good means (next to the devout prayers of the Church) for the decreasing of the plague. And certain it is that upon our weak humiliation (notwithstanding the want of sermons), the plague during all the time of the continuance of the fast did weekly decrease, as was plainly demonstrated by M. Squire in his religious sermon at St. Paul's; and that double increase which Mr. B. mentions (to disparage the fasts) was in a great part to be attributed to the week before the fast began. And however, that could not evidence God's dislike of our fast for want of sermons, no more than the Benjamites prevailing argued their innocency or the injustice of the Israel- ites' cause. God's judgments are *unsearchable and his ways past finding out* [Rom. 11:33], so that (though it be familiar with Master B. to frame arguments for his purpose from them) it is impious presumption peremptorily to assign any particular reason either of their first infliction or their progress or continuance; and there is nothing in the world

---

[23] {On the Venetian Interdict of 1616–17, see W. J. Bouwsma, *Venice and the defense of republican liberty* (U California P, 1968), chap. 7.}

wherein men may and do sooner befool themselves than in reading the obscure characters of God's judgments, if once they pass the bounds of sobriety and presume to be wise above that which is written. But if he would needs point out the cause of the plague and its continuance, why did he not rather impute it to the murmurings & seditious railings against governors and government which he & too many more are guilty of, seeing the Scripture testifies that for the like cause, the like and greater plagues befell the Israelites [Num. 16:3, 41, 46], whereas they never give any example that God did plague any for want of a sermon at a public fast. . . .

   . . .

Chap XVII

Of the sixth pretended innovation in the means of knowledge. The knowledge of God necessary.
The Scriptures the key of knowledge. Impious to take them away or hinder the knowledge of them.
The difference between the Scriptures and sermons. How faith is begotten: of Rom. 10:17.
The word of God must be rightly divided, and what it is so to do.

The sixth innovation (he tells us) is about the means of the knowledge of God and of the mystery of our salvation, wherein he charges the prelates, as our Savior did the Scribes and Pharisees, that they shut up the kingdom of heaven against men, and neither go in themselves nor suffer them that were entering to go in [Matt. 23:13]. Which (saith he) in Luke 11:52 is expressed thus: *Ye take away the key of knowledge.* And then he declares his meaning after a confused clamorous manner, the sum whereof is but this: *they hinder and disgrace preaching, and will not suffer men to preach or catechize as they desire.* For answer to this, I say first: that it is a certain truth (and granted by all that understand anything in religion) that the knowledge of God and of the mysteries of salvation is most necessary for every Christian; so as without a competent measure thereof by some means attained, it is impossible for any man (come to years of discretion) to be saved. Secondly, it is also as certain that it is not in the power of nature to attain unto this competency of knowledge in those things especially that concern the mysteries of our redemption, without the help of a key reached out unto us from God himself, who alone can make known what is that his *good, acceptable, and perfect will,* by believing and doing whereof, he hath determined to bring men to happiness.

Thirdly, it is agreed upon by all Protestant divines that this key of knowledge is the word of God contained in the canonical Scriptures of the Old and New Testament, which contain all things necessary to salvation. . . . And this hath been an old deceit, with which many ministers of his {Burton's} faction have cozened (if not themselves) the people. For whatsoever is spoken concerning the efficacy or necessity of God's word, the same they tie and restrain only unto sermons: howbeit not to sermons read neither (for such they also abhor in the Church), but sermons without book, sermons which spend their life in their birth and may have public audience but once. And hence it is that these great cries are raised, that a minister shall not for any irregularity be suspended or his extravagant fancies restrained or any order for the time or manner of preaching prescribed, but presently they cry out that the *word of God, the Gospel & ordinary means of salvation are taken away or hindered.* The truth is, we have no word of God but the Scripture. Apostolic sermons were, unto such as heard them, his word, even as properly as unto us their writings are.

Howbeit, not so our own sermons, the expositions which our discourse of wit doth gather and minister out of the word of God—and much less every fond opinion which passion or misguided zeal shall utter out of the pulpit. . . .

With these cautions, whatsoever honor men shall give (not to every vain babbling & venting of fables & news & corantos out of the pulpit, but) to preaching rightly so called—that is, the sober and solid explication & application of any portion of the word of God—will never offend the prelates of these times nor any other piously affected Christian. . . . Men do not (we know) bring the saving knowledge of God into the world with them. It must be instilled by some means, and among the rest, it is God's ordinance *that the priest's lips which should preserve knowledge* should in this way *let their doctrine drop as the rain, and their speech distill as the dew* [Mal. 2:7, Deut. 31:1]; and that the people (who have not the like opportunity or ability of knowledge) might *seek the law at their mouths*, who (even in this) *are the messengers* of the Lord of hosts. Yea, if this be not enough, let them prefer this above all other means, and it will easily be granted in regard they are more apt to make impression upon the hearers, more powerful incentives of good affections than other ways of teaching are. But all this notwithstanding, though there be so much of God in this work, yet there is somewhat of man still in the best of them, and that, where ever it be, is not privileged from error, imperfection, and vanity. And hence it comes to pass that many times men (with those in the Prophet) use their tongues and say, *The Lord saith, when God sent them not nor commanded them, but they prophesy false dreams and cause the people to err by their lightness* [Jer. 23:31-2]. Yea, too often (as these sermons here before us), men make the pulpit but a stage to act their passionate distempers and spleen, to ransack the affairs of state and to pick out thence such things as may claw the people's itch, who ever are content to hear those above them taxed. . . .

. . .

. . . If sermons upon the Lord's Day be produced to that length that they jostle out the prayers of the Church, or be become of that esteem as that men shrink up all religion into hearing, or that they be of that strain that the ignorant may be ever learning and never able to come to the knowledge of the truth, it is but reason that they both cut them shorter and provide for the due esteem of other religious duties and for the instruction of the ignorant, by turning sermons into catechizing; and if that be abused too, and that men, instead of laying the foundation and teaching the first principles of the oracles of God (which is the true catechizing), shall soar aloft and adventure upon the most high and abstruse points in divinity and, notwithstanding his Majesty's *Declaration* to the contrary, shall deliver the doctrines of election and reprobation—and that in such wise as to make God the author of sin and obduration in sin, which is blasphemy in the highest degree—if men use to catechize after this manner (as some of late have done), is it not high time to reduce men to the prescribed platform of the church catechism,[24] which (even in the bare questions and answers, as it is there set forth) cannot be denied . . . to contain the principles of Christian religion. . . . Lastly, if sermon-prayers shall be used as libels (as some have used them) or be exalted above the prayers of the Church (as with too many they are), it cannot but be much better to tie men to the form prescribed in the canon

---

[24] {i.e., the catechism included in the Book of Common Prayer: see http://justus.anglican.org/resources/bcp/1559/Confirmation_1559.htm (accessed June 8, 2012).}

. . . and to shut up all in the Lord's Prayer, which is without all contradiction the most absolute pattern of prayer and the sum of all rightly conceived petitions.

My conclusion then is that the reverend bishops, doing these things upon these grounds . . . are unjustly charged to take away the key of knowledge, whose right use by these means is preserved and restored to the singular benefit of Christian souls.

Chap. XVIII

Of the seventh pretended innovation in the rule of faith. What matters of religion are submitted to the bishops' decision. The doctrine of our Articles. The properties of the bishops' decisions. Master Burton's clamors against the bishops in this particular, odious and shameful. Of that speech which he ascribeth to the Lord Archbishop of Canterbury concerning the Catholic Church. What is justly attributed to the Church, and how we, ordinarily, come to know the Scriptures to be Scriptures.

The seventh innovation he makes to be in the rule of faith: *for, whereas the perfect and complete rule of faith is the holy Scripture . . . our new doctors cry up the dictates of the Church—to wit, of the prelates—to be our only guides in divinity: as in Reeve's* Communion book catechism expounded, *pag. 20 & 206, where* [as he saith that author affirms] *all ministers must submit to the judgment of the prelates in all matters pertaining to religion, and all prelates must submit to the judgment of the arch-prelate*—and then adds his own gloss: *as having a papal infallibility of spirit whereby, as by a divine oracle, all questions in religion are finally determined.*

My answer to this shall be very brief. . . . First, it is confessed that the *holy Scripture is the sole and complete rule of faith.* . . . But somewhat sure there is in it—that is, in matters of religion—submitted to the bishops' judgment. True, and so it ever was in the Church of God. But this extends not to matters of faith or manners to be believed and done of necessity to salvation, so as to coin new articles in either kind. The power which by them is challenged, and by all understanding Christians in all ages of the Church ascribed to them, is no other but that which is given them by the tenth Article of our religion, whose words are *that the Church hath power to decree rites and ceremonies, and authority in controversies of religion* [see preface to the Book of Common Prayer referring parties doubting of anything that is contained in that book to the bishop, and the bishop doubting, to the archbishop[25]]. Where by the Church (whoever Master B understands) is meant the heads and governors in the Church, to whom the right of direction and government doth peculiarly belong; and therefore they are called *bishops* or overseers . . . as being, by their office, to judge of things needful and to direct those that are under their charge.

Now this power of theirs hath these properties. 1. It is not supreme, but ministerial; not ruling, but ruled by the Scriptures, by which rule they are to square their determinations in all matters of religion. . . . 2. The things wherein they have power to decree, ordain, alter, and change anything touching religion in the Church is {*sic*} only in matter of ceremony, which are, in comparison of the points of faith, only circumstantial. . . . 3. In these things which they thus order and ordain, they must keep them to those general rules: 1. that things be done decently and in order; 2. that nothing be ordained

---

[25] {It was this passage that Reeve quoted in *The Communion book catechism expounded* (London, 1636), 206.}

contrary to the Scripture; 3. that things beside the Scripture ordained be not enforced to be believed of necessity to salvation, as our Article speaks. 4. Their decisions in matters of religion are not infallible, neither did they ever challenge . . . any papal infallibility of spirit; neither did they arrogate any other ability of right and true judgment in things than is attained by ordinary means, nor any immediate divine inspiration or assistance annexed to their chair—all which the pope doth. Lastly, the submission that is required by those that are under them, ministers and people, is not absolute and such as no inferior priest or Christian can without sin dissent from their judgments; but in regard of external order and for the avoiding of confusion and sects in the Church, as it is not left free for every man to appoint or judge of matters of religion or to have them after their own way, so it cannot but be a great disorder, and consequently a sin, for any man out of his private humor openly to reclaim {censure} or to disobey those who are invested with the power of judicature. . . .

. . .

It is no innovation to admit traditions, which was ever granted in our Church and never denied by any learned Protestant. We baptize infants, receive the Apostles Creed, acknowledge the number, names, and authors of the books of canonical Scripture. . . . Only we do not admit any traditions contrary to the Scriptures, nor do we (as the Council of Trent) receive them with the same reverence and pious affection, or advance them to an equality of authority with Scriptures, but as subservient unto them. Further (though Master B. startle at it), it is no innovation neither to make the Church's testimony to be the means of our knowledge the Scripture to be the Scripture: which is no more than our Articles allow, calling the Church *a witness and a keeper of Holy Writ* [Article 20]. . . .

. . .

Chap XIX

Of the jurisdiction of bishops: how far of divine right given by Christ to his apostles and from them derived by succession. The power given to the apostles divided into several orders. What power ecclesiastical belongs to the king, and the intent of the statutes which annex all ecclesiastical jurisdiction to the Crown. Of Master Burton's quotation of the Jesuit's Direction to be observed by N.N.[26] *Master B. and the Jesuit, confederates in detraction and ignorance.*

But there are two things here which I am unwilling to pass over. The first is that here he saith that the words which he ascribes to the Lord Archbishop of Canterbury were *by him spoken at the censure of Doctor Bastwick for oppugning the jurisdiction of bishops* jure divino *as being nowhere found in the Scripture,* &c. This is one thing which, though here brought in upon the by, I cannot pass, because I find him elsewhere much harping upon the same string. He will not have the bishops derive their succession from the apostles; cries out upon Dr. Pocklington for delivering that doctrine, affirms *their authority and jurisdiction to be only from the king*; that not to derive it thence is against the law of the land, and I know not what danger besides; and that Doctor Bastwick is imprisoned for defending his Majesty's royal prerogative, and much more to the same purpose. Here . . . I will only lay down some brief conclusions. . . .

[26] {On this pamphlet, see the introduction to the Chillingworth readings <*infra*>.}

. . .

That which results from all this is that to affirm the episcopal order or authority, as it is merely spiritual, to be received not from the king but from God and Christ, and derived by continual succession from the apostles, is no false or arrogant assertion, nor prejudicial to the king's prerogative royal, and so not dangerous to those that shall so affirm or that challenge and exercise their jurisdiction in that name.

For the further demonstration hereof, I will also briefly set down what power in causes ecclesiastical is due and challenged by the king and other sovereign civil magistrates, & what ecclesiastical jurisdiction is annexed to the Crown of this realm, which the bishops must acknowledge thence to be received, and exercised in that right.

My first conclusion shall be in the words of our thirty-seventh Article, where the power of *kings in causes ecclesiastical* is described to be only *that they should rule all estates and degrees committed to their charge by God, whether they be ecclesiastical or temporal, and restrain with the civil sword the stubborn and evil-doers.* Other authority than this . . . his Majesty neither doth, ne ever will challenge; nor indeed is it due to the imperial crown either of this or any other realm. Where I observe two things wherein the sovereign authority of princes in causes ecclesiastical doth consist. First, in ruling ecclesiastical persons: under which are comprised, 1. their power to command and provide that spiritual persons do rightly and duly execute the spiritual duties belonging to their functions; 2. to make and ordain laws to that end, and for the advancement and establishing of piety and true religion, and the due and decent performance of divine worship, and for the hindrance and extirpation of all things contrary thereunto. Secondly, in punishing them as well as others (when they offend) with the civil sword. Spiritual or ecclesiastical persons, being offenders, are not exempt from the coercive power of the king, but that he may punish them as well as others; but it is with the civil sword, as that only which he beareth; not with the ecclesiastical, or by sentence of excommunication. *It belongs to bishops, and not to kings, to draw the spiritual sword, yet that is also wont to be unsheathed and sheathed at the godly command and motion of religious kings.* And they may (as pious princes use) second, yea, and prevent {anticipate}, the spiritual sword, and with the civil (as namely with bodily and pecuniary punishment) compel their subjects,[27] as well ecclesiastical as temporal, to the performance of the duties of both Tables.

My second conclusion . . . is that the bishops having any civil power annexed to their places and exercising the same either in judging any civil causes or inflicting temporal punishments, whether bodily or pecuniary, have and use that power wholly from the king and by his grace and favor in his right.

That the episcopal jurisdiction even as it is truly episcopal and merely spiritual, though in itself it be received only from God, yet inasmuch {as} it is exercised in his Majesty's dominions and upon his subjects by his Majesty's consent, command, and royal protection, according to the canons and statutes confirmed by his authority, nothing hinders but that thus far all ecclesiastical authority and jurisdiction may be truly said to be annexed to the Crown and derived from thence.

And this only is the intent of those statutes which annex the ecclesiastical jurisdiction to the Crown. Which notwithstanding, it may truly be affirmed that the bishops

---

[27] {The text has "his subjects."}

have their function and jurisdiction, for the substance of it as it is merely spiritual and so properly ecclesiastical, by divine right and only from Christ, and that it is derived by a continual and uninterrupted succession from the apostles. But if Master Burton conceive that the bishops affirm that they have power to exercise this their spiritual jurisdiction within his Majesty's dominions and over his subjects of themselves and without license and authority from his Majesty; or that their temporalities, their revenues, their dignities to be Barons of the Parliament &c., or the authority that they have and use either to judge in causes temporal or to inflict temporal punishments belong to them by divine right, or otherwise than by the favor of his Majesty and his predecessors, he makes them as absurdly ignorant and presumptuous as himself.

. . .

Chap. XX

The last innovation in the rule of manners. The Scriptures acknowledged to be the sole rule of manners, and how. Old canons, how in force. The act before the Communion Book doth not forbid the use of ancient and pious customs. Master B. incurring the penalty of that statute. Of cathedral churches. The argument from them frees the rites and ceremonies there used from novelty and uperstition. Of the royal chapel. His dangerous insinuations referred to the censure of authority. The close.

‡

Chap. XXI

A brief discourse of the beginning and progress of the disciplinarian faction. Their sundry attempts for their Genevan dearling. Their doctrines new and different from the true and ancient tenets of the Church of England, and they truly and rightly termed innovators.

It was one of the greatest evils that ever happened to this Church that in the infancy of the Reformation (which was happily begun in the reign of King Edward of happy memory), many for conscience sake and to avoid the storm of persecution which fell in the days of Queen Mary, betaking themselves to the Reformed Churches abroad, and especially to Geneva, were drawn into such a liking of the form of discipline then newly erected by Master Calvin there, that returning home they became quite out of love with that which they found here established by authority; insomuch that, set upon by the persuasions and examples of John Knox and other fiery-spirited zealots in Scotland, they attempted and by all means endeavored to advance their strongly-fancied platform of Genevan discipline. For the bringing about whereof, the course they then took for the drawing of the people to a liking of their intentions was to pick quarrels against the names and titles given to the fathers and governors of our Church, apparel of ministers, and some ceremonies in the Book of Common Prayer retained and prescribed, which they taxed of superstition and remnants of popery. And afterwards when T.C. and others (who had also been at Geneva) had drunk in the opinion of Master Beza—who by that time had promoted the discipline there invented by his master and made it one of the especial notes of the true Church, as if it had till then been maimed and imperfect—what books were then written, what seeming humble motions made, what pamphlets, pasquils, libels flew abroad; yea, what violent attempts, plots, conspiracies, and traitorous practices were then set on foot by the men of that faction are at large set forth in divers books of that argument, and are yet fresh in the memories of many alive at this day.

What the care and courageous zeal of the governors of this Church and state then was for the preventing and overthrowing of these men's desperate designs, the flourishing and peaceful estate which this Church hath since by their means enjoyed doth abundantly speak. For the authors of these innovations, troubles, and disorders, receiving just and public censure according to their several demerits, they which remained well-willers and abettors of that cause were glad to lie close and carry themselves more warily than before and to wait some better opportunity for the effecting of their purpose. Which they apprehending to be offered at the coming of King James to this crown, began again to move, but so as beginning as it were at their old A B C, their complaint was principally against the use of ceremonies, subscription, and sundry things formerly questioned by their predecessors in the Book of Common Prayer. And when that learned and judicious King had out of his wise and gracious disposition vouchsafed to take their complaint into his serious consideration and to grant them a solemn and deliberate hearing in the conference held at Hampton Court, *the success {outcome} of that conference* (to use the words of his royal proclamation) *was such as happeneth to many other things which, moving great expectation before they be entered into, in their issue produce small effects.* For (to give the sum of that which there follows) mighty and vehement informations were found to be supported with so weak and slender proofs that that wise King and his Council, seeing no cause to change anything either in the Book of Common Prayer, doctrine, or rites established, having caused some few things to be explained, he by his royal proclamation commanded a general conformity in all sorts, requiring the archbishops and bishops to see that conformity put in practice.

Being thus frustrate of their hopes of bringing in their darling platform, some of the principal among them, remaining stiff in their opinion and opposition to authority, received a just censure and suffered deprivation. Others (grown wiser by the example of their fellows' suffering), that they might save their reputation and yet continue in their places, invented a new course and yielded a kind of conformity, not that they thought any whit better of the things, but for that they held them (though in themselves unlawful) not to be such as for which a man ought to hazard (not his living, that might savor of covetousness, but) his ministry and the good which God's people might, by that means, receive. This project prevailed with many to make them come off to a subscription, and yet gave them liberty—in private and where they might freely and with safety to {sic} express themselves—to shew their disaffection to the things which they had subscribed, resolving not to practice what they had professed nor to use the ceremonies enjoined further than they should be compelled. And for this cause, they did wisely avoid all occasions that might draw them to the public profession of conformity by using the ceremonies, and betook themselves to the work of preaching, placing themselves (as much as might be) in lectures and (where any of them were benefices) getting conformable curates under them to bear the burden of the ceremonies. Thus saving themselves and maintaining their reputation with the people, they gained the opportunity to instill into them their principles, not only of dislike of the church government and rites but also of the doctrine established; and though (through the vigilance and care of those that have sat at the stern in this Church) they have been hitherto hindered from erecting their altars of Damascus publicly in our temples, yet have they (using this art now a long time) in an underhand way brought up the use of their own crochets and erected a new Church, both for doctrine and discipline far differing from the true and ancient English Church; and made, though not a local (as some more zealous among them have, by removing to Amsterdam and New England), yet a real separation, accounting themselves the wheat among the tares and monopolizing the names of *Christians, God's children, professors*, and the like. . . .

. . .

And here, for the better demonstration of their real separation wherewith I charge them and that it may appear that though they are with us they are not of us, give me leave briefly to instance in some of the most remarkable points in difference between us: wherein I shall desire my reader to expect no accurate or elaborately methodical discourse, my intent being only to make a rough draft of them in such order as they shall offer themselves to my present memory.

The ordination of priests and deacons in our Church (as ever in the Church of Christ) belongs to the bishops, which (because they {the puritans} cannot otherwise choose) they are contented to accept from their hands that their seal may protect them from danger of law; but yet think themselves not rightly called to that function unless they have withal gotten the approbation of the people of God and of the godly ministers. And for this end they must give trial of their gifts in some private conventicle or adventure it up at some lecture (without the Church's ordination), where some of the fathers of their order shall be present, and after with the people at a feast pronounce sentence of their gifts and abilities. Which if it happen for them, they doubt not but they are rightly called. . . .

1. I say their faith is new, being (as they imagine) a firm persuasion of God's special love to them in Christ, or an assurance of their election, and consequently of salvation: which is nothing else but to have a good conceit of a man's self in regard of God's favor, to believe themselves to be his dearlings.

2. It is new in the instrumental cause of it: being not wrought by the word of God as it is left written for our learning by the holy men of God moved by the Holy Ghost (that has not power to work conversion), but preached; that is (not always out of the pulpit; a table's end will serve), expounded and applied (as they call it) by them. With this help, the word of God (otherwise insufficient) becomes able to work their conversion and salvation; and (which is more strange) to do it in an instant (for they admit no preparatory acts to precede[28]), and that so powerfully that it is impossible to resist or to defer the work of it for a moment, and so sensibly that every man may—yea, and (if he be rightly) must—know the time of his conversion.

3. It is new in the effects of it. For first, it frees a man from the fear of *him that is able to cast body and soul into hell fire*, so that they are exempted from that precept given by our Savior commanding us to fear him. They look at hell as a danger past, and at heaven

---

[28] {On preparation for grace in puritan theology, see Martyn McGeown, "The notion of preparatory grace in the puritans," www.cprf.co.uk/articles/preparationism.htm (accessed December 26, 2011); Norman Pettit, *The heart prepared: grace and conversion in puritan spiritual life* (Yale UP, 1966); Michael Colacurcio, *Godly letters: the literature of the American puritans* (Notre Dame UP, 2006).}

as if they were in possession of it already, holding the hope of reward a poor incentive to perform duty or endure affliction: a reprobate may go so far as to abstain from evil and do good for fear of hell and with an eye to the recompense of reward; so that a man must go farther than this, or otherwise he can have no assurance that he is the child of God.

Secondly, it gives them a right not to heaven only, but even to the things of this life, which, if others (that want this faith) chance to have, they are in God's sight usurpers, and shall as thieves and robbers be arraigned for them at the dreadful bar of God's severe judgment seat, and be condemned (not for the abuse, but) for the having of whatsoever creatures of God they have had any part in their whole lives, insomuch as every bit of bread they eat shall help to increase their score and aggravate their condemnation. Whereas they having (by virtue of their faith) this right and faculty granted them, may use them securely and without all fear[29]. . . .

Thirdly, it produces a strange kind of justification, whereby at once all their sins past, present, and to come are remitted, and they without more ado as sure of heaven as if they were in it already: and that without any repentance, which (with them) is no cause of the remission of sins, neither indeed can be, as coming too late and when that work is done already by faith; or rather before all faith,[30] which apprehends the free and full remission of their sins ready sealed; before all repentance, which (as they teach) ever comes after faith—though, to say the truth, it seldom either precedes or follows after as it ought; and indeed, I wonder how it should, when they hold that neither it nor good works are of any efficacy in procuring man's salvation. . . . So for good works, though all agree to exclude them from being any means of not only justification but of salvation, yet some do admit them as it were spectators and witnesses of the work done, and in that respect require their presence as necessary, though they contribute nothing to the work. But others are of a more sublime strain, and they think them no way necessary, but rather hinderers of salvation. And whereas vulgar Christians and the under-form or rank of professors do make use of them as signs and evidences of their faith and justification, these teach (as the most new and more refined way) that men should try their works by their faith, and that this is the only way to have constant and untottering comfort, which the commission of no sin can eclipse or diminish; for they, believing that God loves & hath accepted their persons, and that once for all, must believe also that he will take them altogether, with all faults that they are or shall be guilty of.[31] And being his favorites, they may be assured that he will give them more liberty and wink at more and grosser faults in them than in unbelievers and reprobates, who may haply be condemned to hell fire for but looking upon a woman to lust after her, when these scape with actual adultery and many other gross and grievous sins lived and died in without repentance. . . .

---

[29] {This is Wyclif's doctrine of "*dominium* in grace"; see Richard Schlatter, *Private property: the history of an idea* (London: Allen & Unwin, 1951), 37–38, 60–65, 69–70. See also Bayly <117>.}

[30] {That is, on this theology, justification comes before both faith and repentance, for the reasons Dow then goes on to explain.}

[31] {This was apparently the view of Rippertus Sixtus (see Milton, *Catholic and Reformed* 419); moreover, some of the Calvinist divines at the February 1626 York House Conference seem to have held, or at least not denied, that "an unrepentant sinner might still escape eternal punishment because he was numbered among the elect" (Barbara Donagan, "York House Conference revisited," *HR* 64 [1991]: 319–20). Those "of a more sublime strain" sound like antinomians; see Como, *Blown by the Spirit*.}

As their faith is new, so are many acts of God's worship new too. I'll begin with the principal of them all: their prayers, which are far different from the prayers of the Church of England. For, first, our Church appointeth public prayers after a set and solemn form; prayers received from the ancient Church of Christ and venerable for their antiquity; prayers wherein the meanest in the congregation, by reason of the continual use, may join in and help to set upon God with an army of prayers; prayers composed with that gravity, with such pious and soul-ravishing strains, with those full and powerful expressions of heavenly affection that I suppose the world, setting them aside, hath not the like volume of holy orisons. But these are by them slighted and vilified, in whose mouths the short and pithy prayers of the Church are but *shreds and pieces* and not worthy the name of prayers; and the litany accounted conjuring. And instead of these regular devotions, they have brought in a long prayer, freshly conceived and brought forth by the minister, and that (God knows) many times in bald and homely language such as wise men would be ashamed to tell a tale in even to their equals, with many gasping and unseemly pauses and multitudes of irksome tautologies, and (which is none of the least defects of it) in which none of the congregation is able to join with him or to follow him, as not knowing—no, nor the speaker himself sometimes—what he is about to say.[32]

Again, the Church of England hath consecrated certain places to be houses of public prayer, which places so consecrated and appropriated to that holy service, they judge fit that public prayer be there made, as in the places where God is in a more special manner present; but these places are by them contemned, and every place, a parlor, barn, or playhouse, accounted as holy and fit as they for public prayer or any other act of God's worship.

Thirdly, prayers in the Church of England have ever been conceived not only as duties to be performed, but as means also, sanctified by God, for the obtaining of his blessings, whereby he is moved to grant our desires. But with them they are accounted only duties which must be done, in doing whereof men do not so much move God or dispose him to grant their desires as themselves to receive them.

Fourthly, when we (according as our Savior hath taught us in that holy pattern of prayer which he left with his disciples) do pray that God would *forgive our trespasses*, we mean simply and unfeignedly to obtain forgiveness, and that by this means; but they praying for forgiveness of sins intend only continuation of that grace of remission of sins which they have already received, which grace, being immutable, prayer for that purpose is by them judged altogether superfluous. The main end, therefore, that they aim at in their prayers is that they may grow more and more in sense and assurance of the remission of their sins. If we pass from prayer to the sacraments, which, as our Church teaches, are moral instruments[33] to convey these graces unto the receivers which the outward signs visibly represent; and so, that in baptism infants receive remission of their sins and are truly regenerate: these men will allow the sacraments no such virtue, accounting them as bare signs and seals of that grace which they have already received, if they be elect; if otherwise, they hold them to be but as *seals set to a blank*, being to no purpose and of no

---

[32] {See Ramie Targoff, *Common prayer* (Chicago UP, 2001).}

[33] {See T. L. Holtzen, "Sacramental causality in Hooker's eucharistic theology," *Journal of Theological Studies* 62.2 (2011): 607–48.

value; acknowledging no such tie between the act of God and the priest, that what the priest shall do visibly, God should be thought, at the same time and by that means, to effect inwardly by his grace and Holy Spirit. And therefore when (according to our form of ministration of baptism) they are to say that the child baptized is regenerate, some of them are fain to interlace "we hope" and think it true only in the *judgment of charity* or in case they be elected; in which case some think (though others strongly contradict) they may be said truly to be regenerate in baptism. Of the same strain is their doctrine of the blessed Eucharist, wherein they acknowledge no power of consecration in the priest, no other presence of Christ than by way of representation, no other exhibition than by way of signation or obsignation, nor other grace conveyed but in seeming or (at best) the {*sic*} only the assuring of what they had before; which (if they have not) they must want for all that the sacrament can do. Thus have they made these saving ordinances of God of none effect through their traditions.

One thing more I cannot omit . . . which is their manner of observing of fasts and the course they have devised how to have them their own way. The piety of the Church of Christ, in whose steps the Church of England treads, as they have their appointed solemn festivals for the commemoration of God's special mercies by public thanksgivings and rejoicings, so they have also appointed set times for fasting and humiliation, as the time of Lent, the four Embers, &c. These (though the work of fasting seem to please them) they reject and scorn; first, for that they are set times, and perhaps because appointed by authority. For they would, by their good-wills, have them only occasional and in the time of extraordinary calamities, either felt or feared, and to be appointed by the minister when he shall judge the necessities of Christians so to require. A second thing they dislike them for is that they are not enjoined to be kept as Sabbaths extraordinary (which is their doctrine) and so to have the duties of the Sabbaths then observed after an extraordinary manner: as namely, abstinence from bodily labor and the works of men's particular callings, and two or more sermons of a more than ordinary size. . . . Now, because the diligence and care of the Church and state, and the watchfulness of pursuivants, hath frighted them from their private assemblies where they were wont to enjoy themselves and their own way in this kind, they have used in the City of London a new and a quaint stratagem whereby without suspicion they obtain their desires. The course they take is this: some good Christians (that is, professors) intimate their necessities to some minister of note among them and obtain of them the promise of their pains to preach upon that occasion, pitching upon such days and places as where and when sermons or lectures are wont to be; and having given under-hand notice to such as they judge faithful of the day to be observed and the places where they shall meet for that end, thither they resort, and mixing themselves with the crowd, unsuspected have the word they so much desire, with the occasion covertly glanced at, so as those that are not of their counsel are never the wiser. Thus I have divers times known them to begin the day upon a Wednesday, where they had a sermon beginning at six in the morning and holding them till after eight; that being done, they post (sometimes in troops) to another church, where the sermon beginning at nine holds them till past eleven, & from thence again they betake themselves to a third church and there place themselves against the afternoon sermon begin, which holds them till night. And so (without danger of the pursuivants, they observe a public fast, as much as these hard times will give them leave) after their own way and heart.

I should tire my reader if I should at large set down their several tenets and positions: whereof some are besides others, against the Holy Scriptures, the doctrine of the ancient and of our mother Church of England. Among which are the doctrine of the Sabbath, for which of late they have raised such loud cries, as if, without it be established among us, *the glory were departed from Israel and the Ark of God taken.* Of the same strain are their opinions concerning contracts and their necessity, which they use to solemnize in private houses with a sermon and feasting (two usual companions), I will not say to affront and baffle the orders and received customs of our Church (I think that beyond the intention of many among them), though the event proclaim that to be the attendant of their opinion and practice. To these I might add many more, as their assertion of the impossibility of the observation of the law of God, not to the mere natural man, but even to the regenerate and assisted by the grace of God. . . . Omitting then all these, I will only add something of their courses of late undertaken for the propagation of their new Church and Gospel, amongst which the most dangerous and cunning that ever they hatched was that of the buying in of impropriations: a pious & a glorious work and such as, rightly intended, is highly esteemed by all those that sincerely affect the good of this Church and religion. This project so specious in shew had for a long while a fair passage and the approbation of many more than of their own strain, till at length their purposes were unveiled and their aim discovered: which was the erecting of a seminary at Saint Antholin's,[34] subordinated to a classis or clero-laical consistory, who had power (at least in their intentions) to plant there such hopeful imps as should be fit, upon the falling of any of their purchased impropriations, to be removed & transplanted into great & populous places in this kingdom; in which they endeavored so to fasten and fence these transplanted choice ones that no ecclesiastical censure should touch or deprive them of their maintenance, by that means hoping in such places (to use the words of a prime agent in that cause) to establish the *Gospel by a perpetual decree.* . . .

But I find myself digressed. To return therefore and to conclude that which I intended by this brief relation of the doctrine and practices of these men: it may manifestly appear who they are that may rightly be termed innovators and broachers of novel opinions and practices in this Church. . . . What I have written in this kind (God himself knows whom I have served in it), I have written out of love to truth and peace and of them who are misled by these errors; and therefore I say to them (as Saint Augustine concluding an epistle of his to some of Donatus' party), *That this that I have done shall be, if they please, a correction of their errors, but if not, a witness against them.*

FINIS

ᕽ᠊᠊᠊᠊ᕽ

Text: EEBO (STC [2nd ed.] / 7090)

[34] {See the description of this church in *Survey of London* <*supra*>. On the Feoffees for Impropriations, see the entry (under "Impropriations") in *Historical dictionary of Stuart England*, ed. Ronald Fritze and William Robison (Greenwood, 1996).}

Christopher Dow, *Innovations unjustly charged upon the present Church and state, Or an Answer to the most material passages of a libellous pamphlet made by Mr. Henry Burton, and intituled "An Apologie of an Appeale, &c"* (London: Printed by M. F. for John Clark, 1637), 1–5, 7, 10–12, 21, 23–29, 32–34, 38–44, 50–51, 53, 55–59, 66–71, 73, 76–80, 83–86, 88–89, 92–95, 97–98, 102–3, 105–6r, 108r, 109v–110r, 112v–19r, 132–33, 136, 138–39, 141, 145–46, 150–53, 155–56, 160–65, 167–68, 170–71, 175–78, 182, 193–214.[35]

[35] {At p. 106 the text switches to folio numbering, and then back to pagination at 121.}

WILLIAM CHILLINGWORTH
(1602–1644)

The son of an Oxford mercer, Chillingworth had as godfather the thirty-year-old St. John's fellow William Laud—a town-gown relationship rare in early modern Oxford. Chillingworth remained in Oxford, matriculating at Trinity in 1619, where he received his BA a year later, followed by an MA in 1624 and a fellowship in 1628.[1] Widely viewed as a superlative disputant, in 1629 Chillingworth found himself overmatched by the Jesuit missionary priest, John Fisher, with whom Laud had debated in 1624. Persuaded by Fisher's arguments, Chillingworth left England for the Catholic seminary at Douai in 1630, writing to his close friend Gilbert Sheldon (later archbishop of Canterbury) that he had become convinced that "there must be some one Church infallible in matters of faith," which title only the Church of Rome could "challenge to itself" (Maizeaux 5–6). However, he maintained a correspondence with Laud, who a year later convinced him to return to England, although not yet to the English Church. Rather, like the young John Donne four decades earlier, Chillingworth held back from commitment for several years in order to "doubt wisely." Much of his time was spent at Great Tew, the celebrated country-house think tank of his close friend, Lucius Cary, Lord Falkland, whose other regular visitors included Clarendon, Sheldon, Hobbes, Godolphin, Earle, and (at least in spirit) Hales, almost all (Hobbes being the major exception) sharing Falkland's Erasmian commitment to toleration, latitude, and "mere Christianity."

By 1635 Chillingworth had begun working on *The religion of Protestants*, although he had not re-entered the Church of England. A long letter from the mid-1630s defends Arianism on patristic grounds. He wrote Sheldon in 1635 that, while he considered the Church of England a true Church, lacking nothing necessary to salvation, he could not

---

[1] Aubrey charged the young Chillingworth with "the detestable crime of treachery" for sending Laud, then Oxford's Chancellor, weekly updates on University affairs, including, on one occasion, seditious words spoken by one of the fellows. Later historians repeat the charge, but why such reports constitute treachery is never explained. In his *Life in the medieval university*, R. S. Rait notes that "the oath taken by scholars frequently bound them to reveal to the authorities any breach of the statutes" (Cambridge UP, 1918), 69.

subscribe to the Thirty-nine Articles, since he objected to the "damning sentences in St. Athanasius' Creed" and did not think the Fourth Commandment binding on Christians (Maizeaux 93–96). Over the following months however, he came to accept Sheldon's position that subscription did not imply full inward consent to every particular of the fine print, the Articles being rather "general forms of peace" than a confession of faith.[2] He was ordained in 1637, probably shortly after finishing *The religion of Protestants*.

When the war came, and probably since his college days, Chillingworth proved an unwavering royalist. He was with the King's forces in Arundel Castle when it surrendered to Waller's army in 1643. Already seriously ill, Chillingworth was taken as prisoner to what had been the bishop's palace at Chichester, where he was alternately nursed and hectored by the presbyterian zealot, Francis Cheynell, who strove (unsuccessfully) to force the dying man to admit that Turks, Socinians, and Roman Catholics could not be saved. At Chillingworth's burial, Cheynell secured his place in the annals of infamy by hurling a copy of *The religion of Protestants* into its author's grave with the solemn anathema, "Get thee gone, thou cursed book, that hast seduced so many precious souls: Get thee gone, thou corrupt rotten book, earth to earth, dust to dust: Get thee gone into the place of rottenness, that thou mayest rot with thy author, and see corruption."

A handful of Chillingworth's sermons and occasional tracts made their way into print after the Restoration, but *The religion of Protestants* is his magnum opus. The work intervenes in a polemical exchange between the Jesuit Edward Knott and the Laudian provost of Queen's, Christopher Potter, who replied to Knott's 1630 *Charity mistaken* in 1633 with *Want of charity*, to which Knott's 1634 *Mercy and truth*, in turn, responded. Chillingworth's treatise reprints[3] and answers *Mercy and truth*, although its preface deals with Knott's *A direction to be observed by N.N.* (1636), which sought to discredit *The religion of Protestants* by launching a pre-publication attack on its author.

Given Chillingworth's history of intellectual and spiritual independence, Laud apparently felt some concern as to what his godson might be planning to say; hence in early 1637 he asked Oxford's vice-chancellor and its two divinity professors to act as licensers. One of these was the eminent Calvinist John Prideaux, whose imprimatur appears on the first page of the Oxford edition. Chillingworth is clearly not a Calvinist, and at virtually the same time Prideaux licensed *The religion of Protestants* he lectured against positions similar to those the book defends, giving rise to conjectures as to why Prideaux signed off: in particular, whether the imprimatur points to Laudian intimidation.[4] Yet Laud's letter suggests no such thing; he writes Prideaux that

---

[2] This seems to have been the standard high-church position. Bramhall's position re the Thirty-nine Articles was thus that, excepting those restating the fundamental doctrines of the Creed, "neither do we oblige any man to believe them, but only not to contradict them" for the sake of the Church's "peace and tranquility" (Maizeaux 111–12).

[3] The material in the distinctive typeface in the Chillingworth selections below is quoted from Knott's *Mercy and truth*.

[4] Robert Adams argues that Laud must have blackmailed Prideaux, it being "impossible that Prideaux's imprimatur could have been given *bona fide*" since the two men were in "basic contradiction" on the crucial point of the Church's authority in matters of faith and religion, an authority that Prideaux affirmed and

> Mr. Chillingworth is answering of a book that much concerns the Church of England, and I am very sorry that the young man hath given cause why a more watchful eye should be held over him and his writings. But since it is so, I would willingly desire this favor from you in the Church's name—that you would be at the pains to read over this tract, and see that it be put home, in all points, against the Church of Rome, as the cause requires. And I am confident Mr. Chillingworth will not be against your altering of any thing that shall be found reasonable. (Maizeaux 148–49)

Chillingworth had not yet returned to the Church of England, and Laud apparently was unsure of what the "young man" was up to; the letter asks Prideaux to check that the tract really is aimed "against the Church of Rome." Moreover, the letter makes clear that Laud expected Chillingworth to defer to Prideaux (and, presumably, the other licensers) regarding alterations—an authority that Chillingworth's preface acknowledges, noting that the work had "pass[ed] the fiery trial of the exact censure of many understanding judges . . . [who] wanted not sufficiency to discover any heterodox doctrine . . . [and] have been very careful to let nothing slip dissonant from truth or from the authorized doctrine of the Church of England" (Maizeaux 161). It does not follow that Prideaux *liked* Chillingworth's book. Presumably he did not. The puzzlement over his imprimatur rests on a misunderstanding of what such authorization meant. It did not imply that the licenser agreed with a work, just that he found in it nothing directly against the Thirty-nine Articles—or, by 1637, the Caroline injunctions against discussing predestination. Since *The religion of Protestants* neither challenged the Thirty-nine Articles nor handled predestination—and was not, as Laud seems to have feared, a disguised apologia *for* the Church of Rome—Prideaux licensed it, and then gave a series of university lectures disputing some of Chillingworth's positions. The two actions are not inconsistent.

Perhaps the more interesting question with regard to the licensing of Chillingworth's book is why *Chillingworth* did not object, given how close his position is to that of Milton's *Areopagitica* in its rhetoric of heroic liberty versus slavish dogmatism, its faith in the inherent strength of truth, its insistence on the duty of rational creatures to know wherefore they believe. One would have expected Chillingworth to protest the censorial triumvirate Laud set over him rather than vaunt the "exact censure of many understanding judges." Again, one is inclined to suspect intimidation; and again, probably wrongly. Chillingworth's failure to see the contradiction between rational liberty and press controls is not anomalous (and arguably not a failure). It was Laud's stance and fairly typical both of Laudians <*vide* Shelford, *supra*> and of the Great Tew divines, whose relation with Laud seems to have been one of mutual respect. Prior to 1640, the defense of rational autonomy, latitude of belief, and the "unity of charity" <2.84>[5] was an "avant-garde conformist"[6]

Chillingworth denied (*New York Review of Books*, July 21, 1988). This makes no sense. On the question of the Church's authority Laud agreed with *Prideaux*, not Chillingworth.

[5] The references to *The religion of Protestants* follow Chillingworth's division of the work into chapters and numbered paragraphs.

[6] The term, coined by Peter Lake, designates early Stuart anti-Calvinists of a high-church and/or rationalist stripe (see his "Lancelot Andrewes, John Buckeridge, and avant-garde conformity," in *The mental world of the Jacobean Court*, ed. Linda Levy Peck [Cambridge UP, 1991], 113–53).

stance—one incomprehensible to orthodox Calvinists and Romanists who feared that even smallish doctrinal errors often led to damnation—and bound up with the conviction that liberty of conscience required the counterbalance of a strong coercive authority enforcing outward unity and peace. Orr's classic study of Chillingworth describes the latter's view of Milton's party in precisely these terms: "He felt the greatest distaste for those who were pleading conscience to justify rebellion against a lawfully established authority which, in his view, offered a maximum of intellectual tolerance" (130).

Against the Roman Church's claims of infallibility, *The religion of Protestants* holds that there can be no absolute certainties in matters of religion. All we know of the patriarchs, prophets, and apostles, all we know of Christ, comes from the testimony of others, whether passed on by tradition or Scripture. Although such testimony can be wholly trustworthy, it is also inescapably fallible. Since our belief in a proposition should be proportional to the evidence for it, we cannot have absolute but only moral certainty that Scripture is indeed divine revelation, as we have only a moral certainty that men have walked on the moon; both are highly probable and hence deserving of firm belief, but it is not impossible for either to prove false.

The moral certainty argument drew a hostile response from Jesuit and Calvinist divines alike, both accusing Chillingworth of enthroning reason in God's place. Although Chillingworth offers no explicit criticism of Protestant doctrine, he could not but have known that his position constituted a frontal assault on Calvin's claim that "Scripture bears upon the face of it as clear evidence of its truth as white and black do of their color," evidence that the elect, to whom alone the Spirit is given, behold in Scripture with such clarity that they "feel perfectly assured—as much so as if we beheld the divine image visibly impressed on it," and this "every believer experiences in himself" (*Institutes* 1.7). The problem with this, Chillingworth notes (without mentioning Calvin), is that most good Christians experience no such thing <1.9>.

Chillingworth thus breaks with the claims for absolute or infallible certainty common to the Jesuit apologetics and Calvinist orthodoxy of his day; nor does the *OED* find the term "moral certainty" prior to *The religion of Protestants*. The concept, however, has a long and complex pedigree. Recent scholarship has identified, along with the law and medieval philosophy, a third strand deriving from Erasmus woven into the fabric of Chillingworth's argument. Barbara Shapiro has shown that "moral certainty" is one of several precursors for what the law now terms certainty "beyond a reasonable doubt." Courts, like Christians, rely perforce on human testimony for their knowledge of past events, and, as Chillingworth several times points out, judges can be certain enough that their verdicts are correct without claiming infallibility. The legal and epistemic trajectories of moral certainty are intertwined, since the late medieval philosophers, who introduce the distinction among degrees of certainty, use legal examples to illustrate the certainty based on the evidence of testimony, that is, moral certainty. A third strand derives from Erasmus' reworking of ancient skeptical probabilism; for Erasmus, as for Chillingworth, the unbroken consensus of the faithful (i.e., "universal tradition") regarding the fundamentals of Christian belief endows these with as high a probability as matters of past historical fact can attain; it endows them, that is to say, with moral certainty. Chillingworth likewise follows Erasmus in holding that teachings not accepted by the universal Church are best left to the reason and conscience of individuals, and that—since the essential truths are clear and accepted by all, while errors regarding side-matters do not endanger salvation—persecuting men for their beliefs proves either unnecessary or unwarranted.[7]

What seems not to have been noted is that Chillingworth's understanding of faith closely resembles that laid out in Augustine's first post-conversion tract, *De utilitate credendi*, written against the Manichees' claim to afford their disciples knowledge rather than Christianity's mere beliefs. Augustine argues that, indeed, Christians believe rather than know the affirmations of the Creed, nor can it be otherwise, since all claims concerning the past, or any matter outside our immediate ken, require giving credit to another's words—whether purported eyewitness reports, accounts given by earlier historians, common fame, oral tradition, or expert testimony. We cannot know who our father really is, or our mother; for the former, we must believe our mother's word; for the latter, the testimony of the midwife. Both mothers and midwives might be lying, so we can never *know* our true parents, and yet we rightly trust and love those whom we are told to call mother and father. Human society depends on people trusting parents, friends, physicians, teachers, and textbooks. This, Augustine avers, is not credulity, although where grounds for suspicion exist, it may be (21–26).[8]

Augustine's insistence that we have no absolute certainty that Scripture is the word of God but rather believe it for much the same reason we believe any history—namely, "widely extended report . . . strengthened by numbers, agreement, antiquity" (31)—sounds very much like Chillingworth's moral certainty. Yet, although both understand faith as crediting others' testimony concerning past events, they draw surprisingly different conclusions. For Augustine, crediting is primarily a matter of trust—one trusts the Church as one trusts one's friend or mother—not, as for Chillingworth, the rational assessment of evidence. Augustine's point is that belief precedes understanding; one has to trust the map if one is to use it to find one's way home. Chillingworth, by contrast, argues that one should first determine how reliable the map is and then decide how far to trust it, for "faith should be . . . proportionable to the motives and reasons enforcing to it" <1.9>. Something new is going on here.

This newness comes into focus if one contrasts Chillingworth's position with that of Laud and Laud's immediate source, Richard Hooker's *Laws* and his 1586 sermon on the certainty of faith (both which, in turn, draw on Aquinas). Like Chillingworth, Laud and Hooker hold that demonstrative reason trumps tradition and authority; that neither tradition nor authority can lay claim to infallibility, although both have real weight vis-à-vis merely probable arguments. Indeed, Chillingworth several times appeals to Hooker's authority. Yet he quotes selectively, giving Hooker's view that in this life we have no

---

[7] Both Remer and Orr list Acontius, Cassander, and Chillingworth as Erasmians; moreover, his opponents regularly accused Laud of being an English Cassander (e.g., Prynne in *Rome's masterpiece* [1643], 496), and his position in the *Conference with Fisher* <*supra*> bears this out. Laud held that people could rightly be punished for contumacy, disobedience, and troublemaking in church-matters no less than in secular ones, but he sharply distinguishes this from enforcing doctrinal uniformity.

[8] Note that Digby's *A conference with a lady* also defines faith as *traditio*, but then goes on to argue that the Roman Church has handed down, generation by generation, the original teachings of Christ and the apostles, so that its doctrines bear *infallible* witness to the divine truth <*vide infra*>.

certainty of evidence regarding supernatural truths but omitting altogether Hooker's correlative point that faith enables, or rather simply is, the certainty of adherence, whereby "the heart doth cleave and stick unto that which it doth believe" so that "even then when the evidence which he hath of the truth [of God's word] is so small that it grieveth him to feel his weakness in assenting thereto, yet . . . his spirit having once truly tasted the heavenly sweetness thereof . . . he striveth with himself to hope against all reason of believing" (*Works* 3:741). Laud makes the same point, although with his typical dry concision: "faith is a mixed act of the will and the understanding; and the will inclines the understanding to yield full approbation to that whereof it sees not full proof" <896>.[9] For Hooker and Laud, probabilities in religion do *not* rise to the level of moral certainty. Belief requires a striving to hope in excess of, and even against, the evidence. Chillingworth, however, argues that God asks of us no more than "that we believe the conclusion as much as the premises deserve" <1.8>, that our faith be "proportional to the motives and reasons enforcing it," that is, proportional to the evidence <1.9>. What is distinctive about Chillingworth's position is not his claim that the truth of Christianity, resting as it does on the fallible evidence of testimony, cannot be known with absolute certainty, but rather his conviction that the evidence, weighed on the scale of reason, will yield a certainty beyond reasonable doubt.[10]

SOURCES: *ODNB* (q.v., Great Tew, William Chillingworth); St Augustine, "On the profit of believing [*De utilitate credendi*]," in vol. 3 of *A select library of Nicene and post-Nicene Fathers*, ed. Philip Schaff (Buffalo, 1887), 347–66; Alan Crossley, "City and university," in *The history of the University of Oxford*, vol. 4: *seventeenth-century Oxford*, ed. Nicholas Tyacke; Hooker, *Works*; P. des Maizeaux, *The life of William Chillingworth*, trans. James Nichols (London, 1863); Anthony Milton, "Licensing, censorship, and religious orthodoxy in early Stuart England," *Historical Journal* 41 (1998): 625–51; Robert Orr, *Reason and authority: the thought of William Chillingworth* (Clarendon, 1967); Robert Pasnau, "Medieval social epistemology: *scientia* for mere mortals," http://spot.colorado.edu/~pasnau/seminar/pasnau.scientia.pdf (accessed June 8, 2012).; Gary Remer, "Humanism, liberalism, & the skeptical case for religious toleration," *Polity* 25.1 (1992): 21–43; John Robertson, "Hugh Trevor-Roper, intellectual history and 'The religious origins of the Enlightenment,'" *English Historical Review* 124 (2009): 1389–1421; Barbara Shapiro, "Changing language, unchanging standard: from 'satisfied conscience' to 'moral certainty' and 'beyond reasonable doubt,'" *Cardozo Journal of International and Comparative Law* 17 (2009): 261–79; Shuger, "Faith and assurance." See also Robert Adams' review of Hugh Trevor-Roper's *Catholics, Anglicans, and Puritans* in the April 14, 1988, *New York Review of Books* and their subsequent electrifyingly abusive exchanges in the June 16 and July 21 issues.

[9] Note that this passage is not in the 1624 version of *Conference with Fisher*; Laud adds it in 1639, perhaps in response to Chillingworth.

[10] One might in truth be tempted to call Chillingworth's position Socinian were it not the Richard Baxter says much the same. See Shuger, "Faith and assurance."

WILLIAM CHILLINGWORTH

The religion of Protestants a safe way to salvation
1637[1]

The Preface
To the author of *Charity maintained*,[2] with an answer
to his pamphlet entitled *A direction to N. N.*

Sir,

Upon the first news of the publication of your book, I used all diligence with speed to procure it, and came with such a mind to the reading of it as St. Austin, before he was a settled Catholic, brought to his conference with Faustus, the Manichee. For as he thought that if anything more than ordinary might be said in defense of the Manichean doctrine, Faustus was the man from whom it was to be expected, so my persuasion concerning you was, *si Pergama dextra defendi possunt, certe hac defensa videbo*[3]. . . . For I conceived that among the champions of the Roman Church, the English in reason must be the best or equal to the best, as being by most expert masters trained up purposely for this war and perpetually practiced in it. Among the English, I saw the Jesuits would yield the first place to none. . . .

2. Neither truly were you more willing to effect such an alteration in me than I was to have it effected. For my desire is to go the right way to eternal happiness. But whether this way lie on the right hand, or the left, or straight forward; whether it be by following a living guide, or by seeking my direction in a book, or by hearkening to the secret whisper of some private spirit, to me it is indifferent. And he that is otherwise affected and hath not a traveler's indifference, which Epictetus requires in all that would find the truth, but much desires, in respect of his ease or pleasure or profit or advancement or satisfaction of friends or any human consideration, that one way should be true rather than another, it is odds but he will take his desire that it should be so for an assurance that it is so. But I, for

---

[1] {The title page says 1638, but it had come out the year before; see des Maizeaux 237.}
[2] {i.e., Knott's *Mercy and truth, or charity maintained by Catholics*}
[3] {An echo of Virgil, *Aen.* 2.291: "If Troy can be defended by anyone, certainly I shall see you do it."}

my part, unless I deceive myself, was and still am so affected as I have made profession; not willing, I confess, to take anything upon trust and to believe it without asking myself why; no, nor able to command myself (were I never so willing) to follow like a sheep every shepherd that should take upon him to guide me, or every flock that should chance to go before me; but most apt and most willing to be led by reason to any way, or from it, and always submitting all other reasons to this one: God hath said so, therefore it is true. Nor yet was I so unreasonable as to expect mathematical demonstrations from you in matters plainly incapable of them, such as are to be believed and, if we speak properly, cannot be known; such therefore I expected not.[4] For as he is an unreasonable master who requires a stronger assent to his conclusions than his arguments deserve, so I conceive him a froward and undisciplined scholar who desires stronger arguments for a conclusion than the matter will bear. But had you represented to my understanding such reasons of your doctrine as—being weighed in an even balance held by an even hand, with those on the other side—would have turned the scale and have made your religion more credible than the contrary, certainly I should have despised the shame of one more alteration, and with both mine arms and with all my heart most readily have embraced it; such was my expectation from you, and such my preparation which I brought with me to the reading of your book.

3. Would you know now what the event was, what effect was wrought in me by the perusal and consideration of it? To deal truly and ingenuously with you, I fell somewhat in my good opinion both of your sufficiency and sincerity, but was exceedingly confirmed in my ill opinion of the cause maintained by you. I found everywhere snares that might entrap and colors that might deceive the simple, but nothing that might persuade and very little that might move an understanding man and one that can discern between discourse and sophistry. . . .

. . .

7. . . . you stick not . . . to fasten the imputation of *atheism and irreligion upon all wise and gallant men that are not of your own religion.* In which uncharitable and unchristian judgment, void of all color or shadow of probability, I know yet by experience that very many of the bigots of your faction are partakers with you. God forbid I should think the like of you! Yet, if I should say that in your religion there want not some temptations unto and some principles of irreligion and atheism, I am sure I could make my assertion much more probable than you have done or can make this horrible imputation.

8. For to pass by, first, that which experience justifies, that where and when your religion hath most absolutely commanded, there and then atheism hath most abounded; to say nothing, secondly, of your notorious and confessed forging of so many false miracles and so many lying legends, which is not unlikely to make suspicious men to question the truth of all; nor to object to you, thirdly, the abundance of your weak and silly ceremonies and ridiculous observances in your religion, which in all probability cannot but beget secret contempt and scorn of it in wise and considering men and, consequently, atheism and impiety, if they have this persuasion settled in them (which is too rife among you and

---

[4] {Aristotle, *Nic. Eth.* 1.3: "Our discussion will be adequate if it has as much clearness as the subject-matter admits of . . . for it is the mark of an educated man to look for precision in each class of things just so far as the nature of the subject admits; it is evidently equally foolish to accept probable reasoning from a mathematician and to demand from a rhetorician scientific proofs."}

which you account a piece of *wisdom and gallantry*), that if they be not of your religion, they were as good be of none at all; nor to trouble you, fourthly, with this, that a great part of your doctrine, especially in the points contested, makes apparently for the temporal ends of the teachers of it, which yet I fear is a great scandal to many *beaux esprits* among you: only I should desire you to consider attentively, when you conclude so often from the differences of Protestants that they have no certainty of any part of their religion, no not of those points wherein they agree, whether you do not that which so magisterially you direct me not to do, that is, proceed *a destructive way, and object arguments against your adversaries which tend to the overthrow of all religion?* And whether, as you argue thus, "Protestants differ in many things, therefore they have no certainty of any thing," so an atheist or skeptic may not conclude as well, "Christians and the professors of all religions differ in many things, therefore they have no certainty in any thing." Again, I should desire you to tell me ingenuously, whether it be not too probable that your portentous doctrine of transubstantiation, joined with your forementioned persuasion of *no Papists, no Christians*, hath brought a great many others, as well as himself, to Averroes his resolution, *quandoquidem Christiani adorant quod comedunt, sit anima mea cum philosophis?*[5] Whether your requiring men, upon only probable and prudential motives, to yield a most certain assent unto things in human reason impossible, and telling them, as you do too often, that they were as good not believe at all as believe with any lower degree of faith, be not a likely way to make considering men scorn your religion (and consequently all, if they know no other) as requiring things contradictory and impossible to be performed? Lastly, whether your pretence that there is no good ground to believe Scripture but your Church's infallibility, joined with your pretending no ground for this but some texts of Scripture, be not a fair way to make them that understand themselves believe neither Church nor Scripture?

9. Your calumnies against Protestants in general are set down in these words, chap. ii. §2. *The very doctrine of Protestants, if it be followed closely and with coherence to itself, must of necessity induce Socinianism. This I say confidently, and evidently prove by instancing in one error, which may well be termed the capital and mother-heresy from which all other must follow at ease: I mean their heresy in affirming that the perpetual visible Church of Christ, descended by a never-interrupted succession from our Savior to this day, is not infallible in all that it proposeth to be believed as revealed truths. For if the infallibility of such a public authority be once impeached, what remains but that every man is given over to his own wit and discourse? And talk not here of holy Scripture: for if the true Church may err in defining what Scriptures be canonical or in delivering the sense and meaning thereof, we are still devolved either upon the private spirit (a foolery now exploded out of England, which finally leaving every man to his own conceits ends in Socinianism) or else upon natural wit and judgment, for examining and determining what Scriptures contain true or false doctrine and, in that respect, ought to be received or rejected. And indeed, take away the authority of God's Church, no man can be assured that any one book or parcel of Scripture was written by divine inspiration or that all the contents are infallibly true, which are the direct errors of Socinians. If it were but for this reason alone, no man who regards the eternal salvation of his soul would live or die in Protestancy, from which so vast absurdities as these of the Socinians*

---

[5] {Since Christians worship what they eat, let my soul be with the philosophers.}

must inevitably follow. And it ought to be an unspeakable comfort to all us Catholics while we consider that none can deny the infallible authority of our Church but jointly he must be left to his own wit and ways, must abandon all infused faith and true religion, if he do but understand himself right.

In all which discourse, the only true word you speak is, *This I say confidently*; as for *proving evidently*, that, I believe, you reserved for some other opportunity; for the present, I am sure you have been very sparing of it.

10. You say, indeed, confidently enough, that *the denial of the Church's infallibility is the mother-heresy from which all other must follow at ease*. Which is so far from being a necessary truth, as you make it, that it is indeed a manifest falsehood. Neither is it possible for the wit of man, by any good or so much as probable consequence, from the denial of the Church's infallibility to deduce any one of the ancient heresies or any one error of the Socinians, which are the heresies here entreated of. For who would not laugh at him that should argue thus: neither the Church of Rome nor any other Church is infallible; *ergo*, the doctrine of Arius, Pelagius, Eutyches, Nestorius, Photinus, Manichaeus was true doctrine? On the other side it may be truly said, and justified by very good and effectual reason, that he that affirms with you the pope's infallibility puts himself into his hands and power to be led by him at his ease and pleasure into all heresy, and even to hell itself; and cannot with reason say (so long as he is constant to his grounds) *Domine, cur ita facis?*[6] but must believe *white to be black and black to be white, virtue to be vice, and vice to be virtue*; nay (which is an horrible but a most certain truth) Christ to be Antichrist, and Antichrist to be Christ, if it be possible for the pope to say so: which, I say and will maintain, however you daub and disguise it, is indeed to make men apostatize from Christ to his pretended vicar, but real enemy. For that name and no better . . . I presume he deserves, who, under pretence of interpreting the law of Christ (which authority, without any word of express warrant, he has taken upon himself), doth in many parts evacuate and dissolve it, so dethroning Christ from his dominion over men's consciences and, instead of Christ, setting up himself; inasmuch as he that requires that his interpretations of any law should be obeyed as true and genuine, seem they to men's understandings never so dissonant and discordant from it (as the bishop of Rome does), requires indeed that his interpretations should be the laws; and he that is firmly prepared in mind to believe and receive all such interpretations without judging of them (and though to his private judgment they seem unreasonable) is indeed congruously disposed to hold adultery a venial sin and fornication no sin, whensoever the pope and his adherents shall so declare. And whatsoever he may plead, yet either wittingly or ignorantly he makes the law and the law-maker both stales, and obeys only the interpreter. . . . If I should pretend to believe the Bible, but that I would understand it according to the sense which the chief mufti should put upon it, who would not say that I were a Christian in pretence only, but indeed a Mahometan?

11. Nor will it be to purpose for you to pretend that the precepts of Christ are so plain that it cannot be feared that any pope should ever go about to dissolve them and pretend to be a Christian; for, not to say that you now pretend the contrary—to wit, *that the law of Christ is obscure even in things necessary to be believed and done*, and by saying so have made a fair way for any foul interpretation of any part of it—certainly, that which the Church

---

[6] {Master, why doest thou thus?}

of Rome hath already done in this kind is an evident argument that, if once she had this power unquestioned . . . she may do what she pleaseth with it. Who that had lived in the primitive Church would not have thought it as utterly improbable that ever they should have brought in the worship of images and picturing of God as now it is that they should legitimate fornication? Why may we not think they may in time take away the whole communion from the laity as well as they have taken away half of it? . . . And therefore, seeing we see these things done which hardly any man would have believed that had not seen them, why should we not fear that this unlimited power may not be used hereafter with as little moderation. . . . I conclude, therefore, that if Solomon himself were here and were to determine the difference, which is more likely to be mother of all heresy, the denial of the Church's or the affirming of the pope's infallibility, that he would certainly say, *This is the mother, give her the child.*

12. You say again confidently that *if this infallibility be once impeached, every man is given over to his own wit and discourse,* which, if you mean discourse not guiding itself by Scripture but only by principles of nature, or perhaps by prejudices and popular errors, and drawing consequences not by rule but chance, is by no means true. If you mean by discourse, right reason grounded on divine revelation and common notions[7] written by God in the hearts of all men, and deducing according to the never-failing rules of logic consequent deductions from them; if this be it which you mean by discourse, it is very meet and reasonable and necessary that men, as in all their actions, so especially in that of the greatest importance, the choice of their way to happiness, should be left unto it; and he that follows this in all his opinions and actions, and does not only seem to do so, follows always God; whereas he that followeth a company of men may oft-times follow a company of beasts. And in saying this, I say no more than St. John to all Christians in these words, *Dearly beloved, believe not every spirit; but try the spirits, whether they be of God or no.* . . . And though by passion or precipitation or prejudice, by want of reason or not using what they have, men may be, and are oftentimes, led into error and mischief; yet, that they cannot be misguided by discourse truly so called, such as I have described, you yourself have given them security. For what is discourse but drawing conclusions out of premises by good consequence? Now the principles which we have settled—to wit, the Scriptures—are on all sides agreed to be infallibly true. And you have told us in the fourth chapter of this pamphlet that *from truth no man can by good consequence infer falsehood*; therefore, by discourse no man can possibly be led to error; but if he err in his conclusions, he must of necessity either err in his principles (which here cannot have place) or commit some error in his discourse—that is, indeed, not discourse but seem to do so.

13. You say, thirdly, with sufficient confidence, that *if the true Church may err in defining what Scriptures be canonical or in the delivering the sense thereof, then we must follow either the private spirit or else natural wit and judgment, and by them examine what Scriptures contain true or false doctrine and in that respect ought to be received or rejected.* All which is apparently untrue, neither can any proof of it be pretended. For though the present Church may possibly err in her judgment touching this matter, yet have we other directions in it besides the private spirit and the examination of the contents (which latter

---

[7] {The Euclidean term for axioms (e.g., the whole is equal to the sum of its parts); what Hooker calls the "first principles of reason" (*Laws of ecclesiastical polity* 1.8.5).}

way may conclude the negative very strongly, to wit, that such or such a book cannot come from God because it contains irreconcilable contradictions; but the affirmative it cannot conclude, because the contents of a book may be all true and yet the book not written by divine inspiration); other directions therefore I say we have besides either of these three, and that is the testimony of the primitive Christians.

. . .

20. The other part of your accusation strikes deeper and is more considerable: and that tells us that *Protestantism waxeth weary of itself; that the professors of it—they especially of greatest worth, learning, and authority—love temper and moderation, and are at this time more unresolved where to fasten than at the infancy of their Church; that their churches begin to look with a new face, their walls to speak a new language, their doctrine to be altered in many things for which their progenitors forsook the then visible Church of Christ: for example, the pope not antichrist, prayer for the dead, limbus patrum, pictures, that the Church hath authority in determining controversies of faith and to interpret Scripture; about free-will, predestination, universal grace; that all our works are not sins, merit of good works, inherent justice, faith alone doth not justify, charity to be preferred before knowledge; traditions; commandments possible to be kept; that their thirty-nine articles are patient, nay ambitious, of some sense wherein they may seem Catholic; that to allege the necessity of wife and children in these days is but a weak plea for a married minister to compass a benefice; that Calvinism is at length accounted heresy and little less than treason; that men in talk and writing use willingly the once fearful names of priests and altars; that they are now put in mind that for exposition of Scripture they are by canon bound to follow the Fathers, which if they do with sincerity, it is easy to tell what doom will pass against Protestants, seeing, by the confessions of Protestants, the Fathers are on the Papists' side, which the Anwerer to some so clearly demonstrated that they remained convinced.* In fine, as the Samaritans saw in the disciples' countenances that they meant to go to Jerusalem, so you pretend that it is even legible in the foreheads of these men that they are even going, nay, making haste to Rome. Which scurrilous libel, void of all truth, discretion, and honesty, what effect it may have wrought, what credit it may have gained with credulous Papists (who dream what they desire, and believe their own dreams) or with ill-affected, jealous, and weak Protestants, I cannot tell; but one thing I dare boldly say, that you yourself did never believe it.

21. For did you indeed conceive, or had any probable hope, that such men as you describe, men of worth, of learning, and authority too, were friends and favorers of your religion and inclinable to your party, can any man imagine that you would proclaim it and bid the world take heed of them? . . . The truth is, they that can run to extremes in opposition against you, they that pull down your infallibility and set up their own, they that declaim against your tyranny and exercise it themselves over others are the adversaries that give you greatest advantage and such as you love to deal with; whereas upon men of temper and moderation, such as will oppose nothing because you maintain it, but will draw as near to you, that they may draw you to them, as the truth will suffer them; such as require of Christians to believe only in Christ and will damn no man nor doctrine without express and certain warrant from God's word; upon such as these you know not how to fasten. . . .

. . .

22. . . . . For what if out of devotion towards God, out of a desire that he should be worshipped, as *in spirit and in truth* in the first place, so also in the beauty of holiness? what if, out of fear that too much simplicity and nakedness in the public service of God may beget in the ordinary sort of men a dull and stupid irreverence, and out of hope that the outward state and glory of it, being well-disposed and wisely moderated, may engender, quicken, increase, and nourish the inward reverence, respect, and devotion which is due unto God's sovereign majesty and power? what if, out of a persuasion and desire that Papists may be won over to us the sooner by the removing of this scandal out of their way, and out of an holy jealousy that the weaker sort of Protestants might be the easier seduced to them by the magnificence and pomp of their church-service, in case it were not removed? I say, what if, out of these considerations, the governors of our Church, more of late than formerly, have set themselves to adorn and beautify the places where God's honor dwells and to make them as heaven-like as they can with earthly ornaments? Is this a sign that they are warping towards popery? Is this devotion in the Church of England an argument that she is coming over to the Church of Rome? . . .

. . .

26. As for the points of doctrine wherein you pretend that these divines begin of late to falter and to comply with the Church of Rome, upon a due examination of particulars it will presently appear, first, that part of them always have been, and now are, held constantly one way by them: as the authority of the Church in determining controversies of faith, though not the infallibility of it; that there is inherent justice, though so imperfect that it cannot justify; that there are traditions, though none necessary; that charity is to be preferred before knowledge; that good works are not properly meritorious; and, lastly, that faith alone justifies, though that faith justifies not which is alone. And secondly, for the remainder, that they, every one of them, have been anciently, without breach of charity, disputed among Protestants: such, for example, were the questions about the pope's being the antichrist; the lawfulness of some kind of prayers for the dead; the estate of the Fathers'[8] souls before Christ's ascension; free-will, predestination, universal grace; the possibility of keeping God's commandments; the use of pictures in the church. . . . they have been anciently, and even from the beginning of the Reformation, controverted amongst them, though perhaps the stream and current of their doctors run one way, and only some brook or rivulet of them the other.

. . .

30. The third and last part of my accusation[9] was that I answer out of *principles which Protestants themselves will profess to detest*, which indeed were to the purpose, if it could be justified. But besides that it is confuted by my whole book and made ridiculous by the approbations premised unto it, it is very easy for me out of your own mouth and words to prove it a most injurious calumny. For what one conclusion is there in the whole fabric of my discourse that is not naturally deducible out of this one principle, *that all things necessary to salvation are contained in the Scripture*? Or, what one conclusion almost of importance is there in your book which is not by this one clearly confutable? Grant this, and it will presently follow, in opposition to your first conclusion and the argument

---

[8] {i.e., Old Testament patriarchs}
[9] {i.e., Knott's accusation of Chillingworth in *A direction to N. N.*}

of your first chapter, that amongst men of different opinions touching the obscure and controverted questions of religion, such as may with probability be disputed on both sides (and such are the disputes of Protestants), good men and lovers of truth on all sides may be saved; because all necessary things being supposed evident, concerning them, with men so qualified, there will be no difference—there being no more certain sign that a point is not evident than that honest and understanding and indifferent men, and such as give themselves liberty of judgment after a mature consideration of the matter, differ about it.

. . .

CHARITY MAINTAINED BY CATHOLICS[10]
The First Part

The state of the question, with a summary of the reasons for which,
amongst men of different religions, one side only can be saved.

NEVER is malice more indiscreet than when it chargeth others with imputation of that to which itself becomes more liable even by that very act of accusing others. For though guiltiness be the effect of some error, yet usually it begets a kind of moderation so far forth as not to let men cast such aspersions upon others as most apparently reflect upon themselves. Thus cannot the poet endure that Gracchus, who was a factious and unquiet man, should be inveighing against sedition; and the Roman orator rebukes philosophers who, to wax glorious, superscribed their names upon those very books which they entitled *Of the contempt of glory*. What then shall we say of D. Potter, who in the title and text of his whole book doth so tragically charge *want of charity on all such Romanists as dare affirm that Protestancy destroyeth salvation*; while he himself is in act of pronouncing the like heavy doom against Roman Catholics? For, not satisfied with much uncivil language in affirming the Roman Church *many ways to have played the harlot, and in that regard deserved a bill of divorce from Christ and detestation of Christians*; in styling her that *proud and curst dame of Rome which takes upon her to revel in the house of God*; in talking of an *idol* to be worshipped at Rome; he comes at length to thunder out his fearful sentence against her: *for that mass of errors* (saith he) *in judgment and practice, which is proper to her and wherein she differs from us, we judge a reconciliation impossible, and to us (who are convicted in conscience of her corruptions) damnable*. . . . By the acerbity of which censure, he doth not only make himself guilty of that which he judgeth to be an heinous offence in others, but freeth us from all color of crime by this his unadvised recrimination. For if Roman Catholics be likewise convicted in conscience of the errors of Protestants, they may and must, in conformity to the Doctor's own rule, judge a reconciliation with them to be also damnable. And that all the *want of charity* so deeply charged on us dissolves itself into this poor wonder: *Roman Catholics believe in their conscience that the religion they profess is true, and the contrary false*.

2. Nevertheless, we earnestly desire and take care that our doctrine may not be defamed by misinterpretation. Far be it from us, by way of insultation, to apply it against Protestants otherwise than as they are comprehended under the generality of those who

---

[10] {The sections in distinctive typeface reprint Knott's text.}

are divided from the only one true Church of Christ our Lord, within the communion whereof he hath confined salvation. . . .

3. Moreover our meaning is not, as misinformed persons may conceive, that we give Protestants over to reprobation, that we offer no prayers in hope of their salvation, that we hold their case desperate. God forbid! We hope, we pray for their conversion, and sometimes we find happy effects of our charitable desires. Neither is our censure immediately directed to particular persons. The tribunal of particular judgments is God's alone. When any man esteemed a Protestant leaveth to live in this world, we do not instantly with precipitation avouch that he is lodged in hell. For we are not always acquainted with what sufficiency or means he was furnished for instruction; we do not penetrate his capacity to understand his catechist; we have no revelation what light may have cleared his errors or contrition retracted his sins in the last moment before his death. In such particular cases we wish more apparent signs of salvation, but do not give any dogmatical sentence of perdition. How grievous sins disobedience, schism, and heresy are, is well known. But to discern how far the natural malignity of those great offences might be checked by ignorance or by some such lessening circumstance is the office rather of prudence than of faith.

4. Thus we allow Protestants as much charity as D. Potter spares us, for whom, in the words above mentioned and elsewhere, he makes ignorance the best hope of salvation. . . .

. . .

6. And because we cannot determine what judgment may be esteemed rash or prudent except by weighing the reasons upon which it is grounded, we will here . . . present a summary of those principles from which we infer that Protestancy in itself, unrepented, destroys salvation; intending afterwards to prove the truth of every one of the grounds, till by a concatenation of sequels we fall upon the conclusion for which we are charged with want of charity.

7. Now this is our gradation of reasons: almighty God having ordained mankind to a supernatural end of eternal felicity hath, in his holy providence, settled competent and convenient means whereby that end may be attained. The universal grand origin of all such means is the incarnation and death of our blessed Savior, whereby he merited internal grace for us and founded an external visible Church, provided and stored with all those helps which might be necessary for salvation. From hence it followeth that in this Church, among other advantages, there must be some effectual means to beget and conserve faith, to maintain unity, to discover and condemn heresies, to appease and reduce schisms, and to determine all controversies in religion. For without such means, the Church should not be furnished with helps sufficient to salvation, nor God afford sufficient means to attain that end to which himself ordained mankind. This means to decide controversies in faith and religion (whether it should be the holy Scripture, or whatsoever else) must be endued with an universal infallibility in whatsoever it propoundeth for a divine truth—that is, as revealed, spoken, or testified by almighty God—whether the matter of its nature be great or small. For if it were subject to error in any one thing, we could not in any other yield it infallible assent because we might with good reason doubt whether it chanced not to err in that particular.

8. Thus far all must agree to what we have said, unless they have a mind to reduce faith to opinion. And even out of these grounds alone, without further proceeding, it undeniably follows that of two men dissenting in matters of faith, great or small, few or many,

the one cannot be saved without repentance, unless ignorance accidentally may in some particular person plead excuse. For, in that case of contrary belief, one must of necessity be held to oppose God's word or revelation sufficiently represented to his understanding by an infallible propounder; which opposition to the testimony of God is undoubtedly a damnable sin, whether otherwise the thing so testified be in itself great or small. And thus we have already made good what was promised in the argument of this chapter: that amongst men of different religions, one only is capable of being saved.

9. Nevertheless, to the end that men may know in particular what is the said infallible means upon which we are to rely in all things concerning faith, and accordingly may be able to judge in what safety or danger, more or less, they live; and because D. Potter descendeth to divers particulars about Scriptures and the Church, &c., we will go forward and prove that, although Scripture be in itself most sacred, infallible, and divine, yet it alone cannot be to us a rule or judge fit and able to end all doubts and debates emergent in matters of religion; but that there must be some external, visible, public, living judge to whom all sorts of persons, both learned and unlearned, may without danger of error have recourse. . . .

10. If once therefore it be granted that the Church is that means which God hath left for the deciding all controversies in faith, it manifestly will follow that she must be infallible in all her determinations, whether the matters of themselves be great or small; because, as we said above, it must be agreed on all sides that if that means which God hath left to determine controversies were not infallible in all things proposed by it, it could not settle in our minds a firm and infallible belief of any one.

11. From this universal infallibility of God's Church it followeth that whosoever wittingly denieth any one point proposed by her as revealed by God is injurious to his divine majesty, as if he could either deceive or be deceived in what he testifieth; the averring whereof were not only a fundamental error but would overthrow the very foundation of all fundamental points; and therefore, without repentance, could not possibly stand with salvation.

12. Out of these grounds we will shew that, although the distinction of points fundamental and not fundamental[11] be good and useful as it is delivered and applied by Catholic divines to teach what principal articles of faith Christians are obliged explicitly to believe, yet that it is impertinent to the present purpose of excusing any man from grievous sin who knowingly disbelieves: that is, believes the contrary of that which God's Church proposeth as divine truth. For it is one thing not to know explicitly something testified by God, and another, positively to oppose what we know he hath testified. The former may often be excused from sin, but never the latter, which only is the case in question.

. . .

16. We are then to prove these points: first, that the infallible means to determine controversies in matters of faith is the visible Church of Christ. Secondly, that the distinction of points fundamental and not fundamental maketh nothing to our present question. Thirdly, that to say the Creed contains all fundamental points of faith is neither pertinent nor true. Fourthly, that both Luther and all they who, after him, persist in division from the communion and faith of the Roman Church cannot be excused from schism. Fifthly,

[11] {On this distinction, see Laud, *Conference with Fisher* <379–80 *supra*>.}

nor from heresy. Sixthly and lastly, that in regard of the precept of charity towards one's self, Protestants be in a state of sin as long as they remain divided from the Roman Church. And these six points shall be several arguments for so many ensuing chapters.

17. Only I will here observe that it seemeth very strange that Protestants should charge us so deeply with *want of charity* for only teaching that both they and we cannot be saved, seeing themselves must affirm the like of whosoever opposeth any least point delivered in Scripture, which they hold to be the sole rule of faith. Out of which ground they must be enforced to let all our former inferences pass for good. For is it not a grievous sin to deny any one truth contained in holy Writ? Is there in such denial any distinction between points fundamental and not fundamental sufficient to excuse from heresy? Is it not impertinent to allege the Creed containing all fundamental points of faith, as if, believing it alone, we were at liberty to deny all other points of Scripture? . . .

. . .

THE ANSWER TO THE FIRST CHAPTER

Showing that the adversary grants the former question and proposeth a new one; and that there is no reason why among men of different opinions and communions one side only can be saved.

To the first §. Your first onset is very violent. D. Potter is charged with malice and indiscretion for *being uncharitable to you, while he is accusing you of uncharitableness.* Verily, a great fault and folly, if the accusation be just; if unjust, a great calumny. Let us see then how you make good your charge. The effect of your discourse, if I mistake not, is this: *D. Potter chargeth the Roman Church with many and great errors; judgeth reconciliation between her doctrine and ours impossible; and that for them who were convicted in conscience of her errors, not to forsake her in them or to be reconciled unto her is damnable; therefore, if Roman Catholics be convicted in conscience of the errors of Protestants, they may and must judge a reconciliation with them damnable; and consequently to judge so is no more uncharitable in them than it is in the Doctor to judge as he does.* All this I grant, nor would any Protestant accuse you of want of charity if you went no further: if you judged the religion of Protestants damnable to them only who profess it, being convicted in conscience that it is erroneous. For *if a man judge some act of virtue to be a sin, in him it is a sin indeed.* . . . For I shall always profess and glory in this uncharitableness of judging hypocrisy a damnable sin. Let hypocrites then and dissemblers on both sides pass. It is not towards them, but good Christians; not to Protestant professors, but believers, that we require your charity. What think you of those that believe so verily the truth of our religion that they are resolved to die in it and, if occasion were, to die for it? What charity have you for them? . . . Will you grant that, notwithstanding their errors, there is good hope they might die with repentance? And if they did so, certainly they are saved. If you will do so, this controversy is ended. No man will hereafter charge you with *want of charity.* . . . If you will not, but will still affirm as *Charity mistaken* doth, that Protestants, not dissemblers but believers, without a particular repentance of their religion cannot be saved, this, I say, is a want of charity. . . .

. . .

3. *Ad* §3, 4, 5, 6. *That you give us not over to reprobation, that you pray and hope for our salvation*: if it be a charity, it is such a one as is common to Turks and Jews and pagans with us. But that which follows is extraordinary, neither do I know any man that requires

more of you than there you pretend to. For there you tell us *that when any man esteemed a Protestant dies, you do not instantly avouch that he is lodged in hell. . . .*

. . .

5. Thus much charity therefore, if you stand to what you have said, is interchangeably granted by each side to the other: that neither religion is so fatally *destructive but that by ignorance or repentance salvation may be had on both sides. . . .*

6. But, for the present, Protestancy is called to the bar, and though not sentenced by you to death without mercy, yet arraigned of so much natural malignity (if not corrected by *ignorance or contrition*) as to be *in itself destructive of salvation.* Which controversy I am content to dispute with you, tying myself to follow the rules prescribed by you in your preface. Only I am to remember you that the adding of this limitation, *in itself,* hath made this a new question; and that this is not the conclusion for which you were charged with want of charity, but that—whereas according to the grounds of your own religion, *Protestants may die in their supposed errors either with excusable ignorance or with contrition and if they do so may be saved*—you are still peremptory in pronouncing them damned. Which position, supposing your doctrine true and ours false, as it is far from charity (whose essential character it is to judge and hope the best), so I believe that I shall clearly evince this new, but more moderate, assertion of yours to be far from verity, and that it is *Popery, and not Protestancy, which in itself destroys salvation.*

7. *Ad* §7 & 8. In your gradation I shall rise so far with you as to grant *that Christ founded a visible Church stored with all helps necessary to salvation, particularly with sufficient means to beget and conserve faith, to maintain unity and compose schisms, to discover and condemn heresies, and to determine all controversies in religion* which were necessary to be determined. For all these purposes, he gave at the beginning (as we may see in the Epistle to the Ephesians) apostles, prophets, evangelists, pastors, and doctors, who by word of mouth taught their contemporaries and by writings (wrote indeed by some, but approved by all of them) taught their Christian posterity to the world's end how all these ends, and that which is the end of all these ends, salvation, is to be achieved. And these means the providence of God hath still preserved, and so preserved that they are sufficient for all these intents. I say, *sufficient,* though through the malice of men not always effectual (for that the same means may be sufficient for the compassing an end and not effectual, you must not deny, who hold that *God gives to all men sufficient means of salvation, and yet that all are not saved*). I said also, sufficient to determine all controversies which were *necessary to be determined.* For if some controversies may for many ages be undetermined, and yet in the meanwhile men be saved, why should or how can the Church's being furnished with effectual means to determine *all* controversies in religion be necessary to salvation? . . . If I have no need to fly, I have no need of wings. Answer me then, I pray, directly and categorically: is it necessary that all controversies in religion should be determined? or, is it not? If it be, why is the question of predetermination, of the Immaculate Conception, of the pope's indirect power in temporalities so long undetermined? If not, what is it but hypocrisy to pretend such great necessity of such effectual means for the achieving that end which is itself not necessary? Christians therefore have, and shall have, means sufficient (though not always effectual) to determine, not all controversies, but all necessary to be determined. I proceed on farther with you, and grant that this means to decide controversies in faith and religion must be endued with an universal infallibility

in whatsoever it propoundeth for a divine truth. For if it may be false in any one thing of this nature, in any thing which God requires men to believe, we can yield unto it but a wavering and fearful assent in any thing. These grounds therefore I grant very readily, and give you free leave to make your best advantage of them. And yet, to deal truly, I do not perceive how from the denial of any of them it would follow that faith is opinion; or, from the granting them, that it is not so. But, for my part, whatsoever clamor you have raised against me, I think no otherwise of the nature of faith, I mean historical faith, than generally both Protestants and Papists do; for I conceive it an assent to divine revelations upon the authority of the revealer; which, though in many things it differ from opinion (as commonly the word opinion is understood), yet in some things, I doubt not but you will confess that it agrees with it. As first, that as opinion is an assent, so is faith also. Secondly, that as opinion, so faith is always built upon less evidence than that of sense or science, which assertion you not only grant, but mainly contend for in your sixth chapter. Thirdly and lastly, that as opinion, so faith admits degrees; and that as there may be a strong and weak opinion, so there may be a strong and weak faith. These things if you will grant . . . I am well contented that this ill-sounding word, *opinion*, should be discarded, and that among the intellectual habits you should seek out some other genus for faith. For I will never contend with any man about words, who grants my meaning.

8. *But though the essence of faith exclude not all weakness and imperfection, yet may it be inquired whether any certainty of faith under the highest degree may be sufficient to please God and attain salvation?* Whereunto I answer that though men are unreasonable, God requires not anything but reason; they will not be pleased without a down-weight, but God is contented if the scale be turned; they pretend that heavenly things cannot be seen to any purpose but by the mid-day light, but God will be satisfied if we receive any degree of light which makes us leave the *works of darkness and walk as children of the light.* They exact a certainty of faith above that of sense or science; God desires only that we believe the conclusion as much as the premises deserve, that the strength of our faith be equal or proportionable to the credibility of the motives to it. Now, though I have and ought to have an absolute certainty of this thesis, *all which God reveals for truth, is true*—being a proposition that may be demonstrated, or rather so evident to anyone that understands it, that it needs it not; yet of this hypothesis, *that all the articles of our faith were revealed by God*, we cannot ordinarily have any rational and acquired certainty more than moral, founded upon these considerations: first, that the goodness of the precepts of Christianity and the greatness of the promises of it show it, of all other religions, most likely to come from the fountain of goodness. And then, that a constant, famous, and very general tradition, so credible that no wise man doubts of any other which hath but the fortieth part of the credibility of this, such and so credible a tradition tells us that God himself hath set his hand and seal to the truth of this doctrine by doing great and glorious and frequent miracles in confirmation of it. Now our faith is an assent to this conclusion, that *the doctrine of Christianity is true*; which being deduced from the former thesis which is metaphysically certain and from the former hypothesis whereof we can have but a moral certainty, we cannot possibly by natural means be more certain of it than of the weaker of the premises; as a river will not rise higher than the fountain from which it flows. For the conclusion always follows the worser part, if there be any worse; and must be negative, particular, contingent, or but morally certain, if any of the propositions from whence it

is derived be so; neither can we be certain of it in the highest degree, unless we be thus certain of all the principles whereon it is grounded. . . . Or, as if a message be brought me from a man of absolute credit with me, but by a messenger that is not so, my confidence of the truth of the relation cannot but be rebated and lessened by my diffidence in the relater.

9. Yet all this I say not as if I doubted that the Spirit of God, being implored by devout and humble prayer and sincere obedience, may and will by degrees advance his servants higher, and give them a certainty of adherence beyond their certainty of evidence. But what God gives as a reward to believers is one thing; and what he requires of all men as their duty is another; and what he will accept of out of grace and favor is yet another. To those that believe, and live according to their faith, he gives by degrees the *spirit of obsignation and confirmation*, which makes them know (though how they know not) what they did but believe. . . . He requires all, that their faith should be, as I have said, proportionable to the motives and reasons enforcing to it; he will accept of the weakest and lowest degree of faith, if it be living and effectual unto true obedience. For he it is that *will not quench the smoking flax nor break the bruised reed*. He did not reject the prayer of that distressed man that cried unto him, *Lord, I believe; Lord, help mine unbelief.* He commands us to *receive them that are weak in faith*, and thereby declares that he receives them. And as nothing avails with him but faith *which worketh by love*; so any faith, if it be but as a *grain of mustard-seed*, if it work by love, shall certainly avail with him and be accepted of him. Some experience makes me fear that the faith of considering and discoursing men is like to be cracked with too much straining: and that, being possessed with this false principle, that it is in vain to believe the gospel of Christ with such a kind or degree of assent as they yield to other matters of tradition; and finding that their faith of it is to them indiscernible from the belief they give to the truth of other stories, {they} are in danger not to believe at all, thinking 'not at all' as good as 'to no purpose'; or else, though indeed they do believe it, yet to think they do not and to cast themselves into wretched agonies and perplexities, as fearing they have not that without which it is impossible to please God and obtain eternal happiness. Consideration of this advantage which the devil probably may make of this fancy made me willing to insist somewhat largely on the refutation of it.

10. I return now thither from whence I have digressed, and assure you, concerning the grounds afore-laid—which were, that there is *a rule of faith whereby controversies may be decided which are necessary to be decided, and that this rule is universally infallible*—that notwithstanding any opinion I hold touching faith or any things else, I may and do believe them as firmly as you pretend to do. . . .

11. Indeed, if the matter in agitation were plainly decided by this infallible means of deciding controversies, and the parties in variance knew it to be so and yet would stand out in their dissension, this were, in one of them, direct opposition to the testimony of God and undoubtedly a damnable sin. But if you take the liberty to suppose what you please, you may very easily conclude what you list. For who is so foolish as to grant you these unreasonable postulates: that every emergent controversy of faith is plainly decided by the means of decision which God hath appointed; and that, of the parties litigant, one is always such a convicted recusant as you pretend? . . . Methinks with much more reason and much more charity, you might suppose that many of these controversies which are now disputed among Christians (all which profess themselves lovers of Christ and truly desirous to know his will and do it) are either not decidable by that means which God

has provided, and so not necessary to be decided; or, if they be, yet not so plainly and evidently as to oblige all men to hold one way; or, lastly, of decidable and evidently decided, yet you may hope that the erring party, by reason of some veil before his eyes, some excusable ignorance or unavoidable prejudice, doth not see the question to be decided against him, and so opposeth not that which he doth know to be the word of God, but only that which you know to be so, and which he might know were he void of prejudice—which is a fault, I confess, but a fault which is incident even to good and honest men very often, and not of such a gigantic disposition as you make it, to fly directly upon God Almighty and to give him the lie to his face.

12. . . . Neither must you argue thus: *the Church of Rome is the infallible propounder of divine verities, therefore he that opposeth her calls God's truth in question*; but thus rather, *the Church of Rome is so, and Protestants know it to be so, therefore in opposing her, they impute to God that either he deceives them or is deceived himself.* For as I may deny something which you upon your knowledge have affirmed, and yet never disparage your honesty, if I never knew that you affirmed it; so I may be undoubtedly certain of God's omniscience and veracity, and yet doubt of something which he hath revealed, provided I do not know nor believe that he hath revealed it. So that though your Church be the appointed witness of God's revelations, yet until you know that we know she is so, you cannot without foul calumny impute to us *that we charge God blasphemously with deceiving or being deceived.* You will say, perhaps, that this is directly consequent from our doctrine *that the Church may err,* which is directed by God in all her proposals. True, if we knew it to be directed by him, otherwise not; much less if we believe and know the contrary. But then, if it were consequent from our opinion, have you so little charity as to say that men are *justly chargeable with all the consequences of their opinions?* Such consequences, I mean, as they do not own, but disclaim; and if there were a necessity of doing either, would much rather forsake their opinion than embrace these consequences? . . .

13. *Ad §17. Protestants* (you say) *according to their own grounds must hold that of persons contrary in whatsoever point of belief one part only can be saved; therefore it is strangely done of them to charge Papists with want of charity for holding the same.* The consequence I acknowledge, but wonder much what it should be that lays upon Protestants any necessity to do so! You tell us it is their *holding Scripture the sole rule of faith;* for this, you say, obligeth them to pronounce them damned that oppose any least point delivered in Scripture. This I grant, if they oppose it after sufficient declaration, so that either they know it to be contained in Scripture, or have no just probable reason . . . to doubt whether or no it be there contained. For to oppose in the first case, in a man that believes the Scripture to be the word of God, is to give God the lie. To oppose in the second, is to be obstinate against reason; and therefore a sin, though not so great as the former. But then this is nothing to the purpose of the necessity of damning all those that are of contrary belief, and that for these reasons. First, because the contrary belief may be touching a point not at all mentioned in Scripture; and such points, though indeed they be not matters of faith, yet by men in variance are often overvalued and esteemed to be so. . . . Secondly, because the contrary belief may be about the sense of some place of Scripture which is ambiguous and with probability capable of divers senses; and in such cases it is no marvel, and sure no sin, if several men go several ways. Thirdly, because the contrary belief may be concerning points wherein Scripture may with so great probability be alleged on both sides (which is

911

a sure note of a point not necessary) that men of honest and upright hearts, true lovers of God and of truth, such as desire above all things to know God's will and to do it, may, without any fault at all, some go one way and some another, and some (and those as good men as either of the former) suspend their judgment and expect some Elias to solve doubts and reconcile repugnancies. Now in all such questions, one side or other (whichsoever it is) holds that which indeed is opposite to the sense of the Scripture which God intended, for it is impossible that God should intend contradictions. But then this intended sense is not so fully declared but that they which oppose it may verily believe that they indeed maintain it, and have great show of reason to induce them to believe so; and therefore are not to be damned as men opposing that which they either know to be a truth delivered in Scripture or have no probable reason to believe the contrary; but rather in charity to be acquitted and absolved as men who endeavor to find the truth but fail of it through human frailty. . . .

. . .

CHAPTER II

What is that means whereby the revealed truths of God are conveyed to our understanding, and which must determine controversies in faith and religion?

. . .

19. But besides all this, the Scripture cannot be judge of controversies, who ought to be such as that to him, not only the learned or veterans, but also the unlearned and novices may have recourse: for these being capable of salvation and endued with faith of the same nature with that of the learned, there must be some universal judge which the ignorant may understand, and to whom the greatest clerks must submit. Such is the Church, and the Scripture is not such.

20. Now, the inconveniences which follow by referring all controversies to Scripture *alone* are very clear, for by this principle all is finally in very deed and truth reduced to the *internal private spirit*, because there is really no middle way betwixt a public external and a private internal voice; and whosoever refuseth the one, must of necessity adhere to the other.[12]

21. This tenet also of Protestants, by taking the office of judicature from the Church, comes to confer it upon every particular man, who, being driven from submission to the Church, cannot be blamed if he trust himself as far as any other, his conscience dictating that wittingly he means not to cozen himself, as others maliciously may do. Which inference is so manifest that it hath extorted from divers Protestants the open confession of so vast an absurdity. Hear Luther: *The governors of Churches and pastors of Christ's sheep have indeed power to teach, but the sheep ought to give judgment whether they propound the voice of Christ or of aliens.* . . . Whitaker, even of the unlearned, saith *they ought to have recourse unto the more learned, but in the meantime we must be careful not to attribute to them over-much, but so that still we retain our own freedom.* Bilson also affirmeth *that the people must be discerners and judges of that which is taught.*[13] . . . and nothing is more

---

[12] {See Laud's *Conference with Fisher* <384–85>.}

common in every Protestant's mouth than that he admits of Fathers, Councils, Church, &c. as far as they agree with Scripture—which, upon the matter, is himself. Thus heresy ever falls upon extremes; it pretends to have Scripture alone for judge of controversies, and in the meantime sets up as many judges as there are men and women in the Christian world. What good statesmen would they be who should ideate or fancy such a commonwealth as these men have framed to themselves a Church! They verify what St. Augustine objecteth against certain heretics: *You see that you go about to overthrow all authority of Scripture, and that every man's mind may be to himself a rule what he is to allow or disallow in every Scripture. . . .*

. . .

23. Moreover, there was no Scripture or written word for about two thousand years from Adam to Moses, whom all acknowledge to have been the first author of canonical Scripture; and again, for about two thousand years more, from Moses to Christ our Lord, holy Scripture was only among the people of Israel; and yet there were gentiles endued in those days with divine faith, as appeareth in Job and his friends. Wherefore during so many ages the Church alone was the decider of controversies and instructor of the faithful. Neither did the word written by Moses deprive that Church of her former infallibility or other qualities requisite for a judge. . . . Now the Church of Christ our Lord was before the Scriptures of the New Testament, which were not written instantly nor all at one time, but successively upon several occasions, and some after the decease of most of the apostles; and after they were written, they were not presently known to all churches; and of some there was a doubt in the Church for some ages after our Savior. Shall we then say that according as the Church by little and little received holy Scripture, she was by the like degrees divested of her possessed infallibility and power to decide controversies in religion? . . After the apostles' time and after the writing of Scriptures, heresies would be sure to rise, requiring in God's Church, for their discovery and condemnation, infallibility: either to write new canonical scripture, as was done in the apostles' time by occasion of emergent heresies; or infallibility to interpret Scriptures already written; or, without Scripture, by divine unwritten traditions and assistance of the Holy Ghost, to determine all controversies. . . . Certainly such addition of Scripture, with derogation or subtraction from the former power and infallibility of the Church, would have brought to the world division in matters of faith, and the Church had rather lost than gained by holy Scripture (which ought to be far from our tongues and thoughts), it being manifest that for decision of controversies, infallibility settled in a living judge is incomparably more useful and fit than if it were conceived as inherent in some inanimate writing.[14] . . . If Protestants will have the Scripture alone for their judge, let them first produce some Scripture affirming that by the entering thereof infallibility went out of the Church. D. Potter may remember what himself teacheth: that the Church is still endued with infallibility in points fundamental; and consequently, that infallibility in the Church doth well agree with the truth, the sanctity, yea, with the

---

[13] {William Whitaker, head of St. John's, Cambridge (d. 1595) was a prominent Calvinist theologian and controversialist; Thomas Bilson, Bishop of Winchester (d. 1616), a leading moderate churchman, author of *The perpetual government of Christ's Church* (1593), and one of the two supervising editors of the Authorized Version.}

[14] {Plato's *Statesman* is the *locus classicus* for this position.}

sufficiency of Scripture for all matters necessary to salvation. I would therefore gladly know out of what text he imagineth that the Church, by the coming of Scripture, was deprived of infallibility in some points and not in others? He affirmeth that the Jewish Synagogue retained infallibility in herself, notwithstanding the writing of the Old Testament; and will he so unworthily and unjustly deprive the Church of Christ of infallibility by reason of the New Testament? Especially if we consider that in the Old Testament, laws, ceremonies, rites, punishments, judgments, sacraments, sacrifices, &c. were more particularly and minutely delivered to the Jews than in the New Testament is done, our Savior leaving the determination or declaration of particulars to his Spouse, the Church, which therefore stands in need of infallibility more than the Jewish Synagogue. . . .[15]

. . .

25. Besides all this, the doctrine of Protestants is destructive of itself: for either they have certain and infallible means not to err in interpreting Scripture, or they have not. If not, then the Scripture (to them) cannot be a sufficient ground for infallible faith nor a mere judge in controversies. If they have certain infallible means and so cannot err in their interpretations of Scriptures, then they are able with infallibility to hear, examine, and determine all controversies of faith; and so they may be, and are, judges of controversies, although they use the Scriptures as a rule. And thus, against their own doctrine, they constitute another judge of controversies beside Scripture alone.

26. Lastly, I ask D. Potter whether this assertion, *Scripture alone is judge of all controversies in faith*, be a fundamental point of faith or no? He must be well advised before he say that it is a fundamental point, for he will have against him as many Protestants as teach that by Scripture alone it is impossible to know what books be Scripture, which yet to Protestants is the most necessary and chief point of all other. D. Covel expressly saith, *Doubtless it is a tolerable opinion in the Church of Rome . . . to affirm that the Scriptures are holy and divine in themselves but so esteemed by us for the authority of the Church.*[16] . . . If he answer that their tenet about the Scriptures being the only judge of controversies is not a fundamental point of faith, then, as he teacheth that the universal Church may err in points not fundamental . . . so the very principle upon which their whole faith is grounded remains to them uncertain. . . .

27. Since, then, the visible Church of Christ our Lord is that infallible *means whereby the revealed truths of Almighty God are conveyed to our understanding*, it followeth that to oppose her definitions is to resist God himself. . . .

ANSWER TO THE SECOND CHAPTER

Concerning the means whereby the revealed truths of God are conveyed to our understanding, and which must determine controversies in faith and religion.

[15] {For the oddly symmetrical puritan-presbyterian axiom that, since the Old Testament gave the Jews detailed rules for worship and ecclesiastical polity, so the New Testament must give Christians even more detailed rules, see book 3 of Hooker's *Laws* (1593) and the first two chapters of Milton's *The reason of Church government* (1642). Hooker, of course, denies the axiom.}

[16] [In his defense of M. Hooker's books, art. 4. p. 31 {i.e., William Covell, *A iust and temperate defence of the fiue books of ecclesiastical policie written by M. Richard Hooker* (London, 1603)}.]

Ad §1. He that would usurp an absolute lordship and tyranny over any people need not put himself to the trouble and difficulty of abrogating and disannulling the laws made to maintain the common liberty, for he may frustrate their intent and compass his own design as well, if he can get the power and authority to interpret them as he pleases, and add to them what he pleases, and to have his interpretations and additions stand for laws: if he can rule his people by his laws, and his laws by his lawyers. So the Church of Rome, to establish her tyranny over men's consciences, needed not either to abolish or corrupt the holy Scriptures, the pillars and supporters of Christian liberty (which, in regard of the numerous multitudes of copies dispersed through all places, translated into almost all languages, guarded with all solicitous care and industry, had been an impossible attempt); but the more expedite way, and therefore more likely to be successful, was to gain the opinion and esteem of the public and authorized interpreter of them, and the authority of adding to them what doctrine she pleased under the title of *traditions* or *definitions*. For by this means she might both serve herself of all those clauses of Scripture which might be drawn to cast a favorable countenance upon her ambitious pretenses (which in case the Scripture had been abolished she could not have done), and yet be secure enough of having either her power limited or her corruptions and abuses reformed by them, this being once settled in the minds of men *that unwritten doctrines, if proposed by her, were to be received with equal reverence to those that were written; and that the sense of Scripture was not that which seemed to men's reason and understanding to be so, but that which the Church of Rome should declare to be so, seemed it never so unreasonable and incongruous.* The matter being once thus ordered, and the holy Scriptures being made in effect not your directors and judges (no further than you please) but your servants and instruments . . . it is safe for you to put a crown on their head and a reed in their hands and to bow before them and cry *Hail, King of the Jews!* to pretend a great deal of *esteem and respect and reverence* to them, as here you do. But to little purpose is verbal reverence without entire submission and sincere obedience; and, as our Savior said of some, so the Scripture, could it speak, I believe would say to you, *Why call ye me, Lord, Lord, and do not that which I command you?* Cast away the vain and arrogant pretense of infallibility, which makes your errors incurable. Leave picturing God[17] and worshipping him by pictures. *Teach not for doctrine the commandments of men.* Debar not the laity of the testament of Christ's blood. Let your public prayers and psalms and hymns be in such language as is for the edification of the assistants {standers-by}. Take not from the clergy that liberty of marriage which Christ hath left them. Do not impose upon men that humility of worshipping angels which St. Paul condemns. Teach no more proper sacrifices of Christ but one. Acknowledge them that die in Christ to be blessed and *to rest from their labors.* Acknowledge the sacrament after consecration to be bread and wine, as well as Christ's body and blood. Acknowledge the gift of continency without marriage not to be given to all. Let not the weapons of your warfare be carnal, such as are massacres, treasons, persecutions, and, in a word, all means either violent or fraudulent. These and other things, which the Scripture commands you, do, and then we shall willingly give you such testimony as you deserve; but till you do so, to talk of estimation, respect, and reverence to the Scripture is nothing else but talk.

---

[17] {This is not necessarily a criticism of Laudian practice, which seems to have disallowed visual representation of the Father, the Trinity, the Godhead, etc.}

. . .

3. For, whereas you say no cause imaginable could avert your will from giving the function of supreme and sole judge to holy Writ but that the thing is impossible, and that by this means controversies are increased and not ended, you mean perhaps that you can or will imagine no other cause but these. But sure there is little reason you should measure other men's imaginations by your own. . . . For what indifferent and unprejudicate man may not easily conceive another cause which (I do not say does, but certainly) may pervert your wills and avert your understandings from submitting your religion and Church to a trial by Scripture? I mean the great and apparent and unavoidable danger, which by this means you would fall into, of losing the opinion which men have of your infallibility, and consequently your power and authority over men's consciences, and all that depends upon it. . . . As for the impossibility of Scriptures being the sole judge of controversies . . . I cannot but desire you to tell me, if Scripture cannot be the judge of any controversy, how shall that touching the Church and the notes of it be determined? And if it be the sole judge of this one, why may it not of others? Why not of all?—those only excepted wherein the Scripture itself is the subject of the question, which cannot be determined but by natural reason, the only principle beside Scripture which is common to Christians.

. . .

5. In the next words we have direct boy's play, a thing given with one hand and taken away with the other; an acknowledgment made in one line and retracted in the next. *We acknowledge* (say you) *Scripture to be a perfect rule forasmuch as a writing can be a rule; only we deny that it excludes unwritten tradition.* As if you should have said, we acknowledge it to be as perfect a rule as writing can be; only we deny it to be as perfect a rule as a writing may be. Either therefore you must revoke your acknowledgment or retract your retraction of it, for both cannot possibly stand together. For if you will stand to what you have granted, that *Scripture is as perfect a rule of faith as a writing can be*, you must then grant it both so complete that it needs no addition and so evident that it needs no interpretation, for both these properties are requisite to a perfect rule, and a writing is capable of both these properties.

. . .

7. Now, that a writing is capable of both these perfections, it is so plain that I am even ashamed to prove it. For he that denies it must say that *something may be spoken which cannot be written.* For if such a complete and evident rule of faith may be delivered by word of mouth, as you pretend it may and is; and whatsoever is delivered by word of mouth may also be written, then such a complete and evident rule of faith may also be written. If you will have more light added to the sun, answer me then to these questions: whether your Church can set down in writing all these which she pretends to be divine unwritten traditions and add them to the verities already written? And whether she can set us down such interpretations of all obscurities in the faith as shall need no further interpretations? If she cannot, then she hath not that power which you pretend she hath, of being an *infallible teacher of all divine verities* and an infallible interpreter of obscurities in the faith; for she cannot teach us all divine verities, if she cannot write them down; neither is that an interpretation which needs again to be interpreted. If she can, let her do it, and then we shall have a writing not only capable of, but actually endowed with both these perfections

of being both so complete as to need no addition and so evident as to need no interpretation. . . .

8. You will say that *though a writing be never so perfect a rule of faith, yet it must be beholden to tradition to give it this testimony, that it is a rule of faith and the word of God.* I answer . . . that it is one thing to be a perfect rule of faith, another to be proved so unto us. And thus, though a writing could not be proved to us to be a perfect rule of faith by its own saying so (for nothing is proved true by being said or written in a book, but only by tradition, which is a thing credible of itself), yet it may be so in itself, and contain all the material objects, all the particular articles of our faith, without any dependence upon tradition—even this also not excepted, that *this writing doth contain the rule of faith.* Now when Protestants affirm against Papists that Scripture is a perfect rule of faith, their meaning is not that by Scripture all things absolutely may be proved which are to be believed; for it can never be proved by Scripture to a gainsayer that there is a God or that the book called Scripture is the word of God; for he that will deny these assertions when they are spoken, will believe them never a whit the more because you can shew them written. But their meaning is that the Scripture—to them which presuppose it divine and a rule of faith, as Papists and Protestants do—contains all the material objects of faith, is a complete and total, and not only an imperfect and a partial rule.

. . .

10. . . . For Scripture might very well be all true though it contain not all necessary divine truth. But unless it do so, it cannot be a perfect rule of faith, for that which wants anything is not perfect. For I hope you do not imagine that we conceive any antipathy between God's word written and unwritten, but that both might very well stand together. All that we say is this, that we have reason to believe that God *de facto* hath ordered the matter so that all the gospel of Christ, the whole covenant between God and man, is now written. Whereas if he had pleased, he might have so disposed it that part might have been written and part unwritten; but then he would have taken order to whom we should have had recourse for that part of it which was not written; which, seeing he hath not done (as the progress shall demonstrate), it is evident he hath left no part of it unwritten. We know no man therefore that says it were any injury to the written word to be joined with the unwritten, if there were any wherewith it might be joined—but that we deny. The fidelity of a keeper may very well consist with the authority of the thing committed to his custody, but we know no one society of Christians that is such a faithful keeper as you pretend. The Scripture itself was not kept so faithfully by you, but that you suffered infinite variety of readings to creep into it, all which could not possibly be divine, and yet in several parts of your Church, all of them until the last age were so esteemed. The interpretations of obscure places of Scripture, which without question the apostles taught the primitive Christians, are wholly lost; there remains no certainty scarce of any one. Those worlds of miracles which our Savior did which were not written, for want of writing are vanished out of the memory of men; and many profitable things which the apostles taught and writ not (as that which St. Paul glanceth at in his second epistle to the Thessalonians of the cause of the hindrance of the coming of Antichrist) are wholly lost and extinguished, so unfaithful or negligent hath been this keeper of divine verities, whose eyes, like the keeper's of Israel (you say) have never slumbered nor slept. Lastly, we deny not but a judge and a law might well stand together, but we deny that there is any such judge of God's

appointment. Had he intended any such judge, he would have named him, lest otherwise (as now it is) our judge of controversies should be our greatest controversy.

11. *Ad* §2, 3, 4, 5, 6. In your second paragraph, you sum up those arguments wherewith you intend to prove that *Scripture alone cannot be judge in controversies*, wherein I profess unto you beforehand that you will fight without an adversary. For though Protestants, being warranted by some of the Fathers, have called Scripture the judge of controversy; and you, in saying here that Scripture alone cannot be judge, imply that it may be called in some sense a judge, though not alone; yet to speak properly (as men should speak when they write of controversies in religion), the Scripture is not a judge of controversies but *a rule only, and the only rule for Christians, to judge them by*. Every man is to judge for himself with the judgment of discretion, and to choose either his religion first, and then his Church, as we say; or, as you, his Church first, and then his religion. But by the consent of both sides, every man is to judge and choose; and the rule whereby he is to guide his choice, if he be a natural man, is reason; if he be already a Christian, Scripture—which we say is the rule to judge controversies by. Yet not all simply, but all the controversies of Christians, of those that are already agreed upon this first principle, that the Scripture is the word of God. But that there is any man, or any company of men, appointed to be judge for all men, that we deny; and that I believe you will never prove. The very truth is, we say no more in this matter than evidence of truth hath made you confess in plain terms in the beginning of this chapter, *viz.* that *Scripture is a perfect rule of faith forasmuch as a writing can be a rule*. So that all your reasons whereby you labor to dethrone the Scripture from this office of judging, we might let pass as impertinent to the conclusion which we maintain and you have already granted, yet out of courtesy we will consider them.

12. Your first is this: *a judge must be a person fit to end controversies, but the Scripture is not a person nor fit to end controversies, no more than the law would be without the judges; therefore, though it may be a rule, it cannot be a judge*. Which conclusion I have already granted; only my request is that you will permit Scripture to have the properties of a rule: that is, to be fit to direct everyone that will make the best use of it to that end for which it was ordained; and that is as much as we need desire. For as if I were to go a journey and had a guide which could not err, I needed not to know my way; so on the other side, if I know my way or have a plain rule to know it by, I shall need no guide. Grant therefore Scripture to be such a rule, and it will quickly take away all necessity of having an infallible guide. But *without a living judge, it will be no fitter* (you say) *to end controversies than the law alone to end suits*. I answer, if the law were plain and perfect, and men honest and desirous to understand aright and obey it, he that says it were not fit to end controversies must either want understanding himself or think the world wants it. Now the Scripture, we pretend, in things necessary is plain and perfect; and men, we say, are obliged under pain of damnation to seek the true sense of it and not to wrest it to their pre-conceived fancies. Such a law therefore, to such men, cannot but be very fit to end all controversies necessary to be ended. For others that are not so, they will end when the world ends, and that is time enough.

. . . *If the pope's decrees*, you will say, *be obscure, he can explain himself, and so the Scripture cannot*. But the Holy Ghost that speaks in Scripture can do so, if he please; and when he is pleased, will do so. . . . Besides, he can, which you cannot warrant me of the pope or a council, speak at first so plainly that his words shall need no further explanation—and so in things necessary we believe he hath done. . . . For if the Scripture (as it is in things necessary) be plain, why should it be more necessary to have a judge to interpret it in plain places than to have a judge to interpret the meaning of a council's decrees, and others to interpret their interpretations, and others to interpret theirs, and so on forever? And where they are not plain, there if we, using diligence to find the truth, do yet miss of it and fall into error, there is no danger in it. They that err and they that do not err may both be saved. So that those places which contain things necessary, and wherein errors were dangerous, need no infallible interpreter because they are plain; and those that are obscure need none because they contain not things necessary, neither is error in them dangerous.

13. *The law-maker speaking in the law,* I grant it, *is no more easily understood than the law itself,* for his speech is nothing else but the law; I grant it *very necessary that besides the law-maker speaking in the law, there should be other judges to determine civil and criminal controversies, and to give every man that justice which the law allows him.* But your argument drawn from hence to shew a necessity of a visible judge in controversies of religion, I say is sophistical, and that for many reasons.

. . .

16. Thirdly, in civil and criminal causes the parties have for the most part so much interest and very often so little honesty that they will not submit to a law, though never so plain, if it be against them; or will not see it to be against them, though it be so never so plainly; whereas, if men were honest, and the law were plain and extended to all cases, there would be little need of judges. Now in matters of religion, when the question is whether every man be a fit judge and chooser for himself, we suppose men honest and such as understand the difference between a moment and eternity. And such men, we conceive, will think it highly concerns them to be of the true religion, but nothing at all that this or that religion should be the true. And then we suppose that all the necessary points of religion are plain and easy, and consequently every man in this cause to be a competent judge for himself, because it concerns himself to judge right as much as eternal happiness is worth. And if through his own default he judge amiss, he alone shall suffer for it.

17. Fourthly, in civil controversies we are obliged only to external passive obedience, and not to an internal and active. We are bound to obey the sentence of the judge, or not to resist it, but not always to believe it just; but in matters of religion, such a judge is required whom we should be obliged to believe to have judged aright. So that in civil controversies every honest understanding man is fit to be a judge, but in religion none but he that is infallible.

18. Fifthly, in civil causes there is means and power, when the judge hath decreed, to compel men to obey his sentence; otherwise, I believe, laws alone would be to as much purpose for the ending of differences as laws and judges both. But all the power in the world is neither fit to convince nor able to compel a man's conscience to consent to anything. Worldly terror may prevail so far as to make men profess a religion which they believe not (such men, I mean, who know not that there is a heaven provided for martyrs and a hell for those that dissemble such truths as are necessary to be professed), but to force either any man to believe what he believes not or any honest man to dissemble what he does believe (if God commands him to profess it) or to profess what he does not believe, all the powers in the world are too weak, with all the powers of hell to assist them.

19. Sixthly, in civil controversies the case cannot be so put but there may be a judge to end it who is not a party; in controversies of religion it is in a manner impossible to be avoided but the judge must be a party. For this must be the first, whether he be a judge or no, and in that he must be a party. Sure I am, the pope, in the controversies of our time, is a chief party, for it highly concerns him, even as much as his popedom is worth, not to yield any one point of his religion to be erroneous. And he is a man subject to like passions with other men; and therefore we may justly decline his sentence for fear temporal respects should either blind his judgment or make him pronounce against it.

20. Seventhly, in civil controversies it is impossible Titus should hold the land in question and Sempronius too; and therefore either the plaintiff must injure the defendant by disquieting his possession, or the defendant wrong the plaintiff by keeping his right from him. But in controversies of religion, the case is otherwise. I may hold my opinion, and do you no wrong; and you yours, and do me none; nay, we may both of us hold our opinion and yet do ourselves no harm, provided the difference be not touching anything necessary to salvation, and that we love truth so well as to be diligent to inform our conscience and constant in following it.

21. Eighthly, for the deciding of civil controversies, men may appoint themselves a judge; but in matters of religion, this office may be given to none but whom God hath designed for it, who doth not always give us those things which we conceive most expedient for ourselves.

22. Ninthly and lastly, for the ending of civil controversies, who does not see it is absolutely necessary that not only judges should be appointed, but that it should be known and unquestioned who they are? Thus all the judges of our land are known men, known to be judges, and no man can doubt or question but these are the men. Otherwise, if it were a disputable thing who were these judges, and they have no certain warrant for their authority but only some topical[18] congruities, would not any man say such judges in all likelihood would rather multiply controversies than end them? So likewise if our Savior, the king of heaven, had intended that all controversies in religion should be by some visible judge finally determined, who can doubt but in plain terms he would have expressed himself about this matter? He would have said plainly, The bishop of Rome I have appointed to decide all emergent controversies. For that our Savior designed the bishop of Rome to this office, and yet would not say so nor cause it to be written *ad rei memoriam* by any of the evangelists or apostles so much as once, but leave it to be drawn out of uncertain principles by thirteen or fourteen more uncertain consequences, he that can believe it, let him.

23. All these reasons, I hope, will convince you that though we have, and have great necessity of, judges in civil and criminal causes, yet you may not conclude from hence that there is any public authorized judge to determine controversies in religion, nor any necessity there should be any.

24. *But the Scripture stands in need of some watchful and unerring eye to guard it, by means of whose assured vigilancy, we may undoubtedly receive it sincere and pure.* Very true, but this is no other than the watchful eye of divine providence, the goodness whereof will

---

[18] {merely probable}

never suffer that the Scripture should be depraved and corrupted, but that in them should be always extant a conspicuous and plain way to eternal happiness. Neither can anything be more palpably inconsistent with his goodness than to suffer Scripture to be undiscernibly corrupted in any matter of moment and yet to exact of men the belief of those verities which, without their fault or knowledge or possibility of prevention, were defaced out of them. So that God requiring of men to believe Scripture in its purity engages himself to see it preserved in sufficient purity, and you need not fear but he will satisfy his engagement. You say we can have no assurance of this but your Church's vigilance. But if we had no other, we were in a hard case, for who could then assure us that your Church hath been so vigilant . . . there being various lections in the ancient copies of your Bibles. . . . Yet the want of such a protection was no hindrance to their salvation; and why then shall having of it be necessary for ours? But then, this vigilancy of your Church, what means have we to be ascertained of it? First, the thing is not evident of itself—which is evident, because many do not believe it. Neither can anything be pretended to give evidence to it but only some places of Scripture, of whose incorruption more than any other, what is it that can secure me? If you say the Church's vigilancy, you are in a circle, proving the Scriptures uncorrupted by the Church's vigilancy, and the Church's vigilancy by the incorruption of some places of Scripture, and again the incorruption of those places by the Church's vigilancy. If you name any other means, then that means which secures me of the Scripture's incorruption in those places will also serve to assure me of the same in other places. For my part, abstracting from[19] divine providence which will never suffer the way to heaven to be blocked up or made invisible, I know no other means (I mean, no other natural and rational means) to be assured hereof than I have that any other book is uncorrupted. For though I have a greater degree of rational and human assurance of that than this in regard of divers considerations, which makes it more credible that the Scripture hath been preserved from any material alteration, yet my assurance of both is of the same kind and condition: both moral assurances, and neither physical nor mathematical.

25. To the next argument the reply is obvious: *that though we do not believe the books of Scripture to be canonical because they say so* . . . yet we believe not this upon the authority of your Church but upon the credibility of universal tradition, which is a thing credible of itself and therefore fit to be rested on, whereas the authority of your Church is not so. . . . But yet (to return you one suppose for another), suppose I should for this and all other things submit to her direction, how could she assure me that I should not be misled by doing so? She pretends indeed infallibility herein, but how can she assure us that she hath it? What, by Scripture? That, you say, cannot assure us of its own infallibility, and therefore not of yours. What then, by reason? That, you say, may deceive in other things, and why not in this? How then will she assure us hereof? By saying so? Of this very affirmation there will remain the same question still: how can it prove itself to be infallibly true? Neither can there be an end of the like multiplied demands till we rest in something evident of itself which demonstrates to the world that this Church is infallible. And seeing there is no such rock for the infallibility of this Church to be settled on, it must of necessity, like the island of Delos, float up and down forever. And yet upon this point, according to Papists, all other controversies in faith depend.

[19] {apart from}

. . .

27. . . . when Scripture is affirmed to be the rule by which all controversies of religion are to be decided, those are to be excepted out of this generality which are concerning the Scripture itself. . . . Just as a merchant, showing a ship of his own, may say "all my substance is in this ship," and yet never intend to deny that his ship is part of his substance nor yet to say that his ship is in itself. . . . Your negative conclusion therefore, that these *questions touching Scripture are not decidable by Scripture* . . . is evident of itself, and I grant it without more ado. But your corollary from it, which you would insinuate to your unwary reader, *that therefore they are to be decided by your, or any visible Church*, is a mere inconsequence. . . . as if there were nothing in the world capable of this office but the Scripture or the present Church. Having concluded against Scripture, you conceive, but too hastily, that you have concluded for the Church. But the truth is, neither the one nor the other have anything to do with this matter. For, first, the question whether such or such a book be canonical Scripture, though it may be decided negatively out of Scripture by showing apparent and irreconcilable contradictions between it and some other book confessedly canonical, yet affirmatively it cannot, but only by the testimonies of the ancient Churches: any book being to be received as undoubtedly canonical or to be doubted of as uncertain or rejected as apocryphal, according as it was received or doubted of or rejected by them. Then for the question, of various readings which is the true? It is in reason evident and confessed by your own Pope that there is no possible determination of it but only by comparison with ancient copies. And, lastly, for controversies about different translations of Scripture, the learned have the same means to satisfy themselves in it as in the questions which happen about the translation of any other author: that is, skill in the language of the original, and comparing translations with it. . . .

. . .

49. . . . you tell us that *if there be some other means precedent to Scripture to beget faith, this can be no other than the Church.* By the Church, we know you do and must understand the Roman Church, so that in effect you say no man can have faith but he must be moved to it by your Church's authority; and that is to say that the King and all other Protestants to whom you write, though they verily think they are Christians and believe the Gospel because they assent to the truth of it and would willingly die for it, yet indeed are infidels and believe nothing. The Scripture tells us, *The heart of man knoweth no man, but the spirit of man which is in him.* And who are you to take upon you to make us believe that we do not believe what we know we do? But if I may think verily that I believe the Scripture, and yet not believe it; how know you that you believe the Roman Church? I am as verily and as strongly persuaded that I believe the Scripture as you are that you believe the Church, and if I may be deceived, why may not you? Again, what more ridiculous, and against sense and experience, than to affirm that there are not millions amongst you and us that believe upon no other reason than their education and the authority of their parents and teachers and the opinion they have of them, the tenderness of the subject and aptness to receive impressions supplying the defect and imperfection of the agent. And will you proscribe from heaven all those believers of your own creed who do indeed lay the foundation of their faith (for I cannot call it by any other name) no deeper than upon the authority of their father or master or parish priest? Certainly, if they have no

true faith, your Church is very full of infidels. Suppose Xaverius,[20] by the holiness of his life, had converted some Indians to Christianity, who could (for so I will suppose) have no knowledge of your Church but from him, and therefore must last of all build their faith of the Church upon their opinion of Xaverius: do these remain as very pagans after conversion as they were before? Are they brought to assent in their souls and obey in their lives the gospel of Christ, only to be tantalized and not saved . . . because, forsooth, it is a man, and not the Church, that begets faith in them? What if their motive to believe be not in reason sufficient? Do they therefore not believe what they do believe because they do it upon insufficient motives? They choose the faith imprudently perhaps, but yet they choose it. . . . But yet I know not why the authority of one holy man, which apparently hath no ends upon me, joined with the goodness of the Christian faith, might not be a far greater and more rational motive to me to embrace Christianity than any I can have to continue in paganism. . . .

. . .

84. *Ad* 17. §. In this division you charge us with *great uncertainty concerning the meaning of Scripture*—which hath been answered already by saying that, if you speak of plain places (and in such all things necessary are contained), we are sufficiently certain of the meaning of them, neither need they any interpreter; if of obscure and difficult places, we confess we are uncertain of the sense of many of them, but then we say there is no necessity we should be certain, for if God's will had been we should have understood him more certainly, he would have spoken more plainly. And we say, besides, that as we are uncertain, so are you too; which he that doubts of, let him read your commentators upon the Bible and observe their various and dissonant interpretations, and he shall in this point need no further satisfaction.

85. But seeing there are *contentions among us, we are taught by nature and Scripture and experience* (so you tell us out of Mr. Hooker) *to seek for the ending of them by submitting unto some judicial sentence whereunto neither part may refuse to stand.* This is very true. Neither should you need to persuade us to seek such a means of ending all our controversies, if we could tell where to find it. But this we know, that none is fit to pronounce for all the world a judicial definite obliging sentence in controversies of religion, but only such a man or such a society of men as is authorized thereto by God. And besides, we are able to demonstrate that it hath not been the pleasure of God to give to any man, or society of men, any such authority. And therefore, though we wish heartily that all controversies were ended, as we do that all sin were abolished, yet we have little hope of the one or the other until the world be ended, and in the meanwhile think it best to content ourselves with and to persuade others unto an *unity of charity and mutual toleration,* seeing God hath authorized no man to force all men to *unity of opinion.* . . .

. . .

93. . . . God is not defective in things necessary; neither will he leave himself without witness, nor the world without means of knowing his will and doing it. And therefore it was necessary that by his providence he should preserve the Scripture from any indiscernible corruption in those things which he would have known. . . . But now neither is God lavish in superfluities; and therefore, having given us means sufficient for our direction

---

[20] {St. Francis Xavier (d. 1552), cofounder of the Jesuit order and important missionary.}

and power sufficient to make use of these means, he will not constrain or necessitate us to make use of these means, for that were to cross the end of our creation, which was to be glorified by our free obedience, whereas necessity and freedom cannot stand together; that were to reverse the law which he hath prescribed to himself in his dealing with man: and that is *to set life and death before him, and leave him in the hands of his own counsel.* God gave the wise men a star to lead them to Christ, but he did not necessitate them to follow the guidance of this star; that was left to their liberty. God gave the children of Israel *a fire to lead them by night, and a pillar of cloud by day*, but he constrained no man to follow them; that was left to their liberty. So he gives the Church the Scripture, which, in those things which are to be believed or done, are plain and easy to be followed like the wise men's star. Now that which he desires of us, on our part, is the obedience of faith and love of the truth and desire to find the true sense of it and industry in searching it and humility in following and constancy in professing it; all which, if he should work in us by an absolute irresistible necessity, he could no more require of us as our duty than he can of the sun to shine. . . .

. . .

110. *Ad* §20. If by a private spirit, you mean a particular persuasion that a doctrine is true, which some men pretend but cannot prove to come from the Spirit of God, I say, to refer controversies to Scripture is not to refer them to this kind of private spirit. For is there not a manifest difference between saying *the Spirit of God tells me that this is the meaning of such a text* (which no man can possibly know to be true, it being a secret thing)[21] and between {*sic*} saying *these and these reasons I have to show that this or that is true doctrine, or that this or that is the meaning of such a Scripture*—reason being a public and certain thing, and exposed to all men's trial and examination? But now, if by private spirit you understand every man's particular reason, then your first and second inconvenience will presently be reduced to one, and shortly to none at all.

111. *Ad* §. 20. And does not also giving the office of judicature to the Church come to confer it upon every particular man? for before any man believes the Church infallible, must he not have reason to induce him to believe it to be so? and must he not judge of those reasons, whether they be indeed good and firm, or captious and sophistical? Or would you have all men believe all your doctrine upon the Church's infallibility, and the Church's infallibility they know not why?

112. Secondly, supposing they are to be guided by the Church, they must use their own particular reason to find out which is the Church. And to that purpose you yourselves give a great many notes,[22] which you pretend first to be certain notes of the Church, and then to be peculiar to your Church and agreeable to none else; but you do not so much as pretend that either of those pretences is evident of itself, and therefore you go about to prove them both by reasons; and those reasons, I hope, every particular man is to judge of whether they do indeed conclude and convince that which they are alleged for: that is, that these marks are indeed certain notes of the Church, and then that your Church hath them, and no other.

---

[21] {See Laud, *Conference* <384–85>.}

[22] {*Theol.* Any of certain characteristics—as unity, sanctity, catholicity, and apostolicity—by which the true Church may be known (*OED*).}

113. One of these notes, indeed the only note of a true and uncorrupted Church, is conformity with antiquity—I mean the most ancient Church of all, that is, the primitive and apostolic. Now how is it possible any man should examine your Church by this note, but he must by his own particular judgment find out what was the doctrine of the primitive Church and what is the doctrine of the present Church, and be able to answer all these arguments which are brought to prove repugnance between them? Otherwise he shall but pretend to make use of this note for the finding the true Church, but indeed make no use of it, but receive the Church at a venture, as the most of you do, not one in a hundred being able to give any tolerable reason for it. So that instead of reducing men to particular reasons, you reduce them to none at all, but to chance and passion and prejudice and such other ways, which if they lead one to the truth, they lead hundreds, nay thousands, to falsehood. But it is a pretty thing to consider how these men can blow hot and cold out of the same mouth to serve several purposes. Is there hope of gaining a proselyte? Then they will tell you, God hath given every man reason to follow, and if the blind lead the blind, both shall fall into the ditch; that it is no good reason for a man's religion that he was born and brought up in it, for then a Turk should have as much reason to be a Turk as a Christian to be a Christian; that every man hath a judgment of discretion which, if they will make use of, they shall easily find that the true Church hath always such and such marks, and that their Church hath them, and no others but theirs. But then, if any of theirs be persuaded to a sincere and sufficient trial of their Church, even by their own notes of it, and to try whether they be indeed so conformable to antiquity as they pretend, then their note is changed: you must not use your own reason nor your judgment, but refer all to the Church and believe her to be conformable to antiquity, though they have no reason for it; nay, though they have evident reason to the contrary. For my part, I am certain that God hath given us our reason to discern between truth and falsehood; and he that makes not this use of it but believes things he knows not why, I say it is by chance that he believes the truth and not by choice, and that I cannot but fear that God will not accept of this *sacrifice of fools*.

114. But you that would not have men follow their reason, what would you have them follow? their passions? or pluck out their eyes and go blindfold? No, you say, you would have them follow authority. On God's name, let them. We also would have them follow authority, for it is upon the authority of universal tradition that we would have them believe Scripture. But then, as for the authority which you would have them follow, you will let them see reason why they should follow it. And is not this to go a little about? To leave reason for a short turn, and then to come to it again, and to do that which you condemn in others? It being indeed a plain impossibility for any man to submit his reason but to reason; for he that doth it to authority must of necessity think himself to have greater reason to believe that authority. . . .

115. And whereas you say that a Protestant *admits of Fathers, Councils, Church, as far as they agree with Scripture, which upon the matter is himself*; I say, you admit neither of them, nor the Scripture itself, but only so far as it agrees with your Church; and your Church you admit because you think you have reason to do so; so that by you as well as Protestants, all is finally resolved into your own reason.

116. . . . So that the difference between a Papist and a Protestant is this: not that the one judges and the other does not judge; but that the one judges his guide to be

infallible, the other, his way to be manifest. *This same pernicious doctrine is taught by Brentius, Zanchius, Cartwright, and others.*[23] It is so in very deed, but it is taught also by some others whom you little think of. It is taught by St. Paul, where he says, *Try all things; hold fast that which is good.* . . . It is taught by St. Peter in these: *Be ye ready to render a reason of the hope that is in you.* Lastly, this very pernicious doctrine is taught by our Savior in these words: *If the blind lead the blind, both shall fall into the ditch.* . . . All which speeches, if they do not advise men to make use of their reason for the choice of their religion, I must confess myself to understand nothing. . . .

117. But you demand, *what good statesmen would they be who should ideate or fancy such a commonwealth as these men have framed to themselves a Church?* Truly if this be all the fault they have, that they say *every man is to use his own judgment in the choice of his religion, and not to believe this or that sense of Scripture upon the bare authority of any learned man or men, when he conceives he hath reasons to the contrary which are of more weight than their authority,* I know no reason but, notwithstanding all this, they might be as good statesmen as any of the society. But what hath this to do with commonwealths, where men are bound only to external obedience unto the laws and judgment of courts, but not to an internal approbation of them, no, nor to conceal their judgment of them if they disapprove them? As, if I conceived I had reason to mislike the law of punishing simple theft with death, as Sir Thomas More did, I might profess lawfully my judgment, and represent my reasons to the king or commonwealth in a Parliament, as Sir Thomas More did, without committing any fault or fearing any punishment.

. . .

122. And how it can be any way advantageous to civil government that men without warrant from God should usurp a tyranny over other men's consciences and prescribe unto them without reason, and sometimes against reason, what they shall believe, you must show us plainer if you desire we should believe. For to say, *verily I do not see but it must be so,* is no good demonstration. For whereas you say *that a man may be a passionate and seditious creature,* from whence you would have us infer that he may make use of his interpretation to satisfy his passion and raise sedition, there were some color in this consequence if we (as you do) made private men infallible interpreters for others; for then indeed they might lead disciples after them and use them as instruments for their vile purposes. But when we say they can only interpret for themselves, what harm they can do by their passionate or seditious interpretations but only endanger both their temporal and eternal happiness, I cannot imagine; for though we deny the pope or Church of Rome to be an infallible judge, yet we do not deny but that there are judges which may proceed with certainty enough against all seditious persons such as draw men to disobedience either against Church or state, as well as against rebels and traitors and thieves and murderers.

. . .

150. . . . But though we pretend not to certain means of not erring in interpreting all Scripture, particularly such places as are obscure and ambiguous, yet this, methinks,

---

[23] {All three are 16th-century reformers: Thomas Cartwright (d. 1603) a fiery English puritan-presbyterian; Jerome Zanchius (d. 1590) an Italian Reformed biblical exegete and rigid predestinarian; and John Brent (d. 1570), a Lutheran in his sacramental theology, but with a proto-Congregationalist ecclesiology.}

should be no impediment but that we may have certain means of not erring in and about the sense of those places which are so plain and clear that they need no interpreters; and in such, we say, our faith is contained. If you ask me how I can be sure that I know the true meaning of these places, I ask you again, can you be sure that you understand what I, or any man else, says? They that heard our Savior and the apostles preach, could they have sufficient assurance that they understood at any time what they would have them do? If not, to what end did they hear them? If they could, why may we not be as well assured that we understand sufficiently what we conceive plain in their writings?

. . .

152. . . . God be thanked that we have sufficient means to be certain enough of the truth of our faith. But the privilege of not being in possibility of erring, that we challenge not, because we have as little reason as you to do so, and you have none at all. If you ask, seeing we may possibly err, how can we be assured we do not? I ask you again, seeing your eye-sight may deceive you, how can you be sure you see the sun when you do see it? Perhaps you may be in a dream, and perhaps you, and all the men in the world, have been so when they thought they were awake, and then only awake when they thought they dreamt. But this I am sure of, as sure as that God is good, that he will require no impossibilities of us: not an infallible nor a certainly unerring belief, unless he hath given us certain means to avoid error; and if we use those which we have, he will never require of us that we use that which we have not.

153. Now from this mistaken ground, that it is all one to have means of avoiding error and to be in no danger nor possibility of error, you infer upon us an absurd conclusion: *that we make ourselves able to determine controversies of faith with infallibility and judges of controversies.* For the latter part of this inference, we acknowledge and embrace it: we do make ourselves judges of controversies; that is, we do make use of our own understanding in the choice of our religion. But this, if it be a crime, is common to us with you (as I have proved above). . . . But then again I must tell you, you have done ill to confound together judges and infallible judges, unless you will say either that we have no judges in our courts of civil judicature, or that they are all infallible.

. . .

156. Yet when we say the Scripture is the only rule to judge all controversies by, methinks you should easily conceive that we would be understood of all those that are possible to be judged by Scripture, and of those that arise among such as believe the Scripture. For, if I had a controversy with an atheist whether there was a God or no, I would not say that the Scripture were a rule to judge this by, seeing that, doubting whether there be a God or no, he must needs doubt whether the Scripture be the word of God. . . . But among such men only as are already agreed upon this, that the Scripture is the word of God, we say all controversies that arise about faith are either not at all decidable, and consequently not necessary to be believed one way or other, or they may be determined by Scripture. In a word, that all things necessary to be believed are evidently contained in Scripture, and what is not there evidently contained cannot be necessary to be believed. And our reason hereof is convincing, because nothing can challenge {lay claim to} our belief but what hath thus descended to us from Christ by original and universal tradition. Now nothing but Scripture hath thus descended to us; therefore nothing but Scripture can challenge our belief. . . .

. . .

159. Notwithstanding . . . I conceive this doctrine {that Scripture is the rule of faith} not fundamental, because if a man should believe Christian religion wholly and entirely, and live according to it, such a man, though he should not know or not believe the Scripture to be a rule of faith . . . my opinion is he may be saved; and my reason is, because he performs the entire condition of the new covenant, which is that we believe the matter of the gospel—and not that it is contained in these or these books. So that the books of Scripture are not so much the objects of our faith as the instruments of conveying it to our understanding. . . .

160. . . . A judge may possibly err in judgment; can he therefore never have assurance that he hath judged right? A traveler may possibly mistake his way; must I therefore be doubtful whether I am in the right way from my hall to my chamber? Or can our London carrier have no certainty, in the middle of the day, when he is sober and in his wits, that he is in the way to London? . . .

. . .

162. Besides (you say) *among public conclusions defended in Oxford the year 1633, to the questions whether the Church have authority to determine controversies of faith and to interpret holy Scripture, the answer to both is affirmative.* But what now if I should tell you that in the year 1632, among public conclusions defended in Douai, one was *that God predeterminates men to all their actions, good, bad, and indifferent*—will you think yourself obliged to be of this opinion? If you will, say so; if not, do as you would be done by. Again, methinks so subtle a man as you are should easily apprehend a wide difference between authority to do a thing and infallibility in doing it—and again, between a conditional infallibility and an absolute. The former, the Doctor {Potter}, together with the Article of the Church of England, attributeth to the Church, nay, to particular Churches, and I subscribe to his opinion: that is, an authority of determining controversies of faith according to plain and evident Scripture and universal tradition,[24] and infallibility while they proceed according to this rule. As if there should arise an heretic that should call in question Christ's passion and resurrection, the Church had authority to decide this controversy and infallible direction how to do it, and to excommunicate this man if he should persist in error. I hope you will not deny but that the judges have authority to determine criminal and civil controversies; and yet I hope you will not say that they are absolutely infallible in their determinations—infallible while they proceed according to law, and if they do so; but not infallibly certain that they shall ever do so. . . .

‡

ANSWER TO THE THIRD CHAPTER

Wherein it is maintained that the distinction of points fundamental and not fundamental is, in this present controversy, good and pertinent, and that the catholic Church may err in the latter kind of said points.

[24] {This seems considerably weaker than Laud's claim in the 1639 Preface to *Conference with Fisher*, that the Church has authority to determine the doubtful and difficult places of Scripture *<supra>*.}

13 . . . God himself hath told us that *where much is given, much shall be required; where little is given, little shall be required.* To infants, deaf men, madmen, nothing, for aught we know, is given; and if it be so, of them nothing shall be required. Others, perhaps, may have means only given them to believe *that God is, and that he is a rewarder of them that seek him*; and to whom thus much only is given, to them it shall not be damnable that they believe but only this much. Which methinks is very manifest from the Apostle in the Epistle to the Hebrews, where, having first said that *without faith it is impossible to please God,* he subjoins as his reason, *For whosoever cometh unto God must believe that God is, and that he is a rewarder of them that seek him.* Where, in my opinion, this is plainly intimated, that this is the *minimum quod sic,* the lowest degree of faith wherewith, in men capable of faith, God will be pleased; and that with this lowest degree he will be pleased where means of rising higher are deficient.[25] . . . Now it is possible that they which never heard of Christ may seek God; therefore it is true, that even they shall please him and be rewarded by him. I say rewarded, not with bringing them immediately to salvation without Christ, but with bringing them, according to his good pleasure, first to faith in Christ, and so to salvation. To which belief the story of Cornelius in the tenth chapter of the Acts of the Apostles, and St. Peter's words to him, are to me a great inducement. For, first, it is evident he believed not in Christ but was a mere gentile . . . and yet we are assured that *his prayers and alms (even while he was in that state) came up for a memorial before God, that his prayer was heard and his alms had in remembrance in the sight of God. . . .*

. . .

26. . . . Neither is your argument concluding, when you say *if in such things she may be deceived she must be always uncertain of all such things,* for my sense may sometimes possibly deceive me, yet I am certain enough that I see what I see and feel what I feel. Our judges are not infallible in their judgments, yet are they certain enough that they judge aright and that they proceed according to the evidence that is given when they condemn a thief or a murderer to the gallows. A traveler is not always certain of his way but often mistaken; and doth it therefore follow that he can have no assurance that Charing-Cross is his right way from the Temple to Whitehall? The ground of your error here is your not distinguishing between actual certainty and absolute infallibility. Geometricians are not infallible in their own science, yet they are very certain of those things which they see demonstrated; and carpenters are not infallible, yet certain of the straightness of those things which agree with the rule and square. So, though the Church be not infallibly certain that in all her definitions, whereof some are about disputable and ambiguous matters, she shall proceed according to her rule; yet being certain of the infallibility of her rule, and that, in this or that thing, she doth manifestly proceed according to it, she may be certain of the truth of some particular decrees, and yet not certain that she shall never decree but what is true.

‡

---

[25] {cf. Laud, *Conference* <379>.}

THE ANSWER TO THE FOURTH CHAPTER

Wherein is shewed that the Creed contains all necessary points of mere belief

1. *Ad* §1–6. Concerning the Creed's containing the fundamentals of Christianity, this is Dr. Potter's assertion . . . *The Creed of the apostles (as it is explained in the latter creeds of the catholic Church) is esteemed a sufficient summary or catalogue of fundamentals by the best learned Romanists, and by antiquity.*

2. By *fundamentals* he understands not the fundamental rules of good life and action . . . but the fundamental doctrines of faith, such as, though they have influence upon our lives (as every essential doctrine of Christianity hath), yet we are commanded to believe them and not to do them. The assent of our understandings is required to them but not obedience from our wills.

3. But these speculative doctrines again he distinguisheth . . . into two kinds: of the first are those which are the objects of faith in and for themselves; which, by their own nature and God's prime intention, are essential parts of the gospel; such, as the teachers in the Church cannot without mortal sin omit to teach the learners; such, as are intrinsical to the covenant between God and man; and not only plainly revealed by God, and so certain truths, but also commanded to be preached to all men and to be believed distinctly by all, and so necessary truths. Of the second sort are accidental, circumstantial, occasional objects of faith, millions whereof there are in holy Scripture; such, as are to be believed, not for themselves, but because they are joined with others that are necessary to be believed, and delivered by the same authority which delivered these. . . .

. . .

13. . . . For seeing falsehood and error could not long stand against the power of truth were they not supported by tyranny and worldly advantage, he that could assert Christians to that liberty which Christ and his apostles left them must needs do truth a most heroical service. And seeing the overvaluing of the differences among Christians is one of the greatest maintainers of the schisms of Christendom, he that could demonstrate that only these points of belief are simply necessary to salvation wherein Christians generally agree, should he not lay a very fair and firm foundation of the peace of Christendom? Now the corollary which, I conceive, would produce these good effects . . . is this: that what man or Church soever believes the Creed and all the evident consequences of it sincerely and heartily cannot possibly (if also he believe the Scripture) be in any error of simple belief which is offensive to God; nor therefore deserve for any such error to be deprived of his life or to be cut off from the Church's communion and the hope of salvation. . . .

. . .

16. . . . Certainly, if Protestants be faulty in this matter, it is for doing it too much, and not too little. This presumptuous imposing of the senses of men upon the words of God, the special senses of men upon the general words of God, and laying them upon men's consciences together, under the equal penalty of death and damnation; this vain conceit that we can speak of the things of God better than in the words of God; this deifying our own interpretations and tyrannous enforcing them upon others; this restraining of the word of God from that latitude and generality, and the understandings of men from that liberty, wherein Christ and the apostles left them, is and hath been the only fountain

930

of all the schisms of the Church, and that which makes them immortal. . . . Take away these walls of separation, and all will quickly be one. Take away this persecuting, burning, cursing, damning of men for not subscribing to the words of men as the words of God; require of Christians only to believe Christ and to call no man master but him only; let those leave claiming infallibility that have no title to it, and let them that in their words disclaim it, disclaim it likewise in their actions. In a word, take away tyranny, which is the devil's instrument to support errors and superstitions and impieties . . . and restore Christians to their just and full liberty of captivating their understanding to Scripture only, and as rivers when they have a free passage run all to the ocean, so it may well be hoped, by God's blessing, that universal liberty, thus moderated, may quickly reduce Christendom to truth and unity. These thoughts of peace (I am persuaded) may come from the God of peace, and to his blessing I commend them, and proceed.

. . .

39. *Ad*. §16, 17. The saying of the most learned prelate and excellent man, the Archbishop of Armagh[26] . . . {is} as great and as good a truth, and as necessary for these miserable times, as possibly can be uttered. For this is most certain, and I believe you will easily grant it, that to reduce {restore} Christians to unity of communion there are but two ways that may be conceived probable: the one, by taking away the diversity of opinions touching matters of religion; the other, by showing that the diversity of opinions which is among the several sects of Christians ought to be no hindrance to their unity in communion.

40. Now the former of these is not to be hoped for without a miracle. . . . What then remains but that the other way must be taken, and Christians must be taught to set a higher value upon these high points of faith and obedience wherein they agree than upon these matters of less moment wherein they differ. . . . And to such a communion what better inducement could be thought of than to demonstrate that what was universally believed of all Christians, if it were joined with a love of truth and with holy obedience, was sufficient to bring men to heaven? For why should men be more rigid than God? Why should any error exclude any man from the Church's communion which will not deprive him of eternal salvation?

‡

{5.}71. *Ad* §24. *But schismatics from the Church of England, or any other Church, with this very answer, that they forsake not the Church but the errors of it, may cast off from themselves the imputation of schism* {Knott}.—Ans: True, they may make the same answer and the same defense as we do, as a murderer can cry *not guilty* as well as an innocent person, but not so truly nor so justly. The question is not what may be pretended but what can be proved by schismatics. They may object errors to other Churches, as well as we do to

---

[26] {James Ussher, quoted by Knott in *Charity mistaken*: "That in those propositions which without all controversy are universally received in the whole Christian world, so much truth is contained as, being joined with holy obedience, may be sufficient to bring a man to everlasting salvation; neither have we cause to doubt but that as many as walk according to this rule (neither overthrowing that which they have builded by superinducing any damnable heresies thereupon, nor otherwise vitiating their holy faith with a lewd and wicked conversation), peace shall be upon them and upon the Israel of God."}

yours; but that they prove their accusation so strongly as we can, that appears not. To the priests and elders of the Jews imposing that sacred silence mentioned in the Acts of the Apostles {5:28-29}, St. Peter and St. John answered, they *must obey God rather than men.* The three children to the King of Babylon gave in effect the same answer. Give me now any factious hypocrite who makes religion the pretence and cloak of his rebellion, and who sees not that such an one may answer for himself in those very formal words which the holy apostles and martyrs made use of; and yet, I presume, no Christian will deny but this answer was good in the mouth of the apostles and martyrs, though it were obnoxious {liable} to be abused by traitors and rebels. Certainly, therefore, it is no good consequence to say, *schismatics may make use of this answer; therefore all that do make use of it are schismatics.* But, moreover, it is to be observed that the chief part of our defense—that you deny your communion to all that deny or doubt of any part of your doctrine—cannot with any color be employed against Protestants, who grant their communion to all who hold with them, not all things, but things necessary; that is, such as are in Scripture plainly delivered.

TEXT: *The works of W. Chillingworth, M.A., containing his book, entitled, "The religion of Protestants a safe way to salvation"* (Philadelphia, 1840).

Checked against *The religion of Protestants a safe way to salvation, or, an answer to a book entitled "Mercy and truth, or charity maintain'd by Catholics,"* which pretends to prove the contrary (Oxford: Printed by Leonard Lichfield, 1638) (STC [2nd ed.] / 5138.2).

SIR KENELM DIGBY
(1603–65)

The *ODNB* entry on Digby calls him a courtier and natural philosopher. To these labels, one might also add philosopher, diplomat, Son of Ben,[1] Catholic intellectual, and pirate. His friends included Laud and Hobbes. He corresponded with Descartes on philosophy and with Fermat on mathematics. He was simultaneously chancellor to England's exiled Catholic Queen and a favorite of Oliver Cromwell. His relationship with Venetia Stanley is one of the great historical romances of the seventeenth century. What follows is thus a highly selective account of Digby's unusually eventful and multifaceted life.

Raised by his devoutly Catholic mother and Jesuit tutors—his father, Sir Everard Digby, having been executed for his role in the Gunpowder Plot—Kenelm Digby entered Oxford's recusant-friendly Gloucester Hall in 1618, where he so impressed his humanist and Catholic-leaning tutor, Thomas Allen,[2] that Allen willed his magnificent library to his former pupil, whom he termed "the Mirandola of his age." Within two years, Digby departed Oxford for the Grand Tour. In 1623 he received a summons from his cousin, John Digby, Earl of Bristol, to leave Florence for Madrid to help negotiate the Spanish Match; although the negotiations failed, Digby impressed Charles, who, upon their return to England, had him knighted and made gentleman of his privy chamber. In 1624 he secretly married Venetia Stanley, the court beauty and alleged court mistress, whom Digby had loved since childhood, and then, in 1627, "to advance himself in the king's service" (*ODNB*), obtained letters of marque allowing him to seize and plunder French and Spanish ships, England being then at war with these two countries. Digby's foray into piracy proved successful, and he returned a hero and a wealthy man. Upon his return in 1629, Digby, now the father of a growing family, accepted a post on the Navy Board, which required that he take the oaths of supremacy and allegiance. He thus became at

---

[1] He was in fact Ben Jonson's literary executor and edited a 1640/41 folio of Jonson's late plays.

[2] Allen was a principal ally of the staunchly Protestant Sir Thomas Bodley in the founding of the Bodleian Library—a collaboration that would repay further study.

least a nominal Anglican, but not a complacent or merely careerist one, since during the early 1630s he sought out, and formed a close friendship with, William Laud.[3]

Disaster struck in 1633 when Venetia suddenly died, leaving her grief-stricken husband under suspicion of having poisoned her (the *ODNB* says "cerebral haemorrage"). Digby renounced the world, put on monastic robes, and retired to Gresham College, where he threw himself into scientific research, a subject that had long fascinated him. Then, in September of 1635 he left London for Paris, where he found to his surprise and joy that "Gallican Roman Catholicism allowed scientists and natural philosophers to exchange ideas in freedom" (*ODNB*). Within a month he returned to the Catholic fold, although it was only in 1637 that a Carmelite friar resolved his final intellectual difficulties. Shortly thereafter, he wrote his *Conference with a lady* for the daughter of Sir Edward Coke, Lady Purbeck.

Before leaving England, Digby began his life-long friendship with the Roman Catholic priest and philosopher, Thomas White. In Paris, White introduced Digby to Mersenne, a Minim friar connected to all the leading intellectual figures of the day. Digby was already friendly with Hobbes, who was living in Paris in 1635–36; through Mersenne, he also came to know Descartes. When the *Discourse on method* came out in 1637, Digby sent Hobbes a copy.

Digby returned to England in 1638, soon joining the entourage of Henrietta Maria. The Long Parliament did not look favorably upon "Popish recusants" active in the royalist cause, and in November 1642, Digby found himself a prisoner at Winchester House. He spent his eight month's confinement drafting his major philosophical work,[4] *The two treatises* (publ. 1644), whose first volume, *On bodies*, grafts the atomist materialism of the new philosophy on to an Aristotelian metaphysics, creating the earliest "fully developed system of mechanical philosophy" in English (Henry 213). The *Two treatises* share Descartes' systematic dualism, the first volume outlining a materialist physics, the second defending the immortality of the soul. On the basis of experiments he conducted for the first volume, Digby has been termed the father of modern embryology.[5]

On his release from prison in 1643, Digby returned to France, shortly thereafter becoming chancellor to Henrietta Maria at her court-in-exile. He spent the rest of the Interregnum working on behalf of the royal cause, and, after the regicide, seeking to gain toleration for English Catholics. Allowed to return to England in 1654, he developed an improbable friendship with Oliver Cromwell. During these years, he, White, and other English Catholic intellectuals formed the Blacklo group, which sought to fuse theology, Aristotelian philosophy, and mechanistic physics into a coherent system that

---

[3] Laud, *Works* 6:447–55. That friendship resulted in Digby's 1634 gift of over 300 valuable mss, including 200 inherited from Thomas Allen, to the Bodleian.

[4] During the same months, he also sketched some of his key ideas in a commentary on Sir Thomas Browne's *Religio medici* (see Shuger, "Laudian idiot").

[5] He was also the first to note the role oxygen plays in plant life and the inventor of the modern wine bottle, although Digby's best-remembered contribution to science is, alas, the sympathetic powder, which allegedly healed sword wounds when applied to the offending sword, the wound itself being merely kept clean and dry; this proved to be far more effectual than any current treatment, repeated successful experiments winning over numerous skeptics, until someone realized that the secret lay not in the powdered sword but in keeping the wound clean and dry.

could "guarantee that certainty on which they believed human salvation depended," a system forged against the skeptical probabilism championed by Anglican latitudinarian divines (Krook x, 9). After 1660, Digby remained the Queen Mother's chancellor and continued to fight for Catholic toleration and to pursue his philosophical and scientific studies, which included experimental research in alchemy, cosmetics, cookery, and medicine. Digby was among the first members elected to the Royal Society. He died at home in 1665 and was buried in Venetia's tomb in the crypt of Christ Church, Newgate.

A conference with a lady falls into two main parts. The first nine points largely set forth Digby's own distinctive, and probably heterodox, theological position;[6] the remainder of the work, however, develops staple arguments used by Counter-Reformation apologists.

The lady addressed, Francis Villiers, was the daughter of Sir Edward Coke: the daughter whom, at fourteen, her father forced to marry the mentally unstable John Villiers— Coke seeking to further his own career by this alliance with one of Buckingham's kin. The marriage was not a happy one, and by 1625 Lady Purbeck and Lord Robert Howard had entered into a long-term adulterous relationship, for which she was convicted at High Commission. Rather than perform the assigned penance, she escaped, disguised, to Howard's estate in Shropshire; arrested again ten years later, she fled to Paris, where, with Digby as her spiritual guide, she converted to Catholicism.

The more significant context of *A conference* is a series of discussions that probably took place in early 1635 between Digby and White, on the one side, Falkland and Chillingworth on the other.[7] These debates between the Blackloists and the Great Tew circle resonate throughout *A conference with a lady*, but their echo can likewise be heard in *The religion of Protestants*.

In both texts, the argument hinges on the nature, validity, and authority of *traditio*. Against Chillingworth's argument that one can, at best, have moral certainty regarding past events, and then only if one has written eyewitness testimony, White and Digby argue for the infallibility of the Roman Church on the grounds that it alone could point to an "unbroken line of master and disciples" going back to Christ, and this continuous *traditio* sufficed to guarantee "that no false doctrines or errors could have crept in"; whereas reliance on Scripture led merely to the proliferation of competing interpretations, as post-Reformation history amply attested (Henry 218).

Digby's concern with religious epistemology also makes itself felt in his quite striking argument that no testimony, however reliable, of past miracles would prove sufficiently compelling to outweigh our natural tendency to disbelieve claims that go against both our senses and our interests—for example, that eternal joys that await those who renounce the pleasure of world and flesh. Faith in things invisible and inconvenient requires that "some inward and supernatural light be given her {the soul} to disperse all the mists that

---

[6] E.g., the materialist psychology and psychologization of heaven and hell in points #2 through 5; the tendency to depict God less as a divine Person than a first Principle in #7; and the reduction of Christ's role to his teaching office in #9. On Digby's theology, see Shuger, "Laudian idiot."

[7] Versions of these debates were later published as *A discourse of infallibility with Mr. Thomas White's answer to it, and a reply to him by Sir Lucius Cary late Lord Viscount of Falkland . . .* (London, 1660) and *Mr. Shillingworths {sic} letter touching infallibility* (London, 1662).

the senses raise against the truth of the doctrine"; and this infused light, this "giving of the Holy Ghost," as at Pentecost, overcomes all vacillation, all doubt, all coldness <#14>.[8] Digby's claim affirms the Blackloist commitment to the possibility of absolute certainties against the Great Tew position defended in *The religion of Protestants* that the evidence of testimony suffices for moral certainty concerning the truths necessary for salvation, and moral certainty is enough, for God does not require our faith to be stronger than the evidence he affords us of its truth. According to Chillingworth, reason thus can find the historical witness to Scripture's truth sufficiently compelling to support the life of faith— in part because Chillingworth allows a lesser degree of certainty to count as faith, but also in part because he allows a lesser degree of ascetic renunciation to count as a life of faith.

In some respects, however, Digby's "inward and supernatural light" corresponds to Calvinist teaching on assurance. There are crucial differences: the Catholic version does not bring certainty of one's own election, but certitude regarding the actuality of things spiritual and unseen. Yet both Digby and Preston understand true faith as a triumphant, transformative, and absolute knowing;[9] and Digby's argument that it is precisely this supernaturally-infused certitude that makes it possible to resist the pull of "flesh and blood and human nature" and thus to attain the extraordinary sanctity that constitutes, for him, the proof of the Holy Spirit's "inhabiting in the {Roman} Church," <#s 14, 16> endows such certitude with no less pivotal a role in Digby's Catholicism than assurance plays among experimental Calvinists.

An insistence on certainties rather than mere beliefs characterized Reformed and Counter-Reformation theology alike,[10] and sharply distinguishes both from the Erasmian and/or Thomist strains one finds in Hooker, Laud, and the Great Tew cohort.[11] The same line of demarcation separates Digby's argument that, without an infallible Church, religion dissolves into a chaos of private opinions <#16> from the responses of Chillingworth and Laud, which hinge on the claim Digby summarily brushes aside: that all Christians *do* agree on "fundamental doctrine," and differing on matters not fundamental does no harm. Digby's further allegation <#16> that Protestants reject the authority of "the whole current of ancient Fathers and Doctors of the Church, and General Councils" is not new, but at first glance seems scarcely applicable to the Laudian Church. Sixteenth-century Protestants do at times speak slightingly of Christian antiquity, but from the Elizabeth Settlement on, one rarely finds such sentiments among English churchmen; Jewel's semi-official *Apology of the Church of England* (1562) based its case on patristics, and following the Howson-Abbot clash in 1615, King James sent directives to the universities mandating that divinity students study "the Fathers and Councils, Schoolmen, histories and controversies," rather than modern compendia like Calvin's *Institutes* (Wordsworth 4:320). Yet

---

[8] That faith requires an infused supernatural light was traditional and orthodox (so Laud <385>), but this light of faith was not typically held to make its objects so clear and distinct that all doubt vanished.

[9] See, e.g., Preston's "The buckler" *<supra>*.

[10] And, of course, Cartesian philosophy.

[11] Note that in Digby's case, this insistence leads to problems. Much of *A conference* is devoted to defending the Roman Church's infallibility by virtue of its faithful transmission of Christ's original teachings. Yet since Digby also argues that no one believes the Church's testimony without the inner light of the Spirit, who writes "the law of the Gospel . . . in men's hearts and in their minds" <#14>, it becomes hard to see why the Church needs to be infallible or what difference its infallibility makes.

Digby may not be attacking a straw man. The Blacklo-Great Tew conferences, in which Digby and Chillingworth took part, date from around 1634–35, the same years that John Hales, who had close ties to Great Tew, was writing *A tract concerning schism*, which explicitly denies the past any normative authority whatsoever *<vide supra>*.

A conference is thus a transitional work. Some of its arguments do reprise standard anti-Protestant debating-points. Yet often even the standard arguments have been subtly reconfigured to contest the avant-garde skeptical rationalism of Great Tew, and, especially in its opening sections, to contest it along lines that themselves draw freely on cutting-edge modernist thought.

SOURCES: *ODNB*; John Henry, "Atomism and eschatology," *British Journal for the History of Science* 15 (1982): 211–39; Dorothea Krook, *John Sergeant and his circle: a study of three seventeenth-century English Aristotelians*, ed. and intro. Beverley Southgate (Brill, 1993); R. T. Petersson, *Sir Kenelm Digby: the ornament of England, 1603–1665* (London: Jonathan Cape, 1936); Shuger, "The Laudian idiot," in *The world proposed: Thomas Browne quatercentenary essays*, ed. Reid Barbour and Claire Preston (Oxford UP, 2009), 36–62; Stefania Tutino, *Thomas White and the Blackloists* (Ashgate, 2008); Christopher Wordsworth, *Ecclesiastical biography, or, lives of eminent men, connected with the history of religion in England*, 4 vols., 3rd ed. (London, 1839).

SIR KENELM DIGBY

A conference with a lady about choice of religion
1638

Madam,

My being conscious to myself how confusedly and intricately I have delivered my conceptions unto your Ladyship, upon the several occasions of discourse we have had together concerning that important subject of what faith and religion is the true one to bring us to eternal happiness (wherein your Ladyship is so wisely and worthily inquisitive and solicitous), hath begotten this following writing: in the which I will, as near as I can, sum up the heads of those considerations I have sometimes discussed unto you in conversation. And I will briefly and barely lay them before you without any long enlargement upon them, as having a better opinion of the reflections that your Ladyship's great understanding and strong reasoning soul will by yourself make upon the naked subject sincerely proposed than of any commentary I can frame upon it. And indeed, such discourses as these are deeper looked into when they are pondered by a prudential judgment than when they are examined by scientifical speculations.

But with your leave, I shall take the matter a little higher than where the chief difficulty seemeth to be at which your Ladyship sticketh: conceiving that if we begin at the root and proceed on step by step, we shall find our search the easier and the securer, and our assent to the conclusions we shall collect will be the more firm and vigorous.

We will therefore begin with considering why faith and religion is needful to a man before we determine the means how to find out the right faith: for that being once settled in the understanding, we shall presently without further dispute reject what religion soever is but proposed that hath not those proprieties which are required to bring that to pass that religion in its own nature aimeth at. And this must be done by taking a survey of some of the operations of a human soul, and of the impressions made in it by the objects it is conversant withal.

1. Your Ladyship may be pleased then to consider, in the first place, that it is by nature engrafted in the souls of all mankind to desire beatitude (by which word I mean an entire,

perfect, and secure fruition of all such objects as one hath vehement affections unto, without mixture of anything one hath aversion from).

2. In the next place, you may please to consider that this full beatitude which the soul thirsteth after cannot be enjoyed in this life. For it is apparent that intellectual goods, as science, contemplation, and fruition of spiritual objects and contentments, in their own nature are the chief goods of the soul, and affect her much more strongly and violently than corporal and sensual ones can do, for they are more agreeable to her nature and therefore move her more efficaciously when they are duly relished. But such intellectual goods cannot be perfectly relished and enjoyed as long as the soul is immersed in the body, by reason that the sensual appetite maketh continual war against the rational part of the soul, and in most men mastereth it; and in the perfectest, this earthly habitation doth so draw down and clog and benumb the noble inhabitant of it (which would always busy itself in sublime contemplations) as it may be said to be but in a jail whiles it resideth here. And experience confirmeth unto us that the sparks of knowledge we gain here are not pure but have the nature of salt water that increaseth the thirst in them who drink most of it; and we swallow the purest streams like men in a dropsy, who the more they drink are still the greedier of more. Therefore to have this greediness of knowing satisfied . . . we must have patience until she {the soul} arrive unto another state of life, wherein being separated from all corporal feces {dregs}, impediments, and contradictions, she may wholly give herself up to that which is her natural operation and from whence resulteth her true and perfect delight. Besides, even they who have attained to the greatest blessings (both inward and outward) that this world can afford yet are far from being completely happy. . . . The very fear of losing them . . . is such a spoonful of gall to make their whole draught bitter. . . . How little can any man relish the objects of delight which with never so great affluence beset him round about, when he knoweth a sharp and heavy sword hangeth by a slender thread over his head, and at length must fall, and ever after sever him from them? A little distemper, an accidental fever, and ill-mingled draught (such a one as the miracle of wit and learning Lucretius met withal) is enough to turn the brains of the wisest man that is, and in a few hours to blot out all these notions he hath been all his life laboring to possess himself of, and to render him of a more abject and despicable condition than the meanest wretch living that hath but the common use of reason. The Genius that presideth over human affairs delighteth in perpetual changes and variation of men's fortunes, so that he who late sat enthroned in greatest dignity is all of a sudden precipitated headlong unto a condition most opposite thereunto. He that but yesterday had all his joys enlarged and swelled up to their full height by the communication of a perfect and entire friend (without which can there be any true joy?) hath today lost the comfort of all that the world can afford him by the irrecoverable loss of that one friend. In a word, death growing daily upon him and encroaching upon his outworks and by hours reducing him into a narrower circle, at length seizeth upon himself and maketh an eternal divorce between him and what was dearest to him here.

3. Our next consideration then shall be to discover what will result out of our swift passage through this vale of miseries and what impressions we shall carry with us out of this pilgrimage. . . . Therefore to proceed on in this method, our third conclusion shall be that whatsoever judgment the soul once frameth in this life, that judgment and that affection will perpetually remain in the soul, unless some contrary impression be made in it to

blot it out, which only hath power to expel any former one. For judgments and affections are caused in a man by the impression that the objects make in his soul; and all that any agent[1] aimeth at in any operation whatsoever (be it never so forcible in action) is but to produce a resemblance of itself in the subject it worketh upon; and therefore it excludeth nothing that it findeth formerly there (which in our case is the soul), unless it be some such impression as is incompatible with what it intendeth to effect there; or that the subject is not large enough both to retain the old and receive the new, in which case the first must be blotted out to make room for the latter. But of judgments and affections, none are incompatible to one another but those that are directly opposite to one another by contradiction; therefore only such have power to expel one another. And all that are not such are immediately united to the very substance of the soul; which, having an infinite capacity, it can never be filled by any limited objects whatsoever, so that they always reside in the soul—although they do not at all times appear in outward act, which proceedeth from hence: that new and other images are by the fantasy represented to the soul, and she seemeth to busy herself only about what she findeth there, which being but one distinct image at a time (for corporal organs have limited comprehensions and are quickly filled with corporal species), she thereupon seemeth to exercise but one judgment or but one affection at a time. But as soon as the soul shall be released out of the body (which is like a dark prison to wall it in), then she will at one and the same instant actually know and love all those things she knew and loved in the body, with only this difference: that her knowledges will then be much more distinct and perfect, and her affections much more vehement than they were in this life, by reason that her conjunction here with resistant matter was a burden and a clog unto her, and hindered the activity and force of her operations. The difference of these states may in some measure be illustrated by a gross and material example. Represent unto yourself a man walled up in a dark tower that is so close as no air nor light can come into it, excepting only at one little hole, and that hole too affordeth no clear and free passage to the sight, but hath a thick and muddy glass before it. Now if this man would look upon any of the objects that are about this tower, he must get them to be placed over against that hole, unto which he must lay his eye; and then he can discern but one at a time, and that but dimly neither; and if he will see several bodies, it must be by so many several iterated acts as they are in number. But suppose some earthquake or exterior violence to break asunder . . . the walls of this tower, leaving the man untouched and unhurt; then, at one instant and with one cast of his eyes, he beholdeth distinctly, clearly, and at ease all those several objects that with so much labor and time he took but a mistaking survey of before.

4. The fourth consideration shall be, that after the first instant wherein the soul is separated from the body, she is then in her nature no longer subject or liable to any new impression, mutation, or change whatsoever. For that which should cause any such effect must be either a material or a spiritual agent. But a material one cannot work upon it, for that requireth quantity in the patient. . . . Nor can any spiritual agent cause any succession of new alteration, but all that spirits work one upon another is done at once and at one

---

[1] {The "agent" is that which is acting upon something else; that on which an agent acts is the "patient." In the scenario described by Digby, the various sensible and intellectual objects are the agents; the soul, the patient.}

instant—which we shall discern the clearer by examining the reason why there is succession and time taken up in the alterations that are wrought amongst material things: for in them, by reason of their quantity that causeth an extension and distance of the parts, the agent, although it have never so much disposition and efficacy to work, must have his several parts applied to the several parts of the patient by local motion, which requireth time for the performance thereof. And besides, even in the agent itself, the grossness and heaviness of the matter giveth an allay and is a clog to the activity of the form, and as it were pulleth it back whiles it is in action. But this is not so in spiritual substances, and therefore we may conclude that among them, in the same instant that the agent is disposed to work, the action is performed: for on his part there is nothing to retard it, nor is there required any local motion which should take up time; and likewise by the same reason, in the very instant that the patient is disposed to receive any impression, it is wrought in it. And thus, although there were never so many agents, and every one of them to perform never so many actions, they would be all done and ended in one and the same instant.

5. The next consideration shall be, that those persons who in this world had strong and predominant affections to sensible and material objects, and died in that state, shall be eternally miserable in the next, for by what we have said, it appeareth that those affections will eternally remain in the soul . . . and the affections of a separated soul are much more ardent and vehement than whiles it is in the body. But it is impossible they should ever attain, in that state, to the fruition of what they so violently covet and love. . . . they cannot choose therefore but execrate themselves for their fondly misplaced (yet then eternally necessary) affections, and pine away (if so I may say) with perpetual anguish and despair of what they so impatiently and enragedly desire and never can obtain.

6. The sixth consideration shall be, that to be happy in the next life, one must not settle their predominant affections upon any creature whatsoever or any good that we can naturally attain to the knowledge of in this life. For what natural good soever we love or enjoy here, we must by death be divorced from, and (as we have said before) that separation will cause perpetual sorrow, because the affections remain unchangeable. . . .

And thus it followeth that either man was not created for a determinate end and for a state convenient for his nature and able to satisfy the original appetences of his soul; or at the least, no man can by natural means arrive to the end and period of happiness.

7. But now to proceed in the pursuance of this method of reasoning, and to follow hence-forward the conduct of a supernatural guide, since nature quitteth us here, having led us on as long as she was able to see—we may, in the seventh place, consider that God, when he created man, did not assign him to remain in the state of pure nature, but did out of his goodness and liberality confer something upon him that exceeded the sphere of his nature. . . . For as heat, being essential to fire, cannot but produce heat in whatsoever it {fire} hath application unto, so God, being in his own essence goodness itself, cannot choose but do unto whatsoever proceedeth from him all that good which the nature of it is capable of. . . . so that, there wanting an infinite object to satisfy the infinite capacity of the soul, and without which she must be eternally miserable, it remaineth that he who gave that capacity must also afford the object, and assign means how to compass and gain it. All which, we have already proved, is out of the reach of nature to discern, and therefore it followeth of consequence that the author of nature must endow man with some

supernatural gifts, if he be in a fit disposition to receive them, which may bring him to the supernatural end he was created for.

8. Our eighth conclusion shall be that, of these supernatural gifts, the first (and the ground and foundation of all the rest) is faith. For we have already determined that we cannot by any natural means attain to the knowledge of any object that may render us completely happy in the next life; and yet such knowledge must be had, to the end that we may direct our actions to gain the fruition of that object. Therefore there is no way left to compass this but by the instructions and discipline of some master whose goodness and knowledge we can no ways doubt of—by which two perfections in him, we may be secure that he neither can be deceived himself nor will deceive us. Now the doctrine that such a master shall teach for such an end, we call faith.

9. In the ninth place, we must determine that this master must be God and man. For, first, by our discourse upon natural principles, we have proved that to avoid misery in the next life, we must deny our senses the content and satisfaction that they naturally desire in corporal things and that we must withdraw our affections from all material objects. And next we have collected that the object which we must know and love to be happy doth exceed the reach and view of any created understanding to discern. Therefore we may safely conclude that this doctrine ought to be delivered unto us originally by God himself. Forafter {*sic*} the first branch, which is of withdrawing our affections from sensible goods, although out of natural principles that doctrine is to be collected, yet that is not a sufficient means to settle mankind in general in the belief of it. For the discourse that proveth it is such an abstracted one as very few are capable of it. . . . Of those that have both years and capacity to wield such thoughts, there are so few that are not in a manner forced away from such interior recollections by their particular vocations and the natural necessities they are obliged unto, as to beat it out by themselves is not a sufficient means to serve mankind in this case. And to think that those few, who, having great parts, may with much labor have attained to the knowledge thereof, should instruct others that are simpler and are taken up by other employments and courses of life, were very irrational: since no man, be he never so wise, is such but may be deceived; and then how can it be expected that another man should, without sensible demonstration, believe his single word in a matter so contrary to sense and wherein he must forgo so great contentments and present utility?

And for the other branch, which is in the instructing mankind concerning the right object that he is to know and love to be happy, that is altogether out of the reach of any man whatsoever by himself to discover; and therefore much less can he in his own name instruct others therein. And if any man should go about to do so and to introduce a new doctrine of faith not formerly heard of, drawing the arguments for confirmation thereof only out of his own ratiocination and discourse, that alone were enough to convince {convict} him of falsehood, since he should thereby undertake to know what were impossible for him of himself to attain to the knowledge of.

Therefore it is necessary that the author of the doctrine we must believe, the instructor of the actions we must perform, and the promiser of the happiness we may hope for, be God himself. . . .

But because the weakness of our intellectual nature is such, whiles we remain here in our earthly habitations, imprisoned in our houses of clay, as we cannot lift up our heavy and drowsy eyes and steadily fix our dim sight upon the dazzling and indeed invisible Deity, nor entertain an immediate communication with him . . . it was necessary that God himself should descend to some corporal substance that might be more familiar and less dazzling unto us: and none was so convenient as human nature, to the end that he might not only converse freely and familiarly with us, and so in a gentle and a sweet manner teach us what we should do, but also preach unto us by his example and himself be our leader in the way that he instructed us to take. The conclusion then of this discourse is that it was necessary Christ, God and man, should come into the world to teach us what to believe and what to do.

10. The tenth conclusion shall be that those unto whom Christ did immediately preach this faith and unto whom he gave commission to preach it unto others and spread it through the world after he ascended to heaven, ought to be believed as firmly as he himself. The reason of this assertion is that their doctrine, though it be delivered by secondary mouths, yet it proceedeth from the same fountain: which is God himself, that is the prime verity, and cannot deceive nor be deceived. But all the difficulty herein is to know who had this immediate commission from Christ, and by what seal we should discern it to have been no forged one. The solution of this ariseth out of the same argument which proveth that Christ himself was God and that the doctrine he taught was true and divine: which is, the miracles and works he did, exceeding the power of nature, and that could be effected by none but by God himself. . . . In like manner, the apostles' doing such admirable works and miracles as neither by nature nor by art magic could be brought to pass, that must necessarily infer God himself cooperated with them to justify what they said; it is evident that their doctrine (which was not their own, but received from Christ) must be true and divine.

11. The eleventh conclusion shall be that this faith, thus taught by Christ and propagated by the apostles and necessary to mankind to believe (as well that part of it which is written as the whole, which is not), dependeth intrinsically upon the testimony of the Catholic Church, which is ordained to conserve and deliver it from age to age. (By which Catholic Church, I mean the congregation of the faithful that is spread throughout the whole world.) For we have proved before that the way to the true faith ought to be open and plain to all men, of all abilities and in all ages, that have a desire to embrace it; and this cannot be but either by the immediate preaching of Christ or else by the information (either in writing or by word of mouth) of them that learned it from him, and their delivering it over to others, and so from hand to hand until any particular time you will pitch upon. But from Christ's own mouth none could have it but those who lived in the age when he did; therefore there remaineth no other means to have it derived down to after ages than by this delivery over from hand to hand . . . which course of deducing faith from Christ we call *tradition*. So that this conclusion proveth that the Church is the conserver both of the whole doctrine of faith necessary for salvation and likewise of the divine writ dictated by the Holy Ghost and written by the prophets, evangelists and apostles, which we are also bound to believe. And the same assent that we are to give to the truth of Scriptures (that is to say, that the Scriptures we have are true Scriptures), the very same we are to give to other articles of faith proposed unto us by the Church, for they alike depend of the same authority, which is the veracity of the Church proposing and

delivering them unto us to be believed. And we may as well doubt that the Church hath corrupted the Scriptures as that she hath corrupted any article of faith.

12. The twelfth conclusion shall be that into the Catholic Church no false doctrine in any age can be admitted or creep in: that is to say, no false proposition whatsoever can ever be received and embraced by the Catholic Church as a proposition of faith. For whatsoever the Church believeth as a proposition of faith is upon this ground, that Christ taught it as such unto the Church he planted himself, and so it left it in trust to be by it delivered over to the next age. And the reason why the present Church believeth any proposition to be of faith is because the immediate preceding Church of the age before delivered it as such. And so you may drive it on from age to age until you come to the apostles and Christ. Therefore to have any false proposition of faith admitted into the Church in any age doth suppose that all they of that age must unanimously conspire to deceive their children and youngers, telling them that they were taught by their fathers to believe, as of faith, some proposition which indeed they were not. Which being impossible (as it will evidently appear to any prudent person that shall reasonably ponder the matter) that so many men spread throughout the whole world, so different in their particular interests and ends and of such various dispositions and natures, should all agree together in the forgery of any precise lie, it is impossible that any false doctrine should creep into the Church.

. . .

{13.} . . . But this is not enough; our disquisition must not rest here. We must not content ourselves in this divine affair and supernatural doctrine with a certitude depending only upon natural causes. The wisdom of God proportioneth out congruent means to bring on every thing to their proper end; and according to the nobility of the effect that he will have produced, he ordaineth equivalent noble causes. Therefore, man's obtaining beatitude being the highest end that any creature can arrive unto and altogether supernatural, it requireth supernatural causes to bring us to that end and a supernatural infallibility to secure us in that journey. We must not only have a supernatural way to travel in (which is faith) but also a supernatural assurance of the right way, unto the discovery of which all that we have already said doth necessarily conduce: for God's providence, that disposeth all things sweetly, will not in any general affair introduce into the material world any supernatural effect until the natural causes be first disposed fittingly to cooperate on their parts, and then he never faileth of his. As, for example, when a natural creature is to be produced into being, the father and mother must both concur in contributing all that is in their power to the generation of a child; and yet we are sure the soul to be produced hath no dependence of them; yet notwithstanding, without their precedent action, no new soul would be. But when the matter is fittingly disposed in the mother's womb, he never misseth creating of a soul in that body, which is as noble an effect and as much requiring the omnipotency of God as the creating of nothing all the material world. . . . And so in like manner we may rationally conclude that in this high and supernatural business of delivering over from hand to hand a supernatural doctrine to bring mankind to the end it was created for, he will first have all the natural causes fittingly disposed for the secure and infallible performance of that work, and then that he will add and infuse into them some supernatural gift whereby to give them yet further a supernatural assurance and infallibility—which they may with an humble confidence in his unlimited goodness expect and claim at his divine hand when they are reduced {restored} to that state as is convenient for the reception of such a supernatural gift.

14. Our fourteenth conclusion, therefore, shall be that God hath given to his Church, thus composed, the Holy Ghost, to confirm it in the true faith, and to preserve it from error, and to illuminate the understanding of it in right discerning the true sense of those mysteries of faith that are committed to the custody of it, and to work supernatural effects of devotion and sanctity in that Church. And this I prove thus: considering that the doctrine of Christ is practical and aimeth at the working of an effect, which is the reduction of mankind to beatitude; and that mankind comprehendeth not only those that lived in that age when he preached, but also all others that ever were since or shall be till the end of the world, it is apparent that to accomplish that end it was necessary Christ should so effectually imprint his doctrine in their hearts whom he delivered it unto as it might, upon all occasions and at all times, infallibly express itself in action, and in the delivery of it over from hand to hand should, in virtue and strength of the first operation, produce ever after like effects in all others. Now to have this completely performed, it was to be done both by exterior and by interior means, proportionable to the senses without and to the soul within. The outward means were the miracles that he wrought, of which himself saith, *if I had not wrought those works that no man else ever did, they were not guilty of sin; but now they have no excuse* (or to this purpose); and he promised the apostles they should do greater than those. And that miracles are the proper instruments to plant a new doctrine and faith withal, the Apostle witnesseth when he saith that miracles are wrought for the unfaithful not for the faithful. . . . But it is manifest by the fall of the apostles themselves that only {by itself} this exterior means of miracles is not sufficient to engraft supernatural faith deep enough in men's hearts, when as they, upon Christ's passion, not only . . . denied their Master but had even the very conceit and belief of his doctrine exiled out of their hearts and understanding, notwithstanding all the miracles they had seen him work. . . . Therefore it was necessary that some inward light should be given them, so clear and so strong and so powerful as the senses should not be able to prevail against it, but that it should overflowingly possess and fill all their understandings and their souls, and make them break out in exterior actions correspondent to the Spirit that steered them within. And the reason is evident: for whiles, on the one side, the senses discern apparently miracles wrought in confirmation of a doctrine, and on the other side, the same senses do stiffly contradict the very possibility of the doctrine which those miracles testify, the soul within, having no assistance beyond the natural powers she hath belonging originally unto her, is in great debate and anxiety which way to give her assent; and though reason do prevail to give it to the party of the present miracles, yet it is with great timidity. But if it happen that the course of those miracles be stopped, then the particular seeming-impossibilities of the proposed faith remaining always alike lively in their apprehension, and the miracles wrought to confirm it residing but in the memory—and the representations of them wearing out daily more and more, and the present senses and fantasy growing proportionably stronger and stronger, and withal objecting continually new doubts about the reality of those miracles—it cannot be expected otherwise but that the assent of the soul should range itself on the side of the impossibility (as[2] appearing

---

[2] {The text is corrupt here, although the sense is clear enough; this is my conjectural emendation.}

to the present senses) and renounce the doctrine formerly confirmed by miracles, unless some inward and supernatural light be given her to disperse all the mists that the senses raise against the truth of the doctrine. Now the infusion of this light and fervor we call the giving of the Holy Ghost. . . . And this was prophesied long before . . . by Jeremiah, whose authority S. Paul bringeth to prove that the law of the Gospel was to be written by the Holy Ghost in men's hearts and in their minds . . . *the faith of Christ not written with ink, but with the spirit of God; nor graven in stony tables, but in the fleshy ones of their hearts.* And in performance of this prophecy and of Christ's promise, the history telleth us that on the tenth day after the ascension of Christ, when all his disciples (who were then all his Church, and were to preach and deliver it to all the world) were assembled together, the Holy Ghost was given them, and that in so full a measure . . . as they never after admitted the least vacillation therein; but they, immediately casting away all other desires and thoughts, were inflamed with admirable love of God . . . and when, by reason of that zeal of theirs, anything happened to them contrary to flesh and blood and human nature (as persecutions, ignominies, corporal punishments, and even death itself), they not only not shunned it as before, but greedily ran to meet and embrace it, and joyed and gloried in it. . . . Whereupon, by the way, we may note that in what Church soever we find not a state of life for sanctity and near union with God and contempt of worldly and transitory things raised above the pitch of nature and morality, we may conclude the Holy Ghost inhabiteth not there. For every agent produceth effects proportionable to the dignity of it, and the excellency of any cause shineth eminently in the nobleness of its effects. . . .

15. Our next conclusion shall be that this Church or congregation of men spread over the world, conserving and delivering the faith of Christ from hand to hand, is even in its own nature perpetual in time, and cannot fail as long as mankind remaineth in the world. This needeth no further proof than that which we have already made: which is derived from the necessity of supernatural faith to bring mankind to the end it was created for. . . . Yet in this way of reasoning that I use, we are to examine our conclusions as well by the genuine and orderly causes that beget them and by their own particular principles, as to assent unto them for the necessity that we see in them in regard of the end that they are referred unto. . . . Thus then: as philosophers conclude that it is impossible any whole species or kind of beasts should ever be utterly exterminated and destroyed . . . because the amplitude of the universe is greater than the variety of causes can be from which such a general and entire corruption must proceed, in like manner we may confidently conclude that it is impossible any depraved affections should so universally prevail . . . as would be requisite to extirpate and root out a doctrine, universally spread over it all, that was at the first taught and confirmed with such seals of truth as the miracles that Christ and the apostles wrought; that in itself is so pure and agreeable to the seeds that every man findeth sowed even by nature in his own soul; that worketh such admirable effects as the reformation of manners in mankind; that withdraweth men's affections from human and worldly contentments and carrieth them with a sweet violence to intellectual objects and to hopes of immortality and happiness in another life; that prescribeth laws for happy living, even in this world, to all men of what condition soever, either public or private, as working a moderation in men's affections to the commodities and goods of this life, which else in nature is apt to blind men's minds, and is the cause of all mischiefs and evils; and lastly, that is delivered over from hand to hand, from worlds of fathers to worlds of

sons, with such care and exactness as greater cannot be imagined and as is requisite to the importance of that affair, which is infinitely beyond all others, as on which the salvation and damnation of mankind wholly dependeth. . . . It remaineth now that we close up this discourse by applying all these premises unto the question in hand: which is, where we shall find out this infallible Church that by it we may gain the knowledge of the true faith of Christ whereby we are to be saved.

16. For this end, our sixteenth and last conclusion shall be that the congregation of men spread over the world joining in communion with the Church of Rome is the true Catholic Church in which is conserved and taught the true saving faith of Christ.

The truth of this conclusion will . . . appear evidently by reflecting upon what we have said, and only examining whether the Roman Church be such a one as we have determined the true Church of Christ must be. . . . This point, after these grounds laid, requireth no very subtle disquisition, but is discernable even by the weakest sights. . . . For it hath believed in every age all that hath been plainly and positively taught unto it by their fathers as the doctrine of faith derived from Christ, and admitteth no other article whatsoever as an article of faith. Whereas on the other side, all other Christian Churches among us that pretend reformation, having no certain and common rule of faith, but every particular man governing himself in this matter by the collections of his own brain and by his own private understanding and interpretation of Scripture (which only he acknowledgeth as the entire rule of faith), it must consequently follow that according to the variety of their tempers and judgments, there must be a variety and difference of their opinions and beliefs. . . . And accordingly we see by experience that scarce any two authors out of the Roman Church that have written of matters of faith have agreed in their tenets, but rather have dissented in fundamental doctrine and have inveighed against one another in their writings with great vehemence and bitterness. Whereas on the other side, the Doctors of the Roman Church in all times, in all places, and of all tempers have agreed unanimously in all matters of faith, although in the meantime, several of them have, in divers other points, great debates against one another and pursue them with much sharpness: which strongly confirmeth the ground upon which we frame this observation.

But to insist a little further upon this material and important consideration: it is evident that the proceeding of the reformers openeth the gate to all dissention, schism, irreverence, pride of understanding, heresy, and ruin of Christian religion: for to justify the new births of their rebellious brains, the first stroke of their pen must be to lay a taint of ignorance and error upon the whole current of ancient Fathers and Doctors of the Church, and General Councils, and to blast their authority . . . whose names and records ought to be sacred with posterity. Which when they have done, to settle a constant and like belief in all men, they give no general and certain rule; but leaving every man to the dictamens of his own private judgment according to the several tempers and circumstances (as we said before) that sway every single man in particular, there must result (which we see by experience) as great a variety of opinions as those are different. And lastly, since they quarrel at Catholics' belief in those points where they differ from them because they captivate their understandings with reverence to what the Church proposeth and teacheth and thereby admit into their belief articles which may seem absurd to common sense, they may as well with presumptuous hands grasp at and seek to pluck up the very foundations of Christian religion, as namely the doctrine of the Trinity and of the Incarnation of Christ . . . since there are greater seeming contradictions in them . . . than in those mysteries the reformers cavil at.

In the next place we may consider that, as infallibility is pretended by the Roman Church alone, so it is apparently entailed[3] upon it: for we have proved that no means or circumstance, either moral, natural, or supernatural, is wanting in it to beget infallibility in matters of faith. Whereas on the other side, from the reformers' own position we infer by consequence that their doctrine cannot be hoped (even by themselves) to be infallible; and therefore they that shall submit their understanding to their conduct, though they believe without controversy all they say, must needs (even by reason of what is taught them) float always in a great deal of incertitude and anxious apprehension and fear of error. For they, looking upon the Church but with pure human considerations as an ordinary company of men, will have it liable to mistaking according to the natural imbecility of men's wits and understandings . . . against which they produce no antidote to preserve and secure themselves from the infection and taint they lay upon the Church. For, if they will have the conferences[4] of several passages of Scripture to be that which must give light in the several controverted obscurities, what eminency have these few late reformers shewn either in knowledge of tongues, insight into antiquity, profoundness in sciences, and perfection and sanctity of life, which hath not shined admirably more . . . in multitudes of the adverse party? And none will deny but these are the likeliest means to gain a right intelligence of the true and deep sense of Scriptures. And besides, we may observe that the reason why they deny the several articles wherein they differ from the Catholic Church is because it teacheth a doctrine which is repugnant to sense and of hard digestion to philosophy, both which are incompetent judges of divine and supernatural truths. . . .

. . .

And yet further, besides this want of universality in regard of place, the religion taught by the reformers hath yet a greater restriction than that: for even in its own nature it is not for all sorts of persons and for all capacities, whereas the true saving faith to bring men to beatitude ought to be obvious to all mankind, and open as well to the simple as to the learned. For since they lay the Scriptures as the first and highest principle, from whence they deduce all that ought to be believed; and that in all arts and sciences the primary and fundamental principles thereof ought to be thoroughly known by them that aspire to the perfect knowledge of those sciences; it followeth that one must have an exact knowledge of the learned tongues to examine punctually the true sense of the Scriptures, and that one must be perfectly versed in logic to be able to reason solidly and to deduce true consequences from certain principles . . . and lastly, one must be endowed with an excellent judgment and strong natural wit. . . . With which excellencies, how few are there in the world fairly adorned?

Fourthly, it is evident that the Roman Catholic Church only hath had a constant and uninterrupted succession of Pastors and Doctors and tradition of doctrine from age to age, which we have established as the only means to derive down the true faith from Christ. Whereas it is apparent all others have had late beginnings from unworthy causes, and yet, even in this little while, have not been able to maintain themselves for one age

---

[3] {bestowed as an inalienable inheritance (*OED*)}
[4] {collation, comparison}

throughout . . . in one tenor of doctrine or form of ecclesiastical government. Lastly, we may consider how the effect of the Holy Ghost his inhabiting in the Church, in regard of manners, making the hearts of men his living temples, shineth eminently in the Catholic Church, and is not so much as to be suspected in any other whatsoever. For where this Holy Spirit reigneth, it giveth a burning love of God (as we have touched before) and a vehement desire of approaching unto him as near as may be. Now the soul of man moveth towards God . . . by intellectual actions, the highest of which are mental prayer and contemplation; in which exercises, a man shall advance the more by how much he is the more sequestered from the thought and care of any worldly affairs and hath his passions quieted within him and is abstracted from communication with material objects and is untied from human interests . . . living in the world as though he were not in it, wholly intent to contemplation (when the inferior part of charity calleth him not down to comply with the necessity of his neighbors). This form of life we see continually practiced in the Catholic Church by multitudes of persons of both sexes that, through extreme desire of approaching as near unto God as this life will permit, do . . . either retire into extreme solitudes or shut themselves up forever within the narrow limits of a straight monastery and little cell, where having renounced all the interest and propriety in the goods of this world and using no more of them than is necessary for the poor sustenance of their exhausted bodies (which they mortify with great abstinences, watchings, and other austerities, that they may bring them into subjection and root out, as much as may be, the very fuel of concupiscence and passions), and having of their own accord barred themselves of all propriety of disposing of themselves in any action, and renounced even the freedom of their will; and thus, in sum, having taken an eternal farewell of all the joys and delights that this world can afford and that carnal men would be so loath to forgo for any little while, yet by the internal joys that they find in their prayer and contemplation . . . they live so happily and cheerfully and with such tranquility of mind, and upon occasions say so much of the overflowings of their bliss as it is apparent they enjoy there the hundredfold that Christ promised in this life. . . . Whereas on the other side no such examples or supernatural form of life are to be met withal in any other Church whatsoever. Rather, they disclaim from them, and like men of this world (which is the expression that Christ useth in the Gospel to design {designate} those that are not of his Church), not being able to discern things of the Spirit . . . they neglect and disdain them, and imagine that all Christian perfection consisteth in an ordinary human moral life, which is the uttermost period that any among them seek to attain unto. And therefore we may hence conclude that they have no interior worker among them more sublime than their own human discourses and judgments; and that supernatural sanctity (an effect of the Holy Ghost) is confined only to the Catholic Church.

Besides, we may observe by daily experience how those persons that addict themselves to such an extraordinary way of life do absolutely prove either the best or the worst of mankind: the one excelling in admirable piety, fervor of devotion, abstraction and sanctity of life, and some of them soaring up to a pitch even above nature; the other abounding in all sorts of impiety, wickedness, and dissolution of manners, till at length their hearts become even hardened against correction and all sense of spiritual things. . . . And this being a constant and certain effect . . . it must be attributed to a constant and powerful cause, which can be no other than the near approaching of those persons to the original fountain of sanctity and goodness; which, being like a consuming fire, worketh vehement effects in them according to the disposition they are in and to the nearness that they have unto that fire: so that, as the sunbeams (which are the authors of life and fecundity to all plants and vegetables) shining upon a tree that hath taken solid roots in the earth, maketh it bud, flourish, and bear fruit; and on the other side, if it be weakly rooted, their heat and operation upon that tree maketh it the sooner to wither and die[5] . . . in like manner, they who being rooted in charity approach to that divine sun do flourish and bring forth excellent and oft-times supernatural fruits of devotion, fervor, and sanctity, but those who have depraved affections so environing the roots of their hearts as that the soil of charity cannot introduce her nourishing sap into them . . . if they come within the beams of this holy sun . . . they do but wither away the sooner. . . .

And again we see that those who, having addicted themselves wholly to such a course of seraphical life . . . do thereby (as we may reasonably conceive) approach nearest to God Almighty and draw immediately from him (who is the fountain of light and truth) strongest emanations and clearest influences to illustrate their understanding and enflame their affections, those persons (I say) have ever been most earnest in the maintenance of those points of the Roman doctrine which are most repugnant to sense (as in particular, of that of the real presence of Christ's body in the Blessed Sacrament . . .) and adore them with greatest reverence and are enflamed with ferventest devotion unto them. And therefore we may conclude that this confidence, religiousness, and fervor proceedeth from hence: that these men . . . are thus confirmed in this faith and are thus set on fire with this devotion more vigorously and vehemently than ordinary secular men by the immediate working and inspiration of the Holy Ghost. . . . And it were not agreeable to the goodness of God to permit those persons that most affectionately seek him and who for his sake, out of pure devotion and desire of contemplating truth, do abridge themselves of all other worldly contentments, to have their understandings worse blinded with false doctrine than other men that seek him more coldly . . . as of necessity it would follow theirs were, if the doctrine that the Catholic Church professeth were not true, and the Holy Ghost resided not in it to work those effects. Now on the contrary part, let us make a short inquiry whether it be probable that the late pretended reformers have been illuminated by God in an extraordinary manner to discover truth, which they say hath for many ages lain hid. Surely if any such thing were, they would have expressed in their manner of life, by some extraordinary sanctity and excellent actions and supernatural wisdom, that extraordinary communication which they would persuade us they had with the Divinity. . . . The apostles when they were replenished with the Holy Ghost received immediately the gift of tongues and a clear intelligence of all the Scriptures, whereby they made clear unto the auditors the obscurest passages of them, and continually wrought miracles; and all those that ever since them have introduced the Gospel into any country where formerly it was not received have still had their commission authorized by the same seals: and shall our late particular reformers be credited in their pretended vocation and in their new doctrine that shaketh the very foundations of the faith that hath been by the whole Christian world for so many ages believed and delivered over from hand to hand, whenas nothing appeareth in them supernatural and proceeding from a divine cause?

---

[5] {Everard makes the same argument: see <555–56>.}

This, Madam, is as much as I shall trouble your Ladyship withal upon this occasion, which indeed is much more than at the first I intended or could have suspected my pen would have stolen from me. The substance of all which may be summed up and reduced to this following short question: namely, whether in the election of the faith whereby you hope to be saved, you will be guided by the unanimous consent of the wisest, the learnedest, and the piousest men of the whole world, that have been instructed in what they believe by men of the like quality living in the age before them, and so from age to age until the apostles and Christ, and that in this manner have derived from that fountain both a perfect and full knowledge of all that ought to be believed, and likewise a right understanding and interpretation of the Scriptures as far as concerneth faith (the true sense of which, so far, is also delivered over by the same tradition); or whether you will assent unto the new and wrested interpretations of places of Scripture made by late men that rely merely upon their single judgment and wit (too slight a barque to sail in through so immense an ocean) and whose chief leaders for human respects and sinister ends (not to say worse of them) made a desperate defection from the other main body, since which time no two of them have agreed in doctrine, and among whom it is impossible your Ladyship's great judgment and strong understanding should find any solid stay to repose securely upon and to quiet all those rational doubts that your piercing wit suggesteth unto you. And here, Madam, I shall make an end, having sincerely and as succinctly and plainly as I can delivered you the chief considerations that in this affair turned the scale of the balance with me. . . . wherein you will believe I would take the greatest pains I was able to be sure not to be deceived. . . . This I am sure of, that although I have set this down for your Ladyship in 2 or 3 days (for it is no longer since you commanded me to do it), yet it is the production and result of many hours' meditations by myself—or rather of some years; and how dry soever they may appear to your Ladyship at the first, yet . . . you will (I know), by such application of your thoughts upon them, enlarge and refine what dependeth of[6] the main heads far beyond anything I have said. For such is the nature of notions that are wrought, like the silkworm's ball, of one's own substance: they afford fine and strong threads for a good workman to weave into a fair piece of stuff; whereas they that like bees do gather honey from several authors, or that like ants do make up their store by what they pick up in the original crude substance from others' labors, may peradventure in their works seem more pleasant at the first taste, or appear to have a fairer heap at the first view, but the other's web is more useful, more substantial, and more durable.

I beseech God of his grace and goodness, in this life to enlighten your Ladyship's understanding that you may discern truth and to dispose your will that you may embrace it, and in the next to give you part among those glorious Apostles, Fathers, Doctors, and Martyrs that, deriving the same truth from him, have from hand to hand delivered it over to our times.

FINIS

Text: EEBO (STC [2nd ed.] / 6844.4)
Sir Kenelm Digby, *A conference with a lady about choice of religion* (Paris: widow of J. Blagaert, 1638).

[6] {follows from}

WILLIAM HABINGTON
(1605–1654)

The first two months of his life were particularly eventful. His devoutly Catholic father, Thomas, who nearly went to the block for his involvement in the Babington Plot, had retrofitted his Worcester estate, Hindlip Hall, with multiple priest-holes. There was a Jesuit priest in residence on the fourth of November 1605, the night Habington was born—the night before the gunpowder kegs under Parliament were to have exploded (a catastrophe averted because Habington's maternal uncle, Lord Monteagle, passed on the warning letter to the King). In December, four of the plotters, Garnet among them, showed up at Hindlip Hall. The government search parties arrived a month later. It took them twelve days to discover all the hiding places. Garnet and another Jesuit surrendered on the eighth. Thomas Habington was arrested as well, but he had wisely chosen to be elsewhere during Garnet's visit, and this, plus the intercessions of Lord Mounteagle, allowed him to return home, where he spent his remaining years researching the antiquities of Worcestershire.

At thirteen, Habington was sent to abroad to receive a Catholic education, first from the Jesuits at St. Omer (1618–22) and then at the Jesuit Collège de Clermont in Paris. He returned to Hindlip in the mid-1620s, later moving to London, where he became a well-known figure in both literary and courtly circles, numbered among the Sons of Ben and the servants of Henrietta Maria. In 1633 he secretly married Lucy Herbert, granddaughter of the 8th Earl of Northumberland and daughter of William Herbert, 1st Baron Powis. Their courtship and marriage form the subject of Habington's *Castara* (1634; rev. ed. 1635). His one play, *The Queen of Arragon*, was staged at court and at Blackfriars in 1640. The third edition of *Castara*, published the same year, includes for the first time a section of religious lyrics, two of which are reprinted below. Habington's historical works—the *Observations upon history* and *History of Edward the Fourth*—likewise appeared in the early 1640s.

When the war came, Habington joined the royalist forces; he was serving in the Worcester garrison when it surrendered to Parliamentary troops in 1646. His Hindlip estate was sequestered the next year, but Habington continued to reside there until his death in 1654.

One associates early modern Catholic verse with Crashaw, even though Crashaw's lyrics mostly pre-date his entrance into the Roman communion. Habington, who was a cradle Catholic, writes a very different sort of sacred poetry: sans baroque emotionalism, sans Counter-Reformation exceptionalism. The poems are not distinctively Catholic; most of them, including the two reprinted below, are not even distinctively Christian. Although modeled on the Psalms, their witness to the transience and futility of earthly glories fuses the ancient topoi of *memento mori* with biblical *vanitas* and *contemptus mundi* motifs. The finest of Habington's religious poems, *"Nox nocti"* is a darkly powerful rewrite of Psalm 19 that begins with a celebration of divine creation and ends with something close to Pascal's terror before the "eternal silence of infinite spaces." The impending fall of the British monarchies haunts both poems; so too the impending rise of British imperialism. Habington's prophetic indictment seems yet more striking when one recalls that John Denham's *Cooper Hill*, with its famous paean to English mercantile empire, comes out in 1642, just two years later.[1]

SOURCES: *ODNB*; Jerome de Groot, "Coteries, complications and female agency," in *The 1630s: interdisciplinary essays on culture and politics in the Caroline era*, ed. Ian Atherton and Julie Sanders (Manchester UP, 2006), 189–210; W. D. McGaw, "William Habington and the 'Lion of the North,'" *Studia Neophilologica* 49 (1977): 243–46.

---

[1] See Joshua Scodel, *Excess and the mean in early modern English literature* (Princeton UP, 2002), 128–33; as also Christopher Hodgkins, *Reforming empire: Protestant colonialism and conscience in British literature* (U Missouri P, 2002).

WILLIAM HABINGTON

Castara, 3rd ed.
1640

Non nobis Domine[1]

No marble statue nor high
Aspiring pyramid be rais'd
To lose its head within the sky!
What claim have I to memory?
　　God be thou only prais'd!

Thou in a moment canst defeat
The mighty conquests of the proud,
And blast the laurels of the great.
Thou canst make brightest glory set
　　O'th'sudden in a cloud.

How can the feeble works of art
Hold out 'gainst the assault of storms?
Or how can brass to him impart
Sense of surviving fame, whose heart
　　Is now resolv'd to worms?

Blind folly of triumphing pride!
Eternity why buildst thou here?
Dost thou not see the highest tide
Its humbled stream in th'ocean hide,
　　And ne'er the same appear?

---

[1] {Not unto us, O Lord [not unto us, but unto thy name give glory], Ps. 115:1 (KJV)}

That tide which did its banks o'erflow,
As sent abroad by th'angry sea
To level vastest buildings low
And all our trophies overthrow,
    Ebbs like a thief away.

And thou who to preserve thy name
Leav'st statues in some conquer'd land!
How will posterity scorn fame,
When th'idol shall receive a maim,
    And lose a foot or hand?

How wilt thou hate thy wars, when he,
Who only for his hire did raise
Thy counterfeit in stone, with thee
Shall stand competitor, and be
    Perhaps thought worthier praise?

No laurel wreath about my brow!
To thee, my God, all praise, whose law
The conquer'd doth and conqueror bow!
For both dissolve to air, if thou
    Thy influence but withdraw.

Nox nocti indicat scientiam[2]

    When I survey the bright
        Celestial sphere,
So rich with jewels hung, that night
Doth like an Aethiop bride appear,

    My soul her wings doth spread
        And heaven-ward flies,
Th'Almighty's mysteries to read
In the large volumes of the skies.

    For the bright firmament
        Shoots forth no flame
So silent but is eloquent
In speaking the Creator's name.

    No unregarded star
        Contracts its light
Into so small a charactar,
Remov'd far from our human sight

---

[2] {Night unto night sheweth knowledge, Ps. 19:2 (KJV)}

But if we steadfast look,
     We shall discern
In it, as in some holy book,
How man may heavenly knowledge learn.

It tells the conqueror
     That far-stretcht power,
Which his proud dangers traffic for,
Is but the triumph of an hour;

That from the farthest North[3]
     Some nation may,
Yet undiscovered, issue forth
And o'er his new-got conquest sway;

Some nation yet shut in
     With hills of ice
May be let out to scourge his sin
'Till they shall equal him in vice;

And then they likewise shall
     Their ruin have,
For as yourselves, your empires fall;
And every kingdom hath a grave.

Thus those celestial fires,
     Though seeming mute,
The fallacy of our desires
And all the pride of life confute.

For they have watcht since first
     The world had birth,
And found sin in itself accurst,
And nothing permanent on earth.

⤝⤞

Text: EEBO (STC [2nd ed.] / 12585)
William Habington, *Castara the third edition. Corrected and augmented* (London: Printed for Will. Cooke, 1640).

[3] {A possible allusion to Scotland, with which England was then at war; however, prior to the late 17th century, barbarism was typically associated with the far north.}

GEORGE WITHER[1]

Hallelujah: or Britain's second remembrancer
1641

To the thrice honorable, the high courts of Parliament,
now assembled in the triple empire of the British Isles,
Geo. Wither humbly tenders this his
Hallelujah, or second remembrancer

Fifteen years now past, I was in some things of moment a remembrancer to these Islands, which have in many particulars so punctually and so evidently succeeded according to my predictions, that not a few have acknowledged they were not published so long before they came to pass without the special providence and mercy of God to these kingdoms.[2] . . .

For though it were but a bush which burned, God was the inflamer of that shrub; and, as it now seemeth, it was a beacon warrantably fired to give true alarms to prevent those dangers and innovations which then to me appeared near at hand. . . .

I arrogate no more than Balaam's ass might have done: God opened mine eyes to see dangers which neither my most prudent masters nor men as cunning as Balaam seemed to behold. God opened my mouth also and compelled me, beyond my natural abilities, to speak of that which I foresaw would come to pass. . . .

For the better performance of which duty, I do now execute the office of a remembrancer in another manner than heretofore; and have directed unto you, the most honorable representative bodies of these kingdoms, the sweet perfume of pious praises, compounded according to the art of the spiritual apothecary, to further the performance of thankful devotions; hoping that by your authorities they shall, if they so merit, be recommended unto them for whose use they are prepared. And there will be need both of God's extraordinary blessing and of your grave assistance herein.

---

[1] {For the overview of Wither's life and work, see the introduction prefacing his 1623 *Hymns and songs of the Church* <supra>.}

[2] {Wither here refers to his dire prophecies of divine chastisement in the 1628 *Britain's remembrancer*.}

For so innumerable are the foolish and profane songs now delighted in, to the dishonor of our language and religion, that hallelujahs and pious meditations are almost out of use and fashion; yea, not in private only, but at our public feasts and civil meetings also, scurrilous and obscene songs are impudently sung without respecting the reverend presence of matrons, virgins, magistrates, or divines. Nay, sometimes in their despite they are called for, sung, and acted with such abominable gesticulations as are very offensive to all modest hearers and beholders, and fitting only to be exhibited at the diabolical solemnities of Bacchus, Venus, or Priapus.

For prevention whereof, I am an humble petitioner that some order may be provided by the wisdom and piety of your assemblies, seeing, upon due examination of this abuse, it may soon be discovered that as well *censores canticorum* as *librorum* will be necessary in these times;[3] and I am confident your zeal and prudence will provide as you see cause, and accept these endeavors of your humble suppliant and servant, who submitting himself and his remembrances to your grave censures, submissively takes his leave and beseecheth God's blessing upon your honorable designs and consultations.

TO THE READER

. . .

I have observed three sorts of poesy now in fashion. One consisteth merely of rhymes, clinches {puns}, anagrammatical fancies, or such like verbal or literal conceits as delight schoolboys and pedantical wits; having nothing in them either to better the understanding or stir up good affections.

These rattles of the brain are much admired by those who, being men in years, continue children in understanding, and those chats[4] of wit may well be resembled to the fantastical suits made of taffeties and sarcenets, cut out in slashes, which are neither comely nor commodious for sober men to wear, nor very useful for anything, being out of fashion, but to be cast on the dunghill.

Another sort of poesy is the delivery of necessary truths and wholesome documents, couched in significant parables and illustrated by such flowers of rhetoric as are helpful to work upon the affections and to insinuate into apprehensive readers a liking of those truths and instructions which they express.

These inventions are most acceptable to those who have ascended the middle region of knowledge; for though the wisest men make use of them in their writings, yet they are not the wisest men for whose sake they are used. This poesy is frequently varied according to the several growths, ages, and alterations of that language wherein it is worded; and that which this day is approved of as an elegancy may seem less facetious {elegant} in another age; for which cause such compositions may be resembled to garments of whole silk adorned with gold lace; for while the stuff, shape, and trimming are in fashion, they are a fit wearing for princes; and the materials, being unmangled, may continue useful to some purposes for some other persons.

---

[3] {This petition gives substance to Milton's fears in *Areopagitica* that effectual censorship would have to extend to "all the lutes, the violins, and the guitars in every house . . . all the airs and madrigals, that whisper softness in chambers."}

[4] {frivolous prattle}

A third poesy there is which delivers commodious truths and things really necessary in as plain and in as universal terms as it can possibly devise; so contriving also what is intended that the wisest, having no cause to contemn it, may be profitably remembered of what they know, and the ignorant become informed of what is convenient to be known.

This is not so plausible among the witty as acceptable to the wise, because it regardeth not so much to seem elegant as to be useful for all persons in all times; which it endeavoreth by using a phrase and method neither unpleasing to the time present nor likely to grow altogether out of use in future ages; and if it make use of enigmatical expressions, it is to prevent the profanation of some truths or the oppressing of their professors: the commendation of this poesy is not improperly set forth by a mantle or such-like upper garment of the best English cloth; for that continueth indifferently serviceable for all seasons, and may be usefully and commendably worn by men of every degree.

To this plain and profitable poesy I have humbly aspired, and especially in this book, imitating therein, though coming infinitely behind them, no worse patterns than the most holy prophets; and by this means, I hope the memorial of God's mercies shall be the better preserved in our hearts, and things pertinent to our happiness be the more frequently presented to a due consideration.

. . .

Songs and hymns are the most ancient writings of the world, and the most esteemed in pious ages; in them divine mysteries were first recorded, and doubtless to celebrate the honor of God and to stir up men's affections to the love and practice of holiness and virtue was the prime subject and scope of ancient song and music, though at this time they are otherwise overmuch employed. . . .

. . . Nay, poesy hath been so profaned by unhallowed suggestions . . . and by having been long time the bawd to lust, and abused to other improper ends, that some good men, though therein not very wise men, have affirmed poesy to be the language and invention of the devil.

To prevent these errors and offences, Mr. Sandys, Mr. Herbert, Mr. Quarles, and some others have lately to their great commendations seriously endeavored, by tuning their muses to divine strains and by employing them in their proper work. For the like prevention I have also labored according to my talent. . . .

. . .

In all these compositions, I have made use of no man's method or meditations but mine own. Not that I despised good helps, but partly because my fortunes and my employments compelled me to spin them out of my own bowels as occasions were presented unto me; and chiefly because I thought, by searching mine own heart, I should the better find out those musings and expressions which would flow with least harshness and be most suitable to their capacities whom I desire to profit.

. . .

Without more words, I commit these my humble devotions to their use who shall approve and accept of them, and the event {outcome} of my studies and desires to God's gracious providence, whom I beseech to sanctify them to his glory.

June 1, 1641.

THE FIRST PART
CONSISTING OF HYMNS OCCASIONAL[5]

HYMN XXII
When we ride for pleasure.

WE make use of God's creatures, as well for pleasure as for necessity. Therefore when we ride forth for pleasure, it will become us to mix, now and then, such thankful meditations with our lawful pleasures as are in this hymn.

My God, how kind, how good art thou!
Of man, how great is thy regard!
Who dost all needful things allow,
And some for pleasure hast prepar'd.
With what great speed, with how much ease,
On this thy creature am I borne,
Which at my will and when I please
Doth forward go and back return.

2. Why should not I, O gracious God,
More pliant be to thy command,
When I am guided by thy word,
And gently reined[6] by thy hand?
Asham'd I may become to see
The beast, which knows nor good nor ill,
More faithful in obeying me
Than I have been to do thy will.

3. From him therefore, Lord, let me learn
To serve thee better than I do,
And mind how much it may concern
My welfare to endeavor so.
And though I know this creature lent
As well for pleasure as for need,
That I the wrong thereof prevent,
Let me still carefully take heed.

4. For he that willfully shall dare
That creature to oppress or grieve,
Which God to serve him doth prepare,
Himself of mercy doth deprive.
And he, or his, unless in time
They do repent of that abuse,
Shall one day suffer for his crime,
And want such creatures for their use.

---

[5] {Wither's title for these hymns probably derives from the *Occasional meditations* of Joseph Hall, first published in 1630.}

[6] {Here and elsewhere, the terminal "ed" is a separate syllable: e.g., "rein-ed".}

HYMN XLIII
A hymn for a house-warming

THE ancient and laudable use of house-warmings is here insinuated; for in this hymn the friends assembled are taught to beseech God Almighty to make that habitation prosperous and comfortable to them and theirs who are newly come thither to dwell.

Among those points of neighborhood
Which our forefathers did allow,
That custom in esteem hath stood
Which we do put in practice now.
 For when their friends new dwellings had,
Them thus they welcome thither made,
That they the sooner might be free
From strangeness, where they strangers be.

2. To this good end we partly came,
And partly friendship to augment;
But if we fail not in the same,
This is the prime of our intent:
 We come with holy charms to bless
 The house our friends do now possess,
In hope that God *Amen* will say
To that for which we now shall pray.

3. Lord, keep this place, we thee desire,
To these new comers ever free
From raging winds, from harmful fire,
From waters that offensive be,
 From graceless child, from servants ill,
 From neighbors bearing no good-will,
And from the chiefest plagues of life,
A husband false, a faithless wife.

4. Let neither thieves that rove by night,
Nor those that sneak about by day,
Have pow'r their persons to affright,
Or to purloin their goods away.
 Let nothing here be seen or heard
 To make by day or night afeard:
No sudden cries, no fearful noise,
No vision grim, or dreadful voice.

5. Let on this house no curse remain,
If any on the same be laid;
Let no imposture pow'r obtain
To make the meanest wit afraid.
 Let here nor Zim nor Jim be seen,
 The fabled fairy king or queen,
Nor such delusions as are said

To make the former age afraid.
6. Keep also, Lord, we pray from hence,
As much as frailty will allow,
The guiltiness of each offence,
Which to a crying sin may grow.
Let no more want, wealth, hope, or fear,
Nor greater griefs or joys, be here,
Than may still keep them in thy grace,
Who shall be dwellers in this place.
7. But that just measure let them have
Of ev'ry means which may acquire
The blessedness which they most crave,
Who to the truest bliss aspire.
And if well-wishers absent be
Who better wish them can than we,
To make this blessing up entire,
We thereto add what they desire.

HYMN LIII[7]
Another hymn for the Lord's Supper

God's unspeakable favor vouchsafed in the sacrament of the body and blood of Christ is acknowledged; the inexpressibleness of that mysterious communion is confessed, and those blessed effects are hereby desired also which ought to be endeavored for by every worthy partaker of the same.

. . .

12. But if in essence we agree,
Let us in love assay
To erring souls true guides to be
And to the weak a stay.
For love is that strong cément, Lord,
Which us must reunite;
In bitter speeches, fire, and sword,
It never takes delight.
13. Mere carnal instruments these are,
And they are much beguil'd
Who dream that these ordained were
Our breaches to rebuild.
Therefore, we pray thee, by that love
Which us together brought,
That thou all Christian men wouldst move
To love as Christians ought.

---

[7] {Compare with the 1623 version of the same hymn in *Hymns and songs*, #83, st. 17ff. *<vide supra>*}

14. Let not self-will our hearts bewitch
      With pride or private hate,
Or cherish those contentions which
      Disturb a quiet state;
Nor suffer avaricious ends,
      Or ignorant despite,
To hinder those from being friends
      Whom love should fast unite.
15. Let those who, heedless of thy word,
      Suppose that fleshly pow'r
Or that the temporary sword
      Can ghostly foes devour,
Let them perceive thy weapons are
      No such as they do feign,
Or that it is a carnal war
      Which must thy truth maintain.
16. Confessors, martyrs, preachers, Lord,
      Thy battles fight for thee;
Thy Holy Spirit and thy Word
      Their proper weapons be.
Faith, hope, long-suffering, prayer, and love
      For bulwarks are prepar'd,
And will their fittest engines prove
      To conquer and to guard.
17. For Babel, doubtless, may as well
      Thereby be overthrown,
As those accursed walls which fell
      When rams-horn trumps were blown.

      The worldlings' parts to play,
Or to believe God's blessed peace
      Shall come the devil's way.
18. Lord! let thy flesh and blood divine,
      Which now receiv'd hath been,
Our hearts to charity incline,
      Our souls refine from sin.
And by this holy sacrament
      Make us in mind retain
What thou didst suffer to prevent
      Our everlasting pain.
19. Moreover let us for thy sake
      With one another bear,
When we offences give or take,
      That thine we may appear.
And that when hence we called be,

We thither may ascend,
To live and be belov'd of thee,
Where love nor life have end.

HYMN LXXX
When a dear friend is deceased

SOME are so sensible of losing their dearly beloved friends that they are almost swallowed up with grief: therefore this hymn was prepared to mitigate their sorrow by directing them for consolation to him in whom they may find again their deceased friends and better comforts than they lost.

Now my dear friend is gone,
Ah me! how faint my heart appears!
How sad, and how alone!
How swoln with sighs, how drown'd with tears!
 Faint† would I tell,   †gladly
 What griefs, what hell,
Is now within my breast;
 But who doth live,
 That ease can give,
Or bring me wished rest?
2. Those ears which I would fain
Should once more hear what I would say,
Shall never now again
Unto their heart my thoughts convey;
 Nor shall that tongue,
 Whose tones were song
And music still to me,
 To please or cheer
 My drooping ear,
Hereafter tuned be.
3. O dear, O gracious God,
If in ourselves we bliss had sought,
Of passions what a load,
Upon my soul had now been brought!
 How had I found,
 Within that round
Wherein I should have run,
 The joyful end
 Which doth befriend
Affections well begun?
4. Had we our love confin'd
To that which mortal proves to be,
Or had we been so blind
That we death's power could not foresee,

Where had been found,
When under ground
My dear companion lay,
        A fit relief
        To cure that grief
Which wounds my heart this day?
5. But while we liv'd and lov'd,
In thee, each other up we stor'd;
My friend, by death remov'd,
In thee, therefore, I seek, O Lord.
        My loss by none
        But thee alone
Repaired now can be;
        What I endure
        Admits nor cure
    Nor ease except by thee.
6. Be thou to my sad heart
A sweet relief now I am griev'd;
Be to it as thou wert,
When here with me my dearest liv'd.
        That which I lov'd
        Is but remov'd
To thee, our perfect bliss;
        And that I had
        Was but the shade
Of what my darling is.
7. In thee behold I shall,
In thee I shall again enjoy,
What thou away didst call,
And what thou didst by death destroy.
        We by thy grace
        Shall there embrace,
Where friends do never part;
        Which now I mind,
        Methinks I find
Sweet hope relieve my heart.
8. I feel it more and more
My soul of comfort to assure;
And now for ev'ry sore,
I know and feel thou hast a cure;
        For which my tongue
        Shall change her song,
Thy goodness to commend;
        And thou art he

Who still shalt be
My best-affected friend.

HYMN CII
For one upbraided with deformity

To some this is a very great affliction, and they who are sensible of other men's passions will not think it impertinently added, if this hymn be inserted to comfort such as are upbraided or afflicted through their bodily defects in this kind, and to instruct their despisers.

Lord, though I murmur not at thee,
For that in other's eyes
I so deformed seem to be
That me they do despise;
Yet their contempt and their disdain
My heart afflicteth so,
That for mine ease I now complain,
My secret grief to show.
2. Thou know'st, O God, it was not I
Who did this body frame,
On which they cast a scornful eye
By whom I flouted am.
Thou know'st likewise it was not they
Who did their bodies make,
Although on my defects to play
Occasions oft they take.
3. Then why should they have love or fame
For what they have not done,
Or why should I have scorn or shame
For what I could not shun?
Thy workmanship I am, O Lord,
Though they do me deride;
And thou by what they have abhorr'd
Art some way glorified.
4. Therefore since thou this way hast chose
To humble me on earth,
My imperfections now dispose
To help my second birth:
Let me in thee contentment find,
And lovely make thou me,
By those perfections of the mind,
Which dearest are to thee.
5. Since features none in me appear,
To win a fleshly love,

Let those which priz'd by others are,
My passions never move;
But quench thou all those youthful fires
Which in my breast do burn;
And all my lusts and vain desires
To sacred motions turn.
6. So though in secret grief I spend
The life that nature gave,
I shall have comforts in the end
And gain a blessed grave;
From whence the flesh which now I wear,
In glory shall arise,
And fully beautified appear
In all beholders' eyes.

THE SECOND PART
Consisting Of Hymns Temporary.[8]
The Author's Protestation, Petition, And
Charge Concerning These
Temporary Hymns.

Forasmuch as things well intended and good in their own nature may be willfully perverted or misunderstood, and because the great enemy of devotion hath from some of these hymns heretofore published taken occasion to make them unserviceable to others and mischievous to me; yea, and so prevailed, that men contrary in opinion to each other have joined in converting that into a means of my temporal undoing which I prepared for the spiritual profit of others, I do hereby protest that I neither approve nor desire to cherish the observation of Jewish, popish, or of any other superstitious days, times, or seasons; but from the days and times which in our Church and commonwealth are warrantably and piously observed for the furtherance of our sanctification or for the better and oftener commemoration of God's mercies; and from those days and times also whereof general notice is yearly taken for civil ends and purposes, I have rather sought and found opportunities to root out superstition and to bring to remembrance mercies and benefits, past, present, and in hope, which ought to be more thankfully considered.

Our observation of days, times, and seasons in this Church is neither Jewish nor popish; and I unfeignedly believe that if these times of commemoration had not been ordained, fewer by many thousands had heard of those mercies, benefits, and mysteries which we commemorate; and perhaps, if these anniversaries were neglected, many would quite forget them, and the following generations become ignorant of them altogether.

For our Christian festivals and other observable times do give unto us occasion to tell, and unto our children the like occasion to ask, why such times are observed; and this was the prime intent and right use, as well of those Jewish festivals which were observed by divine right, as of the days of Purim, and of such other as were ordained by civil constitution; and I am undoubtingly persuaded that the morality of those observations continues,

---

[8] {pertaining to a specific, limited time}

though their ceremonial part be abrogated; yea, I believe they are so exemplary to us, that we are obliged by their example to take all pertinent and convenient occasions from days, times, and every other good opportunity to commemorate God's mercies and improve our own piety.

. . .

HYMN V
For Wednesday

THE heavens were upon this day first adorned with stars and with those two great luminaries whereby days and nights, times and seasons, are guided and distinguished; and to praise God for these, and for those many blessings of pleasure, profit, and convenience thereby enjoyed, this hymn was composed.

> This day the planets in their spheres
> And those fair stars which night by night
> Have shin'd so many thousand years
> Receiv'd their being and their light.
>   Upon this day were first begun
> Those motions, Lord, by which we know
> How days do pass, how years do run,
> And how the seasons come and go.
> 2. The sun was then ordain'd by thee
> To rule the day and give it light;
> The moon and stars were made to be
> The guides and comforts of the night.
>   For these, therefore, thy praise I sing,
> And for the blessings which to man
> The sun, the moon, or stars do bring,
> Or brought since first the world began.
> 3. For interchange of nights and days,
> For winter, summer, spring, and fall,
> For all of these I give thee praise,
> For thou gav'st being to them all:
>   When sun, or moon, or star, I view,
> Let them so make me think on thee,
> That as days, weeks, and years renew,
> I may renew my thanks to thee.

HYMN XIV[9]
For the King's Day

THE first day of the king's {reign} is yearly solemnized in this kingdom, partly that the people might assemble to praise God for the benefits received by their prince, and partly

---

[9] {This hymn closely resembles its 1623 counterpart (#90), but stanzas 5 & 6 are new.}

to desire God's blessing upon him and his government; which duties being well performed in due time would prevent the mischiefs which attend on tyranny and rebellion.

Lord, when we call to mind those things
　　　Which we should ask of thee,
Rememb'ring that the hearts of kings
　　　At thy disposing be;
And how of all those blessings which
　　　Are outwardly possess'd
To make a kingdom safe and rich,
　　　Good princes are the best:
2. When this we mind, thy name to praise
　　　Our hearts inclined are,
For him, O Lord, whom thou didst raise
　　　The royal wreath to wear;
And we entreat that he may reign
　　　In peaceful safety long,
Thy faith defender to remain,
　　　And shield thy truth from wrong.
3. With awful† love and loving dread　　　　　　　　†reverent
　　　Let us observe him, Lord;
And as the members with their head,
　　　In Christian peace accord.
Then fill him with such princely care
　　　To cherish us for this,
As if his heart did feel we are
　　　Essential parts of his.
4. Let neither party struggle from
　　　The duties it should own,†　　　　　　　　　†owe
Lest each to other plagues become,
　　　And both be overthrown.
For o'er a disobedient land
　　　A tyrant thou wilt set;
And they who tyrant-like command,
　　　Rebellion shall beget.
5. When that ill spirit once is rear'd
　　　Which tyranny doth teach,
Or when that devil hath appear'd
　　　Which doth rebellion preach,
In vain to either party then
　　　Their dangers we foreshow,
Or plead the laws of God or man,
　　　For blind and mad they grow.
6. With willful fury they run on
　　　To execute their will,

Not caring what be said or done,
    Or whom they rob or kill;
And settled peace we seldom see
    Return to them or theirs,
Till rooted from the land they be
    By sickness, death, or wars.
7. Permit not, Lord, so sad a doom
    Upon these realms to fall;
And that on us it may not come,
    Remit our errors all.
Yea, let the party innocent
    Some damage rather take,
Than by self-will or discontent
    A greater schism to make.
8. Teach us who placed are below,
    Our callings to apply,
And not o'er-curious be to know
    What things are done on high.
Teach him uprightly to command,
    Us rightly to obey,
That both in safety still may stand,
    And keep a lawful way.
9. When kings' affairs we pry into,
    Ourselves we oft beguile;
And what we rather ought to do,
    Is left undone the while;
Whereas if each one did attend
    The course wherein they live,
And all the rest to thee commend,
    Then all should better thrive.
10. Our minds, O Lord, compose thou thus,
    And our dread sovereign save;
Bless us in him, and him in us,
    That both may blessings have.
Yea, grant that many years we may
    This hymn devoutly sing,
And mark it for a happy day
    Wherein he first was king.

HYMN XXVII

Another for the same day {Feast of the Nativity}

SINCE the Godhead vouchsafed so to honor the Manhood as to become united thereunto, we are by this hymn remembered not to despise those who are of the same nature with us, but rather humbly to descend to others for their good, and to endeavor the reparation of our nature by striving to conform it unto Christ.

> Since all of us near kinsmen be,
>> Descended from one stem,
> Why brutishly inclin'd are we
>> Our brethren to contemn?
> He that both heaven and earth did frame,
>> Our nature did not scorn;
> But being God, a man became,
>> And of a maid was born.
> 2. This, men and angels wonder'd at,
>> As with good cause they may,
> This, therefore, to commemorate,
>> We set apart this day:
> This day we make an anniverse,
>> That favor to record,
> And to our children to rehearse
>> The mercies of the Lord.
> 3. That moment whereon God decreed
>> To do as he foresaid,
> Enabled was the woman's seed
>> To break the serpent's head;
> And Jesus Christ to satisfy
>> For our accused crimes,
> Vouchsaf'd both to be born and die
>> At his appointed times.
> 4. By him newborn so let us be,
>> To sin so let us die,
> That we may live with him where he
>> Is now enthron'd on high.
> As he the Godhead for our sake
>> With Manhood did array,
> On us his nature let us take
>> As fully as we may.
> 5. Whereto we nearest shall attain,
>> When we do mercy show,
> And strive those longings to restrain
>> Which flesh and blood pursue.
> We are assur'd, O Savior Christ,
>> Thine incarnation may
> Our nature hereunto assist:
>> Assist, therefore, we pray.

THE THIRD PART
CONTAINING HYMNS PERSONAL.
TO THE READER

THESE times are so captious that we otherwhile {sometimes} displease even when we do courtesies, if we prevent not mistakings by some excuses or complements; therefore, without a prologue I dare not proceed to the next part or volume of hymns, lest I might seem burdensome in their number, for some have already given me occasion to suspect that objection.

. . .

I confess I am, for aught I know or have yet heard, the first that did compose personal hymns in this kind; and perhaps, therefore, as it usually fares with new inventions, they will not seem so plausible as occasional and temporary hymns, which have been very anciently in use; yet I am persuaded that when they are better known, no discreet reader will either disapprove them or judge them to be any of those novelties which are justly despicable or impertinent.

. . .

HYMN I
For a Briton

WE that are Britons enjoy many peculiar privileges, and have obtained sundry blessings and deliverances famously observable; we are therefore obliged to a special thankfulness, not only as we are Christian men, but as we are Britons also; and this hymn intends the furtherance of that duty.

> Halellujah now I sing,
> For my heart invites my tongue
> To extol my God, my King,
> In that blessed angel song;
>   And as I enabled am,
> I will sacrifice to God
> Thanks in this whole island's name
> In a joyful praiseful ode:
> You that loyal Britons be,
>   Hallelujah sing with me.
>   *Cho.* Hallelujah sing with me,
>   You that loyal Britons be.
> 2. On her coasts our Maker smiles,
> And vouchsafed her the rule
> Over all the floods and isles,
> From the Midland Straits to Thule;
>   Plenty doth her valleys fill,
> Health is in her climates found,
> Pleasure plays in ev'ry hill,
> And these blessings peace hath crown'd:
>   Hallelujah therefore sing

Till the shores with echoes ring.
    Cho. Till the shores with echoes ring,
    Hallelujah therefore sing.
3. When that blessed light arose
Which dispelled death's black shade,
She was of the first of those
Who thereof was partner made;
    And although she seem a place
To the frozen zone confin'd,
Yet the longest day of grace
In her happy coasts hath shin'd:
    Sing let us to God therefore,
    Hallelujah evermore.
    Cho. Hallelujah evermore,
    Sing let us to God therefore.
4. That no foreign foe may seize
Her dear children evermore,
Ditch'd and wall'd with rocks and seas
Her beloved borders are;
    God Almighty so provides,
That likewise to guard her lands,
She hath clouds, and wind, and tides,
Calms, and storms, and shelves, and sands;
    Now, therefore, my song shall be,
    Hallelujah, Lord, to thee.
    Cho. Hallelujah, Lord, to thee,
    Now, therefore, my song shall be.
5. When we had a darkness here
Worse than what th' Egyptians had,
When we more in bondage were,
And to Babel slaves were made,
    God renew'd again the light
And the freedom which we lost,
That for thanks enjoy we might
What our fathers' lives had cost:
    Therefore, while I have a tongue
    Hallelujah shall be sung.
    Cho. Hallelujah shall be sung,
    Therefore, while I have a tongue.
6. When our Deborah arose
And God's Israel judg'd here,
When confederated foes
Did invincible appear,
    Spain's proud Sisera had thought
To have sunk us with his weight,

But the stars against him fought
And made famous eighty-eight:
    Hallelujah, therefore, cry,
    Till heav'n's vaulted roof reply.
    Cho. Till heav'n's vaulted roof reply,
    Hallelujah, therefore, cry.
7. When of harms we dreamed not,
But at rest securely liv'd,
By a damned powder plot,
Rome our ruin had contriv'd;
    For by thunders from below,
Had not God forbad the doom,
We had perish'd at a blow,
And but few had known by whom:
    Hallelujah, therefore, sound,
    For the grace which then we found.
    Cho. For the grace which then we found,
    Hallelujah, therefore, sound.
8. When by riot and excess
We those times of dearth deserv'd,
Which did bring us to distress
And in danger to be sterv'd,
    Once God sent beyond belief,
Fruits where none did plant or sow,
And at other times relief,
Ere we saw the same in show.
    To our great and gracious King,
    Hallelujah, therefore, sing.
    Cho. Hallelujah, therefore, sing,
    To our great and gracious King.
9. When for our contagious crimes
Sicknesses have raged here,
Such as few preceding times
Therewithal acquainted were;
    When a pestilential breath
Made us from each other fly,
Threat'ning universal death,
God had pity on our cry:
    Therefore, while we breathing be,
    Hallelujah sing will we.
    Cho. Hallelujah sing will we,
    Therefore, while we breathing be.
10. Worst of wars, domestic war,
'Twixt our nations was begun,[10]

---

[10] {A reference to the Bishops Wars of 1639–40 pitting England against Scotland.}

Spreading threats and terrors far
Of more mischief than was done;
    Here it march'd as if it said,
Britain, speedily repent,
Else my fury yet delay'd,
Thee and thine ere long will rent:
Therefore, trumpets, fifes, and drums,
    Hallelujah well becomes.
    Cho. Hallelujah well becomes,
    Warlike trumpets, fifes, and drums.
11. When a general offence
Had almost to ruin brought,
Law, religion, state, and prince,
And a schism among us wrought;
    Yea, when snares for us were laid,
And when avarice and pride
Had our freedoms nigh betray'd,
God protection did provide:[11]
    Hallelujah, therefore, sound,
    Till it reach the starry round.
    Cho. Till it reach the starry round,
    Hallelujah we will sound.

HYMN V
For a Member of the Parliament

It is necessary that the rule whereby things are to be regulated should be straight; and therefore law-makers ought to be wise and upright men, lest the chief remedy of our evils be made worse than the evils themselves. To the members of our High Court of Parliament this is well known; yet this hymn shall perhaps be a means to remember some of them of that which they know.

They no mean place of trust receive,
    Who by free choice have gain'd
That faculty legislative
    Which I have now obtain'd;
For they have ample pow'r from those
    By whom they chosen be,
In temp'ral things to bind and loose
    As they just cause do see.
2. Whoe'er, therefore, they be that shall
    Ambitiously affect
To fill such rooms before those call
    Who freely should elect—

---

[11] {Perhaps a reference to the calling of the Long Parliament.}

Whoe'er those be, they more presume
    Than justice doth permit,
And more unto themselves assume
    Than reason judgeth fit.
3. Whoe'er, likewise, for private ends,
    For favor, fear, or hate;
To harm his foes, to please his friends,
    Or save his own estate;
Yea, whosoe'er his dearest blood
    Or those by him begot
Prefers before the common good,
    This trust deserveth not.
4. Lawgivers personate a part
    Which doth in them require
A prudent brain, an upright heart,
    A rectified desire:
For who believes that they can give
    To others laws upright,
Who lewdly talk, profanely live,
    And in vain things delight?
5. Imprudent legislators may
    Much greater mischiefs cause
And innocency more betray
    Than they that break the laws:
For he that many laws doth break
    May wrong but one or two,
But they which one bad law shall make
    Whole kingdoms may undo.
6. Inspire me, Lord, with grace, therefore,
    With wisdom and stout zeal,
And with uprightness, evermore
    To serve the common weal;
And so to serve, that their offence
    At all times I may shun,
Who serve it so as if the prince
    And kingdom were not one.
7. He that with one of these partakes
    Unto the other's wrong,
What goodly show soe'er he makes,
    Will injure both ere long:
Yea, whatsoever such pretend,
    Whate'er they swear or say,
They will be traitors in the end,
    And one or both betray.

HYMN XXI
For one contentedly married

THE intent of this ode is to show that our natural affections are never fully satisfied in the choice of our helpers until God bring man and wife together by, as it were, making the one out of the other through a frequent conversing together and by observing and approving each other's condition, which is never done till those passions are cast into a sleep, which make them dote on wealth, honor, beauty, and such unfit marriage-makers.

Since they in singing take delight
Who in their love unhappy be,
Why should not I in song delight
Who from their sorrow now am free?
    That such as can believe may know
    What comforts are on earth below,
And prove what blessings may be won
By loving so as I have done.
2. When first affection warm'd my blood,
Which was ere wit could ripen'd be,
And ere I fully understood
What fire it was that warmed me,
    My youthful heat a love begat,
    That love did love I know not what;
But this I know, I felt more pains
Than many a broken heart sustains.

. . .

7. Nor ease nor pleasure could I find
In beauty, honor, love, or pelf;
Nor means to gain a settled mind
Till I had found my second self:
    Thus till our granddame Eve was made,
    No helper our first parent had;
Which proves a wife in value more
Than all the creatures made before.
8. Half tir'd in seeking what I sought,
I fell into a sleep at last;
And God for me my wishes wrought,
When hope of them were almost past;
    With Adam I this favor had,
    That out of me my wife was made,
And when I waked I espied
That God for me had found a bride.
9. How he this riddle brought to pass,
This curious world shall never hear;
A secret work of his it was,
Not fit for every vulgar ear:

Out of each other form'd were we,
    Within a third our beings be;
    And our well-being was begun
By being in ourselves undone.
10. I have the height of my desire,
In secret no dislike I find;
Love warms me with a kindly fire,
No jealous pangs torment my mind:
    I breathe no sigh, I make no moan,
    As others do and I have done;
Nor do I mark, nor do I care,
How fair or lovely others are.
11. My heart at quiet lets me lie
And moves no passions in my breast;
Nor tempting tongue, nor speaking eye,
Nor smiling lip, can break my rest:
    The peer I sought by me is found,
    My earthly hopes by thee are crown'd;
And I in one all pleasures find
That may be found in woman-kind.
12. Each hath of other like esteem,
And what that is we need not tell;
For we are one, though two we seem,
And in each other's heart we dwell;
    There dwells he too, embracing us,
    By whom we were endeared thus;
He makes us rich though seeming poor,
And when we want will give us more.
13. Lord, let our love in thee begun,
In thee, likewise, continuance have;
And if thy will may so be done,
Together lodge us in one grave.
    Thence on the Lamb's great wedding-day
    Raise us together from the clay;
And where the Bridegroom doth remain,
Let us both live and love again.

HYMN XXIV

For a man in general

Few men so consider the privileges of their sex as to be thankful for the same, by which neglect they sometimes abuse their prerogatives; the amendment of which oversights was aimed at by offering this hymn to be sometimes used.

Great, O Lord, thy favor was,
That a being I have gain'd;

Greater was in this thy grace,
That therewith I life obtain'd;
    But in that the soul I had
Thou with reason hast endow'd,
And to reason faith didst add,
Greater mercy hath been show'd.
2. These large favors I confess,
And consider their esteem,
Yet I value ne'ertheless
Those that lower-prized seem;
    Therefore, Lord, in what I can,
Thanks I now to thee return,
That I was brought forth a man,
Rather than a woman born.
3. Not that I their sex despise,
Or too much exalt mine own,
For in these I were unwise,
And more pride than thanks had shown;
    But the truth to thee I'll speak:
Though men strongest counted are,
I confess myself too weak,
Female suff'rings well to bear;
4. For when I observe the pains,
Which pursue a childing womb,
And the torments it sustains
When the hour of birth is come;
    When I heed the nightly care
Which the nursing mouths procure,
Grievous things methinks they are
Which a woman doth endure.
5. To submit my knowing soul,
As they oft are fain† to do,   †obliged
To a churl, a fool's control,
And perhaps dishonest too;
    There my body to subject,
Where I loathe to draw my breath
And by nature disaffect,
Would be worse to me than death.
6. I will thankful therefore be
That at better ease I seem,
And express my thanks to thee
In a due respect of them;
    For as first a woman's blame
Was occasion of our fall,
So first by a woman came
That which makes amends for all.

HYMN LIX

For a prisoner at the place of execution

It is usual for prisoners brought to suffer for death to sing at the place of their execution,[12] that they may testify their hope of a joyful resurrection and of mercy in the world to come; in the expression of which hope, this hymn assisteth and intimateth with what meditations they should be exercised at their suffering.

> When Achan for his lawless prize
>   A censure should receive,
> His pious judge did him advise,
>   To God the praise to give.
> For when our sins we do confess,
>   We make his justice known,
> And praise the ways of righteousness,
>   By blaming of our own.
> 2. Lord, I have well deserv'd the doom
>   By which condemn'd I am,
> And to this place I now am come
>   To suffer for the same;
> In hope through my firm faith in thee,
>   And for thy mercy's cause,
> That this shall my last suff'ring be
>   For breaking of thy laws.
> 3. Behold not, Lord, behold thou not
>   With countenance austere,
> The crimes which do my soul bespot
>   And fill my heart with fear;
> But since I have repented them,
>   Since I in thee believe,
> And do likewise myself condemn,
>   Do thou, O Lord, forgive.
> 4. Though with disgrace cast forth I am
>   And thrust from living men,
> Lord, let me not appear with shame,
>   When I appear again.
> Yea, though this way to thee I come,
>   And have my lot misspent,
> Thy wasteful child receive thou home,
>   Since he doth now repent.
> 5. Them comfort who are fill'd with grief
>   This end of mine to see;

---

[12] {A claim corroborated by the parodic scaffold hymn sung by the kitchen staff at the opening of act 3, scene 2 of George Chapman, Ben Jonson, John Fletcher, and Philip Massinger, *The bloody brother; or Rollo, a tragedy* [ca. 1612–24] (London, 1718).}

Let my sad fall and my lewd life
  To others warnings be;
Oh! let all those who see me climb
  This mountain of disgrace,
Amend their lives whilst they have time,
  And virtue's path embrace.
6. Once more I for myself, O Lord,
  Of thee do humbly crave,
That thou the mercy wouldst afford,
  Which now I seek to have.
But longer why do I delay
  This bitter cup to drink?
Thou knowest, Lord, what I would say,
  Thou know'st what I can think.
7. My heart speaks more than words express,
  And thoughts the language be
By which the sinner in distress
  Speaks loudest unto thee.
The world, therefore, thus turning from,
  Of her I take my leave;
And, Lord, to thee, to thee I come,
  My spirit now receive.

HYMN LXI

For them who intend to settle in Virginia, New England, or the like places

MANY depart every year from this Isle to settle in Virginia, New England, and other parts of America, whose happiness I heartily desire, and whose contented well-being in those places might perhaps be somewhat furthered by such meditations as these; and therefore to those who please to accept thereof, I have recommended my love in this hymn.

Lord! many times thou pleased art,
  Thy servants to command
From their own countries to depart
  Into another land,
That thou mayst there a dwelling-place
  Upon their seed bestow,
Or else to bring thy saving grace
  To those to whom they go.
2. To whatsoever end it were
  That hither I am sent,
To do thy will and serve thee here
  It is my true intent;
And humbly I of thee require,
  That as thy will to do

Thou hast inclined my desire,
    Then grant performance too.
3. From old acquaintance, from my kin,
    And from my native home,
My life anew here to begin,
    I, by thy leave, am come.
And now the place of my abode
    Appeareth unto me
Another world, yet here, O God,
    My God thou still shalt be.
4. This land is thine as well as that
    From which I lately came;
Thy holy Word this light begat,
    The heav'ns are here the same;
Sun, moon, and stars, as well as there,
    The seasons do renew,
The vapors drop their fatness here,
    And thy refreshing dew.
5. Oh, let the Sun of Righteousness,
    Thy truth and grace divine,
Within the uncouth wilderness
    With brightness also shine;
That we and they whom here we find
    May live together so,
That one in faith and one in mind
    We by thy grace may grow.
6. Since to that place we seem as dead
    From whence we be remov'd,
The follies which with us were bred,
    The sins which there we lov'd,
Here let us bury on the shore,
    That they may not be seen
And learn'd by those that heretofore
    So wicked have not been.
7. But innocent, O Lord, and wise,
    Let our demeanors be,
That they whose rudeness we despise
    No ill example see;
But taught as well by deed as word,
    So let their good be sought,
That they may room to us afford,
    As due for what we brought.
8. And let the place from whence we came
    To us be still so dear,

That we nor injure nor defame
    Church, prince, or people there;
But let us pass our censures now
    Upon ourselves alone,
And by our conversation show
    What best is to be done.
9. Make us contented with that lot
    To which we now are brought;
Let that which may not here be got,
    A needless thing be thought;
For this he may suppose with ease,
    Who by the natives heeds
With how few things their minds they please,
    How little nature needs.
10. Let all our labors be for life,
    Our life unto thy praise,
Not needlessly augmenting grief
    Or pain by vain assays:
That though our trash be not so much
    As other countries have,
We may in graces be as rich,
    And inwardly as brave.
11. So when the course of time is run,
    And God shall gather all
That liv'd betwixt the rising sun
    And places of his fall,
Our friends that farthest from us are
    Shall meet with joy again;
And they and we who now are here,
    Together still remain.[13]

TEXT: George Wither, *Hallelujah: or Britain's second remembrancer*, intro. Edward Farr (London, 1857)
    Checked against *Hallelujah, or Britain's second remembrancer, bringing to remembrance (in praiseful and penitential hymns, spiritual songs, and moral-odes) meditations, advancing the glory of God, in practice of piety and virtue: and applied to easy tunes to be sung in families &c / composed in a three-fold volumes by George Wither* (Printed by I. L. for Andrew Hebb, 1641) (Wing / W3162).

[13] {It occurs to me, looking out my study window on a quiet Los Angeles evening, that surely divine providence contrived that the volume should end with this stanza.}

APPENDIX I
List of Authors According to Birth Year

Dod, John 1550–1645

Andrewes, Lancelot 1555–1626

Howson, John 1556/57–1632

Munday, Anthony ca. 1560–1633

Field, Richard 1561–1616

Buckeridge, John ca. 1562–1631

Shelford, Robert ca. 1563–1638/39

Barlow, William ca. 1565–1613

Carier, Benjamin ca. 1565–1614

Bradshaw, William ca. 1570–1618

Donne, John 1572–1631

Laud, William 1573–1645

Hall, Joseph 1574–1656

Bayly, Lewis, ca. 1575–1631

Montagu, Richard ca. 1575–1641

Sibbes, Richard ca. 1577–1635

Corbett, Richard 1582–1635

Fletcher, Phineas 1582–1650

Adams, Thomas 1583–1652

Everard, John ca. 1584–1640/41

Hales, John 1584–1656

Drummond, William 1585–1649

Sparke, Michael ca. 1586–1653

Preston, John 1587–1628

Sanderson, Robert 1587–1663

Wither, George 1588–1667

Sydenham, Humphrey ca. 1591–1650

Quarles, Francis 1592–1644

Cosin, John 1594–1672

?Dow, Christopher fl. 1613–1638

Laurence, Thomas 1597/98–1657

Hoard, Samuel 1599–1658/59

Prynne, William 1600–1669

Strode, William 1600–1645

Earle, John 1601–1665

Chillingworth, William 1602–1644

Digby, Sir Kenelm 1603–1665

Habington, William 1605–1654

Godolphin, Sidney 1610–1643

APPENDIX II
Topical Index*

Absolute & actual power

        Sydenham 1633; Hoard

Adiaphora

        Bradshaw; Buckeridge; Field; Sanderson 1619 (and Christian liberty); Preston 1621; Laud; Montagu; Sanderson 1636; Hales ca. 1619–38

Aesthetics, sacred

        Bradshaw (singing); Strode; Sydenham 1633; *Survey of London*; Dow; Wither 1641

Alsmgiving

        Adams; Cosin 1632–33; *Survey of London*; Hales ca. 1619–38

Altars

        Crashaw (in Shelford); Dow

Animal, treatment of

        Prynne 1629; Hoard; Wither 1641

Anti-Calvinism

        Carier; Howson; Cosin 1621; Montagu 1624, 1625; Hoard; Laurence; Shelford; Dow

Antinomianism

        Sydenham 1622; Everard; Dow (puritan)

---

  * Works will be referred to by their authors' last name or, where appropriate, by their title. If the anthology includes more than one work by the same author, the works will be distinguished by their date: e.g., Wither 1623. The order within each entry follows the volume's more or less chronological ordering.

Anti-popery & popish plots

> Adams; Howson; Fletcher; *The spy*; Cosin 1632–33; Prynne 1636; Dow

Anti-puritanism

> Howson; Sanderson 1619; Corbett ca. 1620–21; Montagu 1624, 1625; Earle; Corbett ca. 1632–33; Sydenham 1633; Shelford; Dow

Apocalypticism

> Corbett ca. 1620–21; Fletcher; *The spy*

Arcana Dei

> *Collegiate suffrage*; Sydenham 1622; Montagu 1624; Everard (and progressive illumination); Laurence; Dow (re divine judgment)

Arminianism & anti-Arminianism

> *Collegiate suffrage*; Preston 1621; Fletcher; *The spy*; Hoard

Asceticism

> Bayly; *Little Gidding story books*; Digby

Assurance

> Dod; Bayly; *Collegiate suffrage*; Sparke; Laud; Preston ca. 1625; Sibbes; Dow

Atonement

> Andrewes 1604; *Collegiate suffrage*; Sydenham 1622 (limited); Andrewes 1623 (*Christus victor*); Preston ca. 1625; Prynne 1629 (limited); Quarles 1632; Hoard; Quarles 1635

Authority (see also "Scripture, authority of")

> Laud (nature and kinds of); *Little Gidding story books* (of Scripture/reason; coercive; of tradition; of individual conscience); Shelford (and autonomy); Sanderson 1636 (of tradition); Hales (nature and kinds of; and autonomy; and individual reason; of tradition); Dow (divine and human); Chillingworth (nature and kinds of; of individual reason; of universal tradition); Digby (of tradition)

Authority of the institutional church (see also "Infallibility")

> Bradshaw; Buckeridge; Field; Carier; Sanderson 1619; Preston 1621; Laud; Cosin 1632–33; Laurence; Sanderson 1636; Hales ca. 1636, ca. 1638; Dow; Digby
>> Vis-à-vis the godly prince: Bradshaw; Buckeridge; Carier
>> Respecting controversies in religion: Laud; Chillingworth; Digby

Autonomy of national churches

> Sanderson 1636

Calvinism & Calvinist consensus

> Carier; Howson; *Collegiate suffrage*; Sydenham 1622; Sparke; Dow

Censorship

> Adams; *Collegiate suffrage*; *The spy*; Hall; *Little Gidding story books*; Prynne 1636; Dow; Wither 1641

Ceremonies

> Bradshaw; Field; Sanderson 1619; Laud; Laurence; Hales ca. 1636; Dow

Charity (see also "Almsgiving")

> Dod (in judging); Adams; Sanderson 1619 (in judging); Earle; *Survey of London*; Shelford

Christian liberty

> Sanderson 1619; Dow; Chillingworth

Church buildings, architecture, monuments, etc.

> Corbett 1609; Adams; Corbett 1632–33; Strode; *Survey of London*; Laurence; Crashaw [in Shelford]

Church, visible and invisible

> Field; Carier; Laud; Dow

Church, vis-à-vis state

> Bradshaw; Buckeridge; Field; Carier; Howson; *Collegiate suffrage*; Sanderson 1619; Laud; Laurence; Shelford; Dow; Chillingworth

Civic piety

> Adams; *Survey of London*; Dow

Civil power, nature and extent of

> Bradshaw; Buckeridge; Field; Carier; Sydenham 1633; Dow; Wither 1641
> Re specifically religious offenses (see also Sabbath): Bradshaw; Adams; *Collegiate suffrage*; Cosin 1632–33

Clergy, role of

> Carier; Earle: Laurence; Shelford

Confession

> Carier; *Little Gidding story books*; Dow

Conformity & non-conformity

> Sanderson 1619; Quarles 1632; Cosin 1632–33; Hales ca. 1636, ca. 1638; Dow

Congregationalism

> Bradshaw

Conscience

> Dod (and moral law); Buckeridge (private; whether human laws bind in); Field (whether human laws bind in); Sanderson 1619 (re adiaphora); Preston ca. 1625 (internal witness); Shelford; Hales ca. 1636, ca. 1638; Chillingworth (liberty of)

Conspiracy theories (see under "Anti-popery and popish plots")

Contemptus mundi

> Bayly; Drummond; *Little Gidding story books*; Quarles 1632; Habington

Conversion, Law to Gospel (see also "Regeneration & sanctification")

> Preston 1625; Hall; Sibbes

Conversion, to Roman Catholicism

> Carier; Digby

Covenant theology

> Preston ca. 1625; Sibbes; Hoard

Crypto-Catholics & Church papists (see also under "Anti-popery and popish plots")

> Howson; Fletcher; *The Spy*; Earle; Prynne 1636

Discipline, Genevan

> Bradshaw; Dow

Divine law

> Dod; Buckeridge; Bayly; Cosin 1632–33; Sanderson 1636

Doctrinal latitude

> Laud; Montagu 1624; Laurence; Godolphin; Hales ca. 1636; Chillingworth

Ecclesiology

> Bradshaw; Buckeridge; Field; Bayly; Carier; Sanderson 1619; Cosin 1621; Dow; Digby

Economic & social justice

> Dod; Adams; *Survey of London*; Hales ca. 1619–38

Emotions

> Andrewes 1604; Donne (holy tears); Sparke; Quarles 1635

English Church, theological identity of

> Carier; Howson; *Collegiate suffrage* Sanderson 1619; Preston 1621; Laud; Montagu 1624, 1625; Dow

English exceptionalism

> Fletcher; *The spy*; Wither 1641

Episcopacy

> Bradshaw; Sanderson; Prynne 1636; Hales ca. 1636, ca. 1638; Dow

Epistemology, religious (see also "Faith, grounds of"; "Infallibility"; "Moral certainty")

> Drummond; Laud; Sibbes; *Little Gidding story books*; Chillingworth; Digby

Ethics, Christian (see also "Almsgiving"; "Charity"; "Economic & social justice"; "Good works")

> Dod; Adams; Sanderson 1619; Sparke; Donne; Preston ca. 1625; Sibbes; *Little Gidding story books* (patience); Hoard; Shelford

Eudemonism

> Dod; Shelford; Drummond; Preston ca. 1625; Everard; Quarles 1632; Hoard; Dow

Faith, temporary

> *Collegiate suffrage*; Prynne 1629

Faith, nature and grounds of (see also "Assurance"; "Epistemology"; "Moral certainty")

> Laud; Preston ca. 1625; Sibbes; Quarles 1632 (and works); Quarles 1635 (and reason); Godolphin; Chillingworth; Digby

Family, marriage, & household

> Donne; *Little Gidding story books*; *Survey of London*; Shelford; Dow; Wither 1641

Fear

> Dod; Buckeridge; Sydenham 1622; Quarles 1632; Hoard; Laurence; Dow

Feasts, fasts, and holy days (see also "Sabbath")

> Andrewes 1604; Cosin 1621; Donne; Andrewes 1623; Wither 1623; Cosin 1632–33; Prynne 1636 (public fasts); Dow; Wither 1641

Friendship

> Wither

Free-will, freedom & necessity

> *Collegiate suffrage*; Drummond; Sydenham 1622; Montagu 1624; Preston ca. 1625; Quarles 1632; Hoard

Fundamentals, foundations, and beliefs necessary for salvation (see also "Doctrinal latitude")

> Dod; Field; Bayly; Laud; Montagu 1624; The spy; Laurence; Shelford; Dow; Chillingworth

Gender

> *Little Gidding story books*; Wither 1641

Gentiles, possible salvation of

> Preston 1621, Laud; Preston ca. 1625; Hoard

Good works & holy living (see also "Economic and social justice"; "Ethics"; "Sanctification")

> Dod; Field; Adams; Hall; Everard; Quarles 1632 (and faith); *Survey of London*; Laurence; Shelford; Dow
>> As signs of election: Bayly; Preston ca. 1625

Grace

> Bayly; Laud (necessary for faith); Sibbes; Quarles 1632 (and human agency); Hoard
>> Effectual: *Collegiate suffrage*; Sydenham 1622; Preston ca. 1625; Prynne 1629; Hoard
>> Irresistible: *Collegiate suffrage*; Preston 1621; Sydenham 1622; Preston ca. 1625; Prynne 1629; Hoard

Great Tew

> Earle; Godolphin; Hales; Chillingworth; Digby

Gunpowder Plot

> Fletcher

Heaven & hell (see also "Relation of the living and the dead")

> Bayly; Drummond; Andrewes 1632 (harrowing of hell); Fletcher; Everard (spiritualized); Digby

Hypocrisy

> Adams; Earle; Corbett ca. 1632–33

Hypothetical universalism

> *Collegiate suffrage*; Preston 1621, ca. 1625; Prynne 1629; Hoard

Images & iconoclasm

> Dod; Carier; Corbett ca. 1632–33; Strode; *Survey of London*; Quarles 1635

Immortality of the soul

> Drummond; *Little Gidding story books*; Digby

Infallibility

> Laud; Preston ca. 1625; Shelford; Hales ca. 1636, ca. 1619–38; Dow; Chillingworth; Digby

Interiority, religious/spiritual

> Dod; Sparke; Preston ca. 1621, ca. 1625; Everard; Sibbes; *Little Gidding story books*; Quarles 1632, 1635

Justification

> Bayly; Field; Preston ca. 1625; Strode

Laity, role of

> Bradshaw (elders); Laud; *Survey of London*; Laurence; Shelford; Hales ca. 1619–38; Chillingworth

Laudianism & anti-Laudianism

> *The spy*; Everard; Corbett ca. 1632–33; Shelford; Strode; Cosin 1632–33; Sydenham 1633; Laurence; Prynne 1636; Dow; Chillingworth

Miracles

> *Little Giddings story books*; Digby

Moral certainty

> Laud; Chillingworth

Mystery

> Andrewes 1604; Sydenham 1622; Everard; Sydenham 1633; Laurence; Godolphin

Mystical union

> Everard

Nature

> Sydenham 1633 (natural law; book of; proto-Romantic); Shelford (book of); Habington (book of)

Pastoral comfort

> Dod; Preston 1621; Sparke; Preston ca. 1625; Everard; Sibbes

Patristics

> Buckeridge; Field; Carier; Quarles 1635; Hales ca. 1636, ca. 1619–38; Dow

Perfectionism (see "Rigorism and the salvation of ordinary Christians")

Perseverance & falling from grace

> Dod; Barlow; Field; *Collegiate suffrage*; Montagu 1624, 1625; Preston ca. 1625; Dow

Prayer

> Dod; Field (for the dead); Bayly (private); Preston 1621 (liturgical); Sparke (private); Dow (for the dead)

Preaching

> Bradshaw; Bayly; Adams; *Collegiate suffrage*; Cosin 1621; Preston ca. 1625; Earle; Shelford; Prynne 1636; Dow

Predestination

> Field; Bayly; *Collegiate suffrage*; Sydenham 1622; Donne; Montag 1624, 1625; Preston ca. 1625; Prynne 1629; Quarles 1632; Hoard; Laurence; Dow

Preparation for grace

> *Collegiate suffrage*; Preston 1621; Dow

Private spirit and individual judgment (see also "Christian liberty," "Conscience")

> Field; Laud; Everard; Hales ca. 1636, ca. 1619–38; Chillingworth; Digby

Providence & providentialism

> Dod; Bayly; *Little Gidding story books*; Sydenham 1633; Prynne 1636; Habington

Reason

> Dod (carnal); Laud; *Little Gidding story books* (versus Scripture); Hoard; Godolphin; Hales (authority of); Laurence; Chillingworth (authority of)

Regeneration and sanctification

> Bayly; *Collegiate suffrage*; Preston 1621; Sydenham 1622; Sparke; Preston ca. 1625; Hall; Prynne 1629; Sibbes; *Little Gidding story book*s; Wither 1641

Relation of the living and the dead

> Field; Corbett 1609; Donne; Drummond; *Little Gidding story books*; Strode; *Survey of London*; Dow; Wither 1641

Repentance/penance

> Carier; Preston 1621, ca. 1625; Hall; Quarles 1632; Godolphin

Reprobation

> Dod; Bayly; *Collegiate suffrage*; Sydenham 1622; Montagu 1624; Prynne 1629; Hoard

Resurrection of the body

> Bayly; Donne; Drummond; Quarles 1632; Strode; *Survey of London*; Laurence

Revenge

> Dod; *Little Gidding story books* (and chivalric romance); Quarles 1632

Rigorism and the salvation of ordinary Christians

> Dod; Bayly; Sanderson 1619; Preston 1621; Cosin 1621; Preston ca. 1625; Laud; Earle; Everard; Hall; Sibbes; *Survey of London*; Shelford; Godolphin; Chillingworth

Royal authority

> Bradshaw; Buckeridge; Carier; Dow (and episcopate); Wither 1641

Royal supremacy (see also "Church/state," "Royal authority")

> Buckeridge: Carier; Prynne 1636

Sabbath

> Dod; Bayly; Howson; Cosin 1632–33; Prynne 1636; Sanderson 1636; Dow

Sacral loci

> Everard (and divine omnipresence); Cosin 1632–33; Sydenham 1633; Laurence; Crashaw [in Shelford]; Shelford; Dow

Sacraments

> Corbett 1609; Bayly; Carier; Andrewes 1623; Wither 1623; Preston ca. 1625; Quarles 1632; Shelford; Dow; Wither 1641
> > Baptism: Donne; Montagu 1625; Dow

Saints

> Field (invocation of); Wither 1623 (feast days); *Little Gidding Story Books*;
> Cosin 1632–33 (veneration of); Quarles 1635 (invocation of); Digby

Sanctification of ordinary Life

> Wither 1641

Scriptural interpretation

> Dod; Field; Bayly; Laud; Everard; Chillingworth
>> Allegorical: Andrewes 1604; Field; Cosin 1621; Andrewes 1623;
>>   Everard
>> Literal: Bradshaw; Field
>> Typological: Andrewes 1604; Cosin 1621; Andrewes 1623; Everard

Scripture, authority of

> Dod; Bradshaw; Chillingworth; Dow
>> As word of God: Laud; Strode; Dow; Chillingworth
>> As rule of faith: Chillingworth
>> Vis-à-vis Church: Bradshaw; Field; Laud; Chillingworth; Digby

Secret and revealed will of God

> Preston ca. 1625; Prynne 1629

Skepticism

> Earle

Sublime

> Sydenham 1633; Laurence

Toleration & religious uniformity

> Carier; Sanderson 1619; *The spy*; Hales ca. 1636, ca. 1638; Chillingworth

Tradition, authority of

> Carier; Laud; Sanderson 1636; Hales 1619–38; Dow; Digby
>> Apostolic: Laud; Dow; Chillingworth

Violence, sectarian/confessional

> Howson (academic factionalism); Wither 1623; Fletcher (militant
> Calvinism); *The spy* (militant Calvinism); Wither 1641

Voluntarism

> Dod; Bradshaw; Sydenham 1622; Prynne 1629; Everard; Cosin 1632–33

Witchcraft

> Cosin 1632–33